THE EXPOSITOR'S BIBLE COMMENTARY

General Editor:

FRANK E. GAEBELEIN
Headmaster Emeritus, Stony Brook School;
Former Coeditor, *Christianity Today*

Associate Editor:

RICHARD P. POLCYN
Zondervan Publishing House

Consulting Editors, Old Testament:

WALTER C. KAISER, JR.
Professor of Semitic Languages
and Old Testament,
Trinity Evangelical Divinity School

BRUCE K. WALTKE
(Consulting Editor, 1972–1984)
Professor of Old Testament,
Regent College

RALPH H. ALEXANDER
(Consulting Editor, 1984—)
Professor of Hebrew Scripture
Western Seminary, Portland, Oregon

Consulting Editors, New Testament:

JAMES MONTGOMERY BOICE
Pastor, Tenth Presbyterian Church,
Philadelphia, Pennsylvania

MERRILL C. TENNEY
Professor of Bible and Theology, Emeritus,
Wheaton College

THE EXPOSITOR'S BIBLE COMMENTARY

with

The New International Version
of
The Holy Bible

IN TWELVE VOLUMES

VOLUME 5

(PSALMS - SONG OF SONGS)

ZondervanPublishingHouse
Academic and Professional Books
Grand Rapids, Michigan

A Division of HarperCollins*Publishers*

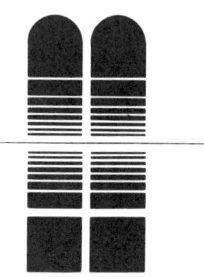

THE EXPOSITOR'S BIBLE COMMENTARY, VOLUME 5

Requests for information should be addressed to:
Zondervan Publishing House
Academic and Professional Books
Grand Rapids, Michigan 49530

Library of Congress Cataloging-in-Publication Data
(Revised for Volume 5)

The Expositor's Bible commentary.
Includes bibliographies.
Contents: v. 1. Introductory articles.—v. 5.
Psalms–Song of Songs—v. 12. Hebrews–Revelation.
1. Bible—Commentaries. I. Gaebelein, Frank Ely, 1899– .
II. Douglas, J. D. (James Dixon) III. Bible. English.
New International 1976.
BS491.2.E96 220.7'7 76-41334
ISBN 0-310-36470-1 (v.5)

Printed in the United States of America

93 94 95 / DH / 10 9 8 7 6

This edition is printed on acid-free paper and meets the American National Standards Institute Z39.48 standard.

CONTENTS

Contributors to Volume 5 vi
Preface vii
Abbreviations ix
Transliterations xv
Psalms 1
Proverbs 883
Ecclesiastes 1137
Song of Songs 1201

CONTRIBUTORS TO VOLUME 5

Psalms: Willem A. VanGemeren

B.A., University of Illinois, Chicago; B.D., Westminster Theological Seminary; M.A., Ph.D., University of Wisconsin

Professor of Old Testament; Chairman, Dept. of O.T. Studies, Reformed Theological Seminary

Proverbs: Allen P. Ross

Th.M., Th.D., Dallas Theological Seminiary; Ph.D., Cambridge University

Professor of Old Testament Studies, Trinity Episcopal School for Ministry

Ecclesiastes: J. Stafford Wright

M.A. Cambridge University

Former Principal of Tyndale Hall, Bristol, and Canon Emeritus of Bristol Cathedral

Song of Songs: Dennis F. Kinlaw

A.B., Asbury College; B.D., Asbury Theological Seminary; M.A., Ph.D., Brandeis University

President, Asbury College

PREFACE

The title of this work defines its purpose. Written primarily by expositors for expositors, it aims to provide preachers, teachers, and students of the Bible with a new and comprehensive commentary on the books of the Old and New Testaments. Its stance is that of a scholarly evangelicalism committed to the divine inspiration, complete trustworthiness, and full authority of the Bible. Its seventy-eight contributors come from the United States, Canada, England, Scotland, Australia, New Zealand, and Switzerland, and from various religious groups, including Anglican, Baptist, Brethren, Free, Independent, Methodist, Nazarene, Presbyterian, and Reformed churches. Most of them teach at colleges, universities, or theological seminaries.

No book has been more closely studied over a longer period of time than the Bible. From the Midrashic commentaries going back to the period of Ezra, through parts of the Dead Sea Scrolls and the Patristic literature, and on to the present, the Scriptures have been expounded. Indeed, there have been times when, as in the Reformation and on occasions since then, exposition has been at the cutting edge of Christian advance. Luther was a powerful exegete, and Calvin is still called "the prince of expositors."

Their successors have been many. And now, when the outburst of new translations and their unparalleled circulation have expanded the readership of the Bible, the need for exposition takes on fresh urgency.

Not that God's Word can ever become captive to its expositors. Among all other books, it stands first in its combination of perspicuity and profundity. Though a child can be made "wise for salvation" by believing its witness to Christ, the greatest mind cannot plumb the depths of its truth (2 Tim. 3:15; Rom. 11:33). As Gregory the Great said, "Holy Scripture is a stream of running water, where alike the elephant may swim, and the lamb walk." So, because of the inexhaustible nature of Scripture, the task of opening up its meaning is still a perennial obligation of biblical scholarship.

How that task is done inevitably reflects the outlook of those engaged in it. Every Bible scholar has presuppositions. To this neither the editors of these volumes nor the contributors to them are exceptions. They share a common commitment to the supernatural Christianity set forth in the inspired Word. Their purpose is not to supplant the many valuable commentaries that have preceded this work and from which both the editors and contributors have learned. It is rather to draw on the resources of contemporary evangelical scholarship in producing a new reference work for understanding the Scriptures.

A commentary that will continue to be useful through the years should handle contemporary trends in biblical studies in such a way as to avoid becoming outdated when critical fashions change. Biblical criticism is not in itself inadmissable, as some have mistakenly thought. When scholars investigate the authorship, date, literary characteristics, and purpose of a biblical document, they are practicing biblical criticism. So also when, in order to ascertain as nearly as possible the original form of the text, they deal with variant readings, scribal errors, emendations, and other phenomena in the manuscripts. To do these things is essential to responsible exegesis and exposition. And always there is the need to distinguish hypothesis from fact, conjecture from truth.

The chief principle of interpretation followed in this commentary is the grammatico-historical one—namely, that the primary aim of the exegete is to make clear the meaning of the text at the time and in the circumstances of its writing. This endeavor to understand what in the first instance the inspired writers actually said must not be confused with an inflexible literalism. Scripture makes lavish use of symbols and figures of speech; great portions of it are poetical. Yet when it speaks in this way, it speaks no less truly than it does in its historical and doctrinal portions. To understand its message requires attention to matters of grammar and syntax, word meanings, idioms, and literary forms—all in relation to the historical and cultural setting of the text.

The contributors to this work necessarily reflect varying convictions. In certain controversial matters the policy is that of clear statement of the contributors' own views followed by fair presentation of other ones. The treatment of eschatology, though it reflects differences of interpretation, is consistent with a general premillennial position. (Not all contributors, however, are premillennial.) But prophecy is more than prediction, and so this commentary gives due recognition to the major lode of godly social concern in the prophetic writings.

The Expositor's Bible Commentary is presented as a scholarly work, though not primarily one of technical criticism. In its main portion, the Exposition, and in Volume 1 (General and Special Articles), all Semitic and Greek words are transliterated and the English equivalents given. As for the Notes, here Semitic and Greek characters are used but always with transliterations and English meanings, so that this portion of the commentary will be as accessible as possible to readers unacquainted with the original languages.

It is the conviction of the general editor, shared by his colleagues in the Zondervan editorial department, that in writing about the Bible, lucidity is not incompatible with scholarship. They are therefore endeavoring to make this a clear and understandable work.

The translation used in it is the New International Version (North American Edition). To the International Bible Society thanks are due for permission to use this most recent of the major Bible translations. It was chosen because of the clarity and beauty of its style and its faithfulness to the original texts.

To the associate editor, Richard P. Polcyn, and to the contributing editors—Dr. Walter C. Kaiser, Jr., Dr. Bruce K. Waltke, and Dr. Ralph H. Alexander for the Old Testament, and Dr. James Montgomery Boice and Dr. Merrill C. Tenney for the New Testament—the general editor expresses his gratitude for their unfailing cooperation and their generosity in advising him out of their expert scholarship. And to the many other contributors he is indebted for their invaluable part in this work. Finally, he owes a special debt of gratitude to Dr. Robert K. DeVries, publisher, The Zondervan Corporation, and Miss Elizabeth Brown, secretary, for their assistance and encouragement.

Whatever else it is—the greatest and most beautiful of books, the primary source of law and morality, the fountain of wisdom, and the infallible guide to life—the Bible is above all the inspired witness to Jesus Christ. May this work fulfill its function of expounding the Scriptures with grace and clarity, so that its users may find that both Old and New Testaments do indeed lead to our Lord Jesus Christ, who alone could say, "I have come that they may have life, and have it to the full" (John 10:10).

Frank E. Gaebelein

ABBREVIATIONS

A. General Abbreviations

A	Codex Alexandrinus
Akkad.	Akkadian
א	Codex Sinaiticus
Ap. Lit.	Apocalyptic Literature
Apoc.	Apocrypha
Aq.	Aquila's Greek Translation of the Old Testament
Arab.	Arabic
Aram.	Aramaic
b	Babylonian Gemara
B	Codex Vaticanus
C	Codex Ephraemi Syri
c.	*circa*, about
cf.	*confer*, compare
ch., chs.	chapter, chapters
cod., codd.	codex, codices
D	Codex Bezae
DSS	Dead Sea Scrolls (see E.)
ed., edd.	edited, edition, editor; editions
e.g.	*exempli gratia*, for example
Egyp.	Egyptian
et al.	*et alii*, and others
EV	English Versions of the Bible
fem.	feminine
ff.	following (verses, pages, etc.)
fl.	flourished
ft.	foot, feet
gen.	genitive
Gr.	Greek
Heb.	Hebrew
Hitt.	Hittite
ibid.	*ibidem*, in the same place
id.	*idem*, the same
i.e.	*id est*, that is
impf.	imperfect
infra.	below
in loc.	*in loco*, in the place cited
j	Jerusalem or Palestinian Gemara
Lat.	Latin
LL.	Late Latin
LXX	Septuagint
M	Mishnah
masc.	masculine
mg.	margin
Mid	Midrash
MS(S)	manuscript(s)
MT	Masoretic text
n.	note
n.d.	no date
Nestle	Nestle (ed.) *Novum Testamentum Graece*
no.	number
NT	New Testament
obs.	obsolete
OL	Old Latin
OS	Old Syriac
OT	Old Testament
p., pp.	page, pages
par.	paragraph
Pers.	Persian
Pesh.	Peshitta
Phoen.	Phoenician
pl.	plural
Pseudep.	Pseudepigrapha
Q	Quelle ("Sayings" source in the Gospels)
qt.	quoted by
q.v.	*quod vide*, which see
R	Rabbah
rev.	revised, reviser, revision
Rom.	Roman
RVm	Revised Version margin
Samar.	Samaritan recension
SCM	Student Christian Movement Press
Sem.	Semitic
sing.	singular
SPCK	Society for the Promotion of Christian Knowledge
Sumer.	Sumerian
s.v.	*sub verbo*, under the word
Syr.	Syriac
Symm.	Symmachus
T	Talmud
Targ.	Targum
Theod.	Theodotion
TR	Textus Receptus
tr.	translation, translator, translated
UBS	Tha United Bible Societies' Greek Text
Ugar.	Ugaritic
u.s.	*ut supra*, as above
v., vv.	verse, verses
viz.	*videlicet*, namely
vol.	volume
vs.	versus
Vul.	Vulgate
WH	Westcott and Hort, *The New Testament in Greek*

B. Abbreviations for Modern Translations and Paraphrases

AmT	Smith and Goodspeed, *The Complete Bible, An American Translation*
ASV	American Standard Version, American Revised Version (1901)
Beck	Beck, *The New Testament in the Language of Today*
BV	Berkeley Version (The Modern Language Bible)
JB	The Jerusalem Bible
JPS	*Jewish Publication Society Version of the Old Testament*
KJV	King James Version
Knox	R.G. Knox, *The Holy Bible: A Translation from the Latin Vulgate in the Light of the Hebrew and Greek Original*
LB	The Living Bible
Mof	J. Moffatt, *A New Translation of the Bible*
NAB	The New American Bible
NASB	New American Standard Bible
NEB	The New English Bible
NIV	The New International Version
Ph	J. B. Phillips *The New Testament in Modern English*
RSV	Revised Standard Version
RV	Revised Version — 1881–1885
TCNT	Twentieth Century New Testament
TEV	Today's English Version
Wey	*Weymouth's New Testament in Modern Speech*
Wms	C. B. Williams, *The New Testament: A Translation in the Language of the People*

C. Abbreviations for Periodicals and Reference Works

AASOR	*Annual of the American Schools of Oriental Research*
AB	*Anchor Bible*
AIs	de Vaux: *Ancient Israel*
AJA	*American Journal of Archaeology*
AJSL	*American Journal of Semitic Languages and Literatures*
AJT	*American Journal of Theology*
Alf	Alford: *Greek Testament Commentary*
ANEA	*Ancient Near Eastern Archaeology*
ANEP	Pritchard: *Ancient Near Eastern Pictures*
ANET	Pritchard· *Ancient Near Eastern Texts*
ANF	Roberts and Donaldson: *The Ante-Nicene Fathers*
A-S	Abbot-Smith: *Manual Greek Lexicon of the New Testament*
AThR	*Anglican Theological Review*
BA	*Biblical Archaeologist*
BAG	Bauer, Arndt, and Gingrich: *Greek-English Lexicon of the New Testament*
BAGD	Bauer, Arndt, Gingrich, and Danker: *Greek-English Lexicon of the New Testament* 2nd edition
BASOR	*Bulletin of the American Schools of Oriental Research*
BC	Foakes-Jackson and Lake: *The Beginnings of Christianity*
BDB	Brown, Driver, and Briggs: *Hebrew-English Lexicon of the Old Testament*
BDF	Blass, Debrunner, and Funk: *A Greek Grammar of the New Testament and Other Early Christian Literature*
BDT	Harrison: *Baker's Dictionary of Theology*
Beng.	Bengel's *Gnomon*
BETS	*Bulletin of the Evangelical Theological Society*
BH	*Biblia Hebraica*
BHS	*Biblia Hebraica Stuttgartensia*
BJRL	*Bulletin of the John Rylands Library*
BS	*Bibliotheca Sacra*
BT	*Babylonian Talmud*
BTh	*Biblical Theology*
BW	*Biblical World*
CAH	*Cambridge Ancient History*
CanJTh	*Canadian Journal of Theology*
CBQ	*Catholic Biblical Quarterly*
CBSC	*Cambridge Bible for Schools and Colleges*
CE	*Catholic Encyclopedia*
CGT	*Cambridge Greek Testament*

CHS	Lange: *Commentary on the Holy Scriptures*
ChT	*Christianity Today*
DDB	*Davis' Dictionary of the Bible*
Deiss BS	Deissmann: *Bible Studies*
Deiss LAE	Deissmann: *Light From the Ancient East*
DNTT	*Dictionary of New Testament Theology*
EBC	*The Expositor's Bible Commentary*
EBi	*Encyclopaedia Biblica*
EBr	*Encyclopaedia Britannica*
EDB	*Encyclopedic Dictionary of the Bible*
EGT	Nicoll: *Expositor's Greek Testament*
EQ	*Evangelical Quarterly*
ET	*Evangelische Theologie*
ExB	*The Expositor's Bible*
Exp	*The Expositor*
ExpT	*The Expository Times*
FLAP	Finegan: *Light From the Ancient Past*
GKC	Gesenius, Kautzsch, Cowley, *Hebrew Grammar*, 2nd Eng. ed.
GR	*Gordon Review*
HBD	*Harper's Bible Dictionary*
HDAC	Hastings: *Dictionary of the Apostolic Church*
HDB	Hastings: *Dictionary of the Bible*
HDBrev.	Hastings: *Dictionary of the Bible*, one-vol. rev. by Grant and Rowley
HDCG	Hastings: *Dictionary of Christ and the Gospels*
HERE	Hastings: *Encyclopedia of Religion and Ethics*
HGEOTP	Heidel: *The Gilgamesh Epic and Old Testament Parallels*
HJP	Schurer: *A History of the Jewish People in the Time of Christ*
HR	Hatch and Redpath: *Concordance to the Septuagint*
HTR	*Harvard Theological Review*
HUCA	*Hebrew Union College Annual*
IB	*The Interpreter's Bible*
ICC	*International Critical Commentary*
IDB	*The Interpreter's Dictionary of the Bible*
IEJ	*Israel Exploration Journal*
Int	*Interpretation*
INT	E. Harrison: *Introduction to the New Testament*
IOT	R. K. Harrison: *Introduction to the Old Testament*
ISBE	*The International Standard Bible Encyclopedia*
ITQ	*Irish Theological Quarterly*
JAAR	*Journal of American Academy of Religion*
JAOS	*Journal of American Oriental Society*
JBL	*Journal of Biblical Literature*
JE	*Jewish Encyclopedia*
JETS	*Journal of Evangelical Theological Society*
JFB	Jamieson, Fausset, and Brown: *Commentary on the Old and New Testament*
JNES	*Journal of Near Eastern Studies*
Jos. Antiq.	Josephus: *The Antiquities of the Jews*
Jos. War	Josephus: *The Jewish War*
JQR	*Jewish Quarterly Review*
JR	*Journal of Religion*
JSJ	*Journal for the Study of Judaism in the Persian, Hellenistic and Roman Periods*
JSOR	*Journal of the Society of Oriental Research*
JSS	*Journal of Semitic Studies*
JT	*Jerusalem Talmud*
JTS	*Journal of Theological Studies*
KAHL	Kenyon: *Archaeology in the Holy Land*
KB	Koehler-Baumgartner: *Lexicon in Veteris Testament Libros*
KD	Keil and Delitzsch: *Commentary on the Old Testament*
LSJ	Liddell, Scott, Jones: *Greek-English Lexicon*
LTJM	Edersheim: *The Life and Times of Jesus the Messiah*
MM	Moulton and Milligan: *The Vocabulary of the Greek Testament*
MNT	Moffatt: *New Testament Commentary*

MST	McClintock and Strong: *Cyclopedia of Biblical, Theological, and Ecclesiastical Literature*
NBC	Davidson, Kevan, and Stibbs: *The New Bible Commentary*, 1st ed.
NBCrev.	Guthrie and Motyer: *The New Bible Commentary*, rev. ed.
NBD	J. D. Douglas: *The New Bible Dictionary*
NCB	*New Century Bible*
NCE	*New Catholic Encyclopedia*
NIC	*New International Commentary*
NIDCC	Douglas: *The New International Dictionary of the Christian Church*
NovTest	*Novum Testamentum*
NSI	Cooke: *Handbook of North Semitic Inscriptions*
NTS	*New Testament Studies*
ODCC	*The Oxford Dictionary of the Christian Church*, rev. ed.
Peake	Black and Rowley: *Peake's Commentary on the Bible*
PEQ	*Palestine Exploration Quarterly*
PNFl	P. Schaff: *The Nicene and Post-Nicene Fathers* (1st series)
PNF2	P. Schaff and H. Wace: *The Nicene and Post-Nicene Fathers* (2nd series)
PTR	*Princeton Theological Review*
RB	*Revue Biblique*
RHG	Robertson's *Grammar of the Greek New Testament in the Light of Historical Research*
RTWB	Richardson: *A Theological Wordbook of the Bible*
SBK	Strack and Billerbeck: *Kommentar zum Neuen Testament aus Talmud und Midrash*
SHERK	*The New Schaff-Herzog Encyclopedia of Religious Knowledge*
SJT	*Scottish Journal of Theology*
SOT	Girdlestone: *Synonyms of Old Testament*
SOTI	Archer: *A Survey of Old Testament Introduction*
ST	*Studia Theologica*
TCERK	Loetscher: *The Twentieth Century Encyclopedia of Religious Knowledge*
TDNT	Kittel: *Theological Dictionary of the New Testament*
TDOT	*Theological Dictionary of the Old Testament*
THAT	*Theologisches Handbuch zum Alten Testament*
ThT	*Theology Today*
TNTC	*Tyndale New Testament Commentaries*
Trench	Trench: *Synonyms of the New Testament*
TWOT	*Theological Wordbook of the Old Testament*
UBD	*Unger's Bible Dictionary*
UT	Gordon: *Ugaritic Textbook*
VB	Allmen: *Vocabulary of the Bible*
VetTest	*Vetus Testamentum*
Vincent	Vincent: *Word-Pictures in the New Testament*
WBC	*Wycliffe Bible Commentary*
WBE	*Wycliffe Bible Encyclopedia*
WC	*Westminster Commentaries*
WesBC	*Wesleyan Bible Commentaries*
WTJ	*Westminster Theological Journal*
ZAW	*Zeitschrift für die alttestamentliche Wissenschaft*
ZNW	*Zeitschrift für die neutestamentliche Wissenschaft*
ZPBD	*The Zondervan Pictorial Bible Dictionary*
ZPEB	*The Zondervan Pictorial Encyclopedia of the Bible*
ZWT	*Zeitschrift für wissenschaftliche Theologie*

D. Abbreviations for Books of the Bible, the Apocrypha, and the Pseudepigrapha

OLD TESTAMENT

Gen	2 Chron	Dan
Exod	Ezra	Hos
Lev	Neh	Joel
Num	Esth	Amos
Deut	Job	Obad
Josh	Ps(Pss)	Jonah
Judg	Prov	Mic
Ruth	Eccl	Nah
1 Sam	S of Songs	Hab
2 Sam	Isa	Zeph
1 Kings	Jer	Hag
2 Kings	Lam	Zech
1 Chron	Ezek	Mal

NEW TESTAMENT

Matt	1 Tim
Mark	2 Tim
Luke	Titus
John	Philem
Acts	Heb
Rom	James
1 Cor	1 Peter
2 Cor	2 Peter
Gal	1 John
Eph	2 John
Phil	3 John
Col	Jude
1 Thess	Rev
2 Thess	

APOCRYPHA

1 Esd	1 Esdras
2 Esd	2 Esdras
Tobit	Tobit
Jud	Judith
Add Esth	Additions to Esther
Wisd Sol	Wisdom of Solomon
Ecclus	Ecclesiasticus (Wisdom of Jesus the Son of Sirach)
Baruch	Baruch
Ep Jer	Epistle of Jeremy
S Th Ch	Song of the Three Child (or Young Men)
Sus	Susanna
Bel	Bel and the Dragon
Pr Man	Prayer of Manasseh
1 Macc	1 Maccabees
2 Macc	2 Maccabees

PSEUDEPIGRAPHA

As Moses	Assumption of Moses
2 Baruch	Syriac Apocalypse of Baruch
3 Baruch	Greek Apocalypse of Baruch
1 Enoch	Ethiopic Book of Enoch
2 Enoch	Slavonic Book of Enoch
3 Enoch	Hebrew Book of Enoch
4 Ezra	4 Ezra
JA	Joseph and Asenath
Jub	Book of Jubilees
L Aristeas	Letter of Aristeas
Life AE	Life of Adam and Eve
Liv Proph	Lives of the Prophets
MA Isa	Martyrdom and Ascension of Isaiah
3 Macc	3 Maccabees
4 Macc	4 Maccabees
Odes Sol	Odes of Solomon
P Jer	Paralipomena of Jeremiah
Pirke Aboth	Pirke Aboth
Ps 151	Psalm 151
Pss Sol	Psalms of Solomon
Sib Oracles	Sibylline Oracles
Story Ah	Story of Ahikar
T Abram	Testament of Abraham
T Adam	Testament of Adam
T Benjamin	Testament of Benjamin
T Dan	Testament of Dan
T Gad	Testament of Gad
T Job	Testament of Job
T Jos	Testament of Joseph
T Levi	Testament of Levi
T Naph	Testament of Naphtali
T 12 Pat	Testaments of the Twe Patriarchs
Zad Frag	Zadokite Fragments

E. Abbreviations of Names of Dead Sea Scrolls and Related Texts

CD	Cairo (Genizah text of the) Damascus (Document)
DSS	Dead Sea Scrolls
Hev	Nahal Hever texts
Mas	Masada Texts
Mird	Khirbet mird texts
Mur	Wadi Murabba'at texts
P	Pesher (commentary)
Q	Qumran
1Q, 2Q, etc.	Numbered caves of Qumran, yielding written material; followed by abbreviation of biblical or apocryphal book.
QL	Qumran Literature
1QapGen	Genesis Apocryphon of Qumran Cave 1
1QH	*Hodayot* (Thanksgiving Hymns) from Qumran Cave 1
1QIsa a,b	First or second copy of Isaiah from Qumran Cave 1
1QpHab	Pesher on Habakkuk from Qumran Cave 1
1QM	*Milhamah* (War Scroll)
1QpMic	Pesher on portions of Micah from Qumran Cave 1
1QS	*Serek Hayyahad* (Rule of the Community, Manual of Discipline)
1QSa	Appendix A (Rule of the Congregation) to 1Qs
1QSb	Appendix B (Blessings) to 1QS
3Q15	Copper Scroll from Qumran Cave 3
4QExod a	Exodus Scroll, exemplar "a" from Qumran Cave 4
4QFlor	Florilegium (or Eschatological Midrashim) from Qumran Cave 4
4Qmess ar	Aramaic "Messianic" text from Qumran Cave 4
4QpNah	Pesher on portions of Nahum from Qumran Cave 4
4QPrNab	Prayer of Nabonidus from Qumran Cave 4
4QpPs37	Pesher on portions of Psalm 37 from Qumran Cave 4
4QTest	Testimonia text from Qumran Cave 4
4QTLevi	Testament of Levi from Qumran Cave 4
4QPhyl	Phylacteries from Qumran Cave 4
11QMelch	Melchizedek text from Qumran Cave 11
11QtgJob	Targum of Job from Qumran Cave 11

TRANSLITERATIONS

Hebrew

א = ʾ	ד = ḏ	י = y	ס = s	ר = r
בּ = b	ה = h	כּ = k	ע = ʿ	שׂ = ś
ב = ḇ	ו = w	כ ך = ḵ	פּ = p	שׁ = š
גּ = g	ז = z	ל = l	פ ף = p̱	תּ = t
ג = ḡ	ח = ḥ	מ ם = m	צ ץ = ṣ	ת = ṯ
דּ = d	ט = ṭ	נ ן = n	ק = q	

◌ָ(ה) = â (h)	◌ָ = ā	◌ַ = a	◌ֲ = ^{a}
◌ֵי = ê	◌ֵ = ē	◌ֶ = e	◌ֱ = ^{e}
◌ִי = î	◌ֹ = ō	◌ִ = i	◌ְ = ^{e} (*if vocal*)
וֹ = ô		◌ָ = o	◌ֳ = ^{o}
וּ = û		◌ֻ = u	

Aramaic

ʾ b g d h w z ḥ ṭ y k l m n s ʿ p ṣ q r ś š t

Arabic

ʾ b t ṯ ǧ ḥ ḫ d ḏ r z s š ṣ ḍ ṭ ẓ ʿ ġ f q k l m n h w y

Ugaritic

ʾ b g d ḏ h w z ḥ ḫ ṭ ẓ y k l m n s s̀ ʿ ǵ ṗ ṣ q r š t ṯ

Greek

α — *a*	π — *p*	αἰ — *ai*
β — *b*	ρ — *r*	αὐ — *au*
γ — *g*	σ,ς — *s*	εἰ — *ei*
δ — *d*	τ — *t*	εὐ — *eu*
ε — *e*	υ — *y*	ηὐ — *ēu*
ζ — *z*	φ — *ph*	οἰ — *oi*
η — *ē*	χ — *ch*	οὐ — *ou*
θ — *th*	ψ — *ps*	υἱ — *hui*
ι — *i*	ω — *ō*	
κ — *k*		ῥ — *rh*
λ — *l*	γγ — *ng*	῾ — *h*
μ — *m*	γκ — *nk*	
ν — *n*	γξ — *nx*	ᾳ — *ā*
ξ — *x*	γχ — *nch*	ῃ — *ē*
ο — *o*		ῳ — *ō*

PSALMS

Willem A. VanGemeren

PSALMS

Introduction

1. The Book of Psalms

    a. The Psalms as windows into Israel's faith
    b. The Psalms as man's word to God and God's Word to man: The inspiration and authority of the Psalms
    c. The study of the Book of Psalms
        1) Hebrew poetry
            a) Rhyme, meter, and strophe
            b) Parallelism
        2) Literary analysis

2. Types of Psalms
3. God, the Psalmist, and the World

    a. The names of God
    b. The perfections of God
    c. The acts of God
    d. The hope of redemption and righteousness
    e. The kingdom of God
    f. The Davidic Messiah
    g. Wisdom from above

4. Composition
5. Structure
6. Appendixes

    a. Literary approach to the Psalms
        1) Parallelism
            a) Synonymous
            b) Antithetic
            c) Synthetic (formal)
            d) Miscellaneous
        2) Literary devices
            a) Standardized phrases or paired synonyms
            b) Acrostic
            c) Alliteration
            d) Apostrophe
            e) Assonance
            f) Chiasm
            g) Ellipsis
            h) Hendiadys
            i) Hyperbole
            j) Inclusion
            k) Merismus

- l) Metonymy
- m) Onomatopoeia
- n) Paronomasia
- o) Refrain
- p) Repetition
- q) Synecdoche

b. Literary Genre
- 1) Praise
- 2) Lament
- 3) Lament and praise
- 4) Other types of psalms
  - a) Enthronement
  - b) Wisdom
  - c) Miscellaneous

c. Psalm titles
- 1) Person or group associated
  - a) David
  - b) The director of music
  - c) Jeduthun
  - d) The sons of Korah
  - e) Asaph
  - f) Solomon
  - g) Heman the Ezrahite
  - h) Ethan the Ezrahite
  - i) Moses
- 2) Background or historical information
- 3) Musical or liturgical information
  - a) With stringed instruments
  - b) For flutes
  - c) According to *sheminith*
  - d) According to *gittith*
  - e) *Selah*
  - f) To the tune of "The Death of the Son"
  - g) To the tune of "The Doe of the Morning"
  - h) To the tune of "Lilies"
  - i) According to *mahalath*
  - j) To the tune of "A Dove on Distant Oaks"
  - k) To the tune of "Do Not Destroy"
  - l) Other tune titles
- 4) Ancient literary categories
  - a) Psalm
  - b) *Shiggaion*
  - c) *Miktam*
  - d) *Maskil*
  - e) Song
  - f) Psalm of praise
  - g) A petition
  - h) For teaching
  - i) For the Sabbath
  - j) For giving thanks
  - k) A prayer

7. Bibliography

a. Commentaries
b. General works

8. Outline

1. The Book of Psalms

a. *The Psalms as windows into Israel's faith*

In the 150 psalms the Holy Spirit has given us more than a book of Israel's prayer and praise. The Book of Psalms is a cross section of God's revelation to Israel and of Israel's response in faith to the Lord.

The Psalms mirror the faith of Israel. In them we receive windows that enable us to look out on our brothers and sisters in the faith of more than twenty-five hundred years ago. The Psalms invite us to experience how God's people in the past related to Him. The Psalms witness to the glory of Zion, to the Davidic covenant, to the fidelity of God, to the Exodus and Conquest traditions, to God the Creator-Redeemer-King, and to Yahweh as the Divine Warrior. We see an interplay of many different motifs and emphases, which, when isolated, help us to understand better the OT as a whole and its bearing on the NT.

The Book of Psalms is God's prescription for a complacent church, because through it he reveals how great, wonderful, magnificent, wise, and utterly awe-inspiring he is (see Kapelrud)! If God's people before the Incarnation could have such a faith in the Lord, witnessing to his greatness and readiness to help, how much more should this be true among twentieth-century Christians! The Book of Psalms can revolutionize our devotional life, our family patterns, and the fellowship and the witness of the church of Jesus Christ.

b. *The Psalms as man's word to God and God's Word to man: The inspiration and authority of the Psalms*

The Book of Psalms is first and foremost God's Word to his people. We hear the voice of God in each individual psalm, through the many moods of the Psalms, and through the manifold themes of the Psalter. The purpose of the Book of Psalms is the same as that of any part of Scripture: the Psalms are "useful for teaching, rebuking, correcting and training in righteousness, so that the man of God may be thoroughly equipped for every good work" (2 Tim 3:16–17).

The Book of Psalms is nevertheless unique. In it God not only speaks to his people, he also encourages us to use the language of the Psalms in our individual and communal prayers and praise. By applying these ancient psalms to a new situation, the life of faith, hope, and love of the individual Christian, the Christian family, and the church may be greatly enhanced.

The Psalms encourage a dialogical relationship between God and his children. Though no OT book has been more important in the history of the church than the Book of Psalms, we are in danger of losing it, partly because of lack of use of the Psalms themselves (Achtemeier, "Preaching from the Psalms," p. 443) and partly because of lack of use of the skills required for understanding them. Our Lord expects his church to incorporate this portion of inspired Scripture into all aspects of Christian living and communication: teaching, preaching,[1] devotions, and living. The values of the Psalms to the individual and to the Christian community are many:

1. *Prayer* is man's communion with God. Prayers in the Psalms take the form of a complaint against the Lord. The individual or community laments the adversity, describes the evil in God's world, or petitions God to be true to his promises.[2] Faith cries out for reality, and lament functions as an expression of authenticity (Brueggemann, "The Costly Loss of Lament," pp. 57–71; Gerleman, pp. 33–49). Truly, the Psalms affect our whole being, or what Calvin (1:xxxvii) called "An Anatomy of all Parts of the Soul":

> for there is not an emotion of which any one can be conscious that is not here represented as in a mirror. . . the Holy Spirit has here drawn to the life all the griefs and sorrows, fears, doubt, hopes, cares, perplexities, in short, all the distracting emotions with which the minds of men are wont to be agitated.

2. *Praise* is man's longing for God and for others to be moved with the same desire for God. The acts of God in the past filled his children with longing for a renewal of his acts, thus intertwining history and eschatology. Israel praised God's acts in the past: Creation, Exodus, Conquest, life of David, victories, and restoration from the Exile. Israel praised the perfections of the Lord, his kingship, his revelation, and his covenant. But they longed for the fullness of redemption, especially when distressed. Any *token* of God's goodness in fulfilling his promise occasioned a greater hope of eschatological fulfillment. Hence praise bridged the two horizons of the past and the future.

3. The Psalms have a distinct place in Christian *liturgy*. Kirkpatrick commented, "From the earliest times the Psalter has been the Church's manual of Prayer and Praise in public worship" (p. xcviii). Perowne wrote, "No single Book of Scripture, not even of the New Testament, has, perhaps, ever taken such hold on the *heart* of Christendom" (1:22).

The above sentiments reflect the nineteenth century. Since that time much has changed. The Psalms are sung and read less. Hymns, gospel songs, and other readings have taken their place in public and private worship. Achtemeier laments, "We are in danger of losing the Psalter in our churches; indeed, many have already lost it, and so it is no accident that many people in our congregations do not know how to pray" ("Preaching from the Psalms," p. 443).

Though the Psalms were first and foremost used liturgically in the temple / synagogue and throughout the history of the church, we ask, with Hustad (p. 417), whether "it is possible that we have lost a significant form of expression that should be captured for the spiritual health of our worship." My answer is an unequivocal yes! The Spirit of God is still witnessing through the Psalms, encouraging the godly to open themselves up for individual and collective transformation, requisite for Christian maturity and the worship of the living God.

4. The Psalms inspire the believer with the *hope* of the kingdom of God: the new

[1] For their value in preaching, see the encouraging article by Achtemeier, "Preaching from the Psalms," pp. 437–49; see also Hull, pp. 451–56; McEachern, pp. 457–60; Wainwright, pp. 34–45.

[2] Brueggemann observes: "Given our privatistic inclination, we do not often think about public disasters as concerns for prayer life. . . . We have nearly lost our capacity to think *theologically* about public issues and public problems" (*Message of the Psalms*, p. 67).

state of justice, righteousness, and bliss.[3] The Psalms guide the Christian into a clearer structuring of worship as the "praise" of the God who has acted in creation, revelation, and redemption, and who will act decisively in establishing his kingdom on this earth. An openness in prayer and praise reveals a longing for God, growing out of a depth of devotional theology, that is, an experiential knowledge of God through his acts, revelation, and communion. How do we develop this "gusto," as C.S. Lewis put it (*Reflections on the Psalms*, p. 52), for the Lord? It may come through liturgical instruction, through a communal excitement with God in Jesus Christ, or through an experiential realization that with the coming of our Lord "kingship" has been democraticized, permitting the most lowly to have hope of exaltation, reward, and dominion. The *study* of the Psalms transforms our perspective on ourselves and on the world.

5. The Psalms reflect the *faith* experience of the "community" of God's people before the coming of Christ. Their expressions of frustration, impatience, anger, and joy reflect the tension between promise and alienation. One of the issues in the lament psalms lies in their definition as petition or complaint. They are both. The emphasis on prayer as petition may emphasize submission to the power of God. The stress on lament will bring out the struggle with God, as the psalmist wrestles with God's freedom, God's promises, and his own inability to understand God. In either case the psalmist cries out in faith for the fullness of redemption.

Now that our Lord has come, the Psalms continue to hold a great value for the Christian community as we, too, cry out for the day of our redemption. What is clearer to us is the NT affirmation that Jesus alone is the Messiah. He alone is the Mediator between God and man. He alone will bring in the fullness of redemption. This means that the richer understanding of the Psalms comes through an empathetic reading of the prayers of our brothers and sisters before Christ as we, too, await the messianic fullness of the kingdom of God and the new heaven and earth.

This use of the Psalms encourages their study as a testimony to the faith of God's people in their historical situation. Perowne wrote, "The Psalter has been, in the truest sense, the Prayer-book both of Jews and Christians" (1:22). Miller concluded, "The Psalter bridges the gap between then and now, the ancient world and the present world, probably better than any other book of the Bible" (*Interpreting the Psalms*, p. 22; see pp. 18–28).

6. God addresses both the *individual* and the *community*. At times it may seem that the Psalms should be limited to Israel in her national existence (community laments) or to the king (royal prayers) and that we may use the Psalms very selectively.

Old Testament scholars have been guilty of emphasizing Israel's collective experiences as a worshiping community to the virtual exclusion of the individual use. Fortunately, several scholars are reassessing the value for individuals. George W. Anderson concludes that the Psalms contain evidence of Israel's private devotional experience ("'Sicut Cervus'"), as individuals call on the Lord to deliver them from adversity, long for his presence, and are involved in dialogue with the Lord (Pss 73; 139).

The Psalms are also most valuable in personal counseling, as in "the therapy of the Psalms . . . (the) symbolic structure speaks to a level of consciousness not touched by textbook propositions. The Psalms speak to the heart and transform it" (Meyer, p. 30).

---

[3]Claus Westermann writes that "hope" in the OT has its root in the Psalms ("Das Hoffen im Alten Testament," in *Forschung am Alten Testament; gesammelte Studien* (Munich: Kaiser, 1964), p. 265.

7. The value of the Psalms lies in their *connection* between the OT and the NT.[4] True, strictly speaking, they belong to the OT and not to the NT, as the psalmists stand among the people of God who served him at the temple and knew only of the kingdom of David and his heirs. Yet the psalmists too longed for the day of redemption, whose light glows ever more brightly in Christ's incarnation, earthly ministry, passion at the cross, ascension to glory, and present rule.

We believe that Jesus is the Messiah of God, in whom all the promises of God are sealed, including his full and glorious messianic rule. This makes us different from the OT saints. But our Lord and his apostles loved the Psalms, which witness to the suffering and exaltation of man and especially to the Son of Man. The early Christians used the Psalms in explaining Jesus' ministry, resurrection, exaltation, and present rule.

From the early church we have inherited a new perspective of reading the Psalms in the light of Jesus' mission and work. Our Lord frequently quoted the Psalms and taught his disciples to interpret the Scriptures in the light of his coming (Luke 24:46–47). From the apostolic usage of the Psalms, it is abundantly evident that they figure prominently in the preaching and teaching of the early church. The apostles established Jesus' suffering (Pss 22; 35; 41; 55; 69; 109), his messianic claims (Pss 2; 72; 89; 110; 132), his priestly ministry (Ps 95), his being the Son of Man (Pss 8; 16; 40), and the coming judgment and redemption (Pss 18; 50; 68; 96–98; 102) on the Psalms (see appendix to Ps 89: The Messianic King).

In the commentary I look at these psalms as God's inspired word that was relevant in the historical context of God's ancient people and is still relevant. The exposition answers the question, What did the Word of God mean to the people who received it as his revelation? But as a Christian expositor, I also keep in mind what the Word means in light of Jesus' advent and in the hope of his coming. Thus all psalms, but especially the messianic psalms, relate to the first coming of Jesus Christ, to his present ministry at the right hand of God, and to his second coming.

c. *The study of the Book of Psalms*

The value of the Psalms increases when we approach them as the Word of God to man in the language of man; study them as literary masterpieces, inspired by the Spirit of God; value the literary forms; and view them as windows into Israel's communion with God. Wilson incisively comments that "the Psalter is a book to be *read* rather than to be *performed;* to be *meditated* over rather than to be *recited from*" (*Editing of the Hebrew Psalter,* p. 207). This leads us to the question of how we study the Psalms.

The books of Psalms, Job, Proverbs, Ecclesiastes, Song of Songs, and Lamentations make up the Poetical Books in the English OT. The limitation of the term "poetical" does not fit the Hebrew forms of poetry, in distinction to narrative and prose. Poetic forms are found throughout the OT, especially in the Prophets. Poetry is so close to prose that one of the issues in OT discussion is the characteristic distinction between prose and poetry (cf. Kugel).

The poetry of the Psalms as a medium of communication is no less adequate than propositions. Through the many artistic forms, the inspired poets communicate the dynamics in the relation between man, God, and the world. Instead of *analysis,* it

[4] See Rose, Old, Kistemaker, Mussner, Müller.

calls for *synthesis*. Instead of giving confidence in established rules of interpretation, the Psalms challenge the Western mind with a view of God so magnificent and so grand that the interpreter is often humbled and awestruck.

1) *Hebrew poetry*

a) *Rhyme, meter, and strophe*

Does Hebrew poetry have meter as in English rhyme? From the outset the definition of meter is important. Both the modern and the biblical artist follow poetic conventions, but the analysis of meter is of a theoretical nature. The student of the poetic work senses a rhythm, analyzes it, and compares it with other works. Meter is "the moulding of a line (or verse) to fit a preconceived shape made up of recurring sets" (Watson, *Classical Hebrew Poetry*, p. 88). It is an abstract way of analyzing poetry in any language, including the Hebrew Bible. However, it is not an easy tool for literary analysis, because no consensus exists on the meter of English poetry, of Akkadian texts (ibid., p. 94), of Ugaritic poetry (ibid., p. 97), and of the poetry of the Psalms.[5] The results are ambiguous and controversial.

The approach to meter varies with the "preconceived shape" of the recurring sets. It is possible to analyze the *stress* (accent) of the lines in the Hebrew text. Each stich (colon) has a set of primary stresses, whether there be 2, 3, or 4. The stress in a bi- or tri-colon may be symmetrical (2 + 2; 3 + 3 + 3; 4 + 4 + 4) or asymmetrical (4 + 4 + 3). For example, the stress in Psalm 10:1 is asymmetric and in v.2 symmetric:

v.1 *lāmāh YHWH taʿᵃmōḏ bᵉrāḥôq taʿlîm lᵉʿittôṯ baṣṣārāh* 4 + 3
(Why, O LORD, do you stand far off? Why do you hide in times of trouble?)

v.2 *bᵉgaʾᵃwaṯ rāšāʿ yiḏlaq ʿānî yittāp̄ᵉśû bimzimmôṯ zû ḥāšāḇû* 4 + 4
(In his arrogance the wicked man hunts down the weak, who are caught in the schemes he devises.)

Syllable counting (scanning) is another method of explaining the ancient meter. In this approach the literary critic counts the number of syllables, regardless of the vowel length, stress, or whether the syllable is open or closed. But the method forces him to reconstruct the meters.[6] Other explanations have been put forward, but all suffer from the problem of reconstructing the text based on a "preconceived shape" of Hebrew meter. The lack of consensus and further research have challenged this premise.[7]

b) *Parallelism*

Distinctive of Hebrew literature is *parallelism*, whether in narrative, prose, or poetry. Parallelism is especially significant in poetry. The classic categories hail from Lowthe (1753): synonymous, antithetic, and synthetic. Today we distinguish between synonymous, antithetic, synthetic, climactic, and emblematic parallelism. Parallelism

---

[5]For a survey of the various approaches, see Stuart, *Studies in Early Hebrew Meter*.

[6]Cross and Freedman, *Studies in Ancient Yahwistic Poetry;* D.N. Freedman, "Pottery, Poetry, and Prophecy," see his note 14 for further bibliography; id., "Acrostics and Metrics in Hebrew Poetry," in *Pottery, Poetry, and Prophecy: Studies in Early Hebrew Poetry* (Winona Lake: Eisenbrauns, 1980), pp. 51–76; Culley, "Metrical Analysis."

[7]Cf. Kugel, pp. 287–304; O'Connor. Craigie (*Psalms 1–50*, pp. 37–38) critically evaluates metrical analysis but in the end adopts it with some reservations. I agree with Tremper Longman, Jr., that a more fruitful approach to Hebrew poetry is that of syntactical parallelism ("A Critique of Two Recent Metrical Systems," *Biblica* 63 [1982]: 230–54). See the discussion on parallelism below and Watson, *Classical Hebrew Poetry*, pp. 114–59.

is a most fundamental Hebrew literary device. Lack of attention results in a multiplication of unrelated facts. The parts of a verse in the Psalms cohere by the principle of repetition, restatement, differentiation, or progression. (For a further treatment of parallelism and literary devices, see Appendix a: Literary Approach to the Psalms.)

Robert Alter argues in favor of "structures of intensification" as a literary approach to poetry.[8] He questions the assumption of synonymity as "no language has entirely true synonyms."[9] Alter goes beyond parallelism by observing the movement from line to line. The literary approach to the Psalms looks for any meaningful movement of "heightening or intensification . . . of focusing, specification, concretization, even what could be called dramatization."[10] According to Alter we can no longer restrict meaning to the narrow confines of the verse. In the "to-and-fro sweep" of the language, the poet moves from man to gaze at God.[11] Analysis of Hebrew poetry thus leads to a meaningful intersection of God and man.

> God exists before and beyond language, and is by no means the product or the captive of the poets' medium. But God manifests Himself to man in part through language. . . . Within the formal limits of a poem the poet can take advantage of the emphatic repetitions dictated by the particular prosodic system, the symmetries and antitheses and internal echoes intensified by a closed verbal structure, the fine intertwining of sound and image and reported act, the modulated shifts in grammatical voice and object of address, to give coherence and authority to his perceptions of the world. The psalmist's delight in the suppleness and serendipities of poetic form is not a distraction from the spiritual seriousness of the poems but his chief means of realizing his spiritual vision, and it is one source of the power these poems continue to have not only to excite our imaginations but also to engage our lives.[12]

2) *Literary analysis*

Literary analysis is a positive application of literary conventions. It is a *positive*, constructive art in that it calls for an attempt to hear the biblical psalm the way it was intended to be heard. All too often the grammatical-syntactic analysis fails in appreciating the *holistic* interpretation of the psalm. The holistic interpretation cannot but point beyond itself to our God and Redeemer, as Torrance put it:

> Since biblical statements indicate more than they can signify at any time, and more than we can express in our interpretation of them, they manifest a predictive quality, for they point above and beyond themselves to the inexhaustible Truth of God. A faithful interpretation of biblical statements, therefore, will not cut short their transcendent reference but will seek to allow their implications to disclose themselves in the light of that reference.[13]

---

[8]*Art of Biblical Poetry*, p. 13; id., "The Psalms-Beauty Heightened Through Poetic Structure," *Bible Review* 2 (1986): 28–41.

[9]*Art of Biblical Poetry*, p. 13.

[10]Ibid., p. 19. Alter proposes various forms of intensification, depending on the distinctive poetics of the psalm or poetic work (p. 84).

[11]Ibid., p. 75.

[12]Ibid., pp. 135–36.

[13]Thomas F. Torrance, *Reality and Evangelical Theology* (Philadelphia: Westminster, 1982), p. 144.

The structure of the Psalms treats the literary units or blocks, called strophes, as carriers of the movement within a psalm. The analysis of strophes has undergone significant refinement in the last fifty years, but I agree with Bratcher that there is little agreement among modern versions and commentators.

The outlines proposed with each chapter are functional. For example, in Psalm 1 we follow this outline:

A. The Discriminating Way of the Godly (vv.1–2)
  B. The Future of the Godly (v.3)
  B′. The Future of the Wicked (vv.4–5)
A′. The Discriminating Way of God (v.6)

This psalm may be read in two ways: sequentially from v.1 through v.6, by strophe (vv.1–2, 3, 4–5, 6), and by literary relationship (AA′ and BB′). The latter manner of reading the psalm allows the reader to sense the balance or closure of the chapter as the psalmist moves from A to A′. The movement may be symmetric (Ps 1) or asymmetric, as in the case of Psalm 3:

A. Lament Over the Enemies (vv.1–2)
  B. Prayer to the Lord (vv.3–4)
    C. Trust in the Lord (vv.5–6)
  B′. Prayer for Deliverance (v.7)
A′. Hope in the Lord (v.8)

Here the focus or emphasis lies in C, as its dissonance creates an element of surprise. The "center" or pivot of the psalm is part of a concentric structure to which the beginning strophes move and on which the later strophes build, as in Psalm 71:

A. Prayer of Confidence (vv.1–4)
  B. Affirmation of Confidence (vv.5–8)
    C. Prayer in Old Age (vv.9–13)
    C′. Hope in Old Age (vv.14–18)
  B′. Affirmation of Confidence (vv.19–21)
A′. Thanksgiving With Confidence (vv.22–24)

Psalm 44 exemplifies the steplike, or ziggurat, movement:

A. God's Past Acts of Deliverance (vv.1–3)
  B. Confidence in God (vv.4–8)
    C. Suffering and Disgrace (vv.9–16)
      D. Claim of Innocence (vv.17–22)
        E. Prayer for Deliverance (vv.23–26)

The various structures are functional devices by which the Western reader can more readily enter into the Hebraic structures of poetry. God has chosen the medium of language in communicating himself and in permitting man to commune with him. The Psalms provide us with God's Word in aesthetic form, as Alter (*Art of Biblical Poetry*, p. 136) observes,

> The psalmist's delight in the suppleness and serendipities of poetic form is not a distraction from the spiritual seriousness of the poems but his chief means of realizing spiritual vision, and it is one source of the power these poems continue to have not only to excite our imaginations but also to engage our lives.

In writing this commentary I have kept in mind the needs of the contemporary reader and the necessity of permitting the biblical ways of poetic expression to be a vehicle of the Spirit to make an impact on our structures of thinking about God, our world, and ourselves, as Torrance writes:

> Nevertheless there are structures of biblical thought and speech found in the Old Testament which have permanent value, both for the New Testament and for the Christian Church. That is why the Church is built upon the foundation not only of the apostles but of the prophets, and in that order, for the Old Testament Scriptures are now assumed within the orbit of the New Testament, for they provide the New Testament revelation with the basic structures which it used in the articulation of the Gospel, although the structures it derived from Israel, were taken up and transformed in Christ.[14]

Patrick D. Miller speaks of an "openness to varieties of application and actualization" on the basis that the language of the Psalms is stylized and metaphorical.[15] In the Psalms three dimensions must be kept together: God-self-enemy.[16] The dynamic element of the psalm lies in its openness, even its ambiguity (Miller, *Interpreting the Psalms,* pp. 43–46). The prayers and praise evoke a response of God's people in a new and concrete historical situation, whether they begin with lament and end on praise or have only ground for praise.[17]

2. Types of Psalms

In the last century OT scholarship has made an attempt at describing the literary forms of the Psalms. Some progress has been made in the investigation of the literary "form" (or "genre"). This discipline is called "form criticism"; as a branch of literary investigation, it has yielded some significant results.

The genius behind form criticism was Hermann Gunkel (1862–1932). He concluded that there were five major literary categories: hymns, community laments, thanksgiving songs of the individual, spiritual laments of the individual, and poems of mixed types (enthronement psalms, victory songs, processional hymns, Zion songs, enthronement songs).[18] Each genre was explained in relation to Israel's worship, hence the term *Sitz-im-Leben* ("original life-situation"; Gunkel, *The Psalms,* pp. 10–25). Gunkel's basic approach has been modified by more recent developments in psalm research, but scholars are still indebted to Gunkel's creative genius.

One of these developments came from Sigmund Mowinckel (1884–1965) with his explanation of how the Psalms had adapted to Israel's liturgical calendar, basing his results on the Babylonian New Year Festival (see Saebø). In the *Psalms in Israel's Worship,* Mowinckel explains the connection between cult, ritual, and psalm types.[19] Out of concern for ritual and comparative religious studies, he sacrificed the principle

---

[14]Thomas F. Torrance, *The Mediation of Christ* (Grand Rapids: Eerdmans, 1984), p. 27.

[15]"Trouble and Woe," p. 35. On p. 42 he writes, "All of this stereotypical language, however, is now placed in a context that serves to give content and reference to the cliches."

[16]See the example of Hannah as portrayed by Miller in "Trouble and Woe," pp. 39–40. Claus Westermann further delineates the stylization of the enemy in *Praise and Lament in the Psalms,* pp. 188–94.

[17]On the resonance between lament and human story, see Patrick D. Miller, Jr., "Interpreting the Biblical Laments" in *Interpreting the Psalms,* pp. 48–63.

[18]Gunkel, *The Psalms;* H. Gunkel and Joachim Begrich, *Einleitung in die Psalmen* (Göttingen: Vandenhoeck & Ruprecht, 1933). For a summary, see Westermann, *The Praise of God,* pp. 16–17; Gerstenberger, "Psalms," pp. 179–83.

[19]"Tradition and Worship: The Role of the Cult in Tradition Formation and Transmission," pp. 101–24.

of diversity, assuming that Israel's religious experience was no different than that of her neighbors. Many approaches to the Psalms are variations of Mowinckel's thesis.[20]

Form criticism, however, has a limited value, as Gerstenberger concludes, "Form critical psalm research is still extremely young and promises to be a very exciting pursuit in the decades to come" ("Psalms," p. 223; id., *Der bittende Mensch*). In the commentary on the Psalms, we shall refer to the literary "form" of each psalm as it more or less corresponds to the formal features of a particular genre. (For a treatment of the literary genres, see Appendix b: Literary Genre.)

Certain cautions, however, are in order. First, rigidity in classification does not permit the literary traditions that may lie behind the psalm to come to their fullest expression. The psalmists often used existing material and incorporated it so well into a new situation that the *creative* end result stands on its own. Second, the connection between literary form and original life-situation is far from clear. This is particularly true when a connection is made between a psalm and a cultic or liturgical situation[21] or between the form and the date (see Hoffman).

Gerstenberger has argued against the cultic interpretation in favor of a more domestic, individual expression of Israelite piety ("Psalms"; id., *Der bittende Mensch*). Childs (IOTS, pp. 508–13) has questioned the critical approach to the Psalms as imposing categories and classifications that are foreign to the canonical shaping of the Psalms. Instead he concludes that the present order is shaped by the placing of Psalm 1 with its emphasis on *Torah* ("law"). The "praise" of Israel, that is, the word of man to God, is the Word of God.[22] Hereby the focus shifts from an anthropological or cultic interest to a *theocentric understanding* (Childs, IOTS, p. 514). Further, the Psalms have an *eschatological orientation*, which Childs defines as

> the final form of the Psalter [that] is highly eschatological in nature. It looks toward to [*sic*] the future and passionately yearns for its arrival. . . . The perspective of Israel's worship in the psalter is eschatologically oriented. . . . When the New Testament heard in the psalms eschatological notes, its writers were standing in the context of the Jewish canon in which the community of faith worshipped and waited. (ibid., p. 518)

Moreover, the individual and the corporate are fused together in the Psalms. Hence the use of the Psalms need not be limited to liturgical purposes; both the devotional and liturgical use of the Psalms have a place as does the corporate and individual use (ibid., pp. 519–20, 522).

Similarly, but distinctively, Brueggemann has proposed a pastorally oriented approach to the Psalms. Building on Westermann's polar lament and praise motifs, Brueggemann approaches the Psalms conscientiously from a postcritical perspective.[23] He categorizes the Psalms as psalms of *orientation* (creation, Torah, wisdom,

---

[20] Namely those of Schmidt, Delekat, and Beyerlin; see Brueggemann, "From Hurt to Joy," p. 11. See also Eaton, "The Psalms and Israelite Worship."

[21] As is the case with Johnson, *Cultic Prophet and Israel's Psalmody*. Haran rightly questions the association between prayer, oracle, and cult in "Cult and Prayer."

[22] Childs, IOTS, pp. 513–15; Mays concludes that the Torah psalms gave a new setting to the use of the Psalms in praise and in prayer.

[23] Brueggemann defines postcritical as a supportive interaction of the scholarly and devotional (*Message of the Psalms*, pp. 16–23). This comes close to Childs's understanding of "canonical approach" (IOTS, pp. 522–23).

retribution, and well-being), *disorientation* (personal and communal lament), and a *new orientation* (individual and communal thanksgiving, royal/enthronement, confidence, and hymns of praise).

Miller coins the term "reinterpretation" as a method of studying how earlier Psalms were reinterpreted in a new context. The Psalms hence cannot be limited to a certain original situation, as its canonical function and meaning may vary from period to period in the progress of redemption.[24]

Greenberg further has set us free from linking the Psalms too exclusively to the temple or to a fixation of genres. In *Biblical Prose Prayer,* he looks at the Psalms as an expression of democratization of religion. Democratization signifies the freeing of the lay Israelite from the bondage of cult, as Greenberg writes, "Constant familiar intercourse with God, unmediated by priests or other ritual expert could have only strengthened the egalitarian tendency . . . that was rooted in Israel's self-conception" (p. 52).

The formal categories are useful as literary designations. I agree with Craigie that the elements of form may not be entirely convincing, but I am even less convinced by the approach he designates as "the recognition of the necessity of the *functional* study of the psalms" (*Psalms 1–50,* p. 47). In approaching the Psalms I am much less inclined to look for the "functional" element, i.e., how the psalm functioned in ancient Israel. I am also skeptical of understanding the Psalms in the light of Ugaritic studies.[25]

In my opinion the expositor is at risk when he explains the text in the context of historical referentiality, liturgy, or cultic *Sitz-im-Leben.*[26]

The language of the Psalms is especially conducive to literary analysis. Instead of searching for the *Sitz-im-Leben,*[27] the interpreter must pay attention to the stylized language, repetitions, and variety of traditions that come together in the Psalms as the prayer book of ancient Israel (see Haran, "Cult and Prayer").

3. God, the Psalmist, and the World

The variety of the themes and moods of the Psalms reflect the depth of Yahweh's revelation to Israel. God is one, but in his unity he loves diversity. The Psalms celebrate the variety in God's creation and in his acts of redemption.[28] They do this in lament, praise, and didactic ways. The Book of Psalms, while not a textbook on OT

[24] *Interpreting the Psalms,* pp. 11–13; Becker, *Israel deutet seine Psalmen;* id., *Wege der Psalmenexegese.*

[25] Dahood's three-volume commentary on the Psalms is a significant contribution of Ugaritica to exegetica, but he has read too much into the psalm material. For a summary of his approach, see his "Hebrew Poetry," IDB supplement, pp. 669–72. For an evaluation, see Smick, "Ugaritic and the Theology of the Psalms," pp. 104–16; and Loretz. K. Luke ("Canaanite Psalms," *Indian Journal of Theology* [1977]: 44–54) has renewed a call to use the Amarna materials for psalm research, but this should be done with great caution in my opinion. See the methodological considerations of Talmon.

[26] Hermann Gunkel coined the phrase *Sitz-im-Leben* to refer to the social context in which a literary form arose. Already in 1950 Nic. H. Ridderbos expressed his reservations with the cultic interpretations of the Psalms in his inaugural lecture, entitled *Psalmen en Cultus;* cf. George W. Anderson, "Enemies and Evildoers."

[27] See the critique by Buss, "The Idea of *Sitz-im-Leben.*" Tate rightly observes that the present situation of psalm study is "rather inchoate" (p. 372).

[28] See the variety of themes touched on by Bonhoeffer (creation, law, holy history, the Messiah, church, life, suffering, guilt, the enemies, the end, petition for the Spirit of life, and the blessing of morning prayer). For a more technical treatment, see Kraus, *Theologie des Psalmen.*

theology or a legal code, is a book to be meditated on. C.S. Lewis, who appears to have deeply studied and loved the Psalms, laments how strange the world of the Psalms appears to the twentieth-century Westerner. He writes:

> In most moods the spirit of the Psalms feels to me more alien than that of the oldest Greek literature. . . . To most of us, perhaps to all of us at most times (unless we are either very uneducated or very holy or, as might be, both) the civilization that descends from Greece and Rome is closer, more congenial, than what we inherit from ancient Israel.[29]

Through the process of meditation and individual and communal celebration, the people of God may become rooted in salvation history.

a. *The names of God*

The most prevalent designation of deity in the Psalms is "the LORD" (*Yahweh,* a little less than 700 times; of which *Yah,* 43 times), followed by God (*Elohim,* 365 times; *El,* 77 times; *Eloah,* only in 50:23), the Lord (*Adonai,* 54 times), Most High (*Elyon,* 22 times; see appendix to Ps 9), Most High (*Shaddai,* only in 68:14; 91:1), Lord Almighty ("Lord of Hosts," Yahweh *Sabaoth,* 15 times; see appendix to Ps 24), and many other names and titles.

The practice of rendering the name of the Lord, Yahweh, by a title ("the LORD") keeps us from sensing the richness of Israel's religious experience and practice. The title lacks the emotive quality affected by the relationship between God and his people. The Lord had revealed his *name* (YHWH or Yahweh) to Israel. They knew not only that God has a name but also the pronunciation of the name: the four sacred letters—*YHWH* (tetragrammaton). Though we are not sure of the precise pronunciation, we accept a common form of pronouncing them as *Yahweh.* This covenant name was holy (Exod 20:7) but also precious. An example of the love of Yahweh is found in Psalm 7:17, where the psalmist, as on so many occasions, uses several references to his beloved God: "I will give thanks to the LORD [Yahweh] because of his righteousness and will sing praise to the name of the LORD [Yahweh] Most High [Elyon]."

> See further the appendixes after Psalms 3: Yahweh Is My God; 7: The Name of Yahweh; 9: Yahweh Is El Elyon; 22: Yahweh Is El; 24: Lord Sabaoth; 98: Yahweh Is the Divine Warrior.

b. *The perfections of God*

The perfections of Yahweh were given to Israel by revelation through Moses. To Moses he revealed his goodness and his glory: "Then the LORD came down in the cloud and stood there with him and proclaimed his name, the LORD. . . . proclaiming, 'The LORD the LORD, the compassionate and gracious God, slow to anger, abounding in love and faithfulness, maintaining love to thousands, and forgiving wickedness, rebellion and sin. Yet he does not leave the guilty unpunished; he punishes the children and their children for the sin of the fathers to the third and fourth generation"

---

[29]*Christian Reflections,* p. 115; see his *Reflections on the Psalms.*

(Exod 34:5–7).[30] The psalms celebrate the constancy of Yahweh's perfections toward Israel (86:15; 103:8; 111:4; 116:5; 145:8).

See the appendix to Psalm 25: The Perfections of Yahweh.

c. *The acts of God*

The perfections of God are always to be correlated with his acts. The people of God did not have a catechism or confessional statement; but if they were to be asked for their *credo* ("I believe"), we could be sure that it would include a recitation of the acts of God in creation and in redemption. The Western tendency to abstract God from his creation is absent in the Psalms, as is any effort to define the Lord in terms of the familiar *omnis* (omnipresent, omnipotent, et al.). God reveals his glory in his self-revelation (perfections) and his acts.

Creation and redemption are held together in constant tension. This tension lies in the activity of God: past and future; national and universal; groaning of creation and hope in the redemption of creation. For Israel the celebration of the acts of God included both "re-presentation" and proclamation (Westermann, *Praise and Lament in the Psalms*, pp. 214–49). Each event was a part of the story of redemption. As Westermann puts it, "History cannot be made to fit into a single moment or into a single event. History always involves a whole range of courses of events; it is never simply an event" (ibid., p. 226).

See the appendixes to Psalms 46: Zion Theology; 132: The Ark of the Covenant and the Temple: Symbols of Yahweh's Presence and Rule.

The people of God also pray for the blessing of Zion (128:5). The glory, splendor, and prosperity of the people of God know no limits; Yahweh himself as their Protector, King, and Warrior is their Creator-Redeemer: "May the LORD, the Maker of heaven and earth, bless you from Zion" (134:3).

See the appendix to Psalm 78: The Mighty Acts of Yahweh; also see the appendixes to Psalms 25: The Perfections of Yahweh; 85: Anger in the Psalms; 98: Yahweh Is the Divine Warrior; 103: Sin and Forgiveness; 119: Yahweh Is My Redeemer; 122: The Praise of Yahweh; 140: the Poor and Oppressed.

d. *The hope of redemption and righteousness*

Redemption is both spiritual and physical. God's people long for his forgiveness and his presence. They also pray for redemption from the afflictions of this body: sickness, death, adversity, famine, persecution, and injustice.

The hope of the redeemed lies in the establishment of God's righteous rule on earth. They long for the full redemption of creation, which includes the body. Redemption is both spiritual and material, because man is not man without his body. In other words, the psalmists have a keen sense of the importance of enjoying God in time and space, the categories of human existence. They await God's demonstration of his sovereignty to all mankind.

The beauty of hope in the Psalms lies in keeping the tension between the present world and the anticipation of the enjoyment of the *visio Dei* together with the *visio*

---

[30]See commentary on Exodus, EBC, 2:486; see also Dentan.

mundi: the beatific vision of God in relation with a renewal of creation. They believe that the Lord will judge evil and reward the godly and that in the end the godly will enjoy the fullness of his splendor in the body. Hence the body is not something to be shed readily but is the instrument of the praise of God!

See further the appendixes to Psalms 85: Anger in the Psalms; 88: Sheol-Grave-Death in the Psalms.

e. *The kingdom of God*

The Psalms celebrate God's present rule over all creation. Yahweh is the Great King over the nations, and God's people have the privilege of petitioning their King on their behalf. He rules in justice and righteousness. He lavishes his bounty on all creation, though it is in rebellion against the Great King. He sustains and governs in accordance with the freedom of his will. The Great King rules especially in and through his chosen people, Israel. They are his instruments of establishing his kingdom on earth. More than that, he has chosen the dynasty of David to lead his people into victory.

Zion is the intersection of space and time, time and eternity, man and God. "Zion" in the Psalms refers to the sweet communion of God and his people. He is present with the citizens of his kingdom in blessing and protection. The kingdom of God was present in Israel, giving God's people the assurance that the Lord, like a king, was with them (cf. Ps 46).

Yet the people also longed for the fullness of God's presence: the restoration of Zion. The restoration of the Jews after the Exile was a *real* expression of his kingdom, as they experienced once again the mighty arm of the Lord: "When the LORD brought back the captives to Zion, / we were like men who dreamed" (126:1; cf. 137:1, 3).

See the appendixes to Psalms 5: Yahweh Is King; 46: Zion Theology; 89: The Messianic King; 98: Yahweh Is the Divine Warrior; 119: Yahweh Is My Redeemer; 132: The Ark of the Covenant and the Temple: Symbols of Yahweh's Presence and Rule. See above for a discussion on the place of imprecations in the Psalms.

f. *The Davidic Messiah*

The presence of the Warrior-King among his people is a comfort to those who trust in him. However, since the days of David, Yahweh has revealed the fact that trust in him is concomitant with trust in his appointed *vassal,* the Davidic king (Pss 2; 72; 89; 132). The Davidic king is his *instrument* of extending his kingdom to all the earth: "The LORD will extend your mighty scepter from Zion; / you will rule in the midst of your enemies" (110:2).

Willis Judson Beecher rightly distinguished between "promise" and "prediction," as the Psalms celebrate the promises of God and anticipate the establishment of the messianic kingdom in its fullness, while enjoying the present stage of the messianic kingdom under the then-reigning Davidic king. Prediction restricts the Psalms to a one-time fulfillment. Hence Beecher concludes that the Psalms, together with the Prophets, point to the promises of God that are eternally valid, as they have their validity in Jesus Christ:

> It is Christ to whom the promise points forward. It is on account of its containing Christ that the promise is cited with so much reiteration, and not for anything it contains apart from Christ. The promise passages connect themselves with everything that is essential in Christian doctrine. They outline the nature and the person of Christ.[31]

See the appendix to Psalm 89: The Messianic King.

g. *Wisdom from above*

The Lord places on the citizens of Zion responsibilities commensurate with their privileges. Psalm 133 enjoins them to uphold unanimity and brotherly love, comparing it to dew from Mount Hermon (v.3):

> It is as if the dew of Hermon
> were falling on Mount Zion.
> For there the LORD bestows his blessing,
> even life forevermore.

The community of the righteous individually and corporately responds wisely to the revelation of God. The righteous often are reviled and persecuted for his name's sake, but they persist in living a life style in obedience to his revelation. They live in the presence of God, seek his presence passionately, suffer grievously, but await his redemption so that others may hear their praises as a witness to the reality of the God who is! In their worship they sing, dance, make loud noise, and use all kinds of instruments, intoxicated by the love of God for his people.

See appendixes to Psalms 1: The Ways of Wisdom and Folly; 19: The Word of God; 122: The Praise of Yahweh; 150: Musical Instruments.

Thus the Psalter opens up dimensions of faith, hope, and love. The people of God before the Incarnation invite us to celebrate, praise, cry, pray, lament, and hope for justice, righteousness, and the kingdom of God and his Messiah. Each psalm is a window that opens up to the faith of Israel and invites us to walk together with the saints before us on the way of God that leads to the establishment of his kingdom on earth.

4. Composition

The Psalms usually carry a heading.[32] The heading or superscription may contain any or all of the following categories of information: identification with a person, association with a historical event, musical and liturgical details, and the type or genre of the psalm.

The practice of adding information to a document or a song was common in the ancient Near East. Scribal practice encouraged the addition of a *colophon* (a note at the end of the piece) containing a summary of the contents, the identity of the author

---

[31] *The Prophets and the Promise*, reprint ed. (Grand Rapids: Baker, 1963), p. 193.

[32] As many as 116 psalms in the MT carry a superscription. The psalms without a superscription have been called "Orphan Psalms": 1; 2; 10; 33; 43; 71; 91; 93–97; 99; 104–7; 111–19; 135–37; 146–50. Of these, most occur in Books III and IV.

or scribe, and at times some musical notation (Gevaryahu). The superscriptions in the Psalms may be interpreted as a colophon, but this does not solve the problem of authenticity. At issue is the time of composition and the authenticity of the information. Critical scholars pay little attention to the titles, assuming that they are later midrashic additions. They point to the variations in the headings between the MT and the LXX. It is true that the headings in the LXX vary both in content and number. One extreme form is the omission of the headings in the NEB. But the issues raised by the superscriptions should not keep us from taking them seriously (Childs, "Psalm Titles and Midrashic Exegesis"; Slomovic).

The study of the headings in the LXX reveals to what extent the superscriptions create problems in the study of the Psalms. First, the translators no longer understood the ancient titles. Second, the LXX has different headings from the MT. It adds "of David" to psalms that do not contain this phrase in the MT (33, 43, 71, 91, 93–99, 104, 137) but deletes "of David" in the superscription of Psalms 122 and 124. It is highly probable that the different liturgical use of the Psalms in Judah and in the Diaspora may account for the variety in the MT and LXX. This matter needs further exploration.

The LXX does not shed direct light on the issue of authenticity of the superscriptions. Essential to the matter of authenticity is the exegetical issue of the meaning of the preposition "of" in the headings, e.g., A Psalm *of* David. The preposition raises two concerns: the ambiguity of meaning and the ambiguity of use. First, the *meaning* of the preposition *l*^{e} is largely determinative. It may be translated in a variety of ways: "to," "of," "concerning," "associated with," or "dedicated to." It is clear that the translation "of David" is significantly different from the rendering "concerning David." Second, the *use* in the Psalter is equally ambiguous. Craigie (*Psalms 1–50*, p. 34) suggests several possible categories of use: individual, group, occasion, or dedication. Let us look at several examples from the NIV:

Psalm 4:	For [*l*^{e}] the director of music. With stringed instruments. A psalm of [*l*^{e}] David.
Psalm 30:	A psalm. A song. For the dedication of the temple. Of [*l*^{e}] David.
Psalm 42:	For the director of music. A *maśkîl* of [*l*^{e}] the Sons of Korah.
Psalm 92:	A psalm. A song. For [*l*^{e}] the Sabbath day.
Psalm 102:	A prayer of [*l*^{e}] an afflicted man. When he is faint and pours out his lament before the LORD.

From these examples it is clear that the ambiguity of the Hebrew particle *l*^{e} ("for" and "of") and its use in the superscriptions raise serious questions regarding the place of the headings in interpretation and their dating. After all, it does make quite a difference if we translate *l*^{e} in our sample as follows:

Psalm 4:	For [*l*^{e}] the director of music. With stringed instruments. A psalm concerning [*l*^{e}] David.
Psalm 30:	A psalm. A song. For the dedication of the temple. Dedicated to [*l*^{e}] David.
Psalm 42:	For the director of music. A *maśkîl* associated with [*l*^{e}] the sons of Korah.
Psalm 92:	A psalm. A song. To be used on [*l*^{e}] the Sabbath day.
Psalm 102:	A prayer for the use of [*l*^{e}] an afflicted man. When he is faint and pours out his lament before the LORD.

Bruce holds that the superscriptions reflect an ancient interpretation, giving a setting to the psalms (p. 52). Craigie assumes that most psalms are anonymous and that only a few may be associated with a Davidic authorship (*Psalms 1–50*, p. 35). The traditional importance of David in his being associated with temple music has received recent confirmation in the study by Sarna. He explains (p. 295) that the variety in superscriptions reflects different "guild" or familial traditions. With the reforms under Josiah and especially after the Exile, the temple worship became centralized and the use of the Psalms developed separately—but not completely independently—from the sacrificial system at the temple. The place of the Psalms in liturgy came to its own after the destruction of the temple (587 B.C.).

Sarna's thesis clarifies the differences and the overlaps in the material of the Book of Psalms. Though reconstruction is almost impossible, each psalm witnesses to its having once been a part of a smaller collection that served God's people in their worship. At the same time each psalm now incorporated in the canonical Psalter perpetuates the prayer and praise of God in new contexts: postexilic Judaism, Judaism at the time of our Lord, and Christianity.

For a brief discussion of the technical words and phrases, see Appendix c: Psalm titles.

5. Structure

The Book of Psalms (*tehillîm*) is the first book of the Writings in the Hebrew Bible and one of the poetical books in the English Bible. At the time of our Lord, people believed that David was the author by the principle of generalization from the many psalms attributed to him (Luke 20:42). The primacy of Psalms in the Writings functioned to mark the division as a whole: the Psalms, i.e., the Writings (cf. Luke 24:44). The English designation "psalm" comes from the Latin *Psalmi* and the Greek *psalmoi* ("songs sung with musical accompaniment"), a translation of the Hebrew *mizmôr* ("a song accompanied by musical instruments"). The Hebrew title (*tehillîm*) signifies the contents of the book: "songs of praise."

The psalms were gathered in separate collections that were eventually brought together into one book under the guidance of the Holy Spirit. Several collections arose over the centuries: smaller ones, such as the psalms associated with the sons of Korah (42–49; 84–85; 87–88), with Asaph (50; 73–83), the second Davidic psalter (51–71), and the Hallelujah psalms (146–50).[33] The larger collections consisted of the psalms associated with David (3–41; cf. 72:20) and the Elohistic psalter (42–83)[34]—itself a collection of smaller collections: the Korahite (42–49) and Davidic (51–71) psalms; the Asaphite psalter (73–83); and the Songs of Ascent (120–34). The process of collection began with smaller collections, to which individual psalms or other collections were added, resulting in a final collection of 150 psalms.[35]

[33] Pierre Auffret argues persuasively for additional collections (Pss 15–24; 135–38) in *La Sagesse dans les Psaumes* (Fribourg: Editions Universitaires, 1982), pp. 407–549.

[34] The *Elohistic Psalter* (Pss 42–83) gets its name from the frequent use of Elohim (204 times) in relation to Yahweh (46 times). Compare this with the first book (Pss 1–41)—Yahweh (272 times) and Elohim (15 times)—and with Psalms 84–150: Yahweh (362 times) and Elohim (13 times).

[35] According to Westermann (*Praise and Lament*, pp. 250–58), the original Psalter may have consisted of Psalms 1–119.

The collection of 150 psalms[36] reflects an external structure, as the Psalms are divided into five "books," of unequal length, paralleling the Five Books of Moses:[37]

Book I: Psalms 1–41; Book II: Psalms 42–72; Book III: Psalms 73–89; Book IV: Psalms 90–106; and Book V: Psalms 107–150.

Each division ends with a doxological refrain (cf. 41:13; 72:18–19; 89:52; 106:48; 150).

The versification of the Psalms presents a small problem. The MT includes the superscription as part of the psalm, beginning the numbering of the verses with the heading. The tradition of the EVV treats the heading separately, sets it off in a different print, and begins the numbering with the text of the psalm. This creates a difference in numbering of one to two verses in most psalms. In this commentary we shall follow the English numbering.

The process of collection may explain duplication, division, and organization. *Duplication* occurs in several psalms (Zimmerli). For example, compare Psalms 14 and 53; 40:13–17 and 70:1–5; 57:7–11 and 108:1–5; 60:5–12 and 108:6–13.[38] *Division* is found in the case of several psalms that reveal some affinity with one another: Psalms 42 and 43.[39] Examples of *organizing* principles are the use of Elohim in preference to the tetragrammaton in the Elohistic Psalter and the linkage of psalms that contain the same or identical words (*Stichwörter*) or motifs (cf. Pss 48–50). A.A. Anderson attempts to explain the process of organization from small units to small collections, from small collections to larger collections, to the final result of the Book of Psalms, beginning with Psalm 1 as an introduction and Psalm 150 as a finale.[40]

6. Appendixes

a. *Literary approach to the Psalms*

Hebrew poetry powerfully uses many literary devices and reveals a strong adherence to literary traditions (forms),[41] with endless variation. Dissonance, variation, and freedom of "playing" with the conventions are as important as adherence to the conventions. The inspired "artist" creates an effect or calls attention to a thought

[36]The LXX has another psalm, Psalm 151. However, it is marked as "outside the number." At Qumran additional psalms not included in the MT, including a Hebrew copy of the LXX Psalm 151, were found. Cf. Sanders, *The Psalms Scroll of Qumran Cave 11;* id., "Cave 11 Surprises." See J. Bjørnar Storfjell, "The Chiastic Structure of Psalm 151," *Andrews University Seminary Studies* 25 (1987): 97–106; Wilson, *Editing of the Hebrew Psalter*, pp. 33–38; Heinz-Josef Fabry.

[37]In the Midrash on the Psalms, the rabbis explain, "Moses gave the Israelites the five books of the *Torah*, and coordinate therewith David gave them the books of the Psalms" (1:1).

[38]A similar phenomenon also occurred in the LXX (the Greek translation). The LXX combines Psalms 9 and 10 and Psalms 114 and 115 but divides 116 (LXX 114–15) and 147 (LXX 146–47). Its numbering consequently varies in Psalms 9–147.

[39]Many also suggest Psalms 9 and 10.

[40]*Psalms*, 1:26–28; see also Westermann, *Praise and Lament in the Psalms*, pp. 250–58; the most prodigious attempt is that of Wilson. He concludes that the breaks in the Psalms were editorially introduced and that different binding techniques exist in Books I–III and IV–V ("Evidence of Editorial Divisions"; id., *Editing of the Hebrew Psalter).*

[41]Freedman affirms that "poetry is the traditional means of expressing and transmitting religious experience" ("Pottery, Poetry, and Prophecy," p. 20). But the issue of the nature of that transmission is as yet unresolved. Culley's approach to oral formulaic language (*Oral Formulaic Language*) has been severely criticized by Watters (pp. 6–19).

or motif (Goldingay, "Repetition and Variation in the Psalms"). Alter (*Art of Biblical Poetry*, p. 205) defines "poetry" as follows:

> Poetry is quintessentially the mode of expression in which the surface is the depth, so that through careful scrutiny of the configurations of the surface—the articulation of the line, the movement from line to poem, the imagery, the arabesques of syntax and grammar, the design of the poem as a whole—we come to apprehend more fully the depth of the poem's meaning.

We shall now consider the basic concept of each form of parallelism.

1) *Parallelism*

a) *Synonymous*

In synonymous (identical) parallelism the members of a line express the same basic idea in several different ways (Boling). For example, Psalm 1:1:

Blessed is the man
who does not walk in the counsel of the wicked
or stand in the way of sinners
or sit in the seat of mockers.

Emblematic parallelism is a form of synonymous parallelism in which one member of the line contains a figurative (metaphor or simile) development of the same thought. For example,

44:19 But you crushed us and made us a haunt for jackals
and covered us over with deep darkness.

44:22 Yet for your sake we face death all day long;
we are considered as sheep to be slaughtered.

b) *Antithetic*

In antithetic parallelism the members of the line are set in contrast to one another. For example:

44:3 It was not by their sword that they won the land,
nor did their arm bring them victory;
it was your right hand, your arm,
and the light of your face, for you loved them.

c) *Synthetic (formal)*

In synthetic parallelism the members of a line complement one another harmoniously to create the desired effect.

12:1

Help,	LORD,	for are no more	the godly
A	B	C	D

have vanished	the faithful	from among men.
C′	D′	E

In this case each colon contains similarities (CC′; DD′) and each contributes one or more unique elements to the whole (A, B, E).

Climactic (step or chain) parallelism is a further development of synthetic parallelism. Not only do the members of the line harmonize, they develop the thought colon upon colon. The finest example of this type is Psalm 44 (see commentary), because each strophe builds on the other to form a grand structure as a whole. This may also be called a ziggurat structure.[42] For example, Psalm 29:3–9:

The voice of the LORD is over the waters;
the God of glory thunders,
the LORD thunders over the mighty waters.
The voice of the LORD is powerful;
the voice of the LORD is majestic.
The voice of the LORD breaks the cedars;
the LORD breaks in pieces the cedars of Lebanon.
He makes Lebanon skip like a calf, Sirion like a young wild ox.
The voice of the LORD strikes with flashes of lightning.
The voice of the LORD shakes the desert;
the LORD shakes the Desert of Kadesh.
The voice of the LORD twists the oaks and strips the forests bare.

d) *Miscellaneous*

Internal parallelism is a kind of parallelism found within a verse, when treated in isolation from other verses. See "external parallelism."

External parallelism denotes the kind of parallelism when two or more verses are compared with one another. For example, Psalm 30:8–10:

A. To you, O LORD, I called; to the Lord I cried for mercy:
B. "What gain is there in my destruction,
B′. in my going down into the pit?
C. Will the dust praise you?
C′. Will it proclaim your faithfulness?
A′. Hear, O LORD, and be merciful to me; O LORD, be my help."

A and A′ form the external parallel, whereas BB′ and CC′ form the internal parallel structure.

2) *Literary devices*

Hebrew poetry employs many literary devices, especially acrostic, anadiplosis, ellipsis, repetition, inclusion, alliteration, assonance, simile, metaphor, paronomasia, and onomatopoeia.[43]

a) *Standardized phrases or paired synonyms*

Standardized phrases or paired synonyms are common in Hebrew poetry. Certain synonyms recur in the same or in a different order.[44] For example,

---

[42] The ziggurat is an ancient Babylonian structure resembling the stepped pyramid in Egypt; cf. Miller, "Synonymous-Sequential Parallelism in the Psalms."

[43] See for further discussion, Soulen; La Sor, "Hebrew Poetry," *Old Testament Survey*, pp. 307–18; id., "Poetry, Hebrew," ISBErev.; Caird, pp. 131–82; Brongers; Nic. H. Ridderbos, "The Psalms: Style-Figures and Structure"; Hugger; Watson, *Classical Hebrew Poetry*, pp. 273–79.

[44] Umberto Cassuto, *The Goddess Anath* (Jerusalem: Magnes, 1953) (Heb.); S. Gevirtz, *Patterns in the Early Poetry of Israel* (Chicago: University of Chicago Press, 1973[2]).

44:24 Why do you hide your face and forget our *misery and oppression?* (cf. Exod 3:7, 9; Deut 26:7; 2 Kings 13:4; 14:26).

In this example "misery and oppression" are found in pairs. At times the break-up of standardized phrases creates a poetic effect.[45] For example, Psalm 45:3b—"clothe yourself with splendor [*hôḏ*] and majesty [*hāḏār*]"—contains the pair *hôḏ* and *hāḏār*, which is usually found in the same sequence (21:5; 96:6). But in Psalm 145:5 the psalmist inverts the order and breaks the standardized phrase *hôḏ wᵉhāḏār* ("splendor and majesty") into *hᵃḏar kᵉḇôḏ hôḏeḵā* (lit., "the majesty of the glory of your splendor"; NIV, "They will speak of the glorious [*kāḇôḏ*] splendor [*hāḏār*] of your majesty [*hôḏ*]").

The psalmists creatively used a tradition of ready-made phrases, or what Watters designates a "stockpile of traditional diction" (p. 80). They were creative artists "freed from the bondage of fixed traditional diction which allowed for no originality" (ibid., p. 144). For example, the word pair "anger . . . wrath" in Psalm 37:8 undergoes a change in Psalm 85:3: "You set aside all your wrath [*'eḇrāh*] and turned from your fierce [*ḥarôn*] anger [*'ap̄*]."[46]

b) *Acrostic*

Acrostic refers to the poetic practice of opening each line, verse, or stanza with a different letter of the alphabet.[47] The acrostics are sometimes complete (Pss 25; 34; 37; 111; 112; 119; 145). Psalms 9 and 10 form an incomplete acrostic. For other examples see Proverbs 31:10–31; Nahum 1:2–10.

c) *Alliteration*

Alliteration is the phenomenon of repetition of similar sounds at the beginning of words. For example:

22:4 *bᵉḵā bāṭᵉḥû . . . bāṭᵉḥû* ("in you . . . put their trust; they trusted"; MT v.5).

d) *Apostrophe*

Apostrophe results from a development of personification (see below). For example, in Psalm 68:15–16 the psalmist describes the mountains and addresses them rhetorically:

The mountains of Bashan are majestic mountains;
  rugged are the mountains of Bashan.
Why gaze in envy, O rugged mountains,
  at the mountain where God chooses to reign,
  where the LORD himself will dwell forever?

[45] Ezra Zion Melamed, "Break-up of Stereotype Phrases as an Artistic Device in Biblical Poetry," in *Studies in the Bible*, ed. C. Rabin, Scripta Hierosolymitana 3 (Jerusalem: Magnes, 1961), pp. 115–53. Menahem Haran, "The Graded Numerical Sequence and the Phenomenon of 'Automatism' in Biblical Poetry," Supplement to VetTest 22 (1972): 238–67.

[46] For more examples see Watters, pp. 81–218.

[47] Craigie, *Psalms 1–50*, pp. 128–31; Freedman, "Acrostic Poems in the Hebrew Bible"; Bazaq, *Structures and Contents in the Psalms*.

e) *Assonance*

Assonance is the phenomenon of repeating similar sounds within words. For example, in 44:7 the sibilant sound (sh, ts, or s) occurs in each word: *hôša‘tānû miṣṣārênû ûm*^{e}*šan’ênû h*^{e}*ḇîšôṯā* (MT v.8).

f) *Chiasm*

Chiasm changes the order of the members of a line. It is a recurring literary device. Its frequency is so great that the commentary cannot call attention to the many occurrences.[48] In the structures of the Psalms, chiasm is often found when the first part corresponds with a part later on in the psalm and the second corresponds to another part. For example, the structure

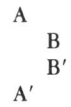

A
  B
  B′
A′

reveals a chiastic arrangement in that A corresponds with A′ and B with B′. The word "chiasm" is derived from the Greek letter *chi* (X), denoting an inversion (crossing) of the parallel members.

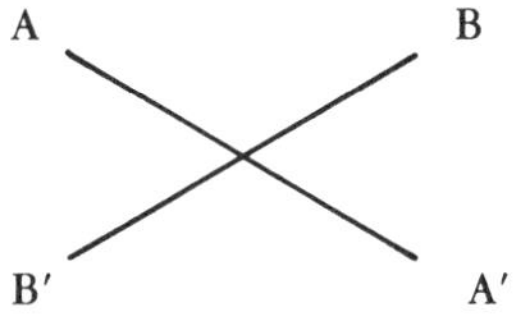

For example,

6:9

The LORD has	heard my cry	for mercy;
A	B	C
the LORD	my prayer	accepts.
A′	C′	B′

In this case BC is in chiasm with C′B′.

g) *Ellipsis*

Ellipsis is the phenomenon of leaving something out of the text that must be read into the colon from the context. The resultant ambiguity forces the reader to involve himself with the text, as he has to choose between two or more options. For example:

12:3 May the LORD cut off all flattering lips and [may the LORD cut off] every boastful tongue.

h) *Hendiadys*

Hendiadys is a figure of speech in which two expressions are intended to be understood as one. For example, Psalm 107:10:

---

[48] See Ceresko; Alden, "Chiastic Psalms," JETS 17, 19, 21.

Some sat in darkness [*ḥōšek*] and the deepest gloom [*ṣalmāwet*], prisoners suffering in iron chains.

Here the two expressions ("darkness," "deepest gloom") intensify the experience of "deep anguish." Another example is found in Psalm 27:1:

The LORD is my light [*'ôr*] and my salvation [*yēša'*]—
whom shall I fear?
The LORD is the stronghold of my life—
of whom shall I be afraid?

Here "light" and "salvation" denote the joy of his beneficent acts and are parallel with the expression "the stronghold of my life."

i) *Hyperbole*

Hyperbole or exaggeration creates a picture in the mind that shuns literalism. Semitic literature reveals an uncanny sense of literary exaggeration, and the OT is certainly not devoid of it. For example, Psalm 40:12:

For troubles without number surround me;
my sins have overtaken me, and I cannot see.
They are more than the hairs of my head,
and my heart fails within me.

j) *Inclusion*

Inclusion is a form of repetition.[49] The beginning and end of the section (verse, strophe, or psalm) *close* the unit by the restatement of the same motif or words[50] or by a contrastive statement. For example, Psalm 70:1 and 5:

Hasten, O God, to save me;
O LORD, come quickly to help me.
. . . .
Yet I am poor and needy;
come quickly to me, O God.
You are my help and my deliverer;
O LORD, do not delay.

k) *Merismus*

Merismus is a coordination of nominal phrases, expressive of totality.[51] For example, in Psalm 105:14, *'āḏām* ("man") and *mᵉlāḵîm* ("kings") denote any and everybody (cf. NIV: "He allowed no one . . . he rebuked kings"). In Psalm 121:2 the psalmist defines Yahweh as "the Maker of heaven and earth," that is, "all created existence." In Psalm 72:8 the phrases "from sea to sea" and "from the River to the ends of the earth" denote the whole created universe.

[49]Alter (*Art of Biblical Poetry*, pp. 116, 118) refers to inclusion as an *envelope* structure.
[50]According to Liebreich nearly half the Psalms begin and end with the same motifs.
[51]See the classic study by Honeyman.

l) *Metonymy*

Metonymy refers to meaning by association. Yahweh's protection is likened to a "shield": "My shield is God Most High, who saves the upright in heart" (7:10). In Psalm 22:15–16 adversity is likened to a "potsherd" and the adversaries to "dogs":

My strength is dried up like a potsherd,
  and my tongue sticks to the roof of my mouth;
  you lay me in the dust of death.
Dogs have surrounded me;
  a band of evil men has encircled me,
  they have pierced my hands and my feet.

Rahab, the dragon, denotes Egypt (Ps 87:4). A related form is *personification*. For other examples see 47:9: "Zion" is the mother of the nations in Psalm 87.

m) *Onomatopoeia*

Onomatopoeia describes a word whose sound creates the effect intended by the speaker. For example, the verb "meditate"—*h-g-h* ("murmur," "mutter," "groan")—may be considered to be onomatopoeic.

n) *Paronomasia*

Paronomasia is a play on words or, better, a use of two or more identical or similarly sounding words with different nuances in meaning. For example, the MT of Psalm 44 begins three verses with the same sounding word, but the first and the third share the same meaning while the second has a different meaning:

v.15 (MT 16) *kol* ("all")
v.16 (MT 17) *qôl* ("sound"; NIV "taunts")
v.17 (MT 18) *kol* ("all").

When the meaning is sharply different, it is an example of *antanaclasis*. For example, in Psalm 69:30–31 the psalmist compares heartfelt obedience, expressed in a "song" (*šîr*), to a sacrifice of the lips (cf. Heb 13:15), being preferable to that of a bull (*šôr*) (cf. Dahood, *Psalms*, 2:165).

o) *Refrain*

Refrain is a form of repetition. The repetition of a whole line or verse throughout a psalm is a most effective device (Goldingay, "Repetition and Variation in the Psalms"). For example:

42:5 Why are you downcast, O my soul?
  Why so disturbed within me?
 Put your hope in God,
  for I will yet praise him,
  my Savior and [6]my God.
 . . . .
[11]Why are you downcast, O my soul?
  Why so disturbed within me?
 Put your hope in God,
  for I will yet praise him,
  my Savior and my God.
 . . . .

43:5 Why are you downcast, O my soul?
Why so disturbed within me?
Put your hope in God,
for I will yet praise him,
my Savior and my God.

p) *Repetition*

Repetition is inherent in the concept of symmetry, according to which words and phrases are repeated in the same, synonymous, or antonymous ways. Repetition is the most important element in Hebrew poetry, as by repetition the artist conveys symmetry and asymmetry, harmony and dissonance. The reader gradually learns to combine the pieces (synthesis) and to see more clearly the internal movement of the psalm. For this purpose he looks for repetition of key words or *Stichwörter* (a repetition of a word or phrase, connecting one part of the psalm with another part). For example, see Psalm 40:

9 I proclaim righteousness [*ṣ-d-q*] in *the great assembly;*
I do not seal my lips,
as you know, O LORD.
10 I do not hide [*k-s-h*] your righteousness [*ṣ-d-q*] in my heart;
I speak of your faithfulness [*'ᵉmûnāh*] and salvation [*y-š-'*].
I do not conceal your love [*ḥesed̲*] and your truth [*'ᵉmet̲*]
from *the great assembly.*
11 Do not withhold [*k-l-'*] your mercy [*raḥᵃmîm*] from me, O LORD;
may your love [*ḥesed̲*] and your truth [*'ᵉmet̲*] always protect me.

q) *Synecdoche*

Synecdoche is a figure of speech in which the part stands for the whole or the whole for the part. The "hand" of the Lord denotes all his being and perfections available to his people: "Let them know that it is your *hand*" (109:27). Similarly "glory," "heart," and "tongue" denote the whole being. In Psalm 24:4 the synecdoche "He who has clean hands and a pure heart" stands for the purity of the whole person.

One special form of synecdoche is *eponymy*. Eponymy takes place when an individual stands for the whole. In Psalm 24:6 two Hebrew MSS and the Syriac read "O God of Jacob," as in the NIV: "Such is the generation of those who seek him, / who seek your face, O God of Jacob." But this verse could well denote the descendants of Jacob: "Such is the generation of those who seek him: Jacob, who seek his face," where Jacob denotes the godly community.

b. *Literary genre*

Subsequent to the works of Gunkel and Mowinckel, "form criticism" has made significant advances. The progress lies in two areas: a movement away from the enthronement ritual (Mowinckel) and a more precise definition of the genres (Gunkel).

Weiser is representative of a covenantal approach to the Psalms. He took the covenant renewal festival as the center of the Psalms. He posited that virtually all genres of the Psalms were related to this autumnal celebration.[52]

---

[52] For a review of Weiser's position, see Gerstenberger, "Psalms," pp. 194–95; Craigie, *Psalms 1–50*, p. 46.

Second, Crüsemann studied the "hymnic" form, explaining the imperatival hymn as a distinctive form in Israel in which the community calls on all its members to praise the Lord for his acts of goodness (Crüsemann, pp. 1–80). Israel developed a strongly polemical element in praising Yahweh for all his acts, perfections, works of creation and redemption, rule in judgment, and vindication. They confessed in hymnic form that "Yahweh (of Hosts) is his name!" (ibid., pp. 81–154; see also the appendix to Ps 7: The Name of Yahweh).

Westermann (*Praise and Lament in the Psalms,* p. 11) also made a serious attempt in modifying Gunkel's categories, concluding that two distinct categories of psalms are polar opposites: lament and praise. His contribution lies in both areas.

1) *Praise*

In his work *The Praise of God,* Westermann significantly modified Gunkel's categories by comparing the structure of the Babylonian psalms (pp. 36–51) and by redefining "hymn" and "thanksgiving songs" into one broad category (*psalms of praise*) with two subcategories: *descriptive* and *declarative praise.*[53] On pp. 102–3 of *The Praise of God,* he defines the hymns of declarative praise as praise of God for specific acts and categorizes them into two forms: *individual* and *communal.* The declarative praise of the individual has these formal similarities:

(1) proclamation;
(2) summary of God's acts;
(3) recollection of the need;
(4) the deliverance;
(5) vow of praise;
(6) descriptive praise.

The declarative praise of the community has these formal similarities (pp. 85–86):

(1) shout of praise or exhortation to praise;
(2) report of God's acts or summary of God's acts;
(3) retrospection of the need;
(4) praise;
(5) report of God's acts.

Distinctive of descriptive praise is the celebration of God's acts in the present. Westermann writes, "The so-called hymn praises God for his actions and his being as a whole" (ibid., p. 31).

2) *Lament*

Westermann has also more clearly defined the formal components of the *lament psalms* (ibid., pp. 64–70):

[53] Ibid., pp. 25–35. In his recent work, *Ausgewählte Psalmen,* Westermann provides a short commentary on Psalms 30; 31:8–9, 20–25; 40:1–12; 66:13–20; 116; and 138 as examples of declarative praise and on Psalms 8; 19; 29; 33; 66:1–12; 103; 104; 113; 139; 145; and 148 as descriptive praise (pp. 121–90). Watts briefly treats Psalms 9–10; 18; 30; 32; 34; 116; 118; and 138 as examples of psalms of thanksgiving or declarative praise and Psalms 100; 113; 134; and 150 as examples of psalms of (descriptive) praise ("Psalms of Trust, Thanksgiving, and Praise," pp. 399–402).

(1) address to God and cry for help;
(2) reference to God's past mighty acts;
(3) description of the distress (concern with the opponents, the psalmist, and God);[54]
(4) confession of trust (confidence)
(5) petition to hear, to deliver, and to vindicate;
(6) questions and/or petition;
(7) vow of praise.[55]

Though few lament psalms include all the elements in the above order and the emphasis of the individual and communal lament psalms differ, the formal structure will help the Western reader to appreciate the movement within these ancient prayers.[56]

Westermann also holds that the lament psalms form the basic rhetorical pattern of Israel's faith, as it includes both lament and praise. Further, he sees three dimensions in the psalms of lament: God, the self ("I"; Gamberoni) or community ("we"; Scharbert), and the "other" (the enemy).[57] Though modern criticism has attempted to identify the "enemy," I agree with Miller ("Trouble and Woe," pp. 33–34) that the stereotypical language should guard against a narrow interpretation or identification of the opponent. Keen interest in historical referentiality or in a cultic interpretation[58] defeats the purpose of the psalm as a prayer to God. (For the theological problem of imprecations, see the appendix to Ps 137: Imprecations in the Psalms.)

3) *Lament and praise*

In the *lament and praise psalms*, the "enemy" is always on the periphery, and in the center is the psalmist and his God. In this relationship there is a movement that leads the one who prays in a *cycle* from prayer to praise.[59] Thus the psalmist addressing the Great King as an individual or on behalf of the community directs his petition in formal categories, reminiscent of a petitioner in the presence of the king. Formal as the structures of the prayers may appear, the relationship signifies a warmth and closeness to God as Yahweh, the Father of individuals and of the people of God. However, Brueggemann ("Loss of Lament," p. 63) rightly insists that the lamenter takes on the responsibility of incurring the consequences if the complaint is trivial.

In the individual lament and praise psalm, the poet confides in his God amid difficulty. In this dialogical relationship the psalmist freely expresses his frustration

[54]The complaint could occur at different points in the development of the lament.

[55]This is a modification of Westermann's form (*The Praise of God*, pp. 53–54). Westermann simplified his own structure: (1) address to God; (2) the complaint; (3) review of God's past acts; (4) petition; (5) divine response; (6) vow to praise (*The Psalms*, pp. 35–43). See also Bellinger, pp. 22–27.

[56]Westermann develops the structure of the *community lament* in a select commentary on Psalm 80 and concludes that Psalms 44; 74; 79; 83; and 89 are related to this genre (*Ausgewählte Psalmen*, pp. 26–38). Similarly, he structures the individual lament in his commentary on Psalms 6; 13; 22; 51; 77; 102; and 130 (ibid., pp. 53–92).

[57]Westermann, *Praise and Lament*, p. 267. Christensen defines a number of national lament psalms (12; 60; 74; 79; 80; 83; 85; 90; 94:1–11; 123; 126; 137) as related to the war oracle (pp. 112–27).

[58]Beyerlin proposes that several individual lament psalms call for protection from the psalmists' accusers at the sanctuary. He and others also explain several lament psalms as arising in sickness; see Klaus Seybold and Ulrich B. Mueller, *Sickness and Healing* (Nashville: Abingdon, 1981).

[59]Cf. Goldingay, "The Dynamic Cycle of Praise and Prayer." See the positive response by Brueggemann, "Response to John Goldingay." See also Brueggemann, "From Hurt to Joy."

with God's slowness in answering him.[60] He also affirms his trust in the Lord (*psalms of confidence*).[61] Miller (*Interpreting the Psalms*, pp. 9–11) concludes that the covenantal understanding was so strong that the psalmist could defend his innocence in the face of God. The confidence of the psalmist in both individual and communal lament and praise psalms arises from a salvation oracle, promising God's protection, victory, and blessing (Bellinger).

While the lament and praise psalms need not be exclusively treated with historical referentiality, Brueggemann rightly relates Israel's "self-understanding" as a polar movement from anguish to celebration, which is experienced in her history from the Exodus to the deliverance from the Exile.[62] Our identification with Israel's history as children of God in Jesus Christ will help us, likewise, to experience the joy of deliverance in our historical context, even though different from the original *Sitz-im-Leben*. Since God is for all who are in Christ, who can be against us (Rom 8:31–39)?[63]

4) *Other types of psalms*

a) *Enthronement*

The hymns celebrating Yahweh's kingship are often designated as *enthronement psalms*.[64] Mowinckel proposed that certain psalms (47; 93; 96–99) arose in a situation similar to the Babylonian New Year's festival, when the king renewed his allegiance to Marduk (the god of Babylon) in an enthronement ritual. Mowinckel saw in the enthronement psalms a literary reflection of an ancient Israelite ritual, borrowed from its environment. He argued that the ritual reenactment of Yahweh's enthronement was a dramatic ritual that helped to assure the presence of God and his gift of victory to Israel. According to this view the people responded to the reenactment with the words "The LORD reigns" (93:1; 97:1; 99:1) or a similar phrase acclaiming his rule (cf. 47:2; 95:3; 98:2). Mowinckel's followers developed these concepts into schools: Myth and Ritual school (S.H. Hooke) and the Scandinavian school (Engnell and Widengren).[65] Some projected from the biblical language that the Davidic king took on himself the role of representative of Yahweh in his suffering, death, and ascension to the throne, as he participated in the reenactment ritual.[66]

---

[60] See Sheila Carney, "God Damn God: A Reflection on Expressing Anger in Prayer," *Biblical Theology Bulletin* 13 (1983): 116–20.

[61] Westermann, *The Psalms*, p. 69. He further develops this genre in a short commentary on Psalms 4; 23; 27:1–6; 62; 73; and 90 in *Ausgewählte Psalmen*, pp. 92–120. Watts ("Psalms of Trust," pp. 395–99) briefly treats Psalms 11; 16; 23; 62; and 121 as examples of psalms of confidence.

[62] "From Hurt to Joy," pp. 71–72. Gerstenberger explores the nature of lament and concludes that all forms of lament contain an element of hope in a breakthrough ("Der klagende Mensch").

[63] See Claus Westermann, "The Role of the Lament in the Theology of the Old Testament," Int 28 (1974): 20–38; John H. Reumann, "Psalm 22 at the Cross. Lament and Thanksgiving for Jesus Christ," Int 28 (1974): 39–58.

[64] Watts designates them as "Hymns to the Lord as King" (Pss 29; 47; 93; 96–99) in his brief treatment in "Psalms of Trust" (pp. 402–4). Westermann observed that the variety of royal psalms does not justify their treatment as a separate genre but as connected by theme. He lists Psalms 2; 18; 20; 21; 45; 61:7–8; 63:12; 72; 89; 101; 110; 132; and 144 as royal psalms and gives a brief commentary on Psalm 72 in *Ausgewählte Psalmen*, pp. 47–53.

[65] Johnson, "The Role of the King"; I. Engnell, *Studies in Divine Kingship in the Ancient Near East* (Oxford: Blackwell, 1967); G. Widengren, *Sakrales Königtum im Alten Testament und im Judentum* (Stuttgart: Kohlhammer, 1955); id., "King and Covenant," JSS 2 (1957): 1–32.

[66] For a sympathetic survey of this view and an argument for a postexilic dating, see Welten. The work of Gray amplifies Mowinckel's position.

Criticism of Mowinckel's model has been slow but is increasing.[67] The following criticisms have been offered. First, the Psalms emphasize God's worldwide rule by virtue of his being the Creator (93:3–4; 96:5). His rule over Israel is a particular expression of his general rule over heaven, the earth, and the seas. The temple and the ark of the covenant were symbolic of his presence, but his presence is a shadowy reality compared with his heavenly rule. Second, Mowinckel's thesis is based on extrabiblical evidence and supported by hypothetical data. The Bible offers virtually no support for his view. It is supposed that the king represented God at the enthronement ritual, on the supposition of a Babylonian ritual, at which the king represented Marduk. The Israelite king did not and could not reenact divine suffering because the hypothesis of divine suffering, death, and victorious ascension is nowhere found in God's revelation in the OT. Third, Mowinckel stressed the annual and thereby the historical reality of God's rule whereas the Psalms also have an eschatological perspective, as Westermann observes: "Borrowing the customs and imagery of the enthronement of an earthly ruler, the community celebrated in these psalms the future inauguration of God's royal rule over the entire world, anticipating the fulfillment of the promise in liturgical jubilation" (*The Psalms*, p. 110; cf. also *The Praise of God*, pp. 146–51).

Watts analyzed the language and the motifs of the psalms ascribing kingship to Yahweh (47; 93; 96–99) and concluded that the number of psalms in this genre can be enlarged by the recognition of two subcategories: (1) psalms celebrating Yahweh's kingship over creation (24; 29; 48; 93; 95; 96; 97; 148); (2) psalms ascribing Yahweh's kingship in giving deliverance to Israel and judgment to the nations (22:27–31; 46; 47; 98; 99).[68] His analysis reveals the difficulty of categorizing the Psalms, as well as the problem of finding the life-setting in the enthronement festival (cf. Clines, "Psalm Research since 1955," p. 125).

No matter what conclusion scholarship may reach on the number of psalms belonging to this category, it is clear that at least Psalms 47; 93; and 96–99 affirm Yahweh's kingship both now and forevermore. These psalms help the Christian reader confess the Lord's universal kingship by enjoying the benefits by virtue of his union with Jesus Christ and by looking forward to the full revelation of his kingdom at the consummation of the ages. In this confession and experience of joy and hope, the Christian identifies himself with the confession, experience, and hope of ancient Israel![69]

b) *Wisdom*

The *wisdom psalms* show clear affinity with the wisdom literature.[70] The wisdom tradition upholds the virtues of godliness (wisdom), the rewards of God, the contrasting way of the righteous and the wicked, and the respective ends of both groups. Wisdom and law are closely related, as both celebrate Yahweh's revelation as

[67] For a discussion on the debate, see Gray, pp. 7–38; Becker, *Messianic Expectation*, pp. 37–47.

[68] Watts, "Yahweh Malak Psalms"; see also Gray's contention (p. 38) that Mowinckel's approach not be judged by a limited number of psalms.

[69] See also Eaton, *Kingship and the Psalms*, and the appendixes to Psalms 5 (Yahweh is King) and 89 (The Messianic King).

[70] See Murphy, "A Consideration of the Classification"; id., *Wisdom Literature and Psalms*. For a recent study, see Perdue, *Wisdom and Cult*. See his excellent historical survey and methodological considerations (pp. 261–68).

the *way* of life. There is no consensus on the wisdom psalms, as the wisdom motif transcends all formal characteristics. We treat the following as wisdom psalms: 1; 10; 12; 15; 19; 32; 34; 36; 37; 49; 50; 52; 53; 73; 78; 82; 91; 92; 94; 111; 112; 119; 127; 128; and 139.[71] Perdue (pp. 269–324) distinguishes between three forms of wisdom hymns: (1) proverb poems: Psalms 1; 19:7–11; 34; 37; 73; 112; 127; 128; (2) *'ashrê* poems: Psalms 32; 119; and (3) riddle poems: Psalms 19:1–6; 49. The wisdom psalms overlap with the psalms of praise and lament, reminding us that the forms of poetry are conventions created for our benefit. The original poets were free in their expression while being bound by certain literary conventions.

c) *Miscellaneous*

Other literary forms are *Zion Songs* (46; 48; 76; 84; 87),[72] *Triumphal Hymn* (68), *Pilgrimage Songs* (120–34), and *Creation Praise* (8; 104; 139). Several other categories are not literary designations but have grown out of the liturgical use of the Psalms.[73] The *penitential psalms* are not a separate literary genre since they include other formal elements. They have in common a strong tradition in Christian liturgy: Psalms 6; 32; 38; 51; 102; 130; and 143 (see the classic study by Snaith).

The *Hallel psalms* too are not to be confused with a literary genre. Instead they form three separate collections: the "Egyptian Hallel" (Pss 113–18); the "Great Hallel" (120–36 or 135–36 or 136; Jewish sources vary on extent); and the concluding Hallel psalms (146–50). The Hallel psalms had a significant part in the praise (*hallel*) of the Lord. The Egyptian Hallel and the Great Hallel (most of which are pilgrimage songs: 120–34) were sung during the annual feasts. The concluding Hallel psalms (146–50) constituted a part of the daily prayers in the synagogues after the destruction of the temple (A.D. 70).

c. *Psalm titles*

The superscription provides us with several categories of information.

1) *Person or group associated*

a) *David*

Seventy-three psalms refer to David (*lᵉḏāwiḏ*).[74] Thirteen psalms are clearly associated with David's life (3; 7; 18; 34; 51–52; 54; 56–57; 59–60; 63; 142).[75]

---

[71] Westermann argues for a broad definition of wisdom genre in his select commentary on Psalms 1 and 119 (*Ausgewählte Psalmen*, pp. 203–6).

[72] Watts, "Psalms of Trust," p. 404. Westermann treats Psalm 46 as an example in his commentary (*Ausgewählte Psalmen*, pp. 197–201).

[73] Westermann treats Psalms 24; 118; and 122 in his commentary (*Ausgewählte Psalmen*, pp. 190–97).

[74] Book I (1–41): 3–9; 11–32; 34–41;
Book II (42–72): 51–65; 68–70;
Book III (73–89): 86;
Book IV (90–106): 101; 103;
Book V (107–50): 108–10; 122; 124; 131; 133; 138–45.
Additional psalms are associated with David in the NT: Psalm 2 (Acts 4:25); Psalm 95 (Heb 4:7).

[75] Many of these psalms portray the anguish due to the enemy attacks. The enemy attacks with plots and abuse of the tongue (Pss 17; 25; 27–28; 31; 35; 41; 52; 54–57; 63–64; 71; 86; 109; 140–41). David was particularly vulnerable when pursued by Saul, when fleeing from Absalom, or when state or personal affairs were not beyond criticism (cf. Pss 25; 35; 41; 71; 86; 109).

However, this does not solve the problem of authorship. On the one hand, the Bible clearly teaches that David was a poet of extraordinary abilities (2 Sam 23:1) and a musician (Amos 6:5; cf. 1 Sam 16:15–23; 18:10; 2 Sam 1:17–27; 3:33–34; 23:1–7) and that he created the temple guilds of singers and musicians (1 Chron 6:31–32; 15:16, 27; 25:1–31; 2 Chron 29:25–26; cf. Neh 12:45–47). The NT writers likewise assumed that David was the author of many psalms (cf. Matt 22:43–45; Acts 2:25–28; 4:25–26; Heb 4:7) and even spoke of the Book of Psalms as being David's (Luke 20:42).

The difficulty of how to understand the preposition *l^{e}* ("for," "belonging to," or "concerning") is crucial in determining authorship (see p. 19). A.A. Anderson (*Psalms*, 1:45) concludes that it signifies "belonging to David" in the majority of psalms.

b) *The director of music*

The notation "For the director of music" (*lam^{e}naṣṣē^{a}ḥ*) appears in fifty-five psalms (also in Hab 3:19) and serves probably as a musical addition, marking the psalm to be a part of temple worship or to be recited by the leader of the choir. The psalms that make up this collection may have been part of an older collection (Briggs, 1:lxxii–iv). The precise use and significance of the phrase is unclear. It occurs in the following psalms:

Book I: 4–6; 8–9; 11–14; 18–22; 31; 36; 39–41;
Book II: 42; 44–47; 49; 51–62; 64–70;
Book III: 75–77; 80–81; 84–85; 88;
Book IV: none;
Book V: 109; 139–40.

c) *Jeduthun*

Jeduthun (Pss 39; 62; 77) was a Levite whom David appointed to be the director of music at the temple together with Heman and Asaph (1 Chron 16:41–42; 25:1, 6; 2 Chron 5:12). He was probably the same as Ethan the Ezrahite (Ps 89), a descendent of Merari, son of Levi. But, according to 1 Chronicles 2:6, Ethan is of the tribe of Judah. It may be that Levites were brought into the lineage of Judah. The identification in not unproblematic.

d) *The sons of Korah*

The sons of Korah (Pss 42; 45–49; 84–85; 87–88) were descendants of Kohath, son of Levi, who served in the temple as musicians (1 Chron 6:22).[76] From them we have the collection of the so-called Korahite Psalms: 42–43; 44–49; 84–85; 87–88.[77]

e) *Asaph*

Asaph (Pss 50, 73–83) was one of David's choirmasters and a descendant of Gershon, son of Levi (cf. 1 Chron 6:39; 15:17; 2 Chron 5:12). The collection is also

---

[76]The Levites had many responsibilities, including singing and playing instruments in the temple (cf. 1 Chron 6:31–47; 15:16, 27; 23:5, 30; 25; 2 Chron 29:25–26; Neh 12:45–47).

[77]Buss, "The Psalms of Asaph and Korah." Wanke placed these psalms in the Jerusalem context; Goulder argues for their original separate existence as a northern (Dan) collection on the basis of vocabulary and content.

known as the Asaphite Psalms. It appears that Psalm 50 became separated from the Asaphite Psalms because of its thematic connections with Psalms 48–49 (Buss, "The Psalms of Asaph and Korah").

f) *Solomon*

Psalms 72 and 127 are attributed to Solomon.

g) *Heman the Ezrahite*

Heman the Ezrahite (Ps 88) was a sage (cf. 1 Kings 4:31) or a leading singer of the family of Kohath, son of Levi (1 Chron 6:16, 33, 39, 43–44; 15:17, 19; 16:41–42; 25:1, 4–6; 2 Chron 5:12; 35:15).

h) *Ethan the Ezrahite*

Ethan the Ezrahite (Ps 89) was a counselor of Solomon (1 Kings 4:31). He may be identified with Jeduthun (Ps 39) or with being a descendant of Jeduthun. (See c above.)

i) *Moses*

Moses (Ps 90) was the great law-giver and the servant of God.

2) *Background or historical information*

Thirteen psalms are related to David's life:

Ps 3: "When he fled from his son Absalom."
Ps 7: "A *shiggaion* of David, which he sang to the LORD concerning Cush, a Benjamite."
Ps 18: "He sang to the LORD the words of this song when the Lord delivered him from the hand of all his enemies and from the hand of Saul."
Ps 34: "When he pretended to be insane before Abimelech, who drove him away, and he left."
Ps 51: "When the prophet Nathan came to him after David had committed adultery with Bathsheba."
Ps 52: "When Doeg the Edomite had gone to Saul and told him: 'David has gone to the house of Ahimelech.' "
Ps 54: "When the Ziphites had gone to Saul and said, 'Is not David hiding among us?' "
Ps 56: "When the Philistines had seized him in Gath."
Ps 57: "When he had fled from Saul into the cave."
Ps 59: "When Saul had sent men to watch David's house in order to kill him."
Ps 60: "When he fought Aram Naharaim and Aram Zobah, and when Joab returned and struck down twelve thousand Edomites in the Valley of Salt."
Ps 63: "When he was in the Desert of Judah."
Ps 142: "When he was in the cave."

One psalm is associated with the dedication of the temple:

Ps 30: "For the dedication of the temple."[78]

[78]Craigie rightly observes that this psalm may have been used generally in dedication liturgies ("Psalms," ISBErev., 3:1031).

3) *Musical or liturgical information*

Several psalms carry a notation on the instruments to be used in accompanying the choir.

a) *With stringed instruments*

Stringed instruments (harp and lyre) accompanied certain psalms (4; 6; 54–55; 61; 67; 76). For background see 1 Chronicles 23:5; 25:1, 3, 6; Psalms 33:2; 43:4; 71:22. A.A. Anderson observes that the note is intended to "exclude percussion and wind instruments" (*Psalms,* 1:48).

b) *For flutes*

Only Psalm 5 carries this note. The meaning is uncertain. Mowinckel (2:210) relates it to the Babylonian "flute psalms of lamentation."

c) *According to* sheminith

This term appears in Psalms 6 and 12 and in 1 Chronicles 15:21. As its form is related to the Hebrew word for eight, it may denote the manner of singing or musical accompaniment ("octave") or possibly an instrument with eight strings.

d) *According to* gittith

The word "gittith" occurs only in the superscription of Psalms 8; 81; and 84. Its meaning is unknown, though several suggestions have been made: a Gittite lyre, a festival song (associated with the wine press), or a musical term.

e) Selah

The word "selah" occurs seventy-one times in the Psalms. Its use particularly in the first three books suggests its antiquity. It was likely used as a musical marker, but its precise significance in Israel's worship remains unclear (for a discussion, see Craigie, *Psalms 1–50,* pp. 76–77).

f) *To the tune of "The Death of the Son"*

In Psalm 9 the phrase "To the tune of 'The Death of the Son' " may be a variant of "According to *alamoth*" (Ps 46). The word *alamoth* is related to the word for "maidens"; and this may signify a female choir, a band of maidens playing tambourines (68:25), or a musical term for a high musical setting (soprano) (Craigie, *Psalms 1–50,* p. 342). The LXX reading is "hidden things."

g) *To the tune of "The Doe of the Morning"*

The LXX rendered the superscription of Psalm 22 by "help of the dawn." The Masoretic reading "deer" or "doe" is preferable. The NIV makes an interpretative addition: "to the tune of."

h) *To the tune of "Lilies"*

This designation occurs in Psalms 45; 69; and 80 in alternate forms. In Psalms 60 and 80 we read "To the tune of 'The Lily of the Covenant.' " The word for "covenant" is here *'ēḏûṯ* ("testimony"). The usage is unknown.

i) *According to* mahalath

Since the word *mahalath* is related to the Hebrew word for "sick" or "sickness," it has been suggested that what is in view is a prayer of a sick person (Ps 53). A similar phrase occurs in Psalm 88: "According to *mahalath leannoth.*" It may denote the instruments used (possibly flutes) or a tune. The significance is obscure.

j) *To the tune of "A Dove on Distant Oaks"*

This tune appears only in Psalm 56.

k) *To the tune of "Do Not Destroy"*

Though this tune occurs in four psalms (57–59; 75), no further illumination can be given on this ancient designation.

l) *Other tune titles*

Because of the problem with the technical use of many of the words in the superscriptions, it is not always clear whether a term denotes a liturgical or a literary category. See the next section.

4) *Ancient literary categories*

a) *Psalm*

A psalm (*mizmôr*) is frequently found in the heading, as many as fifty-seven times. The designation *mizmôr* denotes a song that was accompanied by musical instruments. Both secular psalms (Ecclus 49:1) and religious psalms may have existed at one time, but the Hebrew Bible limits usage to the religious songs. The word *mizmôr* occurs in the heading of Psalms 3–6; 8–9; 12–13; 15; 19–24; 29–31; 38–41; 47–51; 62–68; 73; 75–77; 79–80; 82–85; 87–88; 92; 98; 100–101; 108–110; 139–141; and 143. The root *z-m-r* is often used to denote songs with musical accompaniment (cf. Pss 33:2; 71:22; 98:5; 147:7; 149:3). A more general meaning of "praise" also occurs (Pss 30:12; 47:6–7; 68:4, 32), but the praises may have been accompanied by musical instruments.

The designation "A psalm" also occurs in combination with "A song" (see below). The rabbinic interpretation held that depending on the placing of "psalm" in relation to "song," the psalm was accompanied either by musical instruments or by a choir. It is preferable to consider the title "song" to be more general and the designation "praise" to be more specific.

b) Shiggaion

Shiggaion occurs only in Psalm 7: "A *shiggaion* of David, which he sang to the Lord concerning Cush, a Benjamite." The meaning is uncertain. It could be a musical term or a literary designation, such as a psalm of lamentation (Mowinckel, 2:209) or a psalm with irregular literary features (from the root *š-g-h*, "wander"). The precise meaning and function are unknown to us.

c) Miktam

Miktam appears in six psalm titles (16; 56–60). Its meaning is unknown, though many explanations have been offered: a golden psalm, a private prayer, epigram, an atonement psalm, inscription, and many others. Craigie favors "inscription" on the ground that the form is related to the word "stain" (Jer 2:22) and that the root *k-t-m* is best understood as "inscribe," denoting psalms that celebrate events that had been "inscribed."[79]

d) maśkîl

maśkîl, found in thirteen psalms (32; 42; 44–45; 52–55; 74; 78; 88–89; 142), is equally obscure. It is most likely related to the root *s-k-l* ("be wise," "instruct") and may be a literary designation for a didactic psalm (cf. 32:8). Other suggestions include "a skillful psalm," "a meditation," and "harmony."

e) *Song*

Song (*šîr*) occurs more than thirty times in the title of the psalms: Psalms 18 (*šîrāh*); 30; 45–46; 48; 65–69; 75–76; 83; 87–88; 92; 108; 120–134 (the Songs of Ascent). Several of these have the combined title:

> *šîr mizmôr* ("A song. A psalm"): 48; 66; 83; 88; 108
> *mizmôr šîr* ("A psalm. A song"): 30; 65; 67–68; 75–76; 87; 92
> *maśkîl šîr* ("A *maśkîl.* A wedding song"): 45
> *šîr mizmôr* and *maśkîl:* ("A song. A psalm of the Sons of Korah. . . . A *maśkîl* of Heman the Ezrahite"): 88.

The "song" is a general category of poetry, used elsewhere in the OT to designate a love song (S of Songs), a drinking song (Isa 24:9), a proverbial song (1 Kings 4:32 [5:12 MT]), a lament song (Amos 8:10), a song of triumph (Judg 5:12), and a levitical song with musical accompaniment (1 Chron 6:31–32 [MT 16–17]). The combination of *šîr* with another designation specified the particular nature of the song: for example, "For the director of music. To the tune of 'Lilies.' Of the Sons of Korah. A *maśkîl.* A wedding song" (Ps 45). The pilgrimage songs (Songs of Ascent) constitute a collection of songs that probably was used during the pilgrimage feasts (Pss 120–34).[80]

f) *Psalm of praise*

Psalm of praise (*tᵉhillāh*) occurs only in the superscription of Psalm 145: "A psalm of praise." The word *tᵉhillāh* is more commonly used within the Psalms (9:14 [MT 15]; 22:3 [MT 4], 25 [MT 26]; 71:6, 8, 14; 106:2, 12, 47; 145:21 et al.). It is a nominal form of the root *h-l-l,* from which we get our phrase Hallelujah ("praise Yah[weh]" or "praise the Lord") and which lies behind the Hallel psalms (the Great Hallel, Pss

---

[79] *Psalms 1–50,* p. 154; cf. Miller, "Psalms and Inscriptions."
[80] See the introduction to Psalm 120.

120–36; the Egyptian Hallel, Pss 113–18). The word *tehillāh* came ultimately to be the Hebrew designation for the whole psalter: *tehillîm* ("Psalms").

g) *A petition*

In Psalms 38 and 70 the verbal phrase *lehazkîr* ("to remember"; NIV, "a petition") may be associated with the "memorial portion" (cf. Lev 2:2; 24:7) or with a call to the Lord to remember him. Craigie (*Psalms 1–50*, p. 300) translates it literally: "To bring to remembrance." It is unclear whether or not the term denotes a cultic use.

h) *For teaching*

Only in Psalm 60 do we find this phrase, designating its pedagogical purpose, i.e., for teaching David's fighting men how to function in time and rhythm with one another.

i) *For the Sabbath*

Psalm 92 clearly identifies its use in relation to the Sabbath.

j) *For giving thanks*

This title occurs only in Psalm 100 and creates a difficulty of interpretation, whether or not the psalm was used cultically with a thank offering (Lev 7:12).

k) *A prayer*

The prayer is in the form of a lament and occurs in Psalms 17; 86; 90; 102; and 142. Specific data suggest the use or importance of the "prayer":

> A prayer of Moses the man of God (Ps 90).
> A prayer of an afflicted man. When he is faint and pours out his lament before the LORD (Ps 102).

7. Bibliography

a. *Commentaries*

Alexander, Joseph Addison. *The Psalms. Translated and Explained.* Reprint. Grand Rapids: Zondervan, 1864.
Allen, Leslie C. *Psalm 101–150.* WBC. Waco: Word, 1983.
Anderson, A.A. *The Book of Psalms.* 2 volumes. The New Century Bible Commentary. Grand Rapids: Eerdmans, 1972.
Briggs, C.A., and Briggs, E.G. *A Critical and Exegetical Commentary on the Book of Psalms.* The International Critical Commentary. 2 volumes. Edinburgh: T. & T. Clark, 1906–7.
Brueggemann, Walter. *The Message of the Psalms.* Minneapolis: Augsburg, 1984.
Calvin, John. *Commentary on the Book of Psalms.* Translated by James Anderson. 3 volumes. Reprint. Grand Rapids: Eerdmans, 1963.
Craigie, Peter C. *Psalms 1–50.* WBC. Waco: Word, 1983.
Dahood, Mitchell. *Psalms.* AB. 3 volumes. Garden City, N.Y.: Doubleday, 1966–70.

Delitzsch, Franz. *Biblical Commentary on the Psalms*. KD. Translated by David Eaton. 3 volumes. London: Hodder and Stoughton, 1902.
Eaton, J.H. *Psalms*. Torch Bible Commentaries. London: SCM, 1967.
Goldingay, John. *Songs from a Strange Land. Psalms 42–51*. Downers Grove: InterVarsity, 1978.
Goulder, Michael D. *The Psalms of the Sons of Korah*. JSOTS 20. Sheffield: JSOT, 1982.
Keet, Cuthbert C. *A Study of the Psalms of Ascents. A Critical and Exegetical Commentary Upon Psalms CXX to CXXXIV*. Greenwood: Attic, 1969.
Kidner, Derek. *Psalms 1–72*. Downers Grove: InterVarsity, 1973.
———. *Psalms 73–150*. Downers Grove: InterVarsity, 1975.
Kirkpatrick, A.F. *The Book of Psalms*. The Cambridge Bible for Schools and Colleges. Cambridge: The University Press, 1902.
Kraus, Hans-Joachim. *Psalmen*. Biblischer Kommentar Altes Testament. 2 volumes. Neukirchen Kreis Moers: Neukirchener Verlag, 1960.
Oesterley, W.O.E. *The Psalms*. London: SPCK, 1962.
Perowne, J.J. Stewart. *The Book of Psalms*. 2 volumes. Reprint. Grand Rapids: Zondervan, 1966.
van der Ploeg, J.P.M. *Psalmen uit de Grondtext vertaald en uitgelegd*. De Boeken van het Oude Testament, VII A/B. 2 volumes. Roermond: J.J. Romen & Zonen, 1971–74.
Ridderbos, J. *De Psalmen: Vertaald en Verklaard*. Commentaar op het Oude Testament. 2 volumes. Kampen: Kok, 1955, 1958.
Rogerson, J.W., and McKay, J.W. *Psalms*. The Cambridge Bible Commentary. 3 volumes. Cambridge: The University Press, 1977.
Snaith, Norman. *The Seven Penitential Psalms*. London: Epworth, 1964.
Stuhlmueller, Carroll. *The Psalms*. Old Testament Message. 2 volumes. Wilmington: Michael Glazier, 1983.
Weiser, A. *The Psalms: A Commentary*. OTL. London: SCM, 1959.
White, R.E.O. *A Christian Handbook to the Psalms*. Grand Rapids: Eerdmans, 1984.

b. *General works*

Achtemeier, Elizabeth. "The Use of Hymnic Elements in Preaching." *Interpretation* 39 (1985): 46–59.
———. "Preaching from the Psalms." *Review and Expositor* 81 (1984): 437–49.
Albertz, Rainer. *Weltschöpfung und Menschenschöpfung: Untersucht bei Deuterojesaja, Hiob und in den Psalmen*. Stuttgart: Calwer Verlag, 1974.
———. *Persönliche Frömmigkeit und offizielle Religion: Religions-interner Pluralismus in Israel und in Babylon*. Stuttgart: Calwer Verlag, 1978.
Alden, Robert L. "Chiastic Psalms: A Study in the Mechanics of Semitic Poetry in Psalms 1–50." *Journal of the Evangelical Theological Society* 17 (1974): 11–28.
———. "Chiastic Psalms (II): A Study in the Mechanics of Semitic Poetry in Psalms 51–100." *Journal of the Evangelical Theological Society* 19 (1976): 191–200.
———. "Chiastic Psalms (III): A Study in the Mechanics of Semitic Poetry in Psalms 101–150." *Journal of the Evangelical Theological Society* 21 (1978): 199–210.
———. "The Psalms—Beauty Heightened Through Poetic Structure." *Bible Review* 2 (1986): 28–41.
Aletti, Jean-Noël, and Trublet, Jacques. *Approche poétique et théologique des Psaumes: Analyses et Méthodes*. Paris: Cerf, 1983.
Alter, Robert. *The Art of Biblical Poetry*. New York: Basic Books, 1985.
Anderson, Bernard W. *Out of the Depths. The Psalms Speak for Us Today*. Philadelphia: Westminster, 1983.
Anderson, George W. "Enemies and Evildoers in the Book of Psalms." *Bulletin of the John Rylands Library* 46 (1965): 18–29.
———. "'Sicut Cervus': Evidence in the Psalter of Private Devotion in Israel." *Vetus Testamentum* 30 (1980): 388–97.

Auffret, Pierre. "'Pivot Pattern' Nouveaux Examples (Jon. ii 10; Ps. xxxi 13; Is. xxiii 7)." *Vetus Testamentum* 28 (1978): 103–12.

______. *La Sagesse A Bati Sa Maison.* Fribourg: Editions Universitaires, 1982.

Bazaq, Jacob. *Structures and Contents in the Psalms: Geometric Structural Patterns in the Seven Alphabetic Psalms.* Tel Aviv: Dvir, 1984 (Heb.).

______. "Structural Geometric Patterns in Biblical Poetry." *Poetics Today* 6 (1985): 475–502.

Becker, Joachim. *Israel deutet seine Psalmen. Urform und Neuinterpretation in den Psalmen.* Stuttgart: Verlag Katholisches Bibelwerk, 1966.

______. *Wege der Psalmenexegese.* Stuttgart: KBW, 1975.

______. *Messianic Expectation in the Old Testament.* Translated by David E. Green. Philadelphia: Fortress, 1980.

Bellinger, W.H., Jr. *Psalmody and Prophecy.* JSOTS 27. Sheffield: JSOT, 1984.

Beyerlin, Walter. *Die Rettung der Bedrängten in den Feindpsalmen der Einzelnen auf institutionelle Zusammenhänge untersucht.* FRLANT 99. Göttingen: Vandenhoeck & Ruprecht, 1970.

Boling, Robert G. "'Synonymous' Parallelism in the Psalms." *Journal of Semitic Studies* 5 (1960): 221–55.

Bonhoeffer, Dietrich. *Psalms: The Prayer Book of the Bible.* Translated by James H. Burtness. Minneapolis: Augsburg, 1970.

Botterweck, G. Johannes. "Gott und Mensch in den Alttestamentlichen Löwenbildern." *Wort, Lied un Gottesspruch: Beiträge zu Psalmen und Propheten. Festschrift für Joseph Ziegler.* Edited by Josef Schreiner. Würzberg: Echter Verlag, 1972, pp. 117–28.

Bratcher, Robert G. "Dividing the Psalms Into Strophes." *The Bible Translator* 29 (1978): 425–27.

Brongers, H.A. "Merismus, Synekdoche und Hendiadys in der Bibel-Hebräischen Sprache." *OudTestamentische Studiën* 14 (1965): 100–114.

Bruce, F.F. "The Earliest Old Testament Interpretation." *Oudtestamentische Studiën* 17 (1972): 44–52.

Brueggemann, Walter. "From Hurt to Joy, From Death to Life." *Interpretation* 28 (1974): 3–19.

______. "The Formfulness of Grief." *Interpretation* 31 (1977): 263–75.

______. "Psalms and the Life of Faith: A Suggested Typology of Function." *Journal for the Study of the Old Testament* 17 (1980): 3–32.

______. "Response to John Goldingay's 'The Dynamic Cycle of Praise and Prayer.'" *Journal for the Study of the Old Testament* 22 (1982): 141–42.

______. *Praying the Psalms.* Winona: St. Mary's, 1982.

______. "The Costly Loss of Lament." *Journal for the Study of the Old Testament* 36 (1986): 57–71.

Buss, Martin J. "The Psalms of Asaph and Korah." *Journal of Biblical Literature* 82 (1963): 382–92.

______. "The Idea of Sitz-im-Leben—History and Critique." *Zeitschrift für die alttestamentliche Wissenschaft* 90 (1978): 157–70.

Butler, Trent C. "Piety in the Psalms." *Review and Expositor* 81 (1984): 385–94.

Caird, G.B. *The Language and Imagery of the Bible.* Philadelphia: Westminster, 1980.

Ceresko, Anthony R. "The Function of Chiasmus in Hebrew Poetry." *Catholic Biblical Quarterly* 40 (1978): 1–10.

Childs, Brevard S. "Psalm Titles and Midrashic Exegesis." *Journal of Semitic Studies* 16 (1971): 137–50.

______. *Old Testament Books for Pastor and Teacher.* Philadelphia: Westminster, 1975.

______. *Introduction to the Old Testament as Scripture.* IOTS. Philadelphia: Westminster, 1979.

______. *Old Testament Theology in a Canonical Context.* OTTC. Philadelphia: Westminster, 1985.

Christensen, Duane L. *Transformations of the War Oracle in Old Testament Prophecy. Studies in the Oracles Against the Nations.* Missoula: Scholars, 1975.

Clines, D.J.A. "Psalm Research Since 1955: I: The Psalms and the Cult." *Tyndale Bulletin* 18 (1967): 103–26.

———. "Psalm Research Since 1955: II. The Literary Genres." *Tyndale Bulletin* 20 (1969): 105–25.

Coddaire, Louis, and Weil, Louis. "The Use of the Psalter in Worship." *Worship* 52 (1978): 342–48.

Crenshaw, James L. "The Human Dilemma and the Literature of Dissent." *Tradition and Theology in the Old Testament.* Edited by Douglas A. Knight. Philadelphia: Fortress, 1977, pp. 235–58.

Cross, F.M., and Freedman, D.N. *Studies in Ancient Yahwistic Poetry.* SBL Dissertation 21. Missoula: Scholars, 1975.

Crüsemann, Frank. *Studien zur Formgeschichte von Hymnus und Danklied in Israel.* Neukirchen-Vluyn: Neukirchener Verlag, 1969.

Culley, Robert C. *Oral Formulaic Language in the Biblical Psalms.* Toronto: University of Toronto Press, 1967.

———. "Metrical Analysis of Classical Hebrew Poetry." *Essays on the Ancient Semitic World.* Edited by J.W. Wevers and D.B. Redford. Toronto: University of Toronto Press, 1970, pp. 12–28.

Cullinan, Thomas. "Opening Words on the Psalms." *Clergy Review* 63 (1978): 205–7.

Dahood, Mitchell. "Ugaritic and the Old Testament." *De Mari à Qumrân: L'Ancien Testament: Son Milieu. Ses Ècrits. Ses relectures juives. Hommage á Mgr J. Coppens.* Edited by H. Cazelles. Paris: P. Lethiellieux, 1969, pp. 14–33.

———. "Hebrew Poetry." *Interpreter's Dictionary of the Bible.* Supplementary volume. Edited by K. Drim. Nashville: Abingdon, 1976, pp. 669–72.

De Fraine, J. "'Entmythologisierung' dans les Psaumes." *Le Psautier. Ses Origines. Ses Problèmes littéraires. Son Influence.* Edited by Robert De Langhe. Louvain: Institut Orientaliste, 1962, pp. 89–106.

De Langhe, Robert, ed. *Le Psautier. Ses Origines. Ses Problèmes littéraires. Son Influence.* Louvain: Institut Orientaliste, 1962.

Dentan, R.C. "The Literary Affinities of Exodus xxxiv:6f." *Vetus Testamentum* 13 (1963): 34–51.

Eaton, J.H. *Kingship and the Psalms.* Studies in Biblical Theology. Second Series 32. Naperville: Allenson, 1976.

———. "The Psalms and Israelite Worship." *Tradition and Interpretation: Essays by Members of the Society for Old Testament Study.* Edited by G.W. Anderson. Oxford: Clarendon, 1979, pp. 238–73.

———. *Vision in Worship. The Relation of Prophecy and Liturgy in the Old Testament.* London: SPCK, 1981.

Eichrodt, W. *Theology of the Old Testament.* TOT. Translated by J.A. Baker. 2 volumes. Philadelphia: Westminster, 1961, 1967.

Elwell, Walter A., ed. *Evangelical Dictionary of Theology.* EDT. Grand Rapids: Baker, 1984.

———. *Baker Encyclopedia of the Bible.* BEB. 2 volumes. Grand Rapids: Baker, 1988.

Eissfeldt, Otto. "Die Psalmen als Geschichtsquelle." *Near Eastern Studies in Honor of William Foxwell Albright.* Edited by Hans Goedicke. Baltimore: Johns Hopkins Press, 1971, pp. 97–112.

Fabry, Heinz-Josef. "11Q Psa und die Kanonizität des Psalters." *Freude an der Weisung des Herrn, Beiträge zur Theologie der Psalmen, Festgabe zum 70. Geburtstag von Heinrich Gross.* Edited by Ernst Haag and Frank-Lothar Hossfeld. Stuttgart: Katholisches Bibelwerk, 1986, pp. 45–79.

Ferré, Frederick. "Metaphors, Models, and Religion." *Soundings* 51 (1968): 327–45.

Fischer, James A. "Everyone a King: A Study of the Psalms." *The Bible Today* 97 (1978): 1683–89.

Freedman, D.N. "Pottery, Poetry, and Prophecy: An Essay in Biblical Poetry." *Journal of Biblical Literature* 96 (1977): 5–26.

———. "Acrostic Poems in the Hebrew Bible: Alphabetic and Otherwise." *Catholic Biblical Quarterly* 48 (1986): 408–31.

Gamberoni, Johann. "Der Einzelne in den Psalmen." *Freude an der Weisung des Herrn, Beiträge zur Theologie der Psalmen, Festgabe zum 70. Geburtstag von Heinrich Gross.* Edited by Ernst Haag and Frank-Lothar Hossfeld. Stuttgart: Katholisches Bibelwerk, 1986, pp. 107–23.

Gerleman, Gillis. "Der 'Einzelne' der Klage- und Dankpsalmen." *Vetus Testamentum* 32 (1982): 33–49.

Gerstenberger, Erhard. "Der klagende Mensch." *Probleme biblischer Theologie. Gerhard von Rad zum 70. Geburtstag.* Edited by Hans Walter Wolff. Munich: Chr. Kaiser, 1971, pp. 64–72.

———. "Psalms." *Old Testament Form Criticism.* Edited by John H. Hayes. San Antonio: Trinity University Press, 1974, pp. 179–223.

———. *Der bittende Mensch.* Neukirchen-Vluyn: Neukirchener, 1980.

Gese, Hartmut. "Die Entstehung der Büchereinteilung des Psalters." *Vom Sinai zum Zion: Alttestamentliche Beiträge zur biblischen Theologie.* Munich: Chr. Kaiser, 1974, pp. 159–67.

Gevaryahu, H.M.I. "Biblical Colophons: A Source for the 'Bibliography' of Authors, Texts, and Books." Supplement to *Vetus Testamentum* 28 (1975): 42–59.

Goldingay, John. "Repetition and Variation in the Psalms." *Jewish Quarterly Review* 68 (1978): 146–51.

———. "The Dynamic Cycle of Praise and Prayer in the Psalms." *Journal for the Study of the Old Testament* 20 (1981): 85–90.

Goulder, Michael D. *The Psalms of the Sons of Korah.* JSOTS 20. Sheffield: JSOT, 1982.

Gray, John. *The Biblical Doctrine of the Reign of God.* Edinburgh: T. & T. Clark, 1979.

Greenberg, Moshe. *Biblical Prose Prayer. As a Window to the Popular Religion of Ancient Israel.* Berkeley: University of California Press, 1983.

Gunkel, Hermann. *The Psalms. A Form-Critical Introduction.* Translated by Thomas M. Horner. Philadelphia: Fortress, 1967.

Gunn, George S. *God in the Psalms.* Edinburgh: Saint Andrews, 1956.

Haglund, Erik. *Historical Motifs in the Psalms.* Gleerup: CWK, 1984.

Haran, Menahem. "The Cult and Prayer." *Biblical and Related Studies Presented to Samuel Iwry.* Edited by Ann Kort and Scott Morschauer. Winona Lake: Eisenbrauns, 1985, pp. 87–92.

Hayes, John H., and Miller, J. Maxwell, edd. *Israelite and Judaean History.* IJH. Philadelphia: Westminster, 1977.

Hoffman, Yair. "The Transition from Despair to Hope in the Individual Psalms of Lament." *Tarbiz* 55 (1985/6): 161–72 (Heb.).

Honeyman, A.M. "Merismus in Biblical Literature." *Journal of Biblical Literature* 71 (1952): 11–18.

Hugger, Pirmin. "Alliteration in the Psalter." *Wort, Lied und Gottesspruch. Beiträge zur Psalmen und Propheten. Festschrift für Joseph Ziegler.* Edited by Josef Schreiner. Würzberg: Echter Verlag/Katholisches Bibelwerk, 1972, pp. 81–90.

Hull, William E. "Preaching on the Psalms." *Review and Expositor* 81 (1984): 451–56.

Hustad, Donald P. "The Psalms as Worship Expression: Personal and Congregational." *Review and Expositor* 81 (1984): 407–24.

Interpreter's Dictionary of the Bible. Supplementary volume. IDBS. Edited by K. Drim. Nashville: Abingdon, 1976.

Johnson, Aubrey R. "The Role of the King in the Jerusalem Cultus." *The Labyrinth: Further Studies in the Relation Between Myth and Ritual in the Ancient World.* Edited by S.H. Hooke. London: Society for Promoting Christian Knowledge, 1935, pp. 71–111.

———. *Cultic Prophet and Israel's Psalmody.* Cardiff: University of Wales, 1979.

Joüon, P. Paul. *Grammaire de l'Hébreu Biblique.* Rome: Institut Biblique Pontifical, 1947.

Kaiser, Walter C., Jr. *Toward an Old Testament Theology.* TOTT. Grand Rapids: Zondervan, 1978.

Kapelrud, Arvid S. "Tradition and Worship: The Role of the Cult in Tradition Formation and Transmission." *Tradition and Theology in the Old Testament.* Edited by Douglas A. Knight. Philadelphia: Fortress, 1977, pp. 101–24.

Keel, Othmar. *The Symbolism of the Biblical World. Ancient Near Eastern Iconography and the Book of Psalms.* Translated by Timothy J. Hallett. New York: Crossroad, 1985.

Kistemaker, S. *The Psalm Quotations in Hebrews.* Amsterdam: Van Soest, 1961.

Kraus, Hans-Joachim. *Theologie des Psalmen.* TP. Biblischer Kommentar Altes Testament. Neukirchen-Vluyn: Neukirchener Verlag, 1979.

Kroll, Woodrow Michael. *Psalms. The Poetry of Palestine.* Lanham: University Press of America, 1987.

Kuhlewein, Johannes. *Geschichte in den Psalmen.* Stuttgart: Calwer, 1973.

Kugel, J.L. *The Idea of Biblical Poetry: Parallelism and Its History.* New Haven: Yale University Press, 1981.

L'Heureux, Conrad. "The Ugaritic and Biblical Rephaim." *The Harvard Theological Review* 67 (1974): 265–74.

______. *Rank Among the Canaanite Gods: El, Ba'al and the Repha'im.* Missoula: Scholars, 1979.

La Sor, William Sanford; Hubbard, David Allan; and Bush, Frederic William. *Old Testament Survey.* Grand Rapids: Eerdmans, 1982, pp. 307–18.

______. "Poetry, Hebrew." *International Standard Bible Encyclopedia.* 4 volumes. Revised. Edited by G.W. Bromiley. Grand Rapids: Eerdmans, 1979–88, 3:891–98.

Levenson, Jon D. *Sinai and Zion. An Entry Into the Jewish Bible.* Minneapolis: Winston, 1985.

Lewis, C.S. *Reflections on the Psalms.* London: Geoffrey Bles, 1958.

______. *Christian Reflections.* Edited by Walter Hooper. Grand Rapids: Eerdmans, 1967.

Liebreich, L.J. "Psalms 34 and 145 in the Light of Their Key Words." *Hebrew Union College Annual* 27 (1956): 181–92.

Loewenstamm, Samuel E. "The Trembling of Nature During the Theophany." *Comparative Studies in Biblical and Ancient Oriental Literatures* (CSBAOL). Neukirchen-Vluyn: Neukirchener Verlag, 1980, pp. 173–89.

______. "On Stylistic Patterns in Biblical and Ugaritic Literatures." CSBAOL, pp. 256–61.

______. "The Expanded Colon in Ugaritic and Biblical Verse." CSBAOL, pp. 281–309.

______. "A Ugaritic Hymn in Honour of Il." CSBAOL, pp. 320–32.

______. " 'The Lord Is My Strength and My Glory.' " CSBAOL, pp. 333–40.

______. "The Ugaritic Myth of the Sea and Its Biblical Counterparts." CSBAOL, pp. 346–61.

______. "Ugarit and the Bible. I." CSBAOL, pp. 473–95.

Loretz, O. "Die Ugaristik in der Psalmeninterpretation." *Ugarit-Forschungen* 4 (1972): 167–69; 17 (1986): 213–17.

Magonet, Jonathan. "Some Concentric Structures in Psalms." *The Heythrop Journal* 23 (1982): 365–76.

Mann, Jacob. *The Bible as Read and Preached in the Old Synagogue.* Vol. 1. New York: Ktav, 1971; Vol. 2 with Isaiah Sonne. Cincinnati: Hebrew Union College, 1966.

Mays, James Luther. "The Place of the Torah-Psalms in the Psalter." *Journal of Biblical Literature* 106 (1987): 3–12.

McEachern, Alton H. "Preaching From the Psalms." *Review and Expositor* 81 (1984): 457–60.

Meyer, Stephen G. "The Psalms and Personal Counseling." *Journal of Psychology and Theology* 2 (1974): 26–30.

Miller, Patrick D., Jr. "Synonymous-Sequential Parallelism in the Psalms." *Biblica* 61 (1980): 256–60.

______. "Psalms and Inscriptions." Supplement to *Vetus Testamentum* 32 (1981): 311–32.

______. "Trouble and Woe. Interpreting Biblical Laments." *Interpretation* 37 (1983): 32–45.

______. "Enthroned on the Praises of Israel: The Praise of God in Old Testament Theology." *Interpretation* 39 (1985): 5–19.

———. *Interpreting the Psalms.* Philadelphia: Fortress, 1986.
Mowinckel, Sigmund. *The Psalms in Israel's Worship.* PIW. Translated by D.R. Ap-Thomas. 2 volumes. Nashville: Abingdon, 1962.
Müller, Paul-Gerhard. "Die Funktion der Psalmzitate im Hebräerbrief." *Freude an der Weisung des Herrn, Beiträge zur Theologie der Psalmen, Festgabe zum 70. Geburtstag von Heinrich Gross.* Edited by Ernst Haag and Frank-Lothar Hossfeld. Stuttgart: Katholisches Bibelwerk, 1986, pp. 223–42.
Muilenburg, J. "A Study in Hebrew Rhetoric: Repetition and Style." Supplement to *Vetus Testamentum* 1 (1953): 97–111.
Murphy, Roland E. "A Consideration of the Classification, 'Wisdom Psalms'." Supplement to *Vetus Testamentum* 9 (1963): 157–67.
———. "The Faith of the Psalmist." *Interpretation* 34 (1980): 229–39.
———. *Wisdom Literature and Psalms.* Nashville: Abingdon, 1983.
Mussner, Franz. "Die Psalmen im Gedankengang des Paulus in Röm 9–11." *Freude an der Weisung des Herrn, Beiträge zur Theologie der Psalmen, Festgabe zum 70. Geburtstag von Heinrich Gross.* Edited by Ernst Haag and Frank-Lothar Hossfeld. Stuttgart: Katholisches Bibelwerk, 1986, pp. 243–63.
O'Connor, M. *Hebrew Verse Structure.* Winona Lake: Eisenbrauns, 1980.
Oesterley, W.O.E. *The Psalms, Translated With Text-Critical and Exegetical Notes.* London: S.P.C.K., 1962.
Old, Hughes Oliphant. "The Psalms of Praise in the Worship of the New Testament Church." *Interpretation* 39 (1985): 20–33.
Peifer, Claude J. "Sing for Us the Songs of Zion: the Jerusalem Psalms." *The Bible Today* 97 (1978): 1690–96.
Perdue, Leo G. *Wisdom and Cult. A Critical Analysis of the Views of Cult in the Wisdom Literatures of Israel and the Ancient Near East.* SBLDS 30. Missoula: Scholars, 1977.
Rad, Gerhard von. *Old Testament Theology.* OTT. Translated by J.A. Baker. 2 volumes. Philadelphia: Westminster, 1961, 1967.
Reindl, Joseph. "Weisheitliche Bearbeitung von Psalmen." Supplement to *Vetus Testamentum* 32 (1981): 333–56.
Ridderbos, Nic. H. *Psalmen en Cultus.* Kampen: Kok, 1950.
———. "The Psalms: Style-Figures and Structure." *OudTestamentische Studiën* 13 (1963): 43–76.
———. *Die Psalmen.* Beihefte Zeitschrift für die alttestamentliche Wissenschaft 117. Leiden: Brill, 1972.
Rose, André. "L'Influence des Psaumes sur les Annonces et les Récits de la Passion et de la Résurrection dans les Evangiles." *Le Psautier. Ses Origines. Ses Problèmes littéraires. Son Influence.* Edited by Robert De Langhe. Louvain: Institut Orientaliste, 1962, pp. 297–356.
Sabourin, Leopold. *The Psalms. Their Origin and Meaning.* 2 volumes. Staten Island: Alba House, 1969.
Saebø, Magne. "Sigmund Mowinckel and His Relation to the Literary Critical School." *Studia Theologica* 40 (1986): 81–93.
Sanders, J.A. *The Psalms Scroll of Qumran Cave 11.* Discoveries in the Judean Desert 4. London: Clarendon, 1965, pp. 54–64.
———. "Cave 11 Surprises and the Question of Canon." *New Directions in Biblical Archaeology.* Edited by D.N. Freedman and J.C. Greenfield. Garden City: Doubleday, 1971, pp. 113–30.
Sarna, N.M. "The Psalm Superscriptions and the Guilds." *Studies in Jewish Religious and Intellectual History, Presented to Alexander Altmann on the Occasion of His Seventieth Birthday.* Edited by Siegfried Stein and Raphael Loewe. London: Institute for Jewish Studies, 1979, pp. 281–300.
Scharbert, Jose. "Das 'Wir' in den Psalmen auf dem Hintergrund altorientalischen Betens." *Freude an der Weisung des Herrn, Beiträge zur Theologie der Psalmen, Festgabe zum 70.*

Geburtstag von Heinrich Gross. Edited by Ernst Haag and Frank-Lothar Hossfeld. Stuttgart: Katholisches Bibelwerk, 1986, pp. 297–324.

Schenker, Adrian. "Das Gebet im Lichte der Psalmen." *Bibel und Kirche* 35 (1980): 37–41.

Schneider, Severin. "Das Denken in Bildern als Voraussetzung für das persönliche Psalmenbeten." *Bibel und Kirche* 35 (1980): 47–54.

Shepherd, M.H., Jr. *The Psalms in Christian Worship: A Practical Guide*. Minneapolis: Augsburg, 1976.

Slomovic, E. "Toward an Understanding of the Formation of the Historical Titles of the Book of Psalms." *Zeitschrift für die alttestamentliche Wissenschaft* 91 (1979): 350–80.

Smick, Elmer B. "Ugaritic and the Theology of the Psalms." *New Perspectives on the Old Testament*. Edited by J. Barton Payne. Waco: Word, 1970, pp. 104–16.

———. "Mythopoetic Language in the Psalms." *Westminster Theological Journal* 44 (1982): 88–98.

———. "Israel's Struggle With the Religions of Canaan." *Through Christ's Word. A Festschrift for Dr. Philip E. Hughes*. Edited by W. Robert Godfrey and Jesse L. Boyd III. Phillipsburg: Presbyterian and Reformed, 1985, pp. 108–17.

Snaith, Norman. *The Seven Penitential Psalms*. London: Epworth, 1964.

Soulen, Richard N. *Handbook of Biblical Criticism*. Atlanta: Knox, 1981.

Steck, Odil Hannes. *Friedensvorstellungen im alten Jerusalem: Psalmen, Jesaja, Deuterojesaja*. Zürich: Theologischer Verlag, 1972.

Stendebach, Franz Josef. "Die Psalmen in der neueren Forschung." *Bibel und Kirche* 35 (1980): 60–70.

Stolz, Fritz. *Psalmen im nachkultischen Raum*. Theologische Studien 129. Zurich: Theologischer Verlag, 1983.

Storfjell, J. Bjørnar. "The Chiastic Structure of Psalm 151." *Andrews University Seminary Studies* 25 (1987): 97–106.

Stuart, Douglas K. *Studies in Early Hebrew Meter*. Missoula: Scholars, 1976.

Talmon, Shemaryahu. "Emendation of Biblical Texts on the Basis of Ugaritic Parallels." *Scripta Hierosolymitana* 31 (1986): 279–300.

Tate, Marvin E. "The Interpretation of the Psalms." *Review and Expositor* 81 (1984): 363–75.

Throntveit, Mark A. "The Penitential Psalms and Lenten Discipline." *Lutheran Quarterly* 1 (1987): 495–512.

Van der Ploeg, J.P.M. "Réflexions Sur Les Genres Littéraires Des Psaumes." *Studia Biblica et Semitica: Theodoro Christiano Vriezen qui munere Professoris Theologiae per XXV Annos functus est, ab Amicis, Collegis, Discipulis dedicata*. Wageningen: Veenman, 1966, pp. 265–77.

———. "L'Etude du Psautier (1960–1967)." *De Mari a Qumran: L'Ancien Testament: Son Milieu. Ses Ecrits. Ses relectures juives. Hommage à Mgr J. Coppens*. Edited by H. Cazelles. Paris: P. Lethiellieux, 1969, pp. 174–91.

van 't Spijker, W. "Bucers Commentaar op de Psalmen: Hebraica Veritas cum Christi Philosophia Coniungenda." *Theologia Reformata* 30 (1987): 264–80.

Wainwright, Geoffrey. "The Praise of God in the Theological Reflection of the Church." *Interpretation* 39 (1985): 34–45.

Wanke, Gunther. *Die Zionstheologie der Korachiten in ihrem Traditionsgeschichtlichen Zusammenhang*. Berlin: Töpelmann, 1966.

Watson, Wilfred G.E. "The Pivot Pattern in Hebrew, Ugaritic and Akkadian Poetry." *Zeitschrift für die alttestamentliche Wissenschaft* 88 (1976): 239–53.

———. *Classical Hebrew Poetry: A Guide to Its Techniques*. JSOTS 26. Sheffield: JSOT, 1984.

Watters, William R. *Formula Criticism and the Poetry of the Old Testament*. Berlin: Walter de Gruyter, 1976.

Watts, John D.W. "Yahweh Malak Psalms." *Theologische Zeitschrift* 21 (1965): 341–48.

———. "Psalms of Trust, Thanksgiving, and Praise." *Review and Expositor* 81 (1984): 395–406.

Welten, Peter. "Königsherrschaft Jahwes und Thronbesteigung." *Vetus Testamentum* 32 (1982): 297–310.

Westermann, Claus. *The Praise of God in the Psalms*. Translated by Keith R. Crim. Richmond: Knox, 1965.

———. *The Psalms: Structure, Content, and Message*. Translated by Ralph D. Gehrke. Minneapolis: Augsburg, 1980.

———. *Praise and Lament in the Psalms*. Translated by Keith R. Crim and Richard N. Soulen. Atlanta: Knox, 1981.

———. *Ausgewählte Psalmen*. Göttingen: Vandenhoeck & Ruprecht, 1984.

Wilson, Gerald H. "Evidence of Editorial Divisions in the Hebrew Psalter." *Vetus Testamentum* 34 (1984): 337–52.

———. *The Editing of the Hebrew Psalter*. SBLDS 76. Chico: Scholars, 1985.

Ziegler, Joseph. "Die Hilfe Gottes 'am Morgen'." *Alttestamentliche Studien: Friedrich Nötscher zum 60. Geburtstag gewidmet*. Bonn: Peter Hanstein, 1950, pp. 281–88.

Zimmerli, Walther. "Zwillingspsalmen." *Wort, Lied und Gottesspruch: Beiträge zu Psalmen und Propheten. Festschrift für Joseph Ziegler*. Edited by Josef Schreiner. Wurzberg: Echter Verlag/Katholisches Bibelwerk, 1972, pp. 105–13.

———. *Old Testament Theology in Outline*. OTTO. Translated by David E. Green. Atlanta: Knox, 1978.

8. Outline

Book I: Psalms 1–41

Psalm 1: God's Blessing on the Godly
Appendix: The Ways of Wisdom and Folly
Psalm 2: The Messianic King
Psalm 3: Quietness Amid Troubles
Appendix: Yahweh Is My God
Psalm 4: An Evening Hymn (in Despondency)
Psalm 5: A Morning Prayer (in Anticipation of God's Presence)
Appendix: Yahweh Is King
Psalm 6: A Prayer (in Deep Anguish)
Psalm 7: The Righteous God Loves the Righteous
Appendix: The Name of Yahweh
Psalm 8: The Glory of the Creator and of Man
Psalm 9: Prayer and Praise for God's Just Rule of the Nations
Appendix: Yahweh Is El Elyon
Psalm 10: The Rule of Man and God's Kingship
Psalm 11: Refuge in the Righteous King
Psalm 12: Lying Tongues and the Truthfulness of God's Word
Psalm 13: Waiting for God's Salvation
Psalm 14: God Deals With Foolish Evildoers
Psalm 15: Who May Live in God's Presence?
Psalm 16: Refuge in the Lord
Psalm 17: A Prayer for God's Justice
Psalm 18: Royal Thanksgiving
Psalm 19: God's Perfections Revealed in Work and Word
Appendix: The Word of God
Psalm 20: Prayer for Victory
Psalm 21: The Rule of God Through His King
Psalm 22: Anguish and Joy
Appendix: Yahweh Is El
Psalm 23: The Goodness of God
Psalm 24: The King of Glory Is Our God
Appendix: Lord Sabaoth
Psalm 25: A Prayer for Deliverance, Guidance, and Forgiveness
Appendix: The Perfections of Yahweh
Psalm 26: The Innocent Plea for Redemption
Psalm 27: Confidence in the Lord
Psalm 28: Prayer to the Lord, My Strength and My Shield
Psalm 29: The Victorious Kingship of Yahweh
Psalm 30: Praise for God's Faithfulness in a Time of Need
Psalm 31: How Great Is Your Goodness!
Psalm 32: The Blessing of Forgiveness and Wise Living
Psalm 33: The Lord Is a Sovereign and Gracious Ruler
Psalm 34: Wise Counsel for the Poor of Heart
Psalm 35: A Prayer for Vindication
Psalm 36: The Blessedness of the Wise

Psalm 37: Wise Living in a Crooked Generation
Psalm 38: A Prayer for Reconciliation
Psalm 39: A Stranger to Life and an Alien With God
Psalm 40: The Joyful Experience and Expectation of Salvation
Psalm 41: God's Blessings in Adversity

Book II: Psalms 42–72

Psalms 42–43: Hoping in the Lord's Salvation
Psalm 44: Redeem Us Because of Your Unfailing Love
Psalm 45: The Wedding of a Son of David
Psalm 46: The God of Jacob Is Our Fortress
  Appendix: Zion Theology
Psalm 47: Yahweh Is the Victorious King
Psalm 48: The Beautiful City of God
Psalm 49: The Folly of Riches Without Wisdom
Psalm 50: A Heart of Gratitude
Psalm 51: Forgiveness and the Community
Psalm 52: An Uprooted and a Sprawling Tree
Psalm 53: God Deals With Foolish Evildoers
Psalm 54: Surely God Is My Help!
Psalm 55: The Lord Sustains the Righteous!
Psalm 56: Walking in Darkness With God's Light
Psalm 57: The Exaltation of Yahweh in the Midst of Alienation
Psalm 58: Surely the Righteous Still Are Rewarded
Psalm 59: My God Is My Champion
Psalm 60: Has God Forgotten Us?
Psalm 61: A Prayer From a Fainting Heart
Psalm 62: Rest and Reward
Psalm 63: The Excellence of God's Love
Psalm 64: Prayer for Protection
Psalm 65: The Bounty of Our Savior
Psalm 66: Come and See What God Has Done
Psalm 67: Grant Your Blessing on All Your Creation
Psalm 68: God Is a Father to the Oppressed
Psalm 69: The Zeal for Your House and God's Love for His Own
Psalm 70: See Psalm 40:13–17
Psalm 71: Longing for Yahweh's Righteous Acts
Psalm 72: The Glory of the Davidic Kingdom

Book III: Psalms 73–89

Psalm 73: The Suffering of God's Children and the Goodness of God
Psalm 74: The Destruction of the Temple
Psalm 75: Justice Is the Lord's
Psalm 76: The Lord Is the God of Jacob
Psalm 77: A Remembrance of God's Greatness
Psalm 78: Lessons From Israel's History
  Appendix: The Mighty Acts of Yahweh

Psalm 79: Lord, Remember the Sheep of Your Pasture
Psalm 80: Make Your Face to Shine on Us
Psalm 81: If My People Would But Listen to Me
Psalm 82: The Judgment of God in the Great Assembly
Psalm 83: A Lament Concerning the Presence of Evil
Psalm 84: A Deep Longing for the Presence of God
Psalm 85: Surely His Salvation Is Near!
Appendix: Anger in the Psalms
Psalm 86: Give Me a Sign of Your Goodness
Psalm 87: Glorious Things of Thee Are Spoken
Psalm 88: A Prayer in the Darkness of Despair
Appendix: Sheol-Grave-Death in the Psalms
Psalm 89: Will You Reject Us Forever?
Appendix: The Messianic King

Book IV: Psalms 90–106

Psalm 90: Teach Us to Number Our Days
Psalm 91: In the Shelter of the Most High
Psalm 92: In Praise of the Lord
Psalm 93: Yahweh Reigns Gloriously
Psalm 94: Yahweh Is the Judge of the Earth
Psalm 95: Let Us Kneel Before Our Maker
Psalm 96: Yahweh Will Judge the World in Righteousness
Psalm 97: The Joys of Zion
Psalm 98: A New Song to the Lord
Appendix: Yahweh Is the Divine Warrior
Psalm 99: Yahweh Is the Revealer-King
Psalm 100: The Lord Is God and He Is Good
Psalm 101: Commitment to Excellence
Psalm 102: You Remain, but I. . . .
Psalm 103: His Compassions They Fail Not!
Appendix: Sin and Forgiveness
Psalm 104: Great Is Your Faithfulness to All Creation
Psalm 105: Yahweh's Acts in Salvation History
Psalm 106: Remember Yahweh's Love and Israel's Disobedience

Book V: Psalms 107–150

Psalm 107: Lessons From the Experience of the Saints
Psalm 108: See Psalms 57:7–11 and 60:5–12 (=108:6–13).
Psalm 109: Yahweh Loves the Needy
Psalm 110: The Kingdom of the Lord
Psalm 111: Celebration of God's Faithfulness
Psalm 112: The Triumph of Faith
Psalm 113: Yahweh Is Exalted in His Saving Acts
Psalm 114: We Are the People of God!
Psalm 115: We Are the Servants of God!
Psalm 116: Be at Rest, for the Lord Is Good

Psalm 117: Great Is His Love Toward Us
Psalm 118: Open the Gates of Righteousness
Psalm 119: The Joy of God's Law in Distress
Appendix: Yahweh Is My Redeemer
Psalm 120: Yahweh, I, and They
Psalm 121: Yahweh Is My Guardian
Psalm 122: May There Be Peace in Zion!
Appendix: The Praise of Yahweh
Psalm 123: Have Mercy, O Lord
Psalm 124: Our Helper Is the Maker of Heaven and Earth!
Psalm 125: Peace Be on Israel
Psalm 126: The Restoration Is Here!
Psalm 127: The Blessing of the Lord
Psalm 128: The Family Blessed by Yahweh
Psalm 129: Yahweh Is Righteous
Psalm 130: May the Blessing of the Lord Be on You!
Psalm 131: Contentment With God
Psalm 132: The Tabernacling of Yahweh
Appendix: The Ark of the Covenant and the Temple: Symbols of Yahweh's Presence and Rule
Psalm 133: The Communion of the Saints
Psalm 134: May Yahweh Bless You From Zion!
Psalm 135: Yahweh Is Free in His Marvelous Acts
Psalm 136: Yahweh Is Good!
Psalm 137: If I Forget You, O Jerusalem
Appendix: Imprecations in the Psalms
Psalm 138: Yahweh Delivers the Humble
Psalm 139: Yahweh Knows Me!
Psalm 140: You Are My God!
Appendix: The Poor and Oppressed
Psalm 141: May My Prayer Be Like Incense!
Psalm 142: Yahweh Alone Is My Portion in the Land of the Living
Psalm 143: Lead Me on Level Ground
Psalm 144: Yahweh Is My Warrior
Psalm 145: Great Is Yahweh's Universal Kingdom!
Psalm 146: Yahweh Reigns Forever and Ever
Psalm 147: The Blessedness of the People of God
Psalm 148: Praise to Yahweh, the Wise Creator
Psalm 149: Yahweh Delights in His People
Psalm 150: Praise Yahweh
Appendix: Musical Instruments

Text and Exposition

Book I: Psalms 1–41

Psalm 1: God's Blessing on the Godly

The first psalm appropriately introduces the Book of Psalms with its pronouncement of blessing on all who respond in fidelity to the God of the covenant. The covenant not only forms the background for distinguishing the righteous from the wicked but also provides the basis for the blessing on the righteous and the curse on the wicked.

The placing of this psalm at the beginning of the Psalter is significant because it both invites and encourages God's people to live godly lives. Wilson writes, "While Ps 1 as an introduction sets the 'tone' for an approach to the Psalter, it indicates this is a collection to be read rather than performed. . . . it stresses the importance of the approach (it is a matter of Life or Death)" (*Editing the Hebrew Psalter*, p. 207). It also provides the assurance that the righteous will be rewarded and that, in the end, God "knows the way of the righteous." The first psalm sets the tone for the entire Psalter because of its concern for God, for godly living, and for the hope of the godly in the realization of the promises of the covenant. This psalm contrasts the two life styles set out in the wisdom literature and reminds the readers of the choices of life or death, of blessing or curse (cf. Deut 30:11–20).

Psalm 1 is a *wisdom* psalm and shares many features common to the Book of Proverbs and to other psalms designated as wisdom psalms (34; 37; 49; 73; 111–12; 119; 127–28; 133; see the Introduction). Psalm 1 holds forth the blessedness of godliness, encouraging the godly to pursue the way of God over against the way of the world. The psalm encourages wisdom as the way of life by emphasizing the blessedness of the righteous, the adversity of the wicked, and the contrastive ways between the righteous and the wicked.

As a didactic psalm, Psalm 1 encourages the pursuit of godliness by contrasting God's rewards and his judgment. Therefore, the psalm tends to be idealistic. For example, it does not claim to deal with the totality of human life, such as the problems of suffering (cf. Pss 37; 73; Job) or the meaning of life (Ecclesiastes). The imagery of Psalm 1 resembles Jeremiah 17:7–8, but it differs from it in structure (cf. James A. Durlesser, "Poetic style in Psalm 1 and Jeremiah 17:5–8. A Rhetorical Critical Study," *Semitics* 9 [1984]: 30–48). The contrastive juxtaposition between the righteous and the wicked is heightened by the change from positive (P) to negative (N) verbal forms, as analyzed by Rosario Pius Merendino: NPPNNP ("Sprachkunst in Psalm I," VetTest 29 [1979]: 45–60). For a study on the impact of Psalm 1 on ancient Jewish literature, see Johannes Marböck, "Zur frühen Wirkungsgeschichte von Ps 1," *Freude an der Weisung des Herrn, Beiträge zur Theologie der Psalmen, Festgabe zum 70. Geburtstag von Heinrich Gross*, edd. Ernst Haag and Frank-Lothar Hossfeld (Stuttgart: Katholisches Bibelwerk, 1986), pp. 207–22.

The structural divisions (see also W. Vogels, "Structural Analysis in Psalm 1," *Biblica* 60 [1979]: 410–16; P. Auffret, "Essai sur la Structure littéraire du Psaume 1," *Biblische Zeitschrift* 22 [1978]: 26–45) bring out the discriminating way of the godly who live on earth with a constant consideration of the future, when the Lord shall judge the wicked and reward the godly (see also Miller, *Interpreting the Psalms*, pp. 81–86). The main divisions are as follows:

A. The Discriminating Way of the Godly (vv.1–2)
  B. The Future of the Godly and the Wicked Contrasted (vv.3–5)
A′. The Discriminating Way of God (v.6)

The structural chiasm (ABB′A′) is also found at the beginning and end as an inclusion:

A. Dissociation From the Wicked (v.1)
  B. Association With God (v.2)
  B′. God's Association With the Godly (v.6a)
A′. God's Removal of the Wicked (v.6b)

The first psalm may have consisted of Psalms 1 and 2. According to some ancient MSS, the quotation of Psalm 2:7 in Acts 13:33 is introduced as "the first psalm." In rabbinical traditions the first two psalms were also united as one (Craigie, *Psalms 1–50*, p. 59; b. *Berakoth* 9b). W.H. Brownlee has recently argued in favor of the unity of the two psalms ("Psalms 1–2 as a Coronation Liturgy," *Biblica* 52 [1971]: 321–36). However, the evidence is not decisive. In any case, the matter is of no great importance because the message of the first psalm stands on its own. It is a didactic psalm with an invitation to wise—"godly"—living. The second psalm, a royal psalm, brings out the folly of the nations who do not submit themselves to God and his anointed, concluding with a call for wisdom (2:10–12). The call to respond wisely by dissociation from sinners (1:1) parallels the rebuke to kings and nations to submit themselves to the Lord and his Messiah (2:10). Moreover, the introduction "blessed is" at the beginning of Psalm 1 (v.1) forms an inclusion with Psalm 2:12b by the formula "Blessed" (*'ašrê*). In spite of these factors, the traditional treatment of each psalm as a unit, bound together by the inclusionary motif ("blessed") and by the appeal to wisdom, is sustained (cf. John T. Willis, "Psalm 1—An Entity," ZAW 91 [1979]: 381–401). For a literary evaluation of Psalm 1, see Alter, pp. 114–17.

I. The Discriminating Way of the Godly

1:1–2

1 Blessed is the man
  who does not walk in the counsel of the wicked
or stand in the way of sinners
  or sit in the seat of mockers.
2 But his delight is in the law of the LORD,
  and on his law he meditates day and night.

1 The opening phrase of the psalm ("Blessed is the man") is an appropriate introduction to the Book of Psalms. The Psalms encourage individuals as well as the community of God's people to live for God's glory. The formula "Blessed is the man" evokes joy and gratitude, as man may live in fellowship with his God. Blessedness is not deserved; it is a gift of God. God declares sinners to be righteous and freely grants them newness of life in which he protects them from the full effects of the world under judgment (Gen 3:15–19). Outside of God's blessing, man is "cursed" and ultimately leads a meaningless life (Eccl 1:2). The word "happy" is a good rendition of "blessed" (*'ašrê*), provided one keeps in mind that the condition of "bliss" is not merely a feeling. Even when the righteous do not feel happy, they are still considered "blessed" from God's perspective. He bestows this gift on them. Neither negative feelings nor adverse conditions can take his blessing away.

The blessing of God rested on Abraham (Gen 12:3) and was incorporated into the Abrahamic and Sinaitic covenants (Gen 17:2–16; Deut 7:13; 28:3–6). For the godly blessing is both the experience and the anticipation of the fulfillment of God's promises (cf. Deut 30:15–20). Since man's being is both physical and spiritual (Gen 2:7), God's blessings extend to the whole person (cf. Pss 34, 127).

While man's "happiness" is a free gift of God, it must be promoted by two kinds of activities: *dissociation* from the wicked and *association* with God (v.2). Dissociation is brought out by means of three negative sentences. The godly man does *not* (1) walk (*hālaḵ*) in the counsel of the wicked, (2) stand (*'āmaḏ*) in the way of sinners, or (3) sit (*yāšāḇ*) in the seat of mockers; rather, he reflects on the Lord in his walking, standing, and sitting (cf. Deut 6:7; see Gunnel André, " 'Walk', 'Stand', and 'Sit,' " in Psalm i 1–2," VetTest 32 [1982]: 327; cf. Stefan C. Reif, "Ibn Ezra on Psalm I 1–2," VetTest 34 [1984]: 232–36).

The perfect mood of the verbs in each case emphasizes that the godly are *never* involved with anything tainted with evil (Joüon, par. 112d). These three descriptions do not represent three kinds of activities of the wicked or a climactic development from walking to sitting or an intensification in the depraved activities of the wicked. Instead, the parallelism is synonymous and profoundly portrays the totality of evil. For a contrastive use of complete loyalty to the Lord, see Deuteronomy 6:7.

There are two possible translations of *'aṣaṯ rešā'îm*: "counsel of the wicked" (NIV) and "council of the wicked" (Dahood, *Psalms*, 1:1–2). The context does not determine the meaning because both meanings are possible. The usage of the phrase elsewhere ("schemes [counsel] of the wicked," Job 10:3; 21:16) and of similar phrases ("the plans [counsel] of the nations," Ps 33:10; "the advice [counsel][of] the elders," 2 Chron 10:8, 13) is in favor of the traditional translation: "counsel." The emphasis lies on the folly of the wicked rather than on the act of meeting as a deliberative body. Their whole "way" (*dereḵ*) is corrupt. The "way" is a common metaphor for "manner of life" (TDOT, 3:284–86; TWOT, 1:196–97). The psalm contrasts the two ways: the way of sinners and the way of the righteous (v.6).

The "mockers" (*lēṣîm*) have no regard for God and his commandments. The mocker is a fool in the language of wisdom (Prov 9:8; 14:6). He does not respond to instruction (9:7; 15:12) but stirs up strife by his insults (22:10). He delights in mocking (1:22). Thus the way of folly is comprehensive as it entails a devotion to self and to the group in all areas of life.

In contrast the godly in their walking, lying down, and getting up—whether at home or along the road—are devoted to the Lord (Deut 6:7; cf. Josh 1:7–8). In all their activities they keep distant from the ungodly, lest they get under their influence. They carefully guard themselves in their family, business, and social relations as they set the terms of their relations, while being polite and gracious (cf. Prov 25:21–22; 1 Cor 5:9–13; 2 John 10–11).

2 The righteous man is positively identified by his association with "the law of the LORD." The "law" is not to be limited to the Five Books of Moses or even to the OT as a whole. The Hebrew word *tôrāh* ("law") signifies primarily instruction that comes from God (see the appendix to Ps 19: The Word of God). This is the distinctive difference between revelation and religion (J. Ellul, *A Living Faith*, tr. Peter Heinegg [San Francisco: Harper & Row, 1983], pp. 111–25). Revelation comes from God for the purpose of helping man to live in harmony with God's will, whereas religion is man's attempt to order his path and to explain the world around him. The godly in every age live in accordance with revelation. The contents of the revelation may vary, and Christians may dispute how the OT laws relate to the church today; but there should be an earnest search for and delight in doing the will of God as set forth in Jesus' teaching (Matt 6:10; 12:50; 1 John 3:11–24; 5:2–3; see T.E. McComiskey, *The Covenants of Promise. A Theology of the Old Testament Covenants* [Grand Rapids: Baker, 1985], pp. 66–80).

The psalmist does not speak here about the deadening effects of the law but of its life-giving aspects. Life responds to life, and spirit responds to spirit; so it is with the new life of the believer as he responds joyfully to the living God and to the Spirit who has inspired his word. The believer's delight is not only in knowing, studying, and memorizing the Word of God but especially in *doing* God's will, rather than being deceived by the wicked. C.S. Lewis incisively observed, "The Law's beauty, sweetness, or preciousness, arose from the contrast of the surrounding Paganism, we may soon find occasion to recover it. Christians increasingly live on a spiritual island" ("Sweeter than Honey," in *Reflections on the Psalms*, p. 64).

"Delight" (*ḥeps̱ô*) expresses all that makes the man of God happy. The law is more than his delight; it is his chief desire. The fear of the Lord, as the beginning of wisdom, is expressed as a delight in God's law (112:1; cf. Isa 58:13–14) and not only in pious words or a good feeling about God (cf. TWOT, 1:148–49).

In the wisdom literature the way of *tôrāh* signifies the adherence to, as well as the enjoyment and application of, God's will to everyday life. The delight of the godly in doing God's will on earth (Matt 6:10) is the result of a special relationship with the Lord.

The godly man "meditates" (*hāg̱āh*) in the law of God day and night. The verb *hāg̱āh* is onomatopoeic (TWOT, 1:205); i.e., in its basic meaning ("to murmur" or "mutter"), it alludes to the *sound* of animals (Isa 31:4; 38:14) or a moaning noise (Isa 16:7). Since the Bible, in part or as a whole, was generally not available to God's people, they memorized and "pondered" the word (cf. 119:11), the perfections of the Lord (63:6), and his mighty acts (77:12; 143:5). The alternation of the perfect (v.1) and imperfect (v.2) brings up the habitual aspect of reflection on God's word (Joüon, par. 112d). The one who meditates *continually* reflects God's word in life. H. Ringgren writes that study and practice blend into one: "The zealous study of the law which results in being filled with the will of Yahweh and the doing of his commandments" (TDOT, 3:323).

Meditation is not the setting apart of a special time for personal devotions, whether morning or evening, but it is the reflection on the Word of God in the course of daily activities (Josh 1:8). Regardless of the time of day or the context, the godly respond to life in accordance with God's word. Even where the word is not explicit, the godly person has trained his heart to speak and act with wisdom (Prov 1:1–7). According to Proverbs 3:1–6, the wise man receives instruction (*tôrāh*), writes it on his heart, and wholeheartedly trusts in the Lord with all his heart in all his daily activities. The psalmist exclaims how he loves the law of God because its commandments make him wiser than his enemies and lead him to greater insight and understanding than that of his teachers and elders (119:97–100). On the connection between wisdom and the law of Moses, see Eichrodt, TOT, 2:344–49; Joseph Blenkinsopp, *Wisdom and Law in the Old Testament: The Ordering of Life in Israel and Early Judaism* (Oxford: Oxford University Press, 1983); Childs, OTTC, pp. 210–14.

Notes

1 The phrase אַשְׁרֵי הָאִישׁ (*'ašrê hā'îš*, "Blessed is the man") is a formula of blessing and is a synonym of בָּרוּךְ (*bārûk*, "blessed"; cf. TWOT, 1:80). Walter Käser ("Beobachtungen zum alttestamentlichen Makarismus," ZAW 82 [1970]: 225–50) gives a convincing argument that the expression "blessed is" represents a form of wisdom literature. By this form the author proclaims the blessings of covenantal life and the joy of living continually in the presence of God who is faithful from day to day (cf. 94:12; 112:1; 119:1–2). The formula is found as early as the Pyramid Texts. However, in the covenantal structure of Israel, it was transformed and enriched (cf. TDOT, 1:445–48). Our Lord also used this expression in the Beatitudes (Matt 5:3–12).

Dahood's proposal to read דֶּרֶךְ חַטָּאִים (*derek ḥaṭṭa'îm*, "the way of sinners") as "assembly of sinners" (*Psalms*, 1:2) is based on the parallel construction and on a doubtful etymology.

2 "LORD" is an English translation of the tetragrammaton יהוה (*YHWH*), usually pronounced as "Yahweh." In reading the Psalms, the name of God is an important marker of his presence and his closeness to his people. The significance of the name will receive further attention when important to the exposition of the text (see the appendixes to Ps 3: "Yahweh Is My God," and to Ps 7: "The Name of Yahweh"; cf. Willem A. VanGemeren, "Tetragrammaton," in Elwell, EDB, pp. 1079–80).

Brueggemann treats Ps 1 together with Pss 15; 24; 119 as "Songs of Torah" (*Message of the Psalms*, pp. 38–42).

II. The Future of the Godly and the Wicked Contrasted

1:3–5

3 He is like a tree planted by streams of water,
which yields its fruit in season
and whose leaf does not wither.
Whatever he does prospers.

4 Not so the wicked!
They are like chaff
that the wind blows away.
5 Therefore the wicked will not stand in the judgment,
nor sinners in the assembly of the righteous.

3 The happiness of the godly is likened to a tree. The tree is a familiar metaphor for the blessed life of the godly (Jer 17:7–8). In the wisdom literature the tree is a metaphor for wisdom itself (Prov 3:18); and the wise man is likened to a tree of life in that his speech and activities are life-giving and restorative (Prov 11:30; 15:4). Unlike trees growing wild in wadis or planted in the fields, where the amount of rainfall varies, the tree the psalmist envisions has been planted purposely by irrigation canals (*palgê māyim*, "streams of water"), artificial water-channels made for the purpose of irrigation (cf. Prov 21:1; Eccl 2:5–6; Isa 30:25).

The imagery of the leaves and the fruit assure the godly that they will receive God's blessing and will enjoy life as a gift of God (cf. Ezek 47:12). True to the language used in wisdom literature, the godly are characterized by the success the Lord sends their way. The "prosperity" of the righteous does not necessarily extend to the assurance of great wealth but primarily to God's blessing on their words and works (cf. 90:14–17). The psalmist thus encourages the godly to pursue the way of wisdom. The wise man is characterized by success. Nevertheless, the psalm does not encourage a success-oriented faith. The godly do not seek success for its own sake, but they *do* receive a measure of blessing on their lives. The prosperity of the righteous—guaranteed or limited to the godly—is a gift of God, a by-product of wise living; cf. Joseph (Gen 39:2–3, 23), Joshua (1:8), Solomon (2 Chron 1:11–12), and Hezekiah (2 Chron 32:30). But success is not an infallible token of God's presence, for the wicked may also prosper (Ps 37:7). Rather, the righteous live with the *hope* of God's blessing.

4 How different is the end of the wicked! Whereas Jeremiah compares the lot of the wicked to a bush in the wasteland that dries up, the psalmist compares the wicked to mere "chaff." The imagery of chaff is not uncommon in the Bible (cf. Ps 35:5; Isa 17:13; 29:5; Hos 13:3; Zeph 2:2; Matt 3:12). Malachi compares the end of the wicked on the Day of the Lord both to "stubble" and to a tree consumed by fire from root to branch (4:1). The metaphor of chaff reveals both the uselessness of the wicked and the ease with which God will deal with them. Even as the winnower casts the chaff to the afternoon breeze, so the Lord will drive away the wicked. No one will remember their place.

The brevity of the wicked's description stands in stark contrast to the fuller portrayal of the righteous as a tree with leaves and fruit (v.3). It is also briefly compared to the lengthy description of the wicked in v.1.

5 The conclusion is clearly marked by the word "therefore" (*'al-kēn*). The end of the wicked may not be clear while they are alive and busying themselves with wickedness, but from God's perspective the wicked have no future. They cannot withstand the judgment of God, whether it comes in the present, by means of adversity, or on the Day of the Lord. They are judged by being alienated from the congregation of the righteous. "The assembly of the righteous" (*'ᵃdaṯ ṣaddîqîm*) is composed of those who have a relationship with God and enjoy his presence. They will experience his presence both now and in the life to come. The word "assembly" (*'ēḏāh*) is a collective term for the people of God (TWOT, 1:388), used here in a more spiritual way to indicate that the judgment of God also comes on circumcised Israelites who did not love God or keep his commandments. "Judgment" (*mišpāṭ*) is the whole of the judicial process by which Yahweh will establish his rule on earth. He is the God of justice (Mal 2:17–3:5), who in his wrath and righteous indignation execrates the wicked. Therefore, it is an awful matter to fall under his judgment. The judgment of God *will* strike the wicked so that they will be incapable of rising (cf. Isa 2:12–21). His judgment takes place throughout redemptive history and will come to a climactic end in "the day" of the Lord (Zeph 1:14–18; cf. Matt 13:41–43; 1 Thess 5:1–11).

Notes

3 On the shift from active to passive verbs, see Alter, p. 115; R. Lack, "Le Psaume 1—Une Analyse Structurale," *Biblica* 57 (1977): 154–67.

3–4 The literary approach of holistic interpretation espoused by Meir Weiss adds a new dimension to understanding the text. He integrates the tree imagery in Ps 1 and Jer 17 as descriptive of the nature of the wise (see *The Bible From Within. The Method of Total Interpretation* [Jerusalem: Magnes, 1984], pp. 133–63).

5 The צַדִּיקִים (*ṣaddîqîm*, "righteous") are those who love God and do his will. They have close fellowship (cf. Ps 15) as they practice the will of the Most High in all areas of life. The OT concept of righteousness includes justification by faith but also a relationship of communion with God and of responsiveness to Yahweh in doing his will (see 111:3–4; 112:3–4; see W.A. VanGemeren, "Righteousness," in Elwell, BEB, 2:1860–62; TWOT, 2:752–55; see appendix to Ps 25: The Perfections of Yahweh).

III. The Discriminating Way of God

1:6

6 For the LORD watches over the way of the righteous,
but the way of the wicked will perish.

6 The reason for the certainty of the judgment lies in God's knowledge of the affairs of men. God knows! The knowledge of God involves not only an objective knowledge about the righteous but also a subjective relationship with them, assuring them that he cares for his own, protects them, and will reward them (cf. 31:8; 37:18; 144:3).

The intimate acquaintance with God as an expression of his love and care is expressed by the verb "know" (*yôḏēaʿ*; NIV, "watches over"; cf. KB, p. 365). The verb, also used for the intimate relationship of husband and wife (Gen 4:1), marks the love of God for his children. God heard the groaning of the Israelites in Egypt, and he "knew" (Exod 2:25; NIV, "was concerned"). This knowledge about their miserable condition is the beginning of the magnificent story of the Exodus, because he demonstrated his love for them by many signs and wonders (cf. Exod 19:4). God's "knowledge" is a deep commitment to, love for, and care of his own; hence the translation "the LORD watches over" (cf. Rom 8:29–39). As such it is an expression of his covenantal commitment (see Herbert B. Huffmon, "The Treaty Background of Hebrew *Yadaʿ*," BASOR 181 [1966]: 31–37).

The "way of the righteous" is characterized by a love for God and a readiness to live a godly life. However, there is a second way: "the way of the wicked" (cf. v.1). The Lord offers no protection to those who are not reconciled to him; rather, their end is destruction. Jesus warned us that those who know him must do the will of God as interpreted by him (Matt 5–7). Those who do not produce fruit will come under the judgment of his words: "I never knew you. Away from me, you evildoers!" (Matt 7:23; cf. vv.15–27).

Appendix: The Ways of Wisdom and Folly

Old Testament wisdom writings (Job, Proverbs, Ecclesiastes), other sections of the Old and New testaments, and many psalms contrast the ways of the wise and of the fool. There are only two ways: the way of God and the way of man; the way of wisdom and the way of folly. What is biblical wisdom? Biblical wisdom begins and ends with Yahweh, whose way is evident in his creation (Ps 19) and in revelation (Pss 19; 119). The Lord freely chose to reveal himself to Israel and freely elected Israel. The godly in Israel responded to election and divine grace by living in the presence of God. Zimmerli speaks of a dialogical nature of election and responsible living in the presence of Yahweh (OTTO, p. 46). Responsible or wise living was not systematized into a grid of ethical rules. It was first and foremost a devotion to a living God. Childs puts it so aptly, "The response of faith is so intense and directed so personally to God because the possession or loss of life is measured in terms of his relation to God who both 'kills and makes alive' " (OTTC, p. 210).

The righteous

What is the biblical wisdom that the psalmists speak of so frequently? First, wisdom calls for a *response*. The invitation is open to all (34:11–12; cf. Prov 1:8–9; 2:1–3:10). Regardless of age, social standing, or gender, whether Jew or Gentile, God expects the response of love and submission to him (49:1–3). Those who devote themselves to a loving response may have to undergo fatherly discipline: "It was good for me to be afflicted so that I might learn your decrees" (119:71). Out of the brokenness of heart, the godly learn wisdom; and out of gratitude they seek wisdom. The way of wisdom demands total commitment: "Blessed are they who keep his statutes and seek him with all their heart" (119:2; cf. vv.3, 10). Since God is greater than any treasure, the love for God demands the ultimate sacrifice—total loyalty and discipleship: "I rejoice in following your statutes as one rejoices in great riches" (119:14; cf. vv.20, 127).

Second, wisdom opens the door to living in the imitation of God, the Great King over all creation. Creation unfolds the manifold wisdom of God. Everything coheres in him and through him. Because he is one, there is one way of living in coherence in this world: the way of God. The way of God is shown throughout the Psalms but may be illustrated by reference to Psalms 111 and 112. In Psalm 111 the psalmist sets forth the way of God. The "way" (*dereḵ*) of Yahweh is seen in the variety and magnificence of his works (111:2). They frame the world of human experience, as the Lord maintains order in his world (111:3). He is also *generous* like a father toward his creation, bestowing on it grace, compassion, and provision (111:4–5; cf. 145:9). He cares much for all of his creation, but so much more for his covenant people who respond to him as wise children (111:5b–6)! They are the object of his particular love, communion, and blessing (111:7–9). He has revealed his way in creation, redemption, and written revelation. He looks for those who respond properly to his presence (111:10).

According to Psalm 112 the wise are like their heavenly Father. The wise imitate God as they establish Yahweh's way on earth as their divinely appointed sphere of operation (112:3). Their works are established as they show compassion and are gracious (112:4–5, 9). They are steadfast (112:6–7) and successful (112:8–9). They live in harmony with God's order. Childs rightly observes: "The call to an obedient response which involves honesty, charity and peace is grounded in the prior acts of God" (OTTC, p. 216).

Third, the way of God evidences itself in submission to divine revelation. The Book of Psalms opens with this distinctive way of living in the freedom of divine revelation: "But his delight is in the law of the LORD, / and on his law he meditates day and night" (1:2; cf. 37:31). This seems to be a paradox. The godly is free only when he serves God: "I run in the path of your commands, for you have set my heart free" (119:32; cf. v.45).

This attitude toward God's revelation is never separate from a love for the Lord: "Praise the LORD. / Blessed is the man who fears the LORD, / who finds great delight in his commands" (112:1). "Fear" (*yir'āh*) denotes an attitude of submission and openness to divine instruction. The wise man is not alone. While he shuns the godless way of life, he treasures fellowship with the godly (119:63). In Psalm 111 the psalmist refers to the community of the godly as "the council [*sôḏ*] of the upright" (v.1). The *sôḏ* denotes a group of people who associate together, having a way of living in common (cf. 25:14; Prov 3:32) in distinction from the way of the wicked (Jer 15:17; Ps 64:2).

Fourth, the wise are blessed by the Lord. He rewards them in this life and in the life to come (1:3, 6; 119:1–2, 38, 68, 88; 127; 128; 2 Tim 4:8). He does good to them by delivering them from evil (119:17; cf. Matt. 6:13), by fulfilling his promises (119:123), and by removing the wicked from the earth (1:6; 119:119). The aged psalmist of Psalm 37 encourages the godly to keep life in focus, especially in duress. Trust in the Lord overcomes anxiety and bitterness of heart. Further, God's promises are true and will come true! Hence, he encourages the suffering saints to trust in the Lord and to do good (37:3).

The psalmist further encourages the young people to gain wisdom by learning from the experience of the past: "Taste and see that the LORD is good; / blessed is the man who takes refuge in him. / Fear the LORD, you his saints, / for those who fear him lack nothing" (34:8–9; see Ps 34).

What promises are set before the wise? They are blessed in receiving the goodness of the Lord himself (23:6; 34:8). His presence brings sufficiency in matters of food, clothing, and human needs (34:9–11; cf. Matt 6:33–34). Yahweh promises to deliver and protect them (34:15, 17–19, 22). Such a person lives closer to Yahweh than he can ever imagine: "He who dwells in the shelter of the Most High / will rest in the shadow of the Almighty" (91:1). This God can and will care for his own by day or by night (91:3–13), on account of their devotion to him: "Because he loves me," says the Lord, "I will rescue him; I will protect him, for he acknowledges my name" (91:14; cf. vv.15–16).

The imagery of the first psalm portrays the wise person as successful because God is with him. He is likened to a tree, whose verdancy and fruit are lasting (1:3–4; 92:12–15). This is only because "the LORD watches over the way of the righteous" (1:6a). The future of the wise is bright, even in adversity. He holds on to God and to his promises. He believes that regardless of the suffering, Yahweh is for him (37:4–5). He affirms that in the end "he will make your righteousness shine like the dawn, the justice of your cause like the noonday sun" (37:6).

The promise of God, repeated by our Lord, is that "the meek will inherit the land and enjoy great peace" (37:11; cf. Matt 5:5). Yahweh will never abandon those who suffer on account of his name, even in this present evil existence: "For the LORD loves the just / and will not forsake his faithful ones. / They will be protected forever, / but the offspring of the wicked will be cut off" (37:28; cf. vv.39–40).

Fifth, the godly person (*ḥāsîḏ; ṣaddîq*) is dependent on divine guidance (32:8; 119:24, 34), on God's love (*ḥeseḏ*), and on divine favor (119:29), while humbly walking in reliance on the Lord (119:26–27). He despises the attitude of self-reliance as much as he does the way of those who stubbornly refuse to follow God. But he does recognize his weakness, as he prays, "Oh, that my ways were steadfast / in obeying your decrees!" (119:5; cf. v.9). The wise man is constantly *vigilant*, lest he be tempted and succumb to evil (119:11). Further, he lives in awe of the revelation of God, never assuming that he fully grasps the Word of God, but praying instead, "Open my eyes that I may see / wonderful things in your law" (119:18). This attitude is well-expressed by Ellul as

> authenticity of faith, attentive listening to God's Word, the informing of everyday life by the Christian spirit, and boldness become once more the true face of revelation. . . . [their] names are not written in any historical movement, in any genealogy, in any story of the propagation of the faith, these men and women who are content simply to be true and pious unknown Christians. (Jacques Ellul, *The Subversion of Christianity*, tr. Geoffrey W. Bromiley [Grand Rapids: Eerdmans, 1986], pp. 208–9)

The primary goal of the "righteous" lies with God's honor and the establishment of his kingdom by *orthopraxis*, the *doing* of the will of God. He does not seek to impose his will on others, to restructure society, or to transform his arena of operation by exchanging spiritual values for political, societal, or temporal structures. Yes, the wise confess with the psalmist: "I am a stranger on earth; / do not hide your commands from me" (119:19; cf. v.23). His goal is to operate within God's designs and to persevere in this to the end: "Teach me, O LORD, to follow your decrees; / then I will keep them to the end" (119:33; cf. v.112).

The wise live in anticipation of God's intrusion in human affairs. In doing the will of God, they continually await with great expectation the establishment of God's righteousness on earth: in judgment and in rewards. In Psalm 119 we read, "My soul faints with longing for your salvation, / but I have put my hope in your word. / My eyes fail, looking for your promise; / I say, 'When will you comfort me?' " (vv.81–82; cf. vv.77–79, 174).

Kuntz distinguishes three levels of applicability of divine "retribution" in the wisdom psalms: (1) the ideal or traditional (Pss 1; 25:12–14; 32; 37; 40:5–6; 128; (2) the realistic (Pss 34; 37:39–40; 94:12–15; 112); and (3) the eschatological or futuristic (Pss 49; 73:23–26).

Theology, revelation, ethics, and eschatology are correlatives (1:5–6; 37:34; 119:42–43, 49, 52, 74). Life in hope of the kingdom of God intensifies the desire to do what is right in the present (119:134–63). (Johag persuasively relates "good" to covenantal loyalty in which the righteous person does what is good in the eyes of the Lord; that is, he is faithful [pp. 14–23].) The "fear of the LORD" is the beginning of wisdom in the sense that the wise man desires to order his life in the present in anticipation of the order Yahweh will establish. Wise living is living with "order" (von Rad, OTT, 1:433). The man of hope experiences freedom from fear and great peace because his hope lies in Yahweh: "Great peace have they who love your law, / and nothing can make them stumble. / I wait for your salvation, O LORD, / and I follow your commands" (119:165–66).

Vocabulary of the wise

"poor" and "needy" (*'ānî, 'eḇyôn, dāl, daḵ*, see 9:9, 18; 69:32–33; 129:1–2)

"wise" (*ḥāḵām*, see 49:10; 107:43, esp. in Proverbs [47 times])

"to be understanding" (*b-y-n: bînāh* ["understanding"], *teḇûnāh* ["understanding"])

"faithful" (*ḥāsîḏ*, "godly," "faithful [one/people]," "holy one," "saint," "consecrated one," and "devoted" in NIV; see 4:3)

"upright" (*yāšār*, often used to characterize the "heart" [cf. 7:10; 11:2; 32:11; 36:10 et al.] or the "way" [37:14] of the godly)

"righteous" (*ṣaddîq*, see 1:6)

"understanding" (*ś-k-l: maśkîl* [NIV, "any who understand," 14:2; a Hiphil participle, usually found in superscriptions [see Introduction]; *śēḵel* ["have understanding," 111:10])

"blameless" (*tāmîm*, "perfect"; denotes a life style of integrity; see 15:2)

The fool

The fool is variously referred to as "the wicked," "senseless," "mocker," "arrogant," and "enemy." The fool lives without mystery, without a sense of awe, and without accountability: "How great are your works, O LORD, / how profound your thoughts! / The senseless man does not know, / fools do not understand" (92:5–6). This class of people coexists within the covenant community and outside.

The one group rejects the oracles of God and defines their own style of life in clear contradiction to what they have been taught (50:16). They bring confusion, injustice, greed, competition, slander, and all the evils of this world into the community of the godly (Pss 55; 84:10; 94; 119). Their power could become so overwhelming that they form a threat to those who live godly among the people of God (73:3–4). The other group denotes the enemies of God's people and the king: the nations that live in rebellion to God's kingdom.

The response of the godly to either group is a prayer for the manifestation of God's kingdom in which all unrighteousness will be removed. They clearly distinguish between the way of this world and the way of God (cf. 26:5). Hence, the Psalms open with a clear distinction between the way and the end of the godless mockers and that of the righteous (Ps 1).

The "fool" is a person who lives practically as if God is not there, does not see his actions, and extends his operation on earth by ridding this earth of the godly or by oppressing them (10:2, 4, 13; 11:2; 14; 36:1). C.S. Lewis's insight is worth quoting: "What makes this contact with wicked people so difficult is that to handle the situation successfully requires not merely good intentions. . . . It is therefore . . . mere prudence to avoid it when we can" ("Connivance," in *Reflections on the Psalms*, p. 74).

The "imprecations" on the enemies (see appendix to Ps 137) arise only out of the godly's sense of hope that Yahweh will reject the kingdoms of man: "Arise, O Lord! / Deliver me, O my God! / Strike all my enemies on the jaw; / break the teeth of the wicked" (3:7). Their faith is in Yahweh who has revealed his nature as righteous, loving, and compassionate. They further believe that Yahweh's nature and his kingdom will exclude all who live in opposition to his perfections (cf. 11:5). They cannot have a future (cf. 5:4–5).

The godly also believe that God in his love will bless them (7:9) and that this can only happen when all evil is removed (9:5, 16; 37:10, 13, 17, 20, 28, 34, 38, 40; 58:9; 68:2; 75:8; 92:7; 97:10; 104:35; 106:18; 107:42; 112:10; 125:3; 141:6; 145:20; 147:6).

Vocabulary of the wicked

"sinner" (*ḥaṭṭā'*, see Ps 1)
"wicked" (*rāšā'*, see Ps 1)
"mocker" (*lēṣîm*, see Ps 1)
"arrogant" (*zēḏîm*, see Ps 119:21, 51, 69, 78, 85, 122)
"fool" (*nāḇāl*, see Ps 14:1)
"who do wrong" (*pō'ᵃlê 'āwen*, see Ps 5:5)
Other words denote "enemy" (*'ōyēḇ*, *mᵉrē'îm*, *rōḏep̱*, *śōnē'*, *šôrēr*).

The problem of wisdom in the reality of a world of alienation

The Psalms, like the wisdom books of Job and Ecclesiastes, reflect realistically on the cost of living in imitation of God. On the one hand, the wise man is protected by the shelter of the Almighty while awaiting the fulfillment of God's promises. On the other hand, he experiences the full brunt of evil while in this life. This world seems to be populated and dominated by ungodly squatters who disenfranchise the godly. The purpose of wisdom is to give a balanced perspective. True, life is harsh! But God knows and cares (34:15–22)!

The enemies in the various psalms are real, whatever form they may represent: power, greed, injustice, jealousy, religious orthodoxy, or opportunism. The wise are most sensitive to the great disparity existing between God's rule in justice and righteousness (see appendix to Ps 25: The Perfections of Yahweh) and the twisted way of man. Yet the psalmist encourages the wise not to be afraid whatever may come: "Why should I fear when evil days come, / when wicked deceivers surround me—/ those who trust in their wealth / and boast of their great riches?" (49:5–6).

The commitment of the wise is first and foremost to the Lord, who will reward all who hunger and thirst for righteousness. He will establish his kingdom on earth (see appendix to Ps 5: Yahweh Is King). Yahweh will give his people life in its fullness: "But God will redeem my life from the grave; / he will surely take me to himself" (49:15). But the power, material treasures, and oppression of the wicked will cease forever and ever (49:7–14; cf. Ps 37).

In the lament psalms the king, individuals in Israel, and the community of God's people pray for the light of God's kingdom to dawn. The psalms bring into focus both the life of the individual and the community before God and the opposition experienced in this world. The godly live in tension. Who are the enemies? The identification of the enemy changes, depending on who is praying: the Davidic king, an individual, or the nation. But in general it may be said that the godly experienced the reality of a world in alienation: persecution, opposition, oppression, ridicule, injustice, and death (Miller, "Trouble and Woe," pp. 33–34)!

In this light the psalms encourage the godly to commit their adversities to the Lord (cf. Ps 37), not to be taken by the short-lived pleasures of the fool (49:16–20), and trust in the Father's wisdom (Ps 73). Even during the darkest hours, the wise remember the confession, "Surely God is good to Israel, / to those who are pure in heart" (73:1). It is true that the graver the burdens of this life weigh on the godly, the more precious Yahweh becomes to them: "Yet I am always with you; / you hold me by my right hand. / You guide me with your counsel, / and afterward you will take me into glory. / Whom have I in heaven but you? / And earth has nothing I desire besides you" (73:23–25).

In this knowledge of God's care, the "brokenhearted" and "crushed in spirit" have hope that Yahweh will deliver the righteous from "many troubles" (34:19). Out of this conviction the psalmist encourages the godly to look around themselves and see the ways of God: "Consider the blameless, observe the upright; / there is a future for the man of peace" (37:37).

Texts: 1; 10; 12; 14; 15; 19; 32; 34; 36; 37; 49; 50; 52; 53; 73; 78; 82; 91; 92; 94; 111; 112; 119; 127; 128; 133.

Bibliography: George W. Anderson, "Enemies and Evildoers," pp. 18–29; Michael L. Barré, " 'Fear of God' and the World View of Wisdom," BTB 11 [1981]: 41–43; Paul van der Berghe, "*Àni* et *Ànaw* dans les Psaumes," *Le Psautier*, ed. Robert De Langhe (Leuven: Institut Orientaliste, 1962), pp. 273–95; Georg Braulik, "Law as Gospel. Justification and Pardon According to the Deuteronomic Torah," Int 38 (1984): 5–14; Childs, OTTC, pp. 210–12; Heinz-Josef Fabry, "Der himmlische Thronrat als ekklesiologisches Modell," *Bausteine biblischer Theologie. Festgabe für G. Johannes Botterweck zum 60. Geburtstag dargebracht von seinen Schülern*, ed. H.J. Fabry (Köln: Peter Hanstein, 1977), pp. 99–126; F.C. Fensham, "Common Trends in Curses of the Near Eastern Treaties and Kudurru-Inscriptions Compared with the Maledictions of Amos and Isaiah," ZAW 75 (1963): 155–75; Mervyn Fowler, "The Meaning of *lipnê* YHWH in the Old Testament," ZAW 99 (1987): 384–90; B. Gemser, "Gesinnungsethik im Psalter," OTS 13 (1963): 1–20; Stanley Gevirtz, "West-Semitic Curses and the Problem of the Origins of the Hebrew Law," VetTest 11 (1961): 137–58; Ingeborg Johag, "*tôḇ*-Terminus Technicus in Vertrags- und Bündnisformularen des Alten Orients und des Alten Testaments," *Bausteine biblischer Theologie*, pp. 3–23; Carl Keller, "Les 'Béatitudes' de l'Ancien Testament," *Maqqēl shâqēdh, La Branche d'Amandier. Hommage à W. Vischer* (Montpellier: Causse, Graille, Casteneau, 1960), pp. 88–100; Kraus, TP, pp. 156–203; J. Kenneth Kuntz, "The Canonical Wisdom Psalms of Ancient Israel: Their

Rhetorical, Thematic, and Formal Dimensions," *Rhetorical Criticism. Essays in Honor of James Muilenberg*, edd. Jared J. Jackson and Martin Kessler (Pittsburgh: Pickwick, 1974), pp. 186–222; id., "The Retribution Motif in Psalmic Wisdom," ZAW 89 (1977): 223–33; Roland E. Murphy, *The Psalms, Job* (Philadelphia: Fortress, 1977); id., *Wisdom Literature and Psalms;* id., "Religious Dimensions of Israelite Wisdom," in *Ancient Israelite Religion. Essays in Honor of Frank Moore Cross*, edd. Patrick D. Miller, Jr., Paul D. Hanson, and S. Dean McBride (Philadelphia: Fortress, 1987), pp. 449–58; A. Murtonen, "The Use and Meaning of the Words *l^ebārek* and *b^erākāh* in the Old Testament," VetTest 9 (1959): 158–77; Anthony Phillips, "Nebalah—a term for serious disorderly and unruly conduct," VetTest 25 (1975): 237–42; Gerhard von Rad, *Wisdom in Israel* (Nashville: Abingdon, 1972); id., "'Righteousness' and 'Life' in the Cultic Language of the Psalter," in *The Problem of the Hexateuch and Other Essays* (New York: 1966), pp. 243–66; id., OTT, 1:418–41; Reindl, pp. 333–56; Nic. H. Ridderbos, *De "Werkers der Ongerechtigheid" in the Individueele Psalmen* (Kampen: Kok, 1939); Katherine D. Sakenfeld, *The Meaning of Ḥesed in the Hebrew Bible: A New Inquiry*, Harvard Semitic Monographs 17 (Missoula: Scholars, 1978), pp. 241–45; id., *Faithfulness in Action* (Philadelphia: Fortress, 1985); J. Scharbert, "'Fluchen' und 'Segnen' im Alten Testament," *Biblica* 39 (1958): 1–36; id., "Die Geschichte der *bārûk*-Formel," *Biblisches Zeitschrift* 17 (1973): 1–28; Norman H. Snaith, *Distinctive Ideas of the Old Testament* (London: Epworth, 1944), pp. 51–78; W.S. Towner, "'Blessed be YHWH' and 'Blessed Art Thou, YHWH'—The Modulation of a Biblical Formula," CBQ 30 (1968): 386–99; C. Westermann, *Der Segnen in der Bibel und im Handeln der Kirche* (Munich: Kaiser, 1968); id., "The Blessing God and Creation," in *What Does the Old Testament Say About God?* ed. Friedemann W. Golka (Atlanta: Knox, 1979), pp. 39–52; Zimmerli, OTTO, pp. 107–8.

TDOT, 1:27–41, 140–47; 2:99–107; 3:195–230; 4:309–19, 364–85; THAT, 1:557–66; TWAT, 3:83–87, 1059–70; TWOT, 1:282–84.

Psalm 2: The Messianic King

Since its subject concerns the anointing and coronation of a Davidic king (cf. 2 Kings 11:12), Psalm 2 is classified as a *royal* psalm. There is no general agreement on the historical context of this psalm. Although dates range from the time of David to that of the Maccabees, the language, style, and theology fit an early monarchic date. Any attempt to link the psalm with an actual coronation of a Judean king (see William H. Brownlee, "Psalms 1–2 as a Coronation Liturgy," *Biblica* 52 [1971]: 321–36) finds little support in the text (Craigie, *Psalms 1–50*, p. 65). It is preferable to read the psalm in the light of Nathan's prophecy of God's covenant with David (2 Sam 7:5–16). (On the Davidic covenant, see Kaiser, *TOTT*, pp. 143–64; O. Palmer Robertson, *The Christ of the Covenants* [Grand Rapids: Baker, 1980], pp. 229–69). The structure of the psalm easily unfolds into four divisions, which show good movement from beginning to end: (1) the rebellious nations on earth (vv.1–3); (2) God in heaven (vv.4–6); (3) the decree of the Lord (vv.7–9); and (4) the anointed king on earth (vv.10–12). The structure is as follows:

A. The Rebellious Nations (vv.1–3)
  B. God's Rule in Heaven (vv.4–6)
  B′. God's Decree (vv.7–9)
A′. The Rule of the Messiah on Earth (vv.10–12)

For a detailed structural analysis, see Pierre Auffret, *The Literary Structure of Psalm 2*, translated by David J.A. Clines, JSOTS 3 (Sheffield: JSOT, 1977).

The psalm begins with the turmoil of the nations and ends with the blessing of those who trust in the Lord. As an example of redemptive-historical drama, it gives a theological perspective for interpreting world events. The psalm reflects a deep understanding of God's covenant with David (2 Sam 7:5–16; see Kaiser, *TOTT*, pp. 143–64; Robertson, *The Christ*, pp. 229–69). God's relationship with David and his sons, who were also "anointed," involves the promise that through the Davidic dynasty God will establish his universal rule over the earth. See the challenging discussion in Levenson, pp. 154–56.

The inspired author has made an invaluable contribution to God's people in all generations. As the Word of God to Israel, the psalm functioned to rouse God's people to trust in him and to look for an era that would see the removal of all enemies, the enthronement of the anointed king, the universal rule of God, and peace for God's people (cf. Pss 72; 89; 132; Isa 9:6–7; 11:1–10). In essence God's people could look for an era in which all aspects of the psalm would be fulfilled. On the relevance of this psalm in the OT and on the rule of Jesus, see Miller, *Interpreting the Psalms*, pp. 87–93.

The second psalm is one of the psalms most quoted in the NT. It was favored by the apostles as scriptural confirmation of Jesus' messianic office and his expected glorious return with power and authority. The writers of the synoptic Gospels alluded to Psalm 2 in their account of Jesus' baptism, when the Father proclaimed him to be his son (v.7; cf. Matt 3:17; Mark 1:11; Luke 3:22). With the words of v.7, Jesus introduced the beginning of the messianic age (cf. Donald A. Carson, "Matthew," EBC, 8:109).

The first-century church applied the second psalm to the Messiah as an explanation of the crucifixion of Christ by the rulers (Herod and Pontius Pilate), the nations, and Israel (the priests, scribes, and Pharisees). They had conspired together against the Messiah of God (Acts 4:25–28). Paul applied it to Jesus' ministry: his sonship, resurrection, and ascension to glory, which confirmed God's promises in Jesus as *the* Messiah (Acts 13:32–33).

Psalm 2:8 is similarly applied in Hebrews, where the glory of the Messiah as "the exact representation of his [God's] being" is revealed in Jesus' suffering for sins, in his authority "at the right hand of the Majesty in heaven" (1:3), and in his authority over angelic beings (1:5–6). The apostle John reveals the greatness of the Messiah's victory. He was born of a woman but is destined to "rule all the nations with an iron scepter" (Rev 12:5). He is the Rider on the white horse who will "strike down the nations" in the day of God's wrath (Rev 19:15; cf. 11:16–18).

The apostolic witness makes it clear that the second psalm has a messianic dimension. While it is preferable to understand the psalm first in its historical and literary setting as a "royal psalm," the eyes of faith must look beyond it to the powerful message of the full establishment of God's kingdom in Jesus Christ.

The theological significance of Psalm 2 lies in the hope that it entails. The anointed king rules by God's appointment. The wise response of repentance is a victory for the Messiah (v.12) and a *token* of the final victory over his enemies, the opponents of God's kingdom (cf. Rev 19:19–21; 20:7–10). From the perspective of typology, Jesus is the fulfillment of the psalm (cf. R.T. France, *Jesus and the Old Testament* [London: Tyndale, 1971], pp. 85–86). He is born of David's lineage (Matt 1:1; Luke 2:4, 11), has a right to David's throne (Luke 1:32), is the Son of God in a unique way (Matt 3:17; Luke 9:35; Heb 1:5), and will ultimately subdue all enemies under his feet (1 Cor

15:25–27; Heb 2:5–8). The "ideal" kingdom of God can best be appreciated by the kingdom in Israel, that is, from the perspective of the development of God's promise through David's lineage to the coming of the Messiah.

The psalm offers a special hope for the church of Jesus Christ as we look forward to the day of our redemption, to the era of peace and victory (Isa 65:20–25). When we pray "your kingdom come," we know that at our Lord's return peace will rule over the hearts and lives of all people. At that time the raging of the nations will cease.

In the light of this psalm's message, our prayer should include (1) a petition for the full establishment of the messianic kingdom, (2) thanksgiving that we who are Gentiles have been incorporated into God's kingdom, (3) an entreaty for the nations of the world that continue their rebellion against God, (4) a supplication for our brothers and sisters under governments hostile to Christianity, and (5) intercession for the Jewish people that they may soon be restored to Christ (Rom 11:25–32).

I. The Rebellious Nations

2:1–3

1 Why do the nations conspire
and the peoples plot in vain?
2 The kings of the earth take their stand
and the rulers gather together
against the LORD
and against his Anointed One.
3 "Let us break their chains," they say,
"and throw off their fetters."

1–2 The introductory interrogative "Why" expresses the irony of the tumultuous efforts against the Lord and his anointed (v.1). The psalmist was neither surprised nor worried by the rebellion of the nations. He expressed astonishment that the rulers of the earth even tried to counsel together against God. The same idea can be expressed by "Why do the nations bother?" At the very outset the psalmist makes it clear that the nations' attempt is in vain. They are agitated like the waves of the sea. In their anger they make all kinds of senseless noise. It is not that they plot with any design or purpose but rather that they react emotionally to God's rule (cf. Acts 4:25–28; Rom 1:21–32).

In the ancient Near East, "the kings" (v.2) considered themselves to be "divine" monarchs, who are here portrayed as bringing together all their "sacral" powers and forces against the Lord God and his anointed (see Gary V. Smith, "The Concept of God/the gods as Kings in the Ancient Near East and the Bible," *Trinity Journal* 3 [1982]: 18–38; W.A. VanGemeren, "Kingship," in Elwell, BEB, 2:1264–69). Their rebellion is an outright rejection of the Davidic king, constituting a threat to the universal rule of God (v.2). The united counsel and confrontation is parallel with the folly of the wicked (1:1); but whereas the godly meditate on God's law, the kings "meditate" (NIV, "plot," v.1) on rebellion.

The rebellion is against the Lord and "his Anointed One." At the coronation ceremony the new king first pledged fidelity to the covenant and was then crowned and proclaimed as the legitimate ruler. Only then was he anointed with holy oil (2 Kings 11:12), becoming the "anointed of the Lord" (cf. 1 Sam 16:13; 1 Kings 1:39). The "Anointed One" (*māšîaḥ*, v.2) refers to any anointed king who was seated on the throne of David. Since the psalm has a prophetic dimension, the messianic interpretation must also take the NT evidence into account. Jesus is the Christ ("Messiah," "Anointed One"; cf. J. Jocz, "Messiah," ZPEB, 4:198–207; TWOT, 1:530–31). Regardless of how the king responded to the Lord, the promises of God to Israel and her rulers were unconditional. The actual state of the kingdom in Israel at any age was at best a pale representation of the ideal kingdom. The prophets looked for the day when Israel and Judah would be ruled by a Davidic king from Jerusalem (Isa 9:2–7; Jer 23:5–6; 33:14–16; Ezek 34:23–24; 37:24–28; Hos 3:5) and the nations would be subject to him (Isa 11:10; Mic 4:1–5).

The perspective of promise was so vivid in the eyes of the psalmist that he saw the turbulence of the nations for what it was: a "vain" effort. Nevertheless, this turbulence is still dangerous; and the Bible records the destructive and oppressive forces of nations and rulers (Assyria and Babylonia). The prophets addressed their oracles against these nations, some of which were "oppressors" (Aram, Assyria, and Babylonia), while others were "trouble makers" (Edom, Moab, Ammon, and Philistia) or "seducers" (Phoenicia, Egypt).

The first-century church pointed out Herod, Pilate, the Romans, and even the Jews as rebels against the Anointed when they conspired together to take Jesus' life (Acts 4:25–28). The prophets, the Lord Jesus, and the apostles all witness that the nations will rise up against God and his Messiah as long as the messianic era awaits its fullness (Zech 12:1–9; 14:1–11; Matt 24:7; Luke 21:10; 2 Thess 2:3–4, 8–12; Rev 17:14; 19:14–21).

3 The goal of the rebellion is lordship (v.3). In the ancient Near East there were lords (suzerains) and servants (vassals). The poet, in hyperbolic language, portrays the kings of earth as breaking away from their required allegiance to the King of Kings. "Chains" and "fetters" refer to the manner the yoke of a cart or plow was placed on the necks of animals (Jer 27:2; 30:8; Nah 1:13). Thus the yoke of God's kingship is not merely rejected; it is insolently thrown off (cf. Jer 2:20). The kingdoms of this earth are by nature opposed to the rule of God and his Messiah. The pronoun "their" amplifies the close connection between God and his Messiah. It is impossible to submit to God without submitting oneself to his Messiah. The Father's recognition of the Anointed One was the basis of the authority of the Davidic dynasty, and his enthronement of his Messiah at his right hand constitutes the basis for the apostolic preaching (Acts 2:36).

Notes

---

1 In Acts 4:25 Peter quotes from the LXX: "Why do the nations rage and the peoples plot in vain?" The Hebrew verb רָגְשׁוּ (*rāg^e^šû*, "conspire") is unique and has the meaning of "being restless." The NIV note observes the difference with the LXX rendering, "rage," cited by Peter.

Craigie's proposal that לְאֻמִּים (*l^e^'ummîm*, "peoples") be rendered by "warriors" is a legitimate but unusual parallel for "nations" (*Psalms 1–50*, pp. 62–63).

The root ה־ג־ה (*h-g-h*, "meditate") occurs here in a different, antithetical context to Ps 1:2. The rendering "plot" is suggested by the context. Craigie derives the phrase "murmur murderously" from the "growl" of animals (*Psalms 1–50*, p. 63; see KB[3], 1:228).

2 The rulers of the nations are מְלָכִים (*m^e lāḵîm*, "kings"), the usual word for rulers, whether of a city or an empire, and *rôz^e nîm*, a poetic word for "leader" or "dignitary" (cf. 76:12; 148:11; Isa 40:23). The repetition "kings" and "rulers" in v.10 is misleading because there "rulers" is a translation of *šōp̱^e ṭîm* ("judges," "leaders"), e.g., the "judges" were tribal and/or national leaders. The variety of terms for the nations (v.1) and their rulers (vv.2, 10) brings out the comprehensiveness of the rebellion: all kinds of nations and rulers rebel against the Lord. How dare they!

II. God's Rule in Heaven

2:4–6

4 The One enthroned in heaven laughs;
the Lord scoffs at them.
5 Then he rebukes them in his anger
and terrifies them in his wrath, saying,
6 "I have installed my King
on Zion, my holy hill."

4 The Lord is not perturbed by the turmoil among the nations. On the contrary, a scornful laugh comes from his throne. The scene in heaven gives the reader assurance that God is "a mighty fortress," unassailable by forces of flesh and blood. Yet he graciously involves himself with his people and shares his kingdom with the "anointed" king. This king is not merely a "puppet" or an instrument of his wrath but rather has a special relationship to God as "son" and therefore as "heir" (vv.7–8).

In this section the scene shifts from earth to heaven, where we catch a glimpse of God laughing at and mocking the feeble attempts of the rulers. The OT commonly uses anthropopathic language to describe God in terms of human emotions. Above the turbulence ("rage") of the nations, God sits and reacts to their rebellion against him ("plot," "gather together," vv.1–2) with laughter. His laughter is an expression of ridicule, for he knows their end (cf. 37:13). The confidence of God's people rests in God himself, who is unmoved by the political machinations on earth. As earthly creatures we can hardly avoid becoming involved; yet our hope is in the God who laughs and scoffs at our enemies (cf. 59:6–8). "The One enthroned in heaven" is "Lord" (*'^a ḏōnāy*, lit., "Adonai"), i.e., the Master of the universe.

5 In his appointed time, God speaks with "words" as well as with "acts" so that the nations will be terrified by his anger. The "anger" (*'ap̱*) of God is an expression of his "jealousy" (Nah 1:2–6). He tolerates no opposition, competition, or apathy but requires absolute loyalty to himself and to his will (vv.11–12).

6 The emphatic "I" introduces the words of God's decree to appoint to the throne a Davidic ruler who will bring the nations to submission. God's "I" is emphatic in response to the activities of the rulers. It could be translated "as for me." God's reaction to the stirring on earth is the installation of an anointed king, and his determination to share his rule with a Davidic king is not weakened in the face of opposition. His "decree" stands.

The Davidic king ruled in Zion, God's chosen dwelling place (cf. Ps 132; Deut 12:14, 18; 14:23; 15:20). God had sanctified the city by his presence; therefore Zion was his "holy hill." Israel knew that God could not be limited to a hill or a temple but rather that his kingship extended from heaven as "the throne" to the "whole earth" as his footstool (1 Kings 8:27; cf. Isa 66:1). Yet, in a special and more narrow sense, Zion, the "holy hill," was his "footstool" (1 Chron 28:2; Pss 99:5; 132:7; Lam 2:1; Matt 5:35). The gracious consecration of Zion as his dwelling place was part of the promise to establish the Davidic dynasty (2 Sam 7:5–16; Kaiser, TOTT, pp. 159–64). The designation "Zion" expresses hope, reminding us of God's promise to David, sealed by his presence in the temple. The assurance of victory over the enemies of the kingdom is hereby given to David's dynasty (see Donald E. Gowan, *Eschatology in the Old Testament* [Philadelphia: Fortress, 1986], pp. 4–20; appendix to Ps 46: Zion Theology).

Notes

5 The verbs in the bi-colons are not synonymous in usage. The NIV's "he rebukes," a translation of יְדַבֵּר (*yedabbēr*, "he speaks"), results from the parallelism with יְבַהֵל (*yebahēl*, "terrifies"). The *effect* of God's speech is terror. The words of the speech are given as a *decree* (v.7), which the nations must accept as a "rebuke."

III. God's Decree

2:7–9

7 I will proclaim the decree of the LORD:

He said to me, "You are my Son;
today I have become your Father.
8 Ask of me,
and I will make the nations your inheritance,
the ends of the earth your possession.
9 You will rule them with an iron scepter;
you will dash them to pieces like pottery."

7 The decree of God deals with the Davidic king and the establishment of God's kingdom on earth. These verses interpret God's covenant with David and properly extend David's rule to the ends of the earth.

In accordance with the scene in heaven (vv.4–6), the divinely appointed king speaks about the Lord's promise, publicly proclaiming his own relationship with God, the Great King. The declaration involves the retelling of the revelation of God with great joy (TWOT, 2:1540). "I will proclaim" (*'asapperāh*) together with "the decree of the LORD" (*ḥōq YHWH*) has raised a significant issue of interpretation. G.H. Jones is correct in his caution not to read too much into "decree," such as the terms of God's covenant with David or a copy of the law given to the king. Jones proposes that "the emphasis is on the retelling or the re-counting . . . Yahweh's decree was indeed his glorious work for his people" ("The Decree of Yahweh Ps II, 7," VetTest 15 [1965]: 344). The "decree of the LORD" (*ḥōq YHWH*) involves the act of adoption and the expectation of obligation (TWOT, 3:316–17). Here it also has a sense of privilege (cf. Gen 47:22 ["allotment"]; Exod 29:28 ["share"]; Lev 24:9 ["share"]).

The "decree" of the Lord determines his relationship to the king and to the nations.

The Davidic king is by birth and by promise the "son of God." Here it signifies a legal right (so TWOT, 2:316–17). His commission is to make "the domain of Yahweh visible on earth" (Zimmerli, OTTO, p. 92: see Helmer Ringgren, "Psalm 2 and Belit's Oracle for Ashurbanipal," in *The Word of the Lord Shall Go Forth. Essays in Honor of David Noel Freedman*, edd. Carol F. Meyers and M. O'Connor [Winona Lake: Eisenbrauns, 1983], pp. 91–95).

God is the Davidic king's "father" (cf. 2 Sam 7:14; also cf. Ps 89:27). In actuality this relationship is confirmed at the moment of the coronation: "Today I have become your Father." Therefore the theocratic king must respond to the interests and desires of his father and represent the will of God to his people. Jesus is the Christ, the "Son" of God by the Father's proclamation (Matt 3:17; Mark 1:11; Luke 3:22). He is seated at the right hand of the Father (Acts 2:33; Heb 1:3), the place of kingly rule and authority.

8 The privilege of kingship lies in the relationship between God and the king. After all, he is the "son" of God. As such he may freely ask for an extension of his rule, because it fits within God's planned universal rule. The father graciously grants to his son the promise of the world-wide rule as his "inheritance." Since God is the Ruler of the world, he authorizes the Davidic king to extend his kingdom to "the ends of the earth." This language is not simply hyperbole. In it lies the hope of the saints (cf. Rev 2:26–27; 6:10; 19:15). The world, which was broken up into nations and languages after the rebellion at Babel (Gen 11:1–9), continues in a rebellious state against the Lord. From the moment God gave his promises to David (2 Sam 7:13–16) and sealed them in an unconditional covenant (2 Sam 23:5), God's people have looked for a ruler of David's lineage who would usher in the era of peace and prosperity spoken of by the prophets (Isa 2:2–4; 4:1–6; 9:6–7; 11:1–16; Jer 33:14–26; Ezek 37:24–28; Mic 4:1–5; Zech 9:9–10:1). In a prayer for the king (Ps 72), Solomon prays that he may rule "from sea to sea and from the River to the ends of the earth" (v.8) and that his rule will bring glory to God (vv.18–19) and prosperity to God's people (v.7). The era of David and Solomon gave Israel a taste of the blessings the theocratic kingship could bring.

God's sovereignty extends to the ends of the earth (cf. 72:8–11). Already in his promises to Abraham, Isaac, and Jacob, God made it clear that his concern was beyond the land of Canaan (cf. Gen 22:17–18; 26:4; 28:14; cf. Mal 1:5). The universal rule of God is derived from the authority granted by God to rule with great power over the nations (so Walter C. Kaiser, Jr., "The Davidic Promise and the Inclusion of the Gentiles [Amos 9:9–15 and Acts 15:13–18]: A Test Passage for Theological Systems," JETS 20 [1977]: 97–111).

9 The rule of God's messiah brings stability, even if he has to use force. The Lord's king has power to smash all opposition to his rule. His sovereignty may be expressed as an "iron rule" in which rebels are crushed like fragile clay vessels (cf. Jer 19:11). The authority of the king is derived from God in that the Lord "breaks the spirit of rulers" (Ps 76:12). The context favors "authority" as the proper interpretation. As J.A. Emerton writes, "To confer on a king authority over foreign nations naturally includes the right to use force against them if necessary. A king may need to shatter his vassals if they rebel, even though he will hope that he will not have to resort to such action" ("The Translation of the Verbs in the Imperfect in Psalm II.9," JTS 29 [1978]: 503).

The "scepter" (*šēḇeṯ*) is a symbol of rule. It is the means of discipline and judgment.

As the scepter of a monarch, it symbolizes here the authority granted by God to rule with great power over the nations. It is "an instrument of despotism" (KD, 1:97).

Notes

7 For the king as God's "son," see 2 Sam 7:14; Ps 89:26; TDOT, 2:155–57; F. Charles Fensham, "Father and Son as Terminology for Treaty and Covenant," *Near Eastern Studies in Honor of William Foxwell Albright*, ed. Hans Goedicke (Baltimore: Johns Hopkins Press, 1971), pp. 121–35.

9 The verbal phrase "you will rule them" renders תִּרְעֵם (*tir'ēm*, from *r-'-h*) based on the LXX (cf. Rev 2:27), whereas the MT reads תְּרֹעֵם (*terō'ēm*, "you will break them," from *r-'-'*; so NIV mg.). Emerton correctly appreciates the divinely granted authority in his modal translation of this verse: "Thou mayest break them, . . . thou mayest dash them in pieces" ("The Translation of the Verbs," pp. 499–503). Gerhard Wilhelmi argues in favor of the LXX in "Der Hirt mit dem eisernen Szepter. Überlegungen zu Psalm II 9," VetTest 27 (1977): 196–204.

IV. The Rule of the Messiah on Earth

2:10–12

10 Therefore, you kings, be wise;
be warned, you rulers of the earth.
11 Serve the LORD with fear
and rejoice with trembling.
12 Kiss the Son, lest he be angry
and you be destroyed in your way,
for his wrath can flare up in a moment.
Blessed are all who take refuge in him.

10 The universal rule of God is expressed by his patience, calling for kings and rulers to assess their situation. If they are wise, they will respond favorably. "Therefore" is a good translation of *we'attāh* (lit., "and now"). The phrase, as used in the wisdom literature ("now then . . ."), signals an exhortation to wisdom (Prov 5:7; 7:24; 8:32). The wise response includes both a spirit willing to receive God's revelation about the anointed and his kingdom and a joyous spirit of submission to the Lord (v.11). The Lord expects his creatures and especially the leaders of the nations to make a wise response to the impending day of his wrath.

11–12 Moreover, submission is the only acceptable response to the Great King (v.11). Submission is expressed by "service," which connotes a willingness to become a vassal and thus to recognize God's suzerainty ("lordship"). The "fear" (*yir'āh*) of the Lord in this situation is not a sign of emotional instability but a mark of wisdom. It is expressive of the day of his wrath on the nations. "Lest" (*pen*) controls the two following sentences: "Lest he be angry and [lest] you be destroyed" (v.12). Who will be angry and destroy? The context is ambiguous. Because God requires submission to himself and to his son (vv.11–12a) and blesses those who trust in him (v.12c), Yahweh ("the LORD") may well be the subject of the verbs, "worship the LORD with reverence;

tremble, and kiss the king, lest the LORD be angry with you . . . for his anger flares up in a moment" (NEB). This would fit in with the conclusion of the first psalm. He will most surely bless those who find refuge in him (5:11; 34:8; 118:8–9), whereas the sinners will perish (cf. 1:6).

Notes

---

10 The imperative הַשְׂכִּילוּ (*haśkîlû*, "be warned") with וְעַתָּה (*we'attāh*, "and now"; NIV, "therefore") expresses a logical connection with the preceding verses. It marks a concluding exhortation (Joüon, par. 177m).

12 The command נַשְּׁקוּ־בַר (*naššeqû-bar*, "Kiss the Son") has occasioned much discussion. The two problems are (1) the Aramaic word *bar* for "son" instead of *ben* and (2) the verb *nāšaq* ("kiss") is rarely used to signify submission (1 Kings 19:18; Hos 13:2). No alternate interpretation has been given that makes sense without requiring emendation. William Holladay proposes "Kiss, O Son, . . . you who forget the grave, You who forget him who buries" ("A New Proposal for the Crux of Psalm II 12," VetTest 28 [1978]: 110–12). A. Robinson explains it as a "deliberate haplography": "and remove with trembling weapons of iron" ("Deliberate but Misguided Haplography Explains Psalm II:11–12," ZAW 89 [1977]: 421–22). In favor of the traditional translation (so NIV) are the context of the psalm (submission to the Lord and to the anointed), the proposal by Delitzsch that the sequence *bar pen* ("Son, lest") avoids the dissonance of *ben pen* (KD, 1:98), and the suggestion by Craigie that the usage of the Aramaism may be intentionally directed to the foreign nations (*Psalms 1–50*, p. 64).

Erich Zenger has proposed an original messianic psalter (Pss 2–89) to which Ps 1 with its wisdom motif and "beatitude" was attached (" 'Wozu tosen die Völker. . . ?' Beobachtungen zur Entstehung und Theologie des 2. Psalms," *Freude an der Weisung des Herrn, Beiträge zur Theologie der Psalmen, Festgabe zum 70. Geburtstag von Heinrich Gross*, edd. Ernst Haag and Frank-Lothar Hossfeld [Stuttgart: Katholisches Bibelwerk, 1986], pp. 495–511).

Psalm 3: Quietness Amid Troubles

This psalm is the *first* psalm in many ways. It is the first psalm included in the collection of psalms ascribed to David (Pss 3–41, with the exclusion of Pss 10 and 33). It is also the first of thirteen psalms that bear a superscription relating to an episode in David's life (Pss 3, 7, 18, 34, 51, 52, 54, 56, 57, 59, 60, 63, 142). It is the first of the lament psalms and contains the first occurrence of the word "Selah."

The mood of the psalm is established by its genre. It is an *individual lament* psalm in which the main speaker expresses confidence in personal and individual deliverance by God (vv.3–8). Because of the parallels with Psalm 4 ("sleep," 3:5; 4:8; "glory," 3:3; 4:2), these psalms (3 and 4) may be read together. It has been suggested that Psalm 3 is a morning psalm (cf. v.5) and Psalm 4 is an evening psalm (cf. v.8). Delitzsch (KD, 1:100) calls it a "morning hymn of one in distress, but confident in God." Craigie argues in favor of an evening psalm and further defines it as a "royal protective psalm" (*Psalms 1–50*, p. 71). Kidner rightly states, "Yet this is also an evening psalm for the ordinary believer, who can reflect that his troubles are nothing beside David's, and David's expectations nothing beside his" (p. 54). Yahweh's protection and goodness are available, whether in the morning or the evening.

The psalm is composed of five divisions:

A. Lament Over the Enemies (vv.1–2)
B. Prayer to the Lord (vv.3–4)
C. Trust in the Lord (vv.5–6)
B′. Prayer for Deliverance (v.7)
A′. Hope in the Lord (v.8)

(For a further discussion on structure, see P. Auffret, "Note sur la Structure Littéraire du Psaume 3," ZAW 91 [1979]: 93–106; id., "Notes complémentaires sur la Structure littéraire des Psaumes 3 et 29," ZAW 99 [1987]: 90–93.)

As the psalmist looks over the multitude of enemies (vv.1–2), his eyes of faith are focused on the Lord (vv.3–4) who grants his beloved sleep (vv.5–6). In his prayer he expresses confidence that the Lord will deliver him and, through this, will restore his blessing to his people (vv.7–8).

The historical situation reflected in the psalm finds David at a low moment in his life. Because of his sin with Bathsheba (2 Sam 11–12), his life was torn apart by family troubles (2 Sam 12:15–14:33), and his kingdom was wrenched from his grasp by Absalom's rebellion (2 Sam 15:1–19:43). The hearts of Israel were with Absalom (2 Sam 15:13). The anointed of the Lord (cf. Ps 2:6) was forced to flee Jerusalem and wait out the crisis at an encampment across the Jordan (2 Sam 17:24). Thus the psalm reflects the national situation as well as the personal feelings of David.

There is no internal evidence that brings into doubt the authenticity of the superscription: "A psalm of David. When he fled from his son Absalom." In fact, it suits the motif of the second psalm remarkably well (Kirkpatrick, p. 13). The major difference between the second and third psalms is that the enemies who had risen against the Lord's anointed (2:6) in Psalm 3 were not the nations and kings (2:1–2) but the people of Israel. These internal enemies were numerous (v.1) and doubted God's closeness to David (v.2). David described God in military language as his "shield" and the "Glorious One" (v.3, NIV mg.). He would "arise" and "deliver" David by striking down the enemies. (See the appendix to Ps 119: Yahweh Is My Redeemer.)

The canonical significance of the psalm lies, not in the historical situation and David's confidence in a time of deep trouble, but in its theological message. The Lord will redeem his anointed one, establish his kingdom, and bless his people! The benefit of the Davidic covenant (see Pss 2; 132) for Israel is found in the assurance of God's presence, his promise of deliverance, and his blessings through the anointed king. Though the kingship may be assaulted from within, the Lord's promise to David stands firm. The hope of the godly rests not only in God but also in the anointed. Since Jesus is the Messiah, the Anointed One, the believer joins with Israel in the assurance of God's promise, the reception of the benefits of the people of God through the Messiah, the hope of the Messiah's complete victory, and the desire for the establishment of the age of blessing (v.8).

From a redemptive-historical perspective, the psalm witnesses to the intense opposition of God's enemies to his kingdom and his superior power. Though David had grievously sinned, resulting in the present trouble, the covenant was not broken. Despite the personal and national tragedies that befell David (2 Sam 12–20; 24), the Lord graciously established Solomon's kingdom (1 Kings 2:12, 46). The God who gave the victory to David and the blessing to his people has confirmed his love in Jesus, who identified himself with David's suffering and emerged victorious. Through

Jesus, God extends deliverance, victory, and blessing to all who believe on his name (Eph 1:11–14; 2:8–10; Phil 3:20–21).

I. Lament Over the Enemies

3:1–2

A psalm of David. When he fled from his son Absalom.

1 O LORD, how many are my foes!
How many rise up against me!
2 Many are saying of me,
"God will not deliver him." *Selah*

1–2 David lamented over his many adversaries in three statements. The complaints are in the form of synthetic parallelism, connected by the key word "many." The "many" comprise a united front, composed of three groupings: the enemies, the growing opposition, and the skeptics. The number of the enemy has multiplied. The MT expresses "many" in two ways: a verbal form (*rabbû*, lit., "[how my enemies] have increased"; cf. "how many are my foes," NIV) and a nominal adjective (*rabbîm*, "many" in "many rise up" and "many are saying"). The enemies have existed in the past (verbal form, perfect mood), and they are increasing ("many" as an adjective). There is a development from a covert rebellion to an open and growing rebellion, the intensity of which is also brought out by the pronominal suffixes in the MT: "*my* foes" (*ṣārāy*, v.1a), "against *me*" (*'ālāy*, v.1b), and "of *me*" (*lᵉnap̱šî*, lit., "to my soul," v.2a; for the OT view of man, see Notes on 4:4, 7).

There were many who mocked David and exclaimed that his God would not take care of him! Their power was increasing because many were joining the rebellion. They cursed the king (cf. 2 Sam 16:7–8) or sarcastically concluded that the king had been abandoned by the God whom he had served so diligently and in whom he had put his trust. How the situation had changed! During the era of international peace of David's kingdom (2 Sam 7:1), the enemies had arisen from *within* Israel. They joined together with great ferocity and animosity toward their king.

In the midst of this tragedy, the king prayed, "O LORD." Many understand this form of address to be referring to God as the sovereign Creator, far removed from man and his struggles. Yet here the psalmist addresses God by his revealed covenant name, *Yahweh*. In the language of prayer in the OT, this address has the same connotation as "Abba, Father" in the NT. For the people of God, the name of the Lord was the assurance that his promises to David would be fulfilled (cf. 2:7–9). He is the Father of Israel and particularly of David (and his sons) as the anointed king. Unfortunately, the psalmist's sense of deep spiritual intimacy between him and his God is lost in our customary translation "O LORD."

Notes

For a brief discussion of the technical words and phrases in the superscription, see the Introduction.

1 (2 MT) The exclamatory particle מָה (*māh*, "what," "how") controls all three lines (Joüon, par. 162a): "how many! . . . How many! . . . Many" (vv.1–2). The omission of "how many"

(v.2, NIV) breaks up the verses unnecessarily because "there is an element of climax reached in the third line" (Craigie, *Psalms 1–50*, p. 73).

2 (3 MT) "God will not deliver him" is a translation of the nominal sentence אֵין יְשׁוּעָתָה לּוֹ בֵאלֹהִים (*'ên yᵉšû'āṯāh lô ḇē'lōhîm*, "he has no deliverance in God"). The intent of the sarcasm is that the king cannot expect victories anymore, because his God has forsaken him (cf. NEB, "God will not bring him victory"). The repetition of the root ישׁע (*y-š-'*, "deliver") connects the components of the psalm:

v.2 יְשׁוּעָתָה (*yᵉšû'āṯā*, "deliverance"; for this form, cf. GKC, par. 90g; Joüon, par. 93j);
v.7 הוֹשִׁיעֵנִי (*hôšî'ēnî*, "deliver me," a Hiphil imperative);
v.8 הַיְשׁוּעָה (*hayᵉšû'āh*, "the deliverance").

The word *hayᵉšû'āh* signifies more than spiritual redemption. Its basic meaning is "help" and forms a parallel construction with "arise" (v.7) in order to express the hope of the psalmist that God will intervene by granting him help against the enemies. (See the appendix to Ps 119: Yahweh Is My Redeemer.)

II. Prayer to the Lord

3:3–4

> 3 But you are a shield around me, O LORD;
> you bestow glory on me and lift up my head.
> 4 To the LORD I cry aloud,
> and he answers me from his holy hill. *Selah*

3 God is so different from the "many" who oppose him. David addressed God confidently with an *emphatic* and *contrastive* use of the personal pronoun "you" (*wᵉ'attāh*). How different he is from the rebellious masses! David was certain of God's promises that are confirmed in the covenant (cf. 2:6–9). Therefore, his confidence rested in the nature of God, described here by a metaphor ("shield") and by one of his attributes ("glory"). He was convinced that God's kingship is forever. And although the kingship was forcibly removed from the Lord's anointed, he was still protected by God's kingship. With the metaphor "shield" (*māḡēn;* cf. 7:10; 18:2, 30; 28:7; Gen 15:1), the psalmist places himself under the *protection* of the Great King, who has promised to protect his own (Gen 15:1; Deut 33:29). (See the appendix to Ps 98: Yahweh Is the Divine Warrior.)

The power of the Great King is referred to by the word "glory" (*kāḇôḏî*, lit., "my Glorious One," NIV mg.). The phrase signifies the Lord's glorious rule over his kingdom. He is the Lord of hosts, with tens of thousands of angels at his command. Even as a king can be described as glorious because of his vast armies, so the Lord is glorious because he can marshal the angelic host to aid his children (34:7; 91:11). The king puts his confidence in the protection that God alone can provide, because his glory is greater than any human power. The glory of God is nothing less than the revelation of his hiddenness!

The psalmist explains further that the "Glorious One" gives him reason to lift up his head. The "lifting of the head" is a Hebraism expressive of confidence in the Lord. He has power to raise up the humble and abase the mighty (1 Sam 2:7–8; Ps 103:7–9). He exalts whom he wills and when he wills. The Psalms express confidence that the Lord will "lift up the head" of his people when he is victorious over his enemies (cf. 18:46–50; 27:4–6; 110:5–7).

Even though the king had reason for despondency, his knowledge of God gave him reason for hope. The confidence of the king was not in his knowledge of the future, nor in the might of his forces, but in God who had installed him as king (2:6).

4 Even when he was removed from the presence of God in Jerusalem, the king knew that the Lord would answer him when he called. The king is portrayed as leaving Jerusalem weeping, barefoot, with his head covered (2 Sam 15:30). In this condition he raised up his "voice" (*qôlî*) to the Lord (NIV, "I cry aloud"). The position of *qôlî* is emphatic in the MT and brings out the need of the supplicant (cf. 27:7; 142:1). Notice how he first looks up to God as his King (v.3) to whom he cries for help (v.4) and thereafter quietly submits himself, being able to go to sleep (v.5). The "cry" comes between the expression of reliance on Yahweh's kingship and the declaration of confident sleep. "My voice" is here equivalent to "I": "*I* cry to the LORD" (cf. Joüon, par. 151c). The confidence that God would answer him is based on the father-son relationship that the Lord promised to his anointed (cf. 2:7). In the treaties of the ancient East, the king (suzerain) expected his vassals to protect him, and he promised also to come to their aid. For David, God is more than "Lord," because he calls (on) the Great King (as) his father. David's confidence in prayer lies, not in righteous deeds done in the flesh, but in the gracious promises of God. Even in moments of great despair, when the soul feels itself abandoned by all others, comfort may be drawn from the assurance that God answers. For a discussion of "his holy hill," see the comment on 2:6.

Notes

3 כְּבוֹדִי (*k^e^bôdî*, "my glory") is parallel with "shield" and is a designation of God. The NIV margin is preferable. See Craigie: "But you. . . . are a shield . . . , my glory, and the One who holds up my head" (*Psalms 1–50*, p. 70).

III. Trust in the Lord

3:5–6

5 I lie down and sleep;
I wake again, because the LORD sustains me.
6 I will not fear the tens of thousands
drawn up against me on every side.

5–6 The Hebrew text begins with the personal pronoun "I" as an emphatic way of expressing the inner quietness of the psalmist. In fact, it may be translated "as far as *I* am concerned." Lying down to sleep expresses David's confidence in God's response to his plea. He is the Great King who will come to the aid of his son. Instead of being vexed in his soul or making plans to relieve the pressure, he has learned to console himself with God (e.g., the well-known example of Peter in Acts 12:5–6). Too often plans come before prayers. How many blessings we may miss by conceiving our own schemes only to see God frustrate them later and work out his own plan!

The psalmist knows that God "sustains" (*yismᵉḵēnî;* cf. TWOT, 2:628). The sustenance of God is the psalmist's protection. The life of faith is one of being protected by God's loving care, marking the difference between despair and hope. He looked up to God while he faced the "tens of thousands" who had surrounded him as a city under siege (cf. Isa 22:7; NIV, "posted" [*šāṯû*] is identical to "drawn up" here). The "tens of thousands" (*riḇᵉḇôṯ*) is related, linguistically, to the words for "many" (vv.1–2). Thus vv.1 and 6 form an *inclusio* by the use of cognate forms of the root *r-b-b* ("be many") and by the repetition of the prepositional phrase "against me" (vv.1, 6).

David's commitment to God results in an abandonment of his problem to God. Though David was moved by the "many enemies" (vv.1–2), prayer renewed his confidence in the One who will be victorious over the many. The psalmist knew that his glorious King and Father would take care of him, and with this thought he consoles himself and goes to sleep.

Notes

5 The change from perfect tense in "lie down . . . sleep . . . wake again" to the imperfect יִסְמְכֵנִי (*yismᵉḵēnî,* "sustains") brings out how the psalmist had *habitually* trusted in the Lord. The patterns he had set, over years of experience with the Lord, had led him to rest quietly. For a similar construction see Ps 1:1–2.

IV. Prayer for Deliverance and Expression of Hope

3:7–8

7 Arise, O LORD!
Deliver me, O my God!
Strike all my enemies on the jaw;
break the teeth of the wicked.

8 From the LORD comes deliverance.
May your blessing be on your people. *Selah*

7 At this point the psalm moves with a quickening rhythm. The prayer's intensity is marked by the words "Arise, O LORD! / Deliver me, O my God!" Verse 4 makes a reference to his outcry, while v.7 contains the actual words of the prayer. The prayer is reminiscent of Moses' prayer when the ark of the covenant went ahead of Israel (Num 10:35; cf. Ps 68:1). Moses prayed that the Lord would move the enemies out of the way as the ark, symbolic of God's presence, went ahead of the people. However, God's presence was not limited to the ark of the covenant, which was at this time in Jerusalem (2 Sam 15:25, 29). God's presence was with his anointed. The psalmist freely sought to rouse the Lord to action with "Arise" (*qûmāh,* a Qal imperative from *qûm,* "stand up," "arise"). The Lord's rising is in contrast to the many who have arisen against David (*qāmîm,* Qal participle from *qûm,* v.1b). The repetition of a form of *qûm* forms another closure.

The third closure is in the psalmist's prayer for deliverance: "Deliver me, O my God!" Notice that the skeptics had already concluded, "God will not deliver him" (v.1). Here he calls for deliverance (*hôšîʿēnî,* "deliver me") and uses his enemies' word for God—but in a personalized way ("my God")—as he petitions God to prove his adversaries wrong (v.2). The reason for the usage of the generic "God," rather than Yahweh, lies in the connection with the impersonal use of "God" by the enemies. But in the mouth of the psalmist "my God" becomes equivalent to "my Father."

The striking of the enemies on the jaw (v.7b) is an expression of humiliation (cf. 1 Kings 22:24; Isa 50:6; Lam 3:30; Mic 5:1). The metaphor of the breaking of teeth likens the enemies to wild animals whose strength is taken away when their teeth are crushed (cf. Ps 58:6). This expression of vindication may seem harsh to our ears, but the psalmist is putting before us the hope that, regardless what enemies may arise from within or from without the kingdom of God, God will be victorious. The hope of the church still lies in the coming of Jesus Christ and his victory over all his enemies (1 Cor 15:24–28; 2 Thess 1:5–10). (See the Introduction for a discussion on the imprecations in the Psalms.)

8 The reference to the deliverance of the Lord balances the closure with the beginning observation that many had arisen against the king, taunting him and saying that there was no deliverance for him (v.2b). Victory belongs to the Lord, and he grants it to his beloved. That the psalmist was not only concerned for himself and the security of his kingship is evident by the conclusion. His prayer was that, through the victory granted to the Lord's anointed, God's blessing might return to his people. The spirit of the shepherd-king is revealed by his concern for the welfare of his people.

The blessing of God is the result of his gracious deliverance. He granted the "blessing" of his presence, protection, and prosperity to Abraham (Gen 12:2–3) and confirmed it to Israel (Deut 26, esp. vv.5–10). To David, God promised the removal of wicked people and external enemies as well as the subsequent peace of his people (2 Sam 7:10–11, 29). David looked forward to the time of full blessing. In his hope lies ours, for in Jesus' promises the victory and blessings of God are assured.

Notes

7 The two perfects—הִכִּיתָ (*hikkîṯā,* "you have struck) and שִׁבַּרְתָּ (*šibbartā,* "you have broken")—preceded by imperatives—קוּמָה (*qûmāh,* "Arise") and הוֹשִׁיעֵנִי (*hôšîʿēnî,* "Deliver me") must be rendered as imperatives (Joüon, par. 119l):

Arise, O LORD!
    Deliver me, O my God!
Strike all my enemies on the jaw!
    Break the teeth of the wicked.

Another attractive translation given by Dahood (1:15, 19) is:

Rise up, O Yahweh, save me, my God!
O that you yourself would smite
    all my foes on the jaw!
Smash the teeth of the wicked!

Appendix: Yahweh Is My God

Yahweh is the name by which the God of the patriarchs revealed himself to ancient Israel (Exod 3:15). Though the rendering "the LORD" in the NIV keeps us from feeling the emotive significance of the *name* revelation, the reader may readily substitute Yahweh whenever the phrase "the LORD" (with small capitals) occurs in the English text. Granted that the pronunciation of God's holy name is debated, OT scholars generally hold that the name Yahweh and the shortened form *Yah* (as in Hallelu-jah) are more reliable than the usual designation *Jehovah,* which is the unfortunate result of the use of the consonants of YaHWeH (the tetragrammaton or four letters referring to the divine name) and the vowels of *'adonai* ("Lord").

Apart from the Elohistic Psalter, the name of the Lord is the most common reference to the God of Israel in the Psalms. It is the name of self-communication and covenant love. His name assures his covenantal perfections (Exod 34:6–7) and the fulfillment of his promises (Exod 6:4–7). The people of God felt the closeness of their God as he had promised to be their God and to adopt them as his children. They knew him by name! They prayed in his name and gave thanks to his name! They loved the name Yahweh.

Yahweh is the glorious King, who is close enough to hear and respond to the prayers of his people: "Give ear to my words, O LORD, / consider my sighing. / Listen to my cry for help, / my King and my God, / for to you I pray" (5:1–2; cf. 4:3; 6:9). The promises of Yahweh are summarized in these words: "For the LORD God is a sun and shield; / the LORD bestows favor and honor; / no good thing does he withhold / from those whose walk is blameless" (84:11). The Lord is faithful to his people and to the land: "The LORD will indeed give what is good, / and our land will yield its harvest" (85:12).

Yahweh accepts his people, extends his blessings to his children, and rewards them; but he abhors the wicked: "The LORD examines the righteous, / but the wicked and those who love violence / his soul hates. / On the wicked he will rain / fiery coals and burning sulfur; / a scorching wind will be their lot. / For the LORD is righteous, / he loves justice; / upright men will see his face" (11:5–7; cf. 1:6). His blessings are likened to the "light" of his face: "Many are asking, 'Who can show us any good?' / Let the light of your face shine upon us, O LORD" (4:6). The greatest reward is the invitation to enjoy his hospitality: "Surely goodness and love will follow me / all the days of my life, / and I will dwell in the house of the LORD / forever" (23:6).

Yahweh instructs his children in the *way* pleasing to him. His way is the way of revelation (*Torah,* cf. 1:2), and he watches carefully over the steps of his children so they do not slip: "I will instruct you and teach you / in the way you should go; / I will counsel you and watch over you" (32:8; cf. 16:7–8; 119).

Yahweh is the only and absolute value in this life and in the life to come: "I said to the LORD, 'You are my Lord; / apart from you I have no good thing' " (16:2). In laments and praise Yahweh alone is the focus. Zimmerli has put it well in defining the *distinctive* elements of OT prayers: (1) all prayers are directly addressed to God and not to any other being, in harmony with the first commandment; (2) Yahweh is known by the revelation of his character, his deeds, and his identification with his people; (3) the believer addresses God by his name (Yahweh), which he has freely and graciously revealed to his children (OTTO, pp. 150–55).

Related Concepts: Appendixes to Pss 5 (Yahweh Is King); 7 (The Name of Yahweh); 9 (Yahweh Is El Elyon); 22 (Yahweh Is El); 24 (Lord Sabaoth); 25 (The Perfections of Yahweh); 46 (Zion Theology); 78 (The Mighty Acts of Yahweh); 98 (Yahweh Is the Divine Warrior); 119 (Yahweh Is My Redeemer); 132 (The Ark of the Covenant and the Temple: Symbols of Yahweh's Presence and Rule).

Bibliography: Otto Eissfeldt, "El and Yahweh," JSS 1 (1956): 25–37; David Noel Freedman, "Divine Names and Titles in Early Hebrew Poetry," *Pottery, Poetry, and Prophecy: Studies in Early Hebrew Poetry* (Winona Lake: Eisenbrauns, 1980), pp. 77–129; Kraus, TP, pp. 24–25; L'Heureux, *Rank Among the Canaanite Gods;* Patrick D. Miller, Jr., "El the Warrior," HTR 60 (1967): 411–31; id., "El, The Creator of Earth," BASOR 239 (1980): 43–46; J.A. Motyer, *Revelation of the Divine Name* (London: Tyndale, 1949); E. Noort, "Het Ik—Zijn Van Jhwh. Over de Problematiek Van de Persoonlijke God in de Theologie van het Oude Testament," *Gereformeerd Theologisch Tijdschrift* 85 (1985): 132–51; Marvin H. Pope, *El in the Ugaritic Texts* (Leiden: Brill, 1955); H. Ringgren, *Israelite Religion* (Philadelphia: Fortress, 1966), pp. 66–103; Martin Rose, *Jahwe, Zum Streit um den alttestamentlichen Gottesnamen.* Theologische Studien 122 (Zürich: Theologischer Verlag, 1977); Georg Schmuttermayr, "Vom Gott unter Göttern zum einzigen Gott, Zu den Spuren der Geschichte des Jahweglaubens in den Psalmen," *Freude an der Weisung des Herrn, Beiträge zur Theologie der Psalmen, Festgabe zum 70. Geburtstag von Heinrich Gross,* edd. Ernst Haag and Frank-Lothar Hossfeld (Stuttgart: Katholisches Bibelwerk, 1986), pp. 349–74; M.H. Segal, "El, Elohim, and YHWH in the Bible," JQR 46 (1955): 89–115; P.M. Walsh, "The Gods of Canaan," *The Mighty From Their Thrones* (Philadelphia: Fortress, 1987), pp. 13–28; Zimmerli, OTTO, pp. 150–55l.

THAT, 1:31–38, 142–49, 702–7; TWAT, 3:534–54; TDOT, 1:242–61, 267–84; TWOT, 1:12–13.

Psalm 4: An Evening Hymn (in Despondency)

The psalm is an evening hymn (v.8) and forms, together with the morning psalm (Ps 5; cf. 5:3), avenues for the believer to come to his heavenly Father in prayer. As an expression of confidence in God, the psalm helps the reader to meditate on God's fatherly care and to leave the troubles and causes of anxiety in his hands. Here the psalmist teaches us that in our walk with God he can bring us to the point where we can sleep without fear.

The authorship and the setting of the psalm are debated. The superscription associates it with David. Craigie (*Psalms 1–50,* p. 79) holds that the psalm is anonymous and reflects an early adoption as an evening prayer in the formal worship of Israel. However, internal evidence suggests the author was David. The author speaks of his "glory" having been turned to "shame" (v.2) and authoritatively commands his enemies to be silent and repent. Apparently he was a man acquainted with honor and had come to a period of disgrace in his life. Yet he still felt at liberty to speak to his enemies with the voice of authority.

Dating the psalm in relation to David's life is more problematic. J. Ridderbos connects it with the time of Saul's pursuit of David (p. 35). Delitzsch relates this psalm and the previous psalm (Ps 3) to the period of Absalom's rebellion (KD, 1:104; cf. Calvin, 1:37; Kidner, p. 55). Eaton connects the psalm with a king but does not identify that king (p. 36). Oesterley represents still another point of view. He interprets the "enemies" as a metaphor for harvest failure (p. 129) and argues for a preexilic date (p. 130).

The literary genre of the psalm fits the *individual psalms of lament,* with motifs characteristic of the subgenre, *psalms of confidence.* The mixture of the genres may account for the lack of consensus in determining the structure.

The following expository structure develops the argument in broad outline:

A. Prayer (v.1)
  B. Call for Trust in the Lord (vv.2–5)
A′. Prayer (vv.6–7)
  B′. Expression of Trust (v.8)

The message of the psalmist is that his confidence is in the Lord who will not abandon his beloved in distress but will restore his blessings and joy to them. This confidence gives rise to one blessing that the enemies cannot take away: inward peace (v.8).

The message of confidence is enhanced by the psalm's messianic dimension. The king is representative of a dynasty to whom God has covenanted his loyalty (2 Sam 7:11b–15; cf. Ps 2:6–7). The anointing of David gave rise to expectations of joy and peace. Yet David did not experience the fullness of the blessing, nor did he witness the conversion of all his enemies and skeptics. Throughout the OT the godly awaited that promised era of peace, joy, and restoration. Eventually the postexilic period brought an era of renewed expectation as the people of God experienced a sense of safety (v.8). But it was not until Jesus came that the godly had reason to hope for the fullness of the blessings God had bestowed on them through the Anointed One (see also Otto Wahl, "Du allein, Herr, lässt mich sorglos ruhen—Die frohe Botschaft von Ps 4," *Freude an der Weisung des Herrn, Beiträge zur Theologie der Psalmen, Festgabe zum 70. Geburtstag von Heinrich Gross,* edd. Ernst Haag and Frank-Lothar Hossfeld [Stuttgart: Katholisches Bibelwerk, 1986], pp. 457–70).

I. Prayer

4:1

For the director of music. With stringed instruments. A psalm of David.

1 Answer me when I call to you,
  O my righteous God.
Give me relief from my distress;
  be merciful to me and hear my prayer.

1 In his need the psalmist turns to his "righteous God." The designation "righteous" is much more than a description of God's nature. The psalmist believes that regardless of his innocent suffering, God will act triumphantly on behalf of his servant. He is the God who *does* righteously in the spirit of Psalm 18:46–48. The word "righteous" (*ṣeḏeq*) expresses the relation between God and his people. It signifies more than an absolute standard or norm. True, God is righteous in himself; but his righteousness is expressed as he relates to his people, as a father to his children. He has promised them his presence and victory over adverse circumstances.

Faith in God's righteousness is based on God's covenant promise that he will come to the rescue of his children in need (Ps 25:4–5; Isa 45:13; cf. NEB, "maintainer of my right"). Calling boldly on God is a privilege that belongs to his children. It is to this end that the psalmist calls on God as "my righteous God."

By a series of four imperatives, the psalmist pours out his heart before God: "Answer me," "give me relief," "be merciful," and "hear my prayer." He calls on the Lord in his "distress" (*ṣār*), though the nature of this "distress" is not clear. It could be psychological (25:17) or physical (31:9–10) or both (66:11–12). Boldly, and yet humbly, he casts himself on the "mercy" of God, who has covenanted to be loving and faithful to his own (Exod 34:6). Prayer is a form of communication in which the child of God casts himself on the mercy of God. The verbal phrase "be merciful to me" (*ḥonnēnî*) is related to the noun "favor" (*ḥēn*) and to the divine attribute "gracious" (*ḥannûn*; see TWOT, 1:302–4). The psalmist expresses his need for the favor, grace, and mercy of the covenant God, who stoops down to help needy human beings.

Notes

For a brief discussion of the technical words and phrases in the superscriptions, see the Introduction. See also Hab 3:19.

1 (2 MT) The imperative הִרְחַבְתָּ (*hirḥabtā*, "give me relief") is a perfect that literally means "you have broadened," which in a sequence of imperatives functions as an imperative (cf. Joüon, par. 119l). Some versions differ from this syntactic possibility and render it as a perfect (cf. "You have relieved me," NKJV).

II. Call for Trust in the Lord

4:2–5

2 How long, O men, will you turn my glory into shame?
How long will you love delusions and seek false gods?
Selah
3 Know that the LORD has set apart the godly for himself;
the LORD will hear when I call to him.

4 In your anger do not sin;
when you are on your beds,
search your hearts and be silent. *Selah*
5 Offer right sacrifices
and trust in the LORD.

2 The psalmist's prayer contains a positive contemplation of what his opponents should do. These verses help us to understand his "distress," which was left unspecified (v.1). The focus is not on his past grievances but on the folly of their opposition and their need to repent and trust in the Lord.

The "men" (*b^enê 'îš*, v.2) belong to the class of prominent citizens. As a class they form the landowners, the wealthy, and the powerful in Israel's society (cf. 49:2; 62:9; Isa 2:9; 5:15; note: EVV do not bring out the distinction as in Heb.). The leadership has gone astray. They are opposed to the king and have shown their enmity in two ways.

First, the leaders have scoffed at his "glory"; i.e., they have despised the position of the king. "Glory" (*kāḇôḏ*) is bestowed by God on his anointed king (3:3). Second, they characterize themselves by a diligent pursuit of what is "vain" (NIV, "delusions") and "deceptive" (NIV, "false gods"; NIV mg., "seek lies"). These words explain how they have trodden the king's glory into the ground by betraying it for an unspecified worthless cause.

3–5 In a series of seven imperatives, the enemies are called on to respond in a more constructive way: "Know. . . . be angry [NIV, "in your anger"] do not sin; say [NIV, "search"] . . . be silent . . . offer . . . and trust."

First, the enemies should recognize that the Lord has chosen David to be his friend. He is "the godly" set apart by the Lord, who has bestowed on him his steadfast love, confirmed to him by covenant (v.3; cf. 2 Sam 7:15a).

The interpretation of v.4 affects the meaning of the next four imperatives. This verse is very problematic. How does "on your beds" fit in with the series of imperatives? The NIV gets around the problem by putting "when you are on your beds" before "search your hearts." Ancient and modern versions give interpretative translations (cf. NEB, "though you lie abed resentful, do not break silence"). Another interpretation that is quite attractive is to understand "be angry" in the sense of "tremble" and see it in parallel with "be silent," in the sense of "wail" or "cry" (KB^3, 1:217). The following gives the sense:

> Tremble
> but do not sin, speak in your hearts;
> wail on your beds.

Here David calls on the enemy to repent with a view toward the bringing of righteous offerings and trusting in the Lord (v.5).

Second, the command to be "angry" seems strange in light of Ephesians 4:26 and 31. The verb (*rig^ezû*) could also be translated as "be disturbed" or "tremble." Though the enemies may have strong feelings of enmity, they must learn to submit themselves. Strong emotions are not easily turned in the opposite direction, but the enemies must reflect on the consequences of their continued rebellion. The sense of the clause is "tremble with fear, and stop sinning."

Third, the prohibition "Do not sin" is an exhortation for the enemies to repent from their evil way of life. Hatred of God's people is always wrong (cf. James 3:9), but it is especially reprehensible when directed toward God's anointed.

Fourth, if the enemies persist in their way, David exhorts them to do so secretly, while they lie on their beds. "Search your hearts" (NIV) is an idiomatic translation of "speak to your hearts" and signifies thinking and planning (Pss 10:6, 11, 13; 14:1; 53:1; Isa 47:8, 10). The wicked may think their perverse thoughts to themselves, if they have to, but they should not be expressed publicly.

Fifth, the enemies should wail over their past hostility. "Be silent" (NIV, *dōmmû*) also has the sense of keeping still like a stone (Exod 15:16). Since the verb is parallel with "tremble" (NIV, "In your anger"), it is preferable to assume that David calls on his opponents to "wail" over their sin against him and against the Lord.

A break between v.4 and v.5 is indicated by "Selah" and may mark a change from a call to repentance (vv.3–4) to an exhortation to act. These last two imperatives call for *true* repentance: "Offer right sacrifices and trust in the LORD." The enemies are to present the sacrifices to the Lord in accordance with his ordinances (Deut 33:19; Ps 51:16–17, 19) and with the attitude of commitment, because he does not delight in mere sacrifice (1 Sam 15:22; Ps 50:14). They must be "sincere" sacrifices, presented out of wholehearted trust in Yahweh, as an expression of submission to him. The sacrifices are only "righteous" (*ṣeḏeq*) when they are acts of devotion flowing out of a right relationship with God.

Notes

---

2 (3 MT) The phrase כְּבוֹדִי (k^e*ḇôḏî*, "my glory") receives various treatments. Among them is the LXX's "heavy of heart," presupposing a textual variant. Other versions have "honor become a reproach" (NASB), "pay me not honour but dishonour" (NEB), "how long will you be dull of heart?" (NAB), and "why shut your hearts so long?" (JB).

The words רִיק (*rîq*, "vain") and כָּזָב (*kāzāḇ*, "deception") may refer to idolatrous worship (so NIV; cf. Ps 40:4; Isa 44:20; Hos 7:13; 11:12; Amos 2:4) or to a different ideology, which the psalmist considers worthless. The context, in my opinion, weakly supports it.

3 (4 MT) The BHS proposes that the verb הִפְלָה (*hiplāh*, "has set apart") be emended to הִפְלָא (*hiplā'*, "has done marvelously"). The proposal is based on C and a number of MSS. The emendation requires an emendation of *ḥāsîḏ lô* ("the godly for himself") to *ḥeseḏ lî* ("love to me"), as in NEB's "has shown me his marvelous love" (cf. 31:21). This emendation is unnecessary.

חָסִיד (*ḥāsîḏ*, "godly"), related to *ḥeseḏ* ("love"), is characterized by love for God and man. Out of the twenty-five occurrences, it appears sixteen times in Psalms (cf. TWOT, 1:307). The word for "godly" (*ḥāsîḏ*, "loved one"; NIV, "godly" or "faithful one"; JB, "those he loves"; NAB, "faithful one") is a passive noun from the root *ḥ-s-d* ("to show covenantal love and fidelity"). Its form is similar to "righteous" (*ṣaddîq*) and, therefore, should be translated actively to designate the quality of the relationship between Yahweh and the psalmist: "loyal one" (NIV, "faithful" in 12:1; 18:25; "godly" in 32:6). See TWOT, 1:307–8; Katherine D. Sakenfeld, *The Meaning of Hesed in the Hebrew Bible: A New Inquiry.* Harvard Semitic Monographs 17 (Missoula: Scholars, 1978), pp. 241–45.

4, 7 (5, 8 MT) The words for "heart"—לֵבָב (*lēḇāḇ*) and לֵב (*lēḇ*)—respectively denote the whole being: physical, spiritual, emotional, rational, and volitional. See Eichrodt, TOT, 2:142–45; von Rad, OTT, 1:153; TDOT, 3:606–11; THAT, 1:862–67; TWOT, 1:466–67. See especially the study by F.J. Stendebach, "Die Bedeutung einer alttestamentlichen Anthropologie für die Verkündigung und die theologische Erwachsenbildung," in *Bausteine biblischer Theologie. Festgabe für G. Johannes Botterweck zum 60. Geburtstag dargebracht von seinen Schülern*, ed. Heinz-Josef Fabry (Köln: Peter Hanstein, 1977), pp. 333–49. He concludes that dualism has no place in the OT conception of man and that man is not soul and body but a wonderfully integrated unity of body and soul (p. 340).

4 (5 MT) John S. Kselmann's rendering is close to my proposal: "Tremble, and do not sin; weep bitterly from your hearts, upon your beds" ("A Note on Psalm 4:5," *Biblica* 68 [1987]: 103–5).

III. Prayer

4:6–7

6 Many are asking, "Who can show us any good?"
  Let the light of your face shine upon us, O LORD.
7 You have filled my heart with greater joy
  than when their grain and new wine abound.

6a As a true "shepherd" of Israel, David knew the hearts of the people. It was a time of turmoil and frustration due to unfulfilled expectations regarding the covenant blessings. It is not clear who the "many" were. Were they the skeptics (Craigie, *Psalms 1–50*, p. 81; cf. Ps 3:2), or were they his supporters who honestly questioned what was happening? Whoever they were, David prayed for them also and called on God to make his covenant blessings evident. He did this by an allusion to the priestly benediction (Num 6:24–26). They asked, "Who can show us any good?" David responded by pointing away from himself and to the Lord as the author of blessing.

6b–7 David prays specifically for the nation and for himself (NIV, vv.6b–8). His intercessory prayer for the nation is that the Lord may restore the fullness of his blessing. "The light of your face" (v.6b) is an idiom for the benefits of the covenant resulting from God's *presence* (cf. Num 6:25). The disgrace of the king has brought an end to God's blessings. While the people lamented, David prayed. He prayed because the Lord had "filled [his] heart with greater joy." David had the personal assurance of God's presence. God-given joy is vastly more important than all the food the world can give. It is a fruit of the Spirit (Gal 5:22–23) and therefore cannot be imitated.

Notes

6–7 (7–8 MT) These verses form a chiastic structure. Verses 6a and 7b are to be read in a complementary way, as also vv.6b and 7a. The word "many" (רַבִּים [*rabbîm*]) begins the construction, and the verbal phrase "were many" (רַבּוּ [*rabbû*], untr. in NIV) closes it. Moreover, the "good" for which the people are longing is further explained in v.7a as "their grain and new wine." Because of the complementary construction of vv.6b and 7a, the perfect verb נָתַתָּה (*nāṯattāh*, "you have given"; NIV, "you have filled"), preceded by the imperative "Let the light . . . shine," should be translated as an imperative: "Fill my heart with greater joy" (Joüon, par. 119l, unlike the NIV). The resultant translation forcefully brings out the chiastic structure (ABB′A′):

A. "*Many* . . . any good?" B. "Let the light of your face shine"
B′. "Fill my heart with greater joy." A′. "grain and new wine are *many*."

6 (7 MT) The allusion to the priestly benediction is equally difficult. Are the "many" saying this or is it David's response? What is the meaning of נסה (*n-s-h*)? How should the verse be read? It has been proposed that the root is *n-w-s* ("flee") with the sense "the light of your face has fled from us" (NEB; Dahood, *Psalms*, 1:26) or *n-s-*ʿ ("travel," "depart"; cf. Kraus, *Psalmen*, 1:31). J.H. Eaton supports this latter rendering. The people are lamenting, "Many are saying, 'O that we might be shewn good! The light of thy face, Lord, has fled from over us!' The king responds: 'Thou hast put gladness in my heart more than they had when their corn and wine were plentiful' " ("Hard Sayings. Psalm 4. 6–7," *Theology* 67 [1967]: 356). This translation seems to be most reasonable.

IV. Expression of Trust

4:8

[8] I will lie down and sleep in peace,
for you alone, O Lord,
make me dwell in safety.

8 The enemies diligently pursued "vanity" and "deception" in an attempt to frustrate the king and bring down his glory (cf. v.2). Others may have asked where prosperity had gone (v.6). David was not worried about the outcome. He was concerned, but not anxious, about the people (vv.3–7). He committed his way to the Lord as he went to sleep. The enemies may have vexed themselves on their beds (v.4), but he experienced "peace," the peace that comes as a blessing from God (Num 6:26). His confidence in Yahweh "alone" is the reason for his peaceful sleep. The expression "make me dwell in safety" connotes not only the absence of enemies and hostilities but also the presence of peace (Deut 33:28; Jer 23:6; Ezek 34:25, 27–28; 38:8, 14; Hos 2:18; cf. Mic 7:14). It has an eschatological dimension, as it looks for God to act as the Faithful Shepherd, ensuring the security of his people. He alone can fully restore his people to the full experience of his covenant blessing (cf. Jer 32:37).

Notes

8 (9 MT) The MT's יַחְדָּו (*yaḥdāw*, "together") is an unusual way of expressing that he will both lie down and go to sleep (cf. 3:5). The NIV leaves it untranslated. Kirkpatrick (p. 20) interprets it as an "exquisite expression of absolute confidence" in the Lord.

Psalm 5: A Morning Prayer (in Anticipation of God's Presence)

The reality of life on earth frustrates the full joy of the godly. Fears swell up in our hearts as we contemplate the harshness of life. This psalm is full of encouragement to those who suffer adversity and is appropriately called "a morning prayer" (cf. v.3). The prayer leads the worshiper of God into his presence (v.7) and to a deep realization of God's kingship (v.2) over life's circumstances. David (see below) prayed for himself and his people and prefigured our Lord's concern for his church (John 17). The Christian has boldness through his Savior to approach God (Heb 10:19) and to make his needs known to his heavenly Father in the name of the Son. Even when no answer is forthcoming, it is possible to cling to the affirmation that God is righteous (v.8a).

The authorship and date of this psalm, as in most psalms, are controversial. The answer is determined by how one understands the phrases "I lay" (v.3b), "your holy temple" (v.7b), and the identity of the enemies. Dates range from David's time to the postexilic period. Some critics view the psalm in the context of a highly developed cult and argue that the references to the temple, sacrifices (v.3b, but see below), and the individual enemies fit the situation of the postexilic era when the godly community experienced harassment. Craigie rejects the Davidic authorship on the basis of the content of the psalm (*Psalms 1–50*, p. 85). Eaton associates it with the Davidic dynasty (p. 38), and conservatives argue for a Davidic authorship. Calvin placed the date at a time after David had gained the kingship from Saul and had the opportunity to reflect on his conflicts with Saul (1:52). Delitzsch puts it in the context of the pre-Absalom rebellion, "when the fire which afterwards broke forth was already smouldering in secret" (KD, p. 119). The context may well fit in with the period of Absalom's rebellion (cf. Pss 3, 4) because David was separated from the ark of the covenant (cf. exposition on v.7), experienced animosity, was in great need of deliverance, and was concerned for the godly in his kingdom (vv.11–12). The expressions of fondness for God's "house" (cf. 23:6; 27:4; 84) are often in the context of a separation from God's presence (cf. 42, 43) or in an experience of deep emotional or physical distress (Pss 23; 27; cf. Isa 38:11, 20, 22; Jonah 2:4). In his separation from the ark (cf. 2 Sam 15:24–29) and in his distress caused by enemies, David prayed to experience again the presence of his God and King (v.2).

The psalm is generally categorized as an *individual lament* psalm. It shares elements of the psalms of *confidence* (vv.1–3; 8–12) and also of a *community* lament (vv.11–12). There is no agreement on the original life situation. Critical scholars, who date it to a postexilic time, associate it with the temple cult and suggest a priestly or Levitical author. The psalm functioned as a part of the morning liturgy in the second temple.

The structure of the psalm falls into two main parts with the last verse as a conclusion: (a) prayer for God's justice (vv.1–7) and (b) prayer for God's righteousness (vv.8–11).

A. Prayer for God's Justice (vv.1–3)
  B. Affirmation of God's Hatred of Evil (vv.4–6)
    C. Hope in Fellowship With God (v.7)
A′. Prayer for God's Righteousness (v.8)
  B′. Affirmation of Evil (v.9)
    C′. Hope in God's Righteousness (vv.10–12)

The psalmist moves from the affirmations (B; introduced by the particle *kî* ["truly," "certainly," vv.4, 9, 12; omitted in vv.4, 9 in NIV]) to the expressions of hope (C; vv.7, 10, 11). The whole prayer finds its focus in the faith stated in the last verse.

I. Prayer for God's Justice

5:1–3

For the director of music. For flutes. A psalm of David.

1 Give ear to my words, O LORD,
  consider my sighing.
2 Listen to my cry for help,
  my King and my God,
  for to you I pray.
3 In the morning, O LORD, you hear my voice;
  in the morning I lay my requests before you
  and wait in expectation.

1 The lament is an expression of a great need felt by the psalmist. He expresses himself with audible sounds, whether they be words or groans. In his state of mind he does not think about the formalities of prayer, because he knows that the Lord hears both the inner thoughts (in the form of a "sighing" for the moment of redemption) and the audible prayers. The "words" and the "sighings" (groanings) reveal his need and come to the Lord's ear as a "cry for help." The "sighing" is a nonverbal expression of need (cf. Ps 39:3; Rom 8:26). The word "sighing" (*hāḡîḡ*) is related to the root *h-g-g* ("long for," "burn," elsewhere only in 39:3 [4 MT]; KB^3, 1:228). The cry of dependence and need comes from an oppressed person to someone who is in the position to redeem and deliver. It presupposes that an injustice has been done.

2 Because of the apparent injustice, David prayed to no one other than his "King" (see the appendix to Ps 5: Yahweh Is King). The phrase "my King and my God" (cf. 84:3) recognizes that while God is the sovereign King and able to deliver, he is close enough to his children that they may call him "my God," the equivalent of "Abba."

3 With the dawn of each new day, prayer is renewed with the hope that the Lord will soon respond. The "morning" is symbolic of a renewal of God's acts of love (cf. Lam 3:23). The change from darkness to light brings with it the association of renewed hope. In the early morning hours (cf. 55:17; 88:13; 92:2), the psalmist sought the Lord (his covenant God) in prayer because he knew that Yahweh would not forsake him. It is to this end that he presented him with his "requests" (or "offerings," see Notes). During the day he waited with "expectation" to see what the Lord would do for him.

Notes

For a brief discussion of the technical words and phrases in the superscription, see the Introduction.

3 (4 MT) The verbal phrase אֶעֱרָךְ־לְךָ (*'e'erok-lekā*, "I shall stretch out for you") has no object. The NIV proposes "my requests" as the object of the verb. Other possibilities are "my sacrifice" and "my case" (Anderson, 1:82).

II. Affirmation of God's Hatred of Evil

5:4–6

4 You are not a God who takes pleasure in evil;
with you the wicked cannot dwell.
5 The arrogant cannot stand in your presence;
you hate all who do wrong.
6 You destroy those who tell lies;
bloodthirsty and deceitful men
the LORD abhors.

4–6 Deeply ingrained in Israel's belief system and developed in the wisdom literature is the conviction that the God of Israel hates evil in any form. Whereas other religions brought together good and evil at the level of the gods, God had revealed that evil exists apart from him and yet is under his sovereign control. The religion of Israel was revelatory. The psalmist shows a clear conviction that God hates in the most radical way any form of evil and denies lawless persons any (present or future) right to his presence (v.4). Whoever expects his own people to dissociate from evildoers (Ps 1:1–2; Amos 5:15) and encourages righteous and holy living (Pss 15:2–5; 24:4–6) cannot betray them by having a double standard himself.

The verbal phrases "[you are not a God] who takes pleasure" (*hāpēṣ*, v.4), "you hate" (*śānē'tā*, v.5), and "[the LORD] abhors" (*yeṯā'ēḇ*, v.6) affirm three times God's absolute hatred of evil. In Malachi's days some argued that God "delights" in evildoers (Mal 2:17). But, in response, the Lord revealed how he will quickly judge unfaithful people as well as those who oppress the poor (Mal 3:5). Similarly, the negative statements "cannot dwell" and "cannot stand" (cf. 1:5) are complemented by the phrase "you destroy," having the same root (*'-b-d*) as the verb in 1:6: "but the way of the wicked will perish."

God hates both the sin and those who sin against him (v.5). The particular sins are examples of a way of life. The liar is only a hairbreadth away from the murderer (v.6).

Though the liar may claim that he only goes so far with his deception, when he is caught, the liar is a dangerous man, because he may attempt to cover his tracks. Deception and greed mark the man who is unfaithful to God and man; he is a potential candidate for murder. The "bloodthirsty" man is, therefore, not necessarily one who is guilty of murder, but one who no longer knows the limits between "mine" and "thine" and thus twists and perverts justice, even at the cost of human lives or dignity (cf. Isa 3:13–15; 5:8–10; Amos 6:12). Instead of "taking pleasure" in evil, the Lord "abhors" all who practice wickedness.

III. Hope in Fellowship With God

5:7

> 7 But I, by your great mercy,
> will come into your house;
> in reverence will I bow down
> toward your holy temple.

7 In contrast to the wicked who will not be able to "stand" or "dwell" in God's presence, the psalmist prays with expectation that the Lord will permit him to enjoy his presence. The contrastive phrase "but I" (*wa'ᵃnî*) expresses the psalmist's hope in God's love (*ḥesed*), over against God's certain hatred of all forms of evil.

The hope of fellowship with God is based, not on his righteousness, but on God's sovereign "love" (*ḥesed;* NIV, "mercy," but should be "love" or "unfailing love"). The entrance into the house of God was not limited to the godly, because the priests could not distinguish between the godly in heart and the godly in appearance. It is to this end that the people were reminded of the conditions for entrance into God's presence and fellowship in Psalms 15 and 24. For the psalmist the hope of entering into the temple is much more than the physical walking into the courts of the temple (see the appendix to Ps 132: The Ark of the Covenant and the Temple: Symbols of Yahweh's Presence and Rule). The psalmist seeks the affirmation of God's love for him in an evil world and, hence, the assurance of God's presence with him. Like the psalmist in the "shepherd psalm," he longs to dwell in the house of the Lord (23:6). Because he knows that God is "holy," he prostrates himself in the direction of the temple (cf. 1 Kings 8:35, 38, 42; Pss 28:2; 138:2; Dan 6:10) with the prayer of hope that the Lord will answer him. His submission to his covenant God is further brought out by the manner of his approach. He bows down "in reverence," not in paralyzing fear.

IV. Prayer for and Hope in God's Righteousness

5:8–12

> 8 Lead me, O LORD, in your righteousness
> because of my enemies—
> make straight your way before me.
>
> 9 Not a word from their mouth can be trusted;
> their heart is filled with destruction.
> Their throat is an open grave;
> with their tongue they speak deceit.
> 10 Declare them guilty, O God!

Let their intrigues be their downfall.
Banish them for their many sins,
for they have rebelled against you.

11 But let all who take refuge in you be glad;
let them ever sing for joy.
Spread your protection over them,
that those who love your name may rejoice in you.
12 For surely, O LORD, you bless the righteous;
you surround them with your favor as with a shield.

8–9 The psalmist's reflection on fellowship with the Lord (v.7) renews his prayer that the Lord may *act* on his behalf. He prays for the Lord to "make straight" his path by "leading" the godly in his "righteousness" (v.8). The prayer has two components. On the one hand, he prays for the Lord's presence to guide him (cf. Pss 23:3; 143:11; Prov 3:6; 8:32–34; 12:28) by leveling the obstacles from the way of life (cf. 27:11). On the other hand, he prays for the Lord to show himself "righteous" because his divine order is challenged by the ungodly (cf. 31:1; 71:2; 119:40; 143:1, 11). The removal of evildoers is an act of redemption, giving the godly reason for hope and praise. Both aspects of the prayer for God's righteousness are further developed in vv.9–11.

First, the psalmist prays to be kept safe from evildoers. They are all around, and the psalmist commits his way to the Lord (v.8). The wicked are further described as instruments of destruction and death (v.9). By their reign of terror, they are opposed to the God of life and truth. The heart of the wicked is full of "destruction," as they plot to destroy God's established order (cf. chs. 17; 25; 27–28; 31; 35; 41; 52; 54–57; 59; 63–64; 71; 86; 109; 140–41). Their mouths, filled with lies and deceit, are likened to "an open grave," because of their deadly words (cf. Jer 5:16). They speak words that rob people of their desire to live. With their "slippery" tongues they sow discord, hatred, and death (v.9; cf. Ps 12).

10 At the root of the evildoers' actions is their rebellion against God. Their lack of loyalty on the human plane reveals their essential lack of concern for God and his established order. The chaos caused by the evildoers requires a response from the Lord. For this reason the psalmist prays for their demise. The declaration of their "guilt" also signifies the judgment of destruction. The phrase "declare them guilty" (*ha'ᵃšîmēm,* "you destroy them," Dahood, *Psalms,* 1:35–36) calls on the Lord both to declare a guilty verdict and to judge them with an appropriate sentence (cf. Ps 34:21–22; Isa 24:6; Hos 5:14; 10:2).

Second, the psalmist prays that the Lord's righteousness will triumph by holding the wicked culpable for their acts and, once culpable, that he will remove them from the covenant community. The wicked cannot continue to live as if their way is blessed or condoned by the Lord. The seeds sown in unrighteousness and unfaithfulness must bear their fruits by bringing "calamities" on the wicked. God's justice must cause the schemes of the wicked to backfire on themselves (see the appendix to Ps 137: Imprecations in the Psalms).

11–12 The just acts of God leading to the conviction and the destruction of the wicked give the godly community a reason to rejoice in his righteousness (v.11). The righteous acts of God include the preservation of the godly, "who take refuge" (see 7:1) in him, and their glorification, as they praise him for the establishment of his righteousness and justice on earth. The psalmist hopes that God's judgment of the wicked will provide the righteous with a greater reason to rejoice in the marvelous powers of salvation and victory, which he shares with his own. The "righteous" (v.12; see 1:6) are the same as those "who love your name" (v.11; cf. 69:36; 119:132). The wicked rebelled against his sovereignty, whereas the godly longed for his love and fellowship (cf. v.7). They love the covenant name Yahweh, as it is their shield. Yahweh protects his own under the cover of his wings (cf. 91:4).

The grand conclusion exalts Yahweh as the God who deals graciously with the righteous. Though the word "righteous" is not used with reference to God, the language of "blessing," "protection," and "favor" are all expressions of his righteous acts for his people. The hope of the godly lies in Yahweh, who will constantly guard his own as with a "shield." The affirmative particle *kî* ("for surely," v.12) along with the emphatic use of "you" form a fitting conclusion to the prayer that began with an appeal to God's kingship (v.2). Truly the king will protect and care for his own. It has to be so! (See the appendix to Ps 98: Yahweh Is the Divine Warrior.)

"You surround them" (v.12) may also be translated as "you crown them" (*ta'ṭ^{e}rennû*). On the one hand, the Lord extends his protection and favor, likened to a "shield" (cf. 35:2; 91:4). On the other hand, he bestows his royal glory on the godly (cf. 3:3). The crowning with his "favor" is an integral part of the blessing of the Lord (see A.A. Anderson, 1:86; cf. Deut 33:23; Ps 30:5).

Notes

---

7 (8 MT) חֶסֶד (*ḥeseḏ*, "mercy") is better translated by "faithful love." See Notes on 4:3 and appendix to Ps 25: The Perfections of Yahweh.

9 (10 MT) It is possible that קִרְבָּם (*qirbām*, lit., "their inner being"; NIV, "their heart") and קֶבֶר (*qeḇer*, "grave") are meant to be a play on words.

The verbal phrase יַחֲלִיקוּן (*yaḥ^{a}lîqûn*, "they speak smoothly," "they flatter"; NIV, "they speak deceit") is an idiom for flattery. Dahood's translation, "they bring death" (*Psalms*, 1:35–36), while attractive in the present context, is unnecessary.

10 (11 MT) There may be an intentional contrast between the "great mercy" (v.7) of God and the "many sins" of the wicked by the repetition of the phrase בְּרֹב (*b^{e}rōḇ*, "in much," "in the multitude"; NIV, "for their many"). The one is a ground for fellowship ("by your great mercy"), whereas the other is the reason for God's banishing the wicked from his presence ("for their many sins").

11 (12 MT) The verbal clause וְיִשְׂמְחוּ (*w^{e}yiśm^{e}ḥû*, "and they will be glad," "and let them be glad" [cf. NIV]) preceded by imperatives ("Declare them guilty. . . . Banish them") is best translated as a result clause: "so that all who take refuge in you will be glad" (Joüon, par. 116f).

שֵׁם (*šēm*, "name") denotes the name revealed to Israel: Yahweh. For the significance of this, see the appendix to Psalm 7: The Name of Yahweh.

Appendix: Yahweh Is King

The Psalms celebrate the present kingship of God. In both lament and praise the people of God know that Yahweh is King. In the lament psalms they look forward to his acts of deliverance and vindication as the Divine Warrior. They believe that Yahweh alone can subdue all kingdoms and principalities. In praise psalms the people of God look back to the acts of deliverance and celebrate his majesty in creation and in redemption. For the theology of divine enthronement, see the Introduction. The followers of Mowinckel's emphasis on the annual enthronement ritual have increased the number of royal psalms from the original 47; 93; 96–99 to include also 29; 48; 65; 68; 76; 85; 89; 110; and laments (both communal and individual; cf. Gray, *The Biblical Doctrine of the Reign of God*, pp. 39–116).

The roots for "rule" are *m-l-k* ("be king," a denominative of *melek̲* ["king"]; with derived nouns: *malk̲ût̲* ["kingdom"], *mamlāk̲āh* ["kingdom"], *m*ᵉ*lûk̲āh* ["kingdom"]), *m-š-l* ("rule," derivative: *memšālāh* ["dominion," "kingdom," "governance"]), and *r-d-h* ("rule"). The roots and their derivatives are synonyms. The Psalms, while ascribing kingship to Yahweh, explore the significance of Yahweh's rule for Israel, the nations, and creation (cf. Pss 93; 96–99). In addition, many psalms portray, have confidence in, and long for the full establishment of his kingdom over all the created order.

Needless to say, any discussion of Yahweh's kingship must operate from the assumption that the psalmist uses mythopoetic language. (For an excellent introduction to this concept, see Elmer B. Smick, "Mythopoetic Language in the Psalms," WTJ 44 [1982]: 88–98.) The nations spoke of their deities as kings and described the functions and limitations of their gods. Yahweh revealed himself to Israel as *the* king, as he rules *on behalf of* his people. Thus the Psalms use the language of accommodation but operate from the revelation of Yahweh. He is King and his kingdom is greater, better, and more exalted than any other conception of kingship, whether mythological or political (H. Frankfort, *Kingship and the Gods* [Chicago: University of Chicago Press, 1948]; Smith, "The Concept of God/the gods as King in the Ancient Near East and the Bible," pp. 18–38; VanGemeren, "Kingship," 2:1264–69). The ancients believed in the plurality of gods, where each ruled over separate spheres of interest. When the psalmist exclaims, "For the LORD is the great God ['ēl, 'El'], the great King [*melek̲*] above all gods" (95:3), he declares that there is no other King than Yahweh. When the ancients believed that one god was victorious over other gods or over the powers of chaos, the psalmist confessed his faith in Yahweh who alone is the victorious King:

> The heavens praise your wonders, O LORD,
> your faithfulness too, in the assembly of the holy ones.
> For who in the skies above can compare with the LORD?
> Who is like the LORD among the heavenly beings?
> In the council of the holy ones God is greatly feared;
> he is more awesome than all who surround him.
> O LORD God Almighty, who is like you?
> You are mighty, O LORD, and your faithfulness surrounds you.
>
> You rule [*m-š-l*] over the surging sea;
> when its waves mount up, you still them.
> You crushed Rahab like one of the slain;
> with your strong arm you scattered your enemies.
>
> (89:5–10)

Yahweh alone is King in heaven above and also on earth. He establishes order in the world of creation and hence in human society. The Psalms adumbrate Yahweh's wonderful and wise ordering of all of creation, the preservation of the world, and, in hymnic form, look forward to the righteous establishment of his order in the world. The place of Yahweh in Israelite society is much more prominent in the OT.

Central to the discussion on Yahweh's kingship is the phrase *YHWH malak̲* (93:1; 96:10; 97:1; 99:1; cf. 1 Chron 16:31). The phrase could be translated "Yahweh has become king" (this is the usual translation of those who follow Mowinckel's idea of annual enthronement ritual; for a criticism see Introduction, 4a) or "Yahweh is king." (For the various translations, see J.A. Soggin, "König," THAT, 1:917–18; Karl H. Ulrichsen ["JHWH MALAK: einige Sprachliche Beobachtungen," VetTest 27 (1977): 361–77] favors a contextually related interpretation; John Day, *God's Conflict with the Dragon and the Sea. Echoes of Canaanite Myth in the Old Testament* [Cambridge: Cambridge University Press, 1985], pp. 36–37.) I agree with the rendering "Yahweh is king" for several reasons.

First, the kingdom of God is an everlasting kingdom:

> Your kingdom [*malḵûṯ*] is an everlasting kingdom [*malḵûṯ*],
> and your dominion [*memšālāh*] endures through all generations.
>
> The LORD is faithful to all his promises
> and loving toward all he has made.
>
> (145:13)

Second, the kingdom of God appears in creation and in redemption. On the one hand, Psalm 145 celebrates God's kingdom in creation. Yahweh is King in bestowing blessing and his royal splendor on all creation:

> The eyes of all look to you,
> and you give them their food at the proper time.
> You open your hand
> and satisfy the desires of every living thing.
>
> (145:15–16)

On the other hand, the Lord also establishes his dominion in redeeming his people from oppressors, kings, and the kingdoms of this world. The kingdom of God consists of his acts demonstrating his goodness, love, justice, righteousness, and compassion:

> They will celebrate your abundant goodness [*ṭûḇ*]
> and joyfully sing of your righteousness [*ṣ-ḏ-q*].
>
> The LORD is gracious and compassionate [*raḥûm*],
> slow to anger [*'ap̱*] and rich in love [*ḥeseḏ*].
> The LORD is good [*ṭôḇ*] to all;
> he has compassion [*raḥ^{a}mîm*] on all he has made.
> All you have made will praise you, O LORD;
> your saints will extol you.
>
> They will tell of the glory [*kāḇôḏ*] of your kingdom [*malḵûṯ*]
> and speak of your might,
> so that all men may know of your mighty acts
> and the glorious [*kāḇôḏ*] splendor [*hāḏār*] of your kingdom [*malḵûṯ*].
>
> (145:7–12)

Third, the Lord is King in his judgment: "The LORD reigns forever; / he has established his throne for judgment" (9:7). Though his rule may not be apparent, Yahweh rules sovereignly over the nations; and they will be held accountable to him: "God reigns over the nations; / God is seated on his holy throne" (47:8; cf. v.9; 49:13; 66:7).

Yahweh rules with equity, establishing order on earth through his acts of deliverance and vengeance: "May the nations be glad and sing for joy, / for you rule the peoples justly / and guide the nations of the earth" (67:4). He will protect his own as with a shield: "Indeed, our shield belongs to the LORD, / our king to the Holy One of Israel" (89:18). He will deliver his own completely from whatever oppression and acts of hostility they may encounter: "But you, O God, are my king from of old; / you bring salvation upon the earth" (74:12). This includes Israel, as they have witnessed Yahweh's victory over the king of Egypt, Sihon, and Og (Pss 135; 136). But also the nations, which will submit themselves to his rule, need not be afraid: "Sing to God, O kingdoms of the earth, / sing praise to the Lord" (68:32). Great is the glory, strength, and majesty of the Great King, and the redeemed of the Lord will declare his praise:

> They will tell of the glory of your kingdom
> and speak of your might,
> so that all men may know of your mighty acts
> and the glorious splendor of your kingdom.
> (145:11–12)

The mighty acts of Yahweh evoke *awe* among his people and *dread* among the nations. Brueggemann uses the phrase "psalms of orientation" to denote the psalms celebrating Yahweh's kingship, as he provides for new order, dispenses justice, and sanctifies this world. He recognizes "the old order"—an order of injustice, chaotic forces, and infidelity—but there is hope in the eschatological dimension of the Psalms.

Fourth, the Lord has established his rule among his people: "Judah became God's sanctuary, / Israel his dominion" (114:2). He chose Jerusalem as his dwelling place (Ps 132): Mount Zion (see the appendix to Ps 46: Zion Theology). They experience the bliss of his blessings and protection (cf. Ps 46), as he has chosen Zion for his holy mountain: "Why gaze in envy, O rugged mountains, / at the mountain where God chooses to reign, / where the LORD himself will dwell forever?" (68:16; cf. 146:10). The temple is the palace of Yahweh, wherein he rules over the earth: "The LORD reigns, / let the nations tremble; / he sits enthroned between the cherubim, / let the earth shake" (99:1).

Yahweh's kingdom cannot be restricted to the earth, as he rules over all creation, including heaven. Hence the psalmist also conceptualizes of God's throne as being in heaven: "The LORD has established his throne in heaven, / and his kingdom rules over all" (103:19). Mettinger attempts to explain the presence and parousia of God's kingdom as a paradox. I agree, but he posits this as arising from two different traditions (*Dethronement*, p. 36).

Fifth, Yahweh has ordained the establishment of his kingdom through the dynasty of David (Ps 2). The appointment of the Davidic dynasty is the full establishment of God's kingdom on earth. Kings, princes, and rulers may rebel against God's rule or that of his messiah: "The kings of the earth take their stand / and the rulers gather together / against the LORD / and against his Anointed One" (2:2). However, Yahweh's decree stands: his kingdom will be established! As long as a ruler of David's dynasty reigned in Jerusalem, the kings could praise him for victory: "He gives his king great victories; / he shows unfailing kindness to his anointed, / to David and his descendants forever" (18:50; cf. 21:1, 7). Even in adversity the anointed of the Lord knows that God is king: "for dominion belongs to the LORD / and he rules over the nations" (22:28).

Sixth, the kingdom of David further accentuates the interests of God's kingdom: righteousness, justice, peace, love, and equity. His messiah is the vassal of the Great King and is zealous for the worship of God, executes God's will on earth, extends God's blessings to the people, and will bring all nations to submission to the Great King: "All kings will bow down to him / and all nations will serve him" (72:11).

The hope of the godly lies in the perpetual establishment of Yahweh's reign: "The LORD will extend your mighty scepter from Zion; / you will rule in the midst of your enemies" (110:2; cf. 45:6). Here we meet three correlated concepts: Zion theology, the kingdom of God, and the Davidic royal theology. It is apparent that the goal of the messianic kingdom runs parallel to the purpose of God in redemptive history:

> The nations will fear the name of the LORD,
> all the kings of the earth will revere your glory.
> . . . .
> when the peoples and the kingdoms
> assemble to worship the LORD.
>
> (102:15, 22)

Seventh, the rebellions on earth will cease and Yahweh's kingdom will be established in peace: "Nations are in uproar, kingdoms fall; / he lifts his voice, the earth melts" (46:6; cf. 76:12; 79:6; 110:5–6). From this (eschatological) vantage point the godly know that God's kingdom is already a reality:

> The LORD reigns, he is robed in majesty;
> the LORD is robed in majesty
> and is armed with strength.
> The world is firmly established;
> it cannot be moved.
>
> (93:1; cf. 96:10)

Since he rules over all creation, including his people, Yahweh receives the homage due to him from the created order, from his people, and from the kings of the earth: "Praise the LORD, all his works / everywhere in his dominion. / Praise the LORD, O my soul" (103:22; cf. 138:4; 148).

Texts: 5:2; 9–10; 11:4–6; 18; 24:7–10; 33:12–19; 35:22–28; 44:4; 47:2; 48:2; 50; 58:11; 65; 68; 74:12; 82:1–4; 84:3; 89; 93–100; 143:1–2, 11–12; 149:2.

Related Concepts: Appendixes to Pss 3 (Yahweh Is My God); 7 (The Name of Yahweh); 9 (Yahweh Is El Elyon); 22 (Yahweh Is El); 24 (Lord Sabaoth); 25 (The Perfections of Yahweh); 46 (Zion Theology); 78 (The Mighty Acts of Yahweh); 98 (Yahweh Is the Divine Warrior); 119 (Yahweh Is My Redeemer); 132 (The Ark of the Covenant and the Temple: Symbols of Yahweh's Presence and Rule).

Bibliography: Milos Bic, "Das Erste Buch des Psalters eine Thronbesteigungs-Liturgie," *The Sacral Kingship/La Regalità Sacra* (Leiden: Brill, 1959), pp. 316–32; John Bright, *The Kingdom of God* (Nashville: Abingdon, 1953); Brueggemann, *The Message of the Psalms*, pp. 123–67; Childs, IOTS, pp. 515–18; R.E. Clements, *Isaiah and the Deliverance of Jerusalem. A Study in the Interpretation of Prophecy in the Old Testament.* JSOTS 13 (Sheffield: JSOT, 1980), pp. 72–89; J. Coppens, "La Royauté de Yahvé dans le Psautier," *Ephemerides Theologicae Lovanienses* 53 (1977): 297–362; 54 (1978): 1–50; Keith R. Crim, *The Royal Psalms* (Richmond: Knox, 1962); Walter Dietrich, "Gott als König," *Zeitschrift für Theologie und Kirche* 77 (1980): 251–68; J.H. Eaton, *Kingship and the Psalms.* Studies in Biblical Theology Second Series 32 (Naperville: Allenson, 1976); W. Eichrodt, OTT, 1:124–28; 476–79; Heinz-Josef Fabry, "Der himmlische Thronrat als ekklesiologisches Modell," *Bausteine biblischer Theologie. Festgabe für G. Johannes Botterweck zum 60. Geburtstag dargebracht von seinen Schülern*, ed. H.J. Fabry (Köln: Peter Hanstein, 1977), pp. 99–126; John Gray, "The Kingship of God in the Prophets and Psalms," VetTest 11 (1961): 1–29; id., *The Biblical Doctrine of the Reign of God;* R.H. Hiers, "Kingdom of God," IDBSuppl., p. 516 (up-to-date bibliography); Tryggve B.D. Mettinger, *The Dethronement of Sabaoth. Studies in the Shem and Kabod Theologies* (Lund: Gleerup, 1982); von Rad, OTT, 1: 360–64; H. Ridderbos, *The Coming of the Kingdom* (Philadelphia: Presbyterian and Reformed, 1976); Roy A. Rosenberg, "Yahweh Has Become King," JBL 85 (1966): 297–307; Hans Heinrich Schmid, *Gerechtigkeit als Weltordnung. Hintergrund und Geschichte des* *alttestamentlichen Gerechtigkeitsbegriffes* (Tübingen: Mohr, 1968); Werner H. Schmidt, *Königtum Gottes in Ugarit und Israel. Zur Herkunft und Königsprädikation Jahwes* (Berlin: Töpelmann, 1961); id., "Kritik am Königtum," *Probleme biblischer Theologie. Gerhard von Rad zum 70. Geburtstag,* ed. Hans Walter Wolff (Munich: Chr. Kaiser, 1971), pp. 440–61; Gary V. Smith, "The Concept of God/the Gods as Kings in the Ancient Near East and the Bible," *Trinity Journal* 3 (1982): 18–38; J. Garcia Trapiello, "El Dios 'rey' de Israel," *Studium* 19 (1979): 43–46; Marco Treves, "The Reign of God in the O.T.," VetTest 19 (1969): 230–43; M. Tsevat, "King, God as," IDBSuppl., pp. 515–16; W.A. VanGemeren, "Kingship," in Elwell, BEB, 2:1264–69; Arthur Weiser, "Zur Frage nach den Beziehungen der Psalmen zum Kult: Die Darstellung der Theophanie in den Psalmen und im Festkult," *Festschrift für Alfred Bertholet zum 80. Geburtstag,* edd. Walter Baumgartner, Otto Eissfeldt, Karl Elliger, and Leonhard Rost (Tübingen: J.C.B. Mohr, 1950), pp. 513–31; Peter Welten, "Königsherrschaft Jahwes und Thronbesteigung," VetTest 32 (1982): 297–310; Keith K. Whitelam, *The Just King. Monarchical Judicial Authority,* JSOTS 12 (Sheffield: JSOT, 1979); see also the Introduction to the Psalms.

TDAT, 4:926–958; THAT, 1:908–19; TWOT, 1:507–9.

Psalm 6: A Prayer (in Deep Anguish)

This psalm is one of the seven penitential psalms (6, 32, 38, 51, 102, 130, 143) of the early church. It was the practice of the early Christians to sing and read the psalms on Ash Wednesday as part of their penance for sin. In a strict sense, however, it is not a penitence psalm, for there is no confession of sin or prayer for forgiveness. The psalm is now categorized as an *individual lament* psalm. For the history of Psalm 6, see H.C. Knuth, *Zur Auslegungsgeschichte von Psalm 6* (Tübingen: Mohr, 1971).

The sudden change in tone between vv.1–7 and vv.8–10 has occasioned the question of the integrity of the psalm. Throughout the first part the psalmist speaks of personal suffering that is so intense that he may collapse. He prays that God may heal him and no longer be angry. With a sudden twist he turns to the wicked and, in an assured voice, announces that they, instead, will be disgraced (v.8). The tension between the two parts may be resolved, and several proposals have been made. Oesterley suggests that the first part is the original psalm composed after a period of great physical suffering and that the same author added vv.8–10 after an experience with the enemies (p. 94). Craigie classifies it as a "psalm of sickness" (*Psalms 1–50,* p. 91) and accounts for the change by assuming that the psalmist, after he had received a word from God, could confidently dismiss the enemies. The position of J. Ridderbos (*Psalmen,* pp. 52–53) and Rogerson/McKay (p. 33) understands the language of physical suffering as a metaphor for the anguish of abandonment. This last view is, in my opinion, in harmony with the entire psalm. It is not possible to be certain of the original setting in which the psalm arose. It seems best to take the psalm as an expression of deep, personal anguish, without any additional speculation on the original context (Kraus, "soul pain," *Psalmen,* p. 48; cf. Miller, "Trouble and Woe," p. 39).

There is no general agreement on the structure of the psalm, apart from the broad division: vv.1–7 (prayer for restoration) and vv.8–10 (confidence in the Lord's answer). The first part could be divided into two sections: (1) prayer for grace (vv.1–3) and (2) prayer for deliverance (vv.4–7). We shall follow the outline of the NIV:

A. Prayer for God's Favor (vv.1–3)
B. Prayer for God's Love (vv.4–5)
B′. Need of God's Love (vv.6–7)
A′. Prayer for God's Favor (vv.8–10)

Our Lord Jesus identified fully with the anguish of the soul in his suffering (John 12:27). Therefore the comfort for the Christian does not lie in David's example but ultimately in the victory achieved by our Lord and the greater benefits of grace, love, and the presence of God in the Spirit that are ours in Christ. The Christ who will cast out the enemies of his kingdom (v.8; cf. Matt 7:23; Luke 13:27) will certainly come to the aid of his beloved who suffer depression, despair, and anguish of soul!

I. Prayer for God's Favor

6:1–3

For the director of music. With stringed instruments.
According to *sheminith.* A psalm of David.

1 O LORD, do not rebuke me in your anger
or discipline me in your wrath.
2 Be merciful to me, LORD, for I am faint;
O LORD, heal me, for my bones are in agony.
3 My soul is in anguish.
How long, O LORD, how long?

Verses 1–3 express the perplexity of the psalmist during a period of depression. The tragedy is intensified by the semblance of God's anger; for the psalmist's suffering is nearly more than he can bear, and there is no end in sight. He asks for God's grace to sustain him because he is at the end of his rope.

1 The discipline of the Lord may be so harsh that it seems that he is angry. David prayed that the Lord would not discipline him in wrath. The position of the phrases "not . . . in your anger . . . or . . . in your wrath" in the MT is emphatic, so as to emphasize that the psalmist is not suffering justly because of his sin. The discipline of the Lord is there! But the psalmist does not understand why it has come or how long it is going to last. God's discipline is for the purpose of sanctification; however, in David's present experience it almost works the opposite results. God seems to have forsaken him (v.3) and, therefore, ceased to care for his servant, either dead or alive (v.5).

The verbs "rebuke" (*tôḵîḥēnî*) and "discipline" (*tᵉyassᵉrēnî*) are often synonymous. The "rebuke" of the Lord may be a form of judgment, but it may also be in the form of a lesson in life (Deut 4:36; 8:5; 2 Sam 7:14; Ps 94:10; Prov 3:12; see THAT, 1:739). Eliphaz states the argument that the Lord delivers man from calamities even when he has inflicted them in the process of "maturation" (Job 5:17–26, esp. vv.17–18).

2 In his suffering, the nature of which is only intimated in vv.8–10, David turned to Yahweh as if to say, "Father, my covenant faithful God." He does not confess his sins but asks the Lord to demonstrate his covenant promises: restoration (v.2) and loyalty (v.4). The discipline of the Lord appears to him as too severe. In a manner characteristic of the OT, he identifies suffering with judgment (reproof) and judgment with God's wrath (cf. 38:1–3). The OT describes vividly the terrible effects of God's wrath. When he comes to judge, "the earth trembles; the nations cannot endure his wrath" (Jer 10:10; cf. Isa 66:15–16; Mic 1:2–4; Nah 1:2–4; Zeph 1:14–17). It is terrible to fall into God's angry hands.

Who can stand in the judgment of God? Certainly not a man who is in deep anguish! The verb "faint" (*b-h-l*) may express the process of withering of leaves, crops (grapes, olives, cf. Isa 24:7; Joel 1:10, 12), and verdant regions, such as the Bashan, Mount Carmel, and the Lebanon (Nah 1:4). Metaphorically it signifies the weakness of strong people and of fortifications (Isa 24:4; Jer 14:2; Lam 2:8). For the psalmist it shows how his vigor (spiritual, psychological, and physical) has been brought down.

Though the anguish of his soul is stated in physical language ("faint" and "bones"), the psalmist is using such terms as metaphors for his deep depression. The word "bones" signifies the depth and intensity of his depression, which has affected his most inner being. In fact "being" is expressed in Hebrew by "bone" (*'eṣem*; cf. Gen 29:14 [NIV, "flesh"]; Exod 24:10 [NIV, "itself"]) and "soul" (*nep̱eš*, v.3; cf. Gen 27:4 [NIV, "my (blessing)]"; Lev 24:17 [NIV, "life"]; 1 Sam 18:3 [NIV, "himself"]; 1 Kings 19:10 [NIV, "me"]). In Oriental fashion no clear distinction is made between "soul" and "body" because man suffers in his whole being. The agony of "my bones" means the same as "my soul is in anguish" (v.3), i.e., "I am full of anguish."

3 The "anguish" is even more intense because it seems that the discipline has no regard for man's frailty and has no apparent end in sight. The psalmist cries to the Lord to be gracious (*ḥonnēnî*; NIV, "be merciful," v.2) so as to restore him (*rep̱ā'ēnî*, "heal me," v.2). If not now, when? It seems as if God is carried away with his instruction and has no regard for his frail child. Verse 3 is incomplete with the final cry "how long?" Because of the intensity of his emotions, he cannot complete his thought. Similar language occurs elsewhere in the Psalms (13:1; 35:17; 74:10; 79:5; 89:46; 90:13) but is usually complete. The sense could be rendered as "How long will it be before you heal me?" or "How long will it be before you deliver me?" (in anticipation of v.5).

Notes

For a brief discussion of the technical words and phrases used in the superscription, see the Introduction.

1 (2 MT) For the emphatic position of the negatives, see Joüon, par. 160–61; cf. Ps 38:3 (2 MT).

2 (3 MT) The root ב־ה־ל (*b-h-l*) occurs three times in this context (vv.2, 3, 10), and each occurrence is translated differently in the NIV: "are in agony. . . . is in anguish. . . . dismayed."

3 (4 MT) The Hebrew נֶפֶשׁ (*nep̱eš*, "soul") denotes the whole being. See TWOT, 2:587–91: "It comes as no surprise, then, that in some contexts *nep̱eš* is best rendered by 'person,' 'self,' or more simply by the personal pronoun" (ibid., p. 590). See also Westermann in THAT, 2:71–95.

II. Prayer for God's Love

6:4–5

4 Turn, O LORD, and deliver me;
save me because of your unfailing love.

[5]No one remembers you when he is dead.
Who praises you from the grave?

4 David boldly, not diffidently, called on the Lord: "Return!" (*šûḇāh;* NIV, "Turn"). If he had sinned, he would not wait patiently for the Lord. *At this moment,* in the depth of his suffering, he needed his God—who had promised not to leave him—to extend his "unfailing love" (*ḥesed;* see 5:7) to him and thereby deliver him. Only the Lord can take a man out of deep depression so as to give a sense of well-being in the whole person.

5 What is man when he is dead? This is not to say that the OT denies life after death, but rather it puts the emphasis on the present life as the most important stage in man's relationship with God. The psalmist believes that there is *still* life to live and that there is therefore still time to praise the Creator! (See the appendix to Ps 88: Sheol-Grave-Death in the Psalms.)

The combination of "remember" and "praise" suggests that "remember" is more than an intellectual act of mental representation. It is an intense spiritual act of bringing to the mind what God has done as the basis of gratitude and praise (cf. 111:4; 145:7).

III. Need of God's Love

6:6–7

[6]I am worn out from groaning;
all night long I flood my bed with weeping
and drench my couch with tears.
[7]My eyes grow weak with sorrow;
they fail because of all my foes.

6 The experience of suffering produces tears. David did not know how much longer he could bear the anguish, insomnia, and tears. He was alone at night in his bed; but it seemed that, instead of God's sustaining presence, his foes were there in his thoughts. David could not renew his strength by himself. He was at his wit's end! The hyperbolic expressions in these verses portray the utter despondency of David.

The verb "flood" (*'aśḥeh*) is rare. Its basic meaning is "to swim in," as if to say one is drowning in grief, a hyperbolic expression for deep grief.

7 The verb "grow weak" (*'āšešāh*) is also rare in the OT; it occurs only three times and only in the Psalms (6:7; 31:9, 10). The context suggests that the failing eyesight is not the result of old age but of deep sorrow. The related verb "fail" usually means "grow old" and is not commonly predicated to eyes (38:10). The Aquila and Symmachus texts read "I grow old" (cf. BHS), but theirs seems to be an interpretative translation.

Notes

7 (8 MT) For a rejection of Dahood's rendering of צוֹרְרָי (*ṣôrerāy,* "foes") as "pining," see Craigie, *Psalms 1–50,* pp. 90–91.

IV. Prayer for God's Favor

6:8–10

8 Away from me, all you who do evil,
for the LORD has heard my weeping.
9 The LORD has heard my cry for mercy;
the LORD accepts my prayer.
10 All my enemies will be ashamed and dismayed;
they will turn back in sudden disgrace.

8–10 These verses mark a radical change in tone. Instead of the lament there is a renewal of strength by which the psalmist proclaims to the enemies that the Lord has been victorious in him and that, consequently, they need to prepare themselves for God's vindication of him. The transition from lament to a note of victory is not unknown in the Psalms (cf. 20:6; 22:22; 28:6; 31:19; 56:10; 69:30; 140:13). This is an example of the prophetic element in the individual lament psalms (see Bellinger, pp. 44–47).

The Lord has come to the rescue of his servant. He has heard his child crying for favor. He will now deal with the enemies who "do evil" (v.8; see 5:6) by bringing on their heads the terrible fate they brought on David: shame, agony, and sudden disgrace. Confidence springs up from conditions changed by the Lord and does not result from a mere psychological lift or personal effort. When grace penetrates into the depth of an anguished soul, joy in the Lord anchors faith, which no one can remove. (For the emphasis of confidence in suffering, see Elizabeth Achtemeier, "Overcoming the World," Int 28 [1974]: 75–89.)

Psalm 7: The Righteous God Loves the Righteous

The psalmist puts his case before the Lord, "the righteous judge" (v.11), in the face of the false accusations of the enemies (vv.1–2). He believes in his own heart that he has not done anything to deserve the ill-treatment of his adversaries. It is unclear who the adversaries are and to what period in David's life the heading of the psalm refers. The Bible makes no mention of "Cush, the Benjamite" (cf. superscription). Commentators who hold to the Davidic authorship are divided in opinion, and they date the psalm to the pursuits of Saul the Benjamite (cf. J. Ridderbos, p. 63) or to the time of Absalom's rebellion, when the latent hostility of the Benjamites resurged (cf. 2 Sam 16:5–14; 20:1–22; so Kidner, p. 63). The unity of the psalm has been contested (see Kraus, *Psalmen*, pp. 55–56), but the progression of the contents from lament to thanksgiving is not unusual in the Psalms. Craigie's comment is relevant: "Thus, although one may distinguish between praise and lament in terms of literary categories, the psalms are nevertheless intimately interrelated in the context of religious experience" (*Psalms 1–50*, p. 117).

The situational aspect gives way to an eschatological dimension in David's expectation that the Lord will rule over the nations. When the rule of God is established, the righteous will no longer be harassed by the wicked. On the basis of this faith, the psalmist leads us to rejoice in the righteousness of our God. Christians can join with the spirit of the psalm as they look forward to the rule of Christ over the nations and the execution of justice and righteousness on earth (cf. 2 Thess 1:5–10).

The specific genre of Psalm 7 has been difficult to determine because it contains elements of an individual lament (vv.1–2), an oath (vv.3–5), a psalm of Yahweh's kingship (vv.6–12), and a thanksgiving hymn (v.17).

The structure of the psalm falls into these parts:

A. Prayer for Refuge (vv.1–2)
B. Oath of Innocence (vv.3–5)
C. God's Righteous Judgment (vv.6–13)
B′. Judgment of the Guilty (vv.14–16)
A′. Praise of God's Righteousness (v.17)

I. Prayer for Refuge

7:1–2

A *shiggaion* of David, which he sang to the LORD
concerning Cush, a Benjamite.

1 O LORD my God, I take refuge in you;
save and deliver me from all who pursue me,
2 or they will tear me like a lion
and rip me to pieces with no one to rescue me.

1–2 The first two words in Hebrew ("Yahweh, my God," v.1) contain the expression of confidence that the heavenly Father cares for his child on earth (cf. O. Eissfeldt, "'Mein Gott' im Alten Testament," ZAW 61 [1945/48]: 3–16). The additional expression "I take refuge in you" (*bᵉḵā ḥāsîṯî,* from *ḥ-s-h*) amplifies the closeness of his relationship with God. It functions as an expression of loyalty and trust in lament psalms (7:1; 11:1; 16:1; 25:20; 31:1; 57:1; 71:1; 141:8; cf. TWOT, 1:307–8).

In the deepest need, the anguished soul cries out to the Father in the confidence that only the LORD can deliver him from those who pursue him (cf. 1 Sam 23:28; 24:14; 25:29; 26:18; see the appendix to Ps 119: Yahweh Is My Redeemer). The manner of speaking about his enemies is not to be limited to a metaphorical imagery of false accusers (cf. Craigie, *Psalms 1–50,* p. 100) but encompasses those who are pregnant with evil and conceive trouble and violence (vv.14–16).

The psalmist feels as if he is being mauled by a lion and torn to pieces (v.2; cf. 10:9; 17:12; 22:12–13, 16, 20–21; 35:17; 57:4; 58:6; 124:6). In his utter helplessness he calls on his covenant God who has promised to be ready to help. The psalmist's predicament reveals the tension between knowing that he is innocent (vv.3–5) and experiencing the apparent judgment of God.

Notes

For a brief discussion of the technical words and phrases in the superscription, see the Introduction.

1 (2 MT) The proposal that "all who pursue me" should be read as "him who pursues me" (BHS) may fit in with the singular form of the verbs "tear . . . rip" (MT; NIV uses a plural to be consistent with "all who . . .") in v.2 (3 MT) and with the singular of "foe" (v.4 [5 MT]) and "enemy" (v.5 [6 MT]). However, there is no textual evidence in favor of this change,

and it is not unusual that the enemies are referred to collectively in the singular, such as a lion (cf. 17:12).

II. Oath of Innocence

7:3–5

3 O LORD my God, if I have done this
and there is guilt on my hands—
4 if I have done evil to him who is at peace with me
or without cause have robbed my foe—
5 then let my enemy pursue and overtake me;
let him trample my life to the ground
and make me sleep in the dust. *Selah*

3–4 The psalmist protests in the presence of God: Why is he treated as an offender of the covenant? He, therefore, appeals again to his heavenly Father using the same words as in v.1 ("Yahweh, my God"). The repetition of "if" (*'im*, three times in MT) together with his readiness to suffer for any wrong he may have done show that the psalmist is confused. He is astonished that the Lord permits him to be treated as an evildoer (cf. Deut 25:16). He swears in the presence of God that he is innocent, though not perfect!

The threefold use of "if" (MT; NIV, "if . . . and. . . . if," vv.3–4) introduces with increasing clarity a statement of faithlessness, culminating in a description of wrongs done against friend and enemy. The phrase "him who is at peace with me" is better translated as a noun (Joüon, par. 121k) and is equivalent to a close friend (cf. Ps 41:9; Jer 38:22). The translation "ally" is possible, but Craigie's translation—"if I have repaid my ally with treachery, and rescued his adversary empty-handed" (*Psalms 1–50*, pp. 96, 100–101)—assumes an emendation of the MT, an accusation by the enemies, and a technical use of treaty terms.

5 The psalmist does not argue that these hypothetical statements are actual charges. Instead, he argues that he has not done anything to friend or foe to deserve this treatment! If he were a man of treachery, he would gladly permit his enemy to trample him to death (cf. 2 Kings 7:17). He willingly suffers the curses of the covenant, knowing that the wicked do not deserve "life" and "glory" (see Notes) as do those who are blessed with the covenant promises.

Notes

---

4 (5 MT) The translation "robbed" for אֲחַלְּצָה (*'ªḥallᵉṣāh*) is preferable to "saved" or "delivered" (KB, p. 305).

5 (6 MT) The form יִרַדֹּף (*yiraddōp̱*, "let . . . . pursue") is a mixture of the vowelization of two patterns (Qal and Piel; Joüon, par. 16g). It indicates that the Masoretes were undecided on the preferable vowelization. The meaning is unaffected.

The phrase כְּבוֹדִי (*kᵉḇôḏî*, "my glory") should not be left out for a supposed dynamic equivalent "me" in "and make me sleep." The psalmist knows that the Lord has given him glory (cf. 4:2) and that he may remove it if injustice is found in him (7:5; cf. NEB, "and trample my honor in the dust"). John W. McKay rejects Dahood's "my liver" (*Psalms*, 1:43), concluding that the passages make good sense with the traditional meaning "glory" ("My Glory . . . A Mantle of Praise," SJT 31 [1978]: 167–72).

III. God's Righteous Judgment

7:6–13

6 Arise, O LORD, in your anger;
rise up against the rage of my enemies.
Awake, my God; decree justice.
7 Let the assembled peoples gather around you.
Rule over them from on high;
8 let the LORD judge the peoples.
Judge me, O LORD, according to my righteousness,
according to my integrity, O Most High.
9 O righteous God,
who searches minds and hearts,
bring to an end the violence of the wicked
and make the righteous secure.

10 My shield is God Most High,
who saves the upright in heart.
11 God is a righteous judge,
a God who expresses his wrath every day.
12 If he does not relent,
he will sharpen his sword;
he will bend and string his bow.
13 He has prepared his deadly weapons;
he makes ready his flaming arrows.

6 The psalmist puts forth request after request as he pours out his heart before the Lord. Out of the turmoil of his heart and the conviction of his innocence he calls on God to act *now* in judgment and in wrath. The purpose of the preceding section has been, not only to vent his own feelings of frustration and to express his indignation at the injustice done, but also to move God to have compassion on his child. He appeals to God's sense of justice and integrity (v.8). He believes that when God is provoked, "justice" (*mišpāṭ*) will be done. Hence the repetitive prayer requesting the Lord to act: "Arise, . . . rise up. . . . Awake."

7–8 When the Lord comes in his indignation, the nations can no longer escape their due. He is powerful to call the nations to account because he rules over them. The verb "rule" (*šē̌bāh*, v.7) is a slight emendation of the MT (*šûḇāh*, "return"). This proposal fits the context best; otherwise it would seem that God has been absent from "on high" and has let evil run its course. The judgment of evil will be a vindication of the psalmist's "righteousness" (*ṣeḏeq*) and "integrity" (*tôm*) (v.8). He has searched his heart to see whether he has been disloyal to God or to man. In the depth of his heart, he knows himself not to be sinless but at least to be a man of integrity. Because of the gravity of his suffering and alienation from God, only God can graciously renew their relationship.

9–11 In vv.9–11 David focuses on the Lord's righteous rule in six descriptive phrases: "righteous God" (*'ᵉlōhîm ṣaddîq*, v.9), "tester" (*bōḥēn*, "who searches minds and hearts," v.9 NIV), "my shield" (*māḇinnî*, v.10; cf. 3:3; Gen 15:1), "savior" (*môšîaʻ*, "who saves," v.10 NIV), "righteous judge" (*šôp̄ēṭ ṣaddîq*, v.11), "a God who expresses his wrath" (*'ēl zōʻēm*, v.11) (see the appendix to Ps 98: Yahweh Is the Divine Warrior).

The reader might now expect further development on the theme of judgment on the enemies, but the psalmist returns to the motif of innocence (as in vv.3–5). The Lord, who knows the true character of his people, is called to judge him along with the nations. This self-confidence while in the presence of God reminds us of the Reformation theme, that those who are justified and lead godly lives have a right to present themselves with boldness before the righteous Judge (Heb 10:19–23; 2 Tim 4:8). Faith looks up to God, whose characteristics may be symmetrically arranged:

A. tester
  B. righteous
    C. shield
    C′. savior
  B′. righteous judge
A′. indignant

First, the affirmation of God as "righteous" and as "tester" (v.9; NIV, "searches") is no cause for the righteous (*ṣaddîq*) to be afraid. They have taken "refuge" (v.1) in his grace. Their faults are not hidden from his sight, because he tests "minds and hearts" (v.9). The phrase "minds and hearts" is a translation of "hearts and kidneys" (*libbôṯ ûḵelāyôṯ*), a reference to man's innermost being (cf. Ps 26:5; Jer 11:20; 17:10; 20:12). He tests men because he knows the heart of humans (Jer 17:9). The righteous depend on the gracious relationship initiated and confirmed by God. On the other hand, he will righteously judge and bring an end to "the violence of the wicked."

Second, God is indignant ("expresses his wrath," v.11) against those who have been tested and are found wanting. He is the "righteous judge" who protects the godly with his saving shield and judges the wicked in his wrath. These motifs are developments of his prayer in v.9: "bring to an end the violence of the wicked / and make the righteous secure."

Third, the Lord protects the righteous as with a "shield" (v.10; cf. 3:3; 18:35). After the phrase "my shield," the Hebrew adds "on," giving an awkward rendering: "my shield is on God."

The Lord protects his own, for they are "the upright in heart" (*yišrê-lēḇ*, v.10). The "upright" are those who are full of integrity and who in their loyalty to God can ask him to judge them and search their hearts (vv.8–9). But before the judgment occurs, the Lord takes the judgment seat and gathers the nations around him (vv.7–8a). This is familiar imagery in the Psalms of Yahweh's kingship (95–99).

12–13 David's conviction that God will judge evil grows as he portrays the Lord as a righteous "warrior" with sword, bow, and arrows (vv.12–13). A fuller description of God as a divine warrior is found in Psalm 98. His lightnings are the "flaming arrows" (cf. 18:14). The reference is to arrows dipped in flammable material, such as oil or pitch, and set aflame before being shot. If the wicked do not repent (v.12, see Notes), their judgment is sure. The sharp sword, deadly weapons, and flaming arrows are metaphors of the inescapable judgment. David had felt himself in a deadly predicament (v.2), but the situation will be turned around because God will come to the aid of his children. God is *preparing* himself for judgment at his appointed time. (See the appendix to Ps 137: Imprecations in the Psalms.)

Notes

8, 10 (9, 11 MT) The NIV reads עָלָי (*'ālāy*, "on me") as a divine epithet and alternate form of Elyon ("Almighty"): "O Most High" (so also v.10: "My shield is God Most High"; see the appendix to Ps 9: Yahweh is El Elyon). The BHS proposes a prepositional phrase in v.10: "God is my shield over me" (cf. 3:3; Kraus, *Psalmen*, p. 54). Craigie renders the preposition in v.8 as "Most High" and v.10 as "upon" (*Psalms 1–50*, pp. 97–98).

9 (10 MT) The word כְּלָיוֹת (*k^elāyôṯ*, "kidneys"; NIV, "minds") always occurs in the plural. It denotes the deepest aspect of one's being (see von Rad, OTT, 1:153; TWOT, 1:440–41). The phrase "heart(s) and mind(s)" is a hendiadys for one's inner being (26:2; 73:21; Jer 11:20; 17:10; 20:12; Rev 2:23).

10 (11 MT) Dahood has argued extensively in favor of the meaning "Suzerain" for מָגֵן (*māḡēn*, "shield"). Beginning with 84:11:

For the LORD God is a sun and shield [*māḡēn*];
  the LORD bestows favor and honor;
no good thing does he withhold
  from those whose walk is blameless.

Dahood calls attention to the parallel of "sun" and "shield." He explains the former as being a reference to Pharaoh ("sovereign") and consequently renders "shield" by a synonym: "Suzerain" (*Psalms*, 1:16–17). The argument is more sophisticated but is arbitrary because of its dependence on cognate terminology. His translation of this verse is:

Truly Sun and Suzerain
  Yahweh God
Favors and honors bestows.
Yahweh will not withhold his rain
  from those who walk with integrity.
(*Psalms*, 2:279)

Occasionally the NIV slips into Dahoodian Ugaritic explanations or suggests alternate clarification in the Notes. In v.10 the NIV has "My shield is God Most High, / who saves the upright in heart," but the margin on "shield" reads: "Or *sovereign*." So also are 59:11; 84:11; 89:18. I have rejected this interpretation because the word "shield" is a metonymy for Yahweh, because it requires emendation of the MT, and because the Hebrew metaphor makes sense. (See the appendix to Ps 98: Yahweh Is the Divine Warrior.)

12 (13 MT) The Hebrew is unclear as to the subject of the verb יָשׁוּב (*yāšûḇ*, "he will return"). The NIV makes God the subject and translates *yāšûḇ* as "relent" (cf. mg.). It is possible to translate the verb as a hendiadys rendering "sharpen" as "if he will not again sharpen his sword, he will bend and string his bow" (cf. GKC, par. 120g). BHS proposes a conjectural reading, suggesting that v.12a be read with the preceding colon: "a God who expresses his wrath every day, if he does not repent." A.A. Macintosh comes to quite a different conclusion: "God vindicates the righteous, but God utterly condemns the unrepentant" ("A Consideration of Psalm vii.12f," JTS 33 [1982]: 481–90).

IV. Judgment of the Guilty

7:14–16

14 He who is pregnant with evil
  and conceives trouble gives birth to disillusionment.
15 He who digs a hole and scoops it out
  falls into the pit he has made.

[16]The trouble he causes recoils on himself;
his violence comes down on his own head.

14–16 The psalmist evokes another powerful picture. Evil is metaphorically portrayed as a "lion" (v.2), an army (v.5), and in these verses in the language of conception and birth (v.14). The wicked are filled with evil, as a pregnant woman about to give birth. Once wickedness is born, it grows into a "lie" (*šāqer;* NIV, "disillusionment," v.14), "trouble" (*ʿamālô,* v.16), and "violence" (*ḥamāsô,* v.16). Our Lord warned against having a heart from which come "evil thoughts, sexual immorality, theft, murder, adultery, greed, malice, deceit, lewdness, envy, slander, arrogance, and folly" (Mark 7:21–22). The apostle James speaks of the desire-sin-death cycle (James 1:14–15; cf. Kidner, p. 65).

The certainty of judgment (vv.12–13) and the prevalence of evil (vv.14–15) find their point of contact in the doctrine of the retribution of evil (v.16; cf. Ps 9:15). Sin comes home to roost (Kidner, p. 65) and may be likened to a boomerang (cf. Prov 26:27; Matt 26:52). The Lord is a righteous judge!

Notes

14 (15 MT) G.J. Thierry ("Remarks on Various Passages in the Psalms," *OudTestamentische Studien* 13 [1963]: 77) renders this verse thus:

Lo, he was fecundated with sin,
and is pregnant with evil,
and he beareth lie.

15 (16 MT) The Hebrew has a play on the word וַיִּפֹּל (*wayyippōl,* "falls") and יִפְעָל (*yip̄ʿāl,* "made"); see Craigie (*Psalms 1–50,* p. 99, note on v.16a).

V. Praise of God's Righteousness

7:17

[17]I will give thanks to the LORD because of his
righteousness
and will sing praise to the name of the LORD Most
High.

17 The psalm that began with a prayer (vv.1–2), an oath of innocence (vv.3–5), and an expression of confidence in the Lord's righteous rule (vv.6–13) comes to its conclusion in the conviction that the guilty will be judged (vv.14–16) and the righteous will be secured under the protective shield of God (vv.9–10). Therefore, the righteous rejoice in the righteousness (*ṣeḏeq*) of God. God's righteous judgment affects both the wicked and the righteous. The wicked fall, whereas the righteous experience deliverance in God's acts of judgment. The attribute of God's righteousness is what he does or will do on behalf of his own. He is a victorious God who triumphs over evil and will avenge his children (see N.A. Schuman, "God's Gerechtigheid en de 'Wet' van de Vangkuil [Psalm 7:11–17]," *Loven en Geloven.*

Opstellen van Collega's en Medewerkers aangeboden aan Prof. Dr. Nic. H. Ridderbos, ed. M.H. van Es et al. [Amsterdam: Ton Bolland, 1975], pp. 95–110). Despair is thus transformed into hope, and hope is expressed in the singing of praise to the Lord. Bellinger (pp. 50–53) concludes that the certainty of the psalmist arises from a prophetic insight.

The praise of God is usually accompanied with musical instruments (cf. 71:22). The *name* of the God of Israel is Yahweh (see appendix: The Name of Yahweh). He alone is El Elyon ("God Most High"; see the appendix to Ps 9: Yahweh Is El Elyon). "Most High" is an epithet of deity and first occurs in the interaction between Melchizedek and Abraham, where El Elyon is the "Creator of heaven and earth" (cf. Gen 14:18–20, 22). It occurs with Yahweh in the Psalms (18:13 [= 2 Sam 22:14]; 9:2; 21:7; 77:10). Here, as in Genesis 14:19–22, the "Most High" is descriptive of the universal rule of God, to whom his subjects sing praise (cf. 9:2; 50:14; 92:1; cf. THAT, 2:286). The hope of the godly is in the final removal of evil. In the resurrection and ascension of our Lord Jesus, the church has received great assurance of the realization of the new era (Matt 25:31–31). Therefore, the praise of God's people must include affirmations of God's righteousness and the victory of our Lord Jesus, in the spirit of Revelation 11:15–18; 12:10–12; 16:5–7; 18:1–20; 19:1–8.

Appendix: The Name of Yahweh

The Psalms celebrate or "remember" (cf. Exod 3:15) "the name" of the Lord as the object of thanksgiving, confidence, and prayer. The "name" Yahweh is the revelation of the glory of God in his acts of creation and redemption and in the revelation of his person. The faithful love and rejoice in the name: "But let all who take refuge in you be glad; / let them ever sing for joy. / Spread your protection over them, / that those who love your name may rejoice in you" (5:11; cf. 9:2; 18:49).

The name of God is the name of the Creator-Redeemer-King. He is not the Redeemer of Israel only because Yahweh is the Creator: "O LORD [*YHWH*, 'Yahweh'], our Lord, / how majestic is your name in all the earth! / You have set your glory / above the heavens" (8:1; cf. v.9; 124:8). He is not a national deity but the King of the world. He freely revealed to Israel his "name" when he graciously chose them out of all the nations (Exod 19:5–6). In this unique relationship Israel was privileged to pray to their covenant God, as Zimmerli writes, the OT saints only know one God, and they pray only in his name: "the Old Testament believer . . . may—indeed must—call upon him without hesitation" (OTTO, p. 152).

God's name is reliable, as he promises that all who seek him and call on his name will be saved: "Those who know your name will trust in you, / for you, LORD, have never forsaken those who seek you" (9:10; cf. 33:21). The *name* guarantees Yahweh's blessing and protection. *Blessing* extends all the benefits flowing from God's gracious relationship to his people: "Blessed is he who comes in the name of the LORD. / From the house of the LORD we bless you" (118:26; cf. 115:1). *Protection* extends to all the members of the covenant community, i.e., all who have found refuge in the Lord as the only God: "May the LORD answer you when you are in distress; / may the name of the God of Jacob protect you. /. . . we trust in the name of the LORD our God" (20:1, 7b; cf. 44:5, 20; 91:14).

The name of the Lord is the solemn *guarantee* by covenant that he will fulfill all his promises. The phrase "for his name's sake" is equivalent to the use of "in Jesus' name," as it applies all the promises and assurances given to the saints. He guides (31:3), refreshes, restores, and supplies the need's of his people (23:3); forgives their sins (25:11; 79:9); has compassion (119:132); delivers them from adversity (54:1; 79:9; 106:8; 109:21); and preserves their lives (143:11).

Worship of the "name" consists of remembrance of all God's perfections and mighty acts in creation and redemption. To this end the Psalms refer back to what God has done; to his attributes; to his promises to Abraham, Moses (111:2–9), and David (89:24); and to recent acts; and they project forward to the eschatological hope (69:34–36) of the establishment of his kingdom and of his Messiah in fullness:

> May his name endure forever;
> may it continue as long as the sun.
> All nations will be blessed through him,
> and they will call him blessed.
> . . . .
> Praise be to his glorious name forever;
> may the whole earth be filled with his glory.
> Amen and Amen.
>
> (72:17, 19)

The psalmist believes that God's kingdom will be established when all nations will praise the name of Yahweh: "All the nations you have made / will come and worship before you, O LORD; / they will bring glory to your name" (86:9; cf. Pss 67; 102:15). Rightly does von Rad observe that "Israel did not hide this name of God from the Gentiles in fear, but rather felt herself in duty bound to make it known to them" (OTT, 1:185). The symbol of this covenant is the temple, where the Lord made his name to "dwell" (*š-k-n;* see Mettinger, pp. 38–79).

The act of praise is the harmonious response of the people of God to the revelation of God in word and in act: "Ascribe to the LORD the glory due his name; / worship the LORD in the splendor of his holiness" (29:2; cf. 30:4; 34:3; 44:8; 48:10; 52:9; 54:6; 61:8; 63:4, 11; 66:2, 4; 68:4; 69:30; 75:1; 86:12; 89:12, 16; 92:1; 96:2, 8; 97:12; 99:3; 100:4; 102:21; 103:1; 105:1, 3; 106:47; 113:1–3; 115:13; 116:17; 135:1, 3, 13; 138:2; 140:13; 145:1–2, 21; 149:3). Praise unites all creation together in a sublime act of submission, love, and adoration of the Creator-King-Redeemer, whose name is Yahweh:

> Let them praise the name of the LORD,
> for he commanded and they were created.
> . . . .
> Let them praise the name of the LORD,
> for his name alone is exalted;
> his splendor is above the earth and the heavens.
>
> (148:5, 13)

For Israel "the name" had a place both in and outside their corporate worship. That is to say, they used the sacred name in sacrifice, praise, and blessing but also in court, writing, and war (von Rad, OTT, 1:183). Yahweh is the name above all names; and his name is revealed in the name of Jesus, to whom all power and authority belong (Matt 28:20). Even as Yahweh's name was not to be taken in vain (Exod 20:7), the name of Jesus our Lord is holy!

Texts with "the name of the LORD" (Yahweh): 7:17; 20:7; 102:15, 21; 113:1–3; 116:4, 13, 17; 118:10–12, 26; 122:4; 124:8; 129:8; 135:1; 148:5, 13.

For other names in the Psalms, see the appendixes to Pss 3 (Yahweh Is My God); 5 (Yahweh Is King); 9 (Yahweh Is El Elyon); 22 (Yahweh Is El); 24 (Lord Sabaoth); 98 (Yahweh Is the Divine Warrior); 119 (Yahweh Is My Redeemer).

Bibliography: W. Albright, "The Name Yahweh," JBL 43 (1924): 370–78; 44 (1925): 175–78; 57 (1948): 379–80; Roland de Vaux, "The Revelation of the Divine Name

YHWH," *Proclamation and Presence. Old Testament Essays in Honour of Gwynne Henton Davies*, edd. John I. Durhamn and J.R. Porter (Richmond: Knox, 1970), pp. 48–75; Eichrodt, TOT, 2:40–45; D.N. Freedman, "The Name of the God of Moses," JBL 79 (1960): 151–56; W.C. Kaiser, Jr., "Name," ZPEB, 4:360–66; Kraus, TP, pp. 20–24; L.F. Hartman, "God: Names of," *Encyclopaedia Judaica*, 7:674–79; Tryggve B.D. Mettinger, *The Dethronement of Sabaoth. Studies in the Shem and Kabod Theologies* (Lund: Gleerup, 1982); J.A. Motyer, *The Revelation of the Divine Name* (London: Tyndale, 1956); von Rad, OTT, 1:179–87; Martin Rose, *Jahwe, Zum Streit um den alttestamentlichen Gottesnamen*, Theologische Studien 122 (Zürich: Theologischer Verlag, 1977); R. Tournay, "Le Psaume VIII et la Doctrine Biblique du Nom," RB 78 (1971): 18–30; W.A. VanGemeren, "Tetragrammaton, EDT, pp. 1079–80; Zimmerli, OTTO, pp. 17–32; 151–52.

TDOT, 3:534–54; THAT, 2:949–963; TWOT, 2:934–35.

Psalm 8: The Glory of the Creator and of Man

The hymnic quality of this psalm has been observed by many. The difficulty of classification is due to the many elements woven together in a poetic blend. For our purpose we shall consider it as a *hymn of praise* and, more particularly, a hymn of *creation praise*. Brueggemann treats this psalm together with Psalms 33, 104, and 145 as "Songs of Creation" (pp. 29–38).

The Lord is the object of praise (vv.1, 9). Therefore the praise is not an expression of joy in creation apart from the Creator. Pantheism deifies and glorifies nature as a separate entity from the Creator. Theism joyfully looks at God as the good Creator, Ruler, and Sustainer of the world.

It is not clear how the hymn was used in the worship of ancient Israel. Because it makes mention of the moon and the stars and not of the sun, its cultic place may be associated with evening worship.

The psalm forms a unified whole (see Pierre Auffret, "Essay sur la Structure & Littéraire du Psaume viii," VetTest 34 [1984]: 257–69), but the content may be summarized as follows:

A. Ascription of Praise (v.1a)
  B. The Glory of the Great King (vv.1b–2)
    C. God's Interest in Man (vv.3–4)
    C′. Man's Derived Glory (v.5)
  B′. Man's Glory as Ruler (vv.6–8)
A′. Concluding Ascription of Praise (v.9)

The introductory and concluding ascriptions of praise form an inclusion (see Alter, pp. 117–21). The literary approach of holistic interpretation espoused by Meir Weiss complements our analysis (*The Bible From Within. The Method of Total Interpretation* [Jerusalem: Magnes, 1984], pp. 293–97).

The significance of Psalm 8 lies in its approach to Creation and its application to the Messiah. The psalm is a corrective to the speculative and/or scientific approach to Creation. The biblical account of Creation is phenomenal (focuses on effects rather than causes) and was intended to help Israel to praise Yahweh as the sole Creator of everything in heaven, on earth, and in the sea. The created universe and the account of Creation (Gen 1:1–2:3) should evoke praise of the wonderful Creator. The NT applies the glory of man to the Messiah, as he has subjected everything to himself

(Heb 2:6–9; cf. 1 Cor 15:27; Eph 1:22). In Jesus' victory the Christian has received the glorious renewal the psalmist speaks of (Heb 2:10–11)! Though the psalm is not messianic in the narrow sense (see J. Alberto Soggin, "Zum achten Psalm," *Annual of the Swedish Theological Institute* 8 [1972]: 106–22), it has a messianic application in that Jesus is fully man and has realized God's expectation of man in perfect obedience and holiness. Those who belong to the Messiah have received greater glory and holiness than did God's people in the OT. Hence the significance of the cultural mandate and man's dominion over God's creation are not lessened. The Father expects an even more responsible involvement with his creation by his children in Jesus Christ.

I. Ascription of Praise

8:1a

For the director of music. According to *gittith*.
A psalm of David.

[1]O LORD, our Lord,
how majestic is your name in all the earth!

1a The introductory and concluding ascriptions of praise form an inclusion within which the glory of the Creator is the object of celebration. The Redeemer-God, Yahweh, is Lord over his people. The title "our Lord" (*'ᵃḏōnênû*) is an address to God as king: "our governor" or "our ruler" (as Coverdale's rendering: "O Lorde oure Governoure"; cf. 97:5; 110:1); so to speak of Yahweh as "Lord" was an ascription of kingship in the OT (97:5). The Redeemer-King of Israel is the Creator! His name (Yahweh) is glorious over all the earth, by virtue of his creative activities (cf. Gen 1:1–31). What is marvelous is the Great King's revelation of his glory in, and thereby his self-involvement with, his creation. He, the glorious One, has endowed the earth with glory! A hymn of praise is sometimes the only way man can express his amazement with God's glorious rule. The "majesty" of Yahweh's name radiates from his work on earth and heaven. The word "majestic" (*'addîr*, "mighty") is a royal attribute denoting his victories (Exod 15:6), his might in judgment (1 Sam 4:8; Ps 76:4), his law (Isa 42:21), and his rule over creation (Pss 8:1, 9; 93:4). All creation reveals the power and glory of God's name (Rom 1:20). Only God's people know how to respond to this revelation of his majesty in nature, because he has revealed his "name" to them (Exod 3:14–15). (On the name, see R. Tournay, "Le Psaume VIII et la Doctrine Biblique du Nom," RB 78 [1971]: 18–30.)

Notes

For a brief discussion of the technical words and phrases in the superscription, see the Introduction.

II. The Glory of the Great King

8:1b–2

You have set your glory
above the heavens.
2 From the lips of children and infants
you have ordained praise
because of your enemies,
to silence the foe and the avenger.

1b–2 The glorious rule over heaven is no surprise from a theistic perspective: Heaven declares his glory (19:1). But the marvel of the biblical view of the Creator is that his creation on earth not only reveals but is glorious (cf. Isa 6:3). The discordant note sounded by the enemies (v.2; cf. 44:16) in his creation is silenced by the praise of children (v.2; cf. Matt 21:15–16). Regardless of how the wicked assert themselves, they cannot outdo the evidence of God's glory on earth and in heaven. It is all around us (cf. Rom 1:20). His glory is established (NIV, "ordained"), and no enemy can overcome his kingdom. The translation "you have ordained praise" may also be rendered "you have established a bulwark" ("strength," NIV mg.). The sound of the children is concrete evidence of God's fortress on earth. The continuity of the human race is God's way of assuring the ultimate glorification of an earth populated with a new humanity (Hab 2:14). The sound of opposition is silenced by the babbling and chatter of children. What a contrast! What a King!

Notes

1b (2 MT) The difficulty of v.1b lies in the MT. The NIV reading is possible but conveniently omits a translation of the Hebrew particle "which." The phrase אֲשֶׁר תְּנָה (*'ᵃšer tᵉnāh*) defies translation. What does the particle modify, and how should the verb *tᵉnāh* be parsed? Several proposals have been made. The verb may be emended to *tānāh* ("praise," "celebrate in song"; cf. Judg 5:11; 11:40; see RSV, "whose glory . . . is chanted"). Dahood (*Psalms*, 1:49) has made an acceptable suggestion by joining the two words together into the form of *š-r-t* ("serve" or "worship") with an energic ending: "I shall worship your majesty." The verb may also be emended to *nāṯattā* ("you have given"). This last solution, adopted by BHS and the NIV, makes good sense. The pronoun "which" functions here as an explanatory particle.

III. God's Interest in Man

8:3–4

3 When I consider your heavens,
the work of your fingers,
the moon and the stars,
which you have set in place,
4 what is man that you are mindful of him,
the son of man that you care for him?

3 The Creator has established two spheres of rule: heaven and earth. He has established the celestial bodies in the firmament and has given them the rule over day and night (Gen 1:17–18), whereas he appointed man to govern the earth (Gen 1:28). The psalmist reflects on the grandeur of space with the moon and stars. How space reveals the glory, wisdom, and power of the Great King (cf. 89:11; Job 36:29; 38:33; Isa 40:26)! The heavenly bodies all have their appointed place. They are his "work" (*maʿᵃśēh,* "act"). The reading "work" is preferable to "works" (MT). The Cairo Geniza and a number of Hebrew MSS support the singular form. The "fingers" of God express in a sensitive manner his care as a sculptor. Craigie comments, "In contrast to God, the heavens are tiny, pushed and prodded into shape by the divine digits; but in contrast to the heavens, which seem so vast in the human perception, it is mankind that is tiny" (*Psalms 1–50,* p. 108).

4 In relation to the vastness of space, the order and the importance of the heavenly bodies, what is man! Why did God invest man with glory? Why does God uniquely care for man? The questions are poetic devices to evoke a sense of awe and place a proper perspective on one's self-worth. Inasmuch as God gave shape to the heavenly bodies with his fingers, why should he concern himself with man? The word "man" (*'ᵉnôš*) is a poetic word for man in his frail human existence (9:20; 90:3; 103:15), whereas the idiom "son of man" (cf. 80:17; 144:3) is contrasted with "God" (v.5a; "heavenly beings," NIV mg.). Man is by nature an "earthling," and yet he is the particular object of God's attention. The God who gave shape to heaven with his fingers continues to focus his attention to man. This is brought out by Rui De Menezes, "From Dust to Glory—the Anthropology of the Psalms," *Jeevadhara* 16 (1986): 105–20.

The Creator has invested glory and honor on man. The verbs "mindful"(from *z-k-r,* "remember") and "care for" (*p-q-d,* lit., "visit") convey the care of God, who remembers positively by acting on behalf of man. Instead of "visiting" man with judgment, as his sin deserves, God's goodness extends to all creatures in his care (Matt 5:45). According to B.S. Childs (*Memory and Tradition in Israel* [Naperville: Allenson, 1962], pp. 33–34), God's fatherly compassion motivates him to be continually concerned with mankind. He has not forgotten man (cf. Gen 9:8–17). The imperfect tense of the verbs supports the continuity of God's care (cf. 144:3; Job 7:17; 14:3).

IV. Man's Derived Glory

8:5

5 You made him a little lower than the heavenly beings
and crowned him with glory and honor.

5 Man's significance is not to be limited to his existence before sin came into the world. Man still is "crowned" (*tᵉʿaṭṭᵉrēhû*) with glory. The sequence of verbs (v.6) expresses poetically the status God, by his divine decree, gave to man. The verses could be rendered as "You made [perfect] him a little lower than the heavenly beings and crown [present] him with glory and honor. You make [present] him ruler over the works of your hands; you put [past] everything under his feet."

Man is *still* glorious and continues to govern the earth (cf. 21:5; 45:3; see Walter Brueggemann, *In Man We Trust* [Atlanta: Knox, 1972]). "Glory and honor" are attributes of God's kingship (29:1; 104:1) extended to man's royal status. This is brought out by the two center colons. The structure reveals man's past and present glory. It seems as if the psalmist is unaware of the Fall, being concerned, not with man's sinful condition, but with God's fatherly love and care for mankind.

Yet man is not divine; he is in "the image and likeness of God" (Gen 1:26–27). In this exalted status he may be said to be "less than God" (NIV mg.) or less than "the heavenly beings" (NIV). But in what way is man lower than the heavenly beings? And who are the heavenly beings to whom man's glorious status is likened? The phrase "lower than" (from *ḥ-s-r*, "lack") also has the meaning "to make someone lack" or "deprive someone of something" (KB^3, 1:325). Man is short of being divine because he is an earthling (Gen 2:7). Yet he is not a beast, because he is also "celestial" (Gen 2:7). The Hebrew for "heavenly beings" is simply "God" or "gods" (*'ᵉlōhîm*, "Elohim"). It may refer to angelic beings (cf. 82:1, 6–8); and the LXX, followed by Hebrews 2:7–9, takes it this way. Calvin rejected the angelic reference in our psalm as contrary to the natural meaning: "We know what freedoms the apostles took in quoting texts of Scripture . . . because they reckoned it sufficient to show . . . that what they taught was sanctioned by the word of God, although they did not quote the precise words" (1:103; cf. Richard Longenecker, *Biblical Exegesis in the Apostolic Period* [Grand Rapids: Eerdmans, 1975], p. 181).

Another solution is to consider "god" as a poetic reference to the pagan gods. Man's position is to be compared to the place the pagans give to their gods. Yahweh is above the gods (cf. 86:8), and man is a little below them. Paganism is hereby excluded! Man's position is elevated to "royalty," but a derived royalty. God remains far above man. Man is "a god in small," but this does not mean that he is divine (J. Ridderbos, p. 75).

The dignity of man is a gift of God and requires a relationship of responsibility as well as a response of praise to the good Creator. In his full participation with humanity, Jesus has been "crowned . . . with glory and honor" (Heb 2:7) because of his responsiveness to the Father. He is "the radiance of God's glory and the exact representation of his being" (Heb 1:3). Jesus, the God-Man, has suffered death for man (Heb 2:9) and hence has received greater glory and authority. The Father has subjected everything to the Son (Heb 2:5; cf. Col 1:15–20), and all things must submit to his messianic rule (1 Cor 15:27). For an appreciation of the messianic significance, see Felix Asensio, "El Protogonismo del 'Hombre-Hijo del Hombre' del Salmo 8," *Estudios Biblicos* 41 (1983): 17–51. C.S. Lewis incisively corrects our tendency of restricting the richness of the Christian faith as he comments on this psalm: "We stress the Humanity too exclusively at Christmas, and the Deity too exclusively after the Resurrection; .. The ancient interpretation of Psalm 8, however arrived at, is a cheering corrective" (*Reflections on the Psalms,* p. 134).

V. Man's Glory as Ruler

8:6–8

6 You made him ruler over the works of your hands;
you put everything under his feet:
7 all flocks and herds,
and the beasts of the field,

[8]the birds of the air,
and the fish of the sea,
all that swim the paths of the seas.

6–8 Man's position over creation was granted before the Fall (Gen 1:28), but it was not taken away from him (Gen 9:1–3, 7). Man is God's appointed governor (vassal) over creation. His function on earth is to maintain order, to shine his light on creation, and to keep a beneficent relationship with all that God has created on earth and in the sea: beasts of the field, birds of the air, fish and the creatures of the sea (vv.7–8). The Great King has appointed man to maintain dominion over creation ("put everything under his feet") and not be controlled by creation. All creatures, domesticated and wild, are subject to man's authority and may at his will be used for food (Gen 9:3).

Notes

6 (7 MT) For a study of this verse in the light of Gen 1:28, see Manfred Görg, "Alles hast Du gelegt unter seine Füsse, Beobachtungen zu Ps 8,7b im Vergleich mit Gen 1,28," *Freude an der Weisung des Herrn, Beiträge zur Theologie der Psalmen, Festgabe zum 70. Geburtstag von Heinrich Gross,* edd. Ernst Haag and Frank-Lothar Hossfeld (Stuttgart: Katholisches Bibelwerk, 1986), pp. 125–48.

7 (8 MT) The creature described enigmatically as "the one that passes over the paths of the seas" may be a general reference to marine life (cf. NIV, "all that swim the paths of the seas") or a more specific description of the large sea animals, which, as it were, traverse the seas and whose existence held a spell over the ancients (cf. Craigie, *Psalms 1–50,* pp. 108–9; Kraus, *Psalmen,* 1:71).

VI. Concluding Ascription of Praise

8:9

[9]O LORD, our Lord,
how majestic is your name in all the earth!

9 See verse 1 above.

Psalm 9: Prayer and Praise for God's Just Rule of the Nations

The psalm is an incomplete acrostic psalm (aleph-kaph) and seems to have formally belonged together with Psalm 10 (lamed-taw). There are several arguments given in support of treating these two psalms as a unit: (1) the absence of a superscription in Psalm 10; (2) the continuity of the acrostic device; (3) similar vocabulary; and (4) the LXX and the Vulgate's treatment of Psalms 9 and 10 as one psalm.

Over against this, however, we observe that the acrostic pattern is incomplete and may have been imposed on the psalm. Psalm 9 seems to be a complete unit of itself. Moreover the acrostic moves from kaph (v.18) to qoph (v.19) to shin (v.20), skipping several letters. Psalm 10 also seems to be a unified whole. Its so-called acrostic pattern is incomplete: lamed (v.1), pe (v.7b), ayin (v.8b), and the final four signs of the Hebrew alphabet (vv.12–17). An analysis of the contents and the internal structure of each psalm is indecisive. Psalm 9 is an *individual lament* psalm, combining prayer with praise and telling of God's just rule over the nations. Psalm 10 is an *individual lament* psalm in which prayer focuses on the enemies of the covenant, who have at one time belonged to the faithful. The two elements of praise and prayer are not impossible, but the diverse elements in the two psalms caution us against treating the two psalms as one. Rightly, Kirkpatrick observes, "The two Psalms present an unsolved literary problem" (p. 42; see also Robert Gordis, "Psalm 9–10—A Textual and Exegetical Study," *The Word and the Book* [New York: Ktav, 1976], pp. 114–32).

The internal structure of Psalm 9 seems to form a complete unit:

A. Individual Praise (vv.1–2)
B. Judgment on the Wicked (vv.3–6)
C. Hope in God's Just Rule (vv.7–10)
A′. Communal Praise and Individual Prayer (vv.11–14)
B′. Judgment of the Wicked (vv.15–18)
C′. Hope in God's Just Rule (vv.19–20)

The hope for the godly (vv.7–10, 18–20) lies in the affirmation of God's "just" rule as he executes judgment on the wicked (vv.3–6, 15–17; see the appendix to Ps 1: The Ways of Wisdom and Folly). Bellinger (pp. 39–42) sees the description of "domestic corruption" in Psalms 9–10 as an example of the prophetic spirit in the *individual lament* psalms.

It is impossible to date the psalm to a certain period in David's (Israel's) history. The characterization of the enemy is purposefully ambiguous so as to permit the individual lament to be used as a community lament. A note of praise is found throughout the psalm (vv.1, 2, 11, 14) as an antidote to fear. The psalm gives to the needy child of God a sense of confidence in God's just rule (vv.4, 7–9, 16, 19–20), faithfulness to his promises (vv.9–10, 12, 18), and hope in the acts of God on behalf of his children. Lament changes into praise, and fear becomes victorious joy. Though the need was immediate and God may have responded to that particular need, the psalm looks forward to a time when all wickedness will be removed. There is an eschatological dimension to the psalm, with the expectation of the rule of God on earth and the fear of the nations (v.20). The focus of the psalm is on God's kingship and his goodness to his children who cry out for deliverance from the vexations of this world. (See the appendix to Ps 5: Yahweh Is King.)

I. Individual Praise

9:1–2

For the director of music. To ⌊the tune of⌋ "The Death of the Son."
A psalm of David.

1 I will praise you, O LORD, with all my heart;
I will tell of all your wonders.
2 I will be glad and rejoice in you;
I will sing praise to your name, O Most High.

1–2 In response to a distressing situation, the psalmist brings himself to praise God in anticipation of the hour of deliverance. In vv.13–14 he prays for God's mercy and promises to praise him in public when he has been delivered. In v.19 he prays more particularly for God to strike the enemies. Therefore the psalm must be read as a lament psalm, and the mood of vv.1–2 is set by the context. He exhorts himself to praise the Lord, not only as a therapy to forget his troubles for a moment, but to deepen his trust in the Lord. The depth of gratitude and joy finds expression in five synonymous verbs expressive of praise: "I will praise . . . tell. . . . be glad . . . rejoice . . . sing praise." The cohortative mood is used to convey the determination of the psalmist (NIV, "I will"). The first (*'ôḏeh,* "praise") and last (*'ᵃzammᵉrāh,* "sing praise") verbs, as well as the references to God as "Elyon" ("Most High"), are identical to Psalm 7:17. Compare 7:17: "I will give thanks [*'ôḏeh*] to the LORD . . . and will sing praise [*'ᵃzammᵉrāh*] to the name of the LORD Most High [Elyon]" with 9:1–2, which reads: "I will praise [*'ôḏeh*] you, O LORD . . . I will sing praise [*'ᵃzammᵉrāh*] to your name, O Most High [Elyon]."

The verbs for praise express the intensity of the psalmist's love for God. His God is none other than the God of "wonders," whose "name" is Yahweh and who alone is "Most High." The psalmist is filled with praise on account of the history of God's mighty acts. Praise involves the "self," the story of God's acts, and the community of God's people. (See the appendix to Ps 122: The Praise of Yahweh.)

First, the psalmist praises God with all his mind ("with all my heart," v.1; cf. Deut 6:5), for he loves the Lord without reservation.

Second, the "wonders" (*nip̄lᵉ'ôṯeyḵā*) are the marvelous acts of redemption and judgment. The Lord has delivered his people from many distresses in the past. The Psalms often make mention of the wonderful acts of the Lord (cf. 26:7; 71:17; 75:1; 78:32; 96:3; 105:2; 106:7; 107:8, 15, 21, 24, 31; 111:4; 145:5; see the appendix to Ps 78: The Mighty Acts of Yahweh). They are particularly his acts of creation and redemption and were regularly rehearsed as a reminder of God's goodness and love, especially for comfort in time of need (cf. TWOT, 2:723; KB, p. 760). The psalmist praises the "name" (Yahweh) of God, who is the same as the "Most High" (Elyon; cf. 7:17; 92:1; see appendix below: Yahweh Is El Elyon), in hope that the name of God will protect his servant and that the Lord will manifest again a "wonder" on his behalf.

Third, the verbs for praise also express the communal aspect of individual praise. The psalmist loves the Lord, has confidence in the power and wonder of God's acts, and encourages the community in his expression of praise (cf. Eph 5:19–20).

Notes

For a brief discussion of the technical words and phrases in the superscription, see the Introduction.

In "To the tune of 'The Death of the Son,'" the meaning of עַלְמוּת (*'almûṯ*) is unknown. The NIV rendering is based on a separation of the one word into two words, "on death," and is supported by the Cairo Geniza and a number of Hebrew MSS. Based on Ps 46:1 (MT), it is possible to read *'almûṯ* as a corrupt form of *'al-'ᵃlumôṯ* (cf. LXX). The *'ᵃlumôṯ* ("maidens") could signify a musical term, possibly a choir made up of young girls or "by female (treble or soprano?) voices" (Craigie, *Psalms 1–50*, p. 114) or by maidens playing tambourines (cf. Exod 15:20). The phrase *'al mûṯ labbēn* ("The Death of the Son") could also be a corruption of *binᵉḇālîm 'al-'ᵃlamôṯ* ("to play the lyres according to *'ᵃlamôṯ*"; cf. J. Ridderbos, p. 81), as in 1 Chron 15:20: "to play the lyres according to *alamoth*." The meaning of the phrase remains enigmatic.

II. Judgment on the Wicked

9:3–6

3 My enemies turn back;
  they stumble and perish before you.
4 For you have upheld my right and my cause;
  you have sat on your throne, judging righteously.
5 You have rebuked the nations and destroyed the wicked;
  you have blotted out their name for ever and ever.
6 Endless ruin has overtaken the enemy,
  you have uprooted their cities;
  even the memory of them has perished.

3 The "wonder" continues when the Lord removes the immediate problem and ultimately all enemies of his kingdom. The prayer is that the Lord will "turn back" (6:10; 56:9) the enemies so that they will be no more. The verb "turn back" is an infinitive construct in Hebrew, which may be rendered as causal ("because," Briggs, 1:82) or temporal ("when," Dahood, *Psalms*, 1:55). The temporal reading is the more natural and fits in the context of the prayer for deliverance (cf. Craigie, *Psalms 1–50*, p. 115). When God makes the enemies to flee, they will stumble and perish. "Before you" may be interpreted as "from your presence," "because of your presence," or "in your presence."

4–5 Consistent with the context and the lament genre of the psalm, we propose a reading of the perfect in vv.4–5 as an imperative (precative perfect): "Uphold my right . . . sit on your throne. . . . rebuke the nations . . . destroy the wicked; blot out their name." The prayer contains a request that the Lord will uphold his own (v.4b), rule righteously (v.4c), and rebuke the nations (v.5), so that ruin and destruction will overtake them and their memory may perish (v.6; cf. 1:6). In support is Dahood's discussion of the particle (*kî*, "because"; NIV, "for") before a perfect in v.4: "Oh that you would defend" (*Psalms*, 1:55).

The child of God may freely present his "right"/"cause" (v.4) to his Redeemer-God. The "right" (*mišpāṭ*) is the case lodged against the wicked. The word "cause" (*dîn*, "judgment") is a synonym of "right" (cf. 140:12). Belief in God's justice is liberating because God is both Advocate and Judge. He will free all his own from oppression and harassment (146:7). Freedom from worry is God's gift to his child, because God judges "righteously."

The "righteous" (*ṣeḏeq*, see 4:1) judgment of God is guaranteed by his rule. He is the Great King over all and, thereby, has authority to judge effectively (cf. 93:2; 122:5). To this end the psalmist prays that God will "rebuke the nations and destroy the wicked" (cf. v.5). The "rebuke" of God is an expression both of his wrath (cf. 2:5) against the enemy and of his defense of the righteous. He is the Divine Warrior who "rebukes" in a revelation of his power over the world and of his deep love for his own (cf. Ps 76, esp. v.6). In the end it will seem as if the wicked have never existed. He will blot out their name (v.5). (See the appendix to Ps 98: Yahweh Is the Divine Warrior.)

6 The prayer for the end of the wicked is chiastic (ABB′A′). The enemies and their mighty cities will perish forever:

A. May the enemies be destroyed;
B. May their cities be everlasting ruins;
B′. May you uproot their cities;
A′. May the memory of them perish.

This translation is based on (1) the understanding of "enemy" as a collective singular with the verb "destroy" in the plural; (2) on the ellipsis of "cities" in the second colon; (3) on the Hebrew syntax according to which "everlasting" modifies the cities and not the enemies; and (4) on the plural "ruins" (MT: *ḥᵒrāḇôṯ;* cf. Jer 25:9; 49:13; Ezek 26:20). Their "memory" (*zikrām*) is their fame (cf. Hos 14:7), full of injustice and terror (cf. TWOT, 1:241–43).

Notes

5 (6 MT) On the meaning of גָּעַרְתָּ (*gā'artā,* "you have rebuked") as "to render ineffective" or "destroy," see P.J. Van Zijl, "A Discussion of the Root *gā'ar* ('Rebuke')," *Biblical Essays,* ed. A.H. Van Zyl (Potchefstroom: Pro Rege-Pers, 1969), pp. 56–63.

The purpose of blotting out their name is to remove any remembrance of their acts (Deut 9:14; 25:19; 29:20; cf. Ps 83:4). The Jews still use this idiom in speaking about their enemies of the past in order to bring about both curse and judgment. For example, "Hitler *yimmaḥ šᵉmô* ("may Hitler's name be blotted out").

6 (7 MT) The last word of this verse in the MT, הֵמָּה (*hēmmāh,* "they"), is rendered as "of them" in the NIV. Dahood takes it as the first word of v.7 (8 MT, BHS) and renders it "behold," based on the Ugaritic *hm* ("look," "behold,") (*Psalms,* 1:56). But *hm* functions as a conditional particle ("if"; cf. Craigie, *Psalms 1–50,* p. 115) in Ugaritic. As difficult as the syntax is, the NIV makes good sense (cf. Kraus, *Psalmen,* p. 76) and may be a form of stress (GKC, par. 135f). Craigie emends it to *hinnēh* ("behold") and joins it with v.7 (8 MT) (*Psalms 1–50,* pp. 114–15).

III. Hope in God's Just Rule

9:7–10

7 The LORD reigns forever;
he has established his throne for judgment.
8 He will judge the world in righteousness;
he will govern the peoples with justice.
9 The LORD is a refuge for the oppressed,
a stronghold in times of trouble.
10 Those who know your name will trust in you,
for you, LORD, have never forsaken those who seek
you.

7–10 The ground of hope in prayer is the belief that the Lord rules! In contrast to the temporary threat of the wicked, Yahweh "reigns," having established "his throne for judgment" (v.7)! The hope of the godly during duress remains in the presence of God's kingdom. Though not always transparent, Yahweh is King! Belief in his kingship affects one's outlook in life in two ways. First, the doctrine of God's kingship affirms the conviction of the difference between his rule and that of the nations. His rule is characterized by perpetuity ("forever"), justice ("judgment"), equity (*ṣeḏeq*, "righteousness," v.8; see 4:1), and "uprightness" (*mêšārîm;* NIV, "justice"; cf. 96:10; 98:9). Second, the doctrine of God's kingship gives hope in the biblical teaching that he shall establish righteousness on earth (v.8). Because he reigns (cf. 11:4; 103:10), there is hope. He is the "refuge" and "stronghold" for his children (v.9).

The MT repeats the word *miśgāḇ* ("refuge"; lit., "high place," such as a rock [cf. Isa 33:16] or a wall [cf. Isa 25:12]). The repetition (NIV, "refuge," "stronghold"; cf. 11:1) bears out the dependability of the Lord in the hour of need (cf. 46:7, 11; 59:10, 16–17; 62:2, 7). God as a "refuge" was a significant OT metaphor for the power and goodness of Yahweh for the "oppressed" (*daḵ*), an OT equivalent of "poor in spirit" (cf. 10:17; 74:21) and is synonymous of "afflicted" (cf. v.12). He does not and will "never" forsake those who rely on him (v.10)! The translation "never" for "not" (*lō'*) is appropriate (cf. Joüon, par. 112d).

The psalmist is confident that God's rule is beneficial to the godly, that is, to those who "know" the name of the Lord (v.10). He cares for them (1:6), and they trust in his "name" to deliver them from distress. They "seek" him with their whole being (14:2; 22:26; 34:5, 10) and are not like the nations that forget God (v.17).

Thus the realization of God's judgment on the wicked and deliverance of the godly forms the basis of hope for the godly in any age that the Lord's rule will be established on earth. There is an element of finality in the belief of God's rule. Justice and righteousness will be established. Oppressors will be no more. The paired balance of "justice . . . equity" (v.8; NIV, "righteousness . . . justice") expresses confidence in the *wise* rule of God (67:4; 96:10). God's justice and righteousness have been demonstrated in Jesus' coming, and the hope of the church is in the rule of God on earth. The promise of the Father's care has been confirmed in Jesus' words that he will not leave us or forsake us (Matt 28:20; Heb 13:5).

Notes

7 (8 MT) The waw at the beginning of v.7 should be translated as a disjunctive: "now." David prays for the Lord to rule and judge the wicked (vv.3–6) and affirms that the Lord does indeed rule (v.7). The particle should not be deleted as in the NIV and as BHS proposes.

IV. Communal Praise and Individual Prayer

9:11–14

11 Sing praises to the LORD, enthroned in Zion;
proclaim among the nations what he has done.
12 For he who avenges blood remembers;
he does not ignore the cry of the afflicted.

13 O LORD, see how my enemies persecute me!
Have mercy and lift me up from the gates of death,
14 that I may declare your praises
in the gates of the Daughter of Zion
and there rejoice in your salvation.

11–12 The praise of the godly rises out of their conviction that God cares. The psalmist has already exhorted himself to sing and has encouraged the godly by reminding them of the acts of God (vv.1–2). He now calls on all of them to join with him in singing a hymn, the focus of which is God's just rule. He is "enthroned in Zion" (cf. 2:4, 6). Zion is his "footstool," or the earthly manifestation of his heavenly rule (cf. 2:4; 76:2; 132:13–14). He is present *with* his people in blessing and in protection. This Great King serves his people, vindicating the needy (3:4; 20:2). (See the appendix to Ps 132: The Ark of the Covenant and the Temple: Symbols of Yahweh's Presence and Rule.) His kingship is evidenced in his mighty deeds, recorded in the history of Israel. The history of Israel witnesses to the nations that the God of Israel continuously loves his people (106:1; Isa 12:4–6; 1 Chron 16:8–15). Even when they were in distress and it seemed that God was not present, the nations were to understand that God's nature will never tolerate injustice done to his elect. He does not forget the atrocities suffered by the poor, who depend on him for their daily existence. The "afflicted" (*ʿaniyîm* [Kethiv] also *ʿanāyîm* [Qere]; cf. vv.12, 18; 10:2, 9, 17) are the "poor," "wretched," "weak," "helpless," or "humble." They are overwhelmed by their sense of need and inability to deal with their situation (cf. KB, p. 720; TWOT, 2:683–84; Kraus, *Psalmen,* 1:82–83 [excursus]). But the righteous Judge will vindicate the blood of the innocent (cf. Gen 4:10). He does care for "the cry of the afflicted" (cf. 34:2).

13–14 The psalmist is more particular about the distress and yet obscures the specifics with generalities and a hyperbolic manner of expression (v.13). The plural ("enemies") may also refer to number or to a state of being: "animosity." The enemy causes "affliction" (NIV, "persecute me"; cf. NEB, "look upon my affliction"). The gravity of the experience of affliction often gives rise to a prayerful cry for help (cf. v.12; 88:13) with the hope that God may "see" (25:18; 31:7; 119:153) and have mercy.

The intensity of the suffering is comparable with death. David feels as if hell ("the gates of death") is here. Life has turned into a trial of alienation, affliction, and disaster. He cannot dig his way out but prays that God will show him "mercy" (cf. 4:1). The "gates of death" is a hyperbolic expression, synonymous with great adversity (cf. 118:17–19). It is an antonym of "the gates of the Daughter of Zion" (v.14), characterized by righteousness and salvation (118:19–21). Only in "Zion" may the godly find rest because God dispenses his righteousness to them where he is. The "Daughter of Zion" is a metaphor for God's people (Mic 4:8) or for Jerusalem, the city of God (Isa 1:8; 10:32).

The psalmist reflects on the public praise of God in his courts in Jerusalem. However, the idiomatic expression favors a more general designation of public praise, wherever God's people are willing to listen. Life and the praise of God go together. The praise of God is a recounting of the "salvation" of God (v.14; cf. 118:21; see 3:2). The psalmist looks forward to God's deliverance and to the end of the rule of the wicked. He also looks forward to the time when he will "declare" (v.14a; cf. v.1: "tell" the "wonders") the "praises" (= "praiseworthy acts") of the Lord. The repetition of the verb *ʾasapperāh* ("tell," "declare," vv.1, 14) forms an inclusionary motif of prayer and praise (vv.1–2, 11–14). The public proclamation involves a remembrance of God's "wonders" (v.1), of his "praises" (i.e., his praiseworthy acts; cf. Isa 60:6), and of his glorious acts of "salvation" (v.14; cf. 3:8). The plurals emphasize the *many* acts of God on behalf of his own people (cf. THAT, 1:498–99).

V. Judgment of the Wicked

9:15–18

15 The nations have fallen into the pit they have dug;
their feet are caught in the net they have hidden.
16 The LORD is known by his justice;
the wicked are ensnared by the work of their hands.
Higgaion. Selah

17 The wicked return to the grave,
all the nations that forget God.
18 But the needy will not always be forgotten,
nor the hope of the afflicted ever perish.

15–18 These four verses are to be regarded as the hymn of praise the psalmist spoke of in v.14. The hymn is composed of two parts (vv.15–16, 17–18) separated by two musical notations (*Higgaion, Selah*). The two stanzas show an internal unity, with an ABA′B′ structure:

A. The end of the wicked (v.15)
B. God's justice pertaining to the nations (v.16)
A′. The end of the wicked (v.17)
B′. God's faithfulness to the afflicted (v.18)

Dahood treats the mood in these verses as a precative perfect and renders the verbs consistently as "may" (*Psalms*, 1:57–58). However, in the context the acts of God on behalf of his own form the object of the praise. The trust of the godly is grounded in their conviction that "the needy will not always be forgotten, nor the hope of the afflicted ever perish" (v.18). Therefore they can anticipate the time when the principle of retribution takes effect and the afflicted find relief. Calvin states, "But, in my judgment, David here rather confirms himself and all the godly with respect to the future, declaring that whatever the wicked may attempt, it will have a termination disastrous to themselves" (1:128). The perfect tense ("have fallen," etc.) shows that the praise of God's glorious acts is due to the *expected* victory over the enemies and to his giving full relief to his own. The song includes hope pertaining to the end of the wicked, as if it already had taken place (vv.15–16), much the same as the song "Fallen! Fallen is Babylon the Great!" (Rev 18:2). Victory is viewed as an accomplished fact (Kidner, p. 70).

Notes

15 (16 MT) Stanley N. Rosenbaum explains how the words "proud" and "nations" may have been confused in the MT and that we read גֵּאִים (*gē'îm*, "proud") instead of גּוֹיִם (*gôyim*, "nations") in vv.15, 16, 17, 19, 20 (16, 17, 18, 20, 21 MT); 10:16 ("New Evidence for Reading *Ge'im* in Place of *Goyim* in Pss. 9 and 10," HUCA 45 [1974]: 65–70; following H.L. Ginsberg, "Some Emendations in Psalms," HUCA 22 [1950–51]: 97–104). But Craigie dismisses the proposal as "possible" but improbable (*Psalms 1–50*, p. 115).

15, 17 (16, 18 MT) The "pit" and the "grave" (Heb. "Sheol") refer to the "pit of Sheol," where the wicked finally go. The godly may experience alienation, adversity, and affliction, but they are delivered "from the gates of death" (v.13). See the appendix to Ps 88: Sheol-Grave-Death in the Psalms.

16 (17 MT) The verb "ensnared" is a translation of an emended text—נוֹקַשׁ (*nôqāš*) instead of נוֹקֵשׁ (*nôqēš*). The former is a Niphal perfect of *y-q-š* ("to trap"), whereas the latter is a Qal participial form of *n-q-š* ("to knock down"). The ancient versions read the Niphal form: "the wicked are trapped." This rendering brings out more clearly the principle of retribution (cf. v.15; 7:15–16; 35:7–8; 57:6).

Higgaion is a musical notation (cf. 92:4). Combined with *Selah,* it may indicate a meditative mood in which vv.17–18 are to be sung. Craigie writes, "It might imply *soft* singing or accompaniment and could thus indicate the concluding verses of the psalm (those following the *Higgaion*) should be rendered quietly, as befits the solemn theme" (*Psalms 1–50,* p. 116).

VI. Hope in God's Just Rule

9:19–20

19 Arise, O LORD, let not man triumph;
let the nations be judged in your presence.
20 Strike them with terror, O LORD;
let the nations know they are but men. *Selah*

19–20 The mood changes from pensive meditation on God's faithfulness to the elect (v.18) to a rousing cry for immediate deliverance: "Arise, O LORD. . . . Strike them with terror" (vv.19–20). "Terror" is not an indication of complete alienation and doom; rather it is an act by which the nations may "fear" Yahweh, recognizing their human frailty (*'enôš,* "man," v.19). Weiser correctly notes, "The purpose of the judgment is to reveal the reality of God to the whole world, and that man cannot grasp the revelation of God unless he realizes his own human weakness and helplessness" (p. 152).

The cry comes out of a broken spirit and shows no evidence of enmity or a desire for revenge. The issue is God's justice and faithfulness to his own. If he does not judge the nations (v.19), the nations will never realize that they are revolutionaries against their Creator-King. They are but "men," i.e., weak and human. The choice of word for "man" (*'enôš,* see 8:4) is singularly important. The battle is between man in his "humanness"—characterized by death, weakness, and limitations—and Yahweh. Man's defiance of God requires God's just response.

There is also conflict between the kingdom of God and the kingdom of man. The prayer of the godly must include the petition "Thy kingdom come. Thy will be done on earth as it is in heaven" (cf. Matt 6:10). On the cross God "struck" his own Son. But in Christ's resurrection lies the assurance that God is victorious over sin and death and that the nations too may join in the experience of salvation. Consistent with true repentance, man must confess that he is "man," i.e., sinful, rebellious, and weak. The acts of God inspire awe that may lead to fear or to greater rebellion. The "terror" (v.20) of the acts of God strikes the ungodly with a sense of hopelessness (cf. Deut 4:34; 26:8; 34:12; Jer 32:21), but God's vengeance on the wicked signifies hope and redemption for the godly!

Notes

20 (21 MT) The MT's מוֹרָה (*môrāh*, "teacher") is to be rejected in favor of a number of MSS and ancient versions: מוֹרָא (*môrā'*, "terror," "dread").

Appendix: Yahweh Is El Elyon

In Canaanite religious thought El, the creator, was the supreme deity of the Canaanite pantheon. Melchizedek, the priest-king of Salem, served El Elyon (NIV, "God Most High") whom Melchizedek knew as "Creator of heaven and earth" (Gen 14:19). But the relation between El, Elyon, and Baal in Canaanite religion is far from clear. John Day advances the thesis that Elyon was a separate deity, having "El-like characteristics" (p. 130), and that he also has Baal-like characteristics (p. 133).

Israel believed that only Yahweh is El Elyon ("God Most High," cf. Gen 14:22). The psalmists, too, use the epithet Elyon to refer to Yahweh, and their use has no mythological overtones. Whatever they may say about Elyon is completely adapted to the bounds of revelation from Sinai: "For you, O LORD, are the Most High [Elyon] over all the earth; / you are exalted far above all gods" (97:9). He is Yahweh Elyon and there is no other Elyon than Yahweh! Therefore the psalmist prays, "Let them know that you, whose name is the LORD— / that you alone are the Most High [Elyon] over all the earth" (83:18).

In Psalm 7 the beginning, center, and end form an artistic whole with the several designations for the Lord: Yahweh, Elohim, El, Elyon:

LORD [Yahweh] my God [Elohim], I take refuge in you;
save and deliver me from all who pursue me. (v.10)

. . . .

God [Elohim] is a righteous judge,
a God [El] who expresses his wrath every day. (v.11)

. . . .

I will give thanks to the LORD [Yahweh] because of his righteousness
and will sing praise to the name of the LORD [Yahweh] Most High [Elyon]. (v.17)

Similarly, chapter 9:1–2 reveals an inclusionary motif:

I will praise you, O LORD [Yahweh], with all my heart;
I will tell of all your wonders.
I will be glad and rejoice in you;
I will sing praise to your name, O Most High [Elyon].

(See also 18:13; 21:7.)

Yet the mythopoetic association of Elyon with the sacred mountain becomes transparent in the Zion theology (see the appendix to Ps 46: Zion Theology). For example, "There is a river whose streams make glad the city of God, / the holy place where the Most High [Elyon] dwells" (46:4). He is "the" Rock, "They remembered that God was their Rock, / that God Most High [Elyon] was their Redeemer" (78:35). He is the only God to whom one offers sacrifices, pays one's vows (50:14), and sings praise (92:1), because he alone hears and answers prayers (57:2). His acts are from of old: "Then I thought, 'To this I will appeal: / the years of the right hand of the Most High' " (77:10). The citizens of Zion, the city of Elyon, have their names recorded and live securely in the hope of the glorious future of Zion: "Indeed, of

Zion it will be said, / 'This one and that one were born in her, / and the Most High [Elyon] himself will establish her' " (87:5).

Elyon provides protection for his people: "He who dwells in the shelter of the Most High [Elyon] / will rest in the shadow of the Almighty [Shaddai]" (91:1; cf. v.9).

The preposition *'al* has been understood as an archaic form of *'eli*. The NIV renders the preposition *'al* ("on") by Most High in 7:8 ("let the LORD judge the peoples. / Judge me, O LORD, according to my righteousness, / according to my integrity, O Most High [*'ālāy*]") and 7:10 ("My shield is God Most High [*'al*], / who saves the upright in heart"). It accepts the argument that Dahood has offered that *'al* is a form of *'eli* ("Most High" or Elyon; *Psalms*, 1:45–46). In 62:7 ("My salvation and my honor depend on God; / he is my mighty rock, my refuge") the NIV appends a note, suggesting the alternate reading, "God Most High is my salvation and honor."

Texts: 7:17; 9:2; 18:13; 21:7; 46:4; 47:2; 50:14; 57:2; 73:11; 77:10; 78:17, 35, 56; 82:6; 83:18; 87:5; 89:27; 91:1, 9; 92:1; 97:9; 107:11.

Bibliography: R.E. Clements, *God and Temple* (Philadelphia: Fortress, 1965), pp. 43–48; M. Dahood, "The Divine Name *'Elî* in the Psalms," *Theological Studies* 14 (1953): 452–57; John Day, *God's Conflict With the Dragon and the Sea. Echoes of Canaanite Myth in the Old Testament* (Cambridge: Cambridge University Press, 1985), pp. 129–40; Norman C. Habel, " 'Yahweh, Maker of Heaven and Earth': A Study in Tradition Criticism," JBL 91 (1972): 321–37; Eckart Otto, "El und JHWH in Jerusalem," VetTest 30 (1980): 316–29; Elmer B. Smick, "Ugaritic and the Theology of the Psalms," pp. 113–14; Walther Zimmerli, *The Old Testament World*, tr. John J. Scullion (Atlanta: Knox, 1976), pp. 15–16.

THAT, 2:285–87; TWOT, 2:668–69.

Psalm 10: The Rule of Man and God's Kingship

(A Prayer)

The focus of Psalm 10 lies on the problem of theodicy, i.e., the justice of God in face of the prosperity of the wicked Israelites. The psalm gives a moving picture of the development of evil within the covenant community. First, the hypocrite abandons God, tests him in his evil exploits, and becomes increasingly brazen in his effrontery (cf. Mal 3:15). A rule of terror is unleashed against the godly, who, in response, cry out for Yahweh, their covenant God, to see and deliver them (v.1). When Yahweh does not immediately respond, evil grows more bold; and the wicked curse, lie, threaten, and deal perversely (vv.7–10), convinced that God does not care.

The tone of the psalm changes in v.12, with a prayer for God to act now that the need is so great. The confidence of the psalmist rises when he meditates on God's righteous rule. Yes, Yahweh *is* King. He will uproot evil and defend the rights of his children. (See the appendix to Ps 5: Yahweh Is King.)

It seems that vv.12–18 fit most appropriately conceptually and linguistically with Psalm 9. The acrostic is more complete, whereas vv.1–8 show little evidence of a clear acrostic. Many of the proposals to recover the acrostic pattern are based on changes in colons for reasons of balance (stichometric analysis). It may be that a section of the acrostic poem was lost and that vv.1–11 form a separate psalm that is set between two sections of the acrostic poem (9:1–20; 10:12–18). Because of changes in language, mood, and subject matter, Psalm 10 should be considered separately from Psalm 9 (cf. J. Ridderbos, 1:89). On the proposed unity of Psalms 9 and 10 as one acrostic psalm, see the comments on Psalm 9.

The structure of the psalm divides into five parts:

A. Questions (v.1)
  B. The Rule of the Wicked (vv.2–11)
    C. Prayer for Deliverance (vv.12–15)
  B′. The Rule of God (v.16)
A′. Resolution (vv.17–18)

The mood changes accordingly from amazement (A) to anxiety (B) to boldness in prayer (C) to confidence in God's rule (B′) and, finally, to anticipation of God's deliverance (A′).

The expectations of justice and the fullness of God's rule on earth are more intense since the coming of our Lord. The NT also looks forward to the reign of God over this world: "The kingdom of the world has become the kingdom of / our Lord and of his Christ, / and he will reign for ever and ever" (Rev 11:15). By affirming his rule, God shows that he cares and is able to resolve the problem of the suffering of the righteous (Kraus, *Psalmen,* 1:87).

I. Questions

10:1

[1]Why O LORD, do you stand far off?
  Why do you hide yourself in times of trouble?

1 The assurance of God's kingship and justice is missing in the opening note of the psalm. The tone is set by the interrogative "Why?" (cf. 2:1; 22:1; 42:9; 43:2; 74:1; 88:14). The psalmist does not accuse God of having forsaken his own; rather it seems to him as if "the times of trouble" (cf. 10:1) are too much a burden to carry. His prayers for deliverance are unheard. He needs God's help, but it is as if God keeps his distance by keeping himself well-hidden (cf. Isa 49:14). The question also introduces the riddle of the prosperity of the wicked and the suffering of the righteous (cf. Ps 73). The riddle is not *resolved* but is *refocused* on the God who cares for his own (v.14).

Notes

1 Psalm 2 also begins with the interrogative particle "Why," expressive of the deep concern with the prosperity of the wicked.

II. The Rule of the Wicked

10:2–11

[2]In his arrogance the wicked man hunts down the weak,
  who are caught in the schemes he devises.
[3]He boasts of the cravings of his heart;

he blesses the greedy and reviles the Lord.
4 In his pride the wicked does not seek him;
in all his thoughts there is no room for God.
5 His ways are always prosperous;
he is haughty and your laws are far from him;
he sneers at all his enemies.
6 He says to himself, "Nothing will shake me;
I'll always be happy and never have trouble."
7 His mouth is full of curses and lies and threats;
trouble and evil are under his tongue.
8 He lies in wait near the villages;
from ambush he murders the innocent,
watching in secret for his victims.
9 He lies in wait like a lion in cover;
he lies in wait to catch the helpless;
he catches the helpless and drags them off in his net.
10 His victims are crushed, they collapse;
they fall under his strength.
11 He says to himself, "God has forgotten;
he covers his face and never sees."

2 In their pride the wicked act as "gods" in this world. Their vile words and despotic acts offend and hurt the people of God. But God does not always react swiftly to protect the honor of his name. Moreover, it is a far greater evil when the wicked belong to the covenant community. The people whom the psalmist describes were familiar with God and his law, but they openly rejected the godly way of life in favor of freedom and power.

The ways of evil and righteousness are inconsistent. Evil cannot tolerate godliness but pursues the godly with an unholy zeal. The righteous, whom the wicked attempt to trap, are not "weak" but "afflicted" (see 9:12). They are not yet caught but may be caught (see Craigie: "In arrogance, the wicked hotly pursue the afflicted. Let them be caught up," *Psalms 1–50*, p. 120). The translation "hunts down" (*d-l-q*) brings out the "hot pursuit" (KB^3, 1:214) of the wicked (cf. Lam 4:19). But it is not clear whether the godly are actually caught by their crafty schemes (cf. vv.8–10) or whether the psalmist prays that the wicked may be caught by their own plots (cf. 7:15–16; 9:15).

3–4 The evil man's hatred of the godly expresses a total disregard for the Lord and his commandments. He is filled with self (v.3; NIV, "the cravings of his heart," lit., "the desire of his soul"). The wicked "boasts" that whatever he desires, he can accomplish by his schemings. The phrase "he blesses the greedy" is ambiguous in the MT. The "greedy" (*bōṣēaʿ*, active participle) may be the subject of "blesses," i.e., "the greedy blesses." But this leaves open the question of whom he blesses. On the other hand, "bless" may be a euphemism for "curse" (cf. Job 1:5), thus being a synonym of "revile": "the greedy curses and reviles the Lord." Some close v.3 with "the greedy curses" and read "reviles the Lord" together with "the wicked" in v.4: "the wicked despises the Lord in his pride, he does not seek him" (see Craigie, *Psalms 1–50*, pp. 120–21; A.A. Anderson, 1:114; NEB, "arrogant as he is, he scorns the Lord"). The NIV may be maintained with a change in the second colon of v.3: "the greedy curses."

This greedy man has no regard for God or his commandments (vv.3b–4, 5b, 11). He "praises" (*hillēl;* NIV, "boasts") himself but spurns the covenant God (v.3). His goal in life is a purposeful avoidance of God (v.4). He is not an atheist, but instead he has conveniently chosen to live without God (cf. 14:1; Jer 5:12). Worship of the Creator-covenant God has been exchanged for worship of himself, the creature (Rom 1:23). The rejection of the Lord is evident from the greedy man's warped sense of justice and concern (v.5), his false confidence (v.6), his foul language (v.7), his perverse acts (vv.8–10), and his utter disregard of accountability to God (v.11).

5 Success may crown injustice. The prosperity of the godly (1:3) is guaranteed by God, but the wicked makes every effort to take his share. He flaunts the "judgments" (*mišpāṭeyḵā;* NIV, "laws") of God (v.5). The "judgments" are God's revelation of the just ordering of the society and the life of his people. The wicked also considers God's judgments too far removed from him. Because God has not yet come in judgment, the wicked man becomes more brazen in his selfish, despotic rule. He has contempt for anyone who gets in his way and counts them as "his enemies." As a token of contempt, "he sneers at" (snorts at) anyone who opposes him (cf. Mal 1:13).

6 Success breeds success. In his prosperity the wicked man presumptuously takes to himself the privileges of the righteous. God has promised that they will not be moved (15:5; 16:8; 21:7; 62:2; 112:6). The wicked man does not need God. Moreover, he is "happy" with himself.

In his pride the wicked may live without a sense of accountability as he does not expect retribution (vv.4, 6; cf. v.13). Moreover he takes measures never to experience "trouble" as he autonomously attempts to avoid God's righteous judgment. Bank accounts, associations, board positions, and property give him a sense of self-worth and security.

7–10 The wicked man may appear not to be dangerous, but he uses his tongue as a weapon (v.7). He intimidates with his curses and threats (cf. 59:12); his oath is worthless because it is a lie. But he is so powerful and persuasive in his speech that he always seems to get his way. His speech reflects his schemings (vv.3–4, 6; cf. Rom 3:10–18), and his intent is to work destruction (12:2). "Trouble and evil" are a way of life for him (cf. 7:14). "Trouble and evil" are graphically portrayed by the stealthy behavior of the wicked (vv.8–10). He lies in wait like a wild animal to ambush and gain control over innocent victims. The word "victims" (v.8) translates an obscure Hebrew word that occurs also in v.10 (cf. KB^3, 1:306; and J. Barr, *Comparative Philology and the Text of the Old Testament* [Oxford: Clarendon, 1968], pp. 228–29).

Once the wicked man has his victim, he carries him off like a "lion" (v.9; cf. 7:2; 17:12; 22:13). The psalmist also compares the wicked man to the hunter who pursues his prey and traps it in a net (cf. v.2). Thus the victims are overpowered by brute force. They receive no justice or mercy. Might makes right.

11 The psalmist returns to his starting point (cf. vv.2–4). The arrogance of the wicked expresses itself in injustice, but his root problem is his utter disregard for the Lord. He has rejected the covenant God, not by speculative thought, but by his speech and actions. As soon as he has set out on the road of independence from God, he gains confidence. He mistakes God's patience with evil for God's lack of interest in justice and the innocent victims. His boldness grows as he no longer senses any accountability to God for his actions. Why should he, if God does not even see? The godly, too, experience God's absence (v.1). Anarchy rules when God's patience with the wicked does not bring them to repentance.

Notes

2 The MT is ambiguous. The imperfect may express the jussive mood: "Let them [the wicked] be caught." Another possible reading follows the LXX and the Vulgate: "the afflicted will be caught" (cf. NIV). In support of this rendering is the parallelism with the first colon. On the other hand, 7:15–16 and 9:15 support the belief in divine retribution (see NEB, "may his crafty schemes be his own undoing!").

3 G.J. Thierry renders this verse: "For he (the impious) praises Impiety to his heart's content, / and he extols Profit . . . ! he despises Yahwe!" ("Remarks on Various Passages in the Psalms," *Oud Testamentische Studiën* 13 [1963]: 83).

5 The verb יָחִילוּ (*yāḥîlû*, "are prosperous") may be related to the root *ḥ-y-l*, a denominative of the noun *ḥayil*, "strength" (cf. KB³, p. 298: "to be strong"). The strength of the wicked lies in his wealth. It seems as if his prosperity lasts.

Acrostic analysis has resulted in a correction of the text. The word מָרוֹם (*mārôm*, "haughty"), beginning with the letter mem, is emended to סָרוּ (*sārû*, "they depart"). But a desire to restore the alphabetic acrostic is not enough. The MT, as reflected in the NIV, makes good sense. But see Craigie: "Your judgments are removed from him" (*Psalms 1–50*, p. 121).

6 The MT of this clause is problematic: "which [אֲשֶׁר, *'ašer*] not in evil." The NIV assumes an emendation of the text: "blessed" (אִשֻּׁר, *'aššur*) instead of *'ašer*. The emendation makes good sense and has found wide acceptance (Craigie, *Psalms 1–50*, p. 122; BHS). The NEB's "no misfortune can check my course" is based on another emendation. The NKJV reflects most closely the MT: "I shall never be in adversity."

7 Again for acrostic and/or stichometric reasons, some read the word אָלָה (*'ālāh*, "curse," "swear") with v.6, allowing for the letter peh to begin v.7. So Craigie: "Happiness without misfortune! so has he sworn. His mouth is" (*Psalms 1–50*, p. 121; cf. A.A. Anderson, 1:115).

10 "Under his strength" is an abstract expressed in Hebrew by a plural—עֲצוּמָיו (*'aṣûmāyw*, lit., "his mighty ones"). It may be a metaphor derived from the claws of a lion (cf. BDB, p. 783).

III. Prayer for Deliverance

10:12–15

12 Arise, LORD! Lift up your hand, O God.
Do not forget the helpless.
13 Why does the wicked man revile God?
Why does he say to himself,
"He won't call me to account"?
14 But you, O God, do see trouble and grief;
you consider it to take it in hand.
The victim commits himself to you;
you are the helper of the fatherless.
15 Break the arm of the wicked and evil man;
call him to account for his wickedness
that would not be found out.

12–15 The "why" (v.1), expressive of the psalmist's occupation with the problem of the prosperity of the wicked, changes into a cry for God's help. Because of the increasing oppression and anarchy, "now" is the time for God to act. The prayer also contains both an appeal to God's honor (v.13) and a vindication of God (v.14).

The structure of the prayer is ABB′A′:

A. Prayer for God's intervention (v.12)
  B. The boast of the wicked (v.13)
  B′. The trust of the afflicted (v.14)
A′. Prayer for God's intervention (v.15)

Verses 12 and 15 together form the prayer for God's intervention. The wicked claims that (1) God (El) has forgotten (v.11), that (2) God will not call him to account for his evil deeds (v.11), and that (3) no trouble will overtake him (vv.5–6). The psalmist prays that (1) God (El) will demonstrate his strength ("your hand") so as to help the afflicted ("helpless," NIV; v.12), that (2) God will break the power of the wicked and so demonstrate that he sees evil and holds the wicked accountable (v.15), and that (3) nothing but trouble will come to the evil and that their earthly "kingdom" will thus be broken (vv.12–15).

The prayer for deliverance is in the form of an inclusion (vv.12, 15). In between the psalmist reflects on the folly of the wicked (v.13). He asks with amazement "why" or "how" the wicked dare to revile God (cf. v.3) and imagine that God does not see evil (cf. v.11). He answers his own question, calming his feelings of disturbance and anxiety at the presence of evil (v.14). God does after all see their evil exploits.

The wicked may spurn God and his judgments (vv.3–5), while the innocent victims seek protection from their heavenly Father (v.14b). The emphatic use of "But you" and "you" (v.14) implies that the sole hope of the victims is in their abandonment to their God, who has promised to help the fatherless and all his children in need (cf. vv.17–18; 37:40; 46:6–7; 109:26–28). God's patience explains the delay in justice (cf. Calvin: "It is, however, our duty to wait patiently so long as the vengeance is reserved in the hand of God, until he stretches forth his arm to help us," 1:152).

Notes

12 For "arise" see 3:7; 9:19.

14 "To take it in hand"—לָתֵת בְּיָדֶךָ (*lāṯēṯ beyāḏeḵā*, lit., "to give in your hand")—is an idiom for "to requite" (Briggs, 1:87; cf. Pss 28:4; 120:4).

IV. The Rule of God

10:16

16 The LORD is King for ever and ever;
  the nations will perish from his land.

16 The hope of the righteous in a just world lies in Yahweh. His kingship is established forever and ever. How can the wicked think that he will last "from generation to generation" (cf. v.6)? The wicked, together with the nations, will perish from "his land," so as to leave God's people at rest. The concern of the psalmist here is with the "land" of Israel, where anarchy prevailed. The word "nations" refers to the wicked in Israel, who act like the nations (cf. Dahood's "heathen," *Psalms,* 1:61). Calvin observes: "By *the heathen* he does not mean foreigners. . . . but hypocrites, who falsely boasted that they belonged to the people of God" (1:155).

Notes

16 Dahood (*Psalms,* 1:66) argues in favor of the optative perfect of "perish": "Let the heathen perish from his earth."

V. Resolution

10:17–18

[17] You hear, O LORD, the desire of the afflicted;
you encourage them, and you listen to their cry,
[18] defending the fatherless and the oppressed,
in order that man, who is of the earth, may terrify no more.

17–18 God's kingship was revealed to Israel (Exod 15:18) and came to expression in Israel. Because God is faithful to the covenant, he has promised to judge (NIV, "defending," v.18) the needy. "The fatherless [cf. v.14] and the oppressed" is a reference to the class of people who were most easily wronged (cf. 82:3) but were protected by God's law (Exod 22:22–24; Deut 10:18; 16:11, 14; cf. Isa 1:17; Jer 7:6; James 1:27; cf. F.C. Fensham, "Widow, Orphan, and the Poor in Ancient Near Eastern and Wisdom Literature," JNES 21 [1962]: 129–39; see the appendix to Ps 5: Yahweh Is King).

God gives the needy their "desire" (v.17) by stopping the reign of terror by men who act as gods. The MT has two infinitive constructs: "to judge" and "to terrify," translated in the NIV with God as the subject of the judging and "man" as the subject of the terrorizing. Parallelism requires that God be the subject of *both* verbal forms: "defending . . . and terrifying." However, the negative particle *bal* ("not") changes the second colon into a result clause (as in NIV). Craigie renders *bal* in an affirmative sense: "Once again he will continue to execute judgment for orphan and oppressed, to terrify mere earthlings!" (*Psalms 1–50,* pp. 121, 123; for the basis see C.F. Whitley, "The Positive Force of the Hebrew Particle בל," ZAW 84 [1972]: 213–19).

The idiom "man, who is of the earth" expresses the weakness of man (*'enôš;* cf. 9:19–20). Man is weak and confined to the earth, an "earthling" (Craigie, *Psalms 1–50,* p. 123), whereas God is King. Calvin comments appropriately, "The phrase, *of earth,* contains a tacit contrast between the low abode of this world and the height of heaven" (1:157; cf. Isa 2:22).

Psalm 11: Refuge in the Righteous King

This psalm, as a psalm of David, must have come from a time when David was hunted down by Saul, "as one hunts a partridge in the mountains" (1 Sam 26:20). Its message is not limited by the historical circumstances, however, because the central issue is the persecution of the upright by the wicked. Wherever evil seems to triumph, God's people can take heart in the attitude reflected by David. His confidence was in God!

The psalm is an *individual lament* with an emphasis on confidence in the Lord. See

W.H. Bellinger's treatment of the genre as a complex of lament-trust-thanksgiving ("The Interpretation of Psalm 11," EQ 56 [1984]: 95–101). The lament is expressed in the words of the friends who despair of evil (vv.1c–3). It is possible that the psalmist speaks to himself as he reflects on his situation (vv.2–3), but those speaking (v.1c) are most likely his friends or advisors.

The psalmist encourages his friends to look beyond the immediate, reasonable solution to God who sees both the righteous and the wicked (vv.4–7). This kind of confidence in the Lord can withstand trials, persecutions, and temptations. David knows in his heart that (1) the Lord is King (v.4a), that (2) he examines the works and words of all people, and that (3) he will reward each in accordance with his deeds. The wicked will be destroyed whereas the godly "will see his face" (v.7). Our Lord Jesus also had confidence in the Father when he faced the temptations of Satan and the hostility of people. When our hearts trust in him, he has promised to help us in crisis situations. Confidence in the Lord is a mark of Christian maturity.

The structure of the psalm is in the form of a closure:

A. Refuge in God (vv.1–3)
  B. Yahweh Is the Righteous King (vv.4–6)
A′. God Is the Refuge of the Righteous (v.7)

The central thrust is the nature of God's righteous rule as it affects the upright of heart and the wicked. For a more intricate structural analysis, see Pierre Auffret, "Essai sur La Structure Littéraire de Psaume 11," ZAW 93 (1981): 401–18.

I. Refuge in God

11:1–3

For the director of music. Of David.

1 In the LORD I take refuge.
  How then can you say to me:
  "Flee like a bird to your mountain.
2 For look, the wicked bend their bows;
  they set their arrows against the strings
to shoot from the shadows
  at the upright in heart.
3 When the foundations are being destroyed,
  what can the righteous do?"

1–3 Confidence in the Lord describes the psalmist as he is surrounded by the wicked and receives counsel from his advisors. His confidence is grounded in years of walking with God. Therefore he is amazed at the lack of stability of his advisors. Where is their faith when they counsel him to flee? "Flee like a bird" (v.1) is an expression of quick escape in search of quietness (cf. 55:6; 124:7).

The psalmist quickly dismisses escape, even though it is a viable alternative. His advisors argue against him with facts. First, the wicked slander him as they stalk like predators for the kill (v.2). Their tongues are bent like bows; their words are "arrows" against the string. They lie in ambush and with their "tongues" hurl sudden abuse at the godly.

Second, the wicked lurk in the dark. The battle is not in the open, where one can see it. So it is with evil. It is pervasive and yet not easy to spot. The wicked are deceptive and filled with treachery.

Third, the foundations are destroyed. The word "foundations" (*šāṯôṯ*) occurs only here with this meaning (elsewhere "buttocks," 2 Sam 10:4; Isa 20:4). The "foundations" appear to be a metaphor for the order of society (75:3 [NIV, "pillars"]; 82:5; Ezek 30:4): the "established institutions, the social and civil order of the community" (Briggs, 1:89–90). This order has been established by the Lord at creation and is being maintained, as H.H. Schmid puts it: "All factors considered, the doctrine of creation, namely, the belief that God has created and is sustaining the order of the world in all its complexities, is not a peripheral theme of biblical theology but is plainly the fundamental theme" ("Creation, Righteousness, and Salvation: 'Creation Theology' as a Broad Horizon of Biblical Theology," in *Creation in the Old Testament*, ed. Bernard W. Anderson [Philadelphia: Fortress, 1984], pp. 102–17). God's justice and law are being replaced by human autonomy and its resultant anarchy.

Fourth, the wicked are fully intent on making anarchy the way of life. They haunt the "upright in heart" (*yišrê-lēḇ*), that is, those who are characterized by their integrity. The word "upright" (*yāšār*) denotes the godly, who know and love the Lord (cf. 7:10; 36:10; cf. 73:1). They are not perfect, nor are they "upright" in their own eyes. They love the Lord and, therefore, do his will. They, as the "righteous" (*ṣaddîq*, vv.3, 5), constitute the opposite of the wicked, who are bent on ridding themselves of those who do God's will on earth. The wicked's hatred of righteousness matches their ability with the bow and arrow. The argument holds true because the wicked are likened to archers in ambush. They are treacherous, stealthy, and intent on maligning and making the godly fall (cf. 10:7–10; 37:14).

Perhaps David is disconcerted with his own thoughts, as he speaks to himself. A tension has developed. There are two kinds of responses to the immediate threat: escape or refuge. It seems that reason dictates *escape*. The godly seem to be powerless against such treachery. In view of this, he asks, "What can the righteous do?" This question is a more probable reading than the NIV marginal note: "What is the Righteous One doing?" The psalmist has already answered this counsel by his personal expression of trust: "In the LORD I take refuge" (v.1). The emphatic "in the LORD" is reflected in the NIV. Trust and confidence in the Lord mark this psalm (cf. vv.4, 7), not escape, but asylum with God!

Notes

For a brief discussion of the technical words and phrases in the superscription, see the Introduction.

1 The הַר (*har*, "mountain") is a place of refuge from persecution (cf. 1 Sam 26:20). The MT reads "your" as a masculine plural. The pronoun "you" is absent in the LXX, Targum, and Syriac versions; instead, the one word in Hebrew, הַרְכֶם (*harḵem*, "your mountain"), is divided into two words: הַר כְּמוֹ (*har kᵉmô*, "mountain like"; so J. Ridderbos, 1:96–97; Craigie, *Psalms 1–50*, p. 131). The NEB follows another possible reading, suggested by the LXX (cf. BHS): "Flee to the mountains like a bird" (cf. A.A. Anderson, 1:120).

2 In the Psalms the evil of the tongue is often metaphorically described in terms of deadly weapons such as the sword and the bow and arrow (cf. 37:14; 57:4; 64:3–4; see also Jer 9:8).

II. Yahweh Is the Righteous King

11:4–6

4 The LORD is in his holy temple;
the LORD is on his heavenly throne.
He observes the sons of men;
his eyes examine them.
5 The LORD examines the righteous,
but the wicked and those who love violence
his soul hates.
6 On the wicked he will rain
fiery coals and burning sulfur;
a scorching wind will be their lot.

4–5 The psalmist looks beyond both his advisors and his enemies to the Lord, raising his eyes to heaven. The "holy temple" (v.4) is not the temple of Solomon, which may not have been constructed by this time. God's palace is in heaven (18:6; 29:9; Mic 1:2; Hab 2:20)! God is "holy," and from his throne in heaven he sees all mankind. The "throne" of God is a symbol of his royal rule and authority to judge (cf. 9:7; 47:8; see the appendix to Ps 5: Yahweh Is King). Hence no radical distinction should be made between his dwelling in heaven and in the temple, as suggested by Tryggve B.D. Mettinger (*The Dethronement of Sabaoth. Studies in the Shem and Kabod Theologies* [Lund: Gleerup, 1982], p. 31).

The Lord's eyes "test" mankind as he patiently observes their feverish activities (MT, "his eyes see, his eyelids examine the sons of man," v.4b). The "eyelids" (or "pupils") are here a synonym for eyes (hence NIV, "He observes . . . ; his eyes"). Craigie argues persuasively for retaining the translation "eyelids": "Thus, although it is clear that in prosaic terms the word . . . in this context means 'his eyes,' the poetic brilliance may lie precisely in the fact that the poet used the term 'eyelids' " (*Psalms 1–50*, p. 132).

It may seem that God, by his inactivity, does not care; but he sees and examines the wicked together with the righteous (vv.4–5). The verb "examine" (*b-ḥ-n*, "test") denotes the activity of the smith in the process of purifying gold or silver (cf. Jer 6:27–30; 9:7; cf. Ps 7:9). The holy God may not immediately judge the wicked, but his holiness excludes any love for those who "love violence."

6 In his time God will judge the wicked. Then the examination will be by fire, and they cannot stand through his judgment. The "fiery coals and burning sulfur" (brimstone) will consume them, just as it destroyed Sodom and Gomorrah (cf. Gen 19:24; Deut 29:23; Ezek 38:22). Another image of judgment is the "scorching wind," the *sharab* or *ḥamsin*, as it is known in Israel today. The hot desert wind blows over the Middle East during the changes in season from spring to summer and from summer to fall. Its effects are devastating, as the beauty of vegetation changes over night into parched, withered plants (cf. Isa 21:1; 40:7–8; Jer 4:11). The wicked will be like the flowers of the field, which are here today and gone tomorrow.

Destruction is the wicked's "lot," which translates the Hebrew idiom *meֽnāṯ kôsām,* "portion of their cup"). It is reminiscent of the head of a household who gives each member a cupful to drink at a meal. Thus God gives the wicked a "cupful" of his wrath (cf. Isa 51:17, 22; Ezek 23:31–33). Even our Lord drank the cup of God's judgment like a grievous sinner (Matt 26:39) for our sake. Because of Jesus' work on the cross, God's patience with evil, Peter reminds us, is an expression of his grace, permitting men to repent. But one day he will rain down fire on the earth and destroy the ungodly (2 Peter 3:7–10).

Notes

4 It is possible to interpret the holy temple as a reference to God's dwelling in Jerusalem (see Craigie, *Psalms 1–50,* p. 133). However, parallelism favors his heavenly abode.

5 The MT could be rendered in two ways: "The LORD examines the righteous, but the wicked and those who love violence his soul hates" or "The LORD, the Righteous One, examines the wicked, and those who love violence his soul hates." The contrastive translation is preferable: "The LORD examines the righteous, . . . but the wicked . . . his soul hates."

His "soul" is an expression for God; i.e., *the LORD* hates the violence of the wicked (cf. Isa 1:14–17).

6 The phrase "fiery coals" requires an emendation of the MT (based on Symm.), as the word פַּחִים (*paḥîm,* "snares") followed by אֵשׁ (*'ēš,* "fire") is meaningless in the MT. The Hebrews were not familiar with mineral coal but used charcoal.

III. God Is the Refuge of the Righteous

11:7

> 7 For the LORD is righteous,
> he loves justice;
> upright men will see his face.

7 The "righteous" (*ṣaddîq*) God loves those who do righteous acts (*ṣ^e^ḏāqôṯ;* NIV, "justice"; cf. Isa 33:15–16). He who sees and examines all men promises that only the "upright" (*yāšār*) of heart (cf. v.2) will see him (cf. 17:15; 63:2; Matt 5:8; 1 John 3:2; Rev 22:4). To see the face of God is an expression of deliverance from adversity, of close communion, and of the reality of God's blessed presence (cf. 23:6; 63:2) in this world and in the world to come (cf. Dahood, *Psalms,* 1:71; Hans F. Fuhs, *Sehen und Schauen. Die Wurzel ḥzh im Alten Orient und im Alten Testament. Ein Beitrag zum prophetischen Offenbarungsempfang* [Würzburg: Echter Verlag, 1978], p. 274).

Psalm 12: Lying Tongues and the Truthfulness of God's Word

This psalm is a prayer on behalf of or by the people of God for deliverance from the deceptions and scheming of the godless (vv.1–4). The Lord promises to protect his own (v.5), but he expects his children to live with the tensions resulting from a walk in faith: reliance on his promise (vv.6–7) and the reality of the ever-present vileness of man (v.8).

The genre is that of a *community lament.* The psalm also includes a statement of confidence in God. The structure is a movement from prayer (vv.1–4) to promise (v.5) to a renewed assessment of the present world (vv.6–8). The emotional variation includes prayer (vv.1–3), curse (v.4), promise (v.5), confidence (vv.6–7), and observation of the presence of evil (v.8). The introduction and conclusion form an inclusion that accentuates and explains the unresolved tension created by the conduct of the wicked and focuses the reader's attention on God's promise at the middle of the psalm.

The expository structure may be viewed as follows:

A. Prayer for Deliverance (vv.1–4)
  B. Promise of the Lord (v.5)
  B′. Reflection on God's Promises (v.6)
A′. Prayer for Deliverance (vv.7–8)

I. Prayer for Deliverance

12:1–4

For the director of music. According to *sheminith*. A psalm of David.

1 Help, LORD, for the godly are no more;
  the faithful have vanished from among men.
2 Everyone lies to his neighbor;
  their flattering lips speak with deception.

3 May the LORD cut off all flattering lips
  and every boastful tongue
4 that says, "We will triumph with our tongues;
  we own our lips—who is our master?"

1 The very first word in the Hebrew and English texts is indicative of need: "Help" (cf. 3:7; 6:4). The description of the prevalence of evil is a connecting link with Psalm 11:2–3. The intent of the wicked was to rid themselves of "the upright in heart" (11:2; cf. v.7). The psalmist observes that the godly have vanished (cf. Isa 57:1; Jer 5:1–2; Hos 4:1; Mic 7:2). The godly are characterized by their faithfulness to the Lord, and they are beloved by him (cf. 4:3). The parallelism of "faithful" (*'ᵉmûnîm*) in the plural with "godly" (*ḥāsîḏ*, see 4:3) in the singular requires both nouns to be regarded as descriptions of people: "faithful men" and "godly men" (cf. 31:23). The NEB takes both nouns as abstracts and misses the contrast of the faithful with the deceptive men: "for loyalty is no more; good faith between man and man is over."

Mankind is bereft of the God-fearers. Of course, this is hyperbolic language, but it is a manner of bringing before the covenant God his promise to free his people. What has happened to the covenant community and the promises? One is reminded of Elijah's complaint (1 Kings 19:10). But even then the Lord responded that seven thousand were left (1 Kings 19:18)!

2–4 The wicked disobey God with their tongues. They pervert and twist truth (v.2). Their goal is to gain power by flattery, deception, and clever schemes. They do not tolerate authority but prefer autonomy and anarchy (v.4). The idiom "with heart and heart" or "double-minded" (*bᵉleḇ wālēḇ*, v.2; cf. Prov 26:24–26) is rendered "with deception" in the NIV. The Hebrew idiom brings out the source of the deception: "the heart." The wicked are "double-hearted" by the very way they speak. In other words, they are hypocritical (James 3:10–12). Their inner heart is deceptive and so is their flattery. They are completely taken by falsehood.

Instead of godliness, vileness is exalted (v.8). What a contrast to a godly covenant community in which wisdom and righteousness are to be exalted! The wicked are not necessarily theoretical atheists, but their conduct convicts them of practical atheism. Their aim is power and that end justifies any means (v.4; cf. 10:2–11). They do not shrink from flattery, boasting, denying God's way, and exalting their own way. They desire a Machiavellian victory as did Absalom (2 Sam 15:1–6).

In response to the "fine" speech of the wicked, the psalmist cries out to his covenant God. He prays that perverse speech will cease and that righteousness thereby may be established (v.3; see the appendix to Ps 1: The Ways of Wisdom and Folly).

Notes

For a brief discussion of the technical words and phrases in the superscription, see the Introduction.

1 (2 MT) הוֹשִׁיעָה (*hôšî'āh*, "save"; NIV, "help") is from *y-š-ʿ* ("save," "deliver," "vindicate"); cf. v.5: "I will protect [*y-š-ʿ*] them."

There is a general agreement on the translation "vanished" (פַּסּוּ, *passû*). The root *p-s-h* is a *hapax legomenon*, and the Targum reads "come to an end" from the root *s-w-p*. Several Hebrew MSS have פָּצוּ (*pāṣû*, "are scattered").

3 (4 MT) גְּדֹלוֹת (*gᵉdōlôṯ*, "great") is a noun ("pride") that together with the verb "speak" becomes an adverb, "boastfully" (KB^3, 1:170). Since the verb "speak" is a participial form modified by "tongue," the translation is "a tongue speaking boastfully"; cf. NEB, "and the tongue that talks so boastfully."

4 (5 MT) The verb "triumph" reflects the Hebrew denominative verb גבר (*g-b-r*, "be strong") from the noun גֶּבֶר (*geḇer*, "man"). Dahood (*Psalms,* 1:73) renders it "we are powerful" (cf. NEB, "our tongue can win us the day").

The NIV margin gives an alternate rendering of "we own our lips": "*our lips are our plowshares.*" Dahood (*Psalms*, 1:73–74) has proposed that the MT's אִתָּנוּ (*'ittānû*, "with us") be read as *'ittēnû* ("our weapons" or "plowshares," 1 Sam 13:20–21; Isa 2:4; Mic 4:3). A.A. Anderson (1:126) suggests another possible reading—"with our lips we have worked wonders"—based on the emendation *'ôṯēnû* ("our wonder"). There is no textual evidence against the traditional reading "our lips are with us" in the sense of the NIV's "we own our lips" (cf. LXX).

II. Promise of the Lord

12:5

5 "Because of the oppression of the weak
and the groaning of the needy,
I will now arise," says the LORD.
"I will protect them from those who malign them."

5 The Lord answers the cry of the needy, even as he has promised. He hears their groaning (Exod 2:24; Pss 79:11; 102:20) and prepares himself to act on their behalf. The language of v.5 resembles God's promise in Isaiah 33:10: " 'Now will I arise,' says the LORD. / 'Now will I be exalted; / now will I be lifted up.' " The exaltation of God must bring the abasement and removal of the wicked (Isa 33:11–12). But the psalmist knows that the full deliverance may be a long way off, because he concludes with the realization that for the present time "what is vile is honored among men" (v.8). The protection is a deliverance from the immediate threat.

God protects the afflicted from their oppressors. The last clause of v.5 is not clear in Hebrew. The NIV rendering describes the wicked as "those who malign them." Other versions, including the LXX, and commentators see here a reference to God (cf. "I will shine forth for him," Craigie, *Psalms 1–50*, p. 136). It may also refer to the afflicted as those who "pant for" deliverance (cf. NEB, "I will place him in the safety for which he longs").

Notes

---

5 (6 MT) For an approach to this psalm as a war oracle, see the study by Christensen, pp. 112–27. For other psalms, see 60; 74; 79; 80; 83; 85; 90; 94:1–11; 123; 126; 137.

בְּיֵשַׁע (*b^e^yēša'*, "in deliverance") appears in the NIV as "(I will) protect (them)," an idiomatic rendering of "[I will place] in deliverance." Here "deliverance" (from *y-š-'*) means more than "safety" (Briggs, 1:98). It also signifies a response to the initial cry, translated "help," and could be rendered as in the NIV: "I will protect" or, preferably, "I shall vindicate."

יָפִיחַ לוֹ (*yāpî^a^ḥ lô*) is literally "he will blow at him" (NIV, "malign them"). The LXX rendering, "I shall appear in radiance to him," may represent a textual variant that Craigie adopts: "I will shine forth for him" (*Psalms 1–50*, p. 136). Based on Ugaritic evidence, Patrick D. Miller, Jr., proposes an alternate root, *y-p-ḥ* ("witness"), instead of *p-u-ḥ*, and explains the idiom as "witness on his behalf" or "the witness for him": "I will place in safety the witness on his behalf" ("*Yāpîaḥ* in Psalm XII 6," VetTest 29 [1979]: 495–501).

III. Reflection on God's Promises

12:6

> 6 And the words of the Lord are flawless,
> like silver refined in a furnace of clay,
> purified seven times.

6 The assurance of the godly ultimately lies in God's promises. His "words" (= "promises") are pure (= "flawless"), refined like silver that has been subjected to a sevenfold process of purification (cf. 18:30; 119:140). Over against the lies, deceptions, false honesty, treachery, perverse speech, and scheming of the wicked is God's word! The OT is full of his promises, which have been confirmed by our Lord (2 Cor 1:20). Bellinger concludes that the certainty of the psalmist arises from a prophetic insight (pp. 61–63) and that "salvation is now being actualized; these verses give a prophetic vision of judgment and deliverance from the present crisis and are then clearly to be seen as a prophetic element in the psalm since they anticipate God's deliverance of the worshippers" (pp. 62–63).

Notes

6 (7 MT) The description of the silver is uncertain in the MT. BHS proposes an emended reading resulting in parallel phrases: "And the words of the Lord . . . [like] refined silver; his works [are like] purified gold." The meaning of the word עֲלִיל (*ʿalîl*) is uncertain. If the traditional meaning is maintained ("crucible" or "furnace," BDB, p. 760), it is possible to translate the phrase "to the earth" or "of the earth," giving the NIV rendering "a furnace of clay" (cf. Dahood, *Psalms*, 1:74). For the justification of Craigie's renderings—"silver refined in a furnace, gold purified seven times"—see his commentary (*Psalms 1–50*, pp. 136–37).

IV. Prayer for Deliverance

12:7–8

7O Lord, you will keep us safe
and protect us from such people forever.
8The wicked freely strut about
when what is vile is honored among men.

7 In response to the assurance of God's word, the psalmist brings his lament to a peaceful conclusion. Regardless of the circumstances of life, God's children are assured of the special protection of their heavenly Father from the evil of the world in which they live. The wicked may turn the world upside down, but God will guard his own. He keeps them "safe" from the wicked, "from such people" (lit., "from this generation"; cf. 14:5 ["company"]; Prov 30:11–14; Matt 17:17). The word "generation" signifies here a group of people who live at the same time; i.e., contemporaries (KB^3, 1:209). The NEB expands the meaning: "from a profligate and evil generation." The Lord will "keep safe" and "protect" his children, as promised (Num 6:24–26).

8 God's guarding his people is a reality even when the wicked walk around as kings. When vv.1, 7–8 are read together as an inclusion, the comfort lies in God's protection from an evil generation that is, after all, characterized by human frailty. The repetition "sons of man" (NIV, "men," vv.1, 8) serves to emphasize that the wicked are mortal (cf. Isa 2:22). Therefore the hope of the psalmist lies in Yahweh, his covenant God (vv.1, 7). The psalm contains no resolution to the problem of evil, but it recognizes that evil is under the full sovereignty of the Lord. He will care for his children, because "the words of the Lord" are flawless (v.6).

Notes

7 (8 MT) The pronominal suffixes of the verbs are inconsistent: "you will keep them safe and protect him." Other Hebrew MSS give a consistent reading in the first person plural adopted by the NIV: "you will keep *us* safe and protect *us*" (cf. LXX).

Dahood's rendering of "O Eternal One" for זוּ לְעוֹלָם (*zû leʿôlām*, lit., "this, forever") is possible (*Psalms*, 1:75).

8 (9 MT) The last clause of this verse has occasioned difficulty. Dahood's proposed reading—"digging pits for the sons of man"—is in his own view "hypothetical" (*Psalms*, 1:75). The temporal usage of the participle כְּ (*k*ᵉ, "like") with the infinitive construct רֻם (*rum*, "be high") gives a satisfactory meaning: "when . . . is honored." Moreover, it forms a symmetric inclusion with vv.1–4 by contrasting the vanishing of godliness and the exaltation of evil. The NEB rendering brings this out: "The wicked flaunt themselves on every side, while profligacy stands high among mankind."

Psalm 13: Waiting for God's Salvation

The psalm, which is a deeply moving picture of despair and trust, realistically depicts the anguish of the soul yet is characteristic of a life of deep faith. The fourfold repetition "how long" (vv.1–2) emphasizes the intensity of emotions. The threefold prayer ("look . . . answer . . . give light," v.3) calms the psalmist down to the point where he concludes with a two-part song in the midst of darkness (vv.5–6). Delitzsch (1:199) expressed well the movement of the psalm:

> The Psalm consists of . . . three groups of decreasing magnitude. A long deep sigh is followed, as from a relieved breast, by an already much more gentle and half calm prayer; and this again by the believing joy which anticipates the certainty of being answered. This song as it were casts up constantly lessening waves, until it becomes still as the sea when smooth as a mirror, and the only motion discernible at last is that of the joyous ripple of calm repose.

The psalm is classified as an *individual lament* (see Odil Hannes Steck, "Beobachtungen zur Beziehung von Klage und Bitte in Psalm 13," *Biblische Notizen* 13 [1980]: 57–62), but it is also expressive of the needs of the community of God's people. The situation the psalmist speaks of that brings him to the point of despair may be illness.

The structure is simple and traces the development from despair to quietness, or, in the words of Luther, "hope despairs and yet despair hopes."

A. Expression of Despair: How Long? (vv.1–2)
B. Expression of Prayer: Give Me Light! (vv. 3–4)
C. Expression of Hope and Trust: Let Me Sing! (vv.5–6)

The literary approach of holistic interpretation espoused by Meir Weiss complements our structural analysis (*The Bible From Within. The Method of Total Interpretation* [Jerusalem: Magnes, 1984], pp. 298–314).

I. Expression of Despair: How Long?

13:1–2

For the director of music. A psalm of David.

1 How long, O LORD? Will you forget me forever?
How long will you hide your face from me?
2 How long must I wrestle with my thoughts
and every day have sorrow in my heart?
How long will my enemy triumph over me?

1–2 The depth of the emotions is seen in the repetition of "how long" (four times; cf. 6:3). David looked first at God as the source of his trouble, when he asked, "Will you forget me forever?" Here "forever" is used in the sense of "continually" (cf. 16:11, "eternal," NIV) or "utterly" (A.A. Anderson, 1:128; see NEB, "wilt thou quite forget me?"). The experience of divine alienation is unrelated to his being a sinner. There is no confession of sin, no contrition, and no recognition of personal guilt that keeps God's blessing away from the psalmist.

For some reason unknown to David, God has removed his covenant mercy from him (cf. 10:1, 11). The hiding of God's face is an anthropomorphic expression for alienation and curse (cf. 30:7; 44:24; 88:14). The shining of God's face signifies blessing (cf. Num 6:25–26; Pss 4:6; 31:16; 67:1; 80:3, 7, 19). The psalmist is alone, and suffering in loneliness aggravates the anguish. Where are the blessings of protection, grace, and peace promised by the Lord (Num 6:25–26)? The psalmist is disturbed within himself. He searches his thoughts as to what has happened. The English "counsels" or "thoughts" (NIV), like the Hebrew, may also connote "worry." Calvin wrote: "Especially, upon seeing that they are destitute of all resources, they torment themselves greatly, and are distracted by a multitude of thoughts; and in great dangers, anxiety and fear compel them to change their purposes from time to time" (1:183; see THAT, 1:751; Craigie, *Psalms 1–50,* p. 140).

The depth of the psalmist's being ("my heart," v.2) is nothing but "sorrow" (cf. 6:3). "Every day" is a good translation for *yômām* ("by day"). The Codex Alexandrinus and the Lucian recension of the LXX add "and night." It may well be that "by day" is a shortened idiom for "day and night" (1:2) and, hence, "every day" (NIV; cf. NEB, "day and night").

God is displeased, but why? When the psalmist turns to the people around him, he sees his enemy (v.2). The enemy is on the periphery of his concern (Westermann, *The Psalms,* pp. 61–62), and yet he is always there. Is the enemy death (so Dahood, *Psalms,* 1:77), the presence of evil in the world, or oppressors who have nearly "overcome him" (v.4; cf. 62:3)? There seems not to be sufficient reason for limiting the situation to illness and death, because the clause "sleep in death" (v.3) may be a metaphor for deep depression and suffering. The precise cause of suffering is obscure because the autobiographical context was less important than the prayer (cf. James L. Mays, "Psalm 13," Int 34 [1980]: 279–83). When the Lord has forgotten his covenant child, an opponent becomes a greater threat to that child's well-being. The smallest problem takes on greater significance. The psalmist is disturbed in his deepest being by God's lack of interest, by the adversaries (adversities), and by his own feelings.

Notes

For a brief discussion of the technical words and phrases in the superscription, see the Introduction.

2 (3 MT) The phrase עֵצוֹת בְּנַפְשִׁי (*ʿēṣô*t̲ *bᵉnap̱šî,* "the counsels in my soul"; NIV, "my thoughts") is often emended to עַצֶּבֶת (*ʿaṣṣeḇeṯ,* "grief") to provide a parallel for "sorrow" (v.2b; cf. BHS). Even though the LXX and ancient versions support the MT, the argument is put forward that intellectual activity ("thoughts," "counsels") is not usually associated with the soul, considered to be the seat of the emotions (cf. Craigie, *Psalms 1–50*, p. 140). Dahood's proposal ("how long must I place doubts in my soul," *Psalms*, 1:76–77) has not found acceptance. A more plausible meaning is "anguish" or "pain," a synonym of יָגוֹן (*yāḡôn*, "sorrow"; see THAT, 1:751).

II. Expression of Prayer: Give Me Light!

13:3–4

> [3] Look on me and answer, O LORD my God.
> Give light to my eyes, or I will sleep in death;
> [4] my enemy will say, "I have overcome him,"
> and my foes will rejoice when I fall.

3–4 The three imperatives ("look . . . answer. . . . Give light") present the psalmist's petition in sequence. He believes that God has hidden his face from him; therefore he asks, "Look on me" (v.3). The "look" of God is an indication of his gracious attitude (Isa 63:15). Divine abandonment and alienation made the psalmist experience despair, but God's "look," expressive of favor, renews life. Second, the psalmist asks for God to "answer" him. The answer is a positive message of God's favor by which the Lord frees his servant from the causes of the anguish of soul. Third, the psalmist believes that only by God's favor will he receive "light" for his eyes. This idiom expresses the effect of God's blessings. A man relieved from troubles and blessed with God's protection, peace, and favor shows his inner spiritual condition in his outward appearance (cf. 36:8–9; 1 Sam 14:27, 29). His eyes sparkle with God's grace. On the other hand, the experience of anguish is expressed by the dimness of the eyes (cf. 6:7; 38:10).

The psalmist's prayer contains an urgent appeal for God's covenant favor. If he were to be vexed and overcome by "death," the enemies would have cause to gloat (vv.3–4; cf. 35:19–21; 38:16–17). Their joy expressed not only pleasure in the fall of the godly but also in God's failure to be faithful to his covenant promises. "Death" need not be the separation from this life but may indicate the severity of the misfortune (cf. "when I fall," v.4b). The "fall" is a stumbling under a load too heavy to carry (38:17; cf. 10:10). When the feet "slip" (Deut 32:35), no psychological or spiritual reserve is left; and one can only look for greater troubles. Weiser comments, "His thought is dominated by one anxiety only, the anxiety that he might waver in his faith and lose confidence in God and so might provide for his adversaries the opportunity of gaining an easy victory" (p. 163). Before more trouble comes, and before the godless have reason to rejoice over the defeat of the godly, God must act to protect his honor. In another yet similar setting, Moses pleaded with the Lord to deal kindly with Israel, lest the nations have reason to argue against the power of Israel's God (Num 14:15–16).

III. Expression of Hope and Trust: Let Me Sing!

13:5–6

> [5] But I trust in your unfailing love;
> my heart rejoices in your salvation.
> [6] I will sing to the LORD,
> for he has been good to me.

5–6 Though he has experienced deep despair, the psalmist does not give up. His feet did not slip. He held on to the promise of God's covenant love: "your unfailing love" (*ḥeseḏ*). He is not overwhelmed by his troubles, but in his depression he says, "But I trust." The emphatic "But I" (v.5) is a surprising response from the heart of a depressed person. Because life may be so bitter for some, it is only by God's grace that the heart of faith may groan, "but I." Both v.5 and v.6 react to this confidence in the Lord's faithfulness to his promises by jussive and cohortative forms of the verbs: "Let my heart rejoice. . . . Let me sing" (see Dahood: "Let my heart rejoice. . . . Then shall I sing," *Psalms,* 1:76). The modal usage of the verbs appears to indicate the continuation of his prayer (vv.3–4). Thus we suggest that vv.5–6 be rendered: "But since I trust in your unfailing love, may my heart rejoice in your salvation, may I sing to the Lord, 'He has been good to me.'" Craigie writes, "The actual song of praise would burst forth once deliverance had been accomplished, but the knowledge that deliverance was coming created an anticipatory calm and sense of confidence" (*Psalms 1–50,* p. 143).

The effect of God's love for which the psalmist longs is the experience of salvation (v.5). "Salvation" (*yᵉšûāh,* see 3:2) signifies the *whole* well-being of God's child. He needs the assurance that God cares (v.1), as well as the experience of victory over enemy and the adverse circumstances (vv.2, 4). He also needs the healing in his thoughts of anguish and self-pity (v.2). God's "salvation" takes care of all his needs. He will rejoice in the Lord when God shows his fatherly care. "For he has been good [*gāmal*] to me" (v.6). The verb *gāmal* ("deal bountifully with," "reward"; NIV, "has been good") is fraught with meaning. Yahweh bestows his benefits, not in small measure, but in fullness, so as to give his children the experience of complete and free deliverance (116:7; 119:17). As Calvin states, "The word . . . signifies nothing else here than *to bestow a benefit from pure grace*" (1:187). In contrast to the enemies who rejoice in God's seeming absence and lack of care, the psalmist expects that the godly will ultimately rejoice in God's salvation.

Notes

5–6 (6–7 MT) On the variety of expressions of hope in lament psalms, see the excellent article by Yair Hoffman, "The Transition From Despair to Hope in the Individual Psalms of Lament," *Tarbiz* 55 (1985/86): 161–72 (Heb.).

6 (7 MT) Aare Lauha renders *g-m-l* with a positive element evoking thanksgiving: "he has accomplished his deed in my regard" ("'Dominus benefecit.' Die Wortwurzel *GML* und die Psalmenfrömmigkeit," ASTI 11 [1977/78]: 57–62); so also in 116:7; 142:7.

Psalm 14: God Deals With Foolish Evildoers

This psalm is parallel to Psalm 53. The language is similar except on a few points, which may be explained by the context in which each was finalized. For a discussion of the differences and the specific goal of each, see Psalm 53.

The genre has been disputed. Because of its affinity with the lament psalms against the wicked, it has been categorized as an *individual lament.* However, the contrast between the fool and the one with understanding is representative of the wisdom psalms (Robert A. Bennet, "Wisdom Motifs in Psalm 14 = 53—*nābāl* and *'ēṣāh,*" BASOR 220 [1975]: 15–21; see the appendix to Ps 1: The Ways of Wisdom and Folly). Another representative element is the *prophetic* motif, incorporated in a liturgical prayer. Among commentators there is no general agreement on the genre. Bellinger concludes in favor of a *communal lament*, in which the wisdom and prophetic style permeate the psalm (pp. 70–73). Sh. Weissblueth favors a more philosophical interpretation: the rejection of atheism (cf. 9:17 and 10:3–4; in "Psalm 14 and Its Parallel—Psalm 53," *Beth Mikra* 29 [1983/84]: 133–38 [Heb.]).

The date and authorship are difficult to determine. Those who hold to the Davidic origin often explain v.7 as a post-Davidic addition. Kidner considers the whole psalm as Davidic (1:80). Modern commentators generally posit a postexilic date; however, Craigie does not find the evidence convincing and believes that a preexilic date is likely (*Psalms 1–50*, p. 147). If the psalm is essentially Davidic, its original situation in David's life cannot be determined with accuracy.

The psalm may be divided into four sections in the following structure:

A. The Fool (v.1)
  B. The Lord's Perspective (vv.2–3)
  B′. The Prophetic Perspective (vv.4–6)
A′. The Hope of the Righteous (v.7)

I. The Fool

14:1

For the director of music. Of David.

1 The fool says in his heart,
  "There is no God."
They are corrupt, their deeds are vile;
  there is no one who does good.

1 The "fool" (*nāḇāl*) is neither ignorant nor an atheist. The word "fool" is synonymous with wicked (cf. TWOT, 2:547). It reflects the wisdom tradition where the "fool" aggressively and intentionally flouts his independence from God and his commandments (cf. 53:1; 74:18, 22). The wicked were fools when they acted corruptly, shamelessly (Deut 32:5–6), and in willful disregard for the ways of God. The opposite of "fool" is "wise," or one who understands (v.2). A portrayal of the evil nature and practices of the ungodly "fool" is given in Isaiah 32:4–7.

The denial of God is not an absolute denial of his existence. The pagans around Israel believed in many gods, and the impious in Israel did not rationalistically deny the historic and cultural links between the Lord and Israel. In his impudence the fool disregards God's expectations. God is not important in his life. He shuts off the affairs of this world from divine intervention and denies any personal accountability to God for his actions (cf. 10:4; 73:11; Jer 5:12; Zeph 1:12; Rom 1:28; see THAT, 2:27–28).

The "fool" is a man of convictions, expressing his innermost being in what he thinks ("says in his heart"). In his heart he denies the practical import of God's existence. Within the congregation he may mimic the sounds of faith, but his true self shows disregard for God, his commandments, and his people. He is characterized by an absence of concern or love for others (Craigie, *Psalms 1–50*, p. 147), but he is occupied with himself. He is a humanist/secularist, while holding on to the vestiges of theism. While he thinks "there is no God," he may express his impiety by immorality.

Three verbal phrases describe the perniciousness of the wicked. First, "they are corrupt" signifies the ruinous, destructive acts of the wicked (cf. Gen 6:12; Deut 4:16; Isa 1:4). Second, "their deeds are vile" refers to the detestable acts done out of complete disregard for the majesty of God's kingship and of his revealed law (cf. Ezek

16:49–52). Third, "there is no one who does good" (*ṭôḇ*), a general summary statement, shows the absence of godliness.

Immorality affects the fabric of any society; but within the covenant community of Israel, it affects all the people of God. In a hyperbolic way the psalmist laments the corruption, vileness, and absence of good (*ṭôḇ*) in the land. The corruption of mankind in Noah's time brought on God's judgment in the Flood (Gen 6:12). Now that corruption is prevalent among God's people, will God not judge? In a climactic way the author has set forth the depravity of man. He is "corrupt, . . . vile; there is no one who does good" (cf. Zeph 3:7). The fool ignores accountability to God and the moment of divine judgment (Rom 3:10–12).

Because many in Israel act corruptly, it seems as if the righteous are hidden among the thistles of the wicked (cf. Isa 59:4; 64:7; Jer 8:6). The description of the wicked in Psalm 10:3–11 is a fuller explication of the detestable practices of those who think that God does not see (10:11).

Notes

For a brief discussion of the technical words and phrases in the superscription, see the Introduction.

1 A foreign nation may be called foolish by its disregard for Israel's rights, customs, and the revelation of the Lord (Deut 32:21; NIV, "a nation that has no understanding"; cf. Ps 74:18). The change from singular ("the fool") to plural ("They are corrupt, . . . their deeds") is not unusual in Hebrew, as the word "fool" is a collective for all who act foolishly.

II. The Lord's Perspective

14:2–3

2 The LORD looks down from heaven
  on the sons of men
to see if there are any who understand,
  any who seek God.
3 All have turned aside,
  they have together become corrupt;
there is no one who does good,
  not even one.

2 The Lord sees his creation. The Creator-King looks down on his creatures and observes the affliction of his children (cf. 10:14; 11:4–5; 102:19–20). He "looks down" as witness and judge to observe the actions of mankind (*bᵉnê-'āḏām;* NIV, "sons of men"; cf. 11:4). The God who saw the corruption of man before the Flood (Gen 6:5), who came down to see man's united rebellion against the Creator-King at Babel (Gen 11:5), and who heard the outcry of evil at Sodom and Gomorrah (Gen 18:21) observes mankind to see whether there are wise people among the fools.

The wise are those "who understand [*maśkîl*] and seek [*dōrēš*] after God." The righteous are characterized by their love for God and adherence to his laws. They love to do the will of their covenant God on earth. The man with understanding (*maśkîl;* cf.

Prov 10:5; 16:20; 21:12) is a sharp contrast to the "fool." The wise is not only a man of understanding but one who acts in accordance to his understanding of the nature and revelation of the Lord (cf. TWOT, 1:282–84; 2:877–78). David was such a man (1 Sam 13:14; 16:7; 18:14–15). The wise, therefore, "seek God" (cf. 9:10) and live in accordance with God's absolute standards of holiness, purity, and justice (cf. 24:3–6). But they are often the objects of persecution, abuse, and affliction (vv.4–6). The Lord graciously looks down to see his children with the intent to deliver them (cf. 102:19). (For the problem of evil and theodicy, see Miller, "Psalm 14," *Interpreting the Psalms*, pp. 94–99.)

3 As God observes mankind, he is overwhelmed by the evil he sees. It seems as if "all have turned aside," have "become corrupt," and no one "does good." Again these are three verbal phrases (cf. v.1). The verb "turned aside" (*sār*) is a translation of the MT. Several MSS read with Psalm 53:3 "became apostate" (*sāg*). The verbs are functionally synonymous, and it is impossible to prove which is more original. Briggs suggests that both were in the original and that in time one copyist took one verb and another took the other (1:110). The NIV adopts the same translation in 14:3 and in 53:3: "they have together become corrupt."

It seems as if mankind in totality ("together"), as in the days of Babel (Gen 11:1–9), has "become corrupt" (cf. Job 15:16). The negative picture of the fool (v.1) is reinforced by the totality of human evil: "all," "together," and "no one" (two times). Mankind has become apostate because it has "turned aside" (cf. 53:3). "Become corrupt" (*ne'ᵉlāḥû*) only occurs here, in the parallel passage (53:3), and in Job 15:16. The meaning is derived from Arabic ("to make sour," of milk; KB^3, 1:53).

The apostle Paul quoted from vv.1–3 as a part of a string of OT quotations (Pss 5:9; 140:3; 10:7; Isa 59:7–8; Ps 36:1) to demonstrate that mankind at large is "under sin" (Rom 3:11–18). Several MSS of the LXX add Romans 3:13–18 in between v.3 and v.4. Briggs has correctly explained the addition as a Christian interpolation (1:104).

Notes

3–4 Craigie (*Psalms 1–50*, p. 144) sets these lines off with quotation marks as an oracle from God but admits that only v.4a may be God's reaction to man's corruption. Such marks are unnecessary if the psalmist takes a prophetic role as he reflects on God's word (cf. A.A. Anderson, 1:130–31; Bellinger, pp. 70–73).

III. The Prophetic Perspective

14:4–6

4 Will evildoers never learn—
those who devour my people as men eat bread
and who do not call on the LORD?
5 There they are, overwhelmed with dread,
for God is present in the company of the righteous.
6 You evildoers frustrate the plans of the poor,
but the LORD is their refuge.

4–6 The Lord is the "refuge" (*maḥsēh*) of the wise (v.6), who are called "my people" (v.4), "the company of the righteous" (v.5), and "the poor" (v.6). The fools are not numbered among them because they are "evildoers" who do not "know" (*yāḏᵉʿû;* NIV, "learn"). They do not know the Lord intimately nor do they care about his looking down from heaven. They busily pursue their self-interests and, in so doing, "devour" God's people. Their hatred of righteousness and the vulnerability of the righteous combine to make the wise easy prey (cf. Isa 3:14–15; Mic 3:1–3). The appetite of the godless is insatiable (cf. Isa 9:20–21). They "devour" the possessions of others and add them to their own, completely disregarding the rights of their subjects (cf. Isa 5:8). The people of Isaiah's day likewise had no knowledge (NIV, "understanding," 5:13; cf. 1:3) of God's judgment to come. They ate and satisfied their appetites for a moment, but they did not return to the Lord. They expressed no remorse, no recognition of his judgment, and no request for mercy.

Suddenly, God's judgment will come on the wicked. The power and terrorizing of the wicked will come to an end when the Lord intervenes on behalf of his "people" (v.4), who are "the company of the righteous" (*dôr ṣaddîq,* v.5). Then "dread" will overtake (*pāḥᵃḏû p̱āḥaḏ*) the fools, while the righteous enjoy the presence of their covenant God. Yes, the Lord is with his own, even when it seems as if he is far from them. The wicked may for a time heap abuse on "the plans of the poor." But even in their persecution, God is "the refuge" of his children.

Notes

4 For a refutation of Dahood's rendering "Devour the grain they did not harvest" (1:80), see Craigie (*Psalms 1–50,* pp. 144–45).

5 The particle שָׁם (*šām,* "there") at the beginning of v.5 indicates that an important event is about to take place (cf. 36:12 [13 MT; NIV, "see"]; 66:5 [6 MT; NIV, "come"]; 68:27 [28 MT; NIV, "there"]). Dahood proposes that *šumma* ("behold") in the El Amarna tablets with the meaning "behold" best explains the idiom (1:81; cf. Judg 5:11 [untr. in NIV]; 1 Sam 4:4 ["there," NIV]; 7:6 ["there"]; Ps 66:6 ["come," NIV]; cf. Briggs, 1:110).

The word דּוֹר (*dôr*), usually translated as "generation," may signify "company" or "assembly" (cf. Frank J. Neuberg, "An Unrecognized Meaning of Hebrew *Dôr,*" JNES 9 [1950]: 215–17; KB³, 1:209; Dahood, *Psalms,* 1:82).

6 Dahood proposes "The council of the poor will humiliate it," emending the MT תָּבִישׁוּ (*tāḇîšû,* "frustrate") to *tôḇîšû* ("humiliate," 1:80). The NIV adds "evildoers" to make clear that "you" is not mistakenly read as a reference to God. It may be that the word "plans" (*ʿᵃṣaṯ,* from *ʿēṣāh,* "counsel," "plan") has the meaning of "worry" as in 13:3 (NIV, "thoughts"). This supports Eaton's rendering "In the anguish of the poor you shall meet your downfall, for the Lord is his refuge" (p. 55). Delitzsch gave a modal reading: "Would ye bring to shame the counsel of the afflicted" (1:202; so also J. Ridderbos, 1:111)! Craigie proposes, in his words, a "possible solution, though fairly radical": "*There they caused great fear,* but God is in the assembly of the righteous. *The counsel of the poor they confounded,* but the Lord is his refuge" (*Psalms 1–50,* p. 145). For "poor" see 9:12.

IV. The Hope of the Righteous

14:7

7 Oh, that salvation for Israel would come out of Zion!

When the LORD restores the fortunes of his people,
let Jacob rejoice and Israel be glad!

7 It may be that this verse is an inspired addition to the psalm, a prayer for the redemption of God's people at a time of national disaster, possibly the Exile. The conclusion is a most appropriate prayer for "salvation" (*yᵉšû'āh,* see 3:2). The phraseology "restore the fortunes" is characteristic of the prophets as they describe the era of restoration when Israel, restored to the land, will again enjoy the blessings ("the fortunes") of God (cf. Ezek 16:53; Zeph 2:7). When God's people see the acts of God's redemption, they rejoice. After the Exile God demonstrated his faithfulness by his blessings, by restoring Israel to the land, and by permitting his temple to be rebuilt. The psalmist anticipates an era when God will vindicate his people and deliver them from the fools who oppress and harass them. In Jesus' coming Jews and Gentiles are further assured of God's concern, vindication, and presence with his people. When the Jews are restored to faith in Jesus the Messiah, they will rejoice and all Christians will join with them in giving praise to God's faithfulness (cf. Rom 11:33–36). The redemption of Zion is also referred to by Isaiah (59:20) and quoted by Paul (Rom 11:26).

Notes

7 The phrase בְּשׁוּב שְׁבוּת (*bᵉšûḇ šᵉḇûṯ,* "when . . . restores the fortunes") is an example of a cognate accusative from *šûḇ: šᵉḇûṯ*. The word *šᵉḇûṯ* signifies "restoration" and is not related to the root *š-b-h* ("take captive"), as suggested by the NKJV: "when the LORD brings back the captivity of His people" (cf. 85:1; 126:1 [cf. NIV mg.]; Dahood, *Psalms,* 3:218; TWOT, 2:896; John M. Bracke, "*šûḇ šᵉḇûṯ:* A Reappraisal," ZAW 97 [1985]: 233–44). Gray (pp. 110–16) argues in favor of "restoration" as "rehabilitation."

Psalm 15: Who May Live in God's Presence?

The psalm begins with a question and concludes with God's promise. The question-and-answer method, coupled with the concluding promise, suggests that the psalm is a *wisdom* psalm (so also Dahood, *Psalms,* 1:83). Other exegetes treat it in a liturgical fashion. J.L. Koole connects it with a royal covenant renewal, relating it to 2 Kings 11:12 ("Psalm XV—Eine königliche Einzugsliturgie," *OudTestamentische Studiën* 13 [1963]: 98–111). A.A. Anderson defines the genre as an "entrance liturgy" (1:135). Weiser advances a strong argument in favor of a liturgical reading (pp. 167–68) and shows sensitivity to the emphasis on social ethics expected of the righteous (p. 169). The tension between liturgical/cultic and ethical may be resolved if the psalm, originating in Israel's cult, developed in Israel's wisdom tradition. (See the appendix to Ps 1: The Ways of Wisdom and Folly.)

The narrow question of what God requires of the pilgrims was broadened to include what God expects of *all* who desire to live in his blessed presence. Two other passages have a bearing on this thesis. Psalm 24:3 also contains the double interrogative "Who? . . . Who?" and answers the questions in a cultic way: ritual purity and abstinence from idolatry are requisites for entering into God's presence. A separation from the liturgical/cultic usage is also found in Isaiah 33:14–16. Isaiah, likewise, begins with a twofold "who" and answers it by stressing the requirement of righteous living, similar to our psalm, and concludes with a promise (v.16). The similarity between Psalm 15 and Isaiah 33:14–16, with its emphasis on righteous living and promise, favors the designation of Psalm 15 as a *wisdom psalm.*

The structure of Psalm 15 is as follows:

A. The Question (v.1)
B. The Response (vv.2–5a)
C. The Promise (v.5b)

For a careful analysis and interaction of proposed structural divisions, see Pierre Auffret, "Essay sur la Structure Littéraire du Psaume XV," VetTest 31 (1981): 385–99; Lloyd M. Barré, "Recovering the Literary Structure of Psalm xv," VetTest 34 (1984): 205–10. Levenson has favored us with a fine treatment of this psalm in relation to Zion theology (pp. 172–76). He writes, "The ascent to Mount Zion is a question of increasing ethical perfection as well as geography" (p. 173).

I. The Question

15:1

A psalm of David.

1 LORD, who may dwell in your sanctuary?
Who may live on your holy hill?

1 The repetition of the interrogative particle "who" is not so much a question of the *identity* of those entering into God's presence as it is of *what kind* of a person may enjoy his fellowship. The verbs "dwell" and "live" are synonyms connoting a temporary residence and may be interpreted metaphorically for communion with God. Calvin views it this way: "The meaning of his discourse, to express it in a few words, is this, that those only have access to God who are his genuine servants, and who live a holy life" (1:205). In contrast, the psalmist uses the verbs "dwell" and "stand" to say that the wicked are excluded from fellowship with God (5:4–5). This accessibility is best expressed by the ancient Near Eastern image of hospitality to strangers. In this case the question is "Who may be a guest in your tent?" (cf. Briggs, 1:113; Dahood, *Psalms,* 1:83, or NEB, "Who may lodge in thy tabernacle?").

The complementary usage of "sanctuary" and "your holy hill" suggests the background of a pilgrimage to Mount Zion, God's holy hill. There David had first placed a tent for the ark of the covenant (cf. 2 Sam 6:1–19). On that site the tent was later replaced by the magnificent temple of Solomon. The word "sanctuary" (*'ōhel,* "tent") is a technical term for the tabernacle of God among Israel. (See the appendix to Ps 132: The Ark of the Covenant and the Temple: Symbols of Yahweh's Presence and Rule.)

The presence of God was centralized, in the OT and in Jesus' time, in the tabernacle (temple). The institutions of the tabernacle and the priesthood symbolized God's presence among his people. The people were responsible to prepare themselves to meet with God in Jerusalem during the three great pilgrimage festivals (Passover, Firstfruits, and Booths). As the pilgrims approached Jerusalem—the city of God, where his "sanctuary" was located on the "holy hill"—they had to examine themselves before entering the courts of God's sanctuary.

Of course, the significance of the psalm is broader than that suggested by Gunkel and others. They limit it to an "entrance" or "priestly" liturgy (Eichrodt, TOT, 1:278) in which the pilgrims ask the priests about the requisite preparations for entering the sanctuary. As a wisdom psalm its purpose is to guide God's people into a life of holiness, justice, and righteousness so that they may live in the presence of God, wherever they may reside.

The conclusion—"He who does these things will never be shaken" (v.5b)—confirms the thesis that the psalmist calls for a response of godliness as the way of wisdom. The reward of wisdom is God's pleasure, presence, and blessing in life (cf. Ps 1). The question "who may dwell" received greater significance when Jesus told the woman of Samaria that God is not worshiped in Jerusalem or on Mount Gerizim but at any place where his people come into his presence "in spirit and in truth" (John 4:23–24). The fundamental requirements of holiness, spirituality, and fidelity for anyone who desires to live in the shadow of the Almighty are put before us in this psalm (cf. 61:4).

Notes

For a brief discussion of the technical words and phrases in the superscription, see the Introduction.

1 On "Zion" see the appendix to Ps 46: Zion Theology.

On the "tent" in Israelite and Canaanite traditions, see Richard J. Clifford, "The Tent of El and the Israelite Tent of Meeting," CBQ 33 (1971): 221–27.

II. The Response

15:2–5a

2 He whose walk is blameless
and who does what is righteous,
who speaks the truth from his heart
3 and has no slander on his tongue,
who does his neighbor no wrong
and casts no slur on his fellow man,
4 who despises a vile man
but honors those who fear the LORD,
who keeps his oath
even when it hurts,
5 who lends his money without usury
and does not accept a bribe against the innocent.

2–5a The positive and negative requirements are given as guidelines for self-examination of one's heart. Mowinckel (*Psalms,* 1:179) and, more recently, Craigie (*Psalms 1–50,* pp. 150–51) have proposed that a total of ten positive and negative conditions are set forth in a structure of four categories:

A. Three positive conditions (v.2)
A′. Three negative conditions (v.3)

B. Two positive conditions (v.4)
B′. Two negative conditions (v.5a)

It is questionable whether this is the intent of the psalmist. First, the nature of parallelism requires that the colons be read in relation to one another and not independently. For example, v.2b ("speaks the truth") seems to balance v.3a ("has no slander") in the Hebrew text. Second, whereas the number ten may be symbolic, the conditions are far from complete. The moral law as summarized in the Ten Commandments is only partially represented. The prohibitions against idolatry, divorce, stealing, and murder are not included; nor is the honoring of one's parents. Third, those listings (Ps 24:4–5; Isa 33:14–15) containing similar and different requirements clearly show evidence of parallelism:

Ps 24:

4a. clean hands	b. pure heart
c. no idolatry	d. no falsehood (=idolatry)

Isa 33:

15a. walks righteously	b. speaks what is right
c. rejects extortion	d. does not accept bribes
e. stops his ears against the plots of murder	f. shuts his eyes against contemplating evil

Thus the author of our psalm puts before the godly *representative* expectations of wise living. He assumes the Decalogue as the absolute standard and develops the requirements based on Israel's apodictic laws (Walter C. Kaiser, Jr., *Toward an Old Testament Ethics* [Grand Rapids: Zondervan, 1983], pp. 81, 112–26).

The standard of holiness is summarily represented by key words and representative commandments to evoke a *holistic* response of godliness. The wise are characterized as being "blameless," "righteous," and "faithful" ("truth," NIV). A.A. Anderson distinguishes the requirement of v.2 as the actual response and views the conditions of vv.3–5b as representative examples (1:137).

The psalmist refrains from giving a list of ceremonial requirements. This would be expected if the psalm were an entrance liturgy. But we have seen that his concern is with the encouragement of wisdom; hence, the conditions for wise living are representative. The sage, or wise man, is primarily characterized by the word "blameless" (*tāmîm*). He is a man of integrity in relationship to God and man. In his personal relations, blamelessness finds expression in a righteous and faithful life style.

The "blameless" walk is the manner of life characterized by integrity. The word *tāmîm* signifies a moral way of life. It is not synonymous with "perfect" but with an attitude of the heart desirous of pleasing God (cf. 18:24; 101:2, 6; 119:1; Matt 5:48; Eph 1:4; Col 1:22). Noah was such a man (Gen 6:8), as was Abraham (Gen 17:1). The walk of integrity was required both before the Flood and before the law was revealed at Sinai. Regardless of what God requires, the blameless man does God's will on earth. Such a man is blessed by the Lord (84:11–12).

The words "righteous" (*ṣeḏeq*) and faithful (*'ᵉmeṯ;* NIV, "truth") in Hebrew are synonymous with "blameless." Righteousness is a dynamic term describing God or man in his relations with man. The righteous man *does* what is right; he lives in accordance with God's expectations (see 4:1). The phrase "truth from his heart" reveals the fidelity between the "heart," as the seat of one's being, and the speech ("who speaks"), which expresses one's inner being. The wise man is a man of integrity in all his relationships and activities. For a contrast, see 12:2.

The activities of walking, doing, and speaking are participial forms. As we observed in Psalm 1:1, the three activities are not to be isolated as separate expressions of the righteous path but express synthetically that everything the wise man does is in harmony with the expectations of God and man. There is no guile in him (cf. John 1:47). Calvin wrote, "But he describes the approved servants of God, as distinguished and known by the fruits of righteousness which they produce" (1:206).

The three negative conditions give examples of what a blameless man does not do (v.3; cf. 1:1–2). The idiom for "slander on his tongue" is unique in the OT. The verb "slander" (*rāḡal*, "gossip," Qal pattern) occurs usually in the Piel with the meaning "spy out." Briggs (1:116) suggests that it may have the meaning "play the spy," whereas Dahood translates it, "He who does not trip over his tongue" (1:83). There is no reason to deviate from the traditional meaning (cf. NIV; see also 2 Sam 19:27). The point is clear that the wise man does not slander (gossip; cf. 5:9; James 3:3–8).

The word for "neighbor" (*rēaʿ*, "comrade," "friend") is somebody with whom one frequently associates. The wicked had no sense of loyalty and laid traps for anyone to fall into (10:2). The wise man does not purposely hurt his fellow man, let alone his friend. The argument goes from the general to the more specific as the psalmist explicates the nature of the godly man. He is a man of fidelity (v.2). The words "neighbor" and "wrong" contain a wordplay in Hebrew: *rēaʿ* and *rāʿāh*.

The word for "slur" (*ḥerpāh*, "reproach") together with the verb *nāśā'* ("lift up," cf. 69:7; Jer 15:15; Zeph 3:18) forms an idiom: "casts a slur." The wise man neither initiates nor rejoices in the reproach of his associates. He empathizes in their hurt. Calvin goes a step further in applying it to a receptivity to gossip: "But I think there is also here rebuked the vice of undue credulity, which, when any evil reports are spread against our neighbours, leads us either eagerly to listen to them, or at least to receive them without sufficient reason" (1:207).

The antithetical parallelism contrasts the wise man's reaction to the "vile man" and to "those who fear the LORD" (v.4). The "vile man" (*nim'ās*, "rejected," "scorned," a participial form, Niphal of the root *m-'-s*, "reject") is a "reprobate," known for his evil deeds. The godly are not free to despise any sinner, only those who are hardened in their perversities.

The reason for the wise man's concern lies in his deep respect for others. He "honors those who fear the LORD." In his self-respect he respects the rights, gifts, and status of others. He sees no need for acting in a destructive way in order to express jealousy, judgmentalism, or power. He loves his neighbor as himself (Lev 19:18; cf. Matt 22:39–40). Therefore he habitually neither hurts nor casts slurs on his fellow men (cf. NEB, "who never wrongs a friend and tells no tales against his neighbour"). Yet he is not naïve. He ably distinguishes between those who fear the Lord and those who are reprobates. The "vile man" knows no other way than evil and mischief. He is not the occasional offender who needs restoration (cf. Gal 6:1). Instead, he is determined in his way. The righteous exercises care in his relations with the reprobates. Even when the reprobates exalt themselves (10:2–7), the wise man does not look for their favors. They are unreliable!

When he promises, makes a vow, or swears to do something, the wise man remains true to his word (cf. Eccl 5:1–7; Matt 5:33–37). He has a deep sense of integrity and must often make material sacrifices to be honest. His honor is more important than his wallet. This is brought out more fully in v.5a.

The wise man's concern for people shows up also in his relationship to the poor and those who need justice (v.5). The poor at times needed a loan to keep themselves from being sold into slavery. The idiom "lends his money" (lit., "his silver he does not give") refers to the practice of giving silver as an ancient equivalent for money-lending.

"Usury" was the practice of charging high interest on business loans. According to the law, the Israelite was not to take advantage of the adversities of a fellow Israelite who had fallen on hard times (Exod 22:25–27; Lev 25:35–36; Deut 23:19). Usury was prohibited because of the need of the poor not to get *further* into debt and because of the ancient Near Eastern practice of high interest rates, as much as 50 percent (cf. "Interest," ZPEB, 3:295)! The Israelite was to have regard for his fellow Israelites.

Often the poor were also cast into court and taken advantage of by the well-to-do, who could easily afford to pay a bribe to thwart justice. Bribery was strictly prohibited in the law (cf. Exod 23:8; Deut 16:19). The godly witness or judge should refuse any bribe as being a perversion of justice. Dahood goes beyond this in suggesting that "innocent" should be translated "hungry" (based on Amos 4:6) and that the word for "bribe" be given the broader meaning "compensation": "nor accept compensation from the hungry" (*Psalms*, 1:83–85). Although the law clearly prohibits usury and bribery, it does not, however, prohibit receiving an equitable compensation. Moreover, the legal aspect of the regulations of vv.4b–5a inclines the balance in favor of the usual legal meaning of "innocent" (over against Dahood).

The prophets did not spare words in condemning the practice of bribery (cf. Isa 1:23; 5:23; Amos 5:11–15). The godly person does not discriminate against the poor in favor of the rich, powerful, and influential.

Notes

2 "From his heart" is a good translation of בִּלְבָבוֹ (*bilᵉḇāḇô*) because the preposition *bᵉ* ("in") may denote "from" (cf. Dahood, *Psalms*, 1:83). See the note on "double heart" as expressive of the hypocrisy of the wicked (12:2).

4 The second part of v.4 remains difficult. The literal sense cannot be right: "who swears to do evil and does not change." The LXX and ancient versions read "to do evil" as "to his neighbor" (for the similarity of the words, see comment on "neighbor" in v.3 above). Dahood proposes that the preposition לְ (*lᵉ*, "to") may carry the sense of separation "from" or, here, "not to." "He swore to do no wrong" (*Psalms*, 1:83–84; id., "Note on Psalm 15,4 [14,4]," CBQ 16 [1954]: 302). I agree with A.A. Anderson (1:139) that Dahood's suggestion is not satisfactory and that it is preferable to interpret the sense of the MT, as the NIV does; see NEB, "who swears to his own hurt and does not retract."

4–5 For a study of the poetic balance, see Patrick D. Miller, Jr., "Poetic Ambiguity and Balance in Psalm XV," VetTest 29 (1979): 416–24.

III. The Promise

15:5b

He who does these things
will never be shaken.

5b The reward of God ensures that the wise man will "dwell" with the Lord (v.1; cf. 23:6). He may experience adversities, but he will never fall (cf. 37:31), as will the wicked (1:4–6; 9:17; 37:36). He will never be "shaken" (cf. 16:8). This is God's promise. Clearly the ethics of God's people are not a system of morality independent of the Lord but have a theological basis (see Eckart Otto, "Kultus und Ethos in Jerusalemer Theologie: Ein Beitrag zur theologischen Begründigung der Ethik im Alten Testament," ZAW 98 [1986]: 161–79). This is also our Lord's emphasis in the Sermon on the Mount (Matt 5–7).

Psalm 16: Refuge in the Lord

The confession of *confidence* in God exemplifies a deep trust in the Lord in both life and death. The life-setting of Psalm 16 is difficult to determine, as the psalmist speaks of his condition in general terms. A variety of opinions exists on the origin of the psalm: an expression of devotion to the Lord by a Levitical priest (Kraus, *Psalmen*, 1:119–20); a profession of faith by a Canaanite convert to Yahwism (Dahood, *Psalms*, 1:87); and a confession of confidence in the midst of crisis (Craigie, *Psalms 1–50*, p. 156). Because of these opinions and the indecisiveness of the data, the psalm may at least be viewed as a composition made during a time of peace and quiet. This fits the beginning of David's regime, before the surrounding nations challenged his sovereignty (so J. Ridderbos, 1:126); but see Johannes Lindblom for a date c. 500 B.C. ("Erwägungen zur Psalm XVI," VetTest 24 [1974]: 187–95). The general reference to the wicked and the expectation of death are arguments in favor of an early date.

The focus of the psalmist is on the Lord and all his benefits. He celebrates the goodness of God that he has experienced in life. It may be that he reflects on past troubles, but the thrust is on his confidence in the Lord with respect to the future. He begins with a prayer (v.1), expresses confidence in the Lord (vv.2–4) because of all his benefits (vv.5–8), and rejoices in the expectation of a continued walk on "the path of life" (vv.9–11). The divisions of the psalm follow this progression of the argument. The psalm reveals an inner structure:

A. Confidence in the Lord (vv.1–4)
  B. The Experience of Faith (vv.5–6)
A′. Confidence in the Lord (vv.7–8)
  B′. The Experience of Faith (vv.9–11)

This structure highlights the focus on the Lord and the dynamic experience of his sovereign beneficence. The various expressions of God's goodness (vv.5–6, 9–11) are synthetic to bring out his benefits in both life and death:

v.5a	food and drink	v.9	body secure
v.5b	lot	v.10	grave
v.6a	pleasant places	v.11a	path of life
v.6b	delightful inheritance	v.11b	joy and pleasure

The quotation of vv.8–11 in Acts 2:25–28 and of v.10 in Acts 13:35 (cf. LXX) makes this psalm especially dear to Christians, for it anticipates the resurrection of our Lord (see exposition below). Long before Christ's advent, the psalmist is confident in the quality of life assured by God's presence both now and in the world to come. Such confidence is further guaranteed by the resurrection of our Lord. The life of the believer before Christ was good, but it is even better since the coming of the Messiah!

I. Confidence in the Lord

16:1–4

A *miktam* of David.

1 Keep me safe, O God,
for in you I take refuge.

2 I said to the LORD, "You are my Lord;
apart from you I have no good thing."
3 As for the saints who are in the land,
they are the glorious ones in whom is all my delight.
4 The sorrows of those will increase
who run after other gods.
I will not pour out their libations of blood
or take up their names on my lips.

1 The psalm opens with words of trust in God (El), who alone is able to give shelter. The expectation of safe-keeping is grounded in God's promise to keep and to guard the members of the covenant community who seek "refuge" in him (cf. 7:1; 11:1; 17:7) as an indication of his presence. The psalmist does not clearly state whether the particular occasion is the actions of the godless (v.4) or personal sickness (v.10).

2 The psalmist approaches God as "my Lord" (*Adonai*) and as "my good" (NIV, "I have no good thing"). The designation "my Lord" reveals the psalmist's submission to him as "Master" and "Ruler" (see 8:1) over against those who run after other gods (v.4). Hence his confidence is in God's care for him. He further describes his relationship to his God as the source of all his benefits (cf. 23:6; 73:25). The sovereign God is "my good," i.e., the reason for his existence and joy (cf. v.11). Weiser contends, "The relation to God dominates the whole of human life because God lays claim to the whole man" (p. 173). The spirit of joy and confidence in God's sovereign care is also stated in 73:25: "Whom have I in heaven but you? / And earth has nothing I desire besides you" (cf. v.26).

3 Delight in God also finds expression in a joyful acceptance of "the saints" (*q^e^ḏôšîm*). The "saints who are in the land" are the godly who live on earth, over against angelic beings who are "heavenly." The godly are "saints" (cf. 34:9) in that they are consecrated to the Lord (cf. Exod 19:6). The identity of "the saints" has given rise to many proposals: Canaanite deities (Dahood, *Psalms,* 1:87), Levitical priests (Kraus, *Psalmen,* 1:121), pagan priests (NIV mg.), pagan deities (A.A. Anderson, 1:142; Craigie, *Psalms 1–50,* p. 157), and the godly (Calvin, 1:219; J. Ridderbos, 1:127; and NIV).

Another issue in determining the meaning of the term "the saints" is the identity of "the glorious ones." The "saints" are also known as "the glorious ones," as the Lord himself bestows glory and majesty on his own. He is the glorious One (8:1, 9; 93:1, 4). The psalmist thus expresses the importance of the community of the saints. Calvin writes, "We ought, therefore, highly to value and esteem the true and devoted servants of God, and to regard nothing as of greater importance than to connect ourselves with their society; and this we will actually do if we wisely reflect in what true excellence and dignity consist, and do not allow the vain splendour of the world and its deceitful pomps to dazzle our eyes" (1:219; cf. 119:63).

The psalmist's love for the Lord and the godly is contrasted with his attitude toward the ungodly. The idolatrous Israelites and pagans zealously devoted themselves to their gods by making offerings, but God's judgment would come on them (32:10). He would increase their anguish (cf. NEB, "those who run after them find trouble without end"). God would not deliver them from their troubles (32:10) but instead would increase the intensity of adversity.

4 The ungodly's idolatrous acts are further described as pouring of "libations of blood" and swearing by the names of the idols. The exact nature of the cultic practices is unclear. The prepositional phrase "of blood" may refer to human sacrifices (Isa 57:5–6) or to guilt due to bloodshed (Isa 1:15; 66:3). However the phrase may be interpreted, the psalmist strongly states his antipathy to idolatrous practices. Paganism is a way of life completely inconsistent with trust in God as the sovereign Master. The psalmist makes no mention of their idols, in keeping with his declaration that he will not "take up their names" on his lips (cf. Hos 2:17). He rejects and shows disdain for the alleged powers of the numerous pagan deities. Delitzsch writes, "The expression of his abhorrence attains its climax: even their names . . . he shuns taking upon his lips" (1:224).

Notes

For a brief discussion of the technical words and phrases in the superscription, see the Introduction.

1 The reference "O God" is often found in the Elohistic psalter (42–83), and Ps 16 may have belonged there. One factor in favor of an original place in the Elohistic psalter is the corpus of *miktam* psalms (56–60). Psalm 16, as a *miktam* psalm, stands by itself. On the other hand, the frequent address of the Deity as "LORD" (Yahweh, vv.2, 5, 7–8) is appropriate for its present place in the Yahwistic psalter (1–41).

2–4 There are significant problems in these verses that have a direct bearing on the exposition of the text.

2 The MT's אָמַרְתְּ (*'āmart*, "you [fem. suffix] said") was read as "I said" in the ancient versions. Dahood takes it as a Phoenician form of "I said" (*Psalms*, 1:87). Craigie, however, brackets vv.2–3 as a quotation from the person with whom the psalmist is in dialogue (*Psalms 1–50*, pp. 154–55). He suggests that two separate views are given: the syncretistic view, quoted in vv.2–3, and that of the psalmist (vv.4–5). A number of MSS of the LXX and the Syriac have the first person ("I said"), and this seems to fit best (so NIV).

The translation of בַּל (*bal*) as "not" (Joüon, par. 160m) renders an incomprehensible statement: "my good is not on you." The particle may have an affirmative meaning (cf. R.T. O'Callaghan, "Echoes of Canaanite Literature in the Psalms," VetTest 4 [1954]: 164–76), giving the translation "my good certainly is on you" (cf. A.A. Anderson, 1:142; Craigie, *Psalms 1–50*, p. 155; C.F. Whitley, "The Positive Force of the Hebrew Particle בל," ZAW 84 [1972]: 213–19). The phrase בַּל־עָלֶיךָ (*bal-'āleyk̲ā*, "not apart from you") may be a corruption of בַּל־בִלְעָדֶיךָ (*bal-bil'ād̲eyk̲ā*, "not without you"; cf. Briggs, 1:123; BHS). The NIV adopts this emendation, of which Briggs wrote, "The simpler idea that the psalmist is entirely dependent on Yahweh, the source of all good, for his welfare, and cannot prosper without divine favour, is much more probable" (1:119). Dahood reads the preposition "on" as "above"—"there is none above you"—but takes "my good" as a divine epithet: "my Lord, my Good" (*Psalms,* 1:86–87). Briggs (1:123) has argued against the possibility of "above" (as suggested by Dahood and Delitzsch, 1:220).

3 "The glorious ones" is in construct: וְאַדִּירֵי (*wᵉ'addîrê,* "and the glorious ones of"). Craigie emends the phrase by deleting "and" and by reading the final yod as a pronominal suffix: "my mighty ones" (*Psalms 1–50,* pp. 153, 155). Dahood takes the following phrase as a genitive of relation: "and the mighty ones in whom was all my delight" (*Psalms,* 1:86, 88; cf. GKC, par. 130d). Based on the LXX some emend the text to read as a verb, יַאְדִּיר (*yā'dîr,* "he [Yahweh] will be glorious"; cf. Briggs: "[Yahweh] makes wonderful all his good pleasures in them," 1:117, 124; cf. Kraus, *Psalmen,* 1:119; BHS). The NEB (cf. A.A. Anderson, 1:142) emends the phrase to *wa'ᵃrûrîm* ("and cursed"; cf. BHS): "and cursed are all who make them their delight." The variety of emendations and suggestions is aggravated by the ambiguity of the MT. For purposes of exposition, the NIV reading makes sense and is possible.

4 The meaning of מָהָרוּ (*māhārû*) is obscure. The NIV assumes an emendation of a Piel for a Qal: "run after." The absence of a Qal of the root *m-h-r,* I—other than a unique homonym (*m-h-r,* II: "to pay the bride-price," Exod 22:16)—has given rise to emendations and proposals. Dahood explains the verb as a form of the root *h-r-r,* "to lust" (*Psalms,* 1:88); but Craigie has objected to it as lacking "strong support" in Ugaritic texts (*Psalms 1–50,* p. 155). Instead, he takes the more general meaning "acquire" of *m-h-r,* II: "they have acquired another [god]" (ibid., p. 154). BHS gives several other proposals (see also Briggs, 1:124). A complicating factor is the adjective אַחֵר (*'āḥēr,* "another"). The NIV interprets it as "other gods," but the bicolon is most problematic in the MT. There is no satisfactory solution. At best the interpreter can venture to bring out cautiously the "spirit" of the text, as Calvin does: "But the meaning . . . brings out the spirit of the passage, namely, that unbelievers . . . not only lose what is thus expended, but also heap up for themselves sorrows upon sorrows, because at last the issue will be miserable and ruinous to them" (1:222).

II. The Experience of Faith

16:5–6

5 LORD, you have assigned me my portion and my cup;
you have made my lot secure.
6 The boundary lines have fallen for me in pleasant places;
surely I have a delightful inheritance.

5–6 The psalmist has demonstrated his abhorrence of idolatry. He declared that he would not join in with those who poured out a drink offering. Instead, he recognizes how good the Lord is to his own. Loyalty to the Lord is in response to his acts of beneficence. Using the language reminiscent of the conquest of Canaan ("portion," "lot," "boundary lines," "inheritance"), the psalmist reflects on all that the Lord has done. However, he goes beyond the occupation of Canaan by Israel in considering God's benefits to him. The Lord promised to the members of the priesthood to be their share and inheritance (Num 18:20; Deut 10:9; 18:1). Israel as a whole was his inheritance (Jer 12:7–9). But the godly can join in with the experience of the psalmist, wherever and whenever they live. God deals kindly with his children in that he bestows on them his covenant blessings, promises, and fulfillments in measure. The words "portion" and "cup" (v.5) are metaphors for God's sustenance (23:5). The psalmist is not afraid because God upholds his "lot," i.e., he gives what he has allotted to his loyal servant.

The nature of God's benefits are such that they may be described as "pleasant" and "delightful." Even as God gave his people a pleasant land as an inheritance, so the psalmist rejoices in the bounty of God's goodness to him. However, his joy is not first and foremost in God's gifts but in the Lord himself (cf. NEB, "Thou, LORD, my allotted portion, thou my cup"). Similarly, the psalmist views the Lord as his heritage, as A.A. Anderson writes, "The Psalmist may have intended to point not only to his heritage in Yahweh's land, but also to Yahweh himself, who is the ground of all existence" (1:144). Von Rad sees this as a stage in the process of spiritualization of OT rituals: Yahweh is the asylum (OTT, 1:403).

Notes

5 The translation "you have assigned me" assumes an emendation of מְנָת (*m^enāṯ*, "a share of"; cf. 1 Sam 1:4), a construct form with the noun "portion." These two form an idiom: "my chosen portion" (Craigie, *Psalms 1–50*, p. 154). Together with "my cup" it is a balanced pairing of one word for a "share" of food and one for a "cup" of drink. The psalmist addresses God as his food and drink, i.e., all that he needs (cf. NEB, "Thou, LORD, my allotted portion, thou my cup"). The BHS has no text-critical suggestions or emendations.

The conclusion of v.5a also helps in the reading of the second part. The NIV's "you have made my lot secure" translates a supposed Hiphil of *t-m-k* ("support," "hold fast"). But the root of the verb תּוֹמִיךְ (*tômîḵ*) should be *y-m-k*, a nonexistent root in biblical Hebrew. A number of Hebrew MSS read a Qal participial form: תֹּמֵךְ (*tōmēḵ*, "supporter") as a direct reference to God, as in v.5a: "You are the one who holds my lot" (Craigie, *Psalms 1–50*, p. 154). The emendation to *tāmîḏ* ("forever," so Weiser, p. 171) is unnecessary (cf. Briggs, 1:125).

For a refutation of Dahood's proposal "my cup of smooth wine," see Craigie, *Psalms 1–50*, p. 155.

III. Confidence in the Lord

16:7–8

7 I will praise the LORD, who counsels me;
even at night my heart instructs me.
8 I have set the LORD always before me.
Because he is at my right hand,
I will not be shaken.

7–8 The theocentric focus is further supported by the psalmist's response of praise. He shows his loyalty to the Lord in "praise" and in obedience ("I have set the LORD always before me," v.8). The praise of God consists of "blessing" his wonderful name, rendered by "I will praise" (v.7). The blessing is a grateful expression of acknowledgment of his blessing, hence "praise" (cf. 26:12; 34:1; 63:4; 66:8; 68:26; 103:1–2, 20–22; 104:1, 35; 135:19–20; 145:2; so KB^3, 1:153). In life situations the psalmist is not easily moved by the idolaters (v.4), because his chief goal in life is to love God and live for him. By day he can say that the Lord gives him counsel, which aids him to live wisely. At night God "instructs" him through the meditation with his inner self. God is always present at his "right hand" (v.8; cf. 73:23; 109:31; 110:5; 121:5). Therefore his confidence in the Lord is the result of his experience of God's goodness, grace, and fatherly instruction. As a sage, the psalmist can claim God's promise that the wise (righteous) "will not be shaken" (cf. 15:5; 21:7; 62:2, 6; 112:6; Prov 10:30; 12:3). A restatement of these truths is found in v.11.

Notes

7 "At night" (sing.) may not completely reflect the plural לֵילוֹת (*lêlôṯ,* "nights"). It may be translated as "throughout the nights" (cf. KB³, 2:502; cf. Pss 92:2; 134:1). Briggs (1:126), followed by Craigie (*Psalms 1–50,* p. 155), interprets it as "dark nights." Joüon (par. 136b) takes the plural as an example of the plural of composition and translates the phrase "parts of the night." Dahood (*Psalms,* 1:86), on the other hand, renders it "during the watches of the night."

IV. The Experience of Faith

16:9–11

9 Therefore my heart is glad and my tongue rejoices;
my body also will rest secure,
10 because you will not abandon me to the grave,
nor will you let your Holy One see decay.
11 You have made known to me the path of life;
you will fill me with joy in your presence,
with eternal pleasures at your right hand.

9–10 The ground for the psalmist's joy is twofold. First, his God is the sovereign Master to whom he has fled for protection (vv.1–2). Second, the Lord has been good to him (vv.2b, 5–8). He has not been disappointed in having sought him as the ground of his being. His conclusion to this psalm of confidence begins with "Therefore" (v.9); but the "therefore" introduces additional, though related, reasons for his confidence. The psalmist is filled with joy in his Lord, who cares for him in life and in death. In life the Lord gives him security (vv.5–6) and in death, protection (vv.9b–10). He may die, go into "the grave," but the Lord will not permit his beloved ("Holy One") to suffer eternal alienation. The phrase "see decay" (v.10) is a metaphor for total isolation and abandonment from God's presence. It is not clear whether the psalmist had in mind the experience of God's presence in the life hereafter or specifically in the resurrection of the body. However, in the apostolic preaching this verse did have a particular apologetic significance, as both Peter (Acts 2:27, 31) and Paul (Acts 13:35) quoted v.10 as proof of the resurrection of our Lord. (See the appendix to Ps 88: Sheol-Grave-Death in the Psalms.)

The primary significance of the text lies in the confidence of the psalmist that his relationship with God will not end with death. David, to whom the psalm is attributed, died; but we are confident that in his death he, too, enjoyed the presence of God in some special sense. For Peter and Paul the text spoke of the resurrection. They appropriately argued that since David died and did not rise from the grave, the psalm received a special significance in view of Jesus' death and resurrection. Jesus, as the Son of David, arose from the dead, "because it was impossible for death to keep its hold on him" (Acts 2:24). In the progressive unfolding of God's revelation, Peter saw a prophetic/messianic sense in the psalm (v.31). The resurrection of our Lord gives a ground for the confidence of all believers since they, too, will not suffer corruption. The Father will crown his beloved with life. God is concerned with the whole being, and therefore the body is included in the renewal of life. Calvin observes: "Yet as God defends and maintains not only our souls, but also our bodies, David does not speak groundlessly when he represents the blessing of dwelling in safety as extending to his flesh in common with his soul" (1:230).

11 The psalmist develops further the nature of life with God (see W.A.M. Beuken, "Psalm 16: The Path to Life," *Bijdragen: Tijdschrift voor Filosofie en Theologie* 41 [1980]: 368–85; Klaus Seybold, "Der Weg des Lebens. Eine Studie zu Psalm 16," *Theologische Zeitschrift* 40 [1984]: 121–29). Its origin is with God: "you will make known" (NIV mg.). Its goal is the presence of God, even to be at "your right hand." Its effect is "joy" and "eternal pleasures." Life may be experienced here, as the psalmist is fully aware of his blessings (vv.5–8). "The path of life" signifies the way that leads to life. It is a wisdom term for the fullness of life that only the wise could achieve (Prov 5:6; 6:23; 10:17; 15:24). God's blessing attends the life lived in the presence of God. The psalmist conceives of life in fellowship with God both in this world and beyond (cf. Weiser, p. 178).

Beyond the present experiences and joy in God's "presence" lies the hope of a lasting joy in fellowship with God. Dahood takes the phrase as a reference solely to "life eternal" (*Psalms*, 1:91). Briggs views this as a reference to life everlasting, but not including the resurrection of the body. "Such a hope he could not express for this life; he is thinking of everlasting life in the presence of Yahweh and on His right hand, after he has departed this life and gone to Sheol" (1:122). Craigie excludes any reference to the afterlife and limits the meaning to "the fulness of life here and now" (p. 158). But I agree with J. Ridderbos, who comments: "This verse speaks also in comprehensive expressions. . . . viewed in the light of the NT it contains a clear prediction of the eternal joy of life, received in Christ through his resurrection and further of the eternal bliss of all who are in Christ" (1:132; see Armin Schmitt, "Psalm 16, 8–11 als Zeugnis der Auferstehung in der Apostelgeschichte," *Biblische Zeitschrift* 17 [1973]: 229–48; Léonard Ramaroson, "Immortalité et Résurrection dans les Psaumes," *Science et Esprit* 36 [1984]: 287–95).

Notes

9 "Tongue" is based on the LXX and not the MT's כְּבוֹדִי (*k*[e]*ḇôḏî*, "my glory"). "My glory" refers to the "inner being," translated by "life" in Ps 7:5 (NIV). Dahood takes "my glory" as a corrupt form of "my liver" (כְּבֵדִי [*k*[e]*ḇēḏî*], *Psalms*, 1:90, based on a few MSS). See 7:5.

The doctrine of the two aspects of man is clearly given here. Man is "body" (בָּשָׂר [*bāśār*, "flesh"]) and "spirit" ("heart," "glory"; cf. 84:2; Prov 14:30).

There is no need to emend the Hebrew verbal forms (contra Craigie, *Psalms 1–50*, p. 155). The waw conversive form וַיָּגֶל (*wayyāḡel*, "and he rejoiced") preceded by the stative verb "is glad" has a present meaning (Joüon, par. 118p; GKC, par. 111r).

10 "Me" is an appropriate rendering for "my soul"; see Notes on 6:3.

The word "Holy One" is an interpretative translation based on the NT quotations of the LXX (Acts 2:27; 13:35). The Hebrew חָסִיד (*ḥāsîḏ*, "beloved" or "faithful one," see NIV mg.) is a designation of God's servant; see 4:3. The LXX's use of ἁγίοις (*hagiois*) is ambiguous, as it may be rendered "devout," "pious," "pleasing to God," or "holy." The Vulgate solved this by the translation "*Sanctum tuum*" ("your Holy One," Acts 2:27). This rendering lies behind the EVV: "your Holy One."

The word "decay" likewise shows influence of the NT quotation of the LXX (Acts 2:27; 13:35). The Hebrew שַׁחַת (*šaḥaṯ*, "pit," "grave") designates a place for the dead (cf. Isa 38:17) and is roughly synonymous with Sheol (THAT, 2:839–40). For Sheol see 6:5 and the appendix to Psalm 88: Sheol-Grave-Death in the Psalms.

11 It is possible to take the plural nouns שְׂמָחוֹת (*śᵉmāḥôṯ*, "happy things") and נְעִמוֹת (*nᵉʿimôṯ*, "pleasant things") as abstracts: "rejoicing" and "pleasantness" (GKC, par. 122q) or even as an intensification: "full rejoicing" and "the greatest pleasure" (GKC, par. 124e; cf. Craigie, *Psalms 1–50*, p. 155).

Psalm 17: A Prayer for God's Justice

The concern for righteousness dominates this psalm from beginning to end. It is a prayer directed to the Judge of the whole earth that righteousness may prevail on earth (vv.1–2). The psalm concludes with the hope that the psalmist will see God "in righteousness" (v.15). The prayer is a psalm of innocence (cf. Pss 7; 26; 35) under the general category of lament psalms. Craigie proposes that it is "an innocent person's *prayer for protection*" (*Psalms 1–50*, p. 161).

The psalm's setting is far from clear. There are not unambiguous allusions to the historical, social, or cultic setting in David's life. It is too concerned with the need for vindication to be used as a morning prayer (cf. Craigie, *Psalms 1–50*, p. 162). The prayer to God for examination during the night (v.3) and the hope to see God's face upon waking may be arguments in favor of an evening prayer.

The structure of the psalm is readily discernible:

A. Prayer of a Righteous Man (vv.1–5)
  B. Prayer for Protection (vv.6–9)
    C. The Wicked (vv.10–12)
  B′. Prayer for Deliverance (v.13)
    C′. The Wicked (v.14)
A′. Hope in Righteousness (v.15)

I. Prayer of a Righteous Man

17:1–5

A prayer of David.

1 Hear, O LORD, my righteous plea;
listen to my cry.
Give ear to my prayer—
it does not rise from deceitful lips.
2 May my vindication come from you;
may your eyes see what is right.

3 Though you probe my heart and examine me at night,
  though you test me, you will find nothing;
  I have resolved that my mouth will not sin.
4 As for the deeds of men—
  by the word of your lips
 I have kept myself
  from the ways of the violent.
5 My steps have held to your paths;
  my feet have not slipped.

1 The psalmist uses three intense expressions to call on Yahweh ("Hear . . . listen. . . . Give ear"). Yahweh is the God of the covenant, who made wonderful promises and has sworn to confirm them. But his child is in deep distress, and so he confidently, not diffidently, approaches God in prayer. The reason for the confidence lies both in his trust in the covenant God and in his "righteous" way of life.

The word "righteous" (*ṣeḏeq*) may refer to the Lord ("O righteous LORD"), to the psalmist ("a righteous man"; Briggs, 1:128), or to the nature of the prayer ("a righteous plea," NIV). The parallelism requires a synonym for "my cry," which supports the NIV. The addition of the possessive pronoun "my" is based on the LXX and is in symmetry with "my cry." The NEB offers an alternate possibility: "my plea for justice"; so Dahood, "my plea for vindication" (*Psalms*, 1:93). But it is preferable to see the parallelism of "righteous" and "deceitful lips" as chiastic:

Hear, O LORD,
  my righteousness [or "a righteous man"]
    Listen to my cry,
    Give ear to my prayer
  it does not rise from deceitful lips.

The word "righteous"—whether as "righteousness" or as "a righteous man"—is modified antithetically by the last colon. The psalmist prays as an innocent man who is not to be charged with the deception of his contemporaries.

Thus the psalmist has lived in accordance with God's righteous law, is "righteous," and can say that his prayer "does not rise from deceitful lips." Calvin explained it similarly: "The meaning rather is, that David, confiding in his own integrity, interposes God as a Judge between himself and his enemies, to cognosce [*sic*] or determine in his cause" (1:235; cf. Weiser, p. 180). Prayer requires an attitude of sincerity, without hypocrisy (cf. James 5:16–18).

The psalmist yells for help with a great intensity to the Lord. The "cry" is a desperate call for help (106:44; 119:169; 142:6) and an intense form of prayer (61:1; 88:2) that could be translated "my yell" (Briggs, 1:128).

2 The content of the prayer is twofold: (1) for vindication ("may my vindication come from you") and (2) for investigation ("may your eyes see what is right"). These petitions are subsequently developed throughout the psalm in chiastic sequence:

A. Prayer for Vindication (v.2a)
  B. Prayer for Investigation (v.2b)
  B′. Investigation (vv.3–5)
A′. Vindication (vv.6–15)

The psalm moves from a general prayer for righteousness (vv.1–2) and a declaration of innocence (vv.3–5) to a prayer that hopes in God's covenantal loyalty (vv.6–14). In the belief that God is sovereign and faithful, the psalmist rests his case with God and looks forward to his goodness in this life and in the life to come (v.15).

In his second petition (v.2b), the psalmist prays that the Lord may examine his integrity (*mêšārîm*, "what is right," NIV). He is not claiming perfection but addresses God out of the sincerity of his heart and presses for a resolution to his difficulty.

3 The concessive interpretative translation of the NIV—"Though . . . though"—could also be read as a prayer for examination. The sequence of three perfect verbs ("probe . . . examine . . . test") and a twofold use of the negative particle (*bal*, "not") followed by imperfect verbs ("you will find [nothing]" and "[my mouth] will [not] sin") is interpreted by the NIV as a declaration of innocence. Even if God were to probe, etc., he will find that the psalmist is innocent. The absence of "though" in Hebrew and the sequence of perfects in continuation with the three (!) imperatives (v.1) favor Dahood's proposal that the perfects here are precatives, i.e., to be read as imperatives: "Probe . . . examine . . . test me!" (*Psalms*, 1:94). In support of this suggestion is the connection of vv.3–5 with the prayer "may your eyes see what is right" (v.2). Alternately, the psalmist may appeal to God's past investigations and declare his innocence: "you have probed . . . examined . . . tested me" (cf. Craigie, *Psalms 1–50*, p. 159). He believes that he has done nothing to deserve his suffering (v.3b) and that he has not transgressed with his lips against God's commandments (v.3c). His prayer is confident, but it is a godly confidence, expressive both of the deepest trust in and of a tender walk with God. Therefore he requests God to "test" his "heart" (see 7:9), i.e., to put him through every conceivable examination. The probing (*bāḥan*, see 7:9) of "the heart" (v.3a) is a determination of the purity and integrity of the heart. Even as silver and gold underwent a refining process and were tested until the smith was satisfied with the purity of these precious metals, so the psalmist asks for an examination of his purity of devotion to God.

The psalmist calls on the Lord to examine him especially at night, when he cannot cover up or rationalize his daily activities. Calvin comments appropriately: "When a man is withdrawn from the presence of his fellow-creatures, he sees more clearly his sins, which otherwise would be hidden from his view" (1:238). The examination "at night" suggests a time of isolation from one's occupation and social relations, when one is completely alone with God, so that nothing distracts from the examination (cf. Job 7:18). The examination involves a self-examination, as one reflects on one's attitude, loyalty, and obedience to God's commandments.

4–5 The psalmist is confident of his integrity even when the Lord enlarges the scope of his examination to actions and words (v.4). He has paid careful attention to wise living by not associating with the "violent." He contrasts himself ("I," emphatic) with "the violent" (cf. "I on my part have kept," Briggs, p. 129). The "violent" had no consideration of God or his commands. They were the gangsters of the OT, who robbed and murdered without blinking an eye (cf. Jer 7:11; 18:10). He had held onto the way of God. The "paths" of the Lord refer to the way of godliness (v.5; cf. 1:6a) and are in opposition to the "ways of the violent" (cf. 1:6b). He affirms that he held onto the Lord's way, without slipping into the way of thieves.

Notes

For a brief discussion of the technical words and phrases in the superscription, see the Introduction.

For a study on the problems of this psalm, see J. van der Ploeg, "Le Psaume XVII et ses Problèmes," *OudTestamentische Studiën* 14 (1965): 273–95.

1 Dahood's proposal "Destroy deceitful lips," based on an alternate reading of בְּלֹא (*bᵉlōʾ*, "without," "not") as a Piel imperative of a supposed Ugaritic cognate "to destroy," is unwarranted (*Psalms*, 1:92–93; cf. Craigie's refutation, *Psalms 1–50*, p. 160).

2 The MT shows the chiastic, synthetic parallelism more clearly:

A. from before you	B. my vindication	C. may go out,
A′. your eyes	C′. may see	B′. what is right

Because God's eyes see "right things" (*mêšārîm*, "equity"), the psalmist prays that he may soon be vindicated.

The LXX reading "my eyes" is an attempt to explain the text sequentially, as Briggs does: "that mine eyes may behold it" (1:127).

3 The form זַמֹּתִי (*zammōṯî*, "I have resolved") is not to be taken as a noun (LXX) or to be joined with the preceding colon, as in Briggs: "and Thou findest no evil purpose in me" (1:127; cf. also BHS; Kraus, *Psalmen*, 1:128). Dahood's translation "idolatry" finds little support (*Psalms*, 1:92, 94).

עָבַר (*ʿāḇar*) is "sin" in the sense of "transgress," "pass over" (cf. TWOT, 2:641–42).

4–5 These verses are full of textual and exegetical difficulties. The NIV makes good sense out of the terse phraseology of the MT.

II. Prayer for Protection

17:6–9

6 I call on you, O God, for you will answer me;
give ear to me and hear my prayer.
7 Show the wonder of your great love,
you who save by your right hand
those who take refuge in you from their foes.
8 Keep me as the apple of your eye;
hide me in the shadow of your wings
9 from the wicked who assail me,
from my mortal enemies who surround me.

6–9 David appealed to his covenant God to respond to his petition. The subject ("I") of the clause "I call on you" is emphatic, as if he says, "It is I who call on you." The urgency is based on the confidence that God will answer him (v.6). The boldness in his calling on God expresses the close relationship, which is further described by the metaphors "the apple of your eye" and "the shadow of your wings" (v.8; 36:7; 57:1; 63:7; 91:4; cf. Isa 49:2; 51:16). These metaphors express the love of God in his acts of care and protection for those who are dear to him (cf. Deut 32:10). The "shadow of the wings" is a metaphorical description whose background is to be sought in the Song of Moses, which mentions both the "apple of the eye" and the spreading of the "wings" of the eagle (= vulture) in the same context as metaphors for God's love and care (Deut 32:10–12; cf. vv.13–14). Since the enemies had become a real threat, David called on the God of the Exodus, of Mount Sinai, and of the Conquest to act again on behalf of his beloved. The enemies had risen up against him with the intent to "assail" (v.9) him, aiming at nothing less than the destruction of the righteous (vv.7, 9). The phrase "mortal enemies" renders a unique Hebrew phrase (lit., "my enemies in soul"). "In soul" means here "in greed" (i.e., greedy; cf. 10:3; 27:12 ["the desire"]). They "surround" the psalmist like a flood (cf. 88:17) or a band of robbers (22:16). He has become like a city under siege (2 Kings 6:14).

However, God is a help in trouble. He answers prayer (v.6), provides "refuge" (v.7; see 7:1) to those who seek it, and delivers the godly with his "right hand," which signifies the strength by which he sustains and redeems his own (18:35; 139:10) from trouble (Exod 15:6, 12; Pss 60:5; 108:6; 138:7). But it is not enough to be reminded of what God has done in the past or what he is able to do, because the need is *now*. Therefore the psalmist prays for God's deliverance with great intensity, for God to "set apart your loving acts" (v.7, see Notes) and to deliver the godly "by your right hand." He looks for God to demonstrate his promised acts of love and loyalty, but he is not looking for miracles (Weiser, p. 181). God's acts consist of protection (v.8) and ultimately of deliverance from the assailants. God stoops down to deliver his children. As Calvin put it: "We have here presented to our contemplation a singular and an astonishing proof of the goodness of God, in humbling himself so far, and in a manner so to speak, transforming himself, in order to lift up our faith above the conceptions of the flesh" (1:245). But the wicked seek to destroy the righteous by acts of violence, subterfuge, and deception. For a further description, see vv.10–12.

Notes

---

6 The particle כִּי (*kî*, "for") may be also translated as an emphatic particle, "surely," or with Dahood, "O that" (*Psalms*, 1:96).

"My prayer" is literally "my word," i.e., my plea for vindication.

7 The translation "show the wonder of your great love" is based on an alternate reading of the MT. Several Hebrew MSS read הַפְלֵא (*haplē'*, "do wonders"). However, the MT reading הַפְלֵה (*haplēh*, "treat with distinction," "set apart") makes good sense, as in Ps 4:3: "Know that the LORD *has set apart* the godly [*ḥāsîḏ*] for himself." It is tempting to emend our text—חֲסָדֶיךָ (*ḥ^asāḏeyḵā*, "your acts of love" [NIV, "your great love"])—in conformity with 4:3 to *ḥ^asîḏeḵā* ("your loved one" or "your godly one").

9 The verb שַׁדּוּנִי (*šaddûnî*) comes from a Qal perfect of the root שׁדד (*šdd*, "devastate," "lay waste," "despoil," "deal violently with"; cf. KB, p. 949).

III. The Wicked

17:10–12

10 They close up their callous hearts,
 and their mouths speak with arrogance.
11 They have tracked me down, they now surround me,
 with eyes alert, to throw me to the ground.
12 They are like a lion hungry for prey,
 like a great lion crouching in cover.

10–12 The psalmist has poured out the burden of his heart before his God and asked for fatherly protection. He is overwhelmed by the thought of his foes. Just the mention of the enemies (v.9) leads him to elaborate on their evil.

The wicked are "like a lion" (v.12; cf. 7:2; 22:13) in their pursuit of the one godly person! Their beastlike nature finds expression in their callous hearts (v.10a), arrogance (v.10b; cf 5:9), pursuit to the death (v.11a), and violence (v.11b).

The hearts of the wicked are closed up "in their fat" (NIV, "callous"). The idiom "they close up their callous hearts" (*ḥelbāmô sāg̱rû*, lit., "their fat they close") is unknown elsewhere in the OT. The NIV follows BHS in a conjectural reading of *ḥelbāmô* as *ḥēleḇ libbāmô*: "the fat of their hearts" (cf. KB[3], 1:303). Craigie argues persuasively from the similarity of the metaphors (vv.8, 10) in Deuteronomy 32:10–15 that the idiom signifies rebelliousness and renders it: "They have become rebellious" (*Psalms 1–50*, pp. 159, 160–61). The fat parts of an animal were considered to be the best and were burned on the altar (Lev 4:26). The "fat" of the wicked signifies their greedy, self-loving, and insensitive nature (cf. 73:7; 119:70). Prosperity and success are associated with a rebellious spirit, symbolized by "fatness" (cf. 119:70; Deut 32:15).

The outward expression of the wicked is consistent with their inner being. They speak "with arrogance," which excludes God and concern for others (cf. 10:3–6). It is a dangerous signal, because the arrogant cannot be trusted. Even when he speaks properly, his heart is full of his own ego; and at any time his words may become a torrent of curses in order to accomplish his will.

The wicked's violent pursuit of life (v.11) again betrays their callous hearts. Without mercy they track down, surround, and finally destroy those weaker than themselves. This picture of the wicked may be hyperbolic, but it makes a clear point of the ugliness of sin.

The psalmist follows this verbal picture with the metaphor of the lion (v.12). The "lion," a symbol of brute strength and a ferocious appetite (cf. Judg 14:14), is a powerful picture of the wicked (cf. 7:2; 10:9; 22:13). The "great lion" is an unfortunate translation of *k[e]pîr*, which means "young lion." The words "lion" and "young lion" are often used interchangeably for poetic effect (cf. Isa 31:4; Amos 3:4).

Notes

---

11 The Hebrew text is difficult. Most commentators emend the text in order to make some sense. The noun אַשֻּׁרֵינוּ (*'aššurênû*, "our steps") is emended to read יְשֻׁרוּנִי (*y[e]šurûnî*, "they have tracked down"; cf. LXX, "they cast out"). The *Kethiv* form סְבָבוּנִי (*s[e]ḇāḇûnî*, "they surrounded me") is maintained in favor of the *Qere* ("they surrounded us"). The NIV's "to throw me" assumes either a textual change from לִנְטוֹת (*linṭôṯ*, "to throw," "to cast," "to pitch") to לִנְטוֹתִי (*linṭôṯî*, "to throw me"; cf. Craigie, p. 161) or a syntactic reading of "me" as a double-duty suffix.

IV. Prayer for Deliverance

17:13

> [13]Rise up, O LORD, confront them, bring them down;
> rescue me from the wicked by your sword.

13 The mood shifts as David gazes away from the threat of the wicked (vv.9–12) and looks to his God. He prays that God will act, not in the future, but *now*. The situation is critical ("now," v.11), and he awaits the outcome from under the protective "wings" (v.8). The call to "rise" and act (v.13) in deliverance and vindication is common to other psalms (3:7; 7:6; 9:19; 10:12; 74:22; see appendix to Ps 119: Yahweh Is My Redeemer). Instead of direct confrontation with evil, which may bring death (cf. 18:5), he expects the Lord to "confront" evil in his stead. The Lord will not tolerate their opposition; rather he will make the wicked bow down (NIV, "bring down") before the Great King and even before God's people (cf. 18:39). This is not an act of worship, nor of submission, but of total destruction (cf. 20:8) by the "sword" of the Lord.

V. The Wicked

17:14

14 O LORD, by your hand save me from such men,
from men of this world whose reward is in this life.

You still the hunger of those you cherish;
their sons have plenty,
and they store up wealth for their children.

14 Verse 14 is difficult in the MT. The reading of the NIV is one of many possible interpretations. The verbal phrase "save me" is repeated from v.13 ("rescue me") as an ellipsis. The description of the wicked as "men of this world whose reward is in this life" is an interpretation of an enigmatic Hebrew colon: "from a world their portion in life." It is, however, clear that he prays for God to act against the wicked and to rescue his own.

Whom does the psalmist describe in v.14b? The NIV divides v.14 and interprets v.14b so as to fit with v.15. However, the variety of interpretations in commentaries and versions cautions us to take another look at these colons. The literal reading makes for an obscure translation: "your hidden will be full—their—belly sons will have plenty; and will leave their remains to their children." The crux of the problem is the meaning of "your hidden." If it is "your hidden punishment," then v.14b belongs to v.14a with the sense given in the NEB and Briggs: "their belly fill Thou with Thy stored-up penalty. May their sons be sated, may they leave their residue to their children" (1:127). In its favor is the context and the contrastive phrase "and I" or "but as for me" (v.15). On the other hand, "your hidden" could refer back to the metaphor of the wings under which the psalmist found refuge (cf. "But your treasured ones!—you will fill their belly, sons will be sated, and they will bequeath their surplus to their children," Craigie, *Psalms 1–50*, pp. 160–61). This is close to the NIV reading.

However, we believe v.14b should be seen as a continuation of judgment for three reasons: (1) the contrast between "their" and "I" (vv.14b–15a); (2) the ambiguity of "their" (three times) and the problem of correspondence between "your hidden" (masc. sing.!) and the third masculine plural suffix ("their"); (3) the referent of "their" can be no different than the wicked in v.14a: "their portion" (NIV, "whose reward").

VI. Hope in Righteousness

17:15

15 And I—in righteousness I will see your face;
when I awake, I will be satisfied with seeing your likeness.

15 The phrase "and I" is emphatic and seems to be contrastive with God's judgment on the wicked. He confronted them in judgment, but the godly will see his "face." The wicked will be forced to bow down and will be destroyed, whereas the godly will enjoy God's presence "in righteousness." The word "righteousness" (*ṣeḏeq*) has the sense of victory and joy procured by the Lord and shared with his beloved. The wicked were self-satisfied (v.10) and shared their wealth with their descendants so that they too would "be satisfied" ("have plenty," v.14). But the godly do not comfort themselves with the thought of transitory "blessings." They will be "satisfied" with the "likeness" of God! No more threats will come from those who are "like" a lion (v.12), because the lion's "likeness" will be exchanged for God's "likeness." The apostle John applies this experience to the new era, when all God's people "will see his face" (Rev 22:4; cf. also 1 John 3:2; see Hans F. Fuhs, *Sehen und Schauen. Die Wurzel ḥzh im Alten Orient und im Alten Testament. Ein Beitrag zum prophetischen Offenbarungsempfang* [Würzburg: Echter Verlag, 1978], pp. 272–74).

To "wake" may mean here that the prayer is an evening prayer (4:8) or simply a general expression of abandonment to the Lord (3:5). However, it seems that the psalmist by inspiration is looking for a greater experience with God that can only be a part of the postresurrection world (cf. Dahood: "At the resurrection I will be saturated with your being," *Psalms*, 1:93, 99). This present life may be filled with testings, as at night (v.3), but the newness of life (when we "awake," v.15) will bring the rewards of vindication and glorification. However, the future fulfillment does not exclude a sense of present enjoyment.

Notes

15 On "in righteousness" (*ṣeḏeq*), see 4:1. The psalm begins and closes with the same word; the NIV has two translations: "my righteous plea" (v.1) and "righteousness" (v.15).

Psalm 18: Royal Thanksgiving

The psalm has been variously categorized, depending on one's view of the unity of the psalm and of its authorship. Some have divided the psalm into two units: an individual lament (vv.1–30) and a royal thanksgiving psalm (vv.31–50). However, based on a careful study of the parallel psalm in 2 Samuel 22, scholars today generally agree that the psalm is a composite whole (see F.M. Cross, Jr., and D.N. Freedman, "A Royal Song of Thanksgiving: II Samuel 22 = Psalm 18," JBL 72 [1953]: 15–34; J. Kenneth Kuntz, "Psalm 18: A Rhetorical-Critical Analysis," JSOT 26 [1983]: 3–31;

Robert Alter's analysis of Psalm 18 and 2 Samuel 22 reveals a sensitivity to the poetics of each poem [pp. 29–38]).

The original situation is not entirely clear. According to the superscription David had experienced victories over his enemies, including Saul. The psalm of thanksgiving may have served as a victory hymn on various occasions of victory over the enemies of Israel (see J.-L. Vesco, "Le Psaume 18, lecture davidique," RB 94 [1987]: 5–62).

The structure reveals an inclusionary motif around the praise of and the confidence in Yahweh, the Rock of Israel and the God of David (vv.1–2, 46–50). When his servant is in need, the Lord swoops down to deliver him, because he is just to those who love him (vv.20–29). The focus of the text is the righteousness of God (vv.1–2, 46–50) in relation to David's loyalty (vv.20–29).

The structural divisions of the psalm are as follows:

- A. Yahweh, the Rock of Israel (vv.1–3)
  - B. Affliction (vv.4–6)
    - C. The Lord's Coming to Help (vv.7–15)
      - D. The Lord's Deliverance (vv.16–19)
        - E. God's Faithfulness to the Faithful (vv.20–29)
      - D′. The Divine Perfections (vv.30–36)
    - C′. The King's Victory Over the Enemies (vv.37–42)
  - B′. The Glorious Deliverance (vv.43–45)
- A′. Yahweh, the Rock of Israel (vv. 46–50)

For a structural analysis, see Frank-Lothar Hossfeld, "Der Wandel des Beters in Ps 18, Wachstumsphasen eines Dankliedes," *Freude an der Weisung des Herrn, Beiträge zur Theologie der Psalmen, Festgabe zum 70. Geburtstag von Heinrich Gross,* edd. Ernst Haag and Frank-Lothar Hossfeld (Stuttgart: Katholisches Bibelwerk, 1986), pp. 171–90.

I. Yahweh, the Rock of Israel

18:1–3

For the director of music. Of David the servant of the LORD. He sang to the LORD the words of this song when the LORD delivered him from the hand of all his enemies and from the hand of Saul. He said:

1 I love you, O LORD, my strength.

2 The LORD is my rock, my fortress and my deliverer;
my God is my rock, in whom I take refuge.
He is my shield and the horn of my salvation, my stronghold.
3 I call to the LORD, who is worthy of praise,
and I am saved from my enemies.

1 A unique verb expressive of love for God opens the psalm. Hebrew has various ways to express devotion and love for God, but usually the verb translated here as "love" (from *r-ḥ-m,* "to have mercy") is used to affirm God's compassion for man. The verb implies the need of the one who receives the compassion and is associated with the mother's care for her children. David thus expresses his commitment to the Lord who is his source of strength, comfort, and sustenance. The phrase "I love you" communicates an intimacy of his relationship based on experience (see G. Schmutlermayr, "RḤM—Eine Lexikalische Studie," *Biblica* 51 [1970]: 499–532).

The further description of the Lord as "my strength" supports this argument. David has seen the "strength" of God in his adversity. God is "Yahweh, my Strength" (*YHWH ḥizqî*), i.e., the covenant-keeping and loving God who bares his holy arm on behalf of his children (136:12). (See the appendix to Ps 98: Yahweh Is the Divine Warrior.)

2 The divine epithets are derived from David's familiarity with battle and with the geographical scenery of Canaan. The military terms are "my fortress," "my shield," "my stronghold"—possibly "the horn" (see the appendix to Ps 98: Yahweh Is the Divine Warrior), whereas the geographical references are "my rock" (twice: *sela'*, *ṣûr*). These metaphors convey the intensity of David's love for his God as the all-sufficient One. God is the Great King who is able to deliver those who call on him. He is the "rock" of Israel (Deut 32:4, 15, 18, 31, 37), who is faithful from generation to generation.

The Lord provides a refuge in his "fortress" (31:2–4). The "refuge" was an isolated high place in a mountainous region, whose natural relief provided excellent strategic advantages. Jerusalem (2 Sam 5:7), David's stronghold in the wilderness (1 Sam 22:4; 24:22), and Masada in the Judean wilderness are good examples of an ancient "fortress" (= *meṣûḏāh;* cf. Masada). The metaphor of God as "the rock" is explained by the words "my deliverer" (cf. 40:17 = 70:5; 144:2; see the appendix to Ps 119: Yahweh Is My Redeemer) and "in whom I take refuge." Because he is the Redeemer of his people in physical and spiritual needs (cf. v.48), the psalmist knows that he can always find refuge in him (cf. 2:12; cf. 37:39–40; see the appendix to Ps 119: Yahweh Is My Redeemer).

The Lord protects his servant as with a "shield" (cf. 3:3; Gen 15:1) so that the adversities of life may not penetrate and destroy his child. Instead, he elevates him with "the horn of salvation." The word "horn" (*qeren*) has been variously understood as the protection provided by the horn of a bull (Briggs, 1:141), the asylum of the horns of the altar (A.A. Anderson, 1:155), or a hill shaped like a horn. The "horn" may be a symbol of strength, but as a theological reference it denotes the vertical intrusion of Yahweh's power and victory over against the kingdoms of man (see Margit L. Süring, *The Horn-Motif in the Hebrew Bible and Related Ancient Near Eastern Literature and Iconography*, AUSDDS 4 (Berrien Springs: Andrews University, 1980). The imagery of a high place lies also behind the phrase "my stronghold" (cf. 9:9). It is a place of refuge in the rocks (cf. Isa 33:16). The Lord as "refuge" signifies his presence and protection (Ps 46; see the appendix to Ps 5: Yahweh Is King).

3 The outburst of metaphors affirms David's confidence in the Lord's ability to deliver. Therefore, he is praiseworthy (48:1; 96:4). Whenever he "called" on the Lord in prayer, David tasted the sweetness of his deliverance. This reminder of "the enemies" forms a transition to his reflections on God's deliverance in great adversity (vv.4–19).

Notes

For a brief discussion of the technical words and phrases in the superscription, see the Introduction.

II. Affliction

18:4–6

4 The cords of death entangled me;
the torrents of destruction overwhelmed me.
5 The cords of the grave coiled around me;
the snares of death confronted me.
6 In my distress I called to the LORD;
I cried to my God for help.
From his temple he heard my voice;
my cry came before him, into his ears.

4–6 The psalmist recalls the intensity of his anguish as if ropes were wrapped around him and as if death, personified as "cords of death" and "cords of the grave" (= Sheol), were pulling him downward. Another metaphor is that of the rushing streams that seemed to drag him to his death (cf. 30:1). This metaphor is more fully developed in the parallel poem (2 Sam 22:5). The description of suffering is couched in poetic form that has its background in Canaanite (Ugaritic) literature. In the Ugaritic myths Mot is the god of death and Yam is the god of the sea and chaos. The "torrents of destruction" and "the cords of death" (Mot) are victorious, whereas God's servant is lost in the battle. He cannot escape because he is trapped by "the snares of death" (see the appendix to Ps 88: Sheol-Grave-Death in the Psalms). Paganism seems to triumph, as chaos rules and God's deliverance is not forthcoming. But it is at this point that David turns to the Lord. After his prayer (v.6), he portrays the Lord's coming with great power and glory with the intent to establish order and justice, and thereby to redeem his servant.

David remembered to pray to the Lord in his distress. This was not a prayer characteristic of so many prayers, made only at the moment of great need. David knew how to pray in times of prosperity and adversity (5:3). Prayer was a spiritual response to any situation. He knew that his God, Yahweh, would come to his aid, because he trusted in God's promise to rescue his children. Since "distress" seems to be so contradictory to God's promises of protection, the psalmist cries out for help (cf. 5:2). God, the covenant-faithful God, heard the cry in his heavenly temple (cf. 11:4). The cry from the depths of Sheol (v.5) was heard in the height of heaven. (See the appendix to Ps 132: The Ark of the Covenant and the Temple: Symbols of Yahweh's Presence and Rule.)

Notes

---

4 (5 MT) The phrase "torrents of destruction" (lit., "rivers of Belial") evokes images of the netherworld, as described in Canaanite mythology. The etymology of the word בְּלִיַּעַל (*b^elîya'al*) is unsolved, but its use in the OT is laden with negative associations: evil, vile, devilish. For further discussion, see TWOT, 1:111; J.E. Hogg, "Belial in the Old Testament," AJSL 44 (1927–28): 56–58; D. Winton Thomas, "בְּלִיַּעַל in the Old Testament," *Biblical and Patristic Studies: in Memory of Robert Pierce Casey*, edd. J. Neville Birdsall and Robert W. Thomson (Freiburg: Herder, 1963), pp. 11–19.

4–17 (5–18 MT) For an extensive study of the motif of water and divine warfare, see John Day, *God's Conflict With the Dragon and the Sea. Echoes of Canaanite Myth in the Old*

Testament (Cambridge: Cambridge University Press, 1985). He interprets these verses as an example of the historization of the divine conflict (pp. 122–40).

III. The Lord's Coming to Help

18:7–15

7 The earth trembled and quaked,
and the foundations of the mountains shook;
they trembled because he was angry.
8 Smoke rose from his nostrils;
consuming fire came from his mouth,
burning coals blazed out of it.
9 He parted the heavens and came down;
dark clouds were under his feet.
10 He mounted the cherubim and flew;
he soared on the wings of the wind.
11 He made darkness his covering, his canopy around
him—
the dark rain clouds of the sky.
12 Out of the brightness of his presence clouds advanced,
with hailstones and bolts of lightning.
13 The LORD thundered from heaven;
the voice of the Most High resounded.
14 He shot his arrows and scattered ⌊the enemies⌋,
great bolts of lightning and routed them.
15 The valleys of the sea were exposed
and the foundations of the earth laid bare
at your rebuke, O LORD,
at the blast of breath from your nostrils.

7–15 God is concerned with the "distress" of his children. In order to heighten the affect, David first gives us a glimpse of God's reaction in heaven (vv.7–15), and then he describes the deliverance (vv.16–19). God's reaction in his heavenly glory is couched in the language of theophany (Exod 19:16–18; Deut 33:2–3; Ps 68:7–8; Isa 13:9–10; Joel 3:15–16; Nah 1:3–6). Von Rad observes that "the highest beauty in all creation was Jahweh's condescending to and entering into Israel's historical existence. This comes to expression first and foremost in the description of theophanies" (OTT, 1:366). The psalmist describes the theophany in the language of man.

The earthquake is an expression of his anger (v.7). The smoke and the fire represent his readiness to avenge his enemies (v.8). Thus he mounts the cherubim (v.10), soars as a bird on "the wings of the wind," and swoops quickly downward. The clouds are his chariot (cf. 68:33) and the wind makes up the wings (cf. 104:3–4) with which he flies downward on the rescue mission. The darkness of the clouds heightens the affect of his brightness (vv.11–12; cf. Ezek 1:4). As the Divine Warrior moves closer to the enemies, he announces his coming with "hailstones," "bolts of lightning," and "thunder" (vv.12–13). Then he shoots forth "his arrows" in the form of lightning (v.14; cf. 77:17; 144:6; Hab 3:11) and thus rids himself of his enemies. No opposition can stand his presence because he penetrates even the sea (v.16; cf. 32:6; 66:12) and "the foundations of the earth" (v.15). He is the glorious and victorious King over heaven, earth, and sea (cf. Ps 29). His rule is established, and there is no question as to his sovereignty and supremacy. But because the rebellious forces are on earth, the earth "trembles and quakes" (v.7) as it anticipates the fear of the guilty who are seized with "terror and dread" and tremble with anguish at the prospect of his judgment (cf. Exod 15:14, 16). The psalmist thus portrays God's victory in anthropomorphic language. His descent to earth is a phenomenal and literary expression; it does not support a geocentric universe. The language is an inspired medium to picture God's help. It is not scientific.

Notes

10–11 (11–12 MT) Tryggve B.D. Mettinger argues that the cherubim are symbolic of the divine war chariot, a mythopoetic image, in *The Dethronement of Sabaoth. Studies in the Shem and Kabod Theologies* (Lund: Gleerup, 1982), pp. 33–36.

10 (11 MT) For a discussion on the possible meanings of רָכַב (*rāḵaḇ*, "ride"; NIV, "mounted"), see Craigie (*Psalms 1–50*, p. 169).

11 (12 MT) For textual differences with 2 Sam 22:12, see EBC 3 (in loc.).

13 (14 MT) For Most High (Elyon), see the appendix to Ps 9: Yahweh Is El Elyon.

14 (15 MT) For a criticism of Dahood's reading "he forged his arrows," see Craigie (*Psalms 1–50*, p. 169).

15 (16 MT) On the meaning of מִגַּעֲרָתְךָ (*migga'ᵃrāṯᵉḵā*, "at your rebuke") as "your angry shout," see P.J. Van Zijl, "A Discussion of the root *gā'ar* ('rebuke')," *Biblical Essays*, ed. A.H. Van Zyl (Potchefstroom: Pro Rege-Pers, 1969), pp. 56–63.

IV. The Lord's Deliverance

18:16–19

16 He reached down from on high and took hold of me;
he drew me out of deep waters.
17 He rescued me from my powerful enemy,
from my foes, who were too strong for me.
18 They confronted me in the day of my disaster,
but the LORD was my support.
19 He brought me out into a spacious place;
he rescued me because he delighted in me.

16–19 The portrayal of God's indignation and readiness to vindicate gives comfort to the psalmist. He does not fear God's coming in anger, because his father comes to his rescue. Though the enemy forces are strong (vv.4–5), the Lord prevails over their great strength (v.17). He delivers the psalmist from the adversity and provides a new dimension of life. Instead of "disaster," he experiences the Lord to be his "support" (v.18). Instead of "distress" (v.6), the Lord gives him "a spacious place" (v.19; cf. 4:1; 31:8). Instead of the enmity of his foes, he experienced the redemption of the God who delights in him (cf. 22:8; 41:1). This God is faithful! God's love for his servant is beautifully expressed by a series of verbs: "He reached down . . . and took hold of me; / he drew me out of the deep waters. / He rescued. . . . He brought me out . . . ; / he rescued me." The language is reminiscent of God's great act of deliverance of Israel from Egypt, as they were brought out of Egypt, passed through the Red Sea, and came to the land of Canaan. God's mighty acts of deliverance are always evidence of his tender love (cf. Exod 19:4).

V. God's Faithfulness to the Faithful (vv.20–29)

The triumph of faith is expressed here in the realization that the Lord has been faithful, that he has kept his word, and that he rewards the faithful. Faith tastes the goodness of God. The psalmist has argued that the love of God moves heaven and earth for the sake of his own. Now he instructs the hearers (readers) what God expects of his children. The affirmation of his faith(fulness) evokes a desire in the godly to follow the psalmist in his love for God.

This section is composed of two separate parts: man's faithfulness to God (vv.20–24) and God's faithfulness to man (vv.25–29).

A. *Man's Faithfulness to God*

18:20–24

20 The LORD has dealt with me according to my
righteousness;
according to the cleanness of my hands he has
rewarded me.
21 For I have kept the ways of the LORD;
I have not done evil by turning from my God.
22 All his laws are before me;
I have not turned away from his decrees.
23 I have been blameless before him
and have kept myself from sin.
24 The LORD has rewarded me according to my
righteousness,
according to the cleanness of my hands in his sight.

20–24 Loyalty to the Lord shows itself in practical ways, but in essence it is an internal spiritual response. The attitude to God may be described as "righteous" (vv.20, 24) or "blameless" (v. 23). "Righteousness" is that response to God that, on the one hand, adheres to his decrees (v.22b) and, on the other hand, keeps away from evil (v.21). Righteousness and blamelessness are not to be equated with works-righteousness nor with perfection. It is the joyous expression of love to God for all his mercies. It is a response of gratitude. The psalmist is not saying to God, "Look what I have done for you," but he says, "Lord, I love you so much that I make every effort to please you." Therefore he speaks about his devotion to "the ways of the LORD" (cf. Deut 8:6) and to "his laws" (vv.21–22). God's laws regulate all of life and help his servant to respond appropriately to the challenges of life. His righteousness is contextually defined as "cleanness of my hands" (v.24; cf. 24:4; 26:6) and is reflected by his "integrity" (see 15:2) before the Lord, his devotion to the laws (1:2), and the sincerity of his walk before God (see the appendix to Ps 19: The Word of God). He is not double-hearted. He praises, not so much his own accomplishments, but the goodness of God who has dealt with him faithfully. These verses cannot be regarded as a boast, because they are connected in an argument celebrating God's faithfulness. Therefore the psalmist begins and concludes with a reference to the Lord's loyalty (vv.20, 24).

B. *God's Faithfulness to Man*

18:25–29

> 25 To the faithful you show yourself faithful,
> to the blameless you show yourself blameless,
> 26 to the pure you show yourself pure,
> but to the crooked you show yourself shrewd.
> 27 You save the humble
> but bring low those whose eyes are haughty.
> 28 You, O LORD, keep my lamp burning;
> my God turns my darkness into light.
> 29 With your help I can advance against a troop;
> with my God I can scale a wall.

25–26 The Lord helps his own. His own are those who are concerned with being "faithful" (*ḥāsîḏ*, "beloved," "loyal"; cf. 145:17), "blameless," and "pure" (vv.25–26; cf. vv.20–24). He responds with deep concern to his covenant children, whereas he deals in kind with the "crooked" ("perverse," "twisted"; cf. Lev 26:43; Rom 1:28–32). The psalmist rejoices in God's justice, as he deals with each in accordance with his works. The psalmist does not say that God shows himself "shrewd" (v.26) in the sense that he deals wisely with the wicked but that he "acts corruptly" ("crooked") with those who are "crooked." Even as God deals lovingly with those who love him, he lets the crooked acts of the wicked boomerang on their own heads. They receive their just deserts.

27–29 These affirmations of God's goodness and justice are the ground for hope. Even in adversity the "humble" hope in God; even in "darkness" the saints look to him for light (vv.27–28; cf. 27:1). The "haughty" are those who have little or no regard for the Lord (10:5–6; Isa 2:11–12, 17). He often oppresses or disregards the rights of the godly. The Lord graciously turns the misfortunes of his saints and thus grants them the joy of life. As Calvin expressed it, "[David] but introduces him [God] as armed with impetuous violence, for resisting and overcoming the perverse, according as it is said in the common proverb, A tough knot requires a stout wedge" (1:287). In his newfound deliverance, the psalmist expresses a spirit of confident joy. There is no barrier that the Lord cannot overcome, whether it be a "troop" or the wall of an enemy city (v.29). The presence of the Lord gives confidence of victory (cf. Josh 23:10).

Notes

29 (30 MT) The meaning of this verse is uncertain.

VI. The Lord's Goodness (vv.30–45)

Verse 30 closes off the previous section (vv.25–29) with the repetition of "perfect" (*tāmîm;* NIV, "blameless," v.25) and "perfect" (v.30; cf. v.32) and is a transition to vv.30–45.

The psalmist considers the divine perfections and God's goodness to him (vv.30–36) and God's deliverance from the enemies (vv.37–45).

A. *The Divine Perfections*

18:30–36

30 As for God, his way is perfect;
  the word of the LORD is flawless.
He is a shield
  for all who take refuge in him.
31 For who is God besides the LORD?
  And who is the Rock except our God?
32 It is God who arms me with strength
  and makes my way perfect.
33 He makes my feet like the feet of a deer;
  he enables me to stand on the heights.
34 He trains my hands for battle;
  my arms can bend a bow of bronze.
35 You give me your shield of victory,
  and your right hand sustains me;
  you stoop down to make me great.
36 You broaden the path beneath me,
  so that my ankles do not turn.

30–36 The Lord's ways are "perfect" and his word is "flawless" (v.30). Therefore he is filled with goodness to those he loves. He is a "shield" (cf 3:3) and "the Rock" (v.31), who gets involved in the lives of his children (vv.32–34) with the result that they are victorious, strong, and free (vv.35–36; cf. Prov 30:5).

The Lord's perfections are those qualities by which he relates to his creation. He is full of "integrity" (cf. v.25b) to those who respond to him with "integrity." His word, likewise, is "tested" and found to be "flawless" (cf. 12:6; 119:140). Flawlessness is that quality of perfection the silversmith or goldsmith is only able to obtain after repeating the process of refining to obtain 90+ percent of purity. God's word is "pure" without trials and therefore dependable. Because of God's commitment to protect his loyal subjects, by word and work, he is "a shield" (v.30b). Those "who take refuge in him" are described in vv.25–26; namely, the faithful, blameless, and pure. Faith, loyalty, and sanctification are inseparable. The ascriptions of goodness to God lead the psalmist to exclaim, "Who is God besides the LORD?" The answer is no one. This is more than a rhetorical question. It is a Hebraic form of asseveration, equivalent to "There is absolutely no god besides the LORD! There is no other Rock except our God!" (v.31; cf. Exod 15:11; Deut 33:26, 29; 1 Sam 2:2; Isa 45:5a).

The psalmist explains why God is incomparable in vv.32–36 by using three participial phrases followed by two imperfects that have the sense of a present (Joüon, par. 118r):

32 *m^{e}'azz^{e}rēnî* ("arms me with strength")
  wayyittēn ("and makes," lit., "and he made")
33 *m^{e}šawweh* ("he makes . . . like")
  ya'^{a}mîḏēnî ("he enables me to stand," lit., "he will enable me to stand")
34 *m^{e}lammēḏ* ("he trains") followed by a change in subject:
  "my arms can bend a bow."

The first description is more general than the other two. The Lord surrounds ("girds") him with strength. The verb signifies giving support or strengthening at a time of need (cf. v.39). In Isaiah 45:5 the Lord first identifies himself as "the LORD, . . . apart from me there is no God" and follows it up with an affirmation that he strengthens Cyrus to accomplish his goals. Since he is the Rock of Israel (v.31), he alone can give strength (rather than "arm with strength," NIV). The strength of the Lord results in success. The Lord's way is perfect (v.30a), as he helps his servant to regain his strength. He compares this strength to the sure-footedness of an ibex (NIV, "deer"), whose agility permits it to walk on narrow ledges in mountainous and rocky terrain. He also compares himself to a warrior (v.35; cf. 144:1) with special strength. In God's strength he is free (v.36; cf. v.19; Prov 4:12).

B. *The King's Victory Over the Enemies*

18:37–42

37 I pursued my enemies and overtook them;
I did not turn back till they were destroyed.
38 I crushed them so that they could not rise;
they fell beneath my feet.
39 You armed me with strength for battle;
you made my adversaries bow at my feet.
40 You made my enemies turn their backs in flight,
and I destroyed my foes.
41 They cried for help, but there was no one to save
them—
to the LORD, but he did not answer.
42 I beat them as fine as dust borne on the wind;
I poured them out like mud in the streets.

37–42 With the help of the Great King, the messianic King need not be afraid of the enemies. The emphasis lies on his prowess in battle as he aggressively beats back his enemies. He expects nothing less than their total destruction. The enemy being in dire straits called for help from allied forces, but none dared fight against the divinely anointed King (v.41)! It was apparent that the Lord was with the psalmist, as he strengthened him and gave him the complete victory (v.39). The enemies' strength was reduced so that they were no more than useless "dust" (cf. 2 Kings 13:7), only good for being stepped on, like "mud" (cf. Isa 10:6; Mic 7:10) in the open places ("streets," v.42). It may well be that the battles are those mentioned in 2 Samuel 8:10, but the more general point of the section lies in the confidence that no enemy can stand up against the Lord's anointed. Joshua had encouraged Israel with the words that one Israelite in the strength of the Lord could rout a thousand enemies. Too often Israel was preoccupied in its own problems; thus the Lord graciously raised up David and his house with the intent to establish his kingdom on earth (cf. Ps 2).

C. *The Glorious Deliverance*

18:43–45

43 You have delivered me from the attacks of the people;
you have made me the head of nations;
people I did not know are subject to me.
44 As soon as they hear me, they obey me;
foreigners cringe before me.

45 They all lose heart;
they come trembling from their strongholds.

43–45 With gratitude to the Lord, the psalmist summarizes the effects of his campaigns. First, he was victorious over the enemies. They have responded to him, just as the enemies of God did in earlier times to God's presence as the Divine Warrior (cf. Exod 15:14–16; Josh 2:11, 24). The nations submit themselves to his sovereignty (cf. Ps 2:8–12). Second, the nature of the messianic rule is glorious. The Lord has made his anointed king to be "the head" of nations in fulfillment of his word to Israel (Deut 28:13).

VII. Yahweh, the Rock of Israel

18:46–50

46 The LORD lives! Praise be to my Rock!
Exalted be God my Savior!
47 He is the God who avenges me,
who subdues nations under me,
48 who saves me from my enemies.
You exalted me above my foes;
from violent men you rescued me.
49 Therefore I will praise you among the nations, O LORD;
I will sing praises to your name.
50 He gives his king great victories;
he shows unfailing kindness to his anointed,
to David and his descendants forever.

46–50 The psalmist returns to an affirmation of his confidence in the Rock of Israel (cf. vv.1–3). The Rock described by its many metaphors (v.2) is no other than the Divine Warrior who is the "Savior" (*yiš'î*, "my salvation," v.46; cf. v.50: "victories" [*yešû'ô<u>t</u>*, lit., "acts of salvation," see 3:2]) of the messianic King. The acts of "deliverance" involve complete subjugation of the enemies (v.47) and exaltation above the nations (v.48) as expressions of divine vindication (v.47). He is the God "who avenges" (94:1) and "who saves" (94:19–23). (See the appendix to Ps 119: Yahweh Is My Redeemer.)

The psalmist reflects on the acts of God as celebrated in the psalm for the purpose of encouraging God's people to look at the messianic King as the divinely chosen instrument of deliverance. The Divine Warrior has chosen the anointed King of David's lineage to establish his kingdom (v.50). Every Christian knows that the King is none other than Jesus the Messiah. The Davidic kings in the OT established God's kingdom to a lesser and greater extent. But Jesus is the Gospel (i.e., the Good News) of the kingdom (Mark 1:1). In him we receive God's "love" (*ḥese<u>d</u>*), and in him we are victorious. His salvation involves concern for our whole well-being, spiritual and material.

Instead of exalting himself, David praises the Lord (vv.46, 49). Instead of glorifying his own name among the nations, he speaks about his great King to the nations (v.49). Rightly does Delitzsch conclude: "The praise of Yahve, the God of David, His anointed, is, according to its ultimate import, a praising of the Father of Jesus Christ" (1:269). Calvin encouraged the practice of daily reading of this psalm with Christ in mind: "In conclusion, we shall then only duly profit in the study of this psalm, when we are led by the contemplation of the shadow and type to him [Christ] who is the substance" (1:307).

Psalm 19: God's Perfections Revealed in Work and Word

This psalm reflects, more than any other, the beauty and splendor of the Hebrew poetry found in the Psalter. C.S. Lewis wrote, "I take this to be the greatest poem in the Psalter and one of the greatest lyrics in the world" (*Reflections on the Psalms,* p. 63). Weiser, who questions the unity of the psalm, admits that vv.7–14 reflect an insight that is the "result of great concentration." This insight, when coupled with "powerful metaphorical language," raises the psalmist "to the status of a great poet who has stimulated the creative work of such eminent men as Goethe, Haydn and Beethoven" (Weiser, p. 198). Craigie concludes that this psalm "combines the most beautiful poetry with some of the most profound of biblical theology" (*Psalms 1–50,* p. 183).

The psalm comprises three separate motifs that the author has brought together into a unified *wisdom hymn:* creation praise (vv.1–6), a wisdom psalm (vv.7–11), and a prayer for forgiveness and acceptance (vv.12–14). There is evidence for the independent existence of vv.1–6 and vv.7–11. In the former section the reference to deity is God (El, v.1), whereas in the latter the name Yahweh ("LORD") is common (vv.7–9, 14). The relation between God's revelation in creation and that of the law is so close that Craigie argues, along with Clines, that there are "numerous points of contact between the two portions of the psalm" (*Psalms 1–50,* p. 179). Von Rad speaks of the correlation of creation and revelation as an example of wisdom contemplation (OTT, 1:447). It may be that the author lengthened an existing hymn celebrating God's wisdom in his works and his words (cf. A.A. Anderson, 1:167). Over against paganism, secularism, and humanism, he maintains that God's revelation is sufficient to lead man to seek God's favor (cf. v.14). Paul's argument against paganism assumes the clarity of the natural revelation of God's eternal power and divinity (Rom 1:20). See also Christoph Dohmen, "Ps 19 und sein altorientalischer Hintergrund," *Biblica* 64 (1983): 501–17; D.J.A. Clines, "The Tree of Knowledge and the Law of Yahweh (Psalm XIX)," VetTest 24 (1974): 8–14; James A. Durlesser, "A Rhetorical Critical Study of Psalms 19, 42, and 43," *Studies in Biblical Theology* 10 (1980): 179–97; see also Irmtraud Fischer, "Psalm 19—Ursprüngliche Einheit oder Komposition?" *Biblische Notizen* 21 (1983): 16–25; and Odil Hannes Steck, "Bemerkungen zur thematischen Einheit von Psalm 19,2–7," *Werden und Wirken des Alten Testaments. Festschrift für Claus Westermann zum 70. Geburtstag,* edd. Rainer Albertz, Hans-Peter Müller, Hans Walter Wolff, and Walther Zimmerli (Göttingen: Vandenhoeck & Ruprecht, 1980), pp. 318–24.

From the A.D. perspective, we look at this psalm as an indirect witness to the need for a greater "servant" (vv.11, 13) than David, who could keep the law (cf. vv.12–14), who would be "blameless" (v.13) and "pleasing" in God's sight (v.14). The revelation of God in nature and in the law is truly a revelation of God the Father. However, the incarnation of God in Jesus shows more clearly the divine perfections (vv.7–9). We hear more clearly the voice of our Father by listening carefully to what Jesus said and to how he interpreted God's law. The issue in this psalm is not law versus grace or law versus Jesus but the greater revelation of God in Jesus and, consequently, the greater freedom and maturity of God's children (cf. Heb 1:1–3; Matt 5–7; Gal 3:26–4:27). Leslie C. Allen explains the present position of Psalm 19 (following the royal Ps 18) as an intentional attempt at democratization, as David becomes the type of spiritual struggle for every believer ("David as Exemplar of Spirituality: the Redactional

Function of Psalm 19," *Biblica* 67 [1986]: 544–46). If so, Jesus is now our Guide in our spiritual struggles.

The structural components reveal no apparent symmetry:

A. The Revelation of Creation (vv.1–6)
B. The Revelation of God's Law (vv.7–11)
C. Prayerful Reflection (vv.12–14)

I. The Revelation of Creation (vv.1–6)

The psalmist considers the revelation of God in the world of nature. His belief in God as Creator was not set over against the hypothesis of evolution or the problems of science and the Bible. For him creation reveals the Lord's royal majesty and sovereignty (cf. Rom 1:19–20). It evokes a response of recognition of God's existence, majesty, and wisdom and, therefore, of praise (cf. Rom 10:18). The hymn of creation is composed of two parts: the revelation of the skies (vv.1–4b) and the revelation of the sun (vv.4c–6).

A. *The Revelation of the Skies*

19:1–4b

For the director of music. A psalm of David.

1 The heavens declare the glory of God;
the skies proclaim the work of his hands.
2 Day after day they pour forth speech;
night after night they display knowledge.
3 There is no speech or language
where their voice is not heard.
4 Their voice goes out into all the earth,
their words to the ends of the world.

1 The glory and wisdom of God are evident in the vastness of space. The psalmist calls attention to the word "the heavens" as he begins the first verse and concludes with the synonym "the skies": "The heavens . . . the skies" (in MT). This inclusionary form and the chiastic structure cannot be reproduced in the NIV. It is the author's way of evoking in the reader an immediate response to the words "the heavens" and "the skies" (ABCC′B′A′):

A	B	C
the heavens	declare	the glory of God
C′	B′	A′
the work of his hands	proclaim	the skies

These words signify the place where God put the sun, moon, and stars for the purpose of giving light and for distinguishing "day" from "night" (Gen 1:14–19). For the psalmist "space" is not empty but a revelation of God's creation of the magnificent heavenly bodies, which are characterized by radiance and regularity. The verbs "declare" and "proclaim" are participial forms, expressive of the continuous revelation of the heavens, and could be translated "keep on declaring . . . keep on proclaiming." The wars and disturbances on earth often camouflage God's glory, as they divert attention away from the created heavenly bodies, which show more clearly

God's majesty by their regularity and orderliness. He alone is the Creator, because the magnificence of the heavenly bodies confirms that they are all "the work of his hands" (cf. Deut 4:19; 17:3).

2 The alternation of "day" and "night" reveals the constancy of God's creation: "day after day," "night after night." The cycle of day and night contribute to the regularity of the seasons and thus to the regularity of the agricultural calendar (Gen 8:22). They reveal "knowledge" in their own distinct "speech." The "knowledge" is not only knowledge about God but rather a special kind, best understood as God's wisdom, revealed in his creation (cf. Prov 8:22–31).

3–4b Yet natural revelation is without words and is universal, being unrestricted by the division of languages. It transcends human communication without the use of speech, words, and sounds (cf. NIV mg. on v.3). To those who are inclined to hear, revelation comes with no regard for linguistic or geographical barriers, even to the ends of the world (v.4). Calvin observes, "When a man, from beholding and contemplating the heavens, has been brought to acknowledge God, he will learn also to reflect upon and to admire his wisdom and power as displayed on the face of the earth, not only in general, but even in the minutest plants" (1:308–9).

B. *The Revelation of the Sun*

19:4c–6

In the heavens he has pitched a tent for the sun,
5 which is like a bridegroom coming forth from his
pavilion,
like a champion rejoicing to run his course.
6 It rises at one end of the heavens
and makes its circuit to the other;
nothing is hidden from its heat.

4c–6 Life on earth depends on the regularity of the sun. The psalmist did not know all that we know today about the solar system. His concern was to portray in a phenomenal way how the sun rises, as it were, from "a tent" (v.4c). The sun is metaphorically compared to a "bridegroom" and to a "champion" (v.5). The joy of the bridegroom, coming from the wedding canopy or the bridal chamber, represents the radiance of the sun. The "champion" (= "warrior" or "valiant man"), rejoicing in his strength as he sets out to run his course, represents the power of the sun, as it seems to move through "its circuit" (v.6). From the perspective of this earth, the sun "rises" and "makes its circuit" with radiance and vigor, so that it warms the earth. The sun also reveals God's glory, power, and wisdom. One does not have to listen for words, because the effect of the sun is evident, as "nothing is hidden from its heat."

Notes

For a brief discussion of the technical words and phrases in the superscription, see the Introduction.

2 (3 MT) The verb יַבִּיעַ (*yabbîa'*, "pour forth"), from *n-b-'* ("to bubble forth"), denotes the spontaneity of the revelation. It bubbles forth like a spring. For the connection of "bubbling forth" and knowledge as a wisdom motif, see Prov 1:23 and 18:4.

4 (5 MT) The NIV correctly emends the MT's קַוָּם (*qawwām*, "their line") to קוֹלָם (*qôlām*, "their voice"). From the evidence of the ancient versions (LXX and Peshitta), it is apparent that the lamed ("l" sound) was omitted in the transcription of the Hebrew text. Also the parallelism with "words" (v.4b) supports the emendation. Weiser maintains the MT and reads "their law," proposing the revelation of the law of nature (pp. 197–99). It seems that Weiser is too engrossed with the polemical character of the psalm as directed against "pagan science" (p. 200). NEB's "their music" is too interpretative.

The phrase "in the heavens" is an interpretative addition for the MT's בָּהֶם (*bāhem*, "in them"). It may refer back to v.1: "the heavens" or the "expanse" (NIV, "skies"). It is absent in the LXX.

6 For a refutation of Dahood's rendering "from its pavilion" (*Psalms*, 1:120) instead of "from its heat," see Craigie (*Psalms 1–50*, pp. 178–79).

II. The Revelation of God's Law

19:7–11

7 The law of the LORD is perfect,
  reviving the soul.
The statutes of the LORD are trustworthy,
  making wise the simple.
8 The precepts of the LORD are right,
  giving joy to the heart.
The commands of the LORD are radiant,
  giving light to the eyes.
9 The fear of the LORD is pure,
  enduring forever.
The ordinances of the LORD are sure
  and altogether righteous.
10 They are more precious than gold,
  than much pure gold;
they are sweeter than honey,
  than honey from the comb.
11 By them is your servant warned;
  in keeping them there is great reward.

7–11 The revelation of God's law is clearer than the revelation in nature. Nature "declares," "proclaims," "pours forth," and "displays" the revelation of God's majesty, wisdom, and power. However, the revelation of the law is greater. It is greater because it is given by the covenant God, whose name is Yahweh ("LORD," vv.7, 8, 9), whereas nature reveals the glory of the Creator-God (El, v.1; see the appendix to Ps 22: Yahweh Is El). It is also greater because of the comprehensive nature of the revelation. This is brought out by the choice of the synonyms for God's revelation: "law," "statutes" (v.7); "precepts," "commands" (v.8); and "fear," "ordinances" (v.9; see appendix below). The synonyms are not to be studied in abstraction but give a comprehensive emphasis that *all* of the words of the Lord are beneficial. Although the benefits of natural revelation are with us on a daily basis (day, night, heat [vv.2, 6]), how much greater are the comprehensive benefits of God's revelation in the law! The list of four benefits (vv.7–8) is given to encourage the godly to embrace the law of God as an expression of his wisdom. The rewards (v.11) of responsiveness to the revelation of God are compared to gold (v.10; cf. Prov 3:13–18; 8:19) and to honey (cf. Prov 16:24).

The benefits are set forth propositionally (vv.7–9). First, God's word "revives" (cf. v.7). Its restorative quality gives healing to the whole person by assuring forgiveness and cleansing and by giving life to the godly. It unleashes the promises of God by his gracious redemptive acts (80:3, 7, 19). Second, God's word is the source of "wisdom" to all who are ready to receive it (v.7; cf. 119:130; Prov 21:11). Both the inexperienced ("the simple," v.7; cf. Prov 1:4) and the wise develop as they begin with "the fear of the Lord" (v.9; cf. Deut 4:10; Prov 1:7) and embrace the will of God in all aspects of life (cf. Prov 1:2–6). Third, God's word gives "joy" (v.8a). The heartfelt joy is equivalent to inner peace and tranquility, as one loves God with all his heart, i.e., with his innermost being. Fourth, God's word gives "light to the eyes" (v.8b). The internal joy radiates through the eyes. It expresses the joy of being alive and of receiving God's blessings (cf. 13:3). Thus Yahweh has made the sun for light in creation and has given his word for light in redemption.

The reason the revelation of God in his word is superior to natural revelation lies in its clarity and openness to all. God's written revelation manifests a perfect internal harmony between God and his word. God's word reflects God's integrity, uprightness, and fidelity (cf. 18:25: "blameless," NIV). It is "trustworthy" (v.7b) in the sense that his statutes are true in principle and are verifiable in the situations of life (cf. 93:5; 111:7). It is "right" in the sense of straightforward and just. God's word is not perverse or crooked but encourages the godly to be upright. The Bible is an "open" book; there is no hypocrisy in it. It is "radiant," that is, "pure," and its purity effects the clean and upright way of those who are "pure" (cf. 18:26). It is "pure" or "flawless" (v.9), being "refined" like silver (cf. 12:6). It is "enduring forever" (v.9), as it does not change with the times and the incessant variations in fashion. God's word is always "in." It is "sure" (v.9, "faithful," "true"; cf. 119:151, 160), as it reflects the fidelity and loyalty of God (cf. Rev 16:7; 19:2). It is "righteous" as it reflects God's righteousness. It is sweet like the finest honey (v.10). These metaphors refer to the great value of God's word in terms of its effects on those who observe them. It causes integrity, loyalty, uprightness, purity, and growth in righteousness (vv.7–9).

The efficacy of God's revelation is set forth by the synonyms for law, the characteristics of the word, and the beneficial effects on the godly. The Word of God in itself, in its revelatory qualities and its *transforming* effects in the godly, is, therefore, of greater value than the most valuable objects of man's striving: money (= "gold"; cf. 119:72) and fine food (v.10; cf. 119:103). It keeps the wise man on the narrow path by forewarning him of possible pitfalls (v.11a) and by guiding him on to the rewards of godliness: life, God-given joy, wisdom, and contentment (vv.7–9; cf. Prov 22:4; 1 Tim 4:8; 6:6). The repetitious use of "your servant" (vv.11, 13; cf. superscription of Ps 18) bears out the willingness of the psalmist in doing God's will. The word "servant" (*'ebed*) applies to one who either by appointment, office, or choice commits himself to the execution of someone else's will—in this context, the covenant Lord.

Notes

---

11 (12 MT) Some propose another meaning for נִזְהָר (*nizhār*, "warned") based on a homonym of the root *z-h-r* ("illumine"): "Moreover, your servant is illumined by them" (Craigie, *Psalms*

1–50, p. 178; cf. Dahood, *Psalms*, 1:121, 124; id., "An Ebla Personal Name and the Metaphor in Psalm 19, 11–12," *Biblica* 63 [1982]: 260–63). In support of this view is the uncontestable fact that the psalm contains a description of the sun. But the idea of being "warned" or "instructed" fits very well within the reflection, as he prays to be forgiven of hidden and known sins so as to cleanse his way in the presence of his God.

III. Prayerful Reflection

19:12–14

12 Who can discern his errors?
Forgive my hidden faults.
13 Keep your servant also from willful sins;
may they not rule over me.
Then will I be blameless,
innocent of great transgression.

14 May the words of my mouth and the meditation of my heart
be pleasing in your sight,
O LORD, my Rock and my Redeemer.

12–13 The psalmist reflects on himself in relation to God and his revelation. In Psalm 8 when he reflected on God's glory in the heavens, he was forced to look at the dignity of man (8:4a). Now he reflects on man's sinfulness and limitations. God is perfect; and his revelation in nature and the word reveal his glory, power, and wisdom. But man is such an insignificant part in the vastness of space. Just as nothing is hidden from the heat of the sun (v.6), and even as the "voice" of the natural revelation penetrates to "the ends of the earth" (v.4), so God's word with all its perfections (vv.7–9) penetrates and examines man. The godly man stands, therefore, in fear before his Creator-Redeemer, knowing that he may have "hidden faults" or "errors" (v.12) that he has not yet discovered. Inadvertent sins had to be dealt with by the atonement of these sins (Lev 4:2–35; Num 15:22–31). The psalmist shows even a conscientiousness pertaining to the "hidden faults," because he aims at pleasing God so as to live "blameless" before him (cf. 18:25b; Job 1:1, 4–5). Therefore he asks for forgiveness and an ability to express humility and contrition. He desires true godliness according to which he will not knowingly sin against his God (v.13). The wicked sin in their arrogance and show no awareness of having done wrong. "Willful sins" are those often attributed to the "arrogant" (*zēḏîm*), who have no regard for God (cf. NEB, "sins of self-will," or in Dahood: "keep your servant from the presumptuous ones" [*Psalms*, 1:121]). There is no agreement on whether "the great transgression" (v.13) is idolatry (Dahood, *Psalms*, 1:125), adultery, or any other sin against the moral law of God. For the correlation of land-gift, divine order, and man's responsibility, see Walter Brueggemann, "On Land-losing and Land-receiving," *Crux* 19 (1980): 166–73.

14 The psalmist closes with a prayer that shows a link with the beginning of the psalm by the repetition of "words" (cf. v.2: "speech"). The heavens "declare," "proclaim," "pour forth," and "display" without the benefit of human speech; yet they speak clearly—through the language of nature—of the glory, power, and wisdom of God. The Lord revealed his word in speech and written forms accessible to people. In turn the psalmist, as a redeemed creature of God, prays that his expressed and unspoken words may be acceptable to his God, his Rock (cf. 18:2) and his Redeemer (cf. 78:35; Exod 15:13; Isa 63:9); namely, Yahweh, the covenant-loving God.

Notes

12 (13 MT) The verb נקה (*n-q-h*) may mean "to forgive" or "to declare to be exempt from punishment." The former meaning is given here and the latter in v.13d ("innocent").

13 (14 MT) The verb אֵיתָם (*'ēṯām*, "I shall be blameless") is a form of *t-m-m*: Qal imperfect. It is related to the word "perfect" as an attribute of the law (*t*[e]*mîmāh*, v.7a) and of the Lord (*tāmîm*, 18:30). But it may also describe a human being (*tāmîm*, 18:25b: "blameless"; see 7:8 ["integrity"]; 15:2; see the appendix to Ps 1: The Ways of Wisdom and Folly).

Appendix: The Word of God

Psalms 19 and 119 employ at least eight distinct Hebrew words denoting God's revelation and adumbrate each with divine splendor. The marvel of the ages is that the Lord has revealed his word to Moses and that rebellious Israel was the recipient of God's covenant of grace (99:7; cf. Rom 3:2; 9:3–4). The psalmists witness to the importance of this event and to their responsibility in being loyal to their covenant God and Father. After all, the law is the instruction of God to godly living and as God's word was good news to all who lived by faith and by the grace of God.

These eight words also occur in other parts of the Psalms: (1) "law" (*tôrāh*); (2) "word" (*dāḇār*); (3) "laws" (*mišpāṭîm*); (4) "statute(s)" (*'ēḏôṯ*/*'ēḏûṯ*); (5) "command(s)" (*miṣwāh*/*miṣwôṯ*); (6) "decrees" (*ḥûqqîm*); (7) "precepts" (*piqqûḏîm*); (8) "word" or "promise" (*'imrāh*). For example, notice 147:15–19:

He sends his command [*'imrāh*] to the earth;
his word [*dāḇār*] runs swiftly.
He spreads the snow like wool
and scatters the frost like ashes.
He hurls down his hail like pebbles.
Who can withstand his icy blast?
He sends his word [*dāḇār*] and melts them;
he stirs up his breezes, and the waters flow.
He has revealed his word [*dāḇār*] to Jacob,
his laws [*ḥûqqîm*] and decrees [*mišpāṭîm*] to Israel.

"Law" (*tôrāh*) in the broad sense refers to any "instruction" flowing from the revelation of God as the basis for life and action. The godly is receptive to, communes with, and practices the instruction of God: "But his delight is in the law of the LORD, / and on his law he meditates day and night" (1:2). God's revelation demarcates the *way* of God, and the righteous person delights in staying within its perimeters—Psalm 19:7a: "The law of the LORD is perfect, / reviving the soul." The goal of revelation is the *internalization* of God's word in the heart of man so as to transform his way of life: "The law [*tôrāh*] of his God is in his heart; / his feet do not slip" (37:31; cf. 40:8; cf. Jer 31:33). The expression of internalization is *delight* in God's revelation (1:2; 119:70, 77, 113, 163, 165, 174).

"Word" (*dāḇār*) refers to speech, both human and divine. The psalmist exalts divine speech as everything that proceeds from the mouth of the Lord. The verb *d-b-r* ("speak") is derived from the noun and may also be used to refer to human as well as divine speech. Divine speech is distinct from human speech in that it has the power to create (33:6, 9). Through his word he keeps his covenant: "He remembers his covenant forever, / the word [*dāḇār*] he commanded, for a thousand generations" (105:8; cf. v.42). Moreover, his word powerfully transforms human beings: "How can a young man keep his way pure? / By living according to your word [*dāḇār*]" (119:9). His word is faithful (33:4; 119:43), righteous (119:160), the object of hope (119:74, 81, 147; 130:5), eternal (119:89), and wise, "Your word [*dāḇār*] is a lamp to my feet / and a light for my path" (119:105; cf. vv.130, 169). God's word sustains the godly during adverse times: "You are my refuge and my shield; / I have put my hope in your word [*dāḇār*]" (119:114).

"Laws" (*mišpāṭîm*) denote divinely ordered decisions on all kinds of issues. The wicked have no regard for ordering the details of their lives by God's revelation: "His ways are always prosperous; / he is haughty and your laws [*mišpāṭîm*] are far from him; / he sneers at all his enemies" (10:5). The godly recognize the "laws" of God's kingdom as giving order within the community: "All his laws [*mišpāṭîm*] are before me; / I have not turned away from his decrees [*ḥûqqôṯ*]" (18:22).

"Statute(s)" (*'ēḏôṯ/'ēḏûṯ*), derived from *'-w-d* ("witness," "testify"), is often synonymous with "covenant" (cf. 25:10; 132:12). Observance of God's statutes keeps one from advancing illegitimate ambitions: "Turn my heart toward your statutes [*'ēḏûṯ*] / and not toward selfish gain" (119:36). They are the joy and wonder of the godly (119:111, 129), as they enhance life (119:144) and give wisdom (19:7). They, like the covenant, are to be transmitted from generation to generation: "He decreed statutes [*'ēḏûṯ*] for Jacob / and established the law [*tôrāh*] in Israel, / which he commanded our forefathers / to teach their children" (78:5). Israel regularly celebrated their "distinct calling" in feasts and festivals, when they would make their pilgrimages to Jerusalem by divine statute: "That is where the tribes go up, / the tribes of the LORD, / to praise the name of the LORD / according to the statute [*'ēḏûṯ*] given to Israel" (122:4).

"Command(s)" (*miṣwāh/miṣwôṯ*) designates anything ordained by the Lord. It is a synonym of "law," as well as of "decrees" and "laws"—Psalm 19:8b: "The commands of the LORD are radiant, / giving light to the eyes." Within the path of God's commands there is boundless freedom (119:32, 96), joy (112:1; 119:35, 47, 143), and wisdom (119:66, 73, 98). The attitude toward these commands is that of a servant rushing to please his Master (119:60), because the rewards of doing the will of God are great (119:127).

"Decrees" (*ḥûq-qîm/+ôṯ*, from *ḥ-q-q*, "inscribe") ascribes to God the royal sovereignty of establishing his divine will in nature (148:5–6) and in the covenant community (105:10; cf. Deut 4:1). The decree has the force of a covenant, Yahweh's sovereign administration of grace and promise: "He confirmed it to Jacob as a decree [*ḥōq*], / to Israel as an everlasting covenant" (105:10). Yahweh sanctioned the Davidic dynasty (2:7) as his vassal-king on earth. So he has given also sanctions for his people to serve him as his vassal people, who live in accordance with his "inscribed" laws. The psalmist elects the divine decrees over human orders: "Though rulers sit together and slander me, / your servant will meditate on your decrees [*ḥûqqîm*]" (119:23). After all, human kings edict corruption and oppression: "Can a corrupt throne be allied with you— / one that brings on misery by its decrees [*ḥōq*]?" (94:20). How different are Yahweh's royal orders! Repeatedly the psalmist asks the Lord to instruct him in his way, his decrees (119:12, 26, 33, 64, 68, 71, 124, 135, 171). However, the ungodly have no part in his covenant administration: "But to the wicked, God says: / 'What right have you to recite my laws [*ḥuqqîm*] / or take my covenant on your lips?' " (50:16).

"Precepts" (*piqqûḏîm*) appears to be synonymous with "covenant" (103:18) and with the revelation of God (111:7). This word occurs twenty-four times, exclusively in the Psalms. Yahweh's expectations for his children are to be followed: "You have laid down precepts [*piqqûḏîm*] / that are to be fully obeyed" (119:4). The divine orders provide freedom and joy for the godly (19:8; 119:45), even though they meditate on them and keep them punctiliously (119:15, 27, 56, 69, 78, 87, 93, 94, 100, 104, 110, 128, 134, 141, 168).

"Word" or "promise" (*'imrāh*), derived from *'-m-r* ("say"), may denote any word from God (instruction or promise) or man (prayer; cf. 17:6). Its usage is most frequent in Psalm 119 (nineteen out of twenty-five times in the Psalms). The words of man are deceptive (5:9), but every word that proceeds from God's mouth is sound and of great value: "And the words [*'imrāh*] of the Lord are flawless, / like silver refined in a furnace of clay, / purified seven times" (12:6; cf. 18:30; 119:140; Prov 30:5). The word of "promise" is an encouragement as it provides a divine guarantee even in the most distressing moments: "As for God, his way is perfect; / the word [*'imrāh*] of the Lord is flawless. / He is a shield / for all who take refuge in him" (18:30). The author of Psalm 119 reflects again and again on the life-giving word of God, through which he receives comfort, hope, and poise during his adversity: "My comfort in my suffering is this: / Your promise [*'imrāh*] preserves my life" (v.50; cf. vv.58, 76, 82, 116, 123, 154, 170). He longs for the fulfillment of God's promise-word: "Fulfill your promise [*'imrāh*] to your servant, / so that you may be feared" (119:38; cf. v.41). The hiding of God's word in his heart signifies both his devotion to the Lord and his hope, as his life is lived in anticipation of fulfillment (v.11; cf. v.148). Hence he can say, "How sweet are your words [*'imrāh*] to my taste, / sweeter than honey to my mouth!" (v.103; cf. v.162). (See the magnificent essay "Sweeter Than Honey," by C.S. Lewis [*Reflections on the Psalms*, pp. 54–65].) For the psalmist, Yahweh, his Word, and his perfections amplify one another and evoke worship: "I will bow down toward your holy temple / and will praise your name / for your love and your faithfulness, / for you have exalted above all things / your name and your word [*'imrāh*]" (138:2).

Two other nouns derived from *'-m-r* are *'ēmer* ("word") and *'ōmer* ("word"). For example, "Has his unfailing love vanished forever? / Has his promise [*'ōmer*] failed for all time?" (77:8); "O my people, hear my teaching [*tôrāh*]; / listen to the words [*'ēmer*] of my mouth" (78:1).

In conclusion, the psalmist does not distinguish between the law of God and the word of God, between law and gospel. Von Rad rightly criticizes the earlier Lutheran position, which held that "Israel was compelled by God's law to an ever greater zeal for the Law, and that it was the Law and the emotions it evoked which prepared the way for true salvation in Christ" (OTT, 2:405). The Psalms, instead, reflect a close connection between Yahweh and his revelation, between the perfections of Yahweh and the perfections of his revelation, between the grace of God and the love for God, and between salvation by grace and sanctification in grace.

The Lord's concern appears to be with the heart attitude of his servants, as he expects them to readily practice whatever he requires. The *internalization* of the law is both a motivation from the Spirit of God and a wholehearted expression of love for God. Thus de Pinto writes, "That is why there is so much personal dialogue in the Psalms between God and man. The psalms understand the Torah from within as love, and not merely from without, as law. Or better perhaps: in the psalms law and love are not opposed but complementary" (p. 173). It excludes legalism, working for rewards, justification by works, or Pharisaism. The psalmists hold in dialectic tension two focuses: theological ethics (living for the glory of God) and eschatological ethics (living in preparation of the glorious future Yahweh has prepared for those he loves).

Texts: 1:2; 18:20–26; 19:7–14; 25:4–15; 31:23–24; 37; 40:6–11; 51:13; 56:4, 10; 78:1, 2, 5–10, 56; 81:3–5, 8–16; 89:30–34; 94:10; 99:7; 101:2, 6; 105:45; 106:3; 119; 147:19–20.

Bibliography: Childs, IOTS, pp. 513–14; OTCT, pp. 51–57; Brueggemann, "Songs of Torah," in *Message of the Psalms*, pp. 38–42; R.E. Clements, "The Old Testament as Law," *Old Testament Theology. A Fresh Approach* (London: Marshall, Morgan & Scott, 1978), pp. 104–30; Eichrodt, TOT, 1:70–97; Jon D. Levenson, "The Sources of Torah: Psalm 119 and the Modes of Revelation in Second Temple Judaism," *Ancient Israelite Religion. Essays in Honor of Frank Moore Cross*, edd. Patrick D. Miller, Jr.; Paul D. Hanson; and S. Dean McBride (Philadelphia: Fortress, 1987), pp. 559–74; Walter C. Kaiser, Jr., TOTT, pp. 100–121; id., *Toward an Old Testament Ethics* (Grand Rapids: Zondervan, 1983); id., *Toward Rediscovering the Old Testament* (Grand Rapids: Zondervan, 1987), pp. 147–66; Mays, "The Place of the Torah-Psalms in the Psalter," pp. 3–12; Thomas M. McComiskey, *The Covenants of Promise. A Theology of the Old Testament Covenants* (Grand Rapids: Baker, 1985), pp. 59–137; Basil de Pinto, "The Torah and the Psalms," JBL 86 (1967): 154–74; von Rad, OTT, 2:388–409; W. Zimmerli, "The Theological Relevance of the Law," *The Law and the Prophets. A Study of the Meaning of the Old Testament*, tr. R.E. Clements (New York: Harper & Row, 1965), pp. 46–60, 109–40.

TDNT, 4:91–100, 482–86; 7:802–28; TDOT, 1:328–47; THAT, 1:216–19, 433–42; 2:209–20, 530–35; TWOT, 1:54–55, 178–81, 403–5; 2:649–50, 731–32, 757–58.

Psalm 20: Prayer for Victory

Concern for God's blessing on the king in facing national distress dominates the psalm. It contains a beautiful expression of solidarity between the people and their king, as all are involved in imploring the Lord's favor. The people recognize the anointed leader as God's agent in bestowing his favor on the people. The historical occasion for this prayer is not clear. If it dates from David's time, it reflects the early years when David faced the challenge of subduing the surrounding nations. The prayer calls on God to send help from Zion, where the ark had been placed during David's reign and where Solomon erected a beautiful temple. The confidence in God's help shows a deep theological awareness of God's kingship, as well as the Abrahamic, Mosaic, and Davidic covenants. God is faithful to his promises. The psalm concludes with a response of faith by the people, which is demonstrated by the change from petitions addressed to God (vv.1–4) to the anticipated joy of victory (first person plural "we" and "us," vv.7–9).

The psalm shows balance and development. It is a *royal psalm*, like Psalm 2. The literary qualities are evident. The beginning and end form an inclusion by the words "answer" and "day" (NIV of v.9 obscures it by the idiomatic rendering "when" rather than "in the day"). Several words are repeated: "name" (vv. 1, 5, 7) and forms of the root *y-š-ʿ* ("save," vv.5–6, 9; NIV, "victorious," v.5). See K.A.D. Smelik ("The Origin of Psalm 20," JSOT 31 [1985]: 75–81) for a supposed literary relationship with an Aramaic hymn.

The structure may be set forth thus:

A. Prayer in Need (v.1)
  B. Prayer for God's Royal Help (vv.2–4)

C. Rejoicing in Anticipation (v.5)
B′. Confidence in God's Royal Help (vv.6–8)
A′. Prayer in Need (v.9)

The congregation actively participates in the royal preparations for war. An enemy has attacked or has shown intent to attack. At stake is the royal glory. But more than that, God's honor is threatened. The prayer of intercession is for the king and, therefore, for the kingdom of God on earth. The prayer takes the form of a blessing by the repetitive use of "may" and is an appropriate prayer for the full establishment of the kingdom of the Messiah of David.

At the very heart of the petitions and expressions of solidarity is the hope that soon God will grant victory to his "anointed" (v.6, = messiah) and that the "distress" will turn into rejoicing. The OT saints looked constantly for the fulfillment of this hope. In Jesus' coming we receive further assurance that the kingdom of God is being established. The followers of Jesus may implore the Lord for the full establishment of the messianic kingdom, when every knee will bow (v.8; cf. 1 Cor 15:25–26; Phil 2:10), the kingdom is established in his hand (v.7; cf. 1 Cor 15:27), and the victory is given by the Father to the Messiah of David (v.6; cf. 1 Cor 15:28). In anticipation we may join the OT saints in rejoicing, lifting up the banners (v.5), the assurance of hope (v.6, "Now I know"), and the prayer for Jesus' establishment of the kingdom (v.9).

I. Prayer in Need

20:1

For the director of music. A psalm of David.

[1]May the LORD answer you when you are in distress;
may the name of the God of Jacob protect you.

1 The people pray for God's covenant blessings on the king as their representative. God has promised to protect, to be gracious to, and to give peace to his people (Num 6:24–26), thus placing his "name on the Israelites" (v.27). But now that the "distress" is here, they *invoke* the "name of the God of Jacob" to protect the king. "The God of Jacob" is a reference to the Redeemer who delivered Jacob (= Israel) from Egypt (Exod 19:3–4) and who has promised to deal justly with his people (cf. Ps 146:5–10). The "name of the God of Jacob" is Yahweh, as he revealed it to Moses (Exod 3:14–15; 6:2–3). He is the God who promised to bring about all the promises made to the patriarchs, and one of these is the protection of his people: "I will surely bless you. . . . Your descendants will take possession of the cities of their enemies" (Gen 22:17).

In their present distress, God's people are in danger of coming to a low point, unless the God of Jacob raises up the king. In the prayer for protection, the phrase "protect you" is a translation of "place you high," as on a rock (18:2) for protection and strength (cf. 69:29; 91:14; 107:41).

Notes

For a brief discussion of the technical words and phrases in the superscription, see the Introduction.

1 (2 MT) The verbal phrase יְשַׂגֶּבְךָ (*y^eśaggeb̲^ek̲ā*, "may protect you") is a form of the root *ś-g-b* ("be high"). In the Piel pattern it signifies "to make high, inaccessible" and is related to the noun "refuge" (*miśgāb̲*), a high place in the rocks or on a wall (KB[3], 2:605; cf. 18:2: "stronghold"). Dahood rightly observes, "The psalmist may have employed the verb. . . . to elicit the thought of a *miśgāb̲*, 'retreat, bulwark' " (*Psalms*, 1:127).

II. Prayer for God's Royal Help

20:2–4

2 May he send you help from the sanctuary
  and grant you support from Zion.
3 May he remember all your sacrifices
  and accept your burnt offerings. *Selah*
4 May he give you the desire of your heart
  and make all your plans succeed.

The specifics of the prayer include a petition for the Lord's presence (v.2) and favor (v.3) as well as for the king's success (v.4). Each verse has the form:

imperfect / jussive	object
connective waw + object	imperfect / jussive

The structure is chiastic:

Verb ╲╱ Object
Object ╱╲ Verb

Because of the clear structuring by which vv.2–4 explicate the particular requests, v.1 functions as the introduction to the prayer.

2 The presence of God was symbolized in the "sanctuary" on Mount Zion (see the appendix to Ps 46: Zion Theology). Here he had made his "name" to dwell (Deut 14:23; 16:2, 11) and had promised to be present with David, who had shown concern with his sanctuary (2 Sam 7:1–2). The Lord had also promised to establish the Davidic dynasty (2 Sam 7:12, 16) and to give rest from the enemies (2 Sam 7:11). Cult and kingship were integrally related (cf. Ps 132). The history of the united kingdom and of Judah reveals how the Lord was present with the kings who cared for his sanctuary.

The word "sanctuary" (*qōd̲eš*, "holy thing," "holiness") is not the usual term *miqdāš* ("sanctuary," cf. Exod 25:8). Apparently the psalmist has in mind Zion, God's holy hill, where the temple was located (see the appendix to Ps 132: The Ark of the Covenant and the Temple: Symbols of Yahweh's Presence and Rule). God's holy place was localized at Jerusalem but was not limited to Jerusalem. Jerusalem was an earthly reflection of "his holy heaven" (v.6). The phrase "holy heaven" denotes the universal rule of God, whereas his presence in Jerusalem signified to Israel his kingship over his people, Israel. Jesus' teaching on the universality of God's worship extends the bounds of God's kingship to include Gentiles as well (John 4:21–24).

The provisions and support for the sanctuary brought by the people were tokens of their loyalty to the Lord. When God's people are in distress, they call on the Lord to be present by giving support to the anointed leader. The "help" and "support" are evidence of God's presence as the Great King. The verb "support" ("strengthen") could indicate provision of food and drink (Judg 19:5, 8; Ps 104:15) or a demonstration of God's loving acts (Ps 94:18), by which God strengthens (Ps 18:35), restores (Ps 41:3), and delivers his people (Ps 119:117). The "support" of the Lord takes care of all the king's needs as he goes out to battle. The Lord's presence demonstrates his loyalty to the anointed king and thereby to his people. He would go ahead of the Israelite forces, as in the days of old (cf. Exod 15:13–17; Ps 44:4–8).

3 The favor of God was sought by means of the "sacrifices" and "burnt offerings." The Israelite practice of presenting sacrifices and offerings before a military campaign was an act of devotion and submission to the Lord (1 Sam 7:9–10; 13:9–12). Their purpose was not primarily to atone for sin but to seek God's favor and to consecrate oneself for war. As dedicatory offerings, they were burned on the altar so as to make "an aroma pleasing to the LORD" (Lev 1:13; see Willem A. VanGemeren, "Offerings and Sacrifices," in Elwell, EDT, pp. 788–92). The offerings did not guarantee the Lord's favor (cf. 1 Sam 13:9–12), because he delights in loyalty more than offerings (1 Sam 15:22–23). The "remembrance" may be a sacrificial term for acceptance of the offering, especially in light of the parallelism with "accept." The verb "accept" is an extended meaning from the root *d-š-n* ("be fat"), which in the Piel also takes the meaning of "to deal in a plenteous way" (cf. 23:5, "You anoint my head with oil," lit., "you fatten my head with oil"). The acceptance of the sacrifices guarantees God's favor, as if the plenteous sacrifices, as tokens of loyalty, are "remembered" for good. The Lord demonstrates his remembrance by acts of love and, in accepting the burnt offerings, guarantees to deal bountifully with the offerer.

4 The prosperity of the king is dependent on God's presence and favor (vv.2–3). The king's "heart" had to show a walk of integrity with his God (1 Kings 9:4). Concern for God's honor was a prerequisite for wisdom, and a wise heart would produce "plans" (or "counsel") that would come to fruition (cf. 1:3; Prov 8:14–21). As the king received counsel before battle, it was important to discern the will of God (cf. 2 Sam 16:20; 1 Kings 22:7). The people pray that the Lord will prosper both the deliberations of the heart and the counsel ("plans") in preparation for battle. The "plans" (*ʿēṣāh,* "advice" or "plan") are the results of the deliberations that precede a campaign (2 Kings 18:20; Isa 8:10; 36:5).

Notes

3 (4 MT) The plural of both "sacrifices" and "burnt offerings" is based on several Hebrew MSS and the Syriac, Targum, and Vulgate; the MT has a singular form of "burnt offering."

4 (5 MT) The MT reads כִּלְבָבֶךָ (*kilᵉḇāḇeḵā,* "as your heart") for "the desire of your heart." The verb יְמַלֵּא (*yᵉmallēʾ*, "make succeed") is repeated in v.5b ("may [he] grant").

III. Rejoicing in Anticipation

20:5

> [5]We will shout for joy when you are victorious

and will lift up our banners in the name of our God.
May the LORD grant all your requests.

5 When the Lord responds to the prayer, he will demonstrate his presence and favor by giving victory to the king. The people pledge loyalty to the king by affirming their joy in his victory. They are confident that he is God's chosen servant for the occasion and look forward to his return in victory. They also pledge loyalty to the Lord by raising their banners "in the name of our God." Moses raised a "banner" to the Lord after the war with the Amalekites as a token of perpetual war as long as the Amalekites existed as a people (Exod 17:15–16). Here the raising of the banners signifies God's victory over the enemies (cf. Dahood, *Psalms*, 1:128). They trust that the king who goes out "in the name" of Yahweh (vv.1, 5) will experience his presence and favor. They are prepared to raise the banners as an expression of confidence in the forthcoming victory. The people conclude their prayer with the petition for the Lord's blessing.

Notes

5 (6 MT) The LXX reads "we shall be magnified" from the root גדל (*g-d-l*, "be great") instead of from גלד (*g-l-d*, "raise a banner"). BHS proposes an emendation נָגִיל (*nāg̲îl*, "we shall rejoice"), but the NEB chooses in favor of the LXX: "Let us do homage to the name of our God." The LXX and NEB suppose a synonymous parallelism. In favor of the NIV are the allusions to war (cf. S of Songs 6:4).

IV. Confidence in God's Royal Help

20:6–8

6 Now I know that the LORD saves his anointed;
he answers him from his holy heaven
with the saving power of his right hand.
7 Some trust in chariots and some in horses,
but we trust in the name of the LORD our God.
8 They are brought to their knees and fall,
but we rise up and stand firm.

6–8 How easy it is to rely on one's own abilities! The psalmist reflects on the nature of Israel's warfare in contrast to warfare in the ancient Near East. Kings multiplied for themselves horses and chariots (v.7) to secure victory, power, and control (cf. Isa 31:1–3). The Lord had forewarned Israel that their theocratic kings were to be different from the kingship of the nations (cf. Deut 17:14–20). Israel's kings were prohibited to "acquire great numbers of horses" (v.16) but were required "to revere the LORD" (v.19). Underlying this contrast is the belief in God's sovereign kingship over the nations and his readiness to deliver his own people (cf. Josh 23:6–11).

The psalmist reflects on Israel's strength. The verb "trust in" occurs once in the MT (v.7b; NIV inserts it in v.7a) and is a translation of "we shall mention" (*nazkîr*). To "mention" may have the sense of "to proclaim" (cf. 87:4: "I will record"; cf. B.S.

Childs, *Memory and Tradition in Israel* [Naperville: Allenson, 1962], p. 72). God's people proclaim the name of their God rather than the numbers of chariots and horses. In this sense the verb contains an expression of "trust." The Lord is the source of power, because his name is "Yahweh" (v.7), because he is the Great King who dwells in "his holy heaven" (v.6), and because he is able to deliver with "the saving power of his right hand" (v.6; cf. 17:7; 21:8). (See the appendix to Ps 7: The Name of Yahweh.)

The phrase "Now I know" (v.6) is equivalent to "I have come to the conclusion that" (Exod 18:11; Judg 17:13; 1 Kings 17:24). It does not follow that the victory has already been achieved (cf. Dahood, *Psalms,* 1:128). It is an emphatic expression of confidence in the Lord and in the victory that formed the substance of the prayer (vv.1–5). God's commitment is to "his anointed" by covenant (2 Sam 7; cf. Ps 2:2b, 7–9), and therefore the "anointed" king is the divinely appointed means of Yahweh's deliverance. The outcome will be complete victory, leaving the opposition in total collapse (v.8a), whereas God's people will be victorious (cf. 44:7). (See the appendix to Ps 119: Yahweh Is My Redeemer.)

The verb "saves" (v.6), from the same root as "victorious" (v.5), could yield the translation "the LORD gives victory to his anointed." The perfect form "has delivered" (*hôšîaʿ*) is an example of a prophetic perfect. The victory is viewed from the perspective of having been accomplished. So sure is the psalmist!

Notes

6 (7 MT) For the meaning "when you are victorious" (lit., "in your salvation"), see the Notes on 3:2.

"The saving power" is literally the "powers of salvation." The word גְּבֻרוֹת (*geḇurôṯ,* "powers") is an abstract plural: "power." The noun "salvation" is related to the verb "saves" (v.6) and to the noun "victory" (NIV, "victorious," v.5). The power of the Lord effects victory: "the victorious power" (cf. NEB, "the victorious might").

V. Prayer in Need

20:9

> 9 O LORD, save the king!
> Answer us when we call!

9 The psalm begins and closes with a prayer for the king. The phraseology "Answer us when we call!" forms a symmetric relation with "May the LORD answer you when you are in distress" (v.1). People and king are bound together in seeking the Lord's face as they experience "distress." People and king call on the Lord, await an answer, and are dependent on the Lord's act of salvation. The prayer "save the king" must be understood as a prayer for his victories, as the root *yšʿ* ("save," "give victory") occurs twice as a verb (vv.6, 9) and twice as a noun (vv.5–6).

Psalm 21: The Rule of God Through His King

Psalms 20 and 21 have vocabulary and motifs in common. In Psalm 20 a petition is made for victory, whereas Psalm 21 celebrates the victory already achieved (cf. 20:4; 21:1–2). Both psalms contain the alternation of the first person plural and the third person singular (cf. 20:1–4, 5; 21:1–12, 13). Both psalms speak of the Lord's victory (20:5; 21:1, 5) and of the anointed king (20:9; 21:1, 8).

Psalm 21 contains elements of *thanksgiving* (vv.1–7) and *confidence* (vv.8–12). Dahood views it as "a psalm of thanksgiving for the royal victory" (*Psalms*, 1:131). Weiser, rejecting the connection with Psalm 20, proposes that Psalm 21 is "a fragment of the ritual of the coronation of the king, belonging to the cultic tradition of the royal feast" (p. 212). Kraus views the variety of elements (thanksgiving, oracle, and prayer) as parts of a liturgy that are difficult to ascertain (*Psalmen*, 1:169). Craigie also accepts the liturgical approach and places its life setting in a ceremony celebrating "the anniversary or renewal of the king's coronation in the Davidic tradition" (*Psalms 1–50*, p. 190). It seems likely that the psalm contains elements of a *royal liturgy* that have their setting in the traditions of the Davidic covenant. See W. Quintens, "La Vie du Roi dans le Psaume 21," *Biblica* 59 (1978): 516–41.

The structure of the psalm is balanced by repetition of vocabulary (see Craigie, *Psalms 1–50*, p. 190), the inclusio construction (vv.1, 13), and the alternation in speakers.

The structure is as follows:

A. The King's Joy in the Lord's Strength (v.1)
  B. God's Gifts to His King (vv.2–6)
    C. The King's Response (v.7)
  B′. The People's Expectations of the King (vv.8–12)
A′. The People's Joy in the Lord's Strength (v.13)

The king's expressed commitment to God's love (v.7) is a response of *faith* to God's promises to the Davidic dynasty (vv.2–6) *and* of *hope* in God's final victory through his anointed king (vv.8–12). The psalm has indirect messianic overtones, as it gives ground for hope and joy in the anticipation of the kingdom of our Lord Jesus Christ (see Ps 20).

I. The King's Joy in the Lord's Strength

21:1

For the director of music. A psalm of David.

1 O LORD, the king rejoices in your strength.
How great is his joy in the victories you give!

1 The theocratic king knows that the "victories" are God's gracious "gifts" and that they are the evidence of God's "strength" (*'ōz*). Dahood proposes "your triumph" for "your strength" on the basis of its usage in 1 Samuel 2:10; Psalms 29:11; 68:28; 89:17; and the parallelism with "victories" (*Psalms*, 1:131). Instead of a synonymous parallelism, which Dahood assumes, Briggs is correct in viewing vv.1–3 as synthetic (1:184). The "strength" of the Lord is evidence of his covenant love on behalf of his own, resulting in the victory that he graciously shares with them (59:16; 62:11–12). It is synonymous with "might" (*g^e^bûrāh*, v.13). "Victories" (*y^e^šû'āh*, singular in MT) do not result from chariots and horses but by trusting in "the name of the LORD our God"

(20:7; cf. 3:2; 20:5). In 20:5 God's people were looking forward to the time when they could "shout for joy," when God would give them the victory (*y^ešû'āh*). Here the king leads the people in praise, addressing God as the gracious and victorious King by whose strength the people have been delivered. Therefore the king "rejoices" and even expresses his exuberance. In the conclusion (v.13) the psalmist returns to the theme of God's praise. Verses 1 and 13 constitute an inclusion.

Notes

For a brief discussion of the technical words and phrases in the superscription, see the Introduction.

1 (2 MT) For a rejection of Dahood's rendering "the Grand One" as a divine epithet (*Psalms*, 3:XXVI–XXVIII; contra NIV's "great"), see Craigie (*Psalms 1–50*, p. 189).

II. God's Gifts to His King

21:2–6

2 You have granted him the desire of his heart
and have not withheld the request of his lips. *Selah*
3 You welcomed him with rich blessings
and placed a crown of pure gold on his head.
4 He asked you for life, and you gave it to him—
length of days, for ever and ever.
5 Through the victories you gave, his glory is great;
you have bestowed on him splendor and majesty.
6 Surely you have granted him eternal blessings
and made him glad with the joy of your presence.

2 The king had prayed for victory, and his people had joined in imploring the Lord to give the king the desire of his heart (20:4). Now that the Lord has given the victory (v.1), the king gratefully acknowledges that God has "granted him the desire of his heart" (v.2). He had counseled in his heart, formed his plans, and had spoken about the execution of his plans before the Lord. Now the king witnesses that the Lord had blessed his thoughts and spoken requests. The king's ways were aligned with God's plans; therefore the king was successful.

3–6 The Lord of glory comes to welcome the king as if he were the sole victor. The king is treated as the commander-in-chief of God's army on earth. His victory was the Lord's doing, but the king receives his reward. In reward for his loyalty, the Lord bestows on his servant great gifts: his presence, rich blessings, a crown of pure gold, a long rule, great glory, and honor (vv.3–6). The gifts are symbolic of the divinely decreed rule of David and his descendants, as promised in 2 Samuel 7:12–16. The symmetry of vv.3–6 shows an artistry:

A. Presence of God ("you welcomed him," v.3a)
B. Blessings ("rich blessings," v.3a; cf. Prov 24:25b)
C. Glory ("crown of pure gold," v.3b)
D. Life (v.4)

C′. Glory ("glory," "splendor and majesty," v.5; cf. 96:3)
B′. Blessings ("eternal blessings," v.6a)
A′. Presence of God ("the joy of your presence," v.6b)

In the Lord's blessing of the king with "his presence" (vv.3a, 6b) may be an allusion to Abraham's victory over the kings of the east, when Melchizedek, the priest-king of Salem, came out to bless Abraham (Gen 14:18–20). The Lord himself comes out to bless the king so as to crown the victory "with great joy" (v.6). The presence of God is the central promise of the Abrahamic covenant (Gen 17:7–8), of the Mosaic covenant (Exod 25:8; cf. Gen 9:27), and of the Davidic covenant (2 Sam 7:9, 14). The "blessings" are characterized as "rich" and "eternal" (vv.3a, 6a). They are particularly the promises of the Davidic covenant, but not in isolation from the promises of the Abrahamic covenant. The promises pertain to the welfare and prosperity of God's people (cf. 4:7; 23:6; 34:11–13; 37:4; 85:12).

The assurance of these promises lies in God's recognition of his "messianic" king. He bestows "life" (v.4; cf. v.6), i.e., the establishment of the Davidic dynasty: "Your house and your kingdom will endure *forever* before me; your throne will be established *forever*" (2 Sam 7:16 [emphasis mine]; cf. Ps 72:17). In a symbolic way he guarantees the continuation of the Davidic dynasty by the "crown of pure gold." Kingship is by divine right, and this right is symbolized by the placing of a beautiful crown on David's head (v.3b). The external evidence of God's presence, blessing, and bestowal of kingship is in the victories by which the Lord shared his "glory, . . . splendor and majesty" with his king. The royal glory is not naturally inherited but received by divine grant (90:16; 96:6).

Notes

2 (3 MT) The word אֲרֶשֶׁת (*'ᵃrešeṯ*, "request") is a *hapax legomenon* in the OT. Its meaning is derived from cognate languages (KB³, 1:89).

4 (5 MT) John F. Healey assumes that the Ugaritic and Israelite ideology include references to immortality of the king, which subsequently were democratized ("The Immortality of the King: Ugarit and the Psalms," *Orientalia* 53 [1984]: 245–54).

6 (7 MT) On the meaning of שׁית (*š-y-ṯ*) as "grant," see Briggs (1:187).

Craigie renders תְּחַדֵּהוּ (*tᵉḥaddēhû*, "made him glad") as "you make him see," supposing that the root *ḥ-d-h* is a dialectical variation of *ḥ-z-h* ("see," *Psalms 1–50*, p. 189; cf. Dahood, *Psalms*, 1:133).

III. The King's Response

21:7

7 For the king trusts in the LORD;
through the unfailing love of the Most High
he will not be shaken.

7 The king confirms his loyalty to the Lord. His commitment strengthens his relationship to the Lord. The king declares his loyalty to the Lord as a "trust" or dependency, and the Lord assures him that his "love" will not depart. The "unfailing love" (*ḥesed*) is God's gratuitous expression of loyalty to the king who looks expectantly for his blessing. Therefore, "he will not be shaken."

Notes

7 (8 MT) What is the function of this verse in vv.1–7? Briggs treats it as a chorus (1:185). Weiser proposes that these words are uttered by the congregation "as an acclamation" (pp. 214–15; so Craigie, *Psalms 1–50*, pp. 191–92). I agree with A.A. Anderson (1:182) that the change in address from "you" (vv.2–6) to "LORD" is not sufficient ground for suggesting a change in speaker. F.C. Fensham ("Ps 21—A Covenant Song?" ZAW 77 [1965]: 193–202) has proposed that this verse has a great significance in a covenantal context.

For the phrase "he will not be shaken," see the comment on 15:5b.

For "Most High" (Elyon), see the appendix to Psalm 9: Yahweh Is El Elyon.

IV. The People's Expectations of the King

21:8–12

8 Your hand will lay hold on all your enemies;
your right hand will seize your foes.
9 At the time of your appearing
you will make them like a fiery furnace.
In his wrath the LORD will swallow them up,
and his fire will consume them.
10 You will destroy their descendants from the earth,
their posterity from mankind.
11 Though they plot evil against you
and devise wicked schemes, they cannot succeed;
12 for you will make them turn their backs
when you aim at them with drawn bow.

These verses are to be approached from the perspective of the people as they look for a demonstration of the royal power and glory bestowed on the king by the Lord. The people of God view the anointed king as God's means of establishing God's kingdom on earth by ridding the earth of the enemies. To him belong the blessings of the covenant (vv.3, 6). To him also belong the curses of the covenant.

8–10 The Lord has given the king the "keys" to the kingdom, because it is through the "hand" of his anointed that the foes will be removed (v.8). To the enemy, the king's presence will be like a theophany in which God is described as entering the judgment on the enemies (cf. 18:7–15). The "enemies" (v.8) "plot evil" and "devise wicked schemes" (v.11), and their "descendants" are to be destroyed forevermore (v.10). The covenant curses pertain to the enemies of God's people (cf. Gen 12:3) and to the ungodly within the covenant community (cf. Ps 3:1, 7). The Lord will destroy the king's enemies "in his wrath" (v.9). The execration will be so complete that their offspring will be no more (v.10; cf. 9:6; 37:28; 137:8–9; Isa 14:22; see the appendix to Ps 98: Yahweh Is the Divine Warrior).

11–12 All who do not submit to the rule of God's anointed king are included among those who "plot evil" (v.11). The messianic kingship requires absolute loyalty to the Lord and his anointed King (Ps 2). Whether the adversaries belong to the enemy or to the faithless Israelites, they will be subjugated and annihilated (vv.11–12). The rebellious people will not succeed with their "wicked schemes"; instead they will be routed because of the bow that is aimed at them (v.12). There is no enemy force that can stand up against the king, because God has strengthened his "right hand" by which he delivers his people (v.8; cf. 20:6) into the victorious kingdom of Jesus Christ, by whom all enemy powers and forces—even death—will be "swallowed" (cf. Isa 25:8; 1 Cor 15:54–57). His kingdom will be forever!

Notes

8 (9 MT) For the background of this verse, see Ps 20:6 and Mal 4:1.

9 (10 MT) The root שִׂית (*šîṯ*, "place," "put") is repeated in various forms, in v.3 ("placed"), v.6 ("you have granted"), v.9 ("you will make them"), and v.12 ("you will make them"), so as to emphasize God's gratuitous and sovereign benign acts by which the king's authority is extended over the nations.

Craigie takes לְעֵת (*leʿēṯ*, "time") as a textual corruption of לְעֻמַּת (*leʿummaṯ*, "opposite," "against"): "you will set them against your face like a fiery oven" (*Psalms 1–50*, pp. 188–89).

The ambiguity regarding who is appearing (v.9) is resolved in the NIV. The MT is ambiguous, as it closes the first colon with "LORD": "At the time of your appearing, O LORD." It is preferable to read "LORD" at the beginning of the second colon (NIV). Thus the appearance of the king and the help of the Lord are to one end: the carrying out of the curses on the enemies.

12 (13 MT) The "bow" is an idiomatic rendering of "your bowstrings." "Bowstrings" is a metonymy (part for the whole) for the bow and possibly a reference to "arrows" (A.A. Anderson, 1:183).

"For you will make them turn their backs" is literally "for you will make them shoulder." "Shoulder" is here a synonym for back (see Briggs, 1:188). The language of warfare is an ancient Near Eastern metaphor for victory.

V. The People's Joy in the Lord's Strength

21:13

13 Be exalted, O LORD, in your strength;
we will sing and praise your might.

13 Because messianic kingship is wholly dependent on the Great King for its strength, honor, longevity, and authority, the psalm appropriately concludes with an ascription of praise to the Lord. He is the source of "strength" and "might." The king and his people rejoice in God's kingship and the blessings he has bestowed on them. The king led in praise (v.1), and now the people join in ("we will sing and praise," cf. 20:5).

A greater expression of reality may be experienced since the coming of our Lord. He is our King, and he will bring in the fullness of promise. Calvin insightfully remarks:

> This was no doubt true with respect to the kingdom of David; for God in old time displayed his power in exalting him to the throne. But what is here stated was only fully accomplished in Christ, who was appointed by the heavenly Father to be King over us, and who is at the same time God manifest in the flesh. As his divine power ought justly to strike terror into the wicked, so it is described as full of the sweetest consolation to us, which ought to inspire us with joy, and incite us to celebrate it with songs of praise and thanksgivings. (1:356)

Notes

---

13 (14 MT) The exegetical problem pertains to the translation of רוּמָה (*rûmāh*, "drive"; "be exalted" in NIV). Several commentaries and versions give the active reading, as if calling the Lord to act (cf. Weiser: "Arise, O LORD, in thy strength!" p. 211; see Kraus, *Psalmen*, 2:168). But the imperative may also function as "an emphatic statement: "you shall be exalted" (so A.A. Anderson, 1:184).

Psalm 22: Anguish and Joy

The natural division of this psalm into two distinct parts, lament and thanksgiving (vv.1–21, 22–31), has led some to view it as two separate psalms that were joined (see Peter Weimar, "Psalm 22, Beobachtungen zur Komposition und Entstehungsgeschichte," *Freude an der Weisung des Herrn, Beiträge zur Theologie der Psalmen, Festgabe zum 70. Geburtstag von Heinrich Gross*, edd. Ernst Haag and Frank-Lothar Hossfeld [Stuttgart: Katholisches Bibelwerk, 1986], pp. 471–94). However, similar changes from lament (vv.1–21) to thanksgiving (vv.22–31) are found in other lament psalms, and scholars today are in greater agreement over the literary unity of Psalm 22. Carroll Stuhlmueller ("Psalm 22: The Deaf and Silent God of Mysticism and Liturgy," *Biblical Theology Bulletin* 12 [1982]: 86–90) explains the psalm as the work of a postexilic redactor, who was suffering and drew comfort from existing Scriptures, out of which he composed the present work (cf. Fritz Stolz, "Psalm 22: Alttestamentliches Reden vom Menschen und neutestamentliches Reden von Jesus," *Zeitschrift für Theologie und Kirche* 77 [1980]: 129–48). Both relate the psalm to man's anguish and Jesus' suffering as the "man" of God.

Psalm 22 is an *individual lament* psalm in which the assembly of the righteous is invited to participate both in giving thanks and in the communal meal, associated with the votive offering (vv.25–26). Because of the reference to Psalm 22 in the Passion narrative of our Lord, it is tempting to treat this psalm as messianic, predicting our Lord's suffering (cf. Matt 27:39–46; Mark 15:29–34). Instead of viewing it as messianic prophecy, Calvin treats this psalm first in its original context with David as the sufferer and then applies the psalm to our Lord on the ground that "this psalm was composed under the influence of the Spirit of prophecy concerning David's King and

Lord" (1:362; cf. 1 Peter 1:12; see Johannes Schildenberger, "Psalm 22. Todesleiden und Auferstehung," *Erbe und Auftrag* 57 [1981]: 119–23).

In applying the psalm to human suffering, it is most appropriate for the Christian to be moved to tears when reflecting that Jesus the Messiah has so entered the human condition that he suffered in his humanity, being rejected by God and man. Whereas David's suffering was for himself, Jesus' suffering was on behalf of sinners. Through Jesus' suffering the community of Jews and Gentiles (vv.22–30) may worship the Lord from generation to generation, because the middle wall of partition has been removed (Gal 3:26–29; Eph 2:14). The "descendants of Jacob" (v.23) are joined by "the families of the nations" (v.27) in the worship of God and in submission to his kingdom. The kingdom the psalmist speaks of finds its center in Jesus' messianic kingship (cf. Rev 11:15). The prophetic spirit (Acts 2:30–33) moves the reader of this psalm to look beyond David and his experiences to the fullness of God's kingdom in the Messiah, when sorrow and anguish will give way to joy and worship. May that day come soon (Rev 22:1–6)!

For studies on Psalm 22, its application to the suffering of our Lord, and its canonical function in the church, see P.D. Miller, Jr., "Psalm 22," *Interpreting the Psalms,* pp. 100–111; Ottmar Fuchs, *Die Klage als Gebet. Eine theologische Besinnung am Beispiel des Psalms 22* (Munich: Kösel-Verlag, 1982); John H. Reumann, "Psalm 22 at the Cross. Lament and Thanksgiving for Jesus Christ," Int 28 (1974): 39–58. William L. Holladay explains Jeremiah's soliloquies against the background of this psalm ("The Background of Jeremiah's Self-Understanding. Moses, Samuel, and Psalm 22," JBL 83 [1964]: 153–64). J.P.M. van der Ploeg makes a connection with the Suffering Servant, Psalm 22, and our Lord's suffering ("De Dienaar van YHWH en de Psalmen," *De Knecht. Studies rondom Deutero-Jesaja door Collega's en Oud-leerlingen aangeboden aan Prof. Dr. J.L. Koole* [Kampen: Kok, 1978], pp. 173–77).

The structural divisions are clearly marked by the emphatic use of "my God" and "yet you" (vv.1, 3), "But I" (v.6), "Yet you" (v.9), and "But you" (v.19). For a poetic analysis, see Nic. H. Ridderbos, "The Psalms: Style-Figures and Structure," pp. 43–76. For the purpose of exposition, the two components are structured symmetrically:

- A. God's Abandonment, Rule, and Praise of Israel (vv.1–5)
  - B. Public Spectacle (vv.6–8)
    - C. God's Covenantal Responsibilities (vv.9–11)
    - C′. Abandonment and Prayer for Covenantal Favor (vv.12–21)
  - B′. Public Praise (vv.22–24)
- A′. God's Presence and Rule: The Praise of Israel and the Nations (vv.25–31)

The movement of vv.1–21 is from questions (vv.1–2) to a portrayal of the anguish of suffering (vv.12–18), after which the psalmist concludes this part with a prayer (vv.19–21). The psalmist finds rest in the covenant God, who is his strength and help (v.19) in the adversities of life (vv.20–21). The second part (vv.22–31) is symmetric with the beginning of the psalm but contrastive in two ways: the mocking of the people (vv.6–8) gives way to praise in the congregation of those who fear the Lord (vv.22–24); and the experience of temporary abandonment (vv.1–2) is rewarded by generations who will tell of God's mighty acts of deliverance (vv.30–31) so that his rule (v.3) will be evident to all nations (vv.27–28). They will join with Israel in giving praise (v.3; cf. vv.27, 29) to the Lord, their King. (See the appendix to Ps 119: Yahweh Is My Redeemer.)

I. God's Abandonment, Rule, and Praise of Israel

22:1–5

For the director of music. To ⌊the tune of⌋ "The Doe of the Morning."
A psalm of David.

1 My God, my God, why have you forsaken me?
Why are you so far from saving me,
so far from the words of my groaning?
2 O my God, I cry out by day, but you do not answer,
by night, and am not silent.

3 Yet you are enthroned as the Holy One;
you are the praise of Israel.
4 In you our fathers put their trust;
they trusted and you delivered them.
5 They cried to you and were saved;
in you they trusted and were not disappointed.

1 The prayer begins with a threefold cry to El ("my God," *'ēlî*; see the appendix to this psalm) and with three questions. The psalmist, as a child in the presence of his father, pours out his heart. In the intensity of his suffering, there is no other recourse than to cast himself on God. In the Psalms "my God" is equivalent to "my Father." The individual within the covenant community did not have to be content with God's commitment to his people as a whole. His promises were not only national but also personal. Therefore the psalmist calls on him out of deep despair with the address "my God." But here, at the same time, he shows his amazement by the three questions: Why has the Lord ("my God") "forsaken" me, made no attempt at "saving" me (*yᵉšû'āh*, see comment and Notes on 3:2), and not listened to my "groaning"? As the questions increase in frequency and intensity, God's absence becomes unbearable. The psalmist felt himself "forsaken" by his God.

Abandonment or alienation is the experience of suffering, when one hopes for deliverance but no help is forthcoming. Precisely because the psalmist was a child of the covenant, he had great expectations that his covenant God, who had promised to hear and to deliver, would come to his aid. But he felt himself abandoned by him. In this experience of alienation, prayers become authentic in perseverance, as Calvin wrote:

> The true rule of praying is, therefore, this, that he who seems to have beaten the air to no purpose, or to have lost his labour in praying for a long time, should not, on that account, leave off, or desist from that duty. Meanwhile, there is this advantage which God in his fatherly kindness grants to his people, that if they have been disappointed at any time of their desires and expectations, they may make known to God their perplexities and distresses, and unburden them, as it were, into his bosom. (1:362)

2–3 In his experience of abandonment, the psalmist keeps on bringing his prayers before God "by day" and "by night." He is not silent, but God is (v.2)! Then he reflects on who his God is. He is holy in his kingship (v.3) and is the object of Israel's constant praise (vv.3b–5).

The pronoun "you" (v.3) is emphatic and, together with the contrastive use of the connective particle, sets up the distance between God and the psalmist: "Yet you" ("But you"). One might venture to say that he feels a tension in his experience with

God ("my God," three times) and in God's dealings with Israel. His God has abandoned him and is the object of questions (vv.1–2), whereas God has saved his people and is the object of their praise (vv.3–5). The reference to God's being "enthroned" (*yôšēḇ*, "sitting") is a confessional reference to God's rule (2:4; 9:11; 80:1; 99:1). (See the appendix to Ps 132: The Ark of the Covenant and the Temple: Symbols of Yahweh's Presence and Rule.)

4–5 The history of redemption reveals God as loyal and able to save. Israel's trust (*bāṭᵉḥû*) in him was not put to shame, because when they cried, they were delivered. The act of "trust" was a confession of confident hope in God's love for his people (TWOT, 1:102). The psalmist was familiar with the glorious acts of God in Egypt, the wilderness, and the periods of the Conquest, the judges, and the kingdom. Israel's "praise" came to God in his holy sanctuary as expressions of gratitude. They had praised him for his "holy" justice and righteousness as he vindicated them. They had praised him for his rule over the nations (Exod 15:1–18; cf. Pss 95–99) as he sovereignly dealt with enemies and adversities. But it seems as if God does not care to deliver *him*, as is brought out by the contrastive particle "yet" (v.3). Whereas the "fathers" and Israel had occasion for praise, the psalmist felt himself cut off from God's justice and from the communal experience of Israel. The threefold reference to the "trust" of the fathers is symmetric with the threefold statement of his personal trust in the Lord in the phrase "my God." The faith of the ancestors and the faith of the psalmist are one, but their experience is far different. God delivered his people, but the psalmist is left abandoned. In the MT "you" stands three times in an emphatic position, twice as "in you" (well reflected in NIV) and once "to you."

The psalmist views God in contrastive terms to his situation:

his God has "forsaken" him (v.1a)
    Israel's God is "enthroned" (v.3a)
his God is "far . . . from saving" (v.1b)
    Israel's God is "holy" or the "Holy One" (v.3b)
his God is unresponsive to his "groaning" (v.1c)
    Israel's God receives the "praise of Israel" (v.3c)

It is in this light that we can more deeply appreciate our Lord's cry on the cross, "*Eloi, Eloi, lama sabachthani?*" ("My God, my God, why have you forsaken me," Matt 27:46; Mark 15:34). On the cross our Lord was forsaken by and alienated from the Father. In this experience, symbolized by darkness, he was cut off from God's mighty acts of deliverance done for his people. He was alone, separated from God the Father and from his people.

Notes

For a brief discussion of the technical words and phrases in the superscription, see the Introduction.

1 (2 MT) The syntax of v.1 presents several problems. First, the second line is a translation of the cryptic רָחוֹק מִישׁוּעָתִי (*rāḥôq mîšû'āṯî*, "far from my deliverance"). One edition of the Syriac reads "and you have removed from me my salvation." The NIV is close to this with the elliptic reading of the interrogative to connect all three phrases. The word יְשׁוּעָה

(*yᵉšû'āh*, "saving," "salvation," "deliverance," "victory," "vindication") is the same as in 20:6; 21:1, 5 ("victories"). Second, the third line is a unique expression for an anguished cry: דִּבְרֵי שַׁאֲגָתִי (*dibrê ša'ᵃgātî*, "so far from the words of my roaring"; lit., "words of my roaring"). The "roaring" is that of a lion and is metaphorical for a loud and constant cry for help (32:3; 38:8). The LXX understood "roaring" as "transgressions" (metathesis of שׁאג [*š'g*] to שׁגא [*š-g-'*]).

3 (4 MT) The use of the adjective קָדוֹשׁ (*qādôš*, "holy") is ambiguous, as it may function as an attribute ("Yet you are holy," so Weiser, p. 217), a reference to God as "the Holy One" (NIV; so Kraus, *Psalmen*, 1:174), as a metonym for his "sanctuary" (LXX; cf. 114:2) or for his "holy throne" (Dahood, *Psalms*, 1:138–39). There is no solution on which there is general agreement.

The connection between "sitting" (or "enthroned") and "the praises of Israel" is also subject to interpretation. NIV assumes that "you" is elliptic in its reading: "you are the praise of Israel." Craigie reads "enthroned" with the last phrase: "enthroned upon the praises of Israel" (*Psalms 1–50*, p. 194). The NEB explains the praise as Israel's praise of God: "thou art he whose praises Israel sings" (see Kraus, "you praise of Israel," *Psalmen*, 1:174).

II. Public Spectacle

22:6–8

6 But I am a worm and not a man,
  scorned by men and despised by the people.
7 All who see me mock me;
  they hurl insults, shaking their heads:
8 "He trusts in the LORD;
  let the LORD rescue him.
 Let him deliver him,
  since he delights in him."

6–7 As the psalmist reflects on his own situation, God's absence dwarfs his self-image. In contrast to the emphatic "you" (v.3), he refers to himself emphatically: "But I." God is enthroned, but he is "a worm and not a man" (v.6). The phrase "worm and not a man" is for a heightened poetic effect. It expresses his feeling of being less than human (cf. Job 25:6; Isa 41:14). The sense of human dignity is lost when it seems that God is absent and that people reject him (cf. Isa 52:14; 53:2). God is holy and receives the praise of Israel, but the psalmist is the object of scorn and reviling (v.6b). Unwanted, alone, and full of anguish, he cannot enjoy the presence of his fellowmen, who do not understand his situation. Out of sheer disregard for his feelings, they apply their "theological" measuring sticks to his situation and conclude, that if he truly were to trust God, he would not suffer. They mock him, shaking their heads out of shock and misunderstanding (v.7). The shaking of the head may signify rejection (109:25; cf. Matt 27:39) or astonishment (Ps 64:8; Lam 2:15).

8 The unpious mock the psalmist with their argument against his kind of piety. They question his suffering in the light of their myopic view of God's love, and in the promises of God's deliverance. If the psalmist had trusted the Lord, why then is he suffering? They conclude that either he had boasted of trusting in God but was hypocritical or that God does not love him. These ancient mockers posed the issue of the problem of evil and suffering in a most agonizing way. The hope of the godly was in God's "delight" in his saints, especially during times of adversity (cf. 37:23). The support of the Lord's hand (37:24) is not there, and the mockers make the most of this occasion.

Notes

7 (8 MT) The act of mocking was a form of ridicule (cf. Neh 2:19; 4:1), explained further by two verbal phrases: יַפְטִירוּ בְשָׂפָה (*yapṭîrû* *beśāpāh*, "they hurl insults"; lit., "they open lip"; cf. 35:21) and יָנִיעוּ רֹאשׁ (*yānîʿû rōʾš*, "shaking their heads"; lit., "they shake head"). The first phrase occurs only here and speaks of one facial expression. It is not the insult itself (so NIV) but the insulting facial expression (Briggs, 1:202). Suggested translations are "they wag the head (in mocking)" (KB, p. 603), "gape" (Dahood, *Psalms*, 1:136), and "make mouths at me" (NEB).

8 (9 MT) The imperative form גֹּל (*gōl*, "roll" or "trust") does not fit. The NIV accepts the emendation of גַּל (*gal*, "he rolled" or "he trusted"; cf. LXX; Matt 27:43). Usually an object follows the verb and may here be omitted as understood by the context: "he committed his cause to the LORD" (RSV; cf. A.A. Anderson, 1:188). Dahood renders it "He lived for Yahweh," supposing a homonym of *gîl*, meaning "to live" (*Psalms*, 1:139), but this proposal is unnecessary.

III. God's Covenantal Responsibilities

22:9–11

9 Yet you brought me out of the womb;
you made me trust in you
even at my mother's breast.
10 From birth I was cast upon you;
from my mother's womb you have been my God.
11 Do not be far from me,
for trouble is near
and there is no one to help.

9–11 In reflecting on his own desperate situation, the psalmist moves his eyes from the mockers around him ("but I," v.6) to God with an emphatic "Yet you." The problem of suffering finds some focus in God's sovereignty and love for his own. From birth he has owed his life to God, and from birth the Lord has been his covenant God.

The reflection focuses on God's sovereign and providential acts of giving life and sustaining it by the mother's care. God has a purpose for the life of the psalmist, because he has shown him his love from birth. The covenant relationship, too, has been from birth, because God had promised to be the God of Abraham and of his children (Gen 17:7–10). God was his father by covenant and had taken it on himself to be his guardian and protector (v.10). How can God leave his child alone now that he is in trouble and needs help? The psalmist prays for God not to be far away (v.11). In his past experience the Lord had been close to him (vv.9–10), but now he is distant.

Notes

9 (10 MT) The root בטח (*b-ṭ-ḥ*) in מַבְטִיחִי (*mabṭîḥî,* "you made me trust in you") may be rendered as "inspire trust" (KB, p. 118) or "make tranquil" (Dahood, *Psalms,* 1:139). The NEB follows G.R. Driver's suggestion: "who laid me at my mother's breast" ("Difficult Words in the Hebrew Prophets," *Studies in Old Testament Prophecy,* ed. H.H. Rowley, reprint [Edinburgh: T. & T. Clark, 1957], p. 59). The LXX and several Hebrew MSS presuppose an alternate reading: מִבְטַחִי (*mibṭaḥî,* "my strength," "my hope," "my confidence").

The meaning of the phrase גֹחִי מִבָּטֶן (*gōḥî mibbāṭen,* "brought me out of the womb") depends on the etymology of the word *gōḥî.* The LXX and Targum assume the root גהה (*g-h-h,* "draw forth"): "you drew me forth." The root גיח (*g-y-ḥ,* "burst forth") as in Job 38:8 ("Who shut up the sea behind doors / when it burst forth from the womb") is also possible. The etymology is uncertain.

11 (12 MT) For the possible meaning of "deliver" for the root עזר (*'-z-r,* "no one to help"), see Craigie, *Psalms 1–50,* p. 196.

IV. Abandonment and Prayer for Covenantal Favor (vv.12–21)

A feeling of being abandoned by God means all too often an abandonment to some tragedy. The anguish of his experience was the psalmist's loneliness when the adversaries were closing in. He compares his abandonment to being "poured out like water" (v.14), to melting like "wax" (v.14), and to the dryness of a potsherd (v.15). In his agony he looks up and cries for help from his covenant God. But the enemies are all around.

The enemies are described by their hostile activities and also portrayed by metaphors. The enemies are likened to a multitude of "strong bulls" (v.12), to "roaring lions" (v.13; cf. v.21), to "dogs" (vv.16, 20), and to "wild oxen" (v.21). The enemies are all around (vv.12, 16), making disturbing sounds (v.13) and rejoicing over his misery (vv.16–18).

This section should be considered as a unit, whose structure is evident by the repetition of the metaphors for the enemies (vv.12, 13, 16, 20, 21), by the inclusionary motifs, and by the description of the agony of the psalmist:

A. The Enemies (vv.12–13)
  B. Personal Anguish (vv.14–15b)
    C. Severity of Situation: Life Itself (v.15c)
A′. The Enemies (v.16a)
  B′. Personal Anguish (vv.16b–17)
    C′. Severity of Situation: Life Itself (v.18)
      D. Cry for Help (v.19)
    C″. Severity of the Situation: Life Itself (v.20a)
A″. & B″. Enemies and Cause of Anguish (vv. 20b–21)

A. *The Enemies*

22:12–13

12 Many bulls surround me;
strong bulls of Bashan encircle me.
13 Roaring lions tearing their prey
open their mouths wide against me.

12–13 The strength and ferocity of the enemies compares to that of the "bulls of Bashan" (v.12) and to "roaring lions" (v.13). The bulls of Bashan were proverbial for their size because they were well fed on the lush vegetation of the Bashan (cf. Amos 4:1; Mic 7:14). Bashan is the region known today as the Golan Heights, located north of the Yarmuk, east of the Sea of Galilee, and to the south of the Hermon Range. Its elevation is about two thousand feet above sea level, and it receives an average rain of over twenty-four inches per year. Its productiveness in meat, wheat, and oaks, largely due to its regular precipitation, led to Bashan's becoming symbolic of human pride (Isa 2:13). The enemies in their self-reliance are compared to the bulls raised on the Bashan plateau. As they encircle, their "horns" (v.21) are all too evident and inspire fear in the psalmist.

Similarly, the psalmist is unnerved by the enemies who "open their mouths wide against [him]" (v.13b). This action describes the activity of lions and not of bulls, as the NIV makes explicit. The strength, pride, and deadly intent of the enemies, likened to that of bulls, is matched by their cruelty, abuse of power, and hatred of godliness, which is likened to that of lions (v.13; cf. v.21; 7:2; 10:9; 17:12; cf. Isa 38:13).

Notes

---

13 (14 MT) The description of the lion is more moving in the MT by its brevity and use of participles: "tearing and roaring" (cf. NEB, "ravening and roaring lions"; Dahood, "ravening and raging lion" [*Psalms*, 1:137]; Craigie, "like a lion about to rend and roar" [*Psalms 1–50*, p. 195]).

B. *Personal Anguish*

22:14–15b

14 I am poured out like water,
  and all my bones are out of joint.
My heart has turned to wax;
  it has melted away within me.
15 My strength is dried up like a potsherd,
  and my tongue sticks to the roof of my mouth;

14–15b The psalmist feels the impact of the alienation deep within his inner being. The metaphors of "water" and "wax," expressive of formlessness, bring out the inner feelings of an anguished man (cf. Josh 7:5). He can no longer function as a human being. The "bones," "heart," "strength," and "tongue" fail him, not because of any serious disease, but because of a traumatic response to being hated and alienated. He can go no further. He is in a state of shock.

The metaphorical expressions are worth noting. Great fear is likened to "water" (cf. Josh 7:5; Ezek 7:17; 21:7) and to "wax" (v.14; cf. 2 Sam 17:10). Lack of resilience and inability to cope any longer with the trauma of life is brought out in the image of the dried-out and useless "potsherd" (v.15a). Sherds, found by the thousands at archaeological sites, are pieces of broken pottery. Though almost useless, at times they were used as scoops (Isa 30:14). The psalmist is a "broken" man, whose lack of fortitude affects his ability to speak. It is as if his tongue sticks to the roof of his mouth (v.15b; cf. 69:3; 137:6).

C. *Severity of the Situation: Life Itself*

22:15c

you lay me in the dust of death.

15c Because of his deep suffering, the absence of hope, and the ever-present reality of evil around him, the psalmist prepares himself for death. He is poured out like water and is cast into "the dust of death" (see the appendix to Ps 88: Sheol-Grave-Death in the Psalms). Implicitly he holds the Lord responsible for his suffering ("you lay me"; see Craigie, *Psalms 1–50,* p. 196).

D. *The Enemies*

22:16a

16 Dogs have surrounded me;

16a The psalmist briefly returns to consider the enemies and to reflect on his sufferings in a heightened anticipation of the prayer to God (v.19). The enemies ("a band of evil men") are nothing but "dogs." They, too, surround him like the bulls of Bashan (v.12). They, too, are fierce and powerful (v.20b). But the difference in imagery lies in where dogs may be found. They came in many kinds and in great numbers to garbage dumps, ate whatever was thrown away, carried diseases, and transmitted them to humans. The dog was not man's best friend in the ancient Near East. They prowled about while snarling and looking for food (59:14–15). They licked the blood of those killed or unable to fend for themselves (68:23; cf. 1 Kings 14:11; 16:4; 21:19, 23–24; 2 Kings 9:10, 36; Luke 16:21).

E. *Personal Anguish*

22:16b–17

a band of evil men has encircled me,
they have pierced my hands and my feet.
17 I can count all my bones;
people stare and gloat over me.

16b–17 Just as the imagery of the enemies as bulls and lions (vv.12–13) evokes feelings of fear and powerlessness, so also the imagery of the dogs creates a picture of a powerless, righteous sufferer on the heap of ashes. The dogs viciously attack him, gnawing at and biting into his feet and hands. He is but skin and bones (v.17) and is unable to ward them off. His misery is the source of gloating and entertainment.

Notes

16b (17b MT) כָּאֲרִי (*kā'ᵃrî*, lit., "like the lion") has occasioned much discussion. The LXX reads a verb—"they pierced," as does the NIV, from כָּרָה (*kārāh*) or from כּור II (*k-w-r*, "pierce"). Some suggest a homonym of the root *k-r-h* ("bind") and read "they have bound my hands and my feet" (KB³, 2:473). Others propose another root, כָּלָה (*kālāh*, "consume"), assuming the interchangeability of the resh and the lamed (cf. Craigie, *Psalms 1–50*, pp. 195–96: "my hands and my feet were exhausted"). J.J.M. Roberts proposes a reading based on Akkadian: "shrink" or "shrivel" ("A New Root for an Old Crux, Ps XXII 17c," VetTest 23 [1973]: 247–52). The NEB reads, "and they have hacked off my hands and my feet." The text remains an exegetical problem.

F. *Severity of the Situation: Life Itself*

22:18

> [18] They divide my garments among them
> and cast lots for my clothing.

18 The division of the garments by lots continues the same picture as in v.15c. The psalmist feels as if he is about to die; therefore the wicked are waiting to swoop down on him like vultures. The "garments" ("clothing") are divided up like the spoils from battle.

G. *Cry for Help*

22:19

> [19] But you, O LORD, be not far off;
> O my Strength, come quickly to help me.

19 The scene changes, as the psalmist opens his prayer with an emphatic "But you" (cf. "Yet you," v.3). The sudden shift away from his terrifying condition leads him to confront his covenant God, as he prays, "But you Yahweh." The name Yahweh (= LORD) evokes the memory of God's promises to be near, to support his people, and to protect them from adversities. God is Yahweh, the "Strength" of his needy people. This section forms an inclusion with vv.9–11, because both begin with an emphatic reference to God as "You," allude to God's covenantal responsibilities, and ask him not to be far off: "Do not be far" and "be not far off" (cf. vv.11, 19).

Notes

19 (20 MT) "My strength" translates a *hapax legomenon*, אֱיָלוּתִי (*'ᵉyālûṯî*, KB³, 1:39). It is equivalent to "my help" (BDB, p. 33). For a refutation of Dahood's rendering "O my army" (*Psalms*, 1:114), see Craigie (*Psalms 1–50*, p. 197).

H. *Severity of the Situation: Life Itself*

22:20a

[20]Deliver my life from the sword,

20a The psalmist implores God to listen to his prayer, because of the utter despair and meaninglessness of his situation. There is no way out. In view of the absence of any other alternative, he prays that the Lord may spare his "life" ("my precious life"). Life alone was left in him, because he was to his enemies nothing but skin and bones (v.17) and his inner self was sick from anxiety (vv.14–15). The enemy is about to divide his personal possessions (v.18) as he lies "in the dust of death" (v.15c). But he is not ready to die. Only the Lord can deliver him and restore life to him.

Notes

20a (21a MT) "My precious life" is a good rendering of יְחִידָתִי (*yᵉḥîḏāṯî*), as it brings out the value of life over against death (cf. 35:17). Dahood's translation—"my face"—is ingenious but unnecessary (*Psalms,* 1:137, 141).

I. *Enemies and Cause of Anguish*

22:20b–21

my precious life from the power of the dogs.
[21]Rescue me from the mouth of the lions;
save me from the horns of the wild oxen.

20b–21 The psalmist concludes by returning to the imagery of the enemies as dogs, lions, and oxen, but now in reverse order (cf. vv. 12–13, 16). The enemies caused him great anguish by the show of their "power" (lit., "hand"), "mouth," and "horns." They had succeeded in terrorizing him so as to rob him of any desire to live. Yet, as he concludes with the petition, "answer me" (v.21; *'-n-h,* NIV, "save me"), his hope rests in the Lord who has thus far not answered him (v.2). The imperative "save me" fits in with the imperative sequence "come quickly. . . . Deliver. . . . Rescue . . . save me" (vv.19–21).

Notes

21 (22 MT) The verbal phrase עֲנִיתָנִי (*ʿᵃnîṯānî*, lit., "you have answered me"; NIV, "save me"; mg., "you have heard me") appears to be God's response to the charge in v.1: "why have you forsaken me?" So argue Reumann ("Psalm 22") and Hans Heinrich Schmid, "Mein Gott, mein Gott, warum hast du mich verlassen? Psalm 22 als Beispiel von Krankheit und Tod," *Wort und Dienst* NF 11 (1971): 119–40. The NEB renders it "my poor body," based on the LXX's "my lowliness," i.e., "my afflicted soul." There is no need to suppose that the phrase anticipates an oracle of deliverance and should be therefore translated: "you have answered me!" (Craigie, *Psalms 1–50*, pp. 195, 197). Dahood takes it as a precative perfect and treats it as a synonym of "rescue me": "make me triumph" (*Psalms*, 1:142).

V. Public Praise

22:22–24

22 I will declare your name to my brothers;
in the congregation I will praise you.
23 You who fear the LORD, praise him!
All you descendants of Jacob, honor him!
Revere him, all you descendants of Israel!
24 For he has not despised or disdained
the suffering of the afflicted one;
he has not hidden his face from him
but has listened to his cry for help.

22–24 The mood changes after the cry for deliverance (vv.19–21). This section (vv.22–24) corresponds in contrast to the self-portrayal in vv.6–8. There the psalmist saw himself in an abject state, rejected by God and man; but in these verses he declares "the name" Yahweh in the congregation of the faithful (v.22; cf. 20:1). Yahweh has responded to his prayer and has removed the suffering from his servant (v.24). No longer need he ask why his God has forsaken him (vv.1–2), because the Lord has blessed him by not hiding his face (v.24; cf. 30:7; 104:29). Yahweh is faithful to his covenant-promises (v.8) and to his covenant child, who calls him "my God" (= "my Father," vv.1–2).

The "brothers" (*'eḥāy*) may be the psalmist's relatives (50:20; 69:8), friends (35:14; 122:8), or, better, the members of the congregation (v.22; 133:1; Heb 2:12). The "congregation" (*qāhāl*) is here a technical term for the congregation of the righteous (cf. 107:32; 149:1), which excludes the ungodly and mocking Israelites (cf. vv.7–8). They are further identified as "you who fear the LORD" (v.23; cf. Mal 3:16).

Instead of having to listen to the people who scorned and mocked him, the psalmist calls on the Lord. The taunts of the mockers are thus drowned out by the songs of the faithful (v.23). The true sons of Jacob are those who fear the Lord (cf. 24:6). They will honor him with devoted hearts. The verbs "praise," "honor," and "revere" form the outward expression of the fear of the Lord. Those who love the Lord will rejoice in the Lord with the psalmist as an indication of corporate solidarity. These words constitute an encouragement to all the godly, that Yahweh will never completely hide his face from his covenant children (v.24). He will rescue those who trust in him (v.8).

VI. God's Presence and Rule: The Praise of Israel and the Nations

22:25–31

25 From you comes the theme of my praise in the great
assembly;
before those who fear you will I fulfill my vows.
26 The poor will eat and be satisfied;
they who seek the LORD will praise him—
may your hearts live forever!
27 All the ends of the earth
will remember and turn to the LORD,

and all the families of the nations
will bow down before him,
28 for dominion belongs to the LORD
and he rules over the nations.

29 All the rich of the earth will feast and worship;
all who go down to the dust will kneel before him—
those who cannot keep themselves alive.
30 Posterity will serve him;
future generations will be told about the Lord.
31 They will proclaim his righteousness
to a people yet unborn—
for he has done it.

The psalm opened with an individual cry for help (vv.1–2) and closes with a portrayal of "all the families of the nations" worshiping the Lord (v.27). It begins by affirming God's rule, justice, and mighty acts of deliverance for Israel (vv.3–5) and closes with a glorious anticipation of God's rule over and gracious care of the nations (vv.25–29). It commences with what God has done in past generations (vv.4–5) and ends with the expectation that future generations will serve him because they too will know the story of redemptive history and will join in the proclamation of the good news that Yahweh has acted graciously on behalf of his people (vv.30–31). The psalmist's praise (*tᵉhillāh*) is both caused by and directed toward the Lord (v.25). He may now join in with Israel's praises (pl. *tᵉhillôṯ*, v.3; NIV, "the praise of Israel").

25 The psalmist affirms the importance of public worship (cf. vv.22–23) in terms of praise and the presentation of freewill (votive) offerings. A vow was often made during a period of distress (cf. 50:14; 61:8; 66:13; 116:14, 18; Jonah 2:9) and was fulfilled after God had shown his loyalty (65:1; cf. Eccl 5:4).

26 The psalmist shares the votive offerings (cf. Lev 7:16–21) with the poor and afflicted so as to give them a sense of relief, which he has so recently experienced. The votive offering was enjoyed at the temple as a communal meal. He blesses them with the comfort that even as food has strengthened their bodies, so shall the Lord strengthen their hearts, enabling them to endure the period of their affliction with patience. Those who diligently seek the Lord (cf. 24:6) will praise him for his salvation (cf. v.24).

27–28 The psalmist looks beyond the congregation of the righteous in Israel to "the ends of the earth" (v.27; cf. 2:8; 67:7; Isa 45:22; 52:10). Here the theme of God's lordship over all people is emphasized. To God belongs the rule over the earth (v.3; cf. 24:1–2) and the individual nations that live in it (v.28). Because of his "dominion" (= "kingship"), the nations—included in the Abrahamic covenant as "all the families of the nations" (v.27; cf. Gen 12:3; Ps 96:7)—will "remember" the LORD. The act of remembrance is an act of obeisance and worship (vv.27–28). The nations too will come to worship the Lord. This is the vision of hope, as Calvin wrote, "Christ, we know, penetrated with amazing speed, from the east to the west, like the lightning's flash, in order to bring into the Church the Gentiles from all parts of the world" (1:386).

29 Among the worshiping community the psalmist sees "the rich," i.e., the prosperous, people and nations and all the dying ("all who go down to the dust," cf. 28:1; 30:3, 9; 88:4; 143:7; see the appendix to Ps 88: Sheol-Grave-Death in the Psalms). The participial phrase "all who go down" denotes those who are faint-hearted, sickly, dying, and filled with anguish, even as the psalmist once lay "in the dust of death" (v.15; cf. 30:3). Both well-fed and poor people will join in the worship of God. How great is God's grace in that he does not discriminate between Jew and Gentile, between rich and poor (cf. Gal 3:28)!

30–31 The praise of God will extend from generation to generation. The story of redemption will not only include the nations but also generations yet unborn. The object of the proclamation is God's "righteousness" (*ṣᵉḏāqāh*), i.e., his acts of deliverance whereby he demonstrates his sovereign, gracious, and victorious rule (cf. TWOT, 2:754–55). He has done everything (v.31; cf. NEB, "this was his doing")! Each generation will join in with the telling of the story of redemption and of his kingship (cf. vv.3–5) and will, in the process of transmitting it, add what God has done for them. This is the essence of redemptive history.

Notes

---

29 (30 MT) The MT's אָכְלוּ (*'āḵᵉlû*, lit., "they have eaten," Qal perfect; NIV, "all . . . will feast") should be emended, making the verb into two separate words: *'aḵ lô* ("indeed to him," cf. BHS) followed by the simple imperfect of "they will worship" (without a waw conversive), giving the following result:

> Indeed him [emphatic] all the rich
> of the earth will worship;
> all who go down to the dust will kneel
> before him.

(See Kraus, *Psalmen*, 1:176; Weiser, p. 218; Craigie, *Psalms 1–50*, p. 195.)

Some correct דִּשְׁנֵי (*dišnê*, "the rich," lit., "fat ones") to יְשֵׁנֵי (*yᵉšēnê*, "those who sleep") and thus read a parallelism into v.29a with v.29b: "all who go down to the dust" (Kraus, *Psalmen*, 1:176; Weiser, p. 218; Craigie, *Psalms 1–50*, p. 195). The NEB assumes this conjecture and further introduces an interrogative: "How can those buried in the earth do him homage?" If the MT is correct, and there is no strong evidence to question it, v.29 says in essence what is idiomatically expressed in 115:13: "small and great alike." The "great" are the rich and "the small" are those whose strength fails them.

30–31 (31–32 MT) The LXX correctly reads "the coming generation" (v.31), as does Craigie: "to a generation that will come" (*Psalms 1–50*, pp. 195, 197).

Appendix: Yahweh Is El

El was a common designation for the head of the Canaanite pantheon of gods. The Israelites generally avoided referring to Yahweh by this designation, lest there be any confusion that their God was the same as the Canaanite El. The Canaanite El was king, the father of the gods and of man, and he dwelt in a palace on Mount Zaphon. He was benign, the giver of all good gifts. Further, he was responsible for order among the gods and peace on earth. Israel believed that Yahweh was everything the Canaanites claimed for El and for his son Baal and even more.

In the poetical sections of the OT, the inspired authors freely adapted Canaanite literary expressions to the service of Yahweh. In their hearts the psalmists were committed to Yahweh and knew that El was a figment of the imagination. Yet they borrowed the descriptions, perfections, and acts attributed to El. At times a clear polemical force shines through, as the psalmists defend their faith that only Yahweh is El and that there is no other El than Yahweh! Other times the psalmists creatively employ literary motifs in the service of Yahweh.

Yahweh-El is the Creator of heaven and earth (19:1; 90:2). His glory and power are evident in his creation (29:3). He is King over all creatures, even the heavenly beings: "For the LORD is the great God [El], / the great King [*melek*] above all gods" (95:3).

Yahweh-El is holy, full of love, compassion, and forgiveness: "But you, O LORD, are a compassionate and gracious God [El], / slow to anger, abounding in love and faithfulness" (86:15). His power is great, and the "holy beings" in heaven recognize his supremacy: "In the council of the holy ones God [El] is greatly feared; / he is more awesome than all who surround him" (89:7).

Yahweh-El upholds love, justice, and righteousness, avenging the wicked (52:1, 5; 55:9; 94:1) and delivering (vindicating) the innocent (7:11; cf. 10:11–12; 18:47; 77:9, 13–14). He hates evil (5:4) and sees the hidden things the wicked commit (10:11; 73:11, 17). He knows the needs of his own: "Search me, O God [El], and know my heart; / test me and know my anxious thoughts" (139:23). Yahweh-El protects the needy, righteous, and godly in his palace-fortress on the mountain (16:1; 18:2, 30; 78:35). Even the animals look to him for food (104:21).

Yahweh-El rules with integrity. He loves those who lead their lives with integrity:

> As for God [El], his way is perfect;
>   the word of the LORD is flawless.
> He is a shield
>   for all who take refuge in him.
> ....
> It is God [El] who arms me with strength
>   and makes my way perfect.
>
> (18:30, 32)

Yahweh-El may delay his salvation, giving the impression that he is absent (22:1; cf. 42:9; 83:1). Blessed are those who hope for his deliverance: "Blessed is he whose help is the God [El] of Jacob, / whose hope is in the LORD his God" (146:5; cf. 31:5). Yahweh-El will restore all blessings to his needy people (85:8–13).

Yahweh-El gives meaning in life: 'My soul thirsts for God, for the living God [El]. / When can I go and meet with God?" (42:2; cf. v.8; 43:4; 57:2; 63:1; 84:2). Yahweh-El alone is the 'living" God, for whom the godly yearn:

> My soul yearns, even faints,
>   for the courts of the Lord;
> my heart and my flesh cry out
>   for the living God [El].
>
> (84:2)

Yahweh is *El Shaddai* ("God Almighty"). The meaning of Shaddai is obscure. There have been many proposals: "breasted one," "Mounted One," "Almighty." Yahweh was known to the patriarchs as Shaddai (cf. Gen 17:1; Exod 6:3). Recently the mythopoetic background has come more to the foreground, helping us to see the cultural environment of the ancient Near East. From this background the meaning of "Shaddai" as "Mounted One" or "Mountain God" has been proposed. The Psalms have only two occurrences of this ancient designation:

> When the Almighty [Shaddai] scattered the kings in the land,
> it was like snow fallen on Zalmon.
>
> (68:14)

> He who dwells in the shelter of the Most High [Elyon]
> will rest in the shadow of the Almighty [Shaddai].
>
> (91:1)

Yahweh-El reveals himself from Mount Zion: "The Mighty One [El], God, the LORD, / speaks and summons the earth / from the rising of the sun to the place where it sets" (50:1; see exposition of Ps 50). He is present with the Davidic Monarch (89:26). The godly, too, experienced his support, protection, and blessing (68:19–20) and rejoiced in taking part in the procession of the godly to the temple of Yahweh-El:

> Praise be to the Lord, to God [El] our Savior,
> who daily bears our burdens. *Selah*
> Our God [El] is a God [El] who saves;
> from the Sovereign LORD comes escape from death.
> . . . .
> Your procession has come into view, O God [El],
> the procession of my God and King into the sanctuary.
> . . . .
> You are awesome, O God, in your sanctuary;
> the God [El] of Israel gives power and strength to his people.
>
> Praise be to God!
>
> (68:19–20, 24, 35)

Yahweh-El is the object of praise and devotion: "You are my God [El], and I will give you thanks; / you are my God, and I will exalt you" (118:28; cf. 136:26). All creatures in heaven and earth will praise Yahweh-El: "Praise the LORD. / Praise God [El] in his sanctuary; / praise him in his mighty heavens" (150:1).

Texts: 5:4; 7:11; 10:11–12; 16:1; 17:6; 18:2, 30, 32, 47; 19:1; 22:1, 10; 29:1, 3; 31:5; 42:2, 8–9; 44:20; 50:1; 52:5; 55:19; 57:2; 63:1; 68:19–20, 24; 73:11, 17; 77:9, 13–14; 78:7–8, 18–19, 41; 82:1; 83:1; 84:2, 8; 86:15; 89:7, 26; 94:1; 95:3; 99:8; 102:24; 104:21; 106:14; 107:11; 118:27–28; 136:26; 139:17; 140:6; 146:5; 150:1.

Related Topics: See appendixes to Pss 3 (Yahweh Is My God); 5 (Yahweh Is King); 7 (The Name of Yahweh); 9 (Yahweh Is El Elyon); 24 (Lord Sabaoth); 25 (The Perfections of God); 46 (Zion Theology); 78 (The Mighty Acts of Yahweh); 98 (Yahweh Is the Divine Warrior); 119 (Yahweh Is My Redeemer); 122 (The Praise of Yahweh).

Bibliography: G.B. Caird, *The Language and Imagery of the Bible* (Philadelphia: Westminster, 1980), pp. 219–42; Richard J. Clifford, "The Tent of El and the Israelite Tent of Meeting," CBQ 33 (1971): 221–27; J. De Fraine, " 'Entmythologisierung' dans les Psaumes," *Le Psautier. Ses Origines. Ses Problemes litteraires. Son Influence*, ed. Robert De Langhe (Louvain: Institut Orientaliste, 1962), pp. 89–106; Otto Eissfeldt, "El and Yahweh," JSS 1 (1956): 25–37; id., "My God in the Old Testament," EQ 19 (1947): 7–20; Kraus, *Theologie des Psalmen*, pp. 24–25; M. Dahood, "The Divine Name 'Elî in the Psalms," *Theological Studies* 14 (1953): 452–57; P.D. Miller, Jr., "El the Warrior," HTR 60 (1967): 411–31; id., "Aspects of the Religion of Ugarit," *Ancient Israelite Religion. Essays in Honor of Frank Moore Cross*, edd. Patrick D. Miller, Jr., Paul D. Hanson, and S. Dean McBride

(Philadelphia: Fortress, 1987), pp. 53–66; M. Pope, *El in the Ugaritic Texts* (Leiden: Brill, 1955); Elmer B. Smick, "Mythopoetic Language in the Psalms," WTJ 44 (1982): 88–98; id., "Israel's Struggle With the Religions of Canaan," *Through Christ's Word. A Festschrift for Dr. Philip E. Hughes*, edd. W. Robert Godfrey and Jesse L. Boyd III (Phillipsburg: Presbyterian and Reformed, 1985), pp. 108–17; M.H. Segal, "El, Elohim, and YHWH in the Bible," JQR 46 (1955): 89–115; Zimmerli, OTTO, pp. 41–43.

TDOT, 1:242–61; THAT, 1:142–49; TWOT, 1:41–43.

Psalm 23: The Goodness of God

Psalm 23 is a *psalm of trust and confidence* (see the fine exposition by Patrick D. Miller, Jr., "Psalm 23," *Interpreting the Psalms*, pp. 112–19). Its original setting or situation in life is difficult to determine. S. Gelinder concludes that the psalmist was a king who in his trouble was confident in Yahweh's ability to deliver him ("On the Condition of the Speaker in Psalm 23," *Beth Mikra* 23 [1978]: 642–64 [Heb.]). Jack R. Lundbom suggests that the psalm is set in the wilderness at the time of David's flight from Absalom ("Psalm 23: Song of Passage," Int 40 [1986]: 6–16).

The psalm expresses confidence in God's goodness—in this life and in the life to come. The personal way in which the psalmist speaks of God, the imagery of God's soothing guidance, and the ensuing confidence in God have all been factors in making this one of the most charming and beloved of the Psalms. The universal appeal of this psalm lies in the comfort it gives to those who have confronted the most difficult periods of life: "It is for parents who survive the folly of rebellious children, for people returning from war, for someone recently out of jail" (ibid., p. 16). It is a psalm of God's strength and grace for all ages. The teaching of our Lord that he is the Good Shepherd (John 10:11) who has come for both Jews and Gentiles (John 10:16) gives the Christian a sound reason to apply the benefits of God's goodness to the ancient covenant people and to himself, as a child of Abraham and fellow-heir of Jesus Christ (Gal 3:29; 4:7). Moreover, it causes us to hope in the glory God has prepared for his own (Rev 7:17).

The structure of the psalm is both simple and complex (see Craigie, *Psalms 1–50*, pp. 204–5; Charles O'Connor, "The Structure of Psalm 23," *Louvain Studies* 10 [1985]: 206–30; Siegfried Mittmann, "Aufbau und Einheit des Danklieds Psalm 23," *Zeitschrift für Theologie und Kirche* 77 [1980]: 1–23; Werner Stenger, "Strukturale 'relecture' von Ps 23," *Freude an der Weisung des Herrn, Beiträge zur Theologie der Psalmen, Festgabe zum 70. Geburtstag von Heinrich Gross*, edd. Ernst Haag and Frank-Lothar Hossfeld [Stuttgart: Katholisches Bibelwerk, 1986], pp. 441–55). There are two principle metaphors of the Lord's goodness: he is like a "shepherd" who is interested in each sheep (vv.1–4), and he is like a host who has prepared a lavish banquet (vv.5–6). Each of these has its own peculiar set of metaphors. See Jean Marcel Vincent for a careful analysis of the language and poetic artistry ("Recherches exégétiques sur le Psaume xxiii," VetTest 28 [1978]: 442–54). For the purpose of exposition, we shall analyze the psalm under the two metaphors:

A. The Lord Is My Shepherd (vv.1–4)
B. The Lord Is My Host (vv.5–6)

I. The Lord Is My Shepherd

23:1–4

A psalm of David.

1 The LORD is my shepherd, I shall not be in want.
2 He makes me lie down in green pastures,
he leads me beside quiet waters,
3 he restores my soul.
He guides me in paths of righteousness
for his name's sake.
4 Even though I walk
through the valley of the shadow of death,
I will fear no evil,
for you are with me;
your rod and your staff,
they comfort me.

1 The first word of the psalm, "The LORD" (Yahweh), evokes rich images of the provision and protection of the covenant-God. He promised to take care of his people and revealed himself to be full of love, compassion, patience, fidelity, and forgiveness (Exod 34:6–7). The psalmist exclaims, "Yahweh is *my* shepherd," with emphasis on "my." The temptation in ancient Israel was to speak only about "our" God (cf. Deut 6:4), forgetting that the God of Israel is also the God of individuals. The contribution of this psalm lies, therefore, in the personal, subjective expression of ancient piety. For this reason Psalm 23 is such a popular psalm, because it permits each believer to take its words on his lips and express in gratitude and confidence that all the demonstrations of God's covenant love are his, too.

The metaphor of the shepherd has a colorful history, as it was applied to kings and gods. King Hammurabi called himself "shepherd" (ANET, p. 164b). The Babylonian god of justice, Shamash, is also called "shepherd": "Shepherd of the lower world, guardian of the upper" (ANET, p. 388). The metaphor is not only a designation or name of the Lord, but it points toward the relation between God and his covenant-children (cf. 74:1–4; 77:20; 78:52, 70–72; 79:13; 80:1; Isa 40:11; Mic 7:14). The psalmist moves quickly from "my shepherd" to a description: "I shall not be in want." The people of God were well acquainted with shepherds. David himself was a shepherd (1 Sam 16:11), as the hills around Bethlehem were suitable for shepherding (cf. Luke 2:8).

2–4 The image of "shepherd" aroused emotions of care, provision, and protection. A good shepherd was personally concerned with the welfare of his sheep. Because of this the designation "my shepherd" is further described by the result of God's care: "I shall not be in want"; by the acts of God, "he makes me lie down . . . he leads . . . he restores . . . he guides" (vv.2–3); and by the resulting tranquility, "I will fear no evil" (v.4).

Dahood may stretch the meaning of "I shall not be in want" when he writes, "Implying neither in this life nor in the next" (*Psalms*, 1:146); but so do those commentators who find allusions to the Lord's provisions, guidance, and protection of Israel in the wilderness (cf. A.A. Anderson, 1:196–97; Craigie, *Psalms 1–50*, pp. 206–7). The conclusion of the psalm (v.6) gives at least some support to Dahood's contention; however, the psalm should not be narrowly interpreted in terms of "the eternal bliss of Paradise" (Dahood, *Psalms*, 1:145).

The shepherd's care is symbolized by the "rod" and the "staff" (v.4c). A shepherd carried a "rod" to club down wild animals (cf. 1 Sam 17:43; 2 Sam 23:21) and a "staff" to keep the sheep in control. The rod and staff represent God's *constant* vigilance over his own and bring "comfort" because of his personal presence and involvement with his sheep. Verses 1 and 4, taken as an inclusio, read:

> The LORD is my shepherd. . . .
> Your rod and your staff,
> they comfort me.

The nature of the care lies in God's royal *provisions* of all the necessities of his people (see Richard S. Tomback, "Psalm 23:2 Reconsidered," JNSL 10 [1982]: 93–96, for the background in the ancient Near East). The "green pastures" are the rich and verdant pastures, where the sheep need not move from place to place to be satisfied (cf. Ezek 34:14; John 10:9). The "green pastures" were a seasonal phenomenon. The fields, even parts of the desert, would green during the winter and spring. But in summer and fall the sheep would be led to many places in search of food. God's care is not seasonal but constant and abundant. The sheep have time to rest, as the shepherd makes them to "lie down." The "quiet waters" are the wells and springs where the sheep can drink without being rushed (cf. Isa 32:18). The combination of "green pastures" and "quiet waters" portrays God's "refreshing care" for his own.

As the good shepherd provides his sheep with rest, verdant pastures, and quiet waters, so the Lord takes care of his people in a most plentiful way. He thereby renews them so that they feel that life in the presence of God is good and worth living. He "restores," i.e., he gives the enjoyment of life, to his own (v.3; cf. 19:7; Prov 25:13). The word "soul" is not here the spiritual dimension of man but denotes the same as "me" repeated twice in v.2, i.e., "he restores me."

The nature of the shepherd's care also lies in *guidance* (vv.3b–4b). In the previous verse the psalmist spoke of God as leading ("he leads me"). He develops the shepherd's role as a guide only to conclude with another aspect of his shepherdly care: protection (v.4c). He leads his own in the "paths of righteousness." These paths do not lead one to obtain righteousness. "Righteousness" (*ṣeḏeq*) here signifies in the most basic sense "right," namely, the paths that bring the sheep most directly to their destination (in contrast to "crooked paths"; cf. 125:5; Prov 2:15; 5:6; 10:9). His paths are straight (cf. Aubrey R. Johnson, "Psalm 23 and the Household of Faith," in *Proclamation and Presence. Old Testament Essays in Honour of Gwynne Henton Davies*, edd. John I. Durham and J.R. Porter [Richmond: Knox, 1970], p. 258). He does not unnecessarily tire out his sheep. He knows what lies ahead. Even when the "right paths" bring the sheep "through the valley of the shadow of death" (v.4), there is no need to fear.

The idiom "the shadow of death" has stirred up some discussion. Briggs spoke of the MT punctuation (*ṣalmāweṯ*, "shadow of death") as "a rabbinical conceit" and preferred, instead of a compound phrase, one word (*ṣalmûṯ*, "darkness," 1:211–12). D. Winton Thomas ("צַלְמָוֶת in the Old Testament," JSS 7 [1962]: 191–200) has argued persuasively that the MT text may be correct, with "death" being a superlative image for "very deep shadow" or "deep darkness." This imagery is consistent with the shepherd metaphor because the shepherd leads the flock through ravines and wadis where the steep and narrow slopes keep out the light. The darkness of the wadis represents the uncertainty of life. The "straight paths" at times need to go through the wadis, but God is still present.

The shepherd who guides is always *with* the sheep. The presence and guidance of the Lord go together. He is bound by his name ("for his name's sake"), Yahweh, to be present with his people. Underlying the etymology of Yahweh is the promise "I will be with you" (Exod 3:12). For the sake of his name, he keeps all the promises to his covenant children (cf. 25:11; 31:3; 79:9; 106:8; 109:21; 143:11; Isa 48:9; Ezek 20:44). He is loyal to his people, for his honor and reputation are at stake! (See the appendix to Ps 7: The Name of Yahweh.)

The nature of the shepherd's care lies further in the protection he gives (v.4c). Above we briefly considered the significance of the "rod" and the "staff" as they symbolize his presence, protection, and guidance. They summarize his shepherd role. The effects of his care are expressed in the first person—"I shall not be in want. . . . I will fear no evil" (vv.1, 4)—as an inclusionary motif together with "shepherd" and "rod/staff" (vv.1, 4). Thus the psalmist rejoices that Yahweh is like a shepherd in his provisions, guidance, and protection, so that he lacks nothing and fears not.

Notes

For a brief discussion of the technical words and phrases in the superscription, see the Introduction.

3–4 A.L. Merrill ("Psalm XXIII and the Jerusalem Tradition," VetTest 15 [1965]: 354–60) and John Eaton ("Problems of Translation Psalm 23:3f," *Bible Translator* 16 [1965]: 171–76) give a royal interpretation. Eaton (p. 176) renders these verses:

> He restores my life;
> He leads me on the highroad of salvation for the sake of his Name.
> Even though I enter the chasm of Death's dominion,
> I fear no evil; for thou art with me;
> Thy royal rod and staff bring me to joy again.

G.J. Thierry treats these verses as having reference to a person and not to "sheep" ("Remarks on Various Passages in the Psalms," *OudTestamentische Studien* 13 [1963]: 97), as does also Briggs (1:207). Timothy A. Willis disagrees and argues that these verses relate to three distinct tasks of the shepherd (food, water, and shelter) in "A Fresh Look at Psalm xxiii 3a," VetTest 37 (1987): 104–6.

II. The Lord Is My Host

23:5–6

5 You prepare a table before me
in the presence of my enemies.
You anoint my head with oil;
my cup overflows.
6 Surely goodness and love will follow me
all the days of my life,
and I will dwell in the house of the LORD
forever.

5 The Lord is the host at a banquet (cf. Isa 25:6–8) prepared for his child. The "table" is laden with food and drink. Before entering into the banquet hall, the host would anoint the honored guest with oil (45:7; 92:10; 133:2; Amos 6:6; Luke 7:46). The oil was made by adding perfumes to olive oil. The "cup" symbolizes the gracious and beneficent manner of entertainment. The overflowing pictures the Lord as giving the best to his child. It symbolizes the care and provisions of God, previously represented by "green pastures" and "quiet waters." Moreover, the Lord vindicates his servant "in the presence of my enemies," expressing both the adversities of life itself as well as God's demonstration of his love toward his own. In the presence of God, the fragrance of his rewards ("oil") and the bounty of his provisions ("cup") make one forget troubles and tears. His is "the cup of salvation" (116:13) that pertains to both body and spirit.

6 In view of this picture, the psalmist draws comfort that God's love and presence are constant. His "goodness and love" reflect the attributes of Yahweh, the covenant-faithful God. The "goodness" (*ṭô<u>b</u>*) of God is demonstrated in his abundant care and promises, and these are evidence of his blessing (cf. 4:6). In the words of 4:7, it gives greater joy than the abundance of "grain and new wine." The "love" (*ḥese<u>d</u>*; KJV, "mercy") of God is the covenantal commitment to bless his people with his goodness, i.e., his promises. The psalmist expresses deep confidence in God's loyalty. Instead of being pursued by enemies who seek his destruction, God's "goodness and love" follow him. He need not fear, because God's care will always manifest itself in his provisions, abundance, and protection. His loving care follows him throughout life. The psalmist does not say that our cup shall always be full or that our heads will always be anointed with oil, but we do have the promise that God's beneficence will be our lifelong companion.

The psalmist's experience of God's "goodness and love" is equivalent to dwelling "in the house of the LORD." To eat and to drink at the table prepared by the Lord is a recognition of a covenant bond (cf. Kidner, 1:112). The covenant bond does not cease when one leaves the precincts of the tabernacle or temple. The following psalm (24) deals with the moral requisites for fellowship with the Lord and his blessing (vv.3-6; cf. Ps 15). The saints in the OT had a sense of God's presence in the abundant evidences of his goodness. The "house of the LORD" signifies what Kraus defines as "whoever has experienced Yahweh's *y^ešû'āh* ['deliverance'] may at all times remain in the environs of salvation, in the sanctuary" (*Psalmen,* 1:191; cf. 27:4–5; 52:9; 61:4; 63:2; see the appendix to Ps 132: The Ark of the Covenant and the Temple: Symbols of Yahweh's Presence and Rule).

The "experience" with God takes on a transcendental significance, as it gives the believer a taste of everlasting fellowship with God. Thus Weiser writes, "The hallowed atmosphere of worship is and remains a holy experience whereby the heart feels exalted and becomes more strongly conscious of the nearness of God than is possible in the noise and din of the streets" (p. 231). Similarly Brueggemann writes that "it is not the *place* but the vitality of the *relationship* which transforms" (p. 156). In motifs and metaphors identical to this psalm, the Apocalypse portrays the ministry of our Lord, the Great Shepherd, to all who suffer on earth (Rev 7:15b–17).

Notes

5 The verb דִּשַּׁנְתָּ (*diššantā*, "you anoint," "you revive") has the same root as "the rich" (דִּשְׁנֵי, *dišnê*) in 22:29a and may be a verbal link between these two psalms. The meaning "anoint" is unrelated to the anointing of a king (contra Eaton, *Kingship and the Psalms*, pp. 36–38). Rather it denotes the plentiful pouring out of oil (cf. NEB, "thou hast richly bathed my head with oil").

5–6 The LXX renders the last phrase of v.5 together with the first phrase of v.6 to describe the cup as being filled with "good" wine. Though the phrase "goodness and love" occurs only in 23:6, the MT makes good sense. For the covenantal usage, see Michael Fox, "ṬÔB as Covenant Terminology," BASOR 209 (1973): 41–42; Ingeborg Johag, "טוב Terminus Technicus in Vertrags- und Bündnisformularen des Alten Orients und des Alten Testaments," *Bausteine biblischer Theologie. Festgabe für G. Johannes Botterweck zum 60. Geburtstag dargebracht von seinen Schülern*, ed. Heinz-Josef Fabry (Köln: Peter Hanstein, 1977), pp. 3–23.

6 The phrase וְשַׁבְתִּי (*wᵉšab̲tî*, "and I shall dwell") occasions difficulties. "I shall dwell" requires either *wᵉšib̲tî* or *wᵉyāšab̲tî*. The ancient versions agree on the reading "I will dwell" (LXX, Syriac), but the MT reads, "I shall return," i.e., "I shall continually come back to the house of the Lord as long as I live." Delitzsch reads both verbs as a pregnant construction, i.e., "again, having returned, dwell in the house of Jahve" (1:332; cf. Craigie, "and I shall dwell again in the house of the LORD" (*Psalms 1–50*, p. 204). I opt for Dahood's proposal, according to which the MT may be "a contracted form" of *wᵉyāšab̲ti* ("and I shall dwell," *Psalms*, 1:148). This is consistent with the ancient witnesses, and there is no need to emend the MT.

David Noel Freedman has explained this psalm from the exilic perspective, in which the people of God anticipate a new exodus and a renewal of covenant ("The Twenty-Third Psalm," in *Michigan Oriental Studies in Honor of Georg Cameron*, ed. L.L. Orlin et al. [Ann Arbor: University of Michigan, 1976], pp. 139–66). Michael L. Barré and John S. Kselman have further developed this thesis in the light of ancient Near Eastern parallels, concluding that the original royal psalm has been creatively reworked in the exilic community. They, like the Davidic king, pray that they may enjoy God's covenant blessings and his presence forevermore ("New Exodus, Covenant, and Restoration in Psalm 23," in *The Word of the Lord Shall Go Forth. Essays in Honor of David Noel Freedman*, edd. Carol F. Meyers and M. O'Connor [Winona Lake: Eisenbrauns, 1983], pp. 97–127).

Psalm 24: The King of Glory Is Our God

The psalm consists of three parts. Each part brings out a different consideration of God: (1) the Creator-God (vv.1–2), (2) the holy God (vv.3–6), (3) the glorious King (vv.7–10). Many scholars treat the psalm as a liturgical work (see Delitzsch, 1:332–33; Dahood, *Psalms*, 1:151; Craigie, *Psalms 1–50*, pp. 211–12; et al.), but they are by no means agreed on the original setting. In our approach to the psalm, the hymnic use is more prominent. The allusions to Mount Zion and the Lord's glorious entry are not sufficiently strong to provide the background for a return of the ark from war, the entry of the ark into Jerusalem or into the temple (as Ps 132), or a representation of a cultic ceremony, whether an autumnal festival, a divine epiphany, or a theophany. It seems more likely that the hymn celebrates *God's kingship* as it relates to God's people (see the appendix to Ps 5: Yahweh Is King). God is King by virtue of having created all things (vv.1–2), but he desires to rule over the people who open themselves to him by living clean, pure lives in his presence. He is the Redeemer-God of the elect in Jacob, to whom he appears as the Divine Warrior.

The structure of the psalm reflects the basic divisions:

A. The Great King (vv.1–2)
  B. The Hill of the Lord (vv.3–6)
A′. The Divine Warrior (vv.7–10)

A Jewish tradition, reflected also in the heading of the LXX, suggests Psalm 24's use on Sunday, in celebration of the first day of Creation (cf. b *Rosh Hashanah* 31a). Roy A. Rosenberg relates the Talmudic teaching to each one of the days of the week, explaining that the Jews developed a liturgical tradition in Babylon. There various gods received special worship on the days of the week; so Jews celebrated Yahweh's kingship on each day:

Psalm 24 Sunday	Psalm 81 Thursday
Psalm 48 Monday	Psalm 93 Friday
Psalm 82 Tuesday	Psalm 92 Sabbath
Psalm 94 Wednesday	

(See "Yahweh has become King," JBL 85 [1966]: 297–307.)

In Christian tradition Psalm 24 was sung on Ascension Day. But the hymn of Georg Weissel (*Trinity Hymnal,* tr. by C. Winkworth [Philadelphia: OPC, 1961], p. 146) applies the psalm to Christ's advent:

Lift up your heads, ye mighty gates!
Behold, the King of glory waits;
The King of Kings is drawing near,
The Savior of the world is here.
Life and salvation he doth bring,
Wherefore rejoice and gladly sing.

I. The Great King

24:1–2

Of David. A psalm.

1 The earth is the LORD's, and everything in it,
  the world, and all who live in it;
2 for he founded it upon the seas
  and established it upon the waters.

1–2 The psalm first introduces us to the Creator-King, who rules over the earth. The Lord owns "the earth" and "everything" on it. "Everything" is amplified in the parallel phrase as "all who live in it" (v.1). Animals and people make their home on earth and are therefore under his dominion. His rule is established particularly because he has made the world habitable (Isa 45:18). There is not the slightest hint of some primitive cosmology in the words "he founded it upon the seas," as if the psalmist believes that the earth floats on a cosmic ocean (so A.A. Anderson, 1:201). Rather, these words signify that the Lord has manifested his wisdom in creating an orderly world (cf. 136:5–6; 1 Cor 10:26), and therefore he rules over all. The biblical perspective is opposed to the deification of nature, because, while everything is glorious, its glory is derived from the glorious Creator. So von Rad writes, "When the Old Testament speaks of creation, it sees the world in contrast to God: as a realm with its own splendour, . . . but which is nevertheless created, *i.e.* called into being by the creative word with complete effortlessness" (OTT, 2:339).

Craigie is correct in his argument that the psalmist may use "demythologized" language in order to portray "forcefully the Lord's creation of an ordered world, upon seas and rivers, symbolizing the subdued forces of chaos" (*Psalms 1–50*, p. 212). We are not to assume that the Israelites knew the Canaanite cosmogony, but they may have become familiar with words and phrases that were adapted to Israelite purposes without giving credence to the whole pagan association. Thus "seas" and "waters" (v.2, lit., "rivers") may have reflected the forces of chaos in Canaanite cosmogony; but in Israelite usage they are not hostile, chaotic forces, independent from Yahweh, but fully under his dominion (cf. 136:5–6; Gen 1:1–10). The earth is "established." For the correlation of land-gift, divine order, and man's responsibility, see Walter Brueggemann, "On Land-losing and Land-receiving," *Crux* 19 (1980): 166–73.

Notes

For a brief discussion of the technical words and phrases in the superscription, see the Introduction.

1 "Everything in it" is a dynamic rendering of מְלוֹאָהּ (*melô'āh*, "its fullness"). The phrase occurs with "the earth" (Deut 33:16; Isa 34:1; Jer 8:16; 47:2; Ezek 19:7; 30:12; Mic 1:2), with "the world" (Pss 50:12; 89:11), and with "the sea" (96:11; 98:7).

2 נְהָרוֹת (*nehārôṯ*, "the waters") is literally "rivers." The "rivers" are not bodies of water such as the Jordan or Nile but are here synonymous with "seas," hence "waters" (cf. Isa 44:27; Hab 3:8). Dahood renders it "ocean currents" (*Psalms*, 1:150–51), but this goes beyond its usage here and in Ugaritic. John Day sees in vv.2, 7–10 an allusion to the battle with the sea in *God's Conflict with the Dragon and the Sea. Echoes of Canaanite Myth in the Old Testament* (Cambridge: Cambridge University Press, 1985), pp. 37–38.

II. The Hill of the Lord

24:3–6

3 Who may ascend the hill of the LORD?
Who may stand in his holy place?
4 He who has clean hands and a pure heart,
who does not lift up his soul to an idol
or swear by what is false.
5 He will receive blessing from the LORD
and vindication from God his Savior.
6 Such is the generation of those who seek him,
who seek your face, O God of Jacob. *Selah*

3 Who is acceptable to the Creator-King? How may one prepare himself for fellowship with him? The psalmist expresses the nature of fellowship with God in OT terms; e.g., ascending "the hill of the LORD" and standing in "his holy place." "The hill of the LORD" is a reference to Mount Zion (cf. 2:6), also known as "your holy hill" (15:1) and "his holy place" (24:3). Because God is the great Creator-King (vv.1–2), whose residence on earth was symbolized in Jerusalem's temple (vv.7–10), one who seeks

his favor needs to prepare himself, not only ceremonially, but also by sanctifying his life (cf. 15:2–5). If one were to come into God's presence, it should not be for "curse" but for "blessing" (v.5). (See the appendix to Ps 46: Zion Theology.)

It may be that the instructions on moral purity were originally part of a ceremony before completing the last leg of the pilgrimage to Jerusalem. Such an interpretation, however, is not necessary. The hymn instructs God's people *wherever* they may be to live in the presence of the Creator-King in order to receive his blessing. The verbs "ascend" and "stand," as well as the phrases "the hill of the LORD" and "his holy place," may also be borrowed terms from the pilgrimage ritual. By these words the psalmist impresses on the people the requirements of the Lord in general. In view of the absence of cultic or ritual specifications, the psalm need, therefore, not be interpreted solely as a preparation for the worship of the Lord.

4 The Lord expects purity and singleness of heart from all who seek his presence (cf. Matt 5:8). Purity of "hands" and "heart" is the condition of living before God in accordance with his precepts and out of the desire of his heart. Appearance of holiness is not enough, because the "clean hands" are expressive of "a pure heart" (cf. 73:1). The one who has "clean hands" is "innocent" of wrongdoing and readily asks for forgiveness when he has sinned against God. In contrast is the sinner whose "hands are full of blood" and who needs cleansing, forgiveness, and reconciliation (cf. Isa 1:15–18).

God expects, in addition to loyalty to the Lord in heart and life, a *singleness* of devotion. The godly person does not dishonor the Lord's name by idolatry or by falsehood. The parallel construction of "falsehood" ("vanity"; NIV, "an idol") with "what is false" (i.e., "with deception") and of the verbs "lift up" and "swear" favors the conclusion that the psalmist has only dishonesty in mind without a reference to idolatry as a particular act of dishonesty (cf. Exod 20:16; Mal 3:5). If this be so, the two positive descriptions of integrity (v.4a) are balanced by two negative descriptions (v.4b). The godly man is "pure" and not "false" (or hypocritical). This excludes, of course, idolatry in any form. His yea is yea and his nay is nay (cf. 15:3–4; Matt 5:37).

5 The reward for a walk of integrity is the enjoyment of God's presence by his "blessing" and "vindication." The "blessing" is the status of God's favor extended to his loyal servants, who enjoy the promises of the covenant (cf. Num 6:23–26). The Lord who "lifts up his face" in blessing (Num 6:26) also promises that his loyal ones will "lift up" (NIV "receive") a blessing, wherever they may be. It is the Lord's blessing and is, therefore, not subject to feelings, circumstances, or outside influence (cf. 15:5b). Moreover, he receives "vindication" (*ṣᵉḏāqāh*, see Notes) from his Savior-God. His Redeemer will help, provide justice, and grant the ultimate vindication only to those who are faithful to him (cf. 5:8; 22:31; 36:10; Isa 45:8; 46:13; 51:6). The Savior will not only bless but will also protect his people.

6 The psalmist returns to the nature of the recipients of God's blessings (cf. v.4). The "group" of people (NIV, "generation," see Notes; cf. 12:7 ["such people"]; 14:5 ["company"]; 73:15 [untr.]) with whom God is pleased walks with integrity (v.4), not because of outward constraint, but by an internal desire to please him. To "seek him" is an expression of a sincere desire to live in accordance with God's standards (78:34), so as to live in the presence of his "face." The "assembly" (or "generation") is the descendants of Jacob. The NIV follows several MSS, the LXX, and the Syriac with the addition of "God of" to the MT's "your face, Jacob" (see NIV mg.). Briggs's chiastic rendering based on the reading "his face" (Targum) is an attractive possibility:

This is a generation	which resorts to Him;
Those who seek his face	are Jacob

The "generation" of the upright are, thus, the true descendants of Jacob (cf. 1:213, 216). Clearly, the ethics of God's people are not a system of morality, independent of the Lord, but have a theological basis (see Eckart Otto, "Kultus und Ethos in Jerusalemer Theologie: Ein Beitrag zur theologischen Begründigung der Ethik im Alten Testament," ZAW 98 [1986]: 161–79).

Notes

4 The phrase לֹא־נָשָׂא לַשָּׁוְא נַפְשִׁי (*lō'-nāśā' laššāwe' napšî*, "he does not lift up to vanity my soul") contains two exegetical issues. First, the idiom *n-ś-' nepeš le* signifies "longing for," "relish," or "to set one's heart on" (cf. Jer 22:27; 44:14; Hos 4:8). Second, "my soul" is a text-critical problem. The MSS of the Cairo Geniza and a number of versions support a change to "his soul" (so NIV). Those who prefer the MT's "my soul" take it as a synonym for "my name" (cf. the extensive discussion in Delitzsch, 1:336, note). Third, the meaning of "vanity" is debatable. Dahood argues that it is a term for idolatry (*Psalms*, 1:151; so NIV). However, we agree with Briggs (1:215) that the parallelism of "vanity" and מִרְמָה (*mirmāh*, "deception"; NIV, "what is false") requires the rendering "who does not long for falsehood or swears with deception" (cf. NEB, "who has not set his mind on falsehood and has not committed perjury").

6 The word דּוֹר (*dôr*, "generation") may also refer to a group of people (cf. 14:5), here "the assembly" (cf. A.A. Anderson, 1:203).

The repetitive "seek" reflects two Hebrew participles: דֹּרְשָׁיו (*dōršāyw*, "his seekers") and מְבַקְשֵׁי (*mebaqšê*, "those who seek," construct). To seek the Lord is an idiom for covenant loyalty to and fellowship with him. For a careful study of the textual issues, misgivings of commentators, and a reasonable defense of the MT, see Nic. Tromp, "Jacob in Psalm 24: Apposition, Aphaeresis or Apostrophe," in *Von Kanaan bis Kerala. Festschrift für Mag. Dr. J.P.M. van den Ploeg, O.P. zur Vollendung des siebzigsten Lebensjahres am 4. juli 1979*, edd. W.C. Delsman, A.S. van der Woude et al. (Neukirchen-Vluyn: Neukirchener Verlag, 1982), pp. 271–82.

III. The Divine Warrior

24:7–10

7 Lift up your heads, O you gates;
be lifted up, you ancient doors,
that the King of glory may come in.
8 Who is this King of glory?
The LORD strong and mighty,
the LORD mighty in battle.
9 Lift up your heads, O you gates;
lift them up, you ancient doors,
that the King of glory may come in.

[10] Who is he, this King of glory?
The LORD Almighty—
he is the King of glory. *Selah*

7 It is difficult to be sure of the original setting of the psalm. Some explain it from the perspective of the ark's return from battle (Craigie, *Psalms 1–50*, pp. 213–14). Others relate it to David's bringing of the ark to Jerusalem from Kiriath-Jearim (Delitzsch, 1:334). Weiser posits a cult dramatization of a theophany in the temple (pp. 234–35). This difficulty raises the question of the referent of "heads," "gates," and "doors." Dahood explains "lift up your heads" as an idiom for rejoicing by the godly (*Psalms*, 1:152; cf. Luke 21:28). Similarly, A.A. Anderson proposes that "gates" may be symbolic of the people collectively, as in Isaiah 14:31 (1:204–5; cf. Briggs, 1:216–17). The sense of v.7 would be: "Rejoice greatly, O you people [who live within the gates]" (cf. Zech 9:9). On the other hand, the psalmist may be literally addressing the gates of the temple to open up. Or since the temple itself was not yet erected in David's time, the psalmist may be referring to the "ancient doors" of Jerusalem. Regardless of the referent, the point remains that Jerusalem had been a Jebusite city with a long history (cf. K. Kenyon, *Royal Cities of the Old Testament* [New York: Schocken, 1971], pp. 13–35) over which Melchizedek ruled in Abraham's days (Gen 14:18). It became the city of God, because God chose to dwell in it. Consequently, both the city and the people were called on to receive with joy and anticipation the Great King. The repetition in v.9 of the refrain bears out the importance of proper preparation for "the King of glory." Twice the people ask in antiphonal chorus, "Who is [he] this King of glory?" (vv.8, 10).

8–10 "The King of glory" is "the LORD strong and mighty, / the LORD mighty in battle" (v.8) and "The LORD Almighty— /he is the King of glory" (v.10). He is Yahweh (three times, vv.8, 10), the God of the covenant people. He brings blessing, victory, and vindication to his people, because he is their God and Savior (v.5). He is the Warrior (see the appendix to Ps 98: Yahweh Is the Divine Warrior). The descriptive phrases "strong and mighty" and "mighty in battle" (v.5) portray him as the Warrior *for* his people (cf. Exod 15:2–3; Num 10:35; Deut 10:17; Isa 10:21; Jer 32:18). He is not coming to fight against them but for them. He is "LORD Almighty" (*ṣᵉḇā'ôṯ*, "of hosts") as he commands both the heavenly beings (89:6–8; 103:20–21; 148:2) and the host of stars and constellations (Isa 40:26; Joel 2:10–11) (see the appendix to Ps 24: Lord Sabaoth). The Creator-God is the King of Glory and has come down to dwell in the midst of the city of man.

Notes

7, 9 As discussed above, the expressions "your heads," "gates," and "ancient doors" are subject to a variety of interpretations. Additionally, Kraus considers the possibility of a heavenly temple from which the Lord is coming forth to dwell among his own (*Psalmen*, 1:205). A metaphorical reading calls on God's people to rejoice and to exalt themselves in preparation of God's coming (A.A. Anderson, 1:204; see also above). Cross explains the phraseology based on the Ugaritic (UT, 137:19–37; III AB B:19–37): "Lift up, O gods your heads!" The divine council of the Ugaritic pantheon paid homage to Baal as he returned victoriously. Cross interprets "gates" as a demythologized form of the divine council of the Ugaritic pantheon, which lifted up their heads in homage when Baal victoriously returned home (Frank Moore Cross, Jr., "The Divine Warrior in Israel's Early Cult," in *Biblical Motifs. Origins and Transformations*, ed. A. Altmann [Cambridge: Harvard University Press, 1966], pp. 23–24; cf. Patrick D. Miller, Jr., *The Divine Warrior in Early Israel* [Cambridge: Harvard University, 1973], pp. 29–30). For another interpretation and translation, see Alan Cooper, "Ps 24:7–10: Mythology and Exegesis," JBL 102 (1983): 37–60. See also Tryggve N. D. Mettinger, "Fighting the Powers of Chaos and Hell—Towards the Biblical Portrait of God," ST 39 (1985): 21–38.

John Goldingay rightly explains the differences in the language in vv.7, 9 as arising from artistic variation ("Repetition and Variation in the Psalms," JQR 68 [1977]: 146–47).

Appendix: Lord Sabaoth

Yahweh is the Lord of Hosts ("Almighty"). The Great King has at his command innumerable heavenly "hosts," reflecting the glory and splendor of undisputed lordship. He is the Divine Warrior (see appendix to Ps 98), the Commander of all power in heaven and earth. His battles always win him victory. Psalm 24 celebrates the entrance of this great Warrior into Zion: "Who is he, this King of glory? / The Lord Almighty— /he is the King of glory" (v.10). The presence of the divine Warrior among his people is the ground for tranquility, driving out fear: "The LORD Almighty is with us; / the God of Jacob is our fortress" (46:7, cf. v.11). Thus the foundation, the fortification, and the defense of the City of God, Zion, "God makes her secure forever" (48:8). Unlike man, the mighty Warrior is constant in his vigilance and faithful in his love: "O LORD God Almighty, who is like you? / You are mighty, O LORD, and your faithfulness surrounds you" (89:8). He wards off the attackers and scatters them. The psalmist likens the battlefield, littered with corpses, and the enemy weaponry to "snow" (68:14). In conclusion, Yahweh is the Creator, Judge, and the sole object of worship.

Texts: Pss 24:10; 46:7, 11; 48:8; 59:5; 69:6; 80:4, 7, 14, 19; 84:1, 3, 8, 12; 89:8.

Related Topics: See appendixes to Pss 3 (Yahweh Is My God); 5 (Yahweh Is King); 7 (The Name of Yahweh); 9 (Yahweh Is El Elyon); 22 (Yahweh Is El); 25 (The Perfections of God); 46 (Zion Theology); 78 (The Mighty Acts of Yahweh); 98 (Yahweh Is the Divine Warrior); 119 (Yahweh Is My Redeemer); 122 (The Praise of Yahweh).

Bibliography: J.L. Crenshaw, "YHWH *Ṣᵉḇa'ôṯ Šᵉmô:* A Form-Critical Analysis," ZAW 81 (1969): 156–75; Otto Eissfeldt, "Jahwe Zebaoth," *Kleine Scriften*, vol. 3, edd. Rudolf Sellheim and Fritz Maas (Tübingen: Mohr, 1966), pp. 103–23; Tryggve N.D. Mettinger, *The Dethronement of Sabaoth. Studies in the Shem and Kavod Theologies* (Lund: Gleerup, 1982); id., "YHWH Sabaoth—The Heavenly King on the Cherubim Throne," *Studies in The Period of David and Solomon and Other Essays*, papers read at the International Symposium for Biblical Studies, December, 1979, ed. Tomoo Ishida (Winona Lake: Eisenbrauns, 1979), pp. 109–38; J.P. Ross, "Yahweh *Ṣᵉḇā'ôṯ* in Samuel and Psalms," VetTest 17 (1967): 76–92; B.N. Wambacq, *L'Epithète divine Yahvé Sébaoth* (1947); Matitiahu Tsevat, "Yhwh *Ṣeḇa'oṯ*," *The Meaning of the Book of Job and Other Biblical Studies: Essays on the Literature and Religion of the Hebrew Bible* (New York: Ktav Publishing House, 1980), pp. 119–29; A. Weiser, "Zur Frage nach dem Beziehungen der Psalmen zum Kult: Die Darstellung der Theophanie in den Psalmen und im Festkult," in *Festschrift für Alfred Bertholet zum 80. Geburtstag*, edd. Walter Baumgartner, Otto Eissfeldt, Karl Elliger, and Leonhard Rost (Tübingen: Mohr, 1950), pp. 513–31.

THAT, 2:498–507; TWOT, 2:750–51.

Psalm 25: A Prayer for Deliverance, Guidance, and Forgiveness

This psalm is an *individual lament* with strong similarities to a prayer of confidence, especially vv.1–3, 8–15. The setting cannot be determined with certainty. As a psalm of David, it may fit in the period of his adversities after his sin of adultery; but the internal evidence is not clear. On the one hand, the psalmist refers to the inadvertent "sins of my youth and my rebellious ways" (v.7) while, on the other hand, he speaks in present terms about "my iniquity, though it is great" (v.11). The tone is so unlike Psalms 32 and 51 that the reference to sin may express the guilt feelings of one sensitive to his own shortcomings. Forgiveness forms a motif throughout the psalm (vv.6–7, 11, 18). The adversities, which the psalmist details in vv.15–21, are also of a general nature, so as to function as a *community lament.*

The emphasis lies on the personal effect of adversity in the areas of self-examination, guidance, and submission to the Lord. In his experience the psalmist demonstrates a remarkable desire to conform to God. The repetition of the prayer for forgiveness (vv.4–7, 11) is answered in the assurance of guidance. Thus humility and growth in godliness are two positive effects of divine chastisement. The psalm begins and ends on a note of trust in the Lord (vv.1–3, 21) and a prayer that the Lord will not let him down ("Do not let me be put to shame," v.2; cf. v.20). It is also linked with Psalm 24 by the verb "lift up" (24:7, 9).

The psalm is acrostic with a few irregularities. Two verses begin with the letter resh, the letters waw and qoph are absent, and the last verse, beginning with the letter peh, seems an addition or afterthought. For a poetic analysis, see Nic. H. Ridderbos, "The Psalms: Style-Figures and Structure," *OudTestamentische Studien* 13 (1963): 43–76.

In addition to the problems associated with the acrostic, it is not easy to find a structure. The repetition of themes and vocabulary invite the student of the psalm to discover a structure, and we give the results of our trial as an aid to the psalm's exposition.

A. Prayer for Deliverance and Guidance (vv.1–3)
  B. Prayer for Guidance and Forgiveness (vv.4–7)
    C. Assurance of Guidance (vv.8–10)
  B′. Prayer for Forgiveness (v.11)
    C′. Assurance of Guidance (vv.12–14)
A′. Prayer for Deliverance and Protection (vv.15–22)

I. Prayer for Deliverance and Guidance

25:1–3

Of David.

1 To you, O Lord, I lift up my soul;
2 in you I trust, O my God.
Do not let me be put to shame,
nor let my enemies triumph over me.
3 No one whose hope is in you
will ever be put to shame,
but they will be put to shame
who are treacherous without excuse.

1–3 Distressed by his ever-present adversaries, the psalmist turns to the Lord in prayer. He is confident in coming to God, as is brought out by the emphatic "To you" and "in you" (also in MT), by the address of deity as "LORD" (= Yahweh) and "my God," and by including himself among those who trust ("hope") in the Lord (vv.1–2). The psalmist thus creates a setting of joyful confidence in the Lord, who has not and will not disappoint those who trust in him.

The psalmist turns to the Lord in prayer with the attitude of submission and anticipation. The verbs ("I lift up," "trust") have been carefully chosen as a means to enhance the atmosphere of confidence. He turns to his covenant God with his whole being, out of utter dependency on him. The close relationship between the Lord and the psalmist is set forth by the phrase "O my God." To his God, who cares for him, he can come with confident expectation, as he draws close to him in prayer ("I lift up my soul," cf. 86:4; 143:8).

The psalmist prays that the wicked will not overpower him (v.2). From his perspective evil cannot be victorious, because it is an insult to those who trust in the Lord. His eye of faith is fixed on his covenant God by whose promises he lives. Others have trusted and have not been disappointed (cf. 21:7; 22:4–5; 26:1; 31:6, 14; 52:8; 56:4, 11). For him the "shame" or disgrace of God's people leads to the exaltation of the enemies. Their shouts of triumph would hurt him deeply within his very being, marking him as one whose trust in the Lord was only outward. But he does not worry about this possibility, because he turns his attention to the godly and affirms their confident hope that they will receive God's protection. However, "the treacherous," who have no regard for the Lord, receive their just reward for their faithlessness (v.3b).

Notes

For a brief discussion of the technical words and phrases in the superscription, see the Introduction.

1 Because the second line begins with the letter beth, the second letter of the Hebrew alphabetic acrostic בְּךָ (*b^e^kā*, "in you"), it is preferable to read the preceding phrase ("O my God") with v.1. Verse 1 seems incomplete, lacking metrical and stichometric balance. This may be due to scribal haplography, omission, or transposition. We propose to read vv.1–2: "To you, O LORD, I lift up my soul, O my God, / In you I trust . . ." (cf. BHS).

II. Prayer for Guidance and Forgiveness

25:4–7

4 Show me your ways, O LORD,
teach me your paths;
5 guide me in your truth and teach me,
for you are God my Savior,
and my hope is in you all day long.
6 Remember, O LORD, your great mercy and love,
for they are from of old.

7 Remember not the sins of my youth
and my rebellious ways;
according to your love remember me,
for you are good, O LORD.

The mood changes from confidence in God's justice to submission to God's guidance. The heart of the believer is never confident without also being submissive to his God. Times of adversity bring him to moments of reflection, when he submits his whole way of life to the scrutiny of his God. He prays for guidance and mercy.

4–5 The psalmist needs guidance, because he desires to imitate God. The petitioner reveals an earnest desire to do God's will by praying to know "your ways," "your paths," and "your truth." The "ways" and "paths" of the Lord pertain to the manner of life consistent with God's expectations, as set forth in his law (cf. 25:9; 32:8). The "truth" (*'ᵉmeṯ*, see 15:2) describes how one walks in the paths of the Lord, namely, "in faithfulness" (cf. 26:3). The imitation of God requires a submissive spirit to divine instruction, for which he prays four times: "Show me . . . teach me . . . guide me . . . teach me" in a parallel structure. True godliness is not the outward conformity to God's law but the spiritual application of God's law to one's life by God himself. The psalmist prays for the internalization of God's word (see the appendix to Ps 19: The Word of God). Submission is not to a set of principles or to a legal system but to the "Savior" (v.5). The psalmist "hopes" in his Savior-God and knows that he will not be put to shame (cf. v.3). He desires to live faithfully in accordance to his will and hopes daily and regularly in his God. Submission to God finds expression in constant trust and godliness.

6 The psalmist also needs "forgiveness" in view of his failures. He prays for God's covenant "mercy" (*raḥᵃmîm*) and "love" (*ḥeseḏ*), which he has extended "from of old" (cf. 103:17; 143:5) to his covenant people: Abraham, Isaac, Jacob, and the tribes of Israel (cf. Exod 34:6). The word "love" is plural and in parallel with "mercy," which is always pluralized in Hebrew. "Your love" could also designate "your acts of love," and in this case "your mercy" could be translated "your acts of mercy." The psalmist reflects on the actual demonstrations of Yahweh's mighty acts on behalf of Israel. An expression of God's mercy is his readiness to forgive sin (cf. Exod 34:7).

7 The psalmist prays that the Lord will not remember his past sins, shortcomings, and rebellious spirit. This confession need not imply that he had been a gross sinner but could refer to sins of omission (cf. A.A. Anderson: "the inadvertent errors of his youth," 1:209). He prays that the Lord will deal with him, not in accordance with his lack of loyalty, but according to God's own commitment of loyalty. It is difficult to convey the force of the emphatic *'attāh* ("you") at the end of v.7b (lit., "according to your love remember me you!"). Craigie renders it: "Please remember me according to your lovingkindness" (*Psalms 1–50*, pp. 216–17). In archaic English it would read better: "According to your love remember thou me."

The ground of forgiveness is God's *goodness* toward his people, as guaranteed by his *name* (cf. 23:3, 6). The word "goodness" (cf. 145:7), together with "love," is also found in 23:6. The psalmist petitions God's forgiveness, on the basis of his "love" and "goodness," as expressions of the "name" of God. The symmetry of idiom in vv.7c and 11a requires a consistent translation:

7c: "for the sake of your goodness, O LORD"
11a: "for the sake of your name, O LORD"

Forgiveness is that act of grace whereby God extends his love, as if the sin had never taken place! (See the appendix to Ps 25: The Perfections of Yahweh.)

Notes

5 Though the stichometry is not balanced, there is no textual reason to transpose v.7c to v.5c, as Craigie proposes (following BHS): "And I have waited for you all day long on account of your goodness, O LORD" (*Psalms 1–50*, pp. 215–17).

III. Assurance of Guidance

25:8–10

8 Good and upright is the LORD;
therefore he instructs sinners in his ways.
9 He guides the humble in what is right
and teaches them his way.
10 All the ways of the LORD are loving and faithful
for those who keep the demands of his covenant.

This section develops several themes of vv.4–7: God's guidance, forgiveness, and mercy. It introduces the motifs of wisdom and the rewards of godliness.

8–10 God's acts on behalf of his covenant people are characterized by several qualities. They are "good" (*ṭôḇ*, v.8), "upright" (*yāšār*, v.8), "right" (or "just," *mišpāṭ*, v.9), "loving" (*ḥeseḏ*), and "faithful" (*'emeṯ*, v.10). The Lord's acts are beneficent, gracious, just, and expressive of his love and fidelity. The divine perfections are revealed for the sake of sinners(!) so that sinners may learn the ways of the Lord (v.8). Only by revelation and the gracious work of God may man learn of God, enabling a response to him. The psalmist reflects on the beneficence of his God, as he considers his need for further training in righteousness, for which he had prayed in vv.4–5. But here he looks beyond his own needs, to the grace of God evident to others like himself. The Lord is the Master-Teacher who in a gracious and upright manner teaches sinners his ways (v.8).

The act of instruction is set forth by a repetition of three synonyms: "he instructs. . . . he guides . . . and teaches" (vv.8–9; cf. vv.4–5). The "humble" are those "sinners" who have already submitted themselves to his covenant lordship in the fear of the Lord (vv.12, 14). They are instructed in the practice of godliness, as expressed by three idioms: "his ways," "what is right," and "his way" (vv.8–9). The substance of discipleship in the covenantal community is instruction in the "ways of the Lord" (v.10). His ways are unlike "the way of sinners" (1:1) in that he instructs his own to live in accordance with "what is right" (*mišpāṭ*, v.9) and to practice love and fidelity (v.10). Because he deals with his children justly, lovingly, and faithfully, he expects them to imitate him. The psalmist cannot conceive how one may claim covenantal love without keeping the "demands of his covenant" (v.10).

Notes

---

10 The NIV interprets rightly בְּרִיתוֹ וְעֵדֹתָיו (*berîṯô we'ēḏōṯāyw*, "his covenant and his testimonies") as a hendiadys: "the demands of his covenant" (see Dahood: "who keep his covenant stipulations," *Psalms*, 1:154, 157).

IV. Prayer for Forgiveness

25:11

> 11 For the sake of your name, O LORD,
> forgive my iniquity, though it is great.

11 Even as vv.8–10 develop the prayer for instruction and guidance (vv.4–5), so v.11 develops the prayer for forgiveness (vv.6–7). The petitioner rises to a new confidence as he reflects on the "name" Yahweh. He concludes the previous prayer with the request of forgiveness "for the sake of your goodness" (v.7), and he resumes this phraseology in v.11a: "For the sake of your name" (cf. 23:3; 31:3; 79:9; 106:8; 109:21; 143:11). Great though the sin is, God's forgiveness is greater (103:3–12; Mic 7:18–20; 1 John 2:12). (See the appendix to Ps 7: The Name of Yahweh.)

Notes

---

11 The perfect of וְסָלַחְתָּ (*wesālaḥtā*, "and forgive") is a precative perfect, as it continues in the mood set by the imperatives in vv.6–7 (cf. Dahood, *Psalms*, 1:157).

The noun "iniquity" is complementary to the synonyms for sin used in v.7: "sins," "rebellious ways." The petition for forgiveness and the synonyms for sin link vv.7 and 11.

V. Assurance of Guidance

25:12–14

> 12 Who, then, is the man that fears the LORD?
> He will instruct him in the way chosen for him.
> 13 He will spend his days in prosperity,
> and his descendants will inherit the land.
> 14 The LORD confides in those who fear him;
> he makes his covenant known to them.

12–14 Forgiveness, however, is not an end in itself. Forgiveness and guidance are expressions of God's love and goodness to his own. Assurance of forgiveness develops into responsiveness. The "fear of the LORD" is the OT concept for an inner responsiveness and willingness to learn of the Lord. The "humble" are those who continually seek his mercy, forgiveness, and instruction. Maturity in godly wisdom leads to godliness ("the way chosen for him," v.12a), communion with God ("the LORD confides in those who fear him," v.14a), and covenantal bliss (v.13). How great the benefits are!

First, the Lord has a distinct way for the godly to walk. He guides them on "the paths of righteousness" (cf. 23:3), which he chooses for them (32:8). Second, the godly enjoy his fellowship (v.14). The Hebrew idiom for "the LORD confides" is "the secret of Yahweh," which may here be translated by "intimate circle" (cf. Job 19:19; 29:4; Prov 3:32). Those who do his will are his confidants, as was Abraham (Gen 18:17). They receive the full enjoyment of the covenantal relationship: "he makes his covenant known to them (v.14b). Third, the covenantal blessedness is here summarized by two promises: "prosperity" (Heb. "goodness," v.13; cf. 23:6), as promised (cf. 34:10; 37:28–29), and continuity of "seed" and "land" (Gen 15:7; Deut 1:8, 21, 39; 4:1; 6:1–2; Josh 18:3; cf. Ps 37:18, 22, 26, 28–29, 37). By these promises Israel was assured of the establishment of God's kingdom. In this way the Christian, too, can draw encouragement, because he has received the affirmation of the blessings in the Beatitudes (Matt 5:3–12, esp. v.5).

Notes

---

12 The emphatic Hebrew מִי־זֶה (*mî-zeh*, "who is this") is rendered by "Who, then" (NIV, following Dahood, *Psalms*, 1:157). The same phrase could be similarly translated in 24:8–9: "who, then, is the King of glory?"

13 I prefer Brigg's emphatic translation of נַפְשׁוֹ (*napšô*, "his soul"): "he himself" (1:224). Both he and his descendants are blessed (cf. Gen 15:5–7; Deut 4:1, 40; Ps 37:9, 11; Prov 2:21; Matt 5:5).

14 The rendering "confides" is a dynamic equivalent of סוֹד (*sôd*, "assembly" or "council"). Heinz-Josef Fabry argues that *sôd* is an ecclesiological term, synonymous with "congregation" ("Der himmlische Thronrat als ekklesiologisches Modell," *Bausteine biblischer Theologie. Festgabe für G. Johannes Botterweck zum 60. Geburtstag dargebracht von seinen Schülern*, ed. H.J. Fabry (Köln: Peter Hanstein, 1977), p. 118.

VI. Prayer for Deliverance and Protection

25:15–22

15 My eyes are ever on the LORD,
for only he will release my feet from the snare.

16 Turn to me and be gracious to me,
for I am lonely and afflicted.
17 The troubles of my heart have multiplied;
free me from my anguish.
18 Look upon my affliction and my distress

and take away all my sins.
19 See how my enemies have increased
and how fiercely they hate me!
20 Guard my life and rescue me;
let me not be put to shame,
for I take refuge in you.
21 May integrity and uprightness protect me,
because my hope is in you.

22 Redeem Israel, O God,
from all their troubles!

15–22 In vv.1–3 the psalmist lifted up his eyes to the Lord with expectancy and submissiveness, praying that the "enemies" would have no cause for gloating over his misfortune. In the last section of the psalm he returns to the motif of the enemies as he prays with fervor, heaping up the imperatives: "Turn to me and be gracious to me. . . . free me. . . . Look upon . . . and take away. . . . See how. . . . Guard . . . rescue me; / let me not be put to shame" (vv.16–20).

The petitions are framed between affirmations of trust in the Lord (vv.15, 21). The psalmist pleads continually with the Lord for deliverance from "the snare" (or "net") of his adversities. He is entrapped and cannot untangle himself from his difficulties (v.15; cf. 9:15; 31:4). He hopes longingly for his help (vv.15–16; cf. 123:1–2; 141:8; 1 Thess 5:17), and, while waiting, he has committed himself to "integrity and uprightness" (v.21; cf. 1 Kings 9:4). As he receives God's instruction (vv.9–10) in humble fear of the Lord (v.12), the psalmist develops in godliness. His humble walk with the Lord "in integrity and uprightness" assures him of God's protection, even when he is faced by the realities of life. Commentators disagree over the interpretation of "integrity and uprightness" (v.21). Briggs takes the words as personifications of messengers sent to deliver his afflicted people (1:226; cf. Dahood's discussion, *Psalms*, 1:159). A.A. Anderson is inclined to interpret the qualities as belonging to the Lord (1:213). Craigie finds it "probable" that the idiom refers to the psalmist (*Psalms 1–50*, p. 221), as does Calvin: "The saints, in respect of themselves, always come into the presence of God with humility, imploring his forgiveness: and yet this does not prevent them from setting forth before him the goodness of their cause, and the justice of their claims" (1:435).

The psalmist's dependency on the Lord is also brought out in vv.16–20 by the self-descriptions—"lonely and afflicted" (v.16)—and by his expression of trust: "I take refuge in you" (v.20). "Troubles," "anguish" (v.17), "affliction," "distress" (v.18), and "enemies" (v.19) are the causes of his loneliness. The exact nature of his suffering is not clear, but it seems to be related to his awareness of and sensitivity to his "sins" (v.18; cf. vv.7, 11). The effects of sin are great; and though the psalmist sees a correlation between sin and suffering, he casts himself on his covenant God for forgiveness and deliverance from his troubles. The period of affliction gives an opportunity for self-examination (cf. Calvin, 1:434).

The heart of God's saint shows "integrity and uprightness" by demonstrating a deep concern for the people (v.22). The prayer for their deliverance falls outside the acrostic pattern and is, therefore, unexpected. But that surprise element heightens the effect. Israel, too, had its troubles (cf. v.17); and even though there were many times in the history of Israel and Judah that their troubles were well-deserved forms of discipline, the psalmist prays on behalf of the people. Another effect of the addition is that the faithful in Israel could join in and pray the whole psalm as their own. The inspired psalmist leads God's people in prayer. This transforms the individual lament into a community lament. A similar phenomenon occurs in Psalm 34, also an acrostic psalm. After using the last letter of the Hebrew alphabet (v.21), the psalm adds a prayer for redemption (v.22). Possibly the same author is responsible for both.

Notes

16 For the idiom "turn and be gracious," see 86:16; 119:132.

17 The proposal to emend הִרְחִיבוּ (*hirḥîḇû*, "have made large"; NIV, "have multiplied") to הַרְחֵב (*harḥēḇ*, "make large," "relieve") and to add the final waw to the following clause is attractive for two reasons. First, the MT makes little sense (as is evident from the semantic attempt of the NIV). Second, it provides a parallel for "free me." For a similar usage see 4:1: "Give me relief from my distress."

18 The verse begins with a resh, but one expects a qoph. There is little textual justification for emending the text—cf. Craigie: "meet my affliction," from a hypothetical קִרְאֵה (*qir'ēh*, "meet"; *Psalms 1–50*, pp. 216–17)—or with any one verb beginning in Hebrew with *q* (Kraus, *Psalmen*, 1:208).

Appendix: The Perfections of Yahweh

The perfections of Yahweh are those qualities revealed to Israel through Moses (Exod 34:5–7) by which the Lord maintains a blessed and meaningful relation with his people. The laments and praises of the Psalms express confidence in the Lord, as he remains the same, even when the circumstances of God's people are continually in flux. The ground for hope lies in the perfections of Yahweh, for he is good, upright, full of integrity, righteous, just, gracious, faithful, loving, compassionate, and forgiving.

1. *Good (ṭôḇ)*

The perfection of God's "goodness" extends the benefits of his presence and blessing to his people. It covers all areas of covenant life and as such is a synonym of "love," "forgiveness," and "fidelity" (23:6; 25:7; 86:5; 100:5). When the psalmist prays "do good," he petitions the Lord to bestow on him all the care and love (119:17; cf. v.65). When the psalmist says, "you are good" (v.7), he means more than God's moral goodness. Though as a human he does not and is not in a position of judging God, he knows from the revelation of God and from the history of redemption that Yahweh is faithful (86:5). So also when he hopes to see the "goodness" of God while being alive, the psalmist longs for enjoying the benefits of God's promises (27:13; cf. 31:19; 34:8,10; 65:4).

God's "goodness" is associated with his covenant fidelity, and all perfections of Yahweh are included in his promise of "goodness." But the Lord is free in giving his goodness only to the pure in heart, i.e., those who are the object of his love (73:1; cf. 125:4). The godly praise Yahweh's goodness, because they have seen and tasted that he is good and long for the fulfillment of his promise (52:9; cf. 106:1; 107:1; 118:1, 29; 136:1). They long for enjoying God's goodness forevermore (23:6), because his goodness includes peace, life, love, salvation, vindication, and glory.

2. *Equity (mêšārîm)*

Equity or uprightness (*mêšārîm*) is related to *yāšār* ("upright" or "right") and is a derivative of the root *y-š-r*. To do what is "right" is in contrast to the way of the wicked, marked by crookedness, scheming, and perversion. It denotes moral and legal integrity. The Lord looks for this quality in the godly, as he expects them, too, to evidence integrity, i.e., blamelessness (cf. 119:128). It is related to "justice" (*mišpāṭ*).

The literature of the ancient Near East also discloses the concern for "integrity" (cf. D.J. Wiseman, "The Laws of Hammurabi Again," JSS 7 [1962]: 161–72). Gods were known by the name "integrity." The Mesopotamian god of justice (Shamash) had a son by the name of *Mišarum*. The Ugaritic materials contain the idiom "son of uprightness" (*bn mšrm*). For Israel the standard of integrity was no other than Yahweh: "He will judge the world in righteousness [*ṣeḏeq*]; he will govern the peoples with justice [*mêšārîm*]" (9:8; cf. 75:2). Rulers, kings, and leaders were not always reliable in their judgments, but Yahweh is constant: "Do you rulers indeed speak justly? Do you judge uprightly among men?" (58:1). Regardless of how crooked and corrupt society becomes, the Lord maintains order by being above corruption: "Say among the nations, 'The Lord reigns.' / The world is firmly established, it cannot be moved; / he will judge the peoples with equity" (96:10).

The revelation of God's rule in Israel was intended to make Israel his witness to his rule of integrity. They were called to witness to his indubitable virtues: "The King is mighty, he loves justice— /you have established equity; / in Jacob you have done / what is just and right" (99:4). Through Israel's testimony all the nations were to acknowledge Yahweh as King: "let them sing before the LORD, / for he comes to judge the earth. / He will judge the world in righteousness / and the peoples with equity" (98:9).

3. *Righteous (ṣaddîq, ṣeḏeq, ṣᵉḏāqāh, ṣ-d-q)*

Yahweh is "righteous" in his rule (97:2). The perfection of righteousness extends beyond the judicial or forensic quality. True, Yahweh is a righteous judge (7:11; cf. v.8). But he is more! He establishes a *relationship* with his people, who are called "righteous," and in this relationship Yahweh bestows on his children and on their children the benefits of his righteousness: "But from everlasting to everlasting / the LORD's love is with those who fear him, / and his righteousness with their children's children" (103:17).

First, the Lord answers the prayers of the righteous (4:1). Second, he delivers and vindicates them from their enemies (9:4–5; cf. 5:8; 7:9; 31:1; 34; 35:24; 103:6; 125:3). Third, God's kingdom rule establishes his righteousness (9:8; cf. 11:3, 5, 7; 96:13). Righteousness is the nature of God, revealed through his involvement with creation in the course of human history. The progress of God's redemptive involvement in Old, New, and the present reveal the pattern of his righteous intent to establish a new earth (65:5). Fourth, Yahweh reveals the *way* of righteousness in his Torah, and those who keep on the path of his revelation are "righteous" (19:9). Fifth, the acts of God in salvation and vengeance are hence "righteous acts" and form the basis of praise and proclamation (22:31; cf. 35:28; 40:9–10; 50:6; 51:14; 71:15–16, 19, 24; 89:16; 98:9; 111:3; 118:15; 145:7). Sixth, Yahweh's righteousness extends to all his creation, as he blesses and protects it (36:6). Seventh, Yahweh plans to order the world of creation so that it will reflect his goodness and love (85:11). He will rule until all creation reflects the orderliness, peace, and blessing of his righteous rule (145:17). This is the world of righteousness (37:6; cf. 36:10). To this end he has also appointed the Davidic Messiah: "In your majesty ride forth victoriously / in behalf of truth, humility and righteousness; / let your right hand display awesome deeds" (45:4; cf. Pss 2; 72).

In conclusion, Yahweh establishes his kingdom in righteousness. Jews and Gentiles together are the objects of his beneficent rule (98:2). This quality, together with justice, equity, love, and fidelity, characterizes the rule of God on earth: "Love and faithfulness meet together; / righteousness and peace kiss each other" (85:10; cf. 33:5). Then all creation without any resistance harmoniously will proclaim and praise the Lord for his righteous acts (i.e., blessings): "Like your name, O God, / your praise reaches to the ends of the earth; / your right hand is filled with righteousness" (48:10).

4. *Justice (mišpāṭ)*

The "justice" of God expresses his concern for law and order in his creation. His throne is established, and regularly he dispenses his judgments: "The King is mighty, he loves justice— / you have established equity; / in Jacob you have done / what is just and right" (99:4). He upholds justice against all the wicked, who will be condemned: "Arise, O LORD, in your anger; / rise up against the rage of my enemies. / Awake, my God; decree justice [*mišpāṭ*]" (7:6; cf. 1:5–6; 9:16). Instead, he will vindicate his meek and humble children, who have not fared well because of the injustices of this world: "I know that the LORD secures justice for the poor / and upholds the cause of the needy" (140:12; cf. 9:4).

5. *Gracious (ḥannûn)*

The Lord's favor extends to all the benefits of his people: spiritual (forgiveness, reconciliation) and material (prosperity, health, enjoyment of life and land). In the psalms of lament, the people of God cry out to Yahweh to favor them with answer to prayer: "Turn to me and be gracious to me, / for I am lonely and afflicted" (25:16). The object of the prayer is a renewal of God's blessings: "May God be gracious to us and bless us / and make his face shine upon us" (67:1). The revelation of God is also one of the "graces," because through his Torah Yahweh instructs his people how to walk pleasing to him so that they may continue to enjoy his favors: "Keep me from deceitful ways; / be gracious to me through your law" (119:29). Thus the psalmist could claim the promise of the Lord: "I have sought your face with all my heart; / be gracious to me according to your promise" (119:58).

6. *Faithful and Loving (ʾ^e^meṯ, ʾ^e^mûnāh, ḥeseḏ)*

The individual words *ḥeseḏ* ("love," "unfailing love," "loving-kindness") and *ʾᵉmeṯ* ("truth," "faithfulness") or the phrase *ḥeseḏ wᵉʾᵉmeṯ* ("love and truth") refer to God's constancy and fidelity in love, promised to his covenant people at Sinai. The one word defines the other, and the phrase could well be considered a hendiadys: "faithful love." Other pairings of OT *ḥeseḏ* are *bᵉrîṯ* ("covenant," Deut 7:9, 12); *raḥûm* ("compassion," in 103:4), and *ḥônēn* ("pity," 109:12). In each of these paired phrases, the OT portrays the depth of God's love to his covenant people.

The modern understanding of *ḥeseḏ* goes back to Nelson Glueck (*Hesed in the Bible*), who set God's love in the context of covenant. More recently Sakenfeld (*The Meaning of Hesed in the Hebrew Bible: A New Inquiry*) has challenged Glueck's view by arguing against restricting *ḥeseḏ* to a covenantal context. It is an all-embracing term relating to all God's relations in creation and redemption. Whitley disagrees with Sakenfeld and concludes that she does not substantially differ from

Glueck. Instead, he advances the thesis that *ḥesed* has an extensive range: strength, might, fortitude, confidence, pledge, resolution, and health.

The love of Yahweh is his commitment to those who love him to be unceasingly generous in his forgiveness, compassion, and blessings. His fidelity may also be expressed by the word *'emûnāh* ("faithfulness"; cf. 33:4; 36:5; 89:1–2, 5, 8, 24, 33, 49; 100:5; 143:1). There is no limit to his faithfulness, as heaven and earth reveal his perfections: "Your love, O LORD, reaches to the heavens, / your faithfulness to the skies" (36:5; cf. 57:10; 108:4). "He has remembered his love / and his faithfulness to the house of Israel; / all the ends of the earth have seen / the salvation of our God" (98:3; cf. 33:5).

The quality of God's love guarantees the continual operation of all his benefits (perfections) toward his people, including righteousness, uprightness, justice, forgiveness, patience, and compassion (31:5; 40:11; 85:10; 89:2; 100:5; 117:2).

7. *Compassion (raḥûm, raḥamîm, r-ḥ-m)*

The compassion of God refers to his parental concern for his children. Yahweh is supportive and understanding. He hears the prayers of his children and sees their needs: "As a father has compassion on his children, / so the Lord has compassion on those who fear him" (103:13). The psalmists operate from the credo (belief) that Yahweh is compassionate and that in his compassion he listens to their complaints, questions, and laments: "But you, O LORD, are a compassionate and gracious God, / slow to anger, abounding in love and faithfulness" (86:15; cf. 116:5). In the dynamic of faith and questions, the child of God casts himself into the arms of God's compassion, knowing that he cares: "Have mercy on me, O God, / according to your unfailing love; / according to your great compassion / blot out my transgressions" (51:1). For forgiveness of sin, see the appendix to Ps 103: Sin and Forgiveness.

Texts: 25:6, 8, 10, 16, 21; 31:5, 7, 16, 21–23; 33:4–5, 18, 22; 36:5–7, 10; 40:9–11; 48:9–10; 57:1, 3, 10; 71:2, 15–16, 19, 22; 85:7, 10–11; 86:3, 5–6, 11, 13, 15–16; 89:1–2, 5, 8, 14, 16, 19, 24, 28, 33, 37, 49; 90:13–14; 91:4, 14; 92:2, 15; 96:10, 13; 97:2, 6, 10–11; 98:2–3, 9; 103:4, 6, 8, 11, 13, 17; 106:1, 45; 107:1, 8, 15, 21, 31, 42–43; 111:3–4, 7–8; 116:1, 5; 118:1–4, 19, 29; 119; 136; 143:1, 8, 11–12; 145:7–9, 13, 18, 20.

Related Topics: see the appendixes to Pss 5 (Yahweh Is King); 7 (The Name of Yahweh); 19 (The Word of God); 78 (The Mighty Acts of Yahweh); 98 (Yahweh Is the Divine Warrior); 103 (Sin and Forgiveness); and 119 (Yahweh Is My Redeemer).

Bibliography: Yaakov Bazak, "Towards the Significance of the Pair *mišpāṭ ûṣedāqâ* in the Bible," *Beth Mikra* 32 (1986/87): 135–48 (Heb.); J.A. Bollier, "The Righteousness of God," Int 8 (1954): 404–13; G. Brin, "Concerning Several Biblical Expressions Using *ṭôḇ*," *Beth Mikra* 31 (1985/86): 227–41 (Heb.); R.C. Dentan, "The Literary Affinities of Exodus 34:6ff.," VetTest 13 (1963): 34–51; Eichrodt, OTT, 1:228–88; K.Hj. Fahlgren, "Die Gegensätze von *ṣedaqā* im Alten Testament," ed. K. Koch, *Um das Prinzip der Vergeltung in Religion und Recht* (Darmstadt: Wissenschaftliche Buchgesellschaft, 1972), pp. 87–129; J.J. Finkelstein, "Some New *Misharum* Material and Its Implications," in *Studies in Honor of Benno Landsberger in Honor of His Seventy-Fifth Birthday, April 21, 1965*, edd. Hans G. Gütersbock and Thorkild Jacobsen (Chicago: University Press, 1965), pp. 233–46; Michael Fox, "*ṬÔB* as Covenant Terminology," BASOR 209 (1973): 41–42; Nelson Glueck, *Hesed in the Bible*, tr. Alfred Gottschalk, reprint (New York: Ktav, 1975) with a survey of recent studies by Gerald A. Larue (pp. 1–32); A.E. Goodman, " חסד and תודה in the Linguistic Tradition of the Psalter," in *Words and Meanings. Essays Presented to David Winton Thomas on His Retirement From the*

Regius Professorship of Hebrew in the University of Cambridge, 1968, edd. Peter R. Ackroyd and Barnabas Lindars (Cambridge: Cambridge University Press, 1968), pp. 105–15; Carl Graesser, Jr., "Righteousness, Human and Divine," *Currents in Theology and Mission* 10 (1983): 134–41; L.A. Heerboth, "Der Begriff 'Gerechtigkeit' im Alten Testament, besonderes in den Psalmen," *Concordia Theological Monthly* 7 (1936): 497–508; Ingeborg Johag, "*ṭôḇ*-Terminus Technicus in Vertrags- und Bündnisformularen des Alten Orients und des Alten Testaments," *Bausteine biblischer Theologie. Festgabe für G. Johannes Botterweck zum 60. Geburtstag dargebracht von seinen Schulern*, ed. Heinz-Josef Fabry (Köln: Peter Hanstein, 1977), pp. 3–23; Bo Johnson, "Der Bedeutung zwischen *Ṣādāq* und *ṣedaqa*," ASTI 11 (1978): 31–39; L.J. Kuyper, "Grace and Truth," *Reformed Review* 16 (1963): 1–16; W. Lofthouse, "Ḥen and Ḥesed in the Old Testament," ZAW 51 (1933): 29–35; William L. Moran, "A Note on the Treaty Terminology of the Sefire Stelas," JNES 22 (1963): 173–76; E. Perry, "The Meaning of *'emunah* in the Old Testament," *Journal of Bible and Religion* 21 (1953): 252–56; Gerhard von Rad, OTT, 1:370–83; id., " 'Righteousness' and 'Life' in the Cultic Language of the Psalms," *The Problem of the Hexateuch and Other Essays*, tr. E.W. Trueman Dicken (London: Oliver and Boyd, 1966), pp. 243–66; E.T. Ramsdell, "The Old Testament Understanding of Truth," JR 31 (1951): 264–73; Katherine D. Sakenfeld, *The Meaning of Hesed in the Hebrew Bible: A New Inquiry*, Harvard Semitic Monographs 17 (Missoula: Scholars, 1978); id., *Faithfulness in Action* (Philadelphia: Fortress, 1985); Hans Heinrich Schmid, *Gerechtigkeit als Weltordnung. Hintergrund und Geschichte des alttestamentlichen Gerechtigkeitsbegriffes* (Tübingen: Mohr, 1968); id., "Creation, Righteousness, and Salvation: 'Creation Theology' as a Broad Horizon of Biblical Theology," in *Creation in the Old Testament*, ed. Bernard W. Anderson (Philadelphia: Fortress, 1984), pp. 102–17; G. Schmuttermayr, "RḤM—Eine lexikalische Studie," *Biblica* 51 (1970): 499–525; N.H. Snaith, *The Distinctive Ideas of the Old Testament* (London: Epworth, 1944), pp. 21–78; 94–130; D.R. Ap-Thomas, "Some Aspects of the Root ḤNN in the Old Testament," JSS 2 (1957): 128–48; T.F. Torrance, "The Doctrine of Grace in the Old Testament," SJT 1 (1948): 55–65; W.A. VanGemeren, "Righteousness," in Elwell, BEB, 2:1860–62; C.P. Whitley, "The Semantic Range of *Ḥesed*," *Biblica* 62 (1981): 519–26; Zimmerli, OTTO, pp. 142–48.

TDNT, 1:13–15, 232–38, 335–36, 696–701; 2:212–14; 6:183–91, 194–202; 9:376–81; TDOT, 1:292–323; THAT, 1:177–99, 587–96, 599–622, 652–63, 790–93; 2:507–29; TWOT, 1:52–53, 302–4, 305–7, 345–46, 417–18; 2:752–55, 841–43, 947–49.

Psalm 26: The Innocent Plea for Redemption

In this psalm the psalmist casts himself on the Lord with the request that the Lord pay attention to his circumstances. His troubles are undeserved. Yet he is suffering. Therefore he repeats before the Lord his innocence. He is not denying that he is without sin. Rather he affirms that the whole intent of his heart is to do the will of God.

It has been difficult to categorize this psalm. Because of the strong pleading with God, it has characteristics similar to the *individual lament* psalms. However, the absence of the clear circumstances of his adversity and the emphasis on his innocence have led scholars to view it as a *protective psalm.*

The structure (see also Paul G. Mosca, "Psalm 26: Poetic Structure and the Form-

Critical Task," CBQ 47 [1985]: 212–37) of the psalm falls in several parts, which may be structured for our purposes as follows:

A. Prayer for Vindication and Affirmation of Innocence (vv.1–3)
  B. Dissociation From Evil (vv.4–5)
A′. Affirmation of Innocence and Love for the Lord (vv.6–8)
  B′. Dissociation From Evil (vv.9–10)
A″. Affirmation of Innocence and Prayer for Redemption (vv.11–12)

According to this structure the psalm is framed by a prayer as an inclusionary motif. The ground for the prayer and the confidence of God's response lies in the psalmist's conviction that God is just. He will hear the cry of his devoted servant. The positive statement of his devotion to God and his separation from evil is characteristic of the wisdom psalms.

I. Prayer for Vindication and Affirmation of Innocence

26:1–3

Of David.

1 Vindicate me, O LORD,
  for I have led a blameless life;
I have trusted in the LORD
  without wavering.
2 Test me, O LORD, and try me,
  examine my heart and my mind;
3 for your love is ever before me,
  and I walk continually in your truth.

1a The psalmist is not yet concerned about the adversities in which he finds himself. Essentially vv.1–3 contain a prayer for redemption (cf. vv.11b–12). In this prayer he brings out three elements: the need, his innocence, and God's fidelity. He begins with the prayer for vindication. Vindication is here the act of God whereby he declares his servant to be innocent and avenges himself of the wicked (false accusers, enemies).

In his own heart the psalmist knows that he has walked with God in integrity. The prayer for vindication is connected with a petition for God's examination of his heart (v.2). The verbs "vindicate," "test," "try," and "examine" bear out the psalmist's concern for divine approval. The translation "vindicate me" (lit., "judge me") is contextually justified (cf. 7:8; 35:24; 43:1). The act of vindication is not primarily an expression of God's righteous wrath and indignation against the wicked but rather a reassuring word from God (cf. NEB, "Give me justice, O LORD"). The scrutinizing eye of God penetrates into the deepest and innermost recesses, known as the "heart" and as the "mind" (see 7:9). The psalmist is not thinking about two aspects of his life: spiritual and intellectual or emotional and rational. Rather, he offers himself *completely* for a total examination (cf. 7:9; 11:4; Jer 11:20; 17:10; 20:12).

1b–3 The confidence for vindication is not based on the psalmist's innocence but rather on the fidelity of his God (v.1b). The Lord himself has given his "love" (*ḥeseḏ*) and his "truth" (*'ᵉmeṯ*) to the psalmist (v.3). "Love" and "truth" (or faithfulness) are two aspects of one divine quality (Exod 34:6; Pss 6:4; 25:10; 40:10; 61:7; 86:15; 89:14; Mic 7:20). God's love is always faithful. Therefore the psalmist believes that God has motivated and enabled him to walk with integrity of heart. Even in his distress he is fully aware of God's love and loyalty to him. The presence of God is an authentic experience for the psalmist (v.3). Since God is loving and loyal, and not capricious, the psalmist presents his case humbly before his God and is not afraid of God's scrutiny.

Because of God's loyalty, the psalmist stands before God and asks him to look at him. The psalmist has walked, is still walking, and continues in his determination to walk with God in the "integrity" of his heart (see 7:8; cf. Gen 17:1; Prov 10:9). Clearly the psalmist is not a man of self-confidence, as the emphatic placement of "in the LORD" (v.1b) in the Hebrew text brings out: "in the LORD I have trusted." (For "trusted" as expressive of dependency on the Lord's goodness and love, see 21:7; 33:21–22; 52:8; 143:9.)

The verbal phrase "without wavering" (*lō' 'em'āḏ,* "I shall not slip") is best taken as a circumstantial phrase, describing the kind of trust the psalmist has in his God (cf. NEB, "unfaltering trust"). His claim that he has not wavered should not be considered as an idle boast (cf. Luke 18:9–14). Rather, the Lord has promised to uphold his own (cf. 18:35; 37:24). In the last verse of this psalm, the psalmist returns to this affirmation with the bold hope that he will *stand* in the "great assembly" (v.12).

Notes

1a כִּי (*kî,* "for") may be emphatic: "surely" (cf. Dahood's "on my word," *Psalms,* pp. 160–61). The sentence בְּתֻמִּי הָלַכְתִּי (*beṯummî hālaḵtî,* "I have led a blameless life," lit., "in my integrity I have walked") constitutes an inclusion with v.11: "I lead a blameless life" (lit., "and as for me, I shall walk in my integrity").

2 For the metaphorical use of the verbs "test" and "try," see 7:9; so also for the phrase "my heart and my mind" (lit., "my kidneys and my heart"; cf. Jer 11:20; 17:10; 20:12).

3 The two characteristics of Yahweh, often found in combination with each other (25:10; 40:11; 57:3; 61:7; 85:10; 86:15; 89:14; 115:1; 138:2), are here separated to form an inclusion. The MT begins with the phrase כִּי־חַסְדְּךָ (*kî-ḥasdeḵā,* "for your love," i.e., covenantal love) and concludes with בַּאֲמִתֶּךָ (*ba'amitteḵā,* "in your truth," i.e., "by your fidelity to me").

II. Dissociation From Evil

26:4–5

4 I do not sit with deceitful men,
nor do I consort with hypocrites;
5 I abhor the assembly of evildoers
and refuse to sit with the wicked.

4–5 In his devotion to the Lord, the psalmist has demonstrated a hatred of evil in any shape or form. Both verses are in the form of an inclusionary motif with the repetition of the verb "sit." He does not "sit" (cf. 1:1; Jer 15:17) with wicked people. The wicked are described by several synonyms as "deceitful men," "hypocrites," and an "assembly of evildoers." The "deceitful men" (lit., "men of worthlessness") are those who have given themselves to the pursuit of "vanity" (*šāw'*). They are unreliable, babblers, and, therefore, "scoundrels" (cf. 28:3; 119:37; Job 11:11; Prov 6:12–14).

The "hypocrites" are those whose ways and motives are hidden from others (the word comes from *naʿᵃlāmîm,* "the hidden ones," a Niphal participle). Since they are living in darkness, their ways are hidden from man.

The "assembly" of evildoers (v.5; cf. 22:16) is in stark contrast to the "great assembly" of v.12. The word "assembly" (*qāhāl*) often denotes Israel as the "congregation" (or "community") of the Lord (cf. Exod 12:6; Lev 16:17; Num 14:5; Deut 31:30; 1 Kings 8:14, 55; Pss 89:5; 107:32; 149:1). However, within God's people there was a segment that refused loyalty to Yahweh. They established an "assembly" (or "band" in 22:16) within an assembly. Instead of giving them the full rights of fellowship, the psalmist demonstrates his sensitivity to those who do not belong to the Lord. The line of separation is not based on narrow differences of practices and beliefs but on very clear grounds: apostasy from Yahweh. In poetic fashion the psalmist uses the synonyms, not so much to highlight various forms of evil, but rather to set off his concern for integrity over the rest of humanity that shows little or no concern. As is the case in Psalm 1:1, the activities of sitting and consorting with the wicked are not to be taken in a literal way. They are contrastive to his way of walking with the Lord (vv.3, 11). The psalmist affirms his hatred of evil and his complete dissociation from it.

III. Affirmation of Innocence and Love for the Lord

26:6–8

6 I wash my hands in innocence,
   and go about your altar, O LORD,
7 proclaiming aloud your praise
   and telling of all your wonderful deeds.
8 I love the house where you live, O LORD,
   the place where your glory dwells.

6 The psalmist reflects on the temple worship and on his joy in participating in the worship of God. Another psalmist remembered the times of the joyous procession, when God's people used to go up to Jerusalem but could no longer, because the temple had been destroyed and desecrated by the Babylonians (42:4). The psalmist affirms that in the integrity of his heart he is privileged to draw near to God. The expression "wash my hands in innocence" need not refer to the ritual of washing one's hands (cf. Exod 30:18–21; so Briggs, 1:233). It may also express the purity of heart (cf. 73:13) or a declaration of innocence (cf. 24:4; Matt 27:24).

7 The psalmist reflects on the privilege of bringing sacrifices to the Lord's altar, as a symbolic act of his devotion to him. The offerings and sacrifices are not for the purposes of atonement but for thanksgiving. They are expressions of loyalty. This is made clear by the purpose clauses in Hebrew, translated by circumstantial clauses in the NIV: "proclaiming" and "telling." In spite of his troubles, the psalmist looks forward to bringing his offerings of devotion, while proclaiming to his fellow worshipers the acts of God's goodness. The "praise" consists of words of thanksgiving for what the Lord has done. The phrase "proclaiming aloud your praise" (lit., "to proclaim with a voice of thanksgiving") gives the ground for praise, namely, thanksgiving. Thanksgiving (*tôḏāh*) was associated with the offerings of thanksgiving (cf. 50:14; 107:22; 116:17). The reason for the thanksgiving is stated in v.7b. The substance of the thanksgiving consists of his "wonderful deeds," i.e., the history of salvation in which he shares (cf. 9:1; 40:5; 71:17; 75:1; 145:5; see the appendix to Ps 78: The Mighty Acts of Yahweh).

8 The psalmist's concern with integrity, acts of devotion, and words of praise flows out of a heart filled with love for the Lord and for God's house. It is motivated by a zeal for the Lord. A.A. Anderson (1:217) rightly observes that the OT is reluctant in expressing love to God in a direct way. The psalmist says that he loves the Lord by declaring his love for the house of the Lord. But "the house" consists of more than brick and mortar: the Holy One of Israel lives in the midst of his people. He made his "glory" to dwell among his people (Exod 40:34–35; 1 Kings 8:11). The remembrance of God's glory had associations of his "wonderful deeds" (v.7) on behalf of his people. The glory of the Lord had protected and guided the people of God in the past. The psalmist thus finds comfort in his reflections on God's presence and glory. He is transported out of his misery to a new height, being filled with joy and love for his God.

IV. Dissociation From Evil

26:9–10

9 Do not take away my soul along with sinners,
my life with bloodthirsty men,
10 in whose hands are wicked schemes,
whose right hands are full of bribes.

9–10 The return to a reflection on the wicked (vv.4–5) is for purposes of symmetry. The psalmist is not preoccupied with evil. He rejoices in his God and is thankful for his love and tokens of fatherly fidelity. Rather, as a result of his reflection on God's glory and love, he renews his devotion to the Lord and his hatred of sin. In his prayer he sets himself off from sinners whose lot is in the hands of an angry God. In his anger the Lord may "take away" the lives of sinners. The prayer "Do not take away" is a prayer for divine favor. The psalmist prays that he may not be condemned by God's judgment together with the wicked (v.9; cf. 1 Sam 15:6; Ps 104:29; Zeph 1:2–3; 3:8). The sinners are those who have given themselves to a life of sin and rebellion against God. They are the bloodthirsty (cf. 5:6; 55:23; 59:2; 139:19), the schemers, and the perverters of justice (vv.9–10). But the psalmist is not one of them. Therefore he has a reason to hope that the Lord, in his anger, will yet spare him.

V. Affirmation of Innocence and Prayer for Redemption

26:11–12

11 But I lead a blameless life;
redeem me and be merciful to me.

12 My feet stand on level ground;
in the great assembly I will praise the LORD.

11a In contrast to the bloodthirsty and evil man, the psalmist affirms his determination to continue in his walk with the Lord. The contrast is emphatic; "But I" could be rendered also as "But as for me." He has enjoyed walking in the presence of the Lord's love and fidelity (v.3). He has declared a strong devotion and love for the Lord (vv.6–8). He cannot but continue to do what is right. Evil is no temptation for him. He knows in whom he believes and is determined to cling to him in devotion, regardless of the external circumstances.

11b–12 The prayer for divine vindication and examination (vv.1–2) is symmetrical to the prayer for "redemption." The psalmist prays that the Lord's examination (*beḥānēnî*, v.2) will turn into evidence of his mercy (*weḥonnēnî*, v.11). The similarity in sound between the verbs in v.2a and v.11b is evidence of wordplay; but more than that, it is the expression of a confident hope.

The confident hope rises to a new climax. The psalmist sees himself with the godly in Israel. Among them he will praise the Lord for the evidences of his goodness. Thus he will reassure other believers of what God can do in the lives of his children. The test of faith is public and so should be the celebration of God's sustaining grace. Calvin wrote, "It is highly necessary that every one should publicly celebrate his experience of the grace of God, as an example to others to confide in him" (1:449).

Though the psalmist is still suffering from some adversities, he knows that the one who loves him will not permit his feet to stumble. Therefore he says that his "feet stand on level ground" (cf. 27:11; 143:10). His confidence is in the Lord's ability to keep him. Because of God's love, he stands on "level ground." The word *mîšôr* ("level ground," "uprightness") contains a wordplay by the association with the affirmation of his integrity. Even though he claims to stand on "level ground," the psalmist is at the same time saying that he is standing, i.e., continuing in his integrity. Thus he properly connects the doctrine of the assurance of salvation with the doctrine of the perseverance of the saints. His confidence is in the Lord.

Notes

---

12 The phrase "great assembly"—מַקְהֵלִים (*maqhēlîm*, "assemblies")—translates the plural of "assembly" (related by root to the word "assembly" in v.5). The plural is a Hebraic device of emphasis, properly translated in the NIV as "great assembly" (cf. NEB, "full assembly"). Others prefer to give a more literal rendition: "assemblies" (Craigie, *Psalms 1–50*, p. 223).

Psalm 27: Confidence in the Lord

In Psalm 26 the psalmist expressed his devotion to the Lord and his desire to join the assembly of God's people in the worship of God (v.12). This psalm is related to the previous psalm by a common concern for God's tabernacle (cf. 26:8; 27:6), by an expression of dependence on the Lord (cf. 26:1–2; 27:3–8), by a prayer for vindication (26:1, 9–10; 27:2–3, 12), and by the hope in divine deliverance (26:12; 27:13–14).

Critics have often followed Gunkel's proposal of dividing the psalm into two separate psalms: vv.1–6 (a psalm of confidence) and vv.7–14 (an individual lament). In favor of a literary unity of the two sections, Kraus and Craigie have explained that the differences in mood arise from the subject matter and that the similarity of words connect the two sections (cf. Craigie, *Psalms 1–50*, pp. 230–31). Brueggemann holds that the element of confidence is primary (*Message of the Psalms*, p. 152). Eaton regards this as a royal psalm with features of a lament psalm (*Kingship and the Psalms*, pp. 39–40; *Psalms*, pp. 85–86). Even though there is no general agreement on the genre, Eaton's proposal demands careful consideration. The heading ("of David"), the reference to war (v.3), and the concept of sonship (v.10) favor a royal interpretation.

The structure also supports the unity of the psalm by the expressions of confidence. Throughout the psalmist's search for divine protection and guidance, he remains confident. The expository structure may be set forth as follows:

A. Confidence in God's Presence (vv.1–3)
  B. Prayer for God's Presence (vv.4–6)
  B′. Prayer for God's Presence (vv.7–12)
A′. Confidence in God's Presence (vv.13–14)

(See also Pierre Auffret, "'Yahwé m'accueillera.' Etude structurelle du Psaume 27," *Science et Esprit* 38 [1986]: 97–113.)

I. Confidence in God's Presence

27:1–3

Of David.

1 The LORD is my light and my salvation—
  whom shall I fear?
The LORD is the stronghold of my life—
  of whom shall I be afraid?
2 When evil men advance against me
  to devour my flesh,
when my enemies and my foes attack me,
  they will stumble and fall.
3 Though an army besiege me,
  my heart will not fear;
though war break out against me,
  even then will I be confident.

1–3 The confidence of the psalmist lies, not in his own abilities or in the strength of his forces, but in the Lord. He has experienced the Lord's presence and describes it by two metaphors: "light" and "stronghold" (v.1). The Lord as "light" pertains to the experiences of salvation and the confidence of the joyous and glorious victory God has promised to his people. The Lord is "the light" (*'ôr*) of his people (cf. 4:6; 18:28; 43:3; Isa 9:2; 49:6; 60:1; John 1:4, 9; 8:12; 1 John 1:5). The phrases "my light" and "my salvation" mean essentially the same thing. "Light" and "salvation" (*yēšaʿ*) pertain to the work of God in giving relief and victory, crowning his people with his blessings (TWOT, 1:414–16).

Moreover, God is likened to a "stronghold." The imagery of a stronghold (*māʿôz*, "strength") is familiar in the OT (18:2; 28:8; 31:2, 4; 43:2; cf. "helmet" in 60:7; 108:8). He is the strength of his people, providing a place of refuge for them. The purpose of the stronghold is to protect those who seek refuge. Therefore the psalmist calls the Lord "the stronghold of my life."

The intimate knowledge of God's protecting presence gives confidence. In the synonymous questions "Whom shall I fear?" and "Of whom shall I be afraid?" the psalmist uses two separate roots for "fear": *y-r-'* (vv.1a, 3) and *p-ḥ-d* (v.1b). These verses exude an expression of strong confidence in the Lord. Regardless of how great the adversities, the psalmist looks at the greatness of the Lord in relation to the insignificance of his own problems: "evil men" (v.2) or "an army" (v.3). The "evil men" are individual enemies in contrast with the national enemies ("my enemies," "my foes"; cf. v.3: "army," "war"). The opposition and outright "war" do not touch him because his "heart" is strengthened by keeping a perspective on the Lord. The phrase "my heart" points to the source of personal fortitude. Because of his confidence in the Lord, the psalmist is not afraid. In his inner being there is no fear. This confident confession in God's saving love is similar to Paul's confession in Romans 8:31–39.

Notes

For a brief discussion of the technical words and phrases in the superscription, see the Introduction.

2 The idiom "to devour my flesh" is far from clear. It appears to be a metaphor for oppression. The wicked are often likened to beasts who "devour" their victims (cf. 7:2; 14:4; 17:12). The psalmist believes that evil will come to an end: "they will stumble and fall," or even better in this context, "they shall certainly stumble and fall" (cf. A.A. Anderson, 1:221). The note on "to devour my flesh" in the NIV margin ("to slander me") is based on the usage in Dan 3:8 and 6:24.

3 The noun מַחֲנֶה (*maḥ*^{a}*neh*, "an army," lit., "a camp") denotes the enemy forces and is similar to the verb תַּחֲנֶה (*taḥ*^{a}*neh*, "encamp"; NIV, "besiege").

II. Prayer for God's Presence

27:4–6

4 One thing I ask of the LORD,
this is what I seek:
that I may dwell in the house of the LORD
all the days of my life,
to gaze upon the beauty of the LORD
and to seek him in his temple.
5 For in the day of trouble
he will keep me safe in his dwelling;
he will hide me in the shelter of his tabernacle
and set me high upon a rock.
6 Then my head will be exalted
above the enemies who surround me;
at his tabernacle will I sacrifice with shouts of joy;
I will sing and make music to the LORD.

4 Boldness of faith is not naïve belief. The external difficulties are little in comparison with the psalmist's deep desire to experience more fully the presence of God. In God's presence fear is banished. The longing for God's temple expresses the intensity of the psalmist's seeking after God himself (cf. Matt 6:33). The enjoyment of God's presence assures the evident goodness and love of God (cf. 23:6).

The psalmist desires to dwell in the temple of God for the rest of his life (cf. 15:1; 23:4–6). The temple was the visible expression of God's presence and was sought after by the godly. While sitting in God's temple, he planned to "gaze" on the Lord's beauty and to "seek" (inquire after) him in his temple. In the act of gazing on the Lord's beauty, the psalmist submits himself fully to experience the beneficent fellowship with God. God's "beauty" is an expression of his goodness to his people (cf. 16:11; 90:17). When Moses saw his glory, the Lord revealed his perfections of love and compassion (Exod 34:5–6). The "beauty" of the Lord is his favor toward his own (cf. 90:17; 135:3; see C.S. Lewis's intriguing essay "The Fair Beauty of the Lord," *Reflections on the Psalms*, pp. 44–53, and the appendix to Ps 132: The Ark of the Covenant and the Temple: Symbols of Yahweh's Presence and Rule).

In the experience of God's presence, the psalmist also intends to "seek" him (cf. 73:17). Little consensus exists on the meaning of the verb "seek" (see A.A. Anderson, 1:222–23). Was the psalmist seeking him as in the day of trouble, or does the word have a more technical sense? It is probable that he was looking for a divine word or action that would satisfy the longing in his heart (cf. v.8). The desire for God's presence arose out of a need. The psalmist is not an escapist because he wants to hang onto God until he is fully assured of his glorious presence.

5 Verse 5 clarifies the relation between seeking the Lord and the occasion. The psalmist seeks the Lord in his "trouble" (cf. 41:1); and whenever adversities arise, he need not be afraid (cf. vv.1–3). In this context it may well be that the king thus assured himself of God's presence before he led Israel in battle. The OT makes mention of inquiring of the Lord before battle (1 Kings 22:7; 2 Chron 20:3–14). The king anticipates finding protection for himself and his people in the "dwelling," i.e., the "tabernacle," of God! With this assurance he knows that he is in God's protective hands. He further likens this protection by being placed "high upon a rock." God is that rock (*ṣûr*) for those who trust in him (cf. 18:1–2; 28:1; 31:2; 89:26; see the appendix to Ps 98: Yahweh Is the Divine Warrior).

6 When God protects his own by setting them safely as on a high rock, his people have reason to rejoice. Rejoicing casts out fear. Confident of God's help in trouble, the psalmist anticipates a victory over the enemies that have troubled God's people (cf. vv.2–3). He vows to sacrifice to the Lord as an expression of devotion (cf. 26:6), while singing a hymn of devotion to his God. Doubtless he proclaims the mighty acts of God's redemption (cf. 26:7) in his "shouts of joy" and song. "With shouts of joy" (lit., "sacrifices of a shout of joy) are the cry of victory in anticipation of the actual victory (see Rudolf Schmid, "Opfer mit Jubel," *Theologische Zeitschrift* 35 [1979]: 48–54). His expressions of loyalty result from a trusting heart. He knows that he cannot buy God off with his offerings. He knows that his covenant God cares for his own. Weiser appropriately comments, "We are here confronted with a truly living communion with God, with a mutual receiving and giving" (p. 249).

Notes

4 Since the phrase "that I may dwell" (שִׁבְתִּי [*šiḇtî*, lit., "my dwelling"]) is similar to that in 23:6, critics have concluded that this verse is a gloss. But this need not be because it reflects a liturgical form of expression. The usage of the infinitive construct with a pronominal suffix distinguishes it from the two following infinitives: "to gaze . . . and to seek," which could also be rendered by circumstantial clauses: "that I may dwell . . . while gazing . . . and while seeking."

III. Prayer for God's Presence

27:7–12

7 Hear my voice when I call, O LORD;
  be merciful to me and answer me.
8 My heart says of you, "Seek his face!"
  Your face, LORD, I will seek.
9 Do not hide your face from me,
  do not turn your servant away in anger;
  you have been my helper.
 Do not reject me or forsake me,
  O God my Savior.
10 Though my father and mother forsake me,
  the LORD will receive me.
11 Teach me your way, O LORD;
  lead me in a straight path
  because of my oppressors.
12 Do not turn me over to the desire of my foes,
  for false witnesses rise up against me,
  breathing out violence.

7–10 The mood changes suddenly. Verses 7–12 form the background from which the confidence arose. First there may be a period of searching and doubt, out of which true faith develops and leads to a more determined reliance on God. The depth of anxiety is expressed in the liturgical phraseology "hear my voice" (v.7; cf. 4:1; 5:2–3; 17:1; 28:2), "be merciful to me" (6:2; 26:11; 57:1), "do not hide your face" (v.9; cf. 102:2; 143:7), and "do not turn . . . do not reject" (38:22). The repetitious language communicates the intensity of the soul searching and the greatness of his need. He is praying for immediate deliverance out of the adversity (cf. 102:3; 143:7).

The soliloquy is not an expression of self-pity but of abandonment to the Lord. He is merciful and has promised to be faithful to his servant David (2 Sam 7:5–16). The grounds for the abandonment to the Lord are the covenant name Yahweh (v.7), the devotion of the psalmist to his loving God (v.8), the acts of God's past loyalty as the "helper" and Savior (v.9), and the Father-son relationship (v.10).

Out of the abandonment develops a deeper sense of dependence on the Lord. Adversity often appears as an expression of God's lack of interest or outright anger (v.9). When God hides his face, he removes his blessings (cf. 22:24; 30:7; 143:7; cf. "do not hide your face . . . in anger"). In his abandonment the psalmist knows that Yahweh is his heavenly Father (v.10). He looks for the intimacy of a relationship with his Father in heaven even in the experience of God's wrath. Weiser writes, "The love of God transcends every human standard; it is greater than the love of father and mother" (p. 253). The Lord's act of kindness toward him is described by the verb "receive," a form of *'-s-p̱* ("gather"), which is idiomatic of a father's lifting up his child with the intent of providing for his needs (v.10; cf. Exod 19:4; Deut 32:13–14).

11–12 The psalmist prayed for God's mercy (v.11), which he further explicates in terms of guidance and victory (vv.11–12). First, he prays for *guidance* (v.11). His prayer does not arise out of a confession of sin (cf. 32:8) but out of a great desire to do God's will and to experience his fellowship. In the experience of fellowship, he will again enjoy God's protection. The "straight path" signifies an area from which all obstacles have been removed. The same word is also found in 26:12 and properly translated in the NIV as "level ground." Only the Lord can take the psalmist and God's people out of their distress and lead them into safety.

The second request goes one step further. The psalmist prays for victory over the enemies (v.12; cf. v.2). If God is with his people, there can be no force sufficiently powerful to oppose the Lord. Regardless of who the enemies are, whether personal or national, they have arisen to undo the work of God. Their intent is only to destroy (cf. vv.2–3). At issue is whose "desire" will be granted: the psalmist's or the enemies'? According to 41:2 the Lord protects his own, blesses them, and does not hand them over to "the desire of [his] foes" (cf. 112:8). The submissiveness of the psalmist to God's guidance is quite contrastive to the treachery and violence of the ungodly. There is only one solution: victory over the foes.

Notes

---

8 The MT is difficult. See the NIV margin for an alternate rendering. To "seek the face of the LORD" was an expression of devotion, often attended by sacrifices or acts of loyalty (cf. Jer 50:4–5; Hos 3:5; Zech 8:22). The phrase "my heart says" is an idiom for an internal form of dialogue or soliloquy (cf. 4:4; 10:6, 11, 13; 14:1; 35:25; 53:1; 74:8). For a discussion, see Craigie, *Psalms 1–50,* p. 230.

9 For a parallel in ancient Near Eastern literature, see Shalom M. Paul, "Psalm xxvii 10 and the Babylonian Theodicy," VetTest 32 [1982]: 489–92.

12 "The desire of my foes" is literally "the soul [נֶפֶשׁ (*nep̱eš*)] of my foes." Dahood translates "soul" here by "throat" (*Psalms,* 1:166). The NEB's "the greed of my enemies" is closer to the NIV's rendering.

The phrase וִיפֵחַ חָמָס (*wîp̱ēaḥ ḥāmās,* "and breathing out violence") is awkward in the MT because its singular form does not correspond to the plural subject "witnesses." The LXX and the Syriac interpret it as a plural imperfect verb in the Qal, resulting in a minor emendation: וְיָפִיחוּ (*weyāp̱îḥû,* "and they breathe out"). Craigie takes the MT as a verbal adjective, "witness," and as a parallel of "witnesses": "for false witnesses have arisen against me violent witnesses too!" (*Psalms 1–50,* pp. 229–30).

IV. Confidence in God's Presence

27:13–14

13 I am still confident of this:
  I will see the goodness of the LORD
  in the land of the living.
14 Wait for the LORD;
  be strong and take heart
  and wait for the LORD.

13–14 The psalm concludes on a triumphant note. In spite of the difficulties, the royal psalmist leads his people into a deeper faith. He is strongly convinced that the Lord will come to the rescue of his people. He believes that he will taste God's "goodness" in fellowship, protection, guidance, and victory (v.13; cf. 23:6). The hope is based on the promises of God and on God's covenant name, Yahweh. "The land of the living" denotes "life" on earth over against the state of death (cf. 52:5; 142:5; Isa 38:11; 53:8; Ezek 26:20; 32:23).

In a characteristic way the psalmist does not keep his faith to himself. Even as in 26:7, the psalmist looked forward to "proclaiming aloud" the great acts of God. While these words (v.14) were first addressed as an encouragement to his own heart, they had the intended effect of encouraging each and every godly person to draw courage from these words. Verses 13–14 are an appropriate conclusion to the psalm and constitute an inclusionary motif with vv.1–3. The words of encouragement are reminiscent of Moses' words to Joshua (Deut 31:7), of God's commission of Joshua (Josh 1:6, 7, 9, 18), and of Joshua's words to the people (10:25; see also Paul's words of encouragement in 1 Cor 16:13). Redemptive history did not conclude with the Conquest. It continues as long as God's people "wait for the LORD" and do his will (cf. Hag 2:4–5). As Weiser puts it, "Here faith is the power which enables the faithful to endure the tension between his present afflictions and his future deliverance from those afflictions" (p. 254).

Notes

13 The first word in the MT, לוּלֵא (*lûlē'*, "still") is marked by six dots, three above and three below the word. This marking signified a problem with the word by the Masoretes. A literal rendering of the first two words is "unless I had believed." A.A. Anderson's observation is incisive: "This abbreviated sentence probably amounts to an emphatic statement: 'I *have* believed' " (1:226); the NIV has "I am still confident."

Psalm 28: Prayer to the Lord, My Strength and My Shield

The combination of confidence in the Lord and prayer (cf. Ps 27) occurs also in Psalm 28 but in reverse order. The psalmist begins with an urgent prayer in the form of an individual lament (vv.1–5) and concludes with an expression of confidence in the Lord, his strength (vv.6–9). These two psalms are connected by the words "stronghold" (27:1b; 28:8 [NIV, "fortress"]) and "salvation" (27:1a; 28:8); the reference to the temple ("in his temple," 27:4; "Most Holy Place," 28:2b); and the language of prayer ("Hear my voice when I call. . . . Do not" followed by a motive clause and imperatives, 27:7–11; "I call, . . . do not. . . . Hear my cry [lit., 'hear the voice of my supplications']. . . . Do not" followed by imperatives and a motive clause, 28:1–5).

The hymnic thanksgiving to the Lord (vv.6–9) contains both a blessing and a prayer. The psalmist thanks the Lord in anticipation of the response to his prayer (vv.6–8). In the last verse he concludes his prayer with an intercession on behalf of God's people (v.9; cf. 25:22). The psalm is associated with David and portrays the Lord as caring for his people through his "anointed one" (v.8). It is not clearly a messianic psalm, nor is it a royal psalm (so Eaton, *Psalms,* pp. 86–88). However, it shares with the royal psalms the expectation that the Lord will rule victoriously over his people.

The structure of Psalm 28 follows the main structural division according to genre: lament (vv.1–5) and thanksgiving (vv.6–9). The expository structure permits a further division of each:

A. Personal Prayer (vv.1–2)
  B. Prayer for Justice (vv.3–5)
  B′. Trust in God's Justice (vv.6–8)
A′. Personal Intercession (v.9)

The life-setting is far from clear. Craigie interprets the psalm as a *liturgy of supplication* (*Psalms 1–50,* p. 237) as part of the temple worship. It may also be that the psalmist's prayer arises out of a personal concern for kingship in Israel and for the theocratic rule of God over his people. Bellinger treats the psalm as a whole as exemplifying the *individual lament* genre (pp. 38–39).

I. Personal Prayer

28:1–2

Of David.

1 To you I call, O LORD my Rock;
  do not turn a deaf ear to me.
For if you remain silent,
  I will be like those who have gone down to the pit.
2 Hear my cry for mercy
  as I call to you for help,
as I lift up my hands
  toward your Most Holy Place.

1–2 The prayer is directed most emphatically to the Lord—the Hebrew and the NIV use the phrase "to you." This phrase is symmetric with the last clause of v.2: "toward your Most Holy Place." The beginning and end bring into focus the source of answered prayer. The Most Holy Place is that part of the temple most closely associated with the presence of God. In it stood the ark of the covenant protected symbolically by the cherubim (1 Kings 8:6; cf. the appendix to Ps 132: The Ark of the Covenant and the Temple: Symbols of Yahweh's Presence and Rule).

Prayer is an expression of sole dependence on the Lord for help. He alone is the "rock" who gives strength and sustenance to his people. As the "rock" he also provides refuge for his own (18:2, 31; 19:14; 27:5; 73:26; 92:15; 144:1). Prayer is also a privilege that belongs to his covenant people. The psalmist addresses him as "Yahweh." In the ears of the OT saints, this form of address was equivalent to "to you my father." The Lord had invited his people to call on him in their distress, even when the prayer was in the form of an urgent petition, characterized by boldness. This prayer, like so many other psalms, arose out of an urgent need whose specific nature was not important enough to be remembered. Prayers in the Psalms are sufficiently generalized to help God's people in all ages to share in the spirit of prayer.

In his prayer to the Lord, the psalmist makes two petitions. On the one hand, he calls on the Lord to act *now.* Though he may have suffered for some time, the psalmist calls on him to "not turn a deaf ear" (v.1; cf. 35:22; 39:12). The deafness of God is an anthropomorphic expression. It is equivalent to the prayer "Do not hide your face from me" (27:9). The silence of God is cause for additional anguish because it may be expressive of abandonment and judgment. The psalmist thus calls on his covenant God to vindicate him (cf. 109:1).

The silence of God aggravates the psalmist's suffering to the point of becoming unbearable. It is as if he is ready to die. This does not mean that the psalmist is suffering from some incurable disease. He uses a common phraseology (cf. 30:3; 39:2–3; 83:1; 88:3–7; 143:7) for trouble. The "pit" is synonymous with "Sheol" (cf. 22:29; 30:3–4; 88:4). Instead of blessing, the psalmist experiences adversity. But before the testing becomes too severe, too unbearable, he petitions the Lord to be sensitive to his needs. (See the appendix to Ps 88: Sheol-Grave-Death in the Psalms.)

The second petition underscores the first. The psalmist calls on God's perfection of "mercy." The "cry for mercy" (v.2) is a form of prayer, calling for God's grace to extend to him. The word *taḥ^{a}nûnay* ("my supplication," "my prayer for mercy") is related to the word "gracious," "merciful" (*ḥannûn*), one of the attributes of the Lord (cf. Exod 34:6). As he cries out in his distress, the psalmist prays that the All-Merciful may come to his help. He cannot deliver himself, but he trusts that the Lord will extend his mercy to him. To this end he lifts up his hand in prayer, as a symbolic expression of his utter dependence on the Lord. Solomon had asked the Lord to heed those prayers of his people that are directed toward the temple (1 Kings 8:35, 38, 42), and the psalmist conforms to an ancient practice of raising his hands to the Most Holy Place (cf. 63:4; 134:2; 141:2), the dwelling place of God on earth (cf. 5:7).

Notes

For a brief discussion of the technical words and phrases in the superscription, see the Introduction.

II. Prayer for Justice

28:3–5

3 Do not drag me away with the wicked,
with those who do evil,
who speak cordially with their neighbors
but harbor malice in their hearts.
4 Repay them for their deeds
and for their evil work;
repay them for what their hands have done
and bring back upon them what they deserve.
5 Since they show no regard for the works of the LORD
and what his hands have done,
he will tear them down
and never build them up again.

3 The psalmist's true concern is with God's honor. But the psalmist suffers from the apparent lack of justice. Therefore he prays that the Lord may lift him out of his troubles (cf. 26:9–12) so that he will not be likened to nor judged with the wicked.

The wicked are those whose hearts persist in practicing evil and in speaking deceptively. They care only for themselves and not for the pursuit of godliness.

4–5 The psalmist also prays for God's judgment on the wicked (v.4). His concern for retribution does not arise out of some morbid sense of joy in suffering. He submits himself to the Lord who will requite (Matt 16:27; 2 Tim 4:14; 1 Peter 1:17; Rev 20:12–13; 22:12). (See the appendix to Ps 137: Imprecations in the Psalms.)

The wicked have had their chance; but instead of accepting their responsibility to the Lord, they showed their disregard for him. Their lack of respect is an expression of folly, the opposite of wisdom. They have not learned how to respond to God and to his mighty acts in the history of redemption. Instead they have occupied themselves with the works of their own hands. Since there is no correspondence between the works of God and the works of the wicked, they have no place in God's order of things.

The words for "work" or "deed" bring into focus the evil of the wicked. They do not show a proper regard for the "works" (*pᵉʿullōṯ*) of the Lord or "what his hands have done" (*maʿᵃśēh yāḏāyw*) (v.5). Instead they will be judged for their "deed" (*pōʿal*), "work" (*maʿᵃlāl*), and "what their hands have done" (*maʿᵃśēh yᵉdêhem*) (v.4). Both the Lord and the wicked evidence their nature in their work, but there is a qualitative difference between the two kinds of works (cf. Isa 5:12). In essence the wicked work destructively against the works of God. Their due punishment is destruction. The acts of the Lord in creation, redemption, and Yahweh's rule through David reveal the wonder of God's purpose. The history of redemption condemns the wicked. Justice demands that evil be removed so that its power will be completely broken. But the righteous find comfort in God's acts (vv.6–9). (See the appendix to Ps 78: The Mighty Acts of Yahweh.)

III. Trust in God's Justice

28:6–8

6 Praise be to the LORD,
for he has heard my cry for mercy.
7 The LORD is my strength and my shield;
my heart trusts in him, and I am helped.
My heart leaps for joy
and I will give thanks to him in song.

8 The LORD is the strength of his people,
a fortress of salvation for his anointed one.

6 The just works of God do not cease. In anticipation of his righteous judgment and the experience of vindication, the psalmist bursts out in a hymn of praise to God. He "blesses" the Lord for what he will do in response to his prayer (vv.1–2), in which he asks the Lord to respond to his condition in mercy. He claims that the Lord has heard his prayer "for mercy" (cf. v.2) and looks forward to an even greater deliverance.

7 The psalmist calls the Lord "my Rock" (v.1), "my strength" (cf. Exod 15:2), and "my shield" (cf. 3:3). No longer does he feel threatened to the point of despair. In contrast he confesses that he is overjoyed and jubilant. His confidence has not been put to shame. He trusted in the "rock" of his salvation, and that "Rock" proved to be a reliable, covenant-faithful God. (See the appendix to Ps 98: Yahweh Is the Divine Warrior.)

8 The psalmist's confidence in God's justice goes beyond his own experience. He knows that Yahweh is the God of his people. Since the Lord takes care of the individual, he will most certainly prove himself to be the "strength of his people" (cf. 29:11) and the "fortress" or "stronghold" of his anointed king (cf. 27:1). "Salvation," i.e., the victory, belongs to him (cf. 18:50; 20:6).

Notes

---

7 The MT phrase מִשִּׁירִי (*miššîrî*, "from my song"; NIV, "in song") is rendered "from my will" in the LXX; see the NEB, "I praise him with my whole body." The recent study by A. Gelston supports the MT tradition ("A Note on the Text of Psalm XXVIII 7b," VetTest 25 [1975]: 214–16).

8 A number of the ancient versions support the NIV reading, "his people," for the MT's לָמוֹ (*lāmô*, "to them"). The difference is not significant and may be accounted for by assimilation: לְעַמּוֹ (*le'ammô*).

IV. Personal Intercession

28:9

> [9]Save your people and bless your inheritance;
> be their shepherd and carry them forever.

9 In a truly theocratic fashion, the psalmist prays, not only for himself, but also for the people. People and king, nation and individual belong together. He closes his prayer of lament and thanksgiving with a prayer for deliverance from oppression, for the Lord's blessing on his own people, and for God's royal kingship over his own. The psalmist knows that kingship belongs to the Lord and that, ultimately, the Davidic king is representative of the kingship of God. Therefore he calls on the Great King to be true to his people. They are his chosen "inheritance" (Deut 4:20; 1 Kings 8:51). He is the King-Shepherd of his people (Ps 23:1; Mic 5:4; 7:14). His kingdom is an everlasting kingdom. He cares for his sheep in a tender way so as to "carry them" in his arms. This imagery is reminiscent of Isaiah's language (40:11; 46:3–4; 63:9; cf. Exod 19:4) and, of course, of the words of our Lord (John 10:1–18).

Psalm 29: The Victorious Kingship of Yahweh

In a grand hymn of praise, the psalmist sets forth a portrait of Yahweh as the victorious King. The similarity of phraseology and imagery has led scholars to debate for the last fifty years the exact relationship of Psalm 29 with ancient Canaanite poetry (Aloysius Fitzgerald, "A Note on Psalm 29," BASOR 215 [1974]: 61–63). Some treat the psalm as little more than a Canaanite psalm transformed into a Yahwistic hymn (so

John Day, *God's Conflict With the Dragon and the Sea. Echoes of Canaanite Myth in the Old Testament* [Cambridge: Cambridge University Press, 1985], pp. 57–61). We accept the conclusions of Craigie, who has argued in articles and in his recent commentary that the relationship is not one of complete dependence as some suggest (*Psalms 1–50,* pp. 243–46).

The allusions to the Canaanite background may be a polemic device used by the author to demonstrate the superiority of the Lord of Israel over Baal, who was thought to be the lord of the storms. In the words of Craigie, "the poet has deliberately utilized Canaanite-type language and imagery in order to emphasize the Lord's strength and victory, in contrast to the weakness of the inimical Baal" (*Psalms 1–50,* p. 246; see also Hans Strauss, "Zur Auslegung von Ps 29 auf dem Hintergrund seiner Kanaanäischen Bezüge," ZAW 82 [1972]: 91–101).

The hymn of praise focuses on a particular aspect of the rule of God (see James L. Mays, "Psalm 29," Int 39 [1985]: 60–64). Because of the metaphorical significance of the thunder, it is possible to conclude that the hymn evokes a response of awe at the revelation of God (theophany; so Weiser, pp. 260–61) or at his demonstration of victory over the enemies (so Craigie, *Psalms 1–50,* pp. 245–46). The latter interpretation is particularly attractive because of the similarity of imagery in the Song of Moses (cf. Exod 15:2–3 and Ps 29:1–2) and the Song of Deborah (Judg 5:4–5, 19–21).

The meaning of the word *qôl* ("voice," "noise") depends on the interpretive framework. The sevenfold repetition of the word "voice" probably affected in God's people a sense of awe at the God who, in addition to his mighty works in nature and history, had also revealed himself at Mount Sinai. We are hesitant to expound the text solely as a hymn of victory, because it "is not impossible that the mention of the voice of Yahweh brought to the minds of the Israelites the concept of the Word of Yahweh, so powerful and diverse" (A.A. Anderson, 1:233).

The LXX adds an additional comment in the superscription, associating the psalm with the Feast of Tabernacles. In rabbinic tradition it belonged to the Feast of Weeks instead. Scholarship is divided on the original life-setting of the psalm. But there is a general agreement on its antiquity.

The structure of the psalm unfolds readily into three parts: the beginning (vv.1–2) and end (vv.10–11) have an inclusionary focus on the praise of God's kingship, and the middle section portrays in a highly poetic way the glory and power of God's rule (vv.3–9).

A. In Praise of Yahweh's Kingship (vv.1–2)
B. The Glorious Voice of Yahweh (vv.3–9)
A′. In Praise of Yahweh's Kingship (vv.10–11)

(For a critical structural analysis, see Siegfried Mittmann, "Komposition und Redaktion von Psalm xxix," VetTest 28 [1978]: 172–94; P. Auffret, "Notes complémentaires sur la Structure littéraire des Psaumes 3 et 29," ZAW 99 [1987]: 90–93.)

I. In Praise of Yahweh's Kingship

29:1–2

A psalm of David.

1 Ascribe to the LORD, O mighty ones,
ascribe to the LORD glory and strength.

> [2]Ascribe to the LORD the glory due his name;
> worship the LORD in the splendor of his holiness.

1–2 Three times the "mighty ones" are called on to give praise to Yahweh. The threefold usage of "ascribe" followed by the verb "worship" is also found in 96:7–9 (cf. 1 Chron 16:28–29). It may reflect a liturgical practice of calling the worshipers to present themselves with their sacrifices and offerings before the Lord.

The "mighty ones" are to show due honor to his "glory and strength" and to his "name." By the name of the Lord, Israel had gained victories. The "name" of the Lord, Yahweh, was his seal on the covenantal relationship between the Great King and his people Israel. Moses had celebrated the warriorlike character of Yahweh on behalf of his people in his song: "Yahweh is a warrior; Yahweh is his name" (Exod 15:3). The acts of Yahweh include his acts of redemption but are not to be limited to them. In 66:1–2, the psalmist calls on all the nations of the earth to shout with joy as an act of worship due his name (v.2). In this context the psalmist focuses his attention on the victorious nature of Israel's God (vv.3–7) as well as on his just judgment of Israel's exile and restoration (vv.8–20).

The "name" of God is a respectful reference to Yahweh in the demonstration of his "glory and strength." In the preceding psalm the "strength" of the Lord was the assurance of his presence in blessing and protection on behalf of his people (28:7–8). The combination of "glory" and "strength" brings out the nature of his powerful acts in creation and redemption. His acts reveal his "royal" prerogative.

It seems best to assume that the ascription of praise includes songs as well as acts of submission in recognition of Yahweh's glory, strength, and splendor (vv.1–2). They reflect his holy presence ("holiness") in the affairs of man. Thus the psalmist praises the Lord for his rule, sovereignty, and majesty in relationship to his people and to all his works.

Who are the "mighty ones" (v.1) called on to praise God for his works on earth? The NIV rendering obscures the difficulty of the Hebrew text, which states that the "sons of the gods" must give honor to him. The phrase is used elsewhere to denote "heavenly beings" or angels (cf. Gen 6:2, 4; Job 1:6; 2:1; 38:7; Pss 82:6; 89:6). In this context the phrase may be used as a technical term for the divine assembly of heavenly beings who surround the throne of God. The worship of God has its greatest momentum when God's creatures in *heaven* and on *earth* join together to praise him.

The proper approach of the heavenly creatures, like the earthly creatures, can only be "in holy attire" (NIV, "the splendor of his holiness"). Only when arrayed in a manner fit for the worship of the Great King and when consecrated to him like the priests at the temple are God's servants prepared to serve him.

Notes

For a brief discussion of the technical words and phrases in the superscription, see the Introduction.

2 The meaning of the word הֲדָרָה (*hᵃḏārāh*, "splendor," "attire") has been debated. Dahood thought he found a Ugaritic parallel meaning "theophany," e.g., "when the Holy One appears" (*Psalms*, 1:174). The evidence, however, is questionable (KB[3], 1:230). It is related to the word הָדָר (*hāḏār*, "majestic," v.4) and may best be taken with reference to the garments prepared for the occasion (cf. 110:3; cf. Craigie's "Worship the LORD in holy attire," *Psalms 1–50*, p. 242).

II. The Glorious Voice of Yahweh

29:3–9

3 The voice of the LORD is over the waters;
the God of glory thunders,
the LORD thunders over the mighty waters.
4 The voice of the LORD is powerful;
the voice of the LORD is majestic.
5 The voice of the LORD breaks the cedars;
the LORD breaks in pieces the cedars of Lebanon.
6 He makes Lebanon skip like a calf,
Sirion like a young wild ox.
7 The voice of the LORD strikes
with flashes of lightning.
8 The voice of the LORD shakes the desert;
the LORD shakes the Desert of Kadesh.
9 The voice of the LORD twists the oaks
and strips the forests bare.
And in his temple all cry, "Glory!"

3–4 The glory of God rests on all his creation: sky, sea, land, and wilderness. The psalmist reflects on the thunderstorm as a powerful illustration of the majesty and power of the God of Israel. The glorious God (El) manifests his glory and strength even in a thunderstorm at sea. The region of the sea was considered by the Canaanites to be the battleground between Yam, the god of the sea and of chaos, and Baal, the god of fertility and thunderstorms. El, the chief of the Canaanite pantheon, was the benign father of the gods. The direct reference to Yahweh as the glorious El may contain a polemic allusion to the superiority of Yahweh over Baal. Yahweh rules sovereignly over the "mighty waters." The Mediterranean Sea was known to the psalmist as a mighty force, whose powerful waves could cause great destruction. But the Lord is sovereign over the terrible forces of the sea (cf. 93:3–4). (See the appendix to Ps 98: Yahweh Is the Divine Warrior.)

5–6 The glory of God is also evident in the mountains (114:4, 6). The poet singles out Mount Lebanon and Mount Hermon ("Sirion," v.6; cf. Deut 3:9), the mighty mountains to the north of Canaan. In the presence of Yahweh (theophany), they are shaken like small objects. These mighty mountain ranges, rising far above the surrounding landscape to an altitude of ten thousand feet above sea level, are dramatically portrayed as skipping like a calf and like a wild ox (v.6). By the effect of God's power, the grand cedars on Mount Lebanon (cf. Isa 2:13) are felled and splintered to pieces (v.5).

7 It may be that the psalmist associates the thunder so intimately with the lightning that he reflects on the terrible effects of a lightning bolt. The choice of the mountains in the north may again be purposeful. The Canaanites believed that these mountains were the abode of the gods (cf. Weiser, p. 264). The God of Israel shows little respect by shaking the mountains and by felling the trees. He is greater than any of the Canaanite deities.

8–9 The glory of God reveals itself in the desert regions. It is far from clear which particular desert is the "Desert of Kadesh" (v.8). Some take it as a reference to the region around Kadesh Barnea and associate the setting with the Sinai traditions (cf. Weiser, p. 264). A.A. Anderson represents those who identify it with Kadesh by the Orontes (1:237; cf. Dahood, *Psalms,* 1:178). Craigie seems most balanced in his conclusion that "the reference to desert . . . should be interpreted generally, rather than specifically" (*Psalms 1–50,* p. 248). The "Desert of Kadesh" stands for desert regions in general. Yahweh rules over everything, including the vast desert regions. His "voice" is also heard there.

The "voice of the LORD" resonates in heaven and on earth. The proper response of God's heavenly creatures is their ascription of glory to the Great King. Everyone in his heavenly temple cries out, "Glory!" (v.9c). The majestic effect of the poem leaves one struck with awe having the question, Why is it that earthly creatures are not overcome by the splendor of God's kingship?

Notes

3–9 For a study on the background of these verses, see P.C. Craigie, "Parallel Word Pairs in Ugaritic Poetry: A Critical Evaluation of Their Relevance for Psalm 29," *Ugarit-Forschungen* 11 (1979): 135–40; John Day, "Echoes of Baal's Seven Thunders and Lightnings in Psalm xxix and Habakkuk iii 9 and the Identity of the Seraphim in Isaiah vi," VetTest 29 (1979): 143–51; Klaus Seybold, "Die Geschichte des 29. Psalms und ihre theologische Bedeutung," *Theologische Zeitschrift* 36 (1980): 208–19; Johannes Schildenberger, "Psalm 29. Ein Hymnus auf den machtvollen Gott zu Beginn eines neuen Jahres," *Erbe und Auftrag* 57 (1981): 5–12. Christian Macholz concludes that Yahweh is the *totaliter aliter* ("Wholly Other One") from Baal in "Psalm 29 und 1. Könige 19. Jahwes und Baals Theophanie," *Werden und Wirken des Alten Testaments. Festschrift für Claus Westermann zum 70. Geburtstag,* edd. Rainer Albertz, Hans-Peter Müller, Hans Walter Wolff, and Walther Zimmerli (Göttingen: Vandenhoeck & Ruprecht, 1980), pp. 325–33.

9 The MT's אַיָּלוֹת (*'ayyālôṯ,* "deer," "does"; see NIV mg.: "The voice of the LORD makes the deer give birth") does not fit within this context, filled with geographical and botanical allusions. The BHS proposes a slight emendation to give a balanced parallelism: אֵילוֹת (*'êlôṯ,* "oaks"; so NIV).

III. In Praise of Yahweh's Kingship

29:10–11

> 10 The LORD sits enthroned over the flood;
> the LORD is enthroned as King forever.
> 11 The LORD gives strength to his people;
> the LORD blesses his people with peace.

10–11 Though the storms rage and the mountains quake, Yahweh is king. His enthronement over "the flood" assures his children that great as his power is, he is sovereign. Even as in the days of the Flood, when he destroyed creation with his power but saved his own, so it is at any time that God's glory is expressed in the severity of judgment. He rules over nations and peoples that inhabit and traverse land, sea, mountains, and steppe regions. Weiser expresses this truth, "In the face of the dreadful events and the fearful passing away which are a continual threat to all earthly things man's faith finds comfort in God, the eternal King of heaven" (p. 265).

The subject of the psalm is the demonstration of God's glory in nature, but its impact is the opposite. It gives a sense of tranquility and awe. Yahweh, our God, is powerful in his glory. He can and does protect his people. He opens heaven up so as to unleash his blessings of protection, victory, and peace (cf. 28:8–9; 46:1–3; Num 6:24–26). There is quietness within the storm for those who belong to the people of God. Brueggemann views this psalm as a basis for Israel's new life of hope. He writes: "The new order requires the honoring of God, but it also requires the capacity and power to reorder life. That is cause for singing on earth, as in heaven" (*Message of the Psalms*, p. 143).

Notes

Oswald Loretz cautions against rendering the Hebrew text on the basis of Ugaritic texts. Though the Hebrew may share common vocabulary, the context of each text is of primary importance ("KTU 1.101:1–3a und 1.2 IV 10 als Parallelen zu Ps 29, 10," ZAW 99 [1987]: 415–21).

Psalm 30: Praise for God's Faithfulness in a Time of Need

Praise constitutes the key motif. The first words ("I will exalt you") and the last words ("I will give you thanks forever") form an inclusion, in between which the psalmist describes past suffering and the wonderful restoration from his illness. The manner of description of his suffering and his exhortation to the "saints" (v.4) to praise the Lord suggest that the psalm is an individual psalm of thanksgiving. It has similarities with Hezekiah's psalm of praise after his sickness (Isa 38:10–20).

However, the theme of restoration from sickness and the praise of God hardly fit the superscription: "For the dedication of the temple. Of David." If the psalm is Davidic, it may have been composed at the dedication of his palace or of the building materials (cf. 1 Chron 22:2–19). This may be unlikely in view of the word "dedication," connoting the completion of the temple (cf. 1 Kings 8:63). It is preferable to view the psalm as an *individual thanksgiving psalm*, associated with David, and to consider the superscription a later addition in which the psalm was nationalized as an expression of the suffering of the nation in exile and of the restoration from exile. The "temple" must be a reference to the second temple, dedicated in 515 B.C. The psalm became associated with the feast of Hanukkah, commemorating the dedication of the temple in 165 B.C. (J. Ridderbos, 1:251–53). According to the Talmud the Jews recited Psalm 30 during the Hanukkah Festival (b *Sopherim* 18b).

There is little agreement on the structure of the psalm. The parts follow closely on one another without clearly defined literary markers. For our purposes we shall set up an expository structure:

A. Praise for God's Wonderful Acts (vv.1–3)
B. God's Favor and Anger (vv.4–7)
A′. Praise for God's Wonderful Acts (vv.8–12)

At the heart of the psalm is the contrast between God's anger and his favor. Because of his favor, God acts on behalf of his own. They in turn have reason to praise him individually and as a community (v.4).

I. Praise

30:1

A psalm. A song. For the dedication of the temple. Of David.

[1]I will exalt you, O LORD,
for you lifted me out of the depths
and did not let my enemies gloat over me.

1 The praise of God consists of a declaration of his exalted nature and thanksgiving for his free condescension for the purpose of exalting his children. The psalm is set within an inclusion of "praise." It begins with a verbal phrase—"I will exalt you" (cf. Exod 15:2)—and ends on a verbal phrase—"I will give you thanks." These two verbal phrases form the inclusion and occur elsewhere together in the same verse in 118:28 and Isaiah 25:1.

The psalmist experienced a terrible sickness that brought him to the edge of life. Instead of feeling abandoned by the Lord, he witnessed God's goodness in answering his prayer and by healing him (v.2). He exalts God because he brought him up from near-death, listened to his prayer, and did not allow the wicked to rejoice. (See the appendix to Ps 88: Sheol-Grave-Death in the Psalms.)

First, the Lord spared the psalmist from death. The verbal phrase "you lifted me" is a metaphorical usage of a verb meaning "to draw up out of the water" (cf. Exod 2:16, 19). Like a bucket that was lowered down in a well and then raised to draw water up, so the Lord pulled the psalmist out of the grips of Sheol. Here the phrase means "you saved me."

The choice of verbs may set up a contrast between the imagery of God as the Exalted One and his stooping down to draw his servant out of the pit. The particular circumstances of the trouble are not relevant, but the experience of deliverance was important to the psalmist. In God's act of condescension to his need, the psalmist realized afresh God's love for him. The enemies had no occasion to "gloat" (cf. 35:19, 24–27; 38:16), because the Lord turned the psalmist's mourning into "joy" (v.11). The word "gloat" forms a contrast with "joy" in v.11. Though not obvious in the EVV, the words share the same root (*ś-m-ḥ*, "be happy"): "[You] did not let my enemies be joyous over me. . . . [you] clothed me with joy" (vv.1, 11).

Notes

For a brief discussion of the technical words and phrases in the superscription, see the Introduction.

II. God's Wonderful Acts

30:2–3

2 O LORD my God, I called to you for help
  and you healed me.
3 O LORD, you brought me up from the grave
  you spared me from going down into the pit.

2–3 Second, the psalmist praises the Lord for answered prayer. We must observe here again how the psalmist expresses a close relationship between himself and his God even in the hour of need: "O LORD my God" (v.2). Unfortunately, this phraseology seems still distant to our Western ears. The psalmist calls God by his revealed name: "Yahweh my God," as if to say, "Yahweh, you are my God, and I lay claim on your promises to care for me as your child." In the intimacy of communion lies the secret of answered prayer.

Third, the Lord's act of restoring or healing the psalmist (vv.1–2; cf. 51:12; 60:1; 80:3, 7, 19; 85:4; 107:20) ends the gloating of the enemies. So often the wicked rejoice in the adversity of the godly. To them it was proof that God sees neither good nor evil, that he does not reward righteousness, and, therefore, that he does not judge wickedness. The psalmist was concerned, not only with his own sin, but particularly with the good name of the Lord. Since the Lord has saved him out of the pits, he praises him as the Exalted One.

Notes

---

3 (4 MT) For the meaning of "grave" and "pit," see 6:5; 28:1; see also the appendix to Psalm 88: Sheol-Grave-Death.

The NIV follows the *Qere* reading in "from going down into the pit" instead of the *Kethiv*. The MT reads מִיּוֹרְדֵי־בוֹר (*mîyôrᵉḏê-ḇôr*, lit., "from the ones going down into the pit"), and the *Qere* suggests מִיָּרְדִי (*mîyorḏî*, "from my going down"). In view of the usage of this phrase in 28:1 and the unusual grammatical form of the *Kethiv*, it is preferable to accept the MT without emendation.

III. God's Favor and Anger

30:4–7

4 Sing to the LORD, you saints of his;
  praise his holy name.
5 For his anger lasts only a moment,
  but his favor lasts a lifetime;
weeping may remain for a night,
  but rejoicing comes in the morning.

6 When I felt secure, I said,
  "I will never be shaken."
7 O LORD, when you favored me,
  you made my mountain stand firm;
but when you hid your face,
  I was dismayed.

4–7 These verses are full of contrasts: anger and favor (v.5a), moment and lifetime (v.5a), weeping and rejoicing (v.5b), night and morning (v.5b), firm and dismayed (vv.6–7). They express the depth of God's care and the benefits of dependence on the Lord in life.

The praise of God goes from individual praise to a communal celebration. The "saints" are all those who are loyal to the Lord, the members of the covenant community (v.4; see 4:3). They praise "his holy name" (*zēk̲er*). Though the word *zēk̲er* at times is found in conjunction with "name" (*šēm*), it is not synonymous (cf. Exod 3:15; Ps 135:13). It signifies the proclamation of God's acts in the history of redemption associated with the name Yahweh (cf. 111:2–4; 122:4; 145; B.S. Childs, *Memory and Tradition in Israel* [London: SCM, 1962], p. 72; TWOT, 1:242).

The praise of "his holy name" arises for two complementary reasons: forgiveness and restoration. First, the Lord *forgives*. The psalmist confesses within the assembly that he has sinned against the Lord by a haughty, independent spirit (v.6). When everything was going well with him, he "felt secure," even to the point of self-confidence. The MT sets forth the contrast between the psalmist's folly and the Lord's goodness by a disjunctive waw at the beginning of this verse (*wa'ᵃnî*): "But as for me, I said when I felt secure." The security is due to prosperity. The Hebrew phrase *šalwî* ("my ease," "my prosperity") usually denotes a state of well-being (cf. 122:7–9), resultant of God's blessings (cf. Deut 8:7–10), but these blessings had led to self-confidence. The wicked pride themselves in their boastful words: "I will never be shaken" (cf. 10:6). Apparently the psalmist had come to the same point of practical atheism.

In his "anger" the Lord had afflicted the psalmist, who in his despair cast himself on the Lord. The psalmist had been foolish not to maintain his communion with God. The period of anguish was like "night" (v.5) to him, because of the intense experience of weeping. "Remain" (lit., "will spend the night") is a poetic expression of how weeping personified may spend the night with him, only to be gone by morning (cf. NEB, "Tears may linger at nightfall"). The sorrow resulted both from the suffering and from repentance. The psalmist returned to the Lord his God (cf. v.2) and experienced his forgiveness. Even though the psalm does not contain the language of forgiveness, the resultant description of his restoration implies the assurance that the Lord forgave him.

Second, the Lord *restores*. Great is his faithfulness (Lam 3:22–23). The restoration experience is like morning light (v.5). The light ("the morning") is a metaphor for healing, restoration, and blessing. The effect of restoration changes weeping into joy. The psalmist knows that the change did not result from his own efforts, because he was totally incapable of changing his lot (vv.1–3). Rather, it is by the "favor" of the Lord that he was restored. The phrase "when you favored me" (v.7) is a translation of a nominal phrase "in your favor." The word "favor" (*rāṣôn*, also found in v.5) signifies a renewal of love, forgiveness, restoration, and blessing (cf. 106:4; Isa 49:8; 60:10; 61:2). The Lord's name is emphatic: "O LORD, in your favor."

The psalmist also contrasts the judgment of God according to the extent of his expressions of love. His discipline is painful and may be likened to death, whereas his favor restores life (v.4). Dahood (*Psalms*, 1:182–3) proposes an antithetical rendering of "death" (instead of "moment," v.5) and "lifetime" (lit., "life"). This proposal results in a balanced parallelism:

anger — death
favor — life.

Compare these translations: "In his anger is disquiet, in his favor there is life" (NEB); "For in his anger is death, but in his favor is life" (Craigie, *Psalms 1–50*, p. 250). The Lord does not easily abandon his children who sin against him but renews them with his favor.

By God's grace the psalmist feels himself more secure and likens his renewed dependence on the Lord to a "mountain" (v.7). Translations differ on "you made my mountain stand firm." The Hebrew text is difficult. The NIV is a likely rendering. In his strength, he was weak; but in God's healing, he regained strength like a mountain. In his dependence, he is strong. Such is the logic of faith.

Notes

5 (6 MT) Craigie renders רֶגַע (*rega'*, "moment") by "death": "For in his anger is death" (*Psalms 1–50*, pp. 250–51), based on Dahood (*Psalms*, 1:182).

IV. Praise for God's Wonderful Acts

30:8–12

8 To you, O Lord, I called;
to the Lord I cried for mercy:
9 "What gain is there in my destruction,
in my going down into the pit?
Will the dust praise you?
Will it proclaim your faithfulness?
10 Hear, O Lord, and be merciful to me;
O Lord, be my help."

11 You turned my wailing into dancing;
you removed my sackcloth and clothed me with joy,
12 that my heart may sing to you and not be silent.
O Lord my God, I will give you thanks forever.

8–10 How different is the psalmist's relationship with his God from the time that he felt himself secure! He states emphatically that he looks toward the Lord ("To you, . . . to the Lord"). The imperfect of the Hebrew verbs may be better translated as a frequentative action: "I keep on calling, . . . I keep on crying for mercy" (cf. 28:1; 142:2; Joel 1:19).

The psalmist reflects again on the desperate situation in which he found himself (v.9; cf. vv.1–3; 6:5; 88:10–12; 115:17; Isa 38:18–19). He asked for mercy to be spared from "destruction." In his despair he vowed to praise the Lord and to be faithful to him (v.10). If he had been overcome by his suffering and had died, the wicked would have had an occasion to gloat (v.1). But out of concern for God's name, the psalmist had asked to praise the name of the Lord so that all men might know that he is faithful. This is an expression of true repentance: concern for God's name. Based on the covenant promises of God, he calls on him for mercy and help. His help is from the Lord who has made a covenant with his people. There is no one else (54:4).

11–12 The Lord was faithful in changing circumstances. The psalmist returns to the dominant motif of this psalm: Yahweh the Vindicator. He is the Lord who effectually changed wailing into dancing, mourning into joy, and a deathly cry into a song of joy (v.11). Such is the goodness of God. Notice how Calvin observed this over four hundred years ago: "But however much God may terrify and humble his faithful servants, with manifold signs of his displeasure, he always besprinkles them with the sweetness of his favour to moderate and assuage their grief" (1:489).

Because of the mercy of the Lord, the psalmist vows to continue in the praise of God (v.12b). The NIV translates "glory" (*kāḇôḏ,* see 7:5) as "heart." The word occurs in parallelism with "soul" (7:5; NIV, "life") and so frequently refers to the whole human being or existence. He will glorify the Lord! To this end he was redeemed, because he had argued, "Will the dust praise you? Will it proclaim your faithfulness?" To this end the Lord vindicates his servant in the presence of his enemies (cf. v.1; 23:5; 2 Thess 1:5–10). Alter senses the magnificence of the psalmist's language: "It is through language that God must be approached, must be reminded that, since His greatness needs language in order to be made known to men, He cannot dispense with the living user of language for the consummation of that end" (p. 135).

Notes

8 (9 MT) M. Dahood's symmetric translation is of interest but is not convincing: "To you, Yahweh, I cry, / O El my Lord, I plead for mercy" ("Vocative *waw* in Psalm 30:9," *Biblica* 58 [1977]: 218).

8, 10 (9, 11 MT) These verses form an inclusion around the questions raised in v.9. The repetition of the root חנן (*ḥ-n-n,* "be merciful") connects these two verses together with the emphasis on prayer for help.

9 (11 MT) דָּמִי (*dammî,* "my blood") may be emended to דֹּמִּי (*dōmmî,* "my weeping," from *d-m-m* [II]; cf. NIV mg.: "if I am silenced"). In favor of the marginal reading is the parallelism with the last part of the verse. See Craigie: "What profit is there in my weeping?" (*Psalms 1–50,* p. 250).

12 (13 MT) Craigie again takes the meaning from the root *d-m-m* (II, "weep"; cf. v.9): "so that my soul shall sing your praise and not weep" (*Psalms 1–50,* p. 250). The NIV has "not be silent."

Psalm 31: How Great Is Your Goodness!

The difficulty in determining the literary genre of this psalm has led many scholars to view it as a composite work from anonymous authors. Though it gives the impression of being a composite work, the parallels in language between this psalm and other psalms and the prayers of Jonah, Jeremiah, and Lamentations lead to the conclusion that this composition is an original work. The psalmist creatively uses words and phrases from the biblical writings and liturgical tradition of Israel (Craigie, *Psalms 1–50,* pp. 259–60). Bellinger classifies this psalm as an *individual lament* (pp.

32–33; see also Leo Labérge, "A Literary Analysis of Psalm 31," *Eglise et Théologie* 16 [1985]: 147–68).

The tone of the psalm vacillates between lament and thanksgiving, but the nature of the troubles is unclear. Is the psalmist looking for divine protection (vv.1–8)? Is he sick (vv.9–12)? Or has he been wrongly accused (vv.13–18)? The psalm falls into two parts: prayer (lament) and thanksgiving, and both show extensive use of repetition as a literary device.

I. Prayer (vv.1–18)
 A. Prayer for Yahweh's Righteousness (vv.1–5)
  B. Expression of Trust (vv.6–8)
 A′. Prayer for Yahweh's Favor (vv.9–13)
  B′. Expression of Trust (vv.14–18)
II. Thanksgiving (vv.19–24)

I. Prayer (vv.1–18)

A. *Prayer for Yahweh's Righteousness*

31:1–5

For the director of music. A psalm of David.

1 In you, O LORD, I have taken refuge;
let me never be put to shame;
deliver me in your righteousness.
2 Turn your ear to me,
come quickly to my rescue;
be my rock of refuge,
a strong fortress to save me.
3 Since you are my rock and my fortress,
for the sake of your name lead and guide me.
4 Free me from the trap that is set for me,
for you are my refuge.
5 Into your hands I commit my spirit;
redeem me, O LORD, the God of truth.

1–5 The prayer opens with an emphatic declaration of trust (vv.1–4; cf. 71:1–3). The psalmist has taken refuge in God (see 7:1): "In you, O LORD," i.e., the covenant-keeping God. In these words he pours out his heart before his Father, who has promised to take care of him. He trusts in Yahweh because he knows that he will not be put to shame (cf. v.17; 22:5; 25:2, 20). The phrase "in you, O Lord" closes the Te Deum (Kirkpatrick, p. 156).

The psalmist's confidence rests in two convictions: Yahweh will deliver for the sake of his name (v.3), and he is the "rock" of his covenant people (vv.2–3). The "name" of Yahweh was revealed to Israel as a part of the Mosaic covenant (Exod 3:15; 6:3; Ps 20:1). The Lord identified with his people by covenant; his honor is at stake when his people hurt, whether collectively or individually (cf. 23:3; 106:8). (See the appendix to Ps 7: The Name of Yahweh.)

Yahweh is the Great Shepherd of his people who saves and guides (vv.2–3; cf. 23:2–3). It may well be that the psalmist is reflecting here on Psalm 23:1–3. The Lord is also the strength or "the rock" of his people. The many synonyms for Yahweh's strength ("rock of refuge," "strong fortress," "my rock and my fortress," "my refuge") express confidence in deliverance. The Lord is known as the "rock" of Israel (Deut

32:4; 1 Sam 2:2; 2 Sam 22:47; 23:3), because of his readiness and ability to deliver his people (see 18:2). The repetition and use of synonyms bears out the intensity of the need and the depth of the author's trust in Yawheh. He further expresses this in the alternation between prayer and affirmation of confidence:

v.2: Turn your ear . . . / come quickly . . . / be my rock of refuge, / a strong fortress to save me.
v.3: Since you are my rock and my fortress, / . . . lead me and guide me.
v.4: Free me . . . , / for you are my refuge.

The metaphors for God reveal both the effect and the nature of God's protection (see the appendix to Ps 98: Yahweh Is the Divine Warrior). He first describes the effect of Yahweh's protection in two phrases: "my rock of refuge" (*ṣûr-mā'ôz*) and "a strong fortress" (*bêṯ m^eṣûḏôṯ*, lit., "a house of fortification"). In v.3 he repeats the thought in an incomplete synonymous expression, "my rock" (*sal'î*) and "my fortress" (*m^eṣûḏāṯî*), leaving out "refuge" (*mā'ôz*). But he completes the symmetry in v.4 by repeating the word "refuge," thus forming an inclusion:

v.2	*ṣûr*	*mā'ôz*	*bêṯ m^eṣûḏôṯ*
v.3	*sal'î*		*m^eṣûḏâṯî*
v.4		*mā'ôz*	

In his prayer the psalmist seeks a demonstration of Yahweh's righteousness (v.1). "Righteousness" (*ṣ^eḏāqāh*, see 4:1) is a divine perfection by which the Lord assures his own that he cares for their well-being: salvation, protection, blessing, vindication, and glory (see appendix to Ps 119: Yahweh Is My Redeemer). He is the righteous Judge who rights what is wrong. The nature of the problem is not specified but involves the enemies who are waiting to "trap" him (v.4). The word "trap" (*rešeṯ*, "net") is a metaphor for the treachery of the enemy (cf. 9:15; 10:9; 25:15; 35:7; 57:6; 140:5; Ezek 19:8).

There is an urgency in the request "come quickly" (v.2). In spite of the travail of his soul, the psalmist submits himself to God's righteousness ("into your hands," v.5) because he is "LORD" (Yahweh), i.e., "the God of truth." As the God of "truth," he distinguishes himself by his loyalty ("faithfulness," v.5; see "love" in v.7 below) in being the "refuge" for his people (vv.2–4).

Throughout the prayer the Lord is addressed in covenant terms. Even in his great need, the psalmist has not lost heart, because he knows his God. His trust in the Lord is an act of abandonment: "Into your hands I commit my spirit" (v.5). These words were spoken by our Lord on the cross (Luke 23:46) as an expression of trust, when he had completed his suffering. God's expectation of his people, before and after Christ, remains the same. Since Jesus submitted himself freely to the Father's will unto death, he expects nothing less from his followers when they suffer for his name (cf. 1 Peter 4:19).

Notes

For a brief discussion of the technical words and phrases in the superscription, see the Introduction.

1–4 (2–5 MT) These verses have a formal correspondence in 71:1–3. There is no need to emend the text (cf. BHS), as the psalmist uses a formulaic (liturgical) language with creative freedom.

B. *Expression of Trust*

31:6–8

6 I hate those who cling to worthless idols;
 I trust in the LORD.
7 I will be glad and rejoice in your love,
 for you saw my affliction
 and knew the anguish of my soul.
8 You have not handed me over to the enemy
 but have set my feet in a spacious place.

6–8 Confident in Yahweh, the palmist moves from the need to the act of rejoicing in anticipation of answered prayer. The psalmist's trust is not blind, because it is focused on Yahweh (v.6). The nature of Yahweh as the covenant God is further described by two related perfections: fidelity ("the God of truth," v.5; see 15:2) and love ("in your love," v.7). These two attributes are often found in pairs (25:10; 61:7; 86:15; 89:14), but here the stereotyped phrase is broken up effectively (vv.5, 7; see Ezra Zion Melamed, "Break-up of Stereotype Phrases as an Artistic Device in Biblical Poetry," *Studies in the Bible*, ed. C. Rabin, Scripta Hierosolymitana 3 [Jerusalem: Magnes, 1961], pp. 115–53). The quality of his fidelity ("truth") is in strong contrast to the "worthless idols" (v.6) that are unable to deliver. The phrase "worthless idols" (cf. Jonah 2:8) is composed of a construct word (*haḇᵉlê*, "vanities of") together with the noun (*šāw'*, "vain"): "vanities of vain." This emphasizes the total worthlessness of idolatry. Rather than calling them by their proper name, the psalmist stresses that idolatry is loathsome.

How different is the Lord, whose "love" finds expression in his acts of deliverance from the enemies (vv.7–8; see the appendix to Ps 25: The Perfections of Yahweh)! The psalmist knows in the depth of his being that Yahweh is still the same ("for you saw . . . and knew," v.7; cf. 9:12–13). He is the God who saw the affliction of the Israelites in Egypt (Exod 2:24). That Yahweh sees and knows is enough, because this is the first stage of his deliverance. The rendering "saw . . . and knew" in the past tense may be contextually improved by a present tense: "I will be glad . . . for you see . . . and know [*y-d-'*]." The knowledge of God is comforting, as it connotes his loving care and concern for the anguish of the psalmist (cf. Exod 2:25; Ps 1:6, NIV, "watches over").

The psalmist rejoices in anticipation of God's act of deliverance. The rejoicing is based on his trust in God's love (*ḥeseḏ*, see 5:7). The use of the jussive in both verbal forms indicates the strong determination: "I will be glad and rejoice" (v.8). The psalmist also reflects on the effects of God's righteous acts. The Lord, as the Great Shepherd, delivers from distress and guides his own into "a spacious place" (cf. 4:1; 18:19). The experience of deliverance results in a new freedom, in which one is surrounded by the peace and security that attend God's salvation.

Notes

6 The LXX and Syriac read "you hate" for "I hate." Several modern versions emend the MT, e.g., NEB, "Thou hatest all who worship useless idols." A.A. Anderson expresses his agreement on the basis of the contrastive use of the waw before "I": "you. . . , but I" (1:248). In favor of the MT (and NIV), it is likely that the psalmist sets up a contrast between his hatred of idolatry and his trust in the Lord. Moreover, the contrast between Yahweh and idolatry and the contrastive inclusion of the verbs in the perfect at the beginning and end in the MT ("I hate. . . , but I trust") argue in favor of the MT.

C. *Prayer for Yahweh's Favor*

31:9–13

9 Be merciful to me, O LORD, for I am in distress;
my eyes grow weak with sorrow,
my soul and my body with grief.
10 My life is consumed by anguish
and my years by groaning;
my strength fails because of my affliction,
and my bones grow weak.
11 Because of all my enemies,
I am the utter contempt of my neighbors;
I am a dread to my friends—
those who see me on the street flee from me.
12 I am forgotten by them as though I were dead;
I have become like broken pottery.
13 For I hear the slander of many;
there is terror on every side;
they conspire against me
and plot to take my life.

9–10 Here the feelings of confidence ebb away in a flood of tears. As in the previous psalm, the psalmist details his troubles in the center of his prayer (cf. 30:6–7). The enemies he has thus far alluded to take on a real shape. They create "distress" (v.9) by their ridicule and shunning, whereas Yahweh creates a "spacious place" (v.8). They are agents of death (vv.9–11), but Yahweh is the Author of life!

In his distress the psalmist casts himself on the mercy or favor of the Lord. He knows that by covenant he has a right to expect the Lord to act, but his situation is so desperate that he cannot wait. His cry for mercy is an expression of deep despair. He describes his desperation as a physical collapse. His joy in life is gone, his strength diminished (cf. 6:6–7; 44:25). The poetical expression need not imply that he is physically sick but could mean that his mental anguish has sapped his physical strength to a point approaching death. The references to "soul," "body" (lit., "belly"), "my life," "my years," "my strength," and "my bones" (cf. 6:2) refer to the whole human being, i.e., physical and spiritual (v.9). He experiences divine abandonment, which is the absence of God's blessing of well-being. He is robbed of the enjoyment of life.

11–13 The psalmist's life ebbs away because of his enemies. He knows that the Lord has promised him life. But he is downcast and disgraced (v.11; cf. 44:13–14; Jer

20:7–8). The enemies have deeply affected him by their slanderous schemes (v.13; Jer 20:10). He feels as if he has been completely rejected by his contemporaries. The phrase "I am forgotten by them" (v.12, lit., "I am forgotten . . . from heart") expresses the depth of despair. The psalmist has become useless "like broken pottery" (cf. Jer 22:28). He is the object of mockery (v.13). He is surrounded by troubles, like Jeremiah who spoke of "terror on every side" in his soliloquies (Jer 6:25; 20:4, 10; 46:5; 49:29). Our psalmist's situation is similar. His enemies dread him like a disease and act as if he does not exist. He is a living corpse, and down deep inside he knows that it is not right. The last clause—"and plot to take my life," v.13—sums up his concern with life over against death, with justice in opposition to injustice, and with Yahweh's fidelity in contrast to the treachery of man.

Notes

9 (10 MT) The verb חָנֵּנִי (*ḥonnēnî,* "be merciful to me") is familiar in the lament psalms (6:9; 30:10; 51:1; 56:1; 123:3). It is related to one of the divine perfections: חַנּוּן (*ḥannûn,* "gracious").

10 (11 MT) The word עָוֹן (*'āwōn*) may be rendered as "wrong," "guilt," or "punishment." In this context it occurs together with "distress . . . sorrow . . . grief. . . . anguish . . . groaning" and as expressions of the harshness of the psalmist's present existence without a confession of his guilt. Symmachus reads "distress" instead, explaining the NIV rendering "affliction." The NIV margin ("*guilt*") reflects the MT.

11 (12 MT) It is preferable to consider an emendation of the MT. The NIV makes a heroic attempt at translating a problematic Hebrew phraseology: "I have become a contempt and to my neighbors greatly" (lit.). The word in question is the last word, מְאֹד (*mᵉ'ōḏ,* "greatly," "very"). The BHS gives several reasonable proposals: "shaking" (i.e., of the head), "terror," "fear." Dahood gives a possible explanation, proposing that the word עֵד (*'ēḏ,* "calamity") is prefixed by an enclitic mem (*Psalms,* 1:189). So Craigie renders, "Because of all my adversaries, I have become a reproach and to my neighbors, a calamity" (*Psalms 1–50,* p. 256).

12 (13 MT) J.J.M. Roberts disagrees with Dahood's rendering—"I have shriveled up like a dead man"—in favor of "I have been forgotten"; see NIV's "I am forgotten by them as though I were dead" ("*Niskaḥtî . . . millēb,* Ps XXXI 13," VetTest [1975]: 797–801). See also Craigie (*Psalms 1–50,* p. 258).

D. *Expression of Trust*

31:14–18

14 But I trust in you, O LORD;
  I say, "You are my God."
15 My times are in your hands;
  deliver me from my enemies
  and from those who pursue me.
16 Let your face shine on your servant;
  save me in your unfailing love.
17 Let me not be put to shame, O LORD,
  for I have cried out to you;
but let the wicked be put to shame
  and lie silent in the grave.

[18]Let their lying lips be silenced,
for with pride and contempt
they speak arrogantly against the righteous.

14–18 In broad strokes the psalmist repeats the various elements already introduced as a transition to the hymn of thanksgiving (vv.19–24). Several phrases are repeated and show a direct connection with the other sections:

v.1: "let me never be put to shame" (so also v.17);
v.2: "come quickly to my rescue; . . . save"; vv.15–16: "deliver me. . . . save me";
vv.2–4: "my rock of refuge, a strong fortress. . . . my rock and my fortress. . . . my refuge"; v.14: "You are my God";
v.4: "Free me from"; v.15: "deliver me from";
v.5: "Into your hands I commit my spirit"; v.15: "My times are in your hands";
v.6: "I trust in the LORD"; v.14: "I trust in you, O LORD";
v.7: "in your love"; v.16: "in your unfailing love."

The repetition reveals the psalmist's heightened sense of confidence in his Redeemer. First, he affirms his basic confidence in Yahweh, his God (v.14). The phrase "my God" is an expression of closeness, endearment, and trust (cf. 22:1; 86:2; 143:10). Second, he commits his circumstances to God's sovereign control (v.15). His life is in God's hands, whether in adversity or in prosperity (cf. Isa 33:6). A.A. Anderson (1:252) suggests that the phrase "my times" may be synonymous with that in v.5: "my life" (NIV, "spirit"). Third, he commits himself to the love of God (v.16). The word *ḥeseḏ* is nothing less than Yahweh's commitment to his children (cf. vv.7, 21). Fourth, he prays for a resolution to the drama: the end of his adversaries (v.17; for "the grave" or "Sheol," see the appendix to Ps 88: Sheol-Grave-Death in the Psalms).

The psalmist trusts that the Lord will honor his prayer so that he need no longer stand shamefaced in the presence of his enemies. When the Lord extends his *love* in his covenant blessing ("let your face shine," v.16; see 4:6; 13:1), then the wicked will be disgraced. Their treachery and scheming will come to an end (vv.17–18; cf. 12:3; 94:4). The psalmist need not say any more about the fate of the wicked, because he is more concerned about his own situation. After all, the Lord also is sovereign over his adversaries (see appendix to Ps 137: Imprecations in the Psalms).

Notes

16 (17 MT) Though the NIV has two separate renderings of חֶסֶד in vv.7, 16 ("love," "unfailing love"), *ḥeseḏ* signifies the constancy of God's love, based on his covenantal commitment.

II. Thanksgiving

31:19–24

[19]How great is your goodness,
which you have stored up for those who fear you,
which you bestow in the sight of men
on those who take refuge in you.
[20]In the shelter of your presence you hide them

from the intrigues of men;
in your dwelling you keep them safe
from accusing tongues.

21 Praise be to the LORD,
for he showed his wonderful love to me
when I was in a besieged city.
22 In my alarm I said,
"I am cut off from your sight!"
Yet you heard my cry for mercy
when I called to you for help.

23 Love the LORD, all his saints!
The LORD preserves the faithful,
but the proud he pays back in full.
24 Be strong and take heart,
all you who hope in the LORD.

The hymn of thanksgiving consists of two separate and related elements: an affirmation of Yahweh's "goodness" (v.19a; cf. 23:6) in his acts of righteousness, love, and grace (vv.19–22) and an encouragement for the godly to persevere in trusting Yahweh (vv.23–24).

19–22 First, Yahweh is "good" by working things out righteously for those who fear him (v.19; cf. Rom 8:28). Those who are wise put their confidence in him. They believe that he does not put them to shame (vv.19–20). Even when they are oppressed like a "besieged city" (v.21), they are protected in "the shelter of [his] presence" (v.20). The author uses verbs expressing the "hidden" but full enjoyment of God's benefits by repeating the roots *ṣ-p-n* ("hide," "store") and *s-t-r* ("hide," "shelter") in an inclusionary way:

v.19a: *ṣ-p-n* ("stored up")
v.20a: *s-t-r s-t-r* ("shelter . . . hide them")
v.20b: *ṣ-p-n* ("you keep them safe").

The Lord keeps his goodness for those who fear him (v.19), and he keeps his own safe in his dwelling (v.20). While he may "hide" (root *s-t-r*) them in his shelter (v.20a), he nevertheless makes it clear "in the sight of men" (v.19b) that the godly are under his protection. The godly on earth are under his guarded protection and are assured that the Lord will openly demonstrate the fullness of his love (see appendix to Ps 132: The Ark of the Covenant and the Temple: Symbols of Yahweh's Presence and Rule).

The psalmist reviews the various ways that Yahweh expresses his covenantal concerns. His righteousness comes to expression in the context of injustice and adversity (v.20). He manifests his "wonderful love" in loneliness and abandonment (v.21). He is also a God of compassion and favor, hearing the cries of his children (v.22). The formula of blessing "praise be to the LORD" (*bārûḵ YHWH;* lit., "blessed is the LORD") expresses the joy of the redeemed after having experienced his salvation (cf. 28:6).

Second, Yahweh is "good" to his people (vv.19–22). He relates with love (*ḥesed*) and fidelity (*'emeṯ*) to the godly so that they may enjoy the benefits of his loving acts. However, his people are those who submit themselves in "fear" to Yahweh (v.19). They are his "saints" (*ḥasîḏāyw*, "his beloved," "his faithful ones," "those who love him," see 4:3). The "saints" persevere in the hope of God's "love" (*ḥeseḏ;* cf. vv.7, 16,

21). The godly who persevere in love and loyalty will be the beneficiaries of Yahweh's loving acts.

23–24 The psalmist confesses his frailty in having questioned God by despairing in his "alarm" (v.22). But he was proven wrong, and Yahweh triumphed. He did hear and did come to his rescue! The psalmist thus encourages the godly to learn from his experience. He exhorts them to persevere in trusting Yahweh, regardless of their circumstances in life (vv.23–24). They must respond to him in a commitment of faith and "love" (*ḥesed̲;* cf. 26:8; 119:47; Deut 6:5; 10:12). Faith is not a one-time commitment. It is a radical call for a lifetime of commitment. Commitment is abandonment to the living God, who has promised to guard ("preserve") his own (v.23). Such is the life of faith. The outcome is uncertain; but faith lets God be God—by responding to him in "love," by living in the strength of "faith" (v.24a), by observing his word (see appendix to Ps 19: The Word of God), and by waiting in the hope of redemption (v.24b; cf. 33:18, 22).

Notes

---

21 (22 MT) The verb הִפְלִיא (*hip̄lî'*, "to deal in a wonderful way," "to do something in a surprising way") relates to the outcome of the love of God—"for he showed in a wonderful way his love to me"—rather than a modification of the kind of love: "his wonderful love" (NIV).

Instead of בְּעִיר מָצוֹר (*be'îr māṣôr*, "in a fortified city"), the BHS gives several proposals representative of modern scholarly opinion: בְּעֵת מָצוֹר (*be'ēt̲ māṣôr*, "in a difficult time"; cf. Kraus, *Psalmen*, 1:393) or בְּעֵת מָצוֹק (*be'ēt̲ māṣôq*, "in a time of oppression"). See Craigie: "in a time of distress" (*Psalms 1–50*, pp. 257–58).

23 (MT 24) The word אֱמוּנִים (*'emûnîm*, "faithful") could be translated as "his faithful" on the basis of the double-duty suffix (cf. A.A. Anderson, 1:254) or by the abstract "faithfulness."

Psalm 32: The Blessing of Forgiveness and Wise Living

Psalm 32 has a special significance in the life of the church and the Christian. It is one of the seven penitential psalms (6; 32; 38; 51; 102; 130; 143), and its association with David encourages the Christian to use the psalm as an assurance of God's forgiveness (see Robert W. Jenson, "Psalm 32," *Interpretation* 32 [1979]: 172–76). Yet this psalm is more than a penitential psalm. It includes elements of thanksgiving (vv.3–8) and wisdom (vv.1–2, 9–11). The thanksgiving is structured within the context of wisdom (cf. Prov 28:13). The psalm shares the wisdom language and forms of expression ("blessed," vv.1–2; "instruct," "teach," "way," "counsel," v.8; contrast between righteous and wicked, v.10; and advantages of godliness, passim). We conclude that Psalm 32 is an adaptation of a *thanksgiving psalm* to the wisdom tradition (see Craigie, *Psalms 1–50*, p. 265).

The didactic element also projects the confession of sin into the context of wisdom. Contrition is viewed here in its truly biblical context as a deep sorrow for sin coupled with and followed by confession, forgiveness, and an openness to the wisdom of God. Brueggemann views this psalm together with the other penitential psalms as examples of psalms of disorientation in which God's people are not asking for redress but for renewal in their covenantal relationship (pp. 94–106).

The psalm shows a clear structure. The blessing (vv.1–2) presupposes the experience of sorrow, confession, and forgiveness (vv.3–5). The experience of forgiveness leads into an encouragement of the godly to find refuge in the Lord (vv.6–7) and to be instructed by him (vv.8–10). The last verse is a fitting closure, as the psalmist calls on the righteous to rejoice in the Lord (v.11).

The expository structure may be outlined as follows:

A. Blessing of Forgiveness (vv.1–2)
  B. Lesson From Experience (vv.3–5)
    C. God's Protection (vv.6–7)
      D. Promise of Wisdom (v.8)
  B′. Lesson From Experience (v.9)
    C′. God's Protection (v.10)
A′. Rejoicing in Forgiveness (v.11)

The advantage of this structure is that it sets apart the promise of God (v.8) as the center of the psalm. The assurance of forgiveness and protection is conditioned on a readiness to learn from the Lord. The person who learns from him is blessed (vv.1–2) and has cause for rejoicing (v.11). For another structure see Craigie (*Psalms 1–50*, p. 265). See also Jack Barentsen, "Restoration and Its Blessing," *Grace Theological Journal* 5 (1984): 247–69.

I. Blessing of Forgiveness

32:1–2

Of David. A *maskil*.

1 Blessed is he
  whose transgressions are forgiven,
  whose sins are covered.
2 Blessed is the man
  whose sin the LORD does not count against him
  and in whose spirit is no deceit.

1–2 By a twofold repetition of "blessed," three synonyms for sin, and a threefold expression of forgiveness, the assurance of forgiveness is promised to the person "in whose spirit is no deceit" (v.2). Forgiveness is freely and graciously given, regardless of whether it be of a "transgression," "sin," or "iniquity" (v.2; NIV, "sin"). The three words for sin may in certain contexts connote different reactions to God and his commandments: (1) "transgression" (*peša'*) is an act of rebellion and disloyalty (cf. TWOT, 2:741–42); (2) "sin" (*ḥ^{a}ṭā'āh*) is an act that misses—often intentionally—God's expressed and revealed will (cf. TWOT, 1:277); and (3) "sin" (*'āwōn*, "iniquity") is a crooked or wrong act, often associated with a conscious and intentional intent to do wrong (cf. TWOT, 2:650). The three words here do not signify three distinct kinds of sin, because the synonyms overlap. The psalmist declares that the forgiveness of sin, of whatever kind—whether against God or man, whether great or small, whether conscientious or inadvertent, or whether by omission or commission—is to be found in God.

The nature of the sin is not as important here as is the blessedness of forgiveness. The three verbs express the absoluteness of divine forgiveness: (1) "are forgiven" (*nᵉśûy*, lit., "carried away") is the act of removal of sin, guilt, and the remembrance of sin (cf. TWOT, 2:600); (2) "are covered" (*kᵉsûy*) is the gracious act of atonement by which the sinner is reconciled and the sin is a matter of the past, so that the Lord does not bring it up anymore as a ground for his displeasure (cf. TWOT, 1:448); (3) "does not count" (*lō' yaḥšōḇ*) expresses God's attitude toward those forgiven as "justified" (cf. TWOT, 1:330).

There is an expression of joyous excitement in these verses. The voice of wisdom is heard in the last colon where the blessedness of forgiveness is contingent on integrity. The Lord hates those who purposely sin against him. God knows the "spirit" of man, whether the request of forgiveness is expressive of true repentance and sorrow for sin or of regrets for the consequences. To teach the godly both the blessedness of forgiveness and the way of integrity, David has given us a psalm to lead the godly into the path of wisdom. The joy of forgiveness was a reality among the OT saints (cf. Rom 4:6–8). How great is the blessedness of all who have tasted of God's forgiveness in Christ (cf. 1 John 1:9)! However, God expects no less from those whom he has forgiven than blamelessness (cf. Rev 14:5).

Notes

For a brief discussion of the technical words and phrases in the superscription, see the Introduction.

1 For the use of "blessed," see 1:1.

1–2 Von Rad correctly observes that the OT rarely gives a theological reflection on sin but underscores the necessity of confession (OTT, 1:154). Ronald Youngblood rightly emphasizes the radical nature of sin as being against God and not just against man or society in "A New Look at Three Old Testament Roots for 'Sin'," *Biblical and Near Eastern Studies. Essays in Honor of William Sanford LaSor*, ed. Gary A. Tuttle (Grand Rapids: Eerdmans, 1978), pp. 201–5.

II. Lesson From Experience

32:3–5

3 When I kept silent,
  my bones wasted away
  through my groaning all day long.
4 For day and night
  your hand was heavy upon me;
my strength was sapped
  as in the heat of summer. *Selah*
5 Then I acknowledged my sin to you
  and did not cover up my iniquity.
I said, "I will confess
  my transgressions to the LORD"—
and you forgave
  the guilt of my sin. *Selah*

3–4 To encourage the pursuit of godliness, the psalmist draws from his own personal experience. If David is the author, it does not follow that the psalm arose out of the context of his sin with Bathsheba and Uriah. He learned that unconfessed sin is a festering sore. The description of the anguish of suffering is compared to the wasting away of "bones" (cf. 6:2) and the sapping of strength (cf. 22:15; Prov 17:22). In Ezekiel's vision of the valley of the bones (ch. 37), the bones signify the hopelessness and meaninglessness of life apart from the grace of God. The language may be metaphorical; hence the psalmist need not have been physically sick to have experienced the Lord's heavy hand on him.

God's discipline weighed so heavily that the psalmist nearly succumbed under its pressure. It was also continuous ("all day long," "day and night," vv.3–4). God's discipline, like the hot, dry Mediterranean summer climate (v.4), dries up the psalmist's vigor like a plant in the heat of summer deprived of water. How different is his condition from the description of the wise man, likened to a verdant tree (1:3)! He did not experience relief until he recognized sin for what it was.

5 In a truly repentant spirit, the psalmist confessed his sin. The three words for sin (vv.1–2) are used again in v.5 but in a different order. The three synonyms for sin associated with three synonyms for forgiveness (two positive and one negative) are now associated with three verbs for confession (two positive and one negative): (1) he "acknowledged" (a Hiphil form from the root *y-d-ʿ*, "to make known"); (2) he "did not cover up" from the same root as "atone" or "cover" (cf. v.1); and (3) he did "confess," a Hiphil form of *y-d-h* ("confess," also "praise"). The exact nature of his sin is here not important because he intends to teach the joy of Yahweh's forgiveness.

Notes

5 The phrase עֲוֹן חַטָּאתִי (*'ᵃwōn ḥaṭṭā'ṯî*, "guilt of my sin") is a compound form of two synonyms for sin. The NEB takes "guilt in a possible sense of "punishment": "the penalty of my sin."

III. God's Protection

32:6–7

6 Therefore let everyone who is godly pray to you
while you may be found;
surely when the mighty waters rise,
they will not reach him.
7 You are my hiding place;
you will protect me from trouble
and surround me with songs of deliverance. *Selah*

6–7 Suffering need not be a form of discipline for sin (cf. Job). However, adversity is always an occasion for the wise in heart to draw near to the Lord in prayer (v.6) and to find solace in him (vv.6–7). The psalmist encourages the "godly" (*ḥasîḏ*, v.6; see 4:3) to draw near to God in his affirmation of God's ability to protect and to deliver from adversity. Even in the greatest of adversities, likened to the rush of water pushing through the narrow confines of a wadi, the Lord will protect those who have sought refuge in him. He is their "hiding place" (v.7; "shelter" in 31:20). Their joy in deliverance expresses itself in joyful shouts as a tribute to God's fidelity.

Notes

6 "While you may be found" is literally "at a time of finding only." The MT is problematic, and many emendations have been proposed (see A.S. van der Woude, "Zwei alte *Cruces* im Psalter," *OudTestamentische Studiën* 13 [1963]: 131–35). One attractive emendation is related to the emendation proposed in 31:21 (31:22 MT), changing the phrase מְצֹא רַק (*meṣō' raq,* "finding only") to מָצוֹר (*māṣôr,* "distress") or מָצוֹק (*māṣôq,* "stress"; see Craigie: "at a time of stress," *Psalms 1–50,* p. 264; cf. RSV, NAB, NEB). There is insufficient evidence to warrant the emendation, and the NIV makes as good a sense out of the text; see Weiser: "It depends, however, on the individual man whether or not he finds God. It comes to pass only if the godly man readily and candidly pours out his soul before God in prayer for his grace" (p. 286).

IV. Promise of Wisdom

32:8

8 I will instruct you and teach you in the way you
should go;
I will counsel you and watch over you.

8 The sudden shift from the encouragement of God's protection (vv.6–7) to the exhortation to wise living (vv.9–11) is due to a word from the Lord. The personal pronoun "I" does not come originally from the mouth of the psalmist. He quotes Yahweh, who has promised to instruct his children, give them wisdom, and watch over them.

The pattern of "three" verbs is resumed in the promise of God. The Lord promises to (1) "instruct" (from the root *ś-k-l,* "give insight," "give understanding"; cf. TWOT, 2:877); (2) "teach" (from the root *y-r-h,* "instruct," "teach," derived noun: *tôrāh,* TWOT, 1:403); and (3) "counsel" (from the root *y-'-ṣ,* "give advice," TWOT, 1:390).

Notes

8 "I will . . . watch over you" is literally "on you my eye" (cf. 33:18; 34:15; Jer 24:6). See Craigie: "I will give you counsel with my eye upon you" (*Psalms 1–50,* p. 264).

V. Lesson From Experience

32:9

9 Do not be like the horse or the mule,

which have no understanding
but must be controlled by bit and bridle
or they will not come to you.

9 The psalmist expands on the word from God by alluding to the world of nature. Animals such as horses or mules must be bridled to be useful. God gives the godly freedom on the highway of godliness. Anything other than the road of wisdom is folly and shows lack of understanding. The psalmist reflects gratefully on his response to the grace of God in his life when God's hand pressed hard on him (vv.3–4). He drew near to the Lord and confessed his sin. The godly draw near to him out of a personal desire for holiness. Those who do not draw near to him to find refuge (v.6) are like animals that have to be held in check.

The use of the plural form of "do not be" has occasioned difficulty in the light of the singular pronominal suffix in v.8 ("you"). The plural form also occurs in v.11 and may best be explained as exhortation and encouragement to the community. The exhortation to seek wisdom is supported by the experience of the psalmist (vv.3–5), by the revelation of God (vv.6–7), by the promise of God (v.8), and by a lesson from nature (v.9).

VI. God's Protection

32:10

10 Many are the woes of the wicked,
but the LORD's unfailing love
surrounds the man who trusts in him.

10 This section is symmetric with vv.6–7. It repeats essentially the assurance of God's protection and love (*ḥesed*) to those who trust in him. The requirement of "trust" is dynamically equivalent to the expression of reliance on the Lord in v.7. The psalmist adds to this the familiar wisdom motif, contrasting God's dealings with the righteous and the wicked (cf. Ps 1). The wicked may experience endless adversities, whereas the wise will experience the constancy of God's love and protection.

VII. Rejoicing in Forgiveness

32:11

11 Rejoice in the LORD and be glad, you righteous;
sing, all you who are upright in heart!

11 The assurances of God's love, protection, guidance, and forgiveness mark the way of wisdom. Therefore the godly are "blessed" (vv.1–2). Even when they sin, they do not continue in adversity like the wicked. The Lord protects them and changes their "groaning" (v.3) into loud, joyful "songs of deliverance" (v.7). The encouragement to wise living concludes with an exhortation to rejoice. The exhortation to "rejoice" (cf. 5:11; 33:1; Phil 3:1; 4:1; 1 Thess 5:16) does not call for making a vain effort to be happy when one does not feel like it. The godly who are mindful of all the benefits (forgiveness, protection, guidance) of the Lord will rejoice! The benefits are not indiscriminate gifts but are limited to the "righteous," who are "upright in heart." These descriptions parallel the blessing in v.2 on those "in whose spirit is no deceit."

Psalm 33: The Lord Is a Sovereign and Gracious Ruler

Although Psalm 33 is commonly classified as a hymn of praise to the Lord "as Creator" (Brueggemann, pp. 28–38), Craigie rightly specifies the principal theme as praise of God's creative activities in the realms of nature and human history (*Psalms 1–50*, pp. 270–71). The psalm begins with an ascription of praise to Yahweh (vv.1–3) and moves through a catalog of divine perfections (vv.4–5) to a contemplation of the power, purpose, and love of the Lord (vv.6–19). The conclusion focuses on a trusting expectation of God's goodness on behalf of his own (vv.20–22).

The structure reveals a cyclical pattern by which each generation is encouraged to praise the Lord for past and present evidences of his love. Consequently, each generation is to expect the Lord to give further reason for praise as the eyes of faith are fixed on him and on a renewal of his love.

A. Song of Praise (vv.1–3)

F. Hope in Yahweh's Love (vv.20–22) B. Perfections of Yahweh (vv.4–5)

E. Yahweh's Love for His People (vv.18–19) C. Yahweh Is the Creator-Ruler (vv.6–11)

D. Yahweh Is the Ruler Over Mankind (vv.12–17)

The above structure clarifies the movement of the psalm from praise to hope, which when fulfilled leads into a new chorus of similar praise.

The precise original situation is commonly associated with Israel's congregational worship in the autumnal festival. Weiser posits that the new year celebration was particularly appropriate for the recitation of the history of redemption and therefore for the praise of God in history (p. 289). Often the underlying assumption is a stereotyped view of how Israel's worship developed. Whether the psalm was sung originally at an autumnal festival or at a covenant renewal festival in celebration of the new year is difficult to determine. There is no consensus on the date and the *Sitz im Leben* (see Craigie, *Psalms 1–50*, p. 271; Jean Marcel Vincent, "Recherches exegetiques sur le Psaume xxxiii," VetTest 28 [1978]: 442–54).

I. Song of Praise

33:1–3

1 Sing joyfully to the LORD, you righteous;
it is fitting for the upright to praise him.
2 Praise the LORD with the harp;
make music to him on the ten-stringed lyre.
3 Sing to him a new song;
play skillfully, and shout for joy.

1–3 The singing of praise to the Lord finds expression in loud and jubilant exultation, accompanied by musical instruments. The worship of God's ancient covenant people was a joyous occasion. The community of worshipers (v.1) consisted of the "righteous" (*ṣaddîq*, see 1:6) and "upright" (*yāšār*, see 7:10; cf. 32:11). Apparently musical instruments had their place in worship. The psalmist only selects the harp (or "lyre") and the ten-stringed lyre as samples of the instruments. We need not infer that there were no other instruments (see appendix to Ps 150: Musical Instruments).

The reason it is "fitting for the upright to praise him" must be understood against the background of vv.4–19. The call to praise (vv.1–3) assumes that the godly know the Lord, submit themselves to his lordship, and affirm a renewal of hope and trust in his love and deliverance (vv.20–22). Every time the godly meet together for the praise of the Lord, they have further reasons for singing to him. The renewal of his loving acts on behalf of his own gives rise to a response of gratitude in a "new song" (v.3). A.A. Anderson writes, "the same old words could allude to fresh experiences of God's providence" (1:261).

The new experiences find expression in a shout for joy at the accompaniment of musical instruments, and the musicians were further inspired by those "shouts" (v.3; cf. 27:6). The apparent frenzy was an exuberant expression of ever-increasing activity, much like the Hasidic festivals. Thus God's people encourage one another in spiritual songs (cf. Eph 5:19). Each new act of God in the history of redemption is a new occasion for praise. The "new song" is new in the sense that it celebrates a *new* act of God's redemption (v.3; cf. 40:3; 96:1; 98:1; 144:9; 149:1; Isa 42:10; Rev 5:9; 14:3).

Notes

Psalms 1; 2; 10; and 33 are the only psalms in Book I without a superscription. The LXX and 4QPs add a superscription linking the psalm with David.

II. Perfections of Yahweh

33:4–5

4 For the word of the LORD is right and true;
he is faithful in all he does.
5 The LORD loves righteousness and justice;
the earth is full of his unfailing love.

4–5 The nature of the Lord is the major reason for the celebration. His perfections inspire the godly with hope (vv.20–22). All the expressions of his nature in his word (v.4), in creation, and in his acts reveal the correspondence between his nature and his self-expressions (v.5). The Lord is faithful ("right and true"). The word "right" is the same as "upright" (*yāšār,* cf. v.1) in Hebrew. An upright person is one without deception (32:2), full of integrity of heart, and the opposite of the perverse (Prov 8:8). It is synonymous with "faithful" (cf. 19:7–8; 25:8–10; 92:15). (See the appendix to Ps 25: The Perfections of Yahweh.)

The Lord "loves" righteousness (*ṣᵉḏāqāh*) and justice (*mišpāṭ*). His verdicts, rule, and relationship with his people are all characterized by a working out of his plans. He delivers and judges, rewards and punishes, gives life and levies death, raises up and abases. Whatever he does is righteous (see 22:31) in that it is an expression of his wisdom and conformity to his will. Whatever he does is just in that there is no unfaithfulness with him. The rule of faith is that whatever God decrees is right, and whatever he brings to pass is faithful and true.

The Lord's love (*ḥesed*) is evident in his works on earth. With respect to the rest of creation, he shows the same loyalty, constancy, and love that has found particular expression in the covenant relationship with his people (v.22). The revelation of God's perfections in his word and in the world guarantee the outworking of his plans on behalf of his own!

III. Yahweh Is the Creator-Ruler

33:6–11

6 By the word of the LORD were the heavens made,
 their starry host by the breath of his mouth.
7 He gathers the waters of the sea into jars;
 he puts the deep into storehouses.
8 Let all the earth fear the LORD;
 let all the people of the world revere him.
9 For he spoke, and it came to be;
 he commanded, and it stood firm.
10 The LORD foils the plans of the nations;
 he thwarts the purposes of the peoples.
11 But the plans of the LORD stand firm forever,
 the purposes of his heart through all generations.

6–7 The psalm reflects on God's creative activities "by the word" (vv.6, 9; cf. Gen 1; Ps 104:1–9; 119:89; John 1:1, 3; Heb 11:1–3). By his word he established order on earth and in heaven. The meditation on creation focuses on his creation of the universe. Space with its "starry host" (v.6) is awe-inspiring (cf. Isa 40:26). The Lord has made it all and rules over the stars and constellations. The Lord easily collects water and piles it up as in storehouses. He contains the seas ("the deep," v.7; cf. 77:16) as easily as a farmer keeps the grain in a storehouse. Rainstorms, hurricanes, flash floods, subterranean waters, and the mighty oceans inspire awe because of their power and existence apart from man. How much greater we should stand in awe of the Lord!

8 The God of Israel is the Creator-Ruler by whose power the constellations are held in place and by whose wisdom the water is stored up. Therefore the nations on earth must fear the Great King (cf. Amos 4:13; 5:8; 9:6; see appendix to Ps 5: Yahweh Is King). The nations feared many gods, each of whom ruled over the various heavenly bodies and over the sky, land, and sea. Though the verb "fear" (*y-r-'*) may connote the wise response of submission and devotion to the Lord (cf. v.18), the "fear" of the nations is more like terror. The nations must react with "terror and dread" (Exod 15:16) to God's power in creation and in history. Since the Lord made everything and rules sovereign over the whole universe, the nations should recognize that he alone is the Creator-Ruler.

9 The nations must also know that the order in the world is not the result of a harmonious coexistence of the gods. Nothing is accidental! Everything reflects God's wise decree. He alone is reliable. Whatever he spoke came into being (cf. Heb 11:3).

He is also powerful and wise. Order in the world reflects God's sovereign rule. His sovereignty is no cause for dread but is a comfort to the godly.

10–11 It is also apparent that there is order on earth. The nations that shine like stars on earth are fully under his control (cf. Prov 19:21; 21:30; Isa 8:10; 19:17; 46:10–11; Jer 29:11; Mic 4:12). Creation and providence are the timely operations of God's purposes. Nothing will "thwart" his plans, which he has purposed for the encouragement of the godly.

Notes

---

7 The MT's נֵד (*nē<u>d</u>,* "heap" [NIV mg.] or "pile") is interpreted by Craigie as an allusion to the piling up of the water by the Red Sea (*Psalms 1–50,* pp. 272–73). The LXX and ancient versions presuppose a form like (*nō'<u>d</u>,* "wineskin"). Dahood reads it as כֶּנֶד (*kene<u>d</u>,* "jar"), as does the NIV. For a rejection of Dahood, see Craigie, *Psalms 1–50,* p. 270.

IV. Yahweh Is the Ruler Over Mankind

33:12–17

> 12 Blessed is the nation whose God is the LORD,
> the people he chose for his inheritance.
> 13 From heaven the LORD looks down
> and sees all mankind;
> 14 from his dwelling place he watches
> all who live on earth—
> 15 he who forms the hearts of all,
> who considers everything they do.
> 16 No king is saved by the size of his army;
> no warrior escapes by his great strength.
> 17 A horse is a vain hope for deliverance;
> despite all its great strength it cannot save.

The psalm gradually focuses on God's involvement with his people. It moves from a consideration of his creative activities to reflection on his providential working among the nations. The emphasis in the previous section was on his power and his steadfast adherence to his plans. This section is a meditation on the election of his people out of all the nations.

12 First, the Lord freely chose to be the God of his people and appointed them to be his "inheritance." Israel received a special status out of all the nations (cf. Exod 19:5; Deut 4:20; 9:26, 29; 32:9; Pss 28:9; 74:2; 78:62, 71; 94:5, 14; 106:5, 40).

13–17 Second, Yahweh sees everything that happens on earth (vv.13–15). As he is seated on his throne in "his dwelling place," he quietly observes the doings of man. He not only knows what happens but also understands what humans are doing and planning because he has created them (v.15). Mankind is accountable to him, the Supreme Judge. Moreover, mankind can never collude so as to thwart God's purposes, because in and through all the planning and affairs of man, God works out his own goals (vv.10–11). He controls man's destiny. Man may look at military stratagems ("army," "warrior," "horse," vv.16–17), but the Lord is sovereign over them all. He alone can save and he alone can bring to nothing (cf. Exod 14:17; 15:3; Deut 33:29; see appendix to Ps 98: Yahweh Is the Divine Warrior).

God's favor ("the eyes of the LORD," v.18; cf. 32:8; 34:15) rests on his own people who "fear him" and "whose hope" is in his "unfailing love" (*ḥesed*, v.18). Therefore God's people have reason to celebrate. They and only they are "blessed" by the very privilege of being a covenant people (v.12).

Notes

14 The word מָכוֹן (*māḵôn*, "dwelling place") may be a technical reference to God's "throne" (Dahood, *Psalms*, 1:200: "from the throne where he sits"). Craigie understands the word as a modifier of God's throne: "He has gazed from his established throne" (*Psalms 1–50*, p. 269).

15 The particle יַחַד (*yaḥaḏ*, "all"; lit., "together") in "hearts of all" is syntactically problematic. Craigie follows the LXX in interpreting it "individually" (*Psalms 1–50*, p. 270). A.A. Anderson gives a preferable interpretation of the LXX's "alone," in the sense that the Lord alone fashions the hearts (1:265).

V. Yahweh's Love for His People

33:18–19

18 But the eyes of the LORD are on those who fear him,
on those whose hope is in his unfailing love,
19 to deliver them from death
and keep them alive in famine.

18–19 The nations depend on military power. A king who readies himself for battle is interested in the number of his warriors and horses. Humanism is in essence a dependence on man—his abilities and the probabilities of his success. The nations on earth are known by the Lord for their planning and dependency on their military arsenal. Regardless of how powerful the enemy may be or how threatening, the godly are reminded that the Lord supervises all the affairs of man ("looks down," "sees," "watches," "considers" (vv.13–15). However, they need not fear the nations because "the eyes of the LORD are on those who fear him" (v.18). The "eyes of the LORD" is a metaphorical expression for his loving care (cf. 34:15).

Success is not dependent on brute force. Because of Yahweh's sovereign and providential rule over all creation and all the nations, and because of his special love for his people, his children can rest assured. Instead of worrying they "fear him." The fear of the Lord here is an expression of dependency and waiting. The godly know that he will deal with them in accordance with his promise of "unfailing love" (v.18) and that he will deliver them from any adversity (v.19). (See the appendix to Ps 119: Yahweh Is My Redeemer.)

VI. Hope in Yahweh's Love

33:20–22

20 We wait in hope for the LORD;
he is our help and our shield.
21 In him our hearts rejoice,
for we trust in his holy name.
22 May your unfailing love rest upon us, O LORD,
even as we put our hope in you.

20 The hymn moves to a new height in the act of renewal of trust. Regardless of what circumstances God's people may experience, and regardless of when they live, each generation witnesses to the new acts of God's love. The people of the Lord here express a renewal of their covenant commitment. Yahweh as their God is their "help" and "shield" (cf. 3:3; 28:7). They trust in his "holy name," with which they associate past acts of deliverance (see 30:4). This psalm, too, ends on the upbeat note of hope and expectancy (cf. 31:1, 24). (See the appendix to Ps 98: Yahweh Is the Divine Warrior.)

21–22 The people affirm their loyalty and trust in the God who has made heaven and earth, who has chosen them to be his people, and who has promised his protection ("help" and "shield," v.20). His "holy name" guarantees the well-being of his children (v.21). Trust requires submission to Yahweh, that is, a willingness to let God be God. The hope of the believing community rises to a new height as it looks expectantly to the Lord, who will work out his plans for the establishment of his kingdom and the renewal of the earth in accordance with his plans. The prayer of the godly is an expression of submission to the will of God. Moreover, in the covenantal relationship privilege is not taken for granted. Therefore the hymn concludes with a prayer, requesting that God will refresh his people with his love (*ḥeseḏ*). Calvin's insight (1:555) is appropriate here:

> In the meantime, the Spirit, by dictating to us this rule of prayer by the mouth of the prophet, teaches us, that the gate of divine grace is opened for us when salvation is neither sought nor hoped for from any other quarter. This passage gives us another very sweet consolation, namely, that if our hope faint not in the midst of our course, we have no reason to fear that God will fail to continue his mercy towards us, without intermission, to the end of it.

At this point in the service of praise, it would have been most fitting to renew the praise of God by returning to vv.1–3 and then to continue singing through all the couplets. Each time the people sang through the hymn, the truth of God's loving care would have been more applied to the hearts of the godly.

Psalm 34: Wise Counsel for the Poor of Heart

The acrostic pattern of Psalm 34 resembles that of Psalm 25 by the omission of the waw and the use of a second peh at the end after taw. It is possible that both acrostic psalms were composed by the same author. The psalm is generally categorized as an *individual thanksgiving hymn,* but the wisdom element (vv.8–22) may well argue in favor of its being a *wisdom psalm* (see Anthony R. Ceresko, "The ABC's of Wisdom in Psalm xxxiv," VetTest 35 [1985]: 99–104; see the appendix to Ps 1: The Ways of Wisdom and Folly).

The structure is not clear because of the acrostic pattern. Two basic themes unfold: thanksgiving and wisdom.

I. Thanksgiving for God's Goodness and Justice (vv.1–7)
   A. Individual and Communal Praise (vv.1–3)
   B. Individual and Communal Experiences (vv.4–7)
II. In Praise of Wisdom (vv.8–22)
   A. Exhortation to Wisdom (vv.8–14)
   B. The Rewards of Wisdom (vv.15–22)

I. Thanksgiving for God's Goodness and Justice (vv.1–7)

A. *Individual and Communal Praise*

34:1–3

Of David. When he pretended to be insane before Abimelech, who drove him away, and he left.

1 I will extol the LORD at all times;
his praise will always be on my lips.
2 My soul will boast in the LORD;
let the afflicted hear and rejoice.
3 Glorify the LORD with me;
let us exalt his name together.

1–3 The psalmist opens with personal praise in the form of a hymn (Kraus, *Psalmen,* 2:267). He blesses the Lord for the acts and words that bring him "praise." He calls attention to what God has done rather than boastfully point to his own works and accomplishments (cf. 49:6; 105:3). The praise of God is continual, God-centered, and the product of a grateful heart. This is the kind of an offering the Lord will not reject (cf. 50:14–23; Hos 14:2; Heb 13:15). His own response to adversity and deliverance is to encourage the poor ("afflicted," v.2; cf. 9:12), that is, people of God who seek him diligently (v.11). The great chorus of all God's saints joyfully celebrates what God has done on behalf of his own. The purpose of praise is not to make God's people feel good but to acknowledge in a communal way the greatness of our God (v.3; cf. 30:1; 69:30; 99:5, 9; 107:32; 145:1).

Notes

For a brief discussion of the technical words and phrases in the superscription, see the Introduction.

B. *Individual and Communal Experiences*

34:4–7

4 I sought the LORD, and he answered me;
he delivered me from all my fears.

5 Those who look to him are radiant;
their faces are never covered with shame.
6 This poor man called, and the LORD heard him;
he saved him out of all his troubles.
7 The angel of the LORD encamps around those
who fear him,
and he delivers them.

4–5 The wise and experienced author teaches from his own experience. He knows what fears are. The "fears" (v.4) pertain to the horrid experiences in life as well as the dread of the unknown (cf. 31:13; Prov 10:24; Isa 66:4). In addition to his personal experience, he has witnessed how God's saints radiate confidence and joy (v.5; cf. Isa 60:5). They, too, looked for the light of his countenance and were blessed with the abundance of his goodness and blessing (27:1, 4). Fear, terror, gloom, and shame have no place as they give way to radiance!

6–7 The psalmist may actually point to someone in the audience as he says, "this poor man" (v.6, or "humble"). Members from within the community of God's people can attest to the truth of what has been said, as they know that the Lord has delivered them from all adversities (cf. v.17; 31:7; see appendix to Ps 119: Yahweh Is My Redeemer). From the specific the author returns to the general. He assures all the godly that the "angel of the LORD" protects God's beloved (v.7). The angel of the Lord may be an indirect reference to the Lord, or it may be an allusion to the host of angels God has charged with the protection of his own (vv.5–6; cf. 91:11; Gen 32:2; 2 Kings 6:17; Matt 4:5–6). However, protection and deliverance are not automatic, because God expects evidence of allegiance in the form of "fear of God" instead of "dread of life."

Notes

4 (5 MT) The "fears" the psalmist speaks of are those concerns that terrorize the soul and occupy one's thoughts. The noun מְגוּרוֹת (*m^egôrôṯ*, "horrors" or "dread") occurs only three times (Ps 34:4; Prov 10:24; Isa 66:4). "Dread is in stark contrast to the delights of the righteous (Prov 10:24), as the wicked experience "dread" as divine abandonment (Isa 66:4).

5 (6 MT) The emendations proposed by BHS call for an imperative reading of the verbs and a change in the pronominal suffix from "their" to "your"; cf. NEB, "Look towards him and shine with joy; no longer hang your heads in shame" (cf. Craigie, *Psalms 1–50*, pp. 276–77). Though there is some MS support for the changes, the MT makes good sense. The ambiguity of the subject is contextually defined and may be inherent in the acrostic device.

II. In Praise of Wisdom (vv.8–22)

A. *Exhortation to Wisdom*

34:8–14

8 Taste and see that the LORD is good;
blessed is the man who takes refuge in him.

[9]Fear the LORD, you his saints,
for those who fear him lack nothing.
[10]The lions may grow weak and hungry,
but those who seek the LORD lack no good thing.

[11]Come, my children, listen to me;
I will teach you the fear of the LORD.
[12]Whoever of you loves life
and desires to see many good days,
[13]keep your tongue from evil
and your lips from speaking lies.
[14]Turn from evil and do good;
seek peace and pursue it.

8–10 There is no experience of God's goodness without a corresponding godliness. The three imperatives "taste and see" and "fear" are complementary. The wise "taste" God's goodness for themselves by taking "refuge" (v.8) in him and by submitting their way of life to his ("fear," v.9). "Blessed" is the man who finds refuge in the Lord (v.8; cf. 2:12; 5:11; 7:1; 11:1), because he will taste and see that the Lord is good (cf. 1 Peter 2:3). Blessed are those who "fear" him, because they will lack nothing (cf. 23:1). For a third time the psalmist encourages godliness (v.10), by contrasting the godly with young lions (a metaphor for "the rich" or "the strong"? see Notes) who may suffer want. The whole thrust of this section is an encouragement to seek the Lord, because he provides for all man's needs (cf. Matt 6:33).

11–14 The teacher addresses also the younger members of the community. In wisdom literature the students of the sages are known as "sons" or "children" (v.11; cf. Prov 1:8; 4:1). The first lesson in the school of wisdom is "the fear of the LORD" (v.11; cf. vv.9–10; Prov 1:7). The fear of the Lord expresses itself in a submission to his way. The second lesson in the school of wisdom consists in doing the will of God: integrity of language versus deception (v.13; cf. Jer 4:2), practice of good versus evil (v.14; cf. 37:3, 27), and pursuit of peace versus trouble (vv.14, 17; cf. Rom 14:19; Heb 12:14). The reward of wisdom is already enjoyed in this life (v.12), because God is good to those who seek him (vv.8–10). He looks on them with favor and is responsive to their needs (v.15). He cares for them, protects them, answers their prayers, and delivers them from troubles. But he hates evil and will completely rid the earth of all the wicked. His "face" has turned in anger against them (cf. 80:19) so that they will be no more (v.16).

Notes

9 (10 MT) The use of קְדֹשָׁיו (*qᵉḏōšāyw*, "his saints" or "his holy ones") is distinctive, as it rarely applies to the godly. The Lord and his angels are holy, but so are his people. The word *qāḏôš* ("holy") as an adjective describes the consecration of God's people (cf. Lev 11:44–45; 19:2; 20:7; 21:6; Num 15:40), but the adjective has here a substantial force: "the holy ones," as in NT's "the saints."

10 (11 MT) The LXX ("the rich") may have read כַּבִּירִים (*kabbîrîm*, "mighty ones") for כְּפִירִים (*kᵉp̄îrîm*, "lions"). The MT need not be altered because the word "lions" may be a metaphor for those who are strong, oppressive, and evil (cf. 17:12; 35:17). See J.J.M. Roberts, "The Young Lions of Psalm 34:11," *Biblica* 54 (1973): 256–67.

12 (13 MT) "Whoever" (lit., "who this is the man," MT) is an emphatic manner of calling the attention of people to the importance of wisdom. The interrogative "who" also implies a strong positive response, as if to say, "Who loves life and desires to see many good days?" The answer is everyone! But only those who follow the sage counsel of vv.13–14 may enjoy life.

B. *The Rewards of Wisdom*

34:15–22

15 The eyes of the LORD are on the righteous
  and his ears are attentive to their cry;
16 the face of the LORD is against those who do evil,
  to cut off the memory of them from the earth.

17 The righteous cry out, and the LORD hears them;
  he delivers them from all their troubles.
18 The LORD is close to the brokenhearted
  and saves those who are crushed in spirit.

19 A righteous man may have many troubles,
  but the LORD delivers him from them all;
20 he protects all his bones,
  not one of them will be broken.

21 Evil will slay the wicked;
  the foes of the righteous will be condemned.
22 The LORD redeems his servants;
  no one will be condemned who takes refuge in him.

15–22 The psalmist returns to the main theme of an encouragement to wisdom. The "ears" of the Lord (v.15) hear the cry of the righteous (v.17). His "face" (v.16) is close to his needy children, who are "brokenhearted" (v.18; cf. 51:17; 147:3) and "crushed" (v.18). They need not be overcome by their troubles, even though they are fully aware of their self-limitations as they walk humbly before their God. The psalmist is realistic in his portrayal of life. The righteous do not escape trouble. The way of wisdom assures those who walk by it that God is present (vv.15, 17), even when they suffer "many troubles" (v.19). As many troubles as they experience, they need not be afraid, because they are not alone. The Lord will deliver his own. The protection of "bones" is a metaphor for the Lord's care for his own. Evil will overcome the wicked. They will perish (v.21; cf. 1:6). The godly in contrast find the Lord to be faithful. Those who trust (cf. v.8) in him will not perish (v.22).

Notes

---

17 (18 MT) The NIV follows the LXX, Syriac, and Targum in the addition of "the righteous," absent from the MT. It clarifies what is already understood from the context (v.15).

Psalm 35: A Prayer for Vindication

With great emotion and urgency, David prays this prayer. The context in which the psalm arose is not certain as the language of this psalm shifts between legal and military. Whether the psalmist had been maligned and required vindication of his name or whether the problem was of international proportion (cf. Craigie, *Psalms 1–50*, pp. 285–88) is not clear. There is sufficient ambiguity in the psalm that it may be classified as an *individual lament.*

The varied metaphors (legal, judicial, martial, and hunting) add to the colorful expressions in the psalm. The prayer may be divided into three sections (vv.1–10, 11–18, 19–28), each of which in a repetitive and overlapping manner calls on the Lord to act on behalf of the psalmist. Because of the individual and general nature of the prayer, it expresses in words the feelings of our hearts whenever injustice comes into our lives. Jesus identified with those who suffer without apparent cause, because he applies the words of v.19 (cf. 69:4) to himself (John 15:25). The structure of the psalm follows the sections above with further subdivisions:

A. Call on the Divine Warrior (vv.1–3)
  B. Prayer for Vindication (vv.4–10)
    C. The Troubled Soul (vv.11–18)
  B′. Prayer for Vindication (vv.19–25)
A′. Joy of Deliverance (vv.26–28)

I. Call on the Divine Warrior

35:1–10

Of David.

1 Contend, O LORD, with those who contend with me;
fight against those who fight against me.
2 Take up shield and buckler;
arise and come to my aid.
3 Brandish spear and javelin
against those who pursue me.
Say to my soul,
"I am your salvation."
4 May those who seek my life
be disgraced and put to shame;
may those who plot my ruin
be turned back in dismay.
5 May they be like chaff before the wind,
with the angel of the LORD driving them away;
6 may their path be dark and slippery,
with the angel of the LORD pursuing them.
7 Since they hid their net for me without cause
and without cause dug a pit for me,
8 may ruin overtake them by surprise—
may the net they hid entangle them,
may they fall into the pit, to their ruin.
9 Then my soul will rejoice in the LORD
and delight in his salvation.
10 My whole being will exclaim,
"Who is like you, O LORD?
You rescue the poor from those too strong for them,
the poor and needy from those who rob them."

1 The psalmist boldly opens his case with an appeal to God's justice. The verb "contend" (*rîḇ*) is a legal term, frequently used among the prophets (TWOT, 2:845). Dahood prefers the translation "attack" instead of "contend" and "who fight against me." Even though Hebrew usage permits this translation and it fits well within the context, the NIV and most commentators see two complementary pictures: one legal and the other martial. The legal imagery is further developed in the confession of God's justice in v.10 (cf. vv.22–25).

2–3a In need of help the psalmist casts his burden on the Lord and asks him to represent his case as counselor and prosecutor (v.2). The metaphor of a lawsuit changes to that of warfare. The Lord is likened to a warrior who contends on behalf of his own. He comes with a small shield (*māḡēn*) and a "buckler" (*ṣinnāh*, a large, possibly rectangular, shield often carried by a shield-bearer; cf. 1 Sam 17:7, 41), together with a "spear and javelin" (v.3a). The weapons symbolize God's readiness to defend his own.

3b The psalmist is in need of the reassuring words: "I am your salvation" (*yešû'āh*). The use of the pronoun "I" (*'ānî*) may be an abbreviation of a longer phrase: "I am Yahweh, your salvation" (cf. Isa 49:26; 60:16). In biblical usage the pronoun "I" when referring to the Lord signifies the God who has promised to be the Deliverer of his own, the covenant God, and the God who revealed himself as "I am Yahweh" (Exod 6:6–8). The psalmist is not only looking for divine assurance but also for a new act of God: "salvation" (see appendix to Ps 119: Yahweh Is My Redeemer). Salvation signifies more than reconciliation with God, since God, being reconciled with the psalmist, comes to his defense. The biblical view of life is such that a threat to the well-being of soul or body requires a divine act of deliverance, including vindication of the people of God and vengeance on the enemy.

4–8 Prayer for God's deliverance is followed by a prayer for God's vengeance on the enemies. He calls for God's judgments (imprecations) to fall on the enemies in the forms of "shame" (i.e., military defeat, v.4), "chaff" (i.e., worthlessness, v.5), "dark and slippery" paths (i.e., troubles and uncertainties, v.6), and "ruin" (i.e., sudden and complete desolation, v.8). The imprecations are curses invoked on the enemy. Between a series of four imprecations (vv.4–6) and three imprecations (v.8), the psalmist affirms his innocence of any wrongdoing (v.7). The words "without cause" are repeated for the sake of emphasis. The statement of unjust treatment is followed by three more imprecations (v.8) and a climactic statement of the anticipated deliverance (see the Introduction for a discussion on the imprecations in the Psalms). The apostle Paul applies the execration (v.8) to Israel's hardening toward the gospel (cf. Rom 11:7–10).

9–10 The use of the jussive throughout ("may," vv.4–6, 8)—a total of seven times—is to be connected with v.9 by means of a resultative waw, best translated as "so that" (NIV, "Then"). When the Lord's justice is expressed against the wicked, then the righteous rejoice in the Lord!

The activities of the enemies are realistically portrayed by the usage of the participial forms of the verbs ("who fight against me," "those who pursue me," "those who seek my life," "those who plot my ruin," vv.1, 3–4). Parallel with this is the use of participles expressive of the activities of the angel of the Lord ("driving them away" and "pursuing them," vv.5–6). These participles are distinguished from the use of the perfect and imperfect in vv.7–10. The agent of the judgments is the "angel of the LORD" (vv.5–6). The angel of the Lord protects the godly (34:7) and in so doing works death and disaster on all who plan trouble for God's children (cf. vv.7–8; cf. 7:15; 9:15; 57:6). The Lord has commanded his angels to protect his people who love him (cf. v.5; 34:7; 91:11–16).

When the righteous witness the Lord's salvation, they have cause for rejoicing (vv.9–10). The nature of the rejoicing is such that David exclaims with his whole being, "Who is like you, O LORD?" (v.10). The exclamation arises out of anticipation of the divine deliverance. He knows that the Lord is his Helper and Savior (vv.2–3). He knows that he has to wait; but in the meantime he confesses that Yahweh is just to the needy (v.10). The question in v.10a is a Hebraic way of confessing with deep conviction that there is no other than Yahweh who delivers the "poor and needy" (cf. 37:14) and who is powerful and just (cf. Exod 15:11; Pss 71:19; 89:8; Mic 7:18). Since Yahweh alone is the Powerful Warrior, he will save all his people in need, including the psalmist. David has argued from his own situation to a more general affirmation of God's goodness to all. When the Redeemer-Warrior comes to bring in righteousness, the psalmist, too, will join in songs of praise together with the throngs of those redeemed from their troubles, oppressions, and afflictions. He believes that Yahweh is the Divine Warrior, who rules in his acts of vengeance and deliverance (v.10).

Notes

For a brief discussion of the technical words and phrases in the superscription, see the Introduction.

3 The Hebrew word סְגֹר (*s^eg̱ōr*) is an infinitive construct form of *s-g-r* ("close"). Assumedly this is a loan word with the meaning "double axe" or "(socket of a) javelin," and if so the word should be read as a noun: *sāg̱ār* or *seg̱er* ("javelin," BHS; see Dahood, *Psalms*, 1:210–11). The NIV adds a marginal note reflecting the MT: "Or *and block the way.*"

10 The NIV's "my whole being" is an appropriate idiomatic rendering for the MT's "all my bones" (cf. 6:2; 51:8).

II. The Troubled Soul

35:11–18

11 Ruthless witnesses come forward;
they question me on things I know nothing about.
12 They repay me evil for good
and leave my soul forlorn.
13 Yet when they were ill, I put on sackcloth
and humbled myself with fasting.
When my prayers returned to me unanswered,
14 I went about mourning
as though for my friend or brother.
I bowed my head in grief
as though weeping for my mother.
15 But when I stumbled, they gathered in glee;

attackers gathered against me when I was unaware.
They slandered me without ceasing.
16 Like the ungodly they maliciously mocked;
they gnashed their teeth at me.
17 O Lord, how long will you look on?
Rescue my life from their ravages,
my precious life from these lions.
18 I will give you thanks in the great assembly;
among throngs of people I will praise you.

11–16 The confidence in the Lord and the readiness to call the judgment of God on the psalmist's enemies ebbs away in lament. The lament arises, not because of self-pity, but because of the disruption of order in God's kingdom. The psalmist feels himself betrayed by those he has done good to in the past (vv.11–16). He had shown concern for the affliction of others by tokens of mourning (sackcloth, weeping, and fasting, vv.13–14; cf. 2 Sam 12:16, 20) and by intercessory prayer (vv.13–14). One such expression of concern is recorded in David's mission to Hanun at the occasion of his father's death, when his messengers were disgraced by the Ammonite nobles (2 Sam 10:1–5).

In his adversity (v.15) the psalmist found out that his allies were unreliable friends. They had brought him low ("when I stumbled," v.15; cf. 38:17; Jer 20:10). They used false witnesses to accuse him (v.11), to slander him (v.15), and to express their anger against him (v.16). Over against their wicked challenges to his innocence, he claims that he does not "know those who came forward" with the charges (v.11; see Notes).

17–18 In addition the psalmist also experienced that the Lord was far from him (v.17). His enemies have become like wild animals. He laments to his God, "O Lord, how long will you look on?" The reference to God as "Lord" (= Master) may be deliberate. The Master of the universe must have seen all that the rogues have done, but how long will it be before he will act justly?

The psalmist's question of God's justice is an expression of hope in God's ultimate faithfulness. He has become an international spectacle, and the honor of his people and of his God is at stake. When the Lord has shown his mercy on the king, he will lead the congregation in praise (v.18; cf. 22:22, 25; 40:9–10). To this end he appeals to the Lord for deliverance so that he may proclaim publicly the mighty works of the Lord.

Notes

11 Craigie takes יִשְׁאָלוּנִי (*yiš'ālûnî*, "they question me") in the technical sense of legal interrogation (*Psalms 1–50*, p. 285).

The NIV rendering "things I know nothing about" is possible for the problematic Hebrew phrase אֲשֶׁר לֹא־יָדַעְתִּי (*'ašer lō'-yāḏa'tî*, lit., "who/which I do not know/have not known"). However, in view of the parallelism with "ruthless witnesses" and the repetition of the identical phrase in the MT of v.15, defining the "attackers" as "those I do not know" (NIV, "when I was unaware"), the psalmist denotes the accusers as those who were not known to him. Either he did not recognize his friends because of the ways they had changed, or he means that his former allies had sent messengers whom he did not know. The strain caused by his troubles (v.15) and the malicious acts of his former friends were too much for him.

12 The NIV's "and leave my soul forlorn" is an attempt at giving some sense to a problematic reading of the MT: "childlessness of my soul." The BHS gives several possible emendations, one of which, שָׂכוּ (*śākû*, "they lie in wait for"), underlies the NEB's "lying in wait to take my life" (cf. Kraus, *Psalmen*, 1:426).

13 The emphatic וַאֲנִי (*wa'ᵃnî*, "but I"; NIV, "Yet . . . I") contrasts the concern of the psalmist with the evil of his former allies.

15 The underlying Hebrew text of "attackers" is problematic. Some emend the word נֵכִים (*nēkîm*, "cripples") to כְּנָכְרִים (*kᵉnokrîm*, "like foreigners," cf. BHS). Dahood proposes another emendation: נֹכִים (*nōkîm*, "smiters"; cf. *Psalms*, 1:213). The NIV reflects Dahood's proposed translation: "When I stumbled they gathered with glee, smiters gathered around me" (ibid., 1:209, 213). Craigie reads תֹּכִים (*tōkîm*, "oppressors"), based on 4QPsa (*Psalms 1–50*, p. 285).

The NIV's "slandered me" is a Dahoodian rendering. Dahood gives an explanatory translation: "they . . . tore me to pieces, and did not desist from slandering me" (*Psalms*, 1:209). The verbal phrase "from slandering me" comes from v.16a through a Dahoodian form of etymology and emendation (ibid., 1:214). Craigie is more literal: "they tore me apart and would not desist" (*Psalms 1–50*, p. 283; see his criticism of Dahood, p. 285).

16 The first colon of this verse is highly problematic. The NIV emends the meaningless MT phrase לַעֲגֵי מָעוֹג (*la'ᵃgê mā'ôg*, "derisions of the supply") to לַעֲגֵי לָעַג (*la'ᵃgê lā'ag*, "derisions of the derision") and understands it as a superlative expression: "Like the ungodly they maliciously mocked," as does Allen: "With the profanities of derisive mockery" (p. 283). The NIV margin ("ungodly circle of mockers") is based on Dahood's rendition: "My encircling mockers gnashed their teeth at me" (*Psalms*, 1:209).

III. Prayer for Vindication

35:19–25

19 Let not those gloat over me
who are my enemies without cause;
let not those who hate me without reason
maliciously wink the eye.
20 They do not speak peaceably,
but devise false accusations
against those who live quietly in the land.
21 They gape at me and say, "Aha! Aha!
With our own eyes we have seen it."

22 O LORD, you have seen this; be not silent.
Do not be far from me, O Lord.
23 Awake, and rise to my defense!
Contend for me, my God and Lord.
24 Vindicate me in your righteousness, O LORD my God;
do not let them gloat over me.
25 Do not let them think, "Aha, just what we wanted!"
or say, "We have swallowed him up."

19–25 The psalmist returns with a final portrayal of injustice. He has been innocently betrayed by those who were his allies. They have turned against him in their speech, betrayed their ill-feelings with their eyes, and rejoiced in his misfortunes. They have opposed the king and his people ("those who live quietly in the land," v.20). Their words sound harsh as they claim to have evidence against him. The witnesses (v.11) have stood up and have testified, "with our own eyes we have seen it" (v.21).

In view of the injustice of the former allies, the psalmist trusts his case to the Lord. They are filled with treachery and twist the truth to their advantage (vv.19–21; cf. 38:19). Yahweh, too, has seen (v.22; cf. v.17) and will not remain quiet (v.22; cf. 28:1). Not only has he seen what the psalmist has done, he has also seen the evil done against his anointed servant. Based on his hope in God's justice, the psalmist casts himself on the Lord with the request that he act now by vindicating him (v.24; cf. 26:1; 43:1). The "righteousness" of God, his Lord, the Master of the universe, is at stake (vv.23–24; cf. 9:8; 22:31; 31:1; 33:5). (See the appendix to Ps 5: Yahweh Is King.)

First, the psalmist prays that the Lord may act on his behalf so that the enemies will not be overcome with feelings of victory (vv.22–25). These verses reveal an internal balance with two sets of two negative imperative statements ("be not silent"; "Do not be far"; and "Do not let them think," or "say," lit., "do not let them say," twice). Between the symmetry of vv.22 and 24, he calls on the Lord to stir himself to do justice on earth (vv.23–24; cf. 7:6, 8, 17; 31:1). David is convinced that God's speedy trial will end the irritating joviality of the enemies (cf. the repetition of "let not those gloat over me," vv.19, 24).

IV. Joy of Deliverance

35:26–28

26 May all who gloat over my distress
  be put to shame and confusion;
may all who exalt themselves over me
  be clothed with shame and disgrace.
27 May those who delight in my vindication
  shout for joy and gladness;
may they always say, "The LORD be exalted,
  who delights in the well-being of his servant."
28 My tongue will speak of your righteousness
  and of your praises all day long.

26–28 Second, the psalmist prays that justice and righteousness may triumph. Yet this time (v.26) his prayer goes beyond the series of imprecations cast against those who attacked him personally (vv.4–8). In those verses he looked forward only to personal relief. In these last verses he contrasts the wicked and the godly by praying that the enemies of God may suffer the curses of the covenant (v.26; cf. v.4). He also prays for the Lord's people, who suffered disgrace when their anointed king was disgraced. The psalmist's ultimate hope is in the redemption of God's people.

When justice returns to earth, then God's people will be filled with joy and will express their joy to the glory of God (v.27). Their prayer will be for the enlargement of God's kingdom over against the self-exaltation of the enemies. The triumph of the Lord's justice evidences God's love for his servant David, his concern for his well-being, and—by means of the Lord's anointed—his loyalty to Israel's well-being (v.20, lit., "peace," *šālôm;* NIV, "peaceably").

Then the "tongue," which has thus far been the instrument of petition and imprecation, will again praise the Lord for his "righteousness" (v.28; cf. 71:24). The psalm began with a petition for God to act as a judge and lawyer (vv.1–3) and concludes on a note of personal praise. David had expressed the desire to praise the Lord for his justice (vv.10–11) and to give public thanksgiving in the great assembly (v.18). The psalm ends with the hope that both the godly who have joined him in prayer for vindication and God's anointed king may praise God for showing concern for "peace" (NIV, "well-being," v.27) and for "righteousness" (v.28).

Notes

20 The godly are described here only as "those who live quietly in the land." They are people of peace who "delight" in the peace of the kingdom and the well-being of their king (cf. v.27).

27 "Vindication" is literally "righteousness." Because the word צֶדֶק (*ṣeḏeq*, "righteousness") occurs here as well as in v.28, it is preferable to give a consistent translation. The psalmist prayed for God's righteousness (v.24), and he is joined in prayer by the godly who long for the effective manifestation of God's righteousness (cf. 33:5). The effect of God's righteousness is his "vindication" of his servant (see 4:1).

Psalm 36: The Blessedness of the Wise

Commentators have uncovered a variety of genres in Psalm 36: individual lament, wisdom, and hymnic. It is possible to categorize vv.1–4 as a lament with wisdom overtones, vv.5–9 as a hymn, and vv.10–12 as a prayer. It is not uncommon to have mixed genres in the Psalms, and this phenomenon may well reflect the shortcomings of form-criticism. Dahood has observed, "The coexistence of three literary types within a poem of thirteen verses points up the limitations of the form-critical approach to the Psalter" (*Psalms*, 1:218).

We agree with Craigie that the psalm "must be viewed primarily as a literary and devotional composition, in which the poet has blended different literary types in his creative purpose" (*Psalms 1–50*, p. 291). The final product is best understood as a wisdom psalm, even if it means that the first four verses set the mood for interpretation. (See the appendix to Ps 1: The Ways of Wisdom and Folly.)

The structure shows a balanced, chiastic development of wisdom in contrast to ungodliness:

A. The Nature of the Wicked (vv.1–4)
  B. The Wisdom of God (vv.5–6)
  B′. The Joys of Wisdom (vv.7–9)
A′. Prayer of Protection From Evil (vv.10–12)

(See also R.J. Tournay, "Le Psaume XXXVI: Structure et Doctrine," RB 90 [1983]: 5–22.)

I. The Nature of the Wicked

36:1–4

For the director of music. Of David the servant of the LORD.

1 An oracle is within my heart
  concerning the sinfulness of the wicked:
There is no fear of God
  before his eyes.

2 For in his own eyes he flatters himself
too much to detect or hate his sin.
3 The words of his mouth are wicked and deceitful;
he has ceased to be wise and to do good.
4 Even on his bed he plots evil;
he commits himself to a sinful course
and does not reject what is wrong.

1–4 The ungodly lives with no concern for the fear of God, which is the beginning of wisdom (Prov 1:7). He deceives himself into thinking that God neither knows nor cares about evil in the world (v.1). His speech reflects the total disregard for wisdom or godliness ("the fear of God"; cf. Rom 3:18). Instead, it is evil and deceptive (v.3). Evil is his companion, even when he is alone in bed (v.4). He thinks of getting ahead, of his own good, without concern for justice and righteousness.

Verse 4 explicates v.3b. The phrase "on his bed" is parallel with "on the way" (NIV, "course"). The ungodly considers evil both in his lying down and in his walking, being firmly committed to the way of evil over against the way of God. The wicked man takes "a firm stand" (NIV, "he commits himself," v.4; cf. 1:1; Prov 16:29–30; Isa 65:2) in his commitment to wrongdoing. His speech reflects his inner being in that his words are "wicked and deceitful" (v.3; cf. 5:5–6; 10:7). His thoughts, speech, and acts harmoniously mirror the inner "evil" of his being (vv.3–4). With the rejection of wisdom (v.3), he no longer rejects "what is wrong" (v.4; cf. Prov 2:14).

Notes

For a brief discussion of the technical words and phrases in the superscription, see the Introduction.

1 (2 MT) The expression נְאֻם־פֶּשַׁע (*ne'um-peša'*, "an oracle of transgression") is a *hapax legomenon.* The NIV has made an attempt at interpreting the difficult clause. The ancient versions treat the noun "oracle" as a verb, "say" or "speak," and the noun "transgression" as a participial form of the verb "transgress," giving the resultant possibility: "The rebel speaks wickedly deep in his heart" (A.A. Anderson, 1:287). Craigie takes "oracle" independently as a heading: "An oracle" (*Psalms 1–50*, pp. 289–90). Kraus (*Psalmen*, 1:280–81) gives a good survey of the problems, but we cannot agree with his emendation: *nā'îm* ("pleasant," p. 281; cf. BHS). The word *ne'um* may also be translated as "utterance," and if the phrase "an utterance of transgression" is linked with "within his heart" (instead of "my heart," based on several Hebrew MSS; cf. LXX, Syr.), the resultant translation gives sense to the MT: "An utterance of transgression belongs to the wicked, within his heart" (see NIV mg.: "*heart: / Sin proceeds from the wicked*"). See Dahood: "Perversity inspires the wicked man within his heart" (*Psalms*, 1:217–18).

The word for "fear" is פַּחַד (*paḥaḏ*) instead of the usual יִרְאָה (*yir'āh;* cf. Prov 1:7). See the appendix to Ps 78: The Wonderful Works of Yahweh.

2 (3 MT) This verse is equally difficult. One meaning is given by the NIV (cf. Craigie, *Psalms 1–50*, p. 289). Another sense is suggested by A.A. Anderson: "The general idea of the verse is that the godless person deludes himself in believing that God will neither find out his sin or hate it (or him)" (1:287).

II. The Wisdom of God

36:5–6

5 Your love, O LORD, reaches to the heavens,
your faithfulness to the skies.
6 Your righteousness is like the mighty mountains,
your justice like the great deep.
O LORD, you preserve both man and beast.

5 Before reflecting on the joys of wisdom, the psalmist sets up a contrast between the way of the fools and the way of God. Thus he creates an antithesis from which the wise should deduce the superiority of godliness. The qualities reflecting the Lord's wisdom are "love," "faithfulness," "righteousness," and "justice." God's love and faithfulness are complementary terms, so also his righteousness and justice. The faithfulness guarantees the constancy of his "love" (*ḥesed*) for his own. God's righteous nature will effect justice on earth so that the righteous will experience his salvation and the wicked his judgment. (See the appendix to Ps 25: The Perfections of Yahweh.)

6 God's wisdom affects everything he has created: heaven, mountains, and "the great deep" (cf. 33:7). There is nothing that does not reflect the constancy of his love, his righteousness, and his justice (cf. Rom 8:38–39; 11:33). The Creator-God is wise, as everything is upheld by his wisdom. His wisdom has a particular concern for his own creatures, "man and beast" (cf. Pss 104; 147). By his love and justice they live and enjoy living (see Notes).

Notes

---

6 (7 MT) "Mighty mountains" is a proper translation of the Hebrew superlative הַרְרֵי־אֵל (*harrê-'ēl*, "mountains of God"). Craigie renders it as a superlative of magnificence: "like the marvelous mountains" (*Psalms 1–50*, pp. 289–90).

The verb תוֹשִׁיעַ (*tôšîa'*, from *y-š-'*, "save," "rescue"; NIV, "preserve") signifies the preservation and protection of all life. A.A. Anderson concludes, " 'to save' in this verse may mean 'to preserve the life of. . .' or 'to provide for every need (of both man and beast)' " (1:289).

III. The Joys of Wisdom

36:7–9

7 How priceless is your unfailing love!
Both high and low among men
find refuge in the shadow of your wings.
8 They feast on the abundance of your house;
you give them drink from your river of delights.
9 For with you is the fountain of life;
in your light we see light.

7–9 The wisdom of God explains his goodness toward man. God is truly concerned for man (cf. John 3:16). The use of the phrase *bᵉnê 'āḏām* (lit., "sons of mankind"; NIV, "low among men"; see note on v.7; cf. 14:2) bears out God's universal concern for mankind. God's "love" (*ḥeseḏ*) extends to all his creation: "both man and beast" (v.6). The general reference to him as "God" (Elohim) points to his love as an expression of his involvement as the Creator. The Creator protects, feeds, and gives drink. All creatures exist by the goodness of the royal host (cf. Ps 104).

Yet the psalmist extends the imagery particularly to the godly. From the context it is preferable to limit the privilege of God's special protection to godly people (cf. v.8). (For the imagery of God's serving as host of the godly, see 15:1; 23:5–6; 24:3; 27:4; 65:4; Isa 25:6–8; 33:16; Rev 19:9.) They alone have a right to find protection under the "shadow of his wings" (v.7; cf. 17:8). They alone have access to his "house" (v.8; i.e., the temple), where the godly enjoy the communal meals as a token of God's goodness and provisions for them (Isa 65:13). They are given to drink, as it were, from the "river of delights" and the "fountain of life" (vv.8–9). The terms "abundance," "house," "river," and "fountain" evoke the imagery of the blessedness of wisdom. Wisdom is personified as preparing a banquet of rich foods for the wise (Prov 9:1–5) and as flowing like a river or fountain (Prov 10:11; 13:14; 14:27; 16:22; 18:4; John 7:38). The Lord, the source of wisdom, grants his children all their needs.

The metaphors of food and drink denote the blessings of God for his people, both material and spiritual. Through him the godly have food and drink as well as protection and the full enjoyment of their salvation. The words "life" and "light" speak of the fullness of salvation in the presence of God (cf. 4:6; Isa 60:1–2). The word "delights" in "river of delights" (*'ᵃḏāneyḵā*) evokes the imagery of the Garden of Eden ("delight"). The experience of Eden, from which mankind was exiled, may be enjoyed by the godly in their fellowship with God. The Book of Revelation (21:6) further describes the blessings associated with the River of Life!

Notes

7 (8 MT) The NEB rendering—"Gods and men seek refuge in the shadow of thy wings"—is exegetically possible but cannot be the intended meaning. The NIV modifies this to "Both high [*'ᵉlōhîm*] and low among men." It seems that there is an antithesis drawn between God and man. The psalmist exclaims, "God, how priceless is your unfailing love / [so that] human beings may find refuge in the shadow of your wings." Notice also the ambivalence of the NIV: "Both high and low among men find [Or mg.: *love, O God! / Men find;* or *love! / Both heavenly beings and men / find*] refuge in the shadow of your wings." See Allen: "how precious is your lovingkindness, O God, / that human beings find refuge in the shadow of your wings" (1:289), and Dahood: "O Yahweh, how precious is your kindness! / Gods and men find refuge in the shadow of your wings" (*Psalms,* 1:217).

9 (10 MT) Dahood develops the motif of Elysian fields, rendering אוֹר (*'ôr*) as "field": "Truly with you is the fountain of life, / In your field we shall see the light" (*Psalms,* 1:221–23). For an evaluation of Dahood's view, see Elmer B. Smick, "Ugaritic and the Theology of the Psalms," *New Perspectives on the Old Testament,* ed. J. Barton Payne (Waco: Word, 1970), pp. 104–16.

IV. Prayer of Protection From Evil

36:10–12

10 Continue your love to those who know you,
your righteousness to the upright in heart.
11 May the foot of the proud not come against me,
nor the hand of the wicked drive me away.
12 See how the evildoers lie fallen—
thrown down, not able to rise!

The blessedness of godliness in fellowship with God ("for with you," v.9) is great in comparison with the deceptiveness of evil. The love, fidelity, righteousness, and justice of Yahweh form a contrast to the way of the wicked. The wicked will come to an end (v.12). They will be cast down by God's justice and will have no strength to raise themselves. The Creator-God had overshadowed them with his general love for his creatures, but they did not recognize him for the good gifts.

10–11 The psalmist discerns that the godly live by God's unfailing love and righteousness. Therefore he prays that the qualities of God's wisdom may continue toward the "upright in heart," i.e., those who "know" Yahweh (v.10). The continuation of the Lord's "love" (*ḥesed̠*, cf. v.5) and "righteousness" (*ṣᵉd̠āqāh*, cf. v.6) is limited to those who "know" (*y-d-ʿ*) Yahweh and walk in uprightness of heart with him (v.10; cf. 7:10; 32:1). In these verses the psalmist prays for the godly and exhorts them to persevere in the knowledge of God. The knowledge of God requires both trust in and fidelity to the Lord. The wise response to the goodness evident in his wisdom is the full recognition of the Lord in every area of life. The "upright in heart" desire to be like God (32:11; 33:1). They differ from those who practically deny God in their hearts (v.1). However, godliness expresses itself in dependence on the Lord's favor. To this end the godly pray that they may be kept from evil (v.11; cf. Matt 6:13). Life and home, material and spiritual blessings are gifts. If evil prevails, these "gifts" may be taken away, allowing the "proud" to be victorious and drive the godly from their blessings (v.11).

12 In reality the godly live in the shadow of God's wings. The concluding prayer petitions the Lord to care for his children in the confidence that evil will cease. Evil cannot coexist with God's rule. The biblical hope holds out the overthrow of the kingdom of evil. It must fall (cf. 5:10; 35:5; Rom 16:20). The evildoers (cf. vv.3–4; 6:10; 14:4–5) will not stand in God's judgment (cf. 1:5–6). When that moment comes, the joy of God's blessed presence, protection, and provisions will be much more precious to the godly. Bellinger concludes that the certainty of the psalmist arises from prophetic insight (pp. 47–50).

Notes

12 (13 MT) The particle שָׁם (*šām*, "there") does not seem to fit. Dahood's proposal (*Psalms*, 1:224) has been adopted in the NIV: "See how." See 14:5. Kraus takes it as a form of *š-m-m* ("be desolate," *Psalmen*, 1:432); see Craigie: "the workers of wickedness were desolated" (*Psalms 1–50*, p. 290).

Psalm 37: Wise Living in a Crooked Generation

In a moving way the psalmist deals with the issues of life and death, wisdom and folly, and reward and punishment. He is most sensitive to the question of the future and its rewards and sufferings. The psalmist affirms that the Lord will sustain the righteous and that they will fully enjoy the blessings promised to them. The sage sets before the reader or hearer the highway of wisdom, even as our Lord called on his followers to learn from him the way that pleases our Father in heaven (Matt 5:2–10).

At issue is the power, greed, and prosperity of the wicked and the suffering of the righteous. This issue and the manner of resolution provide us with sound reasons to approach Psalm 37 as a *wisdom psalm* (see appendix to Ps 1: The Ways of Wisdom and Folly). Westermann concludes that the entire psalm is so steeped in the wisdom tradition that it could be included in the Book of Proverbs (*The Psalms*, p. 112). Brueggemann treats songs celebrating Creation, Torah, and Wisdom as expressive of "a well-ordered, reliable world" and concludes that this psalm together with Psalm 14 reflect the wisdom tradition in Israel (pp. 42–45).

The structure of the psalm is not transparent. There is little evidence of a logical progression of thought, as the "proverbs" have been organized alphabetically. The alphabetic acrostic, consisting of twenty-two strophes, was a mnemonic aid in retaining the psalm. Yet we may divide the collection of proverbs into units for the purpose of exposition:

A. Exhortation to Hope in the Lord's Deliverance (vv.1–6)
B. The Comfort of Divine Retribution (vv.7–11)
C. The Contrastive Ways of the Righteous and the Wicked (vv.12–26)
B′. Call for Wise Living in View of the Belief in Divine Retribution (vv.27–33)
A′. Exhortation to Hope in the Lord's Deliverance (vv.34–40)

I. Exhortation to Hope in the Lord's Deliverance

37:1–6

Of David.

1 Do not fret because of evil men
or be envious of those who do wrong;
2 for like the grass they will soon wither,
like green plants they will soon die away.

3 Trust in the LORD and do good;
dwell in the land and enjoy safe pasture.
4 Delight yourself in the LORD
and he will give you the desires of your heart.

5 Commit your way to the LORD;
trust in him and he will do this:
6 He will make your righteousness shine like the dawn,
the justice of your cause like the noonday sun.

1–6 The wise man must carefully watch his response to the wicked (v.1). It is all too easy to be adversely affected by their prosperity. Evil men may get their way and move up. They may gain power and prestige. They may abuse power, causing great suffering to others. Regardless of how well off the evil are, they are nothing but mortals who live on an earth under God's just and sovereign rule. In his kingdom the wicked may thrive like grass and plants, but they will not stand up under adversity (v.2). In the Middle East the lush spring vegetation may lose its beauty in a few days after a hot, dry desert wind (*ḥamsin*) has parched the land (cf. 90:5–6; 103:15–16; Isa 40:6–8). In the same way the wicked will quickly fade away (cf. vv.20, 35–36; Job 14:2). (See the appendix to Ps 137: Imprecations in the Psalms.)

Rather than destroying themselves with negative emotions, the godly must keep things in perspective (v.1; cf. vv.7–8; Prov 3:31; 23:17; 24:1, 19). Anger, resentment, and jealousy destroy "faith" in God's goodness and justice and affect one's inner attitude toward everything (cf. Ps 73).

Instead of giving in to self-pity and hatred, the wise man develops a trust in the Lord (v.3; cf. Prov 3:5; 16:20; 28:25; Isa 26:4). Trusting the Lord means faith, especially the more difficult aspect of faith—submission to his will in the hope of his resolution of the dilemma (cf. v.5; 1 Peter 5:6–7). In this spirit of surrender, the wise person finds joy. He delights himself in the Lord (v.4). This "delight" in the Lord is a more positive reaction than "jealousy," as one learns to enjoy all his benefits, including material provisions (cf. v.11), with contentment (v.16).

Antithetical to the metaphor of the withering vegetation is the description of those who trust in the Lord. They will "dwell in the land" and do their work ("enjoy safe pasture"; see note on v.3) with the assurance that the Lord's blessing rests on them. He will grant the desires of their hearts (v.4; cf. 20:4; 21:2; Matt 6:33; Luke 12:31). The condition of their enjoyment is nothing less than a positive response to a bad situation: To "do good" (v.3; cf. v.27; Prov 14:9, 22) and to take "delight" (v.4) in the Lord is the object of their love and hope.

The psalmist returns to a reflection on the meaning of trusting the Lord (vv.5–6). Trust in the Lord is, on the one hand, expressed in active obedience, in reliance on the Lord (vv.3–4). Trust is, on the other hand, a fervent expectation of his justice that, for the righteous, will mark the revelation of their glory. The exhortation to "commit" one's way to the Lord is not a simple abandonment. It involves a full commitment to "roll away" or to "cast" one's feelings of anger, resentment, and jealousy on the Lord (cf. 55:22; Prov 16:3; 1 Peter 5:7).

The "way" (v.5) pertains to one's whole life, including the negative feelings, nagging questions, and concerns of justice. God expects his children to be children and to put themselves completely under his fatherly care. While in v.3 trust was expressed by "doing good," v.5 expresses trust as a waiting for the Lord to act.

The Lord is righteous and just! Therefore by faith the wise have the assurance that he will extend righteousness and justice to his own. "Righteousness" (*ṣeḏeq*) and "justice" (*mišpāṭ*) refer to the evidences of God's rule over this world, when he establishes the righteous order, and when he glorifies his children. They will enjoy all the covenant promises (A.A. Anderson, 1:294). The glory will be unveiled like the rising sun at dawn and like the bright light at noon (v.6; cf. Prov 4:18; Isa 58:8; Mal 4:2; Matt 13:43). Faith says to this promise, "it is true." The righteous may suffer from evildoers (v.1) but live in the hope of the day when God will deal justly with evil. Then the light of the children of God will be like that of the noonday sun (for a prophetic description of this great day, cf. Isa 58:10b; 60:1–3, 18–21).

Notes

For a brief discussion of the technical words and phrases in the superscription, see the Introduction.

1 The NEB's "Do not strive to outdo the evildoers" is a questionable translation. The root חרה (*ḥ-r-h,* "be[come] hot," "become angry") may have the meaning of competitiveness, but only in the rare *tif'el* pattern (cf. Jer 12:5; 22:15).

2 The "grass" is a favorite metaphor for the weakness of the wicked (Job 14:2; Pss 90:5–6; 103:15; 129:6; Isa 40:6; James 1:10–11).

3 The phrase "enjoy safe pasture" is difficult in the MT. The verb רְעֵה (*r*ᵉ*'ēh,* "shepherd") has been interpreted as "pursue" or "keep" with the object אֱמוּנָה (*'*ᵉ*mûnāh,* "faithfulness"): "protect faithfulness" (Kraus, *Psalmen,* 1:285); cf. Weiser: "keep upright in heart" (p. 312). The proposal provides a parallel for "do good." But it is preferable (Briggs, 1:325–26) to view the ambiguous command "shepherd faithfulness" in parallelism with "dwell in the land." Dahood's suggestion that "faithfulness" be rendered as "riches"—"And feed on its riches"—(cf. LXX) is questionable (*Psalms,* 1:225, 228). The word "faithfulness" may be translated as an adverb "in faithfulness" or "faithfully," resulting in a complementary parallelism with "dwell in the land": "tend the sheep faithfully." The complementary expectations to live and to work were also Jeremiah's counsel to the exiles in Babylon (cf. Jer 29:5–7).

II. The Comfort of Divine Retribution

37:7–11

7 Be still before the LORD and wait patiently for him;
do not fret when men succeed in their ways,
when they carry out their wicked schemes.

8 Refrain from anger and turn from wrath;
do not fret—it leads only to evil.
9 For evil men will be cut off,
but those who hope in the LORD will inherit the land.

10 A little while, and the wicked will be no more;
though you look for them, they will not be found.
11 But the meek will inherit the land
and enjoy great peace.

7–11 The psalmist repeats and further develops the themes set forth in vv.1–6:

1. The wicked may enjoy success, but their successes result from scheming (10:2) and "ways" (v.7; cf. 1:1) that are self-centered rather than God-centered (v.7: cf. v.1). They may even embitter the lives of the faithful (v.12).

2. Wise living deals first with negative emotions—especially anger, fretting, and jealousy (vv.7–8; cf. v.1). These may lead to sin against God, self, or other humans (v.8; cf. 73:2–3, 15; Gal 5:20–21, 26).

3. Wise living resists evil by trusting in the Lord and by doing good. A righteous person begins by being "still before the LORD" and by waiting for his deliverance (v.7; cf. 62:1, 5; Isa 30:15). Living faith knows that God will act (cf. vv.5–6).

4. God's justice against the wicked is their premature end (v.9a) and ultimately the complete annihilation of evil (v.10; cf. v.36; Isa 29:20). They will perish like grass (v.2) on the day God has determined for them (v.13b).

5. God's righteousness on behalf of his own is his commitment to vindicate them and to let them "inherit the land" (vv.9b, 11; cf. v.3). The inheritance of the land refers to Canaan, but the promise of God extends to all God's people and to the whole earth (cf. Isa 57:15; 60:21; 65:9), as Jesus made clear in the Sermon on the Mount (Matt 5:5).

6. The promises of God are only for the "meek," who trust God "in hope" (cf. v.9) of justice and who actively do his will on earth. Theirs is the kingdom (v.11)! They will enjoy great peace. "Peace" (*šālôm*) stands for the beneficence of the godly (cf. 72:7), in contrast with the life of suffering (v.12; cf. 119:165–66). The verb for "enjoy" (v.11) is the same as in v.4. The one who delights himself in the Lord will also be able to delight himself in his goodness: "great peace." True *shalom* is God's gift to his children (cf. Rom 5:1). It brings great benefits to those who wait patiently.

7. The Lord is a sovereign ruler and judge. He laughs in scorn at the folly of the wicked. A living faith learns not to take evil so seriously but commits itself to God's sovereignty. He knows the times and the reasons (cf. 2:4).

III. The Contrastive Ways of the Righteous and the Wicked

37:12–26

12 The wicked plot against the righteous
and gnash their teeth at them;
13 but the Lord laughs at the wicked,
for he knows their day is coming.

14 The wicked draw the sword
and bend the bow
to bring down the poor and needy,
to slay those whose ways are upright.
15 But their swords will pierce their own hearts,
and their bows will be broken.

16 Better the little that the righteous have
than the wealth of many wicked;
17 for the power of the wicked will be broken,
but the LORD upholds the righteous.

18 The days of the blameless are known to the LORD,
and their inheritance will endure forever.
19 In times of disaster they will not wither;
in days of famine they will enjoy plenty.

20 But the wicked will perish:
The LORD's enemies will be like the beauty of
the fields,
they will vanish—vanish like smoke.

21 The wicked borrow and do not repay,
but the righteous give generously;
22 those the LORD blesses will inherit the land,
but those he curses will be cut off.

23 If the LORD delights in a man's way,
he makes his steps firm;
24 though he stumble, he will not fall,
for the LORD upholds him with his hand.

25 I was young and now I am old,
yet I have never seen the righteous forsaken

or their children begging bread.
26 They are always generous and lend freely;
their children will be blessed.

12–17 Futile are the activities of the wicked. They "plot" (vv.7, 12, 32) in an attempt to get the upper hand. Their godlessness finds expression in an obsession with evil and a hatred of good. They "gnash their teeth" in bitter jealousy (v.12; cf. 35:16; 112:10). Like soldiers in a desperate battle, they use any trick to overcome the godly. They rule with "sword" and "bow" (v.14; cf. 11:2), symbolic of their strength and abuse of power (cf. v.32; 10:9–10), and eagerly await the destruction of the godly. Their victims are the "poor and needy," i.e, the destitute and those robbed of justice (v.14; cf. 9:12, 18; 34:6; Amos 8:4). Their goal is a chaotic autonomy, a world in which injustice is law (cf. 11:2–3). There is no place for the "upright of way" (v.14; NIV, "whose ways are upright") in the world of crooked and perverse people.

The rule of the wicked deprives the upright of justice and consequently of a livelihood. They have "little" (v.16). However, the wise man knows that a "little" with godliness is preferable to plenty with godlessness (cf. Prov 15:16; 16:8, 19). Above the wicked is a just God who observes their ways. He does not act immediately but "laughs at the wicked" (v.13; cf. 2:4). He sees the end from the beginning and assures the godly that the day of the wicked is coming (v.13). The "day" is the terrible "day of the LORD," when "the power of the wicked" (symbolized by the piercing swords and broken bows, v.15) will be broken (v.17). They will get their just desert, when they fall by their own scheming (v.15; cf. 7:14–15).

18–22 The Lord knows "the days of the blameless." God's knowledge (*y-d-'*) is his subjective involvement in the affairs of his children ("the blameless," v.18; cf. v.37; 15:2). He cares for them (1:6). He knows their "days," i.e., the many days of their lives. Whereas he sees "the day" (sing.) of the wicked (v.13), he will bestow his covenant favors on his own in the days (pl.) to come. The meaning of "days" is explicated in the following colon: "their inheritance will endure forever" (v.18b; cf. vv.3, 11, 22). They will continue even in the "days of famine" (v.19), but the wicked come to an end (cf. 1:6). They may suffer adversities ("disaster," "famine," v.19), but they are unlike the wicked who "wither" (lit., "are put to shame") because they will "enjoy plenty" (lit., "be satisfied"). The righteous are "blessed" by the Lord (v.22) and are therefore guaranteed his covenant mercies: life and its full enjoyment (vv.18, 22).

The psalmist uses a number of synonyms for the godly: "meek" (v.11), "poor," "needy," "those whose ways are upright" (v.14), "righteous" (v.16), and "blameless" (v.18, = "perfect," "people of integrity"). The godly trust in the Lord with patience and hope and do what is good (vv.3–5, 7). In contrast to the wicked who hoard up everything for themselves, the righteous are like God in being gracious (v.21; cf. 112:4). They help the poor by being "generous" (vv.21, 26; cf. 112:5, 9). They fear no evil, even in adversity (v.19), because they trust in a God who knows them (v.18).

The demise of the wicked comforts the righteous. The wicked are, after all, in God's sovereignty like "grass," like "green plants" (v.2), and like "the beauty of the fields" (v.20). The phrase "beauty of the fields" may refer to animals fattened for slaughter (1 Sam 15:9, 15) or to the beauty of flowers (cf. v.2; 103:15). The wicked are like sacrifices going up in smoke or flowers that readily disappear (cf. Isa 40:6). They certainly will "vanish" (twice in v.20) because of God's curse (vv.20, 22). They may even come to poverty in this life so that they have to borrow to stay alive, being unable to pay back (v.21a); but ultimately they will be "cut off" from the presence of God and all his benefits (v.22).

23–26 The focus moves from the contrasts between the godly and the wicked to the blessings of the godly. First, the Lord establishes the godly, even in times of adversity (vv.23–24; cf. Prov 24:16). He may "stumble" (v.24), either by sinning or by being jealous of the wicked (cf. 73:2) or by the traps laid by the wicked, but he will not fall. The Lord keeps him from falling (v.24), just as he breaks the power of the wicked (cf. v.17).

Second, the Lord takes care of the physical needs of his children. The sage and aged psalmist gives a lesson from his own lifelong experience. He has witnessed that God is faithful. He gives life to his people and supports the righteous with "bread." From elsewhere in the psalm, it is clear that the righteous may experience a variety of adversities at the hands of the evil (vv.7, 12, 14, 32–33, 40; famine, v.19; stumbling, v.24; trouble, v.39). But the Lord comes to the aid of his own. They are not "abandoned." The children of God are not immune to the experiences of alienation and to the groaning of this world, but theirs is God's promise that he will not completely forsake his own (Gen 17:7; 28:15; Matt 28:20). He gives prosperity to those who follow him.

Third, the wicked hoard up for themselves, and God takes away from them. He gives to his own because they, like him, are gracious stewards (v.26; cf. v.21; 112:5, 9). They aid without interest others who are in need (Exod 22:25; cf. Pss 15:5; 112:5, 9). God's blessing also extends to the next generation (cf. 112:2), as "their children will be blessed" (v.26). Consistent with his way from Creation, God deals with man in the family context (Gen 2:24; cf. Acts 2:39).

Notes

---

14 Some treat v.14b ("to bring down . . . ways are upright") as an addition (cf. BHS) on the ground that it interrupts the symmetric inclusion of vv.14a and 15a.

17 The "power" is an idiomatic rendering of **זְרוֹעוֹת** (*zᵉrôʿô*ṯ, "arms"). The arms—symbolic of strength (cf. 10:15)—by which the poor have been oppressed will be broken. Truly this is a moving picture of the strength of the Lord and his just acts against the wicked. Instead he "supports" or "upholds" the limbs of the weak (v.24; Isa 40:29).

18 For **ידע** (*y-d-ʿ*) as an expression of covenantal commitment, see Herbert B. Huffmon, "The Treaty Background of Hebrew *Yādaʿ*," BASOR 181 (1966): 31–37.

19 The root of **יֵבֹשׁוּ** (*yēḇōšû*) may be *b-w-š* ("shame") or *y-b-š* ("be dry," "wither"). Dahood argues for "wither" (*Psalms*, 1:229–30) and assumes that "the times of disaster" refers to drought: "They shall not wither up in a time of drought" (1:226). The usual meaning seems preferable (A.A. Anderson, 1:296) in contrast with "plenty" (v.19b). "Shame" means here the lack of food and provisions. The wicked are pictured as in need (v.21a), whereas the righteous will have plenty (vv.19, 21b).

20 For a criticism of Dahood's rendering "shrivel" for **אבד** (*ʾ-b-d*, "perish"), see Craigie, *Psalms 1–50*, p. 296.

The metaphor "like the beauty of the fields" is unclear. The "beauty" is an interpretive rendering of **יְקָר** (*yāqār*, "precious," "best"), which together with **כָּרִים** (*kārîm*, "pastures") may refer either to animals or to flowers (see Craigie: "like the best of the pasture," *Psalms*

1–50, p. 294). The lack of a uniform translation in the ancient versions cautions us against resolving this problem. The NEB gives another reading: "like fuel in a furnace."

23 The MT reads "from the LORD are the steps of a man established, and he delights in his way." The emphatic position of "the LORD" in the MT throws light on the source of the success of the godly. The preposition "from" may also be read "by" (GKC, pp. 121ff.). Our translation—"A man's steps are established by the LORD, and he delights in his way"—differs from the NIV. The NEB brings out the emphatic position of LORD: "It is the LORD who directs a man's steps." But we leave the problem of subject in the clause "he delights" unresolved. Contextually either the Lord or the godly may be the subject. In favor of the latter is Kirkpatrick's contention that man's delight in doing God's will is the condition of the promise of v.24 (pp. 193–94).

IV. Call for Wise Living in View of the Belief in Divine Retribution

37:27–33

27 Turn from evil and do good;
then you will dwell in the land forever.
28 For the LORD loves the just
and will not forsake his faithful ones.

They will be protected forever,
but the offspring of the wicked will be cut off;
29 the righteous will inherit the land
and dwell in it forever.

30 The mouth of the righteous man utters wisdom,
and his tongue speaks what is just.
31 The law of his God is in his heart;
his feet do not slip.

32 The wicked lie in wait for the righteous,
seeking their very lives;
33 but the LORD will not leave them in their power
or let them be condemned when brought to trial.

27–31 The psalmist has given the godly much reason for encouragement as well as a wise perspective on life. However, the righteous must persevere in doing the will of God (v.27; cf. v.3). Thus they have a responsibility to their children, because God will protect his descendants (v.28) and will permit them to dwell in the land (v.27), whereas the offspring of the wicked will be cut off. The idea of the responsibility for one's children's blessing encourages godliness.

The ground for all the blessings is the love of God. He loves "the just" (Prov 2:8) and therefore will never forsake "his faithful ones" (v.28, = "his saints," *ḥᵃsîḏāyw;* cf. 4:3). Nothing can separate us from the love of God in Christ (Rom 8:38–39). The Lord loves the wise, who promote justice and are loving. True wisdom begins with a heart attitude. It may be imitated, but the imitation will only be skin deep. The wise man, who fears the Lord, has a reverence for God and desires to do God's will. The law is written on his heart (v.31; cf. 40:8; Isa 51:7; Jer 31:33; Ezek 36:27). In harmony with his "heart," he speaks wisely (49:3) and thus establishes justice (v.30; cf. 36:6). (See the appendix to Ps 19: The Word of God.)

32–33 Adverse reaction to true wisdom is always a reality. The ungodly cannot tolerate true piety. They can readily dismiss the hypocrite, the fake, and the enthusiast, but the living faith of the wise evokes furious reprisal. The wicked are pictured as thugs who lie in ambush to destroy the wise (v.32; cf. vv.12–15; 10:8–11; Prov 1:11–18). Not only do they murder, they also steal, acquiring lands and houses (cf. 1 Kings 21:15–16; Isa 3:14–15; 5:8).

Even in times of adversity and under expressions of hostility, the wise man knows how to speak wisely (v.30; Prov 10:31–32) and righteously (cf. 35:28). The word of God establishes his "heart" so that he does "not slip" (v.31) by giving in to the evildoers or by envying them (vv.1, 8). Rather he waits for his Lord, who has promised to sustain him. The promise of God pertains to protection and justice (v.33; cf. v.28). The righteous are not forsaken by the Lord when they need him (cf. v.25). He will not suffer them to be tried unjustly by the unjust of the earth (v.33). Even when it seems that God has forsaken them, when the wicked hold power and pervert justice, as in Nazi Germany, God promises to establish justice and to rid the earth of evil.

God's promise of protection is the object of hope in OT eschatology. The godly hoped to enjoy the land, to keep the inheritance of the land, and to share it with their descendants. These promises are confirmed in vv.28b–29 and stand in contrast to the offspring of the wicked who will come to an end (v.28b). The psalm calls on the godly to dwell in the land by continuing their lives as normally as possible, even in adversity. The godly were not to leave the land God had given them, because they were the legitimate citizens (v.9); the everlasting inheritance is theirs (v.18), and they will "dwell in it forever" (v.29). God gave Canaan to Israel, and he has reserved the earth for all who love him (Isa 65:17–25; 66:22; cf. Rev 21:1). What a promise to all who receive the promises of the Abrahamic covenant in Christ Jesus (cf. Gal 3:26–29; 6:15)!

Notes

27 Compare "Then you will dwell in the land forever" with the literal rendering: "and live [imperative] forever" and also with v.3:

v.3: dwell [*š-k-n*] in the land and shepherd faithfully (see Notes on v.3)
v.27: dwell [*š-k-n*] forever.

The MT has three imperatives: "Turn from . . . do good . . . and dwell." The godly have a responsibility in the present for their offspring (so A.A. Anderson comments, "The Psalmist is thinking of the descendants of the righteous as being in possession of the ancestral inheritance," 1:298).

28 The word מִשְׁפָּט (*mišpāṭ*, "justice") may best be read here as "the just," in parallelism with "his faithful ones." The MT "for the LORD loves justice" could be a shortened form of "for the LORD loves [the doers of] justice" (cf. Prov 2:8, where NIV's "the just" is also a rendering of "justice").

"Faithful ones" is a possible rendering of חָסִיד (*ḥāsîḏ*, "beloved," see 4:3). The stress is on loyalty, even as "the just" brings out the just acts of the godly. The emphasis in vv.3 and 26–27 is on the faithful and wise living of the godly.

The letter ayin of the acrostic psalm is missing, unless לְעוֹלָם (*leʿôlām*, "forever") be considered. It is tempting to emend the MT based on the LXX to עַוָּלִים לְעוֹלָם נִשְׁמָדוּ (*ʿawwalîm leʿôlām nišmāḏû*, "the evildoers will be destroyed forever"), because it provides a parallel with the next colon, it begins with an ayin, and it only assumes that the word "evildoers" has been left out and that a copyist corrected the verb from נִשְׁמָדוּ (*nišmāḏû*, "will be cut off") to נִשְׁמָרוּ (*nišmārû*, "will be protected"; cf. NEB, "the lawless are banished forever and the children of the wicked destroyed"). Craigie accepts this emendation (*Psalms 1–50*, p. 296) and also argues from the symmetry of verbs "be destroyed" and "be cut off" in v.38.

30 The verb "utters" is a rendering of יֶהְגֶּה (*yehgeh*, "utter," "ponder," "plan"). The same form occurs in 1:2: "meditates." The idiom expresses the deliberate act of speech. The choice, manner, and tone all reflect wisdom.

31 "His feet" is literally "his steps" (cf. 17:5). When he walks, his steps are not "wobbly" or "shaky" (cf. vv.23–24). The verb תִמְעַד (*tim'ad*, "wobble" or "shake") is rendered as "without wavering" in 26:1.

V. Exhortation to Hope in the Lord's Deliverance

37:34–40

34 Wait for the LORD
and keep his way.
He will exalt you to inherit the land;
when the wicked are cut off, you will see it.

35 I have seen a wicked and ruthless man
flourishing like a green tree in its native soil,
36 but he soon passed away and was no more;
though I looked for him, he could not be found.

37 Consider the blameless, observe the upright;
there is a future for the man of peace.
38 But all sinners will be destroyed;
the future of the wicked will be cut off.

39 The salvation of the righteous comes from the LORD;
he is their stronghold in time of trouble.
40 The LORD helps them and delivers them;
he delivers them from the wicked and saves them,
because they take refuge in him.

34–40 The psalmist draws together the major emphases of the wisdom psalm. Facing evil in the world, the wise response of the godly comprises these elements:

1. Hope in the Lord (v.34; cf. vv.3–7);
2. Loyal obedience to him ("keep his way," v.34);
3. Faith in God's justice.

On the one hand, God exalts the righteous (v.34; cf. v.11), gives them the land (cf. vv.9, 11, 18, 22, 29), gives them a future (or posterity, v.37; cf. vv.26, 28), delivers them and protects them from troubles (vv.39–40; cf. vv.17, 19, 23, 25, 28b, 33), and crowns them with victory (= "the salvation of the righteous," v.39a; cf. v.6; see the appendix to Ps 119: Yahweh Is My Redeemer). On the other hand, he brings down the wicked, even when it seems as if they would live forever (vv.35–36, 38; cf. vv.2, 9–10, 15, 17, 20, 22, 28b).

The psalmist adds to this his personal observation, as he did in vv.25–26. He has observed how the wicked flourished but were cut down (vv.35–36). Their prosperity is likened to "a green tree" (v.35; cf. 1:3); but because of their wickedness, they could not stand in the judgment (cf. 1:5). He further promises that the godly will "see it," i.e., the judgment of the wicked (v.34; 52:6; 58:10–11; Mal 1:5).

The psalmist invites the godly to draw lessons of wisdom from experience by looking at the "blameless" and "the upright" (v.37) and by observing their children and grandchildren. The godly man is concerned with integrity, uprightness, and peace (v.37) as expressions of wisdom. The psalmist brings the psalm to an appropriate conclusion as he calls on us to look at the Lord for protection, help, deliverance, and victory (vv.39–40). He does not say "The Lord helps those who help themselves," but help is promised to those who "take refuge in him" (v.40). Yahweh is their "stronghold" (v.39; cf. 27:1). The Divine Warrior will sustain ("help") and deliver (*p-l-ṭ; y-š-'*, v.40) all who "take refuge" (cf. 2:12) in him.

Notes

---

34 Hope is marked by eager, longing expectancy. The verb is an imperative of קוה (*q-w-h,* "wait for"). Waiting is an expression of loyalty and submission (25:3). The Lord does not put to shame or disappoint those who wait for him (27:13–14).

35 The second colon of this verse is problematic. The LXX reads "going up like the cedars of Lebanon." The crux is the verb מִתְעָרֶה (*miṯ'āreh,* "shows itself naked"). The NEB makes an attempt, without textual support: "rank as a spreading tree in its native soil" (cf. KJV). Craigie (*Psalms 1–50,* p. 296) accepts a proposal by A. Fitzgerald ("The Interchange of L, N, and R in Biblical Hebrew," JBL 97 [1978]: 486) according to which the l and the r are dialectical variants and gives the unique reading *miṯ'alleh* ("raise oneself"). The argument is somewhat forced. Regardless of how one considers the problems, there is no satisfactory solution. The NIV gives at least a possible interpretation.

37 The word "future," which renders אַחֲרִית (*'aḥ^arîṯ,* "last," "end"), occurs in vv.37–38 pertaining to the righteous and the wicked. In the light of Jer 31:17, it may signify offspring: "There is hope for your future" (NIV) could better be translated as "There is hope for your offspring," because the next colon reads,"Your children will return to their own land." Also v.38 of this chapter makes better sense when read "the offspring of the wicked will be cut off." Notice the NIV margin on "future": *"there will be posterity"* (so also v.38).

39 The word תְּשׁוּעַת (*t^ešû'āṯ,* "salvation") connotes the sense of full deliverance from adversities in the fullest sense: the glorification and vindication of God's people (cf. v.6); cf. Craigie, "The victory of the righteous comes from the LORD" (*Psalms 1–50,* p. 295).

Psalm 38: A Prayer for Reconciliation

In this *individual lament* the psalmist calls on the Lord for healing from a crippling disease. He is overwhelmed with guilt, abandonment, and a desire for renewed fellowship with God. He suffers with a sickness from which he has not yet recovered. All the while he experiences the hand of God's discipline and waits for the Lord to respond to his need. Because of the themes of sin, guilt, judgment, and hope in God's salvation, Psalm 38 has been used as a penitential psalm (cf. Pss 6; 32; 51; 102; 130; 143).

The structure is not transparent because of the lack of movement. It is essentially a lament, ending on a note of hope. For our purposes we shall consider the psalm under the following headings:

A. Prayer for Reconciliation (vv.1–4)
B. Pain of Anguish (vv.5–12)
C. Prayer for Vindication (vv.13–16)

B′. Pain of Injustice (vv.17–20)
A′. Prayer for Reconciliation (vv.21–22)

I. Prayer for Reconciliation

38:1–4

A psalm of David. A petition.

1 O LORD, do not rebuke me in your anger
or discipline me in your wrath.
2 For your arrows have pierced me,
and your hand has come down upon me.
3 Because of your wrath there is no health in my body;
my bones have no soundness because of my sin.
4 My guilt has overwhelmed me
like a burden too heavy to bear.

1–4 The psalmist is fully aware of the sovereign hand of God in his life. In his agony he has come to understand the nature of cause and effect. Not all disease results from individual sin. But this disease is associated with "my guilt" / "my sin" (vv.3–4) and "your anger" / "your wrath" (v.1).

Suffering is a form of God's discipline in the school of righteousness. However, discipline may be harsh. Three synonyms for God's anger—"anger" (*qeṣep̱*; cf. 102:10); "wrath" (*ḥemāh*; cf. 6:1; 88:7; 90:7); "wrath" (*za'am*; cf. 78:49; Jer 10:24)—express the righteous indignation of God over the sin of a member of the covenant (cf. TDOT, 1:356–60; 4:464–65; TDNT, 5:395–409; W.A. VanGemeren, "Wrath of God," in Elwell, BEB, 2:2166–67). The ferocity of Yahweh's anger is so great that the psalmist feels himself to be the object of Yahweh's attacks. It is as if he has been set up to be pierced by God's "arrows" (v.2; cf. 7:12; Job 6:4; Lam 3:12).

The metaphorical use of "arrows" may suggest an Israelite use of a Canaanite metaphor in which Resheph, the god of the archers, is the god of plagues and diseases (cf. Deut 32:23; Lam 3:12). The idiom "your hand has come down upon me" (v.2) symbolizes the extent of alienation, resulting from a severe form of discipline (1 Sam 6:3, 5; Pss 32:4; 39:10). Both the "arrows" and God's hand "come down." Since the same root (*n-ḥ-t*, "descend," "bring down"; cf. TWOT, 2:573) occurs in v.2 (NIV, "pierced . . . has come down"), the psalmist accentuates how God's rebuke penetrates deep into his being so as to bring him down. The first occurrence ("pierced") is a Niphal form and is unique in the OT. The second verb ("has come down") reflects a metaphorical usage of God's hand like an army pressing hard against an enemy (cf. Jer 21:13).

The intensity of God's discipline has affected the psalmist's capacity to enjoy life. There is no part of his being that has not been affected. "Health" (v.3) signifies any unaffected part (Isa 1:6). The evidence of God's displeasure is with him, so that there is no "peace" (NIV, "soundness") in his bones, a metaphor for his body (cf. 6:2). The psalmist does not question God's justice. Throughout the lament he recognizes his own sinfulness. He has come to the breaking point because the consequences of his "sin" (i.e., "guilt," v.4) have "overwhelmed" him like a flood (cf. 18:4–5; 69:2, 15; 124:4–5). They are like an intolerable "burden" from which he cannot escape. Therefore he lifts himself up to the Lord with the prayer for relief, compassion, and reconciliation.

Notes

For a brief discussion of the technical words and phrases in the superscription, see the Introduction.

II. Pain of Anguish

38:5–12

5 My wounds fester and are loathsome
because of my sinful folly.
6 I am bowed down and brought very low;
all day long I go about mourning.
7 My back is filled with searing pain;
there is no health in my body.
8 I am feeble and utterly crushed;
I groan in anguish of heart.

9 All my longings lie open before you, O Lord;
my sighing is not hidden from you.
10 My heart pounds, my strength fails me;
even the light has gone from my eyes.
11 My friends and companions avoid me because
of my wounds;
my neighbors stay far away.
12 Those who seek my life set their traps,
those who would harm me talk of my ruin;
all day long they plot deception.

5–8 The experience of suffering is in and all around the psalmist. He sees and feels the pain of his wounds (v.5), his back aches (v.7), and there is no part of his body that does not have something wrong with it (v.7b; cf. v.3a). It is impossible to diagnose his disease, though some have suggested that the phenomena resemble leprosy. The love for metaphor and hyperbole among the Semites should caution the interpreter not to take the language literally.

The anguish results from his mental and spiritual pain as the psalmist reflects on the reason for his suffering. Pain—physical pain—is terrible, but anguish of soul can be overwhelming. The stench of his wounds (v.5; cf. Isa 1:6) is dwarfed by the folly of his sin. He calls sin "folly" (cf. 107:17–18; Prov 19:3), because his sin has found him out. Folly is so much more evident to the wise in heart. Sin is sin; but when it is done conscientiously, it is "folly."

All joy of life is far from the psalmist. He is bowed down and mourns, partly because of his pain, but also because of the anguish of his soul (vv.6–7; cf. 35:14; 42:9). For that reason he despairs within himself, which throws him into a deeper depression so that he is paralyzed from doing anything (v.8). All he can do is "groan" within himself.

9 In the state of depression, it is not easy to communicate meaningfully. One's thoughts are not coherent. Self-doubt incapacitates the depressed. His emotions, actions, and speech are fused together into a "groan." The word "longings" (*ta'ᵃwāh*, lit., "desire") in this context signifies "sighing" of the heart rather than "desire." Here it is synonymous with "anguish" (v.8) and "sighing" (v.9; cf. Dahood: "all my sighing is before thee" [*Psalms*, 1:233]).

10 However, the psalmist looked up to God with the hope that he would understand the meaning of his groan. Even in his state of depression, the psalmist knew his theology. He did not doubt his relationship with the covenant Lord but called on the one who heard Israel's groaning in Egypt (Exod 2:25) to listen also to him. It was not necessary to verbalize his longing for reconciliation, forgiveness, and full restoration. Though God was far from responding, the psalmist lived in the awareness that nothing is hidden from God's eyes. Calvin well understood the meaning of trial, prayer, and perseverance:

> Nay, even in the prayers which we offer up when our minds are at ease, we experience too well how easily our minds are carried away, and wander after vain and frivolous thoughts, and how difficult it is to keep them uninterruptedly attentive and fixed with the same degree of intensity upon the object of our desire. If this happens when we are not exercised by any severe trial, what will be the case when we are agitated by violent storms and tempests which threaten a thousand deaths, and when there is no way to escape them? (2:62)

In his pain the psalmist received little relief in his environment. Relief may come in the form of the little pleasures of life and in the moments of shared experiences with friends, but the psalmist had none of these. He was like Job, except for the fact that the former knew that he had sinned. The psalmist's heart beats feverishly (Dahood, *Psalmen*, 1:233) and leaves him with no rest. Though he is weak, he wants to do something about his situation, but he cannot. His mind and body are in conflict with each other. In this situation he no longer has the proper perspective—"even the light has gone from my eyes."

11–12 The psalmist's personal sense of abandonment is aggravated by his being shunned. Friends and enemies have nothing to do with him. His friends are afraid of associating with a sick person or with a sinner (v.11; cf. 31:11; 69:8; 88:18; Luke 23:49; contrast this with Matt 11:19). The words "friends and companions" (lit., "those who love me and my neighbors") are synonyms for those with whom he normally has good relations. His enemies do not leave him at peace, because even in his trouble they aggravate the situation by adding to his troubles and speaking lies. Their aim is his total and utter ruination (v.12; cf. 5:9; 35:4, 26).

Notes

10 (11 MT) The verb סְחַרְחַר (*s^eḥarḥar*, "pound"), unique in the OT, is a Pealal form of the root *s-ḥ-r* ("pass through"), with a probable meaning of the palpitation of the heart.

11 (12 MT) The prepositional phrase מִנֶּגֶד (*minneg*e*ḏ*, "far away") is usually translated by "in the presence of." For the meaning "far off," Dahood appeals to 10:5 (*Psalms*, 1:236).

III. Prayer for Vindication

38:13–16

[13]I am like a deaf man, who cannot hear,
like a mute, who cannot open his mouth;
[14]I have become like a man who does not hear,
whose mouth can offer no reply.
[15]I wait for you, O LORD;
you will answer, O Lord my God.
[16]For I said, "Do not let them gloat
or exalt themselves over me when my foot slips."

13–14 In his loneliness the psalmist feels himself isolated from the world like a deaf or mute person (vv.13–14). Part of the reason for this is from his desire to be alone in his depression. It is also because he is being shunned, so that he hears little and is kept from speaking. The usual translation of "reply" (*tôḵāḥôṯ*, v.14) is "reproofs" or "arguments." The psalmist has no words or interest in defending his innocence against the accusers or against God (cf. Job 23:4). How different is this sufferer from Job! This man is silently absorbed in his suffering, whereas Job was all too anxious to protest against his friends and to argue with God. This man knows that he has sinned, and in his sin he waits for God to initiate reconciliation. His waiting in silence is in submission to the Lord, and this is to be interpreted as a prayer for divine vindication. Vindication is God's response to the needs of his children, who in their utter helplessness abandon themselves to him.

15 In his total abandonment the psalmist cries out to God as his sole refuge. Because of his sin, guilt, and the consequences of sin, he has no argument against his foes. His foes would desire nothing better than his destruction. However, even in the darkest moments there is still the glimmer of light borne out of a living faith. He knows that God can answer. In his address to God, he still calls on him as "Lord my God." In the Psalms this form of address is far from being a pious phrase, a liturgical form, or an impersonal manner of address. The psalmist claims that the Ruler of the universe is his God.

16 The psalmist has no other hope left than waiting for the Lord (cf. v.15; 31:24; 39:7). There is little time left. The foes are using every opportunity to remind him of their strength and power and of his weakness. Their boasting and self-exaltation increases at the cost of the psalmist's life. He feels as if he is slipping away.

Notes

---

16 (17 MT) It is possible to render בְּמוֹט (*bᵉmôṭ*) in "when my foot slips," an infinitive construct that literally means "in slipping," as a past, "when my foot slipped."

IV. Pain of Injustice

38:17–20

17 For I am about to fall,
and my pain is ever with me.
18 I confess my iniquity;
I am troubled by my sin.
19 Many are those who are my vigorous enemies;
those who hate me without reason are numerous.
20 Those who repay my good with evil
slander me when I pursue what is good.

17 In this section the psalmist calls on the Lord to execute justice on earth. Justice is important, not only for himself, but also for others. First, he is concerned with the enemies who desire to glory over the death of one of the godly so that they may exalt themselves over God. Second, he is concerned with the promise of God that he would not permit the righteous to stumble (15:5; 37; 112:6). In the previous psalm the promise was stated as "though he stumble, he will not fall, / for the LORD upholds him with his hand" (v.24). His "pain" in forms of physical suffering and anguish of mind is ever-present, inescapable.

18 The psalmist confesses his sins again (cf. vv.3–4). As long as he was still troubled by guilt and the consequences of sin, he clung to the Lord for his assurance. Before the coming of Christ, the godly received forgiveness in "token" through the priesthood and the sacrificial system. As long as the psalmist is suffering, there remains a lingering doubt about the efficacy of God's forgiveness. This is not so different from a Christian who in his suffering from his sins continues to plead with God for full pardon and restoration.

19–20 In his soul-searching experience, the psalmist has found himself to be innocent of wrongdoing against those who gloat over his adversities (cf. 35:19). Instead he has treated them well. Yet he is overwhelmed by the number and the enthusiasm of his opponents. It is possible that he is speaking hyperbolically or that in his distress a few troublers seem to be many. They affect him negatively in that he is overwhelmed by their evil force.

Notes

18 (19 MT) The chiasm begins and ends the verse with a word for sin: "I confess [lit., 'declare'] my iniquity; / I am troubled by my sin." The verb אֶדְאַג (*'ed'ag*, "troubled," "anxious," "worried") expresses the deeply rooted guilt and suffering.

19 (20 MT) The word חַיִּים (*ḥayyîm*, "life") seems to be out of place. The NIV has kept close to the MT in the rendition "vigorous." BHS (et al.) proposes a change to חִנָּם (*ḥinnām*, "in vain"; cf. Craigie: "My enemies without cause are numerous" (*Psalms 1–50*, pp. 301–2). It may be that the psalmist is overwhelmed by the vitality of his enemies. Their increase and joy in living, though contrary to what is expected, is all too evident.

V. Prayer for Reconciliation

38:21–22

21 O Lord, do not forsake me;
be not far from me, O my God.
22 Come quickly to help me,
O Lord my Savior.

21–22 In conclusion the psalmist calls three times on the Lord and addresses him in three different ways. He addresses him as "Lord" (Yahweh, the covenant God who promises to be faithful to his children, even when they have sinned against him), "my God" (an endearing phrase, equivalent to "my Father"), and "Lord my Savior" (Master of the universe, who is powerful and able to save; cf. 62:2). Since Yahweh has promised to be near, the psalmist prays, "Do not forsake me." Since a child of God needs the presence of his heavenly Father, the psalmist prays, "Be not far from me, O my God" (v.21; cf. 22:1). Since he submits himself to the sovereignty of God, the psalmist prays, "Come quickly to help me, / O Lord my Savior." Thus he commits his cause to the covenant-God, his Father, and the Great King. The situation is urgent, both because of the fragile state of the psalmist's mind and because of his enemies (cf. 22:1, 11, 19).

Psalm 39: A Stranger to Life and an Alien With God

In a moving way the author draws us into the reality of life with its vexing problems and the unresolved quest for meaning. The psalm is in the form of an *individual lament*. It has little direct connection with the cult; consequently there is general agreement that the composer authored this psalm as an individual contribution to Israel's piety. He demonstrates a strong interest in wisdom and may reflect the influence of Israel's wisdom tradition.

The structure has two parallel movements from a vow of silence to an expression of hope:

A. Silence Before the Lord (vv.1–3)
B. Prayer for Divine Illumination (vv.4–6)
C. Prayer for Deliverance (vv.7–8)
A′. Silence Before the Lord (v.9)
B′. Prayer for Divine Sustenance (vv.10–11)
C′. Prayer for Deliverance (vv.12–13)

I. Silence Before the Lord

39:1–3

For the director of music. For Jeduthun. A psalm of David.

1 I said, "I will watch my ways
and keep my tongue from sin;
I will put a muzzle on my mouth
as long as the wicked are in my presence."
2 But when I was silent and still,
not even saying anything good,
my anguish increased.

[3]My heart grew hot within me,
and as I meditated, the fire burned;
then I spoke with my tongue:

1 In view of his internal and external circumstances, the sacred author determined not to speak anymore. He made a personal commitment to control ("watch") himself (cf. Prov 16:17; James 1:26). He purposed to scrutinize his behavior to see whether there was any unbecoming action. The phrase "my ways" has in view his whole behavior with particular reference to his speech ("my tongue"). He had found it difficult to "muzzle" his mouth, but he had come to the point where it had become necessary (cf. 141:3). The external circumstances that necessitated his determination were due to the ungodly. As in 38:12, 16, and 19–20, the ungodly surround the godly in their adversities like vultures around a dying body.

2 The psalmist desires to speak forthrightly about his internal problems but fears that he may be misunderstood or that he may speak irreverently and give occasion to the enemy. For the sake of God, he vowed to be silent in his suffering. Silence was an expression of submission and hope rather than anger (37:7).

It is not explicit what bothered the psalmist, whether it was a disease or a spiritual problem. Some have proposed that he was distressed with the problem of aging. Whatever the cause of stress may have been, he became intensely aware of his limitations; and in his self-awareness he became vexed with life. Though he was submitting himself to the Lord, he experienced an agonizing pain within (cf. 32:2).

3 In his silence the psalmist learned more about himself. He learned how difficult it was to control himself. The metaphors "my heart grew hot" and "the fire burned" express anger (cf. Deut 19:6; Jer 51:39; Ezek 36:5). The more he reflected on his situation, the more he became exasperated. The phrase "as I meditated" is rendered in 5:1 as "sighing" (*hāg̱îg̱*), a noun related to the root *h-g-g* ("long for," "burn") and not to *h-g-h* ("meditate"; KB[3], 1:228). His whole being was aflame. He had to speak, and when he spoke he wisely addressed the Lord in prayer (vv.4–8).

Notes

For a brief discussion of the technical words and phrases in the superscription, see the Introduction.

1 (2 MT) The verbal phrases "I will watch . . . and keep" are translations of the same Hebrew phrase: אֶשְׁמְרָה (*'ešmᵉrāh*, "let me guard," cohortative). The cohortative expresses the will to restrain oneself and may be interpreted as a vow. It need not be a scribal error (as Craigie suggests, *Psalms 1–50*, p. 307) and be emended to conform with the LXX: "let me put" in the second occurrence (cf. BHS).

For a refutation of Dahood's rendering "full of glee" (*Psalms*, 1:240) for the MT's עַד (*'ad̲*, "as long as"), see Craigie (*Psalms 1–50*, p. 307).

2 (3 MT) "Not even saying anything good" is literally "I kept from good." The word "good" (טוֹב [*ṭôb̲*]) may here also signify that he kept himself from the good things in life (cf. 23:6) or that he restrained his verbal expression. The latter seems to be in keeping with the wisdom motif (Prov 17:27–28).

II. Prayer for Divine Illumination

39:4–6

4 "Show me, O LORD, my life's end
and the number of my days;
let me know how fleeting is my life.
5 You have made my days a mere handbreadth;
the span of my years is as nothing before you.
Each man's life is but a breath. *Selah*
6 Man is a mere phantom as he goes to and fro:
He bustles about, but only in vain;
he heaps up wealth, not knowing who will get it.

4 Unable to resolve his problem, the psalmist turns to the Lord for instruction. The purpose of knowing life's end is not that he may plan for every day of his life. He does not ask to know all that will happen but only the purpose of life. In the greater awareness of the brevity of life, he hopes that the Lord will guide him in an understanding and acceptance of this brevity. Notice the threefold repetition for the brevity of life: "my life's end," "the number of my days," and "how fleeting is my life" (cf. Ps 90; Job 11:7–9; Eccl 2:3).

Prayer is God's means of instruction. In the quietness of prayer, the psalmist returns to the revealed insights pertaining to his life and to life in general. Because the question was personal, his first insight is personal. However, the sage in him is not content until he has generalized it to be applicable to mankind.

5 Contrary to his feelings of self-worth, the psalmist reminds himself that his life is brief. He compares it to a "handbreadth," one of the smallest units of measurement in ancient Israel. It is equivalent to "a couple of inches." In Jeremiah 52:21 the measurement is given in terms of "four fingers thick." In his heart he feels that life is like a mile, but in reality the Lord has made him to live for a brief span of time.

In a more general way, the psalmist speaks of man who feels himself established (see Notes). Even when it seems that man is strong and self-assured, from God's perspective he is little more than a "breath."

6 This last observation leads the psalmist to a more general and less ambiguous statement: man's existence and future are filled with uncertainties. This sounds like the message of Ecclesiastes, and it is! Man is "a mere phantom." In other words, man's importance is dwarfed in comparison with God. Man's busying about may give him status and wealth, but even in his accomplishments he shares the fate of all men. Man is mortal and cannot control his affairs after his death. His inability to control, to know, and to project himself outside the sphere of human limitations characterizes man's fragile existence (cf. Luke 12:13–21; James 4:13–17).

Notes

4 (5 MT) The verb הוֹדִיעֵנִי (*hôḏîʿēnî,* "show me," "teach me," "make known to me") reflects a wisdom term in Hebrew from the root *y-d-ʿ* ("know," "be intimately acquainted"). It is related to the phrase "let me know" (cohortative). The translation could bear out the syntactic relation between both verbs: "Make known to me . . . so that I may know."

5 (6 MT) The "handbreadth" is less than three inches. The plural in the Hebrew text signifies "several handbreadths," a general statement rather than a precise designation.

Verse 5c (6b MT) is problematic by the duplication of "all" in Hebrew; literally it reads, "Indeed, all vanity (breath) all man standing firm." The first use of "all" may be due to dittography. Several Hebrew MSS omit it. The participle נִצָּב (*niṣṣāḇ*,"standing firm") does not seem to fit. Weiser gives an explanatory translation: "self-assured" (p. 327). A.A. Anderson suggests that "even the life of the man who appears to be firmly established (119:89) is but 'a mere breath' " (1:310). On mortality and the resurrection hope, see Andreas Angerstorfer, "Der Mensch nach Ps 39,6f und Targum Ps 39,6f, Verganglichkeitsaussage und Auferstehungshoffnung," *Freude an der Weisung des Herrn, Beiträge zur Theologie der Psalmen, Festgabe zum 70. Geburtstag von Heinrich Gross* (Stuttgart: Katholisches Bibelwerk, 1986), pp. 1–15.

5–6 (6–7 MT) The insights are clearly marked in the Hebrew by introductory particles: הִנֵּה (*hinnēh*, "behold," v.5a); אַךְ (*'aḵ*, "but," "indeed," vv.5b, 6a, 6b). He returns to an insight on the nature of man introduced by the particle *'aḵ* in v.11b (12b MT).

III. Prayer for Deliverance

39:7–8

7"But now, Lord, what do I look for?
My hope is in you.
8Save me from all my transgressions;
do not make me the scorn of fools.

7–8 The quest for meaning in life (v.4) and the insight on the nature of man brings the inspired psalmist to a most important question: "What do I look for in life?" The phrase "but now" (v.7) serves as a conclusion to his previous prayer and an introduction to his prayer for deliverance. He concludes that nothing in life is important or reliable, unless one's hope is secured in God. In his searching for the meaning of life and of man, he has come to a renewed commitment to God. With the renewal of the yearning for God, he is also more aware of his own shortcomings in the presence of God. For this reason he is no longer satisfied with knowledge of man's condition. He is acutely aware of his own condition. He is a sinner and suffers from the consequences of his sin (cf. Ps 38). He needs God's forgiveness, reconciliation, and healing. His hope is in the Lord, for whose deliverance he waits anxiously (cf. 38:15; 40:1). When Yahweh vindicates his servant, the foolish scoffers will have no more occasion to rejoice (cf. 38:15–16). The intent of his prayer, "save me" (*n-ṣ-l*, v.8), is nothing less than reconciliation with God and divine vindication (cf. 38:21–22).

IV. Silence Before the Lord

39:9

9I was silent; I would not open my mouth,
for you are the one who has done this.

9 The reflections in vv.9–13 parallel the thoughts expressed in vv.1–8. In v.9 the psalmist reflects on his silence (cf. vv.1–3). In his silence he was deeply disturbed and feared that he might say something disrespectful about or to his God. Now he realizes that his condition is the Lord's will. In view of this, he willingly accepts it from God's hand. He does not understand everything; but at least he knows that a personal God, instead of an impersonal force, is in charge over his life.

V. Prayer for Divine Sustenance

39:10–11

10 Remove your scourge from me;
I am overcome by the blow of your hand.
11 You rebuke and discipline men for their sin;
you consume their wealth like a moth—
each man is but a breath. *Selah*

10–11 The psalmist's reflections become the basis on which he renews his appeal to God to sustain him in life (cf. vv.4–5). The Lord has instructed him on the meaning of life as a gift whose limitations vex man. He is also vexed by the discipline of the Lord in his life. Man's frailty and God's discipline hedge him in. The Lord sovereignly limits the wealth and the aspirations of man. He disciplines his children. Those who live for the sake of living may soon be disgusted with the frailty of life. For the child of God, disappointments, adversity, and fatherly discipline are reminders of his father's concern. The experience of discipline is like a "scourge" (v.10; cf. 38:11 "wounds") and appears a harsh treatment ("I am overcome," v.10; cf. v.2). Yet the psalmist learns through anguish the meaning and brevity of life. Man is not God or divine. Yahweh takes away man's own definition of meaning in life and consumes his pleasures and wealth like a destructive "moth" (v.11; cf. Hos 5:12).

Notes

---

10 (11 MT) The word תִּגְרָה (*tigrāh*, "hostility"; NIV, "blow") is a *hapax legomenon*, translated in the LXX by "strength."

11 (12 MT) The metaphor of the moth suggests the brevity of man's life or the destructive power of a moth. The context is not clear. The NIV favors the latter interpretation. The last clause of v.11 makes the former interpretation likely.

The word חֲמוּדוֹ (*ḥ*ª*mûḏô*, "his desired thing") could refer to wealth specifically (NIV) or to the pleasures of life in a more general way (cf. Craigie: "his desires," *Psalms 1–50*, p. 307).

VI. Prayer for Deliverance

39:12–13

12 "Hear my prayer, O LORD,
listen to my cry for help;
be not deaf to my weeping.
For I dwell with you as an alien,
a stranger, as all my fathers were.
13 Look away from me, that I may rejoice again
before I depart and am no more."

12–13 In submission to God's will and in recognition of his humanity, the psalmist returns to the Lord with a renewed spirit. The repetition "hear . . . listen . . . be not deaf" (v.12) is characteristic of the lament psalms (4:1; 54:2; 84:8). He addresses his God as Yahweh, the covenant God. But he feels himself a stranger in God's presence (see W.A.M. Beuken, "Psalm 39: Some Aspects of the Old Testament Understanding of Prayer," *The Heythrop Journal* 19 [1978]: 1–11). He has not yet arrived in "the house of the LORD" (23:6). Even though he is a sinner and suffers adversities, he has no doubts about his belonging to the covenant community. His fathers were sojourners in the land and longed for the fulfillments of the promises. The psalmist is a "stranger" in God's world (v.12; cf. Heb 11:13; 1 Peter 2:11).

In a sincere longing for the blessing of God's presence and fellowship, the psalmist prays for the Lord to remove his judgment (v.13). When suffering is over, then the Lord may again renew his joy. For him "joy" is not an eschatological hope, but he prays that here and now he may have a real foretaste of the covenant presence of Yahweh.

Psalm 40: The Joyful Experience and Expectation of Salvation

Critics have proposed that Psalm 40, like Psalm 27, is composed of two separate psalms combined into one. This conclusion is the result of a form-critical analysis according to which the thanksgiving of the individual (vv.1–10) is followed by an *individual lament* (vv.11–17). Moreover, the last section (vv.13–17) is substantially identical to Psalm 70. Over against the critical postulate, Weiser asserts that the combination of thanksgiving and lament is not unusual (cf. Ps 27) and that Psalm 40 may be a prayer based on God's past acts of deliverance (pp. 333–34). Craigie argues for the interrelationship between the two parts on the ground of similar vocabulary and stylistic features (*Psalms 1–50*, p. 314). In addition, Eaton has proposed a new designation of the form: a royal prayer (pp. 113–14); similarly Craigie: "a royal liturgy of supplication" (*Psalms 1–50*, p. 314).

The relationship to Psalm 70 remains difficult. Craigie postulates that Psalm 70 is a later adaptation for the purpose of a more popular usage of the royal prayer (*Psalms 1–50*, p. 314). It may well be that the royal prayer incorporated the liturgy and established prayer, whose present form (vv.13–17) represents a slightly different tradition from that found in Psalm 70.

The structure of the psalm reflects a remarkable unity, in spite of the change in mood from thanksgiving to lament. The expository schematization is as follows:

A. Personal Experience of Salvation (vv.1–3)
  B. Blessedness of God's Protection (vv.4–5)
    C. Expression of Commitment (vv.6–8)
      D. Proclamation of God's Perfections (vv.9–10)
      D′. Prayer for God's Perfections (v.11)
    C′. Confession of Sin (v.12)
  B′. Prayer for God's Protection (vv.13–16)
A′. Personal Need of Salvation (v.17)

(See Nic. H. Ridderbos, "The Psalms," pp. 43–76; id., "The Structure of Psalm XL," *OudTestamentische Studiën* 14 [1965]: 296–304.)

I. Personal Experience of Salvation

40:1–3

For the director of music. Of David. A psalm.

[1] I waited patiently for the LORD;
he turned to me and heard my cry.
[2] He lifted me out of the slimy pit,
out of the mud and mire;
he set my feet on a rock
and gave me a firm place to stand.
[3] He put a new song in my mouth,
a hymn of praise to our God.
Many will see and fear
and put their trust in the LORD.

1–2 The experience of salvation is the story of what God has done: "he turned . . . and heard. . . . He lifted . . . he set" (vv.1–2; cf. 116:1–2). Psalm 27 concluded on a repeated exhortation to "wait for the Lord" (v.14), and our psalmist recounts what happens when one waits "patiently" for the Lord (v.1; cf. 37:7, 10, 34; 38:15; 39:7). Answer to prayer may not be immediate, but perseverance in prayer expresses itself in humble submission to God's sovereignty and the longing for a "new" expression of God's covenantal faithfulness (cf. 37:34; 38:15; 39:7).

In response to the intense and patient longing of the king, the Lord had rescued him in past crises. The allusions to death and dying in the words "slimy pit," "mud," and "mire" (v.2) suggest that David was seriously sick (cf. Ps 38), even to death. Healing was then a salvation from the netherworld (cf. 69:2, 14), out of which the Lord "lifted" him (see appendix to Ps 88: Sheol-Grave-Death). But the metaphors may also express the threat to Israel's national existence by an enemy attack. The king personified the severity of the crisis by the imagery of his own suffering and the Lord's deliverance. The deliverance experienced personally by the king was representative of the experience of the nation.

3 Instead of defeat and subjugation, the Lord had given the king the sweet experience of victory. God had been faithful to his promises by placing him firmly on "a rock" (v.2), symbolic of God's protection (cf. 27:5). In proper response to God's help, David renewed his praise to him. The "new" (33:3; 96:1; 98:1; 149:1) song was not necessarily a new composition. The newness lies in the event of salvation history. The recent victory is one additional chapter in a long series of God's involvements with his people. An older hymn of praise could well have been used in the expression of thanksgiving. The situation is similar to our singing of psalms with which we associate the deliverance by our Lord with all the benefits provided by him. The magnificence of each act of deliverance in the history of redemption inspired awe (cf. 33:8; 52:6). The fear the psalmist speaks of evokes a response. The acts of God inspire the people of God with the sense of awe for their covenant God (cf. Rev 5:9; 14:3).

Notes

For a brief discussion of the technical words and phrases in the superscription, see the Introduction.

2 (3 MT) The translation "slimy pit" is questionable. The word שָׁאוֹן (*šā'ôn,* "desolation") in the phrase "pit of desolation" has no justifiable etymological connection with the Aramaic word meaning "mud" (cf. NEB, "out of the muddy pit"). It is possible to treat it as a homonym of "roar" (of water, cf. 65:7) and to associate it with a metaphorical portrayal of the waters of Sheol (A.A. Anderson, 1:315).

The words "mud" (69:14; Jer 38:6) and "mire" (69:2) are synonyms and may be rendered as a hendiadys, e.g., Craigie: "slimy mud" (*Psalms 1–50,* p. 312). The words "pit" and "mud" refer to Sheol.

"And gave me a firm place to stand" is literally "establishes my steps." The word אֲשֻׁרָי (*'ašurāy,* "steps") is parallel with "my feet." Since they denote the redemption of the whole person, it is preferable to translate the colons consistently as "he set my feet on a rock and gave my (foot)steps a firm place to stand" or as "he set me on a rock and gave me a firm place to stand on."

3 (4 MT) The words "see" and "fear" form a play on words, from the roots ראה (*r-'-h*) and ירא (*y-r-'*).

II. Blessedness of God's Protection

40:4–5

4 Blessed is the man
  who makes the LORD his trust,
who does not look to the proud,
  to those who turn aside to false gods.
5 Many, O LORD my God,
  are the wonders you have done.
The things you planned for us
  no one can recount to you;
were I to speak and tell of them,
  they would be too many to declare.

4–5 The victory inspired Israel to trust more in the Lord (v.3). David blesses those who put their confidence in the covenant God, whose acts of protection ("wonders," v.5; cf. 9:1) are innumerable. Before he praises the Lord for his mighty deeds, he indirectly exhorts people not to depend on human strength or idolatry.

The mighty acts of the Lord are "wonders" in the sense that they are acts of supernatural and providential deliverance (9:1; 26:7; 71:17; 75:1; 145:5; Neh 9:17). The acts of God are the manifestations of his "thoughts toward his people" (v.5; NIV, "the things you planned for us"; cf. 92:5; Isa 55:8–11). The history of redemption shows an inner cohesiveness and movement, unfolding the "thoughts" of the Lord that will ultimately result in the restoration of heaven and earth. The mighty acts of God are too numerous to recount (cf. 104:24; 106:2; 139:17–18; John 21:25). The blessing of the man who trusts in the Lord is such that he places himself under the protection of Yahweh, whose marvelous acts of redemption are too numerous to mention. He is the Incomparable (cf. note on v.5).

Notes

---

4 (5 MT) In his polemic against paganism, the psalmist uses two words: רְהָבִים (*rehābîm,* "arrogant," "idols") and כָּזָב (*kāzāb,* "falsehood"). Two interpretations are possible: "the proud, . . . falsehood" or "the idols, . . . false gods." The NIV is ambivalent in its translation: "the proud, . . . false gods." Dahood argues for a parallel translation: "Pagan idols, . . . fraudulent images" (*Psalms*, 1:243, 245). Craigie takes another approach: "the defiant, the fabricators of falsehood" (*Psalms 1–50*, pp. 312–13). Both alternatives reflect the Hebrew. The NIV is sensitive to both possibilities: "false gods" in the text with a marginal note, "Or *to falsehood*."

5 (6 MT) The phrase "no one can recount to you" is one possible rendering of the problematic Hebrew: אֵין עֲרֹךְ אֵלֶיךָ (*'ên 'ᵃrō<u>k</u> 'ēley<u>k</u>ā*, "no comparing to you," "none opposing you," "no one arranging for you"). The idea behind the phrase lies in the incomparability of Yahweh over against the proud/idols of v.4 (see C.J. Labuschagne, *The Incomparability of Yahweh in the Old Testament* [Leiden: Brill, 1966]).

III. Expression of Commitment

40:6–8

6 Sacrifice and offering you did not desire,
but my ears you have pierced;
burnt offerings and sin offerings
you did not require.
7 Then I said, "Here I am, I have come—
it is written about me in the scroll.
8 I desire to do your will, O my God;
your law is within my heart."

6–8 These words may have been uttered after the ritual presentation of sacrifices and offerings. The king had already presented his offerings before going out to battle in order to atone for the sins of the people ("burnt offerings and sin offerings") and had offered some fellowship offerings in anticipation of salvation (cf. 1 Sam 13:9). On the successful conclusion of the campaign, he would have presented additional sacrifices (cf. 1 Sam 15:21). David is very much aware that the Lord was not pleased with mere sacrifice, as the accounts of Saul bring out. The kingdom had been torn from him because of his disobedience, not because of his aversion to sacrifice (1 Sam 15:22–23). Some have mistakenly concluded from vv.6–8 that the psalmist was opposed to the sacrificial system. To the contrary, David was opposed to mere formalism and declares his personal commitment to the Lord.

Commitment to the Lord is in the form of "open ears." The psalmist has heard the law of God—especially the requirements of kingship, to which he responds with an open ear (see Notes; see also appendix to Ps 19: The Word of God). Commitment to the Lord is also in the form of a personal preparedness to do the will of God ("Here I am," v.7; cf. Isa 6:8). The servant presents himself to his Lord, submitting himself completely to whatever his Master may require (cf. Heb 10:9). David, the Lord's anointed, presents himself as a dedicatory offering to the Lord (cf. Rom 12:1–2).

Commitment to the Lord is also in the form of a wholehearted desire to conform one's way of life to the will of God, as prescribed in the Word of God ("the scroll," v.7). David had heard with his ears what God required of the king (cf. Deut 17:14–20). The Torah of God was to be his charter for the administration of Yahweh's righteousness and justice on earth. David did not feel coerced, but with sincerity and inner commitment he committed his life to doing God's will. Verse 8 is that expression of the internalization of God's law, which characterizes the "new" covenant and was found also in the Mosaic administration (cf. 37:31; Isa 51:7; Jer 31:33–34). This commitment was typological of the obedience of Christ unto death, as applied by the author of Hebrews (10:5–7; see the LXX).

Notes

6 (7 MT) For a treatment of the kinds and purposes of sacrifices, see W.A. VanGemeren, "Offerings and Sacrifices in Bible Times," in Elwell, EDT, pp. 788–92; Steven R. Boguslawski, "The Psalms: Prophetic Polemics Against Sacrifices," *Irish Biblical Studies* 5 (1983): 14–41.

The NIV's "my ears you have pierced" is a rendering of the MT. The verb כָּרִיתָ (*kārîṯā*, "you have dug") is a metaphor for the opening of the ears to make them receptive to hearing, in contrast to "dull ears" (Isa 6:10) or "closed ears" (Jer 6:10). I agree with Kirkpatrick (p. 211) that the metaphor has no relation to the Hebrew practice of piercing the ears of slaves (Exod 21:6). The LXX offers a different reading: "you prepared a body for me" (cf. Heb 10:5–7). The NIV margin reflects the LXX: "Septuagint *but a body you have prepared for me* (see also Symmachus and Theodotion)." The LXX, however, represents a paraphrastic interpretation of a difficult Hebrew phrase (F.F. Bruce, *The Epistle to the Hebrews* [Grand Rapids: Eerdmans, 1964], p. 232).

IV. Proclamation of God's Perfections

40:9–10

9 I proclaim righteousness in the great assembly;
I do not seal my lips,
as you know, O LORD.
10 I do not hide your righteousness in my heart;
I speak of your faithfulness and salvation.
I do not conceal your love and your truth
from the great assembly.

9–10 In response to so great a salvation, David proclaims the good news of Yahweh's perfections to the congregation assembled for worship (v.9; cf. 35:18). He has already spoken of the mighty acts of the Lord (v.5), vowed to uphold the charter of the kingdom, and devoted himself to a lifetime commitment as Yahweh's servant. The psalmist must speak by an inner compulsion. He cannot be quiet ("I do not seal. . . . I do not conceal," vv.9–10).

The psalmist explains why he is so committed. His commitment is correlative to the perfections of Yahweh's rule: "righteousness . . . faithfulness . . . salvation . . . love . . . truth." The Lord's righteousness (*ṣeḏeq*) is expressed in any act ordered on behalf of his people's welfare and the execution of his kingdom purposes. By his righteous acts they are delivered, prosper, and enjoy the benefits of the covenant relationship (See VanGemeren, "Righteousness," in Elwell, BEB, 2:1860–62). Righteousness in this sense is synonymous with "salvation" in the broadest sense. The nature of God's righteous acts is explicated by the other perfections. He is faithful to his covenant people, in accordance with his promises (33:4), resulting in the "salvation" of his people (see appendix to Ps 119: Yahweh Is My Redeemer).

The faithfulness of God is a corollary to his love in that the Lord's love (*ḥeseḏ*, "covenant love"; cf. 13:5; 18:50; 25:10; 31:7; 32:10) is constant. He is the God of love and "truth," i.e., fidelity (cf. 26:3). Salvation is nothing less than the full enjoyment of God's everlasting goodness.

The proclamation of God's perfections is an occasion of public celebration. The repetition of "great assembly" (vv.9–10) constitutes an inclusion. The fellowship of God's people fully shares in the acts of God (cf. 35:18) (see appendix to Ps 25: The Perfections of Yahweh).

Notes

10 (11 MT) Dahood (*Psalms*, 1:246–47) has satisfactorily explained that the prepositional particle לְ (*lᵉ*, "for") has the meaning "from" in the phrase "from the great assembly."

V. Prayer for God's Perfections

40:11

> [11] Do not withhold your mercy from me, O LORD;
> may your love and your truth always protect me.

11 The preceding celebration and proclamation of God's perfections form the basis of the king's supplication. A new crisis has arisen. He prays that Yahweh will continue to bestow his covenant "love" (*ḥeseḏ*) and fidelity or "truth" (*'ᵉmeṯ*) to his anointed servant and through him to the nation. Because of the great need (cf. v.12), he also implores God to have compassion on him. The word "mercy" (*raḥᵃmîm*) was not listed among the perfections of v.10. Now that the people are in need of salvation, he prays for the heavenly father to show compassion to his children. His compassion moves him to initiate the process of restoration and salvation, which is the object of this prayer (cf. 103:13).

Notes

11 (12 MT) The emphatic "you" in "you, O LORD" (untr. in NIV) corresponds to the emphatic "you" in v.9 (10 MT): "you know." The Lord knows that the psalmist has proclaimed his divine perfections in the great assembly. The psalmist has not "withheld" them from the people. So he prays that the Lord will not withhold the continuance of his mighty acts of mercy, love, and fidelity. Otherwise he shows David to be a liar. Craigie interprets אַתָּה (*'attāh*, "you") as a verb, meaning "come": "Come, O LORD, and do not hold back" (*Psalms 1–50*, pp. 312–13).

VI. Confession of Sin

40:12

12 For troubles without number surround me;
 my sins have overtaken me, and I cannot see.
They are more than the hairs of my head,
 and my heart fails within me.

12 The king is troubled by the adversities caused by his enemies (cf. vv.14–15). The relationship between sin and suffering was well known to the OT saints. However, it is not easy to decide whose sin was responsible for the renewed adversities. Though the king speaks of "my sins," he may personify the national sin as his own. As a theocratic leader he takes on himself the sin of the nation as his own and pleads with the Lord to have compassion on the condition of the nation. The consequences of sin had a paralyzing effect on the king and his ability to rule over God's people. This verse is to be read in the light of his expression of commitment (vv.6–8). So great was the affliction ("troubles without number") that he felt overwhelmed like a flood (cf. 2 Sam 22:5; Jonah 2:5). He was so deeply troubled that he lost perspective ("I cannot see. . . . my heart fails within me"). For the hyperbolic expression "the hairs of my head," see Psalm 69:4; Matthew 10:30.

Notes

12 (13 MT) For a physiological explanation of the relation between trouble, tears, and the inability to see, cf. John S. Kselman, "A Note on *LR'WT* in Ps 40:13," *Biblica* 63 (1982): 552–54.

VII. Prayer for God's Protection

40:13–16

13 Be pleased, O LORD, to save me;
 O LORD, come quickly to help me.
14 May all who seek to take my life
 be put to shame and confusion;
may all who desire my ruin
 be turned back in disgrace.
15 May those who say to me, "Aha! Aha!"
 be appalled at their own shame.
16 But may all who seek you
 rejoice and be glad in you;
may those who love your salvation always say,
 "The LORD be exalted!"

13–15 David prays that the Lord will "quickly" (v.13; cf. 22:19; 38:22; 70:1, 5; 71:12; 141:1) help him out of the crisis. He affirms that it must be God's will ("be pleased") and his act of deliverance ("to save me," "to help me"). His prayer for protection is an expression of trust in the Lord's ability to protect him (cf. vv.4–5). Even though it may have been tempting to find ways of taking care of the problems, the psalmist begins and ends with Yahweh. He also prays that those who rejoiced in his and the nation's misery may be proven wrong in their assumption that Yahweh lacked power to redeem his people.

The psalmist prays for his enemies' fall and shame in accordance with the principles of justice and with the promise of God to curse those who cursed his own (vv.14–15; cf. 35:4, 26; Gen 12:3). It must be remembered that the enemies were probably not known personally. They were Israel's national enemies who hated Israel, David, and Yahweh, the God of Israel. The psalmist no doubt knew the admonition to love one's enemies (cf. Prov 25:21; Matt 5:44), but these enemies destabilized the rule of God on earth! As long as the kingdom of God suffers persecution and harassment, we pray for God's kingdom to come, which includes the petition that the Lord will come to vindicate his own and avenge his enemies (cf. 2 Thess 1:5–10). The enemies liked taking potshots at God's people, shouting contemptibly, "Aha! Aha!" (v.15; 35:21, 25). The psalmist prays that the Lord will quickly and suddenly change their fortunes so that they will know who is God (v.14; cf. 35:4, 26; see the appendix to Ps 137: Imprecation in the Psalms).

16 When the Lord demonstrates anew his righteous act of deliverance, God's people will rejoice in his salvation (cf. 35:27). The anointed of the Lord prays for the sake of God's people. As a shepherd-king, he is concerned about their welfare. He prays that they may taste his salvation and always have reason to bless the Lord for his great acts: "The LORD be exalted!" (cf. 35:27; Mal 1:5). The taunts of the enemy—"Aha! Aha!" (v.15)—are silenced, and the shouts of joy from God's people echo the new acts of salvation.

Those who rejoice in the salvation are characterized by their "seeking" the Lord and "those who love your salvation" (cf. 35:27). In Psalm 35 the righteous are described as those who look for the "vindication" (= "righteousness") and the "well-being" or "peace" of the Lord's anointed (v.27). The shift lies in the emphasis of the psalm. Whereas Psalm 35 is in the form of a personal lament in which David prays for himself, this psalm focuses on the Lord's goodness to his people through his servant. David prays here, not for himself, but for his people who have joined him in waiting for the salvation of the Lord.

VIII. Personal Need of Salvation

40:17

17 Yet I am poor and needy;
  may the Lord think of me.
You are my help and my deliverer;
  O my God, do not delay.

17 The psalmist concludes on a personal note. It must be remembered that he speaks, not of himself only, but by corporate identity of the needs of the nation as a whole. He began by affirming that he waited "patiently" on the Lord, and he ends on a note of urgency. The last three words express the need: "do not delay."

The dependency on the Lord for deliverance is brought out by the contrastive personal pronoun in Hebrew: "Yet I. . . . you." He is in desperate need and humbly (cf. 35:10; 37:1–7) casts himself and his people before the Lord. He does not presume on his rights of deliverance by the covenant relationship but prays that the Lord will consider his needs ("think of me").

The affirmation of God's fidelity and ability, which is found throughout the psalm, concludes the prayer. The Lord remains "my help and my deliverer" and "my God" even in crises. It is on this ground that David prays for the speedy deliverance (cf. v.13). Yet, as before, he would be willing to wait "patiently" for the Lord's time to rescue the king and his people.

Psalm 41: God's Blessings in Adversity

This psalm has elements in common with an individual lament (vv.4–10). Yet the introductory (vv.1–3) and concluding (vv.11–12) verses set the mood of thanksgiving for the psalm in such a way that we shall treat it with the majority of modern commentators as a *thanksgiving of the individual.* The psalm reflects on the blessedness of the godly, even when they are taken by great sickness. The Lord blesses his own with sustenance (v.3), even when they suffer on account of sin (v.4). The psalm affirms that the Lord knows the "integrity" of heart and that he will have compassion on his own (v.12).

The structure of the psalm is straightforward:

A. Affirmation of God's Blessings (vv.1–3)
  B. Prayer for Healing (v.4)
    C. The Words of the Enemies (vv.5–9)
  B′. Prayer for Healing (v.10)
A′. Confidence in God's Blessings (vv.11–12)
A″. Concluding Doxology to Book I (v.13)

I. Affirmation of God's Blessings

41:1–3

For the director of music. A psalm of David.

1 Blessed is he who has regard for the weak;
  the LORD delivers him in times of trouble.
2 The LORD will protect him and preserve his life;
  he will bless him in the land
  and not surrender him to the desire of his foes.
3 The LORD will sustain him on his sickbed
  and restore him from his bed of illness.

1 The phrase "blessed is" (*'ašrê*) begins (see 1:1) and closes the first Book of Psalms. It forms a magnificent envelope structure, enclosing forty-one psalms, representative of the literary variety of the Psalms: lament, prayer, praise, confidence, wisdom, Zion song, and affirmation of Yahweh's kingship.

How blessed are the children of God, as they receive grace upon grace! But God's blessings are not automatically bestowed on his people. The Father in heaven looks for those who wisely conform to his heavenly kingdom on earth: righteousness, holiness, love, and justice. He cares for the oppressed and delights to see his children's concern with the things that are important to him: concern for those in need (cf. 35:13–14; 112:9; Matt 5:7; James 1:27). The need may take many forms: "times of trouble," "his foes," or a "sickbed" (vv.1–3).

2–3 The Lord has promised to help and deliver his people so that they will not be overcome by adversities, enemies, or diseases. Positively, the Lord has promised to protect (*š-m-r*) his people from harm (vv.2–3; cf. 18:35; 37:28) and bless them with a long life of good health (*ḥ-y-h*), prosperity (*'-š-r*) in their promised land (37:22), and sustenance (*s-'-d*) in time of need. These promises are inherent in the Abrahamic covenant (Gen 12:2–3), confirmed in the Mosaic covenant (cf. Lev 26:1–13; Num 6:24–26; Deut 7:13–16; 28:1–14), and ratified in the Davidic covenant (Ps 72) and the new covenant in Jesus Christ (2 Cor 1:20).

Notes

For a brief discussion of the technical words and phrases in the superscription, see the Introduction.

1 (2 MT) The preceding psalm closed on an expression of David's need ("I am poor and needy," v.17). A third synonym is used in 41:1, דָּל (*dāl*, "poor," "weak"). The word signifies here those who are lowly because of whatever adversities have overtaken them. There is no need to emend the text, following the LXX, by the addition of "and poor" (*wᵉ'eḇyôn*, BHS; Craigie, *Psalms 1–50*, p. 318).

The verb מַשְׂכִּיל (*maśkîl*, "has regard for") is associated with the wisdom tradition (cf. 2:10; 14:1–2; 36:3) and may be rendered: "Blessed is he who deals wisely with."

2–3 (3–4 MT) The use of the jussive in these verses could be translated, "May the LORD protect . . . and preserve . . . bless . . . and not surrender. . . . May the LORD sustain . . . and restore" (cf. Dahood, *Psalms*, 1:248).

2 (3 MT) The MT's יְאֻשַּׁר (*y ᵉ'uššar*, "will be blessed," Pual) is a corrupt form of יְאַשְּׁרֵהוּ (*yᵉ'aššᵉrēhû*, "may he bless him," Piel; see a number of Hebrew MSS and the LXX). The verb is related to the formula for blessing (v.1: *'ašrê*, "blessed").

The third person is favored by the LXX, Syriac, and Vulgate, rather than the second person (MT): תִּתְּנֵהוּ (*titt ᵉhû*, "you will surrender him"). So also is v.3: "and he will restore him" (see NIV), instead of "you restore him" (MT).

For the idiomatic use of "the desire of his foes," see 27:12.

3 (4 MT) The NIV omits a translation of כָּל (*kol*, "all") as a modifier with "bed," viz., "his whole bed" (so Craigie, *Psalms 1–50*, p. 318). The word "bed" may denote sickness and could be rendered "all of his diseases" (RSV, "all his infirmities").

II. Prayer for Healing

41:4

4 I said, "O LORD, have mercy on me;
heal me, for I have sinned against you."

4 The prayer for healing and restoration (cf. 6:2–3; Jer 17:14) is based on God's promises (vv.1–3). The emphatic use of "I" is for the purpose of contrasting the words of the prayer with the words of the foes (v.5). There is no note of despair in his prayer. The psalmist is not depressed by the weight of his sin; it is likely that he makes a general confession of unwitting sins that he may have committed. He also confesses that he needs the Lord's mercy (*ḥ-n-n*).

Notes

4 (5 MT) The verb רְפָאָה (*r ᵉpā'āh*, "heal") is synonymous with "deliver" or "restore" (cf. 6:2–3; Jer 17:14).

For חָטָאתִי (*ḥāṭā'ṯî*, "I have sinned"), see 32:1 and the appendix to Ps 103: Sin and Forgiveness.

III. The Words of the Enemies

41:5–9

5 My enemies say of me in malice,
"When will he die and his name perish?"
6 Whenever one comes to see me,
he speaks falsely, while his heart gathers slander;
then he goes out and spreads it abroad.

7 All my enemies whisper together against me;
they imagine the worst for me, saying,
8 "A vile disease has beset him;
he will never get up from the place where he lies."
9 Even my close friend, whom I trusted,
he who shared my bread,
has lifted up his heel against me.

5–6 The psalmist laments over the reaction to his sickness. As he listened to what his enemies had to "say" (v.5) about him, he suffered great anguish. Their words were filled with hatred and without sympathy for his trouble. As in other psalms of adversity (cf. 6; 22; 38; 40), the adversary looms like a dark shadow. Every word, movement, and action reveals hatred, bitterness, and malice. The adversary slanders, hoping that evil will triumph and the righteous and their seed may perish from the earth (v.5; cf. 109:13). He is full of deception, hypocrisy, and selfishness (v.6; cf. 4:6).

7–9 Verses 7–9 focus more sharply on what the enemies say and how his close friend has betrayed him. Even on his sickbed he imagined hearing the whisperings of his adversaries. It was as if everybody was talking about his imminent death. The "whisper" (v.7) of the enemies may have been a magical form of incantation (v.8). They described his sickness as horrid, "a vile disease." The word "vile" is a translation of "Belial" and could also be rendered as "a sickness from the devil" or "an accursed disease." While the psalmist thought of himself as innocent of known transgression (vv.11–12), his adversaries hoped that he would die! They thought that his sins had found him out and that he was like one accursed. It appears that the "enemies" were not devoid of religion but were devoid of true religion. True religion shows itself in a concern for the needy (v.1; cf. James 1:27).

The rumors became so malicious that the psalmist's "close friend" (v.9, lit., "a man of peace"; cf. 7:4; 55:12–14; Jer 20:10; 38:22b; Obad 7), whom he regarded as a member of the family, turned against him. The idiom "has lifted up his heel against me" signifies a treacherous act (cf. Gen 3:15; Ps 55:12–14). Thus both friend and adversary malign his name, believing that his death is justified (cf. Jer 9:4). Our Lord alludes to v.9 when explaining that one of the disciples who has eaten "bread" with him at the last Passover will betray him (John 13:18; cf. Matt 26:23; Mark 14:18; Luke 22:21). Judas, too, thought mistakenly that the cause of God would be served best if Jesus were to die.

Notes

5 (6 MT) The perishing of the name often involved the end of one's family line (cf. Deut 7:24; 9:14; 25:6; 2 Sam 18:18; Ps 109:13; Isa 14:22). See Dahood: "In other words, when will his family vanish from the earth?" (*Psalms,* 1:250).

7 (8 MT) On magical practices see Dahood (*Psalms,* 1:251) and A.A. Anderson: "And it is indeed possible that the enemies resorted to certain dubious practices, just to make sure that the afflicted man did not escape death" (1:324).

8 (9 MT) "A vile disease" is literally "a thing of Belial." The meaning of the word "Belial" is not clearly known because of the problem of identifying the etymology (see on 18:4; 101:3). It is a strongly negative word in the OT (cf. 1 Sam 30:22; see Ps 18:4). Craigie translates it, "A devilish disease" (*Psalms 1–50,* pp. 318–19).

The verb יָצוּק (*yāṣûq,* "is being poured"; NIV, "has beset him") is a passive participle and is a metaphor for pouring out like a liquid. The disease is portrayed as something poured out over his sick body. It is inescapable.

9 (10 MT) The word עָקֵב (*'āqēḇ,* "heel") is related to the root *'-q-b* ("scheme," "cheat," "grasp by the heel"), from which the name Jacob ("schemer") is derived (cf. Gen 3:15).

IV. Prayer for Healing

41:10

10 But you, O LORD, have mercy on me;
raise me up, that I may repay them.

10 The prayers of vv.4 and 10 frame the lies of the enemies (vv.5–9). The psalmist cannot respond to their accusations but wholeheartedly trusts in the Lord and in his promise to protect him against his enemies. He prays that the Lord will be gracious to him and restore him (cf. v.4) and that he may "repay them." This prayer for vindication is not vindictive but shows a concern with the honor and justice of the Lord, who has promised to sustain the godly in sickness and in health (vv.2–3). In maligning the psalmist, they have maligned the God of Israel!

V. Confidence in God's Blessings

41:11–12

11 I know that you are pleased with me,
for my enemy does not triumph over me.
12 In my integrity you uphold me
and set me in your presence forever.

11–12 Even in his adversity the psalmist is confident that the Lord will be true to his promises. Within his heart the psalmist knows himself to be a man of integrity (v.12;

cf. 18:25, "blameless"). He also claims the promise that the Lord supports those who love him—especially in their adversities (cf. 37:23–24). As in the shepherd psalm, he longs for the moment when the Lord will deal kindly with him in the presence of his enemies and that he will enjoy God's presence and the experience of his blessings (vv.1–3) forevermore (cf. 23:5–6). Then he will be reassured ("by this I know," v.11; see Notes) of God's delight in him (cf. 18:19; 22:8; 35:27). He trusts in the Lord and is waiting for a token of divine favor and pleasure. David, God's anointed, hopes in God's promise of his presence in blessing and protection (2 Sam 7:16).

Notes

11 (12 MT) The NIV fails to render בְּזֹאת (*b^e^zō't*, "in this," "thus") before יָדַעְתִּי (*yāḏa'tî*, "I know"). When the Lord is gracious by raising him up (v.10), he will know more deeply and intimately that the Lord loves him (cf. 20:6).

The triumph of the enemy also includes a triumphant shout of victory. The verb יָרִיעַ (*yārî^a^'*, "shout") means any kind of shouting associated with warfare, whether at the outset or at the victorious conclusion. The psalmist prays that the enemies may not have occasion to shout in triumph, because they are wrong about him and about his God (cf. 30:1; 35:19; 38:16).

12 (13 MT) The emphatic form of "I" (not in NIV) is in anticipation of God's response. The psalmist believes that the Lord will deal kindly with him, bestowing on him, too, his blessing (vv.1–3). The verbs תָּמַכְתָּ (*tāmaḵtā*, "uphold me") and וַתַּצִּיבֵנִי (*wattaṣṣîḇēnî*, "set me") continue the prayer of confidence in God's blessings, begun in v.10, and may be translated as imperatives (Joüon, par. 112k; Dahood, *Psalms*, 1:252) with the following result:

But you [emphatic], O LORD, have mercy on me;
 raise me up. . . .
  Thus I know that you are pleased with me. . . .
As for me [emphatic],
 In my integrity uphold me
  and set me in your presence forever.

Concluding Doxology to Book I

41:13

13 Praise be to the LORD, the God of Israel,
 from everlasting to everlasting.
  Amen and Amen.

13 The Lord is "blessed" (*bārûḵ;* NIV, "praise be to") in the sense that he is praiseworthy. He is Yahweh, the God of Israel, who has covenanted to be their God and the God of their children. Since he is blessed forever, God's people have assurance that he will continue in his care. To this doxology Israel responded with a twofold "amen." The doxology was popularized through liturgical use (cf. Luke 1:68; Rom 9:5).

Notes

13 (14 MT) For a study on the doxological conclusions, see Ernst Jenni, "Zu den doxologischen Schlussformeln des Psalters," *Theologische Zeitschrift* 40 (1984): 114–20.

Book II: Psalms 42–72

Psalms 42–43: Hoping in the Lord's Salvation

The literary unity of Psalms 42 and 43 is such that they should be treated as one psalm. Even though the MT and LXX keep them separate, there are internal arguments for their unity: (1) the absence of a superscription above Psalm 43; (2) the repetition of a refrain (42:5, 11; 43:5); (3) development of thought from remembrance (42:4, 6) to a specific hope of restoration (43:3); and (4) the lament form. On the variety of expressions of hope in lament psalms, see the excellent article by Yair Hoffman, "The Transition from Despair to Hope in the Individual Psalms of Lament," *Tarbiz* 55 (1985/86): 161–72 (Heb.).

Each psalm is an *individual lament*. Even though the life-situation remains controversial, it is evident that the psalmist was isolated from the temple worship. He may have been a refugee, but it is more likely that he had been exiled to Aram, Assyria, or Babylon and was in the hands of taunting captors (vv.3, 10).

The structure is built around questions and a threefold refrain (42:5, 11; 43:5). The psalmist questions God (42:2b, 9; 43:2) and himself (42:5, 11; 43:5), as his enemies taunt him, "Where is your God?" (42:3, 10). The refrain responds to the questions and exhorts the psalmist and the reader to faith and hope. The expository structure is as follows:

A. Lament (42:1–4)
  B. Hope (v.5)
A′. Lament (vv.6–7)
  B′. Hope (v.8)
A″. Lament (vv.9–10)
  B″. Hope (v.11)
A‴. Lament (43:1–4)
  B‴. Hope (v.5)

The apparent to-and-fro movement takes us from a remembrance of the past through a reflection on the present sufferings to an anticipation of God's vindication and presence. Luis Alonso Schökel ("The Poetic Structure of Psalms 42–43," JSOT 1 [1976]: 4–11) argues persuasively for the unity and development from the past nostalgia and the present affliction to the hope of restoration. See also James A. Durlesser, "A Rhetorical Critical Study of Psalms 19, 42, and 43," *Studia Biblica et Theologica* 10 (1980): 179–97.

I. Lament

42:1–4

For the director of music. A *maskil* of the Sons of Korah.

1 As the deer pants for streams of water,
so my soul pants for you, O God.

2 My soul thirsts for God, for the living God.
  When can I go and meet with God?
3 My tears have been my food
  day and night,
 while men say to me all day long,
  "Where is your God?"
4 These things I remember
  as I pour out my soul:
 how I used to go with the multitude,
  leading the procession to the house of God,
 with shouts of joy and thanksgiving
  among the festive throng.

1–3 The longing of the psalmist for God's presence is clear from simile and the references to God. First, the simile of the "deer" ("hart") expresses the intense yearning for a taste of God's presence. The deer looks until it finds water and quenches its thirst with great joy. So the psalmist longs for God's presence with his whole being (*nep̱eš*, "soul"). As usual "soul" does not denote the spiritual aspect of man exclusively. He intensely longs for ("pants for. . . . thirsts," vv.1–2; cf. 63:1) fellowship with God and will not be content until he may return to Jerusalem and praise God with great joy (43:4). So strong is his physical longing for God that we may agree with C.S. Lewis, who described the psalmists' craving for God as an "appetite for God" (*Reflections on the Psalms*, p. 51).

Second, in the references to God, the psalmist's longing for God increases in intensity. He addresses him as "God" (v.1), then as "the living God," and finally expresses his profound hope to see "the face of God" (MT; NIV, "meet with God," v.2). It may well be that the phrase "living God" (v.2; 84:2; Deut 5:26; Hos 1:10) is associated with the imagery of God as "living water" (cf. Jer 2:13; 17:13), the fountain of life (Ps 36:8–9). In v.8 the psalmist speaks of him as "the God of my life," water and life being closely associated.

In view of his need of God, the psalmist asks when he can return and experience once again the presence of God. He wants to "meet with God" in the temple on Mount Zion (v.2; 84:7). The question is partly rhetorical and functions as one question in a chain of questions (vv.8–9; 43:1). The rhetorical aspect of the question lies in the problem of how a man who desires God's presence can experience alienation from God. The question finds its resolution in the development of these psalms.

The psalmist is hemmed in by his own question, by his longing for God's presence (v.2), and by his enemies who tauntingly ask, "Where is your God?" (v.3; 10:11; 12:4; 59:7; 64:5; 71:11; 73:11; 94:7; 115:2; Mic 7:10). Living in isolation from the land, he could not experience God's presence in the magnificent structure of the temple. Down deep in his heart he asked the same question, "Where is my God?" For this reason he mourns continually. The depth of his sorrow is hyperbolically expressed by "tears" as his "food" (v.3; cf. 80:5; 102:3–11; Job 3:24). The taunts of the enemies serve to bring him closer to despondency. For the present it seems as if God does not have the power to deliver. With these questions he lives continually ("all day long," vv.3, 10). Not knowing where else to turn, he looks back in remembrance, digs deeply into his own soul, and then looks to God for the final answer to his despairing feeling.

4 Adverse conditions create an optimum context for reflection. The psalmist cannot do much more than to "remember." He remembers "these things." What things did he remember? He meditated on the pilgrimages to the temple, the festive celebrations, and God's triumphs in the history of salvation. During the three annual pilgrimage festivals (Passover, Firstfruits, and Tabernacles; cf. Exod 23:17; 34:18–26; Lev 23:4–44; Deut 16:1–17), the pilgrims gathered in Jerusalem and presented their offerings and sacrifices with great rejoicing. It is true that many people were apostates, as the prophets bear out. However, the godly minority (the remnant) focused their hope on a purification of the people, a catharsis of the temple worship, and a new age. The period of exile was the transition between the old age and the new age. The transition period proved immensely difficult for the godly (cf. Ps 137; Lam 1–5). The pouring out of the soul is an expression of the intensity of one's emotions (cf. 62:8; 142:4–7; 1 Sam 1:15; Job 30:16; Lam 2:19).

Notes

For a brief discussion of the technical words and phrases in the superscription, see the Introduction. See especially the discussion on the Korahite Psalms and the Elohistic Psalter.

See C.S. Lewis's intriguing essay "The Fair Beauty of the Lord" (*Reflections on the Psalms*, pp. 44–53).

2 (3 MT) The Masoretes changed any text suggesting that man could see God. The reading וְאֵרָאֶה (*weʾērāʾeh*, "and I shall be seen"; NIV, "meet") is a Niphal form of the verb "see." Without a change in the consonantal text, it is equally possible to read it as *weʾerʾeh* ("and I shall see"). Several Hebrew MSS, the Syriac, and the Targum support this reading as the original.

3 (4 MT) The NIV accepts an emendation of בֶּאֱמֹר (*beʾemōr*, "in saying," inf. cons.) to בְּאָמְרָם (*beʾomrām*, "in their saying," "while men say"). The emendation is supported by several Hebrew MSS and is the reading of v.11 (10 EV).

The taunt is a stereotypical expression put on the lips of the enemies of God (cf. 79:10; 115:2; Joel 2:17; Mic 7:10).

4 (5 MT) The clause "leading the procession" is problematic. The word סָךְ (*sāḵ*) is traditionally understood as "procession" but could be an alternate form of "tent" or "booth" (*sōḵ* or *sukkāh;* so LXX).

A more difficult issue is the meaning of אֶדַּדֵּם (*ʾeddaddēm;* NIV, "leading"). A few Hebrew MSS have an alternate reading: *ʾaddirîm* ("majestic ones," "exalted ones," BHS); see NEB: "in the ranks of the great" and Weiser: "in the company of the exalted" (p. 346). The BHS prefers a different reading: *ʾaddîr* ("Exalted One"). Dahood looked for another etymology than the traditional Hitpael of the root *d-d-h,* which occurs only in Isa 38:15. He proposed the root *n-d-d* ("to bow down") with an enclitic mem: "and prostrate myself near the temple of God" (*Psalms,* 1:254, 257). Craigie objects to the Ugaritic evidence cited by Dahood and returns to the traditional sense: "I used to walk with them" (*Psalms 1–50,* pp. 323–24). For a lexicographic treatment, see KB^3, 1:205.

II. Hope

42:5–6a

5 Why are you downcast, O my soul?
Why so disturbed within me?

Put your hope in God,
  for I will yet praise him,
  my Savior and [6]my God.

5–6a The psalmist analyzes his feelings and asks questions of himself (vv.5, 11; 43:5). The threefold refrain reflects the emotional state of many of God's people during the Exile and, for that matter, any crisis situation. The inner feelings express themselves in questions, despair, and hope in God. The questions are overtaking him. Yet, while hemmed in by the questions in his desperate situation, he still could engage himself in dialogue. There was no voice from God. In the loneliness of alienation, his faith was tried and triumphed! Faith and doubt are twins; and when doubt seemed to triumph, true faith calmed its questions. Faith answered. Faith despairs and despair hopes!

Hope leads the psalmist away from despair. His hope is in "God, . . . my Savior and my God." Hope, in essence, is waiting for God to act (cf. 38:15; 39:7). Hope is focused on the glorious acts of salvation and victory of which the Law, Historical Writings, and Prophets speak. Hope longs for the "praise" of God for the acts of salvation. Hope says, "You are my God," in anticipation of the fulfillment of the promises, even when help is far off. (For the application of these words, reflecting the LXX version, to our Lord's experience in the Garden of Gethsemane, see Matt 26:38.)

Notes

5 (6 MT) The root of תִּשְׁתּוֹחֲחִי (*tištôḥᵃhî,* "you are downcast") is either from the root *š-y-ḥ* ("melt away," Hitpolel impf.) or *š-ḥ-ḥ* ("stoop," "be low," Hitpolel impf.). The forms occur only in these two psalms. An alternate form occurs in 35:14; 38:6 (7 MT).

The MT elliptically or by scribal mistake omits the second interrogative. BHS proposes the change of the MT to conform the present text to 42:11 and 43:5 with the support of a few Hebrew MSS, the LXX, and the Syriac. The emendation is unnecessary in case of ellipsis.

The verb וַתֶּהֱמִי (*wattehᵉmî,* "disturbed") is a form of *h-m-h* ("make a noise," "roar," "be restless"). A.A. Anderson suggests that the similarity of the verb to the noun הָמוֹן (*hāmôn,* "throng") may be a purposeful contrast between past joy and present despair (1:331).

הוֹחִילִי (*hôḥîlî,* "hope") connotes a patient standing in wait for one greater than oneself (1 Sam 10:8) or for the Lord (2 Kings 6:33; Pss 38:15; 39:7; 130:5; Mic 7:7).

The praise is focused on יְשׁוּעוֹת פָּנָיו (*yᵉšû'ôṯ pānāyw,* "the acts of salvation of his face"; NIV, "my Savior"). The acts of God of the past were remembered (v.4) with the hope that the same God will again perform his mighty acts of deliverance. Compare the NIV margin—"*praise him for his saving help*"—with Craigie: "the victories of my God's presence" (*Psalms 1–50*, pp. 323–24). The NIV reads "my God" (v.6) with v.5, resulting in "my Savior and my God," based on a few Hebrew MSS, the LXX, and the Syriac.

John Goldingay rightly explains the differences in the language in the refrain as arising from artistic variation ("Repetition and Variation in the Psalms," JQR 68 [1977]: 147). For a pastorally oriented exposition of this verse, see D. Martin Lloyd Jones, *Spiritual Depression: Its Causes and Cure* (Grand Rapids: Eerdmans, 1968).

III. Lament

42:6b–7

My soul is downcast within me;
  therefore I will remember you

from the land of the Jordan,
  the heights of Hermon—from Mount Mizar.
7 Deep calls to deep
  in the roar of your waterfalls;
all your waves and breakers
  have swept over me.

6b–7 Yet, in spite of the psalmist's reflections and expression of the triumph of hope, the experience of alienation is still there. He is still "downcast" (v.6). Therefore he returns in his memories to the Promised Land, symbolized here by "the land of the Jordan, the heights of Hermon" (v.6). The upper Jordan Valley, the Hermon Range with its peaks reaching nine thousand feet above sea level, and the unknown Mount Mizar point our attention to the region of the sources of the Jordan River. The psalmist returns to the water imagery with which the psalm began. But this time the memories of water are overshadowed by a deep sense of despair. The waterfalls with its rocks, breakers, and waves, and its awesome noise of the rushing and falling waters metaphorically portray his condition. Instead of enjoying the "living water" of the "living God," he is continually faced with an expression of God's judgment. He has no control over his present circumstances and undergoes the present troubles, not knowing where he will end up. Has doubt triumphed?

IV. Hope

42:8

8 By day the LORD directs his love,
  at night his song is with me—
  a prayer to the God of my life.

8 In his self-doubt the psalmist remembers the covenant love of the Lord. By day and night he experienced the evidences of God's care, protection, and blessing. He sang praises to him and prayed to him morning and evening (cf. 92:2). That was a time of fellowship with a God who was always present. The very experience of communion with God made Yahweh "real" to him as "the God of my life" (cf. 66:9). In contrast to the past experience, his "love" (*ḥeseḏ*) seems to be lost; and the psalmist's praise of God's love has changed into continual mourning for God's absence (cf. v.3). God's continual love is a comfort for the soul continually beset by questions and mourning (cf. v.3).

V. Lament

42:9–10

9 I say to God my Rock,
  "Why have you forgotten me?
Why must I go about mourning,
  oppressed by the enemy?"
10 My bones suffer mortal agony
  as my foes taunt me,
saying to me all day long,
  "Where is your God?"

9–10 In his moments of doubt and reflection on God's absence, the psalmist raises questions to God. He asks these questions in faith, because he remembers who his God is: "God my Rock" (v.9). Regardless of how despairing the situation, the Lord is still "the Rock" of Israel. He is the place of refuge (18:2). He asks twice pointedly "why" God has forgotten him (v.9; cf. 13:1; 22:1; 77:9; 88:14).

In the present situation, the psalmist has no other recourse than mourning in the agony of his own perplexity (cf. 35:14; 38:6). He has been abandoned to godless men, who taunt him continually with the same mocking question, "Where is your God?" (v.10). He is like a dying man, and his God, the Rock, is silent. His whole being ("my bones"; cf. 6:2) is distressed by his foes and by God's silence.

Notes

10 (11 MT) This verse is difficult. The NIV's "My bones suffer mortal agony" is literally "in murder in my bones." Several MSS read "like rot in my bones." Craigie proposes "with a breaking in my bones," based on an Akkadian analogy (*Psalms 1–50*, pp. 324–25). Whatever the exact interpretation, the psalmist feels deeply hurt.

VI. Hope

42:11

11 Why are you downcast, O my soul?
Why so disturbed within me?
Put your hope in God,
for I will yet praise him,
my Savior and my God.

11 These reflections bring the psalmist again to a point of despair, self-examination, and an affirmation of hope in the future saving acts of God (cf. comment and note on v.5).

VII. Lament

43:1–4

1 Vindicate me, O God,
and plead my cause against an ungodly nation;
rescue me from deceitful and wicked men.
2 You are God my stronghold.
Why have you rejected me?
Why must I go about mourning,
oppressed by the enemy?
3 Send forth your light and your truth,
let them guide me;
let them bring me to your holy mountain,
to the place where you dwell.
4 Then will I go to the altar of God,
to God, my joy and my delight.
I will praise you with the harp,
O God, my God.

1–2 Thus far the psalmist has called God "the living God" (42:2), "the saving acts" (NIV, "my Savior," 42:5), "my God" (42:6, 11), "the LORD" (Yahweh, 42:8), "the God of my life" (42:8), and "God my Rock" (42:9). Moreover, he has expressed hope in seeing God's presence (42:2) and the acts of love (42:8) and salvation evidencing his presence (42:5–6, 11). In this last couplet he intensifies his prayer for redemption and for the enjoyment of fellowship with the Lord. He has demonstrated his love (*ḥese*ḏ, 42:8) in the past, but the psalmist is not satisfied until he is fully restored to his God. In his distress he calls the Lord "God my stronghold" (v.2; or "refuge," cf. 27:1; 28:8; 31:3; 37:39). Not only is he the Rock of refuge, but also he is the Deliverer of his people in need. This God is powerful to "vindicate" (v.1, *š-p-ṭ;* cf. 7:8; 26:1; 35:24) him in the sense that Yahweh alone can defend him, prosecute the enemy, and execute his verdict (*r-y-b*, "plead my cause," v.1; 35:1, 23: "contend for") against the enemies.

The psalmist has gone around as in "mourning" (42:9; 43:2) because of the absence of God and because of the antagonism of the ungodly. The questions (v.2) are similar to those of the previous strophe (42:9). But the second question is more forceful. The change from "forgotten" (42:9) to "rejected" (cf.44:9, 23) must be observed. As long as God is silent, anguish becomes unbearable (cf. Lam 5:22).

3–4 In the darkness of the adversities, there is no other way than to ask the covenant God to remain faithful to his promises. In despondency and astonishment, his questions and doubt, the palmist asks God for his "light" and "truth" (v.3). The light of God is the experience of the fullness of his redemption (36:9; Isa 58:8, 10; 60:1, 3). The "truth" (*'ᵉme*ṯ) of God is the expression of his covenantal fidelity (40:10; 57:3). If only God will send these two personified expressions of his love to "guide" him back, then he will experience restoration. This verse leads to the answer of the original petition: "When can I go and meet with God?" (42:2).

Possibly the psalmist reflects on the wilderness experience with the pillar of cloud and smoke guiding Israel through the barren wasteland. Then too the Lord was faithful to his people and brought them to the Promised Land. The psalmist's concern is not with land or possessions but for a return to Jerusalem, "your holy mountain" (v.3; cf. 2:6; 3:4; 15:1; 48:2; 99:9). The anticipation to return to "the altar of God" (v.4) and the temple relates back to his remembrance of the pilgrimage festivals (v.3; 42:4). It is the place of God's "dwelling" (NIV, "the place where you dwell"; see appendix to Ps 132: The Ark of the Covenant and the Temple: Symbols of Yahweh's Presence and Rule).

Redemption will result in great joy. This requires another designation for God. The God who is "my stronghold" (v.2) becomes known as "God, my joy and my delight" (v.4). Hope breaks through in this look to the restoration to come. He can imagine himself already playing the lyre (cf. 33:2; see appendix to Ps 150: Musical Instruments) as an expression of the joy of his redemption.

Notes

---

3 The plural form מִשְׁכְּנוֹתֶיךָ (*miškᵉnôṯeyḵā*, "your dwelling places") is an intensive plural: "your very dwelling place."

4 There is some textual support for a slight emendation resulting in balanced lines. Instead of אֵל שִׂמְחַת גִּילִי (*'ēl śimḥaṯ gîlî*, "the God of the joy of my delight," i.e., "God, my joy and my delight," NIV), the BHS proposes: אֵל שִׂמְחָתִי אָגִילָה (*'ēl śimḥāṯî 'āḡîlāh*, "the God of my joy, I shall rejoice"). The latter verbal clause—"I shall rejoice"—parallels "I will praise you."

VIII. Hope

43:5

> 5 Why are you downcast, O my soul?
> Why so disturbed within me?
> Put your hope in God,
> for I will yet praise him,
> my Savior and my God.

5 The refrain returns to the conflict between faith and doubt, to the contrast between the present and the future, and to the hope that "I will yet praise him."

Psalm 44: Redeem Us Because of Your Unfailing Love

The mood of the two previous psalms also dominates Psalm 44. These three psalms are examples of the lament genre and reflect a period of God's rejection of his people (42:9; 43:2; 44:9, 24). They also express the hardship experienced by the reproach of the nations (42:3, 10; 43:2; 44:13–16). However, the differences are more significant than the similarities. Psalm 44 is a *national lament* reflecting defeat in battle.

Though early church fathers of the Antioch school (Chrysostom) and later exegetes (Calvin) have proposed a Maccabean setting, modern scholarship is in general agreement on a preexilic date (Weiser, pp. 354–55), but Kraus cautions against any historical fixation (*Psalmen*, 1:325–26). Arguments in favor of an earlier date are (1) the national lament before a battle against the Moabites and Ammonites (2 Chron 20:4–17); (2) v.22 gives no grounds to the interpretation of religious persecution; and (3) the omission of any reference to the desecration of the temple, as happened in the Maccabean era. The psalm cannot be exilic—though some of its language fits well (e.g., vv.9–16, 19, 22; as Ralph W. Klein assumes in *Israel in Exile. A Theological Interpretation* [Philadelphia: Fortress, 1979], pp. 18–19)—because of its confession of innocence (vv.17–18, 20–21). For these reasons some argue in favor of a dating to the period of Hezekiah or Josiah, when Judah had experienced some form of spiritual revival.

The interchange of first person plural ("we," "our") and singular ("I," "my," vv.4, 6, 15–16) may best be explained as a literary convention rather than a liturgical alternation between people and king (see Craigie, *Psalms 1–50*, pp. 331–32). Thus the corporate reflection is personalized at critical points in the literary structure. The structure reflects an argument that culminates in a prayer for redemption in the form of a stepped parallelism or ziggurat structure.

A. God's Past Acts of Deliverance (vv.1–3)
  B. Confidence in God (vv.4–8)
    C. Suffering and Disgrace (vv.9–16)

D. Claim of Innocence (vv.17–22)
E. Prayer for Deliverance (vv.23–26)

I. God's Past Acts of Deliverance

44:1–3

For the director of music. Of the Sons of Korah. A *maskil.*

1 We have heard with our ears, O God;
our fathers have told us
what you did in their days,
in days long ago.
2 With your hand you drove out the nations
and planted our fathers;
you crushed the peoples
and made our fathers flourish.
3 It was not by their sword that they won the land,
nor did their arm bring them victory;
it was your right hand, your arm,
and the light of your face, for you loved them.

1–3 God's people were participants in the history of redemption. They had heard the story (v.1; cf. 78:3) of what God had done for their ancestors "in days long ago" (cf. Isa 37:26; Mic 7:20), including the era of the Conquest (v.2). Against all odds Israel inherited the land, because God fought on behalf of his covenant people.

The emphasis in vv.2–3 lies on God's leadership and participation. Yahweh had fought for them, expressed metaphorically by "with your hand. . . . your right hand, your arm" (cf. Exod 15:6, 12). Israel's victories were not their own. Though they used their swords and were valiant in battle, they realized that the fulfillment of the land promise was God's (v.3; cf. 20:7–8; 33:16–17). He had "planted" them (v.2; cf. 80:8–12, 15; Exod 15:17; Amos 9:15) and had let them "spread out" like the branches of a tree or the laterals of a vine (NIV, "flourish"; cf. 80:11; Isa 27:6). They were the recipients of his favor: "for you loved them" (*rᵉṣîṯām,* lit., "you showed favor to them," v.3; cf. Deut 4:37; 8:17–18; 9:4, 6). God's "favor" is "the light" of his face (v.3; cf. 4:6; 31:16; 67:1; 80:3, 7, 19; 119:135; Num 6:25), by which they had been victorious in the past. Israel had been the object of his election, love, and favor.

Notes

For a brief discussion of the technical words and phrases in the superscription, see the Introduction.

3 (4 MT) A contrast is implied by the use of the particle כִּי (*kî,* untr. in NIV) at the beginning of each bicolon. It could be rendered causally ("For it was not . . . , but it was your") or as an asseverative statement ("Truly, it was not . . . , but it was"); so also vv.6–7.

II. Confidence in God

44:4–8

4 You are my King and my God,
who decrees victories for Jacob.

5 Through you we push back our enemies;
through your name we trample our foes.
6 I do not trust in my bow,
my sword does not bring me victory;
7 but you give us victory over our enemies,
you put our adversaries to shame.
8 In God we make our boast all day long,
and we will praise your name forever. *Selah*

4–8 This section begins with an emphatic confession of God as the Great King: "You are my King and my God" (v.4; cf. 10:16; 29:10; 47:6; 74:12; 93; 96–99; see appendix to Ps 5: Yahweh Is King). Yahweh was also the "Commander of Israel's victories" (cf. Notes on v.4; NIV mg). He had helped Israel to be victorious over the enemies (vv.5, 7). Each participant in this prayer confessed his personal reliance on the Lord in the words of v.6 (cf. 20:7; 33:16; 60:11–12). Only when the Israelites had put aside their confidence in weaponry and bravery could they become instruments in the hands of God. They had cause to "boast" (v.8; cf. 34:1–2) in the "name" of Yahweh (v.8, "your name"), when they had fought in his "name" (v.5, "through your name"; cf. 5:11; see appendix to Ps 7: The Name of Yahweh).

Notes

4–8 (5–9 MT) These verses show an external symmetry with vv.1–3:

A. Traditions of the Past (v.1)
  B. Victory Over the Past Enemies (v.2)
    C. Victory Not by Human Strength (v.3a)
      D. Victory by the Lord (v.3b)
        E. Confession of Personal Confidence (v.4)
      D′. Victory by the Lord (v.5a)
    C′. Victory Not by Human Strength (v.6)
  B′. Victory Over Past Enemies (v.7)
A′. Praise of God by the Present Generation (v.8)

The structure is chiastic as well as symmetric. The asymmetry of v.4 suggests its central significance in the poetic development. Yahweh's kingship lies at the heart of the matter, as Israel's defeat raises questions concerning his rule.

4 (5 MT) The rendering "my God" instead of "God" (MT) is based on the LXX, Aquila, and the Syriac (see NIV mg.).

Instead of the imperative צַוֵּה (*ṣawwēh*, "command"), the LXX and the Syriac give an alternate reading: מְצַוֶּה (*meṣawweh*, "who commands," "commander"). Dahood makes a good case for reading "Commander" as "my Commander" on the basis of the double-duty suffix (*Psalms*, 1:265).

The plural יְשׁוּעוֹת (*yešûʿôṯ*, "victories"; lit., "acts of salvation") is a plural of abstraction, to be rendered "victory" (Joüon, par. 136g).

6–7 (7–8 MT) For the twofold use of the particle *kî* at the beginning of each verse, see the note on v.3.

III. Suffering and Disgrace

44:9–16

9 But now you have rejected and humbled us;
you no longer go out with our armies.
10 You made us retreat before the enemy,
and our adversaries have plundered us.
11 You gave us up to be devoured like sheep
and have scattered us among the nations.
12 You sold your people for a pittance,
gaining nothing from their sale.

13 You have made us a reproach to our neighbors,
the scorn and derision of those around us.
14 You have made us a byword among the nations;
the peoples shake their heads at us.
15 My disgrace is before me all day long,
and my face is covered with shame
16 at the taunts of those who reproach and revile me,
because of the enemy, who is bent on revenge.

9–16 The reflections on the traditions of God's past victories (vv.1–3) and on the national and personal confidence in God's triumphant kingship (vv.4–8) is suddenly shattered by the reality of the present. The structural development of this section begins with a contrastive particle (*'ap̱*, "But now," "yet") and is followed with five verses, each beginning with a verbal phrase charging God with abandonment (vv.10–14, "You made us. . . . You have made us"). It concludes with two homonyms (*kol*, "all"; *qôl*, "sound"; NIV, "taunts") at the beginning of each verse (vv.15–16). The beginning (v.9) and end (vv.15–16) form an inclusionary motif around the disgrace of Israel, whereas vv.10–14 amplify God's permission and seeming participation in Israel's humiliation. This is the crux. How can the God of the fathers abandon the children?

From the evidence presented in the charges (vv.10–14), it would seem that the Lord had "rejected" and humiliated his people (v.9). They have been allowed to be conquered (v.10a), plundered (v.10b), scattered like sheep (v.11a), and enslaved (vv.11b–12) by their enemies. Consequently the name of Israel, the people of God, has been disgraced among the nations (v.13; cf. Deut 28:37; 1 Kings 9:7; Jer 24:10). At the heart of the charges is the feeling that the Lord cares little for his people. Why else did he sell them out so easily and cheaply to the enemy (v.12)? The people of God express their consternation, though not in a spirit of confrontation. (For a study on doubt in the OT, see R. Davidson, "Some Aspects of the Theological Significance of Doubt in the Old Testament," *Annual of the Swedish Theological Institute* 7 [1970]: 41–52.)

The law of Moses had forewarned that disobedience to the covenant leads to God's displeasure and ultimately to being defeated, despoiled, exiled, and dispersed among the nations (Deut 28:15–68). But as the next section (vv.17–22) bears out, God's people were innocent of displeasing him. The consternation is an expression of their concern with the present reality. Faith in God, the Divine Warrior-King, whose past glorious acts of deliverance they had heard and believed (v.1), was being tested in the current crisis.

To this situation each godly person could join in a personal expression of his agony (vv.15–16). The disgrace of the nation affected each citizen so that he could speak of "my disgrace" (v.15). The sounds of the "taunts" (*qôl*) of enemies and neighboring nations (v.16) were heard "all [*kol*] day long" (v.15; cf. vv.8, 22).

Notes

16 (17 MT) "At the taunts" is literally "at the noise" or "sound," קוֹל (*qôl*).

IV. Claim of Innocence

44:17–22

17 All this happened to us,
though we had not forgotten you
or been false to your covenant.
18 Our hearts had not turned back;
our feet had not strayed from your path.
19 But you crushed us and made us a haunt for jackals
and covered us over with deep darkness.

20 If we had forgotten the name of our God
or spread out our hands to a foreign god,
21 would not God have discovered it,
since he knows the secrets of the heart?
22 Yet for your sake we face death all day long;
we are considered as sheep to be slaughtered.

In spite of all the defeats and suffering, the hearts of the people were right with God. Even when it seemed that he had abandoned them (v.19), they clung close to him with a strong determination to remain faithful. They were loyal to God by keeping his covenant (v.17), by remaining completely ("hearts," "feet") devoted to his way (v.18), and by not giving themselves over to idolatry (vv.20–21). Yet God continued to permit devastation and darkness to oppress his people (v.19). The adversities are likened to a place made desolate by the ravages of war, i.e., "a haunt for jackals" (v.19; cf. Isa 34:13; 35:7; Jer 9:11; 10:22; 49:33; 51:37). "Deep darkness" (*ṣalmāwe<u>t</u>;* see 23:4) is a metaphor for adversities, often resulting in despair (cf. 107:10, 14; Isa 42:7; 49:9).

The people's suffering is not because of their sins. Rather, they suffer "vicariously" like "sheep to be slaughtered" (v.22; cf. v.11; Isa 53:7). They suffer for God's sake (cf. Rom 8:36). In their fidelity to the Lord, they receive greater abuse than if they had conformed to the pagan world. In suffering for the honor of God, they need reassurance of his love (cf. Rom 8:36–39). Scripture encourages us to accept suffering, as Calvin writes, "In order, therefore, that weariness, or dread of the cross, may not root up from our hearts true godliness, let us continually reflect upon this, that it behoves us to drink the cup which God puts into our hands, and that no one can be a Christian who does not dedicate himself to God" (2:171).

Notes

18 (19 MT) As a figure of speech, "hearts" and "feet" connote the whole being. Briggs sees here a reference to the internal and external aspects of obedience (1:380–81).

A number of MSS read the singular instead of the MT's אֲשֻׁרֵינוּ (*'ašurênû*, "our feet"). The singular form of the verb requires a singular subject. The emendation of the text makes little difference in the English translation.

19 (20 MT) John Day reads תַּנִּין (*tannîn*, "dragon") for the MT's תַּנִּים (*tannîm*, "jackals") in *God's Conflict With the Dragon and the Sea. Echoes of Canaanite Myth in the Old Testament* (Cambridge: Cambridge University Press, 1985), p. 139.

21 (22 MT) The people of God were very much aware of Yahweh's searching powers of investigation. During national and personal times of crises, they would pray for Yahweh to search their hearts (7:9; 17:3; 26:2; 66:10; 139:1, 23).

V. Prayer for Deliverance

44:23–26

23 Awake, O Lord! Why do you sleep?
    Rouse yourself! Do not reject us forever.
24 Why do you hide your face
    and forget our misery and oppression?

25 We are brought down to the dust;
    our bodies cling to the ground.
26 Rise up and help us;
    redeem us because of your unfailing love.

The questions of faith usually do not receive an answer. The reason for and the purpose of suffering for the people of God find no resolution in this psalm. There is neither despondency nor evidence of anger with God. The voice of collective and individual lament expresses the difficulty of suffering without cause. The mood of confidence in the Lord has been set by the two beginning strophes. It is faith that looks up to God for his deliverance.

23 The questions of faith express the conviction that a chasm exists between the promises of God and reality. It is out of their deeply felt need and, to some extent, out of wonder that the people of God ask, "Why do you sleep?" It is not that they believe that their God is asleep (cf. 121:4). It emphasizes their need of his immediate attention to their plight. They plead with him to "awake," i.e., rouse himself up as the Divine Warrior (cf. 7:6).

24–26 The present adversity has created a darkness, because "the light" of God's face, which their forefathers had experienced (v.3), is hidden (v.24; cf. 13:1; 22:24; 88:14). They ask how God can ignore them and fail to see their "misery and oppression." In dependency on God's favor, they prostrate themselves to the ground (v.25). They do not have the power to rise up, but in prayer they implore their covenant God to rise up on behalf of them. The petition begins and ends with two imperatives: "Awake. . . . Rouse yourself!" (v.23); "Rise up and help us; redeem us" (v.25; cf. 94:1–2).

Redemption pertains to the welfare of God's people in body and soul. The people come to Yahweh and petition him to look again at their low estate (v.25; cf. 119:25). In the conclusion of their prayer, they submit themselves to the love of God. He covenanted himself to the people and promised them his "unfailing love" (*ḥesed*, v.26; cf. 6:4; Exod 34:6–7; Mic 7:18, 20). This is also Paul's response to suffering, when he affirms that no adversity can separate us from the love of God in Christ Jesus (Rom 8:36–39).

Notes

24 (25 MT) On the significance of God's hiding his face, see Samuel E. Balentine, *The Hidden God: The Hiding of the Face of God in the Old Testament* (Oxford: University Press, 1983).

Psalm 45: The Wedding of a Son of David

The psalm is a *royal psalm* and functioned as a *wedding song* at the occasion of the wedding of a royal couple. Because of the theological significance of the wedding and the function of the Davidic king within God's order of life in Israel and Judah, the wedding song takes on typological significance. Applicable to any descendant of David, it extols the privileged position of his people and sets forth God's expectations of his appointed vassal on earth (cf. Pss 2; 110).

In a special way the psalm also applies to our Lord, who rules as the Son of David (cf. Heb 1:8). However, the expositor must first listen to the psalm in the context of Israel and restrain himself from reading only the relationship of Christ and the church into this text. In this manner he can appreciate more the blessedness of the rule of the One born of a woman into the lineage of David: Jesus our Messiah. Richard D. Patterson uses the phrase "multiplex approach" ("A Multiplex Approach to Psalm 45," *Grace Theological Journal* 6 [1985]: 29–48). I see this as an example of the progressive-fulfillment hermeneutic. I believe that C.S. Lewis grasped the significance of Christmas: "The birth of Christ is the arrival of the great warrior and the great king. Also of the Lover, the Bridegroom, whose beauty surpasses that of man. But not only the Bridegroom as the lover, the desired; the Bridegroom also who makes fruitful, the Father of children still to be begotten and born" (*Reflections on the Psalms*, p. 130).

The structure of the psalm is dependent on the results of metrical and exegetical analysis because there are several difficult phrases and syntactic constructions (for a poetic analysis, see Nic. H. Ridderbos, "The Psalms," pp. 43–76). For our purposes we shall depend largely on the NIV in our exposition and structural analysis.

A. Introduction (v.1)
 B. Address to the King (vv.2–5)
  C. The Glory of the Bridegroom (vv.6–9)
 B′. Address to the Bride (vv.10–12)
  C′. The Glory of the Bride (vv.13–15)
A′. Conclusion (vv.16–17)

I. Introduction

45:1

For the director of music. To ⌊the tune of⌋ "Lilies." Of the Sons of Korah.
A *maskil*. A wedding song.

1 My heart is stirred by a noble theme
as I recite my verses for the king;
my tongue is the pen of a skillful writer.

1 Having been moved by "a noble theme" (lit., "a good word"), the sacred composer adds his own word of tribute to the king. It may be that he received a word from the Lord and wrote or recited the psalm to bless the royal couple. Gifted with a "golden tongue," he was well prepared. Like the scribe Ezra (Ezra 7:6), he excelled in oral composition, interpretation, and communication. As an artist in his own right, he spoke the words of a "skillful writer." (For the skills of ancient writers, see Giorgio Castellion, "Scribal Velox [Ps XLV, 2]," *Forschung zur Bibel. Wort, Lied, und Gottesspruch. Beiträge zu Psalmen und Propheten*, ed. Josef Schreiner, 2 vols. [Würzburg: Echter Verlag, 1972], 2:29–34.)

Notes

For a brief discussion of the technical words and phrases in the superscription, see the Introduction.

II. The Royal Groom (vv.2–9)

A. *Address to the King*

45:2–5

2 You are the most excellent of men
and your lips have been anointed with grace,
since God has blessed you forever.
3 Gird your sword upon your side, O mighty one;
clothe yourself with splendor and majesty.
4 In your majesty ride forth victoriously
in behalf of truth, humility and righteousness;
let your right hand display awesome deeds.
5 Let your sharp arrows pierce the hearts of the king's
enemies;
let the nations fall beneath your feet.

2 The court poet portrays the king in terms of his physical appearance and the perfections required of a Davidic king. The description is idealized, as the poet projects a conception of kingship based on theocratic expectations. He is the one blessed by the Lord because of the promise given to David (2 Sam 7:11–16). The Lord has anointed the king to shepherd his people. Though the word "shepherd" is not used, the concept of shepherd is apparent (cf. Ezek 34:23–24; 37:24). The king is not to rule in an autocratic way, to seek self-gratification, or to abuse the powers vested in him. The example of Saul, the first king of Israel, was a perpetual reminder of the type of king who ruled the surrounding nations. The Davidic dynasty was to be different.

The poet lists some of the expectations as excellencies (NIV, "You are the most excellent of men"). The royal perfections pertain to his judicial, administrative, executive, and military duties. The king's "excellence" (lit., "beautiful"; cf. 1 Sam 9:2; 10:23; 16:12) lies in God's presence with him. It is God's divine blessing manifested in his speech, his royal valor, his concern for establishing God's kingdom (order) on earth, and the continuity of his dynasty (cf. 132; 2 Sam 7:13, 16, 25, 29).

The king's speech is wise, as his words are "anointed with grace" (cf. Prov 22:11; Eccl 10:12; Luke 4:22–23). When the king speaks, people listen. Absalom was such a golden-tongued individual that he quickly won sizeable support for his rebellion against David (2 Sam 15:1–12). Solomon too acquired a reputation for his wise verdicts, evidencing his particular blessing (gift) from the Lord.

3–5 The king's military capabilities secure peace and prosperity for the nation. The emphasis on his royal valor is not evidence of Israel's belligerence. The poet wishes the king success in his military pursuits. When he goes out with sword on his side (v.3; cf. 2 Sam 20:8), he confidently leads his troops to victory. The "splendor and majesty" speak of his past victories and the confident expectation of additional victories every time he marches at the head of his troops.

The Davidic king is the vassal of the Great King ("mighty one," v.3; cf. Isa 9:6: "Mighty God"), and as his vassal he enjoys the prerogatives of divine kingship: "splendor and majesty" (cf. 96:6; 104:1; 145:5). The success of the king is due to his concern for what is important to the Lord and his covenant people. He is a champion of "truth, humility and righteousness" (v.4). In his concern for loyalty ("truth," *'ᵉmeṯ*), he is faithful and just to God and to his people (cf. 72:2; Isa 11:1–5). His kingship mirrors the kingdom of God in fidelity and righteousness. He does not seek his own advantage to the detriment of his people or to the provocation of God's wrath. His concern for "humility" keeps him continually dependent on his covenant God (cf. Mic 6:8; Zech 9:9). True wisdom is evident in trusting, fearing, and walking with God (Prov 3:3–6). His concern for "righteousness" is demonstrated in his ordering the affairs of state to correspond with God's plans. The kingdom of the son of David is a temporal and spacial expression of the kingdom of God on earth.

In dealing with his subjects, the king's righteousness finds expression in just verdicts. In the realm of international diplomacy and foreign affairs, his zeal for righteousness motivates him to establish his kingdom triumphantly. The nations will be struck with awe by his mighty "deeds" (v.4; cf. 2:10–12; 65:8; 106:22; 145:6). In his concern for "truth, humility and righteousness," he does not rest until his enemies recognize his authority (v.5; 2:8–9; 110:1–2, 5-6; 1 Cor 15:25–27).

Notes

---

3 (4 MT) The phrase "with splendor and majesty" may modify the sword of the king or the king himself. Because there is only one verb in the MT whereas the NIV has two, the latter gives an interpretive addition by an elliptic reading of the verb "gird" in the sense of "clothe yourself with splendor and majesty."

B. *The Glory of the Bridegroom*

45:6–9

6 Your throne, O God, will last for ever and ever;
a scepter of justice will be the scepter of your
kingdom.
7 You love righteousness and hate wickedness;
therefore God, your God, has set you above
your companions
by anointing you with the oil of joy.
8 All your robes are fragrant with myrrh and aloes
and cassia;
from palaces adorned with ivory
the music of the strings makes you glad.
9 Daughters of kings are among your honored women;
at your right hand is the royal bride in gold
of Ophir.

6–7 The throne of David is assured by covenant (v.6). The throne of David was God's trust to the descendants of David. Each king on David's throne was reminded that he was king by "divine right" (vv.6–7). However, the Lord expected the sons of David to establish the throne (cf. 1 Kings 2:12, 46). The establishment of the throne was guaranteed by the active pursuit of justice and righteousness. The "scepter of justice" was a royal symbol of his authority to establish a rule of integrity based on the laws of God rather than on the whims or dictates of the king (cf. 67:4; 75:3; 89:14; 96:10; 98:8–9; 99:4; Isa 9:7; 11:4–5; see J.P.J. Olivier, "The Sceptre of Justice and Ps. 45:7b," *Journal of Northwest Semitic Literature* 7 [1979]: 45–54). In his deep love for "righteousness," he opposes all forms of "wickedness." God's rule will be established on earth (v.7; cf. 11:7; 33:5; 99:1–4). Our Lord as the descendant of David inherited the royal throne (cf. Heb 1:8–9). As the "Son" of God, his kingdom is everlasting.

8–9 The inspired poet turns his attention to the preparations for the wedding ceremony. The descriptions and references to the robes, spices ("myrrh and aloes," v.8; cf. S of Songs 4:14), music, the royal daughters, and the royal bride all reinforce the rightness of the moment and of the anointing of this son of David.

The evident blessing of God on the king assures the continuity of the dynasty. The Lord had promised David that his dynasty was to last forever (2 Sam 7:16). Every successor of David enjoyed a special relationship with God as the theocratic representative of his rule on earth. To secure the effects of his blessing on the people, the king should embody the theocratic ideals: wisdom, valor, and the royal attributes.

Notes

---

6 (7 MT) This verse is the most problematic of the psalm. The combination כִּסְאֲךָ אֱלֹהִים (*kis'ᵃkā 'ᵉlōhîm*, "your throne, God") may be interpreted in a variety of ways:

"your throne, O God" (KJV, NIV)
"your throne is like God's throne" (NEB)
"your throne, O divine king" (Weiser, p. 360)
"your throne is a throne of God" (RSV mg.) (cf. A.A. Anderson, 1:349–50; 1 Chron 29:23; see for a defense of the vocative, Murray J. Harris, "The Translation of Elohim in Psalm 45:7–8," *Tyndale Bulletin* 35 [1984]: 65–89).

Dahood has proposed a verbal reading of the nominal phrase "your throne": "the Eternal and Everlasting God has enthroned you" (*Psalms*, 1:269; cf. Craigie, *Psalms 1–50*, pp. 336–37). The usage in Heb 1:8–9 (cf. NIV) shows how the NT applied the text to Jesus, but the OT text should also be read on its own. The strongest evidence is in favor of the elliptic reading of "throne": "your throne [is a throne of] God." Kingship in Israel was a derived, not a divine, kingship. Therefore the further definition "forever and forever" qualifies the kingship of David's dynasty as by divine grant. More recently C.F. Whitley has argued in favor of "Thy throne O Anointed One is forever and ever" ("Textual and Exegetical Observations on Ps 45, 4–7," ZAW 98 [1986]: 277–82).

8 The king was heavily anointed with fragrant oils made from a mixture of olive oil, myrrh, aloes, and cassia. Myrrh was a resin of a shrub (*Cammiphora Abessinica;* see Michael Zohary, *Plants of the Bible* [Cambridge: Cambridge University Press, 1982], p. 200). It was used for the anointing of the tabernacle and the priests (Exod 30:23–29). Aloe was a product of the aromatic eaglewood tree (see Zohary, p. 204). Cassia was an aromatic oil produced from a steam distillation process of leaves, twigs, and young fruit. This oil was imported from East Asia (ibid., p. 203). The anointing oil dripped onto the royal robes so as to make them fragrant (cf. 133:2).

III. The Royal Bride (vv.10–15)

A. *Address to the Bride*

45:10–12

10 Listen, O daughter, consider and give ear:
Forget your people and your father's house.
11 The king is enthralled by your beauty;
honor him, for he is your lord.
12 The Daughter of Tyre will come with a gift,
men of wealth will seek your favor.

10 The bride was seated to the right of the king and was adorned with the valuable gold of Ophir, a proverbially fine gold (v.9; cf. 1 Kings 9:28; 10:11). The psalmist addresses her with words of wise counsel ("listen"; cf. Prov 1:8). He encourages her to be loyal to the people of God by forgetting her own loyalty to her native land and people. The queen was of foreign descent. Like Abraham, she had left her father's house (cf. Gen 12:1), and like Ruth she had to pledge allegiance to God's covenant people and foreswear allegiance to her own (cf. Ruth 1:16). He also encourages her to submit herself fully to her husband, the king, as a symbolic gesture of her belonging to the people of God.

11 The king was God's anointed representative. Submission to the king implied submission to the God of Israel. So while the king takes delight in the physical beauty of his wife, she respects him as her "lord." The wife of a theocratic king must learn to submit herself to the way of Israel, as symbolized in her husband. It would be wrong for her to compare him to the kings of the nations with their powers of state, cultural refinements, and idolatrous ways. Jezebel apparently accepted Ahab only on her own Phoenician terms and influenced him into acculturation. Apparently Solomon was also entrapped by the religious "refinements" and innovations of his foreign wives (1 Kings 11:1–13).

12 The reward for identification with God's people and for submission to the new way of life is exaltation among the nations. The people of Tyre, the great trading center in Phoenicia, are personified as "the Daughter of Tyre." They, as well as other rich nations, will bring tribute to Jerusalem. During Solomon's regime precious gifts were brought to Jerusalem because of his international reputation. The prophets envision the era of restoration as a time when the nations will bring gifts to signify the special position God's people have among the nations. Even the Book of Revelation portrays the glory of the everlasting state in historical terms—"and the kings of the earth will bring their splendor into it. . . . The glory and honor of the nations will be brought into it" (Rev 21:24, 26). So the young bride is comforted with words that bring out the advantages and the honor of being a member of God's people and, more specifically, of the royal household.

Notes

10–15 (11–16 MT) A.S. van der Woude explains exegetical problems as arising from glosses ("Psalm 45:11–19. Ein Neuere Interpretationsversuch," in *Loven en Geloven. Opstellen van Collega's en Medewerkers aangeboden aan Prof. Dr. Nic. H. Ridderbos,* ed. M.H. van Es et al. [Amsterdam: Ton Bolland, 1975], pp. 111–16). In this case he singles out "the Daughter of Tyre" (v.12), "the princess within her chamber" (v.13), and "of the king" (v.15) as glosses.

12 (13 MT) The word בַּת (*baṯ,* "daughter") may signify the descendant or a member of a group. It is possible that the "Daughter of Tyre" is a direct reference to the princess of Tyre as "the" daughter of Tyre (Craigie, *Psalms 1–50,* p. 336). On the other hand, the parallel phrase would suggest that the people of Tyre as a whole are intended (cf. Isa 1:8). The NIV's marginal reading, "*A Tyrian robe is among the gifts,*" based on Dahood's suggestion (*Psalms,* I:274–75), has not found general acceptance.

B. *The Glory of the Bride*

45:13–15

13 All glorious is the princess within ⌊her chamber⌋;
her gown is interwoven with gold.
14 In embroidered garments she is led to the king;
her virgin companions follow her
and are brought to you.
15 They are led in with joy and gladness;
they enter the palace of the king.

13–15 The scene suddenly shifts from the throne room, where the king and his bride are seated together (v.9), to the beautiful bride as she prepares herself for the wedding and enters the royal palace with her maids of honor. She is adorned in a magnificent gown made of gold-embroidered fabric. She and her wedding party are carried into the palace as if on floats of "joy and gladness" (v.15).

Notes

13 (14 MT) "All glorious is the princess" is a possible rendering of the MT. The NEB renders "honour awaits her." The crux is the translation of כָּל (*kol*, "all"). C.F. Whitley proposes a misreading of *bal* with a positive sense: "indeed resplendent is the princess" ("The Positive Force of the Hebrew Particle," ZAW 84 [1972]: 213–19).

IV. Conclusion

45:16–17

16 Your sons will take the place of your fathers;
you will make them princes throughout the land.
17 I will perpetuate your memory through all generations;
therefore the nations will praise you for ever
and ever.

16–17 The poet moves from the queen to the king as the most prominent member of the wedding party (vv.2–9). After all, he is the son of David and a native of Israel. The bride is most blessed in her being incorporated into Israel and into the royal family. She marries into a family blessed by God's promise of continuity of leadership. Using the masculine singular suffix, the poet speaks words of blessing to the king: "your sons . . . your fathers" (v.16). If the king will fulfill God's expectations, then the Lord himself will "perpetuate" (v.17) the memory of the king for generations. Moreover, the nations will sing his praise as an expression of their continued respect.

The psalm has implicit messianic significance. Jesus the Messiah is of the lineage of David. He fulfills the theocratic ideals in his present rule and in his glorious return. The promise of remembrance, perpetuity, and honor given to the Davidic king is particularly applicable to the kingdom of our Lord Jesus Christ. All nations will submit themselves to him (1 Cor 15:24–26; Heb 10:12–13).

Notes

For an interpretative attempt at integrating the exegesis of the psalm and its NT use, see Allen M. Harman, "The Syntax and Interpretation of Psalm 45:7," in *The Law and the Prophets. OT Studies in Honor of Oswald T. Allis*, ed. John H. Skilton (Nutley: Presbyterian and Reformed, 1974), pp. 337–47. For a comprehensive study on Psalm 45, see the published dissertations of Philip J. King, *A Study of Psalm 45 [44]* (Rome: Pontificia Universitas Lateranensis, 1959), and J.S. Maria Mulder, *Studies on Psalm 45* (Oss: Witsiers, 1972).

Psalm 46: The God of Jacob Is Our Fortress

This psalm has been popularized by Martin Luther's rendition in "A Mighty Fortress Is Our God." As a *song of Zion* (cf. 48; 76; 84; 87; 122), it celebrates the presence of God. The combination of the hymnic and the oracular genres has made it virtually impossible to identify the original life situation. Internal evidence indicates settings as varied as victory after battle, celebration of God's kingship at the autumnal festival (A.A. Anderson, 1:355), or the establishment of David's royal cult in Jerusalem (Craigie, *Psalms 1–50*, pp. 343–44). The change from a hymn to a prophetic oracle (vv.8–10) suggests that the original *psalm of confidence* was transformed into an eschatological psalm.

The structure of the psalm falls into three parts, divided by the word "Selah":

The Presence of God in Cosmic Troubles (vv.1–3)
The Presence of God in Judgment (vv.4–7)
The Presence of God on Earth (vv.8–11)

The first two strophes belong together, as is evident from the repetition of vocabulary ("earth," vv.2, 6; "fall," vv.2, 5; "[up]roar," vv.3, 6); the imagery of water ("sea," v.2; "waters," v.3; "river," v.4), and the similarity of style (hymnic, vv.1–7). The third strophe bears resemblances to the first two but clearly is a further development and shows similarities with the prophetic style ("Come and see. . . . Be still, and know"). The hymn reflects the language of a theophany (vv.2–3). In prophetic oracles as well as in the language of Israel's piety, God's coming down to judge the nations is portrayed as throwing the world of nature into convolution (cf. Mic 1:3–4). In contrast to God's wrath with the nations, the psalmist comforts God's people by stating that "the LORD Almighty is with us" (v.7; cf. Nah 1:2–6). The last strophe encourages God's people to look forward to the final establishment of the kingdom of God on earth (vv.8–9). Based on this understanding of the psalm, we shall follow the following expository structure:

A. Confession (v.1)
  B. Theophany (vv.2–6)
A′. Confession (v.7)
  B′. Prophetic Oracle (vv.8–10)
A″. Confession (v.11)

(For an alternate structural analysis, cf. David Toshio Tsumura, "The Literary Structure of Psalm 46, 2–8," *Annual of the Japanese Biblical Institute* 6 [1980]: 29–55; for an attempt to isolate the traditions, see Lloyd Neve, "The Common Use of Traditions by the Author of Psalm 46 and Isaiah," ExpT 86 [1974–75]: 243–46.) The literary approach of holistic interpretation espoused by Meir Weiss complements our structural analysis (*The Bible From Within. The Method of Total Interpretation* [Jerusalem: Magnes, 1984], pp. 314–52).

I. Confession

46:1, 7, 11

For the director of music. Of the Sons of Korah.
According to *alamoth.* A song.

1 God is our refuge and strength,
an ever-present help in trouble.

7 The LORD Almighty is with us;
the God of Jacob is our fortress. *Selah*

11 The LORD Almighty is with us;
the God of Jacob is our fortress. *Selah*

1, 7, 11 The threefold confessional statement (vv.1, 7, 11) presents God in a very personal way to Israel. In the Hebrew text it reads, he is "for us" (vv.1, 7, 11; NIV, "our") and "with us" (vv.7, 11; so also NIV). His people confess him in his grandeur but also in his closeness to them. They call him "God," "the LORD Almighty" (NIV; MT, "the LORD of Hosts" or "Yahweh of Hosts," or "Jehovah Sabaoth" as in Luther's hymn, vv.7, 11), and "the God of Jacob" (vv.7, 11; see appendix to Ps 24: Lord Sabaoth). The LORD Almighty is the Great King over the world, but he is particularly and fondly confessed as "the God of Jacob" (vv. 7, 11), because he has covenanted himself to be the God of Israel. God's people need not fear the presence of the Great King, because the threefold repetition "for us" and the twofold repetition "with us" assure them that the meaning of his covenant name (Yahweh) signifies that God is "with us," i.e., Immanuel (= "God is with us"; cf. Isa 7:14; 8:8, 10; Exod 3:12).

This great God is "ever-present" with his people. His presence in protecting the people of God is described by three metaphors and one explanatory clause. The metaphors are "refuge," "strength," and "fortress." These three words function as synonyms designating the source and effectiveness of Israel's strength. God is their "strength" (cf. 29:11; 68:35; 71:7; Isa 26:1). As their strength he is like a "refuge" where one finds rest and asylum (cf. 14:6; 61:3; 62:7–8; 71:7; 73:28; 91:2, 9; 142:5; Isa 25:4; Jer 17:17). His strength is also evident when they find protection in him as a "fortress." The "fortress" was an isolated, elevated place (cf. Isa 33:16) where people built a stronghold against the enemy (cf. 9:9; 18:2; 48:3; 59:9, 16–17).

Each one of these metaphors relates to a people in need. Only when they are in distress do they need his special protection (cf. 22:19; 27:9; 40:13; 44:26; 63:7). They always need him, but they experience his presence especially when they go through a period filled with anguish and distress (cf. 23:4). Then he is close to them (v.1; cf. Deut 4:7).

Notes

For a brief discussion of the technical words and phrases in the superscription, see the Introduction.

II. Theophany

46:2–6

2 Therefore we will not fear, though the earth give way
and the mountains fall into the heart of the sea,
3 though its waters roar and foam
and the mountains quake with their surging. *Selah*

4 There is a river whose streams make glad the city of
God,

the holy place where the Most High dwells.
5 God is within her, she will not fall;
God will help her at break of day.
6 Nations are in uproar, kingdoms fall;
he lifts his voice, the earth melts.

2–3 Israel's confession of their God is a comforting doctrine. They will not fear even when God's coming (theophany) in judgment is preceded by radical cosmic phenomena: earthquakes and floods (cf. 18:7–15). The world catastrophes are the "woes" of the Day of the Lord heralding the messianic age (cf. Isa 24:18–23; Jer 4:24; Nah 1:5). Every substantial change in the balance of power was interpreted as God's direct intervention in the form of judgment—an expression of the Day of the Lord. This psalm expresses Israel's confidence in the Lord's protection when he shakes the world so as to affect significant political, cultural, and economic changes. Nations and kingdoms may cause great consternation and create havoc on earth (v.6), but they will fall quickly when he speaks his word of judgment (cf. Rev 11:18).

4–6 Surrounded by a world aflame, the people of God are "the city of God" (v.4; cf. Isa 26:1–6). The imagery of the river and the streams is reminiscent of the description of the river with its four branches in the passage on the Garden of Eden (Gen 2:10–14). The restoration to the presence of God is likened to a restoration to the Garden of Eden of all those who are members of the City of God. They need not fear but have reason to be glad because God has made his dwelling with man. The river is a metaphor of blessing and restoration (cf. 65:9; 87:7; Isa 33:21; 43:19–20; Ezek 47:1–12; Joel 3:18; Zech 14:8; Rev 22:1–5). Levenson comments, "The Temple mount . . . is a bulwark and a guarantee against chaos. Only the waters of life flow there" (p. 154).

The Most High (Elyon; cf. Gen 14:18–24; see appendix to Ps 9: Yahweh Is El Elyon) has consecrated Israel by his presence among them (vv.4–5). The great doctrine of the presence of God, even in the OT, affirms that the Great King has identified himself with his people. Therefore they need not fear. God's people will never fall. They will always be assured of his readiness to help them (v.5). The help of God "at break of dawn" (cf. Exod 14:27) suggests that in the darkness of distress the people of God know that the Lord will not let them suffer unduly long (cf. 30:6–7; 90:14). His acts of unfailing love are renewed each morning (Lam 3:22–23).

Notes

2–3 (3–4 MT) Some interpreters expound these verses quite differently. They interpret the metaphors as mythological symbols rather than eschatological symbols. As mythological symbols they speak of the continual conflict between chaos and order, of Canaanite mythology and Israelite theology (see Dahood, *Psalms*, 1:278–79; A.A. Anderson, 1:356; Craigie, *Psalms 1–50*, p. 344). For an extensive study of this motif, see John Day, *God's Conflict With the Dragon and the Sea. Echoes of Canaanite Myth in the Old Testament* (Cambridge: Cambridge University Press, 1985), pp. 120–40.

3–4 (4–5 MT) David Toshio Tsumara attempts to correlate the twofold image of the sea (the hostility of the sea and the benefits derived from it) with the twofold image of "wine":

judgment and gladness of heart ("Twofold Image of Wine in Psalm 46:4–5," JQR 71 [1981]: 167–75).

4 (5 MT) Dahood is representative of those who follow the LXX in interpreting קְדֹשׁ (*qᵉḏōš*, "holy of") as a verb, קִדֵּשׁ (*qiddēš*, "he consecrated"): "the Most High sanctifies his habitation" (*Psalms*, 1:277). BHS lists several other possible readings, but the general sense is given in the NIV.

6 (7 MT) For a description of the "voice" of God in the context of theophany and judgment, see 18:13–15.

III. Prophetic Oracle

46:8–10

8 Come and see the works of the LORD,
the desolations he has brought on the earth.
9 He makes wars cease to the ends of the earth;
he breaks the bow and shatters the spear,
he burns the shields with fire.
10 "Be still, and know that I am God;
I will be exalted among the nations,
I will be exalted in the earth."

The tone changes from hymnic prose to prophetic prose. The hymn of confidence, celebrating God's presence in Zion, is the reason for the prophetic exhortations.

8–9 First, the psalmist exhorts the godly to be wise and discerning by considering (*ḥ-z-h*) the works of God. The "works of the LORD" include all acts of God in the history of salvation: Exodus, Conquest, the period of the judges, and the monarchy (cf. 66:5). The recitation of the mighty acts of God plants deep in the memory of God's people the evidences of his care, protection, and providential rule. Those who are wise enough to remember and look at the world around them have tokens of God's constancy toward his people. Every victory, every subjugation of a hostile nation, and every stroke on the canvas of the history of redemption bring more clearly into focus that the Lord's very plan for mankind includes the cessation of wars and the era of peace. His wars and his judgments of the nations have as a final end the removal of evil instigators, troublemakers, rebels, and expressions of hostility in whatever form. The God of peace will make "wars cease" (v.9; cf. Isa 2:4; Ezek 39:9; Mic 4:3; Zech 9:10). The instruments of warfare, symbolized by "the bow," "the spear," and "the shields," will become inoperative (cf. Isa 9:4; Ezek 39:9–10; Hos 2:18; Mic 4:1–4).

The psalmist surveys the results of God's theophany (judgment) from the perspective of its benefits on the godly. The effects of the wars of God bring "desolations" to the earth (v.8). Because of the threats to and oppression of the people and city of God, the prophetic oracle encourages God's people with the hope that wars will cease and that the aggressors will be devastated, so that they will be no more. Conversely, the benefits of peace, prosperity, and the blessedness of God's presence are implied in the metaphorical portrayal of the river and city of God (vv.4–5). Since God's people have reason to be glad in distress because of God's presence, how much greater will be their joy when the causes of distress are no more!

10 Second, the psalmist encourages the godly to "know" that the Lord is God. Though it was tempting to ally themselves with foreign powers, to rely on military strength, or to give themselves over to idolatry and pagan ways, the godly must learn to persevere to the end. The exhortation "be still" calls on them to stop doing one thing in favor of something else. What their temptation was may be implied from v.2: "Therefore we will not fear." Throughout the history of Israel and Judah, severe national distress brought the temptation to abandon true religion for the ephemeral security of political alliances, military strength, and worldly paganism (*Realpolitik*). Instead of choosing a negative option, the people of God distinguish themselves by the pursuit of godliness: "Know that I am God." The "knowledge" of God includes a factual knowledge about him, his past acts, and his promises. But in this context the psalmist calls on them to commit themselves to the Lord and to seek his "refuge," "strength," and "fortress" (vv.1, 7, 11). The life of faith is lived continually in commitment to God's sovereignty, rule, and ultimate exaltation over all the nations (v.10; cf. Hab 2:13–14). So Levenson writes, "In Jerusalem, there is peace and bliss" (p. 154; see appendix to Ps 98: Yahweh Is the Divine Warrior).

Notes

8 (9 MT) To "see the works of the Lord" is nothing less than the enjoyment of his acts of deliverance and the response of praise to the evidences of Yahweh's presence (cf. 58:10; see Hans F. Fuhs, *Sehen und Schauen. Die Wurzel* ḥzh *im Alten Orient und im Alten Testament. Ein Beitrag zum prophetischen Offenbarungsempfang* [Würzburg: Echter Verlag, 1978]: 285–88).

9 (10 MT) The word עֲגָלוֹת (*ʿᵃgālôṯ*, "wagons") does not fit in, because it nowhere else signifies "war chariots." Hence many follow the LXX in proposing a minor emendation of the word to read עֲגִלוֹת (*ʿᵃgilôṯ*, "round shields"). The evidence is not conclusive; witness the NIV margin ("*chariots*") and Craigie: "and burns war-wagons in the fire" (*Psalms 1–50*, p. 342).

10 (11 MT) The use of the independent pronoun "I" in "I am God" may be an elliptic form of "I, Yahweh, am God."

The second colon repeats the verbal phrase אָרוּם (*'ārûm*) followed each time by a prepositional phrase "among the nations" and "in the earth" beginning with בְּ/בָּ (*ba/bā*, "in," "among"). The verb connotes the absolute and glorious rule of the God of Jacob (cf. 99:2; Isa 57:15).

Appendix: Zion Theology

Several psalms (46, 48, 76) and numerous allusions in the Psalms proclaim the excellencies of Zion. At the center of Zion theology is Yahweh, the Divine Warrior-King, whose kingdom extends to all creation (99:2) but especially to his children. Psalm 46 helps us to visualize God—the Creator of earth, mountains, and sea—among his people, elevated on a high mountain with a mountain stream—representative of his blessings—flowing throughout his kingdom (46:1–4).

The theology of Mount Zion reflects the language of metaphor, derived from the Canaanite background. The Canaanites held to the mythological concept of a pantheon of gods, whose chief deity was El. El had a palace on Mount Zaphon, and from his rule flowed all good things.

Then they set face
Toward El at the sources of the Two Rivers,
In the midst of the pools of the Double-Deep.
. . . .
Come, and I will seek it,
In the midst of my mountain, divine Zaphon,
In the holy place, the mountain of my heritage,
In the chosen spot, on the hill of victory

(Richard J. Clifford, *The Cosmic Mountain in Canaan and the Old Testament* [Cambridge: Harvard University Press, 1972], pp. 48, 68).

The OT writers zealously proclaimed that Yahweh alone is God, while borrowing Canaanite imagery. The Canaanites believed that the chief deities lived on a high mountain and that their rule brought them prosperity, tranquility, and security. The psalmist affirms that God's beneficent rule belongs only to the godly, the residents of Zion.

Mount Zion stands for the vision of God's kingship. God's kingdom is greater than Jerusalem but receives its visible expression in the temple and palace of Jerusalem. Yahweh and his dwelling (temple) are associated with Zion. Further, David is closely related to the Zion tradition because Yahweh commended him for his desire to build a temple in Jerusalem (Ps 132). Levenson (p. 122) designates the temple "the fulcrum for the universe," as Yahweh, Jerusalem, temple, and monarchy became correlated in Israelite theology.

Yahweh is the Great Warrior who establishes peace for his people. They need not fear because he will avenge their enemies (46:8–11). No power on earth can resist God's kingdom. Israel had witnessed his power in the Exodus, Conquest, and his many mighty acts, including the restoration from the Exile. Israel also looked forward to the fulfillment of God's promises in the future. They believed in his promises and projected a grand and glorious new era: the presence of God among his people. In anticipation of this vision, the psalmists and prophets speak of Yahweh's victory over nations, kingdoms, and enemies (cf. 47:8–10; 48:4–7; 76:1–8, 10, 12). His is the vengeance, the wrath, and the zeal in establishing his kingdom. His is also the deliverance for which the godly wait; "when you, O God, rose up to judge, / to save all the afflicted of the land" (76:9). Redemption focuses on Zion; or, as Martin Buber observes, it is *Zioncentric:* "The renewal of the world and the renewal of Zion are one and the same thing, for Zion is the heart of the renewed world" ("Redemption," *On the Bible. Eighteen Studies by Martin Buber*, ed. Nahum N. Glatzer [New York: Schocken, 1982], p. 165).

Yahweh has chosen to establish his kingdom and delights in those who submit themselves to his rule: "For the Lord has chosen Zion, he has desired it for his dwelling" (132:13). The Zion theology-eschatology inspires God's people with adoration, joy, hope, and commitment to the Great King. The Zion theology inspires them with a vision of the kingdom-to-come. This vision is the ground for ethics. Eschatological ethics holds out the promise of life and joy flowing from Yahweh's presence to all who prepare themselves for the full establishment of his kingdom on earth. Though his kingdom is here, God's people expect a dramatic transformation. The godly are those who live and act in anticipation of the vision of Zion. This hope was the basis for ethics, praise, and evangelism (48:8–14).

The "way" of the Lord is the way of the kingdom. The godly reflect his "way" on earth, as they live their lives in accordance with the standards of the "holy" city, Zion. They may not be citizens of Jerusalem, the city, but they are members of the City of God, Zion. This is clearly brought out in Psalm 87, where the psalmist affirms Yahweh's election of and love for all who find shelter in Zion, including Gentiles (87:2–6).

The godly citizens of Zion are people of integrity. They uphold the standards of God's kingdom with a concern for righteousness, justice, love, and humility. Thus when the psalmist asks, "Who may be God's guest in Zion?" (cf. 15:1), he makes it clear that the

Lord has invited no other than those who imitate his way. As God's kingdom cannot be shaken, so the godly are stable and endure (125:1; cf. 84:4–5, 11–12). "Holiness" too is an integral aspect to the way of the kingdom (46:4; cf. 48:1).

During times of duress the people of God freely pray to the Great King, petitioning him to rouse himself to action on their behalf (59:5). As long as the temple was standing, the focus and orientation was toward the temple because the ark of the covenant, "the" symbol of God's kingship on earth, was in the Most Holy Place. For example, the poet of Psalm 84 rejoices in the presence of the Mighty Warrior among his people (v.1) but is envious of the birds who find physical shelter in the temple (v.3).

The comfort of God's protection is limited to the godly. They are the true citizens of the City of God. They do not fear his presence like the nations; rather, they know themselves to be blessed: "O Lord Almighty, / blessed is the man who trusts in you" (84:12). They find rest for themselves, regardless of what may happen in this world (91:1). They long for fellowship with God, as their hearts draw near to the God who has invited his children to draw near to him. They wait with hope for God's deliverance (69:6). They pray for restoration in trials, believing that God will bless them with his favor (80:4; cf. vv.7, 14, 19; 14:7; 84:8).

The godly also focus their joyous praise toward Zion, as they encourage one another (9:14; 65:1; cf. 102:12; 135:21; 149:2). Since Zion extends beyond the temple and Jerusalem, the benefits also extend to the nations, who need to hear the good news: "Sing praises to the LORD, enthroned in Zion; / proclaim among the nations what he has done (9:11). Their love for Zion is no other than the declaration of loyalty to and adoration of the Great King in the midst of his people: "Praise awaits you, O God, in Zion; / to you our vows will be fulfilled" (65:1).

The Zion theology correlates in a magnificent vision of what God has done, does, and will do. Yahweh is the Divine Warrior-King who is present with the Davidic kings and with his people. This conception lies behind much of the OT theology and in the expectation of the New Zion (Jerusalem), the City of God, of which Paul (Gal 4:26) and John (Rev 27) speak (cf. Heb 11:10). The glory of Zion is nothing less than the adoration of God-with-us (Immanuel). The wonder of the incarnation of our Lord Jesus Christ is anticipated in the wonder of God's presence among his people in the OT. The Incarnation is a mystery, but the revelation of God in human form should never take away from the mystery of God's presence and beneficent rule (48:1–3) in the OT.

See also the appendixes to Pss 3 (Yahweh Is My God); 7 (The Name of Yahweh); 25 (The Perfections of Yahweh); 78 (The Acts of Yahweh); 85 (The Anger of the Lord); 88 (Sheol-Grave-Death); 98 (Yahweh Is the Divine Warrior); 119 (Yahweh Is My Redeemer); 132 (The Ark of the Covenant and the Temple: Symbols of Yahweh's Presence and Rule).

Texts: Pss 20; 24:7–10; 46; 47; 48; 50; 68; 76; 84; 87; 93; 96; 97; 98; 99; 122; 149.

Bibliography: R.P. Carroll, "Psalm LXXVIII: Vestiges of a Tribal Polemic," VetTest 21 (1971): 133–50; R.E. Clements, *God and Temple* (Philadelphia: Fortress, 1965), pp. 55–62; 71–73; id., *Isaiah and the Deliverance of Jerusalem. A Study in the Interpretation of Prophecy in the Old Testament,* JSOTSS 13 (Sheffield: JSOT, 1980), pp. 72–89; Richard J. Clifford, *The Cosmic Mountain in Canaan and the Old Testament* (Cambridge: Harvard University Press, 1972); M. Cogan, " 'The City Which I Have Chosen'—The View of Jerusalem in Deuteronomic Literature," *Tarbiz* 55 (1985/86): 301–9 (Heb.); John Day, *God's Conflict with the Dragon and the Sea. Echoes of Canaanite Myth in the Old Testament* (Cambridge: Cambridge University Press, 1985); Roland de Vaux, "Jerusalem and the Prophets," *Interpreting the Prophetic Tradition* (New York: Ktav,1969), pp. 277–300; William J. Dumbrell, *The End of the Beginning. Revelation 21–22 and the Old Testament* (Grand Rapids: Baker, 1985); Otto Eissfeldt, "Silo und Jerusalem," *Kleine Scriften,* vol. 3, edd. Rudolf Sellheim and Fritz Maas (Tübingen: Mohr, 1966), pp. 417–25; Georg Fohrer, "Zion-Jerusalem im Alten Testament," *Studien zur alttestamentlichen*

Theologie und Geschichte (1949–1966) (Berlin: De Gruyter, 1969), pp. 195–241; Hartmutt Gese, "Der Davidsbund und die Zionserwählung," *Zeitschrift für Theologie und Kirche,* N.F. 61 (1964): 10–26 (= "Der Davidsbund und Die Zionserwählung," *Vom Sinai zum Zion: Alttestamentliche Beiträgezur biblischen Theologie* (Munich: Chr. Kaiser Verlag, 1974), pp. 113–29; Donald E. Gowan, *Eschatology in the Old Testament* (Philadelphia: Fortress, 1986); John H. Hayes, "The Traditions of Zion's Inviolability," JBL 82 (1963): 419–26; Jörg Jeremias, "Lade und Zion. Zur Entstehung der Ziontradition," in *Problemebiblischer Theologie. Gerhard von Rad zum 70. Geburtstag,* ed. Hans Walter Wolff (Munich: Chr. Kaiser, 1971), pp. 183–98; Hans-Joachim Kraus, *Theologie,* pp. 94–103; Stanislaw Lach, "Versuch einer neuen Interpretation der Zionshymnen," Supplements to VetTest 29 (1977): 149–64; Levenson; Gerhard Liedke, "Theologie des Friedens: Literaturbericht zu Arbeiten aus dem Bereich der alttestamentlichen Wissenschaft," in *Lieden-Bibel-Kirche* (Stuttgart: Ernst Klett, 1968), pp. 174–86; Tryggve N.D. Mettinger, *The Dethronement of Sabaoth. Studies in the Shem and Kavod Theologies* (Lund: Gleerup, 1982); id., "Fighting the Powers of Chaos and Hell—Towards the Biblical Portrait of God," ST 39 (1985): 21–38; Marcello Milani, "Salmo 46. Uno Studio strutturale sulle imagini di Guerra e di Giudizio," *Studia Patavina* 27 (1980): 513–37; Patrick D. Miller, Jr., *The Divine Warrior in Early Israel* (Cambridge: Harvard University Press, 1973); Bennie Charles Ollenburger, "Zion, the City of the Great King. A Theological Investigation of Zion Symbolism in the Tradition of the Jerusalem Cult," Ph.D. diss. Princeton University, 1982; Eckart Otto, "Silo und Jerusalem," *Theologische Zeitschrift* 32 (1976): 65–77; id., "El und JHWH in Jerusalem," VetTest 30 (1980): 316–29; J.B. Payne, "Zion," ZPEB, 5:1063–66; Claude J. Peifer, "Sing for Us the Songs of Zion: the Jerusalem Psalms," TBT 97 (1978): 1690–96; Norman W. Porteous, "Jerusalem-Zion: The Growth of a Symbol," *Living the Mystery. Collected Essays* (Oxford: Blackwell, 1967), pp. 93–111; von Rad, OTT, 1:39–48, 366–70; 2:155–69; id., "The City on the Hill," *The Problem of the Hexateuch and Other Essays* (London: SCM, 1984), pp. 232–42; J.J.M. Roberts, "The Davidic Origin of the Zion Tradition," JBL 92 (1973): 329–44; id., "Zion Tradition," IDBSuppl., pp. 985–87; A. Robinson, "Zion and *ṣāphôn* in Psalm XLVIII 3," VetTest 24 (1974): 118–23; J.P. Ross, "Yahweh *Ṣ*^{e}*ḇā'ôṯ* in Samuel and Psalms," VetTest 17 (1967): 76–92; Josef Schreiner, *Sion-Jerusalem. Jahwes Königssitz. Theologie der heiligen Stadt im alten Testament* (Munich: Kösel, 1963); Klaus Seybold, "Volksfrömmigkeit und Zionstheologie," in *Die Wallfahrtspsalmen. Studien zur Entstehungsgeschichte von Psalm 120–134* (Neukirchen-Vluyn: Neukirchener Verlag, 1978), pp. 77–85; Odil Hannes Steck, "Jerusalemer Vorstellungen vom Frieden und ihre Abwandlungen in der Prophetie des Alten Israel," *Lieden-Bibel-Kirche,* ed. Gerhard Liedke (Stuttgart: Ernst Klett, 1968), pp. 75–95; id., *Friedensvorstellungen im alten Jerusalem: Psalmen, Jesaja, Deuterojesaja* (Zurich: Theologischer Verlag, 1972); Gunther Wanke, *Die Zionstheologie der Korachiten in ihrem Traditionsgeschichtlichen Zusammenhang* (Berlin: Töpelmann, 1966); Claus Westermann, "Die Zionslieder," in *Ausgewählte Psalmen* (Göttingen: Vandenhoeck & Ruprecht, 1984), pp. 197–201.

TDNT, 7:292–338; THAT, 2:498–506; TWOT, 2:750–51, 764–65.

Psalm 47: Yahweh Is the Victorious King

The psalm celebrates the kingship of God (cf. Pss 93–100). Within the present context it provides a connection with the two hymns of Zion (Pss 46; 48), as Psalm 47 adumbrates the victorious rule of Yahweh over all the earth (see appendix to Ps 5: Yahweh Is King). Its genre conforms to the psalms celebrating Yahweh's kingship. It also has a prophetic, eschatological dimension as the psalmist longs for the full establishment of God's rule on earth (Kidner, p. 177). The cultic interpretation is possible (A.A. Anderson, 1:361), as is the historical (cf. I. Seeligman, "Psalm 47," *Tarbiz* 50 [1980/81]: 25–36 [Heb.]). Recently W. Beuken ("Psalm XLVII: Structure and Drama," OTS 21 [1981]: 38–54) has argued that "only the eschatological interpretation can account for the varied impact which the functions of time and space have on the structure of psalm 47."

The original situation is far from clear. In later Jewish usage Psalm 47 was utilized as part of the New Year's service. The emphasis on ascension (v.5) gave rise to its use on Ascension Day in Christian liturgy.

The structure unfolds as follows:

A. Praise of Yahweh's Mighty Acts (vv.1–2)
  B. Yahweh's Mighty Acts (vv.3–4)
    C. Yahweh's Victorious Kingship (vv.5–6)
  B′. Yahweh Is King (vv.7–8)
A′. Universal Acknowledgment of Yahweh's Kingship (v.9)

I. Praise of Yahweh's Mighty Acts

47:1–2

For the director of music. Of the Sons of Korah. A psalm.

1 Clap your hands, all you nations;
  shout to God with cries of joy.
2 How awesome is the LORD Most High,
  the great King over all the earth!

1 In anticipation of God's kingship, the nations must joyfully acclaim Yahweh as the Great King by clapping their hands (cf. 2 Kings 11:12; for nature, cf. Isa 55:12). The heavenly beings already sing praises to him (cf. 29:1; Isa 6:3). The kingdom of God will only be established when the "nations" on earth will join with the heavenly choirs, celebrating his universal and everlasting kingship. While clapping the people "shout" joyously a victory cheer (20:5).

2 The people are struck with awe (65:8; 76:7, 12) on account of the mighty works (vv.3–4) of the Great King. Here the emphasis is on God, who is Yahweh Elyon, "the LORD Most High, the great King over all the earth." (See the appendix to Ps 9: Yahweh Is El Elyon.) The movement from v.1 with its reference to God climactically ends on the presentation of Israel's God as "the great King." Kings in the ancient Near East loved to designate themselves by this title because with it were associated superiority, suzerainty, and the power to grant vassal treaties (cf. 2 Kings 18:19; Isa 36:4). Any king assuming this title could not tolerate competition. So it is with Yahweh. He alone is the Great King over all the earth (cf. Mal 1:11, 14)!

Notes

For a brief discussion of the technical words and phrases in the superscription, see the Introduction.

II. Yahweh's Mighty Acts

47:3–4

3 He subdued nations under us,
  peoples under our feet.
4 He chose our inheritance for us,
  the pride of Jacob, whom he loved. *Selah*

3–4 The psalmist reflects on Yahweh's mighty acts in salvation history. Through his acts in the Conquest and through its history, Israel has experienced the power of Yahweh. He subdued the nations (cf. 135:8–11; 136:10–20) and gave their land to his people as an "inheritance" (cf. 28:9; 105:11; 135:12; 136:21–22). He has subdued, chosen, and loved. He has acted on behalf of his people because of his deep love for them (20:1; Deut 4:31–32; Mal 1:2). The use of the term "the pride of Jacob" denotes the reasons for Israel's joy in the Lord, whereas in prophetic usage it denotes Israel's independence and arrogance (cf. Hos 5:5; 7:10; Amos 6:8). We cannot be more specific in identifying the particular reference of the pride, whether land or temple.

Notes

3–4 (4–5 MT) The verbs are imperfect and preferably translated as past events: יַדְבֵּר . . . יִבְחַר (*yaḏbēr . . . yiḇḥar,* "he subdued . . . he chose"). The verb *yaḏbēr* is a Hiphil form of *d-b-r* with the preposition *taḥaṯ,* meaning "subjugate" or "subdue" (KB[3], 1:201). It occurs only here and in 18:47 (cf. the parallel form in 2 Sam 22:28).

4 (5 MT) אָהֵב (*'āhēḇ,* "loves") is a stative form best translated as a present (cf. NIV, "loved").

III. Yahweh's Victorious Kingship

47:5–6

5 God has ascended amid shouts of joy,
  the LORD amid the sounding of trumpets.
6 Sing praises to God, sing praises;
  sing praises to our King, sing praises.

5–6 Yahweh is victorious! He has "ascended" (v.5; cf. 68:18) to his heavenly palace. His victorious ascension was accompanied with "shouts of joy [*r-w-'*]" and "the sounding of trumpets" (lit., "ram's horn"; cf. 98:6; 150:3; see appendix to Ps 150: Musical Instruments). His victory march is acknowledged by his subjects on earth. They could rebel because of the return of the Great King to his heavenly abode. But instead they are encouraged to continue doing homage to him by singing his praises. The fourfold use of the root *z-m-r* (v.6, "sing praises"; see appendix to Ps 122: The Praise of Yahweh) creates a poetic effect, stressing the urgency to respond to his heavenly reception with earthly acclamation, celebrating his mighty acts.

IV. Yahweh Is King

47:7–8

7 For God is the King of all the earth;
sing to him a psalm of praise.
8 God reigns over the nations;
God is seated on his holy throne.

7–8 The psalm returns to the reflection of God's kingship on earth (v.7). His ascension into his heavenly palace and his rule over earth emphasize his universal dominion. (A.A. Anderson [1:364] is probably right in seeing the polemical element, as the Canaanites worshiped Baal as the victorious god.)

Yahweh is King over "the nations" (v.8). They too must acclaim his sovereignty (see the appendix to Ps 5: Yahweh Is King). They too must discern that Yahweh is different from all other gods, as he is "seated on his holy [*q-d-š*] throne." No doubt his throne is in heaven (103:19; Isa 66:1), but his footstool extends to earth (99:5; 132:7; 1 Chron 28:2; Isa 66:1). In his essence and in his relations he is "holy" and demands that those who approach him consecrate themselves. In the Apocalypse, John sees Jesus exalted on the throne (Rev 4:9–10; 5:1, 7, 13; 6:16; 7:10, 15; 19:4). He has received the same prerogatives of kingship and authority as the Father; hence the response of the nations must be the same as the psalmist calls for: submission and praise!

Notes

6–7 (7–8 MT) The psalmist encourages God's people and anyone from the nations to praise (*z-m-r*) Yahweh as the only God over heaven and earth: "For God is the King of all the earth" (v.7 [6 MT]).

7 (8 MT) מַשְׂכִּיל (*maśkîl*, "psalm"; NIV mg.: "*a maskil*") may be a musical or literary designation. See the Introduction to the Book of Psalms.

V. Universal Acknowledgment of Yahweh's Kingship

47:9

9 The nobles of the nations assemble
as the people of the God of Abraham,
for the kings of the earth belong to God;
he is greatly exalted.

9 At this point the prophetic, eschatological element distinguishes itself. Weiser comments, "Thus the history of the divine salvation is consummated within the psalm's field of vision" (p. 378). The psalmist prays that all the "nobles" and "kings" of the earth may acknowledge the Lord's kingship. It is not entirely clear whether they come willingly or as hostages; but from usage elsewhere (cf. 72:8–11), it appears that the psalmist longs for the day when all leaders and nations will freely submit to Yahweh's sovereignty. They are accounted as one with "the people of the God of Abraham." Again our text is somewhat ambiguous as the consonants *ʿm* could be read as "the people" (*ʿam;* so NIV) or "with" (*ʿim;* so LXX). The difference is significant, but the general sense seems unaffected: "The nobles . . . assemble the people of the God of Abraham" or "The nobles assemble with the God of Abraham." Taking the MT reading, the NIV takes the bicolons and joins them together with the addition of the particle "as." The sense of the verse suggests that the Gentiles join together with Israel in the worship of God (cf. Gen 12:3; John 12:32; Rom 4:11; Gal 3:7–9).

The psalmist further explains why the nations must associate with Israel. All nations are the subjects of God's rule, whether they recognize it or not. Brueggemann speaks of a juxtaposition of the nations and Israel as distinctive aspects of God's rule: his "providential rule and election love" (*Message of the Psalms,* p. 150).

The psalm concludes with an inclusion, tying the end to the beginning and center. God is "exalted" (*ʿ-l-h*), as he has ascended (*ʿ-l-h*) into his heavenly palace. Truly he is "the LORD Most High" (Elyon, from *ʿ-l-h,* v.2).

Notes

---

9 (10 MT) BHS proposes an alternate reading for "the God of Abraham": "the tents of Abraham."

Instead of "the kings of the earth," the MT reads, "the shields of the earth." The tradition of reading "kings" is ancient, going back to the LXX: "the rulers of the earth." There is also internal evidence, as in 89:18; "king" and "shield" are synonymous. It may be that the *māḡēn*-shield was associated with royalty, and by metonymy "shield" stands for "kings." BHS proposes סִגְנֵי (*signê,* "rulers of"), as does Craigie: "for the earth's rulers" (*Psalms 1–50,* pp. 346–47). The NIV accepts Dahood's argument that *māḡēn* is a divine epithet ("Suzerain"). He alters the vocalization and ends up with

> The God of Abraham is the Strong One;
> truly God is Suzerain of the earth,
> greatly to be extolled.
> (*Psalms,* 1:283, cf. 286–87)

Psalm 48: The Beautiful City of God

In Psalm 47 the Lord receives praise as "the great King" (v.2). In Psalm 48 the greatness of God is shared with his people, who are likened to "the city of God" (cf. v.1). Whereas Psalm 46 could be categorized as either a song of Zion or a psalm of confidence, Psalm 48 is more clearly a song of Zion (see appendix to Ps 46: Zion Theology). This psalm begins with an ascription of praise to God (vv.1–3) and concludes with an encouragement to enjoy fully the evidences of God's presence (vv.12–14). In the middle section the psalmist reflects on God's past acts and on his attributes (vv.4–11). Though there is a structural resemblance with Psalm 46, the emphasis in Psalm 46 is on exhortation (confidence, perseverance). In Psalm 48 the stress is on proclamation of the good news of God's presence that results in the joy of God's people.

See the introduction to Psalm 24 for Rosenberg's study on the liturgical use of the Psalms in Babylon.

Probably the psalm arose in a cultic setting and was used in one or more of the great pilgrimage festivals. The scholarly tendency of associating this and so many other psalms with the Feast of Tabernacles (A.A. Anderson, 1:367; Craigie, *Psalms 1–50,* p. 352) appears to be a subjective judgment.

There is little agreement on the structure. The beginning (vv.1–3) and end (vv.12–14) constitute an inclusion by the repetition of "our God" (vv.1, 14); language of praise and proclamation (vv.1, 13); "Mount Zion" (vv.2, 11); language of joy (vv.2, 11); description of Zion (vv.2–3, 12–13); and "her citadels" (vv.3, 13). The middle section (vv.4–11) sets forth the benefits provided to the covenant people by the presence and protection of God. The expository structure follows the simple movement of the psalm:

A. Our God Is the Great King (vv.1–3)
B. The Perfections of Our God (vv.4–11)
A′. The Great King Is Our Shepherd (vv.12–14)

I. Our God Is the Great King

48:1–3

A song. A psalm of the Sons of Korah.

1 Great is the LORD, and most worthy of praise,
in the city of our God, his holy mountain.
2 It is beautiful in its loftiness,
the joy of the whole earth.
Like the utmost heights of Zaphon is Mount Zion,
the city of the Great King.
3 God is in her citadels;
he has shown himself to be her fortress.

1–3 The hymn begins with an ascription of praise to God because of his accommodation to man. God is the Lord (LORD [Yahweh]) of his covenant people and the Great King of the universe (see appendix to Ps 5: Yahweh Is King). The Lord is "great" in his royal rule (v.1; 96:4; 145:3; 1 Chron 16:25). He is sovereign, powerful, and glorious; and he alone is worthy of the praise of man. However, God's people who are citizens of "the city of our God" have additional reasons for praising him. These reasons are explicated throughout the psalm: his presence, protection, love, and righteousness.

The Great King has chosen to reside among his own people in "the city" on "the holy mountain" (v.1). The explicit reference is to Mount Zion and the city, Jerusalem. Because he is present, Mount Zion is the holy mountain (2:6; 3:4; 15:1; 43:3; 99:9). Only because of God's condescension to dwell on Mount Zion may she be called beautiful in her elevation (NIV, "loftiness") and "the joy of the whole earth" (v.2; cf. 50:2; Lam 2:15). The beauty and joy are not inherent in Mount Zion, because it is surrounded by higher mountains offering a better panoramic view. The godly had a special feeling about Jerusalem that is beautifully and sensitively expressed in this psalm. They looked on the city, mountain, and temple as symbols of God's presence with his people. Therefore the psalmist uses the geographical/spatial references to express the joy of God's people with the blessed presence of God. Von Rad calls this revelation of God's identification the *kenosis* of the OT: the beauty of Yahweh's condescension to the needs of his people (OTT, 1:367).

Alter significantly observes that the psalmist expresses "a paradox at the heart of biblical religion: the universalistic belief in a single God of all the earth Who had chosen as the medium of His relations with humanity the particularism of a compact with one people. This paradox had a major geographical corollary . . . Jerusalem . . . the 'city of our God'" (p. 121; cf. pp. 121–25).

Whatever other peoples might say about their holy cities, mountains, and temples, Mount Zion was "the city of the Great King" (v.2; cf. Matt 5:35). The people of Ugarit worshiped Baal on the "heights of Zaphon," some twenty-five miles to the northeast of Ugarit. For the godly the glorification of Mount Zaphon meant little because Mount Zion was better than Mount Zaphon. Belief in the superiority of Mount Zion is based on the conviction that God is truly present among his people and that he is their strength (v.3; see appendix to Ps 98: Yahweh Is the Divine Warrior).

Notes

For a brief discussion of the technical words and phrases in the superscription, see the Introduction.

2 (3 MT) The Hebrew idiom "It is beautiful in its loftiness" is a *hapax legomenon:* יְפֵה נוֹף (*y^e^p̱ēh nôp̱*, "beautiful of height," i.e., high rising; KB, p. 604). The theological significance has been well expressed by A.A. Anderson: "It is here that, in a sense, heaven and earth meet" (1:368).

The name "Zaphon" elsewhere may be translated straightforwardly as "north." But in this context it is best to retain it as a proper name. Zaphon was to the Canaanites what Mount Olympus was to the Greeks. The Canaanites (Phoenicians) believed that the chief God of the pantheon, El, dwelt on Mount Zaphon. The psalmist is borrowing the imagery and not the theology. Zion is the holy mountain of God. See A. Robinson, "Zion and *ṣāphôn* in Psalm XLVIII 3," VetTest 24 (1974): 118–23.

II. The Perfections of Our God

48:4–11

4 When the kings joined forces,
  when they advanced together,
5 they saw ⌊her⌋ and were astounded;
  they fled in terror.
6 Trembling seized them there,
  pain like that of a woman in labor.
7 You destroyed them like ships of Tarshish
  shattered by an east wind.

8 As we have heard,
  so have we seen
in the city of the LORD Almighty,
  in the city of our God:
  God makes her secure forever. *Selah*

9 Within your temple, O God,
  we meditate on your unfailing love.
10 Like your name, O God,
  your praise reaches to the ends of the earth;
  your right hand is filled with righteousness.

> [11] Mount Zion rejoices,
> the villages of Judah are glad
> because of your judgments.

The second strophe adumbrates the reasons for God's praiseworthiness. The presence of the "Great King" (v.2) evokes two kinds of responses: terror and joy. First, the enemies of God's people fled in terror when they "saw" the workings of God (vv.4–7). Second, the godly also "saw" his works and rejoiced (vv.8–11). The God of Israel inspires both fear and joy, fear in his enemies and joy in his people. God's protection of "the city" symbolizes the many ways in which he protects his people. Every act of "unfailing love" (*ḥesed̲*) and "righteousness" (*ṣedeq*) spreads the fame ("praise," *tᵉhillāh,* from *h-l-l,* v.10) of God's name (*šēm*) (vv.9–10).

4–7 The description of the hostile forces (v.4) is reminiscent of the description in Psalm 2. The kings of the nations have united together in their warfare against God. Unlike Psalm 2, with its emphasis on the role of his vassal-king of the house of David, this psalm focuses on the magnificence of Yahweh, the Divine Warrior. The united effort of the nations gave them confidence, best expressed by A.A. Anderson: "they stormed furiously" (NIV, "they advanced together," v.4).

The description of the nations' reaction (vv.5–6) and God's response inspire God's people. The bold, confident, and strong opposition against God was broken miraculously. It is likened to the destruction of the "ships of Tarshish" that were the pride and glory of seafaring nations such as Phoenicia (v.7). How strong and majestic they were! But how easily a strong wind (cf. Isa 27:8) could toss them about on the open sea and destroy the vessels, people, and cargo! The "storming" of the nations came to an end as though by a "stormy" wind, ordained by the Lord.

The ease with which the Lord repels and destroys the opposition terrifies the nations. The history of redemption demonstrates how the nations were overcome with fear and how their strength melted away (cf. Exod 15:14; Josh 2:11). They were in panic and overcome by a fear so great that they trembled. There they stood unable to push on, overcome by the awe-inspiring glory of the Lord. It was as if they had seen a theophany (cf. 46:2–3). Their anguish is likened to a woman in labor (v.6; cf. Isa 21:3; 26:17; Jer 4:31; 6:24; 13:21; 49:24), but it too passes. Great is the power of our God. Calvin encourages us to look up to God:

> At the same time, let us remember that a nod alone on the part of God is sufficient to deliver us; and that, although our enemies may be ready to fall upon us on every side to overwhelm us, it is in his power, whenever he pleases, to strike them with amazement of spirit, and thus to make their hearts fail in a moment in the very midst of their efforts against us. Let this reflection serve as a bridle to keep our minds from being drawn away, to look in all directions for human aid. (2:223)

8–11 When God shows himself to be the fortress of the godly (cf. v.3), they "see" what he has done (v.8) and are even more convinced that God makes his city "secure forever." The mighty acts of God evidence the presence of "the LORD Almighty" (YHWH *ṣᵉb̲āʾôt̲;* cf. 24:9–10; 46:7), the Ruler of heaven and earth (see appendix to Ps 24: Lord Sabaoth).

The identification with the history of redemption is expressed by the verbs "hearing" and "seeing" (v.8). God's people over the centuries have witnessed the presence of God in ordering the events of the world and in working out the redemption of his people. They are brought together in the common expressions of "meditation," "praise," and "rejoicing" (vv.9–11) as their appropriate response to the presence of God.

The godly "meditate" on God's mighty acts (v.9). Their meditation was more than a devotional reading. They took comfort in, rejoiced in, and made offerings in gratitude to the revelation of God's perfections. It was a God-given visual aid, encouraging them to imagine and to reflect on the long history of God's involvement with Israel and of the evidences of his "unfailing love" (*ḥesed̲*).

The reaction of "praise" (v.10) is a positive response in contrast to the dread that fell on the nations. To the ends of the earth, the praise of God is heard from the lips of the godly. They declare his "righteousness," i.e., the victorious and glorious rule of Yahweh in which his people share the benefits. The rule of God is symbolized by the "right hand," which includes power, justice, righteousness, and love. He rules in giving deliverance to his own people and by avenging himself on their enemies! (See the appendix to Ps 25: The Perfections of Yahweh.)

"Rejoicing" goes from Mount Zion throughout Judah (v.11). The people rejoice in the "judgments" of God, i.e., the ways in which he establishes his kingdom by bringing defeat and subjugation to the opposing forces (cf. 97:8; Exod 15:1–18).

Notes

4–5 (5–6 MT) A different particle introduces each verse: כִּי־הִנֵּה and הֵמָּה (*kî-hinnēh* and *hemmāh*, "for behold," "truly behold," and "behold" [NIV, "when" and "they"]). Dahood's analysis is quite attractive in that he introduces a shock value to the actions of the kings: "For, behold, the kings assembled, together they stormed; Lo! they looked, were sore astounded, terror-struck they were ready to flee" (*Psalms*, 1:288, 291).

7 (8 MT) A few Hebrew MSS read כְּרוּחַ (*kerûaḥ*, "like a wind"), resulting in the translation "like an east wind that destroys the ships of Tarshish."

11 (12 MT) "The villages of Judah" is literally "the daughters [בְּנוֹת (*benôt̲*)] of Judah," an idiomatic expression for the towns and villages of Judah (97:8).

III. The Great King Is Our Shepherd

48:12–14

12 Walk about Zion, go around her,
count her towers,
13 consider well her ramparts,
view her citadels,
that you may tell of them to the next generation.
14 For this God is our God for ever and ever;
he will be our guide even to the end.

12–13 The psalm concludes with an invitation to walk around in Jerusalem, to count "her towers," and to pay careful attention to "her ramparts" and "her citadels" (vv.12–13). It is possible that the pilgrims made a procession around Jerusalem as part of a sacred rite. Scholars have attempted to explain the cultic significance of the procession but are not in agreement on its meaning and place in Israel's worship. In the light of the tenor of the psalm, it is most likely that the physical defense system of ancient Jerusalem symbolized a far greater strength: the protection of God himself. The kings of Judah received their significance on two counts: their loyalty to the Lord and their concern with the security of Jerusalem and Judah. Because the temple was in Jerusalem, the defense of Jerusalem was an expression of loyalty to the Lord. The close connection between material security and dependence on the Lord-Protector go hand in hand.

14 Those who had seen the defense system of Jerusalem had a picture of a greater truth: the protection of God. They could tell their children and grandchildren about the beauty, strength, and history of Jerusalem; but in the telling of the story lay the truth that the Lord is "our God for ever" and that he, like a good shepherd, will continue to "guide" (or "protect") his own "even to the end."

Notes

---

13 (14 MT) "Consider well her ramparts" is literally "put your heart to her strength." The phrase חֵילָה (*ḥêlāh,* "strength") is given in a number of Hebrew MSS and ancient versions as חֵילָהּ (*ḥêlāh,* "her strength"). The word "strength" probably signifies the sloping bank (glacis) outside the wall, viz., "ramparts." Other renderings are "wall" (Dahood, *Psalms,* 1:289) or "fortress" (Craigie, *Psalms 1–50,* p. 351).

The verb פַּסְּגוּ (*passᵉg̲û,* "view") is a *hapax legomenon* of unknown meaning. The rendering "view" fits in the context (cf. Briggs, 2:403: "consider") as does "traverse" (Craigie, *Psalms 1–50,* p. 351). The NEB has "pass her palaces in review."

14 (15 MT) The Lord is the Shepherd who guides his people by protecting them from evil (23:1). The verbal phrase יְנַהֲגֵנוּ (*yᵉnahᵃg̲ēnû,* "will guide us"; NIV, "will be our guide") is particularly suited to the shepherd imagery of the Bible (77:20; 78:52; 80:1; Isa 49:9–10).

A number of MSS read עוֹלָמוֹת (*'ôlāmôt̲,* "forever"; cf. LXX) instead of the MT's עַל־מוּת (*'al-mût̲;* NKJV, "even to death"; NIV, "to the end"). Some scholars have proposed that the phrase belongs to the superscription of Psalm 49 and was accidentally misplaced. For a similar heading see Pss 9 and 46.

Psalm 49: The Folly of Riches Without Wisdom

The psalm is an encouragement to the godly who are haunted by the power and influence of the rich. The problem of the prosperity of the wicked (cf. Ps 73) is difficult, but the psalmist has given us a ray of light as to the final resolution. He does this by the convention of a *wisdom* psalm. His method includes question (vv.5–6), observation of life (vv.10–11), proverbial conclusion (vv.12, 20), metaphor, and personification (v.14; see Leo G. Perdue, "The Riddles of Psalm 49," JBL 93 [1974]: 533–42; see also the appendix to Ps 1: The Ways of Wisdom and Folly).

The structure of the psalm consists of three units: introduction (vv.1–4), the shortfalls of wealth (vv.5–12), and the folly of riches (vv.13–20).

Introduction (vv.1–4)
- A. Question (vv.5–6)
  - B. The Certainty of Death (vv.7–12)

B′. The Folly of Riches (vv.13–14)
A′. Resolution of the Question (vv.15–20)

I. Introduction

49:1–4

For the director of music. Of the Sons of Korah. A psalm.

1 Hear this, all you peoples;
listen, all who live in this world,
2 both low and high,
rich and poor alike:
3 My mouth will speak words of wisdom;
the utterance from my heart will give understanding.
4 I will turn my ear to a proverb;
with the harp I will expound my riddle:

1–2 The introduction reflects the combination of two traditions: the tradition of the prophets (cf. Mic 1:2) and the tradition of wisdom (cf. Prov 1:8). These traditions are complementary as is evident in the teaching of this psalmist. He invites everybody—rich and poor, wise and foolish—from all nations in the "world" (v.1; *ḥāleḏ*, a rare poetic word; cf. 17:14 and Isa 38:11) to listen to his lesson in godly wisdom. Because the lesson pertains to social distinctions based on wealth, the voice of wisdom goes out to all people: "low" (people without a sizable estate) and "high" (people with a substantial estate, v.2; cf. 62:9). He further clarifies the invitation as open to "rich and poor alike." The universal appeal of the topic to be discussed is made clear in vv.5–20.

3–4 For now the psalmist draws the interest of his hearers (readers). Why should they listen? He keeps them in suspense by impressing on them the importance of the discussion. To this end he uses four words for wisdom: "wisdom," "understanding," "proverb," and "riddle" (vv.3–4; cf. Prov 1:1–6). It is not entirely clear how the words differ in meaning from one another. The first two are pluralized forms and may be used to intensify the meaning: "great wisdom" and "great understanding." The second pair of words may express the means by which wisdom is to be communicated: by "proverb," i.e., more particularly by a reflection on the "riddle" of life and death, accompanied by the music of a "harp" (*kinnôr;* see the appendix to Ps 150: Musical Instruments).

Notes

For a brief discussion of the technical words and phrases in the superscription, see the Introduction.

On the exegetical problems of this psalm, see J. van der Ploeg, "Notes sur le Psaume XLIX," *OudTestamentische Studiën* 13 (1963): 137–72.

2 (3 MT) "Both low and high" is literally "both the sons of man and the sons of man." The two similar phrases in the MT employ a different word for man: אָדָם (*'āḏām*, "mankind") and אִישׁ (*'îš*, "man"). The NIV translation is appropriate because the word *'îš* may signify a man of wealth, whereas the word *'āḏām* may be a general designation for man. The second colon reinforces the correctness of this interpretation. The NEB takes a different approach: "all mankind, every living man."

4 (5 MT) The מָשָׁל (*māšāl*, "proverb") may refer to the psalm as a whole, to the intent of the psalm ("instruction"), or to the short, pithy abstraction of wisdom stated and restated in the refrain (vv.12, 20).

"Expound" is literally "open," from the root פתח (*p-t-ḥ*), i.e., "explain."

The חִידָה (*ḥîḏāh*, "riddle") is a form of wisdom: an enigmatic question (1 Kings 10:1) or a parable (Ezek 17:2). Here it probably means an enigmatic question.

II. Question

49:5–6

5 Why should I fear when evil days come,
when wicked deceivers surround me—
6 those who trust in their wealth
and boast of their great riches?

5–6 Why? The inspired teacher of wisdom begins his lesson on wisdom by asking a relevant question. Why should one not fear old age, the uncertainty of the future, and the rejection of man? People try to cushion themselves by heaping up wealth with the hope that this will continually provide an income and keep one from harm and abandonment. But the response to fear is not found in the fleeting sense of well-being that wealth may provide. Those who put their confidence in wealth are all too often those who trouble and deceive the poor, aged, and lonely. The tone of the question is unlike that of the teacher in Ecclesiastes, who raises difficult issues with the intent to get his students involved in the problems of life and death. This teacher of wisdom is more straightforward. When he asks the question, he is all too ready to provide an answer. There is a certain sense of assurance in his question, as if he is saying, Do not be afraid of those who may take advantage of adversities for selfish gains!

Notes

---

5 (6 MT) "When wicked deceivers surround me" is literally "the guilt of my heels surrounds me" (cf. LXX, NKJV). The NIV assumes appropriately an emendation in the MT's עֲקֵבַי (*ʿ*[a]*qēḇay*, "my heels") to עֹקְבַי (*ʿōq*[e]*ḇay*, "those who cheat me" or "my treacherous enemies"; cf. BHS). Based on this emendation the text could be read as "the wickedness of my treacherous enemies surrounds me" (cf. NEB).

III. The Certainty of Death

49:7–12

7 No man can redeem the life of another
or give to God a ransom for him—

8 the ransom for a life is costly,
no payment is ever enough—
9 that he should live on forever
and not see decay.
10 For all can see that wise men die;
the foolish and the senseless alike perish
and leave their wealth to others.
11 Their tombs will remain their houses forever,
their dwellings for endless generations,
though they had named lands after themselves.
12 But man, despite his riches, does not endure;
he is like the beasts that perish.

7–9 The confident answer begins with an interjection: "surely" (v.7; see Notes). Because "death" is the common experience of mankind, rich and poor alike, the rich cannot boast of any advantages over the poor. He cannot use his money to redeem himself from death or to send a substitute for himself (vv.7–8). He may live on a grandiose scale so as to give the impression that he will live forever; but he too must ultimately face death for what it is: a separation from the land of the living, from the comforts of life, and from social and economic distinctions. It is summed up in one word: "the pit" (v.9; NIV, "decay"). The "pit," as a synonym of "Sheol" (cf. 16:10), signifies death and possibly retribution for the evil done in life (cf. 94:13).

10–11 Another asseverative underscores the inevitable conclusion of the lesson of wisdom: "truly" (rather than "for," NIV, v.10). A careful study of life confirms the conclusion of the sage that death is a leveler. All men die, whether they are wise or foolish. The "foolish and the senseless" are those who have hoarded up wealth for themselves (cf. Luke 12:20). It may also be a general designation of those who have rejected the voice of wisdom (cf. Prov 1:8). Those who have made any attempt to perpetuate their own memory by naming real property after themselves may only be remembered by the names engraved on their tombs (v.11; cf. Isa 22:16). The rich ensured that they would be remembered by having beautiful tombs hewn in rock and by placing inscriptions on their sarcophagi. Archaeologists are grateful to all those who painstakingly provided for themselves in death, as their tombs, inscriptions, and material remains witness to ages long past. Apart from archaeologists few people are interested in the tombs of the rich. Their end is in death, and they are forever cast out from their wealth and real properties.

12 The inevitable conclusion is presented in the form of a "proverb." Man, whoever he is (rich or poor), cannot use wealth to his advantage in death. One end overtakes all mankind and animals alike, viz., "death" (cf. Eccl 3:19). The very nature of "life" (animal and human) is such that it has a built-in obsolescence. The inspired author is not interested in addressing the issues of the life hereafter or the differences between human and animal life. He merely observes that death is a part of earthly existence.

Notes

7 (8 MT) The MT is problematic in the usage of אָח (*'āh*, "brother"; NIV, "no man") at the beginning of the verse (cf. Briggs, 1:413) and the Qal imperfect יִפְדֶּה (*yipdeh*, "will/can redeem"). Most modern versions and commentaries agree with the proposals given in BHS to emend "brother" to אַךְ (*'ak̲*, "surely," "but"), based on a few MSS and the usage in v.15, and to read the verb as a Niphal imperfect יִפָּדֶה (*yippāḏeh,* "will/can redeem himself": "Surely a man cannot redeem himself."

It may be that the word אִישׁ (*'îš,* "man") also signifies here a man of wealth, as in v.2.

8 (9 MT) The verse should be considered as a parenthetical remark in between v.7 and v.9. The thought of v.7 is continued in v.9.

10 (11 MT) "For all can see" is literally "for [or truly] he can see." The subject is ambiguous in the MT. Dahood (*Psalms,* 1:295) interprets the subject as God: "If he looks at the wise, they die." It is preferable to assume that the subject of v.7—"a man"—is still the subject of v.10:

v.7: "Surely a man cannot redeem himself"
v.10: "Certainly he can see."

11 (12 MT) "Their tombs" translates קִבְרָם (*qiḇrām,* "their graves"), a form suggested by the LXX, Syriac, and Targum. The MT has a transposed form: קִרְבָּם (*qirbām,* "their inners"). The NIV accepts the emendation "Their tombs will remain their houses" with a marginal note: "Hebrew: *In their thoughts their houses will remain.*"

12 (13 MT) The generic word אָדָם (*'āḏām,* "man") is further explained as if to say that mankind at large, including those members of mankind who are rich, must die.

בַּל (*bal,* "not") could also be rendered affirmatively: "surely" (see C.F. Whitley, "The Positive Force of the Hebrew Particle בל," ZAW 84 [1972]: 213–19). This would result in "man will surely sleep."

The LXX and Syriac introduce the reading of v.20 in v.12: "have understanding," יָבִין (*yāḇîn*), instead of "endure," יָלִין (*yālîn*); so the NIV margin: "Septuagint and Syriac read verse 12 the same as verse 20." Judah Jacob Slotkin has proposed an alternate reading: "Man is (as) cattle and does not complain; he is comparable to beasts that perish" ("Psalm xlix 13,21 [AV 12,20]," VetTest 28 [1978]: 361–62).

John Goldingay rightly explains the differences in the language in vv.12 and 20 as arising from artistic variation ("Repetition and Variation in the Psalms," JQR 68 [1977]: 148).

IV. The Folly of Riches

49:13–14

13 This is the fate of those who trust in themselves,
and of their followers, who approve
their sayings. *Selah*
14 Like sheep they are destined for the grave,
and death will feed on them.
The upright will rule over them in the morning;
their forms will decay in the grave,
far from their princely mansions.

13 The summary of the previous section (v.12) is the basis for a further discussion of the folly of riches and the care of God for the godly. The Bible is not against riches per se but the attitude of self-sufficiency and self-confidence so often associated with riches. The rich come under condemnation for their insensitivity, scheming, deception, and attitude that they rule the world (v.5; cf. James 5:1–6). Those who agree with their words, often benefiting from their power and prestige, will also die and be no more. Regardless of how great a shadow the rich may cast on their generation, they and those who have found shelter in their branches will be no more.

14 Death is personified as a shepherd who leads the rich as sheep to the slaughter. Those who have cared for themselves in life will waste away in death. A terrible lot befalls the rich, whereas the righteous will be victorious. When his night of darkness (a symbol of suffering) is over, there will be "morning." Then his lot will be changed. The Lord will freely redeem the righteous and see that nothing will hurt his own in death and in the life hereafter. The righteous will triumph over evil.

Notes

13–14 (14–15 MT) These verses are difficult in the MT, as reflected by the marginal notes in the NIV and the differences among the EVV and commentators. Craigie (*Psalms 1–50*, p. 356) renders vv.13–14 thus:

> This is their way, their folly,
> and that of those after them who approve their words.
> *Selah*
>
> Like sheep shipped to Sheol,
> Death shall graze on them.
> The upright shall rule at dawn,
> Their forms for Sheol's consumption,
> rather than their lofty abodes.

V. Resolution of the Question

49:15–20

15 But God will redeem my life from the grave;
he will surely take me to himself. *Selah*

16 Do not be overawed when a man grows rich,
when the splendor of his house increases;
17 for he will take nothing with him when he dies,
his splendor will not descend with him.
18 Though while he lived he counted himself blessed—
and men praise you when you prosper—
19 he will join the generation of his fathers,
who will never see the light ⌊of life⌋.

20 A man who has riches without understanding
is like the beasts that perish.

15 The confidence of hope breaks through in v.15 with the affirmation of the resurrection and of fellowship with God. The Lord will intervene on behalf of the godly and redeem (lit., "take") them from the clutches of "death." No money can buy these privileges (v.7). For a positive statement on the contribution of this psalm to the OT teaching on the hereafter, see T.D. Alexander, "The Psalms and the Afterlife," *Irish Biblical Studies* 9 (1987): 2–17.

16–19 The triumph of faith gives no ground to fear what is transitory (v.16; cf. v.5). Riches, splendor, praise of self, or praise of man makes no difference in the grave (vv.16–18). The tragedy of riches may well be that it gives a false sense of security and life. It protects from the hardness of life. Yet the godless rich will die like animals (vv.12, 14) without the hope of the dawning light (v.19; cf. v.14). Death is described here as a place of absolute darkness, where not a ray of light (hope) penetrates—ever (cf. 88:11–12; see appendix to Ps 88: Sheol-Grave-Death). The surprise element may lie in the reservation of the psalmist in not developing a full-blown doctrine of resurrection. It appears that his silence is significant in the context of the ancient Near Eastern mythological conceptions. For this see M.J. Mulder, "Psalm 49:15 en 16: Twee Problematische Verzen," *Loven en Geloven. Opstellen van Collega's en Medewerkers aangeboden aan Prof. Dr. Nic. H. Ridderbos,* ed. M.H. van Es et al. (Amsterdam: Ton Bolland, 1975), pp. 116–34.

20 The purpose of the psalm was to instruct all men, including the rich, in the path of wisdom. The psalmist did not intend to disparage the godly rich who received their wealth as a blessing from God. The difference between man and beast lies in the degree of "understanding." If man has no understanding of himself as man, of his mortality, and of his God, he lives and dies "like the beasts that perish."

Notes

15 (16 MT) The phrase יִקָּחֵנִי (*yiqqāḥēnî,* "he will take me to himself") may be a conscious allusion to the story of Enoch's translation to glory (Gen 5:24; cf. Ps 73:24). For a critical study of this psalm and its understanding of life and death, see Oswald Loretz, "Ugaritisches und Jüdisches. Weisheit und Tod in Psalm 49," *Ugarit-Forschungen* 17 (1986): 189–92. Léonard Ramaroson concludes that the psalmist knew of the bliss of being with God in death ("Immortalité et Résurrection dans les Psaumes," *Science et Esprit* 36 [1984]: 287–95).

16 (17 MT) The interrogative "why" receives an answer in this verse. The verb is the same and each verse reflects on one aspect of "fear": individual suffering in adversity (v.5) and individual suffering in seeing the prosperity of the wicked (v.16). For a description of the anguish and its negative effects caused by the prosperity of the wicked, see Ps 73:3–14.

Psalm 50: A Heart of Gratitude

This psalm is concerned with true loyalty to God. Loyalty is antithetical to formalism and hypocrisy, as the Lord requires a heart of gratitude (see appendix to Ps 1: The Ways of Wisdom and Folly). The psalm differs from most other psalms by its prophetic character. It encompasses features of theophany, accusation, warning, and an invitation to repent (see the structuralist study of Johanna W.H. Bos, "Oh, When the Saints: A Consideration of the Meaning of Psalm 50," JSOT 24 [1982]: 65–77). L.C. Allen rightly observes, "Psalm 50 is a literary tapestry in which stylistic, thematic and form-critical patterns have been articulately interwoven" ("Structure and Meaning in Psalm 50," *Vox Evangelica* 14 [1984]: 33). Brueggemann views this psalm together with Psalm 81 as examples of psalms of disorientation in which God's people are asking for "a second opinion" (*Message of the Psalms,* pp. 88–94).

The occasion of Psalm 50's use in the cultus is not clear. It may have been associated with the great festivals, accompanied by offerings of thanksgiving and dedication (burnt offerings). The references to the covenant and to the laws (v.17) suggest a setting around the Feast of Tabernacles, but this is not certain. For a full study see Eugenio Lakatos, *La Religion Verdadera: Estudio Exegetico del Salmo 50* (Madrid: Casa de la Biblia, 1972).

The structural components of the psalm are as follows:

A. The Righteous Judgment of God (vv.1–6)
  B. Warning to the Godly (vv.7–15)
  B′. Warning to the Wicked (vv.16–21)
A′. The Righteous Judgment of God (vv.22–23)

(For an alternative structure see Allen, "Structure and Meaning," pp. 17–37.)

I. The Righteous Judgment of God

50:1–6

A psalm of Asaph.

1 The Mighty One, God, the LORD,
 speaks and summons the earth
 from the rising of the sun to the place where it sets.
2 From Zion, perfect in beauty,
 God shines forth.
3 Our God comes and will not be silent;
 a fire devours before him,
 and around him a tempest rages.
4 He summons the heavens above,
 and the earth, that he may judge his people:
5 "Gather to me my consecrated ones,
 who made a covenant with me by sacrifice."
6 And the heavens proclaim his righteousness,
 for God himself is judge. *Selah*

1 None other than God himself summons the inhabitants of the earth to prepare themselves for the great judgment to come. The first three words of the Hebrew text emphasize that it is God who has spoken: El (= God), Elohim (= God), Yahweh (= LORD) (the NIV has "The Mighty One, God, the LORD"). The Creator-God (= Elohim) and the Redeemer-God (Yahweh) are one God (= El). He has made a covenant with creation (Gen 9:8–17; cf. Hos 2:18) and with the nation Israel. His rule extends far beyond Israel to the whole earth, poetically described as "from the rising of the sun to the place where it sets."

2 God's relationship with his people, however, is very special to him, as expressed in the portrayal of Zion: "perfect in beauty" (cf. 48:2; Lam 2:15; see the appendix to Ps 46: Zion Theology). The Lord has vested interests in his covenant people. He has adorned them with his glory. The God who at one time revealed himself at Mount Sinai "shines forth" from Jerusalem, where he had made his name dwell. The "light" of God's presence was evident in the glory-cloud in the desert (Exod 13:21–22; Num 9:15–23). The same God repeatedly showed Israel the "light" of his presence (cf. 4:6; 18:28; 27:1; 36:9; 43:3).

3 This great God, the Ruler of the universe, appears as the Great King (see appendix to Ps 5: Yahweh Is King). His appearance (theophany) is attended by phenomena designed to inspire "fear" in man: fire and a tempest. God is like "a consuming fire" (cf. Deut 4:24; 9:3; Isa 66:16; Heb 12:29) when he comes in judgment. In his anger he may storm like a "tempest" (cf. Isa 66:15).

4 God's message is not consoling to Israel, because he summons "the heaven above and the earth" as witnesses against his own people (cf. Deut 32:1; Isa 1:2; Mic 6:1–2). In the presence of the witnesses to the covenant, the Lord commands all his covenant people to be gathered for judgment. It is not clear how they are brought together. It may be that the heavenly beings are commanded to gather the people or that the heaven and earth are personified as responsible for seeing that all the covenant people are brought together.

5–6 The covenant people are only those who are the "consecrated ones, who made a covenant with me by sacrifice" (v.5). They have been consecrated by covenant (Exod 19:5–6; 24:5–8) and sealed by "the blood of the covenant" (24:8). The earth gathers up all the members of the covenant community while the heavens declare that God is the Righteous Judge, especially of his own people (v.6; cf. Heb 12:23–25). It was a great temptation of God's covenant people in the past, as it is now, to believe mistakenly that everything is in order between them and God. The proclamation of "righteousness" affirms that God, the Righteous Judge (cf. Isa 30:18; Mal 2:17–3:6), will order everything on earth in accordance with his will. He does not tolerate anything that does not satisfactorily meet his requirements. What those requirements are will be made more explicit in vv.7–15.

Notes

For a brief discussion of the technical words and phrases in the superscription, see the Introduction.

1 The forms of the root קרא (*q-r-'*, "call," vv.1, 4) have here the sense of "to summon to a trial," so NIV's "summons."

3 For a study on theophany in Pss 18; 50; 68; 77; and 97, see A. Weiser, "Zur Frage nach dem Beziehungen der Psalmen zum Kult: Die Darstellung der Theophanie in den Psalmen und im Festkult," in *Festschrift für Alfred Bertholet zum 80. Geburtstag*, edd. Walter Baumgartner et al. (Tübingen: Mohr, 1950), pp. 513–31; Nic. H. Ridderbos, "Die Theophanie in Ps L 1–6," *OudTestamentische Studiën* 15 (1969): 213–26.

5 It is probable that the designation חָסִיד (*ḥāsîḏ*, "godly," "devotee," "faithful one," "consecrated one," see 4:3) signifies here the covenant community in general and is not a term for the faithful within the nation Israel.

II. Warning to the Godly

50:7–15

7 "Hear, O my people, and I will speak,
O Israel, and I will testify against you:

I am God, your God.
8 I do not rebuke you for your sacrifices
or your burnt offerings, which are ever before me.
9 I have no need of a bull from your stall
or of goats from your pens,
10 for every animal of the forest is mine,
and the cattle on a thousand hills.
11 I know every bird in the mountains,
and the creatures of the field are mine.
12 If I were hungry I would not tell you,
for the world is mine, and all that is in it.
13 Do I eat the flesh of bulls
or drink the blood of goats?
14 Sacrifice thank offerings to God,
fulfill your vows to the Most High,
15 and call upon me in the day of trouble;
I will deliver you, and you will honor me."

7 The people used to present their sacrifices and offerings to the Lord in Jerusalem. But, unlike pagan religions, God needs nothing from his subjects. God, as the Ruler over his people ("I am God, your God"), has a legitimate right by virtue of the covenant relationship (cf. Deut 29:12–15). The God who spoke to Israel through Moses and the prophets in the words "Hear, O Israel" (Deut 5:1; 6:3–4; 9:1; Isa 39:5; Jer 22:2; Amos 7:16) again speaks to his people of his covenantal rights in this psalm. The words are a prophetic indictment against his own people.

8 The people imagined God as being in need of food, as they presented their sacrifices and offerings. The pagans sacrificed to appease and satisfy the cravings of their gods. Israel too was superstitious; and, in their fear of God's anger, they complied with his requirements (cf. Lev 1–7). He does not "rebuke" them because they did not give. They have! The "burnt offerings" were expressions of thankfulness belonging to the category of "dedicatory offerings" (see my "Offerings and Sacrifices in Bible Times," Elwell, *Evangelical Dictionary*, pp. 788–92).

9–11 However, God does not need offerings—not even dedicatory offerings—if they do not express true gratitude and joy from the hearts of the givers. To this end he reminds the people that he is the Creator-Ruler. Everything belongs to him (vv.9–12)! He does not need the few animals the Israelites have presented with a sense of pride and obligation. What are the tens of thousands of animals from Israel's stalls and pens compared with the millions of animals in the forests and fields, on the hills and mountains (vv.10–11; cf. 104:11, 20), that already belong to him?

There is a note of sarcasm in the use of the pronoun "your" in "your stall" and in "your pens" (v.9). It is as if God has heard them proudly say, "This is my bull / goat from my stall / pen!" To this boastful claim God responds solemnly with an emphatic "mine" (v.10; cf. Notes) and concludes his claim with a restatement of his ownership that would linger in the hearts of the hearers: "mine" (v.11). His rule extends to all creation.

12–13 The next step in the argument presents Israel with the inescapable folly of their thinking. Many thought that they were feeding God and that God needed them to keep him well fed and therefore content. What a naïve and wrong view of God! To this he responds that if he were in need, he could take care of himself, because he is the Ruler of the world (cf. 24:1; 1 Cor 10:26) and of every living creature (v.12; cf. Acts 17:24–25). He did not reveal his laws on offerings and sacrifice in order to be "fed." The "flesh" and "blood" of animals (v.13) had another significance, which had escaped the people.

14 The significance of the offerings was in their heart attitude. The offerings and vows were to be concrete expressions of gratitude and dedication to "the Most High" (Elyon; see appendix to Ps 9: Yahweh Is El Elyon). The "thank offerings" and "vows" (i.e., votive offerings) belong to the category of voluntary offerings, in which the offerers shared by eating from the offering (cf. Lev 7:12; 22:29). God desired communion with his people as they presented and ate the communion offerings. Instead of presenting "dedicatory offerings" in a spirit of pride, the people had to learn that the "Most High" (i.e., the supreme Deity and Ruler of the universe) invites them for a banquet to enjoy his presence. Of course, the offering must reflect the true intent: "thankfulness" (cf. v.23; Heb 13:15). The votive offering was usually presented after the Lord had delivered someone from a difficulty or had answered his prayer.

15 The Lord will graciously move his people to gratitude if they will humble themselves and call on him in their need. When the spirit of pride is broken and their trust in God restored, they will again enjoy the benefits of answered prayer and experience the Lord's deliverance of those who call on him. In response they are expected to give "honor" to God with heartfelt joy. (See the appendix to Ps 119: Yahweh Is My Redeemer.)

Notes

---

7 It is likely that the name Yahweh has been replaced by "God" in the Elohistic psalter and that, therefore, the self-identification should read, "I am Yahweh, your God" (cf. A.A. Anderson, 1:384–85). Even if this is not the case, the last word of the verse is the pronoun אָנֹכִי (*'ānōḵî*, "I"), which is a cryptic form of the self-identification "I am Yahweh" (Exod 6:3, 6–8). He is the covenant God.

10–11 The claim to universal possession is stated in the form of an inclusion: "for mine" (לִי [*lî*]) is every animal of the forest, and the creatures of the field are "mine" (עִמָּדִי [*'immāḏî*, lit., "with me").

The expression "on a thousand hills" is unique. The NEB takes "thousand" as a modification of the cattle, "and the cattle in thousands on my hills." BHS proposes another reading: בְּהַרְרֵי אֵל (*beharrê 'ēl*, "on the mountains of God"), which could be interpreted either literally or as a figure of speech, viz., "on the highest mountains" (cf. Dahood: "in the towering mountain," *Psalms*, 1:307–8).

11 God has also a special relation with nature as he is the legitimate Ruler over it. This truth is expressed by the pregnant verbal phrase from the root ידע (*y-d-'*, "I know"; i.e., "I am concerned about"; cf. 1:6).

For the relation of Sinai, represented by the offerings, and Zion, represented by Yahweh's royal epithets, see Levenson, pp. 208–9.

III. Warning to the Wicked

50:16–21

16 But to the wicked, God says:

"What right have you to recite my laws
or take my covenant on your lips?
17 You hate my instruction
and cast my words behind you.
18 When you see a thief, you join with him;
you throw in your lot with adulterers.
19 You use your mouth for evil
and harness your tongue to deceit.
20 You speak continually against your brother
and slander your own mother's son.
21 These things you have done and I kept silent;
you thought I was altogether like you.
But I will rebuke you
and accuse you to your face.

16–17 The renewal of the promise of deliverance (v.15) is not without obligation. Too many members of the community did not share the faith commitment required of full membership. Therefore there is no hope for the "wicked" (v.16), whom the psalmist addressed in this section. The purpose of these verses is to prick the conscience of God's people so as to make them more responsive to God's requirements of the community. Those who are really interested in being his "consecrated ones" (v.5) will wisely respond, whereas the wicked will foolishly cast God's requirements of faith and repentance aside as not being relevant. The purpose of the rebuke was to purify the people who called themselves "people of God."

God hates the hypocrites who parrot the law yet abandon it instantly at the opportunity to promote their self-interests (v.16). God's words are instructive, making wise those who have a regenerate spirit (v.17). The people who reject the divine instruction are not called "unspiritual" but "wicked" or "foolish" (cf. Prov 10:17–18; 13:18–19; 15:5). One either keeps the covenant or rejects it. The equation of "laws" with "covenant" (v.16) makes the relationship between covenant fellowship and allegiance to the stipulations of the covenant essential (cf. Rom 2:17–29).

18–20 The particular charges are representative of the whole Decalogue. The psalmist specifies several examples of disobedience: disregard for another's property, wife, name, or dishonesty. It is true that the people who have broken the seventh, eighth, and ninth commandments have broken the whole covenant. But it is also true that those who associate with covenant breakers fall under the same condemnation! Sin lies both in the act and in the consent.

21 Too often God's silence is taken as his approval (cf. Mal 2:17; 3:14–15). The people became used to God's patience and mistook it for an inability to do anything about the evil on earth. They did not understand that Yahweh is the Wholly Other One, who is free in his judgment as well as in his grace. He cannot be boxed in by humans. At his own time God will come to rebuke and then to judge his people openly.

Notes

21 The NIV's "you thought I was altogether like you" gives an alternate reading in the margin: "*thought the 'I AM' was.*" "I AM" is suggestive of the divine self-revelation: "I AM WHO I AM" (Exod 3:14).

IV. The Righteous Judgment of God

50:22–23

22 "Consider this, you who forget God,
or I will tear you to pieces, with none to rescue:
23 He who sacrifices thank offerings honors me,
and he prepares the way
so that I may show him the salvation of God."

22–23 The grace of God is manifest in his patience. Though his people have had and will continue to have problems, sometimes very serious problems, he is still patient with them. The Word of God invites his people to repent and to devote themselves once more to a life of godliness. He will reject those members of his covenant community who do not repent and treat them as noncovenant people. His judgment will be inevitable and merciless (v.22; cf. Hos 5:14). He, the only Deliverer of his people (Isa 43:3, 11; 49:26), will have no mercy on them. But the remnant that heed the word of prophecy and honor God in a spirit of gratitude and true devotion (cf. Heb 13:15) will witness the fullness of his salvation (*yēša'*, v.23; cf. v.15, a form of *ḥ-l-ṣ*).

Notes

22 The psalmist uses here a rare form for God, אֱלוֹהַּ (*'ᵉlôᵃh*). For other designations see v.1.

Psalm 51: Forgiveness and the Community

This psalm is classified as one of the seven penitential psalms (Pss 6, 32, 38, 51, 102, 130, 143), a subdivision of the psalms of *individual lament.* The reason for this designation lies partially in the confessional nature of these psalms and partially in its use within the Christian community.

The superscription relates the context of the psalm to David's heinous sin with Bathsheba (2 Sam 11:1–12:25), after David had been rebuked by the prophet Nathan. The lament form of the psalm suitably fits the spirit of contrition and prayer for restoration. Gone are the questions. What remains is a soul deeply aware of sin, of having offended God, and of its desperate need of God's grace.

The structure of the psalm combines both the personal concern as well as concern for the welfare of the community at large (vv.18–19; see also Jack Barentsen, "Restoration and Its Blessing," *Grace Theological Journal* 5 [1984]: 247–69). The psalmist hopes that through the process of confession, contrition, and prayer for restoration, the Lord will deal kindly with him and with the community, Zion.

The structure of the psalm is as follows:

A. Prayer for Individual Restoration (vv.1–2)
B. Confession and Contrition (vv.3–6)
C. Prayer for Restoration (vv.7–12)
B′. Thanksgiving (vv.13–17)
A′. Prayer for National Restoration (vv.18–19)

I. Prayer for Individual Restoration

51:1–2

For the director of music. A psalm of David. When the prophet Nathan came to him after David had committed adultery with Bathsheba.

1 Have mercy on me, O God,
according to your unfailing love;
according to your great compassion
blot out my transgressions.
2 Wash away all my iniquity
and cleanse me from my sin.

1 In desperate need of divine forgiveness, the sinner can do nothing but cast himself on God's mercy. The verb "have mercy" (*ḥonnēnî*) occurs frequently in psalms of lament (cf. 4:1; 6:2; 31:9; 41:4, 10; 56:1; 86:3). The same root (*ḥ-n-n*) is used in the priestly benediction "and be gracious to you" (Num 6:25). When sin disrupts the fellowship with the covenant-Lord, the sinner has no right to divine blessings. However, the Lord has promised to forgive, and his forgiveness is based solely on his love and compassion (Exod 34:6–7). Therefore, the psalmist appeals to the Lord's "love" (*ḥesed*) and his "great compassion" (cf. 25:6; Isa 63:7; Lam 3:32; Luke 18:13; 1 Peter 1:3).

2 Forgiveness is an act of divine grace whereby sin is blotted out and the sinner is "cleansed" by the washing away of his sins (vv.2, 7, 9; cf. Exod 32:32; Num 5:23; Ps 32:2). The OT sacrifices and ritual washing symbolized the removal of sin and the renewal of fellowship with the Lord. The sacrifices by themselves could not affect so great a salvation (v.16), but God is free to give his grace to whomever he wants. The prayer is for forgiveness and cleansing.

Notes

For a brief discussion of the technical words and phrases in the superscription, see the Introduction.

1 (3 MT) A few Hebrew MSS read כַּחֲסָדֶיךָ (*kaḥᵃsāḏeyḵā*, "according to your acts of love" or "according to your great love"), so the LXX.

II. Confession and Contrition

51:3–6

3For I know my transgressions,
and my sin is always before me.
4Against you, you only, have I sinned
and done what is evil in your sight,
so that you are proved right when you speak
and justified when you judge.
5Surely I was sinful at birth,
sinful from the time my mother conceived me.
6Surely you desire truth in the inner parts;
you teach me wisdom in the inmost place.

3–4 In his search for forgiveness, the psalmist opens his sinful heart. To this end he uses the three synonyms for sin: "transgressions," "iniquity," and "sin" (vv.1–3; see 32:1–2). The variety of words for sin is for poetic reasons, as they express the seriousness of sin. The author is fully aware of his condition before God. He confesses "I know" (from *y-d-ʿ*) with an emphasis on "I." He knows himself intimately and sees how rebellious he has been. His confession is more than introspection, as he knows that he has sinned against the Lord: "against you, you only" (v.4; cf. Luke 15:18). A similar contrast is found in vv.5–6: "Surely I was sinful at birth. . . . / Surely you desire truth." Von Rad correctly observes that the OT rarely gives a theological reflection on sin but underscores the necessity of confession (OTT, 1:154). Between these two prayers of contrition is an affirmation of God's justice (v.4b). The psalmist does not reject or argue with divine justice (Rom 3:4), because the Lord's verdict is "right" (*ṣ-d-q*, "be righteous").

5–6 Confronted by God's righteous verdict, the psalmist is more deeply pricked by his own sinfulness. Sin consists here of an overt act of rebellion whereby the creature despises divine laws and flaunts a sinful nature (v.5; cf. Job 14:4; Rom 7:18). The confession of depravity is not an excuse for his treachery but serves to heighten the distance between the Lord and himself. God is just, whereas man is so corrupt that his whole being cries out for help. The Lord expects man to be "loyal" (*'ᵉmeṯ;* NIV, "truth," v.6) and to give an earnest, heartfelt expression of godliness. But man in his sinfulness cannot respond unless the Lord sends "wisdom" from on high. Divine wisdom alone can bring a remedy to the sinful heart condition of man. Man is sinful through and through (vv.3–5; cf. Rom 3:9–20; 7:14). Man cannot help himself or justify his sinfulness but is in need of God's wisdom from on high (v.6; Nic.H. Ridderbos, "Psalm 51:5–6," *Studia Biblica et Semitica: Theodoro Christiano Vriezen qui munere Professoris Theologiae per XXV Annos functus est, ab Amicis, Collegis, Discipulis dedicata* [Wageningen: Veenman, 1966], pp. 299–312).

The relation of the two bicolons in v.6 is subject to interpretation. The verbs "desire" and "teach," not being synonymous, suggest intensification of the second bicolon: "Surely you desire truth in the parts, *therefore* teach me wisdom in the inmost place," as in the RSV: "Behold, thou desirest truth in the inward being; therefore teach me wisdom in my secret heart." Another way of interpreting the intensification is given in the NEB: "Yet, though thou hast hidden the truth in darkness, through this mystery thou dost teach me wisdom." Only by receiving revelation from the outside ("you teach me," from *y-d-ʿ*) can the inside become whole (v.6; cf. 32:8). The godly cry out for God, confess their sins readily, and receive assurance of God's forgiveness (cf. Prov 28:13; 1 John 1:9).

Notes

4 (6 MT) Herbert Haag argues persuasively that sin in the biblical sense is only against God. We may hurt our fellowman, but we sin against God (" 'Gegen dich allein habe ich gesündigt,' Eine Exegese von Ps 51:6," *Theologische Quartalschrift* 155 [1975]: 49–50).

6 (8 MT) The verb "you desire" could have two prepositional phrases: "in the inner parts" and "in the inmost place." The reading of v.6 would not significantly be changed: "Surely [or *since*] you desire truth in the inner parts, in the inmost place; teach me wisdom." See Dahood: "Since you prefer truth to both cleverness and secret lore, / Teach me Wisdom!" (*Psalms*, 2:1).

The meaning of the word בַּטֻּחוֹת (*baṭṭuḥôṯ*, "the inner parts") is largely determined by the context, in parallelism with סָתֻם (*sāṯum*, "the inmost place"). KB[3] gives the rendering "hidden" or "inner." The meaning of the Hebrew is uncertain (see NIV mg.).

III. Prayer for Restoration

51:7–12

7 Cleanse me with hyssop, and I will be clean;
wash me, and I will be whiter than snow.
8 Let me hear joy and gladness;
let the bones you have crushed rejoice.
9 Hide your face from my sins
and blot out all my iniquity.

10 Create in me a pure heart, O God,
and renew a steadfast spirit within me.
11 Do not cast me from your presence
or take your Holy Spirit from me.
12 Restore to me the joy of your salvation
and grant me a willing spirit, to sustain me.

7–12 The prayer for restoration consists of (1) a prayer for God's forgiveness (vv.7, 9), (2) a prayer for renewal of joy (v.8), and (3) a prayer for a heart of wisdom and for full restoration to divine favor (vv.10–12).

First, the psalmist asks for God's forgiveness (vv.7–9). The forgiveness must meet the greatness of his need. He is sinful through and through. In the prayer for forgiveness, the author employs two verbs, used in vv.1–2, in reverse order: "wash" (v.7) and "blot out" (v.9). In these verses the psalmist goes beyond the prayer for forgiveness (vv.1–2). He prays that the Lord, like a priest, may cleanse him from his defilement. The unclean, such as lepers, used to present themselves before the priest on the occasion of their purification. The priest, being satisfied that the unclean person had met the requirements for purification, would take a bunch of "hyssop" and sprinkle the person with water, symbolic of ritual cleansing. Here the psalmist petitions the Lord to be his priest by taking the hyssop and by declaring him cleansed from all sin.

With God's forgiveness and cleansing (v.7) comes newness of life. The metaphor "whiter than snow" applied to clean garments and by extension signified forgiveness, cleansing, and newness (cf. Isa 1:18; Rev 3:4–5; 4:4). Renewal begins with the Lord, who alone can blot out sin, the guilt of sin, and any reminder of sin (v.9; cf. 32:1; 90:8; 103:3, 10–12; Mic 7:18–19).

Second, the psalmist prays for restoration of joy (v.8). Joy is the result of God's work in man (cf. Isa 65:17–18). Even as God's displeasure with sin brings judgment, metaphorically described as broken bones (v.8, cf. 32:3; 42:10), so his pleasure brings joy of heart (vv.8, 12). The joy is more than an emotional expression; it is a contented resting in God. The security of having been reconciled with the Lord and of having peace with him (cf. Rom 5:1) is of the greatest import. This joy is hence known as "the joy of your salvation" (v.12; from *yēša'*; cf. 9:14; 13:5; 35:9).

Third, the psalmist asks for a heart of wisdom. Forgiveness and cleansing are prerequisites for communion with God. Wisdom maintains communion. The sin of which the psalmist has spoken (vv.3–6) clings to his inner parts so that man cannot respond in "truth" (fidelity) and wisdom unless God gives it (v.6). For this reason the psalmist renews his prayer for divine wisdom and sustenance (vv.10–13). This involves a radical transformation, expressed by the verbs "create" and "renew" (v.10). Communion with God and morality are not natural gifts but supernaturally endowed graces (cf. Jer 24:7; 31:33; 32:39; Ezek 11:19; 18:31; 36:26; 2 Cor 5:17; Gal 6:15; Eph 2:10; 4:24). Isaiah uses this language to denote the world of restoration from sin, judgment, and the vexations of life under the condemnation of God (Isa 65:17–18).

In the spirit of true contrition, the psalmist prays for a "pure heart," a "steadfast spirit" (v.10; cf. 57:7; 112:7), the "Holy Spirit" (v.11) and a "willing spirit" (v.12; cf. Exod 35:5, 22). Without the internal renewal (cf. Prov 4:23), the psalmist fears the possibility of divine rejection, as was the case with Saul (cf. 1 Sam 16:14). These verses say little about the doctrine of the Holy Spirit in the OT but much about the necessity of spiritual renewal. Spiritual renewal always leads to godliness and wisdom (cf. Deut 5:29; 30:6; Isa 59:21; Jer 31:33–34; Ezek 36:26–27). While the OT saints knew about regeneration and spiritual renewal, the assurance of the benefits of the covenant were conferred by the symbol of sacrifice. The OT saints had not yet received the fuller assurance of forgiveness and spiritual renewal granted to us in the revelation of Jesus, the Perfect Sacrifice (Heb 10:1–18).

Notes

---

7 (9 MT) אֵזוֹב (*'ēzôḇ*, "hyssop" [Syrian hyssop]) was also used for sprinkling blood (cf. Lev 14:4–8; Num 19:6–8, 17–21; Heb 9:19; see Zohary, *Plants of the Bible*, pp. 96–97).

8 (10 MT) The Syriac suggests the alternate reading תַּשְׂבִּיעֵנִי (*taśbî'ēnî*, "satisfy me"), instead of "let me hear" (MT). So Kraus: "Let me be refreshed with joy and gladness" (*Psalmen*, 2:382).

IV. Thanksgiving

51:13–17

13 Then I will teach transgressors your ways,
and sinners will turn back to you.

14 Save me from bloodguilt, O God,
the God who saves me,
and my tongue will sing of your righteousness.
15 O Lord, open my lips,
and my mouth will declare your praise.
16 You do not delight in sacrifice, or I would bring it;
you do not take pleasure in burnt offerings.
17 The sacrifices of God are a broken spirit;
a broken and contrite heart,
O God, you will not despise.

The psalmist's personal confession of sin (vv.1–3) and the prayer for God's gracious renewal of his inner being (vv.7–12) form the basis of his instruction of sinners (v.13), his praise (vv.14–15), and a deeper commitment to the Lord (vv.16–17).

13 First, the sinner who has experienced a deep sense of his own sinfulness, the forgiveness of God, and the sweetness of restored joy shows concern for others. The psalmist who prayed "restore to me" (v.12, *š-w-b*) also prays that he may be instrumental in restoring (*š-w-b;* NIV, "turn back to you") sinners to the "ways" of the Lord (v.13; see appendix to Ps 1: The Ways of Wisdom and Folly).

14–15 Second, praise is an appropriate response to divine deliverance (see appendix to Ps 119: Yahweh Is My Redeemer). Deliverance here is from "bloodguilt" (lit., "bloods," v.14). "Bloodguilt" could signify either the judgment resulting from a grave sin requiring the death penalty (cf. Ezek 18:13) or the sin that led to the death of an innocent man (cf. 2 Sam 12:5, 13). The man who has tasted the grace of God in life cannot but praise him for a new lease on life. God's righteousness manifests itself, not only in judgment (v.4), but also in forgiveness and fidelity to his covenant (cf. 1 John 1:9), when he sets aside the just penalty for sin (v.14). The sinner looks to his "Lord" (*Adonai,* "master") for renewed favor ("open my lips") so that he may freely praise him for his grace (v.15).

16–17 Third, a deeper commitment results from a heart of gratitude. The Lord does "delight in" (*ḥ-p-ṣ*) truth (fidelity, v.6; NIV, "desire") rather than "sacrifice" (v.16). That the psalmist is not opposed to sacrifices comes out in the conclusion, where the community expresses its longing for the renewal of the sacrificial cult (v.19). Rather, he senses God's concern for inner loyalty as a prerequisite for the presentation of animals for sacrifice. He commits himself unreservedly to the Lord by presenting "a broken and a contrite heart" (v.17; cf. 34:18; Isa 57:15; 66:2). The prerequisite for spiritual renewal (vv.10–12) is humility, which is also the prerequisite for a walk with God (cf. Mic 6:8).

Notes

13 (15 MT) A number of Hebrew MSS and the Syriac have "your way" (sing.).

17 (19 MT) The MT's זִבְחֵי (*zib̲ḥê,* "the sacrifices of") could well be read as "my sacrifice," requiring a minor emendation: *zib̲ḥî,* resulting in the NIV margin: "*My sacrifice, O God.*"

V. Prayer for National Restoration

51:18–19

18 In your good pleasure make Zion prosper;
build up the walls of Jerusalem.
19 Then there will be righteous sacrifices,
whole burnt offerings to delight you;
then bulls will be offered on your altar.

18–19 The canonical significance of these verses lies in the community identification with David's sin, the need for grace, and the anticipation of divinely bestowed joy. Kidner may be right in suggesting an exilic date for these verses, as the people of God pray for another manifestation of God's love. Jerusalem's walls have been breached and the sacrifices have ceased. The Lord's "good pleasure" (v.18; cf. Isa 61:2: "favor") made Zion prosper under the postexilic leadership of Zerubbabel and Nehemiah. In the days of Nehemiah, when these prayers had been answered (cf. Neh 12:43), the people were again filled with joy. The sacrifices were offered as sacrifices from "righteous" hearts ("righteous sacrifices," v.19; cf. 4:5; Deut 33:19).

Notes

18–19 (20–21 MT) Jean L.-Duhaime concludes on the basis of vv.18–19 that Psalm 51 is a *community lament,* dating from the Exile ("Le verset 8 du Psaume 51 et la destruction de Jérusalem," *Eglise et Théologie* 13 [1982]: 35–56). So also concludes H.L. Bosman, "Ps. 51:7 en Erfsonde," *Nederduits Gereformeerde Teologiese Tydskrif* 24 (1983): 264–71.

Psalm 52: An Uprooted and a Sprawling Tree

The contrast between the godless and the godly is cast in the picturesque language of an uprooted tree and a fallen tent over against a rank olive tree in the house of God. Such is the end of folly and wisdom. The superscription relates the psalm to an episode in David's life, when Doeg had betrayed and executed the priests of Nob who had helped David (1 Sam 22:17–23). Doeg serves as a symbol of all evildoers, who will meet their just deserts; whereas David represents the righteous, who will be exalted (see appendix to Ps 1: The Ways of Wisdom and Folly).

The genre of the psalm is complex, as it contains elements of lament (vv.1–7), thanksgiving (v.9), wisdom (vv.6–7), an oracle of judgment (vv.1–7), and a mocking saying (v.7). On the whole, the positive tone at the end sets the tone of the psalm as a *psalm of trust.* The righteous will prevail, regardless of the opposition.

The structure of the psalm is as follows:

A. The Folly of Evil (vv.1–4)
B. God's Complete Judgment (v.5)
B′. Wisdom Derived From God's Judgment (vv.6–7)
A′. The Blessing of Righteousness (vv.8–9)

I. The Folly of Evil

52:1–4

For the director of music. A *maskil* of David. When Doeg the Edomite had gone to Saul and told him: "David has gone to the house of Ahimelech."

1 Why do you boast of evil, you mighty man?
Why do you boast all day long,
you who are a disgrace in the eyes of God?
2 Your tongue plots destruction;
it is like a sharpened razor,
you who practice deceit.
3 You love evil rather than good,
falsehood rather than speaking the truth. *Selah*
4 You love every harmful word,
O you deceitful tongue!

1–2 By means of a question followed by a series of accusations, the folly of evil is shown for what it is. In life the wicked may act as a "mighty man" (*gibbôr*, v.1; cf. Isa 5:22; Jer 9:3). He does autonomously "boast" (Hithpael from *h-l-l*, "praise"; cf. 10:3) of his power, exploits, and accomplishments. Evil appears in acts but also in words: "your tongue. . . . speaking. . . . harmful word, . . . deceitful tongue," vv.2–4). The very words are evil because they express the internal plotting (*ḥ-š-b*) of an evil heart. The wicked plot against the godly (cf. 10:2–11; 11:2; 35:4), speaking words of death and destruction ("like a sharpened razor," v.2; cf. 55:21; 57:4; 59:7; 64:3; Prov 18:21). He is a con artist. Deception is his trademark (v.2), or, as Dahood puts it, he is an "artist of deceit" (*Psalms*, 2:11; cf. 101:7).

3–4 The wicked's values are completely distorted. He loves anything that is twisted, perverted, and corrupt. He loves to think, speak, and do "evil" whenever it is to his own advantage (v.3; cf. Mic 3:2). Falsehood and aggressive words aim at the undoing of others (cf. 35:25; 53:4; 120:2–3). He stands for whatever is against God's standards of *good*ness and "righteousness" (*ṣeḏeq;* NIV, "truth," v.3). In the end the psalmist exclaims: "O you deceitful tongue!" as a rebuke of the wicked, whose whole being reflects the evil associated with the tongue (cf. 120:2; James 3:1–12).

Notes

For a brief discussion of the technical words and phrases in the superscription, see the Introduction.

1 (3 MT) For the MT's חֶסֶד אֵל (*ḥeseḏ 'ēl*, "love of God"), the LXX reads "disgrace all day long." The LXX explains in part the NIV's "A disgrace in the eyes of God?" BHS proposes an alternate reading: אֶל חָסִיד (*'el ḥāsîḏ*, "to [against] the beloved"; see RSV's "against the godly"). Dahood stays closer to the MT: "O devoted of El," with an emendation of *ḥeseḏ* to *ḥāsîḏ* (*Psalms*, 2:13). The last reading is preferred because it stays closest to the MT and is a contrastive inclusion with v.9: "you boast . . . against the beloved of God all day long . . . I will praise you in the presence of your beloved."

2 (4 MT) The MT's הַוּוֹת תַּחְשֹׁב (*hawwôṯ taḥšōḇ*) could be rendered as "[your tongue] plots destruction" (NIV) or as "destruction you plot." The use of the second person אָהַבְתָּ (*'āhaḇtā*, "you love") in v.3 (5 MT) favors the conclusion that the wicked are addressed: "Why do you boast . . . why do you plot destruction?" The RSV combines the last two words of v.1 (MT, "all day long") with v.2: "All the day you are plotting destruction."

II. God's Complete Judgment

52:5

[5]Surely God will bring you down to everlasting ruin:
He will snatch you up and tear you from your tent;
he will uproot you from the land of the living. *Selah*

5 Instead of the asseverative, the optative reading is preferable: "Truly, may God bring you down . . . May he snatch you . . . May he uproot you." The verbs are jussives, expressive of a desire. The prayer concerns the coexistence of evil, deception, and injustice together with the godly. The righteous God cannot forever tolerate evil. In the act of judgment, the righteous have an assurance that righteousness will prevail!

The verbs "bring down," "snatch up," "tear from," "uproot" suggest different word pictures. The wicked will be brought down (demolished) like a structure (cf. Judg 8:9). They will be snatched up like a coal out of a fire (cf. Isa 30:14), which is useless when cold. They will be a castaway and vagabond, homeless and without family ("from your tent"; cf. Deut 28:63; Ps 132:3; Prov 2:22). Moreover, they will be like an uprooted tree (cf. Jer 11:19). In the end they will be no more, as they will be forcibly excised from "the land of the living" (cf. 27:13). With their death, evil thoughts, speech, and acts will cease forever!

III. Wisdom Derived From God's Judgment

52:6–7

[6]The righteous will see and fear;
they will laugh at him, saying,
[7]"Here now is the man
who did not make God his stronghold
but trusted in his great wealth
and grew strong by destroying others!"

6 The reaction of the godly to God's judgment is first characterized by awe and terror. Gradually they realize that the judgment was for their encouragement. Then their fear changes into joy. The "righteous" (see 1:6) are those who align their ways of life with God's revelation. They "see" (*yir'û*) and "fear" (*yîrā'û*) the acts of God (for a similar play on words, cf. 40:3); but in the end they will be filled with a triumphant derision for their former oppressors. Righteousness triumphs over evil! The joy of the righteous is not malicious and vindictive (cf. Job 31:29; Prov 24:17). In seeing the evidence of God's righteousness, they receive personal assurance that God judges between good and evil (cf. 2 Thess 1:5–10).

7 The righteous learn a lesson from the judgments of God (see Ps 49). A man who lives and acts independently from God, trusts in himself, and betters himself at the expense of others will be brought down. He may think of himself as a strong man (*geb̲er*, "man"; cf. v.1: *gibbôr*, "mighty man"). He may trust in his wealth (cf. Prov 11:28) and feel himself strong as he exploits and destroys. The wicked may turn away from the Lord as his stronghold and turn to the fleeting security of power, riches, and ill-gotten gains. But when his riches, house, and power are taken away, his life falls apart.

Notes

7 (9 MT) The taunt plays on the use of two forms from the root עוז (*ʿ-w-z*, "be strong"): מָעוֹז (*māʿûz*, "stronghold") and יָעֹז (*yāʿōz*, "grew strong"). The latter part of v.7 is problematic. The Syriac reads "in his riches" instead of "in destruction" (cf. v.2; NIV, "by destroying others"). For a defense of the MT, see Dahood (*Psalms*, 2:16).

IV. The Blessing of Righteousness

52:8–9

8 But I am like an olive tree
flourishing in the house of God;
I trust in God's unfailing love
for ever and ever.
9 I will praise you forever for what you have done;
in your name I will hope, for your name is good.
I will praise you in the presence of your saints.

8–9 In contrast to the "mighty man" (v.1) is the godly. The mighty man trusts in himself, works evil, and hedges himself with ill-gotten gains and power. The Lord uproots him like a tree, makes him a vagabond, and destroys him like a building (v.5). The godly, on the other hand, is likened to a tree flourishing within the house of the Lord (v.8). The wicked boast in their own abilities, whereas the godly praise the Lord for what he has done (v.9).

The imagery of the tree brings out the blessedness of the godly (cf. 1:3; 92:12–13; Jer 11:16). He is like a luxuriant, productive olive tree. The olive tree may last for hundreds of years and is a symbol of longevity and usefulness. Olives are used for food and oil. A productive olive tree supplies about six gallons of oil per year.

The imagery of the tree in the house of the Lord suggests the blessedness of the godly (cf. 15:1). The godly prosper to the extent that they depend on the "love" (v.8) of God for their nourishment and fellowship. The wicked will be brought "to everlasting ruin" (v.5), whereas the godly will enjoy God's "unfailing love" (v.8).

The godly response to God's righteousness is praise! His boast is in the Lord (cf. Jer 9:23–24; contrast v.1). As long as he trusts in God's love "forever and ever" (v.8), the godly have many reasons to praise the Lord "forever" (v.9). The "name" of the Lord (Yahweh) assures him that God is righteous and loving.

Psalm 53: God Deals With Foolish Evildoers

53:1–6

For the director of music. According to *mahalath*. A *maskil* of David.

1 The fool says in his heart,

"There is no God."
They are corrupt, and their ways are vile;
there is no one who does good.

2 God looks down from heaven
on the sons of men
to see if there are any who understand,
any who seek God.
3 Everyone has turned away,
they have together become corrupt;
there is no one who does good,
not even one.

4 Will the evildoers never learn—
those who devour my people as men eat bread
and who do not call on God?
5 There they were, overwhelmed with dread,
where there was nothing to dread.
God scattered the bones of those who attacked you;
you put them to shame, for God despised them.

6 Oh, that salvation for Israel would come out of Zion!
When God restores the fortunes of his people,
let Jacob rejoice and Israel be glad!

This psalm is a parallel version of Psalm 14. For the introductory, expository, and exegetical observations, see Psalm 14. Here only the differences between the two psalms will be discussed.

One obvious and expected difference is the reference to God as Elohim. In the second book of the Psalms, the term Elohim is used more frequently than LORD (= Yahweh). In Psalm 14 the name Yahweh occurs four times and the term Elohim three times. Elohim occurs seven times in Psalm 53.

Second, Psalm 53's position between Psalms 52 and 54 favors an ancient tradition relating to the life of David. Psalm 52 relates to the story of Doeg (cf. 1 Sam 22) and Psalm 54 to the incident of the Ziphites (cf. 1 Sam 23; 26). The term "fool" (*nāḇāl,* 53:1) is suggestive of Nabal, who acted foolishly to David and his men (cf. 1 Sam 25).

Third, the MT shows minor textual variations.

Fourth, the major significant difference is in 53:5. Compare:

14:5–6	53:5
There they are, overwhelmed with dread, for God is present in the company of the righteous. You evildoers frustrate the plans of the poor, but the LORD is their refuge.	There they were, overwhelmed with dread, where there was nothing to dread. God scattered the bones of those who attacked you; you put them to shame, for God despised them.

The psalm celebrates a victory over the enemy who "attacked you" (v.5; lit., "who encamped against you" or "your besieger"). By the power of God, Israel routed their enemies and rid themselves from disgrace. It may be that the original psalm of David was intentionally changed to celebrate God's victory over the enemies as an evidence that he is sovereign over the acts of fools. But which victory? Even though Dahood finds in the military language allusions to Sennacherib's siege of Jerusalem (*Psalms*, 2:20–21; cf. 2 Kings 18–19), it is impossible to be certain. In the canonical situation the psalm encourages God's people to pray for restoration on the basis of God's historic acts (v.5b).

Finally, the superscription is different. For a brief discussion of the technical words and phrases, see the Introduction.

Psalm 54: Surely God Is My Help!

As in Psalm 52, the superscription connects the psalm with David's flight from Saul. The connection between the Ziphite betrayal (cf. 1 Sam 23:19; 26:1) and the psalm is not clear from the contents. The spirit of the psalm reflects that of an *individual lament* in which the psalmist complains against "strangers" and asks the Lord to come to his rescue. The prayer ends with thanksgiving and a vow. The canonical thrust of the psalm with its expression of confidence in the Lord is sufficiently general that the psalm is a fitting prayer for any believer who is maligned.

The structure of the psalm reflects the various internal movements in the psalm:

A. Prayer for Deliverance (vv.1–2)
B. Occasion of the Prayer (v.3)
C. Affirmation of Trust (v.4)
B′. Resolution of the Prayer (v.5)
A′. Thanksgiving for Deliverance (vv.6–7)

I. Prayer for Deliverance

54:1–2

For the director of music. With stringed instruments.
A *maskil* of David. When the Ziphites had gone to Saul and said,
"Is not David hiding among us?"

1 Save me, O God, by your name;
vindicate me by your might.
2 Hear my prayer, O God;
listen to the words of my mouth.

1–2 The parallel verbs "save me" (*y-š-'*) and "vindicate me" (*d-y-n*, lit., "judge me") express both the source and the nature of the deliverance. "God" alone can deliver him from the troubles stated in v.3. For now the focus is on the Lord. Verse 3 begins in the MT with "O God," an emphatic call on the Lord. The nature of this deliverance is none other than the Lord's arbitration ("judge me"; NIV properly translates the phrase dynamically, "vindicate me"; cf. 26:1; 43:1). The Lord must come to protect and rescue his child from evil. The reason for the psalmist's confidence lies in his reliance on the Lord's revelation of himself in the past. He has revealed his "name" ("LORD"; cf. v.6; 20:1; cf. Exod 3:14–15) and his "might" to Israel (cf. 21:13; 66:7; 145:11). The "name" of the Lord signifies his covenant protection and blessing, which he demonstrates to the enemies of his people with destructive "might" (cf. Zeph 3:17). For the phraseology "hear . . . listen" (v.2), see 4:1; 84:8; 102:1.

Notes

For a brief discussion of the technical words and phrases in the superscription, see the Introduction.

II. Occasion of the Prayer

54:3

> 3 Strangers are attacking me;
> ruthless men seek my life—
> men without regard for God. *Selah*

3 This verse is nearly identical to 86:14 (q.v.). The psalmist's opponents are called "strangers" and "ruthless men," who have no "regard for God." Here "strangers" may denote either those who had become estranged from God and the covenant community (cf. Isa 1:4) or non-Israelites (1 Sam 23:11–12). They had little regard for God (contrast 16:8; 119:30) or man, as they were "ruthless" people who insisted on their rights and desires without empathy or mercy (cf. Prov 11:16; Isa 13:11; 25:3–5).

Notes

3 (5 MT) Instead of the MT's זָרִים (*zārîm*, "strangers"), many Hebrew MSS and the Targum read זֵדִים (*zēḏîm*, "arrogant"; cf. 86:14).

III. Affirmation of Trust

54:4

> 4 Surely God is my help;
> the Lord is the one who sustains me.

4 In a hymnic manner, indicated by "surely" and nominal clauses in the Hebrew, the psalm shifts from worry over the arrogant to a confident trust in the Lord. Triumphantly the psalmist exclaims, "Surely God is my help" (cf. 30:10; 72:12; 118:7). The MT further describes the Lord as one of "those who sustain me" (see RSV). However, the NIV is correct in understanding the preposition *b*ᵉ ("among") as emphasizing the Lord as the only one who grants support to his people: "the Lord is the one who sustains me" (cf. GKC, par. 119i). Dahood puts it well: "The Lord is the true Sustainer of my life!" (*Psalms*, 2:23). Because Yahweh is his only Helper, the psalmist looks forward with alacrity to the enjoyment of his God-given life (cf. 51:12).

IV. Resolution of the Prayer

54:5

[5]Let evil recoil on those who slander me;
in your faithfulness destroy them.

5 The resolution of the prayer lies in the conviction that God is just. He will not permit his children to suffer without vindication. The imprecation is not vindictive but expressive of trust in divine justice. Evil must be repaid. The people of God believed in the boomerang effect of sin: "Let evil recoil." The faithlessness of the opponent stands in contrast to God's faithfulness. They are enemies who defame him. The Lord is faithful in his relationship to his people; therefore the psalmist is calm, trusting that his God will protect him from his adversary. (See the appendix to Ps 137: Imprecations in the Psalms.)

Notes

---

5 (7 MT) The NIV follows the *Kethiv* reading, יָשֹׁב (*yāšō<u>b</u>*, "let . . . recoil"), with "evil" as the subject. The *Qere*, יָשִׁיב (*yāšî<u>b</u>*, "cause to bring") is supported by many MSS and the LXX; see the RSV: "He will requite my enemies with evil"; Syriac: "requite!"

The NIV follows Dahood (*Psalms*, 3:25–26) in "those who slander me," instead of the usual meaning, "my enemies" (cf. 5:8; 27:2; 59:1).

V. Thanksgiving for Deliverance

54:6–7

[6]I will sacrifice a freewill offering to you;
I will praise your name, O LORD,
for it is good.
[7]For he has delivered me from all my troubles,
and my eyes have looked in triumph on my foes.

6–7 The resolution of the psalm shines forth in a victory hymn of thanksgiving. The votive offering was a communal offering presented before the Lord but enjoyed in the fellowship of family and friends (see W. VanGemeren, "Offerings and Sacrifices," in Elwell, EDT, pp. 588–92). Beyond the present tragedy is a future that may be shared with others in the company of God. The godly will hear all the Lord has done for his child, as his praise will resound. His "name" (v.6; cf. v.1) will be exalted, because through his name he has brought deliverance and will continue to bring deliverance. It is only fitting ("good," cf. 52:9; 92:1; 106:1; 135:3) to praise him, because in the face of "troubles" and "foes" the Lord is "good." He is our Helper and Sustainer. The victory is his, but he shares the benefits with his own (v.7; cf. 52:6; 58:10; 59:10; 92:10–11).

Psalm 55: The Lord Sustains the Righteous!

This psalm exemplifies the genre of the *individual lament*. The psalmist pours out his heart before the Lord surrounded by expressions of animosity, not only from old foes, but now even from "friends." The mood of the psalm moves from despair, to complaint, to a note of confidence in the Lord. Some have seen in the psalmist's experience a reflection of that of our Lord as he was betrayed by Judas. This appears to be an ancient tradition, as a MS of Jerome's Latin Version has the title "The voice of Christ against the chiefs of the Jews and the traitor Judas" (Kirkpatrick, p. 308; cf. vv.12–14, 20–21). This psalm as well as others (22; 88) express the anguish of the human soul in which our Lord Jesus shared (Heb 2:17–18).

The structure follows the development of thought and shift in mood from despair to trust:

A. Despairing Prayer (vv.1–3)
  B. Personal Reflections (vv.4–8)
    C. Prayer for Justice (vv.9–15)
    C′. Assurance of Justice (vv.16–21)
  B′. Reflection on the Lord (vv.22–23b)
A′. Hopeful Trust (v.23c)

I. Despairing Prayer

55:1–3

For the director of music. With stringed instruments. A *maskil* of David.

1 Listen to my prayer, O God,
  do not ignore my plea;
2   hear me and answer me.
My thoughts trouble me and I am distraught
3   at the voice of the enemy,
  at the stares of the wicked;
for they bring down suffering upon me
  and revile me in their anger.

1–3 The injustices heaped on our psalmist cry out for divine retribution. This battered victim turns to the Lord, asking him to "listen" (v.1; cf. 5:2; 54:2; 142:6) or "hear" (v.2, cf. 17:1; 61:1) and to "answer" his "prayer" (v.1; cf. 65:2). He does not pretend that there is no problem. Up to this point the Lord has withheld help from him. But God's silence is surprising because the Lord had decreed to Israel that he would not "ignore" ("hide himself," Hithpael of *ʿ-l-m*) their problems (Deut 22:1, 3–4; Isa 58:7). But from the point of view of the psalmist, the Lord himself has not yet shown an interest in this case (cf. 10:1).

The prayer flows out of deep despair. He ("my thoughts") is continually troubled (v.2). He cannot find rest within himself. He is full of inner turmoil ("I am distraught"). Instead of the roaring of the sea, he hears the "noise" (NIV, "voice," v.3) of his enemies threatening his existence. They bring "pressure" on him, resulting in grievous "suffering" (lit., "trouble," v.3) and expressions of animosity.

Notes

For a brief discussion of the technical words and phrases in the superscription, see the Introduction.

2 (3 MT) The verb אָרִיד (*'ārîḏ*, in "my thoughts trouble me") has been variously translated in the ancient versions—LXX: "I was grieved"; Jerome: "I was humiliated." There is little agreement on the etymology, whether from *r-w-d* ("to roam"; cf. NEB, "my cares give me no peace"), *r-d-d* ("to beat down"; cf. RSV, "I am overcome"), or *y-r-d* ("descend"; see Dahood, "descend at my complaint," *Psalms*, 2:28).

3 (4 MT) The noun עָקַת (*'āqāh;* NIV, "stares") is a *hapax legomenon,* possibly an Aramaism, "pressure." G.R. Driver renders it "cry of glee" ("Supposed Arabisms in the Old Testament," JBL 55 [1936]: 111); see the NEB's "the shrill clamour." The NIV follows Dahood in "stare."

The verb יִשְׂטְמוּנִי (*yiśṭ^e^mûnî*) may be rendered "hate me" or "persecute me" (A.A. Anderson, 1:413). The NIV translation "revile me" or "slander me," following Dahood (*Psalms*, 2:32), is questionable.

II. Personal Reflections

55:4–8

4 My heart is in anguish within me;
  the terrors of death assail me.
5 Fear and trembling have beset me;
  horror has overwhelmed me.
6 I said, "Oh, that I had the wings of a dove!
  I would fly away and be at rest—
7 I would flee far away
  and stay in the desert; *Selah*
8 I would hurry to my place of shelter,
  far from the tempest and storm."

4–5 How the psalmist yearns to escape his situation! He is full of anguish, fear, and horror (v.4). He is paralyzed emotionally and physically as he mulls over the present evil. He is weak and helpless. His heart is palpitating like a woman in labor (*ḥ-y-l;* NIV, "in anguish"; cf. Isa 13:8; Jer 4:19). The fear of death (cf. Exod 15:16) overtakes him. The piling up of the synonyms for fear ("anguish . . . terrors. . . . Fear and trembling . . . horror") represents a literary manner of exposing how great and deep-seated his fear is. He trembles within and without as he reflects on his present condition (cf. Job 21:6; Isa 21:4; Ezek 7:18).

6–8 Another manner of expressing the psalmist's deep despair is in the escape imagery. How he wishes to be like a dove, free to fly to a high and far-away place, such as an escarpment in the mountains (v.6; cf. S of Songs 2:14; Jer 48:28)! How he wishes to find quiet serenity in the desert, far away from civilization (v.7)! How he wishes to find protective shelter as in a sudden storm (v.8)!

III. Prayer for Justice

55:9–15

9 Confuse the wicked, O Lord, confound their speech,
for I see violence and strife in the city.
10 Day and night they prowl about on its walls;
malice and abuse are within it.
11 Destructive forces are at work in the city;
threats and lies never leave its streets.

12 If an enemy were insulting me,
I could endure it;
if a foe were raising himself against me,
I could hide from him.
13 But it is you, a man like myself,
my companion, my close friend,
14 with whom I once enjoyed sweet fellowship
as we walked with the throng at the house of God.

15 Let death take my enemies by surprise;
let them go down alive to the grave,
for evil finds lodging among them.

This section begins and ends with a prayer (vv.9, 15), which forms an inclusion. The prayer pertains to the presence of evil and the urgency of the situation. The psalmist apparently alludes to the scattering of the nations at Babel and to the sudden removal of Korah, Dathan, and Abiram. The imagery of the evil city explains why the Lord must come in judgment on the city, whereas the treachery of the friend explains how closely the evil is all around.

9–11 The language for justice is intense and so is the need. The psalmist continually witnesses "violence and strife" (v.9; cf. Hab 1:3), "malice and abuse" (v.10; cf. Hab 1:3), "destructive forces . . . threats [or 'oppression,' cf. KB, s.v.; 10:7] and lies" (v.11; cf. 52:2, 4). Injustice, unrighteousness, and deception in word and deed are prevalent in the city of man. He sees no righteousness wherever he turns (to the walls or the open places [NIV, "streets," v.11, or "market places"]); and wherever he looks ("day and night," v.10), evil is king.

The psalmist's prayer is in the form of a complaint, similar to that of Isaiah 57:1–2 and Habakkuk 1:2–4. He lodges the complaint with the Lord (Adonai), the Master of the world, because he trusts in his vindication. Hence he prays that their evil may boomerang on them and bring utter confusion to the masters of anarchy, oppression, and deception (v.9). The verb "confound" (*p-l-g*) may contain an allusion to the Tower of Babel (Gen 11:1–9), where the Lord confounded the languages of mankind (cf. Peleg in Gen 10:24). Even as the wicked cause harm (*b-l-'*) with their words (cf. 52:4; Eccl 10:12), the psalmist prays that the Lord will bring "harm" (*b-l-'*; NIV, "confuse"; cf. RSV, "destroy") on the ungodly. (See the appendix to Ps 137: Imprecations in the Psalms.)

12–14 The psalmist moves climactically from the general to the more specific: The enemy is none other than his friend (vv.12–13). His pain is more intense because of his personal relationship with those who have betrayed him. The adversary is not "an enemy" or "a foe" from whom he could expect trouble and from whom he could hide (v.12). The psalmist builds up to the climactic point until an emphatic and contrastive "but it is you" (v.13) identifies the betrayer as one equal in status, "a man like myself," a "companion," a "close friend" (cf. 31:11; Prov 16:28; Jer 9:4–5). He has been betrayed by one with whom he has enjoyed "sweet fellowship" (v.14; *sôḏ*, "circle of confidants" or "council" as in Gen 49:6; Ps 89:7) within a circle of like-minded people. He reflects on the pleasant memories of spiritual unity they had among the throngs of pilgrims in the temple.

15 The magnitude of the friends' treachery and apostasy explains the impetuosity of the prayer. The former friends are reckoned together with his enemies as objects of the imprecation. Because evil can no longer be dissociated from the adversaries, they must come to an end, together with the evil perpetrated by them. He prays that the Lord will remove them from the land of the living and bring them down in their physical vigor ("alive") into Sheol ("the grave"). The psalmist may be alluding to the swallowing up of Korah, Dathan, and Abiram into the earth (cf. Num 16:31–40).

Notes

---

14 (15 MT) The phrase בְּרָגֶשׁ (*berāḡeš*, "with commotion") is rendered by the NIV as "with the throng" (see Dahood, *Psalms*, 2:29). See 64:2: "noisy crowd." Other suggestions are בְּרֶגַע (*bereḡa'*, "quietly") or בְּרַעַשׁ (*bera'aš*, "noisily").

Heinz-Josef Fabry argues that סוֹד (*sôḏ*, "council"; NIV, "sweet fellowship," cf. 25:14; 89:7; 111:1) is an ecclesiological term, synonymous with "congregation" ("Der himmlische Thronrat als ekklesiologisches Modell," *Bausteine biblischer Theologie. Festgabe für G. Johannes Botterweck zum 60. Geburtstag dargebracht von seinen Schülern*, ed. H.J. Fabry [Köln: Peter Hanstein, 1977], pp. 99–126).

IV. Assurance of Justice

55:16–21

16 But I call to God,
and the LORD saves me.
17 Evening, morning and noon
I cry out in distress,
and he hears my voice.
18 He ransoms me unharmed
from the battle waged against me,
even though many oppose me.
19 God, who is enthroned forever,
will hear them and afflict them— *Selah*
men who never change their ways
and have no fear of God.

20 My companion attacks his friends;
he violates his covenant.
21 His speech is smooth as butter,
yet war is in his heart;
his words are more soothing than oil,
yet they are drawn swords.

16–18 The perversity of evil by "day and night" (v.10) evokes regular prayer three times a day ("evening, morning and noon," v.17; cf. Dan 6:10), reflecting the Hebrew day, which begins with evening (cf. Gen 1:5, 8, 13, 19, 23, 31). The three temporal references, however, need not be limited to three specific prayers; rather they express totality: "throughout the day." The emphatic use of "I" (NIV, "but I," v.16) contrasts the emphatic "you" denoting the evil and treachery of the wicked (v.13). The psalmist remains loyal to the Lord as he calls on him in prayer, believing that the Lord "saves" (*y-š-'*, v.16). The salvation of the Lord contrasts with his judgment on the wicked (v.15) and is in response to the psalmist's prayer. The prayer need not have been more than groaning for redemption as the MT phraseology (lit., "I moan and groan," v.17; NIV, "I cry out in distress," cf. Rom 8:22–23) resembles v.2b: "my thoughts trouble me and I am distraught." The answer to this prayer brings the wicked to their doom and the godly to their experience of triumph and freedom.

The psalmist is confident that the Lord is just in his acts of deliverance. He "saves. . . . hears my voice. . . . ransoms [*p-d-h*]" (vv.16–18) as acts of the Divine Warrior who fights the "battle" for his own (v.18; see appendix to Ps 98: Yahweh Is the Divine Warrior). The net result will be "peace" (*šālôm;* NIV, "unharmed," v.18), even though the opposition has been great.

19 The basis for hope lies in the confessional statement. The God who is "enthroned forever" (or "from of old," RSV) as the Great Judge (cf. Deut 33:27; Pss 9:7–8; 29:10; 74:12; Hab 1:12) will bring judgment on those who trouble his people and do not respond to him in godly fear. He is faithful (72:14)!

20–21 In contrast to the Lord's fidelity is the treachery of the wicked. He may stab his friends in the back (v.20a; lit., "he stretches his hands against those with whom he is at peace"; NIV, "his friends"; cf. Dahood: "his closest ally," *Psalms*, 2:37). He has no regard for the "covenant," i.e., for any commitments and promises (v.20b). He is unreliable, as "his speech is smooth as butter, . . . his words are more soothing than oil" (v.21; cf. Prov 5:3). This man is a hypocrite in that he knows how to win friends, but in his heart he has no loyalty. Instead he is a bellicose man, loving "war" rather than peace (cf. 52:2).

Notes

---

15 (16 MT) This verse has two difficulties. First, the *Kethiv* יַשִּׁימָוֶת (*yaššîmāweṯ*, "desolation") is best divided into two words as in many versions and in the *Qere* יַשִּׁי מָוֶת (*yaššî māweṯ*, "let death overcome"). Second, the last clause in the MT—viz., "for evils in their dwelling in their midst"—is enigmatic but intelligible; cf. NIV, "for evil finds lodging among them." Several emendations have been proposed; see RSV, "let them go away in terror to their graves"; Dahood, "from their throat and breast" (*Psalms*, 2:29).

17 (18 MT) Hans-Peter Müller concludes that "I cry out" is not limited to the lament genre and that it has the basic sense of a loud, enthusiastic, and emotion-filled form of speaking ("Die hebräische Wurzel שִׂיחַ," VetTest 19 [1969]: 361–71). Together with a form of *h-m-h* ("make noise," "groan"), it is rendered in the NIV as "I cry out in distress" (see 77:3: "I groaned; I mused").

19 (20 MT) The clause "men who never change their ways" could also be read as a further description of the Lord: "because in him there is no variation" (Dahood, *Psalms*, 2:36–37; cf. James 1:17.). The MT is terse and could be read with reference either to the Lord or to the wicked. If the wicked are intended, the clause is parallel with "and have no fear of God."

V. Reflection on the Lord

55:22–23b

22 Cast your cares on the LORD
  and he will sustain you;
  he will never let the righteous fall.
23 But you, O God, will bring down the wicked
  into the pit of corruption;
 bloodthirsty and deceitful men
  will not live out half their days.

22 Out of the confidence that the Lord is enthroned (v.19), the psalmist encourages the godly to reflect on his justice. In contrast to the treachery of man, the Lord will "sustain" the righteous so that they will not be overcome (cf. 37:23–24). The oracle of salvation encourages the godly to "cast" their "cares" (lit., "what he has given you"; cf. 1 Peter 5:7) on the Lord. For a similar expression see 37:5–7. Calvin, after struggling with this text, wrote:

> It is not enough that we make application to God for the supply of our wants. Our desires and petitions must be offered up with a due reliance upon his providence, for how many are there who pray in a clamorous spirit, and who, by the inordinate anxiety and restlessness which they evince, seem resolved to dictate terms to the Almighty. . . . and there can be no question that the only means of checking an excessive impatience is an absolute submission to the Divine will, as to the blessings which should be bestowed. (3:344)

23a–b On the other hand, the justice of God requires vindication on the evildoers (v.23a). After all, they have no respect for life and veracity ("bloodthirsty and deceitful men," v.23b; cf. v.6; 37:35–36; 109:7–8). They shall die in the vigor of life (cf. v.15; 26:9; 59:2; 139:19). Bellinger views this as an example of a prophetic dimension in the psalms (pp. 42–44).

VII. Hopeful Trust

55:23c

But as for me, I trust in you.

23c In conclusion and in poetic balance with the opening strophe, the psalm concludes on a note of confidence in the Lord. The subject is emphatic (*wa'ᵃnî*, "But as for me"; cf. v.16), expressive of the psalmist's submission to the will of God regarding the present circumstances and the future of the ungodly. His trust is in Yahweh, the Redeemer–Divine Warrior (cf. 26:1; 37:5).

Psalm 56: Walking in Darkness With God's Light

This psalm expresses the lament of an individual. The psalmist cries to the Lord on account of the opponents who twist his words against him. His spirit of trust in the Lord is reflected in his composure and tranquility in the face of fear. According to the superscription the psalm is associated with David's asylum in Gath (1 Sam 21:10–15).

The structure of the psalm reveals three parts in a pivotal pattern, with the first and the third strophes enclosing the central strophe.

A. Lament (vv.1–2)
  B. Trust in God (vv.3–4)
    C. Affliction and Imprecation (vv.5–9b)
  B′. Trust in God (vv.9c–11)
A′. Thanksgiving (vv.12–13)

I. Lament

56:1–2

For the director of music. To ⌊the tune of⌋ "A Dove on Distant Oaks." Of David. A *miktam*. When the Philistines had seized him in Gath.

1 Be merciful to me, O God, for men hotly pursue me;
all day long they press their attack.
2 My slanderers pursue me all day long;
many are attacking me in their pride.

1–2 The lament begins with a characteristic prayer for "mercy" (*ḥ-n-n;* cf. 6:2; 51:1; 57:1). Instead of building up gradually to his complaint, the psalmist pours out his heart immediately. He paints his adversity in rapid strokes; it is continual, varied, and hostile. The constancy of adversity is expressed by the threefold use of "all day long" (vv.1, 2, 5). The diversity of the opposition is expressed by the verbs "pursue . . . press their attack. . . . slanderers . . . are attacking." The opposition is fierce and will not be satisfied until its goals are achieved. The verbs "pursue" (*š-'-p,* vv.1–2), also rendered as "trample down," and "press" (*l-ḥ-ṣ*) are legal terms, i.e., language of the courtroom (cf. Amos 3:13–14), whereas the verb "attack" (*l-ḥ-m,* vv.1–2) evokes the imagery of war. The repetition as well as the variation in the verbs communicates the restlessness caused by the many attackers. The opponents are only "men" (*'enôš*), but their strength and violence is not to be underestimated because of their animosity (NIV's "slanderers" should more likely be rendered "enemies," v.2; cf. 5:8; 27:11; 59:10) and "pride" (v.2).

Notes

For a brief discussion of the technical words and phrases in the superscription, see the Introduction.

1–2 (2–3 MT) The root שׁאף (*š-'-p*) has two homonymous meanings: (1) "crush" or "trample" and (2) "pant" or "pursue." The difficulty of determining the meaning is exacerbated by its few occurrences (e.g., Gen 3:15; Ps 57:3; Jer 2:24; 14:6). From the description in vv.5–6, it seems that the psalmist accuses his enemy of injustice and hostile acts; and it would seem

that these two activities are seen in light of vv.1–2. If correct, we prefer the rendering "oppress" or "trample down" (rights) for *š-'-p:* "men trample upon me" (RSV; cf. LXX).
2 (3 MT) The NIV translates שׁוֹרֵר (*šôrēr*) by "slanderer" (see 54:5).

II. Trust in God

56:3–4

3 When I am afraid,
   I will trust in you.
4 In God, whose word I praise,
   in God I trust; I will not be afraid.
   What can mortal man do to me?

3–4 Difficult as life is, the psalmist has learned to "trust" in the Lord. Fear is there, but he expresses it positively. He neither feeds his fear nor stares at his problems but looks to his Redeemer who will deliver him. The variation of "I am afraid"/"I will not be afraid" and "I (will) trust" conveys his confidence in the Lord (cf. v.11; 37:5). He knows the absolute distinction between God and man: man is only "flesh" (*bāśār;* NIV, "mortal man," v.4; cf. 38:3; 78:39; Gen 6:3; Isa 40:6–7; Jer 17:5) and the Lord is God. His promise ("word," v.4) is secure and will come true (cf. Isa 40:8). Putting his fear aside, the psalmist praises the promises of the Lord. After all, trusting in the Lord requires a prior commitment to the revelation of God in his Word. (See the appendix to Ps 19: The Word of God.)

III. Affliction and Imprecation

56:5–9b

5 All day long they twist my words;
   they are always plotting to harm me.
6 They conspire, they lurk,
   they watch my steps,
   eager to take my life.

7 On no account let them escape;
   in your anger, O God, bring down the nations.
8 Record my lament;
   list my tears on your scroll—
   are they not in your record?

9 Then my enemies will turn back
   when I call for help.

5–6 With confidence in the Lord's justice as promised in his Word, the psalmist presents his case more clearly before the Lord. His adversaries "twist" (v.5) his words by distorting his intentions in order to ruin him. The verb "twist" is derived from a root (*'-ṣ-b*) that signifies a laborious, toilsome, unrewarding act. They plot so as to undo whatever the godly man has spoken and has planned to do right. They treat him unjustly (see RSV, "they seek to injure my cause"). Moreover, they set him up like an enemy-at-war. They continually gather together ("conspire," v.6), wait ("lurk"), and prepare for the kill (cf. 2:2; 119:95).

7 The psalmist turns to the Lord in a petition for justice, charging his enemies with injustice and conspiracy to destroy the godly. How could the Lord let them get by ("escape")? The psalmist invokes God's judgment on all who may consider themselves members of the covenant community together with "the nations" (cf. 7:6–9).

8–9b The reason for hope in God's justice lies in his divine nature and in his promise to vindicate his children. For this purpose the psalmist adds a personal note about the extent of his suffering (v.8). His "lament" (or "grief," from *n-w-d;* other versions take it as a form from *n-d-d,* "wander"; see the RSV's "thou hast kept count of my tossings") and "tears" are known to the Lord. He has recorded them in his "record" (lit., "book"; cf. 139:16; Exod 32:32; Mal 3:16). He has also put the tears into a "wineskin," to bring to remembrance all the occasions of suffering (v.8; see NIV mg. and Notes). The record and the collection of tears serve as an assurance to the psalmist that the Lord will vindicate him. He rests his case with the assurance that the Lord will hear and respond in justice. When the Lord comes to the rescue of his people, the enemies will be routed (v.9; contrast 44:10).

Notes

6 (7 MT) This verse contains several problems. First, though it is possible to make sense out of יָגוּרוּ (*yāḡûrû,* "they strive," "assail," KB, p. 176; cf. 140:2 [3 MT]), a number of modern versions (e.g., NIV) and commentators follow Jerome in reading יָגֹדּוּ (*yāḡōddû,* "they conspire, band together," 94:21; KB, p. 169). Second, the NIV follows the *Qere*—יִצְפּוֹנוּ (*yiṣpônû,* "lurk")—rather than the *Kethiv* ("set an ambush").

7 (8 MT) The NIV follows the LXX in reading "on no account" for the MT's עַל אָוֶן (*'al 'āwen,* "because of wickedness").

A common emendation of פַּלֶּט (*pallet,* "deliver") is פַּלֶּס (*palles,* "recompense"), as the RSV's "recompense them" (Kraus, *Psalmen,* 2:408). The MT makes sense, if understood as an interrogative, "on account of their iniquity can they escape?" or positively as in NIV, "on no account let them escape."

8 (9 MT) The usual translation of נֹאד (*nō'ḏ*) is "wineskin" or 'bottle"; see RSV, "put thou my tears in thy bottle." Dahood argues in favor of the interpretation adopted by the NIV: "list my tears on your parchment" (*Psalms,* 2:46), but the usual meaning is preferable.

IV. Trust in God

56:9c–11

By this I will know that God is for me.
10 In God, whose word I praise,
in the LORD, whose word I praise—
11 in God I trust; I will not be afraid.
What can man do to me?

9c–11 These verses are similar to v.4. The emphatic "by this" summarizes the psalmist's confidence in God's acts of vindication. God's majestic acts are compelling proof of the covenant relationship. It is to this effect that the psalmist looks for the demonstration of God's love for him so that he may "know" again how much God cares for him (cf. 1:6; Rom 8:28–39). He rests on the promises ("word," v.10) of the Lord, as he praises the Lord of promise. With this certainty of relationship, fear has no place, because who is man in the presence of God (v.11; cf. 118:6)? Goldingay explains vv.10–11 as a poetic refrain of v.4, explaining the variation ("mortal man" ["man"]) as an artistic device ("Repetition and Variation," p. 148).

V. Thanksgiving

56:12–13

12 I am under vows to you, O God;
  I will present my thank offerings to you.
13 For you have delivered me from death
  and my feet from stumbling,
 that I may walk before God
  in the light of life.

12 Instead of ending with lament and petition, the psalm concludes with a ringing thanksgiving and victory. In anticipation of the deliverance, the suffering saint has made a vow to present a "thank offering" to the Lord (cf. 50:14; 107:22; 116:17). The offering was not a payment for the deliverance but an expression of devotion to the Lord.

13 The Lord receives praise because he is true to his promises. He has promised to not let his beloved stumble on account of the wicked (cf. 37:23–24; 55:22), to avenge himself on the wicked, and to give "the light of life" to his children (v.13). Instead of experiencing the pangs of death in the form of animosity, injustice, and persecution practiced by the enemies of God, the godly man believes that the Lord will be faithful in giving him the joy of life (contrast Job 3:20; cf. Isa 9:3; 58:8; John 8:12; for a similar expression, see Ps 116:8). (See the appendix to Ps 88: Sheol-Grave-Death in the Psalms.) In response to God's goodness, the psalmist desires to walk "before" the Lord (cf. Gen 17:1). This is the goal in godly living, as Calvin writes, "The words, *before God*, which are interjected in the verse, point to the difference between the righteous, who make God the great aim of their life, and the wicked, who wander from the right path and turn their back upon God" (3:359). Only life in God's presence gives meaning to his children. It is as if "the light" of life is shining brightly like the sun!

Psalm 57: The Exaltation of Yahweh in the Midst of Alienation

Psalms 56 and 57 portray confidence in the Lord during adversity. The psalms reflect similar situations and may well be read together. The superscription associates Psalm 57 with David's flight from Saul, whether it be at Adullam (1 Sam 22:1) or En Gedi (1 Sam 24:1). This psalm is an *individual lament* that, like the previous psalm, ends on thanksgiving.

The structure of the psalm has two basic components: lament (vv.1–4) and thanksgiving (vv.6–10). Each component has a refrain (vv.5, 11). Both units are related by motif and vocabulary in the ABCC′A′B′ pattern:

I. Lament (vv.1–4)
A. Prayer for Protection (v.1)
B. Prayer for Vindication, Love, and Fidelity (vv.2–3)
C. The Enemies (v.4)
Refrain (v.5)
II. Thanksgiving (vv.6–10)
C′. The Enemies (v.6)
A′. Thanksgiving for Strength (vv.7–8)
B′. Thanksgiving for Love and Fidelity (vv.9–10)
Refrain (v.11)

I. Lament and Refrain

57:1–5

For the director of music. ⌊To the tune of⌋ "Do Not Destroy." Of David.
A *miktam.* When he had fled from Saul into the cave.

1 Have mercy on me, O God, have mercy on me,
for in you my soul takes refuge.
I will take refuge in the shadow of your wings
until the disaster has passed.

2 I cry out to God Most High,
to God, who fulfills ⌊his purpose⌋ for me.
3 He sends from heaven and saves me,
rebuking those who hotly pursue me; *Selah*
God sends his love and his faithfulness.

4 I am in the midst of lions;
I lie among ravenous beasts—
men whose teeth are spears and arrows,
whose tongues are sharp swords.

5 Be exalted, O God, above the heavens;
let your glory be over all the earth.

1–5 The phrase "have mercy on me" is common to psalms of lament (v.1, twice; cf. 6:2; 56:1). Because his need is great, the psalmist seeks asylum with the Lord. The psalmist goes from a general reference ("the disaster," v.1) to a more specific expression of his need: "those who hotly pursue me" (v.3), "lions . . . ravenous beasts" (v.4). Verse 6 gives a full account of how his adversaries have made life miserable. The enemies have brought about "destruction" (cf. 52:2) and persecute him unjustly (v.3; NIV, "who hotly pursue me," *š-'-p;* see 56:1–2).

But the psalmist seeks God's protection ("refuge," twice, from *ḥ-s-h,* v.1; cf. 11:1; 16:1; 25:20). The "disaster" is like a violent storm (v.1; cf. RSV, "the storms of destruction"; NEB, "the storms"), but the Lord can give him "wings"—a metaphor for protection and refuge (cf. 17:8; 36:7; 61:4; 91:4; Ruth 2:12; Matt 23:37).

Confident in the Lord, the psalmist cries out. After all, the Lord is "God Most High" (Elohim Elyon, v.2; cf. 78:56). The name "Most High" signifies that the Lord is exalted in his rule over all that he has created (cf. Gen 14:22; Pss 46:4; 47:2; see appendix to Ps 9: Yahweh Is El Elyon). The Israelites believed that there was no one like their God (cf. Exod 15:11) and that the chief god of the Canaanite pantheon, El, was just a myth. The psalmist here also affirms that the God of revelation is God (El) and that there is no god capable of helping him but his El (v.2; NIV, "to God"). The combination of Elyon and El also occurs in 73:11 and 78:35.

It is the Creator-Ruler's prerogative to bring judgment on his enemies and to deliver his own (vv.2–3). He "fulfills" his plan in favor of the psalmist ("for me," v.2) by bestowing "his love and his faithfulness" as a positive grace and by delivering him from oppression (v.3). Salvation (*y-š-'*, v.3) in the biblical sense has, therefore, two aspects: salvation to the Lord's favor and salvation from evil and adversity.

The need is great. The enemies "hotly pursue" (v.3; see 56:1), like "lions" greedy to devour (NIV, "ravenous beasts," v.4; cf. 55:21; 64:3). They are on a war path: "spears and arrows, . . . sharp swords" (cf. 55:21; 64:3). In words and acts the enemies are vicious; they delight in cruelty more than in peace.

In spite of the grave problems, the psalmist has learned to be calm. He may be "among" or surrounded ("I am in the midst . . . I lie among," v.4; cf. 4:8) by his enemies; but his trust is in the justice, love, and protection of his God who is "Most High." The psalmist's belief in God's justice is so strong that he magnifies the Lord as exalted in majesty and glory (v.5; cf. 18:46–48; 21:12–13; 46:10; 138:4–5; Isa 2:19; 6:3; Hab 2:14). He is the Great King of heaven and earth, whose glory will be manifest when he comes to triumphantly deliver his servant and to avenge the enemy (cf. Exod 15:11–12). This hymnic refrain (v.5) is repeated in v.11.

Notes

For a brief discussion of the technical words and phrases in the superscription, see the Introduction.

2 (3 MT) For Dahood's understanding of עָלָי (*'ālāy,* "for me") as a form of the divine name Elyon, see the appendix to Psalm 9: Yahweh Is El Elyon.

2–3 (3–4 MT) Dahood's understanding of the phrase "who fulfills [his purpose] for me" as "who avenges me" (*Psalms,* 1:45) makes sense within this context, even though the NIV more literally reflects the MT. The "love" and "faithfulness" of the Lord affirm the continued enjoyment of the benefits of covenantal life (v.3; cf. Exod 34:6; Pss 42:8; 43:3).

4 (5 MT) Yigael Yadin ("New Gleanings on Resheph From Ugarit," *Biblical and Related Studies Presented to Samuel Iwry,* edd. Ann Kort and Scott Morschauer [Winona Lake: Eisenbrauns, 1985], p. 273) advances that David's mercenary soldiers (cf. 1 Chron 12:8) may have included a military unit "whose emblem was the lioness goddess, called *Lebaites*." Here the lionlike enemies or "Lebaites" are mercenaries opposed to the king.

II. Thanksgiving

57:6–11

6 They spread a net for my feet—
  I was bowed down in distress.
They dug a pit in my path—
  but they have fallen into it themselves. *Selah*

7 My heart is steadfast, O God,
  my heart is steadfast;
  I will sing and make music.
8 Awake, my soul!
  Awake, harp and lyre!
  I will awaken the dawn.

[9] I will praise you, O Lord, among the nations;
I will sing of you among the peoples.
[10] For great is your love, reaching to the heavens;
your faithfulness reaches to the skies.

[11] Be exalted, O God, above the heavens;
let your glory be over all the earth.

6–11 The Lord is true to his word. The wicked receive their due punishment, and the righteous draw comfort from God's rule over the earth. Wicked men scheme in order to bring the righteous down. They are like hunters who catch their prey with a net or by digging a pit or hole (see 7:15; 9:15). They use any and every scheme so as to exhaust the righteous. The psalmist readily admits that they had nearly succeeded: "I was bowed down in distress" (v.6). He trusted in the Lord's promise to lift up those who are bowed down (145:14) and to keep the godly from slipping (37:24; 55:22). The psalmist rejoices in God's goodness to him because he has seen the wicked entrapped in their own scheming (7:15; 9:15). Evil returns on its practitioners like a boomerang. Those who commit it come to naught; "in due time their foot will slip" (Deut 32:35).

Over against the fall of the wicked is the newly found security of the psalmist. The wicked did not rely on the Lord and were found out (78:37), whereas the psalmist experienced inner transformation ("a steadfast heart"; cf. v.7; 112:7; Col 1:23). Bellinger explains this steadfast attitude as arising from a prophetic insight (*Psalmody and Prophecy,* pp. 53–55).

In response to having witnessed the mighty acts of God, the psalmist praises the Lord by a sequence of cohortatives and imperatives. Out of a grateful heart, the psalmist sings songs of praise and makes a joyful noise on the instruments ("harp and lyre," v.8; cf. 33:2; 98:5; see appendix to Ps 150: Musical Instruments). He will "awaken the dawn" with the song of the redeemed, signifying a new era of the Lord's salvation. So great is his gratitude that he prays that all the nations may know and fear the Lord (v.9; cf. 9:11). The psalmist articulates his marvel at the vastness of the love (*ḥesed̲,* v.10; cf. v.3; 36:5) and fidelity (*'ᵉmet̲,* "truth," "faithfulness"; cf. v.3; 25:5) of the Lord (cf. Rom 8:39; Eph 3:18). (See the appendix to Ps 25: The Perfections of Yahweh.) For the refrain (v.11), see v.5.

Notes

6 (7 MT) The LXX reads "they bowed down my soul" instead of "I was bowed down." The meaning is not greatly affected.

7–10 (8–11 MT) These verses virtually parallel 108:1–5.

The verbs for the praise of God in vv.7–9 (8–10 MT) are piled up by use of synonyms, alternation in moods, repetition (*'-w-r*) and inclusion (*z-m-r;* NIV, "make music. . . . I will sing," vv.7c, 9b):

cohortatives: "let me sing [*š-y-r*]. . . . make music [*z-m-r*]" (cf. NIV, "I will sing . . . make music");

imperatives: "awake [*'-w-r*]. . . . awake [*'-w-r*]";

cohortatives: "let me awaken [*'-w-r*] . . . let me praise [*y-d-h*]. . . . let me sing [*z-m-r*]" (NIV, "I will awaken. . . . I will praise. . . . I will sing").

8 (9 MT) For the meaning "glory" instead of "soul," see 7:5. The emphasis lies on the joy and glory with which the Lord has endowed his people. See John W. McKay, "My Glory . . . A Mantle of Praise," SJT 31 (1978): 167–72.

Psalm 58: Surely the Righteous Still Are Rewarded

This is one of the seven imprecatory psalms (cf. Pss 6; 35; 69; 83; 109; 137). This is a *lament* psalm, but it is unclear whether it belongs to the individual or the communal type of laments. It may well be classified as a prophetic type of lament in which David speaks prophetically of God's judgment on evil (cf. Ps 14). He charges the earthly system of justice with unfairness (vv.1–5) and commits his case to the Lord's justice (vv.6–8). Confident of God's vindication of the righteous, the psalmist's prophetic understanding is a comfort to God's people ("the righteous") whenever they are harassed or maligned. For an approach to this psalm as a war oracle, see the study by Christensen, pp. 112–27. For other psalms of this type, see 12; 60; 74; 79; 80; 83; 85; 90; 94:1–11; 123; 126; 137.

The structure reveals an inclusion of the first and the last verses by the repetition of cognate words: "rulers" (*'ēlem*, v.1; see Notes) and "God" (*'elōhîm*, v.11); "righteous" (*ṣeḏeq*, v.1; NIV, "justly"; *ṣaddîq*, v.11); "speak" (v.1) and "say" (v.11); "judge" (v.1, *tišpeṭû*) and "judges" (v.11, *šōp̱eṭîm*); "man" (*'āḏām;* NIV, "men"); and "on the earth" (*bā'āreṣ*, v.2; NIV, "the earth," v.11). The psalmist includes a rhetorical question, a response (vv.1–2), a description of the wicked (vv.3–5), and a prayer for justice (vv.6–8). He finds solace in prayer and comfort in the Lord's promise of justice (v.9). Instead of having to tolerate mistreatment, the righteous will experience a new freedom that is illustrated by their joy (v.10) and will know that the Lord rewards the righteous.

The structure of the psalm is as follows:

A. Concern for Justice (vv.1–2)
  B. The Lies of the Wicked (vv.3–5)
    C. Prayer for Justice (vv.6–8)
    C′. Expectation of Justice (v.9)
  B′. The Joy of the Righteous (v.10)
A′. Affirmation of Justice (v.11)

I. Concern for Justice

58:1–2

For the director of music. ⌊To the tune of⌋ "Do Not Destroy."
Of David. A *miktam*.

1 Do you rulers indeed speak justly?
  Do you judge uprightly among men?
2 No, in your heart you devise injustice,
  and your hands mete out violence on the earth.

1 The psalmist confronts the rulers with their lack of sensitivity to justice. They are designated here as "gods" (see Notes; cf. 82:1, 6) to mark the contrast with the "God who judges" (v.11). The wicked judges do not render a judgment characterized by "righteousness" (*ṣeḏeq;* see 4:1) and "equity" (NIV, "uprightly," *mêšārîm*). The Lord's rule, on the other hand, is characterized by "righteousness" and "equity" (cf. 98:9b). The rule of the wicked seldom reflects God's standards of governance and justice. Rather than limiting the sense of "judge" to legal disputes, it may be well to be guided by the usage of the same Hebrew root in v.11 and in 98:9b: "govern" or "rule" (cf. TWOT, 2:947–48).

2 The reason for the unjust rule lies in the nature ("heart") of the wicked judges. They are evil in the very core of their being, as they act out the "injustice" of their hearts and continually cause "violence" (cf. 11:5; 18:48) wherever they go. These men are evil in their hearts and therefore in their speech and actions. Alexander comments, "The meaning then is, that these wicked rulers, instead of weighing out justice to their subjects, weighed out, administered, dispensed the most violent injustice, and that too, devised and practiced themselves" (p. 255).

Notes

For a brief discussion of the technical words and phrases in the superscription, see the Introduction.

1 (2 MT) The word "rulers" is an appropriate translation. The MT's אֵלֶם (*'ēlem,* "in silence") does not fit the context. The LXX, Syriac, and Vulgate assume a different reading, as each of these ancient witnesses understood the consonantal text as having a second emphatic particle: "in very deed" (BHS). A comparison with 82:1, 6 supports the emended reading אֵלִים (*'ēlîm,* "gods," i.e., rulers or judges).

2 (3 MT) Several commentators follow the Syriac and the Targum in reading עָוֶל (*'awel,* "wicked," "unjust") as descriptive of the heart: "a wicked heart" (Weiser, p. 429; Kraus, *Psalmen,* 1:415, 417). In favor of this construction is the parallel phrase "the violence of your hands" (MT).

The particle אַף (*'ap̱,* "but") is emphatic and functions here as in response to the previous questions, hence the NIV's "no."

The verb "mete out" is an idiomatic rendering of the verb פָּלַס (*pālas*), which either means "to be level" (Isa 26:7) or "observe," "give thought to," "examine" (Prov 5:6 ["gives thought to"], 21 ["examines"]). The meaning "mete out" (NIV) is derived from the noun *peles* ("balance"; cf. Prov 16:11; Isa 40:12).

II. The Lies of the Wicked

58:3–5

3 Even from birth the wicked go astray;
from the womb they are wayward and speak lies.
4 Their venom is like the venom of a snake,
like that of a cobra that has stopped its ears,
5 that will not heed the tune of the charmer,
however skillful the enchanter may be.

3 The nature of the wicked is amplified in two ways. First, they are wicked from birth. They begin to devise evil from their very youth in that there is no evidence of good or possibility of change in their hearts. The wicked "go astray" (cf. Hos 5:7) from what is right; they are deceptive, selfish, and bend the rules in their favor.

4–5 Second, the wicked are likened to "the venom of a snake" (v.4). The snake had been trained by a snake charmer but has since become unresponsive to the "tune" (v.5; *qôl*, "voice" or "word") of the "charmer" (cf. Eccl 10:11; Isa 3:3), who is highly skilled (*meḥukkām*, related to "wisdom," *ḥoḵmāh*) as an "enchanter," a professional in using the magic arts (cf. Deut 18:11; see Dahood, *Psalms*, 2:60, for epigraphic background). The wicked are as dangerous as the venomous cobra that bites his trainer when touched and handled by him. He is insensitive to God, justice, and the cries of the poor and needy (cf. 36:1–4; 140:3). (For "cobra" see G.S. Cansdale, "Serpent," ZPEB, 5:356–58; cf. 91:13; Deut 32:33; Job 20:14, 16; Isa 11:8.)

III. Prayer for Justice

58:6–8

6 Break the teeth in their mouths, O God;
 tear out, O LORD, the fangs of the lions!
7 Let them vanish like water that flows away;
 when they draw the bow, let their arrows be blunted.
8 Like a slug melting away as it moves along,
 like a stillborn child, may they not see the sun.

6 Even in his prayer for justice, David illustrates the aggressiveness of the wicked by the metaphor of "the lions" (cf. 10:9; 22:13, 21). The imprecatory nature of the prayer may seem strange to our ears, but the radical nature of evil requires a response from the God of justice. True to the analogy, he prays that the Lord will smash the teeth of the lions and knock out their "fangs." The appeal to God and Yahweh forms an inclusion in the MT, and the whole of v.6 is chiastically structured:

A	B	C
O God,	break	their teeth in their mouths
C′	B′	A′
the fangs of the lions	tear out,	O LORD!

7–8 The author changes his analogy to an inanimate object: "water" (v.7). Fear inspired by God affects the psalmist's opponents with great dread, by which their courage "vanishes" (*m-'-s*, Niphal). They will vanish like water that ebbs away. The following simile is far from clear. The NIV likens the psalmist to an archer who shoots "blunted" arrows. He further prays that the wicked may be "like a slug" (v.8), whose trail is nothing but a slimy track, and like a stillbirth. The slug and the "stillborn child" have in common that they do not see the sun. The slug melts away in the sun, and the stillborn child will never see the light of day. So the psalmist prays that the wicked may perish: "may they not see the sun." (See the appendix to Ps 137: Imprecations in the Psalms.)

Notes

6 (7 MT) The LXX reads the verbs as perfects rather than imperatives: "has broken . . . has torn out" (BHS). The *hapax legomenon* מַלְתְּעוֹת (*malteʿôṯ*, "fangs") is an alternate form of the more usual מְתַלְּעוֹת (*meṯalleʿôṯ*, "fangs"; cf. Job 29:17; Prov 30:14; Joel 1:6).

7 (8 MT) The MT of the second hemistich seems to be corrupt; literally it reads, "He draws his arrows like they are cut off." The usual idiom is "bend and string the bow" (cf. 7:12; 11:2; 37:14); and while the NIV adds "the bow" as an explanatory phrase, others emend the problematic חִצָּו (*ḥiṣṣāw*, "his arrows," *Qere; Kethiv:* "his arrow") to חָצִיר (*ḥāṣîr*, "grass") and completely alter the metaphor; see the NEB, "may they wither like trodden grass" (similarly Weiser, p. 429; Kraus, *Psalmen*, 1:415). Dahood sticks close to the MT but suggests another approach: "may he shoot his arrows like the emaciated" (*Psalms*, 2:56, 61–62). For another proposal see Marina Mannati, who relates the "arrows" to the magical powers associated with speech or execration ("Psaume lviii.8," VetTest 28 [1978]: 477–80).

8 (9 MT) The second hemistich has occasioned some problems. The MT has a construct form for "woman" in the phrase "a stillbirth of a woman" (NIV, "a stillborn child"). The LXX reads "fire" for "woman," whose form in the construct resembles that of "fire"; compare *'ēšeṯ* ("woman," from *'iššāh*) and *'ēš* ("fire"). BHS proposes an emendation to the absolute form of "woman": אִשָּׁה (*'iššāh*). C. Steyl translates the verse, "Let them be like the snail which dissolves into slime, like the miscarriage of a woman that never sees the sun" ("The Construct Noun, *Eset*, in Ps. 58.9," JNSL 11 [1983]: 133–34).

IV. Expectation of Justice

58:9

> 9 Before your pots can feel ⌊the heat of⌋ the thorns—
> whether they be green or dry—the wicked will be
> swept away.

9 This verse is most problematic. It seems to me that the NIV rendering is likely as the mood changes from a prayer to an expectation of justice by the introductory particle "before" (*b^e^ṭerem*). This particle is used in the prophetic word as indicative that something surely is going to happen (cf. Isa 7:16; 8:4). The exact nature of the happening is not so clear because of the present ambiguity of the Hebrew text. I cannot improve on the NIV margin: "The meaning of the Hebrew for this verse is uncertain." Dahood is equally stumped by this verse: "The Hebrew of this verse is unintelligible to me" (*Psalms*, 2:62). Robert Althann has taken up the challenge, using the Ebla materials, in "Psalm 58,10 in the Light of Ebla," *Biblica* 64 (1983): 122–24. He translates the verse thus:

> Before they perceive the thorns
> He will strike them with a bramble,
> like running water, like raging water
> He will sweep them away.

V. The Joy of the Righteous

58:10

> 10 The righteous will be glad when they are avenged,
> when they bathe their feet in the blood of the wicked.

10 The joy of the righteous comes to full expression when they see evidences of God's justice. It is not so much the case that they are bloodthirsty but rather that they delight in justice. The reign of terror must come to an end! Isaiah portrays the Lord as the Divine Warrior coming with red garments, stained by the blood of his enemies (Isa

63:1–6). Here the godly join in the victory march, as they too have been granted victory. The imagery of feet in blood portrays the victory (cf. Isa 63:1–6; Rev 14:19–20; 19:13–14), rather than the gruesome picture of people relishing the death of the wicked. The godly share together with the Lord in his triumph over evil. Hence it is better to understand the word "avenged" as "victorious": "The just will rejoice when he beholds [*ḥ-z-h*] his victory."

Notes

---

10 (11 MT) See Dahood, *Psalms,* 2:56; cf. 18:47–48; J. Bright explains "vengeance" in the sense of "deliverance" in Jer 11:20 (*Jeremiah* [Garden City: Doubleday & Company, 1965], p. 87). To "see" (*ḥ-z-h,* untr. in NIV) the vengeance of the Lord is nothing less than the enjoyment of his acts of deliverance and the response of praise to the evidences of Yahweh's presence (cf. 46:8; see Hans F. Fuhs, *Sehen und Schauen. Die Wurzel* ḥzh *im Alten Orient und im Alten Testament. Ein Beitrag zum prophetischen Offenbarungsempfang* [Würzburg: Echter Verlag, 1978], pp. 285–88).

VI. Affirmation of Justice

58:11

11 Then men will say,
"Surely the righteous still are rewarded;
surely there is a God who judges the earth."

11 With the triumph of God, the righteous are vindicated. Whenever justice prevails, God and his kingdom are being established (see appendix to Ps 5: Yahweh Is King). Mankind (*'āḏām,* cf. v.1), which has experienced the oppressiveness of evil, will testify that God rules ("judges," cf. 98:9) with "righteousness" and "equity" (cf. v.1). It will also be evident that God is concerned with the righteous (*ṣaddîq,* see 1:6) and will reward him for his loyalty. The language of "reward" (lit., "fruit") is reminiscent of Psalm 1:3: "He is like a tree. . . . which yields its fruit in season" (see also Gal 6:9; James 5:1–11). The day will come when the righteous will receive their reward from the Father (cf. 2 Tim 4:8).

Psalm 59: My God Is My Champion

This psalm is one of the more problematic psalms, because of style and vocabulary. Moreover, its categorization has been difficult to define. Is it an *individual lament* or a *community lament?* The motifs of God's rule, the nations, and God's judgment of the nations may argue in favor of a national lament. On the other hand, it may be that the psalmist borrowed from the cultic tradition (A.A. Anderson, 1:435) or that the psalm may be classed as a royal lament (Dahood, *Psalms,* 2:66).

The intertwining of various motifs has created a difficulty in structural analysis. The repetition found in vv.6–7 and vv.14–15 are incorporated in the lament, whereas the repetition of confidence in the Lord (vv.9–10, 17) may well be a part of a thanksgiving liturgy.

The structure of the psalm is as follows:

A. Prayer for Deliverance (vv.1–3)
  B. Innocence and Protestation (vv.4–5)
    C. The Wicked and God (vv.6–8)
    C′. Hope in God (vv.9–10a)
  B′. Imprecation on the Wicked (vv.10b–13)
A′. Confidence in God's Response (vv.14–17)

I. Prayer for Deliverance

59:1–3

For the director of music. ⌊To the tune of⌋ "Do Not Destroy."
Of David. A *miktam.* When Saul had sent men to watch
David's house in order to kill him.

1 Deliver me from my enemies, O God;
protect me from those who rise up against me.
2 Deliver me from evildoers
and save me from bloodthirsty men.

3 See how they lie in wait for me!
Fierce men conspire against me
for no offense or sin of mine, O LORD.

1–3 Common to the language of the lament is the repeated call on the Lord to "deliver" (*n-ṣ-l,* vv.1–2; cf. 7:1; 25:20; 31:2, 15; 39:8; 51:14), to "protect" (*ś-g-b,* v.1; 20:1; 91:14), and to "save" (*y-š-ʿ*, v.2; cf. 3:7; 6:4; 7:1; 22:21; 31:16; 54:1). The beginning and end form an inclusion. The psalm opens with a prayer of lament, petitioning the Lord to deliver and protect the godly from the wicked. In the last verses the psalmist affirms his strong belief that God is his "fortress" (v.17, *miśgāb̲,* from the same root as "protect," v.1) and will show his "love" (*ḥesed̲,* vv.10, 17) by delivering him from the enemies.

The prayer for deliverance discloses both hope in the Lord's ability to fully deliver and the urgent need for deliverance. The occasion for the lament is the presence of the adversary: "my enemies, . . . those who rise up against me. . . . evildoers . . . bloodthirsty men" (vv.1–2). The adversary is evil through and through, having no regard for human life ("bloodthirsty"; cf. 5:6; 55:23; 139:19; Prov 29:10). He thrives on alienation ("rise up against me") and enjoys bringing calamity on others ("evildoers"). Like soldiers in ambush, he secretly waits to catch the godly (v.3; cf. 10:8–9; Prov 1:11; Mic 7:2).

Notes

For a brief discussion of the technical words and phrases in the superscription, see the Introduction.

II. Innocence and Protestation

59:4–5

4 I have done no wrong, yet they are ready to attack me.
Arise to help me; look on my plight!
5 O LORD God Almighty, the God of Israel,
rouse yourself to punish all the nations;
show no mercy to wicked traitors. *Selah*

4–5 The psalmist protests that this trouble is unjust. He has not provoked the adversary ("for no offense or sin of mine," v.3; cf. 1 Sam 20:1; 24:11). Yet his enemies have come out against him as public enemy number one. They prepare for a public assault ("ready to attack," v.4; lit., "they run and make ready"). The situation is critical but not desperate.

The protestation of innocence against their violence serves to intensify the psalmist's reliance on God's intervention. Though man may plan evil and create chaos on earth, God has promised to protect his covenant people. The Divine Warrior is the God of Israel! He is "LORD God Almighty [*ṣᵉḇā'ôṯ*, 'of Hosts']" (v.5; cf. 80:4, 19; 84:8; see appendix to Ps 24: Lord Sabaoth).

This self-examination and realization of evil suddenly bring the psalmist to a glorious recovery of hope in the Lord, expressed in the MT by an emphatic "you" preceded by a disjunctive waw: "but you are LORD [Yahweh] God of Hosts, the God of Israel" or "since Thou art God of hosts" (Kirkpatrick, p. 333). He is the Divine Warrior who has covenanted himself to come to the rescue of Israel. Hope focuses on the Lord, the covenant Suzerain, on whom the psalmist repeatedly calls to act ("arise . . . look. . . . rouse yourself," vv.4b–5b) against the evildoers, i.e., "all the nations" and "wicked traitors" (v.5; *hapax legomenon*, cf. 25:2).

III. The Wicked and God

59:6–8

6 They return at evening,
snarling like dogs,
and prowl about the city.
7 See what they spew from their mouths—
they spew out swords from their lips,
and they say, "Who can hear us?"
8 But you, O LORD, laugh at them;
you scoff at all those nations.

6–8 The wicked are like "dogs" (vv.6, 14; cf. 22:16–17; Phil 3:2) that terrorize the streets of the city. They bring anarchy, enjoy chaos, and speak arrogantly. Their mouths are like "swords" (v.7; cf. 57:4; 64:3), as they mock and scoff, challenge God's sovereignty (and possibly even God's love for his own), and belligerently ask, "Who can hear us?" (v.7; cf. 2:1; 10:4, 11; 64:5; 73:11; 94:7). In spite of the commotion on earth, the Lord is not moved. From his perspective evil is ridiculous; it is self-destructive. He will see to it that the rule of oppression will end and that his own will be vindicated (v.8; cf. 2:4; 37:13). The truth of this gives a new perspective on God's justice in the world.

IV. Hope in God

59:9–10a

[9]O my Strength, I watch for you;
  you, O God, are my fortress, [10]my loving God.

9–10a The Lord is stronger than the enemy. They are "fierce men" (*'azîm*, v.3), but he is the "Strength" of his people (*'ōz*, v.9; cf. 62:11; 63:2). Though evil men may prowl the streets of the city and promote anarchy, the Lord is the "fortress" (cf. v.1). In the face of the hatred shown by the enemies, the Lord is the "loving God" by whose "love" (*ḥeseḏ*) his people thrive (v.10a).

Notes

9 (10 MT) The MT's עֻזּוֹ (*'uzzô*, "his strength") appears to be corrupt. A number of Hebrew MSS, the LXX, and the Targum favor עֻזִּי (*'uzzî*, "my Strength"; cf. v.17).
The root for "fortress" (*ś-g-b*) is the same as the verb of v.1 rendered "protect me."

V. Imprecation on the Wicked

59:10b–13

God will go before me
  and will let me gloat over those who slander me.
[11]But do not kill them, O Lord our shield,
  or my people will forget.
In your might make them wander about,
  and bring them down.
[12]For the sins of their mouths,
  for the words of their lips,
  let them be caught in their pride.
For the curses and lies they utter,
[13] consume them in wrath,
  consume them till they are no more.
Then it will be known to the ends of the earth
  that God rules over Jacob. *Selah*

10b–13 Evil men must be held accountable for the "sins of their mouths, . . . their pride. . . . the curses and lies they utter" (v.12). They are utterly deceptive and crooked; hence the evil they have plotted must come on their own heads. They attempted to create restlessness and anarchy on earth, and consequently they must experience God's judgment as an aimless wandering (v.11; cf. Num 32:13; 2 Sam 15:20), as entrapped by their own devices (v.12), and finally brought to an absolute ruin (v.13). The repetition of "consume them" serves as emphasis, as if to say, "destroy them utterly." Whatever lot befalls the wicked comes to them as an expression of God's "wrath" for their many sins.

Purposefully the psalmist prays that the judgment of the wicked will be gradual and not immediate (v.11) and that the power of the Lord may gradually and progressively be more evident to the righteous as well as to the other adversaries. On the one hand, the mighty acts of God serve to encourage the godly, as they rejoice that the Lord goes "before" them in combat with evil (v.10b), in response to the prayer of v.4. The assurance renews the spirit of God's servant, as the humiliation of the wicked gives him reason to hope (v.10c; cf. 53:5–6; 54:7).

On the other hand, the just judgments of the Lord are also instructive to the nations. The whole world must know that they cannot taunt the God of Israel, as he "rules over Jacob" (v.13; cf. v.5). Anytime God acts on behalf of his people, the acts witness to his sovereignty and his care for his people, even "to the ends of the earth" (cf. 2:8; 67:7; 72:8; 98:3; 1 Sam 2:10). He is the "shield" (v.11; cf. 3:3; 18:2), providing protection for those who submit to his lordship ("O Lord [*Adonai*] our shield"). (See the appendix to Ps 98: Yahweh Is the Divine Warrior.)

Notes

11 (12 MT) For a discussion of the NIV marginal note "*sovereign*," see the note on 7:10.

VI. Confidence in God's Response

59:14–17

14 They return at evening,
snarling like dogs,
and prowl about the city.
15 They wander about for food
and howl if not satisfied.
16 But I will sing of your strength,
in the morning I will sing of your love;
for you are my fortress,
my refuge in times of trouble.

17 O my Strength, I sing praise to you;
you, O God, are my fortress, my loving God.

14–17 The evil men are terrorizing like a pack of dogs (cf. v.6). Their appetite is not easily satisfied; so they growl (from *l-w-n;* NIV, "howl," v.15). But the godly are encouraged by the vision of God's laughter (v.8) and by the assurance of his love (vv.9–10). While the wicked are howling, growling, and snarling (vv.14–15), the servant of God praises the Lord instead. The psalmist creates a clear contrast between the wicked and himself ("But I will sing," v.16), as he also did in v.8: "But you, O LORD." The cause for singing lies in the perspective of God's being the "strength," "love," and "fortress" (v.16; see vv.1, 9–10, 17) of his own during times of adversity. Since the Lord's "love" (*ḥesed*) is new every morning to those he loves, the servant of God can renew his song "in the morning." So the noise of evil "at evening," a metaphor of affliction, will be exchanged for the song of the redeemed in the morning, a symbol for deliverance.

The vision of God's rule over the world, of his love for Israel, and of the protection of his people collectively and individually (vv.6, 8–10, 11, 13) transforms the lament into a song of confidence. The psalm began on a note of lament (vv.1–2), asking the Lord to "protect" by putting him on a high place (see v.1), and concludes on a note of celebration of song to the Lord who is the "fortress" (etymologically related to the verb "protect," see note on v.9) and "strength" of his own (see v.9). Through him he will experience deliverance and vindication (vv.10–13). Truly Yahweh is the Divine Warrior of Israel!

Notes

14 Goldingay rightly explains the differences in the language in vv.5 and 14 as arising from artistic variation ("Repetition and Variation," pp. 148–49).

Psalm 60: Has God Forgotten Us?

There are sad moments in the history of the people of God. God has promised to be with his people; but in his own inscrutable wisdom, he seems to abandon them. This psalm raises the issue of divine abandonment and challenges the godly to abandon themselves to the love and compassion of a wise God. According to the superscription, this psalm alludes to David's success in Aram Naharaim, Aram Zobah, and Edom (cf. 2 Sam 8:1–14; 10:16; 1 Chron 18:1–13). Apparently the successes were not always immediate, as this psalm is a community lament in which the people pray for God's success after an apparent defeat.

The psalm is a *national lament*, composed of two laments (vv.1–5, 9–12) and an oracle (vv.6–8). Verses 5–12 are identical to 108:6–13, with only slight variations. Though it is highly likely that these verses come from another liturgical source, we are concerned here with the final composition in the present canonical shape. The structure is chiastic (ABCC′A′B′):

- A. Rejection (vv.1–3)
  - B. Confidence of Victory (v.4)
    - C. Prayer (v.5)
    - C′. Oracle: God's Response (vv.6–8)
- A′. Rejection (vv.9–11)
  - B′. Confidence of Victory (v.12)

(For an approach to this psalm as a war oracle, see the study by Christensen, pp. 112–27.) For other national lament psalms, see Psalms 12; 74; 79; 80; 83; 85; 90; 94:1–15; 123; 126; and 137.

I. Rejection

60:1–3

For the director of music. To ⌊the tune of⌋ "The Lily of the Covenant."
A *miktam* of David. For teaching. When he fought Aram Naharaim and
Aram Zobah, and when Joab returned and struck down twelve thousand
Edomites in the Valley of Salt.

1 You have rejected us, O God, and burst forth upon us;
you have been angry—now restore us!

[2]You have shaken the land and torn it open;
mend its fractures, for it is quaking.
[3]You have shown your people desperate times;
you have given us wine that makes us stagger.

1–3 It is evident that adversity has strained the covenant relationship between God and his people. The people feel that God's temporary abandonment of them has brought them nothing but trouble. Seven verbs emphasize the divine initiation: "you have rejected . . . [you] burst forth . . . you have been angry. . . . You have shaken . . . and [you have] torn it open. . . . You have shown . . . you have given" (vv.1–3).

Rejection, even though for a brief time, is serious (v.1; cf. v.10; 44:9, 23; 74:1; 77:7; 89:38), because it results from God's anger (v.1; cf. 2:12; 79:5; 1 Kings 8:46). His anger is like "wine that makes us stagger" (v.3; cf. 75:8; Isa 51:17, 22; Jer 25:15–29); its impact is felt throughout. God's people live a meaningless existence without his presence. They take defeat seriously, because divine abandonment is the most miserable condition. The psalmist likens abandonment to a state of war (v.1; NIV, "burst forth"; cf. Judg 21:15 [NIV, "made a gap"]; 2 Sam 5:20; like the breach in a wall; cf. Isa 5:5), to an earthquake (NIV, "you have shaken . . . torn it open; . . . it is quaking," v.2; cf. 18:7; 46:3, 6; Isa 24:18–20), and to a state of intoxication (v.3; cf. 75:8; Isa 51:17, 21–22).

The lament is occasionally interrupted by brief prayers for relief and restoration. The people pray for restoration (v.1) to the favor of God and for healing ("mend its fractures," v.2; cf. Jer 30:17–19).

Notes

For a brief discussion of the technical words and phrases in the superscription, see the Introduction.

For a seeming discrepancy in the number of the slain (eighteen thousand in 2 Sam 8:13 and twelve thousand here in Ps 60), see the comment in this series on 2 Sam 8:13.

II. Confidence of Victory

60:4

[4]But for those who fear you, you have raised a banner
to be unfurled against the bow. *Selah*

4 The Lord has raised a "banner" (*nēs;* cf. Isa 5:26; 13:2; Jer 4:6) designating a place where the godly may find refuge under the protection of the Divine Warrior. The godly, those who "fear" (cf. 34:7, 9) him, will find protection from the attacks of the enemy, who are symbolized by the "bow." The confidence of the godly lies in the Lord, the Divine Warrior (cf. vv.6–8).

III. Prayer

60:5

> [5]Save us and help us with your right hand,
> that those you love may be delivered.

5 The familiar cry of the lament songs is "save us" (or "save me"; cf. 54:1; 59:2). The people pray to be saved out of their desperate situation: "Save [*y-š-'*] us and help [*'-n-h*] us with your right hand, that those you love may be delivered [*ḥ-l-ṣ*]." The petitioner asks for nothing less than divine intervention ("right hand"; cf. 20:6; 89:13; et al.) in avenging the enemy and vindicating the godly. The ground of the petition is God's promise to his people. They are his "beloved" (*yᵉd̲îd̲eyk̲ā;* NIV, "those you love"; cf. Deut 33:12; Jer 11:15). To this end they long for God to initiate their deliverance (*y-š-'* and *ḥ-l-ṣ;* cf. 116:8; 140:1) just as he promised (91:15). (See the appendix to Ps 119: Yahweh Is My Redeemer.)

IV. Oracle: God's Response

60:6–8

> [6]God has spoken from his sanctuary:
> "In triumph I will parcel out Shechem
> and measure off the Valley of Succoth.
> [7]Gilead is mine, and Manasseh is mine;
> Ephraim is my helmet,
> Judah my scepter.
> [8]Moab is my washbasin,
> upon Edom I toss my sandal;
> over Philistia I shout in triumph."

6 Answering the prayers of his people, the Lord gives an oracle of hope. He thunders "from his sanctuary" (lit., "in his sanctuary," or "by his holiness"; cf. 89:35; Amos 4:2). He reminds his people of his promise that the earth is his and that no enemy will survive against him!

God is sovereign over Israel, as he alone "parcel[s] out" the portions: Shechem, Succoth, Gilead, Manasseh, Ephraim, and Judah. The geographical references are a representative list of all the regions that make up the heritage of Israel in Palestine and Transjordan. He is also sovereign over the nations: Moab, Edom, and Philistia.

7 The tribes are represented by the two major tribes: Ephraim and Judah (cf. 78:67–68). Ephraim is called a "helmet" (lit., "the strength of my head"), symbolic of force; Judah is a "scepter" (cf. Gen 49:10), symbolic of dominion and governance. Ephraim represents the northern and eastern tribes, Judah the southern tribes. Thus all tribes share in God's rule over the nations.

8 The Lord's authority over the nations is symbolized by "washbasin," "my sandal," and a victory "shout." The picture of Moab coming with a washbasin for the warrior to wash his feet represents her subjugation to servant status. Edom too will be dispossessed by the victorious Warrior, as is implied by the idiom "I toss my sandal." The authority of the Lord will extend from east (Moab and Edom) to west (Philistia). There is no nation from shore to shore that will not have to submit itself to his rule (cf.

46:8–9; 72:8). To this end he has also established the messianic rule of the Davidic dynasty, by which the hostilities of the nations will cease or be broken (Ps 2). Did not the Lord say that Judah is his "scepter"? Judah represents here the Davidic dynasty (cf. 78:68–72), which he has chosen over Ephraim (78:67).

V. Rejection

60:9–11

9 Who will bring me to the fortified city?
Who will lead me to Edom?
10 Is it not you, O God, you who have rejected us
and no longer go out with our armies?
11 Give us aid against the enemy,
for the help of man is worthless.

9–11 The lament resumes in the light of the oracle of hope. David asks the Lord to lead him in victory (v.9). The pain of the defeat and hence of God's apparent rejection is still real (v.10; cf. v.1). The questions are designed to evoke a strong positive response, as the Lord alone will lead the armies into battle and victory. The experience of divine rejection brings out a renewed faith and confidence in the Lord. The king is not looking for a military solution to his problems, such as alliances with other kings, because he knows that their "help [*t^e šû'āh*, from *y-š-'*] . . . is worthless" (v.11; cf. 33:16–17; 146:3). He looks to the Lord who has abandoned his people in hope that he will bring about the victory over the enemy (v.11).

VI. Confidence of Victory

60:12

12 With God we will gain the victory,
and he will trample down our enemies.

12 Here the confidence of divine protection (v.4) flows over into confidence in victory. The oracle of God (vv.5–8) was sufficient to inspire the people not to fear the enemy or to be troubled by the setback. The Lord is still with them, and he will bring them through this adversity with renewed strength, joy, and victory (cf. 44:5; 118:15–16). The emphatic "with God" stands in contrast to the emphatic position of "God" in v.1. The latter stresses his abandonment and the former his deliverance. The psalm opens with God's treatment of his people as his enemies (vv.1–3) and closes with his enmity against the enemies of his people. Truly the Lord is just in his rule! Bellinger explains the shift as arising from a prophetic oracle of salvation, promising victory (pp. 73–76).

Psalm 61: A Prayer From a Fainting Heart

The psalmist's longing for God (vv.1–5) is a familiar motif in the Psalms as an expression of deep love for God arising out of great adversity (cf. Pss 20; 21; 27; 42; 43; 63). The genre of this psalm is debatable. It may be categorized as an individual lament (Kraus, *Psalmen*, 1:433), a royal psalm (Eaton, p. 156), or a royal lament psalm (Dahood, *Psalms*, 2:83–84). In view of the reference to the king (vv.6–7; cf. 63:11), this psalm may very well be an *individual, royal lament.* Regardless of the original function, any child of God may pray this prayer for himself and for his messianic King.

The structure of the psalm is as follows:

A. Prayer for Protection (vv.1–2)
  B. Expression of Confidence (vv.3–5)
A′. Prayer for Protection (vv.6–7)
  B′. Expression of Confidence (v.8)

I. Prayer for Protection

61:1–2

For the director of music. With stringed instruments. Of David.

1 Hear my cry, O God;
  listen to my prayer.
2 From the ends of the earth I call to you,
  I call as my heart grows faint;
  lead me to the rock that is higher than I.

1–2 In a manner well known in the lament psalms, the psalmist calls on the Lord to answer him (see 17:1; cf. 1 Kings 8:28). The object of the supplication is to find divine protection from adversity. The nature of the misery is not spelled out, but its effect on the sufferer is. It wears him out so that he becomes weary of life to the point of despair ("faint," v.2; cf. 77:3; 142:3; 143:4; Jonah 2:7). It seems that the psalmist is so far from God that he speaks to him from a great distance ("from the ends of the earth"). Though the phrase "from the ends of the earth" may denote a geographical distance away from the land (cf. 46:9; Deut 28:49), it is also a metaphor for despair, alienation, and spiritual distance from the Lord.

The Lord alone can bring deliverance by coming to the aid of his ailing child. The psalmist is in the pit and prays that the Lord will guide and protect him. "The rock" (v.2) is a metaphor for protection, denoting a fortified or strategic place where one could find refuge (cf. 18:2), possibly the sanctuary (27:5). The psalmist looks to no other protection than that promised by the Rock of Israel, Yahweh (cf. 62:2, 6–7). The confession "the rock that is higher than I" expresses faith in the Lord's exalted (*yārûm*) position and his ability to deliver. (See the appendix to Ps 98: Yahweh Is the Divine Warrior.)

Notes

For a brief discussion of the technical words and phrases in the superscription, see the Introduction.

2 (3 MT) The LXX reads, "you exalted me" or "lifted me up," instead of יָרוּם (*yārûm,* "he will exalt"; NIV, "higher than I"). See Kraus: "on a rock lift me up" (*Psalmen,* 2:432; cf. 27:5).

The Syriac has "and you have comforted me" (from *n-ḥ-m*) instead of a form from *n-ḥ-h* ("lead," "guide"). Dahood treats the verb *n-ḥ-h* as a technical term for being ushered into the eternal mansions (*Psalms,* 1:85).

II. Expression of Confidence

61:3–5

3 For you have been my refuge,
  a strong tower against the foe.
4 I long to dwell in your tent forever
  and take refuge in the shelter of your wings. *Selah*
5 For you have heard my vows, O God;
  you have given me the heritage of those who fear your
    name.

3 In the present affliction the psalmist recalls the past ways in which the Lord has come through. The psalmist has found him to be a "refuge" (*maḥseh;* cf. 7:1; 11:1; 16:1; 31:1; 46:1; 57:1; 62:8; 71:1, 7; 73:28; et al.) from trouble and "strong" (*'ōz;* cf. 62:11; 63:2 [NIV, "power"]) like a "tower." "Towers" were used for military purposes; and in the case of a siege, people could find protection in them (cf. Judg 9:51–52; Prov 18:10). Even in the present affliction caused by "the foe," the psalmist encounters the protection of the Almighty. The Lord has been and still is his "refuge" and "strong tower."

4 The psalmist longs for the moment when the Lord will invite his suffering saint to fellowship with him. The imagery of dwelling in the tent goes back to the desert experience (cf. Exod 33:7–11; Num 11:16–17) when the Lord resided among the tribes of Israel in a tent. It is this symbol of faith the psalmist draws on, as if to say, "May I be your invited guest of honor in your tent" (cf. 15:1; Isa 33:20; cf. Ps 27:5). Over against the present affliction is the hope of a lasting joy of communion with the Lord. The psalmist longs to be a welcome guest with the Lord "for ages" (NIV, "forever"; cf. 23:6). Another metaphor for divine protection and recognition is that of "the shelter of your wings" (cf. 36:7; 57:1; 91:4). (See the appendix to Ps 132: The Ark of the Covenant and the Temple: Symbols of Yahweh's Presence and Rule.)

5 The past experience and present longing for redemption may be a cause for apprehension. Yet the psalmist has learned to face the future with confidence. He is confident that the Lord will answer and already has answered his vows. The "vows" were made during times of duress as a part of a prayer for deliverance (cf. 50:14–15). The Lord will be true to his covenant promises in response to the cry of those who fear his name (cf. 34:7, 9; 103:11, 13, 17). Together with the godly, the psalmist will enjoy "the heritage." The "heritage" refers both to the land (cf. Deut 2:19; 3:18) and particularly to the enjoyment of the benefits of covenant life (cf. Ps 37:9, 11, 22, 29, 34). The godly will inherit the earth (cf. Matt 5:5).

Notes

5 (6 MT) Some commentators question the MT's יְרֻשַּׁת (*yᵉruššaṯ,* "heritage") in favor of אֲרֶשֶׁת (*'ᵃrešeṯ,* "desire," of 21:2; Kraus, *Psalmen,* 2:432).

III. Prayer for Protection

61:6–7

> 6 Increase the days of the king's life,
> his years for many generations.
> 7 May he be enthroned in God's presence forever;
> appoint your love and faithfulness to protect him.

6 The prayer for personal protection changes to a prayer for the continuity of the divinely established monarchy (cf. Pss 2; 132). Long "life" (lit., "days") is an idiom for the prosperity of the reigning monarch as well as for the preservation of his dynasty (cf. 2 Kings 20:6; Ps 45:6), similar to the British "God save the queen." The second bicolon in v.6 amplifies and intensifies the former: "days . . . king's life, . . . years . . . generations"; that is, the prayer for the king includes a prayer for the well-being of his family for generations to come.

7 The monarchy in ancient Israel was established and maintained by the promise of God's "love and faithfulness" (2 Sam 7:28; 15:20; Pss 40:11; 89:14; Isa 55:3). The Lord had promised that David's dynasty would be "enthroned . . . forever" (cf. 89:36). The ground and hope of the promise lie ultimately in the relationship between God's kingdom and the ruling monarch of the house of David. The Lord desired to shower his goodness—expressed by the phrase "in God's presence" (cf. 56:13)—and divine protection. The promises of the Lord have found their focus in the messiahship of Jesus the Christ, whose rule is established by the promise and reward of the Father (Eph 4:7–13).

IV. Expression of Confidence

61:8

> 8 Then will I ever sing praise to your name
> and fulfill my vows day after day.

8 The prayer vacillates between lament and expression of confidence. Here again the psalmist bursts forth with the confident expectation of fulfilling his vows. The vows were to be fulfilled as soon as the prayers were answered (cf. v.5; 50:14) as an expression of gratitude. Thanksgiving is the heart response to the mighty acts of God. The "praise" of the Lord is to be "forever" (NIV, "ever"). Here the word "forever" connotes continuity rather than eternity, as is also expressed by the parallel statement "day after day." See the discussion by Pierre Auffret, " 'Alors je joueray sans Fin pour ton Nom.' Etude structurelle du Psaume 61," *Science et Esprit* 36 (1984): 169–77.

Psalm 62: Rest and Reward

While facing calamity, the psalmist shows a strong reliance on the Lord. The Lord is the object of his desire, for rest is found in him, whereas people often prove themselves to be untrustworthy. This psalm arises out of a context of great adversity and may be categorized as a *psalm of confidence*. Kirkpatrick explains the psalm against the background of Absalom's rebellion (pp. 347–48) and relates both Psalms 4 and 62 to the same general period. But the internal evidence is inconclusive. The psalm may also be related by similar motif and vocabulary with 39, 61, and 63.

The structure of the psalm is as follows:

A. Confidence in the Lord (vv.1–2)
B. Man Is Unreliable (vv.3–4)
C. The Lord of My Salvation (vv.5–7)
B′. Exhortation to Trust, Not in Man, But in the Lord (vv.8–10)
A′. Confidence in the Lord (vv.11–12)

I. Confidence in the Lord

62:1–2

For the director of music. For Jeduthun. A psalm of David.

1 My soul finds rest in God alone;
my salvation comes from him.
2 He alone is my rock and my salvation;
he is my fortress, I will never be shaken.

1–2 The psalmist encourages himself by reflecting on who the Lord is. His whole being ("my soul," v.1) receives consolation from the conviction that the Lord is sufficient. He can give "rest" (cf. v.5) to all who are looking for quietness of heart. He is the source of "salvation" (*yᵉšû'āh*, vv.1–2, 6; *yēša'* in v.7) and the strength of his people ("rock," "fortress," vv.1–2, 6–7). "Salvation" signifies the whole process of redemption extending to vindication and to the enjoyment of covenant privileges. The Lord alone will save, because he is faithful and able. The Lord is faithful in giving his "love" (*ḥesed*, v.12) and his rewards, and he is also able in that he is "strong" (*'ōz*, v.11) as a "rock" (cf. 42:9; 61:2) and a "fortress" (*miśgāḇ*; lit., "high place"; cf. 59:9, 16–17). (See the appendix to Ps 98: Yahweh Is the Divine Warrior.)

The psalmist's confidence lies ultimately in the Lord. Resting in God requires waiting and patience (cf. 37:7; Lam 3:26). Even while he has many reasons to fear, the psalmist's faith rises to a new height in believing the promise of God that the righteous "will never be shaken" (v.2; cf. 10:6; 37:24; Prov 24:16).

Notes

For a brief discussion of the technical words and phrases in the superscription, see the Introduction.

1 (2 MT) The asseverative particle אַךְ (*'aḵ*, "truly," "surely") occurs six times in this psalm (vv.1, 2, 4, 5, 6, 9; mainly in the expressions of confidence in the Lord) over against four times in Psalm 39 (vv.5, 6 [*bis*], 11). The NIV renders it adverbially as "alone," "fully," and "but" (v.9).

1–2 (2–3 MT) Goldingay rightly explains the differences between vv.1–2 and 5–6 as arising from artistic variation ("Repetition and Variation," p. 149).

II. Man Is Unreliable

62:3–4

3 How long will you assault a man?
  Would all of you throw him down—
  this leaning wall, this tottering fence?
4 They fully intend to topple him
  from his lofty place;
  they take delight in lies.
 With their mouths they bless,
  but in their hearts they curse. *Selah*

3 In contrast to his great confidence in the Lord, the psalmist has little faith in the kingdom of man. Man in opposition to the Lord is destructive, selfish, and deceitful. Yet faith in the Lord overcomes the strongest opposition, as is borne out in the question "How long?" The question is in the form of an indignant challenge of the confidence of the ungodly. The godly hereby calls on the ungodly to give up their evil (cf. 4:2).

4 The ungodly devise many forms of evil. They attack with words and deeds. Their aggressiveness does not rest until those who were seated on a "lofty place" are toppled and reduced to nothingness. Even in this state of weakness, compared to a "leaning wall" and to a "tottering fence" (v.3; cf. 18:29), the wicked purpose nothing less than a complete destruction.

The question (v.3) changes to an asseveration (v.4; *'aḵ*, "surely"; NIV, "fully"). The intent of the wicked is indeed to bring ruin and destruction by anarchy and insurrection (v.4a), by delighting in deception (v.4b), and by hypocritical speech (v.4c; cf. 12:2; 28:3; 55:21). Facing this enmity the psalmist finds his strength in the Lord alone (vv.5–6).

Notes

3 (4 MT) תְּהוֹתְתוּ (*t^{e}hôṯ^{e}ṯû*, NIV, "assault") could be rendered as "assail" or "overwhelm with reproaches" (NEB, "assail with your threats") depending on the root—*h-w-t* or *h-t-t* (KB^3, 1:233, 247). Dahood favors the association with the Ugaritic *hwt* ("word"): "will you bluster" (*Psalms*, 2:91). Similarly he takes the parallel verb to mean "indulge in gossip."

The verb תְּרָצְּחוּ (*t^{e}rāṣṣ^{e}ḥû*, "you kill") appears to be corrupt. The NIV ("you throw him down") accepts the emendation תְּרוּצוּהוּ (*t^{e}rûṣûhû*, "you run against him") from *r-w-ṣ*.

4 (5 MT) The phrase מִשְּׂאֵתוֹ (*miśś^e'ēṯô*, "from lifting him"; NIV, "from his lofty place") seems to be corrupt. Two major proposals may help: (1) מַשֻּׁאוֹת (*maššu'ôṯ*, "deception"; see Dahood's "craft," *Psalms*, 2:92; Kraus, *Psalmen*, 1:436), and (2) מְשַׂנְאַי (*m^{e}śan'ay*, "my enemies").

III. The Lord of My Salvation

62:5–7

5 Find rest, O my soul, in God alone;

my hope comes from him.
6 He alone is my rock and my salvation;
he is my fortress, I will not be shaken.
7 My salvation and my honor depend on God;
he is my mighty rock, my refuge.

5–7 These verses repeat the motif of confidence in the Lord (cf. vv.1–2). The similarity in vocabulary suggests its function as a refrain. But the refrain reveals creative variation of familiar words. Instead of "salvation" (v.1) we find here "hope" (*tiqwāh*, v.5; cf. 71:5). The psalmist further explains that his hope in "salvation" lies in the Divine Warrior who fights for him. This motif is expressed in the climactic parallelism of vv.6–7:

v.6: "my rock . . . my salvation . . . my fortress"
v.7: "on God . . . my salvation . . . my honor . . . my mighty rock . . . my refuge in God" (Hebrew order; notice the repetition of "God").

The "hope" in the Lord (v.5) receives its proper focus because of the underlying faith in God, who can protect and defend his own (cf. 18:2). Faith is the antidote to despair (cf. 37:7). Silence in the presence of the Lord will speed God's deliverance, as Calvin observes, "Never, as if he had said, will he frustrate the patient waiting of his saints; doubtless my silence shall meet with its reward; I shall restrain myself, and not make that false haste which will only retard my deliverance" (2:423).

Notes

7 (6 MT) The NIV margin—"*God Most High is my salvation and my honor*"—is based on Dahood's rendering of the particle עַל (*'al*, "on") as a divine epithet, "Most High" (*Psalms*, 1:45–46). (See the appendix to Ps 9: Yahweh Is El Elyon.)

IV. Exhortation to Trust, Not in Man, But in the Lord

62:8–10

8 Trust in him at all times, O people;
pour out your hearts to him,
for God is our refuge. *Selah*

9 Lowborn men are but a breath,
the highborn are but a lie;
if weighed on a balance, they are nothing;
together they are only a breath.
10 Do not trust in extortion
or take pride in stolen goods;
though your riches increase,
do not set your heart on them.

8–10 The emphatic confession of trust in the Lord (vv.5–7) transforms into an even bolder proclamation, calling on all the godly to put their trust in God. Mankind is unreliable whereas God alone is unfailing. The distinction of "lowborn men" and "the highborn" is based on the different words for "man" in the MT: *'āḏām* and *'îš* (v.9; cf. 49:2). But it is equally possible to treat both colons of v.9 as a general reference to mankind: "mankind is but a breath; mankind is but a lie."

With the Lord is "salvation" and "refuge" (vv.6–8), whereas man is found wanting "on a balance" (v.9; cf. Prov 16:2; 21:2; 24:12). After all, he is but "breath" (*heḇel,* v.9; cf. 39:11; Isa 41:24), lacking in lasting perfections. Man's riches and power are all too often the result of "extortion" (v.10; cf. 73:8; Jer 6:6; 22:17), deception, and theft (cf. Lev 6:2, 4; Isa 30:12; Ezek 22:29). But even when riches are gained legitimately, there is an inherent danger in self-reliance (cf. Matt 19:22; 1 Tim 6:17). Though man may increase in riches and thereby in power, the godly know that their hope lies in the Lord and not in man. The positive "trust in him" (v.8) and the negative "do not trust in extortion" (v.10) together undergird the psalmist's contention that with the Lord is lasting salvation. Though the godly may have to wait with "hope" for his salvation, they are assured that the Lord provides a "refuge" (v.7) to those who long for his salvation ("pour out your hearts to him," v.8; cf. 142:2; Job 3:24) and who do not set their hearts on the riches of man (v.10; cf. 1 Tim 6:17).

Notes

---

8 (7 MT) The LXX suggests an alternate reading of the MT's "at all times": "Trust in him, O whole congregation." Kraus emends the text accordingly from בְּכָל עֵת (*ḇᵉḵol ʿēṯ,* "at all times") to כָּל עֲדַת עָם (*kol ʿᵃḏaṯ ʿam,* "all congregation of people," *Psalmen,* 2:435).

V. Confidence in the Lord

62:11–12

> 11 One thing God has spoken,
>   two things have I heard:
> that you, O God, are strong,
> 12   and that you, O Lord, are loving.
> Surely you will reward each person
>   according to what he has done.

11–12 The psalmist's confidence probes further into the promises of God to his people. He does this by a Semitic device of a numerical sequence of x and x + 1 (see Wm. W. Roth, "The Numerical Sequence x: x + 1 in the Old Testament," VetTest 12 [1962]: 300–311; id., "Numerical Sayings in the Old Testament," Supplement to VetTest 13 [1965]: 55). He is reminded of two divine promises that he has heard (v.11). He has learned that God is "strong" (*ʿōz;* cf. v.7, "mighty rock," lit., "rock of my strength" [*ʿōz*]) and full of love (*ḥeseḏ;* cf. 63:2–3: "power. . . . love" [*ʿōz. . . . ḥeseḏ*]). God is able to deliver his people, and his deliverance is an act of "love." The covenant God is just in his rewards as well as in his vindication (1 Peter 1:17; Rev 2:23; 20:12–13; 22:12). He will richly reward the godly who trust in him (Matt 16:27) and who shun man's deceptive power. The wicked will also receive their deserts (cf. 1:6; Rom 2:6–7; 2 Tim 4:14). (See the appendix to Ps 119: Yahweh Is My Redeemer.)

Psalm 63: The Excellence of God's Love

The psalm is associated with David's stay in the Judean wilderness, either during his escape from Saul (cf. 1 Sam 23) or, in a later period, from Absalom (cf. 2 Sam 15:13–30; Kirkpatrick, pp. 352–53). In spirit it is close to Psalm 42:1–2 and fits well with Psalms 61 and 62 as a collection of psalms bound by a common concern for closeness and fellowship with the Lord. This psalm reflects the genre of individual laments with its characteristic complaint (v.1), expression of confidence in the Lord's ability to help (vv.2–10), and anticipation of public praise (v.11). The psalm has been used as a morning psalm because of the KJV rendering of v.1, still reflected in the NKJV: "early will I seek You."

The structure of the psalm reveals a symmetry in two strophes (vv.1–5, 6–11):

A. Longing for the Lord (v.1)
  B. Vision of God's Beneficence (vv.2–3)
    C. In Praise of the Lord (vv.4–5)
A′. Longing for the Lord (vv.6–8)
  B′. Vision of God's Judgment (vv.9–10)
    C′. In Praise of the Lord (v.11)

I. Longing for the Lord

63:1

A psalm of David. When he was in the Desert of Judah.

1 O God, you are my God,
  earnestly I seek you;
my soul thirsts for you,
  my body longs for you,
in a dry and weary land
  where there is no water.

1 In the Elohistic Psalter (Pss 42–83), the emphatic "O God" signifies essentially the same as Yahweh ("LORD"), the covenant-faithful God. In the seemingly redundant statement "you are my God [El]," the psalmist affirms that his God is El. For the true believer there is no other El than the Lord (see appendix to Ps 22: Yahweh Is El).

The psalmist yearns for fellowship with the Lord like one who thirsts for water after days in the desert. There is no thirst and sense of fatigue like that of a person who walks around in the desert. The arid climate rapidly saps one of strength. So strong is his physical longing for God that we may agree with C.S. Lewis that the psalmist had an "appetite for God" (*The Psalms*, p. 51).

Notes

For a brief discussion of the technical words and phrases in the superscription, see the Introduction.

1 (2 MT) The longing for God consumes the whole being. The NIV rendering "soul . . . body" reflects the MT, but it should be remembered that the Hebrew for "soul" (*nep̱eš*) signifies one's whole being, as does "body" (lit., "flesh"; cf. 84:2).

The verbal phrase "earnestly I seek" is derived from the root שחר (*š-ḥ-r*), which the noun "dawn" is related to. This etymology gave rise to the tradition of treating Psalm 63 as a morning psalm with the translation "early will I seek You" (NKJV; so also LXX; cf. BDB, p. 1007). The NIV correctly emphasizes the eagerness rather than the time of the "seeking," as the verb denotes a diligent search for godly wisdom as most important to life (cf. Prov 2:1–4; 8:17–21). The "search" for God is also expressed in the metaphors associated with the desert: "thirst" (cf. 42:2; 84:2; 143:6), "longs" (*k-m-h, hapax legomenon,* probably "faint with desire"), and "a dry and weary land" (cf. 143:6; Isa 32:2).

II. Vision of God's Beneficence

63:2–3

> [2]I have seen you in the sanctuary
>   and beheld your power and your glory.
> [3]Because your love is better than life,
>   my lips will glorify you.

2 The search for God arises from the psalmist's past experience of fellowship and enjoyment of God's goodness. The psalmist changes metaphors from that of the desert to that of a prophetic vision. He has had a vision of God's beneficence: holiness ("in the sanctuary"), "power" (*ʿōz*), "glory" (*kāḇôḏ*), and "love" (*ḥeseḏ*). Even as Isaiah had a vision of God's holiness and glory (Isa 6:1–3), so the psalmist confesses that he has had a glimpse of the beatific vision. The God he worships is the Great King who promised to be present among his people in "the sanctuary." The symbol of the presence of the glorious and powerful King was the ark of the covenant (cf. 1 Sam 4:21; Pss 78:61; 132:8). (See the appendix to Ps 132: The Ark of the Covenant and the Temple: Symbols of Yahweh's Presence and Rule.)

3 The psalmist's yearning for God is heightened by the past experience of fellowship, his glorious presence, and the evidences of his covenantal love (cf. 62:11–12). The psalmist knows in whom he has believed and is persuaded that this great God will deliver him. The vision of God inspires him with longing as well as with confidence that the Lord will not abandon him. Hence he seeks his love as more than self-preservation and seeks to "glorify" (*š-b-ḥ;* cf. 117:1; 145:4; 147:12) the Lord.

Notes

2–3 (3–4 MT) The words עֹז (*ʿōz,* "power") and חֶסֶד (*ḥeseḏ,* "love") form a literary connection with 62:11–12 (NIV, "strong, . . . loving"). The same words are used in the MT.

III. In Praise of the Lord

63:4–5

> [4]I will praise you as long as I live,
>   and in your name I will lift up my hands.

5 My soul will be satisfied as with the richest of foods;
with singing lips my mouth will praise you.

4 Even if the psalmist were to endure adversity throughout the rest of his life (cf. 104:33; 146:2), he commits himself to the praise of God and to a life of trust in his deliverance. Praise here anticipates the deliverance and is synonymous with prayer. The phrase "I will praise you" parallels "in your name I will lift up my hands" (i.e., pray; cf. 28:2; 141:2; 1 Tim 2:8). The "name" of the Lord (Yahweh) is the ground of hope and trust, because the Lord has signed and sealed his covenant with his "name" (see appendix to Ps 7: The Name of Yahweh).

5 The prayerful praise of God awaits an answer. "Praise" is the response of faith in God's perfections as they relate to his people. He expects the Lord to come through in time by an abundant provision of his needs. He expresses the bounty of deliverance in the metaphor of a banquet (cf. Isa 25:6; Zech 9:15; Rev 19:9). The MT reads literally "marrow and fat" for the NIV's "richest of foods." The phrase is idiomatic and a metaphor for the joy, greatness, and beneficence associated with the love of the Lord (cf. 36:8). Prayer that is confident of the Lord's fidelity to his promises also expresses praise. The Lord is pleased with the "lips" of men that joyfully emit sounds of praise.

IV. Longing for the Lord

63:6–8

6 On my bed I remember you;
I think of you through the watches of the night.
7 Because you are my help,
I sing in the shadow of your wings.
8 My soul clings to you;
your right hand upholds me.

6 The psalm returns to the motif of longing for the Lord in the metaphor of wilderness and thirst (cf. v.1). The psalmist reflects on the Lord during the "watches" of the night (cf. 119:148). According to OT practice, the night was divided into three watches of four hours each (cf. Judg 7:19; 1 Sam 11:11; Lam 2:19). He remembers the Lord's past activities and draws comfort (cf. 42:4) during the night when the shadows of adversity haunt him. He meditates (NIV, "I think of you," *h-g-h*, as in 1:2) by opening the record of God's acts in his spiritual reflection.

7–8 The psalmist finds protection in the Lord. The metaphor "in the shadow of your wings" (v.7) expresses God's acts of fellowship and protection (cf. 17:8; 36:7; 61:4; see 91:4). The Lord has promised to be close to his own, but he also expects his children to draw close to him. The psalmist's confidence lies in the Lord, whose help and support he seeks. Therefore he draws close to his God. The verbal expression "My soul clings to you" (v.8) is man's response to God's invitation to "hold fast to" him (*d-b-q;* cf. Deut 4:4; 10:20; 11:22; 13:4; 30:20; cf. also 2 Kings 18:6). He knows that the Lord will be true to his promises. He has learned to "sing" (*r-n-n,* "exult"; cf. v.5), while awaiting the Lord's "help" (*'ezrāṯāh,* i.e., deliverance) and a new demonstration of the strength of his "right hand" (cf. 18:35; Isa 41:10).

V. Vision of God's Judgment

63:9–10

> 9 They who seek my life will be destroyed;
> they will go down to the depths of the earth.
> 10 They will be given over to the sword
> and become food for jackals.

9–10 The newly gained perspective of the Lord's power to deliver ("power . . . glory. . . . love," vv.2–3; "shadow of your wings. . . . your right hand," vv.7–8) inspires the psalmist by the hope of the Lord's vindication. The Divine Warrior will triumphantly subdue the enemies. He will destroy them (*šô'āh,* "destruction"; cf. 35:8; Isa 10:3). They had planned to destroy the righteous (cf. Prov 3:25), but the Lord will bring them down, down, down to the lowest parts of the earth (v.9). By the metaphors for holocaust—Sheol, war ("the sword"; cf. Jer 18:21; Ezek 35:5), and abandonment (like a corpse devoured by wild animals; cf. Isa 18:6; Jer 19:7)—the psalmist expresses his hope in the final triumph of divine justice. (See the appendix to Ps 137: Imprecations in the Psalms.)

Notes

---

9 The word for "destruction"—שׁוֹאָה (*šô'āh*)—was understood in LXX as לַשָּׁוְא (*laššāwe'*, "in vain," "without cause"); see Kraus: "they, without cause seek my life" (*Psalmen*, 2:440).

VI. In Praise of the Lord

63:11

> 11 But the king will rejoice in God;
> all who swear by God's name will praise him,
> while the mouths of liars will be silenced.

11 The vision of divine vengeance and justice gives further reason for rejoicing. After all, deliverance consists not only of redemption from evil (cf. vv.9–10) but also of redemption to a life of fellowship and enjoyment of God's beneficence (cf. vv.4–5). In view of the present suffering (vv.1, 6–8), the king longs for his God to come through in triumph. Then he will be happy (NIV, "rejoice") and "boast" (NIV, "praise"; see in contrast 52:1) with all those who swear by the divine "name" (cf. Deut 6:13; 10:20; 1 Sam 25:26). The deception of the adversaries will cease and the praise of the Lord alone will be heard (cf. 52:1–5; 107:42)!

Psalm 64: Prayer for Protection

The psalm is an *individual lament,* expressive of an unwavering belief in divine retribution (lex talionis). The psalm begins with a petition and concludes with a call to rejoice in the Lord's righteousness.

The structure of the psalm is an example of a ziggurat.

A. Petition (v.1)
B. Prayer for Protection From the Enemies (vv.2–6)
C. God's Protection and Vengeance (vv.7–9)
D. Rejoicing and Encouragement (v.10)

I. Petition

64:1

For the director of music. A psalm of David.

1 Hear me, O God, as I voice my complaint;
protect my life from the threat of the enemy.

1 The prayer begins with an emphatic "hear" (cf. 61:1). "God" in the Elohistic Psalter is none other than the God of the covenant, who has promised to be near to his people (Deut 4:7). But the psalmist, as he is surrounded by the provocations of the enemies, experiences that God's presence is elusive (cf. 55:17; 1 Sam 1:16). Hence he prays for God's preservation from "the threat [*paḥaḏ*, lit., 'fear'] of the enemies" (cf. Isa 7:2–9). He greatly fears that his adversary has the power to take his life. But he also knows that the Lord has the power to keep or preserve (*n-ṣ-r;* NIV, "protect") the physical life of his people (cf. 12:7; 59:17).

The Lord can "protect" by hiding (*s-t-r*) his own from evil (v.2; cf. 63:7). Verses 2–6 build up the intense horror of the evildoers, who must be dealt with justly. Verses 7–9 describe God's protection in response to the threat of the evildoer.

Notes

For a brief discussion of the technical words and phrases in the superscription, see the Introduction.

1 (2 MT) It is possible that שְׁמַע (*šᵉmaʻ*, "hear") forms an inclusion and a wordplay with v.10, יִשְׂמַח (*yiśmaḥ*, "let . . . rejoice").

II. Prayer for Protection From the Enemies

64:2–6

2 Hide me from the conspiracy of the wicked,
from that noisy crowd of evildoers.

3 They sharpen their tongues like swords
and aim their words like deadly arrows.
4 They shoot from ambush at the innocent man;
they shoot at him suddenly, without fear.

5 They encourage each other in evil plans,
they talk about hiding their snares;
they say, "Who will see them?"
6 They plot injustice and say,
"We have devised a perfect plan!"
Surely the mind and heart of man are cunning.

2–3 The enemies secretly scheme and plot to undo God's saint (v.2). The "conspiracy" (*sôḏ*) results from their banding together in their council of war (cf. 2:1). The enemies have no regard for God. In their secret assembly and in their noisy provocations they are like an army preparing for war. Their speech is as lethal as a sharpened sword (cf. 55:21; 57:4) and as "deadly arrows" (v.3; cf. 59:7).

4 The wicked, who are intent on exterminating the godly, lie in "ambush" (*mistārîm,* "hidden places"; cf. 10:8; 17:12; an allusion to the verb "hide me," v.2) and wait for the opportune moment to make a kill. They "shoot" (*y-r-h,* twice in v.4) without "fear" (*y-r-',* a play on *y-r-h*) of God or man. The unprovoked, methodical extermination of the "innocent" must come to the attention of God. After all, the "innocent man" is blameless in character, as he lives in fear of God and his commandments (cf. 119:1). How different are the wicked from "the innocent man" (v.2)!

5–6 Verses 5–6 repeat and amplify the portrayal of the wicked given in vv.2–4. Both sections enlarge the simple statement in the complaint "the threat of the enemy" (v.1). Whereas vv.2–4 depict the wicked in their opposition to the innocent, vv.5–6 sketch their united efforts in cunning and scheming. They are rebels who, like gangsters, undermine the establishment. They "encourage" (*ḥ-z-q,* "strengthen") one another with their "evil plans" (v.5). They scheme together secretly to lay snares for the righteous so as to entrap their victims (cf. 35:7; 119:110; 140:5; 142:3; Deut 7:16; Prov 22:24–25; Jer 7:9–10). They foolishly believe that they are not accountable to anyone, as is expressed by their confident question "Who will see?" (from *r-'-h,* a play on *y-r-h* ["shoot"] and *y-r-'* ["fear"]). For this spirit see 10:4, 11, 13.

The wicked are also confident as they scheme in their unjust projects (v.6). In opposition to the "innocent" (v.4, or "perfect," *tām*), they "perfect" (v.6, *t-m-m;* NIV, "we have devised a perfect [plan]") their own schemings and enthusiastically hail their plans as successful. In spite of man's boldness and his invincible spirit, the psalmist trusts in the Lord, who knows "the mind and heart of man." Man is evil through and through (cf. 39:11; 62:9).

Notes

2 (3 MT) For "conspiracy" (*sôḏ*) and "noisy crowd," see the Notes on 55:14.

3 (4 MT) Whereas the NIV takes the word מָר (*mār,* "bitter") as a modifier of the arrows ("deadly arrows"), the RSV is probably more accurate in reading "bitter words." Dahood's creative translation bears out the meaning of the text: "(they) aim their poisonous remark like an arrow" (*Psalms,* 2:103).

4 (5 MT) The Syriac has a Niphal reading of *r-'-h* ("appears," "show oneself") instead of a Qal from *y-r-'* ("fear"); see Kraus: "suddenly they shoot—but one does not see them" (*Psalmen,* 2:445).

5 (6 MT) The Syriac interprets the MT's יְסַפְּרוּ (*yᵉsappᵉrû,* "they tell"; NIV, "they talk") as "and they think." Modern commentaries propose יַחְפְּרוּ (*yaḥpᵉrû,* "they dig"). See Kraus: "they dig, they place snares secretly" (*Psalmen,* 2:445).

The MT has יִרְאֶה לָמוֹ (*yir'eh lāmô,* "will see them"), but the Syriac and Jerome suggest an alternate reading: "Who will see us?" (so also NIV mg.).

III. God's Protection and Vengeance

64:7–9

[7]But God will shoot them with arrows;
suddenly they will be struck down.
[8]He will turn their own tongues against them
and bring them to ruin;
all who see them will shake their heads in scorn.

[9]All mankind will fear;
they will proclaim the works of God
and ponder what he has done.

7–8 Just as the wicked suddenly ambush the godly (v.4), so the Lord will "suddenly" bring his judgment (v.7). Their punishment will be based on the "law of retaliation" (lex talionis), that is, their sins will boomerang on them (cf. 62:12). What they had planned to do, the Lord will do to them (cf. 7:16; Prov 6:27). He will shoot (*y-r-h*) them down, as it were, with "arrows" (v.7; cf. v.3; 7:12–13). The evil they had planned to do with their "tongues" will fall back on them (v.8; cf. v.3) and bring about their "ruin." The shame they had planned to bring on the godly will come on them (cf. 22:7; 52:6–7; 59:10; Jer 48:26).

9 The bold challenge of autonomy and anarchy (v.5) has its counterpart in the fear imposed by God's judgment on mankind. The wicked asked, "Who will see us?" (*r-'-h;* NIV mg., v.5) and were unafraid (*y-r-'*) of the consequences of their acts. When all mankind (*'ādām;* cf. 58:11; Isa 40:5–6) will see the power of God, all will "fear" (*y-r-'*). Then justice will triumph! The psalmist encourages all (*'ādām,* "all mankind") to "proclaim" (*n-g-d*) and to "ponder" (*ś-k-l,* "learn from") the acts of God (cf. 2:10; Isa 41:20).

The history of redemption reveals the "works of God" in judgment of rebellious human beings. The story of redemption proclaims the mighty acts of God. Meditation on what God has done enhances one's knowledge of God. The knowledge of God becomes a comforting doctrine. The godly learn that the Lord of history will vindicate them.

Notes

7–8 (8–9 MT) Bellinger concludes that the certainty of the psalmist arises from a prophetic insight (pp. 55–57).

8 (9 MT) The NIV adopts the reading of two MSS—יִתְנוֹדַד (*yitnôdad,* "he will bring them to ruin")—which differs from the MT's יַכְשִׁילוּהוּ (*yitnōdᵃdû,* "they made to stumble"). But the third line ("all who see them will shake their heads in scorn") is a paraphrastic rendering of the MT's "everyone who sees them." It is preferable to read the last line as a transition to v.9: "and brings them to ruin. All who see them, all mankind will fear."

IV. Rejoicing and Encouragement

64:10

[10]Let the righteous rejoice in the LORD
and take refuge in him;
let all the upright in heart praise him!

10 The psalmist encourages the godly to hope in the Lord during adversity. He will vindicate his servants ("the righteous"; cf. 1:6), who are "upright in heart" (cf. 7:10; 11:2). The "righteous" are those who rely on him by finding protection with him (cf. vv.1–2; cf. 57:1; 58:10–11). The sound of their lament will give way to the sound of praise in honor of the Lord. He alone establishes justice on earth! (See the appendix to Ps 98: Yahweh Is the Divine Warrior.)

Psalm 65: The Bounty of Our Savior

The psalmist ascribes praise to the Lord in this *hymn of thanksgiving.* While it is usually classified as a psalm of public thanksgiving, Dahood may well be right in his conclusion that the latter part of the psalm contains a prayer for God's blessing. He interprets the Hebrew perfect in v.13 (*Psalms,* 2:109), translated in the NIV by a present, as a precative: "Visit the earth. . . . Drench her furrows. . . . Crown. . . . may they jubilate and sing!" (vv.9–13). The NIV maintains the hymnic character by alternating the past tense—describing God's past actions—with the present, descriptive of God's continual involvement.

The occasion of the psalm has been difficult to determine. Delitzsch (2:225) proposed to date the psalm to the retreat of the Assyrians in answer to Hezekiah's prayer (Isa 37:30). Others agree on a liturgical background but are divided as to whether the community used this psalm at the Feast of Unleavened Bread in the spring or at the Feast of Tabernacles in the fall of the year. The psalm offers no clear indicators.

The psalm has been viewed in two parts: vv.1–8 and vv.9–13. Kraus assumes that the psalm originally consisted of two separate psalms that in time coalesced into one (*Psalmen,* pp. 449–50). But there is no good reason to question the authenticity of the psalm. In our analysis the first part is further divided into three sections, the second of which is symmetric with vv.9–13:

A. In Praise of God's Presence (vv.1–3)
B. The Blessedness of God's Presence (v.4)
A′. In Praise of God's Rule (vv.5–8)
B′. The Blessedness of God's Rule (vv.9–13)

I. In Praise of God's Presence

65:1–3

For the director of music. A psalm of David. A song.

[1]Praise awaits you, O God, in Zion;
to you our vows will be fulfilled.
[2]O you who hear prayer,
to you all men will come.

3When we were overwhelmed by sins,
you forgave our transgressions.

1 In an august way the psalm calls on the community of God's people to join together for the purpose of praising the Lord. They have come to "Zion," the city of God (cf. 48:2), to fulfill their vows and to present their offerings. The "vows" are expressions of gratitude in fulfillment of God's promises; as forms of "praise" (*tehillāh;* cf. 100:4), they express joy in the Lord's kind acts (cf. 22:25; 61:8).

2–3 Praise is appropriate because of the Lord's many beneficent acts and because of his unmerited favor to his people. They had sinned grievously against him (v.3). Their guilt and its consequences (NIV, "sins," *'awōnōt,* lit., "guilts"; cf. 51:2) as well as their acts of rebellion ("transgressions"; cf. 51:1) weighed heavily on them (cf. 40:12). Yet the Lord "forgave" (v.3, *k-p-r,* "atone," "cover"; cf. "forgave," 78:38; 79:9) their sins so as to remove both the sin and the consequences of their sin. He had dealt kindly with his people (cf. vv.5, 9–13; see appendix to Ps 103: Sin and Forgiveness).

Praise and vows are forms of thanksgiving for answered "prayer" (v.2). Though undeserved, the Lord does answer prayer. The evidences of his gracious rule witness to "all men" (lit., "all flesh"; cf. Isa 40:5 ["all mankind"]; Joel 2:28 ["all people"]) and lead them to seek God's favor (cf. Isa 2:1–4; Mic 4:1–5).

Notes

For a brief discussion of the technical words and phrases in the superscription, see the Introduction.

1 (2 MT) The NIV margin gives "*befits*" as an alternate rendering for "awaits." The Hebrew word דֻּמִיָּה (*dumîyāh,* "silence") does not fit within this context, as "praise" is not silent. The ancient versions (LXX, Syr.) appear to read דֹּמִיָּה (*dōmîyāh,* "proper," feminine participle from *d-m-h*).

2 (3 MT) The LXX, Syriac, and Jerome render "you who hear prayer" as an imperative: "Hear . . . prayer." The hymnic form of the MT should be retained (Kraus, *Psalmen,* 1:449).

3 (4 MT) The prepositional phrase מֶנִּי (*mennî,* "from me") is inconsistent with the pronominal suffix in "our sins." The NIV is preferable: "[when] we [were overwhelmed by] our sins."

II. The Blessedness of God's Presence

65:4

4Blessed are those you choose
and bring near to live in your courts!
We are filled with the good things of your house,
of your holy temple.

4 The Lord hears particularly the prayers of those whom he has "chosen" (cf. Deut 7:6–7; 14:2) and whom he has brought "near" to enjoy his presence. Who are they? They could be God's priests (Num 16:5; Jer 30:21), but equally well they could be his covenant people, to whom he granted the status of a royal priesthood (Exod 19:6). The

Lord has promised to reward those who are especially devoted to him (cf. Pss 15; 24:3–4; Isa 33:15–16). Whoever is loyal to the Lord is blessed (cf. 1:1) with "good things" (cf. 23:6). God's gifts include spiritual benefits (forgiveness of sins, v.3) and the joys of life (vv.9–13). The elect enjoy God's goodness in this life and in the life to come (cf. 1 Tim 4:8). (See the appendix to Ps 132: The Ark of the Covenant and the Temple: Symbols of Yahweh's Presence and Rule; see also C.S. Lewis's intriguing essay "The Fair Beauty of the Lord" in *Reflections on the Psalms*, pp. 44–53).

III. In Praise of God's Rule

65:5–8

5 You answer us with awesome deeds of righteousness,
O God our Savior,
the hope of all the ends of the earth
and of the farthest seas,
6 who formed the mountains by your power,
having armed yourself with strength,
7 who stilled the roaring of the seas,
the roaring of their waves,
and the turmoil of the nations.
8 Those living far away fear your wonders;
where morning dawns and evening fades
you call forth songs of joy.

5–6 In hymnic language the psalmist calls on the community to reflect on God's majesty and power. He has revealed his "awesome deeds" (v.5; cf. 47:2–4; 76:7; 89:7) in delivering his people from adversity, enemies, and famine. Especially in the Exodus the Lord has revealed his great power (cf. Deut 10:21; 2 Sam 7:23; Isa 64:3; Pss 106:22; 145:6). His mighty acts inspire all with "awe," but the demonstration of his power is not arbitrary. He is righteous and he acts with "righteousness" (v.5). Righteousness as a divine perfection guarantees the establishment of God's rule. He avenges his enemies but crowns his people with glory (cf. Isa 41:10; 43:7; 49:3; 52:1; 55:5; 60:9, 21; 61:3). He is "the God of our salvation" (NIV, "O God our Savior"; cf. 1 Chron 16:35; Pss 79:9; 85:4). But more than that, he is also "the hope" (or "trust," 40:4; 71:5) of all mankind! The universality of the gospel finds expression in the phrases "all the ends of the earth" and "of the farthest seas" (v.5; cf. Isa 66:19). God's rule extends to all the earth; therefore all his creation will experience his beneficent rule. (See the appendix to Ps 78: The Mighty Acts of Yahweh.)

The hymn attributes great powers to "God Our Savior" (v.5), whose works witness to all mankind that he is God our Creator. He formed the mountains (v.6; cf. 18:7; 46:2–3; Amos 4:13) and thus demonstrated his valor (cf. 9:5–6; Amos 5:8). The great Creator-God is still "armed . . . with strength" (cf. 93:1; Isa 51:9–10), protecting his people.

7 God's rule also extends over "the seas." In pagan mythology the "sea" connoted chaotic and life-threatening powers. However, Israel knew that the Lord created everything and established his rule over the "roaring" seas and their waves (cf. 89:9; 93:3). The "nations" represent a challenge to God's sovereignty and the order of his rule (cf. 46:2–3, 6; Isa 17:12–14). The Lord has demonstrated his power to the Egyptians, the Canaanites, and the nations. The reports of his mighty acts inspired the nations with fear (*y-r-'*, v.8; related to "awesome deeds" [*nôrā'ôṯ*], v.5; cf. Exod 15:14–16; Josh 2:11). (See the appendix to Ps 5: Yahweh Is King.)

8 Great and majestic are God's "wonders" in nature and in history. Regardless of how far away people may live, they must recognize God's power and respond in "fear" (cf. 67:7). His rule extends from east ("where morning dawns"; cf. 19:5–6) to west ("evening fades"). The nations will rejoice when the Lord brings justice and peace to earth. Inchoate "songs of joy" (cf. 67:4) will replace the taunts, war cry, and rebellious acts of the nations.

Notes

7 Instead of the noun "turmoil," the LXX and Syriac have a verbal form: "the nations are in turmoil."

IV. The Blessedness of God's Rule

65:9–13

9 You care for the land and water it;
you enrich it abundantly.
The streams of God are filled with water
to provide the people with grain,
for so you have ordained it.
10 You drench its furrows
and level its ridges;
you soften it with showers
and bless its crops.
11 You crown the year with your bounty,
and your carts overflow with abundance.
12 The grasslands of the desert overflow;
the hills are clothed with gladness.
13 The meadows are covered with flocks
and the valleys are mantled with grain;
they shout for joy and sing.

9–11 All the covenantal benefits are blessings of God by which he demonstrates to his people that they are his beloved elect (cf. v.4). Water is one such blessing (v.9). People prepare the land before the fall rains by making "furrows" and "ridges" (v.10). They rejoice when after the gentle rains vegetation (NIV, "crops") grows. They rejoice even more when they see the latter rains (cf. Prov 16:15; Jer 3:3; Zech 10:1) in the spring. These rains permit the crops to mature and to produce abundant harvests (v.9). It is as if God's "carts" (i.e., clouds) overflow (v.11; cf. 36:8). When God's carts overflow, his people rejoice in his bountiful provisions. The expression "with your bounty" (lit., "your goodness") links v.11 with v.4 ("good things").

12–13 God's blessings extend to the cultivated crops and to the flocks. The comprehensiveness of his blessings receives further elaboration by the inclusion of the various geographical regions: the steppe ("desert"), the "hills," and the "valleys." So abundant is his goodness that creation (the fields and the pastures) rejoices together with God's people in the beneficence of his redemption (cf. Isa 55:12–13). Truly Yahweh is Creator and Redeemer!

Notes

9–13 The last section may be understood either as a prayer (Dahood, *Psalms,* 2:109) or as a hymn (Kraus, *Psalmen,* 1:448).

Psalm 66: Come and See What God Has Done

This psalm is composed of two independent but related units. The first unit (vv.1–12) is a hymn, which may be further divided into two separate hymns: a hymn celebrating God's great acts (vv.1–7) and a communal praise (vv.8–12). The second unit (vv.13–20) contains an individual thanksgiving psalm. It may well have been the case that originally each unit served as an independent psalm. However, in the present canonical ordering, the psalm calls on all (individuals, the community of God's people, and the nations) to join together in the universal worship of the Lord. It is impossible to reconstruct the original life-situation in which the psalm as a whole or in its components arose. The structure is in the form of three steplike strophes:

A. Universal Praise of God's Kingship (vv.1–7)
B. Community Praise of God's Kingship (vv.8–12)
C. Individual Thanksgiving (vv.13–20)

I. Universal Praise of God's Kingship

66:1–7

For the director of music. A song. A psalm.

1 Shout with joy to God, all the earth!
2 Sing the glory of his name;
make his praise glorious!
3 Say to God, "How awesome are your deeds!
So great is your power
that your enemies cringe before you.
4 All the earth bows down to you;
they sing praise to you,
they sing praise to your name." *Selah*

5 Come and see what God has done,
how awesome his works in man's behalf!
6 He turned the sea into dry land,
they passed through the waters on foot—
come, let us rejoice in him.
7 He rules forever by his power,
his eyes watch the nations—
let not the rebellious rise up against him. *Selah*

The revelation of God's acts calls forth a response, and this can be nothing less than a joyful submission to Yahweh's Lordship: "Shout with joy to God. . . . Sing the glory of his name; make his praise glorious! Say to God. . . . 'the earth bows down to you; they sing praise to you, they sing praise to your name.'. . . come, let us rejoice in him. He rules forever by his power" (vv.1–7; see appendices to Pss 78 [The Mighty Acts of Yahweh] and 122 [The Praise of Yahweh]).

1–4 The psalmist calls on the whole earth to respond with acclamation (NIV, "shout with joy," v.1; cf. 47:1; 98:4; 100:1) to God's royal majesty (vv.3–4). The occasion of the universal praise is the revelation of his "glory" (*kāḇôḏ*, twice in v.2; NIV, "glory . . . glorious"; cf. 96:3). His glory and his "power" (cf. 46:1; 63:2; 68:33–34) attend his mighty "deeds" (v.3). The works of the Great King evoke "awe" (*nôrā'*, from *y-r-'*, "fear"; cf. 65:5; Rev 15:3) and praise among the worshiping community. But God's "enemies" too will bring homage ("cringe"; cf. 18:44; 81:15), even when not from the heart. All peoples of the earth, whether willingly or unwillingly, will "bow down" (v.4; cf. Phil 2:10–11) before the Lord, singing praise to his holy name.

5–7 The "deeds" of the Lord are the object of man's praise (v.3). The Exodus and Conquest form here the historical illustrations of acts of redemption. When the Israelites came out of Egypt, they crossed through the Red Sea as on "dry ground" (v.6; cf. Exod 14:21–15:18). They had witnessed God's mighty deeds at the Red Sea and, with Moses, responded in acclamation, "The LORD will reign for ever and ever" (Exod 15:18). The Israelites rejoiced in the Lord. Having witnessed his "awesome" acts (v.5; cf. 65:5; Exod 15:11), they were assured that the Lord's "eyes watch the nations" (v.7; cf. 11:4; 33:13; Isa 27:3; 37:17). The praise of the Lord witnesses to the nations the greatness and wonder of Israel's God (v.5; cf. 46:8).

Israel's praise also contains a warning. If the enemies of the Lord, who rebel (NIV, "rebellious," v.7; cf. 68:6, 18) by thwarting God's rule, continue in their opposition and ignore the past, they too will be the object of his terror. The Lord will not tolerate any obstacle to the full revelation of his glorious rule on earth (cf. Isa 2:6–22).

Notes

For a brief discussion of the technical words and phrases in the superscription, see the Introduction.

6 The LXX has a participial form to be expected in a hymnic phrase: "he turns," instead of the MT's הָפַךְ (*hāp̄aḵ*, "he turned"). Since v.7 opens with a participle, both verses appear to be in the form of a hymn: "He turns. . . . He rules" (Kraus, *Psalmen*, 1:456).

The word "waters" (lit., "river") need not be limited to the Red Sea, as it may equally refer to the Jordan (cf. 114:3, 5), through which Israel passed at the end of their time in the wilderness (Josh 3:1–17).

The rendering "come" in the NIV assumes that the MT's שָׁם (*šām*, "there") may also have the meaning "behold" (Dahood, *Psalms*, 2:121). The change is unnecessary (cf. NEB, "there did we rejoice in him"). See 14:5.

II. Community Praise of God's Kingship

66:8–12

[8]Praise our God, O peoples,
let the sound of his praise be heard;
[9]he has preserved our lives
and kept our feet from slipping.
[10]For you, O God, tested us;
you refined us like silver.
[11]You brought us into prison
and laid burdens on our backs.
[12]You let men ride over our heads;
we went through fire and water,
but you brought us to a place of abundance.

8 The goodness of God in the history of redemption occasions a renewed outburst of praise. The community of God's people invokes the "peoples" to listen to the good news of what the Lord has done and to "praise" (*b-r-k,* "bless") his name for his new acts of redemption together with Israel.

9–12 God's people confess that the Lord is sovereign in testing and refining his people like silver (v.10; cf. 17:3; 26:2; Prov 17:3; Isa 1:25). The trials are likened to "prison" (v.11; *meṣûḏāh,* "net" or "mountain stronghold," KB³, 2:588), a metaphor for alienation and duress. They endured great affliction, as if "burdens" (*mû'āqāh,* a *hapax legomenon,* probably meaning "hardship"; see KB³, 2:529) had been placed on their "backs." Sovereign protection was removed from his people, and they were given over to their adversaries (v.12; cf. Isa 51:23). The Lord, nevertheless, had permitted all these things ("fire and water"; cf. Isa 43:2) to take place. It seemed as if mortal man (*'enôš* ; NIV, "men") had prevailed.

The duress, however, was for the purpose of trial. During the testing God's people looked for God's grace with greater zeal. He was faithful, as he "preserved" (v.9a) them (lit., "who keeps us in life," a hymnic participial phrase). He does not permit his own to succumb to the trials (v.9b; cf. 37:24; 1 Cor 10:13). However, faith is not faith unless it has been tried like silver and gold. Persevering faith will receive its own rewards (1 Peter 1:7). Having led his people through adversity, the Lord brings them into "a place of abundance" or "a spacious place" (v.12; cf. 18:19; 23:4–6; 119:45).

III. Individual Thanksgiving

66:13–20

[13]I will come to your temple with burnt offerings
and fulfill my vows to you—
[14]vows my lips promised and my mouth spoke
when I was in trouble.
[15]I will sacrifice fat animals to you
and an offering of rams;
I will offer bulls and goats. *Selah*

[16]Come and listen, all you who fear God;
let me tell you what he has done for me.
[17]I cried out to him with my mouth;
his praise was on my tongue.

[18]If I had cherished sin in my heart,
the Lord would not have listened;
[19]but God has surely listened
and heard my voice in prayer.
[20]Praise be to God,
who has not rejected my prayer
or withheld his love from me!

13–16 As a personal expression of gratitude, the last portion of this psalm leads the individual worshiper to personalize the experience of God's people throughout the history of redemption. The psalmist speaks of himself, as he comes to the temple to present burnt offerings of "fat animals" (vv.13, 15; cf. 40:6) in fulfillment of his "vows" (v.14; cf. 65:1; Lev 22:21), as he praises the Lord before "all . . . who fear God" (v.16; cf. 34:7, 9), and as he tells the story of the acts of deliverance from trouble ("what he has done for me"). Those who "fear" (*y-r-'*) God include Israelites as well as believers from the nations or the God-fearers (v.16; cf. Acts 2:5). Thus the history of redemption includes both the experience of the community of God's people as well as the individual acts of deliverance (cf. 22:22; 34:11–12).

A vow often arose in a period of adversity, when the believer expressed his devotion to the Lord in an action to be accomplished as soon as God had answered one's prayer (cf. Judg 11:30–40; Jonah 2:9). The nature of the sacrifice was carefully specified (Lev 22:18–21), lest inferior animals be presented for offering. The qualifying animals the psalmist makes mention of are rams, bulls, and goats (v.15; cf. Isa 1:11). The largess of the vow is unusual. The psalmist apparently speaks here as a representative of the people who have come together collectively to present their offerings out of devotion to the Lord (Kirkpatrick, p. 371).

17–20 The celebration of deliverance from trouble includes (1) lament ("I cried out," v.17a); (2) a declaration of commitment or fidelity ("his praise was on my tongue," v.17b; cf. 10:7); (3) a declaration of innocence in suffering ("if I had cherished sin," v.18; cf. 17:1–2; 18:20–21; 59:3–4; John 9:31); and (4) praise ("God has surely listened," v.19; cf. v.8; "praise" [*b-r-k*], v.20; cf. 28:6; 31:21; 68:19, 35).

Psalm 67: Grant Your Blessing on All Your Creation

The psalm contains elements characteristic of the psalms of *blessing* and of the psalms ascribing kingship to Yahweh. Its life setting is difficult to determine. Since it contains a prayer for God's blessing (v.1), it seems unlikely that it was a "thanksgiving day" (harvest festival) song or more particularly a harvest festival song associated with the Feast of Tabernacles. S. Weissblueth ("On Psalm 67," *Beth Mikra* 23 [1978]: 458–61 [Heb.]) connects Psalms 65–68 as expressive of God's providence and explains this psalm as God's care for Israel, the nations, and all his creation.

The meter is regular (3 + 3), except for v.5 (3 + 2, 2 + 3) and v.7 (2 + 2 + 2) (see Introduction: Rhyme, meter, and strophe). Frank Cross ("Notes on a Canaanite Psalm in the OT," BASOR 117 [1950]: 19–21) has shown that the variation in meter is a stylistic feature of Ugaritic poetry. Based on the meter and vocabulary, the high degree of parallels with Ugaritic, and the cultic coloring, Helen G. Jefferson ("The Date of Psalm LXVII," VetTest 12 [1962]: 201–5) has argued that Psalm 67 is preexilic.

The evidence for the early date of the psalm challenges the critical supposition that Israel's missionary outlook developed after the Exile. Clearly the psalm is a missionary psalm, since it looks forward to the rule of God over Jews and Gentiles (cf. Acts 28:28). For an eschatological interpretation, see W. Beuken, "Psalm LXVII: Structure and Drama," *Old Testament Studies* 21 (1981): 38–54.

Two refrains (vv.3, 5) function as an "envelope" containing further elaboration of God's kingdom and his plan for the nations (v.4). The beginning (vv.1–2) and end (vv.6–7) also form an inclusion. The structure of the psalm is as follows:

A. Prayer for God's Blessing (vv.1–2)
  B. Prayer for Inclusion of the Nations (v.3)
    C. Prayer for the Rule of God (v.4)
  B′. Prayer for Inclusion of the Nations (v.5)
A′. Prayer for God's Blessing (vv.6–7)

I. Prayer for God's Blessing and for the Inclusion of the Nations

67:1–3

For the director of music. With stringed instruments. A psalm. A song.

1 May God be gracious to us and bless us
  and make his face shine upon us, *Selah*
2 that your ways may be known on earth,
  your salvation among all nations.

3 May the peoples praise you, O God;
  may all the peoples praise you.

The blessing, reminiscent of the priestly benediction (Num 6:24–26), pertains to three aspects of blessing: (1) protection (Num 6:24); (2) favor (grace, v.25); and (3) peace (v.26). The allusion to the benediction was sufficient to remind Israel of God's blessings in their totality. God's blessings brought to fulfillment particular promises. The change from "you" (second masc. sing. in Num 6:24–25) to "us" (first common pl.) applies the priestly benediction to each individual. The psalmist encourages God's people to personalize the priestly benediction on themselves "to us . . . us . . . upon us" (cf. Num 6:24–26, "you").

1 God is the source of all benefits. His grace is the basis of his blessing, an undeserved expression of his love for his children. The blessing of God makes life on earth not only possible but even enjoyable. He removes the curse and judgment characteristic of the created world since the Fall (cf. Rom 8:20–21). He delights in his own ("upon us"). An Oriental monarch revealed in his facial expression either his pleasure or displeasure with the party that sought an audience with him. Similarly, God, the Great King, assures his own that he receives them and cares for them with joy.

2 The purpose of God's blessing is not selfish enjoyment of his love by his people. Rather, all the blessings of God are tokens of his presence and favor so that the nations may "know" (*y-d-'*) his way. Knowledge of the way of the Lord is that intimate acquaintance with the God of Israel. From observing God's blessing on his people, the nations should be able to deduce his royal sovereignty and acknowledge Israel's God as God. Thus they too may enjoy the fullness of his "salvation" (*yᵉšû'āh*). The word *y^ešû'āh* ("deliverance," "victory"; cf. 3:2) is rich, as it pertains to all the benefits of God: his kingship, rule, blessings, and promises (cf. 98:3; Isa 52:10).

3 The blessing of God gives rise to praise (vv.3, 5). The praise of Israel lies in the expectation that the nations too will join in the praise of God. The praise of God is in response to his saving involvement with his people. When salvation is extended to the nations, they too will join in praising God.

Notes

For a brief discussion of the technical words and phrases in the superscription, see the Introduction.

2 (3 MT) The change from "your ways" to "his ways" (see NEB) is supported in some Hebrew MSS and the Syriac Peshitta. The NIV reading ("your ways") is preferable in view of "your salvation" in the next colon.

II. Prayer for the Rule of God

67:4

> 4 May the nations be glad and sing for joy,
> for you rule the peoples justly
> and guide the nations of the earth. *Selah*

4 God relates to his world, and the nature of his rule in creation and history unveils his wonderful character. The psalms ascribing kingship to the Lord (93–99) speak of his sovereign, universal rule, characterized by justice (*mîšôr*), joy, and peace. As he rules the nations, he does not exclude them from sharing in the joy of his presence. The nations must acknowledge God as the Giver of all good things, as the Ruler of the universe, and as the One who has revealed his "way" to Israel. To Israel he granted his oracles (Rom 3:2; 9:4–5); and through the Jews came the Savior, Jesus Christ, as the final revelation of the "way" of God (Rom 9:5; cf. Acts 4:12; 9:2). As the gospel goes out to the nations, they must come to the Father through the Son. Since Pentecost Israel's ancient prayer is being fulfilled more magnificently than they could ever have imagined. However, Israel itself does not share in large numbers in Christ's salvation (Rom 11:25). The prayer of the Christian should include an earnest plea that the Jews too may acknowledge God in Jesus Christ so that the kingdom of God may be more greatly evident (Rom 11:26–27).

Notes

4 (5 MT) The NIV follows the MT: "for you rule the peoples justly and guide the nations of the earth." The LXX divides the second colon into two by the addition of "the world with righteousness" after "rule": "for you rule the world with righteousness, the peoples justly, and guide the nations of the earth." The JB gives a syntactic rendering: "since you dispense true justice to the peoples on earth you rule all nations" (cf. 9:8).

III. Prayer for Inclusion of the Nations

67:5

5 May the peoples praise you, O God;
may all the peoples praise you.

5 For v.5 see the comment on v.3 above.

IV. Prayer for God's Blessing

67:6–7

6 Then the land will yield its harvest,
and God, our God, will bless us.
7 God will bless us,
and all the ends of the earth will fear him.

6–7 The psalm concludes with a prayer for God's blessings. The prayer for blessing (vv.1, 4, 7) reiterates the element of "hope" in God's universal rule. Without pointing to the Messiah, the psalm anticipates a glorious messianic era in which Jews and Gentiles share in the glorious presence of God. When God blesses his people, it is with the goal of provoking the nations to jealousy so that they too might come to know him, share in his blessings, and have reason to praise him. Verse 7 forms a inclusion with vv.1–2:

A. Prayer: "Bless us" (v.1)
  B. Effect: "that your ways may be known [*y-d-'*] on earth, your salvation among *all nations*" (v.2)
A′. Prayer: "Bless us" (v.7a)
  B′. Effect: "and *all the ends of the earth* will fear [*y-r-'*] him" (v.7b)

The phrases "all nations" (v.2) and "all the ends of the earth" (v.7) are synonymous (cf. 2:8; 22:27–28; Jer 16:19), as are the verbs "be known" (*y-d-'*, v.2) and "fear" (*y-r-'*, v.7; cf. 2 Chron 6:33; Ps 9:20). Through the process of empirical observation, all must come to the wise conclusion that the God of Israel is King (cf. 2 Chron 6:33; Ps 22:27–28).

Since the coming of Christ, the roles of the Jews and Gentiles have been reversed. The church of Christ as the people of God is largely composed of Gentiles who have come to know God's "ways" in salvation, in the kingdom of Christ, and in his sovereign rule in the affairs of this world. Our joy is now full in Jesus Christ. We have reason to sing for joy, as our heavenly Father blesses us by providing for our needs (Matt 6:25–34). Our prayer must always include a petition to the Father that Israel too may fear him by believing that Jesus is the Messiah. Then "all the ends of the earth will fear him," and the goal of the messianic kingdom will be closer.

Notes

6 (7 MT) The perfect נָתְנָה (*nāṯ*[e]*nāh*, lit., "has given") should be translated as future (so NIV, "will yield"). The first colon is a quotation from Lev 26:4, in which context—"and the land will yield its harvest"—is one example of God's blessings. The reference to Lev 26:4 serves as a reminder of all of God's blessings with which he will bless his own: rain, food, peace, and his presence (Lev 26:3–13).

Psalm 68: God Is a Father to the Oppressed

This psalm has occasioned extensive discussion on its structure, unity, and purpose. The variety has led some to treat the psalm as a collection of songs (cf. W.F. Albright, "A Catalogue of Early Hebrew Poems [Psalm LXVIII]," HUCA 23 [1950/51]: 1–39) that have been brought together into one psalm. Kraus (*Psalmen*, pp. 469–71) stresses the unity of purpose. A.A. Anderson considers the best explanation the libretto approach, according to which the units of the psalm were sung in the progression of the festival procession (1:481). Similar is John Gray's emphasis ("A Cantata of the Autumn Festival: Psalm lxiii," JSS 22 [1977]: 2–26) that this psalm is a cantata in twelve parts, celebrating covenant renewal. John Day too favors the covenant-renewal approach ("The Pre-Deuteronomic Allusions to the Covenant in Hosea and Psalm lxxxviii," VetTest 36 [1986]: 1–12). The occasion itself may have been the autumnal festival (A.A. Anderson, 1:482) or any other festival procession. The variety of motifs do not permit much concurrence. The genre of the psalm is equally debatable. The dominant hymnic elements led Dahood to call this a "triumphal hymn" (*Psalms*, 2:133). The psalm includes prayers (vv.1–3, 28–31), hymnic praise (vv.4–6, 19–20, 32–35), thanksgiving (vv.7–10, 15–18), and oracles (vv.11–14, 21–23). If there is one unifying theme, it is centered around Yahweh the Divine Warrior, who comes to deliver his people in Mount Zion (see appendix to Ps 98: Yahweh Is the Divine Warrior). Kirkpatrick expressed this well: "The theme of this magnificent Psalm is the march of God to victory. It traces the establishment of His kingdom in the past; it looks forward to the defeat of all opposition in the future until all the kingdoms of the world own the God of Israel as their Lord and pay Him homage" (p. 375).

The structure reflects a closure (AA′) and a symmetric development:

A. Prayer for God's Coming as the Divine Warrior (vv.1–3)
  B. In Praise of Divine Vindication (vv.4–6)
    C. A Reflection of the Divine Warrior (vv.7–18)
  B′. In Praise of Divine Vindication (vv.19–20)
    C′. An Oracle From the Divine Warrior (vv.21–23)
A′. Joyful Anticipation of God's Coming as the Divine Warrior (vv.24–35)

(For a careful study on the exegesis, genre, literary structure, and *Sitz im Leben*, see J. Vlaardingerbroek, *Psalm 68* [Amsterdam: Free University, 1973]; J.P. Lepeau, "Psalm 68: an Exegetical and Theological Study," Ph.D. diss., University of Iowa, 1981.)

I. Prayer for God's Coming as the Divine Warrior

68:1–3

For the director of music. Of David. A psalm. A song.

1 May God arise, may his enemies be scattered;
may his foes flee before him.
2 As smoke is blown away by the wind,
may you blow them away;
as wax melts before the fire,
may the wicked perish before God.
3 But may the righteous be glad
and rejoice before God;
may they be happy and joyful.

The psalm begins with a prayer suggestive of Moses' prayer when the ark of the covenant went ahead of God's people in the desert (Num 10:35). The ark was the symbol of God's presence and protection and served as the symbolic throne of the Divine Warrior (see appendix to Ps 132: The Ark of the Covenant and the Temple: Symbols of Yahweh's Presence and Rule). In the form of the ancient prayer, the covenant community raises its voice to the Lord to act, as in the past, against the enemies.

1–2 In God's presence ("before him," v.1) no foe can stand. The impotence of the opposition is likened to "smoke" (v.2; cf. 37:20; 102:3; Hos 13:3) and to "wax" (cf. 97:5; Mic 1:4). The "wind" (interpretative addition, not in MT), "smoke," and "fire" are manifestations of God's presence (theophany; cf. Exod 19:18; 20:18; Isa 6:4). For a study on theophany in Psalms 18; 50; 68; 77; and 97, see A. Weiser, "Zur Frage nach dem Beziehungen der Psalmen zum Kult: Die Darstellung der Theophanie in den Psalmen und im Festkult," in *Festschrift für Alfred Bertholet zum 80. Geburtstag*, edd. Walter Baumgartner, Otto Eissfeldt, Karl Elliger, and Leonhard Rost (Tübingen: Mohr, 1950), pp. 513–31. Von Rad observes that "the highest beauty in all creation was Yahweh's condescending and entering into historical existence. This comes to expression first and foremost in the description of theophanies" (OTT, 1:366).

3 The theophany does not instill "the righteous" (*ṣaddîqîm;* see 1:6) with dread. Instead, the perishing of the "wicked" (v.2; cf. 1:5–6) is an answer to their repeated prayers. They wait for the coming of the Divine Warrior to avenge them. They will rejoice greatly in that hour of vindication (cf. 2 Thess 1:5).

Notes

For a brief discussion of the technical words and phrases in the superscription, see the Introduction.

2 (3 MT) The MT's כְּהִנְדֹּף (*kehindōp̱*, "as driving") is a mixed form (GKC, par. 51k) that probably should be read as a Niphal infinitive construct: "as is blown [driven] . . . may you blow." BHS proposes a consistent Niphal reading: "as [smoke] is blown, may they be blown"; see "like drifting smoke they are driven" (Dahood, *Psalms*, 2:130). This seems to fit with "as wax melts before the fire, may the wicked perish" (v.2b).

II. In Praise of Divine Vindication

68:4–6

4 Sing to God, sing praise to his name,
  extol him who rides on the clouds—
his name is the LORD—
  and rejoice before him.
5 A father to the fatherless, a defender of widows,
  is God in his holy dwelling.
6 God sets the lonely in families,
  he leads forth the prisoners with singing;
  but the rebellious live in a sun-scorched land.

The prayerful hope that the righteous may "be glad [*ś-m-ḥ*] . . . rejoice [*ʿ-l-ṣ*] . . . be happy [*ś-w-ś*] and joyful [*ś-m-ḥ*]" (v.3; three roots) goes over in an invitation to praise the Lord ("sing [*š-y-r*], . . . sing praise [*z-m-r*] . . . extol [*s-l-l*] . . . rejoice [*ʿ-l-z*]," v.4; four roots; cf. Exod 15:21; Pss 33:3; 44:8; 66:4; 96:1), followed by the rationale for acclamation (vv.5–6).

4 The community is convoked to celebrate the acts of divine vindication. To this end they remember what "God," the one "who rides on the clouds," whose name is "the LORD" (*Yah*), has done for his people. The focus is on the "name" of the God of Israel, Yahweh (abbreviated as Yah, as in Eli*j[y]ah* and hallelu*j[y]ah*). He revealed his name to Israel (Exod 3:15), signifying his fidelity to fulfilling his promises (cf. Exod 6:6–8). This God is all that Israel needs. By the ascription "who rides on the clouds," the psalmist contrasts the all-sufficiency of the God of Israel with the powers of Baal whom the Canaanites worshiped as "the Rider on the clouds." They attributed to him rain, fertility, and prosperity. Here the "clouds" signify the chariot of God racing through the sky bringing blessing and curse, vindication and vengeance (cf. 18:10–19).

5–6 From "his holy dwelling" in heaven (v.5; cf. Deut 26:15; Jer 25:30; Zech 2:13), the Lord watches the families of man. His eyes focus on the destitute and the oppressed, whose rights are trampled by the powerful and the rich. Because Israel experienced oppression in Egypt, Israel's laws specified how they should regard the rights of the powerless (cf. Exod 22:22–24; Pss 10:14; 146:9; Isa 1:17, 23; Mal 3:5; James 1:27).

In hymnic language (nominal and participial clauses), the psalm refers to the Lord as "father," "defender" (vindicator, *dayyan;* cf. 72:2), "restorer" (NIV, "sets," v.6), and the Redeemer ("he leads forth"). He is the God who acts on behalf of those who look for protection and vindication: the fatherless, the widows, the lonely (NEB, "the friendless"), and the exiles ("prisoners"; cf. 69:33; Lam 3:33–36). Wherever there are oppressed people, whether they belong to the people of God or not, the Lord's rule brings transformation from injustice to justice and from oppression to vindication. He changes sorrow to "singing."

Those deprived of their rights taste the Lord's goodness in vindication, because the Lord hates "the rebellious" (v.6). The exile of the wicked, proud, and arrogant to live "in a sun-scorched land" is in clear contrast to the redemptive acts of deliverance and restoration (vv.5–6). From this context it is ambiguous whether the term "the rebellious" denotes all the wicked or only those from within the borders of Israel.

Notes

4 (5 MT) Verses 3–4 contain no less than seven synonyms for joyful laudation, one of which ("extol," from *s-l-l*) is quite unique. The root *s-l-l* usually denotes the act of constructing a road or highway (cf. Isa 57:14; 62:10) but is used here metaphorically with the sense of "lift up" or "extol." The sense of preparation in anticipation of the Lord may still be present, as suggested by KB's "prepare a road (while singing)" (p. 659; cf. "pave the highway," Dahood, *Psalms*, 2:130).

Most recently John Day has expressed his difference with the widespread mythopoetic imagery in favor of "Rider through the deserts" (*God's Conflict With the Dragon and the Sea. Echoes of Canaanite Myth in the Old Testament* [Cambridge: Cambridge University Press, 1985], pp. 31–32; cf. NIV mg.). But he too admits that the psalmist may conceive of him as riding on the clouds through the deserts!

6 (7 MT) The phrase בַּכּוֹשָׁרוֹת (*bakkôšārôṯ*, "with singing") is a *hapax legomenon* in Hebrew. A Ugaritic cognate suggests the meaning "sing" (Dahood, *Psalms*, 2:137), but the usual meaning of the root *k-š-r* (from which we get "kosher") also makes sense: "deal properly with," as in "safe and sound" (NEB).

III. A Reflection of the Divine Warrior (vv.7–18)

The prayer and the hopeful praise (vv.1–6) receive greater intensity as the community reflects on the Lord's past acts on behalf of Israel. They reflect on the wilderness experience, when God went ahead of his people (v.7; see the allusion to the ark of the covenant in v.1). They thank the Lord for having guided them through the wilderness into Canaan (vv.7–10), for having given them the Land of Promise (vv.11–14), and for having made his abode on Mount Zion (vv.15–18). The thanksgiving encompasses several major moments of the history of redemption: (1) Exodus, Wilderness Wandering, Mount Sinai, and settlement (vv.7–10); (2) Conquest (vv.11–14); and (3) the establishment of the theocracy in Jerusalem (vv.15–18) (see the appendix to Ps 46: Zion Theology).

A. *Exodus, Wilderness Wandering, Mount Sinai, and Settlement* 68:7–10

7 When you went out before your people, O God,
when you marched through the wasteland, *Selah*
8 the earth shook,
the heavens poured down rain,
before God, the One of Sinai,
before God, the God of Israel.
9 You gave abundant showers, O God;
you refreshed your weary inheritance.
10 Your people settled in it,
and from your bounty, O God, you provided for the poor.

7–8 The Lord is the Divine Warrior. In great power (cf. Exod 13:21–22) he led Israel out of Egypt and through the desert ("wasteland," v.7; cf. Deut 32:10). He appeared at Mount Sinai in a theophany (v.8), attended by the phenomena of earthquake and storm (cf. Exod 19:16–17; Judg 5:4–5; Ps 18:7–15; Hab 3:3–7). Awesome is his coming. The earth quakes and heaven is full of rain, thunder, and lightning (cf. 77:17–18). The Lord is the God of Mount Sinai by revelation and the God of Israel by covenant (cf. Exod 24:8, 10; Judg 5:5).

9–10 As Israel's covenant King, the Lord also provided for them by the "abundant showers" (v.9; lit., "rain of abundances") of water, manna, and meat (cf. Exod 16:4; Ps 78:24, 27) in the desert and continued to shower the land of Canaan with his blessed rains (cf. 65:9–13). The phraseology "weary inheritance" is ambiguous. Is the inheritance a reference to the people or to the land of Canaan? It seems preferable to take the primary reference as the people whom the psalmist calls "your family" or "band" (cf. 2 Sam 23:13: "band of Philistines"; cf. Dahood, *Psalms*, 2:140; NIV, "your people," v.10) and the secondary reference to the land. The Lord provided abundantly for his people; he established them ("settled") in the land and provided bountifully ("from your bounty," lit., "from your goodness"; cf. 23:6) for all "the poor" (*'ānî*), that is, those who had been afflicted in Egypt.

B. *Conquest of Canaan and Subjugation of the Nations*

68:11–14

11 The Lord announced the word,
and great was the company of those who
proclaimed it:
12 "Kings and armies flee in haste;
in the camps men divide the plunder.
13 Even while you sleep among the campfires,
the wings of ⌊my⌋ dove are sheathed with silver,
its feathers with shining gold."
14 When the Almighty scattered the kings in the land,
it was like snow fallen on Zalmon.

11 The Lord is the Divine Warrior. He spoke and his oracle was realized in the conquest of the land. The women celebrate his great acts in song and dance (cf. v.25; Exod 15:20–21; Judg 5; 11:34; 1 Sam 18:6–7).

12–13 The women sing of how the kings of Canaan fled with their armies, leaving their spoils behind (v.12; cf. Judg 5:28–30). Among the spoils were precious objects of art: a dove covered with silver and gold (v.13). The men who stayed behind did not share in the spoils, whereas the women of the warriors shared in the booty. This interpretation varies a little from the NIV translation, but the reader should be aware that the MT here is difficult in translation as well as interpretation (see Notes).

14 The victory of "the Almighty" (*Shaddai*, see Exod 6:3; only here and in 91:1 in the Psalms) is so great that it resembles "snow" on Mount Zalmon. The identity of Zalmon is debatable. According to Judges 9:48, Zalmon ("the Dark One") is one of the mountains by Shechem. Modern commentators favor the identification with Jebel Druze, to the east of the Bashan (v.15; see Albright, "A Catalogue," p. 23), whose mountains are dark colored from the volcanic rock. In either case the psalmist is metaphorically highlighting the power of the Lord, who is victorious in destroying the opposition. The corpses of the victims and their weaponry are lying like scattered snowflakes on the mountains.

Notes

11 (12 MT) The subject of the NIV reading "the company of those who proclaimed it" is ambiguous. However, little doubt exists in the MT, where the feminine plural participle מְבַשְּׂרוֹת (*mᵉḇaśśᵉrôṯ*, "who proclaim the good news") suggests that the women were in view.

12–13 (13–14 MT) These verses contain some problematic phrases. First, the phrase נְוַת בַּיִת (*nᵉwaṯ bayiṯ*, "abode"—or "pasture"—"of the house"; cf. Dahood: "the country's pasture land," *Psalms*, 2:131) could be explained as a participle: "the one dwelling at home" (cf. RSV, "the women at home"). BHS proposes "and in the abode of the house spoil is divided." Second, the agreement with the verb also has occasioned some problems. The NIV emends the third feminine verbal form—תְּחַלֵּק (*tᵉḥallēq*, "she divides")—corresponding with "abode" to a masculine plural: "men divide"; cf. NEB, "the women in your tents divide the spoil." Kraus reads a dual imperfect third person masculine singular: "spoil is divided" (*Psalmen*, 1:465, 467). Third, the meaning of v.13 is uncertain: "Even while you sleep/stay among the sheepfolds/saddlebags [NIV's "campfires" has no linguistic justification], the wings of a dove [NIV, "(my) dove"] are sheathed with silver, its feathers with shining gold." Taking our lead from Judg 5:16, 30, we interpret these verses in praise of the warriors who returned from battle laden with gold and silver, whereas those who stayed behind lost out. The NEB also makes good sense: "O mighty host, will you linger among the sheepfolds / while the women in your tents divide the spoil—an image of a dove, its wings sheathed in silver / and its pinions in yellow gold." Edward Lipinski concludes that the "dove" was a Canaanite cult object ("La Colombe du Ps LXVIII 14," VetTest 23 [1973]: 365–68). Zahavi Beilin came to quite a different conclusion. The dove is symbolic of Yahweh's revelation at Mount Sinai ("The Wings of the Dove Are Covered With Silver and Her Pinions of Gold [Ps 68:14]," *Beth Mikra* 53 [1973]: 227). Christopher Begg interprets the dove in the light of the Sumerian "Vulture Stele," according to which the dove could have had a place in the covenant-making ceremonies ("The Messenger Dove in Ps 68, 12–14," *Ephemerides Theologicae Lovanienses* 63 [1987]: 117–18; id., "The Covenantal Dove in Psalm lxxiv 19–20," VetTest 37 [1987]: 78–81).

C. *The Establishment of the Theocracy in Jerusalem*

68:15–18

15 The mountains of Bashan are majestic mountains;
rugged are the mountains of Bashan.
16 Why gaze in envy, O rugged mountains,
at the mountain where God chooses to reign,
where the LORD himself will dwell forever?
17 The chariots of God are tens of thousands
and thousands of thousands;
the Lord ⌊has come⌋ from Sinai into his sanctuary.
18 When you ascended on high,
you led captives in your train;
you received gifts from men,
even from the rebellious—
that you, O LORD God, might dwell there.

15–16 Turning his eyes from Mount Zalmon to Mount Bashan ("the Golan Heights"), east of the Sea of Galilee, bordered on the north by the majestic Mount Hermon, the psalmist adumbrates the glory of Mount Bashan, expressing poetically that the glory of Mount Bashan is dwarfed by the holiness of Mount Zion: "the mountain of God [emphatic] is [like] Mount Bashan, a mountain of many peaks is Mount Bashan" (lit. rendering of v.15). The Canaanites associated the dwelling place of their gods with high and lofty mountains, and Mount Bashan qualified from its natural endowments as a primary candidate for being the center of Yahweh's kingship on earth. However, the will of God expressed itself differently from human reasoning. The psalmist dramatizes the grandeur of Mount Bashan as well as her jealousy. He personifies Mount Bashan as looking with "envy" (v.16) at Mount Zion, because the Lord chose to establish his "reign" there (cf. 1 Kings 8:12–17; Ps 132:13–14).

17 The Lord who went ahead of his people (v.7) is portrayed as surrounded by an entourage of thousands of "chariots," representative of his heavenly servants (cf. Deut 33:2; 2 Kings 6:15). He who revealed his "holiness" (*qōdeš;* NIV, "his sanctuary") on Mount Sinai is "the Lord" (*Adonai,* cf. v.11) who also went ahead of his people to protect and to bless them (vv.7–10).

18 On the victorious completion of the Exodus, the Wilderness Wanderings, and the Conquest, the Lord returned as it were to heaven ("on high") to celebrate his kingship on earth (cf. 47:5–7). The Divine Warrior had successfully subjugated the enemies ("the rebellious"), having made them "captives" (cf. Judg 5:12) and having received tribute from the conquered nations (cf. v.6c). In commemoration of his mighty acts, he chose Jerusalem among the mountains to establish his abode "where the LORD himself will dwell forever" (v.16). (For a NT application of this truth, see 2 Cor 2:14 and Eph 4:8.)

Notes

---

17 (18 MT) The MT is enigmatic: "the Lord among them, Sinai in holiness [or 'in sanctuary']." This could mean that Mount Sinai is the Lord's sanctuary (see Dahood: "who created Sinai as his sanctuary," *Psalms,* 2:131) or that Mount Sinai is "holy" or that "the Lord came in holiness from Sinai" (NEB; Kraus, *Psalmen,* 1:465). Of these I favor the approach of the NEB, because the Lord revealed his holy presence at Mount Sinai (cf. Deut 33:2).

IV. In Praise of Divine Vindication

68:19–20

19 Praise be to the Lord, to God our Savior,
who daily bears our burdens. *Selah*
20 Our God is a God who saves;
from the Sovereign LORD comes escape from death.

19–20 The comfort of God's presence occasions a renewal of praise. He is "the Lord" (*Adonai,* vv.19–20 [NIV, "Sovereign"]; cf. vv.11, 17, 22, 32), who promised deliverance and victory (v.11) and has come with his tens of thousands of angels from Mount Sinai to dwell in Jerusalem (v.17). This same Master of the universe is "God our Savior." His nature sets in motion the history of redemption, because "our God is a God who saves" (v.20).

For the believing community God is "the God" (*El*, repeated three times: "to God. . . . Our God . . . a God," vv.19–20). His rule extends over all angels in heaven and to all the earth; he is Lord (*Adonai*). In his rule he vindicates and protects. The activity of protection and vindication finds expression in the repeated use of the root *y-š-ʿ* ("save"): "God our Savior" (v.19; lit., "the God of our salvation") and "a God who saves" (v.20; lit., "God of salvations"; cf. 44:4: "who decrees victories"). He is known to the believing community by his "name," Yahweh ("LORD," v.20; cf. v.4). However, even in his closeness to his covenant people, he is still "the Lord" (*Adonai*), rendered in the NIV "the Sovereign LORD" ("Yahweh Adonai," v.20; cf. 71:5, 16; 73:28; 109:21; 140:7; 141:8).

The people of God "praise" (*b-r-k*, v.19; cf. 104:1; Judg 5:2, 9) him because of the evidences of his care. He shows a daily vigilance over his people. He does not carry merely their burdens, but he cares for them (see NEB, "He carries us day by day"; cf. Exod 19:4; Deut 1:31; Ps 28:9; Isa 40:11). He continually leads his people out of "death" (v.20), as he did at the time of the Exodus. The Hebrew root *y-ṣ-ʾ* ("go out") is used for the Exodus (cf. v.7) and here for the deliverance ("escape") from death. If "death" is taken as a personification of Mot ("death"), the Canaanite god of death, then the psalmist proclaims that Israel's El ("God") is victorious over Mot. Again this may be construed as a polemical note against Canaanite mythology. The God of revelation and history is the Incomparable One!

V. An Oracle From the Divine Warrior

68:21–23

21 Surely God will crush the heads of his enemies,
the hairy crowns of those who go on in their sins.
22 The Lord says, "I will bring them from Bashan;
I will bring them from the depths of the sea,
23 that you may plunge your feet in the blood of your foes,
while the tongues of your dogs have their share."

21 The community also rejoices in having received an "oracle" from the Lord (vv.22–23). They receive comfort from his word, sing, and have hope. The word of the Lord has opened a new vision of his victorious rule. The godly ones believe that the Lord will avenge the enemy. The acts of vengeance are expressed poetically by reference to "the heads of the enemies" (cf. 110:6; Hab 3:13–14) and to "the hairy crowns." By metonymy "the heads" and "the crowns" stand for the enemy. Though the language of vengeance is strong, the acts of the enemies were also vile. After all, they have hated the Lord of the universe and have committed shameful acts.

22–23 The oracle of God pertains to the enemy as well as Israel. The object of the verbal phrases "I will bring" (twice, v.22) is left undefined in Hebrew. Since the thrust of the oracle is comfort in adversity and an assurance of God's vindication, the enemies are the likely objects in v.22: "I will bring them [i.e., the enemies] from Bashan; I will bring them from the depths of the sea." Though the enemy might trouble Israel on land or at sea, though they might escape to the escarpments of the rocks or try to hide at sea, the Lord will bring them down (cf. Amos 9:2–3). He will share his victory with his people, to whom the words of comfort in v.23 are addressed. The shocking language reflects poetically the language of war and victory (cf. 58:10).

Notes

22 (23 MT) Dahood personifies the geographical references and sets the text in a mythological context: "I stifled the Serpent, muzzled the Deep Sea" (*Psalms*, 2:131; see NEB, "I will return from the Dragon, I will return from the depths of the sea"). F. Charles Fensham reads: "From the hole of the snake (or Bashan) I will bring back, / I will bring back from the depths of the sea (or *Yam*)" in "Ps 68:23 in the Light of the Recently Discovered Ugaritic Tablets," JNES 19 [1960]: 293). For a criticism see Day, *God's Conflict*, pp. 113–19.

VI. Joyful Anticipation of God's Coming as the Divine Warrior (vv.24–35)

A. *Processional Hymn*

68:24–27

24 Your procession has come into view, O God,
the procession of my God and King into the sanctuary.
25 In front are the singers, after them the musicians;
with them are the maidens playing tambourines.
26 Praise God in the great congregation;
praise the LORD in the assembly of Israel.
27 There is the little tribe of Benjamin, leading them,
there the great throng of Judah's princes,
and there the princes of Zebulun and of Naphtali.

24–27 The oracle inspires the people with greater hope as they await his "procession" (v.24). Ahead of everybody is the Lord, whom the psalmist addresses personally as "my God and King" (cf. 44:4; 74:12). Previously the whole community was involved in thanksgiving, as they celebrated the mighty acts of "God our Savior. . . . Our God" (vv.19–20). This time the personal pronoun ("my"; MT: "my God and my King") involves each worshiper individually as he anticipates the coming of the procession of his God and King. The Lord is viewed returning victoriously from battle to his "sanctuary" (cf. 47:5–9). The processional language reflects the customs of battle: the king, the singers, musicians, and maidens (vv.24–25; see appendix to Ps 150: Musical Instruments). The princes and leaders of the tribes join in singing the victory hymn (v.26). The fact that there are only four tribes (v.27) may be explained by the principle of poetic selectivity. For purposes of brevity and representation, the poet has selected the southern tribes (Judah and Benjamin) and the northern tribes (Zebulun and Naphtali). Together they form one people, as they are true Israelites, i.e., "from the fountain of Israel" (v.26; NIV, "the assembly of Israel"), though made up of many "companies" (*maqhēlôṯ*, from *q-h-l*, "to assemble"; cf. NIV, "the great congregation").

B. *Prayer*

68:28–31

28 Summon your power, O God;
show us your strength, O God, as you have done
before.

29 Because of your temple at Jerusalem
kings will bring you gifts.
30 Rebuke the beast among the reeds,
the herd of bulls among the calves of the nations.
Humbled, may it bring bars of silver.
Scatter the nations who delight in war.
31 Envoys will come from Egypt;
Cush will submit herself to God.

28 With renewed enthusiasm the people of God call on the Lord to demonstrate his "power" (*'ōz*, nominal form of *'-z-z*) and "strength" (verbal form from *'-z-z*; cf. 62:11; 63:2). He has revealed the terror and majesty of his strength in the past victorious acts; but by his own decree (vv.22–23), and by his nature as the Redeemer-God (vv.5–6, 19–20), the community expects him to act again.

29 The Lord has established his majesty in his temple in Jerusalem. The subject nations, led by their kings, will bring him homage (cf. 76:11; Isa 18:7; 60:3–7; 66:20; Hag 2:7; Zech 2:11–13; 6:15; 8:21–22; Rev 21:24).

30–31 The prayer also contains a petition to strike those nations that will not submit themselves to him. They are likened to "the beast among the reeds" and to a "herd of bulls" (v.30). It is ambiguous whether the "beast" is any particular animal (crocodile or hippopotamus), a generic reference (animals), or a symbol of the nations (i.e., Egypt, v.31). The "beast" and the "bulls" denote the oppressors, troublers, and seducers of the nations. They must come to an end, as the nations that have loved warfare and tribute themselves will be "humbled" and despoiled (v.30). Even mighty Egypt shall submit to the Lord, as she will bring *ḥašmannîm* (v.31, a *hapax legomenon*, usually translated "bronze objects," or "red cloth," KB³, p. 348; "blue cloth," Dahood, *Psalms*, 2:150; NIV's "envoys" is based on the LXX). Cush often formed a power base with Egypt (cf. Isa 18:1–19:15; 20:1–6); and she too will bring tribute to the Lord as token of her submission (cf. Isa 19:21; 45:14; see Dahood, *Psalms*, 2:150–51).

Notes

29 (30 MT) For a criticism of a mythopoetic reading, see Day, *God's Conflict*, pp. 119–20. P.D. Miller, Jr., has argued persuasively that animals are metaphors for rulers in "Animal Names as Designations in Ugaritic and Hebrew," *Ugarit-Forschungen* 2 (1970): 177–86.

30 (31 MT) On the meaning of גְּעַר (*ge'ar*, "rebuke") as an expression of anger, see P.J. Van Zijl, "A Discussion of the Root *gā'ar* ('rebuke')," *Biblical Essays*, ed. A.H. Van Zyl (Potchefstroom: Pro Rege-Pers, 1969), pp. 56–63.

The MT's בְּעֶגְלֵי עַמִּים (*be'eglê 'ammîm*, "the calves among the nations") is a strange phrase. Kraus emends it to בַּעֲלֵי עַמִּים (*ba'ₐlê 'ammîm*, "the lords of the nations," *Psalmen*, 1:467).

C. *Triumphal Hymn*

68:32–35

32 Sing to God, O kingdoms of the earth,
sing praise to the Lord, *Selah*

33 to him who rides the ancient skies above,
who thunders with mighty voice.
34 Proclaim the power of God,
whose majesty is over Israel,
whose power is in the skies.
35 You are awesome, O God, in your sanctuary;
the God of Israel gives power and strength
to his people.

Praise be to God!

32–33 The conclusion to the psalm and to this section is a hymn. Since the kingdom of the Lord extends to all nations, and since the nations must one day submit to him, the Lord calls on the "kingdoms of the earth" to respond appropriately to his sovereignty. The invocation to praise is a complementary expansion of the hymn of v.4:

v.4: Sing to God, sing praise to his name, / extol him who rides on the clouds

vv.32–33: Sing to God, *O kingdoms of the earth,* / sing praise to the Lord, / to him who rides the ancient skies above, / who thunders with mighty voice.

Here the kingdoms of the earth are clearly in view, whereas it was unclear to whom the invocation of v.4 was addressed. Verse 32 refers to the Great King as "God" and "the Lord" (*Adonai;* cf. vv.11, 17, 19), whereas the emphasis lies on "the name" of God ("the LORD," Yahweh). The poetic description of his rule develops that of v.4:

v.4: who rides on the clouds

v.33: to him who rides the ancient skies above, / who thunders with mighty voice.

The phrase "the ancient skies above" suggests the excellency of the Lord whose rule extends to the highest heaven (cf. Deut 10:14; 1 Kings 8:27). The thunder reveals the majesty and power of his rule (cf. Pss 18:13; 29:3) on behalf of his own (cf. Deut 33:26).

34 The praise of the subject nations must include an ascription of his sovereignty ("the power of God"; cf. v.28). He has shown his dominion ("majesty"; cf. Deut 33:26) over Israel. Here the emphasis lies on the sovereignty and power of his rule, whereas the hymn (vv.5–6) stresses the personal dimension of his rule: the Lord delivers the oppressed with justice and compassion.

35 This God is "awesome" (*nôrā'*) in his deeds (cf. 47:2; 65:5; Exod 15:11; Deut 10:17; Rev 15:3–4) but still present with his people ("in your sanctuary"; cf. vv.16, 24). He alone is the source of strength for his people. This God is "blessed" (*bārûk;* NIV, "praise be") and is to be "blessed" (cf. 89:52). Calvin encourages us to hope in God's goodness as a witness to his fatherly care:

> From this the Psalmist argues, that should God liberally supply the wants of his people, the consequence would be, to increase the fear of his name, since all ends of the earth would, by what they saw of his fatherly regard to his own, submit themselves with greater cheerfulness to his government. (3:4)

Psalm 69: The Zeal for Your House and God's Love for His Own

This is one of the *imprecatory* psalms (see appendix to Ps 137: Imprecations in the Psalms). The psalm reflects the *individual lament* genre. Because of the many references to it in the NT, this psalm has been interpreted messianically. The messianic interpretation is in the form of an application to the life of devotion to God by the Lord Jesus Christ. The primary significance is David and his suffering. He calls on the Lord to deliver him (vv.1–21) for the sake of "those who hope in you" (v.6). Moreover, he prays for the fall of the wicked (vv.22–29). The lament changes to a hymn of thanksgiving in anticipation of God's redemption (vv.29–36).

Apart from the general structural variation (lament-hymn), we follow this structure in the exposition:

I. Lament
- A. Prayer Out of Personal Need (vv.1–4)
  - B. Affirmation of God's Knowledge (v.5)
    - C. Disgrace for the Sake of God (vv.6–12)
    - C′. Deliverance for the Sake of God's Servant (vv.13–18)
  - B′. Affirmation of God's Knowledge (vv.19–21)
- A′. Prayer for God's Judgment on the Wicked (vv.22–28)

II. Hymn
- A. Personal and Communal Praise (vv.29–32)
  - B. Affirmation of God's Present Care (v.33)
- A′. Cosmic Praise (v.34)
  - B′. Affirmation of God's Eschatological Deliverance (vv.35–36)

(For a rhetorical critical analysis, see Leslie C. Allen, "The Value of Rhetorical Criticism in Psalm 69," JBL 105 [1986]: 577–98.)

I. Lament (vv.1–28)

A. *Prayer Out of Personal Need*

69:1–4

For the director of music. To ⌊the tune of⌋ "Lilies." Of David.

1 Save me, O God,
for the waters have come up to my neck.
2 I sink in the miry depths,
where there is no foothold.
I have come into the deep waters;
the floods engulf me.
3 I am worn out calling for help;
my throat is parched.
My eyes fail,
looking for my God.
4 Those who hate me without reason
outnumber the hairs of my head;
many are my enemies without cause,
those who seek to destroy me.
I am forced to restore
what I did not steal.

1–3 The psalmist describes his distress in a highly metaphorical manner. The adversity of the wicked is like deep "waters," coming up to his "neck" (v.1), so that he is losing his "foothold" (v.2).

The psalmist is "worn out" from repeatedly calling, "Save me" (vv.1, 3; cf. 6:6; Isa 57:10); for the Lord has not yet responded to his cry. He has cried out so intensely that his "throat" seems to be burning ("parched"). Though he is in deep water, his inner being is ablaze. He can go no farther, because his eyes also "fail" him, on account of his many tears (v.3; cf. 119:82, 123; Lam 2:11; 4:17). He is past "calling" for help, as his throat is burning hot. Even though he will be unable to see when God's salvation approaches, because of his failing eyes, still he is filled with hope ("looking," from *y-ḥ-l*, "look for," "hope in"; v.3; cf. 31:24), waiting for God to act.

4 Only after evoking sympathy by the portrayal of his intense suffering does the psalmist give an idea as to the cause of his distress. He is the object of a fierce hatred. The fierceness is compared to the number of the hairs on his head (cf. 40:12). The enmity is "without reason" (cf. 35:19; Lam 3:52). They also deal in "treachery" (*šeqer;* NIV, "without cause"; cf. 35:19; 38:19), accusing him of stealing and requiring him to restore what he has not taken. They are out to destroy him. This verse is partially quoted in John 15:25 as an encouragement to the disciples that the world may hate them, even as Jesus' contemporaries hated him "without reason."

Notes

For a brief discussion of the technical words and phrases in the superscription, see the Introduction.

1–2 (2–3 MT) Because of the grave difficulty of the situation, it is as if the psalmist is standing in a muddy river whose "depths" (v.1; cf. 130:1; Isa 51:10) and strength ("floods," v.2; cf. 69:15; Isa 27:12) nearly overtake him. For a similar metaphorical expression, see 18:4, 16; 42:7.

The "neck" (v.1) is a translation of נֶפֶשׁ (*nep̱eš*, "soul"; cf. Jonah 2:5). Most commentaries and versions agree that the rendering "neck" or "throat" is appropriate here (cf. NEB; Kraus, *Psalmen,* 1:478: "Kehle").

The first section of the lament closes with the prayer for God's judgment on the wicked (vv.22–29). The first word of the psalm, הוֹשִׁיעֵנִי (*hôšî'ēnî*, "save me," from *y-š-'*), forms an inclusion with the phrase יְשׁוּעָתְךָ (*yešû'āṯeḵā*, "your salvation," from *y-š-'*, v.29). It further forms an inclusion with the latter part of the hymn with the expectation that "God will save [יוֹשִׁיעַ (*yôšîa'*)] Zion" (v.35, for forms of the root *y-š-'*, see 3:2; 27:1).

4 (5 MT) The clause "those who seek to destroy me" has occasioned some problems. The MT's מַצְמִיתַי (*maṣmîṯay*) could be interpreted as a Hiphil of the root *ṣ-m-t* ("bring to silence," KB, pp. 807–8) or "exterminate" (BDB, p. 856). Dahood suggests the reading "my locks" as parallel with "hairs" (*Psalms,* 1:157). The Syriac reads מֵעַצְמוֹתַי (*mē'aṣmôṯay*, "than my bones") (BHS). Weiser (p. 490) and Kraus (*Psalmen,* 1:478) follow the traditional rendering, as does the NIV.

B. *Affirmation of God's Knowledge*

69:5

5 You know my folly, O God;
my guilt is not hidden from you.

5 Suddenly the psalmist turns again to the Lord in prayer with an emphatic expression "you know" (cf. v.19). God knows that the psalmist has acted without wisdom, i.e., foolishly ("folly"; cf. 38:5), and that he has committed "acts of wrongdoing" ("guilt"; NEB, "guilty deeds"; a unique word in the Psalms; cf. Lev 4:3; 6:5, 7). Thus while he humbly admits his humanness in the presence of the Lord, the psalmist also declares his innocence of the accusations, petitioning the Lord to deliver him.

C. *Disgrace for the Sake of God*

69:6–12

6 May those who hope in you
  not be disgraced because of me,
  O Lord, the LORD Almighty;
may those who seek you
  not be put to shame because of me,
  O God of Israel.
7 For I endure scorn for your sake,
  and shame covers my face.
8 I am a stranger to my brothers,
  an alien to my own mother's sons;
9 for zeal for your house consumes me,
  and the insults of those who insult you fall on me.
10 When I weep and fast,
  I must endure scorn;
11 when I put on sackcloth,
  people make sport of me.
12 Those who sit at the gate mock me,
  and I am the song of the drunkards.

6 The psalmist speaks on behalf of all the godly as he addresses the Lord as "Lord, the LORD Almighty." This phrase includes three designations for God. He is the Lord of the universe, the LORD of the covenant, and the Divine Warrior ("Almighty," *ṣ*^{e}*bā'ôṯ*). The "God of Israel" is none other than the Great King, whose rule extends to the whole world, and whose covenant love extends to his people. He, the Divine Warrior, is mighty to save. These names and designations embody the expectation of God's people "who hope" (*q-w-h*) in him and "seek" (*b-q-š*) his face. (See the appendix to Ps 24: Lord Sabaoth.)

7 Because God must be true to his promises, as contained in his names, David prays that God's people will never be overtaken by calumny. No one can deny the general truth of God's fidelity. However, as David turns to the particular, himself, the problem gains a new perspective. He is suffering for the sake of God (cf. 44:22)! For God's sake he is being disgraced with "shame" (cf. Jer 15:15).

8–12 For the sake of God, David has become like a "stranger" (*mûzār*) and an "alien" (*noḵrî*) to his own kin (v.8). The fools and drunkards of the town have made him the object of their gossip ("those who sit at the gate," v.12). While he prays and fasts on account of his adversity and the prevalent godlessness, people respond with laughter, mocking, and drinking songs (vv.10–12). Briggs's suggestion may well be correct: "Doubtless the poet is contrasting in his mind the worship of God with song and music in the temple with this abuse of song and music by the ungodly in the public squares" (2:119). What is dear to the heart of the psalmist is the "house" of the Lord (v.9). He was so desirous of pleasing God in the face of ignominy that his "zeal" consumed him, like "a devouring flame" (Dahood, *Psalms,* 2:158; cf. its application to our Lord in John 2:17; Rom 15:3).

Notes

---

10 (11 MT) "When I weep and fast" was understood as "I am afflicted and fast" in the LXX. Kraus (*Psalmen,* 1:480) follows the LXX as more suitable to the Hebrew idiom (Isa 58:5).

12 (13 MT) Usually those who sit in the gates are the elders and leaders of the city. Here, however, the idiom denotes the same class of people as the parallel phrase "drunkards." Though it is true that the two phrases are alliterative—יֹשְׁבֵי שָׁעַר (*yōšᵉḇê šāʿar,* lit., "dwellers of the gate") and שׁוֹתֵי שֵׁכָר (*šôṯê šēḵār,* lit., "drinkers of wine")—it does not follow that the former need to be translated "feasters," as Dahood does: "The feasters and the drunkards" (*Psalms,* 2:159).

According to Hans-Peter Müller, יָשִׂיחוּ (*yāśîḥû,* "they mock," from *ś-y-ḥ*) may denote a loud, enthusiastic, and emotion-filled form of speaking ("Die hebräische Wurzel שִׂיח," VetTest 19 [1969]: 361–71).

D. *Deliverance for the Sake of God's Servant*

69:13–18

13 But I pray to you, O Lord,
  in the time of your favor;
 in your great love, O God,
  answer me with your sure salvation.
14 Rescue me from the mire,
  do not let me sink;
 deliver me from those who hate me,
  from the deep waters.
15 Do not let the floodwaters engulf me
  or the depths swallow me up
  or the pit close its mouth over me.
16 Answer me, O Lord, out of the goodness of your love;
  in your great mercy turn to me.
17 Do not hide your face from your servant;
  answer me quickly, for I am in trouble.
18 Come near and rescue me;
  redeem me because of my foes.

13 The psalmist casts himself even more forcefully on the mercy of the Lord. With an emphatic "I," he projects himself into the foreground, hoping that his covenant God will at last hear his prayer (lit., "as for me, my prayer to you"; cf. 42:8; 109:4). In the foreground we see the psalmist praying to God, whereas in the background the mockers and drunkards are singing their songs of mockery and revelry. In his prayers he asks that "the time of your favor" be now. The phrase "time of your favor" (*ʿēṯ rāṣôn,* lit., "time of favor") is a technical phrase for God's restorative graces: full forgiveness, deliverance, and restoration to the full benefits of God's relationship with his people (cf. Isa 49:8; 58:5; 61:2).

David further specifies what he understands by "favor" in the following verses: deliverance (vv.14–18); God's "love" (*roḇ ḥasdeḵā,* "your great love," v.13) and blessings (*ṭôb ḥasdeḵā,* "the goodness of your love," v.16; cf. 109:21); "sure salvation" (*'emeṯ yiš'eḵā,* lit., "faithfulness of your salvation," v.13); and "your great mercy" (*rōḇ raḥameyḵā,* v.16). These three attributes ("love," "faithfulness," and "compassion") are the ground of deliverance and are the same as those the Lord had revealed to Moses as he made covenant with his people (Exod 34:6–7; cf. Ps 103:8, 17–18). His fidelity to his covenant guarantees the sureness of "salvation." (See the appendix to Ps 119: Yahweh Is My Redeemer.)

14–18 In contrast to the constancy of God is the psalmist who is slipping and sliding. The "mire" and the "floodwaters" are about to overtake him (vv.14–15; cf. vv.1–3). As he prays, the psalmist becomes more intense: "Rescue me. . . . Do not let the floodwaters engulf me . . . or the pit close its mouth over me" (vv.14–15; "pit" is a synonym for Sheol, cf. 55:23; see appendix to Ps 88: Sheol-Grave-Death in the Psalms). In his misery he renews his petition for God's love and mercy (v.16), as expressions of God's presence (vv.17–18). The time for deliverance is now; hence urgency is expressed in staccatolike terseness: "Do not hide . . . answer me quickly, for I am in trouble. Come near [lit., 'come near to my soul,' i.e., 'to me']" (vv.17–18). For the phrase "I am in trouble," confer 18:6; 59:16; 66:14, 17; 102:2; 106:44; 107:6, 13, 19, 28). Because of the numerous enemies (v.18; cf. 5:8; 27:11) and their deceptiveness and mocking (vv.5, 9–12), he prays that his redemption be near.

Notes

14 (15 MT) The MT has an imperative followed by a cohortative of the root *n-ṣ-l* rather than two imperatives: הַצִּילֵנִי . . . אִנָּצְלָה (*haṣṣîlēnî . . . 'innāṣelāh,* "rescue me . . . deliver me"). This syntactic phenomenon could also be rendered by: "Rescue me . . . so that I shall be rescued" (Joüon, par. 116b).

The multiplicity of synonyms throughout a psalm of this type reflects on the literary artistry. Several synonyms for "deliverance" are הוֹשִׁיעֵנִי (*hôšî'ēnî,* v.1), הַצִּילֵנִי (*haṣṣîlēnî,* v.14), אִנָּצְלָה (*'innāṣelāh,* v.14), גְּאָלָהּ (*ge'ālāh,* v.18), and פְּדֵנִי (*peḏēnî,* v.18). The synonyms are so close to one another in meaning that little semantic differentiation ought to be made. (See the appendix to Ps 119: Yahweh Is My Redeemer.)

E. *Affirmation of God's Knowledge*
69:19–21

19 You know how I am scorned, disgraced and shamed;
all my enemies are before you.
20 Scorn has broken my heart
and has left me helpless;
I looked for sympathy, but there was none,
for comforters, but I found none.
21 They put gall in my food
and gave me vinegar for my thirst.

19–21 As in v.5, David quiets himself with the thought that God knows everything about him, which is a quieting thought in comparison to the maligning of his adversaries. Here he repeats the emphatic phrase "You know" (v.19). He trusts that the Lord knows his "scorn" (v.20; cf. 35:26), disgrace (cf. v.7), shame (cf. vv.7, 9–10, 20), and adversities.

The psalmist looks for those who identify with him, but there is no sympathy or comfort (v.20; a restatement of vv.8, 11). Instead, they made things worse for him (v.21; cf. vv.10–12). They did their best to aggravate his troubles, as is expressed by the metaphors "gall" and "vinegar."

Notes

---

19 (20 MT) The psalmist has introduced three synonyms for enemies: שֹׂנְאִים (*śōn ᵉʾîm,* "those who hate [me]," v.4), אֹיְבִים (*ʾōyᵉḇîm,* lit., "treat as an enemy," v.4 [NIV, "enemies"], v.18 [NIV, "foes"]), and צוֹרְרִים (*ṣôrᵉrîm,* lit., "those who band together," i.e., with the intent to persecute, v.19 [NIV, "enemies"]).

21 (22 MT) The Hebrew word רֹאשׁ (*rōʾš;* NIV, "gall") denotes a poisonous herb of the carrot family ("Poison Hemlock" or *Conium Maculatum;* see Zohary, *Plants of the Bible,* p. 186) and is usually translated by "poison" (cf. KB, p. 866; Lam 3:5, 19; Hos 10:4; Amos 6:12). The NIV has here adopted the LXX as reflected in the account of our Lord's passion on the cross (Matt 27:34). Our Lord's suffering was not a fulfillment of this psalm but rather an application of his identification with the psalmist and with all who suffer. The psalmist felt as if he was about to go into the pit and that no one empathized with him. Our Lord suffered more intensely in rejection and death. Therefore he understands all who suffer disgrace (Heb 2:17–18; cf. 4:15). (For other allusions to v.21, cf. Matt 27:48; Mark 15:23, 36; Luke 23:36; and John 19:29.)

F. *Prayer for God's Judgment on the Wicked*

69:22–28

22 May the table set before them become a snare;
  may it become retribution and a trap.
23 May their eyes be darkened so they cannot see,
  and their backs be bent forever.
24 Pour out your wrath on them;
  let your fierce anger overtake them.
25 May their place be deserted;
  let there be no one to dwell in their tents.
26 For they persecute those you wound
  and talk about the pain of those you hurt.
27 Charge them with crime upon crime;
  do not let them share in your salvation.
28 May they be blotted out of the book of life
  and not be listed with the righteous.

22 Characteristic of the imprecatory psalms, the psalmist hurls God's curses on the enemies. They have made life intolerable for him. As a matter of justice and concern, David prays that the Lord may deal equitably with his enemies. However, David is not primarily concerned for himself but rather for what Calvin calls "a holy zeal for the divine glory which impelled him to summon the wicked to God's judgment seat" (2:67). The imprecations are metaphorical and find their context in the experience of the psalmist. The wicked who had ruined his table (v.21) will find that their table will be "a snare . . . and a trap" (cf. Amos 3:5). Both words denote instruments for catching birds. The "snare" (KB, p. 756) is a self-springing trap, whereas the "trap" (KB, p. 505) may have had a bait in it.

23–28 The psalmist's eyes and strength had been failing because of his long wait for God's redemption (vv.3, 14–15). In contrast to his prayer (v.17) for God's "favor," "love," and "mercy" (vv.13, 16), he prays that his enemies may suffer divine wrath (v.24) and may lose courage and strength (v.23). Since he is forsaken by family and friends, he prays that the wicked may be homeless, childless, and without a future (v.25; cf. 109:9–10). In the end they should have no part in the community of God's people on earth nor in the hereafter. To this end he prays that their names be removed from "the book of life," which is God's record of the "righteous" (v.28; cf. 56:8; 87:6; Exod 32:32–33; Isa 4:3; Dan 12:1; Mal 3:16; Rev 3:5; 13:8; 17:8; 20:12, 15; 21:27).

Throughout the imprecation the psalmist alludes to the wrongs done by the wicked that must be righted. He also explicitly explains the rationale. The wicked outrightly hunt down those who suffer adversity or are disciplined by the Lord (v.26). They have enjoyed their lives and are guilty. Therefore he prays that the Lord may give them their punishment (*'āwōn,* lit., "guilt"; NIV, "crime," v.27; cf. Gen 4:13) in accordance with their crimes (*'ᵃwōnām,* lit., "their guilt"). We differ here a little from the NIV by suggesting that the prepositional phrase "on their guilt" (MT) be understood as "for their guilt": "Give them punishment for their crime" (cf. NEB, "Give them the punishment their sin deserves"). If this is correct, vv.27–28 contain parallel thoughts, as the first hemistich calls for God's punishment and the second in each verse contains an allusion to God's work on behalf of the righteous (v.27: "righteousness," *ṣᵉḏāqāh;* NIV, "salvation," and v.28: "righteous," *ṣaddîqîm*). Moreover v.28 is a more explicit form of judgment than that in v.27.

Notes

---

22 (23 MT) The translation of וְלִשְׁלוֹמִים (*wᵉlišlômîm;* NIV, "retribution") is uncertain; see the NIV margin: "Or *snare / and their fellowship become.*" The ancient versions differ in their renderings: LXX, "for retribution" (cf. NIV); Targum, "sacrificial feasts" or "their peace offerings." The Targumic translation may be preferable as it provides a parallel with "the table": "may their fellowship offerings become a trap" (so also J. Ridderbos, 2:213; Kraus, *Psalmen,* 1:480).

26 (27 MT) The MT's אַתָּה (*'attāh,* "you") is best understood as a corrupt form of the object particle אֵת (*'ēṯ;* cf. LXX, Syriac, Jerome [BHS]). This emendation lies behind the rendering "those" (NIV).

28 (29 MT) Dahood renders "righteous" by "meadow." For a criticism of Dahood's view of the Elysian fields, see on Ps 36:10.

II. Hymn (vv.29–36)

A. *Personal and Communal Praise*

69:29–32

29 I am in pain and distress;
may your salvation, O God, protect me.

30 I will praise God's name in song
and glorify him with thanksgiving.
31 This will please the LORD more than an ox,
more than a bull with its horns and hoofs.
32 The poor will see and be glad—
you who seek God, may your hearts live!

29 Verse 29 forms a transition between the lament and the hymn. It may be rendered as a prayer (KJV, NIV) concluding the lament or as the beginning of the hymn: "Whereas I am in pain and distress, your salvation, O God, will protect me." The "salvation" (*y*e*šû'āh*) of the Lord extends to the complete protection of his own, both body and soul. "Salvation" is a synonym of "righteousness" (*ṣ*e*ḏāqāh*, see comment on v.27). Both words denote a complete vindication of the godly by their righteous God (cf. 51:14; Isa 45:21; 51:8; see TWOT, 2:754–55) who will "protect" (lit., "set high") his own (for the parallelism of "deliver" and "protect," see 59:1–2).

30–32 David looks forward to the time when he can record his deliverance by praising his God in a song of thanksgiving (v.30; cf. 75:9). The sacrifice of the lips in thanksgiving (cf. Heb 13:15) and "song" (*šîr*) is better than the sacrifice of a bull (*šôr*, a play on *šîr;* NIV, "ox," v.31; see Dahood, *Psalms*, 2:165). Each act of deliverance is an encouragement to all those who wait for God's deliverance. Thus the "poor" and those "who seek God" will take heart, join with him in gladness, and be satisfied (v.32; cf. 22:26).

Notes

29 (30 MT) The first phrase in the MT is וַאֲנִי (*wa'*a*nî*, "and I"; cf. v.13). The disjunctive use of the waw may be rendered as an emphatic (Joüon, par. 177n) or by subordinating particles ("but," "while," or "now"; see T.O. Lambdin, *Introduction to Biblical Hebrew* [New York: Scribner, 1971], pp. 162–65). The phrase may be found at the beginning of a strophe (cf. v.13) or within (cf. 109:4b, 25).

32 (33 MT) Instead of the MT's רָאוּ (*rā'û*, "have seen"), some MSS and the LXX have an imperfect ("will see"), as does the NIV: "The poor will see." Others suggest an emendation of one vowel, רְאוּ (*r*e*'û*, "see," imperative; Kraus, *Psalmen*, 1:480); see the NEB's "See and rejoice" (cf. 22:23).

B. *Affirmation of God's Present Care*

69:33

33 The LORD hears the needy
and does not despise his captive people.

33 The connection with the preceding verse is not marked in the NIV. The particle *kî* (untr. in NIV; first word in MT) may be emphatic here: "Surely." Kraus takes this as a hymnic exclamation flowing out of the particular act of deliverance (*Psalmen*, 1:484). The participial use of "hear" supports the contention that the psalmist hymnically affirms God's present care: "Surely, the LORD hears the needy" or "The LORD does hear the needy." The "needy" (cf. 9:18; Jer 20:13), i.e., "his captive people" (22:24; 102:17, 20; 107:10–16), will be assured that the God of the covenant does listen to and answer their prayers.

C. *Cosmic Praise*

69:34

34 Let heaven and earth praise him,
the seas and all that move in them,

34 All creation joins with the salvation of God's people. This interrelationship of the welfare of God's covenant people and nature is also found in Isaiah (44:23; 55:12; cf. Rom 8:18–22).

D. *Affirmation of God's Eschatological Deliverance*

69:35–36

35 for God will save Zion
and rebuild the cities of Judah.
Then people will settle there and possess it;
36 the children of his servants will inherit it,
and those who love his name will dwell there.

35–36 The second hymnic affirmation of God's care is also introduced by the particle *kî* (NIV, "for"; cf. v.33 above). The concern of the psalmist was with the Lord ("zeal for your house consumes me," v.9); and to this end he prays for the speedy deliverance of Zion, her cities, and her people. The suffering of the individual is always related to the prosperity of the whole. The attack of the enemies on one of God's people is a virtual attack on God's kingdom. It is not clear whether Judah was under attack or had just come out of a period of war and desolation. Nor is it clear whether this section is original or an addition, reflective of the exilic situation (cf. Jer 33:10–11; 34:7). What is clear is the hope that the Lord will restore his people ("those who love his name," v.36; cf. 5:11; 119:132; Mal 3:16), strengthen them, and permit them and their children to enjoy his benefits. The hope of the godly must always focus on the full restoration of all things, when the Lord will establish his righteous salvation to his people on this earth (cf. 2 Peter 3:13).

Psalm 70

70:1–5

For the director of music. Of David. A petition.

1 Hasten, O God, to save me;
O LORD, come quickly to help me.

[2]May those who seek my life
be put to shame and confusion;
may all who desire my ruin
be turned back in disgrace.
[3]May those who say to me, "Aha! Aha!"
turn back because of their shame.
[4]But may all who seek you
rejoice and be glad in you;
may those who love your salvation always say,
"Let God be exalted!"

[5]Yet I am poor and needy;
come quickly to me, O God.
You are my help and my deliverer;
O LORD, do not delay.

This psalm is virtually identical with the prayer in 40:13–17. The main differences lie in the absence of the divine name, a characteristic of the Elohistic Psalter, and in the addition "hasten" at the very beginning of the psalm. This psalm carries a superscription. For an exposition of the psalm, see Psalm 40:13–17.

Notes

For a brief discussion of the technical words and phrases in the superscription, see the Introduction.

As to the reason for this psalm's existence, Perowne (1:555) says, "I see no reason to abandon the opinion . . . that this Psalm formed originally a part of Psalm xl., and was subsequently detached and altered for a special occasion." Delitzsch believes that it was placed here, "after P. lxix on account of the kindred nature of its contents" (2:287). Obviously, any solution is sheer speculation.

Psalm 71: Longing for Yahweh's Righteous Acts

The psalmist commits himself to God's care. He has enjoyed a life of faith commitment; and through the experiences of communion with the Lord, he has learned that Yahweh is faithful. The confidence of the psalmist holds the variety of lament and thanksgiving together. As an *individual lament* psalm, the aspect of confidence dawns like the sun over dark mountains.

The structure may be difficult to define because of the ebb and flow of the argument. For expository purposes we set forth this outline:

A. Prayer of Confidence (vv.1–4)
B. Affirmation of Confidence (vv.5–8)
C. Prayer in Old Age (vv.9–13)
C′. Hope in Old Age (vv.14–18)
B′. Affirmation of Confidence (vv.19–21)
A′. Thanksgiving With Confidence (vv.22–24)

I. Prayer of Confidence

71:1–4

1 In you, O LORD, I have taken refuge;
let me never be put to shame.
2 Rescue me and deliver me in your righteousness;
turn your ear to me and save me.
3 Be my rock of refuge,
to which I can always go;
give the command to save me,
for you are my rock and my fortress.
4 Deliver me, O my God, from the hand of the wicked,
from the grasp of evil and cruel men.

1–4 The psalmist repeatedly prays for deliverance from his present affliction: "let me never be put to shame. / Rescue [*n-ṣ-l*] me and deliver [*p-l-ṭ*] me . . . / turn your ear to me and save [*y-š-'*] me. / Be my rock . . . ; / give the command to save me [*y-š-'*], . . . / Deliver [*p-l-ṭ*] me" (see appendix to Ps 119: Yahweh Is My Redeemer). The ground for hope lies both in his trust in the Lord and in his belief that Yahweh is "righteous" (*ṣᵉḏāqāh*).

The emphatic position of "in you" and "in your righteousness" in the MT forms an inclusion: "In you, . . . I have taken refuge. Therefore in your righteousness rescue me" (vv.1–2). This conviction that God rules and acts righteously upholds the psalmist in his faith that Yahweh will deliver him (cf. vv.15–16, 19, 24). (See the appendix to Ps 25: The Perfections of Yahweh.)

Verse 1 also forms an inclusion with the last verse by the repetition of "shame" (*b-w-š*). The duress has caused him "shame," but he is confident that Yahweh will overturn his shame and let his adversaries "be put to shame" (v.24).

The references to God also form an inclusion: "In you, O LORD. . . . O my God" (vv.1, 4). The psalmist trusts in Yahweh to deliver him from the wicked, who in turn are characterized by their devotion to evil and unrighteous acts (cf. Jer 6:7). Yahweh is his rock (*ṣûr, sela'*, v.3), his "refuge" (*mā'ôz*, v.3), and his "fortress" (*mᵉṣûḏāh;* cf. 18:2; see appendix to Ps 98: Yahweh Is the Divine Warrior).

Notes

1–3 Verses 1–3 resemble Ps 31:1–3 (see commentary in loc.).

3 The phrase צוּר מָעוֹן (*ṣûr mā'ôn,* "rock of dwelling"; NIV, "rock of refuge") is unusual in light of 31:2, צוּר מָעוֹז (*ṣûr mā'ôz,* "rock of refuge"). A number of MSS, the LXX, and the Targum prefer the reading of 31:2, also adopted by the NIV.

The LXX supports the change from "to which I can always go; give the command" to "fortress" (לְבֵית מְצוּדוֹת, *lᵉḇêṯ mᵉṣûḏôṯ*), as in 31:2 (Kraus, *Psalmen,* 1:489; A.A. Anderson, 1:511–12).

II. Affirmation of Confidence

71:5–8

5 For you have been my hope, O Sovereign LORD,
my confidence since my youth.

[6]From birth I have relied on you;
  you brought me forth from my mother's womb.
  I will ever praise you.
[7]I have become like a portent to many,
  but you are my strong refuge.
[8]My mouth is filled with your praise,
  declaring your splendor all day long.

5–8 Yahweh has been the psalmist's "hope," "confidence," (v.5; cf. Jer 14:8), "praise" (twice, *tᵉhillāh*, vv.6, 8), "strong refuge" (v.7), and "splendor" (v.8) from "birth" (v.6). The psalmist hereby affirms his long-term devotion to the Lord (v.6; cf. 22:10). This devotion is also reflected by the emphatic position in the MT: "For you. . . . on you. . . . (I will praise) you. . . . but you" (vv.5–7). His God is no other than *Adonai* ("the ruler of the universe," "Master") and Yahweh. The covenant-redeemer God (NIV, "Sovereign LORD") has been close to him in deliverance and protection throughout his life.

The current circumstances, however, create questions within the psalmist himself and within the community. He has become "a portent" (*môp̱ēṯ*, "a wonder") to his contemporaries, i.e., a sign of trouble, chastisement, and divine retribution. Nevertheless he throws himself on God as his refuge (v.7). The God of "hope" and the psalmist's "confidence" from youth (v.5) are the same: his "strong refuge" (v.7). These expressions of faith form an inclusion.

Based on this affirmation of trust, the psalmist prays that he may continually have reasons for declaring Yahweh's "praise" and "splendor" (v.8). The psalmist has had reasons to declare Yahweh's royal praise in the past ("from birth," v.6) and looks forward to ascribing the powers of royalty to Yahweh in the future: "praise . . . splendor" (v.8).

Notes

6 The root גזה (*g-z-h*, "cut off") may be rendered "you brought me forth" (NIV). Some emend גּוֹזִי (*gôzî*, Qal participle) to עוּזִּי (*'ûzzî*, "my strength"; Kraus, *Psalmen*, 1:489). But see 22:9: "you brought me out of the womb" (*gōḥî*).

III. Prayer in Old Age

71:9–13

[9]Do not cast me away when I am old;
  do not forsake me when my strength is gone.
[10]For my enemies speak against me;
  those who wait to kill me conspire together.
[11]They say, "God has forsaken him;
  pursue him and seize him,
  for no one will rescue him."
[12]Be not far from me, O God;
  come quickly, O my God, to help me.
[13]May my accusers perish in shame;

may those who want to harm me
be covered with scorn and disgrace.

9–11 Lament shapes the petition. The psalmist prays that the Lord not abandon him in old age (i.e., "when my strength is gone," v.9). "Cast away" and "forsake" signify a state of condemnation and curse (cf. 51:11; Job 19:13–21). The vile enemies (vv.4, 10) are all too ready to condemn him to death (v.10; cf. 3:2; 5:9; 56:6–7), to accuse him as a sinner worse than them, and to justify their evil course of action (v.11; cf. 3:2; 22:7–8). They do not believe in retribution and rewards and autonomously think that they hold the power of life and death in their own hands. Possibly they believed that they were God's appointed agents of justice (cf. 56:4).

12–13 The prayer calls on Yahweh to vindicate his servant speedily (cf. 35:2; 38:22; 40:13–14) by giving him "help" (v.12) and by bringing retribution ("scorn and disgrace") on God's enemies (v.13; cf. 35:26; 109:29). His enemies are "evil and cruel" (v.4) "accusers" (v.13; cf. "speak against me; . . . conspire together," v.10). Their joy lies in bringing misfortune and disgrace to others. The psalmist cries here for Yahweh's fidelity to his promises in bringing the sanctions of the covenant: blessing and curse. He does not do evil for evil nor does he curse his enemies, but he awaits the Lord's judgment. (See the appendix to Ps 137: Imprecations in the Psalms.)

IV. Hope in Old Age

71:14–18

14 But as for me, I will always have hope;
I will praise you more and more.
15 My mouth will tell of your righteousness,
of your salvation all day long,
though I know not its measure.
16 I will come and proclaim your mighty acts, O Sovereign
LORD;
I will proclaim your righteousness, yours alone.
17 Since my youth, O God, you have taught me,
and to this day I declare your marvelous deeds.
18 Even when I am old and gray,
do not forsake me, O God,
till I declare your power to the next generation,
your might to all who are to come.

14–16 In response to his lament, the psalmist affirms strongly his hope in the Lord. First, the emphatic "but as for me" (v.14) leaves no doubt of his commitment, regardless of what may happen. His "hope" is in the Lord (cf. 130:7). Second, he expects the Lord to vindicate him, resulting in a new declaration of "praise" (*t^e^hillāh*). The nature of vindication will be nothing less than an expression of his "righteousness" (*ṣ^e^ḏāqāh*, v.16; see appendix to Ps 25: Divine Perfections). The "righteousness" of the Lord pertains to the acts of salvation, and salvation consists of all that contributes to the well-being of God's children. Calvin writes:

> *The righteousness of God*, as we have just now observed, does not here denote that free gift by which he reconciles men to himself, or by which he regenerates them to

newness of life; but his faithfulness in keeping his promises, by which he means to show that he is righteous, upright, and true towards his servants. (3:93)

God's acts of "salvation" (*y^e^šû'āh*) are too numerous to count (v.15; cf. 40:5; 139:17–18). His "mighty acts" (*g^e^būrôṯ*, v.16) and "marvelous deeds" (v.17; cf. 9:1; 26:7) establish his "righteous" kingdom ("righteousness," v.16). These are the acts of God (*Adonai*), the psalmist's "Sovereign LORD" (cf. v.5).

17–18 The psalmist has devoted himself to God since his youth (v.17; cf. v.6). He has praised him and anticipates proclaiming his praise to another generation ("till I declare your power to the next generation," v.18). The "power" of God is the demonstration of his "arm" (lit. Heb.; cf. 77:15) and an expression of his fidelity ("your righteousness" [*ṣ^e^ḏāqāh*], v.16, and "marvelous deeds" [*p-l-'*], v.17). All who "come" to listen will hear this gray-haired saint tell and retell the story of Yahweh's mighty deeds (v.18; cf. 22:30). The story of God's fidelity cannot but lead us to persevere.

Notes

15 The MT's סְפֹרוֹת (*s^e^p̄ōrôṯ*, "number"; NIV, "measure") is unique. The LXX and other versions read "books" whereas several Greek MSS read "business" or "skill" (NEB, "although I have not the skill of a poet"). The idiom remains problematic. In the context the psalmist reflects on the acts of God, observing their vastness, which may relate to the number, the magnificence, or both.

18 The NIV's "to the next generation, . . . to all who come" reflects the LXX. The MT reads לְדוֹר לְכָל־יָבוֹא (*l^e^ḏôr l^e^ḵol-yāḇô'*, "to a generation to everyone who comes"; cf. 22:30).

V. Affirmation of Confidence

71:19–21

19 Your righteousness reaches to the skies, O God,
you who have done great things.
Who, O God, is like you?
20 Though you have made me see troubles,
many and bitter,
you will restore my life again;
from the depths of the earth
you will again bring me up.
21 You will increase my honor
and comfort me once again.

19 In hymnic fashion the psalmist praises the Lord for his acts. He has expressed his hope in Yahweh's righteous acts of salvation and has vowed to proclaim to the younger generation his readiness to teach them what the Lord has taught him through his mighty deeds. He believes that Yahweh is all-powerful and that he will vindicate him. Faith triumphs in these verses, as the psalmist leads to a grand vision of Yahweh's "righteousness." His righteousness is nothing less than his perfection as evidenced in the "great things." Yahweh is wise and glorious in his rule, as he demonstrates his righteous rule "to the skies" (cf. 36:5; 57:10). No one can comprehend his ways, and no one is like him. Yahweh is incomparable (cf. C.J. Labuschagne, *The Incomparability of Yahweh in the Old Testament* [Leiden: Brill, 1966])! There is no God in heaven above or being on earth who is like Yahweh (cf. 35:10; 86:8; 89:6, 8; Exod 15:11; Mic 7:18)!

20 Great have been the psalmist's troubles. The adversities are hyperbolically described as "the depths of the earth," which contrasts to the phrase "righteousness . . . to the skies" (v.19). Yahweh's power is so great that he can extend his love into the deepest depths. He alone has the power over life and death (cf. 85:6). (See the appendix to Ps 88: Sheol-Grave-Death in the Psalms.)

21 Instead of shame (v.1), the psalmist will receive "honor" (lit., "greatness"). The word "greatness" alludes to "great things" (v.19), i.e., Yahweh's saving acts. Instead of "troubles, many and bitter" (v.20), he receives Yahweh's "comfort." Thus all his adversaries will see that Yahweh is righteous and that he does reward the righteous.

Notes

20 The NIV adopts the *Qere* reading ("you have made me see, . . . you will again bring me up") instead of the *Kethiv* ("you have made us see, . . . you will again bring us up"; Kraus, *Psalmen*, 1:489).

VI. Thanksgiving With Confidence

71:22–24

22 I will praise you with the harp
for your faithfulness, O my God;
I will sing praise to you with the lyre,
O Holy One of Israel.
23 My lips will shout for joy
when I sing praise to you—
I, whom you have redeemed.
24 My tongue will tell of your righteous acts
all day long,
for those who wanted to harm me
have been put to shame and confusion.

22–24 The psalm concludes on a vow to praise Yahweh publicly for his fidelity (*'ᵉmeṯ*, "faithfulness," v.22) as expressed in his "righteous acts" (*ṣᵉḏāqāh*) of deliverance (v.24; cf. vv.3–4). Yahweh is "righteous" in his holiness, as he delivers his children and avenges ("put to shame"; cf. v.1) those who harm them. Yahweh is "the Holy One of Israel" (v.22; cf. 78:41; Isa 1:4) in his acts of redemption (cf. Exod 15:11; Rev 15:3–4).

The repetition of the verbs for "praise" ("I will praise [*y-d-h*] . . . / I will sing praise [*z-m-r*] to you. . . . / My lips will shout for joy [*r-n-n*] / when I sing praise [*z-m-r*] to you," vv.22–23) and the instrumental accompaniment ("with the harp . . . with the lyre," v.22; see appendix to Ps 150: Musical Instruments) complement his vow to proclaim publicly what Yahweh has done ("My tongue will tell of your righteous [*ṣ^e ḏāqāh*] acts all day long," v.24; cf. vv.16, 18; 35:28).

Psalm 72: The Glory of the Davidic Kingdom

This psalm is a *royal psalm*, wherein petition is made for the prosperity of the Lord's anointed. The psalm is messianic in the sense that Jesus is the "Christ" ("anointed one") who shares in all the promises made to David and to his descendants (cf. 2 Sam 7). While the community of God's people prospered under the descendants of David, God's appointed theocratic leadership (Ps 2), the benefits of the rule of Christ, the son of David, are so much greater. Therefore the prayer for the Davidic king is at the same time an expression of hope in the glorious and just rule of Jesus over the earth. It is as much an expectation now as it was before the coming of Jesus. This hope comes to expression in the familiar hymn "Jesus Shall Reign" by Isaac Watts:

> Jesus shall reign wheree'er the sun
>   Does his successive journeys run;
> His kingdom stretch from shore to shore,
>   Till moons shall wax and wane no more.

The psalm begins with a prayer for the messianic kingship of David's dynasty (vv.1–2) and ends on an ascription of praise to the universal kingship of the Lord (vv.18–19). The petition alternates between a prayer for the king, a prayer for the prosperity and justice associated with the rule, and a prayer for the extent of the rule. These elements constitute the structural analysis:

A. Prayer for Davidic Kingship (v.1)
  B. Hope for Righteousness and Justice (vv.2–4)
    C. Prayer for Longevity and Universal Rule (vv.5–11)
  B′. Hope for Righteousness and Justice (vv.12–14)
    C′. Prayer for Longevity and Universality (vv.15–17)
A′. Praise of God's Kingship (vv.18–20)

I. Prayer for Davidic Kingship

72:1

Of Solomon.

1 Endow the king with your justice, O God,
the royal son with your righteousness.

1 The psalm opens with an emphatic "O God" (MT) and closes with a blessing: "Praise be to the LORD God, the God of Israel" (v.18). Petition and praise well up from the heart of faith, as the psalmist invokes God's blessing on the Davidic dynasty. He knows that through this divinely appointed dynasty, the promises of the Lord will be unleashed on his people, yea to the whole world (cf. 2 Sam 7; Ps 2; see Walter C. Kaiser, Jr., "The Blessing of David: The Charter for Humanity," *The Law and the Prophets: Old Testament Studies Prepared in Honor of O.T. Allis*, ed. J.H. Skilton

[Nutley: Presbyterian and Reformed, 1974], pp. 310–18). To be an instrument of God's kingship on earth, the monarch must conform to the divine standards of justice (*mišpāṭeyḵā*, "judgments"; but LXX, Syr.: "justice") and righteousness (*ṣᵉḏāqāh*). These are expressions of godly wisdom (cf. 1 Kings 3:6, 9; Isa 11:1–5; 16:5; 28:6; 32:1). The king, talented as he may have been, had to live in accordance with the revelation from God. To this end the Israelite king ("the king" = "the royal son") received a copy of the law of God at his coronation (cf. Deut 17:18–20) so as to distinguish between the theocratic rule of Israel and the man-centered rule of the nations.

Notes

For a brief discussion of the technical words and phrases in the superscription, see the Introduction.

There is some question whether Solomon wrote this psalm. Only two psalms are attributed to him (cf. 127). Some commentators feel this psalm was not originally written "by" Solomon but "for" him (the LXX has εἰς [*eis*, "to," "for"]). Calvin states, "After carefully weighing all, I incline to the view that David uttered this prayer as he was dying, and that it was put into the form of a Psalm by his son, that the message thereof might never perish. . . . But as Solomon took the argument from his father, and only clothed it in the garb of poetry, we may regard David as the principal author" (cited in Perowne, 2:564). Perowne disputes Calvin's claim and concludes, "The inscription, beyond all doubt, means to say the Psalm is Solomon's" (ibid.).

II. Hope for Righteousness and Justice

72:2–4

2 He will judge your people in righteousness,
your afflicted ones with justice.
3 The mountains will bring prosperity to the people,
the hills the fruit of righteousness.
4 He will defend the afflicted among the people
and save the children of the needy;
he will crush the oppressor.

2–4 The king was an instrument of God's blessing to his people. As the Lord is a Deliverer-Vindicator (cf. 68:5–6), so is the wise king, having been instructed by the Lord. He will "judge" (*dîn*) the cases before him in accordance with "righteousness" (*ṣeḏeq*) and "justice" (*mišpāṭ*, v.2). Hereby the people will share in the benefits of theocratic rule, knowing that their king is "for" them. The "afflicted" (vv.2, 4), "the children of the needy," and the people at large will benefit from his upholding their rights and by avenging the wrongdoer (v.4). These two activities of his rule parallel God's involvement as the Divine Warrior. He rules in his deliverance (vindication) and in his judgments (vengeance). Vindication ("the fruit of righteousness") brings "prosperity" (*šālôm*) as a sense of well-being (v.3) to the people and relief from "the oppressor" (v.4; for the correlation of justice, righteousness, and peace, see Leonhardt Rost, "Erwägungen zum Begriff *šālôm*," in *Schalom. Studien zu Glaube und*

Geschichte Israels. Alfred Jepsen zum 70. Geburtstag, ed. Karl-Heinz Bernhardt [Stuttgart: Calwer Verlag, 1971], pp. 41–44). (See the appendix to Ps 119: Yahweh Is My Redeemer.)

Notes

2–11 Instead of the future tense, the modal form "may he" could well be read as an expression of hope; so the NIV margin.

III. Prayer for Longevity and Universal Rule

72:5–11

5 He will endure as long as the sun,
as long as the moon, through all generations.
6 He will be like rain falling on a mown field,
like showers watering the earth.
7 In his days the righteous will flourish;
prosperity will abound till the moon is no more.

8 He will rule from sea to sea
and from the River to the ends of the earth.
9 The desert tribes will bow before him
and his enemies will lick the dust.
10 The kings of Tarshish and of distant shores
will bring tribute to him;
the kings of Sheba and Seba
will present him gifts.
11 All kings will bow down to him
and all nations will serve him.

5–6 The hope is that the wise king will remain a blessing for a long time. The duration ("as long as the sun, as long as the moon," v.5) probably refers to the length of the royal dynasty rather than the individual ruler. However, the individual contributes to and shares in the longevity of the dynasty and as such in the prosperity of God's people. The prosperity is likened to rain showers on "a mown field" and on "the earth" (v.6). The metaphor of "rain" (*māṭār, rᵉḇîḇîm*) denotes the refreshing and prosperous effects of the reign of the Davidic king (cf. 2 Sam 23:4; Prov 16:15; Hos 6:3; Mic 5:7). What is the beneficial effect of showers on a mown field (*gēz*)? It is likely that *gēz* denotes young growth on a freshly mown field (cf. Amos 7:1).

7 A wise king brings in a rule of righteousness and peace. As long as the Davidic dynasty is responsive to divine wisdom, the Lord guarantees that righteousness and peace will flourish. The effects of his administration will last ("as long as the sun, as long as the moon," v.5), and its benefits on the population will long be enjoyed ("till the moon is no more").

8 The rule of the Davidic dynasty will not only extend in time ("through all generations," v.5) but also in space (vv.8–11). The extent of the Davidic kingdom is in line with the hope of Psalm 2. Its worldwide dominion is representative of Yahweh's rule over the earth. The messianic government spreads out over seas, rivers, and land. It is unnecessary to restrict the meaning to a particular sea (from the Red Sea [or Persian Gulf] to the Mediterranean, cf. Exod 23:31) or river (Euphrates) because v.8 speaks of his universal rule, encompassing seas, rivers, and lands. So we read in Kirkpatrick: "Extension, not limit, is the idea conveyed. The world belongs to God: may he confer on His representative a world-wide dominion! a hope to be realized only in the universal kingdom of Christ" (p. 420).

9–11 Kings and nations shall submit to the divinely appointed ruler (cf. Pss 2; 29:2). Willingly or unwillingly the nations shall present their tribute as acts of obeisance and submission (vv.8–9, 11). That all shall recognize the sovereignty of the Davidic dynasty finds expression in the language of the court ("bow before him," v.9; cf. v.11) and of battle ("will lick the dust," v.9; cf. Isa 49:23; Mic 7:17).

The source of the recognition, whether from nations near or distant, is irrelevant. The nearby nations are represented by "the desert tribes" and the "enemies" (v.9). The distant nations are the kings of the "distant shores" (v.10): Tarshish (cf. 48:7), Sheba (modern Yemen), and Seba (an African nation; cf. Gen 10:7; Isa 43:3; 45:14). The imagery of these verses reflects the Solomonic era of peace, righteousness, and international diplomacy (cf. 1 Kings 4:21, 34; 10:1–29). The visit of the Magi (Matt 2:11) celebrates the submission and tribute of Gentiles to Jesus our Messiah. But John expresses in a vision the hope that one day all nations shall submit to our Lord (Rev 21:26).

Notes

5–11 Robert Alter correlates the temporal and geographical dimensions: "The reign of justice perfectly implemented has the perdurable solidity of the timeless natural landscape. Nature having been introduced in the third line of the poem, the language of the psalm continually intimates a double relation between the order of justice and the order of nature as cause and effect and as symbolic correspondence" (pp. 131–32).

5 The NIV margin reflects the problem of the MT ("you will be feared"). The LXX has an alternate reading, requiring the MT's יִירָאוּךָ (*yîrā'ûḵā*, "they will fear you") to be emended to וְיַאֲרִיךְ (*w^eya'^arîḵ*, "and he will prolong"; NIV, "he will endure"; cf. 89:36).

7 The NIV reading "the righteous will flourish" correctly renders the MT (צַדִּיק, *ṣaddîq*), but the MT reading is not supported by several Hebrew MSS or by the LXX and Syriac, which instead read "righteousness" (*ṣeḏeq*). The parallel reading of "prosperity" (*šālôm*) and "righteousness" (*ṣ^eḏāqāh*) in v.3 supports the emendation in v.7: "In his days righteousness will flourish; prosperity will abound." Paul D. Hanson ("War and Peace in the Hebrew Bible," Int 38 [1984]: 341–62) contends that the Israelite was God's instrument of bringing his peace and righteousness in a "fragile world" (p. 354).

9 The word צִיִּים (*ṣîyîm*) is related to *ṣîyāh* ("waterless region"), hence NIV's "desert tribes." The ancient versions had trouble with this word: LXX, "Ethiopians"; Syriac, "islands." BHS proposes several emendations: "islands" or "enemies" (Kraus, *Psalmen*, 1:494).

IV. Hope for Righteousness and Justice

72:12–14

12 For he will deliver the needy who cry out,
the afflicted who have no one to help.

[13]He will take pity on the weak and the needy
and save the needy from death.
[14]He will rescue them from oppression and violence,
for precious is their blood in his sight.

12–13 The psalmist returns to the theme of hope in an era of righteousness and justice. The divinely appointed and blessed king does not serve his own interests but those of others. He represents God's concern for the oppressed—"the needy ['*eḇyôn*] . . . afflicted ['*ānî*, cf. v.2]. . . . weak [*dal*] and the needy ['*eḇyôn*] . . . the needy ['*eḇ yônîm*]" (see the appendix to Ps 140: The Poor and Oppressed). The destitute, disadvantaged, and social outcasts were subjects of the king; but more than that, they were also his concern. Those against whom others discriminated ("who have no one to help," v.12; cf. Job 24:12; Ps 107:12) were the very people whose concerns the king took to heart ("he will take pity," v.13). His "pity" is the ground for action, transforming sympathy to empathy. "Pity" is an emotion of love and endearment rather than a detached condescension.

14 Since his subjects look to him for justice, God's representative, the king, loves them and values their very lives as his own ("for precious is their blood in his sight"; cf. 9:12; 116:15; 2 Kings 1:13–14). He will "save/rescue" (vv.13–14; cf. vv.2, 4: "judge. . . . defend . . . save") the destitute from their adversaries and from their prosecutors ("oppression and violence"; cf. 10:7; 55:11; see appendix to Ps 119: Yahweh Is My Redeemer). He will grant them life by taking away the pangs of death (v.13; see appendix to Ps 88: Sheol-Grave-Death in the Psalms).

V. Prayer for Longevity and Universality

72:15–17

[15]Long may he live!
May gold from Sheba be given him.
May people ever pray for him
and bless him all day long.
[16]Let grain abound throughout the land;
on the tops of the hills may it sway.
Let its fruit flourish like Lebanon;
let it thrive like the grass of the field.
[17]May his name endure forever;
may it continue as long as the sun.

All nations will be blessed through him,
and they will call him blessed.

15–17 Reflection on the benefits of the theocratic kingship renews the prayer for the extension in time and space of the Davidic dynasty and its monarch (cf. vv.5–11). First, the prayer includes a petition for the longevity of the king and the perpetuity of the dynasty ("long may he live!" v.15; cf. 1 Sam 10:24; 2 Sam 16:16; 1 Kings 1:25, 34, 39). The concern for the "name" of the king (v.17) relates to the continuity of his regime as well as to the continuation of the blessings of his regime ("may it continue as long as the sun," v.17; cf. v.5). Second, the security and perpetuity of his kingship is advanced by the subject nations that bring him tribute—such as the "gold from

Sheba" (v.15; cf. v.10; 1 Kings 10:14–15, 22)—and pray for his welfare (cf. 1 Kings 8:66).

Third, the prosperity of the king blessed by the Lord extends to all realms, represented here by "grain" and "fruit" (v.16). The interrelation between righteousness and prosperity has been well observed by A.A. Anderson: "This verse, and the Psalm as a whole, shows that what we call the 'moral realm' and the 'realm of nature' form one indivisible whole to the Israelites. A community which lives according to righteousness enjoys not only internal harmony, but also prosperity in field and flock" (p. 525). The metaphor for prosperity is the picture of a land covered from valley to mountaintop with fields of grain and fruit-bearing trees. Fourth, the psalmist petitions the extension of blessing to all the subject nations (v.17). They too will be "blessed" (cf. 1:1; 65:4) in accordance with the promise of the Abrahamic covenant (cf. Gen 12:2–3; 22:18; 26:4).

Notes

16 The phrase פִּסַּת־בַּר (*pissaṯ-bar,* "grain") is unique. The word *pissāh* is a *hapax legomenon* and may signify "plentitude" (Kraus, *Psalmen,* 1:494).

The NIV's "let it thrive" is a questionable rendering of מֵעִיר (*mē'îr,* "from a city"), based on Dahood's proposal (*Psalms,* 2:184). The Hebrew word may be corrected by a consonantal transposition to עֲמִיר (*'amîr,* "grain"), resulting in the rendering: "Let its fruit be like Lebanon; let its grain blossom forth like the grass of the field" (see Kraus, *Psalmen,* 1:494; A.A. Anderson, 1:525–26).

The last section of v.16—"let it thrive like the grass of the field"—is problematic, as the subject of the MT ("let them from the city blossom like grass") is undefined. The prayer could include an entreaty for the prosperity of the population, as suggested by the NKJV: "And those of the city shall flourish like grass of the earth" (cf. RSV). The NIV is preferable in taking the subject of the previous colons (cf. "flourishing like the grass of the earth," Dahood, *Psalms,* 2:179, 184).

17 The Hithpael of *b-r-k* ("bless") could be read as "will be blessed" (NIV) or "will bless themselves." Because of the usage in Gal 3:8–9 and the significance of the passive tense in Israel's active mission of bringing God's blessing to the nations, the passive tense is preferable. But it is somewhat surprising that Calvin prefers the reflexive: "But if it is considered preferable to distinguish between these two expressions, (which is not less probable), *to bless one's self in the king,* will denote to seek happiness from him; for the nations will be convinced that nothing is more desirable than to receive from him laws and ordinances" (3:118).

VI. Praise of God's Kingship

72:18–20

[18] Praise be to the LORD God, the God of Israel,
who alone does marvelous deeds.
[19] Praise be to his glorious name forever;
may the whole earth be filled with his glory.
Amen and Amen.

[20] This concludes the prayers of David son of Jesse.

18–20 The concluding doxology closes Book II. The Lord is "blessed" (*bārûḵ;* NIV, "praise be to"). He is God, the LORD (Yahweh), "the God of Israel," who has done and will continue to do "marvelous deeds" on behalf of his people (v.18; cf. 71:14; 86:10; 136:4). Through his "deeds" he has demonstrated his "glorious name" (v.19; cf. 1 Chron 29:13; Neh 9:5; Isa 63:14) in all the earth (cf. Isa 6:3). Such was also the testimony of Zechariah: "Praise be to the Lord, the God of Israel, / because he has come and has redeemed his people" (Luke 1:68).

The congregational response to the doxology is a twofold "Amen" (cf. 106:48; Neh 8:6). They confess that these words are true (Ernst Jenni, "Zu den doxologischen Schlussformeln des Psalters," *Theologische Zeitschrift* 40 [1984]: 114–20). The final verse (v.20) separates the psalms associated with David from those of Asaph (73–83).

Book III: Psalms 73–89

Psalm 73: The Suffering of God's Children and the Goodness of God

The psalmist struggles within himself as to the appropriate response to evil and injustice in the world. His vivid description of the wicked moves him to greater despair until he reflects on his God. Then he again claims the promises of God's presence and protection and seeks the glory of God reserved for him in this life and in the life to come (see Sheldon H. Blank, "The Nearness of God and Psalm Seventy-Three," *To Do and To Teach: Essays in Honor of Charles Lynn Pyatt,* ed. Roscoe M. Pierson [Lexington: The College of the Bible, 1953], pp. 1–13). This psalm is a moving autobiographical reflection on the suffering of the righteous and the prosperity of the wicked (cf. Pss 37, 49; Job). It can be best categorized as a *wisdom psalm* (so J. Luyten, "Psalm 73 and Wisdom," *La Sagesse de l'Ancien Testament,* ed. M. Gilbert [Leuven: University Press, 1979], pp. 59–81) in which the lament is the vehicle of communication (see James F. Ross, "Psalm 73," in *Israelite Wisdom. Theological Literary Essays in Honor of Samuel Terrien,* ed. J.G. Gammie et al. [Missoula: Scholars, 1978], pp. 161–75). Leslie C. Allen argues in favor of a cultic interpretation ("Psalm 73: An Analysis," *Tyndale Bulletin* 33 [1982]: 93–118; cf. Helmer Ringgren, "Einige Bemerkungen zum LXXIII Psalm," VetTest 3 [1953]: 265–72), but form-critical criteria alone are insufficient. For a national interpretation, see Ernst Würthwein, "Erwagungen zu Psalm 73," *Festschrift für Alfred Bertholet zum 80. Geburtstag,* edd. Walter Baumgartner, Otto Eissfeldt, Karl Elliger, and Leonhard Rost (Tübingen: Mohr, 1950), pp. 532–49. For the interpretation as a *psalm of confidence,* see Claus Westermann, *Ausgewählte Psalmen* (Göttingen: Vandenhoeck & Ruprecht, 1984), pp. 98–107. André Caquot gives an extensive analysis of this psalm in support of dating it to the exilic experience of Israel between 587–538 B.C. ("Le Psaume LXXIII," *Semitica* 21 [1971]: pp. 29–55).

The themes of the psalm are summarized in vv.1–3: God's goodness, personal anguish, and the prosperity of the wicked. The last verse constitutes an inclusion by responding to the issues of vv.1–3 with these insights: God's goodness, personal trust, and hope in the judgment of the wicked (vv.27–28). The structure develops these themes:

A. Experience and Belief (vv.1–3)
  B. Prosperity of the Wicked (vv.4–12)

C. Personal Reaction (vv.13–17)
D. Affirmation of God's Justice (vv.18–20)
C′. Evaluation of the Psalmist's Reaction (vv.21–22)
B′. The Desire of the Godly (vv.23–26)
A′. Experience and Hope (vv.27–28)

The psalm is a prayer arising from anguish on account of the freedom of the wicked. The psalmist deals with his emotions until disorientation brings him to a reorienting vision. The belief in God's justice (D) is at the heart of the psalm. It is the turning point (pivot) and accounts for the shift (vv.21–28). The psalmist experiences a new sense of joy and freedom when reflecting on the joy of fellowship with his God. The problem of the suffering of the righteous has no clear resolution, but the "pain" is relieved by the experience of God's living presence.

I. Experience and Belief

73:1–3

A psalm of Asaph.

1 Surely God is good to Israel,
to those who are pure in heart.

2 But as for me, my feet had almost slipped;
I had nearly lost my foothold.
3 For I envied the arrogant
when I saw the prosperity of the wicked.

1 Though it may seem that God does not care for the elect, the psalmist has learned from his own experience that God is good, i.e., his friend. The affirmation ("Surely," vv.1, 13 ,18) sets the tone, as the psalmist expresses God's justice toward the upright (v.1), states his personal dilemma (v.13), and hopes in God's just dealing with the wicked (v.18).

The psalmist encourages the "pure in heart" to join him in praying through their negative emotions and in hoping in God's goodness. The "pure" are not perfect but live in loyalty to God in speech and action, thus evidencing their "pure" motive. They are without hypocrisy. The "heart" occurs in six instances: "pure in heart" (v.1), "callous hearts" (v.7), "kept my heart pure" (v.13), "my heart was grieved" (v.21), "my heart may fail" (v.26), "God is the strength of my heart" (v.26). The place of the "heart" is most important, as Martin Buber writes, "The state of the heart determines whether a man lives in the truth, in which God's goodness is experienced, or in the semblance of truth. . . . The state of the heart determines" ("The Heart Determines [Psalm 73]," *On the Bible. Eighteen Studies by Martin Buber*, ed. Nahum N. Glatzer [New York: Schocken, 1982], p. 201).

2–3 Life can be very difficult for the godly. At times they seem to get nowhere and are provoked to anger and jealousy. Negative emotions are there but must be dealt with. The psalmist readily and publicly admits his error. He "envied the arrogant" (*hôlᵉlîm;* see 75:4). Everything was going well with the ungodly: prosperity, business relations, and family. They experienced "prosperity" (*šālôm,* lit., "peace").

Why was the psalmist so miserable? Engaged in self-pity and questioning God's justice, he was filled with resentment and could easily have joined those he envied. But he did not, for God upholds his saints (v.2; cf. 37:23–24). The contrastive phrase "but as for me" (*wa'ᵃnî*) occurs four times in the Hebrew (vv.2, 22–23, 28). Each time it is emphatic and appears to be a device by which the psalmist confesses his error ("[I] almost slipped," v.2; "I was senseless," v.22) and emphasizes what God has done for him ("I am always with you," v.23; "But as for me, it is good to be near God," v.28). He nearly failed, but God sustained him and kept him close to himself. That is grace! Brueggemann correctly observes: "The psalm impresses one in its remarkable insight and candor. It is a tale of a heart seduced and then healed, a heart isolated and then restored to fellowship" (*Message of the Psalms*, p. 121).

Notes

For a brief discussion of the technical words and phrases in the superscription, see the Introduction.

1 William L. Moran defines "good" as "friendship" in covenantal terminology, and this seems to fit well here and in v.28 ("A Note on the Treaty Terminology of the Sefire Stelas," JNES 22 [1963]: 173–76).

Some EVV read "upright" instead of "Israel" (יִשְׂרָאֵל, *yiśrā'ēl*), assuming a word division: יָשָׁר אֵל (*yāšār 'el*, "upright to"; cf. NEB, "How good God is to the upright"). However, there is no evidence from the ancient versions; and it is preferable to understand "Israel" as the spiritual Israel, e.g., "those who are pure in heart." The only reason in favor of the proposal is a concern for parallelism: "upright" // "pure in heart" (Kraus, *Psalmen*, 1:502).

James L. Crenshaw observes that the whole psalm contains many allusions to parts of the body: "heart" (a key to Ps 73, as it occurs six times, vv.1, 7, 13, 21, 26 [*bis*]), "hand[s]" (vv.13, 23), "feet" (v.2), eyes (cf. v.3), etc. (*A Whirlpool of Torment. Israelite Traditions on God as an Oppressive Force* [Philadelphia: Fortress, 1984], pp. 97–99).

II. Prosperity of the Wicked

73:4–12

4 They have no struggles;
their bodies are healthy and strong.
5 They are free from the burdens common to man;
they are not plagued by human ills.
6 Therefore pride is their necklace;
they clothe themselves with violence.
7 From their callous hearts comes iniquity;
the evil conceits of their minds know no limits.
8 They scoff, and speak with malice;
in their arrogance they threaten oppression.
9 Their mouths lay claim to heaven,
and their tongues take possession of the earth.
10 Therefore their people turn to them
and drink up waters in abundance.
11 They say, "How can God know?
Does the Most High have knowledge?"

12 This is what the wicked are like—
always carefree, they increase in wealth.

4–12 The psalmist gives a summary of the power and freedom of the wicked (vv.4–9). They seem to be carefree and unconcerned about tomorrow. For them life is now, and now seems to be forever. They are doing well, as their wealth and power increase. The wicked may seem to enjoy greater freedom of movement and speech. They are like "gods" in several ways. First, they do not seem to suffer from the frailties, adversities, diseases, and toilsome labor common to man (vv.4–5; cf. Gen 3:17–19). They seem to live above the frustrations of life. The word for "burdens" (*ʿāmāl*) is usually translated as "toil," i.e., the toilsome activities of making a living for one's family (cf. Eccl 1:3). This toil of life includes frustration, adversity, and the business of life. The wicked prosper in their wickedness. Their eyes sparkle because everything is going well for them (v.7). Though their hearts are full of evil schemes, the wicked succeed and prosper (cf. Mal 3:15).

Second, the wicked do not regard God and his commandments. Instead they are puffed up with "pride" (v.6). Their "necklace"—a token of dignity (cf. Gen 41:42)—is self-importance and pride. They leave behind a trail of violence. Whatever they have is due to scheming and a lawless way of life, disregarding the rights of others. They live at the expense of others.

The wicked scoff, boast, and threaten (v.8). They know how to use their tongue as an instrument of evil (cf. 10:6–7), because the imaginings of their hearts are evil. The phrase "evil conceits" (*maśkîyô<u>t</u>*, "image," v.7) usually denotes images of idols. Here it has the metaphorical sense of "imagination." The hearts of the wicked are full of imaginations or schemings by which they seem to succeed and prosper.

The wicked rule with their "tongues" (v.9). By intimidation they instill fear in others, and in their imagination they act as if they can get by without responsibility to God. They decree how things are to be done on earth and what God can do in heaven. They revile God (cf. 10:11, 15) and beguile man. Such is the power, glory, and prosperity of the wicked from the mistaken vantage point of man in his affliction. It seems as if God lets the wicked get by with their wickedness.

Notes

---

4 The word חַרְצֻבּוֹת (*ḥarṣubbô<u>t</u>*) occurs only twice in the MT. In Isa 58:6 it denotes illegal fetters (NIV, "chains of injustice"), signifying oppression. The word "fetters" may carry a metaphorical meaning here: "struggles" (NIV), "torments" (KB^3, 1:342), or "pain" (NEB).

The phrase לְמוֹתָם (*l^emô<u>t</u>ām*, lit., "to their death") occasions greater difficulty. Modern versions (e.g., NIV; see mg.) and exegetes assume an alternate word and stichometric division: לָמוֹ (*lāmô*, "to them") with the first colon ("they have no struggles") and תָּם (*tām*, "perfect") with the second colon ("healthy [= perfect] and strong"). The wicked, thus defined, have no troubles and enjoy great health.

The phrase אוּלָם (*ʾûlām*, "their bodies") is a *hapax legomenon* in the OT.

7 The NIV margin gives the rendering of the Hebrew with an observation that the text follows the Syriac. The MT reads: "comes out from fat their eyes." Instead of "their eyes" the LXX and Syriac read "their guilt," resulting in "from fat comes forth their guilt" (Kraus, *Psalmen*, 1:501–2). The NIV explains "fat" as "callous hearts."

The verb יצא (*y-ṣ-ʾ*, "go out") may signify "to shine" or "to glisten" (Dahood, *Psalms*, 2:189). Even though Dahood's proposal requires repointing the verb, it is preferable by reason of its simplicity. We propose an alternate reading to Dahood's "their eyes glisten more than milk": "their eyes shine because of their prosperity [fat]." See the NEB: "Their eyes gleam through folds of fat"; NIV margin: *"Their eyes bulge with fat."*

10 The meaning of this verse is difficult because of the underlying Hebrew text. The literal rendering of the MT is unintelligible: "therefore his people will return [or 'he turns his people'] hither and waters of fullness are pressed out by them." The BHS proposes by a series of emendations: "They draw (my) people to them and people drink up their words" (Kraus, *Psalmen,* 1:501–2). Many variations exist in commentaries and modern versions. The thrust of the text is given in the NIV. The power, wealth, and influence of riches pervert. People are drawn by the rich. Power corrupts, not only those who have it, but also those who want to get a piece of the action. Opportunists turn to the right people in order to drink from their abundant waters.

11 It is not clear who the speakers are, but most likely the godless boast of their practical atheism (cf. 10:11; 14:1). They do not deny the existence of God but limit him in his knowledge and wisdom. From their perspective God is only concerned with religion, piety, and good deeds and does not punish those who by their own schemings and plottings take advantage of business and political opportunities. The questions of whether and how God knows imply strong, negative responses: "God does not know!" and "The Most High [Elyon] has no knowledge!" (see appendix to Ps 9: Yahweh Is El Elyon). The confidence of the wicked enticed many who did not have strong convictions.

III. Personal Reaction

73:13–17

13 Surely in vain have I kept my heart pure;
  in vain have I washed my hands in innocence.
14 All day long I have been plagued;
  I have been punished every morning.

15 If I had said, "I will speak thus,"
  I would have betrayed your children.
16 When I tried to understand all this,
  it was oppressive to me
17 till I entered the sanctuary of God;
  then I understood their final destiny.

13 It is not always easy to react honestly to the prosperity of others while suffering adversity. The psalmist knows and confesses his problem. First, he confesses that he doubted the value of his concern with sanctification. Keeping his heart "pure" was an expression of a concern for justice and righteousness (cf. 24:4; 119:9). He had not been guilty of bloodshed or oppressive activities; so he could say that his hands were washed "in innocence" (cf. 26:6; Matt 27:24).

14 Second, the psalmist confesses the turmoil of his own experiences. His emotions express self-doubt and envy. He does not question God but asks questions of himself in the spirit of Ecclesiastes. His being "plagued" and "punished" most probably does not refer to a sickness but to the experience of mental turmoil (cf. v.16). In addition he suffered from adversities that took the form of punishments because he could not understand why he was suffering. The external adversities and internal problems with the outworking of God's justice burned in him day and night. It was always there! Yet these ordeals would result in a greater spiritual maturity. R. Davidson correctly argues in favor of the creative and positive role of doubt ("Some Aspects of the Theological

Significance of Doubt in the Old Testament," *Annual of the Swedish Theological Institute* 7 [1970]: 44–46).

15 Third, the psalmist confesses a deep concern for the people of God ("your children"). If he had let his emotions reign, he may have spoken against the community of faith. He confesses that he thought about removing himself for the sake of the prosperity and peace of his soul, but he could not sever the ties with God's people. The Lord kept him from sliding (cf. v.2). Brueggemann concludes that this thought changed the orientation of the psalmist, as he reflects freely and uncumbered by "the ideology of self-sufficiency, affluence, and autonomy" (*Message of the Psalms*, p. 121).

16–17 Fourth, the psalmist confesses that though he cannot understand the ways of God (v.16), he experienced anew God's peace when he entered into the sanctuary (v.17).

Overwhelmed by the greatness, glory, and majesty of God, the psalmist regained a proper perspective of his situation. He rediscovered something he had known but had forgotten: the Lord is just! In the end evil is not and never will be victorious. The wicked will be severely judged. Walther Zimmerli observes incisively that "faith, assailed by its inability to comprehend God's 'order' in the experiences of everyday life, finds its way to the bold confidence which confesses that it will cleave to God as its 'portion' even when heart and body fail" (OTTO, p. 165).

Notes

14 The NIV agrees with BHS in an emendation of the noun תּוֹכַחְתִּי (*tôkaḥtî*, "my chastisement") to a verbal form, הוּכַחְתִּי (*hôkaḥtî*, "I have been chastised," "punished," Kraus, *Psalmen*, 1:502).

15 The people of God are known as the "sons" or children of God, בָּנֶיךָ (*bāneykā*, "your sons"). The OT knows of adoption to sonship (cf. Rom 9:4).

16 The noun עָמָל (*'āmāl*, "trouble"; NIV, "oppression") occurs in v.5 ("burdens").

17 The literary approach of holistic interpretation espoused by Meir Weiss supports our exposition (*The Bible From Within. The Method of Total Interpretation* [Jerusalem: Magnes, 1984], pp. 260–66).

מִקְדְּשֵׁי (*miqdᵉšê*, "sanctuaries") is a plural construct form in the MT. Dahood interprets this as a reference to God's heavenly temple, based on Canaanite usage and the parallelism of "skies" (pl.) in 68:34–35 (*Psalms*, 2:192). But how could the psalmist enter the heavenly sanctuary? Briggs is probably right in taking the plural as an intensive: "the great sanctuary" (2:146; see appendix to Ps 132: The Ark of the Covenant and the Temple: Symbols of Yahweh's Presence and Rule).

IV. Affirmation of God's Justice

73:18–20

18 Surely you place them on slippery ground;
you cast them down to ruin.

19 How suddenly are they destroyed,
completely swept away by terrors!
20 As a dream when one awakes,
so when you arise, O Lord,
you will despise them as fantasies.

18–19 Whereas the Lord had not permitted the psalmist to slip into sin, the wicked were doomed to fall. Their fall is always characterized by the element of surprise (v.19) and by the evident judgment of God (v.18). The Lord has set them up for the fall. The "when" is not as important as the certainty that they will slip and fall. It may take several generations of their dynastic rule before they are brought down. But the assurance of Scripture is that the wicked will be judged "suddenly" and "completely." All kinds of "terrors" or troubles will overtake them, and finally death itself.

20 The wicked are like "a dream," which has a sense of reality when one is asleep but is gone at the moment of awakening. The wicked are "a phantom": here today, gone tomorrow. The coming of God's righteous judgment brings all things into perspective. In the meantime the godly live with the vision that the wicked are nothing but "fantasies." The experiences of terror and anguish of mind will turn out to be little more than a nightmare, a bad dream.

Notes

19 Marvin J. Pope argues that "terrors" may refer to "death" personified as "the king of terrors" (*Job*, AB [Garden City: Doubleday, 1965], p. 126).

20 This verse is very difficult. The literal translation is "like a dream when awakening, Lord, in the city their image you despise." A slight emendation makes sense and is assumed in the NIV. This involves a change of the MT's בָּעִיר (*bā'îr*, "in the city") to בְּעוּר (*b*^{e}*'ûr*, "when one awakes"). The sense of the verse is probably as suggested by the NIV. When God rouses himself to action, the wicked are nothing but an image in relation to God. Though they have set themselves up as "gods," they are not real and will be dealt with quickly. R.J. Tournay explains this verse in the light of a cultic theophany and relates it to v.24: the hope of the resurrection ("Le Psaume LXXIII: Relectures et Interprétation," RB 92 [1985]: 187–200; so also Léonard Ramaroson, "Immortalité et Résurrection dans les Psaumes," *Science et Esprit* 36 [1984]: 287–95).

V. Evaluation of the Psalmist's Reaction

73:21–22

21 When my heart was grieved
and my spirit embittered,
22 I was senseless and ignorant;
I was a brute beast before you.

21–22 The psalmist again considers his reaction to the prosperity of the wicked (cf. vv.13–17). He was deeply affected by envy and anguish. His "heart" and "kidneys" (NIV, "spirit") are expressive of his inner self (v.21; see 7:9; cf. 26:2). Deep inside he was grieved and embittered, resulting in a state of depression. In this state he was irrational (cf. 94:8), not ruled by wisdom. Not to be ruled by wisdom made him like the fools, who are compared to brute beasts (cf. 49:12, 20; Isa 1:2–3). He was plagued with oppressive questions and self-pity. However, he had to go through the experience before he could more fully enjoy fellowship with God. Questions, anguish, and a sense of stupidity may be used by the Lord to mature his servant—an experience shared by other psalmists and by the prophet Jeremiah.

Notes

21 The root idea of יִתְחַמֵּץ (*yiṯḥammēṣ*, "grieved") is "soured." The Hithpael form of the root (*ḥ-m-ṣ*, "be sour") only occurs here and expresses the intensity with which the psalmist's innermost feelings were affected by the experience. From this root comes the noun "leaven," and one might say that the sour experience has "leavened" him through and through.

VI. The Desire of the Godly

73:23–26

23 Yet I am always with you;
you hold me by my right hand.
24 You guide me with your counsel,
and afterward you will take me into glory.
25 Whom have I in heaven but you?
And earth has nothing I desire besides you.
26 My flesh and my heart may fail,
but God is the strength of my heart
and my portion forever.

23–26 In this section the experience of pain and anguish is transformed to the joy of God's presence. God is the psalmist's chief desire (v.25). Twice he repeats "with you" (vv.23, 25 [Heb.]) to express the joy of fellowship with God. Because of God's presence, the psalmist is also more assured of his protection and guidance. God protects him by holding his "right hand" (v.23; cf. 63:8; Isa 41:10, 13; 42:6; Jer 31:32), by giving him internal fortitude ("rock"; NIV, "strength," v.26; cf. 18:2), and by providing for all his needs ("portion," v.26; cf. 16:5). God guides his servant by giving him wisdom and insight ("counsel") as he travels on the road to everlasting glory (v.24).

The "glory" (*kāḇôḏ*, v.24) of God is his blessed presence, which Moses experienced on Mount Sinai (Exod 33:18–23; 34:6–7, 29–35). The glory of God affects one's whole way of life as one lives in the joy of God's love, mercy, patience, grace, and forgiveness. But hope extends beyond this life to the future, when God takes care of all his children's needs.

The joy of fellowship with God as experienced in his protection and guidance is so intense that the psalmist bursts out with a rhetorical question (v.25). The clear answer is that there is no one but God, his Sustainer in heaven, with whom he longingly desires to fellowship even while in the flesh. Therefore he is more prepared to face his present existence with all its problems. He is prepared to grow older and experience failing health and even adversity because God is his "strength," "portion" (v.26), and "refuge" (v.28). "The Rock" (*ṣûr*, v.26; NIV, "strength") of Israel is present with him in protection, guidance, and confidence (18:1–3).

The Lord is also the psalmist's "portion" (*ḥeleq*, v.26). He cares and provides for his own (cf. 16:5). In ancient Israel the priests enjoyed a privileged status of having the Lord as their "share" and "inheritance" (Num 18:20). Though they were denied the privilege of land ownership, they, along with the Levites, were taken care of by the Lord's tithes and offerings (cf. Num 18:1–32). Similarly the psalmist casts himself on the Lord for all his needs, as Crenshaw has put it, "The Psalmist has stood near the flame and has at least been caught up in it" (*A Whirlpool of Torment*, p. 108).

Notes

---

24 In contrast to the אַחֲרִיתָם (*'aḥ^{a}rîṯām*, lit., "their end,"; NIV, "final destiny," v.17) of the wicked, the psalmist is confident of his אַחַר (*'aḥar*, "end"; NIV, "afterward"). The similarity in expression should be obvious.

VII. Experience and Hope

73:27–28

> 27 Those who are far from you will perish;
>   you destroy all who are unfaithful to you.
> 28 But as for me, it is good to be near God.
>   I have made the Sovereign LORD my refuge;
>   I will tell of all your deeds.

27–28 The observation of God's goodness to Israel (v.1) is applicable to the individual. With the emphatic "I" the psalmist confesses, "But as for me, it is good to be near God" (v.28). What a contrast to another occurrence of the emphatic "I": "But as for me, my feet almost slipped" (v.2)! He had been upheld (v.23) by his God, whose presence he had experienced anew in the sanctuary (v.17). His response was that of a renewed commitment by making God his refuge and by praising God's "deeds" (v.28). In anticipation of God's just acts of vindication, the psalmist declares his hope in his God in song. He hopes in the end of the wicked. They must perish because they are "unfaithful" to God. Their judgment is based, not only on their failure to profess faith in God, but also on their lives of immorality and injustice.

These verses are a fitting conclusion and form a contrastive inclusion with vv.1–3. Envy has turned to hope, and God's goodness (see note on v.1) to Israel is also experienced at the individual level. "It is good to be near God" (v.28). Martin Buber comments on this verse: "It is not, however, from his own consciousness and feeling that he can say this, for no man is able to be continually turned to the presence of God: he can say it only in the strength of the revelation that God is continually with him" ("The Heart Determines: Psalm 73," in *Theodicy in the Old Testament*, ed. James L. Crenshaw [Philadelphia: Fortress, 1983], p. 114).

Psalm 74: The Destruction of the Temple

The community of the godly in exile weeps over the destruction of the temple (586 B.C.). The temple symbolized the presence and the protection of God. The Lord had permitted the nations to ravage the land and to destroy his sanctuary and through these acts had demonstrated that he had abandoned his people. In this *community lament* the godly nevertheless affirm the creative and redemptive powers of their covenant God (vv.12–17) as the ground for their petition to be redeemed (vv.18–23). For background see Ralph W. Klein, *Israel in Exile. A Theological Interpretation* (Philadelphia: Fortress, 1979), esp. pp. 19–20. For an approach to this psalm as a war oracle, see the study by Christensen, pp. 112–27. For other psalms see 12; 60; 79; 80; 83; 85; 90; 94:1–11; 123; 126; and 137.

The psalm develops in two parallel halves (vv.1–9, 10–23), and each part of the lament contains questions (vv.1, 10–11) and prayers for remembrance (vv.2–3, 18–21, 22–23). At its structural center, overlapping the two parts, lies the description of the desolation of the temple (vv.4–8), the consequent feeling of abandonment (v.9), and a moving meditation on God's past involvements (vv.12–17). The following schema represents this movement:

A. Prayer for Remembrance (vv.1–3)
  B. Destruction of the Temple (vv.4–8)
    C. Feeling of Abandonment (v.9–11)
    C′. God's Past Involvements (vv.12–17)
A′. Prayer for Remembrance (vv.18–21)
  B′. Destruction of God's Enemies (vv.22–23)

(See Pierre Auffret, "Essai su la Structure littéraire du Psaume lxxiv," VetTest 33 [1983]: 129–48; Graeme E. Sharrock, "Psalm 74: A Literary-Structural Analysis," *Andrews University Seminary Studies* 21 [1983]: 211–23; Meir Weiss, *The Bible From Within. The Method of Total Interpretation* [Jerusalem: Magnes, 1984], pp. 281–93.)

I. Prayer for Remembrance

74:1–3

A *maskil* of Asaph.

1 Why have you rejected us forever, O God?
Why does your anger smolder against the sheep
of your pasture?
2 Remember the people you purchased of old,
the tribe of your inheritance, whom you redeemed—
Mount Zion, where you dwelt.
3 Turn your steps toward these everlasting ruins,
all this destruction the enemy has brought on the
sanctuary.

1–3 Though the punishment of exile was deserved, the people nevertheless felt as if God had abandoned them forever. The lament begins with a searching question: "Why?"—a question that expresses the depth of the emotions. The "why" arises because of the magnitude of God's anger (cf. 18:8; Lam 2:3), the proximity of their past relationship ("sheep of your pasture," cf. 100:3), and their present alienation. The questioner asks how God can be angry with his own people forever. He does not question the correctness of his judgment but uses the question and the lament as the basis for an appeal to God's fatherly heart.

The appeal itself consists of two imperative clauses: "remember" (v.2) and "lift up" (v.3; NIV, "Turn"). The phrase "turn your steps" (v.3) is unique in the OT. The verb *hārîmāh* (lit., "lift up") petitions the Lord to look with pity on the ruins of the city of God (see NEB, "Now at last restore what was ruined beyond repair"). The psalmist calls on the Lord to remember the relationship of grace. The Lord redeemed his people from Egypt (Exod 20:1), formed them to be his "inheritance," i.e., his own people (cf. Jer 10:16; 51:19), and has "of old" maintained this relationship (v.2; cf. Exod 15:13, 16). Moreover, he has chosen to dwell in the midst of his own people on Mount Zion (cf. 2 Sam 7:12–13; 1 Kings 6:12–13).

At this time, however, God's sanctuary lay in ruins. The psalmist calls on the Lord to investigate for himself the fate of Jerusalem. It seems as if the ruins are "everlasting," because every moment of God's anger seems like an eternity. God's enemies have defiled the "sanctuary" of the Lord. They have also defiled God's own people. The people of God are respectively designated as "the sheep of your pasture" (v.1; cf. 79:13; 100:3; Jer 23:1; Ezek 34:31), "the people" (v.2; *'ēḏāh*, lit., "congregation"), and "tribe." The relationship of the people with their covenant God is thus expressed as sheep and shepherd (protection and guidance), as covenant people ("congregation") and covenant God, and as a nation under the blessed governance of the Great King, by whose choice they had become his inheritance (cf. Exod 19:6; Acts 20:28; see appendix to Ps 5: Yahweh Is King). The blessed status is further amplified by God's dwelling among his people in Zion (v.2).

Notes

For a brief discussion of the technical words and phrases in the superscription, see the Introduction.

II. Destruction of the Temple

74:4–8

4 Your foes roared in the place where you met with us;
they set up their standards as signs.
5 They behaved like men wielding axes
to cut through a thicket of trees.
6 They smashed all the carved paneling
with their axes and hatchets.
7 They burned your sanctuary to the ground;
they defiled the dwelling place of your Name.
8 They said in their hearts, "We will crush them
completely!"
They burned every place where God was worshiped in
the land.

4 The presentation of Jerusalem's destruction is given in moving detail, focusing on the desecration of the temple by hostile forces. The enemies "roared" like lions (v.4;

cf. Jer 51:38) as they captured the temple area itself, where God's "congregation" (v.2; NIV, "people") celebrated the appointed feasts. Instead of hearing the priestly benediction (cf. Num 6:24–26), they heard the roaring of the enemy voices. Instead of witnessing the "signs" (v.4) of God's presence and forgiveness (sacrifices, priestly rituals), they saw the pagan "standards" that may have functioned as tokens of their victory (see NEB: "they planted their standards there as tokens of victory") or as symbols in pagan rituals.

5–7a The enemy was ferocious in its attempt to destroy every vestige of Israel's institutions. They were like mad men as they used their axes on the woodwork of the temple (vv.5–6). They had no respect for Israel's God. Instead they wildly wielded the axe as in a thicket of underbrush (cf. Jer 4:7). The beautiful carved work, described in 1 Kings 6:23–35, was destroyed by pagan axes and crowbars. The gold overlay (1 Kings 6:19–22) was stripped (2 Kings 25:13–17) off the wood. Then they burned the temple to the ground (v.7a; cf. 2 Kings 25:9).

7b–8 The lament focuses on the act of defiling the temple, designated by various expressions: "the sanctuary" (v.3), "your meeting place" (v.4; NIV, "the place where you met with us"), "your sanctuary" (v.7), "the dwelling place of your Name" (v.7), and "the meeting places of God" (v.8; NIV, "every place where God was worshiped"). Thus the psalmist emphasizes that the symbolic place of God's covenant and his mercies among his people was desecrated by hostile forces. In these designations he attempts to evoke a response from God, in that his sanctuary (*qōdeš*, "holy place") had been defiled! The usage of the synonyms seems to support his contention that the relationship between the Lord and Israel goes way back to the days of the wilderness (cf. v.2).

The hostile intent and the determination of the Babylonians is clearly expressed in v.8 by the words "They said in their hearts." Their goal was to destroy, by burning to the ground, the meeting place of God with his people. Thus they planned to change Israel's destiny and to remove any reminder of God's past loyalty and of the true worship of God.

Notes

---

4 A number of MSS read the plural: מוֹעֲדֶיךָ (*mô'aḏeyḵā*, "your meeting places," "your feasts"), as in v.8: מוֹעֲדֵי־אֵל (*mô'aḏê-'ēl*, "the meeting places of God," "the feasts of God"), instead of the MT singular: מוֹעֲדֶךָ (*mô'aḏeḵā*, "your meeting place," "your festival"). Regardless of whether the word is plural or singular, a more basic issue concerns the meaning of the phrase. The LXX favors "your feasts" in v.8, so as to avoid the suggestion of many meeting places. It is preferable to understand the phrase as a technical designation of the "sanctuary" of the Lord. The plural of v.8 may be understood as a plural of local extension or amplification (GKC, par. 124b), requiring it to be treated as a singular, "the meeting place of God." "The place where you met with us" is the sanctuary, also known as the "sanctuary of God" in v.8 (NIV, "where God was worshiped"). For a cultic explanation see Folker Willesen, "The Cultic Situation of Psalm LXXIV," VetTest 2 (1952): 289–306.

5 The sense of this problematic verse is reflected by the NIV. A. Robinson's effort illustrates how emendations have thus far proved to be the only way of understanding this verse. He

proposes "The way the ascent seemed like a tangled mess of timber, a city of desolations" ("A Possible Solution of Psalm 74:5," ZAW 89 [1977]: 120–21).

8 The word נִינָם (*nînām,* "their offspring") is taken as a noun in the LXX, but it may be preferable to read it as a verbal form from the root ינה (*y-n-h,* "to be violent," "to crush"), so also the Syriac. The NIV follows this proposal in the rendering "We will crush them completely."

For a discussion of "every place where God was worshiped in the land," see the note on v.4. A. Gelston concludes that v.8 reflects the preexilic situation, when many cultic sites existed in Judah ("A Note on Psalm lxxiv 8," VetTest 34 [1984]: 82–87).

III. Feeling of Abandonment

74:9–11

9 We are given no miraculous signs;
no prophets are left,
and none of us knows how long this will be.

10 How long will the enemy mock you, O God?
Will the foe revile your name forever?
11 Why do you hold back your hand, your right hand?
Take it from the folds of your garment and destroy
them!

9–11 This section is parallel to the questions raised at the beginning in vv.1–3. It concludes the lament (vv.1–8) and forms a transition to the confession of God's kingship (vv.12–17). God's people are disturbed at his apparent absence. They no longer witness any "signs" (v.9). They no longer see the "miraculous," the "symbols" of Israel's revealed religion (see v.4 above); nor do they see Israel's military standards or hear the oracles. Alienation was aggravated by the absence of the prophetic word. Instead of hearing a word from God, they heard the scoffing of the enemies. Their hatred was directed against the God of Israel. In their abandonment the godly show a deep concern for the honor of God's name, reviled by the pagans. On behalf of the community of God's people, the psalmist asks, "How long?" and "Why?" (vv.10–11).

Notes

9 J.J.M. Roberts defines אוֹתוֹת (*'ôṯôṯ,* "miraculous signs") as referring to the exilic expectation of fulfillment of the prophetic word (the downfall of Babylon, return of the temple vessels, and inauguration of the era of restoration). The disappointment of the exilic community is an example of prophetic dissonance ("Of Signs, Prophets, and Time Limits: A Note on Ps 74:9," CBQ 39 [1977]: 474–810). For the nature of prophetic dissonance, see W.A. VanGemeren, *Interpreting the Prophetic Word* (Grand Rapids: Zondervan, 1989), ch. 2.

11 The MT is difficult: "and your right hand from your bosom destroy." In view of the parallel construction, it is preferable to take the verb כַּלֵּה (*kallēh,* "consume," "destroy") as a form of the root *k-l-'* ("to keep from") instead of from *k-l-h;* e.g., BHS's כְּלֻאָה (*kᵉlu'āh,* "hidden"); cf. NEB, "why keep thy right hand within thy bosom."

IV. God's Past Involvements

74:12–17

12 But you, O God, are my king from of old;
   you bring salvation upon the earth.
13 It was you who split open the sea by your power;
   you broke the heads of the monster in the waters.
14 It was you who crushed the heads of Leviathan
   and gave him as food to the creatures of the desert.
15 It was you who opened up springs and streams;
   you dried up the ever flowing rivers.
16 The day is yours, and yours also the night;
   you established the sun and moon.
17 It was you who set all the boundaries of the earth;
   you made both summer and winter.

12–13a The laments give way to a hymn in which the psalmist represents the community in its worship of the great "king" (v.12; cf. 9:8; 10:16; 44:4–5). He has shown himself to be Israel's king "from of old," i.e., since he redeemed them from Egypt (v.13a; cf. Exod 15:18). He has done "acts of salvation" (pl. in MT; NIV, "salvation," v.12), being victorious over Israel's enemies. As King, God has led his people heroically from victory to victory (cf. vv.13–17).

The psalmist sings a hymnic praise remembering the acts of God in creation. He is Yahweh, the "king" (*meleḵ*), the "doer of acts of salvation" (*pōʿēl yešûʿôṯ*, v.12). He is the Redeemer of Israel who rules over all creation. The acts of creation are correlative to his acts of salvation, or what von Rad calls a "soteriological understanding of creation" (OTT, 1:138).

13b–17 The current victory of the pagans and the seeming power of the pagan deities require a powerful demonstration of the Lord's sovereignty. The absolute character of God's power and control is vividly expressed in the language of crushing the heads and of giving his victims as food to the wild animals (vv.13b–14; cf. Ezek 32:4). The God of salvation history redeemed Israel from Egypt in the past. His powers extend to all creation by virtue of his creative powers. He made and sovereignly rules over the waters (v.15; cf. 104:6–11), the earth (v.17; cf. 104:9), day and night (v.16), the heavenly bodies (v.16), and the seasons of the year (v.17; cf. Gen 8:22; Ps 104:19–23).

The psalmist chose the language of Canaanite mythology to celebrate Yahweh's victory over the nations. In the Ugaritic myths Yam ("the sea god") and Baal fought over supremacy. The "monster" (v.13b) symbolizes the wild, uncontrolled forces of the sea (cf. Job 7:12; Isa 51:9), which is also known as Leviathan (v.14; cf. 104:26; Isa 27:1) or as Lotan in the Ugaritic myths. Yahweh, the Creator-Redeemer, had demonstrated his sovereignty in history by the redemption of his people from Egypt (also symbolized as "the monster" in Ezek 29:3 or "Rahab" in Isa 51:9–10).

Notes

---

13 For Leviathan, a Masoretic reading for the Ugaritic *ltn*, see John Gray, *The Biblical Doctrine of the Reign of God* (Edinburgh: T. & T. Clark, 1979), pp. 75–76; Cyrus H. Gordon,

"Leviathan: Symbol of Evil," in *Biblical Motifs. Origins and Transformations*, ed. Alexander Altmann (Cambridge: Harvard University Press, 1966), pp. 1–9, and J. A. Emerton, "Leviathan and *LTN:* the Vocalization of the Ugaritic Word for the Dragon," VetTest 32 (1982): 327–31. The most comprehensive study is found in John Day, *God's Conflict With the Dragon and the Sea. Echoes of Canaanite Myth in the Old Testament* (Cambridge: Cambridge University Press, 1985). See also Tryggve N.D. Mettinger, "Fighting the Powers of Chaos and Hell—Towards the Biblical Portrait of God," ST 39 (1985): 21–38.

V. Prayer for Remembrance

74:18–21

18 Remember how the enemy has mocked you, O LORD,
how foolish people have reviled your name.
19 Do not hand over the life of your dove to wild beasts;
do not forget the lives of your afflicted people forever.
20 Have regard for your covenant,
because haunts of violence fill the dark places of the land.
21 Do not let the oppressed retreat in disgrace;
may the poor and needy praise your name.

18–21 The confessional hymn, celebrating God's creative and redemptive powers, revitalizes the godly with hope. They petition the Lord to "remember" (v.18; cf. v.2) the conduct of the enemies ("wild beasts," v.19) and the afflictions of his covenant people ("your dove"). The enemies have mocked and reviled the Lord's name, Yahweh. For pious Israel the name of the Lord was sacred, as it was his guarantee that he would fulfill all his covenant promises (cf. Exod 6:6–8). The enemies thought they had autonomy over God's people and therefore over the God of Israel. They are nothing but "foolish people" (v.18; cf. Deut 32:6) for denying the power of the Lord (cf. 14:1).

Over against the taunts of the enemy is the quiet cry of the godly, likened to a "dove" (v.19). The enemies are filled with contempt (v.18) and "violence" (v.20). Their pride stands in stark contrast to the powerlessness of the godly, described as "the oppressed, . . . the poor and needy" (v.21). The vile acts of the enemies of God resulted in bloodshed and darkness in the Land of Promise (v.20). In quiet desperation the psalmist prays that the Lord will have mercy on his own so that they will renew their praise of the Lord. The praise of God's name is in contrast to the desecration of his name (vv.18, 21).

Notes

---

18 The verbs expressive of the pagan desecration of the divine name are similar in meaning to those in v.10: חֵרֵף (*ḥērēp̱*, "mock," "taunt") and נִאֲצוּ (*ni'aṣû*, "revile," "treat irreverently").

19 There is no reason to emend the MT's תּוֹרֶךָ (*tôreḵā*, "your dove") to תּוֹדֶךָ (*tôḏeḵā*, "will praise you"; cf. LXX, Syr.); see NEB: "of the soul that confesses thee." For a review of the proposals and for a positive connection of "dove" with covenant ritual (Gen 15:10), see

Christopher T. Begg, "The Covenantal Dove in Psalm lxxiv 19–20," VetTest 37 (1987): 78–81.

VI. Destruction of God's Enemies

74:22–23

[22] Rise up, O God, and defend your cause;
remember how fools mock you all day long.
[23] Do not ignore the clamor of your adversaries,
the uproar of your enemies, which rises continually.

22–23 In conclusion the lament renews a bold appeal for the Lord to act. The acts of God are primarily a vindication of his name and secondarily of his people. As long as the foolish mocking continues, the enemies have reason to boast in their strength. Their power is nothing compared to the Lord's, when he rises to defend his cause (v.22). As long as their loud noise "rises continually" (v.23), it seems that the Lord has rejected his people "forever" (v.1). But he is the only "one to address who is still credible, who has a known past, who can receive imperatives, and who is therefore the ground of hope" (Brueggemann, *Message of the Psalms,* p. 71).

Notes

23 Meir Weiss interprets this verse in the light of the whole psalm. The conclusion sets the tone for the whole psalm, as it dilutes joy with sorrow (*The Bible From Within,* pp. 278–81).

Psalm 75: Justice Is the Lord's

In view of the strong opposition of the arrogant, the godly community looks to God for deliverance. Thematically the psalm shows several similarities with Hannah's song (1 Sam 2:1–10) and Mary's Magnificat (Luke 1:46–53).

The structural elements represent the several genres found in the psalm: thanksgiving (vv.1, 9–10), oracle (vv.2–5), and a prophetic proclamation of the coming judgment (vv.6–8). The genre of the psalm appears to have characteristics of a communal Thanksgiving hymn. The psalm was probably used as a part of a cultic liturgy (Weiser, p. 521).

A. Thanksgiving (v.1)
  B. Oracle of the Lord (vv.2–5)
  B′. Prophetic Oracle (vv.6–8)
A′. Thanksgiving (vv.9–10)

I. Thanksgiving

75:1

For the director of music. ⌊To the tune of⌋ "Do Not Destroy."
A psalm of Asaph. A song.

1 We give thanks to you, O God,
we give thanks, for your Name is near;
men tell of your wonderful deeds.

1 The community of God's people burst out in a song of thanksgiving. The repetition "we give thanks" (*hôḏînû*) is for the sake of emphasis. The godly recall the "wonderful deeds" (*nip̱le'ôṯeyḵā*) of the Lord. These were his acts in creation and in the salvation of his people (cf. 9:1; 78:4; 105:1–2; see the appendix to Ps 78: The Mighty Acts of Yahweh).

Another reason for the joyful celebration of the community may lie in their awareness of God's presence. It is possible to understand "for your Name is near" (*qārôḇ šemeḵā*) in two ways: (1) in the sense of the ancient versions (LXX, Syr., Vul.): "they who call on your name [i.e., worship you] tell of your wonderful deeds" (cf. 145:18) or (2) in the sense of the NEB, which is close to the MT: "thy name is brought very near to us in the story of thy wonderful deeds." If we stay close to the MT, as the NIV and the NEB do, it is preferable to assume that the reason for rejoicing lies in the manifest presence of God proclaimed and celebrated in the stories of God's mighty acts. In the remembrance and retelling of the history of salvation lies the comforting affirmation of God's closeness to his people.

Notes

For a brief discussion of the technical words and phrases in the superscription, see the Introduction.

1 (2 MT) The indefinite subject with סִפְּרוּ (*sipperû*, "tell," Piel perfect) could be "men" (NIV) or a contextually defined subject, "your wonderful deeds," giving the sense "your wonderful deeds tell that your name is near." Kraus emends the text to "those who call in your name tell" (*Psalmen*, 1:520).

II. Oracle of the Lord

75:2–5

2 You say, "I choose the appointed time;
it is I who judge uprightly.
3 When the earth and all its people quake,
it is I who hold its pillars firm. *Selah*
4 To the arrogant I say, 'Boast no more,'
and to the wicked, 'Do not lift up your horns.
5 Do not lift your horns against heaven;
do not speak with outstretched neck.' "

2 The history of redemption bears out the truth of God's oracle of judgment. He is patient, but at his time he does judge. Though he may let wicked individuals and nations go unpunished and even the godly may pray for their deliverance for long periods of time, the Lord will suddenly introduce "the appointed time" for judgment.

The oracle of God is given here as an assurance to his own. Regardless of how long their adversity may last, he is sovereign and has a time appointed for their vindication. That time is characterized by the coming of "the great I am": "it is I." The emphatic position of "I" in the MT brings out that no one else can "judge uprightly." The "upright" (*mêšārîm*) judgment of God pertains to both aspects of his righteous rule: vengeance on the enemies and vindication of the godly (cf. 9:8–20; 58:11; 98:9; Isa 25:8–9).

3 The Lord is in control, even when it seems that everything is falling to pieces. The emphatic use of "I" is complementary to that of v.2. He is the great Judge-Ruler, who will not permit wickedness, evil powers, and the arrogant to undermine the foundations of his kingdom. The quaking of earth and peoples is a metaphor for the erosive effects of evil. Immorality undermines the stability of earth and society (cf. 11:3). In the experiences of the wickedness and arrogance of a Babylon or a Nazi Germany, the Lord proclaims that he graciously upholds his creation. The pillars (*'ammûḏeyhā*) shore up the moral order, preventing his creation from collapsing (cf. 104:5).

4–5 The Lord's word comes directly to those who cause chaos, anarchy, and immorality on the earth. They are "the arrogant" and "the wicked" (v.4). The "arrogant" (*hôllᵉlîm*) live without regard of God and his commandments (cf. 52:1; 73:3). They speak insolently (31:18; 94:4) and are impatient with the distinction between the divine and mankind. They are no different from the "wicked" (cf. 1:1) who boast in their power and autonomy, expressed metaphorically by the word "horns" (v.5; *qāren*, "horn," MT). Their autonomy expresses itself directly against God, as they lift up their horn "against heaven" (*lammārôm*, lit., "to up high").

Notes

2 (3 MT) "You say" is an interpretive addition for the MT's כִּי (*kî*) and explains that God has spoken the words that follow (vv.2–5 [3–6 MT]). *kî* may be translated as an asseverative, "indeed" (Dahood, *Psalms*, 2:211), or as an adverbial particle, "when" (Briggs, 2:160).

4–5 (5–6 MT) These verses have a chiastic structure, in which v.5 explains the actions of the "arrogant" and the "wicked":

A. Boast of the arrogant (v.4a)	B. Horns of the wicked (v.4b)
B′. Horns against heaven (v.5a)	A′. Arrogant speaking (v.5b)

5 (6 MT) The word עָתָק (*'āṯāq*) is better translated as "with insolence" or "arrogantly" than as "outstretched" (NIV; cf. 31:18; 94:4). See NEB: "nor speak arrogantly against your Creator." Dahood follows the LXX's "against God" (vs. MT's "neck") by assuming that "God" is an interpretive translation of *ṣûr* ("rock"). He further amends *'āṯāq* ("outstretched") to *'attîq* ("ancient") and renders the phrase "against the ancient mountain" (*Psalms*, 2:212).

III. Prophetic Oracle

75:6–8

6 No one from the east or the west
  or from the desert can exalt a man.
7 But it is God who judges:
  He brings one down, he exalts another.
8 In the hand of the LORD is a cup
  full of foaming wine mixed with spices;
 he pours it out, and all the wicked of the earth
  drink it down to its very dregs.

6–8 The transition from God's words to a prophetic reflection is marked by another use of "indeed" (*kî*), repeated at the beginning of vv.6, 7, and 8 (NIV offers no translation [vv.2, 6, 8] or renders it "but" [v.7]). The congregation thanks the Lord (v.1) for God's word of promise to abase the oppressors ("arrogant," "wicked," vv.2–5) and for his oracle of judgment (vv.6–8).

God's judgment will be universal. Since his rule extends "from the east or the west" (v.6) and includes wilderness and mountains, i.e., both the northern and southern regions, no one can escape his judgment (cf. Ps 139). Wherever man may exalt himself, the Lord will bring him down (v.7; cf. 1 Sam 2:6–7; Ps 147:6). He is sovereign in judgment and redemption.

God's judgment is severe (v.8; cf. Rev 14:10). In a stairlike triplet the inspired author likens God's judgment to a cup of wine (cf. 60:3; Isa 51:17, mixed with spices; cf. NEB, "and the wine foams in it, hot with spice"). The Lord pours out his judgment on the wicked like the contents of a bowl, and they cannot escape his judgment (cf. Rev 15:7; 16:19).

Notes

6 (7 MT) The NIV follows the proposal of the BHS, according to which הָרִים (*hārîm*, "mountains") is emended to a verb, רוּם (*rûm*, "exalt," "raise up"), as in vv.4–5 (5–6 MT). The translation adopted in the commentary is based on the MT as is supported by Briggs (2:162) and Dahood (*Psalms*, 2:213).

8 (9 MT) The word מֶסֶךְ (*meseḵ*, "mixed with spices") is a *hapax legomenon* in the MT.

IV. Thanksgiving

75:9–10

9 As for me, I will declare this forever;
  I will sing praise to the God of Jacob.
10 I will cut off the horns of all the wicked,
  but the horns of the righteous will be lifted up.

9–10 The communal form of thanksgiving (v.1) celebrating the "wonderful deeds" of the Lord's rule and judgment over the world (vv.2–8) occasions a personal expression of commitment and joy (vv.9–10). The personal pronoun "I" is emphatic, as is brought out by the NIV's "as for me" (v.9). The individual takes it on himself to "perpetuate" the story of God's acts. In retelling the story of salvation and celebrating his mighty acts in song, the redeemed will forever remember what the Lord has done. Their Redeemer is the "God of Jacob" (cf. 20:1). He is committed to protect and help the descendants of Jacob.

The individual also takes on himself a responsibility in distinguishing right from wrong. Since God is opposed to the "horns" of the wicked (vv.4–5), he vows to bring their destruction. The godly disassociate themselves from the wicked by not incurring their favor and influence or by following their strategies (cf. 1:1).

The hope of the godly lies always in God. They cannot by themselves come to power. The Lord raises up and abases. He will vindicate the righteous (*ṣaddîq*, see 1:6) by raising their "horns."

Notes

---

9 (10 MT) The LXX reads אָגִיל ('*āg̱îl*, "rejoice") instead of אַגִּיד ('*aggîḏ*, "I will declare").

10 (11 MT) Several versions prefer to emend the first person to the third in the expression "I will cut off the horns," assuming that this work belongs to the Lord (v.7; Kraus, *Psalmen*, 1:520). See the RSV: "All the horns of the wicked he will cut off."

Psalm 76: The Lord Is the God of Jacob

Yahweh is the Divine Warrior who dwells in Zion (vv.1–3). He has shown his commitment to his people (vv.4–9), for which reason he is praised among his own and feared by the nations (vv.10–12). The adoration of the Divine Warrior by his own people includes both a reflection on past victories and hope for a full establishment of his kingdom on earth. When all kings and nations submit to him, the earth will be quiet (vv.8, 11–12). The psalm is in the form of a victory hymn.

It is highly unlikely that this hymn is to be associated with any one particular victory, such as those over the Assyrians or the Babylonians. B.Z. Luria has made an attempt at explaining the background in the rescue of the Jews from Hamath, in the days of Jeroboam II (cf. 2 Kings 14:25–27). He further connects this psalm with Psalms 77; 80; and 81 as belonging to an Ephraimite psalter ("Psalms from Ephraim," *Beth Mikra* 23 [1978]: 151–60, Heb.). Otto Eissfeldt held that the author of 2 Samuel 5–8 was a contemporary of the psalmist ("Psalm 76," *Kleine Scriften*, vol. 3, edd. Rudolf Sellheim and Fritz Maas [Tübingen: Mohr, 1966], pp. 448–57). W.A. Beuken rightly appreciates the presence of God as the main motif in this psalm, as he develops the imagery of God as the lion, his theophany at Zion, and his beneficent presence ("God's Presence in Salem: A Study of Psalm 76," in *Loven en Geloven. Opstellen van Collega's en Medewerkers aangeboden aan Prof. Dr. Nic. H. Ridderbos*, ed. M.H. van Es et al. [Amsterdam: Ton Bolland, 1975], pp. 135–50).

The structure falls into four strophes:

A. God's Relationship With His People (vv.1–3)
B. The Divine Warrior (vv.4–7a)
B′. The Divine Judge (vv.7b–9)
A′. The Relationship of the Nations With God (vv.10–12)

I. God's Relationship With His People

76:1–3

For the director of music. With stringed instruments.
A psalm of Asaph. A song.

1 In Judah God is known;
his name is great in Israel.
2 His tent is in Salem,
his dwelling place in Zion.
3 There he broke the flashing arrows,
the shields and the swords, the
weapons of war. *Selah*

1–2 God had graciously established a relationship with his people. They had come to "know" (v.1) him by his gracious condescension to dwell in the Solomonic temple, "the tent" (v.2). The "tent" (*sukkô*, lit., "his hut"; cf. 27:5) is where God had made his home. The Lord has chosen "Salem" (cf. Gen 14:18) as his royal city so that both Judah (the southern kingdom) and Israel (the northern kingdom) may comfort each other with the assurance that the Divine Warrior is in their midst (cf. Ps 46). His "dwelling place" (*meʿônāṯô*) is the temple of Solomon (26:8; 68:5), where his own may find refuge (Deut 33:27).

3 Jacob and Israel experienced the triumphs of the Lord, who made a great name for himself in his victories. He is the Warrior who goes ahead of his people. Nothing can stop him. The collection of weapons taken from the enemy witnesses to his power. He has made an end to war by annihilating the arsenal of the nations: "the flashing arrows, the shields and the swords."

Notes

For a brief discussion of the technical words and phrases in the superscription, see the Introduction.

3 (4 MT) "The flames of the bow" (NIV, "the flashing arrows") is a metaphor, derived from Canaanite mythology. For the background, see 78:48. Dahood may well be right in rendering the Hebrew phrase as an instrument of means: "There *with his thunderbolts* he shattered" (*Psalms*, 2:217; emphasis mine).

II. The Divine Warrior

76:4–7a

4 You are resplendent with light,
more majestic than mountains rich with game.

5 Valiant men lie plundered,
they sleep their last sleep;
not one of the warriors
can lift his hands.
6 At your rebuke, O God of Jacob,
both horse and chariot lie still.
7 You alone are to be feared.

4 This section (vv.4–7a) forms a unit by the inclusionary use of the emphatic "you" in the MT and by the play on the words "resplendent" (*nā'ôr*) and "to be feared" (*nôrā'*, v.7). The Divine Warrior is "resplendent" (i.e., enveloped by light) as he shoots forth the thunderbolts (see Notes on v.3). The Lord is "enveloped" in light (cf. 104:2), from which flashes of lightning shoot forth. He is the "majestic" One.

5–6 God's power is real over against the imaginary power of the nations. The kings and rulers of the nations are the "valiant men" (v.5; cf. v.12) who rebel against God and against his anointed king (cf. 2:1–2). They rely on "horse and chariot"(v.6), a metaphor for political power and military strength (cf. 20:7). But human warriors pass away into "their last sleep" (Dahood, *Psalms*, 2:219) and are powerless to raise their strong "hands." Every victory over the enemies comes because of God's involvement as the Divine Warrior with and for his people. The enemies are felled by the "rebuke" of the Lord (cf. 2:5; 9:5; 18:15).

7a The reflection on the great power of the Divine Warrior leads the psalmist to a hymnic praise. The God of Jacob is "awe-inspiring" (*nôra'*; NIV, "to be feared"; cf. v.12; 47:2; 66:3, 5). (See the appendix to Ps 98: Yahweh Is the Divine Warrior.)

Notes

4 (5 MT) There is no good reason to emend the text here so as to read "to be feared" (BHS) instead of "resplendent"; the textual evidence is not uniform.

הַרְרֵי (*harrê*, "mountains," pl. construct) may be an example of the plural of majesty, as is the case with the word "sanctuary" in the plural (cf. 68:35 with *nôrā'*; 73:17).

"Mountains rich with game [*ṭerep̱*]" is not the best rendering of the MT's הַרְרֵי־טָרֶף (*harrê-ṭarep̱*). Among other explanations proposed are "the mountains of a devouring lion" (see KB[3], 2:365) and "everlasting mountains" (LXX). The latter explanation is based on the assumption that the word עַד (*'aḏ*, "prey" or "everlasting"; cf. Gen 49:26; Deut 33:15; Hab 3:6; KB, p. 681) may have been original instead of טֶרֶף (*ṭerep̱*, "prey"; so BHS; A.A. Anderson, 2:553). A scribe may have clarified an inherent ambiguity in the MT by changing the text into an even more obscure expression. If this proposal is correct, the psalmist compares the "majesty" of the Lord to "the everlasting mountains" (Kraus, *Psalmen*, 1:524), a poetic reference to Mount Zion, the dwelling place of the Lord (see note on 2:6; cf. Deut 33:15; Pss 87:1; 110:2; Hab 3:6; see appendix to Ps 46: Zion Theology).

W.A. Beuken ("God's Presence in Salem," pp. 144–50) suggests that since the psalm focuses on Salem, the psalmist may purposefully develop a wordplay of *Jeru* (-salem) with the root *'-w-r*: *nā'ôr* ("resplendent"). The wordplay further extends to the root *y-r-'*: *nôrā'* ("to be feared," vv.7, 12).

6 (7 MT) On the meaning of מִגַּעֲרָתְךָ (*migga'ărāṯeḵā*, "at your rebuke") as "your angry shout," see P.J. Van Zijl, "A Discussion of the root *gā'ar* ('rebuke')," *Biblical Essays*, ed. A.H. Van

Zyl (Potchefstroom: Pro Rege-Pers, 1969), pp. 56–63. See also Tryggve N.D. Mettinger, "Fighting the Powers of Chaos and Hell—Towards the Biblical Portrait of God," ST 39 (1985): 28.

III. The Divine Judge

76:7b–9

> Who can stand before you when you are angry?
> 8 From heaven you pronounced judgment,
> and the land feared and was quiet—
> 9 when you, O God, rose up to judge,
> to save all the afflicted of the land. *Selah*

7b The hymnic outburst is a response of awe at God's glorious power (v.7a) and forms a transition to a reflection on the "judgment" of the Lord. The rhetorical question "Who can stand?" should shock the reader! In the presence of the Judge of the universe, all nations and kingdoms fall silent. No one can stand before him in his anger (cf. 1:5; 130:3; Nah 1:6; see Ps 2:5, "anger")! See also John's development of the judgment scene in Revelation 6:12–17.

8 The Lord protects Zion (vv.1–3), but his rule is not limited to Zion. He is "more majestic than the everlasting mountain" (v.4, see comment) of Zion. He rules over the nations. To that end the psalmist portrays him as the Great Judge of the universe speaking from "heaven." It is not clear from the MT whether "the land" that heard the judgment of the Lord is Canaan or the whole world. However, the contrastive use of "from heaven" and "land" (*'ereṣ*, no definite article) favors the usual understanding of "heaven and earth" (Gen 1:1; 2:4).

9 The purpose of the "judgment" (*dîn*, v.8) is twofold. First, it lets the nations know that Yahweh is the sovereign King (cf. v.7a). Second, the judgment of God gives comfort to the people of God in that he rises (*qûm*) to help "all the afflicted of the earth" (NIV, "land"). In view of our interpretation of *'ereṣ* as "earth," it seems consistent with the message of the psalm that the Lord expresses concern for all the oppressed people on earth. The "afflicted" (see 9:12) are those who await the deliverance of the Lord (9:13; 10:12, 17; 25:9; 34:6; 69:33; 149:4).

Notes

---

7 (8 MT) The NIV follows the MT in "when you are angry" (lit., "on account of your anger"). The phrase מֵאָז (*mē'āz*, "from then") may be emended to *mē'ōz* ("from the power of," so BHS) on the basis of a similar phrase in 90:11 (Kraus, *Psalmen*, 1:524).

IV. The Relationship of the Nations With God

76:10–12

10 Surely your wrath against men brings you praise,
and the survivors of your wrath are restrained.

11 Make vows to the LORD your God and fulfill them;
let all the neighboring lands
bring gifts to the One to be feared.
12 He breaks the spirit of rulers;
he is feared by the kings of the earth.

10 All acts are under God's sovereign control. Even the most hostile acts against his rule will bring him "praise" (cf. Acts 2:23; Rom 8:28). Yahweh turns man's rebellious expression of anger to his glory. Yes, whatever rebellious expression remains (NIV, "the survivors of your wrath") is to his glory. The Lord has armed himself (see NIV mg.) against man's rebellious hostility ("wrath"). When Yahweh goes out as a man of war (Isa 59:17–18), his opponents with all their wrath (hostile acts) will submit to his lordship (see appendix to Ps 98: Yahweh Is the Divine Warrior).

11–12 In view of the dreaded judgment of the Sovereign over all, all people must respond wisely. The covenant people must be careful in paying their vows to the Lord. Since he is "the LORD your God" (v.11), the people of God must be examples to the nations of loyalty to the Lord. But the nations too have an opportunity to respond to the "awe-inspiring" (*môrā';* NIV, "to be feared"; cf. *nôrā',* vv.7, 12; NIV, "to be feared") nature of the Lord. They must bring tribute symbolic of their submission to his authority.

The Lord is "the awe-inspiring one" (v.12; NIV, "he is feared"; cf. v.7). He will crush "the spirit [*rû^{a}ḥ*] of rulers," meaning the hostile opposition of the nations to his rule (cf. 2:9).

Notes

10 (11 MT) J.A. Emerton's rendering is likely: "Surely the wrath of man shall praise thee" ("A Neglected Solution of a Problem in Psalm lxxvi 11," VetTest 24 [1974]: 136–46). Some propose that "man" and "wrath" be read as geographical references and emend אָדָם (*'āḏām,* "mankind," "men") and חֵמֹת (*ḥēmōṯ,* "wrath") to Edom and Hamath (Kraus, *Psalmen,* 2:524–25); see the NEB: "for all her fury Edom shall confess thee, and the remnant left in Hamath shall dance in worship."

Psalm 77: A Remembrance of God's Greatness

The mood of the psalm changes from lamentation (vv.1–9) to reflection (vv.10–12) and ultimately gives way to a joyful hymn celebrating the greatness of the God of Israel (vv.13–20). The shift in genre and syntax as well as the change in meter from 3 + 3 to 3 + 3 + 3 (vv.16–19; cf. Hab 3:8–10) are often cited as indicators that the psalm is a redaction of several fragments (see Introduction: Rhyme, meter, and strophe). Dahood, on the other hand, concludes that while vv.16–19 may have been inserted into the psalm, the language of the whole psalm is archaic and that a tenth-century date is not unlikely (*Psalms*, 2:224).

The psalm may be read as an *individual lament* psalm. The original situation is not clear. If we assume an early date, the psalm may reflect a national calamity rather than the abandonment by God in the Exile. But B.Z. Luria argues that this psalm, together with Psalms 80 and 81, laments the destruction of Samaria in 722 B.C. ("Psalms from Ephraim," *Beth Mikra* 23 [1978]: 151–60 [Heb.]). William A. Goy sees a representative dimension in this psalm ("Dieu A-T-Il Changé?" *Maqqēl Shâqēdh. La Branche d'Amandier: Hommage A Wilhelm Vischer* [Montpellier: Causse Graille Castelnau, 1960], pp. 56–62). He argues that while we should not repeat the mannerism of the psalmist, the psalm witnesses still in our day to the dilemma of faith.

The structure of the psalm reveals the changes in mood more clearly:

A. Cry for Help (vv.1–2)
  B. Remembrance of God in Hymns of the Night (vv.3–6)
    C. Questions (vv.7–9)
  B′. Remembrance of God's Mighty Deeds (vv.10–12)
A′. Confidence in God's Help (vv.13–20)

I. Cry for Help

77:1–2

For the director of music. For Jeduthun. Of Asaph. A psalm.

1 I cried out to God for help;
I cried out to God to hear me.
2 When I was in distress, I sought the Lord;
at night I stretched out untiring hands
and my soul refused to be comforted.

1–2 Lament is a cry of desperation to God. The psalmist repeats the words "I cried out to God" (v.1; lit., "my voice [*qôlî*] to God") by way of emphasis: "My voice to God, I cry for help, my voice to God" (lit. tr.). His prayer is intense because of the "distress" (v.2). The nature of the distress is not specified, but it must have been of such magnitude as to cause him to wonder whether God would reject him or his people forever (cf. vv.7–9).

The psalmist longs for a renewal of communion with the Lord, inaugurated by new acts of God. The lament continues until God hears (v.1). To this end he "sought the Lord" (Adonai, v.2), since the Lord has authority over all things as "master" of the universe. In Oriental fashion he "stretched out" his hands in prayer (143:6) and continued to lift up his hands "at night" (v.2). Yet even in his laments he cannot find rest. He is restless on account of the distance between him and God. He cannot comfort himself nor can others comfort him. He looks to God as the sole comforter of his soul (cf. Gen 37:35; Jer 31:15).

Notes

For a brief discussion of the technical words and phrases in the superscription, see the Introduction.

2 (3 MT) The MT is problematic because of the unusual phrase נִגְּרָה וְלֹא תָפוּג (*niggerāh welō' tāpûg*, "I stretched out untiring"; lit., "[my hand] is gushed forth and does not grow feeble"). The LXX reads "against him" instead of "gushed forth." The verb "gushed forth" has suggested to some an emendation to "my eye flows," i.e., with tears. Briggs (2:172) favors "My hand is extended without growing numb," p. 170), but see the NEB: "and by night I lifted my outspread hands in prayer. I lay sweating and nothing would cool me." Since the idiom probably is a metaphorical extension of the hands outstretched in prayer, the NIV gives a satisfactory rendering (Kraus, *Psalmen*, 1:529–30).

II. Remembrance of God in Hymns of the Night

77:3–6

3 I remembered you, O God, and I groaned;
I mused, and my spirit grew faint. *Selah*
4 You kept my eyes from closing;
I was too troubled to speak.
5 I thought about the former days,
the years of long ago;
6 I remembered my songs in the night.
My heart mused and my spirit inquired:

3–6 In his remembrance the psalmist recalls the acts of God, celebrated in the "songs in the night" (v.6). The present distress seems contradictory to the history of God's involvement and love for his people. The more he muses on the divine perfections, the louder he speaks, and the more his spirit "grows faint" (*titʿaṭṭēp*, v.3; cf. 107:5; 142:3; 143:4; Jonah 2:7) within him. His active remembrance of God does not give comfort but has the opposite effect: groaning and spiritual exhaustion.

The psalmist reflects on "the former days" as celebrated in the "songs in the night" (vv.5–6). The songs sung at night used to be of comfort, as God's people renewed their loyalty to the God who is mighty to deliver. The remembrance of his great power encouraged them, permitting them to sleep quietly even in great adversity (cf. 3:5–6; 4:8). However, the night hymns no longer seem to work. His eyes are kept "from closing" (v.4).

The psalmist troubled himself further by his disquieting thoughts. He was unable to speak coherently about his distress (v.4). Instead, questions and reflections on the past flooded his thoughts. The images of God's past acts of kindness ("the former days"// "the years long ago") ran past his mind's eye. He thinks, remembers, and inquires. In the end he must verbalize his questions (see vv.7–9).

Notes

3, 6, 12 (4, 7, 13 MT) The root שׂיח (*ś-y-ḥ*, "mused," "consider") is used three times. Hans-Peter Müller concludes that the root is not limited to the lament genre and that it has the basic sense of a loud, enthusiastic, and emotion-filled form of speaking ("Die hebräische Wurzel שׂיח," VetTest 19 [1969]: 361–71). It occurs with a form of המה (*h-m-h*, "make noise," "groan") in v.3 (NIV, "I groaned; I mused") and in 55:17 (NIV, "I cry out in distress") and with זכר (*z-k-r*, "remember") in vv.3, 6, 12 (4, 7, 13 MT).

3–6 (4–7) These verses are set within an inclusionary repetition of אֶזְכְּרָה (*'ezkerāh*), rendered in the NIV by "I remembered" and "My heart mused" (vv.3, 6). The cohortative form favors a different rendering: "let me remember." The section is unified by a series of cohortatives, which could be translated as "Let me remember . . . let me groan. . . . Let me remember. . . . Let me muse." The syntactic alternation between the cohortative and the perfect suggests a temporal translation: "When I remembered. . . . You kept my eyes. . . . When I remembered" (cf. Kraus, *Psalmen*, 1:529).

4 (5 MT) Instead of "eyes" (NIV) the MT has שְׁמֻרוֹת (*šemurōt*, "watches of the eyes" or "eyelids"), a *hapax legomenon*.

6 (7 MT) נְגִינָתִי (*negînātî*, "songs in the night") is emended by many to וְהָגִיתִי (*wehāgîtî*, "and I meditate" or "reflect"), based on the LXX. The NEB assumes another reading: "my spirit was sunk in despair."

III. Questions

77:7–9

7"Will the Lord reject forever?
Will he never show his favor again?
8Has his unfailing love vanished forever?
Has his promise failed for all time?
9Has God forgotten to be merciful?
Has he in anger withheld his compassion?" *Selah*

7–9 The formulation of questions has a therapeutic effect. Doubts and questions are expressed by the greatest men of God in the OT and even by our Lord Jesus on the cross, quoting Psalm 22:1: "My God, my God, why have you forsaken me?" (Matt 27:46). Similarly, the psalmist asks whether God will "reject" (v.7; cf. 44:9) his people forever (*l e'ôlāmîm*) by not extending to them his "favor." The "favor" of the Lord is his willingness to be reconciled with his people by forgiving their sins and by blessing them with his grace (cf. 85:1–3; cf. Isa 61:2). The psalmist continues with the questions as to why the "covenant love" (*ḥesed;* NIV, "unfailing love") of God is gone and why "his promise" (*'ōmer*) has become ineffective (cf. Isa 40:8). He further ponders the question why God does not forgive and show mercy on his people (cf. Exod 34:6–7).

These questions go from the present situation of rejection (v.7) to the cause: the Lord's "anger" (v.9). In asking these questions and in expressing his doubts, the heart of the psalmist comes to rest; for he knows that the God of Abraham cannot deny himself and cut himself off from his own people. In questions there lies hope! The people desperately need his "unfailing love" and "mercy." They long for the new era, marked by forgiveness and reconciliation. They believe that the Lord will remain faithful to "his promise."

IV. Remembrance of God's Mighty Deeds

77:10–12

10Then I thought, "To this I will appeal:
the years of the right hand of the Most High."
11I will remember the deeds of the LORD;

yes, I will remember your miracles
of long ago.
12 I will meditate on all your works
and consider all your mighty deeds.

10–12 The remembrance of the age-old acts of God is the basis for faith. God has been, is, and will always be. The reflection on his acts in the past is comforting to those who need him in the present. The name of God "Most High" (Elyon, v.10) goes back to the patriarch Abraham (Gen 14:22; see appendix to Ps 9: Yahweh Is El Elyon). Though Elyon was one of the epithets of El, the Canaanite God, the Hebrews adapted the language to Yahweh. El Elyon, the Creator and Protector of creation, is none other than Yahweh. The compound name El Elyon is broken up in vv.9–10 in that v.9 attributes "compassion" to El ("God") and v.10 speaks of the power of the right hand of Elyon ("the Most High"). Some argue that v.10 should be included with the previous section, but it all depends on how one understands v.10. Ancient tradition divided the text between v.9 and v.10 by the *Selah,* and the NIV wisely follows this tradition. Though v.10 is like a pivot, it is preferable to see the psalmist calming himself at the end of the six questions of vv.7–9. With the mention of El, he was ready to commit himself to the great power of the Almighty (Elyon, cf. 18:13; 46:4–6).

The psalmist remembers (possibly "proclaims," see 20:7; 30:4) the "deeds," "miracles," "works," and "mighty deeds" of the Lord (vv.11–12). The Hebrew text uses four distinct synonyms, translated in the NIV by three distinct English words. The psalmist chose his words carefully so as to create the impression that he is reflecting on the Lord's works in their great variety: in creation, redemption, judgment, and salvation. The first word ("deeds," *maʿalᵉlê*) and the last ("mighty deeds," *ʿᵃlîlôṯeyḵā*) form an inclusion. The middle two synonyms resemble each other in sound (*pilʾeḵā* and *poʿᵒleḵā*). The semantic differences should not be pressed on any of the synonyms (see appendix to Ps 78: The Mighty Acts of Yahweh). The acts of God in their great variety and number reveal the power of "the right and of the Most High" (v.10). The Most High (Elyon) is none other than "the LORD" (v.11; Yah, a shortened form of Yahweh, cf. 68:4). The reason for God's gracious acts is no less than to sustain us, as Calvin put it:

> The reason why so many examples of the grace of God contribute nothing to our profit, and fail in edifying our faith, is, that as soon as we have begun to make them the subjects of our consideration, our inconstancy draws us away to something else, and thus, at the very commencement, our minds soon lose sight of them. (3:218)

Notes

---

10 (11 MT) Two words have occasioned difficulty in the interpretation of v.10: חַלּוֹתִי (*ḥallôṯî,* "my prayer," "my grief," "my piercing") and שְׁנוֹת (*šᵉnôṯ,* "years of," "changing of"). The differences in the ancient versions bear out the problem of obtaining a satisfactory solution on which there will be a general agreement. For this reason interpreters are guided by the context and particularly by their decision of including v.10 with vv.7–9 or with vv.11–12.

11 (12 MT) The NIV follows the *Qere* reading of אֶזְכּוֹר (*ʾezkôr,* "I will remember"). It is supported by many MSS and versions and is consistent with the forms found in vv.3, 6, and

11b. Others adopt the *Kethiv*, אֶזְכִּיר (*'azkîr*), with the meaning "I shall proclaim" or "make mention of."

V. Confidence in God's Help

77:13–20

13 Your ways, O God, are holy.
  What god is so great as our God?
14 You are the God who performs miracles;
  you display your power among the peoples.
15 With your mighty arm you redeemed your people,
  the descendants of Jacob and Joseph. *Selah*

16 The waters saw you, O God,
  the waters saw you and writhed;
  the very depths were convulsed.
17 The clouds poured down water,
  the skies resounded with thunder;
  your arrows flashed back and forth.
18 Your thunder was heard in the whirlwind,
  your lightning lit up the world;
  the earth trembled and quaked.
19 Your path led through the sea,
  your way through the mighty waters,
  though your footprints were not seen.

20 You led your people like a flock
  by the hand of Moses and Aaron.

13–15 The hymn ascribes "holy power" to God (El, v.13; see appendix to Ps 22: Yahweh Is El). The "holy ways" of God pertain to what he has done on behalf of his people, whom he has redeemed and consecrated to himself. The doctrine of the holiness of God has a dynamic dimension in that God involves himself with his people. The word "holy" is a phrase in Hebrew ("in the holiness," *baqqōdeš*), which could be explained as a reference to his sanctuary or to his people (cf. 114:2). We take it to mean that God's way is on behalf of his people. They exclaim with the psalmist, "What god is so great as our God?" (v.13; cf. Exod 15:11; Deut 7:21; 10:17; Ps 95:3). Only Yahweh demonstrates his holy power "among the peoples" (v.14) on behalf of his people, "the descendants of Jacob and Joseph" (v.15). It is only to Israel that he demonstrated his holy power by performing "miracles" (v.14; cf. v.11b) and by showing his "power" (*'ôz*, "strength"). The nations witnessed his mighty deeds and trembled (cf. Exod 15:14–16; Ps 66:8). All these acts are expressions of the "mighty arm" of the Lord (v.15; cf. v.10; Exod 6:6; Ps 136:12). (See the appendix to Ps 98: Yahweh Is the Divine Warrior.)

16–20 The drama of creation and redemption is depicted with great literary imagination. The waters and the forces of nature receive special powers in the imaginative faculties of the poet. The effect of the hymn should be a deep sense of awe of the great power of God, who overcomes any and all obstacles. The powers of the waters and the mysterious forces of the depths of the seas tremble in the presence of God (v.16). The Lord's appearance is cast in the language of Canaan, where Baal was the storm-god. His power was thought to be displayed in the clouds, rain, thunder, and lightning (vv.17–18). For Israel Baal's alleged power was dwarfed by the awesome powers of the God of Israel (cf. 18:7–15; 29:3–9).

God led his people through the Red Sea. Though his presence ("footprints," v.19) was not "visible" to them (v.9), it was apparent in his awesome power over the sea and the path through which Israel passed to the Sinai. His power cannot be fossilized in space and time but is real to all who look to him in faith. Israel bore witness to his awesome power, because he led them "like a flock by the hand of Moses and Aaron" into and through the wilderness (v.20; cf. Exod 15:13; Isa 63:11–12; Mic 6:4).

Notes

16 (17 MT) For an extensive study of the motif of Yahweh and the sea, see John Day, *God's Conflict With the Dragon and the Sea. Echoes of Canaanite Myth in the Old Testament* (Cambridge: Cambridge University Press, 1985). See also Tryggve N.D. Mettinger, "Fighting the Powers of Chaos and Hell—Towards the Biblical Portrait of God," ST 39 (1985): 21–38.

16–18 (17–19 MT) For a study on theophany in Psalms 18; 50; 68; 77; and 97, see A. Weiser, "Zur Frage nach dem Beziehungen der Psalmen zum Kult: Die Darstellung der Theophanie in den Psalmen und im Festkult," in *Festschrift für Alfred Bertholet zum 80. Geburtstag*, edd. Walter Baumgartner, Otto Eissfeldt, Karl Elliger, and Leonhard Rost (Tübingen: Mohr, 1950), pp. 513–31.

18 (19 MT) It is tempting to understand גַּלְגַּל (*galgal*, "wheel"; NIV, "whirlwind") as a reference to the chariots of God; cf. "He makes the clouds his chariot and rides on the wings of the wind" (104:3; see Kraus, *Psalmen*, 1:529).

Psalm 78: Lessons From Israel's History

The wisdom motif of vv.1–4 introduces a didactic psalm. The psalmist is concerned to show how Ephraim lost its special status of blessing and prominence (cf. Gen 48:15–20; 49:22–26; Deut 33:13–17) in favor of Judah. Out of Judah King David was chosen to shepherd God's people, and in Judah God had chosen to dwell (vv.68–72). On the one hand, the didactic element of the psalm has parenthetic undertones, as it shows the folly of rebellion and disobedience. While on the other hand, it has a kerygmatic purpose, demonstrating the bliss of David's kingship.

The structure of the psalm is not easily determined. The psalmist alternates between Israel's rebellion and God's faithfulness—either in the history of redemption or in forms of discipline: "they . . . and he . . . ,"—between Egypt and the Promised Land, and between God's patience with Israel and his utter rejection of Ephraim in favor of Judah. The psalm explains that David and Jerusalem were chosen out of all the tribes because Yahweh is free in his choice.

The date cannot be determined with certainty; but as a part of the Asaph collection the psalm may have been composed in the northern kingdom during the period of secession. In this case the psalm explains the evil of apostasy and the necessity to submit to Yahweh's election of the Davidic dynasty and of the Jerusalem temple (Calvin, 3:226). On the other hand, Anthony F. Campbell argues persuasively in favor of a tenth-century date, explaining that this psalm represents the literary productivity of the Davidic era ("Psalm 78: A Contribution to the Theology of Tenth Century Israel," CBQ 41 [1979]: 51–79).

For convenience we suggest the following structure:

A. Call to Wisdom (vv.1–4)
  B. Lessons From Israel's History (vv.5–64)
    C. Good News: God Has Chosen David (vv.65–72)

The long block of didactic material may further be structured symmetrically:

1. Past and Future Generations (vv.5–8)
  2. Israel in Egypt and in the Wilderness (vv.9–16)
    3. Israel in the Wilderness (vv.17–31)
    3′. God's Mercy on a Rebellious People (vv.32–39)
  2′. Israel in Egypt and in the Wilderness (vv.40–55)
1′. Judgment on a Rebellious Generation (vv.56–64)

I. Call to Wisdom

78:1–4

A *maskil* of Asaph.

1 O my people, hear my teaching;
listen to the words of my mouth.
2 I will open my mouth in parables,
I will utter hidden things, things from of old—
3 what we have heard and known,
what our fathers have told us.
4 We will not hide them from their children;
we will tell the next generation
the praiseworthy deeds of the LORD,
his power, and the wonders he has done.

1–4 The purpose of the introduction is to arouse attention in the manner used by the sages and prophets of Israel. The importance of the "teaching" (*tôrāh*, i.e., "instruction," v.1) lies in the insights gleaned from Israel's history. Hence the first word of the psalmist in the MT is "hear" (lit., "give ear"; cf. 49:1; Prov 7:24; Isa 28:23, synonymous with "listen," lit., "stretch your ear"). "The words of my mouth" (cf. 19:14; 54:2; Deut 32:1) are words of wisdom, expressed in "parables" (*māšāl*, "proverbial form of teaching," v.2; cf. Prov 1:6, "proverbs" in NIV) and in "riddles" ("hidden things," NIV; cf. Prov 1:6, "riddles of the wise"; 49:4). The "riddles" were not "hidden things" in any esoteric form of teaching because the psalmist claims, "We have heard and known" the parables and riddles (v.3). Rather, the wisdom communicated from the fathers to each new generation pertains to the "praiseworthy deeds" and the demonstration of "his power, and the wonders" (v.4; see appendix).

The history of redemption is revelatory. The Lord's mighty acts reveal his love, mercy, and patience with his people. They also conceal, as humans cannot comprehend that God continues to be merciful and patient with a "rebellious people" (cf. v.8). In this sense we understand that Jesus' use of parables was a form of "hiding" the revelation of God from all who were hardened in their hearts (cf. Matt 13:35). But the revelation of God stirs the true believers, as Calvin wrote: "If in this psalm there shines forth such a majesty as may justly stir up and inflame the readers with a desire to learn, we gather from it with what earnest attention it becomes us to receive the gospel, in which Christ opens and displays to us the treasures of his celestial wisdom" (3:228).

The goal of the wisdom teacher is to open Israel's history from God's perspective. The act of "telling" (*m^e^sapp^e^rîm*, pl. participle) "the next generation" (v.4) is a continuation of the tradition "heard and known" from the fathers (v.3; cf. 44:1). The contents of the tradition of redemptive history are transmitted without further explication so that each generation may draw lessons from the "parables" and "riddles" of God's interaction with the previous generations. The acts of God draw attention to God's deeds and not primarily to man's rebellious spirit. They reveal his "power" (*'^e^zûz*, i.e., strength in battle; cf. 145:6; Isa 42:25 ["anger"]), his "glorious" acts worthy of the praise of Israel ("praiseworthy deeds," NIV; cf. 65:1), and the "wonders" (cf. 105:5). (See the appendix to Ps 1: The Ways of Wisdom and Folly.)

II. Lessons From Israel's History (vv.5–64)

A. *Past and Future Generations*

78:5–8

5 He decreed statutes for Jacob
  and established the law in Israel,
 which he commanded our forefathers
  to teach their children,
6 so the next generation would know them,
  even the children yet to be born,
  and they in turn would tell their children.
7 Then they would put their trust in God
  and would not forget his deeds
  but would keep his commands.
8 They would not be like their forefathers—
  a stubborn and rebellious generation,
 whose hearts were not loyal to God,
  whose spirits were not faithful to him.

5–8 Each generation must remember that the Lord revealed the divine oracles to Israel (v.5; cf. Rom 3:2) as an expression of the covenant relationship that he had sovereignly and graciously established between himself and Israel. He "decreed" and "established" (lit., "established" and "set") and "commanded" (v.5). Israel was expected to teach this revelation to their children from generation to generation (vv.5–6) so that each generation might "put their trust in God" (v.7) by remembering "his deeds" (MT, "deeds of El") and by keeping "his commands."

These were God's purposes for all the tribes of Israel (= Jacob, v.5; cf. 20:1). Through Moses he had commanded all Israelites, regardless of tribal descent, to instruct their children at home (Deut 6:6–9, 20–22; cf. Exod 10:2; 12:26–27; 13:8). The ways of God and of Israel in its formative stages in Egypt, in the wilderness, and in the land were an integral part of legal and covenantal instruction. Each generation must remember who they are, sons of "their forefathers—a stubborn and rebellious generation" (v.8; cf. vv.9–64), and what God expects of them: loyalty (vv.7–8).

The "hearts" of the wilderness generation were "not loyal" (*lō'-hēkîn*, i.e., not established, v.8; cf. 1 Sam 7:3), and their "spirits were not faithful" (*ne'emnāh*, from *'āmēn;* cf. 89:37; 101:6) to God (El, v.8; cf. v.7). Instead, they were thoroughly rebellious, as the following verses attempt to demonstrate. The Scriptures frequently refer to the generation of the wilderness as being "stubborn," "rebellious," and "stiff-necked" (cf. Deut 9:6–7, 13, 24; 31:27; 32:5, 20; Acts 2:40). These terms are also applied to a stubborn son (Deut 21:18, 20; cf. Jer 5:23).

B. *Israel in Egypt and in the Wilderness*

78:9–16

9 The men of Ephraim, though armed with bows,
turned back on the day of battle;
10 they did not keep God's covenant
and refused to live by his law.
11 They forgot what he had done,
the wonders he had shown them.
12 He did miracles in the sight of their fathers
in the land of Egypt, in the region of Zoan.
13 He divided the sea and led them through;
he made the water stand firm like a wall.
14 He guided them with the cloud by day
and with light from the fire all night.
15 He split the rocks in the desert
and gave them water as abundant as the seas;
16 he brought streams out of a rocky crag
and made water flow down like rivers.

9 The spirit of "the men of Ephraim" represents the spirit of Israel as a whole. These men were richly blessed with an extensive patrimony among the tribes of Israel in fulfillment of the blessings of Jacob and of Moses (cf. Gen 48:15–20; 49:22–26; Deut 33:13–17). The psalmist's description "armed with bows" fits well with their aggressiveness as portrayed in the Book of Judges (8:1–3; 12:1–6). However, they also lost because they had to flee in war (v.9). From the description of God's judgment on Israel, on Shiloh (located in the mountains of Ephraim), and, particularly, on Ephraim (vv.56–64, 67), the psalmist may be thinking of the Philistine incursion and victory at Ebenezer, which resulted in the loss of the ark and the destruction of Shiloh (1 Sam 4:1–11). Weiser argues, though not persuasively, that the battle the psalmist refers to is the battle of Gilboa, where Saul lost his life (p. 540).

10–12 The people failed in battle and failed to enjoy the blessings because of flagrant disobedience and disregard of God's covenant, as expressed by their refusal to observe God's "law" (*tôrāh,* "instruction," v.10; see appendix to Ps 19: The Word of God). They were no longer moved by the history of redemption, because they had forgotten God's expressions of loving concern, the "wonders" (cf. v.4) and "miracles" (v.12) performed in Egypt and in the wilderness (vv.12–16). He has demonstrated his power through the Ten Plagues (v.12; cf. vv.43–51; Exod 7:1–13:22) at "Zoan" (v.12). Zoan, representative of the Egyptian cities, was a city in the Nile Delta, also known as Tanis (cf. Isa 19:11, 13; 30:4; Ezek 30:14).

13–16 The Lord had led Israel through the Red Sea (Exod 14–15; Josh 4:23; Neh 9:11; Isa 63:12), whose waters congealed like a wall (cf. Exod 15:8; Josh 3:13, 16). Throughout their wilderness sojourning, he showed his presence with them in the pillars of "cloud" and "fire" (v.14; cf. Exod 13:21; Num 10:34; Ps 105:39). Moreover, he supplied them miraculously and abundantly with water (vv.15–16; cf. Exod 17:6; Num 20:8–11; 1 Cor 10:3).

C. *Israel in the Wilderness*

78:17–31

17 But they continued to sin against him,
rebelling in the desert against the Most High.
18 They willfully put God to the test
by demanding the food they craved.
19 They spoke against God, saying,
"Can God spread a table in the desert?
20 When he struck the rock, water gushed out,
and streams flowed abundantly.
But can he also give us food?
Can he supply meat for his people?"
21 When the LORD heard them, he was very angry;
his fire broke out against Jacob,
and his wrath rose against Israel,
22 for they did not believe in God
or trust in his deliverance.
23 Yet he gave a command to the skies above
and opened the doors of the heavens;
24 he rained down manna for the people to eat,
he gave them the grain of heaven.
25 Men ate the bread of angels;
he sent them all the food they could eat.
26 He let loose the east wind from the heavens
and led forth the south wind by his power.
27 He rained meat down on them like dust,
flying birds like sand on the seashore.
28 He made them come down inside their camp,
all around their tents.
29 They ate till they had more than enough,
for he had given them what they craved.
30 But before they turned from the food they craved,
even while it was still in their mouths,
31 God's anger rose against them;
he put to death the sturdiest among them,
cutting down the young men of Israel.

17–31 In response to the evidences of God's presence, guidance, and provisions (vv.11–16), "they," i.e., the people, rebelled. The psalmist draws a powerful contrast between the Lord's doings and the people's response. In reading the psalm, the reader must see the movement from "he" to "they" as an indictment against Israel. They refused to believe, even in the face of the evidence (v.17; cf. John 6:26–31). They were skeptical about God's ability to provide food in the wilderness (vv.18–20). He demonstrated his powers by giving Israel manna and meat (vv.23–29), but his anger was kindled against them so that "his fire broke out" (v.21) and many were killed (v.31; cf. Num 11). The unbelieving generation was condemned because the people were not overwhelmed by God's ability to deliver (v.22). The prior provision of manna (Exod 16:4) should have been enough. This is brought out in the manner in which the psalmist describes it. It came through "the doors of the heavens" (v.23; for "gate of heaven," see Gen 28:17; "floodgates of heaven," see 2 Kings 7:2, 19). It was to be thought of as "the grain of heaven" (v.24; cf. John 6:31; Rev 2:17) and as "the bread of angels" (v.25). The word translated "angels" is "mighty ones" (*'abbîrîm*), a word related to the "Mighty One" (*'ᵃḇîr*, Gen 49:24; Ps 132:2, 5; Isa 1:24).

Israel was not concerned with God or the wonders of God but was fleshly in its basic orientation to life. The people "craved" (vv.29–30) food and died in their lust (vv.30–31; cf. Num 11:33–34; 1 Cor 10:3–5). True faith looks beyond the gifts to the giver, the Lord of Glory.

D. *God's Mercy on a Rebellious People*

78:32–39

32 In spite of all this, they kept on sinning;
in spite of his wonders, they did not believe.
33 So he ended their days in futility
and their years in terror.
34 Whenever God slew them, they would seek him;
they eagerly turned to him again.
35 They remembered that God was their Rock,
that God Most High was their Redeemer.
36 But then they would flatter him with their mouths,
lying to him with their tongues;
37 their hearts were not loyal to him,
they were not faithful to his covenant.
38 Yet he was merciful;
he forgave their iniquities
and did not destroy them.
Time after time he restrained his anger
and did not stir up his full wrath.
39 He remembered that they were but flesh,
a passing breeze that does not return.

The cycle of rebellion, judgment, outward repentance, and God's mercy is representative of Israel's history. The absence of heartfelt contrition on the part of the people and the readiness to forgive on the part of God goes back to Israel's desert experience.

32–33 The people had seen God's "wonders" (v.32; cf. v.11), but "they did not believe" in them (cf. vv.19–20). They rejected the very evidences that should have led them to faith in him. Consequently he abandoned the generation of the wilderness to "futility" (*hebel*, v.33) and "terror" (*behālāh*, v.33). Life became nothing but "vanity" in the sense expressed by Ecclesiastes (cf. 1:2), filled with sudden catastrophes (*behālāh*, cf. Lev 26:16; Isa 65:23). At the end the generation of the wilderness passed away (Num 14:22–23).

34–35 God punished the people for their sins. They did respond on that particular occasion with all the evidences of true repentance (v.34). They sought him and returned to him "eagerly" but hurriedly. They wanted to get the discipline over with and return to normal life. In their return they made mention ("remembered," v.35) of "God . . . their Rock" and of "God Most High" (El Elyon), "their Redeemer" (cf. 119:154). All too often, however, the sole purpose of recognizing God was to derive benefits such as victory in war and provision of food. (For Most High [Elyon], vv.17, 35, 56, see the appendix to Ps 9: Yahweh Is El Elyon.)

36–39 The people's repentance was not an expression of true contrition but was intentionally deceptive. They may have worshiped the Lord outwardly but not with their hearts. They "would flatter" (v.36) him, thinking that they could entice or lure (*p-t-h;* cf. 2 Sam 3:25; Prov 24:28; Jer 20:7) the God of Israel into their schemes, but their every prayer was deceptive (cf. Isa 1:15). Their deception was expressive of the condition of "their hearts," which were determined not to be loyal to the Lord (v.37; cf. Acts 8:31). Though the Lord knew their hearts, he was true to his character in having compassion on them ("he was merciful," v.38; cf. Exod 34:6). His compassion found expression in his forgiveness (cf. 65:3) of their sins, his forbearance with their stubborn spirits, and his empathy with the human condition, so that the full brunt of his anger did not destroy them. Man is after all "flesh," i.e., mortal (v.39; cf. Gen 6:3; Pss 38:3; 56:4; 103:14–15; Isa 2:22). He is like the grass of the field that is here today and gone tomorrow (cf. Isa 40:6–7).

E. *Israel in Egypt and in the Wilderness*

78:40–55

40 How often they rebelled against him in the desert
and grieved him in the wasteland!
41 Again and again they put God to the test;
they vexed the Holy One of Israel.
42 They did not remember his power—
the day he redeemed them from the oppressor,
43 the day he displayed his miraculous signs in Egypt,
his wonders in the region of Zoan.
44 He turned their rivers to blood;
they could not drink from their streams.
45 He sent swarms of flies that devoured them,
and frogs that devastated them.
46 He gave their crops to the grasshopper,
their produce to the locust.
47 He destroyed their vines with hail
and their sycamore-figs with sleet.
48 He gave over their cattle to the hail,
their livestock to bolts of lightning.
49 He unleashed against them his hot anger,
his wrath, indignation and hostility—
a band of destroying angels.
50 He prepared a path for his anger;
he did not spare them from death
but gave them over to the plague.
51 He struck down all the firstborn of Egypt,
the firstfruits of manhood in the tents of Ham.
52 But he brought his people out like a flock;
he led them like sheep through the desert.
53 He guided them safely, so they were unafraid;
but the sea engulfed their enemies.
54 Thus he brought them to the border of his holy land,
to the hill country his right hand had taken.
55 He drove out nations before them
and allotted their lands to them as an inheritance;
he settled the tribes of Israel in their homes.

40–41 Israel's history of frequent rebellion stands in stark contrast to all the evidences of God's goodness. Humanly speaking Israel as a child caused great trouble to his heavenly Father in the wilderness (*yᵉšîmôn;* NIV, "wasteland," v.40; cf. 68:7;

106:14; 107:4; Deut 32:10). Israel "rebelled," caused grief, tried his patience ("tested"), and provoked ("vexed") "the Holy One of Israel" (v.41; cf. 71:22; 89:18).

42–51 The Lord had shown his fatherly care in Egypt and in the wilderness. In turn the Lord had expected his people to sanctify his holy name in an everlasting "remembrance" (Exod 3:15) in the sense that Israel would proclaim, speak about, and sing praises to his name. They did not "remember his power" (*yāḏô*, "his hand," v.42; cf. Exod 3:20), evidenced in the "miraculous signs" ('*ôṯ*, v.43; cf. Exod 4:9, 28, 30; 7:3) and "wonders" (*môp̱ēṯ;* cf. Deut 29:3; 34:11) in Egypt (v.43; cf. v.12) and in their redemption from their "oppressor" (v.42; cf. Exod 15 for a liturgical response to God's acts of redemption). He had turned their rivers into blood (v.44; cf. Exod 7:17–20; Ps 105:29; Rev 16:4) and had troubled the Egyptians with plagues:

fourth plague: flies (v.45; cf. Exod 8:20–32)
second plague: frogs (v.45; cf. Exod 7:25–8:15)
eighth plague: locusts (v.46; cf. Exod 10:1–20)
seventh plague: hail and lightning ("sleet," *hapax legomenon*, v.47; cf. Exod 9:13–35)
fifth plague: diseased livestock (See Notes, v.48; cf. Exod 9:1–7)
tenth plague: death of the firstborn (vv.49–51; cf. Exod 11:1–12:36)

The sequence is dwarfed by the climactic discussion of the tenth plague. Death in Egypt was an expression of God's "hot anger, his wrath, indignation and hostility. . . . his anger" (vv.49–50). He was sovereign over Egypt's adversities by sending the messengers ("angels") of adversity (NIV, "destroying"; MT, "of evil ones," i.e., of adversities, v.49; cf. Exod 12:23), resulting in the death of the "firstborn" of all the males ("firstfruits of manhood," v.51; cf. 105:36) in Egypt ("in the tents of Ham"; cf. 105:23, 27; 106:22).

52–55 Instead of adversity God brought great blessings to his own people like "a flock"/"like sheep" (v.52), a metaphor for Israel. He drowned the Egyptians in the Red Sea (v.53; cf. Exod 14–15); he guided his people so they needed not be afraid; he brought them safely to the Promised Land ("his holy land," lit., "the territory of his holiness," v.54; cf. Exod 15:17; "the hill country," lit., "this mountain"); he drove out the Canaanites; and he gave each tribe its allotted patrimony (vv.52–55).

Notes

---

48 It may be that בָּרָד (*bārāḏ*, "hail") is a textual corruption of דֶּבֶר (*deḇer*, "plague"; cf. v.50). Similarly רְשָׁפִים (*rᵉšāp̱îm*, "bolts of lightning") may be a metaphor for plagues, as the Canaanite god Resheph was the god of the plague (cf. A.A. Anderson, 2:572). Both words (*deḇer* and *rešep̱*) are found for plague in Hab 3:5 (cf. Deut 32:24). For an exhaustive study, see William J. Fulco, *The Canaanite God Resep* (New Haven: American Oriental Society, 1976). He concludes that "the *OT* passages seem to suggest that Resep represents some more-or-less uncontrolled cosmic force, typically as a bringer of plague and sudden death" (p. 61). He is the god involved with life and death. Yigael Yadin presents an extensive bibliography and new archaeological evidence in "New Gleanings from Resheph From Ugarit," *Biblical and Related Studies Presented to Samuel Iwry*, edd. Ann Kort and Scott Morschauer (Winona Lake: Eisenbrauns, 1985), pp. 259–74. He concludes that the little-known goddess Resheph was the patron deity of the archers, also called the "lion goddess."

By the time of the writing of this psalm, the name of the goddess had become a metaphor of death.

F. *Judgment on a Rebellious Generation*

78:56–64

56 But they put God to the test
and rebelled against the Most High;
they did not keep his statutes.
57 Like their fathers they were disloyal and faithless,
as unreliable as a faulty bow.
58 They angered him with their high places;
they aroused his jealousy with their idols.
59 When God heard them, he was very angry;
he rejected Israel completely.
60 He abandoned the tabernacle of Shiloh,
the tent he had set up among men.
61 He sent ⌊the ark of⌋ his might into captivity,
his splendor into the hands of the enemy.
62 He gave his people over to the sword;
he was very angry with his inheritance.
63 Fire consumed their young men,
and their maidens had no wedding songs;
64 their priests were put to the sword,
and their widows could not weep.

56–58 The psalmist returns to the refrain of Israel's rebelliousness (v.56; cf. vv.40–41). This section seems to be symmetric to vv.5–8 as it also refers to "their fathers" (v.57; cf. v.8: "their forefathers"), the faithlessness of Israel (v.57; cf. vv.7–8), and the law of God (v.56; cf. v.5). The people in the land were essentially no different from the generation of the wilderness. Though the Lord had given them his statutes to live by, they provoked him with cultic "high places" and with "idols" (v.58). In this they were unreliable, like a "faulty bow" that springs wrongly when needed (cf. v.9; Hos 7:16).

59–64 Because of Israel's treachery, God removed his glorious presence from them. The complete rejection of Israel probably does not signify that he broke the covenant with the Twelve Tribes in favor of Judah (so A.A. Anderson, 2:575). The verb "rejected" (*m-'-s*, vv.59, 67) is parallel with the phrase "he did not choose" (v.67). The Lord disregarded their position in favor of Judah. Ephraim could have been a leader among the tribes but turned out to be self-serving, bellicose, and idolatrous (cf. Judg 8; 12; 17). His anger (v.59) came to concrete expression in the destruction of the tabernacle at Shiloh (v.60; cf. Jer 7:12; 26:6), in the capture of the ark, symbolic of "his might" and of "his splendor" (v.61; cf. 132:8; 1 Sam 4; 5), and in great adversities (vv.62–64). Young men and priests (cf. 1 Sam 4:11, 17) were killed in battle, leaving behind unmarried maidens and widows; those who were left behind were too greatly afflicted to "weep" over the dead (v.64).

Notes

56 The MT reads, "But they put to the test and rebelled against God Most High." Instead of the usual formula El Elyon, the MT has Elohim Elyon. Briggs suggests that the phrase is too long and should be divided (2:196); so does the NIV: "God . . . the Most High" (Dahood, *Psalms*, 2:246).

59 David Noel Freedman proposes a divine epithet from the adverb מְאֹד (*m^e'ōḏ*, "very" in "very angry") by emending it to *mā'ēḏ* ("almighty"), resulting in a parallel rendering: "God heard and was enraged; then the Almighty rejected Israel" ("God Almighty in Psalm 78:59," Bib 54 [1973]: 268).

III. Good News: God Has Chosen David

78:65–72

65 Then the Lord awoke as from sleep,
as a man wakes from the stupor of wine.
66 He beat back his enemies;
he put them to everlasting shame.
67 Then he rejected the tents of Joseph,
he did not choose the tribe of Ephraim;
68 but he chose the tribe of Judah,
Mount Zion, which he loved.
69 He built his sanctuary like the heights,
like the earth that he established forever.
70 He chose David his servant
and took him from the sheep pens;
71 from tending the sheep he brought him
to be the shepherd of his people Jacob,
of Israel his inheritance.
72 And David shepherded them with integrity of heart;
with skillful hands he led them.

65–72 While the Philistines prevailed over Israel, it seemed as if the Lord was asleep. The renewal of his acts of mercy to Israel was so overwhelming that the psalmist likens God to a "hero" (*gibbôr;* NIV, "man"), who feels himself more heroic when intoxicated with wine (v.65). In his valor he overcame the enemies of his people (v.66) and gave the honor of victory and peace to David of the tribe of Judah (vv.68, 70–71), rejecting the supremacy of Ephraim (v.67). The favored position of Judah was further symbolized by the choice of Jerusalem (Mount Zion) as the place for his temple (v.69; cf. 46; 87:2).

The temple on earth was "like the heights" (v.69). The MT's "like the high ones" (*rāmîm*) does not specify what the height of the sanctuary is being compared with. It may denote the high mountains or the heavenly temple ("like the high heavens"). In view of the parallel with "earth" in the next colon, it is most probable that the psalmist likens God's temple on earth to the permanence of heaven and earth. Yet the Solomonic temple too was destroyed; and a second temple was rebuilt on its foundations after the Exile, which in turn was replaced by the magnificent Herodian temple. In A.D. 70 the Herodian temple was pillaged and destroyed by the Romans. It seems, therefore, that the psalm is pointing to the enduring way of God's presence with man on earth.

God's presence is connected with the Davidic Messiah, our Lord Jesus. He himself said that he is the temple of God (John 2:19–21) and that God must be worshiped in spirit and in truth (John 4:24). The Book of Revelation gives comfort in the magnificent vision of the presence of God among his people, when there will be no need of any temple: "I did not see a temple in the city, because the Lord God Almighty and the Lamb are its temple" (Rev 21:22). They will be satisfied with the "manna" (Rev 2:17), because those who persevere to the end will have a share in the New Jerusalem (Rev 21:27).

The connection between David, the temple, and the rule of God are set forth in vv.68–72. David was taken from shepherding the flocks to take care of God's flock, "his inheritance" (vv.70–71; cf. 1 Sam 16:11). The nature of his rule fulfilled God's expectations, and, hence, he is a role model for all the godly in Israel. David proved himself wise by being a man who was upright ("integrity of heart," v.72; see 7:8) in the midst of a stubborn people. Unlike bellicose and idolatrous Ephraim, David guided the national, political, and religious interests of Israel with "understanding" (i.e., "wisdom"; NIV, "skillful").

The promises pertaining to God's kingdom, the messianic rule, and the presence of God find their focus in Jesus the Messiah. Those who reject him end up like the generation of the wilderness (1 Cor 10:1–13). But all who receive him as the Messiah of God find in him the "bread . . . from heaven" (John 6:41), the water of life (John 7:37–39), and the life everlasting (John 11:25–26)!

Notes

65 See the NEB: "like a warrior heated with wine"; similarly A.A. Anderson: "the Psalmist daringly compares Yahweh with a mighty warrior who is stirred up to great deeds by strong wine" (2:576). David Toshio Tsumara concludes that this verse should be translated as "like a warrior shouting with joy of wine" ("Twofold Image of Wine in Psalm 46:4–5," JQR 71 [1981]: 167–75).

67–72 R.P. Carroll distinguishes between the Sinai/Ephraimite tradition and the Zion/David/-Judah tradition, treating this psalm as a polemic ("Psalm LXXVIII: Vestiges of a Tribal Polemic," VetTest 21 [1971]: 133–50).

Appendix: The Mighty Acts of Yahweh

The people of God sang about, proclaimed, spoke about, and told the stories of Yahweh's mighty acts of salvation. The story of salvation has its roots in Israel's belief in God's involvement with his creation. Creation is not merely an article of faith to be believed but, as C.S. Lewis put it, "an achievement" (see the essay "Nature" in *Reflections on the Psalms,* pp. 76–89; the citation comes from p. 83). The praise of Israel and the education of Israel spotlighted God's acts because they were revelatory and, more than that, they reflected Yahweh's love for his people. But Israel also lamented the absence of his acts, praying for a new demonstration of his wonderful acts (80:2–4). They called on Yahweh, the Divine Warrior-King, to come to the aid of his struggling people.

The synonyms of God's mighty acts are many.

1. Wonders (*p-l-'—pele', niplā'ôt, pel'î*). The root and its derived nouns in the Psalms celebrate the "wonder" of God's acts in creation and in the history of redemption. The psalmist reflected on the wonders of God as a series of acts:

> Many, O LORD my God,
> are the wonders [*niplā'ôt*] you have done.
> The things you planned for us
> no one can recount to you;
> were I to speak and tell of them,
> they would be too many to declare.
>
> (40:5)

The events from the Exodus to the Conquest set into motion the acts of divine condescension:

> They forgot what he had done,
> the wonders [*niplā'ôt*] he had shown them.
> He did miracles [*pele'*] in the sight of their fathers
> in the land of Egypt, in the region of Zoan.
>
> (78:11–12)

These "wondrous acts" reveal God's perfections: fidelity (89:5), love (107:8; cf. vv.15, 21, 31; 136:4), grace, and compassion (111:4–5).

One psalmist confesses that he has learned from a tender age about God's works: "Since my youth, O God, you have taught me, / and to this day I declare your marvelous deeds [*niplā'ôt*]" (71:17). Yahweh and the history of salvation are so intertwined that when the psalmists reflect on the Lord, they think of Yahweh's many acts! Yahweh, his perfections, his acts, the history of the people of God, and the purposes of God coalesce into a magnificent mosaic:

> Sing to the LORD, praise his name;
> proclaim his salvation day after day.
> Declare his glory among the nations,
> his marvelous deeds [*niplā'ôt*] among all peoples.
> For great is the LORD and most worthy of praise;
> he is to be feared above all gods.
>
> (96:2–4; cf. 86:10)

It is no wonder that the people of God told the story of salvation over and over again:

> We will not hide them from their children;
> we will tell the next generation
> the praiseworthy deeds of the LORD,
> his power, and the wonders [*niplā'ôt*] he has done.
>
> (78:4)

Even in moments of despair, the people of God "remembered" and meditated on what God had done:

> I will remember the deeds of the LORD;
> yes, I will remember your miracles [*pele'*] of long ago.
> I will meditate on all your works [*ma'alāl*]
> and consider all your mighty deeds.
>
> (77:11–12)

Moreover, the celebration of God's past acts leads to hope in the new acts of God. So the cycle of lament and praise continues from generation to generation, "proclaiming aloud your praise and telling of all your wonderful deeds [*niplā'ōt*]" (26:7).

2. Signs and Wonders: *'ōt/'ōtôt* ("sign[s]") and *môpēt* ("wonder"). These two words are often paired together and refer to God's acts in Egypt (Exod 7:3; Deut 4:34; 7:19; 34:11); e.g., "the day he displayed his miraculous signs [*'ōtôt*] in Egypt, his wonders [*môpēt*] in the region of Zoan" (78:43).

3. Great and Powerful: "Great" (*gādôl, gedôlôt*) and forms of the root *'-z-z* (*'ōz, 'izzûz, 'ezûz*, "mighty," "power," "strength") further describe the power of God's works: e.g., "They will tell of the power [*'ezûz*] of your awesome works [*nôrā'*], / and I will proclaim your great deeds [*gedôlôt*]" (145:6; cf 68:28; 106:21). They bring nothing but dread among the opponents of God's kingdom: "How awesome [*nôrā'*] are your deeds! / So great is your power [*'ōz*] that your enemies cringe before you" (66:3).

4. Mighty (*g-b-r—gibbôr, gebûrāh*). The words derived from this root are virtually synonymous with *'-z-z* ("be strong"); e.g., "Be exalted, O LORD, in your strength [*'ōz*]; / we will sing and praise your might [*gebûrāh*]" (21:13). The mighty acts of God are acts of deliverance and vindication: "Save [*y-š-'*] me, O God, by your name; / vindicate [*d-i-n*] me by your might [*gebûrāh*]" (54:1). Notice the use of the verbs "save" and "vindicate" in the context with "might." Yahweh is the *gibbôr* ("hero") from of old, who formed the mountains with his strength (65:6). He rules in the fullness of his strength (66:7), as he establishes righteousness on earth:

> You answer us with awesome deeds [*nôrā'ôt*] of righteousness,
> O God our Savior,
> the hope of all the ends of the earth
> and of the farthest seas.
>
> (65:5)

His saints acclaim his strength and the power of his kingdom:

> They will tell of the glory of your kingdom
> and speak of your might [*gebûrāh*],
> so that all men may know of your mighty acts [*gebûrāh*]
> and the glorious splendor of your kingdom.
>
> (145:11–12)

5. Yahweh's Hand and Arm. "Hand" (*yād*) and "arm" (*zerôa'*) are metaphors for Yahweh's strength in the Pentateuch, Prophets, and Poetical books. Moses attributed the victory over Egypt to the "right hand" of God, a synecdoche (part for the whole) for the Warrior-King (Exod 15:6). The psalmists too believe that Yahweh exercises dominion over the nations, subduing all opposition to his kingship:

> Sing to the LORD a new song,
> for he has done marvelous [*niplā'ōt*] things;
> his right hand and his holy arm
> have worked salvation for him.
>
> (98:1)

See also "Now I know that the LORD saves his anointed; / he answers him from his holy heaven / with the saving power [*bigburôt*] of his right hand" (20:6).

6. The Story of Yahweh's Acts. The revelation of Yahweh throughout the progression of redemption reveals facets of the greatness of Yahweh. Each act reveals a hue of the glorious splendor of our God. His acts reveal the involvement of our God in Creation (see Pss 8; 19; 33; 104; 145); in maintaining order in his world; in forming a people for himself; in vindicating his people; in avenging himself of his opponents; and of providing for his sheep with his goodness, his benefits, and his salvation. They are the object of his compassion and, hence, are assured that

they will be fully liberated, vindicated, and redeemed from whatever anxiety, cause of anguish, or form of alienation or oppression. The psalmists cast themselves on the promises of God in the cycle of lament and prayer, awaiting the day of deliverance. They have tasted of God's goodness and have found it so glorious that they look forward to the greater acts of God on behalf of his creation and his people.

The psalmists present us with Yahweh: the Creator, King, Redeemer, and Divine Warrior. Instead of meditating on his attributes apart from his acts in Creation and redemption, they praise Yahweh for his revelation, acts of rule, vengeance, and condescension and deliverance to Israel. The Great King involved himself with his world! Therefore one psalmist vows to praise the Lord for his mighty acts from his youth till his old age and to keep the story of redemption alive by proclaiming to the new generation what God has done:

> My mouth will tell of your righteousness,
> of your salvation all day long,
> though I know not its measure.
> I will come and proclaim your mighty acts [*g^e^b̲ûrāh*],
> O Sovereign LORD;
> I will proclaim your righteousness, yours alone.
> Since my youth, O God, you have taught me,
> and to this day I declare your marvelous deeds [*nip̲lā'ôt̲*].
> Even when I am old and gray,
> do not forsake me, O God,
> till I declare your power to the next generation,
> your might [*g^e^b̲ûrāh*] to all who are to come.
> Your righteousness reaches to the skies, O God,
> you who have done great things [*g^e^d̲ôlôt̲*].
> Who, O God, is like you?
>
> (71:15–19)

7. The Fear and Dread of God's Acts (*y-r-'* and *p-ḥ-d*). The root *y-r-'* ("fear") with its derived verbal (*nôrā'* [pl.: *nôrā'ôt̲*], "awesome") and nominal forms (*yir'āh*, "fear") denote the reaction to Yahweh's rule: "How awesome is the LORD Most High, / the great King over all the earth!" (47:2). The godly stand in "awe" of their Warrior-King: "You are awesome [*nôrā'*], O God, in your sanctuary; / the God of Israel gives power [*'ōz*] and strength to his people. / Praise be to God!" (68:35). His accomplishments in redemptive history inspire them with fear and the nations to stand in awe:

> You answer us with awesome deeds [*nôrā'*] of righteousness,
> O God our Savior,
> the hope of all the ends of the earth
> and of the farthest seas,
> who formed the mountains by your power,
> having armed yourself with strength,
> who stilled the roaring of the seas,
> the roaring of their waves,
> and the turmoil of the nations.
> Those living far away fear [*y-r-'*] your wonders [*'ōt̲ôt̲*];
> where morning dawns and evening fades
> you call forth songs of joy.
>
> (65:5–8; cf. 68:35)

> You alone are to be feared [*nôrā'*].
> Who can stand before you when you are angry?

. . . .

He breaks the spirit of rulers;
he is feared [*nôrā'*] by the kings of the earth.

(76:7, 12)

Godly fear expresses itself in submission to the Great King. It is the prerequisite for wisdom: "The fear of the LORD is the beginning of wisdom; / all who follow his precepts have good understanding. / To him belongs eternal praise" (111:10; cf. 19:11; 86:11). The wise make up the community of God-fearers (22:22–23, 25), who fear no evil (23:4). They "submit" themselves to Yahweh by being receptive to his instruction: "Who, then, is the man that fears the LORD? / He will instruct him in the way chosen for him" (25:12).

The Lord richly rewards those who fear him (31:19; cf. 103:11, 13, 17). In living in submission to the Lord's will, the godly find their strength in the Lord (56:3; cf. vv.4, 11; 112:7). Thus "fear" is related to God's kingship, because Yahweh is looking for servants who do his will on earth, even as the angels in heaven do his will in heaven (89:7).

The hope of the psalmist lies in the eschatological vision, according to which Israel and all the nations will submit to the Lord. Then the kingdom of God will be fully established: "The nations will fear the name of the LORD, / all the kings of the earth will revere your glory" (102:15). Thus "fear" signifies submission to the Lord in this life and a trust that Yahweh's promises will come true in the future.

The root *p-ḥ-d* ("tremble with fear," "dread") and its derived noun, *paḥaḏ* ("fear"), connote more clearly terror. Yahweh will bring sudden disaster on the wicked:

There they were, overwhelmed with dread [*paḥaḏû paḥaḏ*],
where there was nothing to dread [*paḥaḏ*].
God scattered the bones of those who attacked you;
you put them to shame, for God despised them.

(53:5; cf. 14:5)

But the godly need not be afraid (91:5; cf. 78:53), even though the enemy may terrorize the righteous (64:1). The godly "fear" (*y-r-'; p-ḥ-d*) the Lord (119:120, 161). But they have nothing to fear (*y-r-'; p-ḥ-d;* 27:5; cf. 3:6).

Related Topics: See appendixes to Pss 3 (Yahweh Is My God); 7 (The Name of Yahweh); 25 (The Perfections of Yahweh); 46 (Zion Theology); 98 (Yahweh Is the Divine Warrior); 119 (Yahweh Is My Redeemer); 122 (The Praise of Yahweh); 132 (The Ark of the Covenant and the Temple: Symbols of Yahweh's Presence and Rule); 140 (The Poor and Oppressed).

Texts: 9:1; 26:7; 65:5–6, 8; 66:3, 5; 71:16–17; 75:1; 78:4, 7, 11, 26, 32, 42–43; 86:8, 10, 17; 88:10, 12; 89:5, 7–8, 13; 90:16; 96:3; 105:2, 5, 27; 106:2, 7–8, 22; 107:8, 15, 21, 24, 31; 111:3–4, 6; 118:15–16, 23; 136:4, 12; 145:4–6, 11–12.

Bibliography: Bernard W. Anderson, "Introduction: Mythopoetic and Theological Dimensions of Biblical Creation Faith," *Creation in the Old Testament,* ed. Bernard W. Anderson (Philadelphia: Fortress, 1984), pp. 1–24; Brueggemann, "Songs of Creation," *The Message of the Psalms,* pp. 28–38; Eichrodt, TOT, 2:162–67; Otto Eissfeldt, "Die Psalmen als Geschichtsquelle," pp. 97–112; Kühlewein, *Geschichte in den Psalmen;* E. Noort, "Het Ik—Zijn Van Jhwh. Over de Problematiek Van de Persoonlijke God in de Theologie van het Oude Testament," *Gereformeerd Theologisch Tijdschrift* 85 (1985): 132–51; H.H. Schmid, "Creation, Righteousness, and Salvation: 'Creation Theology' as a Broad Horizon of Biblical Theology," in B.W. Anderson, ed., *Creation in the Old*

Testament, pp. 102–17; Westermann, *Praise and Lament in the Psalms*, pp. 214–49.

TDAT, 3:870–94; TDOT, 3:367–82, 401; TWOT, 1:18–19, 67, 148–49, 151, 254, 362–64, 399–401, 723; 2:720–21, 723.

Psalm 79: Lord, Remember the Sheep of Your Pasture

This is a lament written most probably on the occasion of Jerusalem's fall and the subsequent exile of Judah (586 B.C.). Its concerns resemble those of Psalms 44 and 74. Central to the psalmist's prayer is the question of how long the Lord will remain angry with his people. For background see Ralph W. Klein, *Israel in Exile. A Theological Interpretation* (Philadelphia: Fortress, 1979), esp. pp. 20–21. For an approach to this psalm as a war oracle, see the study by Christensen, pp. 112–27. For other psalms, see 12; 60; 74; 80; 83; 85; 90; 94:1–11; 123; 126; and 137.

The structure of this psalm reflects the characteristic elements of the *national lament*: questions, prayer, and hope. For our purposes we analyze the structure as follows:

A. Lament (vv.1–4)
  B. Question (v.5)
    C. Prayer for Vindication and Forgiveness (vv.6–9)
  B′. Question (v.10a)
    C′. Prayer for Vindication and Restoration (vv.10b–13)

I. Lament

79:1–4

A psalm of Asaph.

1 O God, the nations have invaded your inheritance;
they have defiled your holy temple,
they have reduced Jerusalem to rubble.
2 They have given the dead bodies of your servants
as food to the birds of the air,
the flesh of your saints to the beasts of the earth.
3 They have poured out blood like water
all around Jerusalem,
and there is no one to bury the dead.
4 We are objects of reproach to our neighbors,
of scorn and derision to those around us.

1 The lament focuses on the grief caused by the enemies ("the nations," i.e., "the heathen"; cf. 10:16; Luke 21:24; Rev 10:11). They showed no respect for the land and people of God ("your inheritance"), for the temple ("your holy temple," cf. Lam 1:10), or for the city of God ("Jerusalem," cf. 2 Kings 25:9–10). The issue here is not God's justice in judging his people but the means used by the Lord. The pagans must be held accountable for their desecration of the holy people and the holy temple so that they may be restored and God's people no longer experience defilement and disgrace (cf. Isa 35:8; 52:1). (See the appendix to Ps 132: The Ark of the Covenant and the Temple: Symbols of Yahweh's Presence and Rule.)

2 The psalmist laments over the unburied bodies of those who fell by the ravages of warfare. They were left to the wild animals and the birds of prey (cf. Jer 34:20; Lam 4:19). Because their relatives were too busy trying to survive the siege and were exiled, the dead were left to rot in the sun (cf. Lam 4:14–20). They were remembered but not buried! The lack of burial was considered a terrible fate in the ancient Near East. Yet, though famine, war, death, and exile were deserved punishments for Judah's sins (Lam 1:8–9), the people are still spoken of as the people of God. They are called "your servants" and "your saints." The godly remnant was like leaven, by which the whole nation was protected and consecrated.

3 The enemies of Judah, however, had no regard for God or for his people. The epitome of lack of regard for human life is brought out by the metaphor of "water." Blood, i.e., human lives, was like run-off water (cf. v.10; 106:38). War made no distinction between godly and ungodly (Jer 16:4).

4 Those who were left had no reason to rejoice. They carried the reproach and scorn of their oppressors (cf. 44:14). The remnant was in a state of "living death." The curses of the covenant (cf. Deut 28:15–68; 1 Kings 9:6–9) came to haunt the people of God, as they were forsaken by God and rejected by man.

II. Question

79:5

5 How long, O LORD? Will you be angry forever?
  How long will your jealousy burn like fire?

5 The heart-rending "how long" is a cry from a wounded people (cf. Rev 6:10). Having received a severe blow as a people, they ask not why but how long they must suffer. God is angry because of their sins. With the intensity of his anger bearing down on them, they suffer greatly. His jealous anger (119:139; Nah 1:2) is so great that it is likened to a consuming fire. For a similar question, see 89:46.

Notes

5 עַד־מָה (*'aḏ-māh,* "How long") serves as a double-duty interrogative that affects both colons (see 6:3).

The adverbial phrase לָנֶצַח (*lāneṣah,* "forever") also expresses the idea of a superlative, giving the translation "will you be exceedingly angry" (see A.A. Anderson, 2:578).

III. Prayer for Vindication and Forgiveness

79:6–9

6 Pour out your wrath on the nations
  that do not acknowledge you,
on the kingdoms

that do not call on your name;
[7]for they have devoured Jacob
and destroyed his homeland.
[8]Do not hold against us the sins of the fathers;
may your mercy come quickly to meet us,
for we are in desperate need.

[9]Help us, O God our Savior,
for the glory of your name;
deliver us and forgive our sins
for your name's sake.

6–7 The question (v.5) serves as a transition from lament (vv.1–4) to prayer (vv.6–9). In view of the atrocities of the nations against God's community and in view of the gravity of Judah's suffering, the psalmist prays for divine vindication for his people (cf. Jer 10:25). There is no spirit of raw vengeance but rather of justice. Justice must be done because of the conduct of the heathen. They had no regard for God. They did not know him intimately (NIV, "acknowledge"). They did not call on his name (cf. 75:1). Instead they have desecrated and destroyed God's land and people (v.7), leaving his people desperate (cf. 142:7).

8 The remnant in exile prayed for themselves. They believed that they had been spared for a reason. They approached God in prayer for forgiveness of the sins of the previous generations, "the sins of the fathers" (cf. Jer 31:29; Ezek 18:2–4; Dan 9:4–14). The prayer "Do not hold against us" (lit., "Do not remember") is a humble petition for forgiveness, a request for God to blot out any memory of the accumulation of iniquities of the past generations (cf. 103:3, 10–12; Mic 7:18).

Positively, the people prayed that the Lord, who is sovereign and free, would hasten to bestow his mercy on them. In their "desperate need" they were acutely aware of their need of God's mercy, which brings reconciliation, forgiveness, and restoration. The "mercy" of God is not a singular act; it is plural and should be rendered as "your merciful (compassionate) acts" (Briggs, 2:199).

9 Hope rises to a new height in the prayer for help. Hope looks to God as "our Savior." He is the Deliverer of his children, i.e., those who are his by covenant. However, his children have to submit themselves to their heavenly Father as they await his salvation. They appealed to his glorious name ("the glory of your name"), which he had revealed to Israel. Similarly, Moses had appealed to the glorious name, Yahweh, as the ground for patience with sinful Israel (Num 14:13–19).

In and through the darkness of judgment, hope remains in God's promise that he will never abandon his plan of redemption! Redemption has here two aspects: deliverance from the enemies (vindication) and forgiveness for sins (cf. v.8). The sins are not only those of the "forefathers" (cf. v.8) but also those of the present generation ("our sins"). The solidarity of the people in the present and with their past requires that all sins be forgiven. Then the Lord may act graciously. His grace is not conditioned by man's righteous acts or piety but only "for [his] name's sake" (cf. 20:1). His honor as the covenant God guarantees that he will be faithful, even when man is not.

Notes

6–7 These verses are virtually identical to Jer 10:25 (see EBC, 4:451).

7 The "homeland" is an extended meaning of נָוֶה (*nāweh*, "pasturage," "camping place"; cf. KB, p. 601).

8 The "fathers" are literally those who have gone before: רִאשֹׁנִים (*ri'šōnîm*, "former ones"). In Isaiah the "former" denotes the conditions before the Exile, including the results of the Exile itself (Isa 41:22). The word could also modify "sins": "former sins." However, in this context it is preferable to treat it as a reference back to the ancestors.

9 The technical word "atone" in the imperative occurs once in the psalms: כַּפֵּר (*kappēr;* cf. "forgive," 65:3; 78:38; "atonement," Lev 9:7; Deut 21:8).

On "your name's sake," see 23:3.

IV. Question

79:10a

10 Why should the nations say,
"Where is their God?"

10a The psalmist renews his reflection on the reproach and the scorn caused by the "heathen" nations. He again raises a question, related to the previous question, "How long?" (v.5). In view of the atrocities of the nations and the glory of Yahweh's name, why should their taunt be tolerated any longer? The nations have blatantly challenged the power of God with the question "Where is their God?" (cf. 42:3, 10; 115:2; Joel 2:17; Mic 7:10).

V. Prayer for Vindication and Restoration

79:10b–13

Before our eyes, make known among the nations
that you avenge the outpoured blood of your servants.
11 May the groans of the prisoners come before you;
by the strength of your arm
preserve those condemned to die.

12 Pay back into the laps of our neighbors seven times
the reproach they have hurled at you, O Lord.
13 Then we your people, the sheep of your pasture,
will praise you forever;
from generation to generation
we will recount your praise.

10b The prayer of the godly rose with the increased hope that the Lord may deal justly with those who disgraced his people. His vindication must not be delayed but must be executed speedily: "before our eyes." Those who had witnessed the spilling of the innocent blood of the godly around Jerusalem (v.3) hoped for the speedy expression of God's acts of vengeance on behalf of his "servants." Their delight was not in the turn of events against the heathen. They were not filled with hatred and bitterness. Rather their words express the cry of a needy and suffering people who look toward their heavenly Father for deliverance.

11 At the time of the Exodus, God had seen the affliction of his people and had heard their groanings (Exod 2:24; 6:5). The people in exile were not unlike those in Egypt. They too groaned for the moment of their deliverance and prayed that the Lord would rise up and deliver them with his strong "arm" (cf. Exod 15:16). The fate of the exiles is likened to that of prisoners (cf. 102:20; Isa 42:7; 49:9; 61:1) who are "condemned to die."

12 The sevenfold restitution expresses a concern for full justice. Briggs is incorrect in his judgment that this is an expression of "vindictiveness to the neighbouring nations" (2:200). The judgment must be equal to the severity of the reproach of God's name! Certainly the people of God looked for restoration, but the restoration is directly related to their being a witness to the glory of God. Unlike Lamech who desired to avenge himself (Gen 4:24), the people looked toward the Lord to vindicate them. (See the appendix to Ps 137: Imprecations in the Psalms.)

13 The psalm concludes on a note of hope, as God's people look for the day of their redemption (cf. 2 Thess 1:5–10). They are still "the sheep" of his pasture (cf. 100:3), even though they had been forcibly removed from the land (v.7). They anticipate praising God for their redemption from the oppressors and for their forgiveness. How sweet is the hope of the children of God, even in the hour of deepest distress! Brueggemann comments that "new life is never a gift in a vacuum. It is wrought in profound and dangerous struggle as we bring to visibility the deep incongruity that marks our life. Our life is one in which all that is finally holy is violated, day by day" (*Message of the Psalms,* p. 74).

Notes

11 הוֹתֵר (*hôṯēr,* "preserve") is emended by some (NEB) to *hattēr* ("set at liberty," "free") based on the Syriac; cf. 105:20; 146:7. Kraus favors retention of the MT (*Psalmen,* 1:550).

The word תְּמוּתָה (*temûṯāh,* "death") occurs only here and in 102:20.

12 There are two ways of understanding the word חֵיקָם (*ḥêqām,* "laps"). It may signify the directness of God's judgment so that it "strikes the innermost being" (Dahood, *Psalms,* 2:253), or it may be interpreted in the light of the cultural dress, which permitted one to hide objects in a pocket formed by a fold in the garment below the belt (KB[3], 1:300; so NIV).

Psalm 80: Make Your Face to Shine on Us

The psalm is a *community lament.* Its origin may be associated with the last days of Israel (c. 732–722 B.C.). The psalmist refers to "Israel," "Joseph," and "Ephraim, Benjamin and Manasseh" (vv.1–2). Since the northern kingdom was exiled in 722 B.C. and the psalmist prays for God's mercy on Israel, Samaria had not yet fallen to the Assyrians (722 B.C.; see Otto Eissfeldt, "Psalm 80," *Kleine Schriften,* vol. 3, edd. Rudolf Sellheim and Fritz Maas [Tübingen: Mohr, 1966], pp. 221–32). According to a second view, the author may have been a Judean familiar with the recent events of the northern kingdom. A remnant of the northern tribes may have asked for asylum in the south. The psalmist prays that the same lot may not overtake the southern kingdom. B.Z. Luria explains that this psalm together with Psalms 77 and 81 lament the destruction of Samaria in 722 B.C. ("Psalms From Ephraim," *Beth Mikra* 23 [1978]: 151–60 [Heb.]). The LXX addition "concerning the Assyrians" to the superscription lends further weight to this perspective of interpreting the psalm. This psalm may have later become associated liturgically with days of prayer and fasting.

The structure of the psalm reveals a varying refrain in vv.3, 7, 14, and 19 and an address to the Lord as the "God of hosts" ("God Almighty," vv.4, 7, 14, 19; see appendix to Ps 24: Lord Sabaoth). The psalm reveals the following structural divisions:

A. Prayer for Deliverance (vv.1–3)
  B. The Lord's Present Anger (vv.4–7)
  B′. The Lord's Past Mercy (vv.8–14a)
A′. Prayer for Deliverance (vv.14b–19)

I. Prayer for Deliverance

80:1–3

For the director of music. To ⌊the tune of⌋ "The Lilies of the Covenant."
Of Asaph. A psalm.

1 Hear us, O Shepherd of Israel,
  you who lead Joseph like a flock;
you who sit enthroned between the cherubim, shine forth
2 before Ephraim, Benjamin and Manasseh.
Awaken your might;
  come and save us.

3 Restore us, O God;
  make your face shine upon us,
  that we may be saved.

1–2 God's judgment on Israel ("Joseph") is not because he has not shown his regard or love for them. He has cared for the northern tribes as much as he cared for the southern tribes. He is the Great Shepherd (cf. 23:1) who dwelt in the midst of his people, as symbolized by the cherubim above the ark of the covenant (cf. 18:10; 99:1; 1 Kings 8:7; see appendix to Ps 132: The Ark of the Covenant and the Temple: Symbols of Yahweh's Presence and Rule). It is to the Lord, the "royal Shepherd" of Israel, that the psalmist addresses this prayer most urgently on behalf of the northern tribes. He prays that the Lord may open his ear ("hear," cf. 77:1). He prays that "the royal Shepherd" may appear ("shine forth," NIV; see 50:2; 94:1) in his glorious array as the Divine Warrior. Thus the psalmist rouses God to action ("awaken your might," v.2; cf. 35:23; 44:23). The Lord has the "might" to show his "salvation" (*yᵉšu'āṯāh;* cf. GKC, par. 90g; see 3:2; NIV, "save") to his people (see appendix to Ps 119: Yahweh Is My Redeemer).

3 In the refrains (vv.3, 7, 14, 19) the psalmist repeatedly asks the Lord for his gracious restoration to his covenant mercies. The people have broken the covenant and are the objects of his wrath. Only the Lord can "revive" (v.18) the people by forgiveness of their sins, by renewal of the covenant, and by driving out the enemies. This is not merely a prayer for deliverance from the enemy but an urgent petition for the blessings of God. When the face of the Lord shines on his people, they are blessed with his presence and favor (cf. Num 6:24–26; Pss 31:16; 67:1) and will be "saved."

Notes

1–3 (2–4 MT) The emphasis is on the active involvement of God by the usage of three participial phrases at the beginning of each colon: He is the "Shepherd of Israel" (רֹעֵה יִשְׂרָאֵל [*rō'ēh yiśrā'ēl*]), "the guide" or "leader" (נֹהֵג [*nōhēg*]; NIV, "you who lead") of his flock (cf. 74:1; 107:41), and the "One who sits enthroned" (יֹשֵׁב [*yōšēb*; NIV, "you who sit enthroned"]) between the cherubim.

3 (4 MT) Goldingay rightly explains the differences in the refrain (vv.3, 7, 14, 19) as arising from artistic variation ("Repetition and Variation in the Psalms," pp. 149–50). For an approach to this psalm as a war oracle, see Christensen, pp. 112–27. For other psalms, see 12; 60; 74; 79; 80; 83; 85; 90; 94:1–11; 123; 126; 137.

II. The Lord's Present Anger

80:4–7

4 O LORD God Almighty,
how long will your anger smolder
against the prayers of your people?
5 You have fed them with the bread of tears;
you have made them drink tears by the bowlful.
6 You have made us a source of contention to our neighbors,
and our enemies mock us.

7 Restore us, O God Almighty;
make your face shine upon us,
that we may be saved.

4–7 The God of the Aaronic blessing (v.3) is no one else than the "LORD God Almighty" (lit., "of hosts," v.4). He is the Divine Warrior who can marshal all the hosts of heaven to the aid of his people. However, he can also use the hosts on earth to judge the nations on earth, including Israel. Israel felt the weight of his anger. His "anger smolders" (lit., "you smoke"; cf. 74:1) against the prayers of his own people. They pray for his grace and blessing but without avail. Instead, the people suffer from oppression and ridicule. Their food and drink are nothing but "tears" (cf. 42:3; 102:9) in great abundance ("by the bowlful"; see Dahood, *Psalms*, 2:257). The care of the great Shepherd-King is no longer evident. He does not lead them into plentiful pastures and quiet waters (cf. 23:1–2) but instead has given them up to the enemy (cf. in contrast to 23:5). The enemies "mock" (v.6, "laugh") at Israel, as it has become "a source of contention" (cf. Jer 15:10). The godly ask how long the Lord's anger will linger, as they long for divine salvation (v.7; see v.3).

Notes

6 (7 MT) Several Hebrew MSS and the LXX read לָנוּ (*lānû*, "to us") instead of לָמוֹ (*lāmô*, "to them"; cf. BHS). The NIV follows the emendation. Kraus retains the MT (*Psalmen*, 1:555).

III. The Lord's Past Mercy

80:8–14a

8 You brought a vine out of Egypt;
  you drove out the nations and planted it.
9 You cleared the ground for it,
  and it took root and filled the land.
10 The mountains were covered with its shade,
  the mighty cedars with its branches.
11 It sent out its boughs to the Sea,
  its shoots as far as the River.

12 Why have you broken down its walls
  so that all who pass by pick its grapes?
13 Boars from the forest ravage it
  and the creatures of the field feed on it.
14 Return to us, O God Almighty!
  Look down from heaven and see!

8–11 Jacob likened Joseph to "a fruitful vine near a spring, / whose branches climb over a wall" (Gen 49:22). Israel is frequently likened to a vine (cf. Isa 5:1–7; 27:2–6; Jer 2:21; 12:10; Ezek 15:1–8; 19:10–14; Hos 10:1). Our Lord also compared himself to a vine and his disciples to branches (John 15:1–6). In what is sometimes called "The Parable of the Vine" (vv.8–14a; see Weiser, p. 549), the psalmist goes back to the Conquest as he refers to God's activity on behalf of his "vine." The Lord brought Israel out of Egypt and into the land of Canaan (v.8). The Lord cared for his people like a vinedresser as he cleared the ground (cf. Isa 5:2), planted the vine, and nurtured it (v.9). Israel occupied the land, subdued the people, and controlled the nations from the Euphrates ("the River") in the east and "the mighty cedars" (lit., "cedars of God," an idiom of magnitude) of the Lebanon mountains in the north to the Mediterranean on the west ("the Sea," vv.10–11; cf. Deut 11:24). The people had enjoyed the full possession of the land during the days of David and Solomon (2 Sam 8:3; 1 Kings 4:21; cf. Ps 72:8–11).

12–13 Though God had extended much care to Israel in fulfillment of his promises, he had permitted his vineyard to be taken over by "boars" (v.13; cf. Lev 11:7; Deut 14:8; unclean animals, i.e., foreigners) and by wild creatures.

14a In the refrain the people pray that "God Almighty" may look again with kindness ("watch over"; lit., "visit," v.14a; cf. 106:4) on his vine, which he himself had planted with evidences of his mighty acts of salvation and rule ("your right hand," v.15; cf. Exod 15:6).

Notes

13 (14 MT) יְכַרְסְמֶנָּה (*yᵉkarsᵉmennāh,* "feed on it") is related to the Akkadian *kasāmu* ("to cut in pieces"; see Dahood, *Psalms,* 2:259).

The consonants מיר (*m-y-r*) could be read with an ayin (ע [ʿ]) as מִיַּעַר (*miyyāʿar,* "from a forest") or with an aleph (א [ʾ]) as מִיְאוֹר (*miyyᵉʾôr,* "from the Nile"). The Masoretes clarified this ambiguity in favor of the former by the addition of a suspended ayin.

IV. Prayer for Deliverance

80:14b–19

Watch over this vine,
15 the root your right hand has planted,
the son you have raised up for yourself.

16 Your vine is cut down, it is burned with fire;
at your rebuke your people perish.
17 Let your hand rest on the man at your right hand,
the son of man you have raised up for yourself.
18 Then we will not turn away from you;
revive us, and we will call on your name.

19 Restore us, O LORD God Almighty;
make your face shine upon us,
that we may be saved.

14b–19 Israel was at one time honored like "the man at your right hand" (v.17) in the period of the Conquest, because of Joshua. Israel is like a "root" (v.15, or "shoot"). However, Israel has become a useless vine. The people perished by the "rebuke" of God's anger (v.16).

The people pray that the Lord will sustain Israel in her hour of need (v.17) so that the renewal of his favor (cf. 30:5) will lead to a new commitment for Israel (v.18; cf. 75:1). The ground of hope in restoration lies in "the man at your right hand," also called "the son of man" (v.17). These allusions to the Davidic dynasty (see 110:1) focus the hope of the godly in the continuity of God's redemptive purposes. Regardless of what happened at Samaria and of what may happen to Jerusalem, the Lord will be true to David. God's kingdom will be established by the Messiah of David (see Ps 2).

In the refrain the community boldly petitions the Lord to have mercy on his covenant people so that they may have another opportunity. As Weiser puts it, "At the point of supreme peril the cult community, because of this faith, do not give themselves up for lost, but reach out the more determinedly for the saving hand of God which despite all appearances to the contrary stretches out towards them from the darkness" (p. 551).

Notes

15 (16 MT) The LXX reads a verbal phrase—"and establish it"—for the MT nominal phrase וְכַנָּה (*wᵉkannāh,* "and a stem," "and a root"; NIV, "the root"). Baumgartner's lexicon takes it

as a metaphor for "human beings" (KB3, 2:460) and parallel with "the son" (v.15b). Kraus emends it to *w^egannāh* ("and a garden," *Psalmen*, 1:555).

16 (17 MT) Verse 16 is difficult. First, the MT's "burned [fem. passive participle] with fire like garbage" is problematic. The word "burned" could be read as an active verb with the subject ("enemies") understood from the context: שְׂרָפָה (*ś^erupāh*, "they burned it"; Kraus, *Psalmen*, 1:555). The word כְּסוּחָה (*k^esûḥāh*, "like garbage") may also be read as a verbal phrase, כְּסָחוּהָ (*k^esāḥûhā*, "they have cut it down"). The resultant translation is close to the NIV: "They [the enemies) have burned it [the vine] with fire; they have cut it down." Second, we favor a jussive reading of the second colon: "May they [the enemies] perish at your rebuke" (Kraus, *Psalmen*, 1:554).

On the meaning of גַּעֲרַת (*ga^{ʿa}rat*, "your rebuke") as "to render ineffective" or "destroy," see P.J. Van Zijl, "A Discussion of the Root *gā'ar* ('rebuke')," *Biblical Essays*, ed. A.H. Van Zyl (Potchefstroom: Pro Rege-Pers, 1969), pp. 56–63.

It may be that the prayer begins in v.16b with a jussive form of "perish"—"May they [i.e., the enemies] perish at your rebuke"—because "your people" is not in the MT.

17 The identity of "the man at your right hand, the son of man," is discussed by A. Gelston ("A Sidelight on the 'Son of man,'" SJT 22 [1969]: 189–96) and by David Hill ("'Son of Man' in Psalm 80 v.17," *Novum Testamentum* 15 [1973]: 261–69). Both conclude that the term refers, not to Israel as a nation, but to the king, and that this may denote an early messianic reference.

Psalm 81: If My People Would But Listen to Me

The psalm is associated with a feast appointed by the Lord (vv.3–4). The feast most in question is a part of a complex of festivals beginning with the New Year's festival on the first day of the seventh month (Tishri), at which time the ram's horn was blown (v.3; cf. Lev 23:24; Num 29:1), followed by the Day of Atonement on the tenth day of the month and the Feast of Tabernacles on the fifteenth of the month (cf. Lev 23:34–43; Num 29:12–39).

B.Z. Luria explains that this psalm together with Psalms 77 and 80 lament the destruction of Samaria in 722 B.C. ("Psalms From Ephraim," *Beth Mikra* 23 [1978]: 151–60 [Heb.]). Brueggemann views this psalm together with Psalm 50 as examples of psalms of disorientation in which God's people are asking for and receiving "a second opinion" (*Message of the Psalms*, pp. 88–94). See the introduction to Psalm 24 for a discussion of Roy A. Rosenberg's study on the Jewish liturgical tradition from Babylon and the days of the week.

The psalm unfolds into two distinct parts: a hymn (vv.1–5) and an oracle of the Lord (vv.6–16). The structural components of the oracle may be further analyzed for the purpose of the exposition:

I. Festal Hymn (vv.1–5)
II. Oracle of the Lord (6–16)
  A. God's Past Care (vv.6–7)
    B. Exhortation to Listen (vv.8–10)
      C. God's Judgment on Rebellious Israel (vv.11–12)
    B′. Exhortation to Listen (v.13)
  A′. God's Future Care (vv.14–16)

I. Festal Hymn

81:1–5

For the director of music. According to *gittith*. Of Asaph.

1 Sing for joy to God our strength;

shout aloud to the God of Jacob!
2 Begin the music, strike the tambourine,
play the melodious harp and lyre.

3 Sound the ram's horn at the New Moon,
and when the moon is full, on the day of our Feast;
4 this is a decree for Israel,
an ordinance of the God of Jacob.
5 He established it as a statute for Joseph
when he went out against Egypt,
where we heard a language we did not understand.

1–5 In hymnic form the covenant community was called on to celebrate the festivals corporately (v.1). During these celebrations they remembered their common history, beginning with the Exodus (v.5). The Lord ordained his people to observe the Feast of Tabernacles together with the other festivals in the festival complex. Together they sang joyously to the accompaniment of musical instruments (v.2; cf. 98:4–6; see appendix to Ps 150: Musical Instruments). The mention of the tambourine suggests that the people danced while singing praise. The tambourine was often played by women (cf. 68:25; 149:3; 150:4; Exod 15:20; Judg 11:34; 1 Sam 18:6). The "melodious harp" (lit., "pleasant harp" or "lyre") and "lyre" were played in the procession to the temple as well as in the temple courts. The "ram's horn" (*šôp̱ār*, v.3) was sounded at religious ceremonies, such as at the New Moon Festival. The "full moon" fell on the fifteenth of the lunar month and coincided in the seventh month with the Feast of Tabernacles. This festival was of the greatest import in the OT and was also known as "the feast," here "our Feast" (cf. W.A. VanGemeren, "Feasts and Festivals," in Elwell, EDT, pp. 409–12).

The purpose of the celebration was to proclaim aloud the mighty acts of the Lord in the history of salvation ("Sing for joy to God our strength," v.1). During the feast the congregation remembered God's mighty acts in Egypt (v.5). The "God of Jacob" (vv.1, 4; i.e., "the Mighty One of Jacob," Gen 49:24) had warred against the Egyptians, and he shared his victory with his people. The feast was a holy day set apart for communal rejoicing and celebration. The feast was divinely ordained. It was his "decree" (*ḥōq*, paranomasia with *ḥaggēnû*, "our Feast," vv.3b–4a), "ordinance" (*mišpāṭ*), and "statute" (*'ēḏûṯ*). (See the appendix to Ps 19: The Word of God.)

Notes

For a brief discussion of the technical words and phrases in the superscription, see the Introduction.

5 (6 MT) The LXX and several ancient witnesses read "from Egypt" rather than "against Egypt," and consequently the sense of the verse is altered to "when he went out of Egypt" (cf. NEB, "when he came out of Egypt"). P.A.H. de Boer explains the preposition עַל (*'al*, "against") as "over" in the sense of Joseph's exaltation over the Egyptian bureaucracy ("Psalm 81.6a. Observations on Translation and Meaning of One Hebrew Line," *In the Shelter of Elyon. Essays on Ancient Palestinian Life and Literature in Honor of G.W. Ahlstrom*, edd. W. Boyd Barrick and John R. Spencer [Sheffield: JSOT, 1984], pp. 67–80). He further explains that the unique consonantal spelling of Joseph (*y-h-s-w-p*) contains an allusion to the divine name Yah and that the psalm contains an ancient tradition of the important place of the tribe of Joseph (cf. 78:67).

שְׂפַת לֹא־יָדַעְתִּי אֶשְׁמָע (*śᵉp̱aṯ lō'-yāḏa'tî 'ešmā'*, "a language I did not understand I hear") could be taken as a conclusion to vv.1–5, if "the language" be a reference to Israel's experience in Egypt (so NIV). It could also be a reference to the "voice" of God's judgments against Egypt (NIV mg.: "*and we heard a voice we had not known*"). If so, it functions as a transition to the oracle (vv.6–16).

II. Oracle of the Lord (vv.6–16)

A. *God's Past Care*

81:6–7

6He says, "I removed the burden from their shoulders;
their hands were set free from the basket.
7In your distress you called and I rescued you,
I answered you out of a thundercloud;
I tested you at the waters of Meribah. *Selah*

6–7 The Lord had freed Israel from the oppressive tasks in Egypt, where they had carried "baskets" with clay and bricks in the pharaonic building projects (v.6; cf. Exod 1:11). Israel had groaned under the burdens and prayed for deliverance (Exod 2:23–24; 6:5), and the Lord had delivered them (v.7). Not only that, but he had also spoken to them at Mount Sinai "out of a thundercloud" (cf. Exod 19:18–19; 20:18). The "thunder" is associated with a theophanic experience, whenever the Lord appears to deliver his people (cf. 18:7–15). Without charging Israel explicitly, the Lord reminds his people of the tragic incident at Meribah (Exod 17:1–7; Num 20:1–13; cf. Deut 33:8; Pss 95:8; 106:32).

Notes

6–7 (7–8 MT) See Th. Booij, "The Background of the Oracle in Psalm 81," *Biblica* 65 (1984): 464–75. Booij argues in favor of an affinity with Judg 2:1b–2; 6:8b–10; Jer 7:22–25a; 11:7–8; and Ezek 20:5–8, 10–13, 18–21.

B. *Exhortation to Listen*

81:8–10

8"Hear, O my people, and I will warn you—
if you would but listen to me, O Israel!
9You shall have no foreign god among you;
you shall not bow down to an alien god.
10I am the LORD your God,
who brought you up out of Egypt.
Open wide your mouth and I will fill it.

8–10 The language in this section resembles that of Deuteronomy:

"Hear, O my people" (v.8; cf. Deut 4:1; 5:1; 6:4; 9:1; 20:3);
"I will warn you" (lit., "I will testify against you"; cf. Deut 31:19, 26, 28);

"if you would but" (cf. Deut 5:29; 32:29);
"You shall have no . . . / you shall not bow down" (v.9; cf. Deut 5:7);
"alien god" (cf. Deut 32:12, 16);
"I am the LORD your God" (v.10; cf. Deut 5:6).

The Lord reminds the people that he expected them to conform to his likeness by listening to his commandments. He had consecrated Israel to be his people and had put his name on them, as he redeemed them from Egypt. Throughout the wilderness experiences he had supplied all their needs (Deut 29:5–6; 32:10–14) and had promised rich blessings for those who would respond wholeheartedly to him (Deut 30:1–20). The Lord is always ready to "fill" the needs of his people (v.10).

Notes

---

10 (11 MT) The last line of v.10 is treated as suspect in the BHS and is thought to complete the thought of v.5c: "A language [we] did not understand [we] heard, 'Open wide your mouth and I will fill it.' "

C. *God's Judgment on Rebellious Israel*

81:11–12

11 "But my people would not listen to me;
Israel would not submit to me.
12 So I gave them over to their stubborn hearts
to follow their own devices.

11–12 Instead of loyalty to the Lord, born out of gratitude for their redemption and for the promises of the future, Israel continued in their rebellion. The rebelliousness typical of the generation of the wilderness (cf. Pss 78; 95; 106) was unfortunately all too characteristic for most of Israel's history. Israel was foolish by not responding properly (cf. Isa 1:2–3). They did not listen (v.11) or submit themselves to the Lord (*'āḇāh*, "accept readily"; cf. Isa 1:19–20). Therefore God abandoned his own people. They were treated as stubborn children who had to find out for themselves that they could not make it without their God. The phrase "stubborn hearts" (v.12) is especially found in Jeremiah (3:17; 7:24; 9:14; 11:8; 13:10; 16:12; 18:12; 23:17). They are left to their own "counsels" (NIV, "devices"; cf. Jer 7:23–24).

D. *Exhortation to Listen*

81:13

13 "If my people would but listen to me,
if Israel would follow my ways,

13 The grace of God is so great that he cannot abandon his people completely. He passionately calls them to listen to him again. The problems cannot be resolved by human "devices" but only by the direct intervention of the Lord on behalf of his children. It is to this end that the glorious future is yet held before them as a real possibility (vv.14–16).

The Lord opens a new day of deliverance if only his people respond in faith. The progress of redemption unveils the constancy of the Father's repeated call to return, to repent, and to live by faith, in the Old (Moses, Joshua, Samuel, and the prophets) and in the New (cf. Heb 4:6–11). The "now"ness of redemption is whenever people hear God's word, respond in faith and repentance, and live in accordance with God's will and not their own.

E. *God's Future Care*

81:14–16

14 how quickly would I subdue their enemies
   and turn my hand against their foes!
15 Those who hate the LORD would cringe before him,
   and their punishment would last forever.
16 But you would be fed with the finest of wheat;
   with honey from the rock I would satisfy you."

14 The Lord is able to deliver his people, but he requires them to be committed to his revelation (cf. Isa 49:17–19). He promises to protect them from attacks and subjugate hostile forces. His deliverance is quick and lasting because his "hand" will press hard on the enemies of his people.

15 The godly pray that the Lord may soon bring in the fullness of redemption. They pray that he may bring evil to an end. Their prayer could be translated modally: "May those who hate the LORD cringe before him and may their punishment last forever!"

16 The Lord will richly supply the needs of his people. The blessings of God's shepherding care are expressed in terms of rich foods (cf. Isa 25:6). He lavishes on his own the best care, expressed in the metaphor of "the finest of wheat" (Num 18:12; Deut 32:14; Ps 147:14) and of "honey from the rock" (cf. Deut 32:13).

This psalm summarizes God's concern with a loyal and responsive people, blessed and protected by their covenant Lord (cf. Isa 51:4–16). His instruction leads to life and blessing (Isa 48:17–19; John 15:9–17; Rom 5:17–21). But all who reject his instruction will meet the end of the enemies of God. This psalm was a most appropriate "invitation" to covenant renewal during the feast, when God's people reflected on all his acts in the past. As their hearts longed for the redemption to come, they heard anew God's promise of redemption. But they were also reminded of their responsibility. God's people may hasten that day by perseverance in loyalty to him (Acts 3:19–23)!

Notes

---

15 (16 MT) The word "punishment" is an explanatory translation of עִתָּם (*'ittām*, "their time"). Commentators are not in agreement on the exact meaning of "their time." Briggs interprets it positively as expressive of the blessedness of the covenant community: "but let their fortune be forever" (2:213). Dahood takes it in the opposite: "and their doom be sealed"

(*Psalms*, 2:263). A.A. Anderson thinks that it probably refers to "the time of their subjection" (2:591). BHS proposes two alternate readings: בַּעֲתָתָם (*ba'ᵃṯāṯām*, "in their terror"; cf. Jer 8:15; 14:19) or בִּעֻתָם (*bi'uṯām*, "in their horror"; cf. 88:16).

Psalm 82: The Judgment of God in the Great Assembly

This psalm declares that all powers real and imagined are subject to God, the Ruler of the earth (v.8). He cares for all who observe his requirements for "wise" living. It may well be that the psalm also relates to the issue of theodicy, as Weiser explains, "For the existence of evil is here attributed to the activities of forces hostile to God; but at the same time God's righteousness as such remains untouched by the injustice that exists in the world" (p. 557).

The literary form of the psalm has occasioned much discussion, but little agreement has arisen regarding the original life-situation and the date. (See the discussion of Roy A. Rosenberg's interesting study in the introduction to Psalm 24.)

The structure of the psalm may be represented as follows:

A. God's Judgment Over the Gods (v.1)
  B. Judicial Questioning (v.2)
    C. God's Expectations of Justice (vv.3–4)
    C′. God's Condemnation of Evil (v.5)
  B′. Judicial Sentence (vv.6–7)
A′. God's Judgment Over the Earth (v.8)

I. God's Judgment Over the Gods

82:1

A psalm of Asaph.

[1]God presides in the great assembly;
he gives judgment among the "gods":

1 God (Elohim) is portrayed here as ready to judge. He "presides" (*niṣṣāḇ;* cf. Isa 3:13; Amos 7:7; 9:1) as the Great Judge. God assembles the "gods" together for judgment in "the assembly of El" (MT; NIV, "the great assembly"). The assembly of El is a borrowed phrase from Canaanite mythology, according to which El, the chief of the pantheon, assembled the gods in a divine council (see Dahood, *Psalms*, 2:269).

For Israel there is no other God than Yahweh. He embodies within himself all the epithets and powers attributed to pagan deities. The God of Israel holds a mock trial so as to impress his people that he alone is God. Walther Zimmerli has expressed the superiority of Israel's God well in these words: "Whenever a hymn speaks of those other divine powers, whose existence is by no means denied on theoretical grounds, it can only be with reference to the One who will call their actions to judgment (Ps. 82), or in the spirit of superiority that mocks their impotence (Pss. 115:4–8; 135:15–18)" (OTTO, p. 155).

Notes

For a brief discussion of the technical words and phrases in the superscription, see the Introduction.

1 There are at least three ways of explaining "the great assembly" of the "gods." First, the gods are nothing but human judges who are condemned by the Great Judge for being unjust (Calvin, 3:330; KD, 2:402). In support is the legal language in Exod 21:6 and 22:8–9, according to which the coming "before God" could be interpreted as "before the judges" (see NIV). This reading could also be inferred from our Lord's allusion to 82:6: "If he called them 'gods,' to whom the word of God came . . . what about the one whom the Father has set apart as his very own and sent into the world?" (John 10:35–36).

According to a second interpretation, the "gods" are the principalities and the powers of other nations that oppress Israel (Briggs, 2:215; cf. Eph 6:12). The psalm gives little in support of this interpretation.

A third view, though more difficult, is more likely. The "gods" are pagan deities. The gods of the nations are portrayed in this psalm as being nothing more than subjects of God who must render an account to the God of Israel for all their evil and unjust acts. The imagery of the pagan pantheon of gods is used here dramatically to present God's judgment on the rule of evil and the darkness of the world (see Mattitiahu Tsevat, "God and the Gods in Assembly," HUCA 40–41 [1969–70]: 123–37 [= "God and the Gods in Assembly (An Interpretation of Psalm 82)," *The Meaning of the Book of Job and Other Biblical Studies: Essays on the Literature and Religion of the Hebrew Bible* (New York: Ktav Publishing House, 1980), pp. 131–47]; see Peter Höffken, "Werden und Vergehen der Götter. Ein Beitrag zur Auslegung von Psalm 82," *Theologische Zeitschrift* 39 [1983]: 129–37; Heinz-Josef Fabry, "Der himmlische Thronrat als ekklesiologisches Modell," *Bausteine biblischer Theologie: Festgabe für G. Johannes Botterweck zum 60. Geburtstag dargebracht von seinen Schülern*, ed. H.J. Fabry [Köln: Peter Hanstein, 1977], pp. 99–126). On the mythological background, see Franz Josef Stendebach, "Glaube und Ethos—Überlegungen zu Ps 82," *Freude an der Weisung des Herrn, Beiträge zur Theologie der Psalmen, Festgabe zum 70. Geburtstag von Heinrich Gross*, edd. Ernst Haag, and Frank-Lothar Hossfeld (Stuttgart: Katholisches Bibelwerk, 1986), pp. 425–40.

II. Judicial Questioning

82:2

2 "How long will you defend the unjust
and show partiality to the wicked? *Selah*

2 God has the authority to call "the gods" (v.1) of the nations to account. The question "How long?" is a rhetorical device. God indicts the gods with injustice. The Lord loves justice and hates evil (cf. Exod 23:2–3, 6, 8; Lev 19:15–35; Deut 1:17; 16:18–19; Mal 2:9; 3:5). The "gods" are accused on two counts: they are unjust, and they are evil.

III. God's Expectations of Justice

82:3–4

3 Defend the cause of the weak and fatherless;
maintain the rights of the poor and oppressed.
4 Rescue the weak and needy;
deliver them from the hand of the wicked.

3–4 The four imperatives—"Defend [lit., "judge"] . . . maintain the rights. . . . / Rescue . . . deliver"—summarize what God expects. The Lord accuses the gods of irresponsibility to his just rule. They are charged because they have not shown concern for justice (v.3). The gods of the nations have failed.

These verses may also be considered as a didactic poem, in which Israel is reminded of God's expectations of his covenant people (cf. Isa 1:16–17; Zech 7:7–10; Mal 3:9; James 1:27). Failure to observe God's decrees inevitably leads to his condemnation (cf. Isa 10:1–3).

IV. God's Condemnation of Evil

82:5

5 "They know nothing, they understand nothing.
They walk about in darkness;
all the foundations of the earth are shaken.

5 The requirements of the Lord are clear (vv.3–4). However, in contrast to his just requirements, "the gods" stand condemned by their folly, moral darkness, and destruction of God's order. The gods are nothing but fools. They show no understanding of God's order. It is not that they are ignorant of what God expects but that they reject him and his just rule. Folly consists of a conscious rejection of God rather than ignorance of God (cf. Isa 1:3).

The rule of the gods is nothing but "darkness." Darkness (*ḥ^a^šēḵāh*) here is not the phenomenal experience of the darkness (*ḥōšeḵ*) of night but a moral darkness, i.e., "evil." The "gods" wallow in "evil." They further their own powers by destroying the divinely established order. The "foundations of the earth" is a metaphor for God's rule on earth (cf. 11:3; 75:3; 96:10; see appendix to Ps 5: Yahweh Is King). The wicked are those who destroy righteousness and haunt the godly on earth (see K.Hj. Fahlgren, "Die Gengensätze von *ṣ^e^daqā* im Alten Testament," ed. K. Koch, *Um das Prinzip der Vergeltung in Religion und Recht* [Darmstadt: Wissenschaftliche Buchgesellschaft, 1972], pp. 87–129). Even in pagan nations the Lord has established some order by common grace, and he holds the ungodly accountable for their reign of terror and self-aggrandizement at the expense of his order.

V. Judicial Sentence

82:6–7

6 "I said, 'You are "gods";
you are all sons of the Most High.'
7 But you will die like mere men;
you will fall like every other ruler."

6–7 Finally, the dethronement of the gods! The Lord pronounces sentence with an emphatic "I," which could be rendered as "It is I who says." The condemnation is ironic. Though the gods were known as "the sons of the Most High" (Elyon) in Canaanite mythology, they cannot be! They do not reflect the concerns of God with justice, morality, and order. Condemnation of the "gods" is a condemnation of idolatry, and hence of any way of life that is inconsistent with God's concern for justice, morality, and order (vv.3–4). God's judgment rests on all manifestations of unrighteousness, both in the human world and in the angelic world (cf. Matt 25:41; Rev 20:10, 14–15; 21:8).

In the phantom trial the Lord declares the "gods" to be nothing more than "mortals," i.e., "mere men" (*'āḏām*). Paganism affects every area of life; hence the condemnation of the "gods" as irresponsible despots implies the condemnation of all humans who adopt the pagan way of life. The poetic pairing of "men" and "ruler" is an example of merism, signifying "all mortals" (Dahood, *Psalms*, 2:270). This conclusion confirms that of Herbert Niehr, who posits that both gods and men are addressed in this psalm ("Götter oder Menschen—eine falsche Alternative. Bemerkungen zu Ps.82," ZAW 99 [1987]: 94–98).

Notes

6 Dahood interprets "I say" as an expression of the psalmist and translates it "I had thought" (*Psalms*, 2:270). Though this is grammatically possible, we take it as a divine decree, as in 2:6: "I have installed my king," which also has an emphatic use of "I" and is introduced by a verb of speaking.

VI. God's Judgment Over the Earth

82:8

8 Rise up, O God, judge the earth,
for all the nations are your inheritance.

8 The psalm concludes with a prayer for God's justice to appear on earth. The godly respond with a sense of anticipation that one day the God who judged the nongods to extinction will advance his judgment on earth (cf. 94:1–3; 96:1–6; 98:9). Our Lord's prayer ("your kingdom come") is most appropriate whenever we experience injustice. Calvin comments, "It is therefore our bounden duty to beseech him to restore to order what is embroiled in confusion" (3:336). On the importance of justice in God's world order, see Patrick D. Miller, Jr., "Psalm 82," in *Interpreting the Psalms*, pp. 120–24.

The psalm has a cosmic interest for all nations. The Lord all alone is God; there is no other! Christians have to form a counterculture, even as Israel had to separate itself from Canaanite values. This conclusion fits with what Cyrus H. Gordon has determined to be an Israelite reaction to Canaanite values in "History of Religion in Psalm 82," *Biblical and Near Eastern Studies: Essays in Honor of William Sanford LaSor*, ed. Gary A. Tuttle (Grand Rapids: Eerdmans, 1978), pp. 129–31.

Psalm 83: A Lament Concerning the Presence of Evil

This psalm is a *national lament* in which the psalmist prays for the Lord's intervention against the many enemies. He lists some ten enemies, including Assyria. It may be that the psalm arose in a particular historical context (cf. 2 Chron 20:1–30), but it is more likely that the nations are symbolic of the enemies of God's people. The variety of enemies suggests that the psalmist has in view the "troublers," i.e., nations that caused afflictions on Israel (Edom, Ishmael, Moab, Hagrites, Ammon, Philistia,

Amalek), the "seducers," i.e., the nations that enticed Israel toward acculturation (Gebal, Tyre), and the "oppressors," i.e., the nations that overran Israel and Judah and exiled her population (Assyria).

The psalmist prays that the enemies of the Lord's people may be shamed and that they will instead seek the "name" of the Lord (v.16). For an approach to this psalm as a war oracle, see the study by Christensen, pp. 112–27. For other psalms, see 12; 60; 74; 79; 80; 85; 90; 94:1–11; 123; 126; 137.

The psalm is composed of prayer, lament, and imprecations on the enemies. The structural development is concentric:

A. Prayer for God's Action (v.1)
  B. Plottings of the Enemies (vv.2–4)
    C. Greatness of the Opposition (vv.5–8)
    C′. Great Acts of God in Israel's History (vv.9–12)
  B′. Shaming of the Enemies (vv.13–16)
A′. Prayer for God's Action (vv.17–18)

This is the last psalm in the collection of psalms attributed to Asaph (50; 73–83).

I. Prayer for God's Action

83:1

A song. A psalm of Asaph.

1 O God, do not keep silent;
  be not quiet, O God, be not still.

1 The two Hebrew words for "God" (Elohim and El) at the beginning form an inclusion with v.18: "Yahweh" ("the LORD") and "the Most High" (Elyon). The psalmist addresses the only true God, who is none other than Yahweh ("the LORD"), the "Most High" (Elyon, see the appendix to Ps 9: Yahweh Is El Elyon). With this theological conviction in mind, he prays that God may act on behalf of his people. The negative forms ("do not . . . be not") convey the urgency with which he requests the Lord to act (cf. 35:22; 109:1).

Notes

For a brief discussion of the technical words and phrases in the superscription, see the Introduction.

II. Plottings of the Enemies

83:2–4

2 See how your enemies are astir,
  how your foes rear their heads.
3 With cunning they conspire against your people;
  they plot against those you cherish.
4 "Come," they say, "let us destroy them as a nation,
  that the name of Israel be remembered no more."

2–4 The enemies are the occasion for prayer. They are like the waves of the sea, roaring and foaming. They "are astir" like armies preparing for an attack (v.2; cf. Isa 17:12–13; Jer 6:23). They "rear their heads" as an expression of overt hostility and confidence. Their enmity is against God ("those who hate you," MT; cf. 68:1) and against the people of God ("your people," "those you cherish," v.3). The designation "those you cherish" is unique and may mean God's protection during times of trouble (cf. 17:8; 27:5; 31:2–3) or may refer to the value the Lord attaches to his own (see NEB: "those thou hast made thy treasure").

The enemy keeps on plotting (v.3). The best of the wisdom of this world expresses its covert hostility in cunning and plotting. The enemy's goal is nothing less than the holocaust of God's people. The terms "come . . . let us" express the spirit of humanity that rebelled against the Lord at Babel (Gen 11:3–4). There mankind conspired to make a "name" for themselves, and since that time the nations strive at autonomy and "name" recognition. They aim at sovereignty and freedom, as if they are God. This spirit cannot tolerate the Lord or his people (v.4).

Notes

3 (4 MT) The MT has a plural form—צְפוּנֶיךָ (*ṣᵉp̱ûneyḵā*)—for "your hidden ones." Several ancient witnesses have a singular form—צְפוּנְךָ (*ṣᵉp̱ûneḵā*, "your treasure"). The plural could denote the temple, the temple treasure, or the people themselves (see Dahood, *Psalms*, 2:274). The MT is ambiguous. The NIV adopts the last interpretation: "those you cherish."

III. Greatness of the Opposition

83:5–8

5 With one mind they plot together;
they form an alliance against you—
6 the tents of Edom and the Ishmaelites,
of Moab and the Hagrites,
7 Gebal, Ammon and Amalek,
Philistia, with the people of Tyre.
8 Even Assyria has joined them
to lend strength to the descendants of Lot. *Selah*

5 The psalmist rephrases the intent and the manner of the opposition. The nations are "against" the Lord and not just against God's people ("against you"). Their strength is in their plotting and their solidarity. They have made an "alliance" (*bᵉrîṯ*, "covenant") against the Lord as an expression of solidarity ("with one mind"; cf. 27:3; Gen 11:1).

6–7 The psalmist further specifies the ten nations who "hate" the Lord (vv.6–8; cf. v.2 above). The Edomites (v.6) were Israel's archenemies (cf. 137:7). They were the descendants of Esau (cf. Gen 36), who had settled in the hill country of Seir, to the south of the biblical Negeb and into the mountains of Edom (cf. Num 33:37; Deut

1:2). The Edomites were not tent-dwellers as may be implied from the idiom "the tents of Edom." The phrase designates the nation as a whole: the Edomites.

The Ishmaelites were descendants of Ishmael, the son of Hagar and Abraham (Gen 16:15–16; 25:12–18). Here it may serve as a general term for all the Bedouin tribes who dwelt in tents and invaded Judah from the south or for the seminomads who made their living from the caravan trades, such as the Midianites (cf. Gen 37:25, 28; Judg 8:24).

The Moabites, together with the Ammonites, were descendants of Lot (vv.6–7; cf. Gen 19:36–38). The Ammonites caused much trouble for the tribes in Transjordan during the days of Jephthah the Gileadite (Judg 11:6–33) and during the time of Saul, who rescued the people of Jabesh from the threats of Nahash the Ammonite (1 Sam 11:1–11). The Moabites showed their hostility when Israel had bypassed them on their way to Canaan. Balak, king of Moab, unsuccessfully hired Balaam to curse Israel (Num 22–24). Ehud freed the tribes from their subjugation to Eglon, king of Moab (Judg 3:12–30). In periods of weakness in Israel or Judah, these eastern nations exerted additional pressures on God's people. Moreover, these nations were unreliable. They were the objects of the prophetic oracles because of their bitter hatred of Israel and Judah and because of their arrogance (cf. Isa 15–16; Zeph 2:8–10).

The "Hagrites" (v.6), a nomadic tribe living east of the Jordan (cf. 1 Chron 5:10), also were known from Assyrian sources.

The identity of the people of Gebal (v.7) is uncertain. Most scholars identify them with a region south of the Dead Sea. However, Dahood is probably right that Byblos forms an inclusion with Tyre, as both cities were located close to each other in Phoenicia (*Psalms*, 2:274; see NIV mg.: "That is, Byblos"). Both cities were known for their commercial importance. Israel had been culturally subjugated to the materialism and Baalism of Phoenicia.

The people of Amalek (v.7), a nomadic tribe descended from Esau (Gen 36:12, 16), fought Israel independently (Exod 17:8–13) or joined in with other nations such as the Midianites against Israel (cf. Judg 6:3). They lived by Israel's southern border and were largely destroyed by King Saul (1 Sam 15:3).

The Philistines (v.7) are well known from their frequent incursions from the days of the judges until David, especially from the exploits of Samson (Judg 14–16).

8 Finally, the Assyrians were the dominant power from the middle of the eighth century B.C. till the middle of the seventh century B.C. Their end was marked by the Fall of Nineveh (612 B.C.). Critical scholars have objected to the MT and have given several alternate readings on the assumption that the psalm was postexilic. Briggs reads "Samaria" instead (2:221). Others explain it as a reference to an unknown tribe in North Arabia, but this is unlikely. A.A. Anderson concludes in favor of a loose designation to the Assyrian kingdom (2:598–99). The "symbolic" interpretation of Assyria as representative of the oppressive nations voids this matter as an issue.

Notes

---

7 (8 MT) The Syriac reads "the territory of Ammon" instead of "Gebal, . . . Tyre."

IV. Great Acts of God in Israel's History

83:9–12

9 Do to them as you did to Midian,
as you did to Sisera and Jabin at the river Kishon,
10 who perished at Endor
and became like refuse on the ground.
11 Make their nobles like Oreb and Zeeb,
all their princes like Zebah and Zalmunna,
12 who said, "Let us take possession
of the pasturelands of God."

9–12 The phrase "do to them" (v.9) begins the imprecation on the enemies of God (vv.9–17). The future judgment of God is mirrored in the great acts of the Lord in Israel's history (vv.9–12). The psalmist selects two events from the period of the judges: the victory over the Canaanites (Sisera and Jabin) by Deborah and Barak (cf. Judg 4–5) and the victory over the Midianites and their chiefs (Oreb, Zeeb, Zebah, Zalmunna) by Gideon (cf. Judg 6–8). The omission of the names of the judges indicates that the primary deliverer was the Lord himself!

The victory over Midian is left incomplete (v.9; cf. vv.11–12). The mention of Sisera and Jabin leads to a reflection on Yahweh's mighty acts. He fought victoriously against the Canaanites, led by Sisera (vv.9b–10). Yahweh caused the river Kishon to flood so that the Canaanites "perished." The reference to Endor, located at the foot of Mount Tabor, fits the general vicinity of the battle, even though the city does not figure in the narrative of Judges 4. Some propose an alternate reading: "En Harod" (Judg 7:1; BHS; see NEB). The strength of the warriors was taken, and they became nothing but "refuse," as their corpses were denied an honorable burial (cf. 79:2).

The victory over the Midianites is also a *cause celebre* (vv.11–12). The psalmist develops the thought of v.9. The Midianites had despoiled the land of the crops and had caused great fear among the Israelites. This spoiling of Israel's crops is probably referred to in the bold claim "Let us take possession of the pasturelands of God" (v.12). The Midianite chiefs ("nobles") Oreb, Zeeb, Zebah, and Zalmunna were captured and put to death. The Israelites killed Oreb at a rock and Zeeb at a winepress (Judg 7:25), and Gideon killed Zebah and Zalmunna (Judg 8:21).

V. Shaming of the Enemies

83:13–16

13 Make them like tumbleweed, O my God,
like chaff before the wind.
14 As fire consumes the forest
or a flame sets the mountains ablaze,
15 so pursue them with your tempest
and terrify them with your storm.
16 Cover their faces with shame
so that men will seek your name, O LORD.

13–15 The enemies are the enemies of God. The godly must turn to him for deliverance and submit themselves to his will. The believing heart calls on the Lord to act speedily for his righteousness's sake. The emphatic use of "God" in v.13

expresses the prayerful submission to the will of the heavenly Father: "My God, make them . . . , etc." He prays that the curses of God will overtake the arrogant.

The psalmist likens the enemies' lot to that of "tumbleweed," "chaff," and "forest" (vv.13–14). "Tumbleweed" (*galgal,* lit., "wheel") is a plant of the wild artichoke family (*Gundelia Tournefortii*), a plant with wheel-shaped stems and thistles (see Avinoam Danin, "Plants as Biblical Metaphors," BAR 5 [1979]: 20–21). Others translate *galgal* ("wheel") by "whirling dust." The metaphor of the "chaff" is more common (cf. 1:4; 35:5; Isa 17:13; Jer 13:24). The psalmist prays that the Lord may destroy the enemies like "fire" destroys forests and the vegetation on the mountains (v.14). He also prays that the Lord will confound the plotting of the wicked as by a "tempest" and "storm" (v.15). The enemies are "astir" against the Lord (vv.2–4), but he will "terrify" them. (See the appendix to Ps 137: Imprecations in the Psalms.)

16 The confidence of the nations will be shaken by God's sovereign presence. The nations had boastfully claimed that they would rid themselves of the "name" of Israel forever (v.4). Instead, the psalmist prays for the Lord to change their pride and boasting to "shame." However, he shows a deep awareness of God's gracious nature as he opens a door to those among the nations who will seek the "name" of the Lord (Yahweh). This thought is repeated in v.18. God's mighty acts in judgment must lead to the recognition that Yahweh alone is God (vv.17–18)!

VI. Prayer for God's Action

83:17–18

17 May they ever be ashamed and dismayed;
may they perish in disgrace.
18 Let them know that you, whose name is the LORD—
that you alone are the Most High over all the earth.

17–18 The lament comes to a conclusion here. The imprecations begun in v.9 now come to an end. The psalmist's confidence in the Lord (the Most High) forms an inclusion (see v.1). He trusts that the Lord will confound the wicked who scheme against him and the chosen people of God (v.17; cf. vv.15–16). He also prays that the nations may come to "know" the Lord as sovereign Ruler ("the Most High," v.18; cf. 97:9) as well as "the name" ("Yahweh"; see appendix to Ps 7: The Name of Yahweh). The "name" signifies all the benefits of forgiveness, grace, and mercy to those who love him (Exod 34:6–7) but also the powerful acts of judgment (see appendix to Ps 78: The Mighty Acts of Yahweh).

Psalm 84: A Deep Longing for the Presence of God

This psalm contains a collage of diverse genres: hymn, prayer, lament, and a song of Zion. As to the time of composition or original life-situation, it is equally difficult to come to an agreement. The reference to the "anointed one" (v.9) suggests that the psalm is preexilic. Its setting may reflect a festive procession to Jerusalem during one of the festivals (see Th. Booij, "Royal Words in Psalm lxxxiv 11," VetTest 36 [1986]: 117–20). The concern for the temple has suggested to others an exilic date (cf. v.10) when the temple was in ruins. The structural elements reflect the variations in genres:

A. Longing for the Courts of the Lord Almighty (vv.1–4)
B. The Blessing on the Pilgrims (vv.5–7)
C. Prayer for God's Blessing on the King (vv.8–9)
D. Hymnic Praise (vv.10–11)
E. The Blessing of God (v.12)

I. Longing for the Courts of the Lord Almighty

84:1–4

For the director of music. According to *gittith*.
Of the Sons of Korah. A psalm.

1 How lovely is your dwelling place,
O LORD Almighty!
2 My soul yearns, even faints,
for the courts of the LORD;
my heart and my flesh cry out
for the living God.

3 Even the sparrow has found a home,
and the swallow a nest for herself,
where she may have her young—
a place near your altar,
O LORD Almighty, my King and my God.
4 Blessed are those who dwell in your house;
they are ever praising you. *Selah*

1–4 The love for the "dwelling place" (v.1) of the Lord is foremost in the heart of the psalmist as he exclaims, "How lovely!" He reflects on the temple proper as the place of God's symbolic presence, together with "the courts," where the worshipers and pilgrims assembled and spent their days (v.2; cf. 43:3). He physically longs for the experience of God's presence, as he "yearns/faints" with his whole being ("my soul . . . my heart and my flesh," v.2; cf. 16:9). C.S. Lewis gives fine expression to this desire for God:

> I have rather—though the expression may seem harsh to some—called this the "appetite for God" than "the love of God". The "love of God" too easily suggests the word "spiritual" in all those negative or restrictive senses which it has unhappily acquired. . . . [The appetitie for God] has all the cheerful spontaneity of a natural, even a physical, desire. (*Reflections on the Psalms*, p. 51)

The psalmist's total attention is on the "LORD Almighty" (*YHWH ṣᵉḇā'ôṯ*, vv.1, 3, 8, 12; see appendix to Ps 24: Lord Sabaoth), the Great King (v.2; cf. v.3), whose blessing he seeks. The Lord Almighty has power over all forces in heaven and on earth. His presence transforms adversity into prosperity, affliction into freedom, and death into life. He *is* the "living God" (El, v.2; cf. 42:2). It seems that the psalmist develops both motifs in the following strophes: the blessedness of those who experience the kingship of the Lord Almighty (vv.3–4) and the blessedness of the strength and life of those who long for God (El; see appendix to Ps 22: Yahweh Is El). Having expressed the blessedness associated with the presence of the designations Lord Almighty and God, he makes a petition to the Lord Almighty and to God to bless the "anointed" (vv.8–9). The repetition of "LORD Almighty" at the end of the psalm (v.12) forms an inclusion with v.1.

Reflecting on the temple courts, the psalmist pictures the birds that make their nests in the temple eaves. The "sparrow" and the "swallow" (v.3) are common birds; yet they have their nests and raise their young close to the "altar" of the LORD Almighty. The thought of these lowly birds in such a glorious place overwhelms him and leads the psalmist to express his awe in the form of a blessing (v.4). Since birds are greatly privileged to live in and around the temple of the Great King, whose name is "LORD Almighty" (Yahweh Sabaoth), and who is worshiped as his God ("my God"), how much more "blessed" (see 1:1) are all those who serve the Lord at his temple! The psalmist is mainly concerned about the Lord and his blessed presence. The temple was symbolic of God's presence, but his presence was never to be limited to the temple (cf. 1 Kings 8:23–53; Isa 66:1–2).

Characteristic of the wisdom psalms (cf. Ps 1), the psalmist contrasts in v.10 "the tents of the wicked" and the blessedness of the godly in God's courts. The reason for this blessedness lies in God's protection, rewards, and blessing to those who are wise, "those whose walk is blameless" (v.11). As God's blessing was not limited to the temple courts, the blessing on those "who dwell" in the house of the Lord may well be extended to all who do the will of God. They dwell in his presence, wherever they may live.

Notes

For a brief discussion of the technical words and phrases in the superscription, see the Introduction.

3 (4 MT) The word for "sparrow" is a general word for any bird: צִפּוֹר (*ṣippôr*, "bird"; cf. Gen 7:14; Ps 102:7). The parallelism with "swallow" has suggested that the psalmist has a particular but common bird in mind.

Critical scholars delete "O LORD Almighty, my King and my God" (cf. BHS), arguing that this colon overloads the verse.

4 (5 MT) The MT's עוֹד (*'ôḏ*, "still"; NIV, "ever") is rendered in the LXX as "forever," suggesting an alternate Hebrew reading: לַעֲדֵי עַד (*la'ᵃḏê 'aḏ*, "forever").

II. The Blessing on the Pilgrims

84:5–7

5 Blessed are those whose strength is in you,
who have set their hearts on pilgrimage.
6 As they pass through the Valley of Baca,
they make it a place of springs;
the autumn rains also cover it with pools.
7 They go from strength to strength,
till each appears before God in Zion.

5–7 In the absence from the temple precincts, the presence of God may be experienced. The psalmist blesses all (*'āḏām;* NIV, "those," v.5) who have put their confidence ("strength") in the Lord. They trust the Lord for refuge, especially in times of need (see NEB: "Happy the men whose refuge is in thee"). The second part of the description of the godly is far from clear. The literal rendering "paths [or praises] in their heart" (v.5) has given rise to three interpretations: (1) a pilgrimage to Jerusalem; (2) a procession in and around Jerusalem; and (3) praise of the Lord, parallel with "they are ever praising you" (v.4).

In a related passage (Isa 35) the prophet encourages the weak to strengthen themselves in the thought of God's presence (vv.2–4). The blessedness of God's presence and succor finds expression in the processional imagery of a road (*maslûl*, Isa 35:8; cf. 84:5, *m^esillô<u>t</u>*), a wilderness, and the abundance of water (vv.6–8) as the people of God pass from adversity (exile) to the blessedness of his presence ("Zion," v.10), the place where "gladness and joy will overtake them, / and sorrow and sighing will flee away."

It is not unlikely that the psalmist also speaks of the highway, the Valley of Baca, and the water as metaphors of the experience of fellowship and blessedness after a prolonged period of adversity. The strength and joy of the godly stems from their hope in God. Faith in God is ultimate and transforms weak people into those who "go from strength to strength" (v.7) and the Valley of Baca into springs and pools, as expressive of God's blessings (v.6). The object of the search is communion with God ("in Zion"). As faith approaches the presence of God, it goes from "strength to strength" (cf. 2 Cor 3:18: "with ever-increasing glory," lit., "from glory to glory"). Faith waits for God to reveal himself (see appendix to Ps 46: Zion Theology).

Notes

5 (6 MT) Two MSS have הָעָם (*hā'ām*, "the people") instead of the MT's אָדָם (*'ādām*, "man"; NIV, "those").

6 (7 MT) The Valley of Baca is unknown in the OT and seems to be a poetical reference to any level place through which the highway of the pilgrims passes. The word Baca has been associated with "weeping" (by etymology), and it may well be that the psalmist refers to vegetation (balsam tree?) that grows in arid places and that drips water like tears (cf. KB^3, 1:124). The Valley of Baca appears to be symbolic of affliction.

The word "pools" (NIV)—בְּרֵכוֹת (*b^erēkô<u>t</u>*) is an emendation of the MT's בְּרָכוֹת (*b^erā<u>k</u>ô<u>t</u>*, "blessings"; cf. NIV mg.). A.A. Anderson observes that this may be a play on words, as the pools are considered as evidences of God's blessings (2:604).

7 (8 MT) Instead of "till each appears before God in Zion," BHS proposes a Qal reading and a deletion of "before" (*'el*): "they will see God." The NEB follows the LXX: "and the God of gods shows himself in Zion."

III. Prayer for God's Blessing on the King

84:8–9

8 Hear my prayer, O LORD God Almighty;
listen to me, O God of Jacob. *Selah*
9 Look upon our shield, O God;
look with favor on your anointed one.

8–9 The psalmist now turns to the Lord in a prayer for the king ("your anointed one," *māšîaḥ*) who is the "shield" (i.e., protector) of his people (v.9). It is unlikely that Dahood's translation of "suzerain" for "shield" is a significant improvement (cf. v.11; 89:18; *Psalms*, 2:282). The king is the Lord's "anointed" "shield" for his people. Since he too is dependent on the Lord's blessing, the psalmist prays that the Great King may extend his goodness to the earthly ruler.

Though it is not clear what national tragedy may have occasioned this psalm, tragedy has affected both people and king. He addresses God emphatically as "O LORD God Almighty" and closes the invocation with a reference to him as "O God of Jacob" (v.8). Yahweh is the glorious King who has identified himself with "Jacob," i.e., the descendants of Israel (cf. 20:1; 24:6–10).

Notes

9 (10 MT) For a discussion of "shield" (NIV mg., "sovereign"), see 7:10.

IV. Hymnic Praise

84:10–11

10 Better is one day in your courts
than a thousand elsewhere;
I would rather be a doorkeeper in the house
of my God
than dwell in the tents of the wicked.
11 For the LORD God is a sun and shield;
the LORD bestows favor and honor;
no good thing does he withhold
from those whose walk is blameless.

10 The psalmist sings about the superiority of God's presence. One day of fellowship with God is a thousand times better than anything else. The psalmist esteems service as a temple guard superior to receiving public recognition and wealth.

11 Then the psalmist reflects on God's beneficence. He likens God's favor to "a sun and shield." The "sun" is symbolic of the era of restoration (cf. Isa 60:19; Mal 4:2), which is more usually referred to by the words "light" and "brightness" (cf. Isa 60:1, 3).

The Lord bestows "favor and honor" as expressions of his blessing. Favor is his expression of grace by which he draws near to his own and even shares his "glory" with them. The effect of his fellowship is that he will shower all his "goodness" (*ṭôḇ*, see 23:6; cf. Exod 33:19) on those who walk in a "blameless" (*tāmîm;* see 15:2) manner.

Notes

10 (11 MT) "Elsewhere" is a dynamic translation of בָּחַרְתִּי (*bāḥartî,* "I have chosen"). BHS prefers an emendation to *beḥedrî* ("in my room"; cf. NEB, "at home"). Dahood reads it as a reference to the netherworld: "in the cemetery" (*Psalms,* 2:282–83).

10–11 (11–12 MT) The hymn of praise is set apart by the introductory particle כִּי (*kî*) in the MT at the beginning of these verses.

11 (12 MT) Dahood views both metaphors as titles: "Truly Sun and Suzerain/Yahweh God" (*Psalms,* 2:279). For "shield/suzerain," see v.9 and 7:10.

V. The Blessing of God

84:12

12 O LORD Almighty,
 blessed is the man who trusts in you.

12 In conclusion the psalmist looks up again to his Great King—"O LORD Almighty"—and pronounces the third benediction (cf. vv.4–5). In the beginning of the psalm, he expressed his deep desire for fellowship with the Lord Almighty (vv.1–2). He ends the psalm by encouraging everybody ("the man" [*'āḏām*]; cf. a similar expression in v.5) to seek the Lord by putting their trust in him. The essence of godliness is in submissiveness to the Great King, who will grant his blessings to those who find their refuge in him (cf. v.5 above). In Jesus Christ the faithful may worship the Father, as Jesus is the Father's appointed Mediator, the one in whom heaven and earth come together (so S.J.P.K. Riekert, "Die Sin van die Erediens: 'n Eksegetiese en Opnebarings-historiese Studie van Psalm 84," *Nederduits Gereformeerde Teologiese Tydskrif* 18 [1977]: 186–98).

Psalm 85: Surely His Salvation Is Near!

In the context of some national catastrophe, the people of God cry out for deliverance from adversity. Since they already seem to have experienced the outpouring of God's wrath and the depth of his mercy in forgiveness (vv.1–3), it is most likely, though not certain, that the psalm is a postexilic composition.

The genre of the psalm fits that of a *national lament,* composed in four parts: (1) proclamation of God's past acts (vv.1–3); (2) lament and prayer for restoration (vv.4–7); (3) anticipation of God's salvation (v.8); and (4) the words of hope (vv.9–13). In the first three strophes, we find the repetition of "land" (vv.1, 9); "restore"/"return" (*šûḇ,* vv.1, 4, 6; v.6 in NIV, "again"); "your people"/"his people" (vv.2, 6, 8); terms for anger (vv.3, 5); "our Savior," "your salvation," "his salvation" (*yēša',* vv.4, 7, 9). The last strophe (vv.9–13) has little vocabulary in common with the first three. Verses 10–13 explicate and apply the nature of "his salvation" (v.9). The vocabulary in these verses is also repetitive: "our land" (vv. 9, 12), "faithfulness" (vv.10–11), and "righteousness" (vv. 10–11, 13).

The structure of the psalm is as follows:

A. Proclamation of God's Past Acts (vv.1–3)
B. Laments and Prayer for Restoration (vv.4–7)
C. Anticipation of God's Salvation (v.8)
D. The Oracle of Hope (vv.9–13)

I. Proclamation of God's Past Acts

85:1–3

For the director of music. Of the Sons of Korah. A psalm.

1 You showed favor to your land, O LORD;
you restored the fortunes of Jacob.
2 You forgave the iniquity of your people
and covered all their sins. *Selah*
3 You set aside all your wrath
and turned from your fierce anger.

1–3 Restoration resulted from God's sovereign acts of grace: removal of wrath and his forgiving of sin. The Lord has "set aside" all his wrath (v.3). The "wrath" and "fierce anger" of God are associated with his "jealousy," when his holiness had been offended by the sin and transgression of his people (cf. Exod 32:12; 34:7, 14; Num 25:4). Then he is like a "consuming fire" (Exod 24:17; Heb 12:29). In his wrath the people had been dispossessed of their lands, had become bereft of children and loved ones, and had been despoiled by the enemies. When God's wrath "takes away life" (104:29), his people need to learn to live in complete dependence on his mercy.

The Lord graciously and sovereignly forgave the sins of his people (v.2). Forgiveness implies the removal of both sins and the consequences of sin. The word "iniquity" (*'āwôn*) carries both connotations (cf. 32:2; NIV, "sin"; see appendix to Ps 103: Sin and Forgiveness). Guilt and sin were forgiven by the Lord! He exchanged wrath for his "favor" (v.1; cf. "the year of the LORD's favor," *rāṣôn*, Isa 61:2). The emphatic position of the verbal phrase "you showed favor" (root *r-ṣ-h*) indicates God's freedom in his acts of salvation: forgiveness *and* enjoyment of life. Spiritual and physical life are not divorced but are interwoven as expressions of God's "favor." The "land" is his land and the people his people! He "restored the fortunes" of his own. The "restoration of the fortunes" (*šûḇ šeḇûṯ*) is a technical term for the restoration of the oppressed and harassed people from exile (see 14:7; TWOT, 2:896).

Notes

For a brief discussion of the technical words and phrases in the superscription, see the Introduction.

2 (3 MT) The synonyms for verbs for forgiveness are identical to those in 32:1. Von Rad correctly observes that the OT rarely gives a theological reflection on sin but underscores the necessity of *confession* and forgiveness (OTT, 1:154).

II. Laments and Prayer for Restoration

85:4–7

4 Restore us again, O God our Savior,
and put away your displeasure toward us.
5 Will you be angry with us forever?
Will you prolong your anger through all generations?
6 Will you not revive us again,
that your people may rejoice in you?
7 Show us your unfailing love, O LORD,
and grant us your salvation.

4–7 The situation has since changed. As long as God's people are on earth, they will be subject to the vicissitudes of life. The psalmist laments the recent problems that have deprived God's people from enjoyment of God's favor. He interprets them as expressions of God's "displeasure" (*ka'as*, v.4). *ka'as* may result from God's anger (Ezek 20:28) or be a part of the human situation ("vexations," "grief"; cf. 1 Sam 1:7, 16; TWOT, 1:451). It seems that their grief did not result from God's displeasure because the psalm contains no confession. Instead, God tests his people, and in this test they cry out to him. The prayer includes two sets of petitions and a set of questions:

A. Prayer (v.4)
B. Questions (vv.5–6)
A′. Prayer (v.7)

The lamenting community prays that the Lord may "restore" (v.4; cf. v.1) them by extending the benefits of his love to all of life. They pray (v.7) for renewed expressions of his "unfailing love" (*ḥeseḏ*). The renewal of *ḥeseḏ* is synonymous with the enjoyment of God's "salvation," because "salvation" (*yēša'*, see 27:1) extends the benefits of God to his people: victory, peace, enjoyment of this life and the life to come. The repetition of "our salvation" (v.4; NIV, "our Savior") and "your salvation" (v.7) form an inclusion. (See the appendix to Ps 119: Yahweh Is My Redeemer.)

Between the petitions the people lament the new problems by asking question upon question. The questions are antithetical, as the questions in v.5 pertain to his anger, whereas those in v.6 pertain to the effects of withholding divine favor. From the people's vantage point, the Lord goes from anger to anger (v.5). It seems as if they can do nothing to please him. Yet they confess that God's restoration was the work of his hands, and they cast themselves on his mercy (v.6). The personal pronoun "you" (v.6) is emphatic: "Is it not you who can revive us again?" His favor will result in the change from grief to joy (cf. 104:29–30). They await the renewal of his love (*ḥeseḏ*, v.7). (See the appendix to Ps 25: The Perfections of Yahweh.)

III. Anticipation of God's Salvation

85:8

8 I will listen to what God the LORD will say;
he promises peace to his people, his saints—
but let them not return to folly.

8 In submission to the Lord, the people await his response. The "I" of this verse may be the voice of the psalmist or of a prophet awaiting the Lord's response. He receives assurance that the Lord will "speak" (NIV, "promises") "peace" (*šālôm*) and thus grant his people relief from their grief. After all, they are "his people," i.e., his "loyal people" ("saints" [*ḥᵃsîḏāyw*]; see 4:3). "The saints" are those who do not "return to folly."

Notes

8–9 (9–10 MT) John S. Kselmann proposes an alternate rendering:

> Let me declare what El decrees,
> what Yahweh says—for he promises peace,
> to the devoted ones of his people,
> to the one who dwells in security.
> Surely, near is his salvation to those who fear him;
> near is his glory to him who dwells in our land.
> ("A Note on Psalm 85:9–10," CBQ 46 [1983]: 23–27)

8 (9 MT) Dennis McCarthy applies the hope of "peace" to all who are reconciled with God, seeking to live in harmony with his expectations of fidelity and justice. Peace is both a gift and a way of life ("Psalm 85 and the Meaning of Peace," *Way* 22 [1982]: 3–9).

The LXX reads "who turn to him in their hearts" for the MT's וְאַל־יָשׁוּבוּ לְכִסְלָה (*wᵉʾal-yāšûḇû lᵉḵislāh;* NIV, "but let them not return to folly"). Dahood argues that the MT "defies analysis" and gives this rendering: "and those who again confide in him" (*Psalms*, 2:289).

IV. The Oracle of Hope

85:9–13

9 Surely his salvation is near those who fear him,
 that his glory may dwell in our land.

10 Love and faithfulness meet together;
 righteousness and peace kiss each other.
11 Faithfulness springs forth from the earth,
 and righteousness looks down from heaven.
12 The Lord will indeed give what is good,
 and our land will yield its harvest.
13 Righteousness goes before him
 and prepares the way for his steps.

9 God's "surely" is in response to the questions and the laments (vv.4–7). His "salvation" (cf. vv.4, 7) is "near" (cf. Isa 46:13; 51:5), but not for everyone. The exclusionary language of the previous verse is repeated so as to form a connecting link between the lament and the hope. Only those "who fear him" in the spirit of wisdom (over against "folly," v.8) will inherit his benefits. They will be renewed in spirit, as they are the heirs of the new age of restoration. The age of restoration is described by a variety of words: "salvation," "glory," "love," "faithfulness," "righteousness," "peace," and "good" (vv.9–12). The fullness of salvation brings his people "glory," as they share in the benefits of God's victory (cf. v.7 above). Instead of "displeasure" (v.4) and the consequent humiliation of not experiencing his fatherly care, God shares his glory with his own.

10–11 The era of restoration is in God's hands, as he alone can send "love," "faithfulness," "righteousness," and "peace" as his messengers to accomplish his purpose (cf. 43:3; 89:14). The four divine attributes are portrayed here as meeting and kissing one another. The Lord is the source of unfailing love (*ḥesed*), for which the people have prayed (v.7). His love is faithful (*'emet*) and his faithfulness is expressed in love. The words "love and faithfulness" are often found together as expressive of God's loyalty (Exod 34:6; Pss 25:10; 40:10–11; 57:10; 61:7; see appendix to Ps 25: The Perfections of Yahweh). The new era establishes his "righteousness" (*ṣedeq*, vv.10–11, 13; see 4:1; 22:31), expressive of the evident kingship of God in and over his people.

God's presence in glory and prosperity is nothing less than the opposite of their present adversity: "peace" (v.10). The extent of these benefits is further guaranteed by the contrastive complementary usage of "earth" and "heaven" in the sense of "everything" (v.11). His "faithfulness" and "righteousness" will appear on earth and in heaven. His kingdom will be both in heaven and on earth! So Isaiah proclaimed:

> You heavens above, rain down righteousness;
> let the clouds shower it down.
> Let the earth open wide,
> let salvation spring up,
> let righteousness grow with it;
> I, the LORD, have created it.
>
> (45:8)

12 The psalmist returns to his concern for the land and the people. He began by reminding God of what he had done in restoring the people to the land (v.1). The promises of God extend to the enjoyment of his "earth" (v.11). His blessings result in the enjoyment of "what is good," i.e., the "harvest" (cf. 67:6–7).

13 The enjoyment of God's blessings is evidence of his rule. "Righteousness," personified as a messenger (vv.11, 13), denotes his victory and salvation (vv.4, 6, 9, 10–11). Those who fear him will enjoy the benefits of his kingdom: forgiveness (v.2), reconciliation, renewal of covenant status (v.8–9), and the fullness of restoration (vv.9–13). As they await their God, they experience the firstfruits of "righteousness." Faith in God is the basis of hope in a new age characterized by "righteousness" (Gal 5:5; 2 Peter 3:13).

The psalmist began with a reflection of God's past acts of salvation and leaves a canonical hope in the progression of redemption, as God's "righteousness" advances his kingdom. Bellinger rightly concludes that the certainty of the psalmist arises from a prophetic oracle of salvation (pp. 66–70).

Notes

9 (10 MT) The phrase "his glory," based on an emendation of the MT as suggested by the Syriac, with the verb "dwell" (*š-k-n*) alludes to the glorious presence of God with his people (cf. Exod 24:16; see appendix to Ps 132: The Ark of the Covenant and the Temple: Symbols of Yahweh's Presence and Rule).

10 (11 MT) Ingeborg Johag concludes that God's promise of "peace" is equivalent to his promise of "goodness" (cf. Num 10:29; 1 Sam 25:30) and that this is expressive of covenantal terminology ("*ṭôḇ*—Terminus Technicus in Vertrags- und Bündnisformularen des Alten Orients und des Alten Testaments," *Bausteine biblischer Theologie. Festgabe für G. Johannes Botterweck zum 60. Geburtstag dargebracht von seinen Schülern*, ed. Heinz-Josef Fabry [Köln: Peter Hanstein, 1977], p. 20).

13 (14 MT) The last verse is problematic. The Syriac reads צַדִּיק (*ṣaddîq*, "righteous man") instead of צֶדֶק (*ṣeḏeq*, "righteousness") in the first colon. The second colon is more problematic. Who or what is the subject? BHS proposes "peace" (*šālôm*) or "uprightness" (*yōšer*). See the NEB: "Justice shall go in front of him and the path before his feet shall be peace." The NIV takes the subject from the first colon: "Righteousness goes before him and prepares the way for his steps."

Appendix: Anger in the Psalms

The psalms often reflect on anger. This preoccupation may seem abnormal to us, but anger is a theological concern. The psalmists invite us to deal with anger rather than skirt negative human emotions. Hence the psalms invite us to pray through anger and thus to be cleansed of evil emotions and to be filled with hope in the full inauguration of God's kingdom.

1. Synonyms for Anger

The Hebrew text uses several words for "anger." The nuances in meaning are so small that they may be treated as synonyms. What is of interest is how the psalmist at times piles up one word on the other so as to make a poetic impact. The surprise impact may be felt by a modern form of compounding the Hebrew words, as Eichrodt does: "The inward fire of the emotion of anger is described by *hārōn* and *ḥēmā;* its operation on its environment, when pictured in terms of 'snorting' by *rūaḥ* and *'ap*, of 'foaming' or 'boiling over' by *'eḇrāh, za'am,* and *za'ap*, of the breaking forth of something under pressure by *qesep*" (1:258–59). The word *za'a p*does not occur in the Psalms. All other words will be treated below, except for *rûaḥ* ["spirit"]).

'aḇ has two meanings: face (nostril) and anger. The semantic relation is doubtful, except for the evident physical disturbance in one's facial expression. God's anger is an anthropopathic expression referring to God's aversion to man's sin. Man's anger may be justified. But all too often it expresses inconsiderate, avaricious, and short-sighted behavior.

za'am denotes both the state of being angry as well as the vengeance resulting from indignation. The anger of God is active, leading to judgment and execration (curse). Modern lexicographers (KB^3, 1:265) suggest the translation "curse." Thus the NIV of Psalm 7:11—"God is a righteous judge, / a God who expresses his wrath [*za'am*] every day"— could be translated, "God is a righteous judge, / a God who passes sentence every day."

ḥēmāh appears to be used for excitement or intensification of anger: indignation, wrath, rage, fury, or the KJV translation, "hot displeasure." The last translation is related to the root idea (*y-ḥ-m*, "be hot"). *ḥēmāh* ("excitement") is used of animals, God, and man. The "excitement" of God against man's rebellious ways is an anthropopathic word for "indignation."

hārôn is related to the "glow" of the nose, showing forth anger. Often it occurs together with *'ap̱* to give rise to the translation "fierce anger": "Pour out your wrath [*za'am*] on them; / let your fierce [*ḥārôn*] anger [*'ap̱*] overtake them" (69:24).

ka'as is the "sorrow" (6:7; 31:9), "grief" (10:14), or divine displeasure (85:4) that humans may suffer; but they may also provoke the Lord by their evil deeds (78:58; 106:29).

s-t-r pānîm ("hide the face") occurs twelve times in the lament psalms (10:11; 13:1; 22:24; 27:9; 30:7; 44:24; 51:9; 69:17; 88:14; 102:2; 104:29; 143:7). The psalmist laments that in his devotion to the Lord he has been rewarded with God's abandonment. The cause for the lament is not clear as sin is generally not in view. The consequence of God's separation is much more evident. The psalmist experiences alienation from God, life, and family.

'eḇrāh may be translated by "anger," "fury," or "wrath." For example, Yahweh unleashed his anger against the Egyptians:

> He unleashed against them his hot [*ḥarôn*] anger [*'ap̱*],
> his wrath [*'eḇrāh*], indignation [*za'am*] and hostility—
> a band of destroying angels.
> He prepared a path for his anger [*'ap̱*];
> he did not spare them from death
> but gave them over to the plague.
>
> (78:49–50)

The psalmist piles up the synonyms, each word having a little different shade of meaning, as he moves from the emotion of God's anger to the resultant action.

qeṣep̱ is a word for anger, usually restricted to God's anger against man. Occasionally it occurs with *za'am*, "because of your great wrath [*za'am* + *qeṣep̱*], / for you have taken me up and thrown me aside" (102:10). In Psalm 38 God's anger is nothing less than the act of harsh discipline:

> O Lord, do not rebuke me in your anger [*qeṣep̱*]
> or discipline me in your wrath [*ḥemāh*].
> . . . .
> Because of your wrath [*za'am*] there is no health in my body;
> my bones have no soundness because of my sin.
>
> (38:1, 3)

2. The Anger of the Fools

The way of the fools is rarely described by the synonyms for anger. Treachery and lack of reliability better designate the way of the ungodly. However, this does not rule out his outbursts of anger. David exhorts his opponents to submit themselves rather than scheme angrily: "In your anger do not sin; / when you are on your beds, / search your hearts and be silent" (4:4). Elsewhere the association of anger and sin is clearly brought out: "Refrain from anger and turn from wrath; / do not fret—it leads only to evil" (37:8). Yet people can inflict great suffering to their fellow-man by their expressions of animosity (55:3).

3. Yahweh's Anger as Discipline

The portrayal of Yahweh's anger reflects the Near Eastern understanding of the fury of a king when his will is not obeyed or when his vassals rebel against his sovereignty. God's "anger" is provoked by acts of omission, rebellion, subversion, or disobedience and is more than an emotional outburst. It involves judgment, based on his royal will. The Lord wills to discipline, to subdue, and to be victorious in his rule.

The Lord has every reason to be angry. As long as sin rules on this earth, creation is affected by divine abandonment. The prayer of Moses gives a magnificent expression to the anguish of human existence:

> We are consumed by your anger and terrified by your indignation.
> ....+ 2p...
> All our days pass away under your wrath;
>   we finish our years with a moan.
> ....
> Who knows the power of your anger?
>   For your wrath is as great as the fear that is due you.
>
> (90:7, 9, 11)

Several lament and penitential psalms witness to the severity of God's anger on his own children. When the Lord is angry with his people, he pushes them to the side, sets them up for destruction, and treats them like the rebellious nations.

The whole history of God's dealings with Israel reflects God's patience and Israel's rebelliousness, beginning in the wilderness journey (95:10). There is no better picture in the psalms than Psalm 78:

> When the LORD heard them, he was very angry [*'-b-r*];
>   his fire broke out against Jacob,
>   and his wrath [*'ap̱*] rose against Israel,
> ....
> God's anger [*'ap̱*] rose against them;
>   he put to death the sturdiest among them,
>   cutting down the young men of Israel.
> ....
> Time after time he restrained his anger [*'ap̱*]
>   and did not stir up his full wrath [*ḥēmāh*].
> ....
> He unleashed against them his hot anger [*ḥ^a^rôn; 'ap̱*],
>   his wrath [*'eḇrāh*], indignation [*za'am*] and hostility [*ṣārāh*]—
>   a band of destroying angels.
> He prepared a path for his anger [*'ap̱*];
>   he did not spare them from death
>   but gave them over to the plague.
>
> (78:21, 31, 38, 49–50; see also Ps 106)

The story of God's involvement with Israel reflects the tensions between his compassion and his anger, between their recalcitrance and his readiness to forgive, and between his anger in the form of discipline and his "full" anger. Yet the Lord was determined not to give his people the fullness of his blessings: "So I declared on oath in my anger, / 'They shall never enter my rest' " (95:11).

The wrath of God also affects individuals who have sinned against him. The psalmist prays:

> Do not hide your face from me,
>   do not turn your servant away in anger;
>   you have been my helper.
> Do not reject me or forsake me,
>   O God my Savior.
>
> (27:9; cf. 38:1)

So great may be the experience of anguish that one cannot go on with life (cf. 88:7, 16). The psalmist speaks metaphorically of his strength, his bones, and his body as wasting away in God's anger, like vegetation in the summer heat (32:3–4; 38:3).

Yet the psalmist encourages the godly to look at both aspects of God's perfections: the constancy of his love and his holy anger: "The LORD is gracious and compassionate, / slow to anger and rich in love" (145:8; cf. 103:8). His anger is dwarfed in comparison with his love:

> For his anger lasts only a moment,
> but his favor lasts a lifetime;
> weeping may remain for a night,
> but rejoicing comes in the morning.
>
> (30:5)

Out of the darkness of personal and national anguish, the psalms lead the godly to pray for divine restoration. Only the Lord can restore his people (60:1). Though it may seem that he has rejected his people completely, there is always hope, as the questions imply:

> Why have you rejected us forever, O God?
> Why does your anger smolder against the sheep of your pasture?
>
> (74:1)

> Has God forgotten to be merciful?
> Has he in anger withheld his compassion?
>
> (77:9)

> How long, O LORD? Will you be angry forever?
> How long will your jealousy burn like fire?
>
> (79:5)

> O LORD God Almighty,
> how long will your anger smolder
> against the prayers of your people?
>
> (80:4)

> Will you be angry with us forever?
> Will you prolong your anger through all generations?
>
> (85:5)

> How long, O LORD? Will you hide yourself forever?
> How long will your wrath burn like fire?
>
> (89:46)

Yes, the Lord does respond to his people by setting his anger aside (85:3) and by renewing his mercy and compassion: "But you, O Lord, are a compassionate and gracious God, / slow to anger, abounding in love and faithfulness" (86:15). His fidelity (*ḥesed*, *'emet*) to his promises and to the covenant give reason for a positive response to the above questions: "He will not always accuse, nor will he harbor his anger forever" (103:9). He is the Father-King who welcomes back a repentant child.

4. Yahweh's Anger as Execration

God's kingdom becomes a reality in his acts of deliverance and vindication. The people of God believe that the Lord, like a king, daily dispenses his justice: "God is a righteous judge, / a God who expresses his wrath every day" (7:11). The imprecatory psalms (see appendix to Ps 137: Imprecations in the Psalms) express hope in God's rule of righteousness. The psalmist calls on God as the Divine Warrior to rouse himself to action: "Arise, O LORD, in your anger; / rise up against the rage of my enemies. / Awake, my God; decree justice" (7:6).

Submission to the Lord requires loyalty to him and to his Messiah. The Messiah ("anointed one") in the OT was represented by the descendants of David. Yahweh had appointed his Messiah to subjugate the nations, to put down rebellion, and to rule till all authority is in his hands. Psalm 2 is a magnificent expression of this hope. On the one hand, the messianic rule is a concrete expression of his anger (2:5). While, on the other hand, as long as the final day of vengeance has not come, the invitation to submission and loyalty is still open:

> Kiss the Son, lest he be angry
> and you be destroyed in your way,
> for his wrath can flare up in a moment.
> Blessed are all who take refuge in him.
> (2:12)

The psalms celebrate the mighty deeds of Yahweh in vindication and in deliverance as expressive of his righteous rule (cf. 7:6; 18:6; 21:9). Yet it is a mistake to limit the Psalms to a concern with the here-and-now, because throughout the Psalms the people of God look to the final, climactic, and victorious establishment of God's kingdom on earth:

> Pour out your wrath on the nations
> that do not acknowledge you,
> on the kingdoms
> that do not call on your name.
> (79:6)

This hope is grounded in the conviction that Yahweh alone is King: "You alone are to be feared. / Who can stand before you when you are angry?" (76:7). He will not let the wicked get by with their evil schemes (cf. 56:7; 59:13a; 69:24). Only when Yahweh's righteous rule prevails will his kingdom become visible: "Then it will be known to the ends of the earth / that God rules over Jacob" (59:13b).

Texts: 2:5, 12; 4:4; 6:1, 7; 7:6, 11; 10:11, 14; 13:1; 18:7; 21:9; 22:24; 27:9; 30:5, 7; 31:9; 37:8; 38:1, 3; 44:24; 51:9; 55:3; 56:7; 59:13; 60:1; 69:17, 24; 74:1; 76:7, 10; 77:9; 78:21, 31, 38, 50, 58–59, 62, 79:5; 79:6; 80:4; 85:3–5; 86:15; 88:7, 14, 16; 89:38, 46; 90:7, 9, 11; 95:10–11; 102:2, 10; 103:8; 104:29; 106:23, 29, 32; 119:19; 124:3; 138:7; 145:7–8.

Related Concepts: See also the appendixes to Pss 1 (The Ways of Wisdom and Folly); 25 (The Perfections of Yahweh); 78 (The Mighty Acts of Yahweh); 88 (Sheol-Grave-Death in the Psalms); 98 (Yahweh Is the Divine Warrior); 103 (Sin and Forgiveness); 137 (Imprecations in the Psalms).

Bibliography: Samuel E. Balentine, *The Hidden God: The Hiding of the Face of God in the Old Testament* (Oxford: University Press, 1983); Sheila Carney, "God Damn God: A Reflection on Expressing Anger in Prayer," BTB 13 (1983): 116–20; Eichrodt, OTT, 1:258–69; S. Erlandsson, "The Wrath of Yhwh," *Tyndale Bulletin* 23 (1972): 111–16; J. Gray, "The Wrath of God in Canaanite and Hebrew Literature," *Journal of the Manchester University Egyptian and Oriental Society* 25 (1947/53): 9–19; H.M. Haney, "Einige Schilderungen des gottlichen Zorns," *Tradition und Situation. Studien zum alttestamentlichen Prophetie. Artur Weiser zum 70. Geburtstag am 18.11.1963 dargebracht von Kollegen, Freunden, und Schülern,* edd. Ernst Würthwein and Otto Kaiser (Göttingen: Vandenhoeck & Ruprecht, 1963), pp. 107–13; R.P.C. Hanson, "The Wrath of God," ET 58, pp. 216–18; John L. McKenzie, "Vengeance is Mine," *Scripture* 12, pp. 33–39; L. Morris, "The Wrath of God," ET 63 (1951–52): 142–45; R.V.G. Tasker, *The Biblical Doctrine of the Wrath of God* (London: Tyndale, 1951); Claus Westermann, "Boten des Zorns," in *Erträge der Forschung am Alten Testament,* vol. 3 (Munich: Kaiser, 1984), pp. 96–106.

TDAT, 3:182–88; 4:297–302; TDNT, 5:392–418; TDOT, 1:348–60; 3:106–11, 462–65; THAT, 1:220–24, 581–83, 634–35, 838–42; 2:206–7, 432–60, 663–66; TWOT, 1:58, 247, 322, 374–75, 451; 2:643–44, 808–9.

Psalm 86: Give Me a Sign of Your Goodness

This is the only psalm associated with David in the third book of Psalms. It is an *individual lament* psalm, which has thoughts and expressions in common with many other psalms. The need is only generally stated; it may well be that the references to need (v.1), affliction (v.7), and enemies (vv.14, 17) are stylized expressions for adversity in general.

The psalm may be divided into five strophes, each consisting of a prayer for mercy and a confession of the Lord (vv.1–5, vv.6–10, vv.11–13, vv.14–15, vv.16–17). Each confession begins with an emphatic reference to the Lord: "Truly you" (vv.5, 10; NIV, "you," "for you"), "None like you" (v.8; NIV placed after "among the gods. . ."), "Truly your love" (v.13; NIV, "For . . . your love"), "But you" (v.15). The concluding prayer contains a resolution of hope, as the psalmist focuses on the effect of God's love toward him and a final confession of his confidence in God, beginning with an emphatic form: "for you" (v.17c).

The expository structure of the psalm differs from the above structure by highlighting the hymn of confidence (vv.8–10) and by combining the last two strophes into one larger unit (vv.14–17).

A. Prayer for Mercy and Confession of Confidence (vv.1–5)
  B. Prayer for Mercy (vv.6–7)
    C. Hymn of Confidence in the Lord (vv.8–10)
  B′. Anticipation of Deliverance (vv.11–13)
A′. Prayer for Deliverance (vv.14–17)

I. Prayer for Mercy and Confession of Confidence

86:1–5

A prayer of David.

1 Hear, O LORD, and answer me,
for I am poor and needy.
2 Guard my life, for I am devoted to you.
You are my God; save your servant
who trusts in you.
3 Have mercy on me, O Lord,
for I call to you all day long.
4 Bring joy to your servant,
for to you, O Lord,
I lift up my soul.
5 You are forgiving and good, O Lord,
abounding in love to all who call to you.

1–4 The plea for mercy is based on the needs of the psalmist ("poor and needy," v.1), the lordship (i.e., sovereignty) of God ("Lord," vv.3–5), his unique status as God's "servant" (v.2), and the nature of God (v.5). First, it is not clear what the particular needs of the psalmist are. But in his confession of need, he humbles himself in the presence of his God as a creature in need of his God. The phrase "poor and needy" is a stylized idiom (35:10; 37:14; 40:17; 70:5; 109:16, 22) for the godly. The Hebrew text contains a wordplay of "answer me," "poor," and "I": *ʿᵃnēnî kî-ʿānî wᵉʾeḇyôn ʾānî* (lit., "*answer me* for *poor* and needy *I*," v.1; cf. 88:15). He prays that the Lord will "hear" (v.1; cf. 31:2; 71:2; 102:2; lit., "incline your ear") and answer his prayer by guarding his "life" (*nep̱eš*, lit., "soul," v.2; cf. v.13; 25:20). The word "soul" signifies the whole person, and as such the psalmist is asking the Lord to extend to him his covenant blessing according to which the Lord guards and keeps his people from all harm (cf. Num 6:24–26; Ps 121).

Second, the psalmist calls on his covenant God (Yahweh, "LORD," v.1), who is sovereign over all ("Lord," *Adonai*, vv.3–5). Though the repetitive terms for prayer are stylized, the need is real: "Hear, . . . and answer me. . . . / Guard my life. . . . save. . . . / Have mercy on me, . . . / I call to you. . . . / Bring joy . . . / I lift up my soul" (vv.1–4). The psalmist trusts in the Lord and waits for his gracious response. Hope begins with submitting oneself fully to the protection of God. It is further demonstrated by absolute loyalty to the Lord, expressed in several ways: "servant" (*ʿeḇeḏ*, v.2; see 19:11), "devoted" one (*ḥāsîḏ*; see 4:3), and an emphatic "you are my God!" (see appendix to Ps 3: Yahweh Is My God). Those who wait for the Lord do so because he alone can transform adversity into "joy" (*ś-m-ḥ*, "make me happy," v.4; cf. 90:15).

5 The psalmist confides in the Lord, because he knows the nature of his God. The Lord has promised to extend his benefits to all who call on him (vv.5, 13, 15; cf. Exod 34:6–7; Isa 55:6–7): his goodness (*ṭôḇ*, lit., "good"; cf. 23:6), forgiveness (*sallāḥ*, a *hapax legomenon*), and love (*ḥeseḏ*). The effect of the Lord's extending the evidences of his care will be a renewed "joy" in God's renewed acts of covenant fidelity (v.4; cf. 90:14–16). (See appendix to Ps 25: The Perfections of Yahweh).

Notes

1 For a brief discussion of the technical words and phrases in the superscription, see the Introduction.

2 BHS proposes a transposition of "you are my God" to the beginning of v.3, supposing that v.2 is too loaded and that the expression "your servant who trusts in you" is more natural, compared with the MT: "Save your servant, you are my God, who trusts in you." See the NEB: "save thy servant who puts his trust in thee. O LORD my God."

II. Prayer for Mercy

86:6–7

6 Hear my prayer, O LORD;
listen to my cry for mercy.
7 In the day of my trouble I will call to you,
for you will answer me.

6–7 The language of the prayer is stylized form: "Hear my prayer, . . . listen to my cry for mercy. . . . I will call to you" (cf. 28:2; 55:1–2; 130:2). The prayer is for God's "mercy." The phrase "cry for mercy" (v.6) is a prayer from a needy heart (cf. Jer 3:21;

31:9; TWOT, 1:304). The phrase "day of my trouble" (v.7) is equally stylized (cf. 20:1; 50:15; 77:2). The precise nature of the affliction is left undefined.

III. Hymn of Confidence in the Lord

86:8–10

8 Among the gods there is none like you, O Lord;
no deeds can compare with yours.
9 All the nations you have made
will come and worship before you, O Lord;
they will bring glory to your name.
10 For you are great and do marvelous deeds;
you alone are God.

8–10 The anticipation for God's favorable response—"for you will answer me" (v.7)—leads into a hymnic expression of the greatness of God. The experience of Israel's passing through the Red Sea demonstrated the greatness of Yahweh as the Divine Warrior (Exod 15). In the song celebrating his victory, God's people joined with Moses singing, "Who among the gods is like you. . . ? /Who is like you. . . ?" (Exod 15:11). This question was in effect a strong affirmation of the excellence of Israel's God. The psalmist gives here a positive statement rather than a question: "Among the gods there is none like you" (v.8; cf. 58:1–2; 71:19; 89:6; Isa 45:21). There is no other God like the "Lord," whose "deeds" are "marvelous," reflecting his *great*ness (v.10; cf. 72:18; 77:14).

The psalmist affirms his confidence in his God by proclaiming his great acts, by affirming his wholehearted commitment to the God who "alone" can do these wonders (cf. 2 Kings 19:15; Ps 83:18), and by expressing his belief that all people will one day submit themselves to the Lord (cf. Rev 15:4). They will not merely be "put to shame" (v.17), but they may even join with Israel and worship the Lord together with them (Isa 2:3; 45:23; Zeph 2:11; Zech 8:21–22; Mal 1:11). They too will "bring glory" (v.9) by their offerings (Mal 1:11) and by their obedience (Mal 1:6). What an expression of confidence in the Lord's universal sovereignty and in his saving plan for the nations (cf. 22:27–31)! Yahweh alone is God, and the gods of the nations are worthless (cf. 115:3–7; 135:15–18). (See appendix to Ps 78: The Mighty Acts of Yahweh.)

IV. Anticipation of Deliverance

86:11–13

11 Teach me your way, O LORD,
and I will walk in your truth;
give me an undivided heart,
that I may fear your name.
12 I will praise you, O Lord my God, with all my heart;
I will glorify your name forever.
13 For great is your love toward me;
you have delivered me from the depths of the grave.

11 In the confidence that the Lord will have "mercy" (vv.3, 6) on him, the psalmist looks beyond the present troubles to his own renewed commitment to the Lord, his covenant God ("LORD"). As in vv.5–7, the psalmist expresses his devotion and submission to the Lord (vv.11–12):

> Teach me your way, . . .
> and I will walk in your truth;
> give me an undivided heart,
> that I may fear your name.
> I will praise you, . . . with all my heart;
> I will glorify your name forever.

In his desire to walk wisely in the presence of God, he asks for guidance (cf. 27:11; 32:8) and a new heart ("an undivided heart," v.11; cf. Jer 24:7; 32:39; Ezek 11:19). He longs for inner renewal so that he may walk in God's "truth" (v.11; cf. 26:3) and in the "fear" of the "name" of the Lord. To walk in "truth" (*'emet;* see 15:2) signifies fidelity to the Lord. To "fear" the "name" of the Lord signifies a heart of wisdom (cf. Prov 1:7).

12 The renewed commitment also finds expression in acts and words of praise to the Lord. His wholehearted praise (cf. 9:1; 18:49) consists of a verbal expression of gratitude as well as acts of obeisance and gratitude to the Lord, as expressed by the phrase "I will glorify" (cf. "they will bring glory," v.9). (See appendix to Ps 122: The Praise of Yahweh.)

13 The affirmation of confidence presupposes that this great God will and does deliver those who call on him. He remains true to his nature (vv.5, 13, 15). Yahweh delivers from death to life because of his *ḥesed*. Adversity is like "the depth of the grave" or better "of Sheol" (see NIV mg.). Though "Sheol" may denote the realm of the dead, it may also connote the experience of adversity that ultimately may be likened to death (88:6; cf. TWOT, 2:892–93).

Notes

13 Underlying the NIV's "me" in the phrase "delivered me" is the word נֶפֶשׁ (*nepeš*, "soul"), a reference to "life" (v.14; cf. v.2).

V. Prayer for Deliverance

86:14–17

> 14 The arrogant are attacking me, O God;
> a band of ruthless men seeks my life—
> men without regard for you.
> 15 But you, O Lord, are a compassionate and gracious God,
> slow to anger, abounding in love and faithfulness.
> 16 Turn to me and have mercy on me;
> grant your strength to your servant
> and save the son of your maidservant.
> 17 Give me a sign of your goodness,
> that my enemies may see it and be put to shame,
> for you, O LORD, have helped me and comforted me.

14 The psalmist changes from a general to a more specific description of his affliction. He uses a stylized expression (see 54:3). The "arrogant" and "ruthless men" may be a personification of adversity. In this world of alienation, the godly are unwelcome and often are the object of persecution (cf. Matt 5:10; 1 Thess 3:4; Heb 11:37).

15 Confidence is in the covenant God, who is known by his qualities of compassion, grace, patience, love, and fidelity (cf. vv.5, 13; see Exod 34:6–7).

16–17 The psalmist repeats the prayer for divine "mercy" (v.16; cf. vv.3, 6). Verses 16 and 17 seem to be symmetric with the first petition by the repetition of "save" (v.2), "have mercy on me" (v.3), "your servant" (v.4), and the word "goodness" (*ṭôḇāh*, v.17; cf. v.5: "good," *ṭôḇ*).

The psalmist looks as a "servant" for the "strength" of the Lord (v.16). He is "the son of your maidservant" (cf. 116:16). This phrase may also be translated as "your faithful son" (cf. NIV mg.), in which case it is symmetric with "I am devoted to you" (lit., "your loyal one," v.2; see above).

The "sign" of God's goodness is some evidence of the Lord's care for his servant. He has cast himself on the promises of God's goodness, forgiveness, and love (vv.5, 13); his past great and marvelous acts (v.10); and his attributes (v.15).

The psalmist prays that his faith will triumph and that the enemies of God may witness the evidences of Yahweh's fidelity so as to shame them (cf. 35:4). It may well be that Dahood is correct in translating the last two verbs modally: "O that you yourself, Yahweh, would help me and console me!" (*Psalms*, 2:292).

Notes

The stylization may be seen by looking at the *petitions:*

A. vv.1–4: (1) Hear, . . . and answer me; (2) Guard. . . . save; (3) Have mercy on me, . . . I call to you; (4) Bring joy . . . I lift up my soul.

B. vv.5–7: (6) Hear my prayer, . . . listen to my cry for mercy; (7) I will call to you, for you will answer me.

B′. vv.11–13: (11) Teach me your way, . . . give me an undivided heart.

A′. vv.14–17: (16) Turn to me and have mercy on me; grant your strength; (17) Give me a sign.

The stylization may be seen by looking at the divine perfections and acts:

A. vv.1–4: You are my God.

B. vv.5–7: (5) You are forgiving and good, O Lord, abounding in love.

C. vv.8–10: (8) Among the gods there is none like you, O Lord; no deeds can compare with yours; (10) For you are great and do marvelous deeds; you alone are God.

B′. vv.11–13: (11) your way, . . . in your truth; (13) For great is your love toward me.

A′. vv.14–17: (15) But you, O Lord, are a compassionate and gracious God, slow to anger, abounding in love and faithfulness; (17) a sign of your goodness.

The stylization may be seen by looking at the psalmist's relation to the Lord:

A. vv.1–4: (1) Hear, O LORD, and answer me, for I am poor and needy; (2) for I am devoted to you. . . . your servant who trusts in you; (4) to your servant.

A′. vv.14–17: (16) grant your strength to your servant and save the son of your maidservant.

Psalm 87: Glorious Things of Thee Are Spoken

As rich as the theology of this psalm is, its exegesis has raised many issues. Its brevity of style, the seemingly unconnected thoughts, and the absence of structure have made the psalm "one of the most problematic in the whole Psalter" (A.A. Anderson, 2:618). Weiser writes, "The language of the poet is anything but flowing. He moulds his brief sentences in such a daring and abrupt manner that only a few characteristic features are thrown into bold relief while their inner connection is left in the dark" (pp. 579–80).

It is equally difficult to postulate an original life-situation for the psalm. It may well have been associated with any of the three pilgrimage festivals, when Israel together with proselytes joined together in the worship of God at the temple. Exegetes also differ on its dating, whether preexilic, exilic, or postexilic. That the psalm need not be postexilic is carefully set forth by Weiser: "Proselytes already existed in pre-exilic times (cf. II Kings 5); and it can be assumed that during the great pilgrimage-festival Jerusalem gave shelter within her walls to guests of varied origin who had come to attend the feast" (p. 580).

The psalm is usually associated with the Zion Psalms (Pss 48; 76; 84; 122; 137; see appendix to Ps 46: Zion Theology). It consists of three parts:

A. Hymn in Praise of Zion (vv.1–2)
B. God's Register in Heaven (vv.3–6)
C. The Joy in Zion (v.7)

(For an alternate structure and metrical analysis, see Th. Booij, "Some Observations on Psalm lxxxvii," VetTest 37 [1987]: 15–25.)

I. Hymn in Praise of Zion

87:1–2

Of the Sons of Korah. A psalm. A song.

1 He has set his foundation on the holy mountain;
2 the LORD loves the gates of Zion
more than all the dwellings of Jacob.

1–2 Zion, the city of God, symbolizes God's kingdom presence. He has sovereignly established it (cf. Heb 11:10) by entering into a covenant relationship with Israel (cf. 114:2). He has established it on earth! The expression—"he has set his foundation [*yᵉsûḏāṯô*, or 'its foundation']"—is terse, as the pronoun "his" or "its" has no antecedent (v.1). The term "foundation" is equally ambiguous. It is commonly assumed that the psalm speaks of the foundation of Zion and that the pronoun ("his") refers back to God (see Dahood: "O city founded by him," *Psalms*, 2:298). In view of this being a hymn of Zion and the root *y-s-d* is being used with reference to the Lord's acts of Creation and kingship (24:2; 78:69; 102:25; 104:5; Isa 48:13; 51:16) and of his election of Zion (cf. Isa 14:32; 28:16), it is preferable to understand the enigmatic phrase as "he has set her foundation." (See the appendix to Ps 132: The Ark of the Covenant and the Temple: Symbols of Yahweh's Presence and Rule.)

Jerusalem was located on a mountain, often designated as Mount Zion or "holy mountain" (3:4; 15:1; 99:9; Isa 11:9; 65:25). The plural form of "mountain" (*harᵉrê*, "mountains") may be explained as a reference to the hills on which Jerusalem was built (NEB, "on holy hills"), a plural of majesty, or it may be singular in meaning, as is the case with "your tabernacle," which is plural in the MT (43:3; see Dahood, *Psalms*, 2:299). In fact, the use of the plural with "mountains" seems to be related to the plural in the phrase "the dwellings of Jacob." The "holy mountains" are set over against "the dwellings of Zion." The Lord has "founded" Zion by setting his electing love on her (cf. 132:13). The special quality of Jerusalem did not reside in her natural holiness but in the "love" of God. The use of the participle for "love" (*'ōhēḇ*) bears out the constancy of his love for Zion. The phrase "the gates of Zion" (v.2) is a poetic reference to "Zion" (cf. 122:2). The electing love of God for Zion magnifies the uniqueness of the temple in Jerusalem over any other "sacred" places. The designation "dwellings of Jacob" may denote the Israelite cities that have not been chosen as "the" cultic center (cf. 78:67–68; 132:12–14). More likely is the suggestion that the word "dwellings" (*miškᵉnôṯ*, lit., "tabernacles") is a technical term for "cultic centers." A.A. Anderson states, "Verse 2 probably offers an explanation as to why Yahweh chose Jerusalem rather than any other Israelite shrine" (2:620; see Kraus, *Psalmen*, 2:602).

Notes

1 For a brief discussion of the technical words and phrases in the superscription, see the Introduction.

II. God's Register in Heaven

87:3–6

3 Glorious things are said of you,
O city of God: *Selah*
4 "I will record Rahab and Babylon
among those who acknowledge me—
Philistia too, and Tyre, along with Cush—
and will say, 'This one was born in Zion.' "

5 Indeed, of Zion it will be said,
"This one and that one were born in her,
and the Most High himself will establish her."
6 The LORD will write in the register of the peoples:
"This one was born in Zion." *Selah*

3–6 The psalmist suddenly changes his focus from the earthly Jerusalem to the glorious future of the "city of God" (v.3). In his meditation he may have reflected on the prophetic oracles that portray the "glorious" future of Zion, "the mother-city" of all nations (cf. Isa 2:2–4; 26:1–2; 60:15–22; 61:1–7). The songs of Zion also evoke praise of the city of God. The psalmist's ecstasy is not with the present, earthly city but with "the city of God" as a theological entity, from God's perspective.

The passive verb "are said" (*m^e^d̲ubbār*) has occasioned some difficulty. First, the subject is plural whereas the Hebrew participle is singular. Second, the terse Hebrew phraseology (lit., "glories is spoken in you city of God") requires explication. In view of a similar usage of a plural subject and singular participle in Isaiah 16:8, the NIV makes good sense: "Glorious things are said of you, / O city of God" (v.3). The verb "said" (*m^e^d̲ubbār*) may also signify here "sing" (cf. Judg 5:12; so A.A. Anderson, 2:620). The verse could be rendered: "O city of God glorious things are sung of you."

The Lord himself has revealed the glories of Zion through his prophets to encourage his people. The verb "record" (v.4) is symmetric with "write" (v.6). Among the nations he records are Rahab (a demythologized reference to Egypt; cf. 89:10; Isa 30:7; see NIV mg., "A poetic name for Egypt"), Babylon, Philistia, Tyre, and Cush (= Nubia; cf. NIV mg., "the upper Nile region"). These nations are representative of the various powers that dominated much of Israel's history: oppressors (Babylon), troublers (Philistia), and enticers (Egypt, Cush, and Tyre). Regardless of how the nations may have related to God's people in the past, individuals from these nations may still participate in God's "city." The individuals are "those who acknowledge" him (v.4), that is, who worship Yahweh as the living God. On this confession their names are recorded as having been "born in Zion" (v.6). Dahood writes, "Though born abroad, these converts to Yahweh will become citizens of the spiritual metropolis Zion" (*Psalms*, 2:300).

The psalmist reflects again on Zion as "the mother-city" of the faithful as he places Zion in an emphatic position: "Indeed, of Zion" (v.5). What is Zion? Where is Zion? Zion goes beyond the city on earth to the city of God (cf. Isa 49:20–21; 50:1; 54:1–2; 62:4–5; 65:18–24; 66:7–8; Zech 8:2–13; Gal 4:26), where all the names of the godly are recorded (v.6; cf. Exod 32:32; Ps 69:28; Dan 12:1; Mal 3:16) as belonging to the Lord (cf. Mal 3:16; Rev 21:24–27).

The godly are secure in the city that the "Most High" (Elyon, cf. 46:4; see appendix to Ps 9: Yahweh Is El Elyon) "will establish" (v.5). The verb "will establish her" (in the imperfect) forms an inclusion with "he has set his [or better 'her'] foundation" (v.1) so as to also form an inclusion: the God who has established Zion in the past (v.1) will continue to establish her (v.5)! His purpose includes all the faithful from Israel and the nations who respond to him in acts of loyalty and worship. The guarantee of security and inclusion in Zion lies in the Lord's promise and in his being her builder (cf. Heb 11:10, 16).

Notes

---

3 BHS and many modern commentators emend the Pual participle מְדֻבָּר (*m^e^d̲ubbār*, "spoken," "said") to מְדַבֵּר (*m^e^d̲abbēr*, "speak"), assuming that God is the subject: "He speaks glorious things of you" (Weiser, p. 579). Another solution is given in the NEB transposing the phrase to follow v.7: "proclaiming glorious things of you." Kraus renders the phrase with an impersonal subject: "wonderful things they tell of you" (*Psalmen*, 2:600).

4 The name "Rahab" is associated with pagan mythology as a monster whose powers had to be subdued. Yahweh's victory over Egypt at the time of the Passover and Israel's crossing through the Red Sea were greatly celebrated, and in its celebrations Israel compared Egypt

to that mythological monster. In this context "Rahab" is nothing more than a synonym for Egypt (see 74:14). See Notes on 74:13.

5 The evidence in favor of adding "mother" (Kraus, *Psalmen*, 2:600) as the designation of Zion is unclear. The reading is supported by the LXX, which may also lie behind Paul's metaphor in Gal 4:26: "But the Jerusalem that is above is free, and she is our mother." See the NEB: "Zion shall be called a mother, in whom men of every race are born."

6 Erich Zenger interprets the "register of the peoples" as a register of the citizens of Zion. He further connects this with the tables of the law (Exod 24:12; 31:18; 32:19; see "Psalm 87:6 und die Tafeln von Sinai," *Wort, Lied und Gottesspruch. Beiträge zur Septuaginta. Festschrift für Joseph Ziegler*, ed. Josef Schreiner (Würzberg: Echter Verlag/Katholisches Bibelwerk, 1972), 2:97–103.

III. The Joy in Zion

87:7

7 As they make music they will sing,
"All my fountains are in you."

7 The psalmist concludes with a scene on earth. The crowds in the earthly Jerusalem are celebrating with music, song, and possibly even dance. The verbal phrase "make music" is better translated as "dancing" (*ḥōlelîm*, a Polel participle), which together with "singers" may be a hendiadys; for the ones who sing are the same as those who dance. So Weiser writes, "From the festival dance of the Temple congregation, a song now rises in the poet's ears" (p. 584). The song celebrates the glory (cf. v.3) of Zion: "All my fountains are found in you." Dahood's suggested reading—"And all who have suffered in you will sing as well as dance" (*Psalms*, 2:298)—while attractive theologically is not defensible exegetically. Zion is associated with "the fountain of life" (cf. Jer 2:13), of "salvation" (Isa 12:3), "a river whose streams make glad the city of God" (Ps 46:4; cf. Ezek 47; Rev 22:1–5).

Psalm 88: A Prayer in the Darkness of Despair

This is an *individual lament* psalm in which the psalmist knows nothing but sorrow. However, even in the darkness of his grief, he turns to the Lord for deliverance. The dialogue between the psalmist and his God can only be understood from the perspective of faith, in which the godly are free to share their frustrations with their heavenly Father. As in the other psalms of lament, it is difficult to be sure of the precise circumstances of his suffering. He suffered for a long time (v.15), was ostracized by family and friends (vv.8, 18), and had looked to the Lord regularly for deliverance (vv.9, 13). The emotions and suffering expressed by the psalmist are close in spirit to those of Psalm 22. In the tradition of the church, these psalms were linked together in the Scripture reading on Good Friday.

The structure of the psalm discloses a certain repetitiveness due to the psalmist's preoccupation with his suffering.

A. Prayer for Help (vv.1–2)
  B. The Experience of Dying in Life (vv.3–5)
    C. It Is the Lord's Doing (vv.6–9a)

A′. Prayer for Help (vv.9b–12)
C′. It Is the Lord's Doing (vv.13–14)
B′. The Experience of Dying in Life (vv.15–18)

I. Prayer for Help

88:1–2

A song. A psalm of the Sons of Korah. For the director of music.
According to *mahalath leannoth.* A *maskil* of Heman the Ezrahite.

1 O LORD, the God who saves me,
day and night I cry out before you.
2 May my prayer come before you;
turn your ear to my cry.

1–2 The marvel of faith is that the man of faith calls on the Lord even in the depth of his anguish. This psalm begins with an emphatic position of the Lord's name (Yahweh, "LORD"), accompanied with a descriptive clause: "the God who saves me" (v.1; cf. 89:26; Isa 12:2). In the midst of tribulation, faith holds on to the God who has promised to deliver. In his suffering and perpetual anguish, the psalmist prayed day and night (cf. vv.9, 13; 32:3–4; 42:8) with the hope that the Lord would respond to his prayer (v.2; cf. 65:2). The prayer is a deeply piercing shout (*rinnāh;* NIV, "cry"; cf. 17:1; 61:1). Though *rinnāh* may denote a shout of joy in other contexts (cf. 47:1; 105:43), it is here a loud cry for divine help. The psalmist shouts loudly to the Lord, hoping that he will hear.

Notes

For a brief discussion of the technical words and phrases in the superscription, see the Introduction.

1 (2 MT) The NIV follows the MT in "the God who saves me" instead of the proposal in the BHS: אֱלֹהַי שִׁוַּעְתִּי יוֹמָם (*'elōhay šiwwa'tî yômām,* "my God, by day I call for help"; cf. Kraus, *Psalmen,* 2:601). Though the proposal supports the parallelism (so NEB, "my God, by day I call for help, by night I cry aloud in thy presence"), the MT opens with a glimmer of hope and faith in the Lord as the source of salvation. Yair Hoffman observes that the psalmist's virtual absence of hope may reflect his breaking away from the stereotypical language ("The Transition From Despair to Hope in the Individual Psalms of Lament," *Tarbiz* 55 [1985/86]: 161–72 [Heb.]). Ernst Haag explains the darkness of this psalm in the light of the psalmist's concern with an encounter with the living God ("Psalm 88," *Freude an der Weisung des Herrn, Beiträge zur Theologie der Psalmen, Festgabe zum 70. Geburtstag von Heinrich Gross,* edd. Ernst Haag and Frank-Lothar Hossfeld [Stuttgart: Katholisches Bibelwerk, 1986], pp. 149–70).

II. The Experience of Dying in Life

88:3–5

3 For my soul is full of trouble
and my life draws near the grave.

[4]I am counted among those who go down to the pit;
I am like a man without strength.
[5]I am set apart with the dead,
like the slain who lie in the grave,
whom you remember no more,
who are cut off from your care.

3–5 The adversity has been with the psalmist for so long that he ("my soul," i.e., "I") is satiated (NIV, "is full of," *ś-b-ʿ*, v.3), but not with God's blessings (cf. 65:4). Rather he is so deeply galled that he feels his life ebbing away from him. The "grave" (Sheol) is the state of death with all its negative associations. The psalmist is alive but dead (cf. 6:5; 107:18) as to his contemporaries (cf. 22:29; 28:1; 143:7; Prov 1:12). He exists like a shade, "a man without strength" (cf. Isa 14:9–10). He further compares himself with an unknown soldier who together with "the slain" was buried in a mass grave (v.5; cf. Ezek 32:30). He experiences the absence of God, like those who are dead ("whom you remember no more"). He does not deny God's remembrance and care but speaks phenomenally, that is, the way it appears to people. Since little is known about the state of the dead, they are as if forgotten by God. Because the OT has a high view of life, death is unnatural (cf. vv.10–12, see appendix below).

Notes

5 (6 MT) The word חָפְשִׁי (*ḥop̱šî*, "freed"; NIV, "set apart") usually denotes a freed slave (cf. Exod 21:5). It may be a paradoxical expression, as if death brings freedom. Kraus emends it to הֻשַׁבְתִּי (*hušaḇtî*, "I must live among the dead," *Psalmen*, 2:606).

III. It Is the Lord's Doing

88:6–9a

[6]You have put me in the lowest pit,
in the darkest depths.
[7]Your wrath lies heavily upon me;
you have overwhelmed me with all your waves. *Selah*

[8]You have taken from me my closest friends
and have made me repulsive to them.
I am confined and cannot escape;
[9] my eyes are dim with grief.

6–9a The lament turns into an accusation. The adversities did not just happen. On the one hand, the psalmist stresses God's activity and involvement in his morbid existence. He was like a dead man, having been placed in "the lowest pit" and in "the darkest depths" (v.6; cf. 86:13; 143:3; Lam 3:6, 53, 55). In this regard God has treated him like the wicked (cf. 94:13). He effectively implicates God by four verbal phrases. The first and the last are the same, forming an inclusion: "you have put me" or "you have made me" (vv.6, 8; *šattānî*). In the second phrase, he indicts God with oppressing him unjustly ("you have overwhelmed me," v.7; *ʿ-n-h*, Piel: "oppress," "afflict"). The third phrase charges the Lord with removing even his "closest friends" (v.8), leaving him only with "darkness" (i.e., death) as his "closest friend" (cf. v.18).

On the other hand, the psalmist stresses his hurt in that the Lord, his God, has afflicted him ("upon me" emphatic position, v.7, MT). He is the object of God's wrath (cf. 32:4; 38:2; 85:3) but does not understand God's rationale. God's "wrath" has overpowered him like "waves," leaving him utterly helpless (cf. 42:7). Thus he is totally boxed in ("confined and cannot escape," v.8; cf. 142:7; Lam 3:7). He is without fellowship and encouragement of "close" friends (cf. 31:11–12). His situation resembles that of Job, as his friends did not understand him. More than that, our Lord's suffering on earth was such that his own disciples forsook him (cf. Luke 23:49). The distress arises because of his being forsaken by man and by God. Therefore he is full of "grief" (v.9a; cf. 38:10).

Notes

9 (10 MT) The first line of v.9 contains a play on words: עֵינִי (*'ênî*, "my eye") and עֹנִי (*'ōnî*, "grief"). See 6:7.

IV. Prayer for Help

88:9b–12

I call to you, O LORD, every day;
I spread out my hands to you.
10 Do you show your wonders to the dead?
Do those who are dead rise up and praise you? *Selah*
11 Is your love declared in the grave,
your faithfulness in Destruction?
12 Are your wonders known in the place of darkness,
or your righteous deeds in the land of oblivion?

9b–12 In his "grief" (v.9a) the psalmist continually entreats the Lord (v.9b). True faith is not an apathetic acceptance of whatever comes to pass. True faith lies in wrestling with the Lord in prayer. The depth of faith comes to expression in the form of questions (vv.10–12), arising out of the experience of abandonment. In contrast to his experience, the Lord had shown to his people his "wonders" (vv.10, 12; *pele';* see appendix to Ps 78: The Mighty Acts of Yahweh), "faithfulness" (v.11; *'ᵉmûnāh*), "love" (v.11; *ḥeseḏ*), and "righteous deeds" (v.12; *ṣᵉḏāqāh;* see appendix to Ps 25: The Perfections of Yahweh). He gave them the fullness of life (cf. Deut 30:15, 19) as conspicuous evidence of his faithful love. In response they praised him (cf. 40:9–10; 92:2). However, the psalmist is far removed from God's righteous deeds (cf. 71:24).

Yet the questions raise hope that the Lord will have regard for the psalmist and deliver him from his present distress. If he were to go to "the grave" (v.11, cf. v.5), also known as "Destruction" (Abaddon, the place of the departed; cf. Job 26:6; 28:22; 31:12; Prov 15:11; 27:20; Rev 9:11 ["the angel of the Abyss, whose name in Hebrew is Abaddon"]), he would be unable to praise God (see Dahood, *Psalms*, 2:305). The psalmist speaks about death as a place where there is nothing but "darkness" (v.12; cf.

v.6), also known as "the land of oblivion," because those who die are soon forgotten by men (cf. 6:5; 31:12; Eccl 9:5). The language of "death" is phenomenal. From the perspective of the psalmist, death is far from desirable. He longs for the Lord's full deliverance and his covenant mercy. He is asking how he can praise the Lord for his fidelity if he is to be counted among "the dead" (*r^e^pā'îm,* v.10; see TWOT, 2:858).

Notes

10 (11 MT) The word רְפָאִים (*r^e^pā'îm,* "the dead") occurs in the Ugaritic texts, and its meaning has given rise to three major interpretations: they are (1) gods, (2) shades of dead people, and (3) living human beings. According to Conrad E. L'Heureux (*Rank Among the Canaanite Gods: El, Ba'al and the Repha'im* [Scholars, 1979]), they were major gods in the Ugaritic pantheon (pp. 227–30). In the biblical context the word has undergone a change. In the Hebrew texts it may first have denoted "an aristocracy among the dead" (Isa 14:9) and then become a general designation for "the dead" (Job 26:5; Ps 88:10; Isa 26:14, 19; see *Rank Among the Canaanite Gods,* p. 222).

V. It Is the Lord's Doing

88:13–14

13 But I cry to you for help, O LORD;
in the morning my prayer comes before you.
14 Why, O LORD, do you reject me
and hide your face from me?

13–14 The anxiety of faith comes through in these verses. The psalmist commits himself wholly to the Lord: "but I cry to you" (v.13). Though in his torment he has called on the Lord "every day" (v.9), he keeps on bringing his petitions before him "in the morning" (cf. 5:3; 30:5; 55:17). The very frequency and insistency of prayer marks the psalmist as a godly man who believes in the Lord's righteousness and fidelity toward his own (cf. vv.10–12). The question of faith is "why" (v.14) the Lord has abandoned him to sorrow and grief.

The psalmist raises the question of God's anger, resulting in alienation and the absence of his blessing (cf. 10:1; 13:1; 27:9; 74:1; 77:7; 89:38). The depth of despair is most acutely experienced by those who have tasted the goodness of God and the closeness of communion with him. Those who are strangers to this relationship with God may experience adversity and despair, but their despair is oriented to anthropocentric, not theocentric, concerns.

VI. The Experience of Dying in Life

88:15–18

15 From my youth I have been afflicted and close to death;
I have suffered your terrors and am in despair.
16 Your wrath has swept over me;
your terrors have destroyed me.

17 All day long they surround me like a flood;
they have completely engulfed me.
18 You have taken my companions and loved ones
from me;
the darkness is my closest friend.

15–18 The lament concludes by tying together the major themes. First, the psalmist has suffered for a very long time ("from my youth," v.15). Second, he is completely engulfed by adversity, not seeing any way of escape ("swept over me. . . . surround me . . . completely engulfed me," vv.16–17; cf. 42:7). Third, he is exhausted to the point of "despair" because of his inability to cope with the Lord's "terrors" (v.15; cf. 55:4–5) and acts of "wrath" (v.16). Fourth, he knows that the Lord is sovereign even in calamity (v.18). Fifth, he is abandoned to himself and to his God. All alone he prays for deliverance, having no other recourse, not even his "closest friend" (v.18; cf. v.8).

Though the psalm ends on a lament, faith triumphs, because in everything the psalmist has learned to look to "the God who saves" (v.1). The "darkness" (v.18; cf. v.12) of grief is reminiscent of death; but as long as there is life, hope remains focused on the Lord. Brueggemann is right when he writes, "Psalm 88 stands as a mark of realism of biblical faith. It has a pastoral use, because there are situations in which easy, cheap talk of resolution must be avoided" (*Message of the Psalms*, p. 81).

Notes

---

15 (16 MT) The phrase עָנִי אֲנִי (*ʿānî ʾanî*, "I have been afflicted"; lit., "afflicted I") is a play on words. See 86:1.

16 (17 MT) The word "wrath," in the plural—חֲרוֹנֶיךָ (*ḥarôneyḵā*)—may be an example of the plural of intensification ("great wrath," see GKC, par. 124e) or of specification ("your acts of wrath"). In view of the parallelism with "terrors," the two words are complementary: God's acts of wrath inspire him with terror.

Appendix: Sheol-Grave-Death in the Psalms

What do the Psalms say about death and dying? Some have concluded from the emphasis on living and the sparse references to life after death in the Psalms that the psalmists had little understanding of the life hereafter. It is true that at first glance this conclusion seems justified. But it shows little understanding for the cultural context and for the covenantal understanding of life in the Psalms.

First, the psalmists were opposed to the world of pagan mythology with its system of beliefs. The people of God in the OT continually faced mythological concepts. The nations believed in gods who controlled defined areas in heaven, on earth, and under the earth. One of those areas was the netherworld, Sheol, that is, the place of the dead. Over against the belief that a god or gods have control over Sheol, the OT clearly teaches that man's death is appointed by the Lord, who is King over heaven, earth, and even the deepest recesses of the earth (cf. Ps 139).

Second, the psalmists do not deny existence after death but celebrate life within the covenant fellowship. Covenant life is lived under the umbrella of God's kingship and with the promise of his presence in blessing and protection. Therefore they look expectantly to the Lord to be true to his promises, confirmed to Abraham and to Moses. God had called the covenant community to be a *living* witness: a kingdom of priests and a royal nation (Exod 19:5–6). The witness of Israel in this life was not only polemical in nature but also a defense of their faith in Yahweh. His name was directly connected with the well-being of his people, as their happiness witnessed to the glory of their God.

Israel's sorrows raise questions as to God's ability to care for them. The nations were all too aware of this, as they often taunted Israel with the sarcastic taunt: "Where is your God?" Hence the psalmists affirm the importance of "life" as a witness to the ungodly. Life is important! Each individual in Israel was an important reflection of God's glory. The place of God's people as a witness to the Lord explains the emphasis on the present, the urgency, and the expressions of confidence in Yahweh.

Third, the psalmists face the problem of death. Death is a problem in God's world. Death is appalling and ghastly. The reason for the realistic expression of death in the Psalms must be appreciated, considering that death is morbid and unnatural (55:4).

Fourth, the psalmists show generally little interest in eschatology in the narrow sense, that is, how the future will unfold. The psalmists have a theocentric understanding of eschatology. For them eschatology opens up the future of God's promises. They affirm that Yahweh alone is God and that no other power in heaven and on earth opens up the future. They witness to the hope in the grand fulfillment of God's promises, while faithfully submitting to God's freedom in working out his plans. For them the acts of God in Creation and in redemption reveal a glimpse of the fulfillment of God's promises. They praised the Lord for his acts in Creation and redemption, for his revelation, for his enthronement in Zion, and for his having chosen David's dynasty. They prayed for relief from disaster, curse, oppression, and injustice; for God's vengeance on the wicked; and for the vindication of the godly.

The psalmists help us to look at Yahweh, the great and powerful King. He will completely deliver his oppressed people: "yet for your sake we face death all day long; / we are considered as sheep to be slaughtered" (44:22). He is the Redeemer: "But God will redeem my life from the grave; / he will surely take me to himself" (49:15). So also:

> Though you have made me see troubles, many and bitter,
>   you will restore my life again;
> from the depths of the earth
>   you will again bring me up.
>
> (71:20)

The godly also hope that in the end the wicked will be no more; that the kingdom of God will be fully established; and that theirs will be the freedom, peace, and joys of which they have been deprived in life. The wicked will experience an eternity of time in alienation from God and the godly in God's blessed presence (49:14; cf. 55:15, 23). This explains why the psalmist can say, "No one remembers you when he is dead. / Who praises you from the grave?" (6:5). The children of God may experience a living death, as they experience alienation and vexations of life in God's world: "From my youth I have been afflicted and close to death; / I have suffered your terrors and am in despair" (88:15; cf. 9:13; 31:17; 116:3). Suffering in life may be metaphorically described as a struggle of life and death:

> The cords of death entangled me;
>   the torrents of destruction overwhelmed me.
> The cords of the grave coiled around me;
>   the snares of death confronted me.
>
> (18:4–5; cf. 28:1)

When Yahweh prevails the people of God rejoice in his act of deliverance:

> I will exalt you, O LORD,
> for you lifted me out of the depths
> and did not let my enemies gloat over me.
> . . . .
> O LORD, you brought me up from the grave;
> you spared me from going down into the pit.
>
> (30:1, 3)

The psalms celebrate *life,* redeemed from the dangers of this world and evidencing the victory and power of Yahweh (40:2).

Thus far I have not said much about the OT belief in the world hereafter. The reason is that Scripture, including the NT, says little about it. Both OT and NT affirm the hope of the godly in enjoying God's goodness and presence in greater ways than we can imagine. The OT saints were not bereft of this hope! If we approach the psalms as reflections on life of the people of God in this world, we meet real people, who face suffering, injustice, anguish, despair, and death. Rather than submit passively, as it were to the God of Islam, they wrestled with the Lord, questioning his promises. In the process of wrestling, faith triumphed and gained a many-faceted brilliance. For example, the psalmist exclaims:

> For you have delivered me from death
> and my feet from stumbling,
> that I may walk before God
> in the light of life.
>
> (56:13)

This is the victory of faith, which triumphs through hardship (cf. 69:2; 88:3).

In all their varied expressions of death and life, judgment and vindication, curse and blessing, the psalmists confess that Yahweh is the Author of life, the King, and the Redeemer: "What man can live and not see death, / or save himself from the power of the grave?" (89:48). He does come to the succor of his beloved (94:13–14; cf. 103:4; 116:8). He is the hope of his people in life: "But my eyes are fixed on you, O Sovereign LORD; / in you I take refuge—do not give me over to death" (141:8). Even in death Yahweh is there: "Precious in the sight of the Lord / is the death of his saints" (116:15). Further, the psalmist helps us to long for the everlasting presence with God, when we shall "see" him:

> One thing I ask of the Lord,
> this is what I seek:
> that I may dwell in the house of the LORD
> all the days of my life,
> to gaze upon the beauty of the LORD
> and to seek him in his temple.
>
> (27:4)

The NT affirms the terror of death while denying the sting of death. The sting of death has been removed since the resurrection of our Lord, to whom Peter applies the words of Psalm 16:8–11, saying, "But God raised him from the dead, freeing him from the agony of death, because it was impossible for death to keep its hold on him" (Acts 2:24; cf. 2:25–28). Therefore the Christian has greater reason for living this life in the power of the resurrection of our Lord. Further, he also has a greater confidence in facing that great enemy, death, because of the victory of Jesus Christ: "But thanks be to God! He gives us the victory through our Lord Jesus Christ" (1 Cor 15:57).

The Psalms use several words for death: *šᵉʾôl* ("grave" in NIV), *ʾᵃḇaddôn* ("destruction"), *māweṯ* ("death"), *bôr* ("pit"), *taḥtîyôṯ* ("the lowest parts [depths] of the earth"), *maḥšāḵ* ("darkness"), *dûmāh* ("silence"), and *šaḥaṯ* ("pit," "corruption").

sheol (*šᵉʾôl*, "grave" in NIV)

The essential concept of Sheol is the place of the dead, the grave. The OT does not theorize on the state of life after death. It does not suggest that the godly and wicked dead live together until the Judgment. When the psalmist refers to Sheol, he thinks of the tomb, the place where speaking, laughing, and the praise of God are absent. R.L. Harris describes Sheol correctly as "a typical Palestinian tomb, dark, dusty, with mingled bones and where 'this poor lisping stammering tongue lies silent in the grave' " (TWOT, 2:893).

ʾᵃḇaddôn ("destruction")

The word occurs in parallelism with Sheol (Prov 15:11; 27:20) and "grave" (*qeḇer*, Ps 88:11). From its usage it appears that *ʾᵃḇaddôn* denotes the place of the dead in which the physical body undergoes dissolution. In Revelation 9:11 Abaddon is personified as Satan, the cause of death, destruction, and chaos in this world.

māweṯ ("death")

The Hebrew word is attested in other Semitic languages for the state of being dead, for the place of the dead, and for the god ruling over the netherworld. For example, in the Ugaritic literature Mot is the god over the netherworld. It is uncertain to what extent the Hebrew word for "death" may contain an allusion to the Canaanite conception of Mot as a god. Though Dahood made an attempt (*Psalms*, XVI–XVII), his views have not received general acceptance.

bôr ("pit")

The "pit" is a frequent synonym of Sheol, the grave (88:3; Prov 1:12; Isa 14:15). In the "pit" people are powerless (88:4), held down by the slime and mud (40:2). The word is also found in construct as *bôr taḥtîyôṯ* ("lowest pit," 88:6).

taḥtîyôṯ ("the lowest parts [depths] of the earth")

In the ancient Near East, the lowest parts of the earth were commonly conceived of as a place of the shades or departed spirits. It was a gloomy, cavernous place. However, from the use in the Psalms, elsewhere in the OT, and the synonyms, it appears that the Hebraic use has demythologized the pagan associations. It denotes nothing more than the grave, the place of the dead (88:6).

dûmāh ("silence")

"Silence" denotes "the" place of silence, namely the grave. This word is rare and occurs in 94:17 and 115:17 with this meaning.

maḥšāḵ ("darkness")

This word is synonymous with "lowest pit" (*bôr taḥtîyôṯ*) in 88:6 and the place of the dead in 143:3. As a psychological expression it denotes alienation from friends and acquaintances (88:18).

šaḥaṯ ("pit," "corruption")

The problem of derivation complicates the etymology of this word. Is it related to *š-w-ḥ* ("sink down," BDB, p. 1001), *ḥ-w-h* ("bow down"), or to *š-ḥ-t* ("destroy"). The NIV renders the word generally by "pit." Its frequency (twenty-three times in OT) is mainly in the poetic sections of the OT (nine times in Pss; seven times in Job). Sometimes it has the meaning of "pit" (7:15), by which someone gets trapped, in parallelism with "net" (9:15; 35:7). Other times *šaḥaṯ* takes on the meaning of "destruction" or "corruption," the place of the wicked (49:23 [NIV, "decay"]; 55:23). It is also associated with the biblical doctrine of divine retribution in that the "pit" dug by the wicked to trap the righteous will be their fall: "you grant him relief from days of trouble, / till a pit is dug for the wicked" (94:13). The psalmist affirms hope in Yahweh's ability to deliver him from all human entanglements ("the pit"):

> What gain is there in my destruction,
> in my going down into the pit?
> Will the dust praise you?
> Will it proclaim your faithfulness?
>
> (30:9; cf. 16:10)

Texts: 6:5; 16:9–11; 18:4–5; 22:15; 28:1; 30:3, 9; 49:14–15; 55:4, 15, 23; 56:13; 69:15; 72:13; 88:3–6, 11, 15, 18; 116:3, 8, 15; 143:7.

Related Topics: See appendixes to Pss 7 (The Name of Yahweh); 25 (The Perfections of Yahweh); 78 (The Mighty Acts of Yahweh); 98 (Yahweh Is the Divine Warrior); 119 (Yahweh Is My Redeemer); 122 (The Praise of Yahweh); 137 (Imprecations in the Psalms); 140 (The Poor and Oppressed).

Bibliography: T.D. Alexander, "The Psalms and the Afterlife," *Irish Biblical Studies* 9 (1987): 2–17; Lloyd R. Bailey, Sr., "Death as a Theological Problem in the Old Testament," *Pastoral Psychology,* 22, 218 (1971): 20–32; id., *Biblical Perspectives on Death* (Philadelphia: Fortress, 1979); K.F. Barth, *Die Errettung vom Tode in den individuellen Klage- und Dankliedern des Alten Testamentes* (Zollikon: Evangelischer Verlag, 1947); H. Birkeland, "Belief in the Resurrection of the Dead in the Old Testament," ST 3 (1950): 60–78; J.B. Burns, "The Mythology of Death in the Old Testament," SJT 26 (1973): 327–40; M. Dahood, *Psalms,* 3:41–52; W. Eichrodt, TOT, 210–28, 496–529; Manfred Görg, " 'Scheol'—Israels Unterweltsbegriff und seine Herkunft," *Biblische Notizer* 17 (1982): 26–34; R.L. Harris, "The Meaning of the Word Sheol as Shown by Parallels in Poetic Texts," JETS 4 (1961): 129–35; A. Heidel, "Death and Afterlife in the OT," in *The Gilgamesh Epic* (Chicago: University of Chicago, 1949), pp. 137–223; Conrad L'Heureux, *Rank Among the Canaanite Gods: El, Ba'al and the Repha'im;* id., "The Ugaritic and Biblical Rephaim," pp. 265–74; Walter Kaiser, *Toward Rediscovering the Old Testament* (Grand Rapids: Zondervan, 1987), pp. 141–44; Hans-Joachim Kraus, "Vom Leben und Tod in den Psalmen. Eine Studie zu Calvins Psalmen-Kommentar," in *Biblisch-theologische Aufsatze* (Neukirchen: Neukirchener, 1972), pp. 258–77; Thomas J. Long, "Life After Death: The Biblical View," TBT 20 (1982): 347–53; J. Pedersen, *Israel I–II, Israel: Its Life and Culture* (London: Cambridge, 1926), pp. 99–181; M. Pope, "The Word שַׁחַת in Job 9:31," JBL 83 (1964): 269–78; G. von Rad, OTT, 1:387–91; Léonard Ramaroson, "Immortalité et Résurrection dans les Psaumes, *Science et Esprit* 36 (1984): 287–95; Armin Schmitt, "Der frühe Tod des Gerechten nach Weish 4,7–19, Ein Psalmthema in weisheitlicher Fassung," *Freude an der Weisung des Herrn, Beiträge zur Theologie der Psalmen, Festgabe zum 70. Geburtstag von Heinrich Gross,* edd. Ernst Haag and Frank-Lothar Hossfeld (Stuttgart: Katholisches Bibelwerk, 1986), pp. 325–47; E.B. Smick, "The Bearing of New Philological Data on the Subjects of Resurrection and Immortality in the OT," WTJ 31 (1969): 12–21; Hans-Peter Stähli, "Tod und Leben im Alten Testament," *Theologie und Glaube* 76 (1986): 173–92; Nicholas J. Tromp, *Primitive Conceptions of Death and the Nether World in the Old Testament,* Biblica et Orientalia 21 (Rome: Pontifical Biblical Institute, 1969); W.A. VanGemeren, "Sheol," in Elwell, EDT, pp. 1011–12; Bruce Vawter, "Intimations of Immortality and the Old Testament," JBL 91 (1972): 158–71.

TDNT, 1:146–48; TDOT, 1:19–23; THAT, 1:117–20; 1:893–96; 2:841–43; TWOT, 1:3–4, 87–88, 331, 496–97; 2:892–93, 911, 918.

Psalm 89: Will You Reject Us Forever?

There is little agreement on the type or genre of the psalm. Depending on conclusions on date and nature of the compilation, scholars also vary on the interpretation of the function of the psalm. Dates vary from pre-722 B.C. to late postexilic. Some posit a liturgical use (Weiser, p. 591), whereas others view the psalmist as a borrower of earlier materials, refashioning them into a magnificent celebration of the Davidic monarchy and concluding with a prayer that the Lord soon may restore the dynasty of David (A.A. Anderson, 2:630). R.J. Clifford persuasively concludes in favor of the unity of the psalm as a psalm of lament ("Psalm 89: A Lament Over the Davidic Ruler's Continued Failure," HTR 73 [1980]: 35–47). Timo Veijola concludes from vv.25, 37, 43 that the psalm reflects the royal theology of David and may be dated no earlier than the seventh century B.C. ("Davidverheissung und Staatsvertrag. Beobachtungen zum Einfluss altorientalischer Staatsverträge auf die biblische Sprache am Beispiel von Psalm 89," ZAW 95 [1983]: 9–31; see also his more extensive analysis in *Verheissung in der Krise. Studien zur Literatur und Theologie der Exilszeit anhand des 89. Psalms* [Helsinki: Suomalainen Tiedeakatemia, 1982]).

The psalm falls into three parts: (1) the Lord's kingship (vv.1–18); (2) the covenant with David (vv.19–37); and (3) a lament (vv.38–51). The concluding verse (v.52) forms a doxological conclusion of the third book (Pss 73–89). The first section is in the form of a hymn, the second conforms to that of an oracle, whereas the last section is a lament. Though the psalmist may have made an original contribution, it is not unreasonable to propose that he may have fashioned existing elements into a new whole. For a detailed study, see Dennis Pardee, "The Semantic Parallelism of Psalm 89" (*In the Shelter of Elyon. Essays on Ancient Palestinian Life and Literature in Honor of G.W. Ahlstrom,* edd. W. Boyd Barrick and John R. Spencer [Sheffield: JSOT, 1984]: pp. 121–37).

The structural components of each major division may further be delineated.

I. A Hymn of Yahweh's Kingship (vv.1–18)
  A. Individual Praise of Yahweh's Kingship (vv.1–2)
    B. Yahweh's Fidelity to David (vv.3–4)
      C. Heavenly Praise of Yahweh's Kingship (vv.5–8)
      C′. Yahweh's Universal Rule (vv.9–13)
    B′. Yahweh's Fidelity and Congregational Praise (vv.14–18)

II. The Covenant With David (vv.19–37)
  A. Word of Promise (vv.19–29)
    1. Choice of David (vv.19–23)
      2. Promise of universal reign (vv.24–25)
      2′. Promise of messianic reign (vv.26–27)
    1′. Choice of descendants (vv.28–29)
  B. Word of Warning (vv.30–37)
    1. Warning (vv.30–32)
      2. Affirmation of love (vv.33–34)
        3. Affirmation of promised word (vv.35–37)

III. A Lament (vv.38–51)
  A. Complaints Against God (vv.38–45)
    B. Questions and Petitions (vv.46–51)

IV. Doxology (v.52)

I. A Hymn of Yahweh's Kingship (vv.1–18)

A. *Individual Praise of Yahweh's Kingship*

89:1–2

A *maskil* of Ethan the Ezrahite.

1 I will sing of the LORD's great love forever;
with my mouth I will make your faithfulness known
through all generations.
2 I will declare that your love stands firm forever,
that you established your faithfulness in heaven itself.

1–2 The theme of this portion of the psalm is in praise of the acts of the Lord's "great love" (*ḥeseḏ*, plural in MT, v.1). The love of God is constant ("faithful"), as promised and confirmed in the covenant (cf. v.3; Isa 55:3). His commitment to David is further guaranteed by his rule over "heaven" (v.2). The Lord has established his "faithfulness" to David far from the changes characteristic of this earthly scene. The future lies in God who himself has established his "love" and "faithfulness in heaven itself." (See the appendix to Ps 25: The Perfections of Yahweh.)

Praise is also appropriate because God's fidelity lasts "forever" and is therefore independent of man's responsiveness. Though God holds man responsible (cf. vv.30–32), ultimately the Lord will freely work out his acts of "love" and "faithfulness" (*'ᵉmûnāh*). The promises (vv.33–37), the acts of "love," and the guarantee of fulfillment give rise to an outburst of song. The psalmist sings praise to the Lord, proclaiming ("make . . . known," v.1; cf. 71:15; 109:30; 145:21) the Lord's continuing fidelity (v.1; see appendix to Ps 122: The Praise of Yahweh).

Notes

For a brief discussion of the technical words and phrases in the superscription, see the Introduction.

1 (2 MT) The LXX and Theodotion read "your acts of love" for the MT's חַסְדֵי (*ḥasḏê*, "acts of love"), suggesting a parallel reading with "your faithfulness." The words *ḥeseḏ* ("love," vv.1–2, 14, 24, 28, 33, 49) and *'ᵉmûnāh* ("faithfulness," vv.1–2, 5, 8, 24, 33, 49) occur seven times in Psalm 89.

2 (3 MT) The place and function of אָמַרְתִּי (*'āmartî*, "I said") is disputed. The LXX reads it as God's word: "you said." BHS proposes a transposition at the end of v.3 (cf. RSV). The NIV instead keeps to the MT in v.2 ("I will declare") and adds "you said" to the beginning of v.3.

The LXX and Theodotion read תִּכֹּן (*tikkōn*, "[your faithfulness] is established") instead of the MT's תָּכִן (*tāḵin*, "you established [your faithfulness]").

B. *Yahweh's Fidelity to David*

89:3–4

3 You said, "I have made a covenant with my chosen one,
I have sworn to David my servant,
4 'I will establish your line forever
and make your throne firm through all generations.' "

3–4 Yahweh is committed to David, his "chosen one" (*bᵉḥîrî*) and "servant" (*ʿaḇdî*). The former designation serves to emphasize the special relationship, as the king is elected by Yahweh himself to serve as his vassal (cf. 2 Sam 21:6b; Ps 106:23). The term "servant" emphasizes the special role of being Yahweh's representative to the people (see 19:11). The king is elected by God for the sake of executing his will on earth (vv.3, 20, 39, 50; cf. Pss 2; 72; 78:70–72; 2 Sam 7:5, 8, 19–21, 25–29).

The relationship between David and the Lord was guaranteed by "covenant" (*bᵉrîṯ*), made by oath. Even when the party with whom the Lord makes the covenant breaks the terms, its binding nature obligates the Lord to fulfill its terms (cf. vv.34–35). The pledge to David is also extended to his descendants (v.4) and thereby to the future generations of subjects. The Lord himself will secure the rule of the Davidic dynasty. He will "establish" and "make firm" (cf. v.2).

C. *Heavenly Praise of Yahweh's Kingship*

89:5–8

5 The heavens praise your wonders, O LORD,
your faithfulness too, in the assembly of the holy ones.
6 For who in the skies above can compare with the LORD?
Who is like the LORD among the heavenly beings?
7 In the council of the holy ones God is greatly feared;
he is more awesome than all who surround him.
8 O LORD God Almighty, who is like you?
You are mighty, O LORD, and your faithfulness
surrounds you.

5–8 The Lord has "established" his love "in heaven" (v.2). Heaven is not jealous of the special privileges bestowed on David's rule over the earth because it rejoices in God's kingship (see appendix to Ps 5: Yahweh Is King). The rule of God is unquestioned by "the holy ones" (*qᵉḏōšîm*, vv.5, 7; cf. 82:1), who are the "heavenly beings" (lit., "sons of God," v.6). They praise the Lord for his "wonders" (cf. 77:11; 88:10) and "faithfulness" (cf. v.1).

The threefold rhetorical question—"who . . . can compare," "who is like," and "who is like?" (vv.6, 8)—forces a confession of the undisputable rights, sovereignty, and exaltation of Yahweh (see C.J. Labuschagne, *The Incomparability of Yahweh in the Old Testament* [Leiden: Brill, 1966]). He is "greatly feared," "awesome," and "mighty" (vv.7–8). The heavenly hosts serve him willingly as he is "God Almighty" ("God of Hosts," i.e., the sovereign over the heavenly armies; cf. 24:10; 59:5; see appendix to Ps 24: Lord Sabaoth). The heavenly beings constantly stand in awe of the splendor of the Lord (v.7). Since the heavenly beings inspire humans with awe (cf. Judg 13:22), how much more awesome is the Lord who inspires the heavenly beings with awe!

Notes

7 (8 MT) Heinz-Josef Fabry argues that סוד (*sôḏ*, "council," "sweet fellowship"; cf. 25:14; 111:1) is an ecclesiological term, synonymous with "congregation" ("Der himmlische Thronrat als ekklesiologisches Modell," *Bausteine biblischer Theologie. Festgabe für G.*

Johannes Botterweck zum 60. Geburtstag dargebracht von seinen Schülern, ed. H.J. Fabry [Köln: Peter Hanstein, 1977], pp. 99–126).

The rendering "is greatly feared" is possible. The MT has רַבָּה (*rabbāh*, "great," a feminine form). Kraus proposes a masculine reading: "he is great" (*Psalmen*, 2:614).

D. *Yahweh's Universal Rule*

89:9–13

9 You rule over the surging sea;
when its waves mount up, you still them.
10 You crushed Rahab like one of the slain;
with your strong arm you scattered your enemies.
11 The heavens are yours, and yours also the earth;
you founded the world and all that is in it.
12 You created the north and the south;
Tabor and Hermon sing for joy at your name.
13 Your arm is endued with power;
your hand is strong, your right hand exalted.

9–13 The power and constancy of Yahweh's rule is also found on earth. His rule extends even to the wild and foaming sea, which in Canaanite mythology was under Baal's control (cf. 46:2; 74:13). The sea, personified by the name "Rahab" (v.10; cf. Job 26:12; Isa 51:9), is a fallen hero. Rahab, possibly identical with Leviathan (cf. 74:14; 104:26), represents any overt expression of hostility, such as that of the Egyptians (cf. 87:4; Isa 30:7; Ezek 29:3; 32:2), who were defeated at the Red Sea (cf. Exod 14:15). Yahweh's power is unlimited whether at sea, in heaven, or on earth (vv.10–11). His "love" (*ḥesed*) extends both to creation and to the messianic kingdom, represented by David. God's acts in creation are correlative to his acts in salvation, or what von Rad calls a "soteriological understanding of creation" (OTT, 1:138).

The Lord's sovereignty over the earth was established at Creation. He created everything, that is, the extremities of "the north" (or Mount Zaphon, see 48:2) and "the south" (LXX, "the sea," v.12). Reference is particularly made to "[mounts] Tabor and Hermon." Mount Hermon is located to the north of Israel's northernmost tribe (Dan), reaches an altitude of nearly 10,000 feet, and has abundant sources of water that form streams and waterfalls (cf. 42:6). Some fifty miles to the southwest lies Tabor, which, at the height of only 1,800 feet, is nevertheless majestic in its own geographical landscape. These mounts join together with all creation in praising the Lord. All creation witnesses to his dominion, strength, and victorious rule, symbolized by "your strong arm," "your arm," "your hand," and "your right hand" (vv.10, 13; cf. Exod 15:6, 9, 12, 16). Creation too recognizes his sovereignty (cf. 1 Cor 10:26).

Notes

10 (11 MT) On Rahab and Leviathan, see the Notes on 74:13.

E. *Yahweh's Fidelity and Congregational Praise*

89:14–18

14 Righteousness and justice are the foundation
of your throne;
love and faithfulness go before you.
15 Blessed are those who have learned to acclaim you,
who walk in the light of your presence, O LORD.
16 They rejoice in your name all day long;
they exult in your righteousness.
17 For you are their glory and strength,
and by your favor you exalt our horn.
18 Indeed, our shield belongs to the LORD,
our king to the Holy One of Israel.

14 Not only is the Lord's rule characterized by strength, he is also wise and loving in his exercise of kingship. His rule is full of "righteousness and justice" (cf. 33:5; 97:2). There is no evil, injustice, or despotism in his rule. More than that, he is also full of "love and faithfulness" (cf. vv.1, 8; 88:11; see appendix to Ps 25: The Perfections of Yahweh).

15–18 The subjects of the Lord's rule thrive under his administration. They are the "blessed" (v.15; cf. 1:1) and join with creation in praise of the Redeemer (v.16; cf. v.12). Unlike creation the people of God benefit from his personal presence ("the light of your presence," v.15), his "righteousness" (v.16), exaltation ("you exalt our horn," v.17), and his protection ("our shield belongs to the LORD, v.18). The true subjects are those who have learned to exult in his name (vv.15–16), rely on his favor (vv.15–18), acknowledge his sovereignty ("our king," v.18), and respond to his holy presence ("the Holy One of Israel," v.18; see appendix to Ps 5: Yahweh Is King).

Notes

16 (17 MT) M. Dahood's proposal of changing "they exult" (*yārûmû*) to a divine epithet is largely based on a supposed parallel construction: "Yahweh . . . O Exalted" ("The Composite Divine Name in Psalms 89, 16–17 and 140, 9," *Biblica* 61 [1980]: 277–78).

18 (19 MT) For the dubious meaning "suzerain" or "sovereign" (NIV mg.) for "shield," see 7:10.

II. The Covenant With David (vv.19–37)

These verses share words and thoughts with 2 Samuel 7:4–17. The exact relationship is not clear. Possibly both passages come from a common source. The covenant with David was a further development of the Abrahamic and Sinaitic covenants, in its focus on David and the eternal rule of David's dynasty. Those who are in Christ share in the benefits of his regime and, hence, in the promises.

A. *Word of Promise (vv.19–29)*

1. *Choice of David*

89:19–23

19 Once you spoke in a vision,
to your faithful people you said:
"I have bestowed strength on a warrior;
I have exalted a young man from among the people.
20 I have found David my servant;
with my sacred oil I have anointed him.
21 My hand will sustain him;
surely my arm will strengthen him.
22 No enemy will subject him to tribute;
no wicked man will oppress him.
23 I will crush his foes before him
and strike down his adversaries.

19–20 The Lord revealed through the prophet Nathan "in a vision" (v.19; cf. 2 Sam 7:4) that he had chosen David to be his "servant," anointed with "sacred oil" (v.20; cf. 2:2; Exod 30:25; 1 Sam 16:1, 12–13). The choice of David is not inherent in the man himself but in the Lord's free election (cf. Acts 13:22). The Lord "exalted" him, bestowing on him *'ēzer* (v.19, "help"; NIV, "strength"). The Lord has raised up a mighty man to be a warrior for his people and has encouraged his "faithful people."

21–23 These verses complement Psalm 2, where the Lord's anointed receives full authority to subjugate all resistance of God's enemies on earth. The real source of David's power and authority lies in the Lord's presence and purpose.

The mighty "hand" and "arm" of the Lord (v.21; cf. vv.10, 13) strengthened David (cf. 1 Sam 18:12, 14; 2 Sam 5:10) in all his exploits. No one could say that David was strong by himself. The goal of the Lord's succor was to extend his dominion over earth. Since his purposes stand, no power on earth can thwart him (vv.22–23).

Notes

19 (20 MT) It is not entirely clear who the "faithful" are. The phrase חֲסִידֶיךָ (*ḥ*^a^*sîḏeyḵā*, "your faithful ones") has been interpreted to denote the people of God (so NIV; Kirkpatrick, p. 537), the prophets (Kraus, *Psalmen*, p. 622), or the loyal remnant (NEB, "thy faithful servants"). A number of MSS read a singular form: "your faithful one," which would relate to David (cf. 4:3; NIV, "godly").

Dahood explains עֵזֶר (*'ēzer*) as a Ugaritic form of "lad": "I made a lad king" (*Psalms*, 2:316). See A.S. van der Woude, "Zwei alte *Cruces* im Psalter," *OudTestamentische Studiën* 13 (1963): 135–36. BHS suggests that *'ēzer* is a corruption for "crown" (*nēzer;* cf. v.39).

22 (23 MT) The etymology of the verb יַשִּׁא (*yaššiʾ*, "will subject to tribute") is uncertain. The NIV takes it to be from *n-š-'* (I, "to lend to"), whereas the homonym (II) means "to deceive" (BDB, p. 673b). The NEB follows KB, which lists the form under the root *š-w-'* ("to treat badly," p. 951a): "shall strike at him." This latter usage may be preferable in the light of the context: "oppress. . . . crush . . . strike down" (vv.22–23).

2. *Promise of universal reign*

89:24–25

> 24 My faithful love will be with him,
> and through my name his horn will be exalted.
> 25 I will set his hand over the sea,
> his right hand over the rivers.

24–25 The Lord himself will increase David's regime and cause it to flourish. His love and fidelity (cf. v.14b) will surround David so that the promises of the covenant will come to pass. They mirror on earth the nature and plan of Yahweh, whose name (v.24) reveals his love and fidelity. In his name all his promises toward David will be fulfilled. These divine perfections achieve all God's designs, including the exaltation and glorification of David.

The glory bestowed on David will ultimately be recognized by all nations. The Lord's "hand" (v.21) will set the king's "hand" (v.25) over the nations. The usage of "hand" signifies dominion, expressing that David's governance is by authority of the Lord himself. With "his right hand" (v.25, cf. v.13) David will rule over "the sea" and "the rivers," i.e., everything (cf. 72:8). The references to these bodies of water should not be limited to the Mediterranean to the west of Canaan and the Euphrates-Tigris rivers to the east (so Kirkpatrick, p. 538). It is a metaphorical portrayal of the same truth as given in Psalm 2, namely his dominion extends over the whole world (A.A. Anderson, 2:641).

Notes

24 (25 MT) For "horn" see the appendix to Psalm 98: Yahweh Is the Divine Warrior.

3. *Promise of messianic reign*

89:26–27

> 26 He will call out to me, 'You are my Father,
> my God, the Rock my Savior.'
> 27 I will also appoint him my firstborn,
> the most exalted of the kings of the earth.

26–27 The glory of the messianic ruler will also extend to his relationship with the Lord. He will be treated as a son rather than as a vassal or servant (cf. 2:7; 2 Sam 7:14). In this relationship he would more fully experience God's power of deliverance as "the Rock my Savior" (v.26; see 18:2; cf. 95:1; Deut 32:15). The uniqueness and success of the messianic reign lies precisely in the close relationship between the Lord and the Davidic ruler. In Jesus Christ this relationship has been made even firmer in that Jesus is "the" Son of God. Hence his rule will prosper (cf. Rev 1:5).

The primacy over the nations is given to the Davidic king. He is recognized as "my firstborn" (v.27), even as Israel is the "firstborn" of the Lord (Exod 4:22; cf. Jer 31:9; Rev 1:5). As the foremost leader David received special glory associated with his position. He is "the most exalted" (Elyon) among the nations, even as Yahweh is "the

Most High" (Elyon), Creator of heaven and earth (cf. Gen 14:19; Pss 18:13; 46:4; see appendix to Ps 9: Yahweh Is El Elyon).

In a special sense the privileges, promises, and covenants of Israel are conferred on David. Allegiance to David and acceptance of his position as the Lord's anointed is requisite for one's enjoyment of the covenant benefits. So it is also since the coming of our Lord. There can be no acceptance with the Father except through Jesus the Son.

4. *Choice of descendants*

89:28–29

28 I will maintain my love to him forever,
and my covenant with him will never fail.
29 I will establish his line forever,
his throne as long as the heavens endure.

28–29 The Lord renews his commitment to David in affirming, on the one hand, his "covenant" (*berît*) of "love" (*ḥesed*) and of "faithfulness" (*ne'emenet*, from '-*m*-*n*, as in '*emûnāh*, "faithfulness"; NIV, "will never fail"; cf. vv.14, 24). The fidelity and love of God extend "forever" (vv.28–29; emphatic in MT), from generation to generation ("his line," v.29; lit., "his seed") and "as the heavens endure" (lit., "as the days of the heavens"; cf. vv.36–37; Isa 65:17; 66:22; Deut 11:21; Matt 24:35). There can be no doubt in the choice of these words that the psalmist hereby stresses the lasting character of the rule of David's dynasty ("his throne").

B. *Word of Warning (vv.30–37)*

The Davidic covenant is a divine grant, assuring David's dynasty of glory, divine support, and continuity. The promises are conditional. The responsibility lies on each king of David's dynasty to fulfill his role as a representative of God's rule on earth.

1. *Warning*

89:30–32

30 "If his sons forsake my law
and do not follow my statutes,
31 if they violate my decrees
and fail to keep my commands,
32 I will punish their sin with the rod,
their iniquity with flogging;

30–32 Verses 30–31 form the protases (conditions), each verse beginning with "if" ('*im*). The apodasis (conclusion) is found in v.32. The Lord expects the Davidic king to be loyal to him. The expectation of keeping the law, statutes, decrees, and commands were imposed on all of Israel (cf. Deut 4:1, 14, 45; 6:1–9), but the Davidic king had to exemplify a godly walk (cf. Deut 17:14–20). If he was not steadfast in his devotion, he broke covenant (see appendix to Ps 19: The Word of God). "Sin" and "iniquity" (v.32) are expressions of rebellion against the Lord and hence deserving of divine judgment. The penalty for disobedience was severe. The Lord would not withhold "the rod" (cf. 2:9), a symbol of authority and an instrument of inflicting wounds. In light of the reference to the "mace," the "flogging" should be understood as "blows" or "assaults."

2. *Affirmation of love*

89:33–34

[33]but I will not take my love from him,
nor will I ever betray my faithfulness.
[34]I will not violate my covenant
or alter what my lips have uttered.

33–34 Yet the love of God outweighs his judgment. Though he may discipline even acrimoniously, his "love" (*ḥesed*, v.33; cf. v.28) will still extend to the offspring of David. Though man may show contempt for the covenant, the Lord will never "violate" (*ḥ-l-l*, v.34; cf. v.31) his own covenant. What he has promised by oath stands (v.34). In view of the emphasis on God's commitment to the covenant, the psalmist returns to this motif in the next section.

3. *Affirmation of promised word*

89:35–37

[35]Once for all, I have sworn by my holiness—
and I will not lie to David—
[36]that his line will continue forever
and his throne endure before me like the sun;
[37]it will be established forever like the moon,
the faithful witness in the sky." *Selah*

35–37 The emphasis lies on the fidelity of God. His commitment to David's place in the history of redemption is such that it is on a par with the heavens (cf. v.29), i.e., "the sun" and "the moon" (vv.36–37). The covenant with David is so important to the Lord that he swore by himself ("by my holiness," v.35; cf. Isa 45:23; Amos 6:8) that David's lineage will be seated on the "throne," symbol of divinely granted authority over the earth (cf. John 12:34).

Notes

36–37 (37–38 MT) E. Theodore Mullen, Jr., ("The Divine Witness and the Davidic Royal Grant: Ps 89:37–38," JBL 102 [1983]: 207–18) argues from the Near Eastern background that the "sun" and the "moon" are here demythologized to serve as witnesses to the covenant (cf. vv.5–8). Paul G. Mosca further develops Mullen's argument in favor of the function of the Davidic throne (with heavenly and immortal associations) as a witness ("Once Again the Heavenly Witness of Ps 89:38," JBL 105 [1986]: 27–37).

III. A Lament (vv.38–51)

The tone of the psalm changes with the introduction of an emphatic "but you" (v.38). Though the Lord had shown his "love" to David and his descendants and had promised to be like a father to David's offspring, the lamenter speaks of God as having judged his people too strongly. The lament contains both complaints and petitions, and the nature of the lament must always be appreciated in the light of the covenant promises.

A. *Complaints Against God*

89:38–45

38 But you have rejected, you have spurned,
you have been very angry with your anointed one.
39 You have renounced the covenant with your servant
and have defiled his crown in the dust.
40 You have broken through all his walls
and reduced his strongholds to ruins.
41 All who pass by have plundered him;
he has become the scorn of his neighbors.
42 You have exalted the right hand of his foes;
you have made all his enemies rejoice.
43 You have turned back the edge of his sword
and have not supported him in battle.
44 You have put an end to his splendor
and cast his throne to the ground.
45 You have cut short the days of his youth;
you have covered him with a mantle of shame. *Selah*

The verbs used in the complaint against the Lord betray the depth of emotions: "rejected," "spurned," "very angry," "renounced," "defiled," "broken through," "reduced to ruins," "put an end to," "cast . . . to the ground," "cut short," and "covered with shame." The precise historical context is unclear, whether it be exile or a period of national humiliation. In the experience of disgrace, the believer asks challenging questions, stating his case as strongly as possible. Perhaps the Lord will listen and respond to his petitions.

38–40 The primary concern lies with the broken covenant relationship. Whatever the occasion or however Israel or David's descendants may have sinned against the Lord seems not to be germane to the argument. The psalmist is deeply convinced that the Lord is more faithful than man, as the opening words serve to remind us of "the LORD's great love" (v.1). The God who decreed the Davidic covenant (v.19) has now "rejected" (v.38; cf. 43:2; 44:23; 77:7; 88:14) his "anointed one" (*māšîaḥ*). In his anger he seems completely unconcerned with "the covenant" made with David and with the glory associated with "his crown" (v.39; cf. Jer 13:18–19; Lam 5:16; Ezek 21:26–27; cf. also 2 Sam 1:10).

The acts of casting the crown into the dust, spurning the covenant, and destroying the fortifications (vv.39–40) would usually be associated with the activities of Israel's enemies. Here, however, God is the perpetrator of the hostile acts. How can these deeds be reconciled with his "love," "fidelity," and "covenant" celebrated in the hymn and oracle (vv.1–37)? The destruction of Israel's fortification system (v.40) and the cries and scorn of the enemies' victory leave God's people with little hope. God has abandoned his people; more than that, he has rejected the covenant of "love," i.e., the covenant with David.

41–44 Instead of coming to the support of his own people, the Lord has given victory to Israel's enemies. They "plundered" (v.41) and were irresistible because the Lord had raised their "right hand" (v.42; cf. Lam 2:15–17). With Israel's defeat David's crown and honor ("his throne," v.44; cf. in contrast 93:2) are cast to the ground.

45 It appears that the Lord flouts every promise made to David, including the perpetuity of his dynasty. With the disgrace caused by the enemies, the Davidic king as well as the future of the dynasty are cut short (cf. 102:23; Hos 7:9). The image of the "mantle of shame" denotes the disgrace of the Davidic dynasty, in contrast to the "garment of praise" (Isa 61:3; cf. 61:10; 62:3).

From the passion of the language and metaphors, one may associate the lament with the Exile (see Lamentations). Had not the Lord forewarned Solomon that if he or his descendants violated the covenant, the temple would be destroyed and the enemies would ridicule Israel (1 Kings 9:7–8)?

Yet the psalmist gives little hint of the destruction of the temple and Jerusalem's ultimate fall to Nebuchadnezzar. The spirit of the psalm may also express the postexilic frustration with the enemies and with the absence of the Davidic leadership.

Notes

---

44 (45 MT) Kraus gives an attractive reconstruction of the parallelism, though it is not convincing. Instead of הִשְׁבַּתָּ מִטְּהָרוֹ (*hišbattā mitṭ^ehārô*, "you have put an end to his splendor"), he proposes שָׁבַרְתָּ מַטֵּה הוֹדוֹ (*šābartā maṭṭēh hôḏô*, "you have broken the rod of his glory") or הִשְׁבַּרְתָּ מַטֵּה עֹז (*hišbartā maṭṭēh ʿōz*, "you have destroyed the mighty rod," *Psalmen*, 2:615).

B. *Questions and Petitions*

89:46–51

46 How long, O LORD? Will you hide yourself forever?
How long will your wrath burn like fire?
47 Remember how fleeting is my life.
For what futility you have created all men!
48 What man can live and not see death,
or save himself from the power of the grave? *Selah*
49 O Lord, where is your former great love,
which in your faithfulness you swore to David?
50 Remember, Lord, how your servant has been mocked,
how I bear in my heart the taunts of all the nations,
51 the taunts with which your enemies have mocked,
O LORD,
with which they have mocked every step of your
anointed one.

46–51 The questions are interchanged with a petition to "remember":

How long. . . ?
Will you hide. . . ?
How long will your wrath burn. . . ?
Remember. . . .

What man can live. . . ?
Where is your former great love. . . ?
Remember.

The questions bring out the intensity of the agony (cf. 79:5; 88:10–12, 14). If the Lord continues to hide his face (v.46) and to maintain his displeasure ("wrath"), faith and hope may become despair. Hence he asks "How long?" and prays to the Lord to remember that his people are human (v.47).

The phrase "how fleeting is my life" (v.47) underscores the need, as the psalmist prays that the Lord renew his "love" during his lifetime. Instead of enjoying God's acts of his "former great love" (*ḥ^asāḏeyḵā*, v.49) sworn to David (cf. vv.2–3), the people are perishing ("death," "grave" or Sheol, v.48; cf. 88:3–4, 10–12; see appendix to Ps 88: Sheol-Grave-Death in the Psalms). In his prayer he reminds the Lord of the mocking enemies (cf. v.41) by the repetition of the root *ḥ-r-p* (NIV, "has been mocked," "mocked," "have mocked," vv.50–51). The lament began with a description of the disgrace of God's "servant" (vv.38–41) and concludes with a reference to the present state of "scorn" (*ḥ-r-p*, vv.41, 50–51) and an allusion to God's promises by a repetition of the phrase "your anointed one" (vv.38, 51).

The psalmist believes that God's love is forever (cf. vv.1–4); yet he is fully aware that man, a creature of God, is subject to God's freedom. The psalm ends on a note of disorientation, a paradox with the opening affirmation of God's love. What a shocking contrast! Peter applies this truth to the suffering of the followers of the Messiah (1 Peter 4:14), who while heirs of the promises suffer persecution on earth.

Notes

---

50 (51 MT) The MT reading עֲבָדֶיךָ (*'^aḇāḏeyḵā*, "your servants") is supported by the LXX. A number of MSS and the context ("your anointed one," v.51) favor the singular, as in NIV's "your servant" (cf. Kraus, *Psalmen*, 2:615). If the plural is to be maintained, it could be a plural of excellence (Dahood, *Psalms*, 2:320). R. Tournay also concludes in favor of a singular but associates the "servant" with Jehoiachin ("Notes sur le Psaume LXXXIX, 51–52," RB 83 [1976]: 380–89).

IV. Doxology

89:52

52 Praise be to the LORD forever!
Amen and Amen.

52 The third book concludes on a doxology. In spite of the concluding questions raised by Psalm 89, the doxology affirms the necessity to praise the Lord as an appropriate response to all the circumstances in life (cf. 41:13; see Ernst Jenni, "Zu den doxologischen Schlussformeln des Psalters," *Theologische Zeitschrift* 40 [1984]: 114–20).

Appendix: The Messianic King

The "messianic psalms" celebrate the divine promises granted to the Davidic dynasty. The anointed king of David's dynasty represented God's kingdom on earth, as Zimmerli writes, "The king of Israel makes the domain of Yahweh visible on earth" (OTTO, p. 92). The Davidic representative of the Lord was the primary carrier of God's promises. Yet whatever is attributed to the Davidic king also applies to God's son, our Messiah! Calvin carefully interprets the text within its context, avoiding allegorical and typological exegesis (S.H. Russell, "Calvin and the Messianic Interpretation of the Psalms," SJT 21 [1968]: 37–47); but he also insists on relating the psalms to the progression of fulfillment. He writes: "If we attentively consider the nature of the kingdom, we will perceive that it would be absurd to overlook the end or scope, and to rest in the mere shadow . . . it is plainly made manifest from all the prophets, that those things which David testified concerning his own kingdom are properly applicable to Christ" (1:11–12). Beecher writes that the promises of God pertaining to David and his dynasty are eternal and hence cannot be restricted to any one fulfillment: "In their presentation of it the promise is not a mere forecast of a distant future, but is spiritual food for immediate use" (p. 394).

Kirkpatrick writes, "Poetry was the handmaid of prophecy in preparing the way for the coming of Christ. . . . The constant use of the Psalms for devotion and worship familiarised the people with them. Expectation was aroused and kept alive" (p. lxxvi). He defines the elements of hope in terms of (1) the Messiah being king and priest (Pss 2; 18; 20; 21; 45; 61; 72; 89; 110; 132); (2) the suffering of the Messiah (Pss 22; 35; 41; 55; 69; 109); (3) the Messiah as the Son of Man (Pss 8; 16; 40); and (4) the coming of Yahweh for the purposes of judgment and redemption (Pss 18; 50; 68; 96–98; 102), affecting the nations and all creation (8:1; 22:27–28; 24:1; 33:14; 46:10; 47:2, 8–9; 49:1; 65:5; 66; 67; 68:29–35; 72; 86:9; 94:10; 96:13; 98:9; 99:2; 102:15, 21–22; 103:4; 117; 138:4; 150:6). In these psalms the king prays, speaks, or is spoken about.

J.H. Eaton interprets the psalms from the perspective of the "royal ideal" by combining the prophetic and royal traditions: "In the end, then, we see prophecy and the royal institutions intertwined . . . for the people of the OT both were complementary appointments of God" (pp. 200–201). The "royal ideal" bears on the close relationship of Yahweh to the Davidic king, the privileged status of the king, his responsibilities to his people and to the world, and his role in worship, atonement, and witness (p. 199). The "royal ideal" also points to and applies to the life and ministry of our Lord on earth, his present heavenly ministry, and his appointed goal: the establishment of God's kingdom on earth.

Yes, hope was kept alive through the psalms. The godly awaiting the messianic age knew little as to how to bring the divergence together, but they awaited the coming of the Messiah, the Son of David, who alone could bring peace to this earth, establish the kingdom of God, deliver the righteous, and avenge the wicked. Since the kingdom of God and his Messiah are correlative, what pertains to the kingdom of God affects the kingdom of his Messiah.

1. The Relationship Between the Messiah and Yahweh

The OT writers freely adopted the mythopoetic language pertaining to the king, his rule, and his closeness to Yahweh; but he was not considered a divine king. Several psalms bear out the close relationship between Yahweh and his vassal-king. He is "the son" of God in a unique sense: "You are my Son; / today I have become your Father" (2:7; cf. 22:9–11; 71:6; 89:26–27; 139:15–16). He is a "son," but not divine. The fulfillment of God's promises is inseparable from his commitment to David (89:3, 20, 35; 132:1, 10, 17; 144:10; cf. 2 Sam 7). The Psalms and Prophets often speak of the messianic ideal and hence rouse hope in the Messiah, whose reign would bring in all the benefits Yahweh had promised to David. Philip J. King argues persuasively in favor of the messianic interpretation of Psalm 45. Beginning with 2 Samuel 7, which he designates "the Magna Charta of messianic interpretation," he develops the thesis of "an indissoluble union between the dynasty of David and the future Messiah" (p. 117).

The messianic King was receptive and responsive to the execution of the will of God on earth. He was instructed from his youth (71:17–18; cf. 27:1). The messianic King was wise and desired to increase in wisdom (72:1–3; cf. Isa 11:1–9). He desires to do the will of the Lord on earth (cf. 40:6–8; 143:10; Heb 10:5–10). So great is his zeal for Yahweh's kingdom that it "consumes" him with an all-consuming passion (69:9). He loves the Lord (18:1; 116:1), enjoys life by God's grace (63:1–4), and lives with the hope of constant communion with his covenant King (27:4; 73:28).

The failure, breach of covenant, and rebellion against the Suzerain occasion discipline (118:19), confession, and renewal of commitment (Pss 32; 51). The king too is subject to the discipline of Yahweh as his Father (2 Sam 7:14). Above all, the king recognizes the importance of constant transformation by the Spirit of God (51:11–12; cf. Isa 11:2; 42:1).

The Davidic king "administers" the kingdom of God as a vassal. He rules "in the name" of Yahweh. The royal administration of the Davidic king is representative of God's kingdom to the extent that the king brings in the kingdom in glory and power in accordance with the divine grant. Yahweh has revealed his name to his people, but in a more distinctive way to his king. All that the name signifies (the perfections, presence, blessings, and victorious deliverance) are given to the king by divine grant (72:18–19; cf. 54; 89:24; 91:14–15; 118:10–16). The Lord has endowed his messianic King with all that he needs to rule as his vassal.

The Lord is with his messianic King in protection and blessing. The king goes out in battle under the "banner" of Yahweh and returns victoriously with his banner (18:19; 72:8–11; 132:17–18). When not victorious he returns to his covenant Lord, praying for his favor (cf. 5:11–12; 86; 89).

Psalm 72 adumbrates in the most glowing terms the kingdom of David, but neither David nor any of his sons ever achieved the ideal. It is a prayer for the realization of a kingdom of righteousness and justice in which the people of God experience blessing, prosperity, and the very presence of God through his vassal-king. Eichrodt comments on this distinctive phenomenon: "In him (i.e., the Davidic king) men have before their eyes both the pledge and the beginning of the divine work of salvation" (TOT, 1:478). Kirkpatrick observes that the covenant with David is a further development of God's commitments to Abraham: "In glowing colours it depicts the ideal of his office, and prays that he may fulfill it as the righteous sovereign who redresses wrong, and may rule over a world-wide empire, receiving the willing homage of the nations to his virtue, and proving himself the heir of the patriarchal promise" (p. lxxviii).

Yahweh has made a covenant (*b*^{e}*rîṯ*, 89:3, 34, 39) with David and his descendants to grant them his "faithful love" (*'*^{e}*mûnāh; ḥeseḏ;* 89:2, 14, 24, 28, 33, 49). Even when he suspends the covenant privileges in his freedom, Yahweh reassures the king that his covenant is lasting (89:33–37).

God's covenant with David, and as such his commitment to the messianic kingdom, is also established in his covenant with creation. The psalmist in Psalm 89 correlates God's "love" (*ḥeseḏ*) and "faithfulness" (*'*^{e}*mûnāh*) revealed in creation to that granted to David's dynasty (vv.1–8). The continuity of creation witnesses to the certainty of God's commitment to David. This verity is still true, as all things created and sustained by and for our Lord Jesus witness to his present rule (Col 1:15–23)! I believe that C.S. Lewis grasped the significance of Christmas, for he wrote on Psalm 45: "The birth of Christ is the arrival of the great warrior and the great king. Also of the Lover, the Bridegroom, whose beauty surpasses that of man. But not only the Bridegroom as the lover, the desired; the Bridegroom also who makes fruitful, the Father of children still to be begotten and born" (***Reflections on the Psalms***, p. 130).

2. The Suffering Messiah

The messianic King suffers reproaches and humiliation in the process of executing the will of God on earth. He prays for divine deliverance, sustenance, and victory (Pss 18; 22; 89). He commits himself to the will of his heavenly Father, as he longs for an end to his humiliation. In a marvelous way he identifies himself with the lot of man: life in alienation awaiting the redemption of this world in fulfillment of the promises of God.

Both individual and communal lament psalms give expression to the frustration with the messianic ideal. The king and/or his people lament the power of the enemies and the frustration with God's lack of fulfillment of his promises. The lament psalms express the "human" aspect of the king (89:48). He too comes to Yahweh in prayer, is oppressed by enemies, and has to await a divine answer. He is not a demigod or divine. Herein lies a paradox. The one who was called to bring in justice and righteousness into this world suffers humiliation, unable to help himself! Kirkpatrick observes correctly that the suffering of the Davidic kings prepared the godly for the suffering of the Messiah: "Men's minds had to be prepared not only for the triumphant King, but for a suffering Saviour" (p. lxxix). When we read Psalms 18; 20; 21; 22; 27; 33; 35; 40; 41; 54; 55; 57; 61; 69; 89; 91; 92; 109; 118, we receive an insight into the suffering of God's people and also of the messianic King. The king knows God as "his Savior," and in this dynamic relationship of promise and alienation the king grows in his confidence in Yahweh's ability to deliver (89:26–28).

In his alienation the king experiences the depth of despair and divine abandonment. Forsaken by friends and relatives, he is also forsaken by God (Pss 22; 69). Nevertheless he is sustained by the hope of the Resurrection, of God's fidelity, and of his fulfillment of the promises affirmed in the covenants (69:33–36).

Our Lord and the apostles readily applied the words of the Psalms (22; 35; 69) to the passion of our Lord. Jesus experienced complete alienation from man and from God; yet he persevered even to death. Death could not contain him. When he arose, he arose for us—even as when he died, he died for us! This is the gospel (Acts 2:25–28; 13:35; 1 Cor 15:1–3). Thus in our afflictions we can turn to the language of the Psalms in our prayers, reflecting on our Lord's suffering in his intercessory prayers for us (Heb 2:6; 10:5–18). These psalms should not be restricted to being a mere prediction of the Messiah's suffering, because these words are also given for our encouragement. They function canonically in the Christian church to lead us to the Father through the Son, who understands our weakness and who serves us as the Priest-King (Col 1:24; Heb 2:17–18; 4:15).

3. The Messianic Role in Shepherding the People of God

The messianic King is God's appointed "shepherd" over his people. As a shepherd he upholds the pillars of the kingdom of God: justice and righteousness. Further, he rules in the name of Yahweh for the sake of the people. He redresses wrong, protects his people from evil, and blesses them.

The messianic King—as "priest-king"—is the patron of the worship of Yahweh. Though not an Aaronic priest, the Davidic king has sacerdotal functions. He prays for his people and blesses them with God's blessing (20:1–5; 40:16; 72:19). He also serves as God's "priest" in his concern with God's temple, sacrifices, and offerings (66:13–15; 69:9; 132); with set times of prayer (55:17); and with leading God's people in the worship of Yahweh (Pss 118; 144; 145). Psalm 110 brings the offices of king and priest under one head. The psalmist refers to the exalted position of the king, as ruling in his stead ("Sit at my right hand," v.1), giving him victory over the enemies (vv.2–3, 5–7) and bestowing on him a royal "priesthood, like that of Melchizedek" (v.4; cf. Heb 7).

4. The Messianic Role in Extending the Rule of God to this Earth

The messianic King has a twofold role: judgment and deliverance. He is the divinely appointed "Warrior" (see appendix to Ps 98: Yahweh Is the Divine Warrior), by whose reign all things will be brought to submission to the Great King. The hope of the Psalms and of the prophetic writings comes together in the vision of the establishment of God's righteous kingdom with peace, justice, and joy for the godly. They receive their rewards for their suffering and perseverance in the experience of complete liberation, having been vindicated by the Messiah-King. Further, they need never again fear, because evil will have no place in this kingdom.

The royal grant to David includes clear provision for the nations (22:27–28; 72:8–17). They owe him allegiance:

> The earth is the LORD's, and everything in it,
>   the world, and all who live in it;
> for he founded it upon the seas
>   and established it upon the waters.
>
> (24:1–2)

Great joy belongs to the Gentiles who submit themselves to Yahweh's Messiah. The Psalms proclaim the gospel of Israel to the nations, declaring what Yahweh has done and calling on Gentiles to worship the King together with them.

> Praise the LORD, all you nations;
>   extol him, all you peoples.
> For great is his love toward us,
>   and the faithfulness of the Lord endures forever.
> Praise the LORD.
>
> (117:1–2; cf. 66:1–8)

Jews, Gentiles, and the whole of creation will enjoy the messianic King's beneficent rule. However, in any discussion on the messianic rule, we must guard against two extremes. The first is the position that virtually eliminates any future of the Jewish people in the messianic kingdom. The second extreme is the position that virtually limits the messianic kingdom to the Jews to the exclusion of the Gentile church. The apostolic revelation brings both entities together as separate flocks into one flock. The Good Shepherd knows his own; and his sheep, whether from Jewish heritage or from the nations, hear his voice! The challenge in our day is to use the words of Israel in calling Israel to recognize Jesus as the Messiah by declaring what God has done for us through his Messiah. This message must be motivated by love and presented with forbearance and understanding of what has happened to the Jewish people in the last two thousand years and with a deep understanding that in some sense they are still God's beloved and holy to him (Rom 11:16). Bridges can be built if we are sensitive to the apostolic injunction to be humble in our enjoyment of the covenant privileges (Rom 11:20–21).

Hope lies in the vision of Zion, built by the Lord and prepared for his servants, whether Jews or Gentiles:

> Indeed, of Zion it will be said,
>   "This one and that one were born in her,
> and the Most High himself will establish her."
>   The Lord will write in the register of the peoples:
> "This one was born in Zion."
>
> (87:5–6; cf. 102:15–16)

Those who have this hope look forward to the fullness of his kingdom (96:11–13). This hope comes to expression in the familiar hymn by Isaac Watts:

> Jesus shall reign wher-e'er the sun
> Does his successive journeys run;
> His kingdom stretch from shore to shore,
> Till moons shall wax and wane no more.

The sign of the hope of the coming kingdom of justice and righteousness lies in the resurrection and ascension of Jesus Christ. The "royal psalms" proclaim the coming of God. That "coming" is here in the person of the Son (Pss 2; 45; 72; 96–99; 110). Jesus has gone up with acclamation (47; 68:18; cf. Eph 4:8–10), and the assurance of his exaltation lies in his having given us the gift of the Spirit. Further, the assurance of the Father's acceptance lies in the inclusion of the Gentiles in the expansion of the messianic kingdom. Gentiles too are the recipients of the Spirit of Christ (cf. Joel 2:28–32; Gal 5:16–18)!

The King is God's witness to his people and to the nations. He admonishes (2:10–12; 75:4–7), encourages (62:7–8), and declares what God has done in his mighty acts of salvation and vindication (40:10; 71:22–24; 72:18–19). Eaton writes: "But the king's exaltation is not a separation from the people. He is their representative. . . . What God has done for him displays the principles of God's dealings with mankind as a whole. The personal story is thus extended to a universal application" (p. 190).

The unanimous teaching of the NT is that the fulfillment of all OT promises finds its focus in Jesus Christ (2 Cor 1:20). So von Rad concludes:

> No special hermeneutic method is necessary to see the whole diverse movement of the Old Testament saving events, made up of God's promises and their temporary fulfillments, as pointing to the future fulfillment in Jesus Christ. This can be said quite categorically. The coming of Jesus Christ as a historical reality leaves the exegete no choice at all: he must interpret the Old Testament as pointing to Christ, whom he must understand in its light. (OTT, 2:374)

Texts: 2; 3; 4; 5; 7; 8; 9; 10; 11; 16; 17; 18; 20; 21; 22; 23; 27; 28; 31; 33:14; 35; 36; 40; 41; 45; 46; 47; 49; 50; 51; 52; 54; 55; 56; 57; 59; 61; 62; 63; 65; 66; 67; 68; 69; 70; 71; 72; 73; 75; 77; 86; 89; 91; 92; 94; 96; 97; 98; 99; 101; 102; 103; 108; 109; 110; 116; 117; 118; 132; 138; 140; 141; 142; 143; 144; 150.

Related Topics: Appendixes to Pss 5 (Yahweh Is King); 24 (Lord Sabaoth); 25 (The Perfections of Yahweh); 46 (Zion Theology); 78 (The Mighty Acts of Yahweh); 98 (Yahweh Is the Divine Warrior); 132 (The Ark of the Covenant and the Temple: Symbols of Yahweh's Presence and Rule).

Bibliography: Joachim Becker, *Messianic Expectation in the Old Testament;* Willis Judson Beecher, *The Prophets and the Promise* (Grand Rapids: Baker, 1963, reprint of 1905 ed.), pp. 241–62, 365–86; W.H. Bellinger, Jr., *Psalmody and Prophecy;* Milos Bic, "Das Erste Buch des Psalters eine Thronbesteigungsliturgie," *The Sacral Kingship/La Regalità Sacra* (Leiden: Brill, 1959), pp. 316–32; R.E. Clements, "Messianic Prophecy or Messianic History," *Horizons in Biblical Theology* 1 (1979): 87–104; Gerald Cooke, "The Israelite King as Son of God," ZAW 73 (1961): 202–25; J. Coppens, "La Royauté de Yahvé dans le Psautier," *Ephemerides Theologicae Lovanienses* 53 (1977): 297–362; id., 54 (1978): 1–50; Keith R. Crim, *The Royal Psalms* (Richmond: Knox, 1962); John I. Durham, "The King as 'Messiah' in the Psalms," *Review and Expositor* 81 (1984): 425–35; Eichrodt, TOT, 1:124–28, 476–79; J.H. Eaton, *Kingship and the Psalms;* Georg Fohrer, "Der Vertrag zwischen König und Volk in Israel," *Studien zur alttestamentlichen Theologie und Geschichte (1949–1966)* (Berlin: De Gruyter, 1969), pp. 330–51; John F. Healey, "The Immortality of the King: Ugarit and the Psalms,"

Orientalia 53 (1984): 245–54; J. Jocz, "Messiah," ZPEB, 4:198–207; Aubrey R. Johnson, "The Role of the King in the Jerusalem Cultus"; Walter C. Kaiser, Jr., TOTT, pp. 152–64; id., "The Davidic Promise and the Inclusion of the Gentiles (Amos 9:9–15 and Acts 15:13–18): A Test Passage for Theological Systems," JETS 20 (1977): 97–111; id., "The Blessing of David: The Charter for Humanity," in *The Law and the Prophets: Old Testament Studies Prepared in Honor of O.T. Allis*, ed. J.H. Skilton (Nutley, N.J.: Presbyterian and Reformed, 1974), pp. 310–18; id., "Messianic Prophecies in the Old Testament," in *Dreams, Visions and Oracles. The Layman's Guide to Biblical Prophecy*, edd. Carl Edwin Armerding and W. Ward Gasque (Grand Rapids: Baker, 1977), pp. 75–88; id., *Toward Rediscovering the Old Testament* (Grand Rapids: Zondervan, 1987), pp. 101–20; A.F. Kirkpatrick, *Psalms*, pp. lxxvi–lxxxv; Hans-Joachim Kraus, *Theologie des Psalmen*, pp. 134–55; Heinz Kruse, "David's Covenant," VetTest 2 (1985): 139–64; C.S. Lewis, "Second Meanings in the Psalms," in *Reflections on the Psalms*, pp. 120–38; Dennis J. McCarthy, "Compact and Kingship: Stimuli for Hebrew Covenant Thinking," *Studies in The Period of David and Solomon and Other Essays*, papers read at the International Symposium for Biblical Studies, December 1979, ed. Tomoo Ishida (Winona Lake: Eisenbrauns, 1979), pp. 75–92; S. Mowinckel, *The Psalms in Israel's Worship*, 1:42–80; Gerhard von Rad, OTT, 1:306–54; id., "The Royal Ritual in Judah," in *The Problem of the Hexateuch and Other Essays* (London: SCM, 1984), pp. 222–31; Heinz Reinelt, "Gottes Herrschaftsbereich nach den Aussagen der Psalmen," *Freude an der Weisung des Herrn, Beiträge zur Theologie der Psalmen, Festgabe zum 70. Geburtstag von Heinrich Gross*, edd. Ernst Haag and Frank-Lothar Hossfeld (Stuttgart: Katholisches Bibelwerk, 1986), pp. 265–74; Leonhardt Rost, "Sinaibund und Davidsbund," *Theologische Literaturzeitung* 72 (1947): 129–34; id., "Erwägungen zum Begriff *šālôm*," in *Schalom. Studien zu Glaube und Geschichte Israels. Alfred Jepsen zum 70. Geburtstag*, ed. Karl-Heinz Bernhardt (Stuttgart: Calwer Verlag, 1971), pp. 41–44; S.H. Russell, "Calvin and the Messianic Interpretation of the Psalms," SJT 21 (1968): 37–47; Werner H. Schmidt, "Kritik am Königtum, *Probleme biblischer Theologie. Gerhard von Rad zum 70. Geburtstag*, ed. Hans Walter Wolff (Munich: Chr. Kaiser, 1971), pp. 440–61; Elmer B. Smick, "Ugaritic and the Theology of the Psalms," pp. 110–16; Odil Hannes Steck, *Friedensvorstellungen im alten Jerusalem: Psalmen, Jesaja, Deuterojesaja* (Zurich: Theologischer Verlag, 1972); S. Talmon, "Typen der Messiaserwartung um die Zeitenwende," *Probleme biblischer Theologie. Gerhard von Rad zum 70. Geburtstag*, ed. Hans Walter Wolff (Munich: Chr. Kaiser, 1971), pp. 571–87; Marvin E. Tate, "War and Peacemaking in the Old Testament," *Review and Expositor* 79 (1982): 587–96; Timo Veijola, *Verheissung in der Krise. Studien zur Literatur und Theologie der Exilszeit anhand des 89. Psalms* (Helsinki: Suomalainen Tiedeakatemia, 1982); Ernst-Joachim Waschke, "Das Verhältnis alttestamentlicher Überlieferungen im Schnittpunkt der Dynastiezusage und die Dynastiezusage im Spiegel alttestamentlicher Überlieferungen," ZAW 99 (1987): 157–79; Claus Westermann, "Die Königspsalmen" and "Die Psalmen und Jesus Christus," in *Ausgewählte Psalmen*, pp. 47–53; 206–8; Keith K. Whitelam, *The Just King. Monarchical Judicial Authority*, JSOTS 12 (Sheffield: JSOT, 1979); Gerald H. Wilson, "The Use of Royal Psalms as the 'Seams' of the Hebrew Psalter," JSOT 35 (1986): 85–94; Walther Zimmerli, "The Hope of Israel and the Hope of the World," in *The Old Testament and the World*, tr. John J. Scullion (Atlanta: Knox, 1976), pp. 122–50; id., OTTO, pp. 86–93.

TDOT, 9:496–509; THAT, 1:907–20; TWOT, 1:530–31.

Book IV: Psalms 90–106

Psalm 90: Teach Us to Number Our Days

This psalm is a reflection on the transience of life. It contemplates the nature of life under God's wrath and affirms the necessity of living aright in the presence of the Lord. The superscription attributes Psalm 90 to Moses. The spirit of Moses' concern is certainly present in the psalm's deep sense of life's furtive passing; the connection between sin, suffering, and the wrath of God; and the submission of man in prayer for God's favor.

The psalm is composed of three major parts: (1) a hymn of praise (vv.1–2); (2) a lament on the transience of life (vv.3–12); and (3) a prayer for restoration of God's favor (vv.13–17). These divisions reflect a wide variety of literary genres, leading scholars to study the composite nature of the psalm. There is no sufficient ground to dispute the essential unity of Psalm 90 (Kraus, *Psalmen,* 2:629). The expository structure is as follows:

A. The Lord Is God (vv.1–2)
  B. God's Authority Over Man (vv.3–6)
    C. God's Wrath (vv.7–10)
    C′. Proper Response to God's Wrath (vv.11–12)
  B′. Prayer for God's Mercy (vv.13–16)
A′. May the Lord Be Our God (v.17)

For structural analyses see Stefan Schreiner, "Erwägungen zur Struktur des 90. Psalms," *Biblica* 59 (1979): 80–90; P. Auffret, "Essai sur la Structure Littéraire du Psaume 90," *Biblica* 61 (1980): 262–76. For an approach to this psalm as a war oracle, see the study by Christensen, pp. 112–27. For other psalms see 12; 60; 74; 79; 80; 83; 85; 94:1–11; 123; 126; 137.

I. The Lord Is God

90:1–2

A prayer of Moses the man of God.

1 Lord, you have been our dwelling place
  throughout all generations.
2 Before the mountains were born
  or you brought forth the earth and the world,
  from everlasting to everlasting you are God.

1 The psalm begins with and ends on an affirmation of God as "the Lord" (Adonai), the Creator and Ruler of the universe. The difference between these two affirmations is that toward the conclusion the general recognition of God as the Lord and as the shelter of his people is the basis for the prayer that he may again bless his people with his favor in the future (v.17). The Lord himself has been the "dwelling place" (cf. 91:9; Deut 33:27), the oasis of refreshment and encampment for his people for many generations (cf. Deut 32:7). The metaphor is related to the imagery of God's protection (cf. 91:9), and it is not surprising that several MSS and the LXX read here "refuge" (*mā'ôz*) instead of "dwelling place" (*mā'ôn*).

2 The love of God is eternal. The psalmist expresses the greatness of God's fatherly care in the imagery of birth. It is not entirely clear who is giving birth; is it God (NIV, "you brought forth the earth") or the earth ("before the earth and the world gave birth"; cf. Prov 8:25)? The metaphor of God's giving birth is possible (cf. Deut 32:18; P.D. Miller, Jr., "Psalm 90," *Interpreting the Psalms*, pp. 125–30). It is more likely to render the phrase in favor of the earth giving rise to mountains, while not denying the creative role of the Lord in the process of the formation of the earth (cf. Gen 1:11, 20).

The confessional statement "you are God" (v.2) affirms both God's kingship over creation and his otherness. The designations for the Lord in these verses have been carefully chosen, as the psalmist sings praise to "the Lord," the Ruler of the world, who alone is "God" (El; cf. Isa 44:6; 48:12). The Canaanites believed in El as the father of the gods whose supremacy had gradually been taken over by Baal, his son. The psalmist states that there is no other Lord than the God who is eternal and who is the "dwelling place" of his own.

Notes

For a brief discussion of the technical words and phrases in the superscription, see the Introduction.

II. God's Authority Over Man

90:3–6

3 You turn men back to dust,
saying, "Return to dust, O sons of men."
4 For a thousand years in your sight
are like a day that has just gone by,
or like a watch in the night.
5 You sweep men away in the sleep of death;
they are like the new grass of the morning—
6 though in the morning it springs up new,
by evening it is dry and withered.

3–6 In comparison with God, man is nothing but "dust" (v.3). Man in his being is weak (*'enôš;* NIV, "men"; cf. 8:4; 103:15). Man is subject to the Eternal, who alone has power over all his creation, including the life and death of humans. Man is dust and will return to the dust (v.3; cf. Gen 3:19). In comparison with God's eternity, man's brief span of life may be likened to "new grass" (v.5), which shoots up only shortly to be parched (v.6). The analogy comes out of the context of the dry summer climate in Canaan, where the green landscape of the winter and spring could be changed to a brown, parched scenery within a few days of hot weather. The time designations "morning" and "evening" are metaphors for the brevity of life and are not to be taken literally.

Even when man may live to a thousand years—Methuselah lived 969 years (Gen 5:27)—in God's reckoning it is but "a day" (v.4; cf. 2 Peter 3:8) or, even less, "a watch in the night," i.e., a four-hour period (cf. Lam 2:19). Man looks at his fellow beings as strong; but as far as God is concerned, they may be swept away by the waters of the flood (v.5). Each human being is a drop in the giant stream of time.

Notes

5 This verse is quite difficult. The MT's זְרַמְתָּם שֵׁנָה (*zeramtām šēnāh*, "you sweep sleep"; NIV, "you sweep men away in the sleep of death") is ambiguous. Kraus suggests an emendation based on haplography and on the LXX translation "year" (*šānāh*): "[you sow them] year by year" (*Psalmen*, 2:628). Though the emendation makes sense, it enjoys little support. Matitiahu Tsevat emends the text and explains the phrase as an Akkadian calque, resulting in the following rendering:

> You pour sleep on them,
> and they are like grass which fades away.
> In the morning, it sprouts and grows,
> in the evening it withers and is parched.
> ("Psalm xc 5-6," VetTest [1985]: 115–17)

Charles Whitley renders vv.5–6 as follows:

> Their offspring changeth, as grass undergoing change,
> In the morning it sprouts and flourishes,
> In the evening it fades and withers.
> ("The Text of Psalm 90:5," *Biblica* 63 [1982]: 557)

III. God's Wrath

90:7–10

> 7 We are consumed by your anger
> and terrified by your indignation.
> 8 You have set our iniquities before you,
> our secret sins in the light of your presence.
> 9 All our days pass away under your wrath;
> we finish our years with a moan.
> 10 The length of our days is seventy years—
> or eighty, if we have the strength;
> yet their span is but trouble and sorrow,
> for they quickly pass, and we fly away.

7–10 Verses 7–10 develop man's wretched condition in two strophes of two verses each in such a way that vv.7–8 parallel vv.9–10:

A. "we are consumed" (*kālînû*, v.7)
B. "by your anger . . . by your indignation" (v.7)
C. "in the light of your presence" (*pāneyḵā*, v.8)
D. "all our days" (v.9)
B′. "under your wrath" (v.9)
C′. "pass away" (*pannû*, v.9)

A′. "we finish" (*killînû*, v.9)
D″. "our years" (v.9)
D‴. "the length of our years" (lit., "the days of our years," v.10)

The order follows that of the MT. In vv.7–8 the stress lies on God's anger and in vv.9–10 on the brevity of human life. (See the appendix to Ps 85: Anger in the Psalms.)

The psalmist further develops the distance between God and man. The Lord is eternal and sovereign, whereas man is weak and dependent. He explains that man's frailty and anxiety is an expression of God's judgment on man. The Lord's "anger" and "wrath" (vv.7–9) create a barrier between the Lord and man, as man becomes "terrified" (v.7), becoming more aware of his "iniquities" and "secret sins" (v.8). The Lord knows all man's open and hidden sins. The "iniquity" of man denotes his awareness of sinfulness, and the "secret sins" (cf. 44:21) are those acts hidden from the public eye but seen by the Lord. Since he develops the motifs of God's wrath and judgment, the psalmist does not focus on the nature of sin or on the possibility of forgiveness. (See the appendix to Ps 103: Sin and Forgiveness.) The connection of sin, God's wrath, and judgment is prominent in Moses' teaching, especially in Deuteronomy (cf. 4:25–28; 5:9–11; 7:10; 9:19–26; 11:16–17, 28; 17:2–5, 12; 18:19; 21:18–21; 27:15–26; 28:15–68).

The emphasis on the Lord's wrath arises out of a certain context, but the psalm gives no indication of which context. At most it may be said that this psalm is a prayer that God's people pray at times of adversity and that the prayer underscores God's rightful indignation at the offenses of his people. They had sinned grievously against him in the desert and continued a history of vexation. Man, even redeemed man, is sinful and deserves the full impact of God's anger. God's "indignation," however small, is so great that God's people are easily shaken (*b-h-l*, "terrified," v.7; cf. 6:2 ["in agony"]; 83:17; Exod 15:15).

Even more disquieting is the thought that man's very existence characterizes itself as sinful and that God sees nothing but man's sin ("before you," "in the light of your presence," v.8). Because of this, God's wrath is always there ("all our days," "our years," v.9). Man's life is therefore marked by brevity ("seventy years—or eighty") and by vexation ("trouble and sorrow," v.10; cf. Eccl 6:12). Man is "consumed" (v.7; = "we finish," v.9) by God's wrath.

Notes

8 Because the root עלם (*'-l-m*) occurs in the phrase "secret sins" (*'ªlumēnû*, lit., "our secrets"), Dahood argues in favor of the alternate meaning ("be young"), as in *'almāh* ("young woman"): "the sins of our youth" (*Psalms*, 2:321). The rarity of the phrase should caution against confidence of interpretation.

IV. Proper Response to God's Wrath

90:11–12

11 Who knows the power of your anger?
For your wrath is as great as the fear that is due you.

12 Teach us to number our days aright,
  that we may gain a heart of wisdom.

11–12 The two previous motifs of "wrath" and "days" lead into a prayer for wisdom as the only legitimate and wise response to the human condition. Man generally does not pay attention to the divine law of sin and retribution. One reason for this is that the full brunt of God's anger is withheld and unknown to man. The frustrations in life are explained away or accepted as long as there are not too many problems. The greatness of God's wrath should evoke fear, and that fear should be commensurate with God's wrath (v.11). Thus the psalmist calls for a wise response to the previous teaching on the nature of God in contradistinction to the nature of man. His question "Who knows. . . ?" is to be understood as a strong affirmation: "Nobody knows the power of your anger!"

Though no one knows how God's full anger will affect human existence, those who fear the Lord are more aware of the fierceness of his anger. The wise pray for "a heart of wisdom" (v.12). Since no one "knows" (*yôḏēaʿ*, v.11) how great God's rage may be, the wise man is receptive to divine revelation/instruction: "teach us" (*hôḏaʿ*, v.12). The prayer consists of two parts. First, the wise man asks to apprehend the brevity of life. The numbering of "days" (v.12) is an act of recognition of the vast difference between God and finite man. Though life may have many pleasant surprises, God's anger may come at any time; and the wise man reckons continually with God's existence and man's accountability. Second, the wise man applies himself to obtaining a "heart of wisdom" (cf. Deut 5:29; 32:29). Brueggemann observes that this heart "attends to the persistent reality of Yahweh's Lordship" (*Message of the Psalms*, p. 113). Wisdom begins and ends with the Lord, as the wise man seeks the Lord in all his ways (cf. Prov 1:7), and true wisdom begins with the petition for revelation and illumination: "Teach us."

Notes

11–12 Gerhard von Rad treats the whole psalm as a wisdom psalm ("Psalm 90," *God at Work in Israel*, tr. John H. Marks [Nashville: Abingdon, 1980], pp. 210–23).

11 The MT is difficult, as the phrase וּכְיִרְאָתְךָ (*ûḵeyirʾāṯeḵā*, "and your fear") could be understood as in the NIV: "the fear that is due to you" or "who feels your wrath like those that fear thee?" (NEB). The sense seems to be that no one knows the terror of God's displeasure and that therefore man must appropriate wisdom (v.12).

V. Prayer for God's Mercy

90:13–16

13 Relent, O LORD! How long will it be?
  Have compassion on your servants.
14 Satisfy us in the morning with your unfailing love,
  that we may sing for joy and be glad all our days.
15 Make us glad for as many days as you have afflicted us,
  for as many years as we have seen trouble.

[16] May your deeds be shown to your servants,
your splendor to their children.

13–16 These four verses are connected in the MT in that the first two verses consist of four bicolons, of which the first three have an imperative and the last a cohortative, which must be translated as "relent. . . . Have compassion. . . . Satisfy . . . (so) that we may sing" (so NIV, vv.13–14). Similarly, vv.15–16 begin with an imperative and end on a jussive: "Make us glad. . . . (so that) your deeds may be shown." The combination of the imperatives with the result clauses brings out the psalmist's concern with God's mercy ("relent. . . . satisfy. . . . make us glad"), that the effects of his mercy may rest on his people ("that we may sing") and on the succeeding generations ("may your deeds be shown to your servants, . . . to their children"). (See the appendix to Ps 78: The Mighty Acts of Yahweh.)

The prayer consists of three elements. First, the psalmist prays for restoration to God's favor. His anger consumes (v.7), but he may "relent" (lit., "return," v.13; cf. Exod 32:12; Deut 32:36; Ps 80:3) by showering his favor again on his people (cf. 80:4). They are waiting for his divine act of full salvation, asking, "How long?" (cf. 80:4; 89:46). Though his people are suffering, they are still his "servants" (v.13), as they wait patiently for the compassion of their Master. The favor of God is particularly known as his "unfailing love" (*ḥeseḏ*, v.14) or covenantal love. The renewal of his love is associated with "the morning" (cf. 30:5; 49:14; 143:8; Lam 3:23), as the light of day is contrastive with the darkness (gloom) of the night. Thus the psalmist prays for a new beginning, which the Lord alone can open up for his people. (See the appendix to Ps 25: The Perfections of Yahweh.)

Second, the prayer calls on the Lord to restore the joy of his people's salvation. The act of rejoicing is set in contrast to the "trouble and sorrow" of human existence (v.10). The act of salvation finds expression in his restoration of favor and in his deliverance. The people of God have sung and will continue to sing of God's "deeds" (lit., "work," i.e., the work of salvation, v.16; cf. 92:5; Deut 32:4; Hab 3:2), longing for a renewed demonstration of his "deeds." The "work" of God on behalf of his people reveals his "splendor" (cf. Isa 40:5).

Third, God's people long for the continuity of divine blessings rather than an occasional evidence of his love. The phrases "all our days," "many days," and "many years" (vv.14–15) are symmetric with "all our days," "our years," and "the length of our days" (vv.9–10) so as to bring out the contrast between a whole life of sorrow under the rage of God and the life of rejoicing because of his favor.

VI. May the Lord Be Our God

90:17

[17] May the favor of the Lord our God rest upon us;
establish the work of our hands for us—
yes, establish the work of our hands.

17 In conclusion the psalmist prays for God's beneficence, asking that his "beauty" (i.e., "favor"; cf. 27:4) may rest on his people. The Lord's acceptance of his own assures a certain permanence of their work. Life under the sun may be vain. The man under God's judgment can accomplish no ultimate good. However, the godly and wise pray that the Lord will accept their work and "establish" [*kôn^{e}nāh*] it as having value (cf. Deut 2:7; 14:29: 16:15). Frail, limited, and sinful as man is, the love of God can transform what is weak to his own glory. Robert Alter senses the climactic conclusion, as he writes, "The special force of the reiteration of this verb (*kônēn*) at the end of Psalm 90 must be felt as a reversal of the imagery of withering grass, sighs, things burnt up by God's wrath, and . . . humanity flooded or engulfed by sleep" (pp. 128–29).

Psalm 91: In the Shelter of the Most High

Psalm 91 contains both a wisdom psalm (vv.1–13) and a divine oracle (vv.14–16). The wisdom psalm encourages the godly to pursue the path of godliness and holds out the many promises of God's protection and blessings. In this it resembles the wisdom psalms. The conclusions support the place of *wisdom,* as the Lord renews the promises to those who love him.

The psalm is closely connected with Psalms 90 and 92 in thought and language: e.g., "dwelling (place)" (90:1; 91:9); "spring up" (90:6; 92:7), "make glad. . . . your deeds" (90:15–16; 92:4), "Most High" (91:1, 9; 92:1). The prayer of Psalm 90 is for blessing and divine favor. This prayer is confirmed by the promise and oracle of God in Psalm 91. The godly respond to the promises in praise and trust in Psalm 92. Of these psalms only Psalm 91 lacks a superscription. The LXX adds a heading ("Praise. A Song of David"), but its authenticity is doubtful.

Apart from the twofold structural division, the psalm unfolds a distinct progression.

A. Invitation to the Protection of God (vv.1–2)
B. Forms of Protection (vv.3–8)
A′. Invitation to the Protection of God (vv.9–10)
B′. Forms of Protection (vv.11–13)
C. The Oracle of Salvation (vv.14–16)

I. Invitation to the Protection of God

91:1–2

1 He who dwells in the shelter of the Most High
will rest in the shadow of the Almighty.
2 I will say of the Lord, "He is my refuge and
my fortress,
my God, in whom I trust."

1–2 By using the third person impersonal ("he who dwells," v.1), the psalmist directs himself to anyone seeking wisdom (see appendix to Ps 1: The Ways of Wisdom and Folly). The blessings of godliness and the pursuit of wisdom are for all who seek God as their highest good in life. To this end he employs several names for God: Most High (*Elyon;* cf. 18:13; 46:4; 47:2; see appendix to Ps 9: Yahweh Is El Elyon), the Almighty (*šadday,* cf. 68:14), "the Lord" (*Yahweh*), and "my God" (*'ᵉlōhay*). He also encourages the reader by proclaiming that God is "my refuge and my fortress; / my God in whom I trust" (v.2). The names of God evoke confidence, as they connote the power of the Creator-God as well as the endearing love of the covenant-God ("the Lord"). Each of these characteristics are brought together in the confession "He is my refuge and my fortress, / my God, in whom I trust" (v.2; see appendix to Ps 3: Yahweh Is My God).

The description of the protection is also couched in metaphorical language: "shelter," "shadow," and "refuge and . . . fortress." The first two words suggest the imagery of a bird under whose wings the baby birds find safety (cf. v.4; 17:8; 36:7; 57:1; 63:7). The other two words suggest a stronghold or military installation (cf. 18:2; 61:3).

But who may enjoy the hospitality and protection of God? Unlike Psalms 15:1 and 24:3, this psalm gives the answer in a personal, experiential manner: "I will say of the LORD, . . . my God, in whom I trust." Whoever takes on his lips this confession walks in the path of wisdom.

Notes

---

1 For the names of God, see the appendixes referred to and Otto Eissfeldt, "Jahwes Verhältnis zu 'Eljon and Shaddaj nach Psalm 91," *Kleine Schriften*, vol. 3, edd. Rudolf Sellheim and Fritz Maas (Tübingen: Mohr, 1966), pp. 441–47.

2 The MT's אֹמַר (*'ōmar*, "I will say") could also be read as יֹאמַר (*yō'mar*, "he will say," or as in the NIV mg., "*He says*"; cf. LXX). The latter reading corresponds with the general nature of the opening: "He who dwells. . . . he says." The former is preferable because of the wisdom element. The teacher gives a personal account of his faith experience (cf. 34:4–11).

II. Forms of Protection

91:3–8

3 Surely he will save you from the fowler's snare
and from the deadly pestilence.
4 He will cover you with his feathers,
and under his wings you will find refuge;
his faithfulness will be your shield and rampart.
5 You will not fear the terror of night,
nor the arrow that flies by day,
6 nor the pestilence that stalks in the darkness,
nor the plague that destroys at midday.
7 A thousand may fall at your side,
ten thousand at your right hand,
but it will not come near you.
8 You will only observe with your eyes
and see the punishment of the wicked.

3–4 The emphatic pronoun "he" ("Surely he," v.3) amplifies the care of the Lord. He gets wholly involved with the welfare of his people. He protects them from any adversity by evil men, likened to "the fowler's snare" (cf. 119:110; 124:7; 141:9; 2 Tim 2:26) and "the deadly pestilence." He protects them as with feathers, i.e., "his wings" (v.4; cf. 17:8; 36:7; NEB, "pinions"; lit., "his ligament"; cf. v.1; Deut 32:11; Isa 31:5; Matt 23:37; Luke 13:34). Divine protection is likened to that of a bird ("feathers," "wings") that is kept from being trapped by the "fowler's snare." The "shield" and "rampart" (cf. 35:2) develop the imagery of "refuge" and "fortress" (v.2). Yahweh's care is both tender and sufficient because he is faithful, i.e., "true" to his people.

5–7 The protection of God extends to both day and night (vv.5–6). The Lord gives security from all natural and supernatural causes of "fear" (*paḥad*, v.5; cf. 53:5), whether war or disease. These afflictions came on the wicked as just expressions of God's provocation (cf. 53:5), but those who fear the Lord need not be afraid of the "arrow" that brings diseases ("pestilence" and "plague," v.6), whether in broad daylight or in the darkness of the night (cf. 121:5–6). There is no limit to his protection because he has full authority over all things that happen on earth. The greatness of God's protection is further amplified by the ratio of "a thousand" or even "ten thousand" to one (v.7; cf. Josh 23:10).

8 Seeing God's salvation with the eye of faith will further encourage the godly, whom the Lord has promised his protection and blessing. The godly will witness the righteousness, justice, and fidelity of the Lord as well as the punishment of the wicked. (See the appendix to Ps 25: The Perfections of Yahweh.) No power in heaven or earth is greater than that of Yahweh, the Divine Warrior!

Notes

3 The LXX, Symmachus, and the Syriac read דָּבָר (*dᵉḇar*, "word," "a deadly [destructive] word," so BHS) instead of the MT's דֶּבֶר (*deḇer*, "pestilence"). In view of the references to "arrow" and "diseases" in vv.5–6, the MT is preferable.

4 The *hapax legomenon* סֹחֵרָה (*sōḥērāh;* NIV, "rampart") has posed to be an exegetical crux. For a survey of views, see A.A. Macintosh, "Psalm XCI 4 and the Root *sḥr*," VetTest 23 (1973): 52–62.

5–6 The references to "arrow" and "plague" may well be understood against the Canaanite mythological background. The goddess Resheph was the goddess of the archers and brought troubles on her enemies. For background see the note on 78:48.

6 The usual meaning of שׁוד (*š-w-d*) is "devastate" or "overpower," rendered here as "destroy": "the plague that destroys at midday." Robert Gordis proposes a questionable etymology from the Syriac, resulting in "the pestilence that rushes on at noon" (*The Word and the Book* [New York: Ktav, 1976], p. 329).

III. Invitation to the Protection of God

91:9–10

9 If you make the Most High your dwelling—
even the LORD, who is my refuge—
10 then no harm will befall you,
no disaster will come near your tent.

9–10 The invitation is more explicitly extended to all the godly. The psalmist's personal experience serves as an encouragement to embrace the way of wisdom by making "the Most High," i.e., the LORD, one's "dwelling" (v.9). He is the "dwelling" (cf. 90:1) of his people, under whose shelter they find "refuge." The Lord does not guarantee that no evil will befall those who trust him ("make the Most High your dwelling"). All who find "refuge" (cf. v.2) in him will rest with the confidence that whatever happens on earth is with his knowledge. Nothing happens outside his will, whether "harm" (lit., "evil," v.10) or "disaster" (lit., "disease" or "wound"; cf. 38:11; Lev 13;14; Isa 53:8).

Notes

9 The MT is difficult in that a literal translation would result in "When you, O LORD, [are] my refuge; the Most High you have made your dwelling place." The NIV gets around the difficulty by reversing the colons; thus making the personal pronoun "you" in the first colon the subject of the second colon. The promise stands: Yahweh will protect his own! This promise is further elaborated below (vv.11–13). The LXX reads "your stronghold" (*mā'ôz*) for the MT's מָעוֹן (*mā'ôn*, "dwelling place"). Parallelism favors the LXX, similarly 71:3.

IV. Forms of Protection

91:11–13

11 For he will command his angels concerning you
to guard you in all your ways;
12 They will lift you up in their hands,
so that you will not strike your foot against a stone.
13 You will tread upon the lion and the cobra;
you will trample the great lion and the serpent.

11–13 The promises of these verses are conditioned on an appropriate response to v.9. The kinds of divine protection are again brought out to assure God's care and all-sufficiency. The benefits and the requirements are secondary at this point because the emphasis is on the invitation to seek the Lord.

The negative statements ("no harm . . . no disaster," v.10) have their complement in a positive declaration ("he will command his angels . . . to guard you," v.11). The Lord charges his angels with the protection of the godly and of their "tent" (v.10), i.e., all that belongs to them, wherever they may be ("in all your ways," v.11; cf. 34:7; Matt 4:6; Luke 4:10–11; Heb 1:14). Instead of experiencing disaster, stumbling, or dangers along the way ("a stone. . . . the lion . . . the cobra," vv.12–13), the angels will lift the godly out of danger and deliver them (cf. Exod 19:4; Isa 63:9).

In life the Lord may permit many terrible things to happen to his children (cf. Job), as he did to his own Son, our Lord. But his children know that no power is out of God's control. They trust their heavenly Father, while they act responsibly. Hence they do not test the Lord to see to what extent he will deliver them from troubles. Satan tempted our Lord to act presumptuously, but Jesus rebuked Satan, rightly responding that man may not test the Lord (cf. Luke 4:10–12).

V. The Oracle of Salvation

91:14–16

14 "Because he loves me," says the LORD, "I will rescue
him;
I will protect him, for he acknowledges my name.
15 He will call upon me, and I will answer him;
I will be with him in trouble,
I will deliver him and honor him.
16 With long life will I satisfy him
and show him my salvation."

14–16 The Lord announces his salvation oracle to all who love him, i.e., to those who "know" (NIV, "acknowledge") his name. The word "love" signifies here a deep longing or desire for the Lord (v.14; cf. Deut 7:7–8; 10:15). The fullness and depth of his redemption finds reality in those who long for his redemption (vv.14–15; see appendix to Ps 119: Yahweh Is My Redeemer).

The relationship finds expression in communion, in answered prayers (cf. 50:15, 23), and in the "honors" (rewards) due to wise living (vv.15–16). The Lord assures that his own will enjoy themselves as his children in this life and in the life to come (cf. 1 Tim 4:8–9). They will see his "salvation" (*yᵉšû'āh,* v.16; cf. 149:4). The Lord assures us, as Brueggemann observes, that "it is the ground for confidence that the last word is not spoken by us, but to us" (*Message of the Psalms,* p. 157).

Psalm 92: In Praise of the Lord

Psalms 90–92 are united by the development of concepts and the repetition of vocabulary. These psalms lead the worshiper from a meditation on the transiency of life (Ps 90), a call for wisdom (Ps 91), to a climactic celebration of divine deliverance and protection (Ps 92). Psalm 92 embodies a *hymn* (vv.1–3) and an individual thanksgiving (vv.4–15), which are symmetrical with the hymn (vv.1–2) and complaint (vv.3–17) of Psalm 90. Between the complaint of Psalm 90 and the thanksgiving of Psalm 92 stands the wisdom poem (91:1–13) and the divine oracle of promise (91:14–16). These psalms could be structured concentrically.

A. Hymn (90:1–2)
  B. Complaint (90:3–17)
    C. Wisdom Poem (91:1–13)
    C′. Divine Oracle (91:14–16)
A′. Hymn (92:1–3)
  B′. Individual Thanksgiving (92:4–15)

The structure of this psalm may be further divided:

I. Hymn in Praise of the Most High (vv.1–3)
II. Hymn of Thanksgiving (vv.4–14)
  A. Joy in God's Works (vv.4–5)
    B. Judgment on Folly and Exaltation (vv.6–8)
    B′. Judgment and Exaltation (vv.9–11)
  A′. The Prosperity of the Righteous (vv.12–14)
III. Praise of the LORD (v.15)

Though not so evident in the NIV, vv.1–3 and 15 form an inclusion by the phrase *l^ehaggîḏ* (vv.2, 15 [3, 16 MT]), translated as "to proclaim" and "proclaiming," thus bringing both parts of the psalm together into one harmonious whole. For a concentric structural analysis of Psalm 92, see Jonathan Magonet, "Some Concentric Structures in Psalms," *The Heythrop Journal* 23 (1982): 369–72.

I. Hymn in Praise of the Most High

92:1–3

A psalm. A song. For the Sabbath day.

1 It is good to praise the LORD
   and make music to your name, O Most High,
2 to proclaim your love in the morning
   and your faithfulness at night,
3 to the music of the ten-stringed lyre
   and the melody of the harp.

1–3 The Lord is pleased with the praise from his people. The meaning of "good" (v.1) here must be interpreted in the light of 147:1: "appropriate and pleasant." The emphatic use of "good" in the MT precedes three infinitive clauses: "to praise . . . make music . . . to proclaim" (vv.1–2). Each infinitive accents the place of praise as an external response to the acts of God. The Lord expects his people to respond in exclamation of his "name" with which all of his beneficent acts are associated. His name is "the LORD" (Yahweh), and he is "the Most High" (Elyon) whom the patriarchs knew (v.1; cf. 91:1; see appendix to Ps 9: Yahweh Is El Elyon).

As always, the occasion for praise is the evidence of the Lord's "love" (*ḥeseḏ*) and "faithfulness" (*'^emûnāh*)(v.2; see 89:1, 24; see appendix to Ps 25: The Perfections of Yahweh). As the priests and Levites prepared the morning and evening sacrifice (cf. Exod 29:39–41), the Levitical singers led God's people with musical instruments in worship. To this end they used a "ten-stringed" instrument, a "harp," and a "lyre" (see appendix to Ps 150: Musical Instruments).

Notes

For a brief discussion of the technical words and phrases in the superscription, see the Introduction.

The psalm was used by the Levites in the temple worship on the Sabbath day (M *Tammid* 7.4). See the introduction to Psalm 24. Matitiahu Tsevat concludes that the Sabbath sign is essentially an "acceptance of the sovereignty of God" and that it was the most important festival, not being bound by the annual cycle ("The Basic Meaning of the Biblical Sabbath," ZAW 84 [1972]: 447–59, esp. 455–59).

1 (2 MT) The lamed before "the LORD" could also be rendered as a vocative, paralleling "O Most High": "O LORD" (see Dahood, *Psalms*, 2:335–36).

3 (4 MT) The phrase "to the music of" is an interpretive addition, based on הִגָּיוֹן (*higgāyôn*, "the melody of," from *h-g-h*, "meditate"; cf. 1:2).

II. Hymn of Thanksgiving (vv.4–14)

A. *Joy in God's Works*

92:4–5

> 4 For you make me glad by your deeds, O LORD;
> I sing for joy at the works of your hands.
> 5 How great are your works, O LORD,
> how profound your thoughts!

4–5 For the psalmist there is no clear distinction between praise and thanksgiving. He praises the Lord for his "deeds" (v.4) with the voice of thanksgiving. The acts of God are not to be separated from his nature ("love," "faithfulness"; cf. v.2), because his "deeds" are expressive of his nature (cf. 89:1, "loving acts"; NIV, "great love"). What the psalmist prayed for in 90:14–16 ("Satisfy us in the morning with your unfailing love [*ḥeseḏ*], that we may sing for joy [*r-n-n*] and be glad [*ś-m-h*]. . . . / Make us glad [*ś-m-ḥ*]. . . . / May your deeds be shown") becomes reality within the covenantal community, as our psalmist confirms: "For you make me glad [*ś-m-ḥ*] by your deeds, O LORD; / I sing for joy [*r-n-n*]."

The thanksgiving differs from the complaint (90:3–17) in many respects. The repetitive "for" (90:4, 7, 9, omitted from NIV in vv.7, 9) has its counterpart in 92:4 ("for you"). The mood is unlike that of Psalm 90, where the psalmist lists one complaint after another. Here he exclaims, "Surely [an alternative translation of *kî*, as in v.9; cf. 91:3] you make me glad by your deeds."

The "deeds" (pl. in a number of MSS, sing. in MT) of the Lord and the "works" of his hands (v.4; cf. v.5) are his mighty acts of deliverance (vv.7–11, 12–15; cf. Rev 15:3). He abases the wicked and exalts the righteous (cf. 113:7–9; 1 Sam 2:3–8; Luke 1:46–55). In the last verse the psalmist will return to this understanding of redemptive history, as he proclaims "the LORD is upright" (v.15). The Lord reveals the greatness of his love by mighty works ("How great are your works!"), all of which witness to a grand design ("how profound your thoughts!" cf. 40:5; Jer 51:29). Here lies the difference between God and man: man can neither penetrate the mind of God nor fully comprehend the acts of his love (cf. Isa 55:8; Rom 8:39; 11:33–34).

B. *Judgment on Folly and Exaltation*

92:6–8

> 6 The senseless man does not know,
> fools do not understand,
> 7 that though the wicked spring up like grass
> and all evildoers flourish,
> they will be forever destroyed.
>
> 8 But you, O LORD, are exalted forever.

6–8 There are two responses to the works of God in redemptive history. The psalmist first describes the response of the wicked; then he accentuates the wise response in vv.8–15. The fool is like a wild beast. The word "senseless" (*ba'ar*, v.6; cf. 49:10; 73:22; Prov 12:1; 30:2) is expressive of animallike behavior. As an animal shows no perception or analytic ability, so the fool has no common sense (cf. Isa 1:2). He begins and ends with himself, without any respect for God. In his insensitivity to God or in his lack of discernment, he is a brute. Even when he increases in power and prestige, he is nothing but grass, which readily perishes in the heat of summer (v.7; see 90:5–6). The constancy of God's love has no effect on him, because he may flourish for a time, but in the end he must perish (cf. 1:6; 37:35–36).

In contrast to the wicked, the psalmist leads the people of God in a response of faith. The emphatic "but you" (v.8) is in contrast to the fool, as if the psalmist is saying, "In contrast to the short-lived self-exaltation of the fools on earth, you, O LORD, are exalted forever!" "Exalted" connotes the Lord's authority as the supreme Judge, a theme more fully developed in the psalms ascribing kingship to the Lord (Pss 93–100). Because of the conviction that the Lord rules and judges, the psalmist sings praise to the Lord for bringing down the wicked (vv.6–7, 9, 11) and for sharing his exalted glory with his saints (v.10; cf. vv.12–15). These two aspects are further developed in the next sections: judgment on the enemies (v.9) and the exaltation of the righteous (vv.10–11).

C. *Judgment and Exaltation*

92:9–11

9 For surely your enemies, O LORD,
surely your enemies will perish;
all evildoers will be scattered.
10 You have exalted my horn like that of a wild ox;
fine oils have been poured upon me.
11 My eyes have seen the defeat of my adversaries;
my ears have heard the rout of my wicked foes.

9 The downfall of the wicked is portrayed in a hymn consisting of three colons. The repetition in the MT of *kî hinnēh* (NIV, "for surely . . . surely") is a form of hymnic stress on the enemies whose doom comes gradually into focus:

> For surely your enemies, O LORD,
> surely your enemies will perish ['-*b*-*d*, see 1:6];
> all evildoers will be scattered [*p*-*r*-*d*, cf. Job 4:11].

Yahweh's exaltation will bring his vindication of his people, removing completely and suddenly any opposition to his sovereignty (cf. vv.6–7).

10 In contrast to his judgment on the evildoers, the Lord exalts the "horn" of the godly. The verb "exalted" (*rûm*) comes from the same root as the adjective "exalted" (*mārôm*, v.8) and expresses how the people of God are rewarded richly by the supreme Judge. The exaltation of the "horn" expresses the bestowal of divine favor (cf. 89:17, 24; see appendix to Ps 98: Yahweh Is the Divine Warrior). It is uncertain what kind of an animal the "wild ox" is. The word *r*ᵉ'*êm* occurs in poetic contexts (cf. Num 23:22; Deut 33:17; Ps 22:21) and is recently rendered by "wild ox" (KB, pp. 864–65, *Bos primigenius Bojanus;* cf. LXX, "unicorn"). The power and ferocity of this animal was proverbial. The imagery of "horn" also evokes the metaphor of "oil," as oil was poured from a horn (cf. 1 Sam 16:13). (For the imagery of oil as a token of divine blessing and succor, see 23:5; 104:15; and 133:2.) The "oil" is derived from the olive tree, which is indirectly referred to as "oil of a luxuriant tree" (*šemen ra*'ᵃ*nān;* NIV, "fine oils"; cf. 52:8, "olive tree flourishing").

11 God's justice in life is one aspect of the hope of the godly. The psalmist confesses his joy in knowing and in having witnessed God's justice by the downfall of the wicked (cf. 54:7; 112:8; 118:7; 119:84). Another aspect of hope is the ultimate and complete cessation of evil. This hope finds expression in the final exclamation: "there is no wickedness in him" (v.15). Evil and God cannot coexist. Therefore this verse has also been rendered in the future tense. Even in the affirmation of God's past acts lies hope for a greater future! (See the appendix to Ps 1: The Ways of Wisdom and Folly.)

Notes

---

10 (11 MT) The LXX supposes an alternate reading of the MT's בַּלֹּתִי (*ballōṯî*, "I am anointed"; NIV, "have been poured"): "my failing strength." Preferable is the emendation based on the Syriac and Targum: בַּלֹּתָנִי (*ballōṯānî*, "you have poured out"; cf. BHS). In view of the use of the second person in the first colon, I prefer to follow the Syriac and Targum: "you have exalted . . . you have poured out."

D. *The Prosperity of the Righteous*

92:12–14

12 The righteous will flourish like a palm tree,
they will grow like a cedar of Lebanon;
13 planted in the house of the LORD,
they will flourish in the courts of our God.
14 They will still bear fruit in old age,
they will stay fresh and green,

12–14 How different is the tone of these verses from the lament of 90:5–6! The wicked are easily swept away whereas the "righteous" (*ṣaddîq;* cf. 1:6) are likened to a "palm tree" and to "a cedar of Lebanon" (v.12). Both trees are symbolic of strength, longevity, and desirability (cf. v.14; Isa 2:13; 65:22; Hos 14:5–6; Zech 11:2). The metaphorical representation of trees growing and bearing fruit "in the courts" of the Lord (v.13; cf. 84:2, 10) suggests the closeness of the righteous to their God (cf. Isa 61:3; Jer 32:41). For a similar expression, see 52:8, where the psalmist compares himself to "an olive tree flourishing in the house of God." For the imagery of fruitfulness and vigor, see 1:3. Whereas the wicked perish prematurely, the godly rejoice in the promise that the Lord's favor rests on them even in old age. Their vigor lies in God's presence in blessing and protection (see appendix to Ps 132: The Ark of the Covenant and the Temple: Symbols of Yahweh's Presence and Rule).

Notes

---

14 (15 MT) The descriptive phrase "stay fresh and green" (lit., "fat and rank") refers back to the blessing of God, by whose favor the godly are anointed with "oil of rank trees" (see v.10). By the Lord's favor they are sustained, even in old age. For date palm and cedar tree, see Zohary, *Plants of the Bible*, pp. 60–61, 104–5.

III. Praise of the Lord

92:15

[15]proclaiming, "The Lord is upright;
he is my Rock, and there is no wickedness in him."

15 The psalm comes to a close by summarizing the major motif and by returning to the beginning. As we have observed in v.2, the phrase "proclaiming" is identical in form to "to proclaim" in the MT. The godly "proclaim" in hymns of praise and thanksgiving the mighty deeds of the Lord. His deeds reflect his "upright" character, as the wicked are abased and the righteous are exalted. Therefore they exclaim that he is their "Rock" (cf. 28:1; 42:9; 62:2; Deut 32:4), on whom they rely for sustenance and stability. He does not disappoint his children, because, unlike man, there is no "wickedness" in him (cf. 119:3; Zeph 3:5). He alone is reliable!

Psalm 93: Yahweh Reigns Gloriously

This psalm belongs to a group of psalms (47; 93–100) that affirm Yahweh's rule over the earth. Psalm 93 praises the Lord as King over the earth, the powerful seas (for a similar poetic expression, see Ps 29), and even Israel (v.5; see appendix to Ps 5: Yahweh Is King).

This psalm was sung before the Sabbath in the second-temple period (cf. *Tamid* 7.4 and the superscription in the LXX). (See the introduction to Psalm 24 for the liturgical use of the Psalms.) The canonical shape of the psalm in the MT bears no reminder of an original cultic situation. The date of the original composition may have been in the tenth century (Dahood, *Psalms*, 2:338).

The psalm moves rapidly from an ascription of praise to Yahweh's kingship to his rule through his temple (v.5). The 4 + 4 meter changes to a 3 + 3 + 3 meter after v.1 (see Introduction: Rhyme, meter, and strophe). The structure is as follows:

A. Yahweh's Glorious Kingship (v.1a–b)
  B. Yahweh's Kingship on Earth (vv.1c–2)
  B′. Yahweh's Kingship Over the Seas (vv.3–4)
A′. Yahweh's Glorious Kingship in Jerusalem (v.5)

I. Yahweh's Glorious Kingship

93:1a–b

[1]The Lord reigns, he is robed in majesty;
the Lord is robed in majesty
and is armed with strength.

1a–b The exclamation "The Lord reigns" is a proclamation of Yahweh's glorious rule (K.A. Kitchen, *Ancient Orient and Old Testament* [Chicago: InterVarsity, 1966], p. 103; see appendix to Ps 5: Yahweh Is King). The emphatic position of "the Lord" in the MT leaves no ambiguity in the affirmation that it is Yahweh, and no other deity, who reigns in glory (cf. Rev 19:6).

God's reign is evident in his creation (i.e., both earth and sea) and in his acts of redemption. The rule of God is visible, as his glorious mantle spreads out all over his kingdom. "Robed in majesty" is a poetic expression for the glory associated with all of Yahweh's works. His works reveal the nature of the Great King: his glory and strength. His "strength" is a metaphor for his power in subduing all things to his control and is derived from military language (cf. 18:39; see Dahood's rendering: "belted with victory," *Psalms,* 2:340; see appendix to Ps 98: Yahweh Is the Divine Warrior).

II. Yahweh's Kingship on Earth

93:1c–2

The world is firmly established;
it cannot be moved.
2 Your throne was established long ago;
you are from all eternity.

1c–2 The Lord established his kingship on earth when he created the "world" (*tēḇēl;* cf. 24:1). The doctrine of God the Creator stands in stark contrast to the pagan teachings on chaos, primordial forces, and random happenings. Yahweh is the Creator-God. He has "established" (*tikkôn*) the world, and it will not reel and totter under the duress of hostile forces (10:6; 104:5), because Yahweh has established his rule over it. The nations may rage against his rule, but it will not fall (2:1–4; 46:6). His throne is "established" (*nāḵôn,* v.6, from *kûn,* as is *tikkôn* above). Yahweh is "from all eternity" (90:2), but his rule over earth has a historical dimension ("long ago"; cf. Isa 44:8; 45:21; 48:3, 5, 7–8). Therefore the psalmist associates the "throne" as established when Creation took place.

III. Yahweh's Kingship Over the Seas

93:3–4

3 The seas have lifted up, O LORD,
the seas have lifted up their voice;
the seas have lifted up their pounding waves.
4 Mightier than the thunder of the great waters,
mightier than the breakers of the sea—
the LORD on high is mighty.

3–4 The threefold repetition of "the seas have lifted up" has an overwhelming effect. The "seas" (lit., "rivers"; cf. 46:4; 72:8) are the "ocean currents" (Dahood, *Psalms,* 1:151; 2:340) whose powers were feared by the pagans, as in the myth of Baal's victory over Yamm ("the sea god"), also known as "the Judge River" (see Norman C. Habel, *Yahweh Versus Baal: A Conflict of Religious Cultures* [New York: Bookman Associates, 1964], pp. 53–54). The "sea" or "river" is also a metaphor of the nations (cf. Ps 89:9–10; Isa 8:7–8; Jer 46:7–8). Though the waters rise up and "pound" with great force, destroying seashores and property, the Lord is "mightier" (v.4). He has also established his kingship over the seas. The seas are not conceived of as independent forces but as controlled by the power of Yahweh. He is "on high" and therefore not subject to the powers of the sea.

Notes

3 The verb sequence of perfect, perfect, followed by the imperfect of the verb "lifted up" corresponds to Ugaritic poetic practice (Dahood, *Psalms*, 2:341) and should not be interpreted as a reference to a past and a future rebellion: e.g., Weiser's rendering: "The floods once rose up . . . the floods lift up their roaring" (p. 617).

4 Verse 4 may be translated in several ways. The NIV renders it as a comparative: "[Yahweh is] mightier than . . . , mightier than." The NEB clarifies the comparative by restructuring the verse: "The LORD on high is mightier far than the noise . . . , mightier than the breakers." A.A. Anderson gives a literal rendering of the MT: "Above the thunderous noise of the great waters, (above the thunderous noise of) the majestic surgings of the sea, majestic on high is Yahweh" (2:669). Dahood's proposal is highly attractive: "Stronger than thundering waters, Mightier than breakers of the sea, Mightier than high heaven was Yahweh" (*Psalms*, 2:339).

IV. Yahweh's Glorious Kingship in Jerusalem

93:5

5 Your statutes stand firm;
holiness adorns your house
for endless days, O LORD.

5 The Lord's kingship finds particular expression in the covenant community. He has given them his "statutes" (*'ēḏôṯ*, lit., "testimonies," used thirteen times in Ps 119; cf. TWOT, 2:649) and has placed his "house" (*bayiṯ*) in their midst. The "statutes" are symbolic of the covenant relationship, as they "testify" to the people of Israel of the revelation entrusted to them. Even as he has established his sovereignty over the created order so that his "throne was established long ago" (v.2), he has made a firm covenant with Israel ("your statutes [i.e., testimonies] stand firm" [*ne'emnû*, from which we get "amen"]).

Yahweh rules among his people. He has placed his dwelling in their midst (Deut 12:5, 11). Covenant and presence are twin concepts (cf. Exod 29:45–46). His presence as a revelation of his glory evokes awe. God's glory ("majesty," v.1) radiates throughout the created order, as the revelation of his hiddenness, that is his "holiness." The wholly other God makes his "dwelling" among his people! Therefore, they must respond with awe as the appropriate expression of wonder that God is dwelling among man.

God's covenant is "firm," as is his presence, "for endless days" (cf. 23:6). Though the covenant could be broken by man and God could remove his presence, his promises extend to all time. This was confirmed in Jesus Christ, by whom the covenant was renewed and the presence of God was in him (Immanuel = God is with us). The vision of the believer extends to the eschatological reality of God's presence on earth (cf. Rev 21:22–22:5; see appendix to Ps 46: Zion Theology).

Psalm 94: Yahweh Is the Judge of the Earth

This psalm is a prayer for God's kingdom to shine forth so that the oppressed and the downtrodden saints may experience the light of his rule. The use of the perfect as an imperative (v.1) is not unusual in the light of the use of the imperatives in v.2 and the use of the imperfect in lament. The central section (vv.8–15) with its rebuke and blessing relates this psalm to the wisdom tradition in Israel, as argued by F. de Meyer, "La Sagesse Psalmique et le Psaume 94," *Bijdragen: Tijdschrift voor Filosofie en Theologie* 42 (1981): 22–45.

Psalm 94 functions as a fitting transition between Psalms 93 and 95. It is made up of two parts: a *national lament* (vv.1–15) and an *individual lament,* which bring together the individual and the community in their common concern. See the introduction to Psalm 24 for the liturgical use of this psalm.

The structure of the psalm shows a concentric development:

A. The God of Vengeance (vv.1–2)
  B. The Arrogant Words of the Wicked (vv.3–7)
    C. Rebuke of the Wicked (vv.8–11)
    C′. Blessing of the Wise (vv.12–15)
  B′. The Lament on Account of the Wicked (vv.16–21)
A′. Confidence in the Vengeance of the Lord (vv.22–23)

(See also Pierre Auffret, "Essai sur la Structure littéraire du Psaume 94," BN 24 [1984]: 44–72.)

I. The God of Vengeance

94:1–2

1 O Lord, the God who avenges,
O God who avenges, shine forth.
2 Rise up, O Judge of the earth;
pay back to the proud what they deserve.

1–2 Yahweh, the covenant God, is "the God [El] who avenges" (v.1)! The repetition of El in v.1 is symmetric with the use of Elohim ("God") in vv.22–23, forming an inclusion. He alone is God, and as the Ruler-God he will bring his vengeance (*n-q-m*). God's vengeance (pl.) is not vindictive but a response to the evil perpetrated by the wicked. Evil has its own rewards, namely, "what they deserve" (*g^e^mûl*, v.2). The root *g-m-l* may signify rewards of the godly (see 13:6) or God's righteous judgment (cf. 28:4) on the wicked oppressors (Deut 32:35; Isa 34:8; 35:4; Ezek 24:8; 25:14–17; Nah 1:2; Rom 12:19; 1 Thess 4:6).

The prayer for Yahweh to "shine forth" (*y-p-'*, v.1) is a prayer for a theophany, when the Lord appears in his royal splendor to bring justice into a world of anarchy (cf. Deut 33:2; Ps 80:1). When he appears, he will "rise up" (*n-ś-'*) in judgment as the "Judge of the earth" (v.2). His splendor will bring down all who have made themselves rulers over God's earth (cf. Isa 2:20–21; 3:13–14; 6:1). To this end the psalmist employs the liturgical prayer for divine redress of wrongs, resembling the prayer of Psalm 7:6: "Arise [*qûm*], O Lord, in your anger; / rise up [*n-ś-'*] against the rage of my enemies. / Awake [*'ûr*], my God; decree justice" (cf. 35:23–24; 58:11; 76:8–9; 82:8; Isa 51:1). The just Judge cannot tolerate "the proud" (*gē'îm*), who act autonomously without regard for God, his people, or the orderly rule of God (cf. 10:2; 31:18; Prov 29:23; Isa 2:12). He will bring them what they "deserve" (*g-m-l;* cf. 28:4; Lam 3:64).

Notes

This psalm is an orphan psalm, not bearing a superscription. The LXX adds a superscription: "A psalm of David, for the fourth day of the week." It reflects a later liturgical usage, as in the Talmud (b. *Rosh Hashanah* 31a).

1–2 For an approach to these verses as a war oracle, see the study by Christensen, pp. 112–27. For other psalms, see 12; 60; 74; 79; 80; 83; 85; 90; 94:1–11; 123; 126; 137.

1 The plural נְקָמוֹת (*neqāmôṯ,* "vengeances") is a plural of intensification (GKC, par. 124a). Since the psalmist is concerned with the redress of wrongs done to God's people, the word "vengeance" may better be rendered by "vindication" (see Dahood, *Psalms,* 2:346). The effect of God's vindication brings full salvation to the suffering people of God (cf. 2 Thess 1:5–10).

2 The verb הָשֵׁב (*hāšēḇ,* "pay back") forms an inclusion with v.23: וַיָּשֶׁב (*wayyāšeḇ,* "repay them").

II. The Arrogant Words of the Wicked

94:3–7

3 How long will the wicked, O LORD,
how long will the wicked be jubilant?

4 They pour out arrogant words;
all the evildoers are full of boasting.
5 They crush your people, O LORD;
they oppress your inheritance.
6 They slay the widow and the alien;
they murder the fatherless.
7 They say, "The LORD does not see;
the God of Jacob pays no heed."

3–7 The questions bubble forth as the psalmist reflects on the arrogance of the wicked. I agree with the KJV and Dahood (*Psalms,* 2:345) that vv.3–4 be read as a series of questions: "How long will the wicked, O LORD, how long will the wicked be jubilant? How long will they pour out arrogant words; how long shall all the evildoers be full of boasting?" (see also Kirkpatrick, p. 567). The stairlike parallelism is evident as the psalmist develops the evil of the wicked: "How long will the wicked . . . be jubilant? . . . pour out arrogant words; . . . [be] full of boasting?" Further, the use of the synonyms "wicked" (twice in v.3) and "evildoers" (v.4) forms a transition from the words of the wicked (v.3) to their acts (vv.5–6).

The wicked excel in boastful rejoicing (*'-l-z,* "be jubilant," v.3) in their power. There is irony in the use of the root *'-l-z* ("be jubilant"), usually denoting the joy of the righteous in their God because of salvation granted by him (cf. 28:7; 149:5; Hab 3:18; Zeph 3:14). Instead the wicked rejoice. They autonomously grasp at every opportunity of making life meaningful for themselves at the expense of others. Their jubilation is an autosoteric expression.

The arrogant words the psalmist alludes to (vv.3–4) come to clear expression at the end of this strophe, forming an inclusion: "They say, 'The LORD does not see; / the God of Jacob pays no heed' " (v.7; cf. 10:11, 13; 59:7; Job 23:13–14). They "pour out arrogant words" and continuously "are full of boasting" (v.4). Their speech is like a spring, gushing forth nothing but insolent words. The verb "gush forth" (*n-b-'*; NIV, "pour out") may denote the words of the wise (78:2; 119:171; Prov 1:23; 18:4) and the words of folly (59:7; Prov 15:2; Eccl 10:1). The context clarifies that we are dealing with fools, whose speech distinguishes itself in a continual tirade, scolding, and arrogant words (*'āṯāq;* cf. 31:18; 75:4; 1 Sam 2:3); as in 59:7: "See what they spew from their mouths— /they spew out swords from their lips, / and they say, 'Who can hear us?' "

When the ungodly harass God's children, they brazenly affront the Lord, whom the psalmist identifies as "the LORD" (*Yah*) and "the God of Jacob" (v.7)—names that go back to the covenantal relationship that forms the basis of the complaint against the acts of the oppressors. Their words find a match in their acts as they "crush [cf. Prov 22:22] . . . oppress [cf. Exod 22:21]. . . . slay . . . murder" (vv.5–6). The strong language may contain hyperbole, but the bitter truth is that any deprivation, prejudice, injustice, or trampling on the rights of God's people is a throwback on the Lord, who had promised to care for his people ("inheritance," v.5; cf. 28:9; Deut 4:20), among whom are "the widow and the alien; . . . the fatherless" (v.6). They need God's special protection because of their vulnerability (cf. Exod 22:21–22; Deut 10:18; 24:19; Ps 10:14; Mal 3:5; James 1:27).

Notes

---

4 The interrogative particles are missing in v.4, permitting the NIV reading "They pour out arrogant words; / all the evildoers are full of boasting." But an elliptic reading permits the full force of the lament to come to expression. For a similar use see 3:1.

The two verbs יַבִּיעוּ יְדַבְּרוּ (*yabbî'û yedabberû,* "they gush forth; they speak") may be taken as a hendiadys; viz., "They pour out arrogant words" (NIV).

III. Rebuke of the Wicked

94:8–11

8 Take heed, you senseless ones among the people;
  you fools, when will you become wise?
9 Does he who implanted the ear not hear?
  Does he who formed the eye not see?
10 Does he who disciplines nations not punish?
  Does he who teaches man lack knowledge?
11 The LORD knows the thoughts of man;
  he knows that they are futile.

8–11 The psalmist addresses the folly of evil by a rebuke, arising from the heart of wisdom. The wicked are "senseless" like animals (92:6), "fools" (*kesîlîm,* v.8; 49:10; 92:6), lacking in understanding. They foolishly establish their little kingdoms on earth, believing that there is no God who calls them to account. They must know that the Lord knows the hearts ("thoughts," v.11) of humans (*'āḏām*). All humans have the common property of being like a "breath" (*heḇel*, "futile," v.11; cf. 39:5; 78:33; Eccl 1:1), even though they pretend to be powers to be reckoned with.

The questions (vv.9–10) call for a strongly affirmative answer. Yahweh, the Creator, who has "implanted the ear," "formed the eye," "who disciplines nations," and "who teaches man" is the ground of human existence. He does "hear . . . see . . . punish" and know what happens on his earth. The Lord's hearing and seeing may result in judgment (v.11; cf. Gen 18:20–21) and in deliverance, as in Exodus 2:24–25: "God heard [*š-m-'*] their groaning and he remembered his covenant with Abraham, with Isaac and with Jacob. So God looked on [*r-'-h*] the Israelites and was concerned about [*y-d-'*] them." But even before the final judgment, the Lord graciously disciplines and instructs those who respond to him (v.10). But when the fools continue in their folly (v.11; 1 Cor 3:20), the judgment of God will find them out. The vindication of his people will result in their deliverance!

Notes

8 The first three words are connected by the "b" sound in the MT: *bînû bō'ᵃrîm bā'ām*. The word כְּסִילִים (*kᵉsîlîm*, "fools") and the phrase תַּשְׂכִּילוּ (*taśkîlû*, "when will you become wise") form a play on words.

10 The noun דַּעַת (*da'aṯ*, "knowledge") could also be read as an infinitive construct from *y-d-'*: "knowing."

The negative particle הֲלֹא (*hᵃlō'*, "not"), repeated before each verbal phrase in vv.9–10a, is omitted in v.10b and may be explained as an ellipsis or a defective reading. Proposals to correct the reading are *hᵃlō' midda'aṯ* or *hᵃlō' yēḏa'*, which may be rendered as "does not he know?" The verb *y-d-'* has the sense of "care about" (see 1:6).

11 Our comments differ from the NIV on account of the ambiguity of the MT. The pronoun הֵמָּה (*hēmmāh*, masc. pl.) most naturally refers back to "man," though singular (so Kirkpatrick, p. 569). It could refer back to the "thoughts" (fem. pl.) of man (so Kraus, *Psalmen*, 2:656; Dahood, *Psalms*, 2:345). For a similar use see 39:11: "each man is but a breath" (cf. 39:5).

IV. Blessing of the Wise

94:12–15

12 Blessed is the man you discipline, O LORD,
the man you teach from your law;
13 you grant him relief from days of trouble,
till a pit is dug for the wicked.
14 For the LORD will not reject his people;
he will never forsake his inheritance.
15 Judgment will again be founded on righteousness,
and all the upright in heart will follow it.

12–15 In stark contrast to the rebuke of the fools, the psalmist proclaims God's blessing on all who respond to divine instruction. The verbs for divine instruction ("discipline, . . . teach") are identical to those used in v.10: "Does he who disciplines [*y-s-r*] nations. . . . Does he who teaches [*l-m-d*] man. . . ?" All wisdom comes from God, even the wisdom found among the nations. However, the Lord has given his own people a clearer form of revelation: his "law" or, better, "instruction" (Torah; see 1:2 and appendix to Ps 19: The Word of God). Those who respond wisely to his instruction (see Ps 1 and the appendix to Ps 1: The Ways of Wisdom and Folly) are "blessed" (*'ašrê*, v.12; see 1:1). They receive his protection from whatever disasters humans may plot against them, that is, "from days of trouble" (v.13; cf. 49:5) until the wicked receive their just deserts ("till a pit is dug for the wicked"; cf. 7:15; 35:7; 57:6; Prov 26:27; Eccl 10:8).

The wise live in the hope of justice, vindication, and the full experience of God's blessings. This hope is grounded in the promises of God (v.14; cf. 1 Sam 12:22; Jer 12:7; Rom 11:1–2). His commitment extends to "his people" ("his inheritance"; cf. v.5) by covenant. Theirs is the promise of the kingdom, characterized by the order of God ("righteousness"), which "all the upright in heart" (v.15; see 7:10) seek (cf. Matt 5:6; 6:33). This resolution is to be seen in contrast to the lot of the wicked who are a mere breath (v.11).

Notes

15 Several MSS, Symmachus, and the Syriac read "righteous" (צַדִּיק, *ṣaddîq*) in parallel with "the upright in heart," instead of "righteousness" (צֶדֶק, *ṣeḏeq*).

The phrase וְאַחֲרָיו (*we'aḥărāyw*,"and after it") is rendered in NIV as "will follow it." Kraus emends it to *we'aḥărîṯ* ("a good end," *Psalmen*, 2:653), which could also be read as "there will be a reward to the upright in heart." The NIV follows the MT, supposing that the pronoun "it" refers back to "righteousness": "on righteousness, and all the upright in heart will follow it [i.e., righteousness]."

V. The Lament on Account of the Wicked

94:16–21

16 Who will rise up for me against the wicked?
Who will take a stand for me against evildoers?
17 Unless the LORD had given me help,
I would soon have dwelt in the silence of death.
18 When I said, "My foot is slipping,"
your love, O LORD, supported me.
19 When anxiety was great within me,
your consolation brought joy to my soul.

20 Can a corrupt throne be allied with you—
one that brings on misery by its decrees?
21 They band together against the righteous
and condemn the innocent to death.

16 The psalmist returns to the prayer for divine vindication, occasioned by the wicked (vv.3–7). The questions of vv.3–4 lead into another set of questions, from "how long?" to "who?" Both sets of questions call on the Lord to act in judgment against "the wicked . . . evildoers" (cf. vv.3–4), who plot the overthrow of the godly. He knows that Yahweh alone will "rise up" (*qûm*) and "take a stand" (*y-ṣ-b*) as the royal Judge (v.15).

17–19 In this personal expression of the lament, the psalmist confesses that he is deeply troubled by the evildoers, even so that he nearly slipped away into the netherworld ("the silence of death," v.17; cf. 115:17; see appendix to Ps 88: Sheol-Grave-Death in the Psalms). Yet he has experienced the presence of the Lord (cf. 124:1) by his support ("help," v.17; "support," v.18) of "love" (*ḥeseḏ*). He further confesses that he was nearly overwhelmed with despair (v.19). Disturbing thoughts ("anxiety"; cf. 139:23) had nearly crushed the spirit within him. But the Lord came to his rescue, transforming doubt and death into "consolation" and "joy" (cf. 2 Cor 1:5).

20–21 The occasion of despair receives further attention in vv.20–21. It seemed as if the reign of corruption, unjust decrees, and oppression of the righteous coexist with the reign of God. He had asked, "How long" (vv.3–4); and in the absence of an answer from the Lord, it seemed as if Yahweh did not care. But he knew that human autonomy can never exist together with God's purpose of establishing his kingdom on earth (cf. Ps 93). The kingdom of man is destructive, whereas the kingdom of God is restorative. His kingdom brings life and his statutes bring order (93:5). The questions of these verses brought the psalmist to an unwavering answer. The Lord will never tolerate evil to be victorious for long.

Notes

20 For a study on the various interpretations of this verse, see Arthur Allgeier, "Psalm 93 (94), 20. Ein Auslegungs- und Bedeutungsgeschichtlicher Beitrag," *Festschrift für Alfred Bertholet zum 80. Geburtstag*, edd. Walter Baumgartner, Otto Eissfeldt, Karl Elliger, and Leonhard Rost (Tübingen: Mohr, 1950), pp. 15–28.

VI. Confidence in the Vengeance of the Lord

94:22–23

22 But the LORD has become my fortress,
and my God the rock in whom I take refuge.
23 He will repay them for their sins
and destroy them for their wickedness;
the LORD our God will destroy them.

22–23 The closure of the psalm restores harmony to an otherwise disturbing psalm. The psalmist has posed many questions and has asked God to respond by bringing in the fullness of his kingdom. In these verses the psalmist calls on the godly to cast their lot with his God, who alone is the fortress of his people and to whom alone belongs vindication. He is the "fortress, . . . the rock" (v.22; cf. 18:1–2; 59:1) for all who "take refuge" in him (see appendix to Ps 98: Yahweh Is the Divine Warrior). He, the God of vindication (vv.1–2), will repay the wicked for "their sins" and "their wickedness" (v.23), that is, their boastful words and oppressive acts (vv.3–7). He will "destroy them . . . destroy them." The repetition of the verb "destroy" (*ṣ-m-t*) is reminiscent of the repetitive opening: "the God who avenges, O God who avenges" (v.1). In response to the prayer for vindication, the godly hold firm that the kingdom is the Lord's and that he will vindicate them by destroying the wicked and by removing all forms of evil from this world.

Notes

23 The LXX suggests a future act—"and he will bring back"—for the MT's וַיָּשֶׁב (*wayyāšeḇ*, "and he brought back"). The MT could be interpreted as a past act—"He made their malice recoil upon them" (Dahood, *Psalms*, 2:346, 351)—or as a future act (GKC, par. 111w).

Psalm 95: Let Us Kneel Before Our Maker

Though this psalm is not explicitly a psalm ascribing kingship to the Lord (Pss 93–100), its theme is nevertheless in harmony with the spirit of these psalms. The parenthetic section (vv.7d–11) throws doubt on this contention, and it is small wonder that critics have argued for treating vv.1–7c and vv.7d–11 as two separate compositions. G. Henton Davies attempts to give a liturgical explanation as to how the psalm became unified: a summons (vv.1–2) and choral response (vv.3–5) outside the temple court; a summons (v.6) and choral response (v.7a–c) inside the temple court (v.7a–b); and an oracle (vv.7d–11) ("Psalm 95," ZAW 85 [1973]: 183–95). A.A. Anderson too assumes that the psalm shows a coherent unity of composition (2:676).

The original situation is far from clear. The psalm correlates creation and redemption, with a special emphasis on redemption (see C.B. Riding, "Psalm 95 1–7c as a Large Chiasm," ZAW 88 [1976]: 418). The structure of vv.1–7c is chiastic (AB–B'A'), followed by a response and a sermon:

A. Call to Worship (vv.1–2)
  B. Hymn to Yahweh the Creator-King (vv.3–5)
A'. Call to Worship (v.6)
  B'. Hymn to Yahweh the Covenant-God (v.7a–c)
    C. Response and Reflection on Yahweh's Judgment (vv.7d–11)

(See also Marc Girard, "Analyse Structurelle du Psaume 95," *Science et Esprit* 33 [1981]: 179–89; Pierre Auffret, "Essai su la Structure littéraire du Psaume 95," *Biblische Notizen* 22 [1983]: 47–69.)

I. Call to Worship

95:1–2

1 Come, let us sing for joy to the LORD;
  let us shout aloud to the Rock of our salvation.
2 Let us come before him with thanksgiving
  and extol him with music and song.

1–2 The community is summoned to come together for the purpose of celebration. The object of the joyous ceremony is no other than "the LORD" (Yahweh), the covenant God, whose relationship is further explicated in vv.6–7. The occasion is an act of "deliverance." The designation "the Rock of our salvation" (v.1) is applied to the Lord in his role as the Divine Warrior. He defends and delivers his people (cf. 98:2). The designation "Rock" for the Lord is not uncommon in the OT (see 18:2, cf. 18:31, 46; 19:14; 28:1; Deut 32:4; 1 Sam 2:2; 2 Sam 22:3; Hab 1:12). The response to the Lord's presence in deliverance is "thanksgiving" (v.2; cf. 50:14, 23; 100:1, 3; Mic 6:6). Praise and thanksgiving focus on God's mighty acts of salvation. The community worships the Lord in word and music ("with music and song"). The praise consists of a popular outburst of joy using all the available means of expressing love and loyalty to the Lord, their Redeemer.

Notes

1–2 After the introductory "come" the psalmist employs a jussive form in each colon:

"let us sing for joy to the LORD" (*n^e^rann^e^nāh;* cf. 92:1)
"let us shout aloud" (*nārî'āh;* cf. 98:4)
"let us come before him" (*n^e^qadd^e^māh;* cf. Deut 23:5)
"and extol him" (*nārî^a^';* several MSS have a form identical to 1b).

1 A number of MSS have a plural "of our salvations" for the MT's יִשְׁעֵנוּ (*yiš'ēnû,* "our salvation").

II. Hymn to Yahweh the Creator-King

95:3–5

3 For the LORD is the great God,
the great King above all gods.
4 In his hand are the depths of the earth,
and the mountain peaks belong to him.
5 The sea is his, for he made it,
and his hands formed the dry land.

3–5 The exaltation of the Lord is due him, because he is "the great King" (v.3) who alone rules over all his creation (see appendix to Ps 5: Yahweh Is King). The nations have their deities whose sovereignty is limited by the sphere of their rule: "the depths of the earth," "the mountain peaks," "the sea," and "the dry land" (vv.4–5). However, the God of Israel is exalted over all the "gods" of the nations (cf. Exod 15:11). The poet exults in Yahweh, as he alone is "the great God" and "the great King," who rules over the whole world. By affirming faith in the Lord, God's people express loyalty to the Lord and deny the existence of any other deity (cf. 96:4–5). This is the language of hymnic praise, in which the "gods" are contemptible fictions of the imaginations of man (von Rad, OTT, 1:212).

The creative acts ("he made . . . his hands formed") constitute the ground of Yahweh's kingship (cf. 24:1; 89:11). Since he has made everything, no one may isolate a single aspect of God's creation to be his god. The Lord rules over the seas (93:3–4) and the great mountains (90:1–2). They belong to the Lord by creative fiat. Creation and dominion are hereby established as corollary to each other.

III. Call to Worship

95:6

> [6]Come, let us bow down in worship,
> let us kneel before the LORD our Maker;

6 The renewal of the call to worship parallels the form of vv.1–2. Three jussives ("let us worship and let us bow down [NIV: 'let us bow down in worship'], let us kneel") follow the imperative ("come"). Worship is a concrete act of obeisance, expressive of one's devotion to the Lord. The reason for worship is self-understood, as the call for worship is placed within the context of God's universal kingship (vv.3–5) and his covenant love for his people (v.7).

IV. Hymn to Yahweh the Covenant-God

95:7a–c

> [7]for he is our God
> and we are the people of his pasture,
> the flock under his care.

7a–c The hymnic "for" (*kî*) is not so much a reason (NIV, "for") as an exclamation: "truly!" (cf. v.3; 91:3; 92:9). The people of God approach him with a hymn celebrating God's commitment. He is "the LORD" (Yahweh), their God (cf. Exod 19:5–6; Jer 31:33; Ezek 11:20; 14:11; 34:31), their "maker" (cf. 100:3), because he has sovereignly elected Israel and has brought them into being as a covenant people (cf. Deut 32:6, 15, 18; Isa 44:2; 54:5). As their "Maker" he is also their shepherd, and they are "the people of his pasture," i.e., "the flock under his care" (cf. 79:13; 100:3; John 10:11–14).

Notes

7 The phrase יָדוֹ (*yāḏô*, "his hand"; NIV, "under his care") does not quite fit. BHS proposes an emendation based on the use of the imperative in vv.1, 6: דְּעוּ (*dᵉʿû*, "know"): "know today." However, this does not fit with the next clause: "if you hear his voice." The MT is preferable.

Rudolf Schmid suggests that v.7 prepares the ground for Israel's responsibility (cf. v.7d, in *Wort, Lied und Gottesspruch. Beiträge zur Psalmen und Propheten. Festschrift für Joseph Ziegler*, ed. Josef Schreiner (Würzberg: Echter Verlag/Katholisches Bibelwerk, 1972), 2:91–96).

V. Response and Reflection on Yahweh's Judgment

95:7d–11

Today, if you hear his voice,
8 do not harden your hearts as you did at Meribah,
as you did that day at Massah in the desert,
9 where your fathers tested and tried me,
though they had seen what I did.
10 For forty years I was angry with that generation;
I said, "They are a people whose hearts go astray,
and they have not known my ways."
11 So I declared on oath in my anger,
"They shall never enter my rest."

7d The relationship between the Lord and his people had been marred by apathy and outright disobedience. The new era calls for a different response. "Today" is still the moment of grace. "Today" is reminiscent of Moses' insistence that "the moment" of hearing the word evokes a response (cf. Deut 4:40; 5:3; 6:6; 7:11; 9:3; 11:2).

8–9 The past history was associated with "Meribah" ("contending") and "Massah" ("testing"). At these historical places Israel had acted wantonly against the Lord (cf. Exod 17:1–7; Num 20:1–13; 27:14; Deut 6:16; 9:22; 32:51; 33:8; Ps 81:7). These places also symbolize a whole generation of faithless Israelites (cf. 78:18, 41, 56; Heb 3:7–11) who dared to challenge ("test") the Lord. They had witnessed all the mighty works in Egypt, by the Red Sea, and in the wilderness. In response to the Lord's evidences of his care (Exod 19:4), the people grumbled, complained, and challenged outright the Lord's right to take them away from Egypt.

10–11 The generation of the wilderness was representative of many generations of Israelites. The Lord cared for them for "forty years" (v.10, emphatic position). They demonstrated a deviant spirit from the beginning and were consistent in their apostasy. Their "hearts," a metaphor for their inner being, were corrupt; and the people repeatedly proved that they did not love ("know") the ways of God. Though the biblical record testifies to God's continual care for his people during those forty years, the psalmist reminds his audience of the Lord's anger with his people. The verbal phrase "be angry" signifies more than the occasional expression of anger. The verb is rare, and only here is the Lord the subject. The Lord was so greatly disturbed with the negative reaction from his people that he "loathed" them, even as man under God's judgment may come to loathe his own corruption (cf. Ezek 6:9; 20:43; 36:31) and as a righteous man may loathe sin (cf. 119:158; 139:21).

The objects of God's loathing were the rebels, "that generation" that perished in the wilderness. They could not and did not enter into the Promised Land ("my rest," v.11; cf. Deut 12:9; Ps 132:8, 14). The Lord swore that they were aliens to his benefits. Hebrews 4:7 applies these words from a canonical perspective. Joshua and David did not succeed in providing "rest" for God's people. In Jesus the Messiah "rest" is still being offered. This is the "today" of the gospel proclamation (Heb 4:7).

Notes

11 See Walter C. Kaiser, Jr., "The Promise Theme and the Theology of Rest," BS 130 (1973): 135–50, for a fruitful study of the rest motif in Scripture. He concludes appropriately that God offers the eschatological rest in the contexts of creation and redemption. It is here and is still to come. For an interpretation of "rest" as the presence of God as symbolized in the temple, see Georg Braulik, "Gottes Ruhe—Das Land oder der Tempel? Zu Psalm 95,11," *Freude an der Weisung des Herrn, Beiträge zur Theologie der Psalmen, Festgabe zum 70. Geburtstag von Heinrich Gross* (Stuttgart: Katholisches Bibelwerk, 1986), pp. 33–44.

Psalm 96: Yahweh Will Judge the World in Righteousness

This psalm belongs to a group of psalms (93–100) united by genre and motif. These psalms affirm Yahweh's rule over the earth (see appendix to Ps 5: Yahweh Is King). He delivers his people while judging the nations. Though the genre as well as the classification has occasioned a great deal of discussion, we follow the approach suggested by Westermann. These psalms are hymns celebrating Yahweh's kingship and form a subcategory of the descriptive praise psalms. The linguistic similarities between Psalms 96–99 may suggest that the same author has composed these psalms. By being incorporated into a larger unit in 1 Chronicles 16, the psalm became associated with the glorious entry of the ark of the covenant into Jerusalem. The LXX also reflects a temple tradition by adding a superscription: "When the house was built after the exile. A song of David." However, these traditions have little bearing on the original life-situation.

The relationship of Psalm 96 to Isaiah has become a matter of scholarly discussion because of common motifs: polemics against idolatry (Isa 40:18–31; 41:21–24; 44:6–8), creation (40:22; 42:5; 44:24; 45:12), nature's response to God's redemption (49:13; 55:12), and the nations (45:20; 49:7; 56:3–8; 60:9–12, 14, 16; 66:18). Kraus holds that Psalm 96 is dependent on Isaiah 40–66 and hence must date to after the Exile (2:666). A.A. Anderson rightly posits the possibility that Isaiah (40–66) and Psalm 96 are heirs of a similar theological heritage (2:681).

The structure of the psalm falls into several parts:

A. Proclamation of Universal Praise (vv.1–3)
  B. The Majesty of the Lord (vv.4–6)
A′. Proclamation of Universal Praise (vv.7–9)
  B′. The Rule of the Lord (vv.10–13)

I. Proclamation of Universal Praise

96:1–3

1 Sing to the LORD a new song;
  sing to the LORD, all the earth.
2 Sing to the LORD, praise his name;
  proclaim his salvation day after day.
3 Declare his glory among the nations,
  his marvelous deeds among all peoples.

1–3 The threefold call "sing to the LORD" is symmetric with the three imperatives: "praise" (lit., "bless"), "proclaim" (lit., "proclaim good news"), and "declare" (or "tell"). The contents of the praise is "the new song" (v.1; cf. 144:9; 149:1; Rev 5:9; 14:3), that is, the fresh outburst of praise to God. The occasion of praise is a new act of "salvation" (*yᵉšûʿāh,* v.2; cf. 3:2–3), also known as "his marvelous deeds" and "his wonders" (see 9:1). The acts of the Lord are acts of deliverance whereby he assures his people of deliverance and victory (see appendix to Ps 78: The Mighty Acts of Yahweh).

The exact nature of the salvation is not specified here, but it may include all acts in redemptive history: creation and redemption (vv.2, 11–12; cf. 136:4–25). The people of God must give leadership by giving "praise" to his name every day ("day after day"). Thus the "nations" (*gôyîm,* v.3) and the "peoples" (*ʿammîm*) will hear the "good news" (v.2; *b-ś-r,* "declare the good news"; NIV, "proclaim"; cf. Isa 40:9; 41:27; 52:7) of who Yahweh is and what he has done for his people (see appendix to Ps 122: The Praise of Yahweh).

II. The Majesty of the Lord

96:4–6

4 For great is the LORD and most worthy of praise;
he is to be feared above all gods.
5 For all the gods of the nations are idols,
but the LORD made the heavens.
6 Splendor and majesty are before him;
strength and glory are in his sanctuary.

4–5 The psalmist more explicitly sets forth the reasons for the universal proclamation of Yahweh's praise in the form of a hymn. The hymn exclaims his greatness (v.4; cf. 48:1; 145:3), his being "worthy of praise" (*mᵉhullāl,* cf. 48:1), and his awe-inspiring nature (*nôrāʾ;* NIV, "he is to be feared"; cf. 99:3). Yahweh alone is God and all other deities are "fakes." They cannot be gods, because Yahweh alone has made heaven. The pagans may claim that their gods have power over the heavenly realms, but this is excluded by virtue of Yahweh's sole claim to having created "the heavens" (v.5).

6 God's royal glory is evident in creation. Humans are surrounded by the evidences of his royal presence: "splendor and majesty" (cf. 21:5; 45:3–4; 104:1; 111:3), "strength and glory" (cf. v.7). Yahweh is glorious, especially because he relates to his world as King (cf. 21:3) and Creator (104:1–3).

Notes

5 A.A. Anderson renders אֱלִילִים (*ʾᵉlîlîm;* NIV, "idols") as "nobodies" (2:683; cf. Lev 19:4; 26:1; Ps 97:7; Isa 2:8, 18, 20; 10:10–11).

III. Proclamation of Universal Praise

96:7–9

7 Ascribe to the LORD, O families of nations,
ascribe to the LORD glory and strength.
8 Ascribe to the LORD the glory due his name;
bring an offering and come into his courts.
9 Worship the LORD in the splendor of his holiness;
tremble before him, all the earth.

7–9 The psalmist has a renewed urgency in proclaiming the divine name (vv.7–9; cf. 29:1–2). The threefold imperative "ascribe" (vv.7–8a) is symmetric with the threefold use of "sing" (vv.1–2a). However, the object of the imperative as well as the following imperatives show a clear development.

Praise takes the form of concrete expressions of submission to Yahweh. He expects that proper honor be given to his name in recognition of his greatness, majesty, and strength (cf. Mal 1:6, 11). The ascription of "glory" may be in the form of the praise in worship or presentation of a tribute-offering (cf. 20:3; Isa 60:5–6) in the temple courts (v.8; cf. 65:4; 84:10; 92:13; 100:4). The combination of "glory" and "strength" brings out the nature of his powerful acts. They reveal his "royal" splendor. Thus the psalmist calls on all to praise the Lord for his rule, sovereignty, and majesty in relationship to his people and to all his works. All the "clans" (NIV, "families"; cf. Gen 10:32) of the nations (cf. v.3), i.e., of "all the earth," are invited to participate. The universal allusion of v.3 is made more explicit by an allusion to the promise pertaining to the nations in the Abrahamic covenant. All may worship him, but the motivation is as important as the manner. Yahweh expects reverence, submission, holiness, and awe of his divine majesty and presence. (See the appendix to Ps 46: Zion Theology.)

Notes

9 The meaning of the word הֲדָרָה (*hᵃdārāh*, "splendor," "attire") has been debated. Dahood found a Ugaritic parallel meaning "theophany," e.g., "when the Holy One appears" (*Psalms*, 1:176; 2:358). The evidence, however, is debatable, and KB^3 (p. 230) returns to the more traditional meaning: "attire," "garment." It is related to the word הָדָר (*hādār*, "majesty") but is not the same. Craigie translates the colon in 29:2: "Worship the LORD in holy attire" (*Psalms 1–50*, p. 242).

The word חִילוּ (*ḥîlû*, "tremble") could be translated as a pilgrim "dance" (Briggs, 2:304), but the more usual translation (NIV) is preferable.

IV. The Rule of the Lord

96:10–13

10 Say among the nations, "The LORD reigns."
The world is firmly established, it cannot be moved;
he will judge the peoples with equity.
11 Let the heavens rejoice, let the earth be glad;
let the sea resound, and all that is in it;

[12] let the fields be jubilant, and everything in them.
Then all the trees of the forest will sing for joy;
[13] they will sing before the LORD, for he comes,
he comes to judge the earth.
He will judge the world in righteousness
and the peoples in his truth.

10 The second hymn ascribes dominion to the Lord. The proclamation "the LORD reigns" is characteristic of this type of psalm (cf. 93:1; 97:1; 99:1). He has established his rule on earth by the fact of his creation ("the world is firmly established"; cf. 93:1) and by the evidence of his rule with "equity" (*mêšārîm;* cf. 9:8; 17:2; 58:1; 75:2; 98:9; 99:4).

11–12 The coming of God to judge is here a cause for joy. All nature is called on to celebrate his coming: heaven, earth, sea (v.11; cf. Isa 42:10–12; 44:23; 49:13; 55:12–13), sea creatures (cf. 24:2; 98:7; Isa 42:10), fields and wild animals ("everything in them," v.12; cf. 24:1), and "trees of the forest" (cf. Isa 55:12–13). C. Houtman may well be right in his extensive argument that "forest" is an inadequate translation. He renders it as "thicket" or "wilderness" and concludes that the psalmist longs for a transformation of creation at the coming of Yahweh, in which even the jungle and thicket will have a share ("De Jubelzang van de Struiken der Wildernis in Psalm 96:12b," in *Loven en Geloven. Opstellen van Collega's en Medewerkers aangeboden aan Prof. Dr. Nic. H. Ridderbos,* ed. M.H. van Es et al. [Amsterdam: Ton Bolland, 1975], pp. 151–74).

13 The Lord comes to establish "righteousness" and "truth" ("faithfulness") on earth. The hymn closes on the same motif that it began with: the affirmation of God's rule ("governs"; NIV, "will judge") with "equity" (synonymous with "righteousness" and "truth"). The judgment of God includes both vengeance of the ungodly and a deliverance of the godly. The judgment "serves to restore his order in the world" (Weiser, p. 630). Though the focus of the psalm lies on the present, the theological and canonical function stretches to the eschatological hope, when God's rule is fully established.

Psalm 97: The Joys of Zion

This psalm belongs to a group of psalms (93–100) united by genre and motif. These psalms affirm Yahweh's rule over the earth (see appendix to Ps 5: Yahweh Is King). He delivers his people, while judging the nations. Though the genre as well as the classification has occasioned a great deal of discussion, we follow the approach suggested by Westermann, according to whom these psalms are hymns celebrating Yahweh's kingship and form a subcategory of the descriptive praise psalms.

The psalm contains many allusions to other parts of the OT, all of which have been shaped into a magnificent hymn. The structure of the psalm is as follows:

A. The Revelation of Yahweh's Glory (vv.1–6)
  B. Exhortation to Worship (v.7)
  B′. Zion's Worship (vv.8–9)
A′. The Effects of Yahweh's Glorious Rule (vv.10–12)

I. The Revelation of Yahweh's Glory

97:1–6

1 The LORD reigns, let the earth be glad;
let the distant shores rejoice.
2 Clouds and thick darkness surround him;
righteousness and justice are the foundation of his throne.
3 Fire goes before him
and consumes his foes on every side.
4 His lightning lights up the world;
the earth sees and trembles.
5 The mountains melt like wax before the LORD,
before the Lord of all the earth.
6 The heavens proclaim his righteousness,
and all the peoples see his glory.

1 The psalm opens on a positive affirmation of the reign of Yahweh (cf. 93:1; 96:10; 99:1; Rev 19:6). The reign of Yahweh is not limited to Israel but extends to all "the distant shores" (cf. 72:10; Isa 41:1, 5; 42:4, 10; Jer 31:10; Ezek 27:10; Zeph 2:11) and to "the earth" (cf. Isa 49:13). The nature of the Lord's reign is much more important than the fact that he reigns. This psalm, together with the other hymns affirming Yahweh's kingship (Pss 93; 95–99), proclaims the righteous, just, and loyal rule of Yahweh ("righteousness and justice are the foundation of his throne," v.2). He will make righteousness abound on the earth. His rule benefits the development of godliness and brings an end to godlessness. He will establish order on earth.

2–5 The magnificent portrayal of Yahweh's coming in "clouds and thick darkness" (v.2) is reminiscent of the OT metaphors for theophany (cf. 18:9–11). These metaphors go back to Israel's experience at Mount Sinai (cf. Deut 4:11; 22) and were also used to designate the awesome nature of the Day of the Lord (cf. Joel 2:2; Zeph 1:15; Rev 11:5). Out of the darkness fire shoots forth (v.3; cf. 18:8, 12–13; 50:3) like arrows (cf. 18:14; 68:2; 77:17; 106:18; 144:6; Hab 3:11) against his enemies. The intensity and brightness of his coming is so great that it "lights up the world" (v.4; cf. 77:18). The theophany shakes the earth like an earthquake (cf. 77:16; Hab 3:10) and melts the mountains like wax (cf. Mic 1:4; Nah 1:5) in the presence of the Great King (v.5). The parallelism of "LORD" (*YHWH* [Yahweh]) and "Lord" (Adonai) affirms that Yahweh is the Lord ("great King") of all the earth (cf. Josh 3:11, 13; Mic 4:13; Zech 4:14; 6:5).

6 The revelation of God's glory is overwhelming. The heavens already "proclaim his righteousness" and "his glory" (cf. 19:1). When he comes to establish his kingdom in righteousness, all the nations will see his glory (cf. Isa 40:5). (See the appendix to Ps 98: Yahweh Is the Divine Warrior.)

Notes

2–5 Von Rad observes that "the highest beauty in all creation was Yahweh's condescending and entering into historical existence. This comes to expression first and foremost in the description of theophanies" (OTT, 1:366). For a study on theophany in Pss 18; 50; 68; 77; and 97, see A. Weiser, "Zur Frage nach dem Beziehungen der Psalmen zum Kult: Die Darstellung der Theophanie in den Psalmen und im Festkult," in *Festschrift für Alfred Bertholet zum 80. Geburtstag,* edd. Walter Baumgartner, Otto Eissfeldt, Karl Elliger, and Leonhard Rost (Tübingen: Mohr, 1950), pp. 513–31.

II. Exhortation to Worship

97:7

7 All who worship images are put to shame,
those who boast in idols—
worship him, all you gods!

7 The nations must come to the true worship of Yahweh. If they persist in idolatry (cf. 96:5; 115:4–8; Isa 42:17; 45:16), they will be put to shame. Idols are worthless on the day of Yahweh's coming because they will be unable to deliver (cf. 25:3; 37:20; Isa 1:29; Mic 3:7). Instead of the idle praise ("boast") of the idols, the Lord alone is worthy of worship. Hence the psalmist calls on all the gods to worship Yahweh alone. Who are the "gods"? The reference could be to "images" or to creatures of God that occupy "the heavens" (v.6), namely, the angels (so Heb 1:6; LXX), or to both. The "gods" are contemptible fictions of the imaginations of man (von Rad, OTT, 1:212). Yahweh alone is great and above "all gods" (cf. 95:3; 96:4). Since all creatures in heaven must worship him, how much more should worship be the response of his people on earth!

Notes

---

7 On "gods" see Heinz-Josef Fabry, "Der himmlische Thronrat als ekklesiologisches Modell," *Bausteine biblischer Theologie. Festgabe für G. Johannes Botterweck zum 60. Geburtstag dargebracht von seinen Schulern,* ed. H.J. Fabry (Köln: Peter Hanstein, 1977), pp. 99–126.

III. Zion's Worship

97:8–9

8 Zion hears and rejoices
and the villages of Judah are glad
because of your judgments, O LORD.
9 For you, O LORD, are the Most High over all the earth;
you are exalted far above all gods.

8–9 The people of God ("Zion," "the villages of Judah," v.8) rejoice in God's rule. (For an exposition of v.8, see on 48:11.) The new canonical setting of this verse amplifies the response of God's people in the worship of God on earth. They confess that "truly" (NIV, "for," v.9) the Lord is "the Most High" (Elyon) over the earth and above all the angels (v.7; cf. 47:2, 9).

Notes

---

9 The translation "Most High" is one of two possible readings of the MT's עֶלְיוֹן (*'elyôn,* "most high," "exalted"). The word may designate God as "the Most High" (cf. 47:2; 57:2), or it may be a synonym of the parallel expression ("you are exalted," v.9b): "exalted." The latter seems to be preferable because *'elyôn* and the verb *na'ᵃlêṯā* ("you are exalted") are derived from the same root: *'-l-h.* (See the appendix to Ps 9: Yahweh Is El Elyon.)

IV. The Effects of Yahweh's Glorious Rule

97:10–12

10 Let those who love the LORD hate evil,
  for he guards the lives of his faithful ones
  and delivers them from the hand of the wicked.
11 Light is shed upon the righteous
  and joy on the upright in heart.
12 Rejoice in the LORD, you who are righteous,
  and praise his holy name.

10 The practical outworking of the confession (v.9) evidences itself in a profound realization of the kingdom of God on earth. The godly are "those who love the LORD." They are wise in that they hate anything tainted by evil (cf. 1:1–2). They need not fear the day of the Lord's appearance, because he will protect them from the wicked: they are "his faithful ones" (*ḥᵃsîḏāyw,* see 4:3; cf. 30:4; 86:2), who have shown their "loyalty" to him.

11–12 The godly will enjoy the benefits of the rule of God: "light" and "joy" (v.11). Light signifies the blessed state of redemption and victory (cf. Isa 60:1–3). The "righteous" and "upright in heart" (i.e., the godly; cf. 32:11) will enjoy the new age of restoration as the dawning of light (cf. Isa 58:8, 10; Mal 4:2). The exhortation to rejoice (v.12) anticipates the Lord's coming with his blessings. He renews his people. They already experience some evidences of his kingship here on earth but eagerly await the fullness of his kingdom, even while praising him. His "name" (*zēḵer,* lit., "remembrance," as in Exod 3:15) signifies all the promises of the Lord, as fulfilled in the history of redemption, as well as those to be accomplished in the future. The godly rejoice in his past acts, his present rule, and his blessings, as well as in the eschatological beatific vision of God's reign on earth. The last verse ties in with the first, where the nations were invited to rejoice (*ś-m-ḥ*). The "righteous" are God's light to the Gentiles (Isa 42:6).

Notes

---

10 The MT is problematic. The NIV reflects the MT's שִׂנְאוּ (*śin'û*, "hate," imperative) with a minor adjustment, as it renders the imperative by a jussive: "let those . . . hate." Without altering the consonantal structure, it is also possible to adopt the reading proposed by BHS: שֹׂנְאֵי (*śōn*[e]*'ê*, "those who hate"): "those who love Yahweh hate evil." By emending אֹהֲבֵי (*'ōh*[a]*b̲ê*, "lovers of") to a singular construct, אֹהֵב (*'ōhēb̲*), assuming that the yod is a dittography, an alternate reading is proposed: "The Lord loves those who hate evil" (NEB).

11 The phrase "light is shed" (*z-r-ḥ*) is suggested by the LXX, Targum, and several versions (cf. 112:4), instead of the MT's זָרֻעַ (*zāru*[a]*'*, "sown").

Psalm 98: A New Song to the Lord

Like Psalm 96, this psalm reflects on the reasons for God's universal praise. The themes are so similar that some have proposed a common authorship. It is more likely that the psalms have a common literary heritage. Tremper Longman persuasively argues in favor of the psalm being "a Divine Warrior victory song celebrating the return of Yahweh the commander of the heavenly hosts who is leading the Israelite army back home after waging victorious holy war" ("Psalm 98: A Divine Warrior Victory Song," JETS 27 [1984]: 267–68). The historical situation was "dehistoricized," and the psalm has now an eschatological dimension. We agree with Weiser that the many saving events are "represented" as one event, with an eschatological focus (p. 637).

The "representative" significance of the psalm may have found a special place in the worship of postexilic Israel when the Lord had redeemed his people from Babylon. Yet the psalm goes beyond a reflection on the past to a joyful anticipation of the universal restoration of all things, when God's kingdom will be established on earth (see appendix to Ps 5: Yahweh Is King). Our Lord Jesus is the Great Warrior who will overcome the rebellious kings and their armies (Rev 19:11–21), redeem his people, and judge the entire earth (Matt 25:31–46). He is the "KING OF KINGS AND LORD OF LORDS" (Rev 19:16).

The psalm is divided into three stanzas:

A. Joyful Celebration of Past Acts of Deliverance (vv.1–3)
B. Worship of the Great King (vv.4–6)
A'. Joyful Anticipation of God's Coming (vv.7–9)

I. Joyful Celebration of Past Acts of Deliverance

98:1–3

A psalm.

1 Sing to the LORD a new song,
for he has done marvelous things;
his right hand and his holy arm
have worked salvation for him.
2 The LORD has made his salvation known
and revealed his righteousness to the nations.
3 He has remembered his love
and his faithfulness to the house of Israel;

all the ends of the earth have seen
the salvation of our God.

1 The "new song" (cf. 33:3; 40:3; 96:1; 144:9; Isa 42:10; Rev 5:9; 14:3) celebrates the Lord's victory. The psalmist does not explicate the historical details of the victory. The purposeful ambiguity of the background moves the worshiper from a reflection of one event to the worship of the Redeemer-God, by whom his people have been delivered many times. It is possible that the language of "new" well fits Isaiah's conception of the redemption from Babylon as the second Exodus, when the Lord showed his mighty power (cf. Isa 51:9–11; 59:16; 63:5). The "marvelous things" (cf. 106:7) are the acts of the Lord done in his own power, metaphorically represented by "his right hand" and "his holy arm" (cf. Exod 15:11–12; Isa 52:10).

2 Through his power the Lord has obtained victory—"salvation" and "righteousness." In Isaiah these two words are synonyms for the establishment of God's just order on earth in fulfillment of the prophetic word (cf. Isa 46:13; 51:5–6, 8). The nations witness that the Lord is victorious as he blesses his people. However, the saving events are not only for the sake of Israel but also for all the nations (cf. Isa 40:5; 52:10; see appendix to Ps 119: Yahweh Is My Redeemer).

3 The motivating factors for the demonstration of God's power in redemption and vindication are his "love" (*ḥesed*) and his fidelity to his covenant people (cf. 92:2). They who asked to be "remembered" in love and compassion at the time of the Exile (74:2, 18; 89:50) had experienced that the Lord does remember, i.e., he works out the provisions of the covenant (see appendix to Ps 25: The Perfections of Yahweh). God's "marvelous" acts are not limited to Israel. Though the primary focus was on Israel, the Lord provoked the "ends of the earth" (cf. 2:8; 22:27; 59:13; 67:7; 72:8; Isa 45:22; 52:10) to jealousy. Weiser states, "The history of his people as the *Heilsgeschichte* of God reaches its ultimate universal goal with God's recognition by the world, with the coming of the Kingdom of God on earth" (p. 638; see also Tryggve N.D. Mettinger, "Fighting the Powers of Chaos and Hell—Towards the Biblical Portrait of God," ST 39 [1985]: 21–38).

Notes

For a brief discussion of the technical words and phrases in the superscription, see the Introduction.

2 The NIV places "to the nations" at the end of v.2 whereas the MT puts it in between the first and the last colons. It forms a "pivot pattern," as it may be read with the first and the last; cf. T. Longman: "The LORD has made known his salvation—in the presence of the nations—he has revealed his righteousness" ("Psalm 98," p. 268; cf. W.G.E. Watson, "The Pivot Pattern in Hebrew, Ugaritic, and Akkadian Poetry," ZAW 88 [1976]: 239–53).

II. Worship of the Great King

98:4–6

4 Shout for joy to the LORD, all the earth,
burst into jubilant song with music;

[5]make music to the LORD with the harp,
with the harp and the sound of singing,
[6]with trumpets and the blast of the ram's horn—
shout for joy before the LORD, the King.

4–6 The previous stress on the universal extent of God's salvation evokes a response. All life on earth must join the joyful celebration of God's kingship. The earth must prepare itself for his coming by an open welcome, shouting "for joy," bursting "into jubilant song," and making "music" with a variety of instruments. The earth responds with a shout for joy (v.4). The victory of the Lord evokes submission on the part of his subjects (cf. 47:1–2; Zeph 3:14; Zech 9:9). The "earth" signifies here the inhabitants of the earth (cf. 47:2; 66:1; 100:1). The earth bursts into jubilant song. The verb "burst" (*piṣḥû*, "break forth") is also found in Isaiah 44:23 and 55:12 as an appropriate expression to God's acts of salvation. The NIV combines three Hebrew imperatives—"burst out," "rejoice," and "sing"—into a loaded expression: "burst into jubilant song with music" (cf. Isa 52:9). The outburst of joyful praise is in response to the expectation that his salvific acts will benefit all who rejoice. They who welcome their Great King need not fear, because they are the recipients of his victories. He has gone to great length to save them. (See the appendix to Ps 122: The Praise of Yahweh.)

The particular form of the joyful expectation of the Great King expresses itself in a great variety of musical instruments. The "new song" celebrating the "marvelous" acts of the Great King is accompanied by instruments used in the worship of God in the temple (vv.5–6; cf. 47:5; 1 Chron 16:5–6; see appendix to Ps 150: Musical Instruments).

The people of God respond with joyful singing to the accompaniment of musical instruments in celebration of Yahweh's universal kingship. Moses and Miriam led Israel in song in celebration of his victory over the Egyptians and of his deliverance of Israel (Exod 15:1–21). The phrases "shout for joy to the LORD" (v.4) and "shout for joy before the LORD, the King" (v.6) form an inclusion with the latter phrase explaining the particular reason for the celebration: the Lord (Yahweh) is King:

A. Shout for joy [*hārî'û*] to *the Lord,* all the earth,
B. burst into jubilant song . . .
B′. make music
. . . .
A′. shout for joy [*hārî'û*] before the LORD, *the King.*

Notes

5 The repetition of "harp" at the end of the first and at the beginning of the second colons is an example of anakypdosis.

III. Joyful Anticipation of God's Coming

98:7–9

[7]Let the sea resound, and everything in it,
the world, and all who live in it.

8 Let the rivers clap their hands,
let the mountains sing together for joy;
9 let them sing before the LORD,
for he comes to judge the earth.
He will judge the world in righteousness
and the peoples with equity.

7–8 The Creator-Redeemer-King has made the world to be inhabited and will restore everything to himself. The restoration of his people creates an anticipation of the final restoration of all things. The arena of God's "marvelous" acts is the world; and nature forms the stage on which God, the Great King, acts. Nature echoes and reverberates the joy of God's people as they anticipate the coming of the Great King (cf. Isa 55:12). The rejoicing of animal and plant life in the sea and on earth (v.7) constitutes the totality of all of created life (cf. 24:1; 96:11), as does the contrastive pair "rivers" and "mountains" (v.8). The "groaning" of nature (Rom 8:19–21) will give way to rejoicing at his coming.

9 At his coming, the Great King will fully establish his dominion over the created world in "righteousness" and "equity." He will establish his victory ("righteousness") on earth by his judgment and will continue to rule over his subjects with "uprightness," i.e., equity (see 9:9; cf. 17:2; 58:2; 96:10; 99:4). Oesterley comments appropriately, "The reign of universal peace, justice, and happiness has begun in the psalmist's prophetic vision" (p. 428).

Appendix: Yahweh Is the Divine Warrior

The ancient people of God looked to him for all the benefits of kingship. Other nations in the ancient Near East looked to a human king for protection and security. A human king had to be valiant in battle to secure victory over the enemies and to grant peace to his people. But the Israelites looked to Yahweh as their mighty Warrior-King. They believed that he alone gives peace and protects his people. Yahweh is the Royal Protector of his people!

The imagery of war and warfare seems strange to our Western ears. We like to think of peace, whereas the Psalms, together with the prophets, long for God to swoop down and terrify the enemy forces. A glance at Psalm 18 illustrates the strange conception that the ancient psalmist had of God. He portrays God's appearing (theophany) as being attended by smoke, dark clouds, burning coals, and darkness, as Yahweh mounts the cherubim like horses and flies as a bird on the winds. Further, he fights with hailstones, bolts of lightning, and rain. This imagery is an example of mythopoetic language. (For a further discussion of mythopoetic language, see in bibliography below Elmer Smick, "Mythopoetic Language," and Lynn Clapham, "Mythopoetic Antecedents.") Mythopoetic language employs culturally conditioned metaphors, ways of speech, and conceptions with an adaptation to Israelite traditions. For example, the language of God's kingship is culturally conditioned but also transformed by Yahweh's revelation. The mythopoetic language of the Psalms is not surprising, because Israel used the literary heritage of her neighbors to the greatest advantage to demonstrate the superiority and uniqueness of Yahweh, the God of heaven, the seas, the depths, and the earth. All creation serves at the command of Yahweh, the Commander-in-Chief, in gaining a victory to redeem his people. Yahweh "rides the ancient skies above, who thunders with mighty voice" (68:33).

Psalm 98 clearly illustrates the "Yahweh, the Commander-in-Chief" motif, as Israel celebrates the mighty acts of God, the Divine Warrior. All creation (sun, moon, and stars; heaven and earth; cf. 148:8) is at Yahweh's disposal in the establishment of his kingdom. No wonder the psalms abound with war imagery. This imagery depicts the sufficiency and power of Yahweh in all of life's situations.

1. Yahweh as a Shield

The word "shield" (NIV) is represented by two Hebrew words: *māḡēn* (from *g-n-n*) and *ṣinnāh*. The *ṣinnāh* shield denotes a large rectangular shield, protecting the body of the warrior. The Lord's protection and copious blessings are like a *ṣinnāh* shield, as the psalmist exclaims, "For surely, O LORD, you bless the righteous; / you surround them with your favor as with a shield" (5:12). God is good to his children, even as a bird is tender to her young, but yet strong like a warrior with a *ṣinnāh:* "He will cover you with his feathers, / and under his wings you will find refuge; / his faithfulness will be your shield and rampart" (91:4). When in distress the people of God may call on him to prepare himself for the battle. His battle is against the enemies but for his children. So the psalmist freely calls on the Lord to vindicate him from his adversaries, "Take up shield and buckler; / arise and come to my aid" (35:2).

The *māḡēn* shield occurs more frequently. It was significantly smaller and could easily be used by infantry men to protect their chests in sword fights. For the psalmist the *māḡēn* is no less significant: e.g., "But you are a shield around me, O LORD, / you bestow glory on me and lift up my head" (3:3). It provides him with the assurance of protection, deliverance, and victory. Underlying this metaphor is the conviction that Yahweh is King: "Indeed, our shield belongs to the LORD, / our king to the Holy One of Israel" (89:18). David rejoiced in victory because he knew that the Lord was with him, fighting his battles for him: "You give me your shield of victory, / and your right hand sustains me; / you stoop down to make me great" (18:35).

The Lord promises his protection only to those who seek his safekeeping: "My shield is God Most High, / who saves the upright in heart" (7:10; cf. 115:9–11). Even though in despair, the godly hope in Yahweh and rejoice in his promise:

> The LORD is my strength and my shield;
>   my heart trusts in him, and I am helped.
> My heart leaps for joy
>   and I will give thanks to him in song.
>
> (28:7)

Hope requires a patient waiting on the Lord to come to the rescue with his *māḡēn* (33:20; cf. 119:114).

It is clear in the above examples that "shield" signifies more than protection. Associated with protection is the experience of full deliverance, victory, and the full enjoyment of his kingship. One psalm compares the Lord to a sun and a shield in the same breath: "For the LORD God is a sun and shield; / the LORD bestows favor and honor; / no good thing does he withhold from those whose walk is blameless" (84:11).

2. Yahweh as the Warrior

We shall be brief at this point because in the commentary (cf. 5:4–6; 18; 68:1–8; 77:16–19; 98; et al.) we develop the imagery of Yahweh as the Divine Warrior. This tradition goes back to the Song of Moses (Exod 15), when Moses led Israel in a victory song:

> The LORD is my strength and my song;
>   he has become my salvation.
> He is my God, and I will praise him,

my father's God, and I will exalt him.
The LORD is a warrior;
the LORD is his name.

(Exod 15:2–3)

The psalmists look for Yahweh's order in his kingdom. Since the kingdom of God extends to all his creation, not only Canaan, they long for the establishment of justice (*mišpāṭ*), righteousness (*ṣᵉḏāqāh*), peace (*šālôm*), and fidelity (*ḥeseḏ* ["love"], *'ᵉmeṯ* ["truth," "faithfulness"]) on earth.

The godly expect the Lord to vindicate his children by redeeming them from all adversity and by avenging their enemies. His retribution will bring "equity" (*mēšārîm*) to this world. In utter despair and in total abandonment to his Redeemer, the psalmist cries out for action, "Rise up, O LORD, confront them, bring them down; / rescue me from the wicked by your sword" (17:13; cf. 59:5). When Yahweh comes to deliver, nothing can stand in his way. He will use his creation in accomplishing his end (18:12–14). The psalmist portrays Yahweh as fighting with a sword and bow (7:12–13; cf. 21:12; 60:4; 64:7; 135:7; 144:6) in his war with evil. In the end he will establish peace in this world: "He makes wars cease to the ends of the earth; / he breaks the bow and shatters the spear, / he burns the shields with fire" (46:9). The godly need not fear (91:5), because Yahweh is with them.

3. Yahweh as the Fortress

The language of the Psalms employs many metaphors for Yahweh's protection: "rock," "fortress," "stronghold," and "refuge." He is all his people need, regardless of the adversity in life. David said:

I love you, O LORD, my strength.
The Lord is my rock [*sela'*], my fortress [*mᵉṣûḏāh*] and my deliverer;
my God is my rock [*ṣûr*], in whom I take refuge.
He is my shield [*māḡēn*] and the horn [*qeren*] of my salvation,
my stronghold [*miśgaḇ*].

(18:1–2)

The Lord himself is the strength of his people. In the various contexts the presence and power of God receive the preeminence. He protects his people during adversities and sets them "high" (*ś-g-b*), far from the reach of the enemy. In Psalm 31:1–4 we read:

In you, O LORD, I have taken refuge;
let me never be put to shame;
deliver me in your righteousness.
Turn your ear to me,
come quickly to my rescue;
be my rock [*ṣûr*] of refuge [*mā'ôz*],
a strong fortress [*mᵉṣûḏāh*] to save me.
Since you are my rock [*sela'*] and my fortress [*mᵉṣûḏāh*],
for the sake of your name lead and guide me.
Free me from the trap that is set for me,
for you are my refuge [*mā'ôz*].

(cf. 28:8; 46:7; 48:2–3; 94:22)

4. Yahweh as the Rock

Yahweh is the Incomparable One. The deities of the nations were called "rock" or "mountain" as an appellation of strength, reliability, and protection. However, for the people of God, Yahweh was everything they needed. He is *the* Rock: "For who is God besides the LORD? / And who is the Rock [*ṣûr*] except our God?" (18:31). He is the Father, the God, the "totality" of all the epithets and powers attributed to deities, whom the Davidic Messiah confesses, saying, "You are my Father, my God, the Rock my Savior" (89:26).

The word "rock" brings up vivid associations in the poetic literature. Yahweh is strong in being able to deliver: "He alone is my rock and my salvation; / he is my fortress, I will never be shaken" (62:2; cf. 18:46; 19:14). Yahweh protects his people as if they were in a secret hideout, enjoying his protection:

> For in the day of trouble
> he will keep me safe in his dwelling;
> he will hide me in the shelter of his tabernacle
> and set me high upon a rock.
>
> (27:5)

The Lord is the Rock who hears and responds to his afflicted people: "To you I call, O LORD my Rock; / do not turn a deaf ear to me" (28:1; cf. 31:2; 40:1). The Rock of Israel "guides" his people: "Since you are my rock and my fortress, / for the sake of your name lead and guide me" (31:3). He is their hope in despair (42:9; 61:2; 62:2, 6). He shares his glory and the spoils of victory with his people (62:7); so they have reason to rejoice only because of the fullness of Yahweh's salvation: "Come, let us sing for joy to the LORD; / let us shout aloud to the Rock of our salvation" (95:1).

5. Yahweh as the Horn

The metaphor of "horn" (*qeren*) is complex by its varied usage in the OT and in the ancient Near East. The study by Margit L. Sųring (see bibliography) reveals the variety of the horn motifs: animal, musical, vessels, and altar. What is the meaning of "horn" in "He is my shield [*māḡēn*] and the horn [*qeren*] of my salvation, my stronghold [*miśgāḇ*]" (18:2b)?

Sųring concludes that "horn" has a horizontal and a vertical dimension. The horn metaphor begins at the horizontal level with the "bull" tradition, according to which power, fertility, and prosperity are associated with the "horn." But the metaphor is extended vertically into a prophetic-eschatological metaphor for the Davidic dynasty. Yahweh promised to exalt the kingdom of David with power, peace, and prosperity.

The psalms witness to the power struggle between the "power" bases of the enemies on the horizontal level and the intrusion of God's kingdom and of his Messiah on a vertical level. Hence the usual meaning "strength" (see NIV mg. on 18:2) has been amplified by Sųring,

> We, therefore, suggest that the ultimate meaning of the term "horn" . . . is to be found in the unfolding of these two diametrically opposed traditions: the tradition concerned with . . . astral cults and bull-worship, and the "horn" tradition on the vertical level where it is connected with messianic, eschatological, and apocalyptic realities that are said to bring about something totally new. (p. 462)

6. Conclusion

The godly long for the Lord's "redemption." He is their Redeemer, and his redemption extends to all facets of their well-being: reconciliation, forgiveness, communion with God, freedom, and the glorious experience of unrestrained and joyous celebration of being the children of God. This hope, even when not fully realized, gives ground for confidence in despairing life situations, gives reason for hope in the victorious establishment of God's kingdom, and gives cause for rejoicing, as expressed in Psalm 59:16–17:

> But I will sing of your strength [*'ôz*],
> in the morning I will sing of your love;
> for you are my fortress [*miśgāḇ*],

my refuge [*mānôs*] in times of trouble.
O my Strength [*'oz*], I sing praise to you;
you, O God, are my fortress [*miśgāb̲*], my loving God.
(cf. 71:2–4; 91:2–4)

The dimension of hope comes out even more clearly in Psalm 62:2, 6–8:

He alone is my rock [*ṣûr*] and my salvation;
he is my fortress [*miśgāb̲*], I will never be shaken.
. . . .
He alone is my rock [*ṣûr*] and my salvation;
he is my fortress [*miśgāb̲*], I will not be shaken.
My salvation and my honor depend on God;
he is my mighty [*'ôz*] rock [*ṣûr*], my refuge [*maḥᵃseh*].
Trust in him at all times, O people;
pour out your hearts to him,
for God is our refuge [*maḥᵃseh*].
(cf. 144:1–2)

Texts: 3:3; 5:11–12; 7:10–13; 18; 21:12; 24:7–10; 28:7–8; 29; 31:1–3; 33:16–22; 46; 48; 59:9, 11, 16–17; 62:2, 6–8; 64:7–10; 68:1–8, 21–23, 28–35; 71:1–3; 76; 77:13–20; 93:1; 97; 98; 132:8; 144.

Related Topics: See appendixes to Pss 3 (Yahweh Is My God); 7 (The Name of Yahweh); 25 (The Perfections of Yahweh); 46 (Zion Theology); 98 (Yahweh Is the Divine Warrior); 119 (Yahweh Is My Redeemer); 122 (The Praise of Yahweh); 132 (The Ark of the Covenant and the Temple: Symbols of Yahweh's Presence and Rule); 140 (The Poor and Oppressed).

Bibliography: Dianne Bergant, "Yahweh: A Warrior-God?" TBT 21 (1983): 156–61; Lynn Clapham, "Mythopoetic Antecedents of the Biblical World-View and Their Transformation in Early Israelite Thought," *Magnalia Dei. The Mighty Acts of God*, edd. Frank Moore Cross, Werner E. Lemke, and Patrick D. Miller, Jr. (Garden City: Doubleday, 1976), pp. 108–19; Christensen; C. Kenny Cooper, "The Lord of Hosts," *Biblical Illustrator* 12 (1986): 60; Peter C. Craigie, *The Problem of War in the Old Testament* (Grand Rapids: Eerdmans, 1978); Frank Moore Cross, Jr., "The Divine Warrior in Israel's Early Cult," *Biblical Motifs. Origins and Transformations*, ed. A. Altmann (Cambridge: Harvard University Press, 1966), pp. 11–30; W. Eichrodt, TOT, 1:194–200; Paul D. Hanson, "War and Peace in the Hebrew Bible," Int 38 (1984): 341–62; C. Herzog and M. Gichon, *Battles of the Bible* (New York: Random House, 1978); Gwilym H. Jones, "'Holy War' or 'Yahweh War'?" VetTest 25 (1975): 642–58; Millard C. Lind, "Paradigm of Holy War in the Old Testament," *Biblical Research* 16 (1971): 16–31; id., *Yahweh Is a Warrior: The Theology of Warfare in Ancient Israel* (Scottdale: Herald, 1980); Tremper Longman III, "The Divine Warrior: the New Testament Use of an Old Testament Motif," WTJ 44 (1982): 290–307; id., "Psalm 98: A Divine Warrior Victory Song," JETS 27 (1984): 267–74; Tryggve N.D. Mettinger, "Fighting the Powers of Chaos and Hell—Towards the Biblical Portrait of God," ST 39 (1985): 21–38; Patrick D. Miller, Jr., "El the Warrior," HTR 60 (1967): 411–31; id., *The Divine Warrior in Early Israel* (Cambridge: Harvard University, 1973); R. Nysse, "Yahweh Is a Warrior," *Word and World* 7 (1987): 192–201; Gerhard von Rad, *Der heilige Krieg im alten Israel* (Göttingen: Vandenhoeck & Ruprecht, 1969); Elmer Smick, "Mythopoetic Language in the Psalms," WTJ 44 (1982): 88–98; Margit L. Suring, *The Horn-Motif in the Hebrew Bible and Related Ancient Near Eastern Literature and Iconography*, AUSDDS 4 (Berrien Springs, Mich.: Andrews University, 1980); Marvin E. Tate, "War and Peacemaking in the Old Testament," *Review and Expositor* 79 (1982): 587–96; Joseph Thuruthumaly, "Waiting for Yahweh," BTh 8

(1982): 94–103; Moshe Weinfeld, "Divine Intervention in Ancient Israel and in the Ancient Near East," *History, Historiography, and Interpretation. Studies in Biblical and Cuneiform Literatures*, edd. H. Tadmor and M. Weinfeld (Leiden: Brill, 1984), pp. 121–47; W. Weippert, "'Heiliger Krieg' in Israel und Assyrien," ZAW 84 (1972): 460–93; Y. Yadin, *The Art of Ancient Warfare in Biblical Lands in the Light of Archaeological Discovery* (New York: McGraw-Hill, 1963).

TDOT, 2:373–77; THAT, 1:398–402; 2:221–24, 538–43; TWOT, 1:148–49, 169; 2:627, 652, 756, 761, 771, 871.

Psalm 99: Yahweh Is the Revealer-King

This psalm belongs to a group of psalms united by genre and motif, variously designated as the enthronement psalms or the psalms celebrating Yahweh's kingship (Pss 93–100). These psalms affirm Yahweh's rule over the earth (see appendix to Ps 5: Yahweh Is King). He delivers his people, while judging the nations. The structure is somewhat problematic because of the presence of two refrains: "He/The LORD is holy" (vv.3, 5, 9) and "exalt the LORD" (vv.5, 9; cf. "he is exalted," v.2). For the present purpose we shall follow the following expository outline:

A. The Exaltation of the Lord in Israel (vv.1–5)
  B. The Revelation of the Lord to Israel (vv.6–7)
A′. The Exaltation of the Lord in Israel (vv.8–9)

I. The Exaltation of the Lord in Israel

99:1–5

1 The LORD reigns,
  let the nations tremble;
he sits enthroned between the cherubim,
  let the earth shake.
2 Great is the LORD in Zion;
  he is exalted over all the nations.
3 Let them praise your great and awesome name—
  he is holy.
4 The King is mighty, he loves justice—
  you have established equity;
in Jacob you have done
  what is just and right.
5 Exalt the LORD our God
  and worship at his footstool;
  he is holy.

1–5 The psalmist opens with the proclamation "The LORD reigns" (v.1; cf. 93:1; 96:10; 97:1). He is highly exalted in heaven, as he "sits enthroned between the cherubim." The imagery of the cherubim derives from the ark of the covenant, whose lid was a gold slab ("the atonement cover," Lev 16:13) on which two cherubs with spread wings stood. The significance of the cherubim becomes clear in the traditions of Israel, as they spoke of God's dwelling between the cherubim (cf. 1 Sam 4:4; 2 Sam 6:2). The ark of the covenant signified the establishment of God's kingdom on earth and as such became known as his "footstool" (v.5; 132:7–8; 1 Chron 28:2). By extension the "footstool" also referred to the temple (Isa 60:13) and Jerusalem (cf.

Lam 2:1). The Lord's throne in heaven was likened to the "footstool" on earth, as his "enthronement" was likened to being surrounded by the cherubim. The imagery arouses the metaphor of God's being the Divine Warrior: "you who sit enthroned between the cherubim, shine forth. . . . come and save us" (80:1; cf. Ps 98). The cherubim protect the glory of God (cf. Gen 3:24) and are his emissaries (Ps 18:10 = 2 Sam 22:11; Ezek 10:18–22).

The sovereign and glorious rule of the Lord should inspire all inhabitants of the world to "tremble" and "shake" (v.1). The inhabitants of "the earth" respond with awe to God's holy presence. Brueggemann comments, "God's enthronement makes holy presence accessible and makes righteous will more urgent" (*Message of the Psalms*, p. 149). If they do not respond, they are still responsible. However, the psalmist does not develop what will happen if they do not respond. The nations must praise the "name" with which the acts of redemptive history are associated: "great and awesome" and "holy" (v.3). Everything, whether it be God's revelation or his acts of creation and redemption, reveals his greatness, awesomeness, and holiness!

The name "Yahweh" was particularly revealed to Israel to be proclaimed and remembered through festivals, songs, and the stories of redemption. Hence the nations must submit themselves to the Great King who, while being "exalted [*rām*] over all the nations" (v.2), has established his "great"ness in Zion, Jerusalem! As the incarnation of our Lord is a great mystery, so is the dwelling of God in Jerusalem a great mystery. Too often the nations scoffed at Zion and thereby ridiculed the God of Israel, the Great King of the world (48:2). The nations must know that Zion is "his footstool" (v.5; see appendix to Ps 46: Zion Theology).

The nature of the King's rule is no different from his character. He is "holy" (*qāḏôš*, v.3), "mighty" (*ʿōz*, v.4), and "loves justice [*mišpāṭ*]." He is holy in his perfections and awe-inspiring in his glorious presence. The very revelation of his otherness ("holy") is the glory of the Great King. His acts further reveal his majestic power. He is "mighty" in judgment and deliverance. He is "just" in his judgment and deliverance (cf. 11:7; 33:5; 37:28; 97:2). Because of his nature the Lord has "established equity" (*mêšārîm*) and "done what is just [*mišpāṭ*] and right [*ṣeḏāqāh*]" (v.4; cf. 98:9) for the sake of "Jacob," i.e., the people of God or "Zion."

Because the Lord is "exalted" (*rām*, v.2) over the nations and "holy" (vv.3, 5) in his awe-inspiring presence, the people of God must lead the nations in "exalting" (*rômemû*, v.5) the Lord. The object of the exaltation and "worship at his footstool" is to submit oneself to his sovereignty and to respond properly to his holy presence. He has established his kingdom on earth in the election of Israel, in the consecration of Jerusalem, and in this holy temple ("his footstool"; cf. 110:1; 132:7). The acts of God in Israel reveal the nature of the Great King and confirm his universal rule. His rule over the nations will be no different from what he has done on behalf of Israel. They too may benefit from his just and righteous rule (see appendix to Ps 132: The Ark of the Covenant and the Temple: Symbols of Yahweh's Presence and Rule).

Notes

4 Modern commentators find the MT phrase וְעֹז מֶלֶךְ (*weʿōz meleḵ*, lit., "and might of the king"; NIV, "the King is mighty") problematic. Though the ancient versions support the MT and

BHS has no critical note, it is argued that the phrase *wᵉʿōz* ("and mighty") belongs together with "he is holy" and should be read: "he is holy, he is mighty" (NEB). The MT may be retained.

II. The Revelation of the Lord to Israel

99:6–7

6 Moses and Aaron were among his priests,
Samuel was among those who called on his name;
they called on the LORD
and he answered them.
7 He spoke to them from the pillar of cloud;
they kept his statutes and the decrees he gave them.

6 The reminders of what God has "established" and "done" in and for his people (v.4) occasion an elaboration of the acts of the Lord and of his revelation to Israel in the history of redemption through his servants Moses, Aaron, and Samuel. The word "priests" (v.6) should not be taken too narrowly, because in the strict sense Moses was not a priest. The noun is a participial form from the verb "serve" and is here loosely used for "servants" or "intercessors." Moses, Aaron, and Samuel interceded on Israel's behalf. They "called" (*qōr(')îm*, part.) on his "name" (Yahweh) in intercessory prayer, and he responded to their prayers (cf. Exod 14:15; 17:11–12; 32:11–13, 30–32; Num 12:13; 14:13–19; 16:22; 21:7; 1 Sam 7:5, 8–9; 12:16–18; Jer 15:1).

7 Not only did the Lord perform mighty wonders on behalf of his people, he also revealed himself as "he spoke to them from the pillar of cloud." To whom did he speak from the cloud? The text is not clear, whether he spoke to each of the three mediators or to Israel. If he spoke to all three mediators, it would not be appropriate to refer to the Lord's speaking from a cloud to Samuel. If the "pillar of cloud" be a metaphor for God's speaking, then Samuel may be included. But if the psalmist refers to God's response to the prayers of his saints, then his revelation pertains to the special status of these leaders in the eyes of all Israel (Delitzsch, 3:102–3).

III. The Exaltation of the Lord in Israel

99:8–9

8 O LORD our God,
you answered them;
you were to Israel a forgiving God,
though you punished their misdeeds.
9 Exalt the LORD our God
and worship at his holy mountain,
for the LORD our God is holy.

8 The psalmist restates that the Lord has been good to Israel, as he "answered them" (cf. v.6). His deeds showed forth his "great and awesome name" (v.3) and his "mighty" kingship (v.4). Moreover, he revealed his "justice," "equity," and righteousness (v.4) to Israel in avenging himself on those who rebelled and broke his covenant. He inflicted the rebels with plagues, fire, and serpents; he opened the earth and let the generation of the wilderness perish (cf. Num 11:33; 14:37–38). His judgment is an act of "vengeance" on the wicked who have had no respect for his "holy" presence. Yahweh is "jealous" of his royal and divine prerogatives: "for the LORD, whose name is Jealous, is a jealous God" (Exod 34:14). He is a consuming fire to those who deprive him of his rights (cf. Deut 4:24; 9:3). But he is also gracious in his holiness and justice, as he readily forgave the people: "you were to Israel a forgiving God" (cf. Exod 34:6–7).

9 Because of the Lord's greatness, holiness, and justice as demonstrated in his acts of mercy, forgiveness, and vengeance, Israel as the people of God must submit themselves to his lordship by exalting him (see v.5). Thus they may give leadership to the nations. In the many references to his mighty acts, revelation, and forgiveness, the nations may find comfort. Yet there is a warning implied in the affirmation of his vengeance (v.8). If Israel or the nations do not exalt him as holy, they too will perish! Worship is an act of submission to his kingship and is a proper response to his awe-inspiring presence.

Notes

---

8 The MT has been satisfactorily explained by C.F. Whitley. The word נֹקֵם (*nōqēm*, "avenging" or "avenger") does not fit in with "misdeeds," though the NIV makes an admirable attempt: "though you punished their misdeeds," with a marginal rendering: "*an avenger of the wrongs done to them.*" Whitley explains the form as resulting from verse stress and assumes the root *n-q-h* ("cleanse") instead of *n-q-m* ("avenge"): "cleansed them from their wrongdoings" ("Psalm 99:8," ZAW 85 [1973]: 227–30).

Psalm 100: The Lord Is God and He Is Good

In hymnic form the worshipers sing about the Lord and his covenant relationship with his people. It seems likely that the hymn was sung during one of the festivals, but it lacks specifics other than an adumbration of the Lord. Its position after the psalms proclaiming Yahweh's kingship (96–99) suggests the classification with these psalms. More than likely it functions as a hymnic conclusion of this collection.

The structure of the psalm is simple. It divides naturally into two parts (vv.1–3, 4–5), each of which consists of a call to give thanks and a rationale for thanksgiving:

A. Call to Give Thanks (vv.1–2)
  B. Celebration of the Covenant (v.3)
A′. Call to Give Thanks (v.4)
  B′. Celebration of the Covenant (v.5)

(See Pierre Auffret, "Essai su la Structure littéraire du Psaume 100," BN 20 [1983]: 7–14; Walter Brueggemann, "Psalm 100," Int 39 [1985]: 65–69.)

I. Call to Give Thanks

100:1–2

A psalm. For giving thanks.

1 Shout for joy to the LORD, all the earth.
2 Worship the LORD with gladness;
come before him with joyful songs.

1–2 These verses resemble 95:1–2 in form and mood. The psalmist calls on "all the earth" (v.1) to come before the Great King (see appendix to Ps 5: Yahweh Is King). The invocation resembles that of 98:4, where the whole earth too is summoned to "shout for joy to the LORD." The nations must recognize who the Lord is. He is Yahweh (NIV, "the LORD"), by whose grace and blessings his people exist. The nations too are invited to sing hymns to the Lord and to worship him (cf. Isa 56:6–7). The invitation is a free offer. The submission to his rule comes out of a heart response of joy and gratitude for his covenant promises (cf. in contrast 2:11). The "gladness" (*śimḥāh*) reflects the joy in living in harmony with the Creator, Redeemer, and King. The sacrifices of "joyful songs" (v.2; cf. Heb 13:15) are proper as one approaches his presence (cf. 95:6; 96:8; Isa 1:12).

Notes

For a brief discussion of the technical words and phrases in the superscription, see the Introduction.

II. Celebration of the Covenant

100:3

3 Know that the LORD is God.
It is he who made us, and we are his;
we are his people, the sheep of his pasture.

3 This verse shares the language of 95:7. The imperative "know" (from *y-d-'*) signifies acknowledgment or confession (cf. Deut 4:39; Isa 43:10). They confess him as covenant Lord ("the LORD"), their only true God (cf. 1 Kings 18:39). In addition they confess their accountability to him ("It is he who has made us"; cf. Deut 32:6, 15; Isa 43:1, 21; 60:21) and their privileged position ("his people, the sheep of his pasture"; cf. 74:1; 79:13; Isa 40:11; Ezek 34:31). The lordship of God connotes benefits, also clearly brought out by the shepherd imagery of "sheep" and "pasture" (cf. Ps 23; Luke 15:3–6; John 10:1–18).

III. Call to Give Thanks

100:4

4 Enter his gates with thanksgiving
and his courts with praise;
give thanks to him and praise his name.

4 The communal confession arouses another invocation to give thanks to the Lord. The worshiping community entered the temple courts (cf. 96:8) through the gates. The verb "enter" (*bō'û*), identical to the verb in v.2 translated "come," resumes the invocation to praise. In fact, when vv.1, 2, and 4 are read as a unit, the imperatival parallelism is clearer:

vv.1–2: "Shout for joy. . . . Worship . . . come"
v.4: "Enter ['come' in v.2] . . . give thanks . . . praise."

Verses 1–2 bring out the joyful acclamation of God's kingship, whereas v.4 stresses the communal act of worship. They come "with thanksgiving" and "with praise." These are the appropriate sacrifices of "thanks" to his name for all the benefits. Thanksgiving and praise (*b-r-k*) go together, because the Lord reveals himself both in his perfections and acts (cf. 139:1; cf. Jer 33:11).

IV. Celebration of the Covenant

100:5

5 For the LORD is good and his love endures forever;
his faithfulness continues through all generations.

5 God's people adumbrate God's name on account of his goodness to them. He is "good" (106:1; 107:1; 136:1), full of "love" (*ḥesed*) and "faithfulness" (*'emûnāh*) (for these covenantal perfections, see Exod 34:6–7). He remains faithful to his people because he has covenanted to do so (see appendix to Ps 25: The Perfections of Yahweh).

Psalm 101: Commitment to Excellence

The king solemnly vows to administer justice and to live up to the theocratic ideal in Israel. In Deuteronomy 17:14–20 the Lord had instructed the priests to prepare a copy of his law for the king so that he would learn to live rightly and manage his affairs of state as Israel's chief executive. The Davidic king was the Lord's vassal and as such was appointed to execute the wishes of his sovereign, the Suzerain. The vow is reminiscent of the treaty form of the ancient Near East.

The qualities of Jesus the Messiah, as given in Isaiah 11:1–5 and in this psalm, reveal a fulfillment of the theocratic ideal: concern for integrity, justice, and devotion. Similarly, the followers of Jesus must conform to his high standards (v.6; cf. 1 Tim 3:1–16; 2 Tim 2:14–26; Titus 1:6–9). In Europe the psalm came to be known as the "prince's psalm," owing to the concern for the proper conduct of a Christian magistrate, prince, or king.

Clearly the psalm belongs to the *royal psalms,* and further it is in the form of a declaration of commitment. But Allen concludes that Psalm 101 may best be interpreted as a royal complaint instead of a declaration of loyalty (p. 4). The close association of loyalty and wisdom are not uncharacteristic. The wise king abstains from evil and dissociates himself from evildoers or rebels. The parallels in language with wisdom, especially Proverbs 1–9, have been observed by commentators.

Several words are repeated in the psalm: "blameless" (vv.2, 3, 6), "in my house" (vv.2, 7), "before my eyes" (vv.3, 7; NIV, "in my presence"), "put to silence" (vv.5, 8). The psalm opens with a personal expression of devotion to the Lord (v.1) and ends with a commitment to remove evil from the city of the Lord (v.8). The structure is as follows:

A. The King's Commitment to God's Kingdom (vv.1–3a)
  B. Hatred of Evil (vv.3b–5)
    C. Love for God's People (v.6)
  B′. Hatred of Evil (v.7)
A′. The King's Commitment to Justice (v.8)

I. The King's Commitment to God's Kingdom

101:1–3a

Of David. A psalm.

1 I will sing of your love and justice;
  to you, O Lord, I will sing praise.
2 I will be careful to lead a blameless life—
  when will you come to me?

I will walk in my house
  with blameless heart.
3 I will set before my eyes
  no vile thing.

1–3a The motivation for the king's loyalty comes from the Lord's acts of "love and justice" (v.1; cf. Hos 12:6; Mic 6:8; Matt 23:23). He is constant in his "love" (*hese͟d*) and full of "justice" (*mišpāṭ*) in his administration. The Lord's covenantal acts on behalf of his covenant people bring the psalmist to thanksgiving ("I will sing . . . I will sing praise"). These qualities are also the motivating factors for his commitment to lead "a blameless life" (v.2). The verbal phrase "I will be careful to lead" (*ś-k-l*) derives from the wisdom tradition. It expresses the concern for wise living and acting (cf. 2:10) and attentiveness to the lessons of wisdom, by observation or education (cf. Prov 19:16; Isa 41:20). With diligence, having observed the ways of the Lord, the godly leader gives himself to a life of integrity ("blameless," *tāmîm;* cf. 15:2; 119:1; Gen 17:1) in the presence of God as well as in his personal affairs ("in my house with blameless [*tom*] heart"; cf. 18:23; 78:72; 1 Kings 9:4; Prov 20:7). Below in v.7 the theme of personal integrity will be further developed to include all those who form the "house." Both verses together affirm his commitment to keep himself and his environment free from deviation from the practice of love and justice.

The brief prayer "when will you come to me" (v.2) suggests a need, either personal or for the people. It is not uncommon for a vow (affirmation of innocence, declaration of devotion to the Lord) and prayer to originate in a time of lament and duress. However, there is no indication of the original situation. What is clear is the king's dependence on his God.

The king swears before Yahweh that his administration will be characterized by integrity: "I will walk in my house [administration] with blameless [*tom*] heart" (v.2b). The commitment to excellence implies a difference in administration from the manner in which kings ruled in the ancient Near East. The godly king affirms that his loyalty is to Yahweh and not to the ways of this world (*Realpolitik*). This may explain the negative manner in which the vow finds expression. He vows to have nothing to do with any "vile thing" (v.3; lit., "a thing of Belial"), with "the deeds of faithless men," with "men of perverse heart" (v.4; cf. Prov 11:20; 17:20, contrastive with "blameless heart," v.2), or with "evil."

Notes

For a brief discussion of the technical words and phrases in the superscription, see the Introduction.

3 "Vile thing" (NIV) is a rendering of בְּלִיַּעַל (*b^e^lîya'al*, "Belial"). Its meaning is obscure, but from its use Belial appears to be associated with evil. In the OT people could be "vile" or "wicked" (Deut 13:13). In Ps 18:4 the phrase "torrents of destruction" (lit., "rivers of Belial") evokes images of the netherworld, as described in Canaanite mythology. In this psalm the Davidic king vows to keep clear distinctions between his rule of justice and the rule of evil in this world. For further discussion see TWOT, 1:111; J.E. Hogg, "Belial in the Old Testament," AJSL 44 (1941): 56–58; D. Winton Thomas, "בליעל In the Old Testament," *Biblical and Patristic Studies: in Memory of Robert Pierce Casey*, edd. J. Neville Birdsall and Robert W. Thomson (Freiburg: Herder, 1963), pp. 11–19.

II. Hatred of Evil

101:3b–5

The deeds of faithless men I hate;
they will not cling to me.
4 Men of perverse heart shall be far from me;
I will have nothing to do with evil.

5 Whoever slanders his neighbor in secret,
him will I put to silence;
whoever has haughty eyes and a proud heart,
him will I not endure.

3b–5 The godly leader shuns evil in any form. He cultivates purity of mind, heart, and associations: "I will not set. . . . I hate; . . . not cling. . . . shall be far [depart]. . . . I will have nothing to do." The Lord required his people to put him before their eyes, to cling to him with all their heart, and to know him (cf. Deut 11:18, 22; 30:20); hence the negatives are a manner of affirming his devotion (cf. Ps 1:1–2; Prov 3:1–7).

The vow to separate from evildoers (vv.3b–4) calls forth a royal judgment on them. It is not enough for the king to shun evil; in his kingdom he must deal with it harshly. The theocratic king upholds here, not the outer limits of the law, but the inner. He is concerned with what happens "in secret" and with the spirit of his people who have "haughty eyes and a proud heart" (v.5).

The royal concern for integrity within the king's rule evokes a just protestation against those who malign others in secret, because a false testimony may injure someone's reputation or even bring a wrong verdict. Hebrew law dealt severely with false witness-bearing (Exod 23:7; Lev 19:15–18). By way of contrast Psalm 15 praises the righteous because of their truthful speech and their refusal to cast a slur on their fellow man (vv.2–3). Slander, gossip, and false witness bring out the heart condition of man. It is here directly related to "haughty eyes" (v.5; cf. 18:27; Prov 21:4) and "a proud heart" (lit., "a broad heart" or, better, "a greedy heart"). Greed, pride (i.e., lack of respect for others), and slander often go hand in hand, as do the virtues of self-denial, love for others, and fidelity in the godly person (15:2–5) (see appendix to Ps 19: The Word of God).

The royal judgment will rest on evil. The king will root out those who are not acting rightly within the covenant community. The silencing (*ṣ-m-t*, "put to silence," v.5; cf. v.8) and the declaration "him will I not endure" are judicial acts (cf. Isa 1:13–15). He does not merely shun evildoers but execrates them whenever it is in the best interest of God's kingdom (cf. 73:27; 94:23; 143:12).

Notes

3 The expression "the deeds of faithless men" is difficult on two counts. First, the word עֲשֹׂה (*ʿaśōh*, "doing"; NIV, "deeds") is rendered in the LXX as a plural participial phrase *ποιοῦντας* (*poiountas*, "those who do"), instead of an infinitive absolute ("to do"). Second, סֵטִים (*sēṭîm*, "the faithless men") is a *hapax legomenon*, from *s-w-ṭ* ("to depart"), hence, "faithless" or "apostate."

III. Love for God's People

101:6

6 My eyes will be on the faithful in the land,
  that they may dwell with me;
he whose walk is blameless
  will minister to me.

6 Verse 6 is a balanced contrast with the previous verse. The king recognizes—"my eyes will be on" (cf. 33:18; 34:15)—all those who are "faithful" (*'-m-n*) and "blameless" (*tāmîm;* the phrase is here identical to v.2; NIV, "blameless life"). The "faithful in the land" (cf. 35:20) are antithetical to "all the wicked in the land" (v.8). Even as the Lord has invited all who are faithful and blameless to approach him (Ps 15), so the king invites only people of integrity to "dwell" with him and to serve in his presence as appointed courtiers. Only by surrounding himself with the best and most capable men who will advance the interests of God can the king rest assured that the kingdom of God is strengthened.

IV. Hatred of Evil

101:7

7 No one who practices deceit
  will dwell in my house;
no one who speaks falsely

will stand in my presence.

7 Verses 7–8 relate both to the king's personal commitment to integrity (vv.1–3a) and to his commitment to keep all who do not share his commitment away from the inner circle of power (vv.3b–5). The king who vows to walk blamelessly in his house and who invites the faithful of the land to "dwell" with him (vv.2, 6) excludes from dwelling in his house all who do not conform to God's high standards of integrity. The deceptive and greedy (cf. 52:2–3) cannot join his administration. The phrase "stand in my presence" is symmetric with "minister to me" (v.6). Thus the vow for blessing (v.6) requires consistency for the personal life style of the king at his court. He cannot permit the righteous to serve him together with the wicked, regardless of how talented they may be otherwise (cf. Prov 29:12).

V. The King's Commitment to Justice

101:8

8 Every morning I will put to silence
all the wicked in the land;
I will cut off every evildoer
from the city of the LORD.

8 The king further vows that in his daily routine of dispensing justice (lit., "morning by morning"; cf. Zeph 3:5) he will further advance the theocratic goals. The "wicked" (cf. 1:1; 28:3) and the "evildoer" (cf. 28:3) have no place in Jerusalem, "the city of the LORD" (cf. 46:4). He will bring an end to their reign of terror.

Notes

8 The verbs of execration—אַצְמִית (*'aṣmîṯ,* "I will put to silence") and לְהַכְרִית (*lᵉhakrîṯ,* "I will cut off")—are parallel with those in v.5: אַצְמִית (*'aṣmîṯ,* "I will put to silence") and לֹא אוּכָל (*lō' 'ûkāl,* "him will I not endure").

Jerusalem is parallel with "the land." Jerusalem was the religious-political center of God's "land." What happened in Jerusalem affected the whole land.

Psalm 102: You Remain, but I. . . .

This psalm is classified as one of the seven penitential psalms (Pss 6; 32; 38; 51; 102; 130; 143). Some of these psalms are so designated because of their confessional nature; others are classed in this category because of their use within the Christian community. Psalm 102 is an example of the latter. It emphasizes the suffering and discipline often associated with sin (cf. vv.10, 23–24). The psalm exemplifies the literary genre of an individual lament. This lament arises out of an exilic situation, when the godly together with the wicked had been exiled from the land. For other exilic psalms, see 42, 43, 74, 79, 137; see Ralph W. Klein, *Israel in Exile. A Theological Interpretation* (Philadelphia: Fortress, 1979, esp. pp. 21–22). The Mishnah lists this psalm as one of those used while fasting (*Taanith* 2.3).

The structure of the psalm reveals two basic literary elements: lament and prophetic-hymnic. Kraus explains the prophetic-hymnic section as a special exilic development. The godly felt that they too had been rejected by the Lord and that the fulfillment of all the prophetic promises was in doubt. The purpose of the prophetic-hymnic section was to set ablaze a fire of hope in the promises of the Lord within the hearts of the godly (*Psalmen*, 2:695). We shall follow this expository structure:

A. Introductory Prayer (vv.1–2)
B. Lament (vv.3–11)
C. Promises (vv.12–22)
B′. Lament (vv.23–27)
A′. Concluding Perspective (v.28)

I. Introductory Prayer

102:1–2

A prayer of an afflicted man. When he is faint and pours out his lament before the LORD.

1 Hear my prayer, O LORD;
let my cry for help come to you.
2 Do not hide your face from me
when I am in distress.
Turn your ear to me;
when I call, answer me quickly.

1–2 Briggs rightly saw in the vocabulary of the introductory prayer "a mosaic of terms of supplication" by which the psalmist roots his prayer in the liturgical traditions of his time (2:318; cf. 39:12; 65:2 ["my prayer"]; 18:6 ["my cry for help"]; 13:1; 27:9; 69:17 ["do not hide your face"]; 59:16 ["in times of trouble," lit., "in the day of my distress"]; 31:2; 71:2; 88:2 ["turn your ear"]; 56:9 ["when I call"]; and 69:17 ["answer me quickly"]).

Notes

For a brief discussion of the technical words and phrases in the superscription, see the Introduction.

II. Lament

102:3–11

3 For my days vanish like smoke;
my bones burn like glowing embers.
4 My heart is blighted and withered like grass;
I forget to eat my food.
5 Because of my loud groaning
I am reduced to skin and bones.
6 I am like a desert owl,
like an owl among the ruins.

7 I lie awake; I have become
like a bird alone on a roof.
8 All day long my enemies taunt me;
those who rail against me use my name as a curse.
9 For I eat ashes as my food
and mingle my drink with tears
10 because of your great wrath,
for you have taken me up and thrown me aside.
11 My days are like the evening shadow;
I wither away like grass.

3–11 The lament moves from metaphorical expressions of personal anguish (vv.3–7) to the causes of his misery (vv.8–10) and concludes on a brief restatement of his anguish (v.11). The psalmist compares his life ("my days," vv.3, 11) to "smoke," "glowing embers" (v.3), withered "grass" (vv.4, 11), birds (vv.6–7), and "an evening shadow" (v.11). The metaphors express the transitoriness of life. He is and he is not. *He is* as long as he has physical existence (cf. 38:3): "bones" (vv.3, 5), a "heart" (v.4), and "skin" (v.5). But in his physical existence, he is also very much aware that he *is not.* Life has a shadow side, as it vanishes like "smoke" (v.3; cf. 37:20; 68:2; Isa 51:6; Hos 13:3; James 4:14) and like "the evening shadow" (v.11; cf. 144:4; Jer 6:4).

In the tension of being and not-being and of meaning and meaninglessness, the psalmist despairs. He is full of feverish anxiety ("my bones burn," v.3; cf. 22:14; 31:10; Job 30:17, 30; Lam 1:13), experiences adversity ("blighted," "withered like grass," vv.4, 11; cf. 90:5–6; Isa 40:7–8; Hos 9:16; James 1:11), and is alone in his suffering ("like a desert owl, . . . among ruins," v.6; "like a bird alone on a roof," v.7); yet he awaits a change in his lot. In his condition of being and not-being, he has no delight in life or in the joys of life. He forgets to eat and drink (vv.4, 9; cf. 1 Sam 1:7–8; Job 33:20), being most miserable (v.9; cf. 42:3; 80:5).

Consequently the psalmist wastes away to a mere "skin and bones" existence (v.5; cf. 32:3; Job 19:20). His enemies revile him (v.8). They look at him as having been abandoned by his God, and it may well be that the taunt of his enemies includes the question "Where is your God?" (cf. 22:7–8; 42:3, 10). Instead of blessing him and his God, they curse him and curse the God of the covenant people (v.8; cf. Gen 12:3; Isa 65:15; Jer 29:22).

Yet the psalmist knows that the Lord has not rejected him because of his sin. He suffers from the full brunt of God's "great wrath" (v.10; lit., "your wrath and your anger"). In God's anger the psalmist feels as if the Lord were like a hurricane, taking him up and throwing him aside (cf. Job 27:21; 30:22; Isa 64:6).

The lament brings out the depth of despair and the question of personal existence. The psalmist concludes that his existence is little more than a passing shadow or withering vegetation (v.11). He returns to the motifs of the transitoriness of life in alienation (cf. vv.3–4).

Notes

---

3 (4 MT) The phrase כְּמוֹקֵד (*kᵉmôqēḏ*, "hearth" [KB, p. 505: "glowing embers"] is divided unnecessarily by a *maqqef* in the Leningrad Codex (*kᵉmô-qēḏ*), contra a number of MSS and

editions (BHS). It denotes the place as well as the contents and may therefore be translated by "glowing embers" (NIV) or "oven" (NEB).

6 (7 MT) The identification of the birds is uncertain. For a discussion on "desert owl," "owl," and "bird," see ZPEB, 4:555. The owl was an unclean bird (Lev 11:16–18) and was associated with isolated places. These birds were found in ruins and deserted areas ("among the ruins"; cf. Isa 34:10–15; Zeph 2:13–15).

7 (8 MT) שָׁקַדְתִּי (*šāqadtî*, "I lie awake") is literally "I watch out for." The verb *š-q-d* signifies watchfulness (cf. 127:1: "stand guard") to prepare oneself for an upcoming catastrophe (war; cf. Jer 1:12) or for an act of God's deliverance (Jer 1:12; cf. 31:28). Since the psalmist is already experiencing adversity, he is watching for God's help, like a lonely bird on a roof.

III. Promises

102:12–22

12 But you, O LORD, sit enthroned forever;
your renown endures through all generations.
13 You will arise and have compassion on Zion,
for it is time to show favor to her;
the appointed time has come.
14 For her stones are dear to your servants;
her very dust moves them to pity.
15 The nations will fear the name of the LORD,
all the kings of the earth will revere your glory.
16 For the LORD will rebuild Zion
and appear in his glory.
17 He will respond to the prayer of the destitute;
he will not despise their plea.

18 Let this be written for a future generation,
that a people not yet created may praise the LORD:
19 "The LORD looked down from his sanctuary on high,
from heaven he viewed the earth,
20 to hear the groans of the prisoners
and release those condemned to death."
21 So the name of the LORD will be declared in Zion
and his praise in Jerusalem
22 when the peoples and the kingdoms
assemble to worship the LORD.

12 Over against the psalmist's condition is the Lord, whom he addresses with an emphatic "But you." The psalmist is reduced to little more than a fleeting existence, an object of hatred. On the other hand, the Lord's fame ("your renown," lit., "your remembrance") remains from generation to generation (cf. v.24). It is unaffected by the adversities of individuals or even of groups of people (Lam 5:19). As long as his rule lasts, his fame will be told and retold. The Lord's rule is established forevermore (cf. 2:4; 9:7; 99:1).

13–14 In the psalmist's recollection of God's "renown" (v.12) lies hope, as the psalmist reflects on the Lord's "compassion" and "favor" (v.13). The Lord's sovereignty extends over all creation and time. In his freedom he will rise from his throne (cf. 9:19; 76:9; Zeph 3:8) and show mercy to his people (cf. 7:6). The Lord had decreed seventy years for Babylon's hegemony, and thereafter it would fall. With the Fall of Babylon, the "time" ("the appointed time") of God's favor would begin the era of restoration. The psalmist looks at the Lord and is encouraged by the prophetic word, which speaks of a new age (cf. Isa 40:2–4; 61:1–4; Jer 29:10; 30:18; Hab 2:3; Zech 1:12–17). The new era is marked by forgiveness, renewal of the covenant, and the restoration of the people to the land. All this is in view when the psalmist hopes in the promises of the Lord.

The psalmist believes that God loves Zion (vv.13–14; see appendix to Ps 46: Zion Theology). "Zion" is a symbol of the covenant relationship and all the privileges entailed by it, material and spiritual. Zion, as an eschatological symbol, was real in the well-being of God's people, who treasured God's kingship over them. They are the "servants," the faithful remnant, who yearn for the reestablishment of Jerusalem: her walls, homes, and the temple of the Lord. Hyperbolically the "stones" and "dust" of Zion are dear to these saints (cf. 137:5–6).

15–16 In his hope for the prophetic fulfillment, the psalmist goes beyond the dust to reflect on the restored city, characterized by glory and honor among the nations. Its future is completely dependent on the Lord, who has promised to "rebuild" it and to endow it with the glory of his personal and royal presence (v.26; cf. 147:2; Isa 40:5; 60:10; Jer 31:38–40; Mic 7:11). The evidence of God's favor comes to expression on the one hand in the universal worship of the Lord (v.15; cf. 105:8; Isa 59:19). On the other hand, the new era will also mark a renewal of his covenant love as evidenced in answered prayers (cf. 22:24; 69:33; esp. Isa 65:24). While this psalmist prays for the restoration to happen, the writer of Psalm 147 thanks the Lord that he has made it happen! And yet the new acts of God's compassion in the era of the postexilic restoration are foreshadowings of a greater glory to come.

17 Verses 12–17 speak of God's rule (v.12), compassion (vv.13–14), and glory (vv.15–16) in response to the prayers of his servants, "the destitute" (*ʿarʿar*, "naked," "stripped"). The next section (vv.18–22) assures the godly of the glorious hope, regardless how they have been stripped of their dignity. The themes of the former are paralleled in the second section: remembrance, deliverance, restoration, and universal worship.

18–22 The hymnic promises of vv.12–17 must be recorded ("let this be written," v.18) for the sake of all generations to come (cf. 22:31; 48:13; 78:4, 6). The psalmist looks forward with eagerness to the fulfillment of the promises. The realization of the promises in God's acts of redemption will be the ground for greater confidence on the part of "a people not yet created" (cf. Isa 43:15), as they will "praise the LORD" (MT: *Yāh*). The reason for confidence and praise lies in God's acts of deliverance (vv.19–20), the restoration of Zion (v.21), and the universal worship of the Lord (v.22).

The response of the Lord to the suffering of his servants is a reenactment of the Exodus. He heard the groans of his people, burdened under the yoke of the Egyptians (Exod 2:23–25; 3:7–8; 6:5), and remembered his covenant (Exod 6:4–5). In the Exile he "looked down from his sanctuary on high" to respond to the needs of his own (vv.19–20; cf. Deut 26:15; Pss 14:2; 33:13; Isa 57:15; 63:15). Those who were oppressed are likened to "prisoners" and "those condemned to death" (v.20; cf. 79:11; Isa 42:7; 61:1). Out of the ruins of Zion/Jerusalem (v.21) and the "groans" (v.20) of the exiled population, the Lord would raise up a new people, resettled in Zion, who would declare praises to his "name" (vv.18, 21).

Together with the "praise" (v.21; cf. 65:1; 119:171) of the people of God, the nations will join in the worship of the "the name of the LORD" (vv.15, 21–22; see appendix to Ps 7: The Name of Yahweh), in fulfillment of the many prophetic oracles (cf. 47:9; Isa 2:2–4; 60:3–7; Mic 7:12; Zech 14:16). The extent of the prophetic vision takes us from the restoration from exile till the full restoration of God's kingdom. As Calvin observes, "But as the prophets are wont, in celebrating the deliverance from the Babylonish captivity, to extend it to the coming of Christ, the inspired bard in this place, does not lay hold on merely a part of the subject, but carries forward the grace of God, even to its consummation" (4:118).

IV. Lament and Concluding Perspective

102:23–27

23 In the course of my life he broke my strength;
he cut short my days.
24 So I said:
"Do not take me away, O my God, in the midst
of my days;
your years go on through all generations.
25 In the beginning you laid the foundations of the earth,
and the heavens are the work of your hands.
26 They will perish, but you remain;
they will all wear out like a garment.
Like clothing you will change them
and they will be discarded.
27 But you remain the same,
and your years will never end.

23 The psalmist briefly returns to the present situation of grief and trouble. His vitality ("my strength") is cut off "in the course of my life" (lit., "in the way"; cf. Isa 38:10: "in the prime of my life"). These words echo the lament of vv.3–11, where he again was occupied with the brevity, vanity, and anguish of life ("my days"; cf. vv.3, 11).

24–26 In his prayer the psalmist spoke of his transitory existence (v.24), in comparison with the great work of creation (v.25), and with the Lord himself and the certainty of his promises (vv.24b, 27–28). He restates the prayer of v.23, which in itself is a recapitulation of the lament of vv.3–11. He believes that only God has the power to cut short his ordeal rather than his life. God's existence is "through generations" (v.24; cf. v.12); and to this God he prays for deliverance: "O my God." He is the Creator of heaven and earth (v.25; cf. 8:3; Isa 44:24; 48:13), and they are established by him (78:69; 104:5; 119:90; 148:6; Eccl 1:4). Grand and old as they are, they are like nothing in comparison with the Lord himself (v.26). He will be forever (vv.24b, 27), whereas they will "perish" (*'-b-d*, v.26; cf. 1:6; 90:4 [cf. 2 Peter 3:8]) and be of no use like a rag (cf. Isa 51:6).

27 In contrast to all created existence, the Lord "remains the same" (cf. Heb 13:8). He is the "first and last" (Deut 32:39; Isa 41:4; 46:4; 48:12). The phrase "But you" is an emphatic contrast to "they" (v.26), that is, all of created existence (v.25). He remains the same, not undergoing any change over the "years" (cf. v.24). He is the Creator (v.25; cf. Heb 1:10–12) who remains forever.

Notes

23 (24 MT) This verse is textually problematic. The LXX reads עָנָה (*'ānāh*, "he answered") instead of the MT's עִנָּה (*'innāh*, "he broke"), suggesting an alternate reading of the vowels. BHS proposes a still different reading: עֻנָּה (*'unnāh*, "is broken"), assuming that "my strength" is the subject of the verb. The noun כֹּחוֹ (*kōḥô*, "his strength") is a *Kethiv*, also found in the LXX. But the *Qere* (*kōḥî*, "my strength") reading enjoys extensive support, among which are the Qumran Psalm scroll 4QPsb, a number of MSS, the Syriac, and the Targum. The emended MT's "he broke in the way my strength" explains the NIV rendering: "In the course of my life he broke my strength."

BHS proposes another change from an active reading, "he cut short my days," to a passive: "my days are shortened" (*quṣṣ^{e}rû*). Allen favors the numeral form קֹצֶר (*qōṣer*, "a short life," pp. 8, 10).

27 (28 MT) אַתָּה הוּא (*'attāh hû'*; lit., "it is you"; NIV, "you") is an allusion to God's name (TDOT, 3:344).

V. Concluding Perspective

102:28

28 The children of your servants will live in your presence;
their descendants will be established before you."

28 The future of the godly is tied up with God himself and with his promises. The psalmist praises the Lord in that he will be true to "the children of your servants." They and their descendants will "dwell" (*š-k-n;* NIV, "live"; cf. 15:1; 23:6) and be "established" (*k-w-n*) in the Lord's presence (cf. 69:35–36; Isa 65:9; 66:22). Such is the confidence in the covenant care of the Lord.

The Lord magnificently showed his fidelity to his promises when he restored the people from exile under Cyrus and when he sent Jesus the Messiah to restore mankind to himself. God the Father is able to bring "many sons to glory"; and to this end he sent Jesus, his Son, to be the author of our salvation. As the Savior is perfect (cf. Heb 2:10–11), so is his salvation. What the psalmist longed for has been experienced in time as the faithful servants of God have testified. But as long as God's servants suffer, this psalm is appropriate for all who long for the fullness of salvation, whether they be Jews or Gentiles.

Psalm 103: His Compassions They Fail Not!

In hymnic fashion the psalmist praises the Lord for the many benefits bestowed on him, his covenant people, and all creation. The genre is characteristic of the *individual thanksgiving.*

The structure of the hymn may be analyzed as follows:

A. Individual Praise (vv.1–2)
  B. Praise for the Lord's Goodness to Individuals (vv.3–5)
  B′. Praise for the Lord's Kingship Over Israel (vv.6–19)
A′. Universal and Individual Praise (vv.20–22)

The hymn reveals an inclusion motif of individual praise (A and A′) in vv.1a and 22c: "Praise the LORD, O my soul." The latter has been expanded to embrace also the universal praise, as in 148:1–4.

I. Individual Praise

103:1–2

Of David.

1 Praise the LORD, O my soul;
all my inmost being, praise his holy name.
2 Praise the LORD, O my soul,
and forget not all his benefits—

1–2 Praise of God begins with the self. As the psalmist exhorts himself to praise the Lord with his "soul" (*nep̱eš*, vv.1–2) and "inmost being," he has nothing else in mind than a full commitment to the act of giving thanks. There is no thought of a separation between "soul" and "inmost being" (lit., "my inner parts") or between "soul" and "body," because in Hebraic usage the worshiper praises the Lord with his whole being.

The praise of God is focused on "his name." The "name" of the Lord calls to remembrance all his perfections and acts of deliverance ("all his benefits," v.2; see appendixes to Pss 25 [The Perfections of Yahweh] and 78 [The Mighty Acts of Yahweh]). The Lord had revealed his name Yahweh to Israel (Exod 6:6–8; cf. 3:18) so that they might witness his benefits in the redemption from Egypt, in the giving of the land, and in the fulfillment of his promises. The psalmist recites many of the Lord's blessings to the covenant community (vv.3–22). Praise is the response of awe for God, while reflecting on what the Lord has done for the people of God throughout the history of redemption, for creation at large, for the community, and for oneself.

Praise also has an eschatological dimension, as the psalmist reflects on the ultimate righteousness that the Lord will establish (vv.6, 15–19; cf. 2 Peter 3:13). In and through the divine acts in history, the Lord reveals his "holiness" on earth (v.1). Far from separating himself from the evil in this world, God's acts of redemption are significant steps in reclaiming this world by and for "his holy name" and in fulfilling the ultimate plan of dwelling in the midst of his holy people (cf. Ezek 48:35; Rev 22:3). The opposite of "praise" is "forgetfulness." To "forget" (v.2) the "benefits" (*g-m-l;* cf. v.10) of the Lord is to disregard his covenantal lordship (cf. Deut 4:9, 23; 6:12; 8:11; 32:18).

II. Praise for the Lord's Goodness to Individuals

103:3–5

3 who forgives all your sins
and heals all your diseases,
4 who redeems your life from the pit
and crowns you with love and compassion,
5 who satisfies your desires with good things
so that your youth is renewed like the eagle's.

The participles and nominal phrases of the MT express in hymnic form the blessings of covenant life. The Lord "forgives . . . heals. . . . redeems . . . crowns. . . . satisfies" (vv.3–5). The repetitive use of the pronouns ("who" and "your") personalizes the acts of God in that he forgives and restores individuals. These graces flow out of the covenant promises (Exod 34:6–7), according to which the Lord sustains the relationship by being forgiving, loving, and full of compassion but also just.

3 The forgiveness of "sins" (*'āwōn*, lit., "guilt") is God's gracious act of removing the consequences of sin as well as the sin itself (cf. 32:1; 51:2; 90:8). It is synonymous with "heals all your diseases." The "diseases" may be forms of sickness (cf. Mark 2:7); but more likely it is a metaphor for adversities or setbacks (cf. Deut 29:22; Jer 14:19; 16:4), similar to punishment ("sins"). For "healing" as an act of restoration, see 147:3 and Jeremiah 30:12–17; 51:8–9.

4 Instead of letting his beloved be taken by adversity ("the pit"; cf. 16:10; 49:9), the Lord redeems (*g-'-l*) by exalting him to royalty ("crowns") with his "love and compassion." Though humiliation may be rightly deserved, God bestows on his people the largess of his favors, whereby he "makes you feel like a King on the day of his enthronement" (A.A. Anderson, 2:713). "Love" (*ḥese<u>d</u>*) is the assurance of the constancy of his fidelity toward his own (cf. v.11). The complement of "love" is divine "compassion" as that quality by which God as the heavenly Father empathizes with man's frailty (cf. vv.13–14; cf. 40:11; 51:1; 119:77, 156).

5 The Lord forgives, redeems, sustains, and fully restores all the covenantal benefits, even though sin had breached the covenant. The Lord "satisfies" and "renews." He "satisfies" his children with all the blessings of the covenant (cf. 23:6; Jer 32:40; 33:9, 11) so as to "renew" them like an "eagle" (Isa 40:31; cf. Deut 28:49; Jer 4:13). The "eagle" serves as a symbol of vigor and freedom associated with the benefits of restoration to divine favor and covenantal status.

Notes

4 For the Hebrew concept of death, see the appendix to Psalm 88: Sheol-Grave-Death in the Psalms.

5 The meaning of the word עֶדְיֵךְ (*'e<u>d</u>yē<u>k</u>*, "your ornament") is troublesome. The NIV has rendered it like the LXX by "your desires." BHS lists several emendations, among which is עֹדֵכִי (*'ō<u>d</u>ē<u>k</u>î*, "your being"; lit., "as you still are"). This proposal is less dubious than the MT or the LXX. See Allen's "the one who has filled your existence with good" (p. 17).

III. Praise for the Lord's Kingship Over Israel

103:6–19

6 The LORD works righteousness
and justice for all the oppressed.

7 He made known his ways to Moses,

his deeds to the people of Israel:
[8]The LORD is compassionate and gracious,
slow to anger, abounding in love.
[9]He will not always accuse,
nor will he harbor his anger forever;
[10]he does not treat us as our sins deserve
or repay us according to our iniquities.
[11]For as high as the heavens are above the earth,
so great is his love for those who fear him;
[12]as far as the east is from the west,
so far has he removed our transgressions from us.
[13]As a father has compassion on his children,
so the LORD has compassion on those who fear him;
[14]for he knows how we are formed,
he remembers that we are dust.
[15]As for man, his days are like grass,
he flourishes like a flower of the field;
[16]the wind blows over it and it is gone,
and its place remembers it no more.
[17]But from everlasting to everlasting
the LORD's love is with those who fear him,
and his righteousness with their children's children—
[18]with those who keep his covenant
and remember to obey his precepts.

[19]The LORD has established his throne in heaven,
and his kingdom rules over all.

6 From the specific and personal observations of the Lord's goodness (vv.3–5), the worshiper reflects on God's concern with the establishment of "righteousness" in his world and especially in Israel (vv.7–14). The Lord does not tolerate injustice in the world (cf. 33:4–5). His rule is characterized by "righteousness" as he rights what is wrong. "Righteousness" (lit., "righteous acts," pl.; cf. Judg 5:11; Mic 6:5) relates to two aspects of divine activity: "salvation" (Isa 51:6, 8) and "justice" or vindication (Isa 63:1, 4). He delivers from evil and oppression (*mišpāṭîm*, "justice for all the oppressed"; lit., "judgments for all the oppressed," cf. 36:6; 119:7; 146:7). He also avenges the oppressors.

7–10 The psalmist reflects on God's "ways" and "deeds," revealed to Moses (v.7; cf. Rom 3:2). After the sin of the golden calf, Moses had prayed for a greater revelation of the love, mercy, and forgiveness of the Lord as a manifestation of the "ways" of the Lord (Exod 33:13). Then the Lord revealed his perfections to Moses (Exod 34:6–7). The revelation to Moses reveals the grace in the Mosaic covenant, a grace to which the OT attests continually (86:15; 145:8; Neh 9:17; Jer 3:12; Joel 2:13; Rom 9:4–5). Though the Lord may be justly angry because of sin, he does not keep on criticizing ("accuse," v.9; cf. Isa 57:16) or maintain his anger for long (cf. Isa 3:13; Jer 2:9; Mic 6:2). Great as his wrath may be, his mercy is greater (v.8; cf. Isa 54:7–8; James 5:11).

God's covenant and rule over Israel are characterized by grace and divine fidelity. Even when the Great King expresses his righteous anger at Israel's sin, he upholds the covenant by his grace. He does not respond to human infidelity in kind (v.10).

11–14 Through Moses the people received the covenant and the grace of the Lord. Through Moses they have received the adoption to become his children. Through Moses they have received the unique privilege of becoming a holy nation and a royal priesthood (Exod 19:5–6). Though the Lord rules over the whole world, he has chosen one people to become his nation. His rule is vast, extending from heaven to earth and from east to west (cf. 36:5; 57:10; Isa 55:9). God's commitment to his people is not diminished. Rather, it is "great" (lit., "strong," *g-b-r*, v.11; cf. 117:2; Luke 1:50) to all who respond to him.

The love of God is not indiscriminate. He loves those "who fear him" (vv.11, 13; cf. 34:7, 9; 85:9; 102:15; Rom 8:28). He will forgive them, have compassion for them, and treat them as his children (vv.12–14; cf. Exod 4:22; Isa 1:2; 63:4; 64:8; Hos 11:1; Mal 1:6; 2:10; 3:17; Rom 9:4). Though he expects godliness, he is also understanding of the frailty of his children. All of them are but "dust" (*'āp̄ār*, v.14; cf. Gen 2:7; 3:19; Job 4:19; 10:9; 34:15; Eccl 3:20; 12:7), having been shaped by the divine Builder-King (Gen 2:7). Man as a created being is truly man when sustained by divine mercy (v.14; cf. 78:38; 89:47). Our hope lies in the constancy of God's fatherly compassion.

15–18 Forgiveness is a gift. Humans can never take it for granted, because they are and remain human. From the perspective of God's universal rule (v.19), "man" is nothing more than human, i.e., weak (*'ᵉnôš*, v.15; see 8:4). In his transitory existence and subjection to God's judgment, man is "like grass" (cf. 90:6; 92:7; Isa 51:12) or "like a flower of the field" (cf. Job 14:2; Isa 40:6–7). Over against the brevity and weakness of man's existence is the greatness of God's love for those who fear him. His "love" (*ḥesed̠*, v.17) and his "righteousness" (*ṣᵉd̠āqāh;* cf. v.6) last forever.

Those who respond wisely to the Lord, in "fear" (v.17; cf. vv.11, 13; Prov 1:7), will not only enjoy the fullness of the covenant relationship, but their children will also see the salvation of the Lord (cf. 102:28; Luke 1:50). Wise living in the presence of the Great King and covenant God requires responsiveness from the heart. The keeping of "the covenant" implies nothing but obedience to "his precepts" (v.18; cf. Exod 20:6; Deut 7:9). There can be no enjoyment of the covenant unless there is a responsiveness to doing the will of God (cf. Matt 6:9–15).

19 The psalmist calls on the community to recognize the Lord's kingdom. His "throne" is in heaven (cf. 11:4; 93:2), but his kingdom extends to all creation (cf. 93:1; 96:10; 99:1; 1 Chron 29:11–12). This affirmation is both the conclusion of the hymn (vv.3–18) and the transition to a universal, communal, and individual call to worship the Lord (vv.20–22).

IV. Universal and Individual Praise

103:20–22

20 Praise the LORD, you his angels,
you mighty ones who do his bidding,
who obey his word.
21 Praise the LORD, all his heavenly hosts,
you his servants who do his will.
22 Praise the LORD, all his works
everywhere in his dominion.

Praise the LORD, O my soul.

20–22 In language quite similar to 148:1–4, the angelic host is called on to join with God's people in worship of the Lord. The heavenly creatures are his "angels" (cf.

91:11), his "mighty ones" (v.20; lit., "warriors of strength," from *g-b-r;* cf. NEB, "creatures of might"), "his heavenly hosts" (v.21; cf. 24:10; Dan 7:10), and "his servants" (or "ministers"; cf. Heb 1:14). They are always loyal to the Lord: "who do his bidding, who obey his word. . . . who do his will"; and the Lord expects nothing less from his creatures on earth (vv.7, 18; cf. Matt 6:10). The psalm concludes with the inclusionary repetition "praise the LORD, O my soul" (v.22; cf. v.1). Thus the psalmist calls on all creatures in heaven, serving the Lord on high, to join together with creation ("all his works") in the praise of God.

Appendix: Sin and Forgiveness

The people of God find themselves between two poles of fellowship with God. They affirm loyalty and trust in the Lord, and they confess their failure in being faithful to him. The psalms use several words to express the human intrusion into communion with God: *peša'* ("transgression"), *'āwōn* ("sin," "guilt"), and *ḥēṭ'/ḥaṭṭā'ṯ/ḥᵃṭā'āh* ("sin"). Psalm 32 illustrates how the synonyms alternate without noticeable change in meaning.

Blessed is he
  whose transgressions [*peša'*] are forgiven,
  whose sins [*ḥᵃṭa'āh*] are covered.
Blessed is the man
  whose sin [*'āwōn*] the Lord does not count against him
  and in whose spirit is no deceit.
. . . .
Then I acknowledged my sin [*ḥaṭṭā'ṯ*] to you
  and did not cover up my iniquity [*'āwōn*].
I said, "I will confess
  my transgressions [*peša'*] to the Lord"—
and you forgave
  the guilt [*'āwōn*] of my sin [*ḥaṭṭā'ṯ*].

(vv.1–2, 5)

The sinful condition troubles the godly because of its breach of fellowship with God (see the penitential psalms: 6; 32; 38; 51; 102; 130; 143); e.g., "I confess my iniquity [*'āwōn*]; / I am troubled by my sin [*ḥ-ṭ-'*]" (38:18). The effects are often so devastating that it brings the psalmist to despair:

My guilt [*'āwōn*] has overwhelmed me
  like a burden too heavy to bear.
My wounds fester and are loathsome
  because of my sinful folly.
I am bowed down and brought very low;
  all day long I go about mourning.
My back is filled with searing pain;
  there is no health in my body.
I am feeble and utterly crushed;
  I groan in anguish of heart.
All my longings lie open before you, O Lord;
  my sighing is not hidden from you.
My heart pounds, my strength fails me;
  even the light has gone from my eyes.

(38:4–10; cf. 6:2–7; 32:3–4; 40:12; 102:3–11)

The Lord does forgive those broken in spirit (65:3). But the Lord had also prescribed for the godly to follow his regulations for forgiveness and reconciliation. He had revealed to Israel those rituals by which they could be reassured of his forgiveness: expiatory offerings, dedicatory or thank offerings, and communal or fellowship offerings. There could be no communion unless his people had first presented *expiatory offerings* (sin and guilt offerings). Moreover, the expiatory offerings were often attended by *dedicatory offerings* (burnt, cereal, and drink offerings) as expressions of the joy of forgiveness and of consecration of oneself (cf. 20:3; 50:14, 23; 51:19; 54:6; 56:12; 66:13–15; 96:8; 107:22; 116:17).

The offerings and sacrifices presented to the Lord with a heart of faith (4:5) were acceptable to him: "The sacrifices of God are a broken spirit; / a broken and contrite heart, / O God, you will not despise" (51:17). The efficacy of the offering did not lay in the offering but in God's love (*ḥeseḏ*):

> Have mercy on me, O God,
> according to your unfailing love [*ḥeseḏ*];
> according to your great compassion
> blot out my transgressions.
>
> (51:1)

This love anticipated the gift of God in the sacrifice of Christ (John 3:16), but it was no inferior love! The psalmist even calls on Yahweh to be his high priest so as to forgive and purify him (51:2, 9). Another ground for the appeal to divine forgiveness is the "honor" of the Great King, whose commitments and promises were sealed in the covenants. Though the people are not worthy of this glory, they pray that the Lord will act favorably toward them for his glorious name's sake:

> Help us, O God our Savior,
> for the glory of your name;
> deliver us and forgive our sins
> for your name's sake.
>
> (79:9; cf. 25:11)

Truly, Yahweh is gracious and forgiving. The Psalms use a number of phrases to denote divine forgiveness: *š-l-ḥ, n-ś-', k-s-h,* and *k-p-r*.

Š-l-ḥ is an act of God, as he alone can forgive sins: "For the sake of your name, O LORD, / forgive [*š-l-ḥ*] my iniquity, though it is great" (25:11). Yahweh's forgiveness is concomitant with his demonstration of love. All who are the objects of his *ḥeseḏ* received freely his forgiveness: "You are forgiving [*š-l-ḥ*] and good, O Lord, / abounding in love [*ḥeseḏ*] to all who call to you" (86:5; cf. 103:3). The godly respond to his forgiveness by expressing a desire for following the way of the Lord: "But with you there is forgiveness [*š-l-ḥ*]; / therefore you are feared" (130:4).

N-ś-' and *k-s-h* occur twice as synonyms, possibly for poetic effect: "Blessed is he / whose transgressions are forgiven [*k-s-h*], / whose sins are covered [*n-ś-'*]" (32:1; cf. v.5); cf. "You forgave [*n-ś-'*] the iniquity of your people / and covered [*k-s-h*] all their sins" (85:2).

The technical verb "atone" (*k-p-r*) occurs several times in the psalms: "When we were overwhelmed by sins, / you forgave [*k-p-r*] our transgressions" (65:3). "Yet he was merciful; / he forgave [*k-p-r*] their iniquities / and did not destroy them" (78:38). "Deliver us and forgive [*k-p-r*] our sins / for your name's sake" (79:9). The root in the Qal occurs only in Genesis 6:14 as a denominative of the noun *kōp̱er* (II, "bitumen"): cover with pitch. The Piel is more commonly used and signifies the act of covering of sin by which God's wrath is appeased, the guilt is removed, the punishment is revoked, and the sinner is reconciled to God (Exod 32:20; Lev 16:1–34; 17:11).

Forgiveness is the theme of Psalm 103. Man is weak and, thus, could so easily be destroyed by God's wrath. But the Lord is like a father, having compassion on his children. The truth is, there is no limit to God's forgiveness: "as far as the east is from the west, / so far has he removed our transgressions from us" (103:12; cf. v 3). However, he expects those who have tasted his forgiveness to direct their way in accordance with his way (119:11, 133).

Texts: 4:5; 5:10; 7:3; 19:13; 20:3; 25:7, 11, 18; 27:6; 32:1–2, 5; 38:4, 18; 39:8; 40:6, 12; 50:5, 8, 14; 51:1, 3, 14, 16–17, 19; 54:6; 56:12; 59:3, 12; 65:3; 66:13, 15, 18; 68:21; 69:5; 73:7; 78:17, 38; 79:9; 85:2; 89:32; 90:8; 94:23; 96:8; 103:10, 12; 106:28, 38; 107:22; 109:7, 14–15; 116:17; 119:11, 133; 130:3–4; 141:2.

Related Topics: See Appendixes to Pss 7 (The Name of Yahweh); 25 (The Perfections of Yahweh); 119 (Yahweh Is My Redeemer); 122 (The Praise of Yahweh); 132 (The Ark of the Covenant and the Temple: Symbols of Yahweh's Presence and Rule); 140 (The Poor and Oppressed).

Bibliography: Steven R. Boguslawski, "The Psalms: Prophetic Polemics Against Sacrifices," *Irish Biblical Studies* 5 (1983): 14–41; Menahem Haran, "The Cult and Prayer," *Biblical and Related Studies Presented to Samuel Iwry*, edd. Ann Kort and Scott Morschauer (Winona Lake: Eisenbrauns, 1985), pp. 87–92; W.A. VanGemeren, "Offerings and Sacrifices in Bible Times," in Elwell, EDT, pp. 788–92.

TDAT, 4:272–77, 303–18; TDOT, 4:309–19; TWAT, 4:304–18; TWOT, 1:277–79, 452–53; 2:626, 650–51, 741–42.

Psalm 104: Great Is Your Faithfulness to All Creation

The theme of Psalm 104 is God's greatness in ruling and sustaining his vast creation. The form is a *descriptive psalm of praise.* Its theme and form are complementary to Psalm 103. Both psalms have similar beginnings and endings; indeed, both are hymnic in form. Psalm 103 praises the Redeemer-King, whereas this psalm magnifies the Creator-King. However, there is no internal ground for arguing that both psalms were written by the same author, as Kirkpatrick cautiously suggests (p. 604).

The poetic version of Creation is complementary to the prosaic of Genesis 1. Von Rad likens the teaching of Creation to an ancient Near Eastern literary form (*onomasticon*) describing the wonders of nature (OTT, 1:361). This begs the question of the interrelation of this psalm with Egyptian literature, particularly the Hymn of Atum, an Egyptian creation hymn. Though this matter has received extensive treatment (see Allen, pp. 28–30), any discussion on the literary association is complicated by the insufficient evidence of the cosmological framework and literature of the surrounding nations and, hence, by the tentativeness of any theory explaining the relations and possible polemical use of these materials. Zimmerli has analyzed the difference well by explaining that the sun is a part of Yahweh's creative order and, instead, that Yahweh alone is resplendent in glory (OTTO, p. 39). Brueggemann treats it together with Psalms 8; 33; and 145 as "Songs of Creation" (*Message of the Psalms*, pp. 28–38).

The structure is as follows:

A. In Praise of God's Royal Splendor (vv.1–4)
  B. The Material Formation of the Earth (vv.5–9)
    C. The Glory of the Animal Creation (vv.10–18)

D. The Regularity in the Created World (vv.19–23)
C′. The Glory of the Animal Creation (vv.24–26)
B′. The Spiritual Sustenance of the Earth (vv.27–30)
A′. In Praise of God's Royal Splendor (vv.31–35)

I. In Praise of God's Royal Splendor

104:1–4

1 Praise the LORD, O my soul.

O LORD my God, you are very great;
  you are clothed with splendor and majesty.
2 He wraps himself in light as with a garment;
  he stretches out the heavens like a tent
3 and lays the beams of his upper chambers
    on their waters.
He makes the clouds his chariot
  and rides on the wings of the wind.
4 He makes winds his messengers,
  flames of fire his servants.

1 The exclamation "praise [lit., 'bless,' from *b-r-k*] the LORD" arises out of the heart of those who consider themselves blessed to know the covenant Redeemer-God, whose name is Yahweh (NIV, "the LORD"). The psalm begins and ends on the same note of praise (cf. v.35). The Lord evokes praise by his works. Praise may take two forms of expression: direct ("you") and indirect ("he"). The first occurs in the direct address of v.1, where the focus is on the acts of God: "you do very greatly" (NIV, "you are very great") and "you clothe yourself" (NIV, "you are clothed"; cf. 1 Tim 6:16). Both verbal expressions are active verbs, signifying God's active involvement in the world and his expectation of recognition by his creation. The nouns "splendor and majesty" (cf. 96:6) amplify the royal nature of his rule. Yahweh is the Great King, who is known for his mighty acts and whose splendor is evident to all (cf. 8:1; 21:5; 93:1; 96:6).

2 The second form of expression of praise is in hymnic form, characterized by participles of the Hebrew verbs and the use of the third person. This preferably may be translated by relative sentences: "you . . . who wraps . . . who stretches," etc. Thus the majesty of the Great King is revealed in his acts, and the acts of God occasion the hymn of Creation.

God is light. Light is vital to life; hence its primary importance places it as the first of the creative acts. In poetic fashion the psalmist portrays God as covered with light (cf. Hab 3:4). The light reveals something of the divine glory, because God is light (1 John 1:5). The second creative act is "the firmament" or "the heavens" described here as a "tent" stretched out over the earth (cf. Isa 40:22). As a camper readily pitches his tent somewhere, so God without exertion prepared the earth for habitation.

3–4 The imagery of the firmament gives occasion to reflect on the divine glory above the firmament (cf. Ps 29). The poet imagines how the Lord placed his palace in a choice location. The beams on the water above the firmament (cf. 29:3; 148:4; Gen 1:7) provide the support for his royal palace ("upper chambers," v.3). The "chambers," built above the first story of a house for the purpose of privacy and seclusion (cf. 1 Kings 17:19; 2 Kings 4:10), represent God's involvement with and separation from his world (Amos 9:6). This metaphor gives rise to the expression "The LORD sits enthroned over the flood; / the LORD is enthroned as King forever" (29:10).

The Lord's involvement with the world of creation comes to expression in the imagery of the chariot, the clouds, the wind, and the flames of fire (vv.3–4). He sovereignly controls the elements, as if he "rides" on a "chariot" (cf. 18:10), using the wind (cf. 18:10; Heb 1:7 [LXX]), clouds, and lightning ("flames of fire") for his purposes. The winds and the lightning are his "messengers." Since the Hebrew has the same word for "messengers" and "angels," it is apparent that this psalm forms a whole with Psalm 103 (esp. vv.20–22). The Lord is surrounded by his servants, whether they be created like the angels or be powers inherent in his created order (winds, lightning). The Creator-King is, as it were, driving his chariot, symbolic of his governance of his creation. All his created works reveal the splendor and wisdom of the Creator, because he remains constantly involved with his handiwork.

Notes

3 On the theological background, see Tryggve B.D. Mettinger, *The Dethronement of Sabaoth. Studies in the Shem and Kabod Theologies* (Lund: Gleerup, 1982), p. 34. On the mythopoetic imagery, see John Day, *God's Conflict with the Dragon and the Sea. Echoes of Canaanite Myth in the Old Testament* (Cambridge: Cambridge University Press, 1985), pp. 32–34.

II. The Material Formation of the Earth

104:5–9

5 He set the earth on its foundations;
it can never be moved.
6 You covered it with the deep as with a garment;
the waters stood above the mountains.
7 But at your rebuke the waters fled,
at the sound of your thunder they took to flight;
8 they flowed over the mountains,
they went down into the valleys,
to the place you assigned for them.
9 You set a boundary they cannot cross;
never again will they cover the earth.

5–6 These verses focus on the third day of Creation: the formation of the land (cf. Gen 1:9–10; cf. Job 38:8–11). The waters covered the whole earth (v.6; cf. Gen 1:2), forming a vast "deep" (*t^ehôm*). The mountains and valleys, characteristic of the dry land, were as yet covered as with "a garment." The "foundations," i.e., the solid material, were already there by divine creation (v.5; cf. 24:2), but they awaited God's act of separating the waters so as to make the dry land appear. The inspired poet is giving, not a scientific, but a poetic portrayal of Creation. He imagines the magnificence and splendor of God in his reflection on the vastness and depth of the physical creation.

7 The word God spoke at Creation is poetically transformed to a "rebuke" and to the "sound of your thunder" to maintain unity with the previous stanza, where the psalmist spoke about the clouds, winds, and lightning. He continues the phenomenal language of God's theophany. The difference in language between Genesis 1 and this psalm is not the issue. Here he imagines the power of God in the familiar language of nature. The Lord limited the power of the water by a show of his power. This language may be an allusion to the Baal myth, according to which Baal was victorious over the sea god (Yamm); the God of Israel did not fight, because the sea fled like a routed warrior at the mere "rebuke" (9:5; Isa 50:2; Nah 1:4) and presence—"thunder" (cf. 18:13)—of the Lord. Yahweh is sovereign over all powers, even that of the primeval opposition to which several psalms allude (see 74:13; 89:10; cf. von Rad, OTT, 1:150–51).

8–9 Verse 8 poses the problem of subject. According to the NIV, "the waters" (v.7) flee over the mountains, down the valleys, into their allotted place (so also NEB; Dahood, *Psalms*, 3:31). According to the RSV, "The mountains arose, the valleys sank down to the place which thou didst appoint for them." Since the latter interpretation breaks the imagery and "the waters" are most likely the subject, the NIV is preferable (so also Day, *God's Conflict*, pp. 34–35). If this is correct, there are two alternative interpretations of the action. If the military metaphor be retained, the waters run away to the sea, their home territory. It is also possible that the psalmist speaks of mountain springs and valley streams as the allotted place of the water (so also v.9; cf. Job 26:10; 38:10; Prov 8:29). Since the Flood the Lord determined that water should never again cover the earth (v.9; cf. Gen 9:9–17).

Notes

---

7 On the meaning of גַּעֲרָתְךָ (*gā'ªrāṯᵉḵā*, "at your rebuke") as "your angry shout," see P.J. Van Zijl, "A Discussion of the Root *gā'ar* ('Rebuke')," *Biblical Essays*, ed. A.H. Van Zyl (Potchefstroom: Pro Rege-Pers, 1969), pp. 56–63.

III. The Glory of the Animal Creation

104:10–18

10 He makes springs pour water into the ravines;
it flows between the mountains.
11 They give water to all the beasts of the field;
the wild donkeys quench their thirst.
12 The birds of the air nest by the waters;
they sing among the branches.
13 He waters the mountains from his upper chambers;
the earth is satisfied by the fruit of his work.
14 He makes grass grow for the cattle,
and plants for man to cultivate—
bringing forth food from the earth:
15 wine that gladdens the heart of man,
oil to make his face shine,

and bread that sustains his heart.
16 The trees of the LORD are well watered,
the cedars of Lebanon that he planted.
17 There the birds make their nests;
the stork has its home in the pine trees.
18 The high mountains belong to the wild goats;
the crags are a refuge for the coneys.

The inner structure of this section opens up an ABA′ arrangement:

A i. Water in the Mountains (v.10)
ii. Wild Animals (v.11)
iii. Birds (v.12)
B i. Water in the Mountains (v.13)
ii. Domesticated Animals, Plants, and Man (vv.14–15)
A′ i. Water in the Mountains (v.16)
iii. Birds (vv.16)
ii. Mountain Animals (vv.17–18)

10–12 Through the bountiful rain the Lord provides richly for his creation (cf. 65:9–13). God is the source and sustainer of life! Apparently the psalmist reflects on the splendor of mountain rain with its powerful impact on the landscape: plant and animal life. The central section (B) is asymmetric and pivotal. All creation—domesticated animals and plant life—are in the service of man. Man does not live for the purpose of work, because the Lord especially takes care of him (Matt 6:25–34). Yahweh is the Giver of water, which flows out of mountain springs, giving rise to rivers (v.10). The "ravines" (wadis) formed natural carriers for the runoff from rain (v.12) and from mountain springs (v.10). In relation to the surrounding desert regions, the Land of Promise was magnificently well-watered (cf. Deut 8:7). Water provides drink for the wild animals ("the beasts of the field," v.11), of which "the wild donkeys" are representatives. Water provides for growth of trees and shrubs, in whose branches the birds nest and sing (v.12; cf. Matt 13:32).

13–15 Water also provides for domesticated animals and especially for man. The Lord satisfies all of his "works" (v.13), because he has the power and wisdom to water mountains and to sustain plant and animal life. His watering is as effortless as that of a man watering plants or irrigating a garden. He supplies man's needs indirectly through providing fodder for "the cattle" and directly through supplying him with "food" (v.14), i.e., "wine . . . oil . . . and bread" (v.15). Though the earth is cursed (Gen 3:17), the Lord in his free grace richly blesses "man" (*'āḏām*) with ample provision for his daily needs. His blessing extends to all mankind (*'āḏām*), and if so, how much more to his own people (cf. Deut 11:14–15)! "Wine" (cf. Judg 9:13; Eccl 10:19) is given for the uplifting of man's spirit, oil for his appearance (92:10; Luke 7:46), and food for his being (cf. Deut 7:13).

16–18 In the third section our attention is drawn again to the bigger world of nature: the cedars, birds, and wildlife (cf. Job 38:39–39:30). Verse 16 continues the thought of vv.10, 13. The Lord waters the mountains so that the lofty trees ("the trees of the LORD"), i.e., "the cedars of Lebanon," have their needs fully provided for ("well watered," lit., "are satisfied," as in v.13). The region of Lebanon was proverbial for its cedars, growing in the mountains at an altitude of several thousand feet above sea level (cf. 1 Kings 4:33). The birds find nesting places in the trees (v.17; cf. v.12). Even as the cedar and pine are selectively chosen as samples of majestic trees, so the "stork" is a stately bird. The stork is not native to this region but spends the winters in North Africa and in the region of Palestine and Lebanon. The mountains are also a hideout for "the wild goats"—a kind of ibex (1 Sam 24:2; Job 39:1)—and the "coneys"—not a kind of rabbit, but a Syrian coney or rock badger (v.18; cf. ZPEB, 1:937).

Notes

15 On God's gift of wine, see O.H. Steck, "Der Wein under den Schöpfungsgaben. Überlegungen zu Psalm 104," *Trierer Theologische Zeitschrift* 87 (1978): 173–91.

17 Instead of "in the pine trees," the LXX reads "in their tops"; so also the NEB: "the stork makes her home in their tops."

IV. The Regularity in the Created World

104:19–23

19 The moon marks off the seasons,
and the sun knows when to go down.
20 You bring darkness, it becomes night,
and all the beasts of the forest prowl.
21 The lions roar for their prey
and seek their food from God.
22 The sun rises, and they steal away;
they return and lie down in their dens.
23 Then man goes out to his work,
to his labor until evening.

19–23 Even as the rains are in God's hands, so are the moon and the sun. Canaanites attributed rain, sunlight, and the lunar cycle to specific deities. For Israel the Lord sovereignly rules over all creation and establishes order by his wise administration. The "moon" represents the lunar calendar by which the "seasons," the festival days of Israel (cf. Gen 1:14; Lev 23:2, 4, 37, 44), were determined. Sun and moon denotes the regular order of day and night (cf. Gen 1:14), when animals and man have an opportunity to provide for themselves (vv.20–23).

V. The Glory of the Animal Creation

104:24–26

24 How many are your works, O LORD!
In wisdom you made them all;
the earth is full of your creatures.
25 There is the sea, vast and spacious,
teeming with creatures beyond number—
living things both large and small.
26 There the ships go to and fro,
and the leviathan, which you formed to frolic there.

24–26 The world of creation reveals the power, wisdom, and creative diversity of the Lord (v.24). In vv.5–9 the psalmist was in awe of God's majestic power. Verses 10–18 reflect on the variety of his creatures and on his wisdom in sustaining all of them. Verses 19–23 evoke a response of gratitude, because the Lord is in control over the seasons and the alternation of day and night. In verses 24–26 the psalmist calls on the reader to worship with him the Lord's wisdom and creative diversity. He has multiple "works" (v.24; cf. v.13) all over his world. All of life belongs to him ("your creatures," lit., "your possession"), whether on "the earth" (v.24) or in "the sea" (v.25).

The emphasis on sea creatures magnificently complements the mention in vv.10–18 of wild and domesticated animals, birds, and man. The Lord provides for the great number of sea creatures that inhabit the seas in equal variety (v.25). Wherever ships have plied the seas (v.26), reports have come back on the interesting variety of animal life in the sea, among which is the "leviathan." The "leviathan," a creature feared by the Canaanites because of its power represented by seven heads (Baal legend, 1, i:1–3; see Notes on 74:13), is here only a large sea animal, a creature of God ("which you formed"), the Lord's pet (v.26). For an extensive study of this motif, see Day, *God's Conflict*.

The literary approach of holistic interpretation espoused by Meir Weiss adds a new dimension to understanding v.26. He proposes that the sea is the playground of Leviathan "to sport therein." He derives from the etymology of the root *l-w-h* ("accompany") an associative meaning: "a fish accompanying the vessels" (*The Bible From Within. The Method of Total Interpretation* [Jerusalem: Magnes, 1984], pp. 78–93).

VI. The Spiritual Sustenance of the Earth

104:27–30

27 These all look to you
  to give them their food at the proper time.
28 When you give it to them,
  they gather it up;
 when you open your hand,
  they are satisfied with good things.
29 When you hide your face,
  they are terrified;
 when you take away their breath,
  they die and return to the dust.
30 When you send your Spirit,
  they are created,
  and you renew the face of the earth.

27–30 The very source of the material well-being of God's creation (cf. vv.5–26) is the Lord. Nature is dependent on the Creator, looking to him for regular provision (v.27). All creatures on earth and in the sea, wild and domesticated, birds and sea creatures, as well as man, have a sense of the spiritual power by whose favor they live (cf. 145:15–16; 147:9). They have their being in God (cf. Acts 17:24–25). The emphasis in vv.28–30 is on God who acts: "you give . . . you open your hand. . . . you hide. . . you take away. . . . you send . . . you renew." These acts reveal divine favor (also known as common grace) and disfavor ("hide your face"). The Lord gives and sustains life by his life-giving Spirit (v.30). But he also takes away the life-spirit from his creatures (v.29; NIV, "their breath," lit., "their spirit"; cf. Gen 2:7; 6:17). This is what Bernard W. Anderson calls *creatio continua:* "Creation is not just an event that occurred in the beginning, at the foundation of the earth, but is God's continuing activity of sustaining creatures and holding everything in being" ("Introduction: Mythopoetic and Theological Dimensions of Biblical Creation Faith," *Creation in the Old Testament,* ed. Bernard W. Anderson [Philadelphia: Fortress, 1984], p. 14). More usually this activity of God is referred to as Providence.

VII. In Praise of God's Royal Splendor

104:31–35

31 May the glory of the LORD endure forever;
may the LORD rejoice in his works—
32 he who looks at the earth, and it trembles,
who touches the mountains, and they smoke.

33 I will sing to the LORD all my life;
I will sing praise to my God as long as I live.
34 May my meditation be pleasing to him,
as I rejoice in the LORD.
35 But may sinners vanish from the earth
and the wicked be no more.

Praise the LORD, O my soul.

Praise the LORD.

31–32 The praise with which the psalm begins (vv.1–4) forms the conclusion. The Lord, who appears in all of his splendor and reveals himself in creation (vv.1–4), has bestowed his "glory" on his creation (v.31; cf. 19:1; Isa 6:3). His handiwork will flourish as long as he sustains it, as expressed in the prayer "May the LORD rejoice in his works" (cf. Gen 1:31; Prov 8:31). The Lord's presence with his creation is suggested by the association of the noun "glory" and the theophanic language of v.32 (cf. 144:5; Exod 19:18; Amos 9:5).

33–34 The response to the Lord's presence should be like that of the psalmist: praise (v.33), devotion ("as long as I live"; cf. 146:2), and concern with pleasing the Lord (v.34; cf. 19:14). The psalmist prays that the Lord may be pleased with him, as God looks at his creation.

35 Those who do not join in with a grateful response, who do not recognize the Lord as the source of all their material benefits, are outside the covenant of grace. They have no right to his grace and hence have no place on God's earth. The psalmist is not vindictive in his prayer against the wicked but longs for a world fully established and maintained by the Lord, without outside interference.

The hymn concludes on the same note of thanksgiving and praise with which it began (cf. v.1): Hallelujah! ("Praise the LORD").

Psalm 105: Yahweh's Acts in Salvation History

The hymnic celebration of the history of redemption from Israel's sojourn in Egypt to the Conquest is the theme of this psalm. Its motif complements the creation hymn

(Ps 104) and the hymn of God's faithfulness (Ps 106). These three psalms have in common the motif of God's fidelity as Creator-Ruler and as the Redeemer of his people. The use of Psalm 105 was very appropriate for cultic celebration, as is clear from its association with David's bringing the ark to Jerusalem in 1 Chronicles 16:8–36.

The structure follows a historical pattern from covenant to fulfillment of the covenant. The emphasis in each section is the fidelity of the Lord, for which reason the historical reflection leads to a reflection of "his wonderful acts" (v.2; cf. v.5).

A. Invocation to Praise (vv.1–6)
  B. The Covenant of Promise (vv.7–11)
    C. The Protection of the Lord (vv.12–15)
      D. The Providence of the Lord (vv.16–23)
    C′. The Protection of the Lord (vv.24–36)
  B′. The Fulfillment of Promise (vv.37–45b)
A′. Concluding Praise (v.45c)

I. Invocation to Praise

105:1–6

1 Give thanks to the LORD, call on his name;
make known among the nations what he has done.
2 Sing to him, sing praise to him;
tell of all his wonderful acts.
3 Glory in his holy name;
let the hearts of those who seek the LORD rejoice.
4 Look to the LORD and his strength;
seek his face always.

5 Remember the wonders he has done,
his miracles, and the judgments he pronounced,
6 O descendants of Abraham his servant,
O sons of Jacob, his chosen ones.

1–6 The call to praise the Lord consists of six verses. The first five contain imperatives whose frequency decreases from three verbs (vv.1–2), to two verbs (vv.3–4), to one verb (v.5); v.6 has no verb. Each verb is different and adds its own connotation to the harmonious blending of synonyms for praise. Verses 1–2 stress the act of verbal communication: "Give thanks . . . call on his name; make known" (cf. Isa 12:4), "Sing . . . sing praise . . . tell." The following five verbs connote the reflective element. The heart of the devotees is filled with the Lord and his acts: "Glory . . . let . . . rejoice. . . . Look [lit., 'seek' (*d-r-š*) as in v.3] . . . seek [*b-q-š*]. . . . remember." The variety of verbs for "praise" adds an important dimension to the aesthetic wholeness of worship.

The psalmist also interweaves several other motifs: the object of worship, the subjects of worship, and the goal of worship. The Lord is the *object* of worship (cf. 1 Tim 6:16). From the phraseology we learn about "what he has done" (v.1, lit., "his deeds"), "all his wonderful acts" (v.2), his holiness and "strength" (vv.3–4), and "the wonders . . . his miracles, and the judgments" (v.5). The reference to "holy" and "strength" must not be divorced from the acts of God. In other words, for the psalmist the acts of God reveal his being. God is the One who acts, and his acts reveal how marvelously (vv.2, 5, "wonders"; cf. v.27; 9:1; 96:3; Deut 4:34) he acts on behalf of his people, so as to pass "judgments" (v.5; cf. vv.28–36; Exod 6:6; 7:4; 12:12) on their enemies—in this case the Egyptians. His acts reveal the Divine Warrior in his holiness and strength (vv.3–4; cf. 99:3–4; Exod 15:11, 13). The name of the God who acts for his people and against their enemies is none other than Yahweh ("the LORD"), on whose "name" the people call with shouts of joy and with deeply felt gratitude (vv.1, 3) (see appendix to Ps 78: The Mighty Acts of Yahweh).

The *subjects* of worship are none other than the people for whom the Lord has done wonderful and mighty acts: the descendants of Abraham and Jacob (v.6). The Lord has established graciously a relationship with Abraham by covenant (cf. vv.8–11, 42) and committed himself to Abraham's children, as confirmed to Jacob, to whom the tribes looked as their patriarch. Abraham is here called "his servant" (v.6; cf. v.42), a term of closeness and of special appointment (see 19:11, 13). Through Abraham his descendants have become God's "chosen ones" (v.6; cf. v.43; 106:5; Deut 4:37). They became his own people out of all the nations (Exod 19:5–6). However, mere physical descent was not enough. The descendants of Abraham and Jacob were also expected to "seek the LORD" (v.3) in his holy temple with a true spirit of devotion (cf. v.4). In the acts of praise, public rejoicing, and remembrance of God's acts in redemptive history, the people of God would express a unity, as heirs of the Abrahamic covenant, and of Jacob's election over against Esau (cf. Mal 1:2–3).

The goal of *praise* is threefold. First, praise magnifies the Lord. When the people of God reflect on him and what he has done, they ascribe power, holiness, and glory to his name. His perfections and mighty acts are so closely interrelated that no separation can be made between praise and thanksgiving. Second, praise intensifies an appreciation of the history of redemption as it affects God's people in the present. They receive consolation and encouragement, reflecting on what he has done in the past. Third, praise also witnesses to those outside the covenant community ("the nations," v.1). Even as the mighty acts of God were to inspire the nations with awe (76:7, 12), so the recounting of God's acts in the past witnesses to his power over the nations.

Notes

6 The LXX and a MS from Qumran read the plural "his servants," and the Qumran MS also gives a different reading for "his chosen ones": "his chosen one" (so also several Hebrew MSS). The parallelism favors either a singular or plural reading: "his servants, . . . his chosen ones" or "his servant, . . . his chosen one" (Kraus, *Psalmen*, 2:718). However, in view of the singular and plural reading of vv.42–43, the MT of v.6 is preferable: "his servant, . . . his chosen ones."

II. The Covenant of Promise

105:7–11

7 He is the LORD our God;
his judgments are in all the earth.

8 He remembers his covenant forever,
the word he commanded, for a thousand generations,

9 the covenant he made with Abraham,
the oath he swore to Isaac.
10 He confirmed it to Jacob as a decree,
to Israel as an everlasting covenant:
11 "To you I will give the land of Canaan
as the portion you will inherit."

7–11 In hymnic language the psalmist ascribes covenant fidelity to "the LORD" (Yahweh). He is the "God" of Israel by covenant, but his authority extends to "all the earth" (v.7; cf. Gen 18:25). He made a "covenant" (*b^e^rîṯ*, vv.8–10), which is equivalent to "the oath" (v.9) and to "a decree" (v.10), with Abraham, Isaac, and Jacob (cf. Gen 15:18; 17:2–8; 22:16; 26:3–5; 28:13–15; 35:12). The covenant is a sovereign administration of grace and promise in this context the promise of the land of Canaan ("the portion you will inherit," v.11; cf. 78:55).

The covenant is also eternally valid: "for a thousand generations" (v.8; cf. Deut 7:9); an "everlasting covenant" (v.10; cf. Gen 17:7). After all, God has made the oath (v.9; cf. Gen 22:16; 26:3), and as such the covenant fulfillment is not dependent on man (cf. Lev 26:42–45). He has remembered his covenant in sending his Son, through whom we are heirs of the new covenant (Luke 1:72–73).

III. The Protection of the Lord

105:12–15

12 When they were but few in number,
few indeed, and strangers in it,
13 they wandered from nation to nation,
from one kingdom to another.
14 He allowed no one to oppress them;
for their sake he rebuked kings:
15 "Do not touch my anointed ones;
do my prophets no harm."

12–13 The protection of God is transparent in the patriarchal narratives. Israel's beginnings are described by the stage when there were few members of the covenant ("when they were but few in number," v.12) and when the covenant community was not stable ("strangers," "they wandered," vv.12–13). Genesis gives the background to this harsh existence, as the patriarchs migrated to and from Egypt, and within the land, including the territory of Abimelech, king of Gerar. They were continually vulnerable to the jealousy of the kings, subject to pagan immorality, and contingent on the ever-changing political environment (Gen 12–35).

14–15 Nevertheless, Abraham's descendants did not succumb to political and moral pressures. Their strength did not lie in numbers (v.12) but in the Lord's protection. "No one" could undo his purposes, whether "man" or "king" (a merism in the MT: *'āḏām* ["man"] and *m^e^lāḵîm* ["kings"], v.14). He had promised to curse all those who curse Abraham and his seed (Gen 12:3), as they were in the Lord's eyes his "anointed ones" (v.15, pl. of messiah), i.e., his "holy people" (cf. Exod 19:5–6). They constitute his kingdom. As such "my anointed ones" is equivalent to "his chosen ones" (v.6). They are also designated as "my prophets." Though the term "prophet" is only loosely used of Abraham as God's "prophet" (cf. Gen 20:7), the psalmist generalizes it to apply to all three patriarchs. By plagues and dreams the Lord "rebuked" kings.

Therefore kings like the Pharaoh (Gen 12:17), Abimelech, and his son (Gen 20:3; 26:11) did not prevail against Abraham. The Lord was evidently with Abraham and Isaac.

IV. The Providence of the Lord

105:16–23

16 He called down famine on the land
and destroyed all their supplies of food;
17 and he sent a man before them—
Joseph, sold as a slave.
18 They bruised his feet with shackles,
his neck was put in irons,
19 till what he foretold came to pass,
till the word of the LORD proved him true.
20 The king sent and released him,
the ruler of peoples set him free.
21 He made him master of his household,
ruler over all he possessed,
22 to instruct his princes as he pleased
and teach his elders wisdom.

23 Then Israel entered Egypt;
Jacob lived as an alien in the land of Ham.

16 The episode of famine, Joseph's enslavement and exaltation in Egypt, and Israel's migration to Egypt evidence divine providence. Yahweh was as much involved in their protection (vv.12–15) as he was in bringing the adversity ("he called down"; cf. Amos 5:8; 9:6) of famine on the land (cf. Gen 41:54). For "supplies of food" (lit., "staff of bread"), see Leviticus 26:26; Isaiah 3:1; and Ezekiel 4:16; 14:13. However, the adversity was for the purpose of working out his good plan for Israel.

17–19 To this end the Lord led Joseph into enslavement in Egypt (v.17; cf. Gen 45:5, 7; 50:20). Joseph was humiliated in his unjust imprisonment (v.18; Gen 39:20), but he was finally greatly exalted through his God-given ability to interpret dreams (v.19; cf. Gen 40:5–23; 41:12–13). The earlier dreams of his exalted status, of which he had spoken to his brothers, proved to be God's word of promise ("what he had foretold . . . the word," v.19; cf. Gen 37:5–11). The fulfillment came only after a lengthy period of trial ("the word of the LORD purified him"; NIV, "proved him true," cf. Job 23:10).

20–22 Through the order of Pharaoh, Joseph was released from prison and elevated to the high office of "master of his household" (vv.20–21; cf. Gen 41:14, 40). This office is comparable to secretary of state (cf. 1 Kings 16:9; 2 Kings 15:5; 18:18, 37; Isa 22:15), as Joseph was Pharaoh's administrator over all his possessions (cf. Acts 7:10). The king by his own volition became an instrument of God's plan. This again is providence. All recognized the wisdom given to Joseph so that he, a Hebrew, was given full liberty ("as he pleased") to instruct leaders ("princes") and "elders" (v.22).

23 Through divine providence Israel, the ancestor of the Israelites, entered Egypt, also known as "the land of Ham" (cf. v.27; 78:51) as "an alien" (cf. Gen 46:1–7).

Notes

20 The NIV has "the king" as subject of the verbs. This is consistent with v.21 and with Gen 41:14. Kraus, however, takes the Lord to be the subject, as in vv.16–17 (*Psalmen*, 2:716–18). The NIV is preferable because it is consistent with Gen 41:14.

V. The Protection of the Lord

105:24–36

24 The LORD made his people very fruitful;
he made them too numerous for their foes,
25 whose hearts he turned to hate his people,
to conspire against his servants.
26 He sent Moses his servant,
and Aaron, whom he had chosen.
27 They performed his miraculous signs among them,
his wonders in the land of Ham.
28 He sent darkness and made the land dark—
for had they not rebelled against his words?
29 He turned their waters into blood,
causing their fish to die.
30 Their land teemed with frogs,
which went up into the bedrooms of their rulers.
31 He spoke, and there came swarms of flies,
and gnats throughout their country.
32 He turned their rain into hail,
with lightning throughout their land;
33 he struck down their vines and fig trees
and shattered the trees of their country.
34 He spoke, and the locusts came,
grasshoppers without number;
35 they ate up every green thing in their land,
ate up the produce of their soil.
36 Then he struck down all the firstborn in their land,
the firstfruits of all their manhood.

24–25 The first two verses summarize Exodus 1: Israel's multiplication (Exod 1:7) and Pharaoh's jealousy, resulting in hatred. The Lord blessed (v.24), providentially created Israel's adversity (v.25), and was all too ready to protect his "people." The psalmist nearly passes over the adversity because he is filled with the theme of God's protection, as evidenced by his mighty acts. Israel, after all, was his people, whom he considered to be "his servants" (cf. vv.6, 15).

26–27 Out of his servants, the Israelites, the Lord chose Moses and Aaron. Moses is called "his servant" (Exod 14:31), and Aaron (Exod 4:14–16) is the "chosen" one of the Lord (v.26). For the close relationship of "servant" and "chosen one," see v.6. Both these men were instruments of redemption and of demonstrating his power in the form of "miraculous signs" and "wonders" (v.27; cf. 78:43; Exod 10:2; Jer 32:20).

28–36 The psalmist selects eight out of the ten plagues. He also changes the order, as he poetically rewords the account of God's mighty acts in Egypt. The omission of the fifth and sixth plagues as well as the variation in order have no bearing on the historicity of the traditions of what happened in Egypt. The plagues are framed between the ninth (v.28) and the tenth (v.36) affliction on the Egyptians: darkness (Exod 10:21–28) and the death of the firstborn (Exod 11:4–8; 12:29; cf. Ps 78:49–51).

The order in Exodus 7–12 is:	The order in Psalm 105 is:
1. blood	1. darkness (#9)
2. frogs	2. blood (#1)
3. gnats	3. frogs (#2)
4. flies	4. flies (#4)
5. plague	5. gnats (#3)
6. boils	6. hail (#7)
7. hail	7. locusts (#8)
8. locusts	8. death of the firstborn (#10)
9. darkness	
10. death of the firstborn	

Compare also the order in 78:44–51: blood, flies, frogs, locusts, hail, plague (see 78:48), death of firstborn. For a commentary on the plagues, see Exodus 7–12 and Psalm 78:44–51.

Notes

30 The plural form "of their rulers" may best be explained as a plural of majesty—"the chambers of their king" (Dahood, *Psalms*, 3:61)—or as a genitival form—"the royal apartments" (Allen, p. 36).

VI. The Fulfillment of Promise

105:37–45b

37 He brought out Israel, laden with silver and gold,
and from among their tribes no one faltered.
38 Egypt was glad when they left,
because dread of Israel had fallen on them.
39 He spread out a cloud as a covering,
and a fire to give light at night.
40 They asked, and he brought them quail
and satisfied them with the bread of heaven.
41 He opened the rock, and water gushed out;
like a river it flowed in the desert.

42 For he remembered his holy promise
given to his servant Abraham.
43 He brought out his people with rejoicing,
his chosen ones with shouts of joy;
44 he gave them the lands of the nations,
and they fell heir to what others had toiled for—
45 that they might keep his precepts
and observe his laws.

37–39 The interlude in Egypt began with the conclusion of section IV: "Then Israel entered Egypt" (v.23). The fulfillment motif comes out by a twofold use of the verb "brought out" (vv.37, 43). The Lord delivered his people with supplies of silver and gold to provide for their needs in the Promised Land (v.37; cf. Exod 3:21–22; 11:2; 12:35–36). As they were redeemed from Egypt, Israel was very joyous (v.43). The people whom he had chosen ("his chosen ones," v.43; cf. v.6) were filled with joy and laughter, as they shouted clamors of victory (v.43; cf. Exod 15; Isa 35:10; 51:11; 55:12). Egypt too was happy when Israel left, because with the departure of Israel came the end of the plagues (v.38; cf. Exod 12:33).

The Lord took marvelous care of his people. This is expressed by the phrase "from among their tribes no one faltered" (v.37; cf. Deut 8:3–4; Isa 5:27). The Lord sustained his people by his presence, protection, and provisions in fulfillment of the covenant with Abraham. He revealed his presence in the "cloud" and "fire" (v.39; cf. Exod 13:21–22). The Lord was present for guidance (Exod 13:21; Ps 78:14) and protection (Exod 14:19–20; Num 10:34–36). Here the presence of God serves as protection from the sun ("covering," cf. Isa 4:5–6) and from the darkness of the night ("fire to give light," v.39). In addition the Lord provided his people with food and drink ("quail . . . bread of heaven. . . . water," vv.40–41; cf. 78:15–16, 24, 27–28; Exod 16:13–16; 17:1–6).

40–41 The stress in this section is on God's responsiveness to his people. This comes to expression in the verbs "they asked, and he brought them . . . and satisfied them" (v.40; cf. John 6:31). The presence of the Lord assures fulfillment of the promises and the satisfaction of his people. The abundance of his provision also comes to expression in the picturesque language of v.41: "He opened the rock, and water gushed out; / like a river it flowed in the desert" (cf. 78:15–16, 20; Isa 41:18; 48:21). A.A. Anderson rightly observes, "It is noteworthy that in verses 40f. the author emphasizes only what Yahweh has done, without mentioning the murmuring of the people" (2:734).

42–44 The exodus from Egypt and God's presence, protection, and provision reveal his concern for the covenant ("his holy promise," v.42; lit., "his holy word"). He "remembered." Not that he had forgotten it, but the remembrance serves as a prompt to involve himself actively in fulfilling his promises (cf. Exod 2:24). Abraham is God's "servant," and his descendants are God's "chosen ones" (v.43; cf. v.6). It is to this end that he brought them with great joy (see above) out of Egypt into the Promised Land, whose indigenous population consisted of as many as seven nations ("the lands of the nations," v.44; cf. 78:55; Gen 15:19–21). By right of conquest they freely inherited from the Canaanites cities, vineyards, orchards, cisterns, and all kinds of material benefits (cf. Deut 6:10–11).

45a–b However, God's purpose for his people in the covenant with Abraham, in their being chosen, in their redemption from Egypt, and in their living in the Land of Promise was nothing less than to have a responsive people. The emphasis throughout the psalm lies on God's goodness: his promise, protection, providence, and presence. He is true to his word. And as an afterthought, the author reminds God's people of their responsibility. Keeping the precepts of the Lord is, therefore, an expression of joyous gratitude for all the benefits the Lord has provided for his people (cf. 78:7).

Law is not apart from gospel. Law in response to the gospel is no law in the legalistic sense (see appendix to Ps 19: The Word of God).

VII. Concluding Praise

105:45c

Praise the LORD.

45c The psalm begins with a call to praise and ends on a fitting conclusion: "Hallelujah."

Psalm 106: Remember Yahweh's Love and Israel's Disobedience

This psalm complements Psalm 78 in its thematic approach to Israel's history, revealing Israel's unresponsiveness to all the mighty and good acts of the Lord. In its stress in Israel's failure, it contrasts with Psalm 105, where the psalmist records the fidelity of God in his presence, protection, and providence.

The canonical place of this psalm after 105 moves the reader to reflection on the tenacity of human rebellion. The variation of hymn (vv.1–2, 8–12, 43–46) and lament (vv.6–7, 13–21, 24–39) moves the worshiper to praise the Lord. Kraus sees the hymnic element as setting the tone for the psalm (*Psalmen,* 2:727), but Allen interprets it as "a communal complaint strongly marked by hymnic features" (p. 50).

The structural framework favors the hymnic genre because the history of Israel's rebellion is set within a theological context of praise, prayer, and a look at God as the Savior and Judge. As in Psalm 105 the historical development is placed in a theological framework. The interpretation must reflect on the theological and canonical significance of the psalm rather than on the historical referentiality, even though some make a good case for an early exilic dating (Walter Beyerlin, "Der Nervus Rerum in Psalm 106," ZAW 86 [1973]: 50–64; A.A. Anderson, 2:735–36). The structure reinforces the theological interpretation:

A. Invocation to Praise (vv.1–2)
  B. Prayer for God's Salvation (vv.3–5)
    C. Acts of God's Love: Salvation (vv.6–12)
      D. History of Israel's Unbelief and God's Judgment (vv.13–43)
    C′. Acts of God's Love: Restraint (vv.44–46)
  B′. Prayer for God's Salvation (v.47)
A′. Invocation to Praise (v.48)

In language Psalm 106 shares linguistic and formal elements with prayers in Nehemiah 9, Isaiah 63:7–64:12, and Daniel 9. The beginning and conclusion (vv.1, 47–48) also occur in 1 Chronicles 16:34–36.

I. Invocation to Praise

106:1–2

1 Praise the LORD.

Give thanks to the LORD, for he is good;
  his love endures forever.

[2]Who can proclaim the mighty acts of the LORD
or fully declare his praise?

1 The formal inclusionary call to praise ("Praise the LORD," or "Hallelujah") frames the psalm (vv.1, 48). The doctrine of God shines through significantly even in the complaint, prayer, and history of rebellion. The doxology ("praise the LORD"; cf. 104:35; 105:45) and invocation (vv.1b–2) extol the Lord for his being "good" and for his enduring "love" (cf. 23:6). For the liturgical formula ("Give thanks . . . forever"), see 100:5 (cf. 107:1; 118:1; 136:1; Ezra 3:10–11; Jer 33:11).

2 The Lord is faithful to the covenant, as his administration reveals the prosperity of his people. They enjoy the evidences of his benevolent and constant love (see appendix to Ps 25: The Perfections of Yahweh). He does not change, though his people do (cf. vv.12–13). He has shown his love throughout their history in "mighty acts" (cf. v.8 [NIV, "mighty power"]; 20:6; 71:16; 145:4, 12; 150:2). Praise is linked to the revelation of God in history, as "his mighty acts" evoke the response of praise. This God is none other than the Divine Warrior (*gibbôr*), whose acts are mighty (*g*^{e}*b̲ûrôt̲*). The interrogative ("Who can . . . ?) is a Hebraic form of making an asseveration: "no one can proclaim . . . or fully declare" (cf. Exod 15:11).

II. Prayer for God's Salvation

106:3–5

[3]Blessed are they who maintain justice,
who constantly do what is right.
[4]Remember me, O LORD, when you show favor
to your people,
come to my aid when you save them,
[5]that I may enjoy the prosperity of your chosen ones,
that I may share in the joy of your nation
and join your inheritance in giving praise.

3 In view of the goodness, love, and mighty acts of the Lord, "blessed" are all those who enjoy his benefits (cf. 1:1). As in Psalm 1, the blessing is conditioned on pleasing the Lord. Here the psalmist singles out two qualities of a life of integrity: "justice" (*mišpāṭ*) and "right" (*ṣ*^{e}*d̲āqāh*). The Lord expects his children to persevere in maintaining righteousness and justice (v.3), because in so doing they establish his kingdom (cf. 15:1–5; 99:4; Isa 11:3–5; 33:15–17).

4–5 Underlying the prayer for restoration and blessing is the confession of sin (v.6, to be developed in vv.13–39). The people have rebelled against God's kingdom. They suffer on account of the kingdoms of this world. In desperation and in a spirit of contrition, the author prays that the Lord may again bestow his blessing on the godly (v.3) and "remember" (v.4) his covenant. Remembrance signifies, on the one hand, God's commitment by covenant and, on the other hand, God's active involvement. The synonym for "remember" is "visit with blessing" (NIV, "come to my aid"). The effect of God's remembrance is "salvation" and restoration. The object of God's remembrance is the individual ("me . . . my aid. . . . I . . . I," vv.4–5) as a member of the covenant people: "your people. . . . your chosen ones . . . your nation . . . your inheritance" (vv.4–5; cf. 105:6, 43). These synonyms convey the special status of Israel (cf. 33:12; 105:6, 43; Deut 4:20; 9:29).

The Lord has promised to "save" (lit., "with your salvation," *yᵉšûʿāh*) his people. They look to the change from alienation to salvation and from wrath to "favor." The "favor" of the Lord denotes the time for renewal of blessing, restoration, and forgiveness (v.4; cf. Isa 49:8; 61:3). "Salvation" and "favor" are apparently synonymous expressions: "In the time of my favor I will answer you, / and in the day of salvation I will help you" (Isa 49:8) (see appendix to Ps 119: Yahweh Is My Redeemer).

God's salvation results in renewal of his blessing (lit., "goodness"; NIV, "prosperity"; cf. Deut 30:15; Jer 29:32), "joy," and participation in the worship of the Lord ("in giving praise," v.5; cf. Deut 26:19; Jer 33:9). The complement of this prayer is toward the end (v.47).

III. Acts of God's Love: Salvation

106:6–12

6 We have sinned, even as our fathers did;
  we have done wrong and acted wickedly.
7 When our fathers were in Egypt,
  they gave no thought to your miracles;
 they did not remember your many kindnesses,
  and they rebelled by the sea, the Red Sea.
8 Yet he saved them for his name's sake,
  to make his mighty power known.
9 He rebuked the Red Sea, and it dried up;
  he led them through the depths as through a desert.
10 He saved them from the hand of the foe;
  from the hand of the enemy he redeemed them.
11 The waters covered their adversaries;
  not one of them survived.
12 Then they believed his promises
  and sang his praise.

6–7 The Divine Warrior reveals his authority in salvation (vv.7–12) and judgment (vv.40–46). He is known to Israel for his mighty acts, as from the beginning of Israel's history ("when our fathers were in Egypt," v.7) he displayed his power to deliver and fulfill by "miracles" (lit., "wonders" or "wonderful works"; cf. 105:2, 5): the plagues in Egypt and the Exodus (cf. 78:43–51; 105:27–36). But from the beginning too Israel has gone astray and acted corruptly (v.6; notice three synonyms for "sin": *ḥ-ṭ-ʾ*, *ʿ-w-h*, *r-š-ʿ*). Moreover, instead of constancy and vigilance (v.3), they have a history of infidelity: "we . . . , even as our fathers" (v.6).

The contrast between the loving acts (v.7, pl. of *ḥesed̲*; NIV, "kindnesses") of the Lord and Israel's lack of responsiveness dramatizes the greatness of God's love and salvation. He delivered a people who did not respond to his love! More than that, they resisted his authority and kingship even as Egypt had done, for "they rebelled" (cf. vv.33, 43; Isa 1:20; for the language of rebellion, cf. Isa 1:2–4) against him by the Red Sea immediately after their deliverance from Egypt.

8–12 The Lord's deliverance from Egypt discloses his fidelity to his covenant ("for his name's sake," v.8; cf. Isa 48:9), his rule over the nations (cf. Ezek 20:9, 14), and his "mighty power" (cf. v.2; 77:14). His power extends also to his word, because by his "rebuke" (cf. v.9; cf. 104:7; Isa 50:2; Nah 1:4) he brought the sea to submission (cf. 65:7; 104:7). The Red Sea became an instrument of judgment and deliverance. First, the Lord led his people to freedom (cf. Isa 63:13), when the sea bed was dry (cf. 104:6–7), "as through a desert" (cf. Exod 14:21). The Divine Warrior freed ("saved," "redeemed") them (v.10; cf. Luke 1:71) from their "foe," who vanished in their sight (vv.10–11). Second, the sea was also a means of judgment. None of the Egyptians ("their adversaries") survived (Exod 14:28; 15:5). Israel saw the hand of the Lord in the great wonders and acknowledged him as the Divine Warrior in a song of victory. They praised his power in deliverance, judgment, and rule (Exod 15:1–18), even though this faith in "his promises" and their "praise" (v.12) was momentary.

Notes

---

7 The MT's עַל־יָם בְּיַם־סוּף (*ʿal-yām b^eyam-sûp̱*, "by the sea, by the Red Sea") occasions some difficulty. The LXX reads, "they went up to the Red Sea," suggesting an alternate reading for the MT's *ʿal-yām*: viz., *ʿōlîm* ("going up"; see BHS). Two alternate proposals provide for an object to the verb "they rebelled": "but they rebelled against the Most High [*ʿelyôn*] at the Red Sea" (RSV; so also Allen, p. 45) and "they rebelled against you at the Red Sea" (BHS). The NEB makes its own attempt in understanding the MT: "but in spite of all they rebelled by the Red Sea." The evidence is insufficient to make a final judgment against the MT.

IV. History of Israel's Unbelief and God's Judgment (vv.13–43)

The history of Israel's apostasy, also the longest section within this psalm, is framed by the acts of God (vv.6–12; 40–46). The historical reflection essentially goes back to Israel's early history in the wilderness (vv.13–33) and after the conquest of the land (vv.34–39). The chronological sequence is secondary to the theological motifs of rebellion and judgment. The causal relationship between disobedience and judgment (vv.16–34) comes to a climax in the last section (vv.35–43): Israel's apostate life in Canaan and the Exile.

A. *Impatience: Wasting Disease*

106:13–15

13 But they soon forgot what he had done
and did not wait for his counsel.
14 In the desert they gave in to their craving;
in the wasteland they put God to the test.
15 So he gave them what they asked for,
but sent a wasting disease upon them.

13–15 Israel's faith faltered quickly (v.13). Having seen the great acts of the Lord, they readily gave in to impatience when he did not anticipate their needs. In his "counsel" the Great King knew what to do and when, but Israel's refusal to submit to his counsel signified an independence that would develop into the spiritual anemic condition of being stiff-necked and stubborn. They murmured about food and water (Exod 15:22–25; 16:1–17:7). In their lust they devoured the quail without proper preparation (Num 11; Ps 78:28–29). Thus they "put God to the test" (v.14; cf. 78:18) with their selfish spirit, as expressed in Numbers 11:5–6. He gave them what they wanted; but their craving ended in sickness, and their impatience rushed them to a premature death (v.15; cf. Num 11:34).

B. *Jealousy: Death and Fire*

106:16–18

16 In the camp they grew envious of Moses
  and of Aaron, who was consecrated to the LORD.
17 The earth opened up and swallowed Dathan;
  it buried the company of Abiram.
18 Fire blazed among their followers;
  a flame consumed the wicked.

16–18 Korah (a Levite), Dathan and Abiram (both Danites), and 250 leading men of Israel ("their followers," v.18) challenged the special status of Moses and Aaron (cf. Num 16:1–3) in a most insolent manner. They were "envious" (v.16) of the closeness of Moses to the Lord and of the sanctity of Aaron and the priesthood. They argued in favor of the sanctity (priesthood) of all believers, but their argument was grounded in bitterness and jealousy (v.16). Korah, whose involvement receives no mention in this psalm (cf. Deut 11:6), Dathan, and Abiram went down into the earth, whereas the company of 250 wicked men were destroyed by fire (Num 16:35). So jealousy was uprooted from Israel.

C. *Idolatry: Near Destruction*

106:19–23

19 At Horeb they made a calf
  and worshiped an idol cast from metal.
20 They exchanged their Glory
  for an image of a bull, which eats grass.
21 They forgot the God who saved them,
  who had done great things in Egypt,
22 miracles in the land of Ham
  and awesome deeds by the Red Sea.
23 So he said he would destroy them—
  had not Moses, his chosen one,
 stood in the breach before him
  to keep his wrath from destroying them.

19–20 This section and the next are inspired by Deuteronomy 9:7–29, where Moses reminds Israel of two special occasions when they rebelled against the Lord (at Horeb, at Kadesh Barnea, and an allusion to testing—Deut 9:22; cf. vv.13–15). This time Israel's sin is a direct affront of the God who revealed himself at Mount Sinai. They made the golden calf as a symbolic representation of deity, in violation of the second commandment (Exod 20:4–6). They worshiped the material ("metal," "eat grass," vv.19–20) rather than the resplendent "glory" of God, whose glory they had witnessed above Mount Sinai (Exod 24). "Their Glory" (*kāḇôḏ*, v.20; cf. 3:3; Jer 2:11; Hos 4:7; Rom 1:23) is none other than their Savior-God (v.21).

21–22 Idolatry denies the nature of the God of revelation and the God of salvation ("they forgot," v.21; cf. v.13). Too easily did they overlook the manifestation of his mighty acts of salvation and judgment ("great things"; cf. vv.7–11; 71:19; Deut 10:21; "miracles . . . and awesome deeds," v.22; cf. 78:11) in Egypt (i.e., "the land of Ham"; cf. 105:23) and by the Red Sea. The praise of God and expression of faith (v.12) was short-lived. (See the appendix to Ps 78: The Mighty Acts of Yahweh.)

23 In his anger the Lord was ready to "destroy them" (cf. Deut 9:25). He declared his intent to Moses, who interceded for Israel. The metaphor "stood in the breach" derives from military language, signifying the bravery of a soldier who stands in the breach of the wall, willing to give his life in warding off the enemy (cf. Ezek 22:30). So Moses stood bravely in the presence of Almighty God on behalf of Israel. Moses' position was unique, being God's "chosen one" (a synonym of "servant"; cf. 89:3). The Lord responded to Moses' intercession by not destroying the people.

Notes

20 The Sopherim emended the text for theological reasons from "his glory" or "my glory" to "their glory" (see BHS).

D. *Unbelief: Death*

106:24–27

24 Then they despised the pleasant land;
they did not believe his promise.
25 They grumbled in their tents
and did not obey the LORD.
26 So he swore to them with uplifted hand
that he would make them fall in the desert,
27 make their descendants fall among the nations
and scatter them throughout the lands.

24–25 At Kadesh Barnea the people rebelled again. This time they did not believe that the Lord could lead them into the Promised Land ("the pleasant land," v.24; cf. Jer 3:19; Zech 7:14). "His promises," which Israel believed by the Red Sea (v.12), no longer seemed valid (Deut 1:32). Instead of praising him (v.12), they "grumbled" (v.25; cf. Deut 1:27; 1 Cor 10:10). They "despised" and rejected his promise of the land (v.24).

26–27 The oath of God (v.26; cf. Num 14:30; Ezek 20:23) pertained both to that generation and to the generation of the Exile (cf. 95:8–11). The generation of the wilderness died without entering into the Promised Land (cf. Num 14:28–35). The generation of the Exile knew that they too were included in God's oath, as they, who were also the descendants of the generation of the wilderness, were scattered "throughout the lands" (v.27; cf. Lev 26:33; Deut 4:27; 28:64; Ezek 20:23).

E. *Idolatry: Plague*

106:28–31

28 They yoked themselves to the Baal of Peor
and ate sacrifices offered to lifeless gods;
29 they provoked the LORD to anger by their wicked deeds,
and a plague broke out among them.
30 But Phinehas stood up and intervened,
and the plague was checked.
31 This was credited to him as righteousness
for endless generations to come.

28–29 In their idolatrous practices the Israelites even devoted themselves ("yoked themselves," v.28; cf. Num 25:3) to "the Baal of Peor," a local Moabite god. At Mount Peor the Israelites fully participated in the communion sacrifices devoted to "lifeless gods" (lit., "sacrifices of the dead"; cf. 115:4–8; Lev 26:30). Thus they made God jealous and provoked his wrath (cf. Deut 4:25; 31:29), resulting in his immediate judgment: "plague" (v.29; cf. Num 25:8–9).

30–31 Instead of Moses, who had interceded on Israel's behalf at Horeb and at Kadesh Barnea, Phinehas, the grandson of Aaron, killed an Israelite who had joined with a Midianite woman (Num 25:7–8). This heroic act of devotion checked the plague (v.30; Num 25:8). His faith was richly rewarded ("credited to him as righteousness," v.31; cf. Gen 15:6; Heb 11:7) with a covenant promising a perpetual priesthood (cf. Num 25:13; Mal 2:4–6).

F. *Rebellion: Trouble*

106:32–33

32 By the waters of Meribah they angered the LORD,
and trouble came to Moses because of them;
33 for they rebelled against the Spirit of God,
and rash words came from Moses' lips.

32–33 Less than a year before Israel was to enter the Promised Land, Moses too provoked the Lord. At Meribah (cf. 81:7; 95:8) Israel complained about water, and Moses was to speak to the rock. Instead, he hit it, having been thoroughly provoked by Israel. Israel had already "angered the LORD" (v.32) and had "rebelled against the Spirit of God" (v.33). However, Moses' act of hitting the rock was not justifiable, nor were his "rash words" against Israel (cf. Num 20:10–11). Moses could not intercede on his own behalf, though he tried to no avail (cf. Deut 1:37; 3:26). Consequently Moses was punished in not being permitted to enter the land. This is what the psalmist calls "trouble" (v.32).

G. *Idolatry and Acculturation: Exile*

106:34–43

34 They did not destroy the peoples
as the LORD had commanded them,
35 but they mingled with the nations
and adopted their customs.
36 They worshiped their idols,

which became a snare to them.
37 They sacrificed their sons
and their daughters to demons.
38 They shed innocent blood,
the blood of their sons and daughters,
whom they sacrificed to the idols of Canaan,
and the land was desecrated by their blood.
39 They defiled themselves by what they did;
by their deeds they prostituted themselves.

40 Therefore the LORD was angry with his people
and abhorred his inheritance.
41 He handed them over to the nations,
and their foes ruled over them.
42 Their enemies oppressed them
and subjected them to their power.
43 Many times he delivered them,
but they were bent on rebellion
and they wasted away in their sin.

Apostasy, idolatry, and readiness to adapt to pagan cultures became a way of life in Israel. As soon as the land had been largely conquered, the tribal allotments were made, and Joshua charged the Israelites to be faithful to the Lord (Josh 13:1–7; 23:9–11). He would give them success in taking the whole land. However, they readily intermarried and adjusted themselves to Canaanite forms of worship and life (cf. Judg 2:1–3). Immediately on the death of Joshua and his generation, Israel was on a cycle of apostasy from which she would only occasionally turn (cf. Judg 2:6–3:6).

34–38 Because of her commitment through marriage to the indigenous Canaanite population ("they mingled with the nations," v.35; cf. Judg 3:5–6; Ezra 9:1–2), Israel could not be faithful to doing what "the LORD had commanded" (v.34; cf. Exod 34:11–16; Num 33:50–56; Deut 7:1–5, 16; 20:10–18). The Canaanite "customs" (v.35)—idolatry, sacrificial rites, human sacrifice, murder (cf. vv.36–39)—entrapped ("a snare," v.36; cf. Exod 23:33) the Israelites away from the revealed religion of Sinai. Their loyalty was to paganism. They "worshiped" (lit., "served," *'-b-d;* cf. Judg 2:19; Ps 97:7) the gods of the nations ("their idols," v.36) even when those gods required the sacrifices of Israelite children (vv.37–38; cf. Lev 18:21; Deut 12:31; 2 Kings 16:3; 21:6; 23:10; Jer 7:31; Ezek 16:20–21; 20:31; 1 Cor 10:20). The death of the children was nothing less than murder, the shedding of "innocent blood" (v.38; cf. Jer 19:4–5). In addition to human sacrifice, the pagan practices often contradicted the law of God and at times allowed for murderous practices and judgments. They shed "innocent blood" (cf. Isa 1:15–17; Jer 22:3).

39 These various practices "defiled" the people, rendering them ritually unclean for the worship of God. The pagan way of life was a form of religious prostitution (cf. Isa 1:21; Hos 2:2–13), as Israel was divided in its devotion to paganism and Yahwism. The people were unclean, and the land was equally defiled (cf. Num 35:33–34; Isa 24:5; Jer 3:1–2, 9) by the sinful practices of her inhabitants.

40–43 Consequently Israel suffered the greatest humiliation in her history: the Exile. The Exile was God's expression of anger and resentment ("was angry . . . and abhorred," v.40). He had sworn to scatter them among the nations (v.27) but had patiently waited for hundreds of years. Then he became angry. The anger of God is nevertheless no emotional outburst, because of his prior decree, forewarning, pleadings, judgments, and endless endurance with the willful disobedience of his own people. After all, he had helped them many times in their distresses, but without any apparent change in Israel's spiritual condition (v.43). Their ancestors had not waited for his "counsel" (v.13) in the wilderness, and the generation of the Exile rebelled by following their own "counsel" (lit., "they rebelled by their counsel"; NIV, "they were bent on rebellion"; cf. NEB, "and rebellious still"). Even in his anger the Lord still considered Israel to be his own people ("his people . . . his inheritance," v.40; cf. v.5; 28:9)!

V. Acts of God's Love: Restraint

106:44–46

44 But he took note of their distress
when he heard their cry;
45 for their sake he remembered his covenant
and out of his great love he relented.
46 He caused them to be pitied
by all who held them captive.

44–46 The Lord treated his "inheritance," on the one hand, as a nonentity. He permitted nations to invade, control, and oppress his people from time to time, as he did during the period of the Judges (vv.41–42). On the other hand, he lovingly "delivered them" (v.43), as is evident from reading the history of redemption. He still heard their "cry" of "distress" (v.44) and acted on their behalf ("he remembered . . . relented. . . . caused them to be pitied," vv.45–46; cf. Lev 26:41–42; Luke 1:72). Solomon had prayed that the Lord would have mercy on his people when they were scattered among the nations, and the Lord heard this prayer (cf. 1 Kings 8:50; Neh 1:11; Dan 1:9). His "great love" (*ḥeseḏ*) is grounded in the "covenant" with the patriarchs (v.45). He is faithful, even when his people have a record of resistance. His anger is restrained by his great love. This is mercy!

VI. Prayer for God's Salvation

106:47

47 Save us, O LORD our God,
and gather us from the nations,
that we may give thanks to your holy name
and glory in your praise.

47 The psalmist returns to the prayer of vv.4–5. A shift has taken place from the first person singular to plural, as the individual is a part of the community. The whole community has sinned (v.6). The individual cannot fully enjoy God's benefits until he restores his favor to the "chosen ones, . . . nation" (v.5).

To this end the psalmist prays, "Save us" (cf. 54:1; 118:25). God alone is able to restore his people from adversity and affliction, because he is "LORD [Yahweh] our God," i.e., he has covenanted himself to be the God of Abraham and his descendants. The triumph of the Lord results in thanksgiving and praise (cf. Isa 12; 43:21), even as

Israel of old had done in the wilderness (v.12). The new act of God will renew the praise of the Lord.

VII. Invocation to Praise

106:48

48 Praise be to the LORD, the God of Israel,
from everlasting to everlasting.
Let all the people say, "Amen!"
Praise the LORD.

48 The last verse forms an inclusion with vv.1–2 and an appropriate conclusion to the fourth book of the Psalms (90–106; see 41:13). The doxology declares the praise of God as "the God of Israel" (cf. Luke 1:68). As his "love endures forever" (v.1), so will his praise from his people be "from everlasting to everlasting." In hope of deliverance and prosperity (vv.4–5, 47), the people of God respond with an "Amen!" (cf. 1 Chron 16:35–36; see Ernst Jenni, "Zu den doxologischen Schlussformeln des Psalters," *Theologische Zeitschrift* 40 [1984]: 114–20).

Book V: Psalms 107–150

Psalm 107: Lessons From the Experience of the Saints

The introductory verse of this psalm is identical with Psalm 106. But that is where the similarity ends. This psalm is the first of the fifth book of psalms, a thanksgiving-wisdom psalm, and complements the confession of sin and prayer for divine favor and restoration (Ps 106). After an introductory invocation (vv.1–3), the psalmist enumerates cases where the Lord delivered all kinds of people in need (vv.4–32) and concludes on a hymnic praise of the Redeemer-God (vv.33–42). The hymn encourages the godly to observe wisely how great God's love is for his creation and especially for his own people (see Jorge Mejia, "Some Observations on Psalm 107," *Biblical Theology Bulletin* 5 [1975]: 56–66).

The hymnic praise of the Lord (vv.33–42) together with the reference to the gathering of the redeemed (vv.2–3) suggest a postexilic date. Psalm 106:47 contains a prayer for the gathering of God's people out of the nations, and 107 appears to be in the form of thanksgiving and praise for God's answer to prayer.

The structure is self-evident:

A. Invocation to Give Thanks (vv.1–3)
B. Reasons for Thanksgiving (vv.4–32)
B′. Reasons for Praise (vv.33–42)
A′. Invocation to Gain Wisdom (v.43)

I. Invocation to Give Thanks

107:1–3

1 Give thanks to the LORD, for he is good;
his love endures forever.
2 Let the redeemed of the LORD say this—

those he redeemed from the hand of the foe,
3 those he gathered from the lands,
from east and west, from north and south.

1–2 The congregation is called on to confess God's covenant fidelity, affirming his goodness and love toward the redeemed (v.1; cf. 106:1). This is a common liturgical formula, much like a confession of faith. However, its significance was not empty, because "the redeemed of the LORD" (v.2; cf. Isa 62:12) have experienced adversity in exile and have been delivered by the Lord (cf. Isa 35:9; 51:10–11; 63:4). The permanent significance of the psalm lies in the variety of ways in which and from which the Lord redeems his people. He does deliver people from all kinds of afflictions and is not restricted by spacial or temporal limits (vv.4–32). All who have experienced God's love may join together with God's ancient covenant people to give thanks for their deliverance, whether spiritual, psychological, or material.

The Lord delivers from "adversity" (*sār*, v.2; NIV, "foe," but preferably "trouble"; cf. vv.6, 13, 19, 28). Whatever the nature of one's "trouble," the Lord is able to "redeem" (*g-'-l*), and those whom he delivers are "the redeemed" (*g-'-l*). But it is equally clear from the experiences of the redeemed (vv.4–32) that not all who have been delivered from trouble are redeemed in the soteriological sense. Therefore the psalmist calls on everyone who has experienced an act of God's "redemption" to be wise by confessing that he is good, loving, and faithful! (See the appendix to Ps 119: Yahweh Is My Redeemer.)

3 In 106:47 the people of God prayed that the Lord would gather them from the nations. This prayer has been heard in Israel's restoration to the land after a period of exile. The Lord gathered them, as it were, from all directions, wherever his people were found, whether east or west, by land ("the north") or by sea (cf. Isa 11:11; 49:12; Matt 8:11).

Notes

---

3 The MT reads "from the north and from the sea" (cf. NIV mg.). The word יָם (*yām*, "sea") is generally emended to יָמִין (*yāmîn*, "south"; Kraus, *Psalmen*, 2:735), but Isa 49:12 supports the MT.

II. Reasons for Thanksgiving (vv.4–32)

Verses 4–32 complement Israel's history of rebelliousness and divine judgment (106:13–46). The stress of Psalm 106 was on man's unresponsive—even defiant—spirit and God's judgment on sin, whereas the emphasis in Psalm 107 lies on God's goodness in spite of man's sin. These circumstances are divided into two: suffering due to man's limitations (those lost in the desert or on the sea) and suffering due to man's sin (prisoners and sick). The structure reveals a chiastic pattern (ABB'A'):

A. Wanderers in the Desert (vv.4–9)
  B. Prisoners (vv.10–16)

B′. Sick People (vv.17–22)
A′. Sailors on the Sea (vv.23–32)

A. *Wanderers in the Desert*

107:4–9

4 Some wandered in desert wastelands,
finding no way to a city where they could settle.
5 They were hungry and thirsty,
and their lives ebbed away.
6 Then they cried out to the LORD in their trouble,
and he delivered them from their distress.
7 He led them by a straight way
to a city where they could settle.
8 Let them give thanks to the LORD for his unfailing love
and his wonderful deeds for men,
9 for he satisfies the thirsty
and fills the hungry with good things.

4–5 The reference to the "desert wastelands" could be an allusion to the Wilderness Wanderings or to the exilic experience. Though the root *t-ʿ-h* ("wander") occurs in the context of physical lostness (Exod 23:4), it may also denote profligate living (95:10; 119:110). The desert is a place to cross through, not to aimlessly wander in (*t-ʿ-h*). There is no city for protection, and one's supplies of food and water may readily be depleted (vv.4–5). Life loses its meaning as one experiences purposelessness (v.5b; cf. Job 6:18–21).

6–9 God hears the prayer of people in "trouble" (v.6; cf. vv.13, 19). His deliverance is full of surprises, as he supplies all the needs of his people. He straightens the way; leads them into the city; and provides for their shelter, food, and drink (vv.7, 9; cf. Isa 58:10–11; Jer 31:25; Luke 1:53). This God is the object of the thanksgiving hymn, because he manifests his "unfailing love" (*ḥesed̲*) in his "wonderful deeds" (v.8; for parallel see 106:7 [NIV, "miracles . . . kindnesses"]; see appendix to Ps 78: The Mighty Acts of Yahweh). His mercy is not limited to the covenant people, because the Creator-God is kind to "men" (v.8, *beʿnê ʾād̲ām*, "sons of man" or "mankind"; for refrain cf. vv.15, 21, 31). Since he is so gracious to all peoples, how much more to his own covenant children!

Notes

4 The subject of the perfect verb תָּעוּ (*tāʿû*, "wandered") is not supplied. It may be supplied from vv.2–3, but this is unlikely. It is far more possible that the form is to be understood as having an indefinite subject, as in vv.1, 10, 23. Kraus (*Psalmen*, 2:735–36) proposes an emendation to a plural active participle, תֹּעֵי (*tōʿê*, "those who wander"; so also vv.10, 23).

8 For the association of love with God's acts of redemption, see Katherine D. Sakenfeld, *The Meaning of* ḥesed̲ *in the Hebrew Bible: A New Inquiry*. Harvard Semitic Monographs 17 (Missoula: Scholars, 1978), p. 218.

B. *Prisoners*

107:10–16

10 Some sat in darkness and the deepest gloom,
prisoners suffering in iron chains,
11 for they had rebelled against the words of God
and despised the counsel of the Most High.
12 So he subjected them to bitter labor;
they stumbled, and there was no one to help.
13 Then they cried to the LORD in their trouble,
and he saved them from their distress.
14 He brought them out of darkness and the deepest gloom
and broke away their chains.
15 Let them give thanks to the LORD for his unfailing love
and his wonderful deeds for men,
16 for he breaks down gates of bronze
and cuts through bars of iron.

10–12 Suffering also comes in the form of captivity. The language of "darkness," "gloom," and "iron chains" (lit., "iron") connotes despair, deprivation of rights, and judgment of God (v.10; cf. Isa 5:30; 8:22; 9:2; 42:7; 49:9; Mic 7:8; for "iron" as a symbol of oppression, see 2:9; Deut 28:48). Their misfortune was not accidental but resulted from an intentional breach of faith with the Lord. They "rebelled" (v.11; cf. v.17; 106:43) against the revelation of God ("the words of God" or "the law of God"; cf. 106:7, 33, 43) and autonomously despised his royal authority ("his counsel"; cf. 106:43). The reference to "God . . . Most High"—an example of the broken-up stereotyped phrase "God Most High" (El Elyon)—denotes the Creator-God who sovereignly rules over his creation (cf. Gen 14:22; Pss 18:13; 47:2). Israel had defied his authority. He broke their rebellious spirit, forcing them to submit to his sovereignty by "bitter labor" (v.12; cf. 106:42). When they could not endure their lot, they "stumbled" like people without God. The Lord who had promised to sustain his people so that no one would falter (37:24), and who had graciously supported them (cf. 105:37), left his people to themselves so that they would find out what life is like without his love (cf. Isa 3:8). There was no God "to help" (cf. 22:11; 72:12; 2 Kings 14:26; Isa 63:5).

13–16 Yet the Lord who heard the cry of those in distress (v.6) cannot forget the lament of his own people (v.13). He delivered them too regardless of their rebellious spirit. He delivered them from every adverse condition, symbolized here by "darkness . . . deepest gloom . . . chains. . . . gates of bronze . . . bars of iron" (vv.14, 16; cf. Isa 45:2). For this the "redeemed" may give thanks (v.15; cf. v.8).

Notes

---

10 For צַלְמָוֶת (*ṣalmāweṯ*, "gloom"), see 23:4.
11 On Most High (Elyon), see the appendix to Psalm 9: Yahweh Is El Elyon.

C. *Sick People*

107:17–22

17 Some became fools through their rebellious ways
  and suffered affliction because of their iniquities.
18 They loathed all food
  and drew near the gates of death.
19 Then they cried to the LORD in their trouble,
  and he saved them from their distress.
20 He sent forth his word and healed them;
  he rescued them from the grave.
21 Let them give thanks to the LORD for his unfailing love
  and his wonderful deeds for men.
22 Let them sacrifice thank offerings
  and tell of his works with songs of joy.

17–18 This is another description of God's judgment on all who are "rebellious" (v.17; see v.11) against him. They are "fools" (cf. Prov 1:7), because they go astray in their love of wrong ("their iniquities," cf. 32:1). Their "affliction" is a sickness to death, when food and pleasure are no longer relevant. They "loathe" their "food," as they feel that death is nearby (v.18). Death is metaphorically described as "the gates of death" (cf. 9:13; 88:3).

19–20 What the people deserved they did not get. The Lord "saved" them too when they cried to him in their "distress" (v.19; cf. v.6). The "word" (v.20, *dāḇār*) against which they rebelled (cf. v.11) and which had condemned and cursed them became the word of promise, comfort, and restoration (cf. Isa 55:11; John 1:1; Acts 10:36). The "word" is personified here as God's messenger of healing and deliverance from "the grave" (cf. Job 33:23; John 1:1).

21–22 The people too must render thanks to the Lord (v.21; cf. v.8). The form of thanksgiving receives further definition here and in v.31. Thanksgiving was not an empty platitude but consisted of a concrete expression of loyalty to the Lord by the giving of "thank offerings" (v.22), a kind of communal offering, accompanied by "songs of joy." For a prophetic statement of the joy of restoration after the Exile, see Jeremiah 33:11.

Notes

20 The word "grave" renders the rare Hebrew word שְׁחִיתוֹתָם (*š^{e}ḥîṯôṯām*, "their traps" or "their pits"). It seems to be related to שַׁחַת (*šaḥaṯ*, "destruction"), and some emend the form to שַׁחַת חַיָּתָם (*šaḥaṯ ḥayyāṯām*, "their life from the pit"; cf. 103:4) or to מִשַּׁחַת תְּמִים (*miššaḥaṯ tāmîm*, "from the destruction of the perfect," Kraus, *Psalmen*, 2:736). However, the occurrence of the same form in Lam 4:20 argues against an emendation. "Pit" is a poetic form for "the grave."

D. *Sailors on the Sea*

107:23–32

23 Others went out on the sea in ships;
they were merchants on the mighty waters.
24 They saw the works of the LORD,
his wonderful deeds in the deep.
25 For he spoke and stirred up a tempest
that lifted high the waves.
26 They mounted up to the heavens and went down to the depths;
in their peril their courage melted away.
27 They reeled and staggered like drunken men;
they were at their wits' end.
28 Then they cried out to the LORD in their trouble,
and he brought them out of their distress.
29 He stilled the storm to a whisper;
the waves of the sea were hushed.
30 They were glad when it grew calm,
and he guided them to their desired haven.
31 Let them give thanks to the LORD for his unfailing love
and his wonderful deeds for men.
32 Let them exalt him in the assembly of the people
and praise him in the council of the elders.

23–24 Verses 23–32 parallel the section of the wanderers in the desert (vv.4–9) and complement it because "desert" and "sea," being contrastive, denote the farthest regions (cf. Isa 42:10–11). The merchants who cross the seas (v.23) in search of fortune witness the marvels ("works . . . wonderful deeds," v.24) of God's creation at sea (cf. 104:24–26) as well as his ability to calm a storm on "the mighty waters" (v.23; cf. 65:7; 77:19). The Lord's power is so great that he easily stirs up a storm (vv.25–27; cf. Jonah 1:4) and can calm it (vv.29–30).

25–27 By the word of the Lord, all things happen (v.25; cf. 105:31, 34; Gen 1:3; et al.). He lifts up the waves of the sea, which frightens the merchants on the ships as they rise "up to the heavens" and go "down to the depths" (v.26). As the ship is being tossed about as a plaything, the seafarers, unable to do anything about their lot, become dispirited and terrified. As they are being tossed about on board, they hold on to something solid, like "drunken men" who stagger and try to find some stability (v.27; cf. Isa 19:3). All their skills at navigation are ineffective so that they become desperate ("at their wit's end," lit., "all their wisdom was swallowed up"; cf. 55:9).

28–30 The sailors too prayed in their distress (v.28; cf. v.6), and the Lord responded to their prayer. He silenced the sea (v.29; cf. Jonah 1:15; Matt 8:26), brought the seamen safely to their destination ("their desired haven," v.30), and made them "glad" when they saw "the works of the LORD" (v.24).

31–32 The joy of the sailors and merchants brings them to expressions of devotion to the Lord. The proper response of thanksgiving finds its fullest development here. The liturgical refrain (v.31; cf. v.8) is further developed into liturgical participation. The merchants must publicly declare what God has done in communal worship ("in the assembly of the people") and in places of leadership ("in the counsel of the elders," v.32).

Notes

23–32 For a study of this section in the light of Jesus' calming the sea, see Franz Schnider, "Rettung aus Seenot: Ps 107:23–32 und Mk 4:35–41," *Freude an der Weisung des Herrn, Beiträge zur Theologie der Psalmen, Festgabe zum 70. Geburtstag von Heinrich Gross*, edd. Ernst Haag and Frank-Lothar Hossfeld (Stuttgart: Katholisches Bibelwerk, 1986), pp. 375–93.

30 The word מָחוֹז (*meḥôz*, "port" or "city") is a *hapax legomenon* in the OT.

III. Reasons for Praise

107:33–42

33 He turned rivers into a desert,
flowing springs into thirsty ground,
34 and fruitful land into a salt waste,
because of the wickedness of those who lived there.
35 He turned the desert into pools of water
and the parched ground into flowing springs;
36 there he brought the hungry to live,
and they founded a city where they could settle.
37 They sowed fields and planted vineyards
that yielded a fruitful harvest;
38 he blessed them, and their numbers greatly increased,
and he did not let their herds diminish.

39 Then their numbers decreased, and they were humbled
by oppression, calamity and sorrow;
40 he who pours contempt on nobles
made them wander in a trackless waste.
41 But he lifted the needy out of their affliction
and increased their families like flocks.
42 The upright see and rejoice,
but all the wicked shut their mouths.

33–35 The hymn of praise ascribes to the Lord the power to change things. His authority is limitless, extending over water ("rivers, . . . flowing springs," v.33), "fruitful land" (v.34), "desert," and "parched ground" (v.35). He can reverse the condition of anything and therefore the way of life of everybody! The wicked who prosper in their God-given land may find their land useless, parched, and "a salt waste," as happened to the area of Sodom and Gomorrah (vv.33–34; cf. Gen 19; Deut 29:23; Isa 50:2; Jer 17:6).

36–38 The Lord can also transform the wilderness into a well-populated area (vv.36–38). The "desert" (v.35) was so because of aridity and not always because of poor soil. It was "thirsty ground" (v.33) that, when supplied by the abundance of the Lord's "pools of water" and "flowing springs" (v.35; cf. Isa 35:7; 41:18; 43:19–20; 44:3), blossomed into fields of harvest. Where there is water and good land, people may come, find protection in cities, cultivate the fields, plant vineyards, and benefit from God's good land (vv.36–37; cf. vv.4–5). Their bounty is by the blessing of God, even as is their increase in number (v.38; cf. Lev 26:20, 22; Isa 49:19–20; 54:1; Ezek 36:30, 33–37).

39–40 In accordance with the chiastic pattern (curse, blessing, blessing, curse; ABB′A′), the psalmist returns to the motif of curse. The people whom the Lord has blessed with fields, home, and family (vv.35–38) are not dependable. In their prosperity they may exalt themselves. But in time God's judgment will find them out. The people may suffer from "oppression, calamity, and sorrow" (v.39). Their princes will be abased (v.40; cf. Job 12:21, 24).

41–42 Verses 33–40 are an encouragement to "the needy," i.e., those who wait for the Lord (v.41). They draw comfort from seeing the justice of God (v.42; cf. Job 22:19). In his power he blesses them and silences the ruthless power and great evil of "the wicked" (v.42; cf. 1:6; Job 5:16).

IV. Invocation to Gain Wisdom

107:43

43 Whoever is wise, let him heed these things
and consider the great love of the LORD.

43 The conclusion to this psalm transforms the hymn of thanksgiving and praise to a wisdom psalm. The righteous will become wise by studying the acts of the Lord in the affairs of man. Even in adversity, he learns to know his God better and to trust that he will make all things well. His acts of love (NIV, "the great love") are constant. The fool rages against God, but the wise will keep these things in his heart.

Psalm 108

108:1–13

A song. A psalm of David.

1 My heart is steadfast, O God;
I will sing and make music with all my soul.
2 Awake, harp and lyre!
I will awaken the dawn.
3 I will praise you, O LORD, among the nations;
I will sing of you among the peoples.
4 For great is your love, higher than the heavens;
your faithfulness reaches to the skies.
5 Be exalted, O God, above the heavens,
and let your glory be over all the earth.

6 Save us and help us with your right hand,
that those you love may be delivered.
7 God has spoken from his sanctuary:
"In triumph I will parcel out Shechem
and measure off the Valley of Succoth.
8 Gilead is mine, Manasseh is mine;
Ephraim is my helmet,
Judah my scepter.
9 Moab is my washbasin,
upon Edom I toss my sandal;
over Philistia I shout in triumph."

10 Who will bring me to the fortified city?
Who will lead me to Edom?

[11]Is it not you, O God, you who have rejected us
and no longer go out with our armies?
[12]Give us aid against the enemy,
for the help of man is worthless.
[13]With God we will gain the victory,
and he will trample down our enemies.

This psalm consists of two parts (vv.1–5, 6–13), each of which has its duplicate in another psalm. Verses 1–5 derive from Psalm 57:7–11 and vv.6–13 are parallel with Psalm 60:5–12. For an exposition see these psalms.

Psalm 109: Yahweh Loves the Needy

This is one of the imprecatory psalms (see appendix to Ps 137: Imprecations in the Psalms). The genre of the psalm reflects the *individual lament* type. Brueggemann observes that this psalm reveals a delicate balance by keeping two polar expressions in tension: "faithful covenantal speech" and "free, unrestrained speech of rage seeking vengeance," but always such that the latter is subordinated to the former (*Message of the Psalms,* p. 85).

The expository structure is as follows:

A. Invocation to the God of Praise (v.1)
B. The Words and Acts of the Ungodly (vv.2–5)
C. Imprecation (vv.6–15)
B′. The Acts and Words of the Ungodly (vv.16–20)
C′. Prayer for God's Love and Judgment (vv.21–29)
A′. Benediction of the God of Praise (vv.30–31)

I. Invocation to the God of Praise

109:1

For the director of music. Of David. A psalm.

[1]O God, whom I praise,
do not remain silent,

1 The psalmist invokes the Lord to help him by reflecting on God's past acts. He is "the God of my praise" (*t*[e]*hillāṯî;* NIV, "God, whom I praise"). The noun "praise" (MT) is not an attribute of the Lord but serves as a catch-all for all the reasons he is worthy of the praise of his people (cf. 22:3; Deut 10:21; Jer 17:14). He prays that the God who has responded in the past will act again on behalf of his covenant child by not remaining silent (cf. 35:22; 39:12; 83:1).

The word "praise" forms an inclusion with vv.30–31, and as such we agree with Dahood that, "though the burden of the psalm is lament, the poet is so confident that his complaint will be heard (cf. vv.30–31) that he proleptically calls it a 'song of praise' " (*Psalms,* 3:100).

Notes

For a brief discussion of the technical words and phrases in the superscription, see the Introduction.

II. The Words and Acts of the Ungodly

109:2–5

2 for wicked and deceitful men
  have opened their mouths against me;
  they have spoken against me with lying tongues.
3 With words of hatred they surround me;
  they attack me without cause.
4 In return for my friendship they accuse me,
  but I am a man of prayer.
5 They repay me evil for good,
  and hatred for my friendship.

2 Hardly has David opened his mouth before he begins to accuse his enemies. It is not because he hates so easily but rather because the ungodly have been so cruel. He charges them on two counts. First, their words are untrustworthy. The MT emphasizes the "mouth" of the wicked by placing the word "mouth" at the beginning of each phrase: "the mouth of the evil and the mouth of deceit they have opened against me." The repetition of this charge in the next colon reveals the gravity of the situation. The verbal phrases are parallel to each other: "(they) have opened against me" and "they have spoken against me" (lit., "with me"). The threefold description of the speech of the wicked seems to be uppermost in his mind. The speech of the wicked is "wicked," "deceitful," and "lying" (cf. 10:7; 50:19; 52:4).

3–5 Second, the deceptiveness of the wicked comes out of a heart of "hatred" (v.3). The psalmist has done everything to show his "friendship" (v.4; MT, "love"). In his friendship he had done acts of kindness ("good," v.5), but they had been unnoticed. Instead the wicked had returned evil for "good" (cf. 38:20). The depth of his "friendship" (vv.4–5) is set in contrast to the intensity of their "hatred" (vv.3, 5). During his friendship and even in his adversities he remained "a man of prayer" (v.4), given to a life of communion with God and not preoccupied with one-upmanship or vindictiveness. He presents his problem to the Lord awaiting a solution (cf. 35:13–14). They had attacked him as an enemy and did "accuse" (*yiśṭᵉnûnî*, from which we get our word "Satan," i.e., "accuser") him falsely.

The wicked have upset the moral order by their deceptions and exchange of evil for good and hatred for friendliness (v.5). Will the Judge of the universe not pay attention to this?

III. Imprecation (vv.6–15)

For a discussion on the motivation and theological place of the imprecation, see the appendix to Psalm 137: Imprecatory Psalms. Our treatment of the imprecation falls into five parts: (1) guilty on earth (vv.6–8); (2) family (vv.9–10); (3) possessions (v.11); (4) family (vv.12–13); (5) guilty before God (vv.14–15).

A. *Guilty on Earth*

109:6–8

6 Appoint an evil man to oppose him;
let an accuser stand at his right hand.
7 When he is tried, let him be found guilty,
and may his prayers condemn him.
8 May his days be few;
may another take his place of leadership.

6–8 The psalmist calls on evil to be punished by evil (v.6). He hopes that an evil man may be found guilty by "an evil man," whom he also calls "an accuser" (*śāṭān,* from which comes the proper name "Satan," cf. v.4). It is not clear whether the "evil man" is a judge or a person who acts in some authoritative capacity. Anyway, he hopes that the system of justice on earth will not be so corrupt as to twist any and all forms of justice (vv.6–7). Through the instrumentality of human institutions and by means of wicked men, other wicked men are condemned, and in this process God's righteousness is vindicated. The "evil man" and the "accuser" are identical, standing "at his right hand" (cf. Zech 3:1, but cf. v.31) for the purpose of bringing accusations against one of their kind.

The verdict must be "guilty" (*rāšā',* v.7). The word "guilty" is the same word for "evil man" (vv.2, 6; cf. 1:1; 28:3; 92:7). Even if he falls on his knees and asks for mercy, his laments and pleading ("prayers," *t^e^p̱illāh,* singular in MT of v.7 like in v.4) must go unheard. Thus powerful but evil men will be removed from office ("place of leadership," *p^e^quddāṯô,* v.8, related in root to "appoint," *hap̱qēḏ,* v.6) by others who are equally evil.

The psalmist prays that the days of the wicked may be "few" (v.8; cf. 37:35–36; 55:23). In the brevity of corruption lies hope. When oppression, evil, and godlessness are cut short, the Lord establishes his rule over the earth by a built-in obsolescence of human structures.

Notes

6 It is unnecessary to assume with Dahood that the psalmist is calling for a judgment after death and to take the references to the "evil one" as personifications of Satan: "Appoint the Evil One against him, / and let Satan stand at his right hand" (*Psalms,* 3:97, 101). Martin J. Ward views Psalm 109 as an imprecatory psalm in which the psalmist prophetically prays for the end of evil ("Psalm 109: David's Poem of Vengeance," *Andrews University Seminary Studies* 18 [1980]: 163–68).

7 The idiomatic rendering "may his prayers condemn him" explains an enigmatic Hebrew phrase: "and his prayer to sin [לַחֲטָאָה (*laḥ^a^ṭā'āh,* 'to sin')]." The word "sin" may also signify in its basic sense "a miss," i.e., "may his prayer be a miss."

8 A reference to this verse is made in Acts 1:20, as a part of the argument for the filling of the vacancy left by Judas. The word for "office"—פְּקֻדָּה (*p^e^quddāh*)—could also be translated as "goods" or "possessions"; but in view of the usage in Num 4:16; 1 Chron 26:20; 2 Chron 23:18, and the NT quotation (Acts 1:20, "leadership"), "office" best fits here.

B. *Family*

109:9–10

> 9 May his children be fatherless
> and his wife a widow.
> 10 May his children be wandering beggars;
> may they be driven from their ruined homes.

9–10 The psalmist further prays that the family of the wicked man may be without support and comfort. The reduction of his wife to widowhood and his children to being orphans (v.9) is a disgrace to the family name, as they would be at the mercy of their fellow men. The orphans and widows received special protection in Israel, being in need of food and clothing for their daily existence (cf. 82:3; Deut 10:18; 24:17; Isa 1:17; Jer 7:6; Ezek 22:7; Hos 14:3; Mal 3:5). The guilt of the father affected his whole family. Out of destitution they would have to be "wandering beggars" (v.10; cf. Jer 18:21) and homeless.

Notes

---

10 The NIV reflects an emendation of וְדָרְשׁוּ ($w^e\underline{d}\bar{a}r^e\check{s}\hat{u}$, "and seek") to יְגֹרְשׁוּ ($y^e\underline{g}\bar{o}r^e\check{s}\hat{u}$, "may they be driven") based on the LXX. The LXX may reflect a misreading of the text (Allen, p. 74); the MT makes sense, as "seek" is parallel with "beg," resulting in a chiastic stich:

May indeed be wandering	his children	and beg,
A′	B	C′
and seek		away from their ruined homes
C		A

Dahood's proposal, though more ingenious, also attempts to maintain the MT: "Let his children ever roam and beg, / may their houses be investigated by an appraiser" (*Psalms*, 3:97, 103).

C. *Possessions*

109:11

> 11 May a creditor seize all he has;
> may strangers plunder the fruits of his labor.

11 The psalmist also prays that the family of the guilty man may never enjoy "the fruits of his labor." The estate of the guilty is properly "his," as he has toiled for it. The word $y^eg\hat{\imath}^{a\text{'}}$ signifies the gain from labor (TWOT, 1:362), even when improperly obtained. The forfeiture of the family fortune by equally ruthless men ("strangers," cf. 54:3) would further reduce the survivors to dependency and indebtedness. The indebtedness of the family would result in the creditor's removing whatever is left. For the power of the creditor, see 2 Kings 4:1.

D. *Family*

109:12–13

12 May no one extend kindness to him
or take pity on his fatherless children.
13 May his descendants be cut off,
their names blotted out from the next generation.

12–13 In their destitute state (without breadwinner, bankrupt, and homeless), the widow and orphan had legal rights and claims on expressions of "love" (*ḥesed̲*; NIV, "kindness," v.12). The imprecation extends to any who extend a helping hand to the survivors of the guilty. No "kindness" or "pity" (*ḥônēn*, related to *ḥēn*, "favor") was to be shown. The disgrace should even be greater, as the psalmist prays in OT fashion that the curse of God will overtake his family so completely that the family name will be removed off the face of the earth (see B.S. Childs, *Memory and Tradition in Israel* [London: SCM, 1962], p. 71).

Covenant loyalty was rewarded with long life in the land, i.e., longevity and a long line of family (Lev 26:9; Deut 6:2). A breach of the covenant resulted in the execution of the curses, including famine, sickness, exile, and death (Lev 26:14–39). Thus the psalmist prays that the Lord's word will be fulfilled with regard to the profligate. After all, the Lord had commanded Israel to cut off the hardened sinner (Num 9:13; 15:30; 19:13, 20) and at times called for the execution of a whole family (Josh 7:24–25). Sin does have consequences (Exod 20:5)!

Because of the greatness of the sin, the judgment must come, and soon! The children cannot survive their fathers long because of their being reduced to poverty, begging, and loneliness (vv.9–12).

E. *Guilty Before God*

109:14–15

14 May the iniquity of his fathers be remembered
before the LORD;
may the sin of his mother never be blotted out.
15 May their sins always remain before the LORD,
that he may cut off the memory of them from the
earth.

14–15 The psalmist asks God to be just by always remembering the guilt of the whole family. The plural form "his fathers" explains how the guilt of the parents, including one's "mother," affects the children (v.14; cf. Exod 20:5; Deut 5:9). Even when "their names" are "blotted out" (*yimmāḥ*, v.13), the psalmist prays that the Lord will never permit the memory of their sins to be "cut off" (*kārat̲*, v.15). While forgiveness is possible for the repentant sinner (51:1), the hardened sinner is beyond salvation. The unforgiven sins are viewed as "memorials" that "remain before the LORD," even when the "memory" of the names has been forgotten.

Notes

14 The MT's אֲבֹתָיו (*'ᵃb̲ōt̲āyw*, "his fathers") is often emended to אָבִיו (*'āb̲îw*), but unnecessarily so. Dahood assumes that "his fathers" is singular in meaning though plural in form: "May his father's iniquity be recorded" (*Psalms*, 3:97, 105).

IV. The Acts and Words of the Ungodly

109:16–20

16 For he never thought of doing a kindness,
  but hounded to death the poor
  and the needy and the brokenhearted.
17 He loved to pronounce a curse—
  may it come on him;
 he found no pleasure in blessing—
  may it be far from him.
18 He wore cursing as his garment;
  it entered into his body like water,
  into his bones like oil.
19 May it be like a cloak wrapped about him,
  like a belt tied forever around him.
20 May this be the LORD's payment to my accusers,
  to those who speak evil of me.

16 The harshness of the psalmist's attitude to the wicked must be understood in the context of his time. The wicked were evil in that they hated, cursed, oppressed, and harassed the poor and needy. The wicked have no "kindness" (*ḥeseḏ*; cf. v.12). His failure to "remember" (*z-k-r;* NIV, "thought of doing") to practice "kindness" is a serious sin, because it is a breach of the covenantal stipulations (Lev 19:18; Mic 6:8).

The wicked "hounded" (*r-d-p,* "pursue"; cf. 71:11; TWOT, 2:834) the "poor and the needy" (34:2; 35:10) and "the brokenhearted" (cf. "broken of spirit," Prov 15:13; 17:22; 18:14; Isa 66:2). The above references to the needy refer primarily to the psalmist himself (cf. v.22). He is "poor," "needy," and "brokenhearted" and is the object of the attack! The purpose of the hounding is the "death" of the righteous.

17–20 The wicked reject "friendship" (v.4, from the root *'-h-b*) and "love" (*'-h-b,* v.17) in favor of "curse." The "curse" (*qᵉlālāh*; cf. 58:6–9; 69:22–28) was intended to destroy a human being, his position, his family, and the remembrance of his name. The wicked's love for cursing became so much a part of him that the psalmist describes it as if "he wore cursing as his garment," as if "it entered into his body like water, into his bones like oil" (v.18). "Water" and "oil" may have been a part of an ordeal or magic ritual (A.A. Anderson, 2:764). The wicked man is evil through and through. It is "wrapped about him" and "tied forever around him" (v.19).

The psalmist repeats the need for justice and vindication on the principle of lex talionis (retaliation). Instead of a continuation of the imprecation, I prefer reading vv.19–20 as a prophetic statement; i.e., "This is the LORD's payment to my accusers" (Kidner, 2:390).

Notes

---

17 Compare Dahood's rendering:

since he loved cursing,
  it has come to him,

Has not taken delight in blessing,
  it has gone far from him.
(*Psalms*, 3:98)

V. Prayer for God's Love and Judgment

109:21–29

21 But you, O Sovereign LORD,
  deal well with me for your name's sake;
  out of the goodness of your love, deliver me.
22 For I am poor and needy,
  and my heart is wounded within me.
23 I fade away like an evening shadow;
  I am shaken off like a locust.
24 My knees give way from fasting;
  my body is thin and gaunt.
25 I am an object of scorn to my accusers;
  when they see me, they shake their heads.

26 Help me, O LORD my God;
  save me in accordance with your love.
27 Let them know that it is your hand,
  that you, O LORD, have done it.
28 They may curse, but you will bless;
  when they attack they will be put to shame,
  but your servant will rejoice.
29 My accusers will be clothed with disgrace
  and wrapped in shame as in a cloak.

21 With the emphatic "But you" (cf. 22:3, 9, 19), David, in his desperate need, turns to the Lord. He attempts to move the Lord on the basis of three grounds: the nature of the Lord, his own need, and a reminder of the wicked. First, the nature of the Lord is unlike that of the wicked. He is "good" and full of "love" (*ḥese<u>d</u>*). The "name" (see appendix to Ps 7: The Name of Yahweh) of the Lord is no other than Yahweh ("LORD"), and he is the "Sovereign" (MT: *'ᵃ<u>d</u>ōnāy*, "Lord") over all of life. Out of the greatness of his covenantal love for his needy children, the powerful love of the Great King is invoked: "deal well with me" (lit., "do with me"; cf. Allen, "act on my behalf," p. 71) and "deliver me." For a similar phraseology, see v.26.

22–24 Second, the psalmist reminds the Lord of his need. He is "poor and needy" and his "heart is wounded within" him (v.22; cf. v.16). His heart is "pierced" with grief (cf. 55:4–5). It is as if life flows out of him, like the disappearance of "an evening shadow" (v.23; cf. 102:11). He is shaken "like a locust." The locust was proverbial for its ferocious appetite. Because of this farmers would shake locusts off trees and shrubs and destroy them, like we do with other insect plagues (TWOT, 2:828–29; ZPEB, 2:376). The harassment has taken its toll on the psalmist, both psychologically and physically. His body no longer sustains him, as his "knees give way" and his "body is thin and gaunt" (v.24).

25–29 Third, the psalmist reminds the Lord of the adversaries. The emphatic "I" (v.25) stands in contrast to the emphatic "But you" (v.21) and forms a closure of this section. The Lord is good and loving, but the psalmist is haunted by the accusers.

They seek his downfall by heaping on him "scorn" (cf. 31:11; 79:4; 89:41) and by rejecting him ("they shake their heads"; cf. 22:7; Matt 27:39). He prays for relief (v.26; cf. v.21) by particularly asking for God's judgment on the wicked (vv.27–29). The principle of the judgment is clearly that of just retribution: shame and disgrace (v.29; cf. v.25). Their "garments," "cloak," and "belt," signifying a life given to bring "curse" (vv.18–19), will be exchanged for their being "clothed with disgrace" (cf. 35:26). They will be "wrapped in shame as in a cloak" (cf. 71:13). They must know that the deliverance of God's "servant" (v.28; see 19:11) is the Lord's doing and that their judgment is also his work (v.27; cf. 86:17)! He will change the curse of the enemies to a blessing for his people (v.28; cf. 1 Cor 4:12).

VI. Benediction of the God of Praise

109:30–31

30 With my mouth I will greatly extol the LORD;
in the great throng I will praise him.
31 For he stands at the right hand of the needy one,
to save his life from those who condemn him.

30–31 David concludes his prayer for deliverance and judgment with a fervent expectation of standing among the throngs of worshipers (cf. 22:22), filled with praise for the Lord. The Lord stands "at the right hand of the needy one" (v.31; cf. vv.16, 22) as his protector, not as his accuser (cf. v.6). He protects and delivers his children from wicked adversaries (cf. vv.21, 26). To this end the psalmist concludes on the note he began: the praise of God (vv.1, 30).

Notes

---

31 The last phrase in the MT has occasioned some difficulty: מִשֹּׁפְטֵי נַפְשׁוֹ (*miššōp̱ᵉṭê nap̱šô*, "from the judges of his soul"). The LXX reads "from the pursuers of my soul." The RSV explains the nature of the condemnation by the addition of "to death." The NIV gives a satisfactory sense.

Psalm 110: The Kingdom of the Lord

This psalm may be classed with the royal psalms, but the *Sitz im Leben* is unclear. H.H. Rowley has argued that the psalm celebrates David's authority over all twelve tribes, his enthronement in Jerusalem, and the appointment of the Zadokite priesthood ("Melchizedek and Zadok," *Festschrift für Alfred Bertholet zum 80. Geburtstag*, edd. Walter Baumgartner, Otto Eissfeldt, Karl Elliger, and Leonhard Rost [Tübingen: Mohr, 1950], pp. 461–72). Though scholarship is greatly divided on the origin, date, and purpose of the psalm (Allen, pp. 83–84), apostolic usage reveals a strongly messianic motif (cf. Matt 22:44; 26:64; Mark 12:36; 14:62; 16:19; Luke 20:42–44; 22:69; Acts 2:34–35; Rom 8:34; 1 Cor 15:25; Eph 1:20; Col 3:1; Heb 1:3, 13; 5:6; 7:17, 21; 8:1; 10:12–13; 12:2). See David M. Hay, *Glory at the Right Hand. Psalm 110 in Early Christianity*, SBL Monograph 18 (Nashville: Abingdon, 1973).

Further, the psalm has eschatological overtones, as the community of the faithful looks forward to an even greater victory (Kidner, 2:396).

The structure falls into two oracles (vv.1–3, 4–7), each comprising two parts:

A. Promise (v.1)
    B. Victory (vv.2–3)
A′. Promise (v.4)
    B′. Victory (vv.5–7)

I. Promise

110:1

Of David. A psalm.

1 The LORD says to my Lord:
"Sit at my right hand
until I make your enemies
a footstool for your feet."

1 In an oracular statement ("the LORD says," *n*[e]*'um;* cf. 36:1; Allen, "Yahweh's oracle," p. 79), the psalmist speaks of the promise of God pertaining to David and his dynasty. The promise pertains to the covenant between the Lord (*'*[a]*ḏōnî*) and the one in authority over the people of God, the Davidic king. His authority is by divine grant. The Davidic king is a theocratic ruler in the sense that he rules over God's people under the Lord and yet is very close to him (cf. 1 Chron 28:5; 29:23; 2 Chron 9:8; Ps 45:6), at his right hand (cf. 1 Kings 2:19).

The authority belonging to the Davidic king is derived from the Lord. He promises to extend his dominion by subjugating the enemies. To make the enemies a "footstool" is an ancient Near Eastern metaphor for absolute control. Originally the victorious king placed his feet on the necks of his vanquished foe (cf. Josh 10:24; 1 Kings 5:3; Isa 51:23). From this practice arose the idiom to make one's enemy one's footstool. In Psalm 2 the Lord also promises the full authority over the earth to the Davidic king (vv.8–9), and Paul alludes to this when speaking about Jesus' authority as the Messiah of God (1 Cor 15:25). The promise is further developed in the victorious and eschatological language of vv.2–3, 5–7.

Notes

For a brief discussion of the technical words and phrases in the superscription, see the Introduction.

1 The MT uses the phrase אֲדֹנִי (*'*[a]*ḏōnî*, "my master") to denote the lord-vassal relationship between the king and his people (cf. 1 Sam 22:12; 26:18; 1 Kings 1:13; 18:7), whereas the usual reference to deity is אֲדֹנָי (*'*[a]*ḏōnāy*, "Lord" or "my Lord").

II. Victory

110:2–3

2 The LORD will extend your mighty scepter from Zion;
you will rule in the midst of your enemies.

[3]Your troops will be willing
  on your day of battle.
Arrayed in holy majesty,
  from the womb of the dawn
  you will receive the dew of your youth.

2 The Lord will give strength to his king (cf. 1 Sam 2:10), symbolized by the "scepter from Zion" (see 2:6, 9). He has decreed that the Davidic king shall "rule" (imperative from *r-d-h*) over the enemies (see Pss 2; 132:18). The Lord will extend the authority of the king so that enemies will have to recognize him, as was the case to some extent during the reigns of David and Solomon.

3 The text of v.3 is most difficult. Its economy of language and the nominal construction have given rise to different interpretations and textual traditions (see Notes). In spite of the textual problems, we may infer from the military language that the royal troops are numerous. The people come voluntarily on the day of battle, as in the days of Deborah (Judg 5:2, 9). They consecrate themselves, are fully prepared, and place themselves at the service of the king. They will be as abundant as "dew" (cf. 2 Sam 17:12) at dawn. They are youthful and hence valiant for battle. The king's army is prepared, strong, and numerous.

Notes

3 The MT's עַמְּךָ נְדָבֹת (*'amm^ekā n^edāḇōṯ*, lit., "your people voluntary offerings"; NIV, "your troops will be willing") is emended to *'imm^ekā n^edîḇōṯ* ("around you the nobles," Kraus, *Psalmen*, 2:753), suggested by the LXX: "with you is the rule." Allen is right in taking the word *n^edāḇōṯ* ("votive offerings") as a plural of intensification: "your people will volunteer" (pp. 79–80; cf. GKC, par. 141c).

Some propose an emendation of חֵיל (*ḥayil*, "strength"; NIV, "battle") to a verbal form חולל (*ḥôlal*, "be born," BHS). See the NEB: "At birth you were endowed . . . since your mother bore you."

The phrase "in holy majesty" is unique in the MT, as the plural of הָדָר (*hadar*, "majesty") occurs nowhere else. Some MSS read בְּהַרְרֵי (*b^eharrê*, "on mountains of"). See the RSV: "upon thy holy mountains." The association of dew and dawn fits the mountain imagery. The MT is consistent in using a military-royal imagery. The king's subjects are clothed in splendor, devoted ("holy") to the service of their king. John Gray's proposal is much more radical. He emends the bicolon to "On the day you were born you were my chosen one, / Sacrosanct from the womb" (*The Biblical Doctrine of the Reign of God* [Edinburgh: T. & T. Clark, 1979], p. 83).

The phrase "from the womb of the dawn" is highly poetic and unusual.

The last colon is the most difficult: cf. NIV's "you will receive the dew of your youth" and the marginal note, "*your young men will come like the dew.*" The MT reads, "to you dew of your youth." The LXX omits "to you dew" and renders יַלְדֻתֶיךָ (*yalduṯeykā*, "youth") as a verb, as does the Syriac. BHS proposes יְלִדְתִּיךָ (*y^elidtîkā*, "I have begotten you") as in 2:7 (also MSS and Syr.). The NEB reads similarly, "your mother bore you." Kraus has "I have borne you like dew" (*Psalmen*, 2:752–53).

III. Promise

110:4

> [4]The LORD has sworn
>   and will not change his mind:
> "You are a priest forever,
>   in the order of Melchizedek."

4 This verse opens up the question of whether Israel had a sacerdotal kingship. From the priestly laws it appears that there is a clear distinction between Israel's three theocratic officers: king, prophet, and priest. However, David was dressed as a priest (2 Sam 6:14), was in charge of the sacrifices (2 Sam 6:17–18), and gave a priestly blessing to the people (2 Sam 6:18). This was also true of Solomon (1 Kings 8:14, 55, 62–64), as his authority extended over the high priest (1 Kings 2:27, 35). It would be highly unlikely to posit Zadok here as the recipient of the promise, because the promised victory (vv.5–7) speaks of the king's special relationship to the Lord (contra Rowley).

The irrevocable oath is none other than what the Lord has promised to David pertaining to his dynasty (2 Sam 7:13; Pss 89:3, 28–29, 34–35; 132:11). David had shown a deep concern for the Lord's dwelling place; and with the divine appointment of Jerusalem as the focal point of his earthly rule, the Lord made great promises to David (see 132:13–18). Here the Davidic king serves as God's priest "in the order of Melchizedek" (see M. J. Paul, "The Order of Melchizedek [Ps 110:4 and Heb 7:3]," WTJ 49 [1987]: 195–211). Melchizedek was a priest-king over Jerusalem (cf. Gen 14:18), who worshiped the Creator-God as supreme Deity (El Elyon). The Davidic king is after the order of Melchizedek only in so far as the sacerdotal kingship is concerned. He is charged with responsibility over the true worship of the Lord. For a prophetic vision of the glorious union of the Messiah-Priest, see Zechariah 6:13; for the NT application, see Hebrews 5:6–10; 7:22.

IV. Victory

110:5–7

> [5]The Lord is at your right hand;
>   he will crush kings on the day of his wrath.
> [6]He will judge the nations, heaping up the dead
>   and crushing the rulers of the whole earth.
> [7]He will drink from a brook beside the way;
>   therefore he will lift up his head.

5–6 When the king goes out to war, "the Lord" (*'ᵃḏōnāy*), as the Master of the universe, supports him by being at his right hand (v.5; cf. 16:8; 109:31; 121:5). He will further the king's power by crushing the resistance of kings. There is a day of accountability appointed, and that day will be a time of vindication ("the day of his wrath"; cf. 2:5, 12; 21:9; Isa 13:9, 13; Zeph 2:3). On that day the Lord will "judge the nations" (v.6; cf. 2:9; 7:8; 9:8; 76:9; Rev 19:11–21), causing a great defeat for the inimical nations, symbolized by their "corpses" and "heads" (*rō'š*, or as the NIV, "the rulers").

7 The subject of v.7 is ambiguous, whether the king or the Lord. The psalm brings out the effects of God's acts. The theocratic king enjoys victory because of the God who fights for him. The reason for the king's lifting up of his head in triumph (cf. 3:3; 27:6) is because of God's help. The king will tire himself out in battle but will be refreshed by a brook along the way of pursuit. Allen (p. 82) is right that a mere drink from a brook cannot account for the victorious language of v.7b, introduced by "therefore." We must look at the motivation of the king, similar to that of Gideon and his three hundred men who drank from the water at Ein Harod (Judg 7:6). The royal drink may be ceremonial, as the psalmist expresses his confidence in the Lord in the presence of his troops.

Notes

7 Joachim Becker gives an elliptic reading based on ancient Near Eastern military annalistic idiom for a great victory: "He will drink blood" ("Zur Deutung von Ps 110:7," *Freude an der Weisung des Herrn, Beiträge zur Theologie der Psalmen, Festgabe zum 70. Geburtstag von Heinrich Gross* [Stuttgart: Katholisches Bibelwerk, 1986], pp. 17–31).

Psalm 111: Celebration of God's Faithfulness

Psalms 111 and 112 form a unit and may have been written by the same author or originated from within the same general approach to piety. Psalm 111 is a hymn of praise of God's involvement in history and revelation. According to some it belongs to a cultic setting (Kraus, Weiser, Dahood) in which an individual singer teaches Israel to praise the LORD with him, but there is no further agreement on which festival. Others consider the unity of 111 and 112 and argue that the psalms arose in an educational setting: school, synagogue, or wisdom teaching.

This psalm, celebrating the wonders of Yahweh, is in the form of a hymn but has a clearly defined concern with wisdom. The acrostic structure reveals a careful and artistic composition. The psalm consists of 23 bi- and tricolons, each beginning with a successive letter of the Hebrew alphabet, except for the introduction (v.1a). Acrostic poems in general do not show logical development because of the arbitrary imposition of the alphabetic form. The author shows twice that he had difficulty in finding an appropriate word: teth (*ṭerep̱*, "prey" for "food," v.5), tsade (*ṣiwwāh*, "commanded"; NIV, "ordained," v.9). He demonstrates a skillful development by inclusion, repetition of vocabulary, and attention to the historical progression from the Exodus to the Conquest.

The expository outline is as follows:

A. Public Praise for God's Mighty Acts (vv.1–3)
  B. The Works of the Lord in Redemption (vv.4–9)
A′. Response to God's Mighty Acts (v.10)

The structure unfolds the grounds for the praise of God, as both his revelation ("precepts") and his acts reveal that the Lord is "great. . . . glorious and majestic . . . righteous[ness]. . . . gracious and compassionate. . . . faithful and just . . . trustworthy. . . . steadfast . . . faithful[ness] and upright[ness]. . . . holy and awesome." For a detailed structural analysis in favor of the unity of Psalms 111 and 112, see Pierre Auffret, "Essay sur la Structure littéraire des Psaumes cxi et cxii," VetTest 3 (1980): 257–79; Johannes Schildenberger, "Das Psalmenpaar 111 und 112," *Erbe und Auftrag* 56 (1980): 203–7.

I. Public Praise for God's Mighty Acts

111:1–3

1 Praise the LORD.

I will extol the LORD with all my heart
  in the council of the upright and in the assembly.

2 Great are the works of the LORD;
  they are pondered by all who delight in them.
3 Glorious and majestic are his deeds,
  and his righteousness endures forever.

1 The psalm opens and closes with a call to praise God (vv.1, 10c). The opening "hallelujah" sets the mood for the entire psalm as a hymn of praise. The psalmist calls on the community to join in and to respond to his public praise of the Lord. His praise is from the heart and encourages the people of God to join in. The people of God belong to the wise, as they are "the council [*sôḏ*] of the upright" (cf. 107:32; see 25:14), "the assembly" (*'ēḏāh;* see 1:5). The "upright" are "good men" (NEB), only because they do not belong to the category of "the wicked" (112:10). The "assembly" is the gathering of Jacob's descendants who fear the LORD (22:22–23).

2 The praise of God consists of meditation on and proclamation of the works of God on behalf of his people. His acts are "great" in the sense of marvelous and awe-inspiring (cf. 106:21–22; Deut 10:21; Rev 15:3). All his acts from Creation (136:4–9) throughout the history of redemption are "great" and are, therefore, wonders (cf. Job 5:9: "wonders"; lit., "great things"). They bear further investigation, not to be fully comprehended (cf. Job 5:9), but to "ponder" (*d-r-š;* cf. Eccl 1:13) and to "delight in" (*ḥ-p-ṣ*) the works of the LORD.

3 God's works are also "glorious and majestic." Psalm 104:1 uses similar expressions in celebrating the divine acts as his personal involvement with his world of creation, describing his fatherly and royal care of creation. His royal splendor is clearly evident in all his works (8:1–2; 19:1–4a) but particularly in his great acts of redemption on behalf of his people. They had seen his wonders and, thus, his kingship. When Pharaoh's forces drowned in the Red Sea, Moses led Israel in a song of Yahweh's kingship (Exod 15:18). Yahweh is "majestic in holiness, awesome in glory, working wonders" (Exod 15:11).

God's acts of redemption (more than his work of creation) reveal his "righteousness" (*ṣᵉḏāqāh*). The word "righteousness" refers to God's orderly rule over creation, his victorious rule over the nations, and his redemption of his own (103:6). He is the God who is loyal to his covenant and will always—"his righteousness endures forever"—be committed to the redemption of his children (cf. Rev 15:4)! (See the appendix to Ps 25: The Perfections of Yahweh.)

Notes

1 The phrase הַלְלוּ יָהּ (*hallû yāh*, lit., "Hallelu Yah" ["Praise the LORD"]) introduces both Psalm 111 and Psalm 112 and is not a part of the acrostic. Some psalms reveal an inclusionary pattern (113; 117; 135; 146–150), others end on "hallelujah" (115:18; 116:19), and only Psalms 111 and 112 begin with "hallelujah" without the concluding repetition. The emphasis on praise sets the mood for each psalm.

The word לֵבָב (*lēḇāḇ*, "heart") needs no pronominal suffix in Hebrew and is properly translated as "my heart" (Dahood, *Psalms*, 4:122). Thanksgiving with all one's heart expresses the voluntary and complete nature of the praise of God. The phrase "with all your heart" is often found in Deuteronomy in the sense of complete allegiance to the Lord (4:29; 6:5; 10:12; 11:13).

The act of praise and thanksgiving need not be private. The deepest, heartfelt feelings of love and devotion to God find natural expression with those who love the Lord. They are the "council of the upright," "the assembly." For "council" see the note on 25:14; for "upright" see 7:10; and for "assembly" see 1:5. Heinz-Josef Fabry argues that סוֹד (*sôḏ*, "council"; cf. 25:14; 55:14 ["sweet fellowship"]) is an ecclesiological term, synonymous with "congregation" (see "Der himmlische Thronrat als ekklesiologisches Modell," *Bausteine biblischer Theologie. Festgabe für G. Johannes Botterweck zum 60. Geburtstag dargebracht von seinen Schulern*, ed. H.J. Fabry (Köln: Peter Hanstein, 1977), pp. 99–126.

2 "By all who delight in them" renders לְכָל־חֶפְצֵיהֶם (*lᵉḵol-hep̄ṣêhem*, "to all their delights"). The emendation of *hep̄ṣêhem* to *ḥᵃp̄ēṣêhem* explains the NIV rendering: "all who delight in them" (see KB³, 2:326–27; Dahood, *Psalms*, 3:122–23). But see the NEB: "all men study them for their delight"; so also the LXX and the Vulgate.

3 The pairing הוֹד־וְהָדָר (*hôḏ-wᵉhāḏār*, "glorious and majestic") is an example of stylized assonance; cf. 21:5; 45:3–4; 96:6; 104:1; 145:5. They are epithets of the Lord's royal power, as reflected in the works of creation and redemption.

II. The Works of the Lord in Redemption

111:4–9

4 He has caused his wonders to be remembered;
the LORD is gracious and compassionate.
5 He provides food for those who fear him;
he remembers his covenant forever.
6 He has shown his people the power of his works,
giving them the lands of other nations.
7 The works of his hands are faithful and just;
all his precepts are trustworthy.
8 They are steadfast for ever and ever,
done in faithfulness and uprightness.
9 He provided redemption for his people;
he ordained his covenant forever—
holy and awesome is his name.

4–9 The Lord has ordained the remembrance of his redemptive acts in the cult and liturgical calendar of Israel. The word *zēḵer* ("remembrance"; NIV, "to be remembered") is a noun in Hebrew. It connotes the act of "proclamation." Israel not only remembered but proclaimed what God had done (cf. 9:2, 14; 47; 96:3; 117; 145:6). The specific events to be proclaimed are not mentioned, but they include the redemption from Egypt and possibly "the transmission of the salvation history" (A.A. Anderson, 2:774).

The particular acts in redemptive history are the Exodus, the Wilderness Wanderings, the Conquest (vv.5–7a, 9), and the revelation at Sinai ("precepts," *piqqû*<u>*d*</u>*îm*, v.7). The recitation of redemptive history begins with and ends on a truly theocentric focus of redemptive history. The Lord is "gracious and compassionate" (v.4) and his name is "holy and awesome" (v.9).

These preceding epithets make allusions to the Exodus and the revelation at Mount Sinai. The Lord revealed his "awesome" (or "awe-inspiring") nature in the plagues of Egypt and particularly in Israel's crossing of the Red Sea (Exod 15:11). His acts were to inspire "terror and dread" on the nations (Exod 15:16). At Mount Sinai he revealed his "holiness" (Exod 19:6, 14, 22) and his "awesome" glory to his people (Exod 19:18–19; 20:18) so that they might fear him. He revealed the depth of his love, grace, and compassion to Moses after Israel had made the golden calf (Exod 34:6–7; cf. James 5:11).

The great acts of redemption are interwoven with covenant language and references to divine revelation: "he remembers his covenant forever. . . . all his precepts are trustworthy. They are steadfast for ever and ever, done in faithfulness and uprightness. . . . he ordained his covenant forever. . . . all who follow his precepts have good understanding" (vv.5–10). The first mention of his acts are particular: the Exodus, the Wilderness Wanderings, and the Conquest (vv.5–6). The second mention reminds God's people of the acts during the periods of the judges, the kings, and even after the Exile (v.9). The mention of these acts instills the hope that the Lord, who has redeemed his people in the past, will redeem his people in the future.

The acts of God reveal his commitment to the "covenant" (*b*^{e}*rî*<u>*t*</u>) made with the patriarchs (vv.5, 9; cf. Gen 15:18; 17:2–8; 22:17–18; 26:3–5; 28:13–15; 35:12) and confirmed to Israel at Mount Sinai (Exod 24:1–11). It is not clear whether the covenant refers back to the Abrahamic covenant or to the Sinaitic. It seems that since the acts of God in the Exodus and in the conquest of Canaan were fulfillments of his promises to the patriarchs, as restated to Israel, the ground of all the promises is his commitment to the patriarchs. Dahood terms this "the theological foundation of the Exodus event" (*Psalms,* 2:123).

In the covenants God has promised to be present with his people in blessing and protection. The blessings of God were experienced in the provision of "food" (v.5). He protected them and gave them "redemption" (*p*^{e}<u>*d*</u>*û*<u>*t*</u>) from adversity, oppression, and exile (v.9). Whatever their needs were, he took care of his children. The reference to "redemption" refers to the Exodus but need not be limited to it. The allusion may well include all events from the Exodus to the postexilic restoration (Isa 50:2). So A.A. Anderson says, "The psalmist may have had in mind, not only the Exodus events, but also the successive deliverances of God's people" (2:775).

The covenant bond assured God's people of his continuing loyalty, even when they had failed him. His acts of provision and redemption revealed that he is "faithful and just" (*'*^{e}*me*<u>*t*</u>*, mišpāṭ,* v.7), reliable ("trustworthy" [*ne'*^{e}*mān*]; "steadfast" [*sāmû*<u>*k*</u>], vv.7b–8a), and "faithful and upright" (*'*^{e}*me*<u>*t*</u>*; yāšār,* v.8b). His relationship with his children is not based on their fickleness. He himself is faithful ("true") to his covenant promises. His acts of love are "constant."

God's acts also reveal his concern with "justice." He rules as a "just" king over the earth (v.7; cf. 99:4). In his justice he establishes "equity" (98:9; 99:4) by upholding justice for the oppressed, feeding the hungry, freeing the imprisoned, and taking care of the needs of his own (146:7–9; cf. 113:7–9).

The fidelity of the Lord to his promises assures the godly that he is their God for all seasons because he is also powerful to establish justice. His acts in the past proclaim that he can do it, as he has "shown [*n-g-d*, lit., 'declare'] his people the power of his works" (v.6). The biblical revelation brings out the sovereign power of our Redeemer. God works out everything according to his will (cf. Isa 40:28–29; 41:2–4; 44:24–45:7). Allen concludes that these words "mark him as faithful to his own and their just defender from all who would oppress them" (p. 92). To Christians these words are assurances that the covenant has been confirmed in our Lord Jesus and that the faithfulness and justice of the heavenly Father are so much more true today. His covenant is "forever" (vv.5, 9). Paul assures us that no adversity can separate the elect from the love of God in Christ Jesus as he works out his purposes on earth (Rom 8:28–39).

The "precepts" (v.7; cf. 19:7–10; 119:4) also reveal the nature of the covenant God. The word of God was not a burden. It was to give order to God's people, that they might reflect the nature of their King in their national existence. The precepts too are characterized as "trustworthy," "steadfast," and done in "faithfulness and uprightness" (vv.7–8).

God's word is "true" in that all of his promises come to pass. They reflect his "faithfulness" in his relationship to his people. They support ("are steadfast") his rule on earth, as the word is the foundation of the growth and development of his people (v.8). God executes his own word by upholding "faithfulness and uprightness." This phrase is partly identical and clearly synonymous with the description of "the works of his hands" (v.7).

"Done" (v.8) is preferable to a more activistic translation "to be performed." The psalmist is not yet addressing God's expectation of Israel to "perform" the precepts but reflects on God's keeping of his word. Kraus's rendering "to fulfill" is helpful in this regard (*Psalmen*, 2:765). God keeps his own "precepts." It seems that the psalmist is widening the semantic range of "precepts" from laws given at Mount Sinai (v.7b) to God's promises or word-revelations. For a similar emphasis see Psalm 119 and the appendix to Psalm 19: The Word of God.

Thus the inspired author brings out the coherence between the Lord's acts and words. They all reflect his divine nature as a Father-King in relationship to his children-subjects. The precepts with their encouragements, promises, threats, blessings, and curses are true! The God of Israel is Yahweh. Since this psalm celebrates God's wonderful works (vv.2–4), splendor (v.3), and holiness (v.9), the "name" is "to be hallowed and revered in worship and life" (so Briggs, 2:383). The holy and awe-inspiring works, words, and self-revelation (v.8) of Yahweh had a transforming effect on his people (cf. Luke 1:49, 60). They were called to fear him and to be holy (cf. v.10; Ps 112).

Notes

5–6 The verbs used for the acts and the remembrance of his acts are in a chiastic structure:
He provides (*n-t-n*) . . . he remembers (*z-k-r*)

He has shown (*n-g-d*) . . . giving (*n-t-n*) them.

5 The word טֶרֶף (*ṭerep̱*, "prey") may also denote food (Prov 31:15; Mal 3:10). He provided manna, quail, and water for his people in the wilderness (Exod 16; Num 11).

"Those who fear him" does not fit the historical circumstances, as Israel was a rebellious generation in the wilderness (95:8–11). It reflects the didactic aspect of the psalm. The truth is that God cares for those who fear him (*lîrē'āyw*, lit., "to his fearers"; cf. 22:25; 25:14; 33:18; 34:9; 85:9; 103:11, 13, 17; 145:19; 147:11).

6 "The power of his works" is idiomatic for "his powerful works" or possibly even "his mightiest works" (A.A. Anderson, 2:774). His power effected the dispossession of the Canaanites and the Israelite conquest. Dahood takes "power" (כֹּחַ [*kōaḥ*]) as the object of "shown" and translates: "his power by his works he manifested" (*Psalms*, in loc.).

The verbal phrase "He has shown" is an interpretative translation of הִגִּיד (*higgîḏ*, "declared"). God declares his power by his works. Psalm 29 speaks of his "voice" in a dynamic way. Similarly, his declaration of his might is therefore equivalent to a manifestation. Allen makes a good attempt at connecting both colons while preserving the "declarative" act of God: "He declared his mighty deeds to his people, that he would give them the possessions of the nations" (p. 88).

7 The pairing אֱמֶת וּמִשְׁפָּט (*'emeṯ ûmišpāṭ*, "faithful and just") is rare (cf. Jer 4:2). BHS proposes that either the one or the other be read. It is roughly synonymous with "faithfulness and uprightness" (*'emeṯ weyāšār*, v.8). The Lord's acts are characterized by fidelity and by advancing justice in accordance with his decrees. For "faithful" see the comment on 19:10; for "justice" see on 7:6; and for "uprightness" see on 25:21.

8 The NIV, instead of accepting the MT's יָשָׁר (*yāšār*, "upright," an adjective), adopts a minor emendation of a few MSS: יוֹשֶׁר (*yôšer*, "uprightness," a noun).

9 The verb "ordained" is a translation of צִוָּה (*ṣiwwāh*, "commanded"). The acrostic required a tsade; and the psalmist, desiring to bring to conclusion the effects of God's covenant (vv.5–9), chose a verb that is related to covenant terminology (A.A. Anderson, 2:775) but that is secondary to the main idea: God made a covenant to be lasting. See the NEB: "he decreed that his covenant should always endure."

III. Response to God's Mighty Acts

111:10

> 10 The fear of the LORD is the beginning of wisdom;
> all who follow his precepts have good understanding.
> To him belongs eternal praise.

10 The psalmist now evokes a response. The revelation of the Lord's character and his fidelity to the covenant as demonstrated in his acts of redemption and his precepts bring out the royal character of God's rule over his people. He calls for a response of wisdom in which God's people will express "fear" for him, submitting themselves to his rule and following his precepts. The fear of the Lord is "the beginning of wisdom." Even as God began and completed his work of creation (Gen 2:1), man must begin life with the fear of the Lord and complete it by doing his precepts. The wise man has "good understanding" (cf. Prov 3:5–6) (see appendix to Ps 1: The Ways of Wisdom and Folly).

Another response is that of praise. The godly have been exhorted to "praise the LORD." Since he is the Great King, as revealed in his character, rule, works, and words, his subjects who fear his name must respond in perpetual praise. God's covenant is forever (vv.5b, 9), and his praise from the members of the covenant community must be forever (cf. Rev 5:13b; 7:12).

The last colon forms an inclusion with v.1a: "Praise the Lord. . . . To him belongs eternal praise" (v.10c). Dahood takes the last line as a prayer: "May his praise endure forever!" (*Psalms*, 3:125). The psalmist has concluded in hymnic form the ground for godly wisdom and praise. He takes up the theme of wisdom in the next psalm.

Notes

---

10 For the importance of "wisdom" and "fear of the LORD," see the comments on 19:9; 37:30; and 112; and see the appendix to Psalm 1: The Ways of Wisdom and Folly.

"Good understanding" is synonymous with "wisdom" (Prov 3:5).

The NIV adds "his precepts" by ellipsis. The MT reads "to all who do them" and leaves undefined what "them" refers to. The third masculine plural suffix occurs as a third feminine singular in the LXX, Syriac, and Vulgate, referring back to "wisdom," "to all who do it." The use of the verb *'-ś-h* ("done," v.8; "follow," v.10) forms an inclusion, permitting an elliptic reading as in the NIV: "all who follow his precepts."

Psalm 112: The Triumph of Faith

Psalm 112 is an acrostic development of a sage. It is a *wisdom psalm*. As such it shares the formal literary characteristics of the wisdom psalms: it is an acrostic; it uses the "blessed is the man" formula, the vocabulary and concerns of wisdom literature, the contrast between the righteous and the wicked, and the blessings of wisdom. However, the psalm gives a realistic portrayal of wisdom as it brings out, not only the blessings of honor, children, and riches, but also the reality of adversities ("darkness," v.4; "bad news," v.7; "foes," v.8).

This kind of wisdom is Torah wisdom (v.1; see appendix to Ps 1: The Ways of Wisdom and Folly). Both psalms focus on the commands/precepts of the Lord as the revelation of his character ("trustworthy," "steadfast," "faithfulness," "uprightness," vv.7b–8). In addition both psalms consist of bicolons and have similar words and phrases: "delight" (111:2; 112:1); "upright" (111:1; 112:2, 4); "steadfast" (111:8; 112:7); "secure" (112:8); "fear" (111:10; 112:1); "his righteousness endures forever" (111:3; 112:3); and "gracious and compassionate" (111:4; 112:4).

The original context and date are difficult to determine. Many suggest a cultic setting in the postexilic era. However, there is no clear evidence of a cultic setting. The wisdom context provides for the best explanation of the origin of the psalm.

The structure and development of this psalm are not as clearly marked as in the previous psalm. After the initial blessing (v.1), the psalmist describes the blessings of the upright man (vv.2–3) even in adversity (v.4a), because of his evident concern to be "gracious and compassionate" (vv.4b–5). The theme of God's presence and help in difficulty is repeated in vv.7–8, and the wise man is further described as a generous man (v.9). He will be exalted (v.9c), but the wicked will "waste away" (v.10). We shall give an expository structure to the material (see Allen, pp. 96–97, for other suggestions):

A. Blessedness of Those Who Delight in Wisdom (v.1)
B. Blessings of Righteousness (vv.2–3)
C. Blessing in Adversity (v.4)
B′. Blessings of Being Gracious and Compassionate (v.5)
C′. Blessing in Adversity (vv.6–8)
B″. Blessings of Righteousness (v.9)
A′. Curse on the "Longings" of the Wicked (v.10)

The structuring brings out the great advantage of godly wisdom (three times) even in adversity. The author moves back and forth between the ideal and the real. At the heart of his concern is not so much the getting of God's blessings as much as encouraging conformity to God in righteous acts, in cultivating qualities (gracious and compassionate, loyal and steady), and in developing a strong faith in the Lord. The wise person is one of faith, hope, and love!

I. Blessedness of Those Who Delight in Wisdom

112:1

1 Praise the LORD.

Blessed is the man who fears the LORD,
who finds great delight in his commands.

1 The person "blessed" (*'ašrê*, see 1:1) by the Lord shows himself to be in active pursuit of godly wisdom. He begins with the fear of God and ends with finding "great delight in his commands." As an expression of nomic wisdom, the psalm sets forth wisdom as a pattern of behavior based on the revealed will of God. In the previous psalm the inspired author has prepared the reader for the importance of observing God's law by demonstrating that the law is a reflection of God's nature. The precepts are "trustworthy," "steadfast for ever and ever," and expressive of "faithfulness and uprightness" (111:7b–8). As a reflection of God's nature, the commands take on a different quality. They reflect "grace and truth" as exemplified by Jesus (John 1:14). The child of God who loves God is also desirous of doing God's will on earth. He is a wise child, who has "good understanding" (111:10). He not only ponders the works of God with great delight (111:2) but applies himself with equal delight to know God's will (1:2; 119:24, 77, 92, 143, 174).

Notes

1 On "Praise the LORD," see the comment on 111:1.

"The man who fears the LORD" is a synonym for "upright" (יָשָׁר [*yāšār*], vv.2, 4) and "righteous" (צַדִּיק [*ṣaddîq*], vv.4, 6), i.e., the person "who does not walk in the counsel of the wicked" (1:1). Psalm 1 gives a portrayal of the wise man by negation and affirmation whereas 111:1 gives a positive portrayal.

"Who finds great delight in his commands" is equivalent to "But his delight is in the law of the LORD" (see 1:2; see also 111:2).

II. Blessings of Righteousness

112:2–3

> 2His children will be mighty in the land;
> the generation of the upright will be blessed.
> 3Wealth and riches are in his house,
> and his righteousness endures forever.

2–3 The blessed man is a righteous man (v.3b). He practices "righteousness," is concerned with it, and makes every effort to establish God's righteous kingdom on earth. His character and acts are marked by godlikeness (111:3b). Because his way of life shows a concern for God's majesty, glory, and greatness (111:2–3), he builds up the kingdom of God on earth. Therefore, the Lord rewards him with success on his labors. The fruits of success are put in OT terms: many and blessed descendants, wealth, and honor. He enjoys success granted by the bestowal of God's blessing of riches and honor, and his children share in the blessing of their godly parents (cf. 2 Tim 1:5). Thus godliness has its rewards in this life, in future generations, and in the life to come (1 Tim 4:8).

Notes

2 The word "mighty" may be understood as "valiant," "wealthy," or "influential." גִּבּוֹר (*gibbôr,* "hero") is a noun, used in an adjectival sense. In the context of vv.2–3, the association is that of "wealth." It may be that Dahood is right in his argument that "mighty" here means "numerous": "Numerous in the land shall be his seed" (*Psalms,* 3:126–27).

דּוֹר (*dôr,* "generation") may also signify a group of people who are contemporaries (see 12:7; cf. 24:6; Kraus, *Psalmen,* 2:773). A.A. Anderson suggests "family" (2:777), and Dahood extends it to "abode" (*Psalms,* 3:127).

For "upright" see 7:10; cf. 111:1.

3 In 111:3 the psalmist speaks of God's "righteousness" (*ṣᵉḏāqāh*) as enduring forever. Righteousness has there the sense of his acts of redemption and vindication. The wise man as an imitator of God also does "righteous" acts. The importance of this quality of godliness is brought out by repetition (cf. v.9b): "Righteousness" means in the context of the description of his acts (vv.4–9) those works done by man in accordance with the law of God, out of a loving concern for man, in grateful response to God's benefits, but yet not meritorious of salvation. In another sense "righteousness" may also denote the reward (not "merit") of God on the godly, i.e., the promised blessings to those loyal to the covenant (so Kraus, *Psalmen,* 2:773). These blessings are developed throughout this psalm. Briggs limits the blessings to prosperity (2:385–86).

III. Blessing in Adversity

112:4

> 4Even in darkness light dawns for the upright,
> for the gracious and compassionate and
> righteous man.

4 The realism of the psalm breaks through. Wisdom does not always seem to be beneficial. Adversity also comes on the path of the godly. "Darkness" is a metaphor for adversity. It is not clear whether the wise man or the Lord is the source of the light. This verse could be read as "even in darkness [the] light [of the Lord] dawns for the upright" or as "even in darkness [the] light [of the wise] dawns for the upright." The Lord may use the wise as a means toward giving blessing to the upright in their adversity (Weiser, p. 703). The righteous man is "gracious and compassionate" like God (cf. 111:4b). His godly character is a "light" in darkness. "Light" is a metaphor for redemption and the joy of life (cf. 27:1; 36:9; 56:13; Isa 9:2; 10:17). However, when adversity comes in his way, he too like "the upright," will receive light. The latter may experience "darkness" (cf. 107:10) in the forms of "bad news" (v.7) and "foes" (v.8). The promise is that the Lord delivers the righteous from adversities. Therefore the wise man is a gracious and compassionate man who will do his utmost to relieve the suffering of other upright people.

Notes

---

4 The ambiguity of v.4a lies in the problem of identifying the meaning of "light." "Light" may denote the help given by the righteous (Weiser, Eaton, NEB, JB) or the help given by the Lord to the righteous (27:1; Isa 58:8, 10; Mal 4:2). The NIV reading is preferable because the wise man belongs to the group of the "upright" (cf. v.2) and because the Lord is most frequently the source of light (cf. 43:3).

The Hebrew of v.4b is equally ambiguous: "gracious and compassionate and righteous." Several MSS of the LXX add "the Lord" to clarify that the Lord is gracious, compassionate, and righteous (cf. 111:4b; Dahood, *Psalms*, 3:128). Several Hebrew MSS omit the connective between "compassionate" (BHS). Because 112 celebrates the virtues of the wise man and calls him "righteous" (v.6) and his acts "righteousness" (vv.3, 9), it is preferable to take "righteous" as a reference to the godly. He "mirrors" the Lord's attributes in his way of life (Kraus, *Psalmen*, 2:773; see A.A. Anderson, 2:778; Allen, p. 94). An alternate to the NIV is "the righteous man is gracious and compassionate"; parallel to 111:4b: "The LORD is gracious and compassionate."

IV. Blessings of Being Gracious and Compassionate

112:5

> 5 Good will come to him who is generous and
> lends freely,
> who conducts his affairs with justice.

5 The nature of God's grace and compassion (v.4b) is further explicated in this verse. It is possible to maintain the NIV reading, in which "good" functions as "blessed" (v.1). God is good (cf. Jer 33:11; Lam 3:25). Here, however, "good" is the quality of the righteous man. He is "good" in that he "is generous and lends freely." The "good man" (see Notes) is concerned with those in need and generously lends out money (cf. 34:8–10; 37:21). He need not give his money away but invests it in the unfortunate with the expectation that they will repay him, of course, without interest (cf. 15:5; cf. 37:26). With respect to all men, he shows himself a man of "justice." All his expressions of self, whether in words or deeds, are in strict accordance with his heartfelt sense of "justice." He knows what is "just" because he finds "delight in his commands" (v.1), which reflect the "uprightness" of the Lord himself (111:8). The Lord is "faithful and just" in all his acts (111:7). The upright man is not without guidance. He has God's revealed will, which he interprets and applies according to the spirit of the law.

Notes

---

5 "Good will come" may be read as "a good man." It is true that טוֹב־אִישׁ (*ṭôḇ-'îš*, "good man") is not the usual expression, but alphabetic psalms at times use grammar and syntax a little more freely (Dahood, *Psalms*, 3:128). The proposal of the inclusion "a good man . . . a righteous man" in the MT is also a strong argument in favor of an alternate reading.

"His affairs" is a rendering of דְּבָרָיו (*d*e*ḇārāyw*, "his words," "his acts").

For "justice" see comment on 7:6.

V. Blessing in Adversity

112:6–8

6 Surely he will never be shaken;
  a righteous man will be remembered forever.
7 He will have no fear of bad news;
  his heart is steadfast, trusting in the LORD.
8 His heart is secure, he will have no fear;
  in the end he will look in triumph on his foes.

6–8 Because the wise man holds to the precepts of God that are "steadfast forever and ever" (111:8), he is "steadfast" (v.7) in that "he will never be shaken" (v.6), "he will have no fear," "his heart is steadfast" (= *nāḵôn*, "established," v.7), and "his heart is secure" (*sāmûḵ*, "steadfast," v.8, as in 111:8). The emphasis is on the dependable character of the wise man. He may experience all kinds of surprises in life, but he will persevere in doing good. He does not waver or is not easily tossed about (James 1:6–8), but he "perseveres under trial, because when he has stood the test, he will receive the crown of life that God has promised to those who love him" (James 1:12). Whether he received "bad news," reason for "fear," or has problems with his opponents (vv.7–8), his trust is in the Lord (v.7). The Lord has promised that his children "will never be shaken" (10:6; 15:5; 16:8), that they will be remembered (Prov 10:7), and that they will triumph over their enemies (91:8; 118:7).

The wise man has deep "faith" in his commitment to a sovereign and gracious God, whose acts have been described as "great," "glorious," "majestic," and full of "righteousness" (111:2–3) in general, and full of "power," "faithful and just" (111:6–7) to his children, because his covenant with them is forever (111:5–9)! He knows that "in the end" (v.8) God will turn the gloatings and fortunes of the wicked (vv.8, 10). Godliness has its rewards in this life and has its hope fixed in God who will permit his saint one day to "look in triumph on his foes" (cf. 118:7; 2 Thess 1:9–10).

Notes

6 For the confident hope that the godly "will never be shaken," see on 10:6 (cf. 13:5; 15:5; 16:8; 21:7; 30:6).

The emphatic כִּי (*kî*, "surely") with the negative לֹא (*lō'*, "not") may simply be rendered as "never" (Allen, p. 94) or "Nothing shall ever" (NEB). Dahood gives a causal interpretation: "For never" (*Psalms*, 3:126).

The remembrance of the righteous lies in the recounting of his gifts and good deeds (see comment on 111:4; cf. Prov 10:7). His name will be remembered for blessing; in Jewish practice the formula "may his memory remain a blessing" follows the name of the deceased.

Dahood has observed the inclusion of vv.5–6 by the opening phrase "a good man" (NIV, "good"; see note on v.5) and the concluding noun "righteous" in the MT (*Psalms*, in loc.).

8 "Secure," a passive participle of סמך (*s-m-k*, "support") harks back to God's "steadfast" precepts; see on 111:8.

"He will look in triumph" is literally "he will see." The idiom רָאָה בְּ (*rā'āh b^e*, "look at") signifies a victory over the enemies (54:7; 59:10; 91:8; 118:7). The addition "in triumph" is a correct interpretative rendering (NIV). The verb is used as a play on "fear": לֹא יִירָא (*lō' yîrā'*, "he will have no fear") and יִרְאֶה (*yir'eh*, "he will look").

VI. Blessings of Righteousness

112:9

> 9 He has scattered abroad his gifts to the poor,
> his righteousness endures forever;
> his horn will be lifted high in honor.

9 The psalmist briefly restates his thesis. He has singled out generosity and compassion (v.4) as the hallmark of wise living. Wise living is characterized by lasting success, unlike many human endeavors that fail or are short-lived. Therefore, he repeats "his righteousness endures forever" (cf. v.3). The work of the godly endures (cf. 1:3). The apostle Paul refers to this text to give NT support for the principle that "whoever sows generously will also reap generously" (2 Cor 9:6, 9). Since God is gracious and compassionate (111:4), he supplies all that is necessary for his children and expects them to sow so that they may receive a "harvest of . . . righteousness" (2 Cor 9:10).

The quality of godlikeness expresses itself first in generosity. Doing the will of God is motivated by a desire to be like God. A delight in his commands (112:1) presupposes a grateful and generous attitude. This is the spirit of wisdom, the fruit of the Spirit (Gal 5:22–23; 6:8–10; James 3:17–18). God will reward them with an enduring harvest of righteousness. Yes, the righteous can practice righteousness, as Calvin readily admits, "It may, therefore, with propriety be said, that it is a uniform course of liberality which is here praised by the prophet, according to what he formerly observed, *that the righteous manage their affairs with discretion*" (4:329).

The godly man's reward is in the exaltation and honor of his children. The apostle Paul exhorted the believers to lay up a treasure for themselves by generous giving (1 Tim 6:18–19), in accordance with Jesus' teaching (Matt 6:33). He held out the promise that the believers may have "a firm foundation for the coming age," which is "truly life" (1 Tim 6:19). God will exalt and give strength (= "horn") to his own. This is his promise. The enjoyment of this life is not excluded. However, lest God's people give generously only to be rewarded in this life, the Bible holds out before us the greater motivating factor: the final exaltation of God's people and the rejection of the wicked. Only the fullness of the messianic age will witness the separation of the goats from the sheep and the full reward of God's children.

Notes

---

9 קַרְנוֹ (*qarnô*, "his horn") is a symbol of God's rewarding the righteous with "honor" (cf. NIV mg.: "*Horn* here symbolizes dignity"; cf. 75:5; 132:17; Luke 1:69). The "horn" denotes peace, prosperity, and God-granted success, instead of the competitive, greedy aspirations of the wicked (see Margit L. Süring, *The Horn-Motif in the Hebrew Bible and Related Ancient Near Eastern Literature and Iconography*, AUSDDS 4 [Berrien Springs, Mich.: Andrews University Press, 1980]).

VII. The Curse on the "Longings" of the Wicked

112:10

10 The wicked man will see and be vexed,
he will gnash his teeth and waste away;
the longings of the wicked will come to nothing.

10 The psalmist returns to the thought he began with but in a contrastive way: the "delight" of the blessed man (v.1) and "the longings" of the wicked (v.10). The wise man is blessed because his righteousness remains (vv.3, 9). But the wicked, as he sees God's reward on the righteous, will melt away. He is filled with anger, bitterness, and jealousy (cf. Acts 7:54; Gal 5:20). However, his anger will not last, as he destroys himself in his resentment. Though he is full of aspirations ("longings") that motivate him to do great things on earth, he will not succeed. All his schemings and plans "will come to nothing" (cf. 1:6).

Notes

---

10 The reaction of the wicked is a typical way in which they react to the godly in their adversity (35:16; 37:12). But when adversity turns into the prosperity of the righteous, they are "vexed" and "gnash" their teeth in hatred and jealousy. This expresses their rage and intent to overturn the Lord's doing—but in vain! They "waste away," as Briggs puts it, "melting as it were from [their] own heart" (2:387). The NEB gives a helpful rendition: "The wicked shall see it with rising anger and grind his teeth in despair."

The psalm concludes with an antithetical picture as a part of the inclusion: "Blessed is the man . . . who finds great delight in his commands [v.1]. . . . the longings of the wicked will come to nothing" (v.10; see 1:6).

The Hebrew for "longing" is תַּאֲוָה (*ta'ᵃwāh*, "desire," "longing") and denotes here the coveting and scheming of the wicked. There is no need to emend the text to "hope," as in the NEB: "The hopes of the wicked men shall come to nothing."

The Egyptian Hallel: Psalms 113–118

The *Hallel* psalms are found in three separate collections: the "Egyptian Hallel" (113–118), the "Great Hallel" (120–136), and the concluding Hallel psalms (146–150). The Hallel psalms had a significant part in the praise (*hallel*) of the Lord. The Egyptian Hallel and the Great Hallel (most of which are pilgrimage songs: 120–134) were sung during the annual feasts (Lev 23; Num 10:10). The Egyptian Hallel psalms received a special place in the Passover liturgy, as 113–114 were recited or sung before and 115–118 after the festive meal (cf. Matt 26:30; Mark 14:26). The concluding Hallel psalms (146–150) were incorporated in the daily prayers in the synagogue after the destruction of the temple (A.D. 70).

Psalm 113: Yahweh Is Exalted in His Saving Acts

Psalms 113 and 114 are both in the form of *descriptive praise* psalms and belong to the *Egyptian Hallel* psalms (see above). The threefold repetition—at the beginning (v.1) and the conclusion (v.9)—of "Praise the LORD" forms an inclusion and a magnificent opening of the Hallel collection.

The structure is simple:

A. Call to Praise the Lord (vv.1–3)
  B. The Sovereignty of the Lord (vv.4–6)
A′. Call to Praise for His Acts of Deliverance (vv.7–9)

(For a similar structure and exposition, see Peter C. Craigie, "Psalm 113," Int 39 [1985]: 70–74.)

I. Call to Praise the Lord

113:1–3

1 Praise the LORD.

Praise, O servants of the LORD,
  praise the name of the LORD.
2 Let the name of the LORD be praised,
  both now and forevermore.
3 From the rising of the sun to the place where it sets,
  the name of the LORD is to be praised.

1–3 The "servants of the LORD," his loyal people together with the priests and the Levites, come together for the worship of the Lord (v.1). The people of God comprise all, that is, "from the rising of the sun to the place where it sets," who know "the name" Yahweh (v.3; cf. 50:1; Zeph 2:11b; Mal 1:11; see appendix to Ps 7: The Name of Yahweh). The worship of the Lord is not limited to the land of Canaan but is to be universal. Through the witness of faithful Jews, many proselytes joined in the praise of God in the Diaspora. With the coming of our Lord and the preaching of the gospel to the Gentiles, the true worship of God has been gradually extended to all parts of the globe.

The worship of the Lord shows reverence for his "name." The threefold repetition of the "name of the LORD" (vv.1–3) calls attention to the acts and the self-revelation of the Lord, by which he declares the significance of the covenantal relationship to his people, in accordance with his promise (Exod 3:16; 6:7; Ezek 36:28; 37:23). The "name" of the Lord was to be proclaimed so that each generation might remember what he had done and how he had revealed himself (Exod 3:16).

The praise of the Lord was to be a lasting *hallel* ("praise"). The God who acted and revealed himself in creation and in redemption desired each generation to declare to the next generation the story of redemption so that he might have a loyal people on the earth. The emphasis on the continuity of praise is a corollary of the emphasis on the continuity of God's loyalty to his people. Thus the psalm begins with praise and focuses on God's merciful accommodation to the needs of his people (vv.6–9). Furthermore, he is to be praised "both now and forevermore" (v.2; cf. 121:8; 125:2; 131:3).

II. The Sovereignty of the Lord

113:4–6

4 The LORD is exalted over all the nations,
his glory above the heavens.
5 Who is like the LORD our God,
the One who sits enthroned on high,
6 who stoops down to look
on the heavens and the earth?

4–6 The Lord is sovereign over all the "nations" (*gôyîm;* cf. 99:2); over all the "heavens" (cf. 8:1; 57:5, 11); and, by implication, over everything. This bold statement of the glorious rule of the Lord over heaven and earth evokes a rhetorical question, used as a way of stressing the uniqueness and the victorious rule of the Lord: "Who is like the LORD our God?" (v.5; cf. 35:10; Exod 15:11; Deut 3:24; Isa 40:18, 25; 46:5).

The Lord is exalted in his "rule," as he is "enthroned on high" (v.5; cf. 29:10; 103:19). This last affirmation of his rule is symmetric with the opening statement, "The LORD is exalted [*rām*]" (v.4a) and forms an inclusion (cf. Isa 6:1). The participial usage in the phrase "who sits enthroned" (v.5) is a transition to a series of participial phrases. The psalmist creatively calls attention to the contrasting motifs: the exalted rule of Yahweh and his accommodation to the needs of his people; the universal rule of Yahweh (v.3) and his special interest in his people. He is exalted and yet he cares. Or, better, the Lord is exalted; therefore he is able to deliver. The "One who sits enthroned on high" stoops down to his needy children! His acts of redemption are acts of his freedom.

Notes

5 Instead of extending the rhetorical question to vv.5–6, it is more usual to limit the question to the first colon: "Who is like the LORD our God?" (so most versions and commentators).

5–9 See Avi Hurvitz, "Originals and Imitations in Biblical Poetry: A Comparative Examination of 1 Sam 2:1–10 and Ps 113:5–9," *Biblical and Related Studies Presented to Samuel Iwry*, edd. Ann Kort and Scott Morschauer (Winona Lake: Eisenbrauns, 1985), pp. 115–21; David Noel Freedman, "Psalm 113 and the Song of Hannah," *Pottery, Poetry, and Prophecy: Studies in Early Hebrew Poetry* (Winona Lake: Eisenbrauns, 1980), pp. 243–61.

III. Call to Praise for His Acts of Deliverance

113:7–9

7 He raises the poor from the dust
    and lifts the needy from the ash heap;
8 he seats them with princes,
    with the princes of their people.
9 He settles the barren woman in her home
    as a happy mother of children.

Praise the LORD.

7–9 Verses 7–8a are a quote from Hannah's Song (1 Sam 2:8; cf. Mary's Magnificat, Luke 1:52). The Lord takes care of the needs of the "poor" (v.7; cf. 82:3) and "needy" (chiastic structure; cf. 35:10; 86:1) by moving them from outcasts of society ("the dust," cf. Isa 47:1, or "ash heap," cf. Lam 4:5) to a position of prominence ("with princes, with the princes," v.8; cf. 1 Sam 2:8; Job 36:7). The afflicted man will receive recognition and the oppressed woman will receive honor in being a woman. In the ancient Near East, and especially in Israel, motherhood was a crowning achievement of any woman. A barren woman was a social outcast; she was a disappointment to her husband, to other women, and especially to herself (cf. Gen 16:2; 20:18; 1 Sam 1:6; Luke 1:25). However, the goodness of the Lord also extends to the relief from the judgment pronounced in Genesis 3:16. His people are to be blessed with children (cf. 115:14; Isa 48:19; 54:1–3).

The psalm concludes on the note it began with. The final call to praise is so much more conclusive, as the psalmist has developed two reasons for the praise of the Lord: his sovereignty (vv.4–5) and his loving acts of care (vv.6–9a)

Notes

6–9 The pronominal suffix *î* with the participial phrases and with the infinitive construct in v.8 has occasioned critics to emend the text to *ô*. However, the recognition that this is an archaic genitive case ending no longer requires this emendation (cf. Dahood, *Psalms*, 3:132).

9 M. Caspi concludes that the "barren" woman has already suffered from several miscarriages ("môšîḇî ʿaqereṯ habbayiṯ ʾēm-habbānîm śemēḥāh," *Beth Mikra* 25 [1980]: 365–66 [Heb.]).

The LXX and the Vulgate transfer the concluding call to praise to the beginning of Psalm 114.

Psalm 114: We Are the People of God!

Psalm 114 is one of the Egyptian Hallel Psalms (113–118; see introduction to Ps 113). According to the LXX, Syriac, and Vulgate, 114 and 115 form a composite; but the mood and genre vary too greatly for this to be the case. By genre this psalm is a hymn of descriptive praise. The theme is God's theophany to Israel in the wilderness when he committed himself to his people by covenant. He had redeemed Israel from Egypt, consecrated them to be his royal nation, and brought them across the Jordan into the Promised Land. This motif made it an appropriate hymn for the annual Passover ceremony. Brueggemann writes, "Psalm 114 is an invitation for each new generation to participate in this world-transforming memory, to be identified with the tradition and given life by it" (*Message of the Psalms*, p. 142). Norbert Lohfink argues that Psalms 114 and 115 reveal the marks of a deuteronomic theology ("Ps 114/115 [M und G] und die deuteronomische Sprachwelt," *Freude an der Weisung des Herrn, Beiträge zur Theologie der Psalmen, Festgabe zum 70. Geburtstag von Heinrich Gross*, edd. Ernst Haag and Frank-Lothar Hossfeld [Stuttgart: Katholisches Bibelwerk, 1986], pp. 199–205).

The structure of Psalm 114 reveals a chiasm constructed of three stanzas:

A. The Covenant People (vv.1–2)
  B. The Witness of Nature (vv.3–6)
A′. The Covenant God (vv.7–8)

The literary approach of holistic interpretation espoused by Meir Weiss complements our structural analysis (*The Bible From Within. The Method of Total Interpretation* [Jerusalem: Magnes, 1984], pp. 352–78).

I. The Covenant People

114:1–2

1 When Israel came out of Egypt,
the house of Jacob from a people of foreign tongue,
2 Judah became God's sanctuary,
Israel his dominion.

1–2 Kirkpatrick calls the Exodus "the birthday of Israel" as the covenant people (p. 679). They were marvelously delivered out of a foreign land (cf. 105:23), from a people who spoke a different language ("foreign tongue," v.1; cf. Gen 42:23). The reference to the "foreign tongue" evokes the association with oppression (cf. Isa 28:11; Jer 5:15) and is synonymous with "the house of bondage" (cf. Exod 20:2). The nation Israel came out of a foreign land, having been oppressed in Egypt.

Yet it was this nation that the Lord chose for his "sanctuary" and "dominion" (v.2). But whom did he choose for his "sanctuary?" The interchange of Judah and Israel differs from the synonymous use of Jacob and Israel in v.1. It is possible that the two kingdoms are intended: the southern (Judah) and the northern (Israel). The different designations may also be explained as a form of parallelism, signifying the whole of the people (Kirkpatrick, p. 681; Dahood, *Psalms*, 3:134) or the whole nation with a particular honor given to Judah as holy by virtue of her association with the temple in Jerusalem (Allen, p. 103). The resolution to this issue depends to some extent on how one interprets "sanctuary" and "dominion."

If the "sanctuary" denotes the guardianship of the Lord's temple in Jerusalem, it may be a reference here to the privileged position of Judah (cf. 78:68–69; see Allen, p. 105). However, the words "sanctuary" and "dominion" also echo God's promises to all the Twelve Tribes (cf. Exod 19:6). In Exodus 19:5 he promised the covenant-keeping people that they would become his "special people" (*s*ᵉ*gullāh;* NIV, "treasured possession"), his "kingdom-nation" (*mamlāḵāh, gôy*). He called them to serve him as "holy" (*qāḏôš*) servants (*kōhănîm,* "priests," i.e., "those who serve"). The whole people became "holy" (cf. Jer 2:3) to the Lord so that he had one nation over which he ruled ("dominion"). Israel had become his "sacred dominion" (consecrated by the covenant of law).

In conclusion, the references to Judah and to Israel are not contrastive but parallel. All Twelve Tribes had become the "sacred dominion" of the Lord by covenant at Mount Sinai. The Lord covenanted himself to his people so as to dwell among them, and the nation became his sanctuary and the instrument as well as the place of his rule (cf. Deut 4:20; 7:6–8; 32:9–11; 1 Kings 8:51; Hos 13:4; Amos 3:1–2).

Notes

1 Meir Weiss argues for an association of "foreign tongue" with "stern," suggesting to him oppression in Egypt in the meaning "barbarian tongue" (*The Bible From Within,* pp. 93–101).

II. The Witness of Nature

114:3–6

3 The sea looked and fled,
the Jordan turned back;
4 the mountains skipped like rams,
the hills like lambs.

5 Why was it, O sea, that you fled,
O Jordan, that you turned back,
6 you mountains, that you skipped like rams,
you hills, like lambs?

3–6 The wonder of Israel's election as the covenant people has its effect on the world of nature. The psalmist chooses the motif of Israel's miraculous passing through the Red Sea and the Jordan and the theophanic signs at Mount Sinai (Exod 19:18; Judg 5:4; Ps 68:8) as the background for a hymnic celebration of the wonder of God's revelation to Israel. Nature opened a path for the redeemed of the Lord (cf. 29:5).

The Lord was victorious over the power of the sea so that the waters fled like a routed army (vv.3, 5). The mountains and hills "skipped" (vv.4, 6) at the hearing of the word of the Lord (cf. 29:6). Truly Yahweh appeared to Israel and established his kingdom in Israel. That is why nature as it were responded with a twofold response: fear and great joy.

Nature had witnessed the victorious power of the Lord in the crossing through the Red Sea, the Jordan, and the phenomena at Mount Sinai. The motif of the reaction of nature (vv.3–4) is reworked by means of a series of rhetorical questions (vv.5–6). It is as if the psalmist calls on the sea, the Jordan, and the mountains to witness to that great redemptive, historical event, when God established his kingdom on earth, in Israel!

Notes

Meir Weiss shows an appreciation of the Israel-centered theology of this psalm. Creation responds with joy to Yahweh's redemption of his people ("The Exodus From Egypt in Ps 114. Toward the Study of the Hymns of Psalms," Tarbiz 51 [1981/82]: 527–35 [Heb.]).

III. The Covenant God

114:7–8

7 Tremble, O earth, at the presence of the Lord,
at the presence of the God of Jacob,
8 who turned the rock into a pool,
the hard rock into springs of water.

7 The repetition of the prepositional phrase "at the presence of" (*millip̱nê*) introduces the answer to the questions (vv.5–6) and the climactic conclusion. The God of Israel is "Lord" (*'āḏôn*), and the Master of the universe is no other than "the God of Jacob." He is the Lord of the universe (cf. 97:4–6; Rev 20:11), who has freely associated himself to be Israel's God!

8 The powerful and marvelous way of the God of Israel has not ceased. Though the epochs of the Exodus and Conquest were long passed, the psalmist purposefully uses the hymnic participle so as to declare the continuity of God's mighty acts. The God of Israel is he "who [turns] the rock into a pool, the hard rock into springs of water" (cf. Isa 41:18). As Kirkpatrick observes, "He Who made water flow from the rock at Rephidim and the cliff at Kadesh . . . can still provide streams of blessing for His people" (p. 682).

Notes

7 BHS follows Kraus in emending חוּלִי (*ḥûlî*, "tremble") to כָּל (*kol*, "all"), resulting in "at the presence of the Lord of all the earth" (*Psalmen*, 2:778). Bernard Renaud combines the two readings: "all" as the original and the MT "tremble" as a purposeful rereading, resulting in an eschatological orientation ("Les deux Lectures du Ps 114," *Revue des Sciences Religieuses* 52 [1978]: 14–28). Though I disagree with the double reading, I agree with Renaud that the psalm has a clearly prophetic message: the God of the Exodus will establish his kingdom on earth! Nothing can resist him. See also Tryggve N.D. Mettinger, "Fighting the Powers of Chaos and Hell—Towards the Biblical Portrait of God," ST 39 (1985): 21–38.

Psalm 115: We Are the Servants of God!

Psalm 115 is one psalm with Psalm 114 in the LXX and the Vulgate. However, there is little doubt that they form two separate psalms. The motifs and genre of the psalms are too different. Psalm 114 is in the form of a hymn describing the wonder of Israel's redemption from Egypt, whereas the literary forms of Psalm 115 are quite varied and include lament, liturgy, and confidence.

Psalm 115 may be classified as a psalm of *communal confidence.* The psalms of communal confidence are closely related to communal thanksgiving songs and to communal laments. The psalms of communal confidence convey a sense of need as well as a deep trust in the Lord's ability to take care of the needs of the people. There are three such psalms (115, 125, 129). Kraus prefers to include Psalm 46 and to exclude Psalm 115 from this threesome (*Psalmen,* 1:iii).

Psalm 115 had a liturgical place in the worship of ancient Israel. It was one of the Egyptian Hallel psalms (113–118; see introduction to Ps 113). The alternation between the first and second persons suggests the variation between communal recitation and priestly blessings. The expository structure of the psalm is as follows:

A. Community Prayer for Help (vv.1–2)
B. Impotence of Idols (vv.3–8)
C. Confidence in the Lord (vv.9–11)
C′. Blessing of the Lord (vv.12–15)
B′. Power of the Lord (v.16)
A′. Community Praise (vv.17–18)

I. Community Prayer for Help

115:1–2

1 Not to us, O LORD, not to us
but to your name be the glory,
because of your love and faithfulness.

2 Why do the nations say,
"Where is their God?"

1 The community protests against the Lord. They protest because they have suffered. The cause of the suffering is not important, as is the general spirit of the prayer. With the adversity of God's people, the glory of the Lord is at stake. Therefore they begin with a repetition that they do not pray for themselves ("not to us," v.1). Instead, they are concerned about the honor and glory of the name of the Lord (cf. Isa 48:9, 11; Ezek 20:9, 14; 36:21–23; Dan 9:18–19; see appendix to Ps 7: The Name of Yahweh). God's "glory" is directly related to the prosperity of his covenant people. Only after making their protest with an appeal to his glory do the godly remind the Lord of his promised "love and faithfulness" (*ḥeseḏ, 'ᵉmeṯ;* cf. Exod 34:6–7; Ps 138:2).

2 The present adversity casts a doubt on the power of Israel's God. It is not that the godly doubt his power but that the "nations" (*gôyim*) were quick in casting aspersions on the honor of Israel's God, asking, "Where is their God?" (cf. 42:3, 10; 79:10; Joel 2:17; Mic 7:10). The godly firmly believe that God is and that he is able; but out of concern for God's reputation among the nations, they raise this argument. Moses had used this argument when pleading for Israel, when God in his anger was ready to destroy his people (Exod 32:12; Num 14:13–15).

II. Impotence of Idols

115:3–8

3 Our God is in heaven;
he does whatever pleases him.
4 But their idols are silver and gold,
made by the hands of men.
5 They have mouths, but cannot speak,
eyes, but they cannot see;
6 they have ears, but cannot hear,
noses, but they cannot smell;
7 they have hands, but cannot feel,
feet, but they cannot walk;
nor can they utter a sound with their throats.
8 Those who make them will be like them,
and so will all who trust in them.

3 The confident faith of God's people finds expression in the credo "Our God is in heaven; he does whatever pleases him." They affirm that he is still their God ("our God"), that he rules sovereignly ("is in heaven"; cf. v.16), and that he is free in his acts of love and judgment ("whatever pleases him"; see appendix to Ps 5: Yahweh Is King). In this regard he is totally other than the idols. He is powerful and free to act at any time; but he is also free to delay, as Calvin explains, "Because he knows that delay and procrastination are profitable to us; it being his will to wink at and tolerate for a while what assuredly, were it his pleasure, he could instantly rectify" (4:346).

4–7 The confession of confidence in Yahweh has a corollary confession of doubt in idols and in the lasting effect of the charges of Israel's enemies (vv.4–8). It is to this effect that the contrast is drawn between "our God" and "their idols" (vv.3–4). This is the language of faith, in which the "gods" are contemptible fictions of the imaginations of man (von Rad, OTT, 1:212, 217).

The description of the impotence of idolatry resembles those given in Psalm 135:15–18; Isaiah 44:9–20; 46:6–7; Jeremiah 10:1–9; and Habakkuk 2:18–19. Whereas the Lord has the creative powers ("does," v.3; "Maker," v.15), the idols are "made" by man, whose habitation is of "the earth" (v.16). The idols are limited in power because they are human artifacts, share in human limitations, and are made of materials that come out of the earth ("silver and gold," v.4; cf. Isa 40:18–20; 44:9–17; Rev 9:20). Zimmerli has expressed the superiority of Israel's God well: "Whenever a hymn speaks of those other divine powers, whose existence is by no means denied on theoretical grounds, it can only be with reference to the One who will call their actions to judgment (Ps. 82), or in the spirit of superiority that mocks their impotence (Pss. 115:4–8; 135:15–18)" (OTTO, p. 155).

The psalmist amplifies the image of the utter worthlessness of idols, as he delineates how human they look but how inhuman they are. They have "mouths," "eyes," "noses," "hands," "feet," and "throats" but cannot do anything. The first word of v.5 ("mouths") and the last word of v.7 ("throats") in the MT form an inclusion, to emphasize that the idols, unlike the God of Israel, do not speak, reveal, promise, or utter any spoken word. Ultimately divine revelation is the difference between the religions of man and the true religion of the Lord.

8 Not only are idols worthless, those who worship them are also vain (cf. 2 Kings 17:15; Isa 44:9–20; Jer 2:5; Rom 1:21–32). False worship is not innocent but demoralizing, and ultimately the worshipers will perish together with their perishable idols. Von Rad speaks of an "enlightened rationalism which pokes fun at idols" (OTT, 1:217).

Notes

3 Verse 3 begins with a waw before "our God" in the MT. The disjunctive usage of the waw may be here for the purpose of contrast of Israel's credo with the question of the nations. The question, like a catechetical question, gets an unexpected response. A.A. Anderson is probably right in his translation: "Truly our God" (in loc.).

III. Confidence in the Lord

115:9–11

9 O house of Israel, trust in the LORD—
he is their help and shield.
10 O house of Aaron, trust in the LORD—
he is their help and shield.
11 You who fear him, trust in the LORD—
he is their help and shield.

9–11 How different is the religion of revelation! The people of God, led in worship by the priests ("house of Aaron," v.10), do not come to him with images. He comes to them with the promise of blessing and protection: "he is their help and shield" (v.9; see 33:20; cf. Deut 32:30; Pss 3:3; 28:7). In response to his promissory covenant, he expects nothing but loyalty from his people. No idolatry, but monolatry, i.e., the trust and worship of Yahweh alone!

The threefold call "trust in the LORD" has a corresponding threefold assurance of God's protection ("he is their help and shield"). The interchange of second person, implied in the imperative, with the third person ("he is their") may have arisen out of a liturgical setting in which the one group called for trust in the Lord and the other group sang about God's being the help of Israel (e.g., antiphonal choirs).

The threefold division ("house of Israel," "house of Aaron," "You who fear him") occurs elsewhere (118:2–4; 135:19–20 [with "house of Levi"]). It is unclear whether those "who fear him" are a separate class from the house of Israel, namely the "God-fearers" known in the OT (1 Kings 8:41; Isa 56:6) and in the NT (Acts 13:16, 26; 16:14; 17:17; 18:7) as the proselytes or a synonym for "house of Israel" (34:7, 9; 85:9) or all of Israel, i.e., laity as well as priests (cf. v.13). The conclusion is the same, as the psalmist calls on everyone to "trust in the LORD" by abandoning false worship.

IV. Blessing of the Lord

115:12–15

12 The LORD remembers us and will bless us:
He will bless the house of Israel,
he will bless the house of Aaron,
13 he will bless those who fear the LORD—
small and great alike.

14 May the LORD make you increase,
both you and your children.
15 May you be blessed by the LORD,
the Maker of heaven and earth.

12–15 The threefold call to trust the Lord, the three groups of people, and the threefold assurance of God's protection find their symmetric complement in vv.12–15a with a threefold formula of blessing ("will bless us") and a restatement of the three groups ("house of Israel," "house of Aaron," and "those who fear the LORD").

The assurance of the godly is always that the Lord will deal beneficently with his own. Though they may experience affliction and testing, he "remembers" those with whom he has made a covenant (v.12; cf. 98:3; 136:23; Isa 49:14–15) so as to bless them with his deliverance and the fulfillment of his promises. The Lord does not discriminate between the tribes of Israel or between the laity and the priesthood or between the important ("great") and the social outcasts ("small," v.13; cf. Jer 6:13; 16:6; 31:34; Rev 19:5). He is the God of his people, and all his own will be the recipients of his blessing.

The blessing as a word of promise holds out a great future for God's people. In accordance with his promise to Abraham (Gen 12:2), the Lord would bless his people with fruitfulness in descendants. During periods of adversity, whether famine or war, many lost their lives. The concern was with the future of God's people and hence God's promise. The Lord renews the promise through these words of benediction (v.14; cf. 127:3–5; Deut 1:11; Isa 54:1–3; Zech 10:8–12).

V. Power of the Lord

115:16

16 The highest heavens belong to the LORD,
but the earth he has given to man.

16 The certainty of blessing, increase, and protection lies in the belief in who God is. He is "the Maker of heaven and earth" (v.15b). Yahweh is the Creator-God, who sovereignly rules over everything he has created (cf. 121:2; 124:8; 134:3; 146:6) as the "Father" of all his creation (Calvin, 4:355). He is not limited in power or in rule but is enthroned in "the highest heavens" (cf. 2:4; 136:26). How different is he from the idols, who are made with human hands (vv.3–8)! They are earthy whereas the Lord is in heaven, i.e., heavenly (vv.3, 15–16). These verses form a symmetric contrast with the impotence of idolatry (vv.3–8) so as to emphasize the unlimited power and freedom of the Lord. Yet this verse also confirms God's concern with "the earth," the world of his creation. He has graciously given the dominion of this world to humans, not to the aggrandizement of humans, but in the service of the Lord. So Calvin writes,

> The prophet says that the earth was given to mankind, that they might employ themselves in God's service, until they be put in possession of everlasting felicity. True, indeed, the abundance of the earth belongs also to the brutal tribes; but the Holy Spirit declares that all things were created principally for the use of men, that they might thereby recognize God as their father. (4:358)

VI. Community Praise

115:17–18

17 It is not the dead who praise the LORD,
those who go down to silence;
18 it is we who extol the LORD,
both now and forevermore.

Praise the LORD.

17 Humans ("man," v.16b; lit., "the sons of man [*b^enê-'ādām*]") rule over earth by divine right (cf. Gen 1:28). Therefore man must be submissive to the Lord alone. In their submission humans must praise the Lord as the only and true God. However, the nations have gone astray. They do not worship the Lord (cf. vv.3–8). But the people of God, who trust in him and with whom he has made a covenant, love to praise him. If the adversities persist, more and more may die. The dead go down to "silence" (a euphemism for Sheol; cf. 94:17) and can no longer join in the processions, annual feasts, and liturgies (cf. 6:5; 30:9; 88:4–5, 10–12; Isa 38:11, 18; see appendix to Ps 88: Sheol-Grave-Death in the Psalms).

18 Those who protested, "Not to us, O LORD, not to us" (v.1), pray that they will be given an opportunity to fulfill their calling to praise the Lord: "it is we" (emphatic). They do not pray for themselves but for the glory of God (v.1). With the deliverance of God's people, the name of the Lord will be celebrated and the taunting of the enemies (v.2) will cease. Regardless of the outcome of the present dilemma, the people of God know that their God will deliver them (vv.9–15a), because he has elected them to praise him on his earth. They affirm their commitment to "extol" (*b-r-k*, "bless") him "both now and forevermore" (cf. 113:2). The concluding exhortation "Praise the LORD" is the usual conclusion of each of the Egyptian Hallel psalms (cf. 113:9; 116:19; 117:2, with the exception of 114; 118). The LXX and Vulgate add these words as the opening to Psalm 116.

Psalm 116: Be at Rest, for the Lord Is Good

This psalm is the fourth of the Egyptian Hallel psalms (see introduction to Ps 113). By genre the psalm belongs to the classification of *individual thanksgiving* hymns. The psalmist thanks the Lord for delivering him from a great trouble, the nature of which is not specified.

Structurally the psalm has been difficult to analyze. It contains thanksgiving with prayer, lament, confidence, and vows. It seems that the two major motifs throughout the psalm are suggested by several repetitions: "I will call on him [the name]" (vv.2, 13, 17), and "I will fulfill my vows to the LORD" (vv.14, 18); "death" (vv.3, 8, 15); "O LORD" (*'ānnāh YHWH*, vv.4, 16); and forms from the root *g-m-l* ("has been good," v.7;

"his goodness," v.12). In these colons the psalmist alternates between the experience of deliverance (vv.3–4, 7–11, 15–16) and his outbursts of thanksgiving (vv.1–2, 12–14, 17–19). A pivotal point in the psalm is the confession of the perfections of Yahweh, the Deliverer (vv.5–6). The development of the psalm argues against its division, as is the case in the LXX and Vulgate, where vv.1–9 constitute one psalm and vv.10–19 another psalm. The expository structure is complex and may best be viewed with Auffret as three overlapping concentric symmetries, whose centers occur in vv.3, 8–11, and 15–16:

I: A. Thanksgiving (vv.1–2)
 B. The Need for Deliverance (v.3)
  C. God the Deliverer (vv.4–6a)
II: A′. Thanksgiving (vv.6b–7)
  C′. God the Deliverer (vv.8–11)
 B′. Vows of Thanksgiving (vv.12–14)
III: B″. Vows of Thanksgiving (vv.13–14)
  C″. God the Deliverer (vv.15–16)
 A″. Vows of Thanksgiving (vv.17–19)

(Pierre Auffret, "'Je marcherai à la Face de Yahvé,' Etude structurelle du Psaume 116," *Nouvelle Revue Théologique* 106 [1984]: 383–96; id., "Essai sur la Structure littéraire du Psaume 116," *Biblische Notizen* 23 [1984]: 32–47; Robert L. Alden, "Chiastic Psalms (III): A Study in the Mechanic of Semitic Poetry in Psalms 101–150," JETS 21 [1978]: 206).

I. Thanksgiving

116:1–2

1 I love the LORD, for he heard my voice;
 he heard my cry for mercy.
2 Because he turned his ear to me,
 I will call on him as long as I live.

1–2 An emphatically placed "I love" (*'āhaḇtî,* v.1; cf. 18:1) opens the psalm. From the context it is clear that "the LORD" is the object (NIV transposes the object from the next sentence "the LORD heard my voice"). The psalmist's reason for the expression of endearment is motivated by the Lord: answered prayer. He has heard the "cry for mercy" (*taḥ*[a]*nûnāy;* cf. 28:2, 6; 31:22; 130:2; 140:6). For a similar expression of God's care and man's love, see 1 John 4:19: "We love because he first loved us." God's attentiveness to prayer is restated in v.2: "Because he turned his ear to me" (cf. 17:6; 86:1).

The psalmist gives public thanks as an encouragement to the godly to imitate him. For this reason he began with the emphatic "I love" (perfect) and continues with two imperfects and a perfect and concludes with an imperfect: "he heard" (imperfect, *bis*), "he turned" (perfect), "I will call on him" (imperfect). Because the Lord always "hears" the prayers of his people, the psalmist "loves" the Lord, being encouraged to call on him "as long as I live" (lit., "in my days"; cf. Isa 39:8, "in my lifetime"; similarly Ps 63:4; cf. 116:9, "in the land of the living").

Notes

1 The LXX transposes the conclusion of Psalm 115 to the beginning of this psalm: "Praise the LORD."

The syntax of this verse is somewhat complex. The MT literally reads: "I love, because Yahweh hears my voice, my cry for mercy." This could be rendered as ellipsis (so the NIV, with the addition of "he heard") or as emphasis (see Dahood: "Yahweh did hear my plea for mercy" [*Psalms*, 3:110]). I favor the latter because of the idiomatic usage of "voice" (*qôl*) with "cry for mercy" (*taḥ^a^nûnîm*, cf. references in the exposition).

Needless to say, the syntactic and grammatical peculiarities have resulted in many emendations. Two are of note: the imperfect form יִשְׁמַע (*yišma'*, "he hears" or "he heard") is emended as dittography to שָׁמַע (*šāma'*, "he heard") and וּבְיָמַי (*ûḇ^e^yāmay*, "and in my days") to the more usual וּבְיוֹם (*ûḇ^e^yôm*, "on the day," Kraus, *Psalmen*, 2:793).

II. The Need for Deliverance

116:3

3 The cords of death entangled me,
the anguish of the grave came upon me;
I was overcome by trouble and sorrow.

3 The reason for the gratitude is now more graphically set forth in the language of great peril (see 18:4–6). "Death" (*māweṯ*) and the "grave" (*š^e^'ôl*) are personified as hunters lying in wait with "cords" to entangle the godly. From the references to "death" and "the grave," one should not conclude that the psalmist was on his deathbed. Rather, he had been in great distress, as is brought out in the next colon: "I was overcome by trouble and sorrow." Life had become like "hell" (see appendix to Ps 88: Sheol-Grave-Death in the Psalms).

Notes

3 The idiomatic use of מְצָרֵי (*m^e^ṣārê*, "straits," "distress," "anguish") together with "the grave" (Sheol) in parallelism with "the cords of death" is not clear. In Acts 2:24 Peter makes an allusion to this phrase: "freeing him from the agony of death." A.A. Anderson favors the weight of the parallel construction: "the bonds of Sheol" (2:791). In support of this meaning is an allusion to his distress in v.16: "you have freed me from my chains [*môsēray*]." Death personified has the power to entrap, to bind, and to keep its victims enchained.

III. God the Deliverer

116:4–6a

4 Then I called on the name of the LORD:
"O LORD, save me!"
5 The LORD is gracious and righteous;
our God is full of compassion.
6 The LORD protects the simplehearted;

4 In this terrible situation the psalmist resorted to his only hope. He called on God's "name." The "name" of the Lord signifies everything a human needs in life and death, as the Lord has promised to be the God of those who call on him (Joel 2:32) and to deliver his children in their distress (see appendix Ps 7: The Name of Yahweh).

5–6a The perfections of the Lord are those attributes revealed to Israel, in need of his grace (Exod 34:6–7). The psalmist is fully aware that the Lord alone can help him, because he is "gracious," "righteous," full of "compassion," so as to protect (*šōmēr*, participle, lit., "guarding"; cf. 121:3–8) the needy. He is "gracious" (*ḥannûn*) in his forgiveness and in sustaining his children (cf. 103:8; 111:4). He is "righteous" (*ṣaddîq*) in keeping the covenant and all the promises. He is "full of compassion" (*meraḥēm;* cf. Exod 34:6: *raḥûm*) in his tenderness and understanding of the limits of his children (cf. 103:13–14). This affirmation of the character of God is the reason for his thanksgiving, as the Lord is reliable and faithful. At the same time, the psalmist hereby encourages all the godly to call on the Lord in their various distresses! (See the appendix to Ps 25: The Perfections of Yahweh.)

IV. Thanksgiving

116:6b–7

when I was in great need, he saved me.

7 Be at rest once more, O my soul,
for the LORD has been good to you.

6b The affirmation of the character of Yahweh (vv.5–6a) leads the psalmist back to his story of how the Lord delivered him (vv.3–4). The second colon of v.6 restates and develops vv.3–4: "when I was in great need, he saved me." The psalmist called on the Lord, "Save me" (*m-l-ṭ,* v.4); and the Lord was true to his promise: "he saved me" (*y-š-ʿ;* cf. v.13). In v.8 the experience of deliverance is expressed by another verb: "you, O LORD, have delivered" (*ḥ-l-ṣ;* cf. 6:4; 18:19; 34:7; 50:15; 81:7; 91:15; 119:153; et al.; see appendix to 119: Yahweh Is My Redeemer). The variety of the synonyms reveal the fullness of deliverance. Though the Lord has promised to be with his own, the psalmist does not take his deliverance for granted. He is astounded by the marvel of full and free salvation.

7 Because of the goodness of God, the psalmist can speak words of comfort to himself. Unlike the psalmist in 42:5, who comforted himself in despair, and like 103:1–2, the psalmist can reflect on his misery and on the acts of God's goodness (*g-m-l;* see 13:6; cf. 119:17; 142:7). He may be "at rest" (cf. 23:2; 1 Kings 5:4), disregarding the turbulence around him, because he knows his God (vv.5–6).

V. God the Deliverer

116:8–11

8 For you, O LORD, have delivered my soul from death,
my eyes from tears,
my feet from stumbling,

> [9]that I may walk before the LORD
> in the land of the living.
> [10]I believed; therefore I said,
> "I am greatly afflicted."
> [11]And in my dismay I said,
> "All men are liars."

8–9 Only the Lord can change "death," "tears," and "stumbling" (v.8; see 56:13, a close parallel) to a "walk before the LORD" and to a joyful celebration of life "in the land of the living" (v.9; see also 56:13).

10–11 Even in his distress, or especially in his distress, the psalmist learned the lesson of true faith. This experience of living faith comes out more clearly with the NIV margin: "I believed *even when* I said, 'I am greatly afflicted' " (v.10; cf. 2 Cor 4:13). He admits that in his "dismay" (cf. 31:22) he became more aware of human limitations as he saw mankind (*hā'āḏām;* NIV, "men") for what it is: "vain" (*kōzēḇ,* i.e., "lying"; NIV, "liars"; cf. 60:11; 62:9; Rom 3:4; Allen: "unreliable," p. 112). Walter Kaiser remarks from Paul's quotation of Psalm 116:10 in 2 Corinthians 4:13 that it was the same Holy Spirit who worked in the psalmist, Paul, and all other Christians to believe (*Toward Rediscovering the Old Testament* [Grand Rapids: Zondervan, 1987], p. 137).

VI. Vows of Thanksgiving

116:12–14

> [12]How can I repay the LORD
> for all his goodness to me?
> [13]I will lift up the cup of salvation
> and call on the name of the LORD.
> [14]I will fulfill my vows to the LORD
> in the presence of all his people.

12 In his need the psalmist held on tenaciously to God's promises (vv.5–6a), rejecting a human solution (vv.10–11). The Lord was faithful, and the psalmist responds to the Lord's acts of goodness with the question, "How can I repay the LORD for all his goodness [*g-m-l,* cf. v.7] to me?" The answer to the rhetorical question is not given because there is no way to "pay" or "repay" the Lord.

13–14 As a token of his thanksgiving, the psalmist brings "a thank offering" (v.17) together with a drink offering (cf. Num 28:7), which he calls "the cup of salvation" (v.13). At the time of the thank offering, he called again "on the name of the LORD" (cf. vv.2, 17); but this time, not to ask for deliverance, but to thank the Lord and praise his holy name for his fidelity to his promises. The thank offering was a fulfillment of the "vows" made during the distress. The OT saints regularly made vows, especially in periods of great adversity (cf. 50:14; 56:12; Jonah 2:9). The public presentation ("in the presence of all his people," v.14) of the thank offering was not intended for show but for an encouragement of the godly.

Notes

14 The authenticity of this verse is questioned because it is identical with v.18 and is missing in the LXX. The omission may be due to a "deliberate abbreviation of repeated material at some stage in the history of the text" (Allen, p. 113).

VII. God the Deliverer

116:15–16

15 Precious in the sight of the LORD
is the death of his saints.
16 O LORD, truly I am your servant;
I am your servant, the son of your maidservant;
you have freed me from my chains.

15–16 These verses may be read as a public confession and encouragement. The psalmist confesses the great love of the Lord for his "saints" (*ḥāsîḏ*, v.15; see 4:3), in that he does not lightly permit adversity ("death"; cf. vv.3, 8) or an early death (cf. 79:11; 102:20). They are "precious" (cf. 72:14) to him. Since this is true for all the godly ("saints," pl.), it is also applicable to the psalmist as an individual. He too is God's "servant" (*'eḇeḏ*, v.16; see 19:11), born within the household of faith ("the son of your maidservant"; cf. 86:16; Eph 2:19). The Lord has been faithful to his "servant," as he has delivered him from his "chains." The "chains" signify the "imprisonment" (cf. 107:10, 14), a metaphor for his adversity (cf. v.3).

Notes

15 John A. Emerton explains יָקָר (*yāqār*, "precious") as "grievous." The death of his beloved creates sadness to our Lord ("How Does the Lord Regard the Death of His Saints in Psalm cxvi 15," JTS 34 [1983]: 146–56).

16 The NIV margin gives an alternate but less preferable reading of "the son of your maidservant," suggested by Dahood (*Psalms*, 3:150). Dahood argues that בֶּן־אֲמָתֶךָ (*ben-'amāṯeḵā*, "the son of your maidservant") be emended to *ben-'amiṯeḵā* ("your faithful son"; so NIV mg.).

VIII. Vows of Thanksgiving

116:17–19

17 I will sacrifice a thank offering to you
and call on the name of the LORD.
18 I will fulfill my vows to the LORD
in the presence of all his people,
19 in the courts of the house of the LORD—
in your midst, O Jerusalem.

Praise the LORD.

17–19 In the presence of the godly, the psalmist will show his love (v.1) and his gratitude to the Lord for his deliverance. He will present a "thank offering" (v.17; see v.13) as a fulfillment of his "vows" (v.18; see v.14). As was prescribed in the priestly laws, he had to present his offering in the courts of the temple in Jerusalem (v.19; see 84:2, 10; 96:8; 2 Kings 21:5; see appendix to Ps 132: The Ark of the Covenant and the Temple: Symbols of Yahweh's Presence and Rule).

Psalm 117: Great Is His Love Toward Us

Psalm 117 is the fifth of the Egyptian Hallel psalms (113–118; see introduction to Ps 113). It is the shortest psalm, consisting of only two verses. Its genre resembles that of the hymns of descriptive praise. The motif of the praise concerns the love of God, and its cosmic applicability makes this psalm a little jewel. The apostle's quotation of v.1 (Rom 15:11) reveals that the love and plan of God has always included Gentiles, as promised to the patriarchs (Gen 12:3; Gal 3:8).

Great Is His Love Toward Us

117:1–2

1 Praise the LORD, all you nations;
extol him, all you peoples.
2 For great is his love toward us,
and the faithfulness of the LORD endures forever.

Praise the LORD.

1–2 The usual phrase "praise the LORD" (*hallû-yāh,* v.2; 116:19) in the Egyptian Hallel psalms is directed to the covenant community, as they are called on to give praise to their covenant God. However, this time the psalmist calls on the Gentiles (*gôyim,* "nations"; *'ummîm,* "peoples") to praise Yahweh (*hallû 'et-YHWH,* v.1).

The reason for the universal praise of the Lord lies in his dealings with the covenant people. In his relationship to Israel, he reveals a constancy of "love" (*ḥesed*) and "faithfulness" (*'emet;* cf. 115:1; Exod 34:6). These two perfections are often paired, as God's love is always faithful (cf. Exod 34:6–7; Ps 36:5). The love of God is great (*g-b-r,* "be mighty," "be strong"; cf. 103:11). Not only is his love so great in depth and height (cf. Rom 5:20; 1 Tim 1:14), it is also lasting ("endures forever"; see appendix to Ps 25: The Perfections of Yahweh).

In Christ the love of God has been more powerfully demonstrated both to Jews and to Gentiles so that all might praise him for his love (Rom 15:8–9).

Psalm 118: Open the Gates of Righteousness

Psalm 118 is the last of the collection known as the Egyptian Hallel psalms (113–118, see introduction to Ps 113). Originally the psalm may have been used in a liturgical setting, when a Davidic king led the procession of pilgrims in a thanksgiving service (vv.5–21) after a period of anxiety (cf. 2 Chron 20:27–28; see Eaton, pp. 270–71). Possibly the psalm reflects a postexilic situation, when the pilgrims came together for a grand celebration, at which occasion a priest or Levite spoke on behalf of the congregation (vv.5–21). The psalm was readily adapted to other celebrations. Apart from its use during the Passover Seder, Psalm 118 was also sung during the Feast of Tabernacles, according to the Talmud (b. *Sukkoth* 45a–b). The psalm is replete with thanksgiving to the Lord for being the succor of his people.

The genre of Psalm 118 has been difficult to classify, as it exhibits features of *communal* (vv.1–4, 22–25, 27, 29) and *individual thanksgiving* (vv.5–19, 21, 28), as well as verses that are reminiscent of liturgical forms (vv.20, 26). Westermann classifies the psalm as a liturgical psalm (*The Psalms*, p. 98). Allen concludes that it is a thanksgiving liturgy used in religious processions (pp. 122–23). B.J. Oosterhoff concludes that this is an old psalm that received a new interpretation after the Exile and that with the coming of Christ its significance is even more enhanced ("Het Loven van God in Psalm 118," *Loven en Geloven. Opstellen van Collega's en Medewerkers aangeboden aan Prof. Dr. Nic. H. Ridderbos*, ed. M.H. van Es et al. [Amsterdam: Ton Bolland, 1975], pp. 175–90).

Structurally the psalm is also complex. The variety is created by the elements representative of the different genres, by the interchange of individual and communal elements, by the different speakers, and by the collage of motifs. The structure is as follows:

A. Call to Communal Thanksgiving (vv.1–4)
  B. Thanksgiving (vv.5–21)
A′. Thanksgiving Liturgy (vv.22–29)

I. Call to Communal Thanksgiving

118:1–4

1 Give thanks to the LORD, for he is good;
his love endures forever.

2 Let Israel say:
"His love endures forever."
3 Let the house of Aaron say:
"His love endures forever."
4 Let those who fear the LORD say:
"His love endures forever."

1–4 The refrain of v.1 is a familiar one (v.29; see 106:1; 107:1; cf. Ezra 3:11). All Israel had enjoyed the benefits of God's "goodness" (*ṭôḇ*) and "love" (*ḥeseḏ*): the congregation of Israel, the priests ("house of Aaron"), and "those who fear the LORD" (vv.2–4; cf. 115:9–11) (see appendix to Ps 25: The Perfections of Yahweh). The people of God's kingdom (Exod 19:5–6; Ps 114:1) and the priests, the descendants of Aaron, confess that Yahweh is King and that he is "good" and "loving" in his covenant fidelity. From these verses Calvin rightly deduces the reality of God's kingdom in the OT: "[the] kingdom [of Christ], no doubt, extended to the Gentiles, but its commencement and first-fruits were among God's chosen people" (4:378).

Notes

1–4 The LXX differs by the addition of "house of" before "Israel" (cf. 115:9) and "for he is good" (vv.2, 3, 4) after "say."

II. Thanksgiving

118:5–21

5 In my anguish I cried to the LORD,
and he answered by setting me free.
6 The LORD is with me; I will not be afraid.
What can man do to me?
7 The LORD is with me; he is my helper.
I will look in triumph on my enemies.

8 It is better to take refuge in the LORD
than to trust in man.
9 It is better to take refuge in the LORD
than to trust in princes.

10 All the nations surrounded me,
but in the name of the LORD I cut them off.
11 They surrounded me on every side,
but in the name of the LORD I cut them off.
12 They swarmed around me like bees,
but they died out as quickly as burning thorns;
in the name of the LORD I cut them off.

13 I was pushed back and about to fall,
but the LORD helped me.
14 The LORD is my strength and my song;
he has become my salvation.

15 Shouts of joy and victory
resound in the tents of the righteous:
"The LORD's right hand has done mighty things!
16 The LORD's right hand is lifted high;
the LORD's right hand has done mighty things!"
17 I will not die but live,
and will proclaim what the LORD has done.
18 The LORD has chastened me severely,
but he has not given me over to death.

19 Open for me the gates of righteousness;
I will enter and give thanks to the LORD.
20 This is the gate of the LORD
through which the righteous may enter.
21 I will give you thanks, for you answered me;
you have become my salvation.

5 As one who has experienced the "goodness" and "love" of the Lord, an individual gives testimony of how the Lord has delivered him. Who is the individual? Among the suggestions are the king, Israel as a corporate body, or a priest/Levite. Because of the lack of royal references and the interplay between the individual and communal thanksgiving, I favor the view that an individual worshiper represents the people in giving testimony to the Lord's goodness. Originally the worship leader may have been the king or a priest, but the canonical function permits any individual of God's people to recite the acts of God in response to the prayers of God's people in affliction.

The worshiper thanks the Lord because he has heard his cry when he experienced "anguish" (*mēṣar;* see 116:3; cf. Lam 1:3). He was without perspective and in dire straits, but the Lord answered him by bringing him into a "broad place" (NIV, "by setting me free;" see 18:19; 31:8). The trouble is more fully explained in vv.10–12 (see below). The joy of faith lies in answered prayer.

6–7 The psalmist knew that the Lord was with him in all circumstances of life (v.6; cf. Rom 8:31), and based on this conviction he was not afraid of troubles caused by his fellow beings (see 56:9, 11; cf. Heb 13:6). The presence of the Lord is personal ("the LORD is with me," twice, vv.6–7). He comforts with his support ("he is my helper," *'-z-r*, vv.7, 13). He also gives a new perspective on the future ("I will look in triumph on my enemies," v.7; cf. 54:7; 59:10; 92:11; 112:8).

8–9 In a hymnic celebration, the individual worshiper confesses his confidence in the Lord (cf. 116:11; 146:3) rather than in mankind. The mention of "man" (*'āḏām*) in parallelism with "princes" (*neḏîḇîm*) is an example of merismus (cf. 146:3), a literary manner of including all of mankind, both lowly and exalted. The psalmist has learned from experience and hereby encourages the congregation that confidence in the Lord ("to take refuge," twice, vv.8–9; *ḥ-s-h*) is far superior to relying (*b-ṭ-ḥ;* NIV, "to trust"; cf. 78:22) on flesh and blood (cf. 33:16–19).

10–12 The emphasis in the psalmist's thanksgiving has been on the Lord. The allusions to his adversity have been few ("anguish," v.5; "enemies," v.7). The enemies are dwarfed in significance in relationship to the One who helps, provides refuge, and gives victory. Then he briefly encourages the godly by sharing with them how bad the trouble was.

The language of the troubles (vv.10–12) may be interpreted literally or metaphorically. If a king is the speaker, the reference to "All the nations" (v.10), the repetition of "surrounded me" and "I cut them off" (vv.10–11), as well as the metaphorical comparison ("bees," "burning thorns," v.12) could be interpreted as a great victory over the enemies. On the other hand, vv.10–12 could also be interpreted as a poetic borrowing from the royal psalms and as hyperbole of great adversity. The adversity is likened to "all the nations" that "surrounded him" and "swarmed around . . . like bees" and "died out as quickly as burning thorns" (see Kraus, *Psalmen*, 2:805). Within the present context I favor the metaphorical interpretation.

Great as the adversity was, the psalmist overcame his feeling of anguish "in the name of the LORD" (vv.10, 11, 12). The threefold repetition of "the name of the LORD" and the phrase "I cut them off" together with the fourfold use of "surrounded me" (NIV three times, one time "they swarmed around me," vv.10–12) demonstrate that regardless of how great the trouble, the Lord's name was sufficiently powerful (see appendix to Ps 7: The Name of Yahweh). The metaphor for numerousness ("bees," v.12; cf. Deut 1:44) is balanced by a metaphor for the ease in which the problem was dealt with ("as burning thorns"). However, it is not altogether clear what happens to the thorns. The general thrust seems to be that the Lord quickly reduced the fierce opposition.

13–14 Verses 13–14 return in thought to the beginning of the thanksgiving section (v.5): need and deliverance. The adversity was so great that the psalmist felt himself pushed and was "about to fall" (v.13; cf. vv.17–18). However, the help of the Lord was equal to the challenge (vv.5–7). The Lord had shown himself to be faithful to the promise that he would keep his own from falling or stumbling (121:3).

In response to the mighty act of God's deliverance, the psalmist reflects in v.14 on the Lord's help in the light of the ancient witness of God's deliverance in the Song of Moses (Exod 15:2). At that time the Lord had delivered Israel from the Egyptians, as they had crossed through the Red Sea and the waters had covered the Egyptian horses and chariots. Moses had sung a victory song to the Lord, as he ascribed to him the power of being the Divine Warrior.

The Lord is the "strength," "song," and "salvation" of his people (v.14). The word "strength" denotes his power in saving (68:28; 86:16; 89:10; 132:8; Isa 51:9) while "salvation" (*yešû'āh;* cf. v.15, "victory" [*yešû'āh*]) suggests the whole process of his mighty acts, his judgment on the adversaries, and his help to his children, including the final climactic celebrations of his victory. The second word ("song") occurs three times in the bound phrase "my strength and my song" (here; Exod 15:2; Isa 12:2). In these contexts "song" could mean "victory song," but some have suggested a cognate meaning of "protection," related to a Ugaritic idiom (P.C. Craigie, "Psalm 29 in the Hebrew Poetic Tradition," VetTest 22 [1972]: 145–46). The traditional translation (NIV) is preferable in this context, as "shouts of joy" (v.15) is symmetric with "song," before *yešû'āh* (NIV, "my salvation," v.14; "victory," v.15; see appendix to Ps 98: Yahweh Is the Divine Warrior).

15–16 The victory of the Lord is the occasion for communal rejoicing. The psalmist reflects here on the effect of God's mighty works of "salvation" on all the people of the Lord. He is still the speaker, but in his testimony he builds up a longing to participate in the act of thanksgiving to the Lord. He thus draws his audience in.

The "tents of the righteous" (*'ohᵒlê ṣaddîqîm;* see 1:6) are filled with "shouts of joy and victory" (see on v.14) as the godly join in the celebration of God's mighty acts. It is not clear whether the "tents" denote the dwellings of God's people or are the "tents" set up in Jerusalem during the pilgrimage festivals. They sing, possibly, a chorus or refrain whose subject is the Lord's "right hand" (v.16; cf. Exod 15:6, 12).

17–18 Thanksgiving begins with the individual. The psalmist has individually experienced the Lord's power to restore and sustain life by having been delivered out of his troubles. The troubles are likened to "death" (v.18; cf. 116:3, 15), but the Lord's favor is "life." The meaning of "live" (v.17) signifies here the joyful proclamation of "what the LORD has done": his acts of discipline ("the LORD has chastened me severely" and in his controlled discipline: "he has not given me over to death," v.18; cf. 66:9–10; Jer 30:11; 46:28; Hab 1:12; 2 Cor 6:9). His discipline is fatherly in nature, harsh though it may seem (cf. Heb 12:5–11). (See the appendix to Ps 78: The Mighty Acts of Yahweh.)

19–20 The worship leader leads the festal procession of the "righteous" (*ṣaddîqîm,* v.20; cf. v.15) into "the gates of righteousness" (v.19). Only the "righteous" are permitted entrance to the presence of the Lord, symbolically guarded by "the gates of righteousness" (cf. 24:7). The Lord required his people to be "righteous," i.e., to respond to his goodness and love with loyalty (vv.1, 29), even though adversity might give cause for wavering and anguish (v.5). The psalmist has strongly confessed his unswerving loyalty to and trust in the Lord, his "refuge" and "help" (vv.1–9, 13–16). Those who enter into the presence of the Lord must meet this requisite of covenant loyalty and trust in the Lord.

21 In this company of "righteous" people, the psalmist shares his testimony of "thanks" (cf. 18:49; 30:12) for the Lord's "victory" (*yešû'āh;* NIV, "salvation," see v.14). The emphasis on the Lord's "salvation" is consistent with the emphasis in this psalm on the gracious and complete deliverance, freely given to those who "take refuge in the LORD" (vv.8–9) and depend on "the name of the LORD" (vv.10–12). The Lord has been with the individual as he was with Israel of old, in the days of Moses (see v.14).

Notes

5 The shortened, poetic form יָהּ (*Yāh,* instead of Yahweh) occurs here and in vv.14 and 17–19. It may be that the psalmist is influenced by the usage in Exod 15:2 (Allen, p. 120).

10–12 The verbal phrase כִּי אֲמִילַם (*kî 'amîlam,* "I cut them off") may be rendered in either of two ways: (1) *m-w-l* I: "circumcise" (so Dahood: "indeed I cut off their foreskins," *Psalms,* 3:154); the NIV also reflects this meaning but leaves ambiguous what was cut off; (2) *m-w-l* II: "ward off" (KB, p. 502b). The latter usage was understood by the ancient versions and most of the recent versions and commentators. The particle *kî* ("indeed," "truly" as emphatic) is not translated in the NIV but could be rendered as "in the name of the LORD, truly, I warded them off."

12 The MT's דֹּעֲכוּ (*dō'akû* ("they quenched") is problematic because it does not relate directly to the "thorns" or to the "bees." The LXX suggests an alternate reading: "they blazed like fire among thorns." The LXX also changed the first metaphor of the verse: "they surrounded me like bees around wax"; but according to L.H. Brockington (*The Hebrew Text of the Old Testament* [Oxford: Oxford University Press, 1973], p. 151), the LXX hopelessly misunderstood the text. The MT makes sense if the dictionary meaning "quenched" be extended to "be put out," "die out" (NIV).

13 The verbal phrase "I was pushed back" reflects an emendation of the MT's דַּחֹה דְחִיתַנִי (*daḥōh deḥîtanî,* "you certainly pushed me back"). The NIV rendering is based on the textual evidence of the LXX, Syriac, and Vulgate: דַּחֹה נִדְחֵיתִי (*daḥōh nidḥêtî,* "I was indeed pushed back").

The infinitive construct form לִנְפֹּל (*linpōl,* "to fall") may have the meaning of "about to fall" (Dahood, *Psalms,* 3:158).

III. Thanksgiving Liturgy

118:22–29

22 The stone the builders rejected
has become the capstone;
23 the LORD has done this,
and it is marvelous in our eyes.
24 This is the day the LORD has made;
let us rejoice and be glad in it.

25 O LORD, save us;
O LORD, grant us success.
26 Blessed is he who comes in the name of the LORD.
From the house of the LORD we bless you.
27 The LORD is God,
and he has made his light shine upon us.
With boughs in hand, join in the festal procession
up to the horns of the altar.

28 You are my God, and I will give you thanks;
you are my God, and I will exalt you.

29 Give thanks to the LORD, for he is good;
his love endures forever.

22–23 The community of the righteous join in with thanksgiving. In the metaphorical language derived from construction, they praise the Lord for his wonderful ways. He has given prominence to his suffering servant like a "capstone" (v.22). The "capstone" was an important stone that held two rows of stones together in a corner ("cornerstone") or stabilized the stones at the foundation or elsewhere (cf. Isa 28:16). Though the spokesperson (king, priest, Levite, or individual) spoke of adversity and rejection, likened here to the throwing away of a capstone (cf. vv.10–12), the Lord has changed his adversity into a "marvelous" demonstration of himself (vv.22–23). Therefore the emphasis is on the Lord: "the LORD has done this" (v.23).

How appropriate is the application of these verses to the suffering and glory of our Lord (cf. Matt 21:42; Mark 12:10; Luke 20:17; Acts 4:11; Eph 2:20; 1 Peter 2:7)! He suffered in his rejection by man, but the Father demonstrated his acceptance of the Son by making him the "chief cornerstone" (Eph 2:20). Yet all who suffer in this life may draw comfort from this communal testimony.

24–25 The day (v.24) of thanksgiving in the "marvelous" act of the Lord (vv.22–23; cf. 71:17; Jer 32:17, 27) is the "day of salvation." The songs of rejoicing encourage the godly to renew their prayers for God's help: "O LORD save us; / O LORD, grant us success" (v.25). The verbal phrase "save us" (*hôšîʿāh nāʾ;* cf. "Hosanna" in Matt 21:9; Mark 11:9–10) is related to the noun *yᵉšûʿāh* ("salvation," "victory," vv.14–15, 21). The congregation requests the Lord to continue to do his wonderful acts in their midst so that they will "prosper" (have "success") as the people whom the Lord has blessed (cf. 1:3).

26 In response to this attitude of submission and trust in the Lord, the king or priest speaks a word of blessing to all who come to the Lord in his "name" (cf. Mark 11:9; Luke 13:35; 19:38). The blessing is limited to those who meet the basic requirement for entrance, that is, they come "in the name of the LORD" (cf. vv.10–12; see Allen: "with Yahweh's name," p. 120).

27 The people respond to the blessing with a confession of confidence in the Lord. They confess that he alone "is God," by whose "light" (*ʾôr*, an allusion to the priestly blessing, Num 6:25) they exist and are protected from the darkness of famine, war, and exile (cf. 43:3). They also respond to the words of blessing by renewing their commitment and thanksgiving to the Lord in making a procession to the temple in Jerusalem (see appendix to Ps 132: The Ark of the Covenant and the Temple: Symbols of Yahweh's Presence and Rule). The interpretation of v.27b is far from easy;

but the thrust is clear that they demonstrated their commitment in concrete acts, whether they came with "boughs in hand" during the Feast of Tabernacles (M *Sukkah* 3.4; based on Lev 23:40) or with "festal sacrifices" (see NIV mg.).

28–29 The worship leader leads the community in the affirmation that Yahweh alone is God ("You are my God," v.28; cf. v.27a), similar to the confession of Moses (Exod 15:2). Israel, individually and corporately, must give thanks to the Lord, because "he is good, his love endures forever" (vv.1, 29). The psalm concludes with a repetition of the opening lines (inclusionary device).

Notes

---

23 Ernst Jenni explains the analogy in the context of Israel's wisdom tradition ("'Vom Herrn ist dies gewirkt,' Ps. 118:23," *Theologische Zeitschrift* 35 [1979]: 55–62).

24 Adele Berlin explains v.24 in the light of v.23 as a parallel construction, resulting in an alternate translation:

> This is the Lord's doing;
>   it is marvelous in our sight.
> This is what the Lord has done;
>   let us exult and rejoice in it.
>   ("Psalm 118:24," JBL 96 [1977]: 567–68)

25 The repetition of אָנָּא (*'ānnā'*, "please") is left untranslated in the NIV but should be rendered to stress the intensity of the congregation's prayer as well as their dependence on the Lord (cf. NEB: "We pray thee, O LORD . . . we pray thee, O LORD"). Jakob J. Petuchowski sets the psalm in this context and explains "save us" as a prayer for rain ("'*Hoshi'ah Na*' in Psalm CXVIII 25, A Prayer for Rain," VetTest 5 [1955]: 266–71).

26 The MT's בֵּרַכְנוּכֶם (*bēraknûkem*, "we bless you [pl.]") suggests that the people encourage one another with God's blessing. The royal interpretation explains the plural pronoun "you" as having reference to the king: "We (the people) bless you (the king)" (Dahood, *Psalms*, 3:160).

27 The difficulty of this verse lies in the word עֲבֹתִים (*'ᵃbōtîm*, "boughs," "ropes"). Depending on the meaning chosen, the whole line is interpreted in terms of the bunches of branches from the myrtle, willow, and palm trees that the worshipers carried in the festal procession or in terms of the ropes used for binding the sacrifice on the horns of the altar. See NIV margin: "*Bind the festal sacrifice with ropes / and take it*" to the horns of the altar.

1–29 For Luther's interpretation, see Ronald M. Hals, "Psalm 118," Int 37 (1983): 277–83.

Psalm 119: The Joy of God's Law in Distress

The longest psalm in the Psalter, Psalm 119, is well known for its teaching on God's law. Yet the beauty of this psalm lies, not only in the recitation of devotion to the law, but in the psalmist's absolute devotion to the Lord. Most likely writing in the postexilic era, the psalmist knows firsthand the oppression of evil. He has been surrounded by wickedness, pursued by the arrogant and proud, humbled by sorrow and disgrace; yet his refuge is in God. He constantly cries out to God, retreats into his shadow, and finds solace in his strength. This is a psalm, not only of law, but of love, not only of statute, but of spiritual strength, not only of devotion to precept, but of loyalty to the way of the Lord. The beauty in this psalm resounds from the relationship of the psalmist and his God.

The genre of the psalm corresponds most closely to that of the *wisdom psalms:* the blessing formula (vv.1–3), proverbial style, and the concern with the law of God (see J.P.M. van der Ploeg, "Le psaume 119 et la Sagesse," in *La Sagesse de l'Ancien Testament,* ed. M. Gilbert [Leuven: University Press, 1979], pp. 82–87). Yet the psalm also reflects elements of other genres: lament (vv.25, 51, 94; 137; 143; 149; 153–60; W.M. Soll, "Psalm 119: The Hermeneutic of an Acrostic Lament," Ph.D. diss., Vanderbilt, 1982); thanksgiving (v.7); innocence (vv.30, 61; 97–106); praise (vv.33, 44, 57); and confidence (vv.20, 105). All these motifs have been blended into a most beautiful mosaic, celebrating the God who revealed himself to man so that man may live harmoniously with God and man (see Johannes Schildenberger, "Psalm 119. Das grosse Bekenntnis der Liebe zu Gottes Weisung," *Erbe und Auftrag* 57 [1981]: 360–62). Brueggemann treats Psalm 119 together with Psalms 1, 15, and 24 as "Songs of Torah" (*Message of the Psalms,* pp. 38–42).

Psalm 119 is an alphabetic acrostic psalm (as 111, 112), consisting of twenty-two stanzas of eight verses each. The acrostic manner in which the psalmist develops the theme of the law required a sacrifice in structural development. The net effect is what A.A. Anderson terms "a monotonous repetition, which is, nevertheless, impressive even in its repetitiveness" (2:806). Allen calls it "a randomness or more precisely a kaleidoscopic patterning of a certain number of motifs" (p. 139; see also Raymond F. Surburg, "Observations and Reflections on the Giant Psalm," *Concordia Theological Quarterly* 42 [1982]: 8–20). Brueggemann comments that the creation of this psalm "is in fact a massive intellectual achievement. It is an astonishingly crafted poem" (*Message of the Psalms,* p. 39).

The psalmist uses eight words for God's law:

1. "Law" (*tôrāh*) occurs twenty-five times. The word "law" has both a broad and a narrow meaning. In the broad sense it refers to any "instruction" flowing from the revelation of God as the basis for life and action. In the narrow sense it denotes the Torah of Moses, whether the Pentateuch, the priestly law, or the Deuteronomic law. The former meaning is often supposed in the wisdom writings but also in Deuteronomy and the prophets (cf. Deut 17:11; Ps 78:1; Prov 1:8; 3:1; Isa 1:10; 8:16; Mal 2:6). The godly instruction is based on all revelation from God, Mosaic and prophetic. God himself is the source of that revelation, and his instruction comes through his various servants, as Kirkpatrick observes, "Here, as in Pss. i and xix, it must be taken in its widest sense, as synonymous with the 'word' of Jehovah (Is.i. 10; ii. 3), to include all Divine revelation as the guide of life" (p. 703).

2. "Word" (*dāḇār*) occurs twenty-four times. Any word that proceeds from the mouth of the Lord is *dāḇār,* whether it pertains to the Decalogue (Deut 4:13), the law of Moses (Deut 4:2, 10), or the word revealed through the prophets. It is a most general designation for divine revelation, whether of expectation or promise.

3. "Laws" (*mišpāṭîm*) occurs twenty-three times. The "laws" denote cases or legal decisions pertaining to particular legal issues. The "laws" of God are those "case laws" that form the basis for Israel's legal system. In Psalm 119 the word "laws" often denotes the revelation given by the supreme Judge, God himself. He is the Great Judge, and the verdicts rendered by him are authoritative and liberating (cf. "righteous laws," vv.7, 62, 106, 164).

4. "Statute(s)" (*'ēḏûṯ/'ēḏôṯ*) occurs twenty-three times, only once in the singular. The word *'ēḏûṯ* is derived from *'-w-d* ("witness," "testify") and occurs in the

idiomatic usage: "the two tablets of the Testimony" (Exod 31:18) and "the ark of the Testimony" (Exod 25:22). The "tablets" and the "ark" were symbols of the covenant relationship, and hence "testimony" is often synonymous with "covenant" (cf. 25:10; 132:12). The observance of the "statutes" of the Lord signifies loyalty to the terms of the covenant made between the Lord and Israel (cf. 99:7; Deut 4:45; 6:17, 20).

5. "Command(s)" (*miṣwāh/miṣwôṯ*) occurs twenty-two times. The word "command" is a frequent designation for anything that the Lord, the covenant God, has ordered. It is a synonym of "law" as well as of "decrees" and "laws."

6. "Decrees" (*ḥuqqîm*) occurs twenty-one times. The noun is derived from the root *ḥ-q-q* ("engrave," "inscribe"). God, being the Author of his decrees, reveals his royal sovereignty by establishing his divine will in nature (148:6) and in the covenant community (50:16; 105:10; cf. Deut 4:1).

7. "Precepts" (*piqqûḏîm*) occurs twenty-one times. The word occurs only in the Book of Psalms and appears to be synonymous with "covenant" (103:18) and with the revelation of God (111:7). The root *p-q-d* ("visit," "appoint") has a similar significance as "command" (*ṣ-w-h*) in that both roots connote the authority to determine the relationship between the speaker and the object. The Lord "commanded" (NIV, "laid down") precepts, and the response of the psalmist is that of "guarding" (*š-m-r*, vv.63, 134, 168; *n-ṣ-r*, vv.56, 69, 100), responding positively to (128:1), "loving" (v.159), "choosing" out (v.173), "longing" for (v.40), "seeking" (*d-r-š*, vv.45, 94), "meditating" on (vv.15, 78), and "gaining understanding" (v.104) from the precepts of the Lord so as never to "forget" (vv.93; 141), "forsake" (v.87), or "stray" (v.110) from the precepts of the Lord. Essentially the God who orders man to respond to his revelation expects an appropriate response of submission and loyalty to and love of his commands.

8. "Word" or "promise" (*'imrāh*) occurs nineteen times. The "word" (derived from *'-m-r*, "say") may denote anything God has spoken, commanded, or promised (cf. v.140).

I. The Aleph Strophe

119:1–8

א Aleph

1 Blessed are they whose ways are blameless,
who walk according to the law of the LORD.
2 Blessed are they who keep his statutes
and seek him with all their heart.
3 They do nothing wrong;
they walk in his ways.
4 You have laid down precepts
that are to be fully obeyed.
5 Oh, that my ways were steadfast
in obeying your decrees!
6 Then I would not be put to shame
when I consider all your commands.
7 I will praise you with an upright heart
as I learn your righteous laws.
8 I will obey your decrees;
do not utterly forsake me.

1–8 The blessing of God (*'ašrê*, see 1:1) rests on those who give themselves to wise living. The wise are people of integrity (*t^e^mîmê-ḏāreḵ*, "blameless," v.1; cf. Gen 17:1;

Prov 11:20; 13:6). Their walk follows the path set out in God's revelation, "the law" (*tôrāh;* see 1:2). Blessed are all who live for the sake of God, by seeking (*d-r-š,* v.2) him with all their heart (cf. Deut 4:29; 6:5; 10:12; 11:13). The love for God receives expression in doing the will of God. In his "statutes" (*'ēdôt*) he sets down how he is to be loved, and his loving children respond to his wishes. Negatively, the people of integrity "do nothing wrong" (*'awlāh,* v.3), and in this they reflect the nature of God, who in his justice does no wrong (cf. Zeph 3:5).

The hope of the godly lies in the Lord. The psalmist submits himself to God's freedom. He prays that his response to God's revelation may be acceptable (v.5). The walk in God's ways (v.3) requires steadfastness, regularity, and discipline rather than a haphazard response. The "decrees" (*ḥuqqîm,* vv.5, 8) of the Lord give order to human lives, even as they uphold order in the created world.

The psalmist further prays that no "shame" or ultimate disgrace may overtake him (v.6). "Shame" in OT usage connotes a state of being abandoned by the Lord and condemned to utter ruin, such as becomes the enemies of God (cf. vv.31, 46, 80; 6:10; 25:2; 83:17). In this prayer he intimates that he lives with adversity while walking in the way of the Lord. His lament is like a sobbing, as he prays that the Lord will have mercy on his servant. In this spirit we must also understand the prayer "do not utterly forsake me" (v.8). Since he is careful in "fully" (*me'ōd,* v.4) obeying the Lord, he prays that the Lord will not "utterly" (*'ad-me'ōd*) abandon him to his troubles (v.8; cf. 27:9; 71:9, 18; Deut 31:17; Isa 49:14; 54:7).

The psalmist looks for God's favor by which he may again praise his God "with an upright heart" (v.7; cf. 9:1; 111:1; 138:1) for his "righteous laws." The "laws" (*mišpāṭîm*) of God are "righteous" (*ṣedeq;* cf. vv.62, 75, 106, 123, 144, 160, 164, 172; 19:9) in that they establish divine order in this world, granting the godly a sense of deliverance and freedom (cf. v.40: "Preserve my life in your righteousness"). Hence he praises the Lord for his "righteous laws" (cf. vv.62, 164).

As a final expression of commitment to the revelation of God, the psalmist stresses that he will "guard" (NIV, "obey") the "decrees" of God (v.8; cf. v.5). The psalmist hopes that the Lord will deal kindly with his loyal servant by not leaving him abandoned.

II. The Beth Strophe

119:9–16

ב Beth

9 How can a young man keep his way pure?
By living according to your word.
10 I seek you with all my heart;
do not let me stray from your commands.
11 I have hidden your word in my heart
that I might not sin against you.
12 Praise be to you, O LORD;
teach me your decrees.
13 With my lips I recount
all the laws that come from your mouth.
14 I rejoice in following your statutes
as one rejoices in great riches.
15 I meditate on your precepts
and consider your ways.
16 I delight in your decrees;
I will not neglect your word.

9 The psalmist as a wisdom teacher asks the rhetorical question, "How can a young man keep his way pure?" as a teaching device (34:11), similar to that found in Proverbs (1:4; 25:12–13; Eccl 11:9; 12:1). The "young man" is the disciple, also known as "my son" in Proverbs. The young man may keep his way "pure," an equivalent for "blameless" (v.1) and "steadfast" (v.5), by the practice of godliness. As the wise "guard" (*š-m-r*, "keep," vv.4–5, 8, rendered in NIV as "obey") the revealed will of God, so must the disciple "guard" (*š-m-r;* NIV, "by living") God's "word" (*dāḇār*).

10–16 The teacher exemplifies the wise response to God's revelation in vv.10–16. He is sincere in his love for God ("I seek you with all my heart," v.10; cf. v.2) and demonstrates his love for God by treasuring his "word" of promise (*'imrāh*) in his "heart" (v.11). The act of "hiding" God's word is not to be limited to the memorization of individual texts or even whole passages but extends to a holistic living in devotion to the Lord (cf. Deut 6:4–9; 30:14; Jer 31:33). The inner devotion to the Lord also finds expression in a teachable spirit (v.12) and in contentment (vv.14, 16).

The teachable spirit begins with a proper regard for God (v.12). The psalmist confesses his adoration for the Lord ("Praise be to you, O LORD"; cf. 28:6) as an introduction to his petition (see "hallowed be your name. . . . Give us," Matt 6:9, 11). Also in v.7 he connects praise with instruction. This demonstrates that little instruction in godliness takes place unless the heart is full of praise.

Contentment is a true expression of inner godliness. The psalmist declares repeatedly that his inner delight and joy is in God and his revelation: "I have hidden" (i.e., "I treasure," v.11), "I rejoice" (v.14), "I delight" (v.16; cf. vv.24, 47, 70). What brings joy to his life is not material acquisition ("great riches," v.14) but the Lord himself (cf. vv.72, 111, 162; Prov 3:13–14; 8:10–11; 16:16; Matt 6:33).

The external expression of the psalmist's inner loyalty to the Lord is joyful obedience (vv.10, 15–16). Joyful obedience finds expression in seeking the Lord with all one's heart (v.10), lest he "stray" (*š-g-h*, "wander," "err"; cf. Prov 19:27) from God's "commands" (*miṣwôṯ*). His "delight" is not only in knowing the "ways," the "decrees" (*ḥuqqîm*), and the "word" (*dāḇār*), but also in the careful practice (vv.15–16). As part of the practice of godliness, he speaks openly and positively about God's revelation of his will. With his "lips" he "recounts" (*s-p-r*, "count"; cf. NEB, "I say them over, one by one") the "laws" (*mišpāṭîm*), which he treasures as having come out of the "mouth" of the Lord (v.13).

The root *ś-y-ḥ* ("meditate," vv.15, 23, 27, 48, 78) has the basic meaning of a loud, enthusiastic, and emotion-filled form of speaking; but in Psalm 119 it has the sense of a wise, pensive concentration (see Hans-Peter Müller, "Die hebräische Wurzel שׂיח," VetTest 19 [1969]: 361–71). The psalmist may quietly meditate on what the Lord expects of him, controlling his emotions as an expression of absolute loyalty to the Lord.

The love for God's word is love for God (v.16; cf. vv.47, 70), expressed in a heart attitude, in actions, and in words. In his whole being the godly man cries out for God and delights in his will. This kind of a teacher can guide "a young man" to "keep his way pure" (v.9).

III. The Gimel Strophe

119:17–24

ג Gimel

[17]Do good to your servant, and I will live;
I will obey your word.
[18]Open my eyes that I may see
wonderful things in your law.
[19]I am a stranger on earth;
do not hide your commands from me.
[20]My soul is consumed with longing
for your laws at all times.
[21]You rebuke the arrogant, who are cursed
and who stray from your commands.
[22]Remove from me scorn and contempt,
for I keep your statutes.
[23]Though rulers sit together and slander me,
your servant will meditate on your decrees.
[24]Your statutes are my delight;
they are my counselors.

17–20 In difficulty and distress, the Lord and his word are a comfort to the godly. The prayer for help ("do good," *g-m-l,* v.17; cf. 13:6; 116:7; 142:7) presupposes a close relationship between the Lord and the psalmist, as he speaks of himself as "your servant"—a designation of loyalty and submissiveness (cf. 36:1 [MT])—and as "a stranger [*gēr*] on earth" (v.19), a designation of a pilgrim's existence on earth (cf. 39:12–13). As the servant of God and a stranger, his yearning for God and his word is so strong that he feels as if crushed and broken in his alienation from God ("My soul [i.e., "I"] is consumed [lit., 'broken'; cf. Lam 3:16] with longing"). He prays that he may "live" a life of fellowship with God and in obedience to his "word" (*dā<u>b</u>ār,* v.17). He longs to see the "wonderful things" in God's "law" (*tôrāh,* v.18), while being illumined by his "commands" (*miṣwô<u>t</u>,* v.21) "at all times" (v.20). The word of God has the power to reveal, sustain, assure of God's presence, and illumine. The word of God is the psalmist's comfort because of the close connection between the Lord and his word!

21–24 God's blessing rests on those who submit themselves to the law of God (vv.1–3), whereas his curse comes on all those who "stray" (*š-g-h,* v.21; cf. v.10) deliberately from the revealed will of God (cf. v.118). The "arrogant" (*zē<u>d</u>îm;* cf. vv.51, 69, 78, 85, 122; cf. 10:2–11; Prov 21:24; Mal 3:15; 4:1) despise God and godliness with their "scorn and contempt" (v.22; cf. 71:13; 79:12; 89:50). Over against "the arrogant" is "the servant" (v.23, cf. v.17) who shows his loyalty to God's "statutes" (*'ē<u>d</u>ô<u>t</u>,* v.22) by observing (*n-ṣ-r,* "keep"; cf. vv.33–34, 69, 115, 145) them and by "meditating" (*ś-y-ḥ,* v.23; see v.15) on his "decrees" (*ḥuqqîm*). Though the opposition of the community and her "rulers" may be great, the psalmist receives his joy ("delight," v.24; cf. v.16), comfort, and guidance from God's "statutes" (*'ē<u>d</u>ô<u>t</u>*) as his "counselors."

Notes

21 On the זֵדִים (*zēḏîm*, "arrogant"), see Felix Asensio, "Los Zëdin del Salmo 119 en el área 'Dolo-mentira,'" *Estudios Biblicos* 41 (1983): 185–204.

24 On divine guidance in Psalm 119, see Josef Schreiner, "Leben nach der Weisung des Herrn—Eine Auslegung des Ps 119," *Freude an der Weisung des Herrn, Beiträge zur Theologie der Psalmen, Festgabe zum 70. Geburtstag von Heinrich Gross*, edd. Ernst Haag and Frank-Lothar Hossfeld (Stuttgart: Katholisches Bibelwerk, 1986), pp. 395–424.

IV. The Daleth Strophe

119:25–32

ד Daleth

25 I am laid low in the dust;
preserve my life according to your word.
26 I recounted my ways and you answered me;
teach me your decrees.
27 Let me understand the teaching of your precepts;
then I will meditate on your wonders.
28 My soul is weary with sorrow;
strengthen me according to your word.
29 Keep me from deceitful ways;
be gracious to me through your law.
30 I have chosen the way of truth;
I have set my heart on your laws.
31 I hold fast to your statutes, O LORD;
do not let me be put to shame.
32 I run in the path of your commands,
for you have set my heart free.

25 The circumstances of the psalmist forces him even closer to the Lord. He experiences his earthiness and mortality as he is "laid low in the dust" (cf. vv.28, 50, 67, 71, 75, 83, 92, 107, 143, 153; cf. 7:5; 22:15, 29; 44:25). Only the Lord can deliver him and thus give him a new lease on "life" (cf. v.17; 71:20; 80:18; 85:6; 138:7; 143:11). The anticipation of renewal is based on the "word" (*dāḇār*) of God (cf. vv.42, 51, 65, 69, 78, 85, 95, 110, 134, 141, 150, 154, 157, 161; Deut 8:3; 30:6, 15, 19–20; 32:47).

26–27 In adversities the psalmist becomes more teachable, and so his spirit is renewed within him. He opened his life, including his troubles, to the Lord ("I recounted my ways," v.26; cf. 37:5; 49:13; 139:3), believing that the Lord answers prayer (cf. 3:4; 34:4; 118:5). Devoted to his God, the psalmist's concern goes beyond his immediate situation of adversity to understand and apply God's word. It is to this end that he prays for divine instruction ("teach me your decrees"; cf. vv.12, 64, 68, 108, 124, 135, 171) and illumination ("let me understand the teaching [lit. 'way,' *dereḵ*] of your precepts [*piqqûḏîm*]," v.27; cf. vv.18, 34, 73, 125, 169; Isa 40:14).

God's instruction and illumination deepen man's dependence on the Lord. The psalmist prays that he may "meditate" (see v.15) on the "wonders" (*nip̱lā'ôṯ*) of the

Lord (cf. v.18). The word opens up the greatness of God's acts in creation and in redemption.

28–29 The word of God has the power to comfort ("strengthen") those overwhelmed with sorrow ("my soul is weary with sorrow," v.28; see Allen: "I have collapsed with intense sorrow," p. 127). The "sorrow" (*tûg̱āh*) is not a casual tear but the sense of grief and vexation (cf. Prov 10:1; 14:13; 17:21). The word of God is also a means of grace, as it keeps man from the ways of the world ("deceitful ways," v.29; LXX, "the way of iniquity"), and as it renews an inner, burning desire to live a life of devotion to God (vv.30–32).

30–32 Devotion to God focuses on doing his will. The psalmist affirms his deep commitment in the language of action: "I have chosen . . . I have set. . . . I hold fast. . . . I run" (vv.30–32). On the one hand, he fully depends on the Lord for life, sustaining grace, and illumination (vv.25–29), as he alone can deliver us from evil (v.29; cf. Matt 6:13). On the other hand, man is fully responsible in "seeking" the kingdom of God by choosing and living a life of loyalty to God and to his word. The "deceitful ways" (v.29) are set in contrast to "the way of truth" (*'ᵉmûnāh*, i.e., "fidelity," "faithfulness," v.30; cf. 36:5). The latter reflects the faithfulness of God over against the evil of this world. The psalmist's choice (cf. 25:12) is shown in a strong determination to do what is right, beginning with his "heart." Though the word "heart" is not in the MT, the NIV properly assumes an ellipsis (Allen, p. 135). Determination also found expression in an affirmation of love and devotion: "I hold fast" (*d-b-q*, "cling," v.31; cf. Deut 10:20; 11:22; 13:4; 30:20).

The psalmist further prays that his life style—in response to the revealed will of God—will keep him from anxiety and further adversity ("shame," v.31; cf. v.6; 25:2). His prayer reflects faith in the promises of the Lord (v.28). In his hope toward the future, he is supported by a new freedom. He will not only "walk" (vv.1, 3) in the "path of your commands," but he will "run" (v.32; Prov 4:12). The Lord has given him a sense of freedom from anxiety and care (cf. v.28: "My soul is weary with sorrow"). The "heart" (v.32) may denote the inner being filled with joy and happiness (cf. Isa 60:5) or may be an inner understanding as in the language of wisdom (cf. 1 Kings 4:29; Allen: "since you enlarge my understanding," p. 127).

V. The He Strophe

119:33–40

ה He

33 Teach me, O LORD, to follow your decrees;
then I will keep them to the end.
34 Give me understanding, and I will keep your law
and obey it with all my heart.
35 Direct me in the path of your commands,
for there I find delight.
36 Turn my heart toward your statutes
and not toward selfish gain.
37 Turn my eyes away from worthless things;
preserve my life according to your word.
38 Fulfill your promise to your servant,
so that you may be feared.

39 Take away the disgrace I dread,
for your laws are good.
40 How I long for your precepts!
Preserve my life in your righteousness.

33–37 This strophe contains a series of petitions united by the use of the Hiphil imperative: "Teach me. . . . Give me. . . . Direct me. . . . Turn my heart. . . . Turn my eyes. . . . Fulfill. . . . Take away" (vv.33–39). In these petitions a tone of humility and dependence comes through. It is, after all, the LORD who must interpret his own revelation ("teach," v.33; see v.26; cf. 25:4, 9; 27:11; 86:11; Isa 48:17; "give me understanding," v.34; see v.27). It is also the Lord who can provide the spiritual direction and motivation to direct man's steps (v.36; cf. Prov 4:11–19) and incline his "heart"(cf. 141:4) to do his will. It is also the Lord who keeps man from evil, by dimming the luster of this world ("Turn my eyes away from worthless things [*šāw'*]," v.37, i.e., "valueless" [Allen, p. 128]) and by keeping him from greed ("selfish gain," v.36; cf. Isa 33:15).

The purpose of God's positive direction and protection from evil (cf. 32:8) is to encourage the psalmist to keep the law. Keeping the law was not a matter of external conformity in the OT but required "a heart" of absolute devotion to God (cf. Deut 5:29). By God's help he will "keep" (*n-ṣ-r,* v.33; cf. v.2) his "decrees" (*ḥuqqîm*) and receive God's reward (NIV, "to the end"; see Notes) and "obey" (*s-m-r*) his "law" (*tôrāh*) with all his "heart" (v.34). His "delight" of radical loyalty from the heart is a work of grace, as he can only take pleasure in the law of the Lord having been renewed in his mind (v.35; cf. 112:1; Rom 12:2). To this end the psalmist prays that the Lord may "preserve" him (v.37; cf. vv.25, 40) as he walks in the way of God.

38–40 The mood of the prayer changes abruptly to a call for action. The psalmist asks the Lord to "fulfill" his "word" or "promise" (*'imrāh,* v.38) of "righteousness" (*ṣᵉḏ āqāh,* v.40) to his servant (cf. vv.17, 23). In his "righteousness" God delivers, frees, preserves life (v.40; cf. vv.17, 25, 37), and removes a dreaded "disgrace" (v.39; see v.22). The Lord's grace to him will remove disgrace and will promote the fear of God ("so that you may be feared," lit., "your fear," v.38; cf. 130:4). The delight in God's laws ("your laws are good," v.39; "how I long," v.40) is in direct relationship to his prayer that the Lord's righteousness be established for him and for all of God's servants (cf. Gal 5:5–6).

Notes

33 The idiomatic use of עֵקֶב (*'ēqeḇ,* "to the end," "reward") may be understood as "continually" (so LXX, RSV, NIV) or in the sense of "reward." From the usage in v.112; 19:11; Prov 22:4, it is preferable to understand the idiom "as a reward" (so most modern commentators, A.A. Anderson, 2:819).

37 The NIV margin calls attention to the textual difficulty: "your way" (MT), "your ways" (C and a number of MSS), or "with your word" (2 MSS, Targ.; so NIV) (cf. BHS). The last reading may have been influenced by the similar phraseology of v.25. We favor keeping the MT with the sense that the Lord gives life to those who walk in his way (see Allen: "Give me life in your ways," p. 127).

VI. The Waw Strophe

119:41–48

ו Waw

41 May your unfailing love come to me, O Lord,
your salvation according to your promise;
42 then I will answer the one who taunts me,
for I trust in your word.
43 Do not snatch the word of truth from my mouth,
for I have put my hope in your laws.
44 I will always obey your law,
for ever and ever.
45 I will walk about in freedom,
for I have sought out your precepts.
46 I will speak of your statutes before kings
and will not be put to shame,
47 for I delight in your commands
because I love them.
48 I lift up my hands to your commands,
which I love,
and I meditate on your decrees.

41–42 This strophe continues the elements of prayer and commitment. The words "unfailing love" (*ḥ^{a}sāḏîm,* pl., "acts of love," v.41; cf. Isa 55:3) and "salvation" (*t^{e}šû'āh,* a synonym of *y^{e}šû'āh;* cf. vv.123, 166, 174) explicate the prayer for renewal "in your righteousness" (v.40). The "righteousness" of God extends to deliverance and vindication from the adversaries. When the Lord extends his "love" by delivering him according to his "promise" (*'imrāh,* v.41; cf. v.38), then the dreaded "disgrace" (*ḥerpāh,* from *ḥ-r-p,* v.39) will be removed; and he will rebuke the one who "taunts" (*ḥōr^{e}p̱î,* from the root *ḥ-r-p*) him (v.42). Hope in salvation is grounded in God's word of "promise," and his promise calls for "trust" (*b-ṭ-ḥ,* v.42; cf. 26:1) (see appendix to Ps 119: Yahweh Is My Redeemer).

43 The affirmation of trust in the Lord receives further emphasis in v.43. By use of a disjunctive waw at the beginning (properly translated by Dahood as "So do not remove" [*Psalms,* 3:163]), the psalmist contends that hope in God's salvation keeps him from "answering" those who taunt him. He pleads with the Lord to be true to his promises: "the word of truth" (*'^{e}meṯ,* "faithfulness"; cf. v.30: "the way of truth").

44–45 The psalmist promises to remain loyal to the Lord throughout life (v.44). His devotion is a free expression of his love for God (v.45), and in this walk he experiences the Lord's blessing and bounty (cf. v.32; 18:19; 118:5).

46–48 The psalmist vows to speak about God's "statutes" (*'ēḏôṯ*) unashamedly, even in the presence of "kings" (v.46; cf. Matt 10:18; Acts 26:1–2). He is so full of love for God and so filled with joy in the prospect of salvation that he concludes this section with a strong statement on "love" and "delight" (vv.47–48; cf. vv.16, 70, 97, 113, 119, 127, 140, 159, 163) as he prays ("I lift up my hands," v.48; cf. 28:2) and meditates (cf. vv.15, 23, 27).

Notes

41–48 In this section every bicolon begins on a waw, often followed by an aleph prefix of the first person singular imperfect: "I will answer. . . . I will always obey. . . . I will walk. . . . I will speak. . . . I delight. . . . I lift up . . . I meditate" (vv.42, 44–48).

VII. The Zayin Strophe

119:49–56

ז Zayin

49 Remember your word to your servant,
for you have given me hope.
50 My comfort in my suffering is this:
Your promise preserves my life.
51 The arrogant mock me without restraint,
but I do not turn from your law.
52 I remember your ancient laws, O LORD,
and I find comfort in them.
53 Indignation grips me because of the wicked,
who have forsaken your law.
54 Your decrees are the theme of my song
wherever I lodge.
55 In the night I remember your name, O LORD,
and I will keep your law.
56 This has been my practice:
I obey your precepts.

49–56 The word of God provides hope and comfort even in suffering. The psalmist prays that the Lord will "remember" (v.49, *z-k-r*) his word and affirms twice that even in his troubles he himself will "remember" God and his laws ("I remember your ancient laws. . . . In the night I remember your name," vv.52, 55). He knows that the Lord's promises are sure; therefore he has "hope" (v.49; cf. v.43). However, if he expects God to be true to his covenant by "remembering" his promises, his "servant" (v.49; cf. v.38; 9:12; 74:2; 115:12; 136:23) must constantly remember the Lord.

In the process of waiting for deliverance, the law becomes a symbol of hope and a means of comfort. The word of God gave "comfort" (*n-ḥ-m*, vv.50, 52) in the psalmist's "suffering" (v.50). He suffers disgrace, taunting by his adversaries (vv.22, 39, 42, 51, 69, et. al.), and persecution (vv.61, 87, 109). The word of the Lord sustains and restores life ("your promise preserves my life," v.50; cf. v.40). It consoles him even in the pressures of life (vv.51, 53) so that he can sing the praises of God's "decrees" (*ḥuqqîm*, v.54). The "songs" (*z*ᵉ*mîrô*<u>*t*</u>; NIV, "the theme of my song") praise God even in adversity. He feels like a pilgrim (v.54), but in his pilgrimage God is there. Even at night his remembrance of the Lord's "name" evokes songs of praise and thanksgiving (v.55; cf. v.62; see appendix to Ps 7: The Name of Yahweh).

Adversity strengthens hope. The "arrogant" (*zē*<u>*d*</u>*îm*, v.51; cf. v.21) "mock" him (cf. Prov 21:24), but he gets more provoked at their apostasy from God than at the suffering they cause him (v.53; cf. 11:6 ["a scorching wind"]; Lam 5:10 ["feverish"]). They drive him to greater loyalty ("but I do not turn from your law," v.51). The spirit of the psalmist may best be described as loyal rather than zealous, God-centered rather than law-centered, and hopeful and humble rather than filled with pride.

This section is full of confidence in God and of comfort to those who are waiting for his deliverance. Difficult as life may be, God's word can help the suffering sing, even at night (v.55)! This life style does not develop overnight but comes from habitual practice (v.56). The psalmist guarded carefully the "precepts" (*piqqûḏîm*) of God, because in them he found life, restoration, and comfort (cf. v.49).

Notes

---

54 בְּבֵית מְגוּרָי (*b*ᵉ*ḇêṯ m*ᵉ*ḡûrāy*, "Wherever I lodge"; cf. v.19) could also be translated as "in the house of my pilgrimage."

VIII. The Heth Strophe

119:57–64

ח Heth

57 You are my portion, O LORD;
I have promised to obey your words.
58 I have sought your face with all my heart;
be gracious to me according to your promise.
59 I have considered my ways
and have turned my steps to your statutes.
60 I will hasten and not delay
to obey your commands.
61 Though the wicked bind me with ropes,
I will not forget your law.
62 At midnight I rise to give you thanks
for your righteous laws.
63 I am a friend to all who fear you,
to all who follow your precepts.
64 The earth is filled with your love, O LORD;
teach me your decrees.

57–64 The strophe begins with a familiar formula of trust: "[the LORD] is my portion" (v.57; cf. 16:5; 73:26; 142:5). It ends on an exclamation of God's cosmic "love" (*ḥeseḏ*). The world of creation witnesses to his love (v.64; cf. 104:10–30; 136:1–9). Since his love is so great for the created order, how much more wonderful is it for all who are loyal to him!

In recognition of God's goodness, the psalmist promised a deeper commitment "to obey" God's words (cf. vv.55–56) and to do so willingly and quickly (v.60), giving thanks to the Lord in the middle of the night (v.62; cf. vv.7, 55). He shows his love by attentiveness to the word of God (v.60; cf. 1:2) and by associating with the godly, who "fear" (*y-r-'*) the Lord and "who follow [his] precepts" (v.63).

The psalmist petitions the Lord to be gracious to him (v.58). His petition is urgent and corresponds to his diligence toward the law of God (cf. vv.10, 60). Prayer and obedience go hand in hand. Even if the Lord delays his redemption, permitting the wicked to triumph for a while, the psalmist affirms his loyalty as being of primary importance ("Though . . . I will not forget your law," v.61). Faith in God's "righteous" laws (v.62; cf. v.7) triumphs and brings out a song of thanksgiving even when the Lord has not yet dealt with his request! Faith in Yahweh frees the psalmist spiritually from the "ropes" of the wicked, a metaphor for the reign of terror of the wicked who rule with their tongues, schemes, and repressive ways (v.61).

Notes

57 The MT's חֶלְקִי יהוה (*ḥelqî YHWH*, "my portion, O LORD") is usually rendered "the LORD is my portion" (cf. 73:26; 142:5). Some take this as an indication that a priest or Levite was the author of this psalm (cf. Num 18:20).

IX. The Teth Strophe

119:65–72

ט Teth

65 Do good to your servant
according to your word, O LORD.
66 Teach me knowledge and good judgment,
for I believe in your commands.
67 Before I was afflicted I went astray,
but now I obey your word.
68 You are good, and what you do is good;
teach me your decrees.
69 Though the arrogant have smeared me with lies,
I keep your precepts with all my heart.
70 Their hearts are callous and unfeeling,
but I delight in your law.
71 It was good for me to be afflicted
so that I might learn your decrees.
72 The law from your mouth is more precious to me
than thousands of pieces of silver and gold.

65–72 This strophe begins five times on the word "good" (*ṭôḇ*) in the MT. The Lord has done "good" to his servant (v.65, rather than "do good," NIV). He is the source of "good judgment" (v.66). He is "good" (v.68), the ordeal of affliction has been "good" (v.71), and his law is "good" in relation to material possessions (v.72; NIV, "precious"). Thus the psalmist ascribes "goodness" to God in his past and present dealings, to the positive values of his troubles, and to the ultimate value of God's law and divine illumination.

The Lord is good (v.65) because he is faithful to his word (cf. v.9; Deut 6:23; 10:13; 30:9, 15). The Lord is good in his relations and actions (cf. 25:8; 34:8; 73:1; Matt 7:11). He does good particularly to those who align their lives with his will; therefore the psalmist prays again, "Teach me your decrees" (v.68; cf. vv.12, 26, 64).

Good is the experience of humiliation and affliction (v.71; cf. 94:12; Job 5:17; Prov 3:11–12; Lam 3:25–30; Heb 12:4–11), caused by "the arrogant" (*zēḏîm*, v.69; cf. v.21). They are filled with falsehood (cf. vv.29, 78) and "callous" (v.70; see 17:10).

Because of "affliction" the psalmist gives himself more to the "learning" (v.71; cf. vv.7, 66), application (v.69), and love (v.70; cf. v.47) of God's "precepts" (*piqqûḏîm*, v.69), "law" (*tôrāh*, v.70), and "decrees" (*ḥuqqîm*, v.71). He confesses that the discipline of the Lord has changed his life, because he used to "go astray" (v.67; cf. vv.10, 21). Straying from God's commandment was serious because it might lead to being accursed (v.21). Instead of being a covenant breaker, the psalmist is now restored in fellowship and is a covenant keeper ("but now I obey your word," v.67).

Good judgment is requisite for godly living in an evil world (v.66). The psalmist prays that the Lord may give him wisdom. "Knowledge" (*da'aṯ*) primarily denotes the knowledge of God in one's communion with him and secondarily the "response" to the life of fellowship with the Lord. The psalmist prays for discernment and proper actions, flowing forth out of a living relationship with his God.

Good is God's revealed ("from your mouth") "law" (*tôrāh*, v.72). It is "better than" any monetary value (cf. vv.14, 57, 103, 111, 127, 162). The expression "pieces of silver and gold" denotes a large amount of money, but the precise value is not specified. The "law" is only profitable when internalized by the Spirit of God, as Calvin rightly observes:

> Besides, it is certain that he does not here treat of external teaching, but of the inward illumination of the mind, which is the gift of the Holy Spirit. The law was exhibited to all without distinction; but the prophet, well aware that unless he were enlightened by the Holy Spirit, it would be of little advantage to him, prays that he may be taught effectually by supernatural influence. (4:449)

Notes

65–72 "Good" is a covenantal term; see Ingeborg Johag, "טוֹב—Terminus Technicus in Vertrags- und Bündnisformularen des Alten Orients und des Alten Testaments," *Bausteine biblischer Theologie. Festgabe für G. Johannes Botterweck zum 60. Geburtstag dargebracht von seinen Schülern*, ed. Heinz-Josef Fabry (Köln: Peter Hanstein, 1977), pp. 3–23.

66 The MT phraseology is somewhat difficult in v.66: "goodness of taste and knowledge" (NIV, "knowledge and good judgment"). "Taste" has here a metaphorical significance of "judgment" (cf. superscription of Ps 34; Prov 11:22) so that "goodness of taste" signifies "good judgment" (KB^3, 2:361).

X. The Yodh Strophe

119:73–80

Yodh

73 Your hands made me and formed me;
give me understanding to learn your commands.
74 May those who fear you rejoice when they see me,
for I have put my hope in your word.
75 I know, O LORD, that your laws are righteous,
and in faithfulness you have afflicted me.
76 May your unfailing love be my comfort,
according to your promise to your servant.

77 Let your compassion come to me that I may live,
for your law is my delight.
78 May the arrogant be put to shame for wronging me
without cause;
but I will meditate on your precepts.
79 May those who fear you turn to me,
those who understand your statutes.
80 May my heart be blameless toward your decrees,
that I may not be put to shame.

73–74 The psalmist believes in God's election and purpose for his servant. God has "made" him for the purpose of having "understanding" to fulfill his "commands" (*miṣwōṯ*, v.73). Since he has initiated the relationship, the psalmist is confident ("I know," v.75) that the righteous may soon rejoice (v.74).

75–80 The psalmist looks up to God to grant him deliverance because his "laws" (*mišpāṭîm*) are "righteous" (*ṣeḏeq*, v.75; cf. v.40). The Lord works out his plans victoriously so that the godly are exalted and the ungodly will perish. In this regard there is no question as to God's "faithfulness" (cf. 36:5; 89:28–37; Deut 32:4; Isa 11:5) even in affliction (vv.67, 71, 75). God's purpose for affliction is to refine the relationship with his children (cf. Deut 8:16; Lam 3:33; Heb 12:7–11). The other side of God's "faithfulness" is his "love" (*ḥeseḏ*), usually translated as "unfailing love" (v.76; see 5:7). In his deepest needs the psalmist knows that God is still there and that he cares, because of his "faithfulness" (*'ᵉmûnāh*) and "unfailing love" (*ḥeseḏ*). Faith in God's "love" "comforts" him as does the "promise" (*'imrāh*) of God (cf. vv.50, 82). In addition he prays for an evidence of God's "compassion" (v.77) as a token of God's fatherly care for his child in great need (cf. Exod 34:6; 103:13–14). The "compassion" of the Lord gives and sustains life (cf. v.156); hence, comfort is found in the belief that God is compassionate (cf. Deut 13:17–18; Isa 49:13; 54:7; Zech 1:16; see appendix to Ps 25: The Perfections of Yahweh).

The psalmist can say, "I know" that God is righteous and faithful (v.75; cf. 96:13; 143:1). He has an experiential knowledge of God, of his "unfailing love" and "compassion" (vv.76–77). When he looks at humans, the psalmist sees the "arrogant" (*zēḏîm*, v.78; cf. v.21). They have wrongfully dealt with him and must get their just deserts ("may [they] be put to shame," v.78; cf. 6:10; 31:17; 35:4, 26; 83:17). He has already prayed that his present shame may be removed (v.80; cf. vv.6, 22). Even while waiting he continues to "delight" in God's "law" (*tôrāh*, v.77; vv.16, 24), to "meditate" (see v.15) on the Lord's "precepts" (*piqqûḏîm*, v.78; cf. vv.15, 23), and to walk in a "blameless" way (v.80; cf. v.1) in the presence of his Lord.

The psalmist also considers the godly. He prays that they who "fear" the Lord (vv.74, 79) may be encouraged and rejoice (v.74) at God's vindication.

Notes

79 The *Qere* וְיֹדְעֵו (*wᵉyōḏᵉʿēw*, "and those who know"), supported by a number of MSS and the LXX, is the basis for the NIV reading ("understand"). For a similar construction, see v.63. The *Kethiv* וְיֵדְעוּ (*wᵉyēḏᵉʿû*, "that they may know"; cf. v.125) has been accepted by the RSV and A.A. Anderson (2:830).

XI. The Kaph Strophe

119:81–88

כ Kaph

81 My soul faints with longing for your salvation,
but I have put my hope in your word.
82 My eyes fail, looking for your promise;
I say, "When will you comfort me?"
83 Though I am like a wineskin in the smoke,
I do not forget your decrees.
84 How long must your servant wait?
When will you punish my persecutors?
85 The arrogant dig pitfalls for me,
contrary to your law.
86 All your commands are trustworthy;
help me, for men persecute me without cause.
87 They almost wiped me from the earth,
but I have not forsaken your precepts.
88 Preserve my life according to your love,
and I will obey the statutes of your mouth.

81–88 The last strophe of the first half of Psalm 119 brings to climactic expression the psalmist's need for God by a threefold use of the root *k-l-h* ("faints," v.81; "fail," v.82; "wiped [out]," v.87); a "longing" for God's intervention (vv.81–82); a series of insistent interrogatives ("When. . . . How long . . . When," vv.82, 84); prayers for help ("help me. . . . Preserve my life," vv.86, 89); affirmations of his love of God and his word ("in your word. . . . for your promise. . . . I do not forget your decrees. . . . All your commandments are trustworthy. . . . but I have not forsaken your precepts. . . . I will obey the statutes of your mouth," vv.81–82, 86–88); and an existential anguish at the present success of the "arrogant" who are lawless and without reason (vv.85–86).

Because of the long wait for God's salvation, the psalmist's endurance of the "arrogant" (vv.85–86) is wearing down (vv.81–82). His soul "faints" (*k-l-h,* "pines," v.81; cf. 84:2) and his "eyes fail" (*k-l-h,* v.82; cf. v.123; 6:7; 13:3; 69:3); and he feels as if he is near the end of his strength ("they almost wiped [*k-l-h*] me," v.87). As he waits for God's intervention, the psalmist is being persecuted "without cause" (v.86). He feels himself to be "like a wineskin in the smoke" (v.83), i.e., useless, shriveled, and unattractive because of being blackened with soot (cf. Lam 4:8). In his loneliness he laments honestly in the presence of the Lord, asking his questions and making his petitions.

In his despair the psalmist looks only to the Lord for his "salvation" (v.81; cf. 37:39; 62:2; Isa 12:2–3; 45:17; Jer 3:23), as promised in his "word" (v.81; cf. 123; 130:5–6; Lam 4:17) of "promise" (v.82; see *'imrāh*). Therefore he freely asks God several questions. First, he wonders when God will comfort him (v.82; cf. Isa 12:1; 49:13; 51:3, 12; 52:9; Jer 31:13; Zech 1:17). Second, he asks when the Lord will execute "justice" (*mišpāṭ;* NIV, "will you punish," v.84). The "arrogant" (v.85; cf. vv.21, 78, 85) have no regard for God or his word. They persecute (*r-d-p,* vv.84, 86; cf. v.161) and hunt down ("dig pitfalls," v.85) the godly. In contrast the psalmist loves God and his word. Therefore he also submits himself to the Lord's "help" (v.86; cf. vv.173, 175; 30:10; 37:40; 54:4) and for preservation of life (v.88; cf. v.25). The "love" (*hese<u>d</u>;* cf. v.76) is great and so is the need. But the love of God is sufficient for his great need.

XII. The Lamedh Strophe

119:89–96

ל Lamedh

89 Your word, O LORD, is eternal;
it stands firm in the heavens.
90 Your faithfulness continues through all generations;
you established the earth, and it endures.
91 Your laws endure to this day,
for all things serve you.
92 If your law had not been my delight,
I would have perished in my affliction.
93 I will never forget your precepts,
for by them you have preserved my life.
94 Save me, for I am yours;
I have sought out your precepts.
95 The wicked are waiting to destroy me,
but I will ponder your statutes.
96 To all perfection I see a limit;
but your commands are boundless.

89–91 The nature of the Lord is also reflected in everything he has created: heaven and earth (vv.89–90). There is constancy and order in all of creation, reflecting the "faithfulness" (*'ᵉmûnāh*) of the Lord (v.90; cf. vv.75, 86; 89:2; 104; 147:7–9). The order in creation reveals the love, care, and fidelity of the Lord. He is Lord in his created universe, as "all things serve" him (v.91; lit., "all things your servants"). The regularity of day and night witnesses to the constancy of the Lord. Nature serves and abides by the "word" (*dāḇār*, v.89) and the "laws" (*mišpāṭîm*, v.91) of the Lord.

92 The psalmist confesses that he too wants to be included among those who serve the Lord by keeping his "law." He has found "delight" (*š-'-'*; cf. vv.16, 24, 47, 70, 77, 92, 143, 174) in the "law" (*tôrāh*, instruction) of the Lord, and this has given him a sense of being so as to align his life with the revealed will of the Lord. If he had not found meaning in his experience of "affliction," he felt that he would have perished. He would have been like a falling star.

93–96 Therefore the psalmist will not forget the "precepts" (*piqqûḏîm*, v.93) of the Lord, because they give order and preservation of life ("for by them you have preserved my life"; cf. vv.25, 37, 40, 50, 88, 107, 149, 154, 156, 159). The preservation of life is related to the covenantal relationship, as the psalmist knows that he belongs to God ("I am yours," v.94; cf. v.125). Therefore he prays that the Lord may continue to sustain his life ("save me," *y-š-'*; cf. 54:1), in spite of the opposition of "the wicked" (v.95). As long as his hope is fixed on the Lord, he does not "perish" (*'-b-d*) in his affliction (v.92). The wicked may attempt "to destroy" (*'-b-d*) him (v.95; cf. Ezek 22:27); but as their violence increases, the psalmist seeks refuge in a diligent study (*b-y-n*, "ponder"; cf. vv.73, 104) of the "statutes" (*'ēḏôṯ*) of the Lord. The "commands" (*miṣwôṯ*) of the Lord liberate him and give him a new lease on life (lit., "very broad"; NIV, "boundless," v.96; cf. v.32; 118:5). Everything else, perfect as it may be, is limited.

XIII. The Mem Strophe

119:97–104

מ Mem

97 Oh, how I love your law!
I meditate on it all day long.
98 Your commands make me wiser than my enemies,
for they are ever with me.
99 I have more insight than all my teachers,
for I meditate on your statutes.
100 I have more understanding than the elders,
for I obey your precepts.
101 I have kept my feet from every evil path
so that I might obey your word.
102 I have not departed from your laws,
for you yourself have taught me.
103 How sweet are your words to my taste,
sweeter than honey to my mouth!
104 I gain understanding from your precepts;
therefore I hate every wrong path.

97–104 This strophe is a hymn in praise of the law of the Lord. Like the sin/shin strophe, it has no petitions. The strophe is full of repetitions: "how" (*māh*, vv.97, 103), the root *y-r-h* ("law," "taught," vv.97, 102), the phrase "I meditate" (*śîḥah*, vv.97, 99), the prepositional phrases *lî* ("with me," "I," vv.98–99) and *mikkol* ("more than all," v.99; "from every," v.101), the verb *'eṯbônān* ("I have understanding," v.100, "I gain understanding," v.104), and the nouns "path" (*'ōraḥ*, vv.101, 104) and "precepts" (vv.100, 104). The strophe begins with an expression of love for the law and ends on an affirmation of hatred of every form of evil.

The love of God's law (v.97; cf. vv.47, 113, 163) comes out of love for God, the Teacher (v.102). A rejection of God's instruction implies a rejection of the Lord. "Meditation" (vv.97, 99) is a form of devotion to the Lord himself, and hence its practice is regularly cultivated ("all day long," v.97; cf. vv.15, 23, 27, 48, 148). He delights in his understanding of God's law as he reflects on his devotion in relation to the "enemies," "teachers," and "elders" (vv.98–100). The comparison is not a prideful assertion of superiority but a form of exultation in the Lord himself, whose wisdom is more direct and superior (cf. v.102; Jer 9:23–24). The word of God together with divine illumination is superior to any human interpretation. However, in setting forth the excellence of divine illumination, the psalmist would not have been so arrogant as to shun instruction from the teachers and elders!

Because of his love for God, the psalmist devotes himself to the practice of the law, rejecting the way of the wicked (vv.100–102; cf. 1:1–2). The path of the righteous is wholly opposite to the path of the wicked (cf. 1:6; Prov 4:14, 18). Therefore he was obedient (vv.100–101) and did not "depart" (v.102; cf. Deut 9:16; 17:11, 20; 28:14) from God's laws.

The "words" of promise (*'imrāh*, v.103) are not separate from the keeping of the laws. The promises, likened to "honey" (cf. 19:10; Job 23:12; John 4:32, 34), are sweet only when God's instruction is received and leads to understanding as well as an obedient life style (vv.102, 104; cf. vv.29, 128).

Notes

103 אִמְרָה (*'imrāh*, "word") is singular in the MT, but the NIV reading "words" has the support of a number of MSS, the LXX, Syriac, and Targum.

XIV. The Nun Strophe

119:105–12

נ Nun

105 Your word is a lamp to my feet
and a light for my path.
106 I have taken an oath and confirmed it,
that I will follow your righteous laws.
107 I have suffered much;
preserve my life, O LORD, according to your word.
108 Accept, O LORD, the willing praise of my mouth,
and teach me your laws.
109 Though I constantly take my life in my hands,
I will not forget your law.
110 The wicked have set a snare for me,
but I have not strayed from your precepts.
111 Your statutes are my heritage forever;
they are the joy of my heart.
112 My heart is set on keeping your decrees
to the very end.

105–12 The psalmist who hates "every wrong path" (v.104; cf. v.100) thanks the Lord that he has given him his "word" (*dāḇār*, v.105) to be a guide and life-sustaining source ("light," *'ôr;* cf. 97:11; 112:4; John 8:12) as he walks on the "path" of life (cf. Prov 6:23). The "word" assures the believer of the covenant relationship between the Lord and man ("heritage," v.111; cf. Exod 32:13), gives "joy" to the heart, and rewards those who persevere in doing right (v.112, "to the very end"; see v.33).

The "laws" (*mišpāṭîm*) of God are "righteous" (v.106) and are comforting even in adversity. In suffering they speak of the righteousness of the Lord (see v.7) and of his care for the suffering. The psalmist affirms that the Lord alone can "preserve" life (v.107; cf. v.25). He is "righteous" and has given his promise.

Godly living is far from easy. Even in affliction the psalmist has learned to give the Lord "willing praise" (v.108; cf. 50:14; 51:17; Heb 13:15), praying that the Lord may accept his offering (cf. 19:14; Lev 7:18; 19:7), his praise, his thanksgiving, and his receptivity to divine instruction ("teach me," v.108; see v.12).

The nature of the affliction is such that the psalmist is continually at risk (v.109; cf. Judg 12:3; 1 Sam 19:5; 28:21; Job 13:14). He is determined to be loyal to the Lord, even when the wicked attempt to hunt him down and catch him (v.110; cf. vv.85–87; Amos 3:5). Thus far he has not yet strayed from the way of God (cf. 58:3). His joy and determination to please the Lord are much greater than the affliction with which he lives constantly.

XV. The Samekh Strophe

119:113–20

ס Samekh

113 I hate double-minded men,
but I love your law.
114 You are my refuge and my shield;
I have put my hope in your word.
115 Away from me, you evildoers,
that I may keep the commands of my God!
116 Sustain me according to your promise, and I will live;
do not let my hopes be dashed.
117 Uphold me, and I will be delivered;
I will always have regard for your decrees.
118 You reject all who stray from your decrees,
for their deceitfulness is in vain.
119 All the wicked of the earth you discard like dross;
therefore I love your statutes.
120 My flesh trembles in fear of you;
I stand in awe of your laws.

113–20 The ways of the righteous and the wicked are clearly divergent. The wicked are "double-minded" (a Hebrew *hapax legomenon,* v.113), "evildoers" (v.115; cf. 6:8; Isa 1:4), disobedient to God's word ("stray from your decrees," v.118; cf. vv.10, 21), and deceptive ("deceitfulness," v.118). The psalmist dissociates himself completely from them. The language of dissociation itself is a form of commitment to God. He "hates" the "double-minded" but "loves" the law of the Lord (v.113). He calls on the evildoers to stay away from him (cf. 6:8; 139:19) so that he may draw closer to the observance of God's commands (v.115).

The psalmist draws comfort that the Lord is his "refuge" and "shield" (v.114). The "refuge" is associated with the "shelter" that could be found at the tabernacle (cf. 28:7; 33:20; 84:11; 115:9). His "hope" (v.114; cf. v.81) lies in the promised word of the Lord; therefore he draws near to God for "refuge." The Lord is also his "shield," which signifies his protection (see 3:3; cf. 28:7; 33:20; 84:11).

The psalmist prays that the Lord will "sustain" (v.116) and "uphold" (v.117) him so that he may "live" and "be delivered." Since the Lord is his "refuge" and "shield" and has promised to "sustain" (cf. 3:5; 37:17, 24; 54:4; 145:14) him, he prays that the Lord may deliver him so as to enjoy his beneficence in life, lest he be discouraged in waiting (v.116; cf. v.6). The Lord's "upholding" leads to deliverance from all troubles (cf. 20:2; 41:3; 94:18).

The psalmist also believes that the Lord's righteous judgment will come on the wicked. Even as he has rejected them, the Lord will "reject" and "discard" all evildoers like "dross" (vv.118–19). "Dross," the scum that forms on the top when a precious metal is being refined, is discarded by the metalsmith (cf. Isa 1:22; Jer 6:28–30; Ezek 22:18–19).

How different from the ungodly are the godly! They have hope. They draw near to God and find delight in his word: "I love your law" (v.113), "I have put my hope in your word" (v.114), "that I may keep the commands of my God" (v.115), "I will always have regard for your decrees" (v.117), and "therefore I love your statutes" (v.119).

The psalmist concludes this strophe on a final affirmation of godly fear in contrast to the ungodly who "stray" (v.118) from God's decrees. He stands in "dread" of the Lord (v.120; NIV, "awe"). In his reflection of God he "trembles" (*s-m-r*). This is a physical reaction to a psychological state and could be translated by "my skin has goose bumps," or as Allen translates, "Dread of you makes my flesh creep" (p. 131). See also Job 4:15: "A spirit glided past my face, / and the hair on my body stood on end [*s-m-r*]." The presence of God is so real for the psalmist that he responds to his God in spirit and body. His life of obedience is lived in the presence of the living God, whereas the wicked act as if God does not see or care.

Notes

---

119 The verb הִשְׁבַּתָּ (*hišbattā*, "you discard") is a Hiphil perfect from *š-b-t* ("cease"): "you have caused to cease." A few Hebrew MSS and some versions suggest an original Hebrew חָשַׁבְתָּ (*hāšaḇtā*, "you consider"; cf. LXX, "I consider"). There is no reason to reject the MT.

XVI. The Ayin Strophe

119:121–28

ע Ayin

121 I have done what is righteous and just;
do not leave me to my oppressors.
122 Ensure your servant's well-being;
let not the arrogant oppress me.
123 My eyes fail, looking for your salvation,
looking for your righteous promise.
124 Deal with your servant according to your love
and teach me your decrees.
125 I am your servant; give me discernment
that I may understand your statutes.
126 It is time for you to act, O LORD;
your law is being broken.
127 Because I love your commands
more than gold, more than pure gold,
128 and because I consider all your precepts right,
I hate every wrong path.

121–28 The psalmist, who commits himself to the care of the Lord, has done what is "righteous and just" (v.121; cf. 33:5; 89:14). Now he expects the Lord to conform to his "righteous promise" (v.123; cf. vv.81–82), according to which the godly will be delivered from all adversities. As long as the Lord does not intervene, it seems as if the psalmist is left to the "arrogant oppressors" (vv.121–22; cf. vv.21, 51; 72:4; 105:14; Prov 14:31; Jer 12:12). He is innocent of doing the same thing that the oppressors have done because he has lived in accordance with God's expectations.

Godliness is the response of faith to the promises of God, by which the godly act in accordance with the "law-word" by doing what is "righteous and just" (v.121). It is also the response of "hope," waiting and enduring adversity, even to the point of exhaustion ("my eyes fail, looking for your salvation," v.123; cf. v.82). The "salvation" (*yᵉšûʿāh*) extends to all the needs of God's people, as they look for a renewal of God's "love" (*ḥeseḏ*, v.124; cf. 5:7) as well as a deliverance from the "arrogant" (vv.121–22).

Hope in the fullness of "salvation" is the object of faith. Finally, godliness also reveals itself in a teachable spirit. The psalmist prays repeatedly for God to "teach" him (v.124; cf. vv.12, 26, 64, 66, 71, 73, 99, 108, 135, 171) and to give him "discernment" (v.125; cf. vv.27, 34, 73, 144, 169).

Godliness also shows zeal for the honor of God and his laws and a hatred of an ungodly way of life. To this end the psalmist affirms his love for the Lord's "commands" (*miṣwōṯ*, v.127; cf. v.47; Prov 8:17) and compares them favorably with "gold, more than pure gold" (cf. Job 22:25; 28:15–16; Prov 3:14; 8:10, 19; 16:16). "Pure gold" designates a higher degree of purity than "gold." He also expresses his commitment to the Lord by expressing loyalty to his "precepts" (*piqqûḏîm*, v.128).

Together with the psalmist's affirmation of devotion is a righteous indignation at the way of the ungodly who have broken God's "law" (*tôrāh*, v.126). The verb "broken" (*p-r-r*) together with *tôrāh* may well be understood in the prophetic sense as "they have broken covenant" (cf. Isa 24:5; 33:8; Jer 11:10; 31:32; A.A. Anderson, 2:839). Zealous for the honor of God, the psalmist prays that the Lord may soon deal justly with the ungodly: "It is time for you to act, O LORD" (v.126; cf. Jer 18:23).

Notes

127–28 Both verses begin with עַל־כֵּן (*'al-kēn*, "therefore"; NIV, "because"). Though the NIV makes sense, we prefer the usual rendering as an affirmation of devotion. The NEB makes excellent sense: "truly."

128 The phrase כָּל־פִּקּוּדֵי כֹל (*kol-piqqûḏê ḵōl*, "all precepts of all") violates Hebrew syntax and contains a duplication of "all." An acceptable emendation requires a minor reconstruction: לְכָל־פִּקּוּדֶיךָ לְיִשָּׁרְתִּי (*l^e ḵol-piqqûḏeyḵā l^e yiššārtî*, "all your precepts I consider truly right," with an emphatic lamed (Dahood, *Psalms*, 3:168, 187).

XVII. The Pe Strophe

119:129–36

פ Pe

129 Your statutes are wonderful;
therefore I obey them.
130 The unfolding of your words gives light;
it gives understanding to the simple.
131 I open my mouth and pant,
longing for your commands.
132 Turn to me and have mercy on me,
as you always do to those who love your name.
133 Direct my footsteps according to your word;
let no sin rule over me.
134 Redeem me from the oppression of men,
that I may obey your precepts.
135 Make your face shine upon your servant
and teach me your decrees.
136 Streams of tears flow from my eyes,
for your law is not obeyed.

129–31 The psalmist considers the many benefits of God's word. His "statutes" (*'ēḏôṯ*) are "wonderful" (v.129). Through them he gains insight into the "wonderful" acts and perfections of the Lord (cf. v.18; Exod 15:11; Ps 77:11, 14). God's revelation (v.130; NIV, "unfolding"; lit., "opening," from *p-t-ḥ,* "open") illumines (cf. v.105) so that even those not experienced in the realities of life ("the simple"; cf. 116:6; Prov 1:4; 14:15) may gain wisdom ("understanding"; cf. 19:7). Because of these and other benefits, the psalmist uses the metaphor of "mouth," suggesting that he has a great appetite for the "commands" (*miṣwôṯ*) of the Lord (v.131). He "pants" for them as he waits with great anticipation (cf. Job 29:23). Thus he expresses his satisfaction with God's word, which fulfills and refreshes the godly.

132–36 The psalmist prays with great zeal for the Lord's blessing. His blessing (cf. Num 6:24–26) brings "grace" (*ḥ-n-n;* NIV, "have mercy," v.132; cf. 25:16; 86:16), directs and protects from sin and adversities (vv.133–34), and extends God's favor to all of life ("make your face shine," v.135; cf. 31:16). His prayer for God's blessing is in accordance with God's own promises "to those who love your name" (v.132; cf. 5:11). The psalmist asks for the Lord to be faithful to his word and to his past fidelity to his people ("as you always do," v.132; cf. Heb 6:10). The psalmist too gives himself with greater commitment to do God's will ("let no sin rule over me," v.133; "that I may obey your precepts," v.134; "and teach me your decrees," v.135; cf. v.124). So great is his zeal for God's law that he weeps over the continuation of rebellion and transgression (v.136). The idiom "streams [lit., 'irrigation canals,' see 1:3] of tears" is a hyperbole for deep sorrow and anguish of soul.

XVIII. The Tsadhe Strophe

119:137–44

צ Tsadhe

137 Righteous are you, O LORD,
and your laws are right.
138 The statutes you have laid down are righteous;
they are fully trustworthy.
139 My zeal wears me out,
for my enemies ignore your words.
140 Your promises have been thoroughly tested,
and your servant loves them.
141 Though I am lowly and despised,
I do not forget your precepts.
142 Your righteousness is everlasting
and your law is true.
143 Trouble and distress have come upon me,
but your commands are my delight.
144 Your statutes are forever right;
give me understanding that I may live.

137–44 The strophe begins on an affirmation of the Lord's righteousness ("righteous [*ṣaddîq*] are you," v.137) and ends on an affirmation of his word ("your statutes are forever right," *ṣeḏeq,* "righteous," v.144). In between the psalmist laments his troubles (vv.139, 141, 143). The excellence of the Lord and his word is adversely affected by the troubles and disgrace of his saints. The psalmist calls attention to his need, praying that the Lord will establish righteousness in his world.

The Lord is "righteous" in the distribution of rewards and punishments, as well as in his vindication of the godly (v.137; cf. 116:5–6; 147:17–20; Isa 11:4; Rev 16:5, 7; 19:2). Everything reveals that he is "righteous" and that therefore his revelation is just and true; likewise they guarantee that the Lord will be just and true: his "statutes" (*'ēḏôṯ*) are "righteous" (*ṣeḏeq*, vv.138, 144; cf. v.7), "right" (*yāšār*, "upright," v.137; cf. v.7), "trustworthy" (*'emûnāh*, v.138; cf. vv.75, 86), "tested" (*ṣerûpāh*, v.140; cf. 12:6; 18:30), "true" (*'emeṯ*, "faithful," v.142; cf. vv.151, 160; 19:9; John 17:17), and "everlasting"/"forever" (*le'ôlām*, vv.142, 144; cf. Matt 5:17–18).

Trust in the reliability of God's word is directly proportionate to one's trust in the Lord himself. The conviction that the Lord is righteous and faithful, as is his word, evokes a response of great devotion ("zeal," *qin'āh*, v.139; cf. 69:9). The "zeal" increases as the adversities increase so that it wears one out (cf. 69:9). The psalmist takes seriously the presence of sin in this world (cf. v.136). His adversaries "ignore" (*š-k-ḥ*, v.139) God's laws, whereas he does not "forget" (*š-k-ḥ*, v.141) them. Instead, he "loves" (v.140) and finds his "delight" (v.143; cf. vv.16, 24, 47, 70, 77, 92, 174) in them. Yet he feels himself to be insignificant and rejected by men ("lowly and despised," v.141; cf. Judg 6:15; Ps 22:7). Moreover, his loyalty to the Lord and his devotion to godliness have been unrewarded. Instead, troubles have come his way (v.143).

In his anguish the psalmist holds on to faith in the Lord. He is able to help and has confirmed it in his promises (v.140). Though he does not yet see the outcome of his present troubles, the psalmist knows his God to be "righteous," his word to be "righteous" and "faithful," and his promises to have been tested over and over again in redemptive history. He knows in whom he has put his trust. Therefore, he does not challenge the Lord's integrity but prays humbly that he may "understand" (v.144; cf. v.125) so that he may be revived in his inner being ("live"; cf. 116).

XIX. The Qoph Strophe

119:145–52

ק Qoph

145 I call with all my heart; answer me, O LORD,
and I will obey your decrees.
146 I call out to you; save me
and I will keep your statutes.
147 I rise before dawn and cry for help;
I have put my hope in your word.
148 My eyes stay open through the watches of the night,
that I may meditate on your promises.
149 Hear my voice in accordance with your love;
preserve my life, O LORD, according to your laws.
150 Those who devise wicked schemes are near,
but they are far from your law.
151 Yet you are near, O LORD,
and all your commands are true.
152 Long ago I learned from your statutes
that you established them to last forever.

145–46 Out of the conviction of God's righteousness (vv.137–44), the psalmist cries out (*q-r-'*) for God's help. Verses 145–46 begin (in the MT) with "I cry" (*q-r-'*; NIV, "call"). He feverishly presents his lament before the Lord that he may "answer" (v.145; cf. v.26) him in delivering him from adversity ("save me," *y-š-'*, v.146; cf. v.94). While waiting for God's deliverance, he faithfully holds to God's expectations ("obey," *n-ṣ-r,* cf. v.2; "keep," *š-m-r,* cf. v.4).

147–49 The psalmist's intensity in prayer ("with all my heart," v.145; cf. v.58) is matched by his intense loyalty to obedient living ("with all my heart," vv.34, 69). So intense is his longing for God's salvation that he prays "for help" (v.147; cf. 22:24; 28:2) "before" (*q-d-m*) dawn and "through" (*q-d-m,* lit., "before," v.148) the night watches. Throughout the night he loves to "meditate" (*ś-y-h;* cf. vv.15, 23, 27, 48, 99) on God's "promises" (*'imrāh*). He waits for the Lord to come through, having put his "hope" in God's word (v.147; cf. v.81). The focus of his hope lies in the renewal of God's "love" (*ḥesed,* v.149), by which the Lord will justly (NIV, "according to your laws") transform the present adverse conditions to "life."

150–52 Verses 150–51 both begin with the verb "be near" (*q-r-b*) so as to more clearly contrast the closing in of the wicked (v.150) and the closeness of the Lord (v.151). Though the wicked hunt the psalmist down, the Lord is nearby (cf. 69:18; 73:28). Moreover, his relationship with the Lord has been well established. His "statutes" (*'ēdôṯ,* v.152) are constant, unlike the cabalas of the wicked.

Notes

145–46 Verses 145–46 begin with the root קרא (*q-r-'*, "call"); vv.147–48 begin with the root קדם (*q-d-m,* "I rise. . . . stay open").

149 The MT's מִשְׁפָּטֶךָ (*mišpāṭeḵā,* "your laws"; Allen, "your rulings," p. 133), in parallelism with "with your love," could also be read as מִשְׁפָּטְךָ (*mišpāṭ*ᵉ*ḵā,* "your justice").

150 The phrase רֹדְפֵי זִמָּה (*rōḏ*ᵉ*pê zimmāh,* "those who devise wicked schemes") was read differently in a number of MSS, the LXX, and Symmachus: רֹדְפַי זִמָּה (*rōḏ*ᵉ*pay zimmāh,* "my persecutors [are near] with wicked schemes"). The latter alternative seems preferable in view of the many references to the psalmist's adversaries (cf. vv.87, 95, 109) and the use of *rōḏ*ᵉ*pay* ("who persecute me") in the next section (v.157).

XX. The Resh Strophe

119:153–60

ר Resh

153 Look upon my suffering and deliver me,
for I have not forgotten your law.
154 Defend my cause and redeem me;
preserve my life according to your promise.
155 Salvation is far from the wicked,
for they do not seek out your decrees.
156 Your compassion is great, O LORD;
preserve my life according to your laws.
157 Many are the foes who persecute me,
but I have not turned from your statutes.
158 I look on the faithless with loathing,
for they do not obey your word.

159 See how I love your precepts;
preserve my life, O LORD, according to your love.
160 All your words are true;
all your righteous laws are eternal.

153–60 The lament intensifies as the psalmist prays for deliverance, mercy, and life. The strophe is united by a repetition of *rᵉ'ēh* ("look," v.153; "see," v.159), *ḥayyēnî* ("preserve [renew] my life," vv.154, 156, 159), *rabbîm* ("great," v.156; "many," v.157), and the use of the particle *kî* ("for," vv.153, 155, 158) before a statement of loyalty to God's law or absence thereof. The psalmist prays that the Lord will see how great his devotion to him has been and that his life will be preserved.

The psalmist affirms his loyalty to the Lord in contrast to the godless. The protestation of innocence is not to be understood as an expression of pride but rather as an appeal to God's fatherly heart: "I have not forgotten your law" (v.153), "I have not turned from your statutes" (v.157), and "see how I love your precepts" (v.159). The godless haunt him. They flaunt the commandments of the Lord: "for they do not seek out your decrees" (v.155); "for they do not obey your word" (v.158). More than that! As he looks at them, he again affirms his innocence in that he has purposefully avoided their influence (cf. 1:1). They are "the faithless"; that is, they are people who have broken the covenant relationship and whose words and acts are unreliable (cf. 25:3; Isa 48:8; Jer 5:11; Mal 2:10–11). That is what the psalmist means when he says that he has looked on the "faithless with loathing" (v.158; cf. 139:21).

The psalmist's protestation of innocence, the reminder of his affliction, and the mention of the perfidy of the wicked are to move God to action. There is the deep cognizance that only the Lord can "deliver" (v.153) and "redeem" (v.154). Therefore he hands over his case to him, praying for the Lord to "defend my cause." The verb "defend" (*rîḇāh*) as well as the noun "cause" (*rîḇ*) represent a technical legal jargon (35:1; 43:1; 74:22), often used by the prophets as God's covenant prosecutors (cf. Hos 4:1). The Lord alone can vindicate (cf. 43:1). The very nature of the psalmist's existence is in jeopardy. Therefore he repeatedly prays that the Lord will preserve his full enjoyment of covenant life (vv.154, 156, 159; cf. vv.25, 37, 40, 50, 88, 93, 107, 149).

The ground for the redemption is the covenant relationship. Renewal of life is God's gracious "promise" (v.154). It is to this effect that he reminds the Lord of his "compassion" (*raḥᵃmîm*, v.156; cf. 69:16; 103:13; 106:45; Neh 9:19, 27, 31). His "love" (*ḥeseḏ*, v.159; cf. v.88) is a "just" ("according to your laws" or "according to your justice," v.156; cf. v.149) response to his servant. "Many" (*rabbîm*) are the adversaries (v.157), but God's "compassion" is also "great" (*rabbîm*, v.156).

The strophe concludes on an asseveration of God's fidelity in his word. The expression "all your words" (v.160) is an idiomatic rendering of the MT (lit., "the head of your word"), which means "from the beginning God's word is true ['ᵉ*meṯ*, 'faithful']," even as his "laws" (*mišpāṭ*, the MT is sing. but pl. in a number of MSS, the LXX, Syr., Targ.) are forever "righteous" (*ṣeḏeq;* cf. vv.7, 62, 164). The fidelity and righteousness of his word sustain the psalmist in believing that the Lord will vindicate him. He rests his case with the Lord (cf. v.154).

XXI. The Sin and Shin Strophe

119:161–68

ש Sin and Shin

161 Rulers persecute me without cause,
but my heart trembles at your word.

162 I rejoice in your promise
like one who finds great spoil.
163 I hate and abhor falsehood
but I love your law.
164 Seven times a day I praise you
for your righteous laws.
165 Great peace have they who love your law,
and nothing can make them stumble.
166 I wait for your salvation, O LORD,
and I follow your commands.
167 I obey your statutes,
for I love them greatly.
168 I obey your precepts and your statutes,
for all my ways are known to you.

161–63 The joy, devotion, and benefits of a godly life radiate through this strophe. The context of adversity is unchanged, as the "rulers" (v.161; cf. v.23) of the people continually "persecute" (cf. vv.150, 157) "without cause" (cf. 35:7, 19; 69:5; 109:3; Prov 1:11). But instead of anger the psalmist rejoices in the "promise" of the Lord. He is like a warrior returning from battle with "great spoil" (v.162; cf. vv.14, 72, 111; Isa 9:3). His joy does not lie primarily in the immediate rewards but in the heartfelt love for God's instruction ("law," *tôrāh,* v.163; cf. 1:2) and hatred of evil.

164–65 The psalmist praises (*h-l-l,* as in "Hallelujah") the Lord many times a day (symbolized by the number seven) for his "righteous laws" (v.164; cf. v.7). The godly magnify God's name because they know that in his righteousness he will vindicate them. Therefore they have "peace" (*šālôm,* "shalom"). Though surrounded by adversity, they are confident of God's loving care and of his promise that they will not "stumble" (v.165; cf. Prov 4:12; 1 John 2:10).

166–68 In anticipation of that great day of "salvation" (*yᵉšûʿāh*), the psalmist gives himself to hopeful waiting (cf. Gen 49:18) and to the practice of godliness (v.166). Obedience to God's revelation proceeds from a heart committed to the Lord and his word. The psalmist keeps God's laws out of "love" (v.167; cf. vv.47, 119), for God discerns all his activities, emotions, hopes, and fears (v.168; cf. 38:9; Heb 4:13).

XXII. The Taw Strophe

119:169–76

ת Taw

169 May my cry come before you, O LORD;
give me understanding according to your word.
170 May my supplication come before you;
deliver me according to your promise.
171 May my lips overflow with praise,
for you teach me your decrees.
172 May my tongue sing of your word,
for all your commands are righteous.
173 May your hand be ready to help me,
for I have chosen your precepts.
174 I long for your salvation, O LORD,
and your law is my delight.

175 Let me live that I may praise you,
and may your laws sustain me.
176 I have strayed like a lost sheep.
Seek your servant,
for I have not forgotten your commands.

The last strophe of this lengthy psalm contains a prayer for the Lord's salvation. The issues have not been resolved, but the design of the psalm is such that it raises the spirit of expectation in those who love God's word. The psalmist prays for deliverance and grace so that he may sing the praise of his loving and faithful covenant God.

169–72 The psalmist comes before the Lord with a broken spirit, as he offers his prayer to the Lord (v.169). The verb *q-r-b* in the Hiphil is a technical term for the act of presenting an offering (NIV, "may come"; lit., "may . . . come near"). He has nothing left to present but a "cry" (*rinnāh;* cf. 1 Kings 8:28) and "supplication" (*t*ᵉ*ḥinnāh,* related to the word *ḥen,* "favor"; cf. 86:6) for God's mercy (vv.169–70). In this relationship of total dependency, he appeals for understanding (v.169) and deliverance (v.170). He needs "understanding" to know God's word and to discern how he may best respond to the adversities with hope in the promises. He also needs the experience of authentic faith, as he asks, "Deliver me" (v.170; cf. 120:2: "save me," *n-ṣ-l*). He trusts in the "promise" of the Lord, but faith in the promise is nurtured by concrete tokens of God's goodness. In anticipation of that moment of redemption, he contemplates on the joyful expressions of thanksgiving (vv.171–72). Then he will bubble forth ("overflow"; cf. 19:2; 145:7) with "praise" (*t*ᵉ*hillāh,* from *h-l-l*) and will respond in song to God's fulfilled "word" of promise (*'imrāh,* v.172, usually translated as "promise"; cf. v.170). The fulfillment of the "promise" testifies that God and his "commands" are "righteous" (vv.172; cf. v.7), when he triumphs in establishing justice.

173–75 Verses 173–75 repeat these motifs: prayer, a commitment to God's word ("precepts," "law," and "laws"), and an anticipation to praise the Lord for his redemption. God's "hand" (v.173) is a metaphor for his powerful deliverance (cf. Deut 32:36), for which the psalmist "longs" (v.174; cf. vv.77, 81), because God's deliverance preserves life (v.175; cf. v.159). Then he will also "praise" (*h-l-l,* v.175) his Redeemer.

176 The last note of the psalm is a cry from a broken spirit rather than a confession of apostasy. The psalmist feels helpless, like a "lost sheep" (cf. Jer 50:6; Ezek 34:4–6, 16) and cries to his Good Shepherd to "seek" (*b-q-š*) him (cf. Luke 15:4–7). The psalmist's lostness is a result of the adversities he has so frequently mentioned and not because of his neglect of God or his word.

Appendix: Yahweh Is My Redeemer

Divine deliverance is an expression of God's kingship and particularly of his perfections: strength, righteousness, and justice. In lament, confession, and adversity, the psalmists call on Yahweh to reach down from on high and rescue the needy.

Yahweh, the Divine Warrior, is the Redeemer-King (33:16). He rules for the sake of bringing in the fullness of his blessing and protection to his children. Yahweh will vindicate his own and avenge the enemy. Again and again the psalmist leads the godly to affirm their confidence and trust in the Lord as the sole Deliverer: "He fulfills the desires of those who fear him; / he hears their cry and saves [*y-š-'*] them" (145:19). His own people are likened to the poor and the orphans, people without legal status in society: "He will take pity on the weak and the needy / and save [*y-š-'*] the needy from death" (72:13). The Great King cannot tolerate any imbalance in his world, especially when it involves his own children (72:14). The world is God's, and he will bring his righteousness into a perverse world:

> Save [*y-s-'*] me, O God, by your name;
> vindicate me by your might.
> . . . .
> But I call to God,
> and the Lord saves [*y-š-'*] me.
> Evening, morning and noon
> I cry out in distress,
> and he hears my voice.
> He ransoms [*p-d-h*] me unharmed
> from the battle waged against me,
> even though many oppose me.
> God, who is enthroned forever,
> will hear them and afflict them— *Selah*
> men who never change their ways
> and have no fear of God.
> (54:1; 55:16–19; cf. 57:3)

The nature of God is the ground for hope in deliverance. He is compassionate and gracious and, hence, concerned for his children:

> But you, O Lord, are a compassionate and gracious God,
> slow to anger, abounding in love and faithfulness.
> Turn to me and have mercy on me;
> grant your strength to your servant
> and save [*y-š-'*] the son of your maidservant.
> Give me a sign of your goodness,
> that my enemies may see it and be put to shame,
> for you, O LORD, have helped me and comforted me.
> (86:15–17)

The acts of deliverance form the story of redemption. The story is a part of a long history of redemption, stretching back to the Exodus event, and is relived by each successive generation, which also adds to that story by telling of the mighty acts of God's victory. The history of redemption inspires God's people to praise, proclaim, and hope (71:14–18).

The acts of deliverance apply the goodness and blessing of Yahweh to his people. The redeemed of the Lord experience no want, because their Great King satisfies them completely—materially and spiritually. He establishes his victorious kingship so that they may witness to his sovereignty, lordship, and love for his people (106:47–48).

Yahweh's deliverance is promised to the godly, those whose ways align with his. Since he is righteous and just, he delivers those who concern themselves for his standards of justice and righteousness. The Lord favors his beloved with his loving protection as a form of his redemption:

Show the wonder of your great love [*ḥesed*],
you who save [*y-š-'*] by your right hand
those who take refuge in you from their foes.
Keep me as the apple of your eye;
hide me in the shadow of your wings.
(17:7–8; cf. 20:6)

Yahweh's deliverance extends all the benefits of his kingship to his people. He is their Shepherd-King, who will richly bless them with all good things (28:9; 31:16).

The righteousness of God manifests itself in acts of deliverance. His acts of deliverance are righteous because they establish God's righteous rule on earth. The psalmist exclaims, "Your righteousness [*ṣ-d-q*] reaches to the skies, O God, / you who have done great things. / Who, O God, is like you?" (71:19) The "righteousness" of God pertains to his dynamic relationship with his creation in his acts of redemption:

Sing to the Lord a new song,
for he has done marvelous things;
his right hand and his holy arm
have worked salvation [*y-š-'*] for him.
The Lord has made his salvation [*yešû'āh*] known
and revealed his righteousness [*ṣ-d-q*] to the nations.
He has remembered his love
and his faithfulness to the house of Israel;
all the ends of the earth have seen
the salvation [*yešû'āh*] of our God.
(98:1–3)

Yahweh will bring in the victory. In the act of deliverance he permits the godly to share in the joys of victory (60:11–12). In hope of divine justice, the godly hope in Yahweh alone (69:1–3; cf. vv.13–18). Yahweh is the hope of all who long for his redemption. As long as evil is in this world, the godly will be characterized by hope and longing for God (71:4–5). Every day is the day of the Lord's salvation, as the children of God await his deliverance (118:24–25).

The vocabulary in the Psalms is unusually rich with words for deliverance. This is not surprising because in between the poles of prayer and praise is the cry for deliverance. The roots for "deliverance" are *ḥ-l-ṣ*, *y-š-'*, *m-l-ṭ*, *n-ṣ-l/p-ṣ-h*, *p-d-h/g-'-l*, and *p-l-ṭ*. For example, Psalm 71:2–4 has three synonyms, two of which recur twice:

Rescue [*n-ṣ-l*] me and deliver [*p-l-ṭ*] me in your righteousness;
turn your ear to me and save [*y-š-'*] me.
Be my rock of refuge,
to which I can always go;
give the command to save me [*y-š-'*],
for you are my rock and my fortress.
Deliver [*p-l-ṭ*] me, O my God, from the hand of the wicked,
from the grasp of evil and cruel men.

1. *ḥ-l-ṣ*. This word occurs primarily in poetic materials (Job, Proverbs, and Psalms). The Phoenicians called Baal *yḥlṣb'l* ("Baal rescues"). In contrast Israel confessed that Yahweh delivers, as he protects his needy people. So the psalmist encourages us to look in faith at the angel of Yahweh, surrounding his people and protecting them, being prepared to deliver them at any time: "The angel of the LORD encamps around those who fear him, / and he delivers [*ḥ-l-ṣ*] them" (34:7).

The psalmist further affirms several times that Yahweh delivers all who find themselves in trouble (50:15; 81:7; 91:15).

2. *y-š-ʿ*. The root and the derivative nouns *yēšaʿ*, *y^{e}šûʿāh*, *t^{e}šûʿāh*, and *môšāʿāh* form the common stock of terms for deliverance in the Psalms. The original meaning of "be broad" or "be spacious" and the derived meaning "to care for richly" (KB^{3}, 2:427) may still manifest itself in the use of *r-ḥ-b* ("enlarge") as a synonym of *y-š-ʿ*, as in

You give me your shield of victory [*yēšaʿ*],
and your right hand sustains me;
you stoop down to make me great.
You broaden [*r-ḥ-b*] the path beneath me,
so that my ankles do not turn.
(18:35–36)

The "broad" place is in contrast to the "distress" (*ṣar*, lit., "narrow"); compare 4:1:

Answer me when I call to you,
O my righteous God.
Give me relief [*r-ḥ-b*] from my distress [*ṣar*];
be merciful to me and hear my prayer.

It is, therefore, no surprise that God's act of deliverance affects one's whole being and that it is attended by his rich blessings; cf. "From the Lord comes deliverance [*y^{e}šûʿāh*]. / May your blessing be on your people" (3:8).

3. *m-l-ṭ*. This term turns up in contexts of deep despair. The Lord can redeem his beloved from an impossible situation, as in Psalm 124:7–8:

We have escaped [*m-l-ṭ*] like a bird
out of the fowler's snare;
the snare has been broken,
and we have escaped [*m-l-ṭ*].
Our help is in the name of the Lord,
the Maker of heaven and earth.
(cf. 89:49; 107:20; 116:3–4)

Confidence in Yahweh's ability to deliver is a prerequisite. Often the psalms of lament contain a verse or two in which the psalmist confides his trust in the Lord and in his ability to help.

4. *n-ṣ-l*. This word has the basic significance of extrication: "drawing" or "pulling" out. For example, Psalm 144 has two occurrences of the root with the prepositional phrase beginning with "from":

Reach down your hand from on high;
deliver [*p-ṣ-h*] me and rescue [*n-ṣ-l*] me
from the mighty waters,
from the hands of foreigners
. . . .
Deliver [*p-ṣ-h*] me and rescue [*n-ṣ-l*] me
from the hands of foreigners
whose mouths are full of lies,
whose right hands are deceitful.
(vv.7, 11; emphases mine)

In this context we also find the root *p-ṣ-h* ("open up"). It only occurs in Psalm 144 (vv.7, 10, 11) with the meaning "deliver": "to the One who gives victory to kings, / who delivers [*p-ṣ-h*] his servant David from the deadly sword" (144:10).

5. *p-d-h* and *g-'-l*. Both terms have the meaning "ransom" or "payment." Ownership of property or people could be transferred for an agreed upon price. Instead of exacting payment for redemption, Yahweh delivers freely: "The LORD redeems [*p-d-h*] his servants; / no one will be condemned who takes refuge in him" (34:22). The reason lies in the value he places on all who love him. He identifies himself with them and with their distresses. He promises to freely deliver his servants from bondage to others: "He will rescue [*g-'-l*] them from oppression and violence, / for precious is their blood in his sight" (72:14). When they are falsely accused, he is their only defense: "Defend my cause and redeem [*g-'-l*] me; / preserve my life according to your promise" (119:154).

6. *p-l-ṭ*. This term is found frequently in the Psalms in the prayers for Yahweh's deliverance (88:2; 144:2) and in affirmations of trust (22:4, 8). It is synonymous with "help" (*'-z-r*; 37:40; 40:17; 70:5). For example, in 37:40 the verb is found twice and appears together with "help" (*'-z-r*): "The Lord helps them and delivers [*p-l-ṭ*] them; / he delivers [*p-l-ṭ*] them from the wicked and saves them, / because they take refuge in him." Instead of "deliver," *p-l-ṭ* could better be rendered as "to bring to safety."

Conclusion

The words "save," "salvation," "Savior," "redeem," "redemption," and "Redeemer" in the Psalms are pregnant with meaning. Regrettably, the phrase "I have been saved" has become identical to "I have become a Christian." The Hebraic concept is much richer than our modern usage. It is not richer than the NT, because there we come face to face with our great Redeemer, Jesus Christ. However, we have robbed the NT of its rich OT background. From the usage of "deliver" and "deliverance," we have learned that Yahweh will completely redeem his people from all adversity, remove their troubles and tears, vindicate them, honor them, and bestow a new quality of life on his beloved. This involves forgiveness of sin, reconciliation, covenant fellowship, divine compassion in the present, but also the expectation of God's holistic care for his people (in body and spirit, individuals and community, Jews and Gentiles, present and future). The Lord alone is the Savior, and no one or nothing else can give meaning to life. He is the All-Sufficient One!

Yahweh requires faith, commitment, and loyalty from his children. Faith is radical, as it calls for an absolute trust in him, even if the whole world were to be burning: "The Lord is my strength and my song; / he has become my salvation" (118:14). Moreover, hope undergirds the prayers of the saints and is the reason for hopeful praise, because the godly affirm in the Psalms that Yahweh is faithful to his promises (91:14–16; cf. 107:6–9).

Praise is that act of proclamation in which the godly articulate in song and word what God has done, does, and will do. Throughout the Psalms the people of God celebrate his fidelity to the covenant. Salvation comprises all the acts of God, the resurrection and ascension of our Lord Jesus Christ, and the establishment of God's kingdom. While awaiting his kingdom, we praise our Lord for sharing his salvation with us. Further, we must witness to his ability to deliver by proclaiming to all nations the good news of the history of redemption, God's kingdom, and the hope of "righteousness":

> that your *ways* may be known on earth,
> your *salvation* among all nations.
>
> (67:2)

> My mouth will tell of your *righteousness*,
> of your *salvation* all day long,
> though I know not its measure.
>
> (71:15)

But you, O God, are *my king* from of old;
you *bring salvation upon the earth.*

(74:12)

Sing to the Lord a new song,
for he has done marvelous things;
his right hand and his holy arm
have worked *salvation* for him.
The LORD has made his *salvation* known
and revealed his *righteousness* to the nations.
He has remembered his love
and his faithfulness to the house of Israel;
all the ends of the earth have seen
the *salvation* of our God.

(98:1–3; emphases mine)

Redemption is never complete until the people of God enjoy the fullness of God's love without disgrace, adversity, or causes for despair: "O Israel, put your hope in the LORD, / for with the LORD is unfailing love / and with him is full redemption" (130:7).

Texts: 3:2, 8; 7:1–2, 10; 17:7, 13–15; 18:2–3, 17, 19, 27, 41, 43, 48; 20:6, 9; 22:1, 4–5, 8, 21; 31:1–2, 15–16; 33:16–17, 19; 34:4–7, 17–19; 35:3, 9–10; 37:39–40; 40:10, 13, 16–17; 50:15, 22–23; 51:12, 14; 62:1–2, 6–7; 69:13–14, 18, 27, 29, 35; 70:1, 4–5; 71:2–3, 11, 15; 72:4, 12–14; 80:2–3, 7, 19; 85:7, 9; 86:2, 13, 16; 91:3, 14–16; 98:1–3; 106:4, 8, 10, 21, 43; 107:6, 13, 19–20; 109:21, 26, 31; 116:4, 6, 8, 13; 118:14, 21, 25; 119:41, 81, 117, 123, 146, 153, 166, 170, 174; 144:2, 7, 10–11.

Related Topics: See the appendixes to Pss 5 (Yahweh Is King); 7 (The Name of Yahweh); 25 (The Perfections of Yahweh); 46 (Zion Theology); 98 (Yahweh Is the Divine Warrior); 132 (The Ark of the Covenant and the Temple: Symbols of Yahweh's Presence and Rule); 140 (The Poor and Oppressed).

Bibliography: David Hill, *Greek Words and Hebrew Meanings* (London: Cambridge, 1967); Leon Morris, "The Idea of Redemption in the Old Testament," *Reformed Theological Review* 11 (1952): 94–102; Hans Heinrich Schmid, *Gerechtigkeit als Weltordnung. Hintergrund und Geschichte des alttestamentlichen Gerechtigkeitsbegriffes* (Tübingen: Mohr, 1968); id., "Creation, Righteousness, and Salvation: 'Creation Theology' as a Broad Horizon of Biblical Theology," in *Creation in the Old Testament,* ed. Bernard W. Anderson (Philadelphia: Fortress, 1984), pp. 102–17; Werner Schmidt, *Königtum Gottes in Ugarit und Israel. Zur Herkunft und Königsprädikation Jahwes* (Berlin: Töpelmann, 1961); Gary V. Smith, "The Concept of God / The Gods as King in the Ancient Near East and the Bible," *Trinity Journal* 3 (1982): 18–38; W.A. VanGemeren, "King, Kingship," in Elwell, BEB, 2:1264–69; R. Yaron, "A Document of Redemption From Ugarit," VetTest 10 (1960): 83–90.

THAT, 1:383–94, 785–90; 2:96–99, 389–406, 420–27; TDOT, 2:350–55; 3:1035–59; 4:436–41; TWOT, 1:144–45, 292, 414–16, 507; 2:594, 716–17, 724–25.

Psalm 120: Yahweh, I, and They

Psalms 120–134 form a collection known as the "Songs of Ascents," which in turn is a major part of the Great Hallel psalms (120–36). The meaning of the designation "song of ascents" is not clear, whether "Pilgrim Songs," "Song of Degrees," or

"Gradual Psalms." The Mishnah links the collection of fifteen songs with the fifteen steps of the temple where the Levites sang these songs of ascents (*Middoth* 2.5). It is more likely that the songs were sung in the three annual festival processions, as the pilgrims "ascended" (*ʿ-l-h*) to Jerusalem (cf. Exod 23:14–17; Deut 16:16), hence the designation "songs of ascents" (*maʿalôṯ*).

The psalms need not have been composed originally for this purpose. Clearly some reflect other original uses, but they became canonically significant in a new liturgical adaptation, when they were incorporated together in a small collection of fifteen hymns. The Mishnah teaches that in the period of the second temple they were incorporated into the temple liturgy. Richard Press held that they were composed during the Exile ("Der zeitgeschichtliche Hintergrund der Wallfahrtspsalmen," *Theologische Zeitschrift* 14 [1958]: 401–15). Hans Seidel goes beyond the evidence by concluding that Psalms 120–134 represent the Levitical preaching in the early period of the second temple (514–400 B.C.; see "Wallfahrtslieder," in *Das lebendige Wort. Festgabe für Gottfried Voigt*, edd. Hans Seidel and Karl-Heinrich Bieritz [Berlin: Evangelische Verlagsanstallt, 1982], pp. 26–40). On the history of interpretation of the phrase "Song of Ascents," see Cuthbert C. Keet, *A Study of the Psalms of Ascents. A Critical and Exegetical Commentary Upon Psalms CXX to CXXXIV* (Greenwood: Attic, 1969). The most comprehensive study is that of Klaus Seybold, *Die Wallfahrtspsalmen. Studien zur Entstehungsgeschichte von Psalm 120–134* (Neukirchen-Vluyn: Neukirchener Verlag, 1978).

Depending on the reading of *qārā'ṯî* ("I call" or "I called," v.1), scholars are divided in their opinion on the genre of this psalm: *individual lament* (so RSV) or *individual thanksgiving hymn* (Kraus, *Psalmen*, 2:830–31; A.A. Anderson, 2:848). The crux is the rendering of v.1 as a present ("I call") or as a past (Allen: "I called—and he has answered me," p. 145). Allen views the psalm as an individual lament, which anticipates thanksgiving, based on God's response (pp. 147–48; cf. 6:1–10). In our exposition we shall follow this conclusion.

The structure of the psalm is difficult because the psalm has "a disjointed ring on first reading" (Allen, p. 148). We suggest an expository outline:

A. Assurance of Answered Prayer (v.1)
  B. Prayer for Help (vv.2–4)
  B′. Expression of Desperation (v.5)
A′. Longing for Peace (vv.6–7)

I. Assurance of Answered Prayer

120:1

A song of ascents.

1 I call on the LORD in my distress,
and he answers me.

1 The language resembles other individual lament psalms (cf. 3:4; 18:6; 22:21; 66:14; 118:21). The position of "on the LORD" is emphatic in the MT and thus expresses the sole dependence on God in the hour of distress. The "distress" is not specified until vv.2–4. It is more natural to understand v.1 as having taken place in the past: "I called on the LORD in my distress, / and he answered me." The psalmist has already received assurance that the Lord will deal with his problem. The source of the assurance is not given, whether it was a priestly or prophetic oracle. Most likely it is the word of assurance that God would act (see 130:5). In hope he waits now for the Lord to fulfill his promises.

Notes

For a brief discussion of the technical words and phrases in the superscription, see the Introduction to the Psalms and also to Psalm 120. The crux is the meaning of the word הַמַּעֲלוֹת (*hamma'ᵃlôṯ*, "ascents"). Evidence from 11QPs[a] Zion, 14, suggests an alternate reading that Dahood renders as "Song of Extolments" (*Psalms*, 3:195), but in his translation he retains the traditional "A song of ascents."

1 Meir Weiss concludes that v.1b refers to a past act of deliverance and that the psalm should be interpreted as a lament (*The Bible From Within. The Method of Total Interpretation* [Jerusalem: Magnes, 1984], pp. 275–77).

II. Prayer for Help

120:2–4

2 Save me, O LORD, from lying lips
and from deceitful tongues.

3 What will he do to you,
and what more besides, O deceitful tongue?
4 He will punish you with a warrior's sharp arrows,
with burning coals of the broom tree.

2–4 The psalmist details his present adversity. Though he has been assured that the Lord will respond favorably, he still suffers. He prays for deliverance ("save," *n-ṣ-l*) from false accusations and treachery (v.2). He prays that the Lord's word of judgment may bring him relief. The formula "What will he do to you, and what more" (v.3) is a kind of an oath formula (1 Sam 3:17; 2 Sam 3:35; 19:13; 1 Kings 2:23; cf. Weiser, p. 742). As the wicked have spoken deceptively, the psalmist, calling on God to judge them, prays that God will bring on them the fulfillment of their own words.

The "deceitful" tongue is compared to a bow whose arrows are the words (cf. 57:4; 64:3; Prov 25:18; Jer 9:3, 8) and to a fire (Prov 16:27; James 3:6). By the law of lex talionis, the adversaries must receive God's judgment, likened to a "warrior's sharp arrows" and to "burning coals" (v.4; cf. 11:6; 140:10). The "burning coals" were charcoal produced from the "broom tree," whose charcoal was the finest. The tree grows in the desert and may grow twelve feet high (ZPEB, 1:658). The wicked, who had intended to set up their own order based on lying and deception, must be uprooted for the sake of God's honor.

III. Expression of Desperation

120:5

5 Woe to me that I dwell in Meshech,
that I live among the tents of Kedar!

5 The psalmist laments his present condition, as he still dwells as a stranger "in Meshech," "among the tents of Kedar." Meshech is located in Asia Minor by the Black Sea (cf. Gen 10:2; Ezek 38:2). Kedar denotes the Arab tribesmen who lived in the Arabian Desert (cf. Isa 21:16–17; Jer 2:10; 49:28; Ezek 27:21). But how can the psalmist live in two very separate geographical regions at the same time? Attempts at textual changes are many (Allen, p. 146) but unnecessary. I agree with Allen that "the most common interpretation is to judge the ethnic references to be simply metaphorical: the psalmist's enemies are no better than hostile barbarians" (p. 146).

It is unclear whether the psalmist lived in the Diaspora (A.A. Anderson, 2:850) or in Israel (Allen, p. 146; Weiser, p. 743). It is not necessary to infer from the metaphorical references to these foreign regions that the psalmist was actually living in the Diaspora. He lived among a people that were acting like pagans. Dahood may well be right in explaining the verse as conditional: "Even were he to reside as far away as Meshech or Kedar, the psalmist would still feel too close to the hater of peace" (see his translation of v.5: "Woe to me, whether I sojourn near Meshech, / or dwell near the tents of Kedar!" [3:194, 197]).

The verbs "dwell" (*gartî*, "sojourn") and "live" (*šāḵantî*, "tabernacle," "dwell") are significantly chosen. Even though the psalmist may have enjoyed a permanent residence, he felt as if he was no more than a sojourner among his contemporaries. He did not feel at home among an ungodly people. Hence he admits "woe to me" as an expression of his personal misery: "How wretched I have been" (Allen, p. 145).

IV. Longing for Peace

120:6–7

> 6 Too long have I lived
> among those who hate peace.
> 7 I am a man of peace;
> but when I speak, they are for war.

6 The psalmist reminds the Lord that he has suffered long enough in his present situation (v.6). He has "lived" (*šāḵᵉnāh*, fem. form, with "soul" as the subject; lit., "my soul has lived long enough") among apostates who "hate peace." One must assume here that the metaphors of "arrows" and "fire" (see v.4 above) portray the bellicose nature of his adversaries. They malign, slander, and make every aspect of life difficult for the godly. The psalmist is tired of his affliction.

7 The psalmist prays that the Lord may establish peace. The clause "I am a man of peace" translates a nominal phrase: "I peace." In his whole being the psalmist longs for the establishment of peace (cf. 109:4; 119:165; Matt 5:45; Rom 12:18). It may well be that the psalmist is a Davidic king, concerned with a peaceful administration of God's kingdom on earth. The godly have nothing in common with the wicked. The godly speak words of peace, whereas the ungodly sow discord and adversity (cf. Gal 5:19–21; James 3:14–15). Only the Lord can intervene in this situation.

Psalm 121: Yahweh Is My Guardian

Psalm 121 is one of the fifteen "Songs of Ascents" (120–134; for a description, see Ps 120). The psalmist develops an argument, beginning with God the Creator (vv.1–2) and Israel's confession of Yahweh (vv.3–4) and ending with a personal trust in his protection (see W.S. Prinsloo, "Psalm 121: 'n Triomflied van Vertroue," *Nederduits Gereformeerde Teologiese Tydskrif* 21 [1980]: 162–68). The movement of the psalm leads to an encouragement of the reader (so also H.W.M. van Grol, "De Exegeet als Restaurateur en Interpreet. Een Verhandling over de bijbelse Poëtica met Ps. 121 als Exempel," *Bijdragen: Tijdschrift voor Filosofie en Theologie* 44 [1983]: 350–65). The literary features are inclusion ("come," "coming," vv.1, 8) and extensive repetitions ("help," vv.1–2), "watches" (vv.3–4), and "will keep" = "will watch" (vv.7–8).

From the interchange of the first ("I," "my," v.1) and the second person singular ("you," "your," vv.3–8), it would seem that the psalmist uses some form of dialogue; but it is unclear whether the dialogue is between two parties or between the godly man and his inner self, as in Psalms 42 and 43. Because of the lack of decisive criteria and because of the ambiguity of the life situation, we shall treat the psalm as a monologue. The structure reflects a "stairlike" parallelism, divided into four strophes:

A. Yahweh Is the Creator (vv.1–2)
B. Yahweh Is the Guardian of Israel (vv.3–4)
C. Yahweh Is "Your" Guardian (vv.5–6)
D. Blessing (vv.7–8)

I. Yahweh Is the Creator

121:1–2

A song of ascents.

1 I lift up my eyes to the hills—
where does my help come from?
2 My help comes from the LORD,
the Maker of heaven and earth.

1–2 The psalmist, in a situation known only to him, is looking with great anxiety or longing (cf. 123:1) to the hills. He may have looked with anxiety if he expected robbers to be hiding in the hills. The hills provided cover for mobs and vagabonds who caused great harm to travelers. He may also have looked with great anticipation to the hills if he were on a pilgrimage to Jerusalem. Hidden among the hills was the Holy City, Jerusalem (125:2). Both thoughts may well have occupied the ancient traveler: anxiety and anticipation.

A question enters the psalmist's mind: "Where does my help come from?" (v.1). The "help" (*'ēzer*) with which he is concerned pertains to protection, guidance, and blessing (vv.3–8). He desires to prosper in his pilgrimage as well as in life so that he may enjoy a sense of harmony in all his endeavors.

As soon as the question (v.1b) floods his soul, the psalmist comforts himself with the thought that Yahweh, the covenant God, has committed himself to provide "help" to his own (v.2). In addition Yahweh is "the Maker of heaven and earth." This confession goes beyond the modern controversy of evolution and creationism. The creedal statement, also taken up in the Apostles' Creed, originally signified an apologetic statement on Yahweh's sovereignty over all realms: heaven and earth, thereby excluding any claims by pagan deities. Yahweh alone is God (cf. 115:4–7; 124:8; 134:3; 146:6; Jer 10:11)! The sole source of "help" comes from Yahweh, who, as Creator, has unlimited power.

Notes

For a brief discussion of the technical words and phrases in the superscription, see the Introduction.

1 The translation of מֵאַיִן (*mē'ayin*, "from where?" "where from") is the crux of the interpretation of v.1. If it is read as a direct question, it may suggest a negative emotive connotation (anxiety, so NIV). If it is read as a relative pronoun ("from where"), it has a positive emotive connotation (KJV). Allen posits a third alternative: an indirect question—"to see where my help is to come from" (pp. 150–51).

II. Yahweh, the Guardian of Israel, Is "Your" Guardian

121:3–6

3 He will not let your foot slip—
he who watches over you will not slumber;
4 indeed, he who watches over Israel
will neither slumber nor sleep.

5 The LORD watches over you—
the LORD is your shade at your right hand;
6 the sun will not harm you by day,
nor the moon by night.

3–6 The psalmist further develops the contents of the "help" of the Lord in an alternation of negative (two times *'al*, "not," v.3; two times *lō'*, "not"; NIV, "neither . . . nor," v.4; *lō'*, v.6, with ellipsis) and positive descriptions (vv.5, 7–8).

The psalmist reflects on the promises of God as he speaks to his own soul in the second person ("you," "your"). The ground for confidence lies in the further development of the doctrine of God: the guardian (*šômēr;* NIV, "he who watches") of Israel is the guardian (*šōmreḵā*, i.e., "your guardian"; NIV, "he who watches over you") of every believer (vv.3–5)! The repetition of "our guardian" is symmetric and stairlike, as it develops from the particular to the general and returns to the particular:

A. "he who watches over you" (v.3)
B. "he who watches over Israel" (v.4)
A'. "the LORD watches over you" (v.5)

Each of these phrases has the same participle (*šômēr*, "guardian," "watch") in common.

What does the doctrine of Yahweh's guardianship mean? He protects, guides, and blesses his own. He will not permit them to totter and stumble (v.3, "slip"; cf. 55:22; 66:9). He will be the "shade" (v.5; cf. 91:1; Num 14:9; Jer 48:45; Lam 4:20) of his own as he protects them from the dangers of the day and night, represented here by "the sun" and "the moon" (v.6). He protects them throughout the day, as he is at their "right hand" (cf. 16:8; 109:31). The intensity of his care is further amplified by the emphasis on his watchfulness, as he never sleeps nor slumbers (vv.3–4). Pagans permitted their gods to sleep, but the God of Israel is not like any god—he does not need to recreate, eat, or sleep. He is always there to "help." He is the "shepherd" of Israel (cf. Ps 23) who protects, guides, and blesses his own sheep. Regardless of the happenings in life, whether at work or at home, whether asleep or awake, the Lord is "there" to help and to protect. What a God!

III. Blessing

121:7–8

7The LORD will keep you from all harm—
he will watch over your life;
8the LORD will watch over your coming and going
both now and forevermore.

7–8 The change from the participial use of "guardian" or "watch" (*šômēr*) to the imperfect (*yišmōr*, three times, vv.7–8) marks the new emphasis from the present to the future. This is the proper conclusion of the stairlike parallelism, where the psalmist has built up the conviction that the Lord is present to deliver now and forevermore. This conclusion is such a comfort to the believer that he cannot but be assured of the Lord's beneficent care.

The Lord's care extends to all adversities, as he is sovereign over all affairs of life, especially the "life" (*nep̱eš*, lit., "soul") of his own child (cf. 1 Thess 5:23). Whatever he does—whether he arrives at Jerusalem, goes on a far journey, or returns home—the Lord will "watch" over his affairs (cf. Deut 28:6; 31:2; Josh 14:11; 1 Kings 3:7; Ps 139:2–3). The extent of his care is both "now and forevermore" (v.8; cf. 113:2; 115:18).

Psalm 122: May There Be Peace in Zion

This is one of the "Songs of Ascents" (120–134; for a discussion, see the introduction to Ps 120). The psalm is a Song of Zion by genre, though Westermann defines it as the only true "Song of Pilgrimage" (IDBSup., p. 708). The Songs of Zion (46; 48; 76; 84; 87; 132) have much in common with the royal psalms as they celebrate the glories associated with Jerusalem: temple and kingship. Unlike the royal psalms, the Songs of Zion proclaim the glories of Zion in universal and eschatological terms. Together with Psalm 84, this psalm expresses the joy in Zion, with what Allen calls "a pilgrim's warmth of religious emotion" (p. 157).

The significance of this psalm extends from the focus of Zion as the goal of the pilgrimage (vv.1–2) to the eschatological vision of Zion as the center of God's judgment and peace (vv.5–9). The worshipers are hereby continually encouraged to pray for the welfare of Jerusalem (see appendix to Ps 46: Zion Theology).

The structure of the psalm has been analyzed in terms of three and five strophes (Allen, p. 158). The hymn employs a "stairlike" parallelism ("Jerusalem," vv.2–3; "tribes," v.4; "thrones," v.5; "peace," vv.6–8) and an inclusionary motif ("house of the LORD," vv.1, 9). We suggest the following expository structure:

A. The Pilgrim's Joy (vv.1–2)
B. The Pilgrim's Praise (vv.3–5)
C. The Pilgrim's Prayer (vv.6–9)

I. The Pilgrim's Joy

122:1–2

A song of ascents. Of David.

1 I rejoiced with those who said to me,
"Let us go to the house of the LORD."
2 Our feet are standing
in your gates, O Jerusalem.

1–2 In his reflection of the joy of being or having been in Jerusalem, the psalmist mixes the perfect mood ("I rejoiced") with participles "in saying" (NIV, "those who said to me") and "are standing." The choice of verbs is significant, as the psalmist is reflecting on the many times that he has heard the call to go to the house of the Lord. Verse 1 may well be translated as "I rejoice whenever they say to me." At this point he is standing in Jerusalem and rejoicing—with the thousands of other pilgrims—that he has arrived at the goal of his pilgrimage. His feet are standing in Jerusalem!

The pilgrimages were held only three times in the year, during the great feasts of Passover, Firstfruits, and Booths. These feasts held a special redemptive-historical significance, as they commemorated God's goodness in the Exodus, the Conquest, and his continual care throughout the history of Israel (cf. Deut 16:16). As the psalmist looks at Jerusalem and stands within her gates (v.2), he rejoices. His rejoicing goes over into praise, his praise into hope, and his hope into a prayer for the prosperity of God's kingship on earth, blessing his people with his presence (vv.3–9).

Notes

For a brief discussion of the technical words and phrases in the superscription, see the Introduction.

1 Dahood (*Psalms,* 3:204) is correct in his grammatical analysis of נֵלֵךְ (*nēlēk̲,* "we shall go"). The verbal phrase is not a cohortative ("let us go," so NIV) but an imperfect and should be rendered "we will go."

II. The Pilgrim's Praise

122:3–5

3 Jerusalem is built like a city
that is closely compacted together.
4 That is where the tribes go up,
the tribes of the LORD,
to praise the name of the LORD
according to the statute given to Israel.
5 There the thrones for judgment stand,
the thrones of the house of David.

3 In praise of Jerusalem the psalmist looks at the throngs of worshipers who are contained within the city. The city is "closely compacted together" in comparison with the multitudes of pilgrims. Above the heads of the throngs, the walls and buildings of the city rise, giving the sense of buildings and walls being joined together.

4 The unity of the city reflected the unity of the tribes on these special occasions. The Israelite tribes came together for the purpose of praising the "the name of the LORD" (see appendix to Ps 7: The Name of Yahweh). It was an act of loyalty, as the Lord had commanded them to present themselves before him ("statute"; cf. Exod 23:14–17; Deut 16:16–17) during the annual feasts in Jerusalem at the central shrine (cf. Deut 12:5–6; Ps 81:3–5).

5 Jerusalem was not only the religious center, symbolized by the "house of the LORD" (vv.1, 9), but also the political center, symbolized by "the thrones for judgment." The kings of Judah ruled by divine right. They upheld God's kingship to the extent that they were faithful in dispensing justice (for "justice" as a characteristic of the messianic era, see Isa 9:7; 11:3–5).

III. The Pilgrim's Prayer

122:6–9

6 Pray for the peace of Jerusalem:
"May those who love you be secure.
7 May there be peace within your walls
and security within your citadels."
8 For the sake of my brothers and friends,
I will say, "Peace be within you."
9 For the sake of the house of the LORD our God,
I will seek your prosperity.

6–9 The thought of the thrones and the justice associated with the rule of David suggests another association. Justice and peace belong together, as two expressions of the Davidic rule (Isa 9:7). Whether the present era was marked by adversity or not, the psalmist longs for "the peace of Jerusalem" (v.6). The city whose name has a popular etymology of "city of peace" did not always experience peace; nor did she provide "security" (v.7) to her population. The psalmist thus prays that Jerusalem ("the city of peace," cf. Heb 7:2) may truly be a city of peace, providing security and "prosperity" (v.9; lit., "good"; cf. 23:6; Neh 2:10; Jer 23:6) to all who love her. In this prayer Jerusalem is transformed into an ideal, an eschatological expression. The present situation may have reflected a "token" of the reality that God had planned for his people. The psalmist prays that promise may become fulfillment and that token may become reality.

"Peace" (*šālôm*), "security" (*šalwāh*, v.7), and "prosperity" (*ṭôḇ*, v.9) will benefit all the people of God, as it was in the days of David. It is a prayer for "those who love" Jerusalem (v.6), i.e., for "my brothers and my friends" (v.8). In his reflective prayer on the peace of Jerusalem, the psalmist mentions her "walls" and "citadels" (v.7; cf. 48:13), as well as "the house of the LORD" (v.9). In these references he combines the civil, political, and religious significance of Jerusalem. Thus the present experience of joy in going up to "the house of the LORD," the manner in which Jerusalem is "closely compacted together," the mixing together of all of the tribes, and the establishment of "the thrones for judgment" in Jerusalem find their symmetry in the prayer for Jerusalem's peace.

Notes

The exegesis and linkage with Luke 19:41–44 and Rev 20:11–15; 21:11–21 provided by L. Alonso Schökel and A. Strus, "Salmo 122: Canto al Nombre de Jerusalém," *Biblica* 61 (1980): 234–50, is helpful. They relate this psalm to Christ's entry into Jerusalem (Luke 19:41–44) and the apostolic teaching on the glory of the New Jerusalem (Rev 21:11–21) for all whose names are in the Book of Life (20:11–15).

Appendix: The Praise of Yahweh

The praise of God sets the Psalms apart from other books. The Psalms express gratitude for God's acts of condescension to the needs of his people, while hoping in his ultimate act of deliverance. Individual and corporate praise focuses on his mighty acts of creation, on God's involvement in the history of redemption, and on the fulfillment of God's promises.

The godly know in whom they put their trust. Even in despair they see the light coming through because they have already experienced something of his wonder. Hence they are strongly motivated in joyfully submitting themselves to him who is King over all the nations, exalted, holy, and glorious.

The Hebrew roots for praise are many: *'-m-r* ("say"), *b-r-k* ("bless" or "extol"), *b-ś-r* ("proclaim"), *g-y-l* ("rejoice"), *h-l-l* ("praise" and related forms), *z-m-r* ("bring praise"), *y-d-h* ("praise"), *n-g-d* ("proclaim"), *š-y-r* ("sing" and related forms), *s-p-r* ("tell"), *'-l-z* ("leap for joy"), *'-l-ṣ* ("rejoice"), *r-n-n* ("sing for joy"), *r-w-'* ("shout for joy"), *św/y-ś* ("exult"), *d-b-r* ("speak"), *ś-m-ḥ* ("be glad"). Some times three (or more) synonyms occur in the same context:

> I will praise [*y-d-h*] you, O LORD, with all my heart;
>   I will tell of all your wonders.
> I will be glad [*ś-m-h*] and rejoice [*'-l-ṣ*] in you;
>   I will sing praise [*z-m-r*] to your name, O Most High.
> . . . .
> that I may declare [*s-p-r*] your praises [*tᵉhillāh*]
>   in the gates of the Daughter of Zion
>   and there rejoice [*g-y-l*] in your salvation.
> (9:1–2, 14; cf. 33:2–3)

Joy (*ś-m-ḥ*, "be happy," and its derived noun *śimḥāh*, "joy," "happiness") flows from the contentment of the heart, *regardless* of the occasion. Israel rejoiced during national festivals, weddings, at home, at work, in the sanctuary, and especially during the feasts and festivals ordained by the Lord. God's people had reason to rejoice, because God was with them!

Joy led to praising the Lord. Listen to the words of Psalm 66 (vv.1–8; cf. 68:3–4; 104:1):

> Shout with joy [*r-w-'*] to God, all the earth!
>   Sing [*z-m-r*] the glory of his name;
>   make his praise [*tᵉhillāh*] glorious!

Say to God, "How awesome are your deeds!
    So great is your power
    that your enemies cringe before you.
All the earth bows down to you;
    they sing praise [*z-m-r*] to you,
    they sing praise [*z-m-r*] to your name."

Come and see what God has done,
    how awesome his works in man's behalf!
He turned the sea into dry land,
    they passed through the waters on foot—
    come, let us rejoice [*ś-m-ḥ*] in him.
He rules forever by his power,
    his eyes watch the nations—
    let not the rebellious rise up against him.

Praise [*b-r-k*] our God, O peoples,
    let the sound of his praise [*tᵉhillāh*] be heard.

The root *y-d-h* occurs frequently in the Psalms, both in verbal form and in a nominal form (*tôḏāh,* "praise" or "thank-offering"). Westermann has effectively argued that the primary meaning is "praise" and that thanksgiving is implied in the act of praise (*Praise of God,* pp. 25–30). The Psalms' praise focuses on Yahweh, his revelation, his acts in creation and redemption, and his personal and communal acts of deliverance. The OT never distinguishes the nature of God (his perfections) from the acts of God. In an outburst of praise the poet of Psalm 33 leads the people of God to wait hopefully for the Lord's salvation. He is the Great Creator (vv.6–7) and the Sovereign King over the nations (vv.8–11, 13–17). He delights in his people and promises to deliver them to the uttermost. So we read in 33:2–3:

Praise [*y-d-h*] the LORD with the harp;
    make music [*z-m-r*] to him on the ten-stringed lyre.
Sing [*š-y-r*] to him a new song [*šîr*];
    play skillfully [*n-g-n*], and shout for joy [*r-w-ʿ*].

Clearly the psalmist sets the mood for a victory song.

z-m-r ("sing praise") is the root from which we get the word *mizmôr* ("psalm," see Introduction, 6.a.4)a)). Its basic meaning is to sing with accompaniment of instruments. But it is not always clear whether the instruments accompanied the song, were substituted by choirs, or what instruments were particularly designed for this use. Music, dancing, and playing of instruments were incorporated in Israel's worship: "Let them praise [*h-l-l*] his name with dancing / and make music [*z-m-r*] to him with tambourine and harp" (149:3; cf. 33:2; 98:5; 144:9). In Psalm 47:6–8, the psalmist repeatedly uses the root *z-m-r*:

Sing praises [*z-m-r*] to God, sing praises [*z-m-r*];
    sing praises [*z-m-r*] to our King, sing praises [*z-m-r*].
For God is the King of all the earth;
    sing to him a psalm of praise [*z-m-r*].
God reigns over the nations;
    God is seated on his holy throne.

The root *h-l-l* lies behind the anglicized form "hallelujah" ("praise Yah[weh]") and the word *tᵉhillāh* ("praise"), from which the Book of Psalms derives its name: *tᵉhillim* ("Praises"; see the treatment under the superscriptions above). The very last psalm (150) uses only this root throughout, in praise of Yahweh:

Praise [*h-l-l*] the LORD.
Praise [*h-l-l*] God in his sanctuary;
praise [*h-l-l*] him in his mighty heavens.
Praise [*h-l-l*] him for his acts of power;
praise [*h-l-l*] him for his surpassing greatness.
Praise [*h-l-l*] him with the sounding of the trumpet,
praise [*h-l-l*] him with the harp and lyre,
praise [*h-l-l*] him with tambourine and dancing,
praise [*h-l-l*] him with the strings and flute,
praise [*h-l-l*] him with the clash of cymbals,
praise [*h-l-l*] him with resounding cymbals.
Let everything that has breath praise [*h-l-l*] the LORD.
Praise [*h-l-l*] the LORD.

Another common form for praise is *b-r-k,* from which is derived the noun *b*^{e}*rāḵāh* ("blessing") and the passive participle *bārûḵ* ("blessed," or in NIV, "praise").

The LORD has established his throne in heaven,
and his kingdom rules over all.
Praise [*b-r-k*] the LORD, you his angels,
you mighty ones who do his bidding,
who obey his word.
Praise [*b-r-k*] the LORD, all his heavenly hosts,
you his servants who do his will.
Praise [*b-r-k*] the LORD, all his works
everywhere in his dominion.
Praise [*b-r-k*] the LORD, O my soul.

(103:19–22)

The root *g-y-l* and the nominal form *gîlāh* ("rejoicing") may express a variety of settings: from contentment amid sorrow to the festive expressions associated with weddings and Oriental processional dances. The focus of Yahweh's acts of deliverance transforms inner "gladness" into an outward, community celebration.

Praise was a most important dimension in the worship of ancient Israel in personal and communal praise; in liturgical and private praise; in the variety of music, songs, and instruments; and even in dancing. Joy may express itself in quiet musing as well as in victory celebrations. The praise of Israel was also in the form of public *proclamation* that Yahweh alone is King and that he alone rules through his acts of judgment and deliverance. In Psalm 40 we see how close the *praise* and the *proclamation* of God are intertwined:

Many, O LORD my God,
are the wonders you have done.
The things you planned for us
no one can recount to you;
were I to speak [*n-g-d*] and tell [*d-b-r*] of them,
they would be too many to declare [*s-p-r*].

. . . .

I proclaim [*b-ś-r*] righteousness in the great assembly;
I do not seal my lips,
as you know, O LORD.
I do not hide your righteousness in my heart;
I speak [*'-m-r*] of your faithfulness and salvation.
I do not conceal your love and your truth
from the great assembly.

(40:5, 9–10)

In ancient Israel singing, making music, and joyous shouting were for the purposes of remembering the long history of God's involvement with his people. The history of redemption is the focus of Israel's praise: Creation, the Exodus, the Wilderness Wanderings, the Conquest, the victories over the enemies, David's enthronement, etc. Each new act is an occasion to praise Yahweh. Here lies a significant difference between ancient Israel and modern Christianity. Christians tend to individualize God's acts to the virtual exclusion of God's involvement with the community of his people over the millennia. Moreover, we tend to focus on the new acts of God in Christ and in the Spirit, disregarding the vital connection with God's acts before (OT) and after Christ (church history). Finally, we tend to focus in on the work of God in Christ, often disconnecting the ministry of Christ from the vital hope in the completion of his work at his coming. Individual and communal praise brings encouragement, religious excitement, celebration, and hope in the final redemption (cf. Eph 5:19–20; Col 3:16–17).

The Psalms do not restrict praise to the limited circle of Yahweh and his people. Yahweh expected his people to praise him by proclaiming his kingship to the next generation, as well as to other nations. Praise demands communication, as C.S. Lewis persuasively sets it forth: "My whole, more general, difficulty, about the praise of God depended on my absurdly denying to us, as regards the supremely Valuable, what we delight to do, what indeed we can't help doing about everything else we value. I think we delight to praise what we enjoy because the praise not merely expresses but completes the enjoyment" (*Reflections on the Psalms*, p. 95). We "complete" the enjoyment by sharing the witness to God's acts with the new generation. Thus the psalmist gives his inspired reason for educating the future generations in the things of the Lord: the history of redemption:

> One generation will commend [*š-b-ḥ*] your works to another;
> they will tell [*n-g-d*] of your mighty acts.
> They will speak [*d-b-r*] of the glorious splendor of your majesty,
> and I will meditate on your wonderful works.
> They will tell [*'-m-r*] of the power of your awesome works,
> and I will proclaim [*s-p-r*] your great deeds.
> They will celebrate your abundant goodness
> and joyfully sing [*r-n-n*] of your righteousness.
>
> (145:4–7)

We also "complete" the enjoyment by proclaiming to the nations the story of redemption and God's kingship. Yahweh gave Israel the responsibility of sharing the good news of his kingdom:

> Give thanks [*y-d-h*] to the LORD, call [*q-r-'*] on his name;
> make known [*y-d-'*] among the nations what he has done.
> Sing [*š-y-r*] to him, sing praise [*z-m-r*] to him;
> tell of all his wonderful acts.
> Glory in his holy name;
> let the hearts of those who seek the LORD rejoice [*ś-m-ḥ*].
> Look to the LORD and his strength;
> seek his face always.
> . . . .
> He brought out his people with rejoicing [*ś-w/y-ś*],
> his chosen ones with shouts of joy [*r-n-n*];
> he gave them the lands of the nations,
> and they fell heir to what others had toiled for—
> that they might keep his precepts
> and observe his laws.
>
> (105:1–4, 43–45; cf. 108:1–4; 117)

All nations are expected not only to submit to the Lord and his Messiah but to do so joyfully: "Serve [*ʿ-b-d*] the LORD with fear [*y-r-ʾ*] / and rejoice [*g-y-l*] with trembling" (2:11).

Even nature gets involved in praise, as it responds to God's kingship with joy and gratitude:

> Shout for joy [*r-w-ʿ*] to the LORD, all the earth,
> burst into jubilant song with music [*z-m-r*];
> make music [*z-m-r*] to the LORD with the harp,
> with the harp and the sound of singing [*z-m-r*],
> with trumpets and the blast of the ram's horn—
> shout for joy [*r-w-ʿ*] before the LORD, the King.
> Let the sea resound, and everything in it,
> the world, and all who live in it.
> Let the rivers clap their hands,
> let the mountains sing together for joy [*r-n-n*].
>
> (98:4–8)

All creation is the temple of the Great King. Mount Zion is a microcosm of his temple. Hence it was a special privilege to be invited into his inner circle. This privilege was limited to the people of God and, more particularly, to those who drew near to him. How difficult it is for our Western ears to enter into the joy of this ancient psalm:

> Shout for joy [*r-w-ʿ*] to the LORD, all the earth.
> Worship the LORD with gladness;
> come before him with joyful songs.
> Know that the LORD is God.
> It is he who made us, and we are his;
> we are his people, the sheep of his pasture.
> Enter his gates with thanksgiving [*y-d-h*]
> and his courts with praise [*tᵉhillāh*];
> give thanks [*y-d-h*] to him and praise [*b-r-k*] his name.
> For the Lord is good and his love endures forever;
> his faithfulness continues through all generations.
>
> (100:1–5)

Texts: 2:7, 11; 4:7; 6:5; 7:17; 8:2; 9:1–2, 11, 14; 13:4–6; 14:7; 16:7, 9, 11; 18:3, 49; 19:1, 8, 14; 20:5; 21:6, 13; 22:3, 22, 25–26; 24:5; 26:7, 12; 27:6; 28:9; 30:4, 9, 11–12; 31:7, 20; 32:11; 33:1–3; 34:1–2; 35:9, 15, 18, 27; 37:3, 19; 39:13; 40:3, 9; 41:2; 42:4–5, 11; 44:8; 47:1, 5–7; 48:1–2, 10; 49:18; 50:1, 6; 51:8, 12–15; 52:9; 53:6; 54:6; 55:14; 56:4, 10; 57:7, 9; 59:16–17; 63:4–5, 7, 11; 64:9; 65:10, 13; 66:1, 4, 6, 8; 67:1, 3, 7; 68:3, 6, 11, 25–26, 32; 69:30, 34; 70:4; 71:6, 8, 14, 16; 72:15; 74:21; 75:9; 76:10; 77:13; 78:4, 39; 79:13; 84:4; 85:6; 86:4, 12; 87:7; 88:10; 89:5, 12, 16, 42; 90:14; 92:1–2, 4, 15; 94:19; 95:1–2; 96:1–2, 4, 11–13; 97:1, 6, 8, 11–12; 98:4–6, 8–9; 100:1–2, 4; 101:1; 102:18, 21; 103:1; 104:1, 12, 31–34; 105:2–3, 43; 106:2, 5, 47; 107:22, 32, 42; 108:1, 3; 109:17, 28, 30; 111:1, 10; 113:1; 115:13, 17–18; 117:1; 118:26; 119:7, 14, 74, 108, 111, 171, 172, 175; 122:1, 4; 126:2–3, 5; 129:8; 132:9, 16; 134:3; 135:1, 3, 19–20; 137:3–4; 138:1–2, 4–5; 139:14; 140:13; 142:7; 144:9; 145:1–3, 6–7, 10, 21; 146:2; 147:1; 148:1–3, 5, 14; 149:1–3, 5–6; 150:1–6.

Related Subjects: See appendixes to Pss 7 (The Name of Yahweh); 25 (The Perfections of God); 78 (The Mighty Acts of Yahweh); 25 (The Perfections of Yahweh); 150 (Musical Instruments).

Bibliography: Patrick D. Miller, Jr., "Enthroned on the Praises of Israel: The Praise of God in Old Testament Theology," Int 39 (1985): 5–19; A.E. Goodman, "חסד and תודה in the Linguistic Tradition of the Psalter," in *Words and Meanings. Essays Presented to*

David Winton Thomas on His Retirement from the Regius Professorship of Hebrew in the University of Cambridge, 1968, edd. Peter R. Ackroyd and Barnabas Lindars (Cambridge: Cambridge University Press, 1968), pp. 105–15; Norman E. Wagner, "רִנָּה in the Psalter," VetTest 10 (1960): 435–41; Claus Westermann, *The Praise of God*, pp. 26–27.

TDAT, 3:455–74; TDOT, 2:279–308, 313–16, 469–95; 3:404–10; 4:91–98; THAT, 1:353–76, 415–18, 493–502, 674–82; 2:31–37, 782–86, 828–35, 895–98; TWOT, 1:132–33, 135–36, 159, 217–18, 245, 365; 2:549–50, 670, 673, 839, 851, 873, 879, 920.

Psalm 123: Have Mercy, O Lord

This is one of the "Songs of Ascents" (see the introduction to Ps 120). The literary genre reflects a combination of *individual lament* (v.1, "I") and *community lament* (vv.2–4: "our," "us," "we"). The life situation as well as the date of composition are uncertain. The psalm reflects a time of oppression and possibly persecution and was a fitting prayer for relief and deliverance.

The psalmist employed simile ("as the eyes of slaves . . . as the eyes of a maid"), a stairlike parallelism ("eyes," vv.1–2; "he shows us mercy," "have mercy on us," vv.2–3; "endured," vv.3–4; "much," vv.3–4; and "contempt," vv.3–4), and a contrastive inclusion of "to you" (first phrase in MT, emphatic, v.1) and "the arrogant" (last phrase, the cause of the trouble being unspecified to the very last, v.4). The expository structure is as follows:

A. Dependence on the Lord (vv.1–2)
B. Prayer for Mercy (vv.3–4)

I. Dependence on the Lord

123:1–2

A song of ascents.

1 I lift up my eyes to you,
to you whose throne is in heaven.
2 As the eyes of slaves look to the hand of their master,
as the eyes of a maid look to the hand of her mistress,
so our eyes look to the LORD our God,
till he shows us his mercy.

1–2 The first strophe is held together by an inclusion and a chiastic structure. The inclusion is made by the first phrase in the MT, "to you," and the next-to-the-last phrase of v.2: "the LORD our God." The chiastic structure is seen in the use of "eyes" and the references to the Lord. Verses 1–3 may be schematized as follows:

To you . . .	eyes
A	B
B′	A′

eyes . . . to the LORD our God, till he shows us mercy.
Have mercy on us.

The expression of dependence on the Lord is similar to that in 121:1. Both in Psalm 121:1 and 123:1 the psalmist creates a suspense by drawing out the use of the divine name. In 121:1 he makes mention of "the hills" and then portrays the Lord as the Maker of heaven and earth. Here he speaks about him first by "you," then as he "whose throne is in heaven," and concludes on a specific address: "the LORD our God." The intent of both poetic references is to dramatize the awesome power of God, the Ruler of the universe. Yahweh is "the Maker of heaven and earth" (121:2), "whose throne is in heaven" (123:1).

The Lord, to whom the psalmist looks dependently, rules sovereignly. He is on the throne (cf. 2:4; 11:4; 102:12; 115:3), even when the "arrogant" (v.4) trouble his people. Though he is exalted, the name of the God of Israel is Yahweh ("LORD," v.2), i.e., the God who is faithful to his people.

God's people, however, look for his intervention. They are threatened by the arrogant. In utter dependence, like "slaves" and "a maid," they look to "their master" and "mistress" (respectfully) for acts of kindness (v.2). The strophe concludes with a prayer for mercy and thus anticipates the prayer of v.3 (cf. Isa 30:18).

Notes

For a brief discussion of the technical words and phrases in the superscription, see the Introduction.

II. Prayer for Mercy

123:3–4

3 Have mercy on us, O LORD, have mercy on us,
for we have endured much contempt.
4 We have endured much ridicule from the proud,
much contempt from the arrogant.

3–4 The psalmist's prayer for "mercy" (*ḥ-n-n*) is repeated for the sake of emphasis. The need for divine favor (cf. 6:2; 57:1; 86:3) arises out of a deep awareness of injustice done to God's children. They have unjustly "endured" (*ś-b-ʿ*, "to be sated with") great ("much," twice) "contempt" (twice; cf. 119:22) and "ridicule" (cf. 44:13; Neh 2:19; 4:1).

The evildoers are called "the proud" (v.4, lit., "the one at ease"; Dahood: "nonchalant," *Psalms*, 3:208; cf. Isa 32:9, 11; Amos 6:1; Zech 1:15) and "the arrogant." The children of God often find themselves mocked by the "proud" and "arrogant" of the world who rely on and seek only themselves and not God. Whoever these troublemakers are, the godly do not look to them for favor and relief. Though the psalmist portrays the godly as "slaves" (v.2), they serve the Lord alone. Their cry goes up to Yahweh, their heavenly Father. This contrast is clearly brought out in the MT, as the psalm begins with "to you I lift up" and ends on "the arrogant."

Notes

For an approach to this psalm as a war oracle, see the study by Christensen, pp. 112–27. For other psalms see 12; 60; 74; 79; 80; 83; 85; 90; 94:1–11; 126; 137.

4 The MT *Kethiv* גַּאֲיוֹנִים (*ga'ᵃyônîm*, "arrogant," "proud") is maintained in favor of the *Qere*: גְּאֵי יוֹנִים (*gᵉ'ê yônîm*, "proud oppressors"; cf. 17:12; 94:2).

Psalm 124: Our Helper Is the Maker of Heaven and Earth!

This is one of the "Songs of Ascents" (see introduction to Ps 120). In this psalm the community of God's people reflects on the possible and real disasters from which the Lord has delivered them (vv.1–5) as the ground for giving thanks (vv.6–8). Its genre reflects that of the *communal thanksgiving songs.*

Repetition of phrases characterizes this psalm: "If the LORD had not been on our side" (vv.1–2), "then" (*'ᵃzay,* deleted for stylistic reasons in NIV: "[then] they would have . . . [then] the flood would have . . . [then] the raging waters"), "us" / "we" (*nap̱šēnû,* lit., "our soul," vv.4–5, 7: "over us, . . . us away. . . . We have escaped"), "we have escaped" (v.7, twice), and "snare" (*paḥ,* twice, v.7). The repetition is in the form of a stairlike parallelism:

if the LORD had not been on our side [*lānû*]
if the LORD had not been on our side [*lānû*]
  [then] they would have. . . , when their anger . . . against us [*bānû*]
  [then] the flood . . . swept over us [*nap̱šēnû*]
  [then] the raging waters . . . us away [*nap̱šēnû*]. . . .
    We [*nap̱šēnû*] have escaped . . . snare;
    the snare . . . and we have escaped.

The development in the structure is best seen when the first colon in vv.1–2, 6, 8 is read sequentially: "If the LORD . . . if the LORD. . . . Praise be to the LORD. . . . Our help is in the name of the LORD." The confession of the name Yahweh is prominent as an inclusion (vv.1–2, 8) and as a linkage device (v.6) between the two stanzas (vv.1–5, vv.7–8). The expository structure develops as follows:

A. The Presence of the Lord (vv.1–2a)
  B. Protection From Dangers (vv.2b–5)
    C. Praise to the Lord (v.6a)
  B′. Protection From Dangers (vv.6b–7)
A′. The Presence of the Lord (v.8)

I. The Presence of the Lord

124:1–2a

A song of ascents. Of David.

1 If the LORD had not been on our side—
  let Israel say—
2 if the LORD had not been on our side

1–2a The repetition of "If the LORD had not been on our side" (vv.1a, 2a) is for the purpose of emphasis (cf. 129:1–2). Because the Lord has been with his people, they have not perished (cf. 94:17; 119:92) and have hope instead (cf. Neh 4:20). The OT saints had a grateful awareness of God's presence in their midst, even though they had not yet seen the Messiah. The phrase "had been on our side" (*hāyāh lānû*) is the past tense of Immanuel ("God is with us"). Thus the community confesses that God has been with them in their past history.

The confession is a national confession in that all Israel is invited to join together in saying or singing this psalm. The psalm is a recitation of redemptive events, as the people remember how the Lord has delivered them in the history of redemption.

Notes

For a brief discussion of the technical words and phrases in the superscription, see the Introduction to the Psalms and to Psalm 120.

II. Protection From Dangers

124:2b–5

when men attacked us,
3 when their anger flared against us,
they would have swallowed us alive;
4 the flood would have engulfed us,
the torrent would have swept over us,
5 the raging waters
would have swept us away.

2b The presence of God results in his blessings. His blessing includes protection from enemies and dangers, even as he had promised to Abraham and confirmed to Jacob and Moses (Gen 12:3; 28:14; 35:11–13; Lev 26:2–13). His presence had protected Israel from destruction on many occasions, either by their own sins or by the threats of nature or enemies. Throughout her short history Israel was attacked from all sides. God's people confess that the battle is not between them and the nations but between God (Yahweh) and mankind (*'āḏām;* NIV, "men").

3 Often it seemed as if mankind at large was against God's people and that they vented their anger with the living God against his people (cf. 2:1–3; 3:1–2; 66:12). The nations intended to destroy "life" (*ḥayyîm*), which God had given to his people. The verb "swallowed" is a metaphor for "death." Death is often portrayed by "*Sheol*" that devours its victims (cf. 55:15; Prov 1:12). Those who ally themselves with it are instruments of "death," as they, as it were, swallow up those who are alive. However, life granted by the Lord cannot be smothered to death.

4–5 The violent acts are likened to "the flood," "the torrent," and "the raging waters." The metaphor of water as a destructive force is common in the OT (cf. 18:16; 42:7; 69:1–2, 15; Isa 8:7–8; Lam 3:54) because of the destructive torrential rains known to that part of the world (cf. Judg 5:21; Matt 7:27). The "waters" came, as it were, "over our soul" (*napšēnû,* twice; NIV, "over us," "us"). The circumstances so exhausted God's people that they nearly succumbed. The word "raging" (*hazzêḏônîm,* v.5) is a *hapax legomenon,* a word related to *zēḏîm* ("arrogant" or "insolent" people; cf. 86:14; 119:21, 51, 69, 78, 85, 122; TWOT, 1:239–40). Yet in spite of all these troubles, the Lord had been with his people (cf. 56:9, 11).

III. Praise to the Lord

124:6a

> 6 Praise be to the LORD,

6a The praise of the Lord is a transition between the confession of God's past acts of protection (vv.1–5) and the confession of confidence in the Lord (vv.6b–8). He alone is to be praised, because he has been with his people in protecting them.

IV. Protection From Dangers

124:6b–7

> who has not let us be torn by their teeth.
> 7 We have escaped like a bird
> out of the fowler's snare;
> the snare has been broken,
> and we have escaped.

6b–7 The song of thanksgiving praises God for delivering his own from the ungodly. The wicked are like wild animals who devour their prey, but the Lord protects his people from becoming "prey." He also did not let them be like a "bird" caught by a trapper with his "snare" (*paḥ;* cf. 119:110). Throughout v.7 there is a note of triumph, because of the repetition "we have escaped" and the observation that "the snare has been broken." It is the Lord's doing; therefore he is to be praised!

Notes

6 The word טֶרֶף (*ṭerep̱,* "prey") is preferable to the NIV verbal rendering, "who has not let us be torn by their teeth"; cf. NEB, "to be the prey between their teeth" (so most commentators and translations). For a parallel see 7:2.

V. The Presence of the Lord

124:8

> 8 Our help is in the name of the LORD,
> the Maker of heaven and earth.

8 The motif of God's presence begins and concludes this magnificent psalm. The future lies in God's caring hands. He is our "Help." By his "name" (Yahweh; cf. 122:4) we will be protected; so we need not fear. After all, the Maker of heaven and earth is in full control over *'āḏām* ("mankind"; NIV, "men," v.2), which he has created.

Psalm 125: Peace Be on Israel

This is one of the "Songs of Ascents" (see the introduction to Ps 120). The psalm speaks of unshakable confidence in the Lord by whose judgment the power of the wicked over the righteous will be removed. Because of the mixture of confidence and lament, scholars are divided in classifying the genre between a *communal psalm of confidence* and a *communal lament* (Dahood, *Psalms*, 3:214). The psalms of communal confidence are closely related to communal thanksgiving songs and to communal laments. As a psalm of communal confidence, this psalm conveys a deep trust in the Lord's ability to take care of the need of the people (cf. Pss 115, 129). Kraus prefers to include Psalm 46 and to exclude Psalm 115 from this threesome (*Psalmen*, 1:lii).

The structure of this psalm unfolds as follows:

A. Internal Strength (v.1)
  B. Confidence in the Lord's Help (v.2)
    C. Confidence in the Triumph Over Evil (v.3)
  B′. Prayer for the Lord's Help (vv.4–5b)
A′. Peace (v.5c)

I. Internal Strength

125:1

A song of ascents.

1 Those who trust in the LORD are like Mount Zion,
which cannot be shaken but endures forever.

1 Confidence in the Lord strengthens the nation. The people of God in their communal expression of "trust in the LORD" (cf. 37:5; 78:22) are like Mount Zion, celebrated in the Songs of Zion (cf. Pss 46; 48; 76; 84; 87; 122). Mount Zion is more than a hill. It symbolizes God's help (cf. 121:1–2; 124:8), his presence in blessing and protecting his people (76:6–9; 132:13–16), and the privileges of the covenantal relationship. Because of this unshakable confidence in the Lord, the people who trust in him are strong like Mount Zion, "which cannot be shaken but endures forever" (cf. 16:8; 46:5; 93:1; 112:6–7; Isa 28:16; 54:10; see appendix to Ps 46: Zion Theology).

Notes

For a brief discussion of the technical words and phrases in the superscription, see the Introduction.

1 The phrase "endures forever" is a rendering of לְעוֹלָם יֵשֵׁב (*l*[e]*'ôlām yēšēḇ*, "forever sits"; NIV, "endures forever"). Some understand "sit" to be a technical term for "be enthroned" (cf. 9:11; 48:2–3; 91:1) and render it "Jerusalem sits enthroned" (Briggs, 2:454) or "the

Enthroned of Jerusalem" (Dahood, *Psalms,* 3:214). The LXX has an alternate reading, in which "Jerusalem" is a part of the reading of v.1: "he who dwells in Jerusalem" (cf. BHS).

II. Confidence in the Lord's Help

125:2

2 As the mountains surround Jerusalem,
so the LORD surrounds his people
both now and forevermore.

2 Mount Zion is not the highest peak in the mountain range around Jerusalem. To its east lies the Mount of Olives, to its north Mount Scopus, to the west and south are other hills, all of which are higher than Mount Zion. Surrounded by mountains, Mount Zion was secure, by its natural defensibility. So the psalmist compares the Lord to the hills around Jerusalem and the people to Mount Zion. The hills connote endurance (cf. v.1) and a sense of assurance and protection. God is "around" and present with his people (cf. 34:7; Zech 2:5) "both now and forevermore" (cf. 113:2; 115:18; 121:8).

III. Confidence in the Triumph Over Evil

125:3

3 The scepter of the wicked will not remain
over the land allotted to the righteous,
for then the righteous might use
their hands to do evil.

3 The "scepter," a symbol of foreign rule (cf. Isa 14:5), cannot coexist with the protecting presence of God (vv.1–2). The enemies of God's people had made incursions into the land, had occupied it, and at times had even annexed parts or all of Israel and Judah (cf. 124:2–5). But Israel's hope was always in the Lord. Regardless of how evil the times, they knew that the Lord had promised never to permit the wicked to prevail over the righteous, and this promise included the promise of "the land" (*gôral,* "lot," here "land") of Canaan. The "righteous" are those who belong to the covenant community (cf. 1:6). If evil were to prevail, it might be an occasion for some of the godly to be tempted, to lose heart, and to fall away. For the sake of God's people, wickedness must come to an absolute end!

Notes

---

3 'The scepter of the wicked" is a rendering of "the scepter" of הָרֶשַׁע (*hāreša',* "wickedness"). But the LXX and the Syriac read "the wicked" (so NIV). The difference is only one vowel; compare *hāreša'* ("wickedness") and *hārāšā'* ("the wicked").

IV. Prayer for the Lord's Help

125:4–5b

4 Do good, O LORD, to those who are good,
to those who are upright in heart.
5 But those who turn to crooked ways
the LORD will banish with the evildoers.

4–5b Though confident in the Lord's protection (cf. v.2), the people pray for his help. What a beautiful combination: confidence and urgency in prayer! The people ask the Lord to remember them by doing good. The contrastive expressions of God's rule are in deliverance and judgment. He delivers "those who are good," i.e., "those who are upright in heart" (v.4). The ones who do good are the same as those who are upright. Good works are here expressions of an "upright heart" (cf. 7:10). The "evildoers" are apostates who have turned "to crooked ways" (v.5), i.e., paths that twist and turn away from the main road (cf. Judg 5:6). The psalmist prays that the Lord will deal kindly with his people for the sake of the godly, disregarding and judging the apostates together with the wicked.

V. Peace

125:5c

Peace be upon Israel.

5c The benediction of God rests only on those who trust in him (v.1). They will receive God's "peace" (*šālôm;* cf. 122:6–9; 128:6; Num 6:26; Gal 6:16).

Psalm 126: The Restoration Is Here!

This is one of the "Songs of Ascents" (see introduction to Ps 120). In this psalm the community reflects with thanksgiving on God's beneficent acts in the past while praying for his continued goodness. Its form reflects the genre of the *community laments*. Though there is no agreement on the date, the situation of the psalm is closely associated with the return of the small exilic community to the land (after 538 B.C.; Kraus, *Psalmen*, 2:855) and resembles the gratitude and prayer of Psalm 85.

The structure of the psalm is in the form of a stairlike parallelism with the repetition of "then" (twice v.2: "[then] our mouths. . . . Then it was said"), "has done great things" (vv.2b, 3), and the use of the infinitive absolute ("he who goes out . . . will return," v.6), the participle "carrying" (*nōśē'*, v.6), and the praise "songs of joy" (vv.2, 5–6).

A. Joy of God's People (vv.1–2a)
B. Proclamation Among the Nations (v.2b)
C. Thanksgiving (v.3)
D. Prayer (v.4)
E. Assurance of Answered Prayer (vv.5–6)

I. Joy of God's People

126:1–2a

A song of ascents.

1 When the LORD brought back the captives to Zion,
we were like men who dreamed.
2 Our mouths were filled with laughter,
our tongues with songs of joy.

1–2a The psalm begins with a reflection on the kind acts of God in the past. The restoration of "the captives to Zion" (v.1) took place in 538 B.C., in fulfillment of the prophetic word (Isa 14:1–2; 44:24–45:25; 48:20–21; Jer 29:14; 30:3; 33:7, 10–11; Amos 9:14). The people knew about the promises of restoration; but when the actual moment of restoration came, it was an overwhelming experience. They were like those "who dreamed." It all happened too quickly and seemed like a mirage.

The people were exuberant with "laughter" (v.2; cf. Job 8:21) and cried out "songs of joy" (*rinnāh;* cf. vv.5–6; Isa 44:23; 48:20; 49:13; 51:11; 54:1; 55:12). The "song" was a "ringing cry" or "shouts of joy" (TWOT, 2:851). Great had been the sorrow of God's people in exile (cf. Pss 42–43; 79; 89; 137; Lam 3:1–21); but the restoration from exile soon quieted and comforted the hearts of the returnees, as they were filled with happiness and proclaimed with laughter and shouts of joy what God had done for them.

Notes

For a brief discussion of the technical words and phrases in the superscription, see the Introduction.

1 The phrase שִׁיבַת צִיּוֹן (*šîḇat ṣîyôn,* "captives to Zion") has occasioned extensive discussion. BHS et al. emend it to שְׁבוּת (*šᵉḇûṯ,* "fortunes") or to שְׁבִית (*šᵉḇîṯ,* "fortunes," cf. v.4) from the root *š-w-b* ("return"). Dahood argues against this emendation on the ground that the Sefire Inscription has the word *sybt* as a cognate of the Hebrew *šîḇaṯ* with the meaning "fortunes" (*Psalms,* 3:218). For a discussion of this phrase, see 14:7; cf. 53:6; 85:1; Jer 29:14; 30:3; 33:7, 11; Hos 6:11; Joel 3:1; Amos 9:14). Walter Beyerlin explains the phrase as *restitutio in integrum,* as promised by the preexilic prophets, especially Joel (*"Wir sind Trämende," Studien zum 126. Psalm* [Stuttgart: Katholisches Biblewerk, 1978]). For a critical review of his work, see Allan M. Harman, "The Setting and Interpretation of Psalm 126," *The Reformed Theological Review* 44 (1985): 74–80.

The NIV's "like men who dreamed" renders the MT participial phrase כְּחֹלְמִים (*kᵉḥōlᵉ mîm,* "like dreaming"). The NIV margin contains another interpretation: "men restored to health," which assumes a homonymous form of *ḥ-l-m* ("to be strong," "to be healed"). The evidence for this is relatively weak (so A.A. Anderson, 2:864–65). Baumgartner lists only one meaning, excluding the homonym.

For an approach to this psalm as a war oracle, see the study by Christensen, pp. 112–27. For similar psalms see 12; 60; 74; 79; 80; 83; 85; 90; 94:1–11; 123; 137.

II. Proclamation Among the Nations

126:2b

Then it was said among the nations,
"The LORD has done great things for them."

2b So great was the act of restoration that the "nations" (*gôyim*) heard about it, too (cf. 98:2; Isa 52:10; Ezek 36:36). Whenever the Lord acts, his mighty works witness to his glorious ability to deliver his own. For the phrase "has done great things" (cf. Joel 2:21), see the appendix to Psalm 78: The Mighty Acts of Yahweh.

III. Thanksgiving

126:3

3 The LORD has done great things for us,
and we are filled with joy.

3 The nations recognize the greatness of God. The wonder of deliverance is precious to God's people. First, they are in shock, as if in a dream. Then the shock wears off and changes into "joy." This glorious transformation comes out clearly in the MT: *hāyînû kᵉḥōlᵉmîm. . . . hāyînû śᵉmēḥîm* ("we were like dreaming. . . . we were happy"; NIV, "we were like men who dreamed. . . . and we were filled with joy").

IV. Prayer

126:4

4 Restore our fortunes, O LORD,
like streams in the Negev.

4 The new experience of laughter, shouts of joy, and happiness has to be balanced with the reality of life in Canaan. It was a harsh existence (cf. Ps 85; Ezra-Nehemiah; Haggai). Out of the ashes of Judah's destruction and out of the land that had lain fallow, the returnees had to eke an existence.

The returnees' prayer reflects on the harshness of their existence and on the disappointment with the limited fulfillment of the prophetic word. Though they were restored, "nature" was not smiling kindly on the people. They pray for a continuation of the restoration: restoration of their well-being in the land ("fortunes," see 14:7). God's answer to their prayer is a second outburst of blessing, compared to "streams in the Negev." The wadis in the steppe south of Hebron, around Beersheba, were generally dry; but on the rare occasions when during the winter months it rained even as little as one inch, the water ran down its "streams" with great rapidity and often with destructive force. I have seen roads and bridges destroyed by the force of these torrential streams. The "streams in the Negev" are not ordinary phenomena, as much as they represent proverbially the sudden unleash of God's blessing.

V. Assurance of Answered Prayer

126:5–6

5 Those who sow in tears
  will reap with songs of joy.
6 He who goes out weeping,
  carrying seed to sow,
will return with songs of joy,
  carrying sheaves with him.

5–6 Suddenly the short but intensive prayer of v.4 is answered, as if by a prophetic assurance. Yes, God has promised, and he will be true to his promise (cf. Hag 2:19)! The psalm contains a perpetual assurance to God's people that his word is true. The Lord will turn the "tears" into "songs of joy" (v.5). Though work may be laborious and the results uncertain, the Lord will be with his people in their various endeavors, so as to bless them.

The assurance of God's blessing is also an encouragement to be responsible. The people were not to sit by idly, waiting for God to come through. They had to go out and sow, praying that the Lord would be true. The phrase "seed to sow" (v.6) is reminiscent of Haggai's encouragement to the people to sow whatever little they had left, because the Lord will bless them. With our abundance of seed companies and supplies, we forget that the ancient Israelite had to "lose" his seed before he could gain. He had to put his fortune into the soil, hoping for an increase, but was uncertain of the outcome. If his sowing did not pay off, he might not have enough to sow the next season, and he might suffer greater financial loss.

The words of assurance bring us back to the "songs of joy" with which the psalmist opened his psalm (v.6b). The psalm began with expressions of joy and wonder at the restoration from exile. It concludes on the expectation of another miracle to take place: the people will "return" (or "come home") singing "songs of joy," because of the plentiful harvest ("carrying sheaves with him"). The God who has acted with love and fidelity to his people will continue to be with them. Thus the psalm attests to God's lovingkindness and assures God's people in any age of his abiding faithfulness. His promises are secure, as Calvin reminds us:

> In order then that joy may succeed our present sorrow, let us learn to apply our minds to the contemplation of the issue which God promises. Thus we shall experience that all true believers have a common interest in this prophecy, That God not only will wipe away tears from their eyes, but that he will also diffuse inconceivable joy through their hearts. (5:103)

Notes

5–6 Bellinger (pp. 63–66) concludes that the psalm is a prophetic liturgy, consisting of an oracle of salvation and a community lament.

Psalm 127: The Blessing of the Lord

The futility of life and the blessing of God are two contrastive themes in this wisdom psalm. On the one hand, the psalmist shows the anxiety of life without God (vv.1–2). On the other hand, he encourages the godly to trust in the Lord in all matters of life. This psalm is closely related to the following psalm, revealing an internal cohesiveness and unity of purpose (see the careful study by Patrick D. Miller, Jr., "Psalm 127—The House That Yahweh Builds," JSOT 22 [1982]: 119–32; id., "Psalm 127," *Interpreting the Psalms*, pp. 131–37). Both psalms reflect the *wisdom* tradition and may be viewed as examples of the *wisdom genre*.

The original situation is less clear. Mowinckel argued that the wisdom motif is so strong that he posited a midrashic connection between the phrase "unless the LORD builds the house" with the consecration of the temple (2:103). Kirkpatrick favors a postexilic situation, when houses and the temple needed rebuilding (p. 751). A.A. Anderson associates it with the Feast of Tabernacles (2:866). In Jewish practice the psalm is recited as a part of a thanksgiving service after childbirth.

The structure reveals two constrastive parts:

A. Futility and Blessing (vv.1–2)
B. God's Blessing on the Family (vv.3–5)

I. Futility and Blessing

127:1–2

A song of ascents. Of Solomon.

1 Unless the LORD builds the house,
its builders labor in vain.
Unless the LORD watches over the city,
the watchmen stand guard in vain.
2 In vain you rise early
and stay up late,
toiling for food to eat—
for he grants sleep to those he loves.

This section is marked by two conditional clauses and a statement of the vanity of human efforts. Each conditional clause begins with an affirmation of the Lord's involvement in one's work. Each concluding phrase begins in the Hebrew text with the phrase translated in the NIV as "in vain" (*šāw'*). This emphasis calls attention to the place of God's blessing on all human efforts.

1 As a wisdom psalm, Psalm 127 evokes a response of wisdom in the wise in that they would desire to be more God-centered in their everyday lives (see appendix to Ps 1: The Ways of Wisdom and Folly). The problem of the Israelites is the same as that of Western man today. It was too tempting to busy oneself with the construction of a house and the protection of the city. The building of the house may refer to construction of a house within the protective walls of the city. It may also signify the raising of a family, especially because this section precedes a unit in which the family is emphasized as a reward from the Lord (vv.3–5). In the OT it is usual to speak of a family as a "house" even as we speak of a prominent family as a "dynasty" (cf. Gen 16:2; 30:3; Exod 1:21; Ruth 4:11; 1 Sam 2:35; 2 Sam 7:27).

A second concern that the psalmist touches is the protection of the city. In ancient

Israel the city was walled in against enemy attacks. In times of political uncertainties, a city may expend much energy in guarding itself from possible enemy attacks. The psalmist, familiar with the anguish of a nervous population, encourages God's people with the thought that the Lord himself guards the city (cf. 121:4; 132). Thus he rebukes the human efforts in the construction of one's house and involvement in the welfare of the community, unless one trusts in the Lord. The Lord's sovereignty is evident in his blessings on the individual and the community.

2 The psalmist extends God's sovereignty to man's fragile existence. Even as he did not depreciate the importance of the construction of the house and the protection of the city (v.1), so he does not depreciate the importance of hard work. Hard work may involve rising early in the morning and going to bed late at night. But the psalmist decries this as an inferior way of life if the hard work is only for the purpose of providing daily food and clothing for oneself and the family. The higher way of life begins with trusting the Lord in one's work. The blessing of God on the labor of the godly is such that his own are provided with all that they need and can rest without anguish. Anguish is that experience by which work is turned into toil. Human labor under the sun becomes toil when God's blessing is absent.

Notes

For a brief discussion of the technical words and phrases in the superscription, see the Introduction.

II. God's Blessing on the Family

127:3–5

3 Sons are a heritage from the LORD,
  children a reward from him.
4 Like arrows in the hands of a warrior
  are sons born in one's youth.
5 Blessed is the man
  whose quiver is full of them.
They will not be put to shame
  when they contend with their enemies in the gate.

3 The psalmist applies the principles developed in the first two verses to the family. The blessings of the Lord on the godly family are many. First, he gives children as an inheritance. The perpetuity of the believing family is hereby assured, both in number and in membership within the covenant family of faith. The concern of the Israelite was not only that he would have children but particularly that he would have sons, and more particularly that they would be godly sons. The psalmist assures the godly that their inheritance is from the Lord, who will give them godly sons (v.3).

4–5 Second, God gives a sense of security and protection in the godly family. Blessed (*'ašrê*, v.5; see 1:1) is such a man. The psalmist uses a metaphor of war as he likens the children of one's youth to "arrows" (v.4). As the arrows protect the warrior, so the godly man need not be afraid, when blessed with sons. Continuing the metaphor of arrows, the psalmist speaks of the quiver. A house full of children, born before one becomes old (cf. Gen 37:3), is a protection against loneliness and abandonment in society. They have received a godly example at home; and when they come together in the city gate, the place where court was held (69:12; Deut 17:5; 21:19; 22:15, 24; Amos 5:12), they will speak on behalf of their aging father in the presence of their enemies (v.5).

Notes

5 The NIV interprets the MT's כִּי־יְדַבְּרוּ (*kî-yeḏabberû*, "when they speak") in its legal setting: "When they contend." Briggs (2:459) argues that the advantage of sons was particularly experienced in warfare, when the stalwart sons could defend the city and thereby the houses against the enemy (similarly Dahood: "[he] shall drive back his foes from the gate," *Psalms*, 3:222). But the metaphor of war should not extend to the latter part of v.5, because the blessing of a godly father is experienced when his sons help him to succeed even in times of adversity.

Psalm 128: The Family Blessed by Yahweh

This psalm is also a *wisdom psalm* (see introduction to Ps 127). It begins with a blessing (*'ašrê*, see 1:1). The psalm reflects an application of the priestly blessing (Num 6:24–26).

The structure divides into two parts:

A. The Blessing of a God-Fearing Family (vv.1–4)
B. The Benediction (vv.5–6)

I. The Blessing of a God-Fearing Family

128:1–4

A song of ascents.

1 Blessed are all who fear the LORD,
who walk in his ways.
2 You will eat the fruit of your labor;
blessings and prosperity will be yours.
3 Your wife will be like a fruitful vine
within your house;
your sons will be like olive shoots
around your table.
4 Thus is the man blessed
who fears the LORD.

This section heaps image on image and blessing on blessing. It expresses the felicity of the man who fears the Lord. The fear of God is a life of wisdom (cf. 25:12; Job 1:1, 8; 2:3; see appendix to Ps 1: The Ways of Wisdom and Folly).

1–2 The wise man primarily was concerned with walking in the ways of the Lord (v.1; 25:9–10; cf. Prov 14:2), characterized by an observance of love, fidelity, and uprightness. The man who fears the Lord is a man of integrity (cf. 26:1). He receives a blessing from the Lord in all his labors (v.2; cf. 127:2).

The first two verses begin and conclude with a declaration of blessing in order to emphasize the bliss of fearing God. In godly living the judgment of God on man (Gen 3:17–19) is alleviated in that labor is truly blessed by God. It is as if the psalmist wants to say, "You most certainly will be blessed," so as to leave not the slightest doubt that the fear of the Lord has its appropriate rewards.

3–4 In addition to the personal blessing on one's labors, the blessing extends to wife and family (v.3). The dutiful man will enjoy the warmth of wife and family around his table when he eats the fruit of his labors. He sees how the blessing of God extends to wife and children. His wife is compared to a fruitful vine within his house. The children are likened to olive shoots. How contrastive is the man who toils hard without fearing the Lord and who eats alone in anguish (cf. 127:2)!

The imagery of vine and olive tree are reminiscent of the eras of David and Solomon (1 Kings 4:25) and the blessings associated with the messianic era (Mic 4:4; Zech 3:10). To sit under one's vine and fig tree was an expression of a state of tranquility, peace, and prosperity. Even when the country faces adversity, the man who fears the Lord is insulated against adversity by wife and children as the blessings of the Lord are found under the roof of his house. The metaphor of the fruitfulness of the vine extends, not only to the bearing of children, but also to everything the wife contributes to the welfare of family (cf. Prov 31:10–31).

The children, who are likened to olive shoots, are strong and in due time will continue the work that their father has begun (cf. 52:8; Jer 11:16; Hos 14:6). Though the olive tree may not bear after it has been planted for forty years, it is a symbol of longevity and productivity. So are children within the household of faith! They are not like grass, which is here today but is gone tomorrow. Rather, they are olive trees that in due time bear their fruit. The blessedness of the godly man will extend to other generations. What a privilege God bestows on his children in this life that we may already taste the firstfruits of our heritage!

Notes

For a brief discussion of the technical words and phrases in the superscription, see the introduction.

II. The Benediction

128:5–6

5 May the LORD bless you from Zion
all the days of your life;
may you see the prosperity of Jerusalem,
6 and may you live to see your children's children.
Peace be upon Israel.

5–6 The psalmist further delineates the blessedness of the godly. Blessing is not to be limited to a few days or years but rather is experienced throughout life. The psalmist is here not concerned about the problem of the suffering of the righteous (cf. Pss 37, 73) but encourages godliness by showing how God's blessing will ultimately rest on the one who walks in his way. The presence of God extends to his faithful servant wherever he may live.

For the OT saints to be in Jerusalem during a pilgrimage festival was an assurance of God's blessing on their lives. But v.5 clearly teaches that God's blessing goes with his people even when they are not in Jerusalem. For the NT people of God, it signifies so much more clearly the blessing of God on all those who are indwelt by his Holy Spirit.

The blessing of God also extends to the prosperity of Jerusalem. The godly person in the OT was not only concerned about his personal well-being or the well-being of his family; but, while away from the temple, he was concerned also about the worship of God, the defense of the city of Jerusalem, and the welfare of the Davidic dynasty. He knew that if a godly king were ruling over Jerusalem, and if godly priests were serving in the temple, God's blessing would extend to his people. He prayed for the peace of Jerusalem (cf. 122:6–9).

The godly person receives assurance that if he seeks the welfare of God, God sends his blessing. The Lord who blesses his faithful servant will extend his blessing to all the people of God. His blessing extends to individuals and to the people of God (v.6). To see one's children's children is equivalent to "all the days of your life" (v.5).

The final blessing, "Peace be upon Israel," is equivalent to the prayer that the godly may see "the prosperity of Jerusalem" (v.5). The psalmist thus applies the blessing of God from the individual to the prosperity of God's people at large. The psalm therefore encourages the individual to contribute to the building up of the kingdom of God by living a righteous life in the presence of God. Through him his family will be established and through him God will extend his blessing to all the people of God.

Psalm 129: Yahweh Is Righteous

This is one of the "Songs of Ascents" (see the introduction to Ps 120). The psalm reflects the genre of a *communal confidence*. The psalms of communal confidence (115; 125; 129) are closely related to communal thanksgiving songs and to communal laments, especially the imprecation against the enemies (vv.5–8).

The structure falls into two main parts:

A. Prayer for Divine Deliverance (vv.1–4)
B. Prayer for Divine Judgment (vv.5–8)

I. Prayer for Divine Deliverance

129:1–4

A song of ascents.

1 They have greatly oppressed me from my youth—
let Israel say—
2 they have greatly oppressed me from my youth,
but they have not gained the victory over me.

3 Plowmen have plowed my back
and made their furrows long.
4 But the LORD is righteous;
he has cut me free from the cords of the wicked.

1–2 The repetition—"They have greatly . . . they have greatly"—(vv.1–2) with "let Israel say" is identical to that of 124:1–2. The individualized language "oppressed me from my youth" is reminiscent of Jeremiah 2:2; Ezekiel 23:3; and Hosea 2:3, 15; 11:1. The psalmist has very effectively brought together the individual in relation to the people of God. Difficult as certain moments in Israel's history had been, the people had been miraculously spared. The enemy did not prevail (cf. 2 Cor 4:8–10).

3–4 In Psalm 124 the psalmist likened the enemies to destructive floods and to a hunter. Here he likens them to a farmer who plows the fields with long rows. The "plowmen" are the warriors, the long furrows are the wounds and adversities, and the field is "the back" of Israel (v.3). The "back" is a metaphor of Israel's history of suffering, as its enemies attempted to destroy its national life.

In spite of all troubles, the Lord has delivered his own. He is "the righteous One" (see Notes) who has snapped the yoke of the wicked. The "cords" denote the yoke as a whole, which was fastened to the neck of an animal (v.4; cf. Jer 30:8).

Notes

For a brief discussion of the technical words and phrases in the superscription, see the Introduction.

4 The phrase יהוה צַדִּיק (*YHWH ṣaddîq*, "Yahweh righteous") may be understood in two ways: "Yahweh, the Righteous One" or "the righteous Yahweh." In each case Yahweh is directly the subject of the next clause: "has cut me." The NIV divides the verse into a nominal and a verbal clause: "The LORD is righteous" and "he has cut me free."

II. Prayer for Divine Judgment

129:5–8

5 May all who hate Zion
be turned back in shame.
6 May they be like grass on the roof,
which withers before it can grow;
7 with it the reaper cannot fill his hands,
nor the one who gathers fill his arms.
8 May those who pass by not say,
"The blessing of the LORD be upon you;
we bless you in the name of the LORD."

5–8 The confidence in the Lord is based on his past acts of deliverance (vv.1–4). The curse (imprecation) arises out of a dire need and a concern for God's kingdom, not out of individual pettiness. The enemies who "hate Zion" (v.5) are those who have no regard for God and his promises. "Zion" denotes here the Lord's presence among his people, his covenant and blessing, and the hope in the victorious establishment of God's kingdom (cf. 125:1–2; 132; see appendix to Ps 46: Zion Theology). The enemies of Zion include not only "the wicked" of the world but also the Israelites who do not fear the Lord (cf. 125:5).

The psalmist particularly singles out the godless Israelites who benefited from God's blessings without showing love for the covenant God. They enjoyed hearing the greetings "The blessing of the LORD be upon you" and "we bless you in the name of the LORD" (v.8; see appendix to Ps 7: The Name of Yahweh). They even may have casually greeted their fellow-Israelites with the same words (cf. Ruth 2:4), similar to the greeting of "peace" in Israel today. However, their lives were far from the Lord.

Those who "hate Zion" are traitors to man and God. They may feign a certain piety, but in reality they are against God. The imprecation is not filled with personal indignation. The community prays for the sake of the Lord's Zion, asking for God's righteous vindication of the godly (cf. v.4). God's righteousness demands that the wicked and apostates be "turned back in shame" (v.5; cf. 9:3; 35:4; 40:14; see appendix to Ps 137: Imprecations in the Psalms).

Consistent with the agricultural language of the psalm, the people pray that the wicked may wither like "grass on the roof" (v.6; 2 Kings 19:26; Isa 37:27). Roofs were flat; and during periods of moisture or precipitation, grassy weeds might sprout and grow in the shallow dirt. However, the plants soon withered when deprived of moisture (cf. Matt 13:5–6). The grass may grow, but it is so useless that a reaper need not cut it down with a scythe nor bind it into sheaves (v.7). It is a wasted growth. So it will be with the wicked. They will no longer hear God's blessings (v.8), because they will perish (cf. 1:4–6).

Psalm 130: May the Blessing of the Lord Be on You!

This psalm is classified as one of the seven penitential psalms (6; 32; 38; 51; 102; 130; 143). Part of the reason for the designation lies in the confessional nature of these psalms and part of the reason lies in its use within the Christian community. Psalm 130 also belongs to the "Songs of Ascents" (see introduction to Ps 120). Its genre reflects some features of the *individual lament*.

Because of its strong expression of trust in the Lord, Luther called this psalm, together with other penitential psalms, "Pauline Psalms." The weight of sin, confession of guilt, and confidence in God form an individual expression on behalf of others. The Chronicler incorporated v.2 together with 132:8–9, 10b, and 16 into the conclusion of Solomon's prayer (2 Chron 6:40–42).

There is little consensus on the date of this psalm. Dahood argues in favor of a preexilic date (*Psalms*, 3:235), whereas Allen favors a postexilic date (p. 195). It would seem that the usage of v.2 in Chronicles, the word "forgiveness" (v.4; cf. Neh 9:17; Dan 9:9), and the greater awareness of sin and the need of forgiveness in the postexilic era could provide the context in which this psalm arose.

The structure of the psalm falls into four parts (couplets). The relationship between the first three couplets (vv.1–6) and the last has been problematic. Allen's arguments, favoring the unity of the psalm (pp. 193–94), that vv.7–8 may be understood as an encouragement of "the community at large to continue in their larger hope, in view of his own positive experience" (p. 194), are convincing. The structural divisions are as follows:

A. Lament (vv.1–2)
B. Confession of Sin (vv.3–4)
A′. Waiting for the Lord (vv.5–6)
B′. Confidence in Redemption (vv.7–8)

I. Lament

130:1–2

A song of ascents.

1 Out of the depths I cry to you, O LORD;
2 O Lord, hear my voice.
Let your ears be attentive
to my cry for mercy.

1 To the godly, sin, guilt, and God's fatherly discipline are like being cast into "the depths" of the sea, a metaphor of adversity and trouble (cf. 69:1–2, 14; Isa 51:10; Ezek 27:34). Jonah's prayer in the belly of the big fish expresses the anguish of being cast into "the depths of the grave," as "the engulfing waters threatened . . . the deep surrounded . . . [and] seaweed was wrapped around" his head (Jonah 2:2, 5). The metaphor of "the depths" connotes a feeling of alienation from God.

2 In his dire situation the psalmist calls on the "LORD" (Yahweh), his covenant God, in whose sovereignty ("Lord," *Adonai*) is life and death. In his distress he prays that the Lord (*Adonai*) may "be attentive" (cf. 2 Chron 6:40; 7:15; Neh 1:6, 11) to his petition for "mercy" (*taḥᵃnûnāy;* see 28:2; cf. 68:6). Though no reference is made here explicitly to sin or to confession of sin, the adversity is related to sin. The word "mercy" presupposes a servant-master relationship in which the "servant" petitions his "master" (*Adonai*) for a particular favor (see Allen, p. 192).

Notes

For a brief discussion of the technical words and phrases in the superscription, see the Introduction.

1–2 The alternation between LORD and Lord is also found in vv.5–6; hence vv.1–2 and 5–6 form an inclusion.

II. Confession of Sin

130:3–4

3 If you, O LORD, kept a record of sins,
O Lord, who could stand?
4 But with you there is forgiveness;
therefore you are feared.

3 The mercy of the Lord is found in forgiveness. He does not "keep" (*š-m-r;* NIV, "kept a record") all "sins" (cf. v.8; *'ᵃwōnô*t̲, "iniquities") in mind. If he were to keep tally of all "sins" and continue to hold people accountable for all past sins, even the most godly could not "stand" in the presence of the Lord! The question "who could stand?" (*'-m-d*) may be understood in the sense of passing through his judgment (cf. 1:5) or of the enjoyment of the benefits of his presence (cf. 24:3). Though both senses may be implied in the psalmist's rhetorical question, the latter seems to be preferable here. There is hope when the godly cry for mercy (cf. v.2), because God does not keep a record of the iniquities of his people.

4 God is full of "forgiveness" (*sᵉlîḥāh;* cf. Dan 9:9; also cf. Exod 34:7; Pss 86:5; 103:3; 1 John 2:1–2). He is feared, not only because of his great judgment and harshness, but also because of his great love in forgiving. The godly respond with godly fear and love (cf. Deut 5:29; 1 Peter 1:17).

III. Waiting for the Lord

130:5–6

5 I wait for the LORD, my soul waits,
and in his word I put my hope.
6 My soul waits for the Lord
more than watchmen wait for the morning,
more than watchmen wait for the morning.

5 With great anticipation the psalmist hopes in the Lord: "I wait [*qiwwît̲î*] . . . my soul waits [*qiwwᵉt̲āh*] . . . I put my hope [*hôḥāltî*]." The repetition of the verbs for "hope" reveal the longing of his heart for a positive sign and word from the Lord. In his desperate state (vv.1–2) he has learned to be submissive to the sovereign Lord, who is the fountain of grace. In patient waiting faith looks up to the Lord to grant his grace (cf. Lam 3:25–26).

The "word" the psalmist is waiting for may be a salvation-oracle (Kraus, *Psalmen,* 2:872) or an act of salvation in fulfillment of his word of promise (cf. 107:20). From the concern with waiting like a watchman and from the concluding assurance that the Lord will redeem his people from their sins, we deduce that the "word" denotes a new act of salvation by which the godly man is upheld in his faith.

6 The psalmist waits with great anticipation for God's salvation. He is like the watchmen who wait to be released from duty at the dawning of a new day. The watchmen guarded the city (127:1) during the night from sudden attacks, while the population slept peacefully. The Targum understands by "watchmen" the Levitical guards who long for the offering of the morning sacrifices. A.A. Anderson is right that ultimately it makes little difference whether the guards are military or Levitical, as "the point is their waiting for the morning, and the certainty that it will come" (2:877). The twofold repetition "more than the watchmen" is highly effective after a fourfold expression of "hope" in the Lord. The inspired psalmist thus creates a deep sense of longing, dependence, and assurance.

Notes

6 The verb "waits" is missing and may be supplied by ellipsis from the previous verse.

IV. Confidence in Redemption

130:7–8

7 O Israel, put your hope in the LORD,
for with the LORD is unfailing love
and with him is full redemption.
8 He himself will redeem Israel
from all their sins.

7–8 The confidence in the Lord inspired the psalmist to call on all of Israel to renew their submission to the Lord. The call "put your hope [*yahēl*] in the LORD" (v.7) flows out of his own experiences ("and in his word I put my hope," *hôḥāltî,* v.5; both verbs are from the root *y-ḥ-l*). His encouragement resembles that of the psalmist in 131:3. God's "unfailing love" (*ḥesed*) and his "redemption" (*pᵉdûṯ;* cf. 111:9) are unmerited favors, which he sovereignly bestows on his children. The expression "full redemption" relates his favor to many different circumstances as well as the many objects of his grace. His "redemption" is so great that he can even forgive his people from all their "sins" (*ʿᵃwōnōṯāyw,* v.8; cf. v.3) and free them from whatever adversities they suffer from as a result of their sins (see H. Wheeler Robinson, *Redemption and Revelation in the Actuality of History* [London: Nisbet, 1942], p. 223; Miller, "Psalm 130," *Interpreting the Psalms,* pp. 138–43).

Psalm 131: Contentment With God

This is one of the "Songs of Ascents" (see introduction to Ps 120). The writer shares his own experience with God as an encouragement to the community (v.3). In form it is an *individual psalm of confidence.*

131:1–3

A song of ascents. Of David.

1 My heart is not proud, O LORD,
my eyes are not haughty;
I do not concern myself with great matters
or things too wonderful for me.
2 But I have stilled and quieted my soul;
like a weaned child with its mother,
like a weaned child is my soul within me.

3 O Israel, put your hope in the LORD
both now and forevermore.

1 The psalm begins with an emphatic reference to Yahweh in the MT: "O Yahweh, my heart." In the presence of the covenant God, the psalmist has experienced how wonderful complete submission to God is. Submission implies an attitude of humility (cf. Mic 6:8). The opposite of humility is "haughty eyes" and a preoccupation "with great matters" (v.1). The proud person looks, compares, competes, and is never content. He plans and schemes in his heart as to how he can outdo and outperform. The godly knows that true godliness begins in the "heart" that is not proud (cf. Prov 18:12), with eyes that do not envy (cf. 18:27; 101:5; Prov 16:5), and with a walk of life (MT, "I do not walk" for NIV, "I do not concern myself") that is not preoccupied with "greatness" (cf. Jer 45:5) and with accomplishments ("wonderful," i.e., "difficult" or "arduous"; cf. Deut 17:8; 30:11).

2–3 The psalmist has been like a child in the presence of God. Oh the wonder of quiet contentment with God! He has enjoyed the walk with God in which he "stilled" ("composed") himself and "quieted" (i.e., "silenced" or "found rest," 62:1, 5) his soul (v.2).

The psalmist was also like "a weaned child." The age of the child in the simile of the "weaned child" (*gāmul*) should not be stressed. The word *gāmul* may also mean "contented" (W.A. VanGemeren, "Psalm 131:2—*k^e^gāmul*. The Problem of Meaning and Metaphor," *Hebrew Studies* 23 [1982]: 51–57). The suggestion is sometimes made that a weaned child is no longer restless when it is with its mother because it no longer frets for milk. However, a baby satisfied with its mother's milk can also lie contented on its mother's breast. The essential picture is that of contentment, regardless of the age. So the psalmist feels a deep sense of peace, tranquility, and contentment with his God. Gottfried Quell suggests that the psalmist speaks of the experience of children being carried by their mothers on the pilgrimage to Jerusalem ("Struktur und Sinn des Psalms 131," *Das Ferne und Nahe Wort: Festschrift Leonhard Rost zur Vollendung seines 70. Lebensjahres am 30. November 1966 gewidmet*, ed. Fritz Maas [Berlin: Topelmann, 1967], pp. 173–85). Based on his wonderful relationship and walk with the Lord, David calls on Israel to trust in the Lord forevermore (cf. 130:7).

Notes

For a brief discussion of the technical words and phrases in the superscription, see the Introduction.

Psalm 132: The Tabernacling of Yahweh

This is one of the "Songs of Ascents" (see introduction to Ps 120). The psalm is a tenth-century composition, celebrating the bringing of the ark of the covenant into Jerusalem (cf. 2 Sam 6:12–19; Ps 132:6–10). The procession from the house of Obed-Edom to Jerusalem lies in the background of this poetic version of that grand moment in the history of redemption, when Zion was chosen as the capital of David's kingdom and the center of worship. The Chronicler incorporates vv.8–10 in Solomon's prayer at the dedication of the temple (cf. 2 Chron 6:41–42). Others interpret the psalm in the context of a coronation ceremony of a Davidic king (see Delbert R. Hillers, "Ritual Procession of the Ark and Ps 132," CBQ 30 [1968]: 48–55).

The literary genre falls between the Songs of Zion and the royal psalms (see Allen, pp. 204–9). Because of its emphasis on the temple and on God's election of Zion, the psalm is here classified as a Song of Zion. The Songs of Zion have much in common with the royal psalms, as they celebrate the glories associated with Jerusalem: temple and kingship. Unlike the royal psalms, the Songs of Zion proclaim the glories of Zion in universal and eschatological terms (see appendix to Ps 46: Zion Theology).

The exegesis of the psalm is complex because of critical, linguistic, literary, and theological issues. These need not be solved in this exposition (see Allen, pp. 204–9; Kraus, *Psalmen,* 2:877–83; Terence E. Fretheim, "Psalm 132: A Form-Critical Study," JBL 86 [1967]: 289–300). Because of its length and archaic features, the psalm's place among the Songs of Ascents is clearly an enigma.

The literary structure divides into three stanzas (vv.1–5, 6–10, 11–18); but, as Fretheim has demonstrated, the elements of liturgy, narration, and dissonance come together into one meaningful whole. The first stanza begins with a prayer and the second ends on a prayer, forming an inclusion (vv.1, 10). The third stanza is a further development in response to the prayers for David.

A. Prayer for David (v.1)
  B. David's Devotion (vv.2–5)
    C. David's Concern for God's Presence (vv.6–9)
A′. Prayer for David (v.10)
  B′. God's Reward to David (vv.11–12)
    C′. God's Presence in Zion (vv.13–18)

(Bibliography: J.R. Porter, "The Interpretation of 2 Samuel VI and Psalm CXXXII," JTS, NS 5 [1954]: 161–73; C.B. Houk, "Psalm 132, Literary Integrity, and Syllable-Word Structures," JSOT 6 [1978]: 41–48; C. Brekelmans, "Psalm 132: Unity and Structure," *Bijdragen: Tijdschrift voor Filosofie en Theologie* 44 [1983]: 262–65.)

I. Prayer for David

132:1, 10

A song of ascents.

1 O LORD, remember David
and all the hardships he endured.

10 For the sake of David your servant,
do not reject your anointed one.

1, 10 The psalmist or a grateful congregation prays that the Lord will kindly remember all the acts of David's devotion (for a similar prayer or expression, cf. Neh 5:19; 13:14, 22, 31). The act of remembering (*z-k-r*) may denote a special kind of remembering, as God does when his covenant is seriously threatened by a third party. He remembered the Abrahamic covenant when Israel was in Egypt (Exod 6:5) and when Israel had sinned against the Lord (cf. Exod 32:13; Lev 26:42; Deut 9:27). It is more likely that the prayer is for God's continual remembrance of his covenant with David (v.10; cf. 89:49–50). The Lord's remembrance is for "blessing" his people (Allen, p. 201). David had endured great "hardships" (v.1; lit., "self-affliction"; cf. Lev 23:27, 29) in the conquest of Jerusalem (2 Sam 5:6–12) and in bringing the ark to Jerusalem.

Verse 10 forms an inclusion with v.1. The prayer upholds David by the special designations "your servant" (*'eḇeḏ;* cf. 27:9) and "your anointed one" (*māšîaḥ;* cf. 2:2;

84:9; 89:20). These designations apply to David and to all his descendants who were anointed as kings over Israel or Judah. The prayer also petitions the Lord to deal kindly with David's descendants and, consequently, with the people. The expression "do not reject" (lit., "do not turn away the face"; cf. 1 Kings 2:16) is the same as that in 84:9: "look with favor on your anointed one."

Notes

For a brief discussion of the technical words and phrases in the superscription, see the Introduction.

1 The LXX and Syriac read "his humility" instead of "his hardship," suggesting an alternate reading of the MT (cf. BHS). This alternate reading is suggestive of David's humiliation before the ark and his rebuke by his wife (cf. 2 Sam 6:16, 20–22). Allen has "his painstaking effort" (p. 200).

II. David's Devotion

132:2–5

2 He swore an oath to the LORD
and made a vow to the Mighty One of Jacob:
3 "I will not enter my house
or go to my bed—
4 I will allow no sleep to my eyes,
no slumber to my eyelids,
5 till I find a place for the LORD,
a dwelling for the Mighty One of Jacob."

2 Though the "oath" and "vow" have not been recorded in Samuel or Chronicles, David was determined to bring the ark to Jerusalem and to have a temple built. When David heard that God had blessed Obed-Edom, the guardian of the ark (2 Sam 6:12), David immediately made efforts to bring the ark to Jerusalem.

The "LORD" (Yahweh) is "the Mighty One of Jacob" (vv.2, 5; the repetition is an inclusionary motif). The designation "Mighty One of Jacob" derives from Genesis 49:24 and signifies the marvelous manner in which the Lord had protected, guided, and blessed Jacob. The epithet connotes the great strength of the Lord as the Divine Warrior (see appendix to Ps 98: Yahweh Is the Divine Warrior) rather than a possible rendering "the Steer of Jacob." The Lord had granted David his victories (cf. 2 Sam 5:12; 7:1), and David planned to erect an edifice to this Great King, the Divine Warrior.

3–4 David vowed not to enter his "house" or to go to "bed" until the temple was built. The MT reads, "the tent of my house" and "the couch of my bed." Both expressions may refer to the same object, namely, that he would not enter his inner chamber (bedroom) to lie down on his bed. These expressions are further clarified in v.4 (cf. Prov 6:4). Some have concluded from the phraseology of v.3 that David vowed to abstain from marital relations (A.A. Anderson, 2:881). However, this is unlikely if v.3 and v.4 are read together.

5 David's goal was to establish a "place" for God's "dwelling" (*miškānô<u>t</u>,* pl.; cf. 43:3; cf. 2 Sam 6:17). David made a temporary structure for the tabernacle and only later desired to build a more permanent structure. The former he was granted, but the latter had to wait until Solomon's reign. David's concern was with the glory of the Lord and with the blessedness of the presence of the covenant God, who had promised to "dwell" (*š-k-n,* "tabernacle") in the midst of his covenant people (cf. Exod 25:8–9).

Notes

---

5 Nahum M. Sarna concludes that אָבִיר (*'ā<u>b</u>îr,* "Mighty") and אַבִּיר (*'abbîr,* "bull") are etymologically unrelated and existed separately from the beginning ("The Divine Title *'abhîr ya'aqôbh,"* in *Essays on the Occasion of the Seventieth Anniversary of the Dropsie University [1909–1979],* edd. Abraham I. Katsh and Leon Nemoy [Philadelphia: Dropsie, 1979], pp. 389–96).

III. David's Concern for God's Presence

132:6–9

6 We heard it in Ephrathah,
we came upon it in the fields of Jaar:
7 "Let us go to his dwelling place;
let us worship at his footstool—
8 arise, O LORD, and come to your resting place,
you and the ark of your might.
9 May your priests be clothed with righteousness;
may your saints sing for joy."

6 David and his men ("we") heard of the whereabouts of the ark when they were at Ephrathah. The location of Ephrathah is further defined by "in the fields of Jaar." Ephrathah by itself could refer to the vicinity around Bethlehem (Ruth 4:11; Mic 5:2) or to Kiriath Jearim (cf. 1 Chron 2:19, 24, 50); but with the further description of "the fields of Jaar"—a reference to Kiriath Jearim (Jearim is a plural of "Jaar")—the identity of Ephrathah is further delimited in favor of Kiriath Jearim, where the ark was located (cf. 1 Sam 6:21–7:2; see F.M. Cross, Jr., *Canaanite Myth and Hebrew Epic* [Cambridge: Harvard, 1973], p. 94).

7–8 The "find" of the ark was well received by the people. Together with David and his men, they desired to worship the Lord in Jerusalem. The people joined in the festal procession as the ark was led from Obed-Edom's house in Kiriath Jearim to Jerusalem, "his dwelling place" (*miškānô<u>t</u>,* v.7, pl., as in v.5), also known as God's "resting place" (v.8). With the choice of Jerusalem and the final transportation of the ark to Jerusalem, the period of the desert wanderings came to an end. The ark had been transported by the priests until it was placed in the Shiloh tabernacle (1 Sam

4:3). With the capture of the ark by the Philistines, it went from city to city (1 Sam 4–6) until David brought it to Jerusalem. The placement of the ark in Jerusalem ushered in a new era in God's rule over Israel: the Davidic era.

The ark after all was the "footstool" of the Lord's throne (see 99:5). The temple and, more particularly, the ark symbolized the earthly rule of God (99:1–2; cf. Num 10:35–36; 2 Chron 6:41–42). God had extended his kingdom to Israel and through Israel to the ends of the earth.

The worship of the Lord signified a reception of and submission to his kingship (v.7). The Great King is the Divine Warrior, whose "might" (*'ôz*, v.8) was represented by the ark (cf. 78:61). It had been "the" symbol of Yahweh as the Divine Warrior during the wilderness journey (cf. Num 10:35–36). To this end the people repeat the words of Moses ("arise, O LORD"; cf. Num 10:35–36) as they bring the ark to Jerusalem, praying that the Lord will grant them deliverance from their enemies and will rule over them (v.8). (See appendix to Ps 98: Yahweh Is the Divine Warrior).

9 The priests who served in the presence of the Lord were his instruments for dispensing "righteousness" (*ṣeḏeq*, v.9). "Righteousness" here signifies more than a relationship with God. It is synonymous with "salvation" (*yēša'*, v.16; see 2 Chron 6:41), signifying victory, blessing, and deliverance (see 4:1; 22:31; 24:5). The blessedness of his presence, represented by the priests "clothed" in their priestly garments, resulted in great joy to God's loyal servants (*ḥ^{a}sîḏîm;* NIV, "saints," v.9; see 4:3).

IV. Prayer for David

132:10

10 For the sake of David your servant,
do not reject your anointed one.

10 See the comments on v.1.

V. God's Reward to David

132:11–12

11 The LORD swore an oath to David,
a sure oath that he will not revoke:
"One of your own descendants
I will place on your throne—
12 if your sons keep my covenant
and the statutes I teach them,
then their sons will sit
on your throne for ever and ever."

11–12 The Lord responds to David's "oath" (v.2) with his own "oath" (v.11). Though the narrative in Samuel pertaining to the promises to David (2 Sam 7:12–16) makes no mention of an oath, here it is a poetic expression for the certainty of God's promise to David (cf. 89:3, 35). His word is "a sure oath" (*'^{e}meṯ*, lit., "faithful"; see 15:2; cf. 2 Sam 7:28, "your words are trustworthy"). The word of God relates to David's oath (vv.2–5) and also to his prayer (vv.1, 10). The verbal phrase "do not reject" (v.10, from *š-w-b*) is related to the promise that he will not "revoke" (*š-w-b*) his "sure oath" (v.11).

David's concern and effort in establishing a "dwelling" (v.5) for the Lord is symmetric with the Lord's concern to establish the throne of David (vv.11–12). With these two foci (God's presence and the Davidic dynasty) the restlessness characteristic of Israel from Moses to David comes to an end. The promises to Abraham came to a specific fulfillment during that grand era of the Davidic-Solomonic kingship.

The Lord established David's dynasty ("one of your own descendants," "your sons," "their sons," vv.11–12). The promise of kings coming out of Abraham's seed is thus being fulfilled in David's dynasty (Gen 17:6). The promises focus on David, as he is the divinely appointed "seed" by whom the promises of the covenants are to be fulfilled.

The promises are balanced by responsibility. The king by his unique office is the guardian of the theocracy and hence of the covenant. He must keep the "covenant" (*berîṯ*, v.12; cf. 55:20; 89:34), i.e., "the statutes" (*'ēḏôṯ*; cf. 25:4–5, 9; 71:17; 119:2, 12) of the Lord. The sovereignty of God decrees that the dynasty of David will rule. The holiness and justice of the Lord require that David and his descendants be loyal to the covenant God. The promise belongs to David and his seed forevermore (cf. 89:4, 29; Jer 33:20–22)!

VI. God's Presence in Zion

132:13–18

13 For the LORD has chosen Zion,
he has desired it for his dwelling:
14 "This is my resting place for ever and ever;
here I will sit enthroned, for I have desired it—
15 I will bless her with abundant provisions;
her poor will I satisfy with food.
16 I will clothe her priests with salvation,
and her saints will ever sing for joy.

17 "Here I will make a horn grow for David
and set up a lamp for my anointed one.
18 I will clothe his enemies with shame,
but the crown on his head will be resplendent."

13–14 The presence of the Lord is related to his choice of Zion (v.13) and to David's concern for God's presence in the midst of his people (vv.2–5). Temple and kingship are corollary concepts (Kraus, *Psalmen*, 2:879–83). Zion is chosen as the earthly city of the Great King, where he makes his "dwelling" (*môšāḇ*) and "resting place" (vv.13–14; cf. vv.7–8). David prayed that the Lord might establish a "place" for "his footstool" in Jerusalem (vv.5, 7); and the Lord assured him that he "has chosen" (*b-ḥ-r*, v.13) and "desired" (*'-w-h*, vv.13–14) to establish his kingdom there: "here I will sit enthroned" (*y-š-b*; cf. v.12: "[they] will sit," *y-š-b*, i.e., "their sons will sit on the throne"). The divine rule and the divinely appointed ruler were hereby concentrated in Jerusalem before the coming of our Lord Jesus.

15–16 The Lord will bless his people abundantly in his royal presence (v.15). The presence of the Divine Warrior (cf. v.8) guarantees his beneficence in "salvation" (i.e., "deliverance," v.16), "provisions" (v.15), and "joy" (v.16; cf. Deut 15:4–6). The "poor" (*'ebyôn*, v.15; cf. 35:10; 86:1) and the "priests" (v.16; cf. v.9) will share in this new age.

17–18 These verses continue the promises made to David in vv.11–12 and also are God's response to the prayer for David (vv.1, 10). The Lord's promise that he will "make . . . grow" (*š-m-ḥ*, v.17) brings to our mind the many promises that he will raise up a "shoot" of David (cf. Jer 23:5; Zech 3:8; 6:12)—the messianic King (see Briggs, 2:472). The "horn" denotes the great vigor of the Davidic dynasty, by whom the Lord had planned to rule over the earth (89:24–29). Even after the Exile, the promise of the "sprouting horn" was kept alive (cf. Ezek 29:21). Zechariah, the father of John the Baptist, understood v.17 as a messianic reference (Luke 1:69–75).

David, who is also called "the lamp of Israel" (2 Sam 21:17), is further assured that his "lamp" (*nēr*) has been "set up" by the Lord (v.17). The Lord has established his dynasty like a "lamp" that is kept burning and gradually lightens everything from darkness to full light (cf. 18:28). Through David's dynasty God's kingship will be established, because God will subdue his enemies. The glory of David's dynasty is further summed up by the "crown" (v.18), a symbol of his glorious rule (89:39). The priests will "be clothed with righteousness," i.e., "salvation" (v.16), as a symbol of God's blessings and rule over his people. Through David the Lord will "clothe" his enemies with the shame of defeat and judgment (v.18; cf. 35:26; 109:29). This word of promise contains the Christian hope in the majesty, rule, and dominion of our Lord Jesus Christ. He will put down all of God's enemies (cf. 1 Cor 15:25–28; Rev 19:17–21).

Appendix: The Ark of the Covenant and the Temple: Symbols of Yahweh's Presence and Rule

Yahweh's rule extends to all spheres: heaven, earth, seas, and below the earth. His kingdom is both universal and outside of time, while at the same time it is local and within time. For example, the psalmist easily portrays his rule in heaven above: "The One enthroned in heaven laughs; / the Lord scoffs at them" (2:4) and in Zion below: "Sing praises to the LORD, enthroned in Zion; / proclaim among the nations what he has done" (9:11). Both references also bear out his universal kingdom: so also:

> The LORD reigns,
> let the nations tremble;
> he sits enthroned between the cherubim,
> let the earth shake.
>
> (99:1)

and "But you, O LORD, sit enthroned forever; / your renown endures through all generations" (102:12). Another psalm reveals how in Israel eternity and time and space intersect: "The LORD sits enthroned over the flood; / the LORD is enthroned as King forever" (29:10; cf. 113:5; 146:10).

The center of the world is Zion, and the focus of Zion is Yahweh. He "dwells" among his people. The "dwelling" (*š-k-n*) of Yahweh signifies both his freedom and his commitment. The use of *š-k-n* ("tabernacle" or "dwell," from which *miškān*, "tabernacle," "dwelling," "the place where the Lord dwells") in distinction from *y-š-b* ("reside," "abide") expresses the Hebraic concept of Yahweh's independence. Man resides (*y-š-b*), but God's "name" "tabernacles" (*š-k-n*) among man. When God is the subject of the root *y-š-b*, it is best to understand it as God's *enthronement* rather than his location (see Mettinger, pp. 78–79; 94–95). He is free, because nothing can bind, restrict, or limit God. He may enter into time and space, but he is not bound to it. His throne is in heaven (2:4), but his footstool is in Jerusalem: "Exalt the LORD our God / and worship at his footstool; / he is holy" (99:5).

The people of God rejoice that Yahweh is with them: "How lovely is your dwelling place [*miškān*], / O LORD Almighty!" (84:1). Yet his people can never take his presence for granted, because he is holy in his freedom. This means that Yahweh can never coexist with evil. Though he may tolerate evil, his holiness excludes evil; and in the end he wills to consecrate everything by his very presence. On the other hand, he is committed to his people. He chose Israel and has consecrated them to himself. These two emphases (freedom and commitment) present us with the OT dialectic. God is free to be present with his people but at the same time free to remove his presence from his people. Jerusalem is "the holy [*q-d-š*] place where the Most High dwells [*miškān*]" (46:4), but Yahweh may also abandon his earthly habitat.

The token of the Lord's presence is Jerusalem, Mount Zion, the holy mountain. The psalmists expect the Lord to respond to their prayers from Zion: "To the LORD I cry aloud, / and he answers me from his holy hill" (3:4). They long to be God's invited guests on his holy mountain: "LORD, who may dwell in your sanctuary? / Who may live on your holy hill?" (15:1; cf. 24:3). The hope of the righteous was to enjoy the closeness of communion no matter where they might be:

> One thing I ask of the LORD,
> this is what I seek:
> that I may dwell in the house of the LORD
> all the days of my life,
> to gaze upon the beauty of the LORD
> and to seek him in his temple [*hêḵāl*].
> (27:4; cf. 23:6)

Zion became the symbol of the Garden of Eden, the New Creation: "They feast on the abundance of your house; / you give them drink from your river of delights" (36:8; cf. 46:4). This explains the metaphor of the tree in Psalm 52:8:

> But I am like an olive tree
> flourishing in the house of God;
> I trust in God's unfailing love
> for ever and ever.
> (cf. 92:13)

The sanctuary is also the focus of the pilgrimage feasts, as Israel made its way toward Jerusalem:

> Send forth your light and your truth,
> let them guide me;
> let them bring me to your holy mountain,
> to the place where you dwell [*miškān*].
> (43:3; cf. 42:4; 55:14)

The tribes of Israel rejoiced in the presence of the Lord: "Great is the LORD, and most worthy of praise, / in the city of our God, his holy mountain" (48:1; 99:9). Though Jerusalem was only some two thousand feet above sea level, the mountain motif coalesces the real with the mythological, as the psalmist speaks of Yahweh's protection:

> For in the day of trouble
> he will keep me safe in his dwelling;

he will hide me in the shelter of his tabernacle
  and set me high upon a rock.

(27:5)

Yahweh has elected to dwell in Jerusalem. He has freely chosen Mount Zion as his "holy" mountain out of all the mountains: "He has set his foundation on the holy mountain" (87:1). All mountains are his (95:4), because he has created them (65:6; 90:2). But in a singular decision he has decreed that David's desire for a temple be granted and that he would bless his people with his presence (Ps 132): e.g.:

The LORD has chosen Zion,
  he has desired it for his dwelling [*y-š-b*].
"This is my resting place for ever and ever;
  here I will sit enthroned [*y-š-b*], for I have desired it."

(132:13–14)

The psalmist acclaims the significance of this choice by poetically ascribing the excellence of Zion: "Why gaze in envy, O rugged mountains, / at the mountain where God chooses to reign, / where the LORD himself will dwell forever?" (68:16; cf. v.15). Hence the people of God looked for Yahweh's protection and blessing, as they thought of the temple as God's dwelling place: "As the mountains surround Jerusalem, / so the Lord surrounds his people / both now and forevermore" (125:2; cf. 31:20; 121:1). The "mountain" motif brings together Yahweh's dwelling (the temple) and the covenant relationship, as well as the messianic dimension, as Yahweh decreed: "I have installed my King / on Zion, my holy hill" (2:6). One psalmist prays for the continual communion of David's dynasty with Yahweh: "May he be enthroned [*y-š-b*] in God's presence forever; / appoint your love and faithfulness to protect him" (61:7).

The "temple" was God's sanctuary (*miqdāš*, from *q-d-š*, "be holy"), his palace on earth. The OT recognizes gradations of holiness; while the whole land was holy, Jerusalem was more sacred. The outer court was holy, the Holy Place was holier, and the Most Holy Place was Yahweh's "dwelling," the *d^e^b̲îr* ("the Most Holy Place"; cf. 1 Kings 6:5, 16, 19–20; 7:49; 8:6, 8; 2 Chron 3:16 [NIV mg.]; 4:20). The *d^e^b̲îr* was cubicle in shape, in which the ark of the covenant symbolized the presence of Yahweh. The word occurs only once in the Psalms, in 28:2:

Hear my cry for mercy
  as I call to you for help,
as I lift up my hands
  toward your Most Holy Place [*d^e^b̲îr*].

God's palace (*hêḵāl*) is also known simply as his "house," where God's people desired to present themselves for an audience with the Great King:

But I, by your great mercy,
  will come into your house [*bayiṯ*];
in reverence will I bow down
  toward your holy temple [*hêḵāl*].

(5:7)

The "glory" (*kāb̲ôḏ*) of the Lord "dwelt" among Israel! The Gospel of John outlines the brilliance of God's glory in the Christ tabernacling on earth (John 1:14), but in the OT the people of God experienced Yahweh's glory: "I love the house where you live, O LORD, / the place where your glory dwells" (26:8).

The LORD's earthly palace is a replica, a microcosm, of his heavenly palace:

The LORD is in his holy temple [*hêkāl*];
the LORD is on his heavenly throne.
He observes the sons of men;
his eyes examine them.
(11:4; cf. 33:14; 103:19; 113:5; 123:1)

He rules, sees, judges, and rewards his creation from his holy temple in heaven as he does from his earthly sanctuary. He loves his people and responds to their prayers (18:6). His people are blessed, because they prosper on account of his presence:

Blessed are those you choose
and bring near to live in your courts!
We are filled with the good things of your house [*bayit*],
of your holy temple [*hêkāl*].
(65:4)

Hence the psalmist calls on God's people to proclaim to the nations that Yahweh, the King of the world, rules from Zion: "Sing praises to the LORD, enthroned [*y-š-b*] in Zion; / proclaim among the nations what he has done" (9:11). The people also present their offerings in gratitude for his deliverance: "Then there will be righteous sacrifices, / whole burnt offerings to delight you; / then bulls will be offered on your altar" (51:19; cf. 27:6; 66:13). They looked forward to joining together in the worship of Yahweh. The pilgrims' psalms ("Songs of Ascent," Pss 120–34) give a sense of the excitement, longing, and intensity of Israel's religion. For example, Psalm 122:

I rejoiced with those who said to me,
"Let us go to the house of the LORD."
Our feet are standing
in your gates, O Jerusalem.
Jerusalem is built like a city
that is closely compacted together.
That is where the tribes go up,
the tribes of the LORD,
to praise the name of the LORD
according to the statute given to Israel.
. . . .
For the sake of my brothers and friends,
I will say, "Peace be within you."
For the sake of the house of the LORD our God,
I will seek your prosperity.
(vv.1–4, 8–9)

The righteous looked beyond the superficiality of the organized cult, the hypocrisy of some priests and individuals, and all the frailty associated with people serving at the temple and reflected instead on Yahweh: his wonders, his salvation acts, and his love: "Within your temple, O God, / we meditate on your unfailing love" (48:9). Further, the godly desired to serve Yahweh as a member of his entourage:

Better is one day in your courts
than a thousand elsewhere;
I would rather be a doorkeeper in the house of my God
than dwell in the tents of the wicked.
(84:10)

Heaven is the Lord's palace (*hêkāl*), as is Jerusalem; but so, also, is God's creation on earth:

> The voice [*qôl*] of the LORD twists the oaks
> and strips the forests bare.
> And in his temple [*hêkāl*] all cry, "Glory [*kābôd*]!"
> The LORD sits enthroned [*y-š-b*] over the flood;
> the LORD is enthroned [*y-š-b*] as King [*melek*] forever.
>
> (29:9–10)

There is no limit to God's freedom to dwell wherever he so desires. The Jerusalem temple is a microcosm, a token, a symbol of his presence; but it can never confine the glorious majesty of the awesome Creator-Redeemer-King: "You are awesome, O God, in your sanctuary [*miqdāš*]; / the God of Israel gives power and strength to his people. / Praise be to God!" (68:35; cf. 96:6).

The ascription of praise and the perfections of God support the thesis that Yahweh's sanctuary was a concrete token of his kingdom. Prayer in the direction of the temple was not a superstitious act but showed submission to and love of the Great King, who dwelt among his people:

> I will bow down toward your holy temple
> and will praise your name
> for your love and your faithfulness,
> for you have exalted above all things
> your name and your word.
>
> (138:2)

Yahweh will secure the deliverance of all oppressed wherever they may be: "A father to the fatherless, a defender of widows, / is God in his holy dwelling" (68:5; cf. 9:7).

However, the people of God must always be mindful that Yahweh is holy (*q-d-š*): "Yet you are enthroned [*y-š-b*] as the Holy One; / you are the praise of Israel" (22:3). He was separate from evil and had consecrated his people to himself to be his holy people (Exod 19:5; cf. 1 Peter 2:9–10). But when his people desecrate the covenant and his sanctuary, Yahweh is free to abandon his people (cf. Ezek 10). In 586 B.C. Judah experienced traumatic shock as the temple was desecrated and destroyed by the Babylonian forces. The Israelites believed that they had a right to Yahweh and that he was bound to them; but they should have learned from the experience of Shiloh that Yahweh is free in his dwelling: "He abandoned the tabernacle [*miškān*] of Shiloh, / the tent he had set up among men" (78:60). When his people sin against his holy presence, his presence extricates himself from the institutions of man. So also it was in 586 B.C., when "they burned your sanctuary to the ground; / they defiled the dwelling place [*miškān*] of your Name" (74:7; cf. 79:1). Because of the correlation of Yahweh's dwelling among his people, the temple, and the Davidic dynasty, the psalmist also makes reference to Yahweh's alienation from David: "You have put an end to his splendor / and cast his throne to the ground" (89:44).

The symbol of God's eternal (meta-historical) and temporal rule is the ark. The Israelite had no problem of conceptualizing his rule, as he envisioned Yahweh's being enthroned on earth, in the temple, on the ark, and in between the cherubim: "Hear us, O Shepherd of Israel, / you who lead Joseph like a flock; / you who sit enthroned between the cherubim, shine forth" (80:1). Compare this sentiment with "God, who is enthroned forever, / will hear them and afflict them" (55:19).

To a certain degree the Davidic dynasty shared in this symbolism. For that reason David's concern for the ark (Ps 132) was such a significant matter. The vassal-king secured the kingdom of the suzerain by protecting and honoring the symbol of

Yahweh's lordship over the earth and over his people. David secured Jerusalem as the symbol of God's presence, his resting place (132:8), which Yahweh authorized with promise: "This is my resting place for ever and ever; / here I will sit enthroned, for I have desired it" (132:14). David prays that he and his defendants "may . . . be enthroned in God's presence forever" and that God would appoint his "love and faithfulness to protect" them (61:7). This is what Eichrodt calls the actualization of the presence of God:

> But its deepest value lies in the fact that here *the firm foundations of the earthly national community in a reality which is living and eternal, the roots of all earthly existence in a redeeming divine grace* which condescends to meet men in these concrete forms, are now brought home to the consciousness with a directness of impact that makes visible the inner organic connection between belief in God and the actions with which he is worshipped. (TOT, 1:421)

Texts: 5:7; 9:11; 15:1; 18:6; 22:3; 27:4–6; 31:20; 60:6; 61:4, 7; 63:2; 65:4; 73:17; 74:7; 79:1; 80:1; 87:2; 92:13; 100:4; 116:19; 118; 132; 138:2.

Related Topics: See appendixes to Pss 5 (Yahweh Is King); 7 (The Name of Yahweh); 9 (Yahweh Is El Elyon); 24 (Lord Sabaoth); 25 (The Perfections of Yahweh); 46 (Zion Theology); 78 (The Mighty Acts of Yahweh); 89 (The Messianic King); 98 (Yahweh Is the Divine Warrior); 103 (Sin and Forgiveness); 119 (Yahweh Is My Redeemer); 122 (The Praise of Yahweh); 137 (Imprecations in the Psalms); 140 (The Poor and Oppressed); 150 (Musical Instruments).

Bibliography: G.W. Ahlstrom, "Der Prophet Nathan und der Tempelbau," VetTest 11 (1961): 113–27; R.E. Clements, *God and Temple* (Philadelphia: Fortress, 1965); Richard J. Clifford, "The Tent of El and the Israelite Tent of Meeting," CBQ 33 (1971): 221–27; G. Henton Davies, "The Ark of the Covenant," *Annual of the Swedish Theological Institute* 5 (1967): 30–47; Eichrodt, TOT, 1:392–456; Jörg Jeremias, "Lade und Zion. Zur Entstehung der Ziontradition," in *Probleme biblischer Theologie. Gerhard von Rad zum 70. Geburtstag,* ed. Hans Walter Wolff (München: Chr. Kaiser, 1971), pp. 183–98; H.-J. Kraus, "Die Kulttraditionen Jerusalems," *Psalmen,* 1:197–205; id., "Die Verherrlichung der Gottesstadt," *Psalmen* 1:342–45; id., "Königtum und Kultus in Jerusalem," *Psalmen,* 2:879–83; id., *Theologie,* pp. 88–94; M. Haran, *The Temple;* id., "The Ark and the Cherubim: Their Symbolic Significance in Biblical Ritual," IEJ 9 (1959): 30–38, 89–94; Jean Ouellette, "The Solomonic Debir According to the Hebrew Text of I Kings 6," JBL 89 (1970): 338–43; Aubrey R. Johnson, "The Role of the King in the Jerusalem Cults," *The Labyrinth: Further Studies in the Relation Between Myth and Ritual in the Ancient World,* ed. S.H. Hooke (London: Society for Promoting Christian Knowledge, 1935), pp. 73–111; Mervyn Fowler, "The Meaning of *lipnê* YHWH in the Old Testament," ZAW 99 (1987): 384–90; Tryggve N.D. Mettinger, *The Dethronement of Sabaoth. Studies in the Shem and Kabod Theologies* (Lund: Gleerup, 1982); id., "YHWH Sabaoth—The Heavenly King on the Cherubim Throne," *Studies in The Period of David and Solomon and Other Essays,* papers read at the International Symposium for Biblical Studies, December 1979, ed. Tomoo Ishida (Winona Lake: Eisenbrauns, 1979), pp. 109–38; Bennie Charles Ollenburger, "Zion, the City of the Great King. A Theological Investigation of Zion Symbolism in the Tradition of the Jerusalem Cult," Ph.D. diss., Princeton University, 1982; G. von Rad, OTT, 1:234–41; Konrad Ruprecht, *Der Tempel von Jerusalem. Gründung Salomos oder jebusitsches Erbe? Beihefte zur Zeitschrift für die Alttestamentliche Wissenschaft* 144 (New York: Walter de Gruyter, 1977); Josef Schreiner, *Sion-Jerusalem. Jahwes Königssitz. Theologie der heiligen Stadt im Alten Testament* (München: Kösel, 1963); Roland de Vaux, "Arche d'Alliance et Tente de Réunion," *Bible et Orient* (Paris: Cerf, 1967), pp. 261–76; M. Weinfeld,

"The Concept of God and the Divine Abode," in *Deuteronomy and the Deuteronomic School,* pp. 191–209; Zimmerli, OTTO, pp. 70–81.

TDAT, 3:1012–32; 4:23–40; TDOT, 1:363–74; 2:107–16; 3:382–88; THAT, 2:903–9.

Psalm 133: The Communion of the Saints

This is one of the "Songs of Ascents" (see the introduction to Ps 120). The formula of "blessing" ("how good and how pleasant," see below) has suggested that Psalm 133 is a liturgical song of blessing or a wisdom psalm (A.A. Anderson, 2:885; Kraus, *Psalmen,* 2:889). The metaphors, images, and blessing formula favor the classification of *wisdom psalms* (see J.P.M. van der Ploeg, "Psalm CXXXIII and Its Main Problems," in *Loven en Geloven. Opstellen van Collega's en Medewerkers aangeboden aan Prof. Dr. Nic. H. Ridderbos,* ed. M.H. van Es et al. [Amsterdam: Ton Bolland, 1975], pp. 191–200; see appendix to Ps 1: The Ways of Wisdom and Folly). The date and origin of the psalm are uncertain. Stig Norin has proposed a context in which the tensions between Israel and Judah were still felt and concludes in favor of dating it to some time during the reign of Hezekiah (see "PS.133. Zusammenhang und Datierung," *Annual of the Swedish Theological Institute* 11 [1978]: 90–95).

The structure of the psalm reflects the patterns of blessing and comparison:

A. Blessing (v.1)
  B. Comparison With Oil (v.2a)
    C. Aaronic Ministry (v.2b)
  B′. Comparison With Dew (v.3a)
A′. Blessing (v.3b)

I. Blessing

133:1

A song of ascents. Of David.

1 How good and pleasant it is
  when brothers live together in unity!

1 The psalmist pronounces a blessing on those who "live together in unity." During the pilgrimages, the Jews enjoyed an ecumenical experience on their way toward and in Jerusalem. The pilgrims came from many different walks of life, regions, and tribes, as they gathered for one purpose: the worship of the Lord in Jerusalem. Their unity was in conformity with the regulations for the three annual feasts (Exod 23:14–17; Lev 23:4–22, 33–43; Num 28:16–31; 29:12–39; Deut 16:1–17). During the feasts the Jews celebrated their common heritage: redemption from Egypt and their encampment around the tabernacle in the wilderness (cf. Num 2).

Notes

For a brief discussion of the technical words and phrases in the superscription, see the Introduction.

II. Comparison With Oil and the Aaronic Ministry

133:2

> [2]It is like precious oil poured on the head,
> running down on the beard,
> running down on Aaron's beard,
> down upon the collar of his robes.

2 Fellowship of God's people on earth is an expression of the priesthood of all believers (cf. Exod 19:6), promised to Israel and renewed to the church in Christ (1 Peter 2:9–10). The psalmist compares the expression of harmonious unity to sacerdotal oil. The oil prepared for the use in the tabernacle was a special, fragrant oil, whose recipe was not to be imitated (cf. Exod 30:22–33). In addition to being used for the consecration of the Tent of Meeting, only the high priest and the priests could be anointed with this oil, associated exclusively with priestly service (cf. Exod 30:30–33).

The specific reference to "Aaron" should not be limited to him, as the whole priesthood was anointed with oil. Here Aaron is the "head" of the priestly clan. His name is representative of all the priests. Through the priestly institution the Lord assured his people of forgiveness and blessing (Exod 29:44–46; Lev 9:22–24; Num 6:24–26). At the same time the allusion back to primitive Israel in the wilderness conjures up the association of the unity of the tribes around the tabernacle, receiving the high priestly ministry of Aaron after he had been consecrated by "oil" (Lev 8:30).

The simile further compares the unity of the brotherhood to the plentiful oil, which runs down, down, down from the head, to the beard, and to "his robes."

Notes

2 It is not entirely clear whether it is the "beard" that is flowing down "upon the collar of his robes" (so MT; Allen, pp. 211–12) or the "oil." The latter suggestion seems more likely in view of the simile (see Kirkpatrick, p. 771; Dahood: "Like the precious oil . . . , which flows over the collar of his robes," *Psalms*, 3:250, 252). W.G.E. Watson treats the beard as a simile: "like Aaron's beard" ("The Hidden Simile in Psalm 133," *Biblica* 60 [1979]: 108–9). D.T. Tsumara's criticism is well taken. He argues that there are two, not three, similes and renders these verses thus:

> 2. Like the sweet oil on the head
> flowing on the beard,
> (the sweet oil) on Aaron's beard,
> flowing down on the collar of his robes;
> 3. Like the dew on Mt. Hermon
> flowing down on Zion's mountains.
> ("Sorites in Psalm 133, 2–3a," *Biblica* 61 [1980]: 416–17)

III. Comparison With Dew

133:3a

> [3]It is as if the dew of Hermon
> were falling on Mount Zion.

3a Because of the high altitude of Mount Hermon (nearly ten thousand feet above sea level) and the precipitation in the forms of rain, snow, and dew, Mount Hermon was proverbial for its lush greenery even during the summer months (cf. 89:12; "Hermon," in ZPEB, 3:125–26) and for its dew that sustained the vegetation. The experience of the pilgrims is like that of the refreshing dew of Hermon. During the summer months (from May to October) virtually no precipitation falls on Jerusalem, even in the form of dew. During these months at least two pilgrimages were held: the Feast of Firstfruits in May/June and the Feast of Booths in September. Regardless of how harsh the conditions of the pilgrimage, life, or nature, the fellowship of the brotherhood of God's people was refreshing.

IV. Blessing

133:3b

For there the LORD bestows his blessing,
even life forevermore.

3b The psalmist returns to the note of blessing (cf. v.1). Where God's people are living together "in unity," "there" the Lord sends blessing by his "command" (*ṣ-w-h;* NIV, "bestows"). The nature of the blessing is specified in the second part of this verse: "even life forevermore." "Life" with its fullness of enjoyment in the presence of God is a gift of God. Brueggemann comments, "Psalm 133 reflects Israel's capacity to appreciate the common joys of life and to attribute them to the well-ordered generosity of Yahweh" (*Message of the Psalms*, p. 48).

The referent of "there" is ambiguous. Some exegetes relate it back to "Mount Zion" (Kirkpatrick, p. 771). Dahood more properly associates the brotherly concord (v.1) with Zion (*Psalms*, 3:252). Yet it makes little difference whether "there" refers to those having fellowship or to Jerusalem, because in both cases "life" is enjoyed, not as an end in itself, but in communion with the people of God. (See the appendix to Ps 46: Zion Theology.)

Psalm 134: May Yahweh Bless You From Zion!

This is the last of the "Songs of Ascents" (see introduction to Ps 120) and forms a magnificent conclusion to this collection of psalms. It is a liturgical hymn by genre and consists of two strophes:

A. Call to Worship (vv.1–2)
B. Priestly Benediction (v.3)

I. Call to Worship

134:1–2

A song of ascents.

1 Praise the LORD, all you servants of the LORD
who minister by night in the house of the LORD.

[2]Lift up your hands in the sanctuary
and praise the LORD.

1–2 The psalmist calls on the priests to lead the people in worship. The priests are "the servants of the LORD," who "minister" (lit., "stand") in the temple. Though there is some disagreement on the identification of the "servants," the further descriptions denote the priests and possibly the Levites. They were chosen to "serve" (*'-b-d;* TWOT, 2:639) him in the temple ("the house of the LORD"). The priestly and Levitical ministry is often designated by the verb "stand" (*'-m-d;* cf. 135:2; Deut 10:8). The priests praised the Lord in song and with musical instruments both day and "night" (v.1; cf. 1 Chron 9:33; 23:26, 30).

In addition to praise in music, the Levites and priests also offered up prayers with hands lifted up (cf. 28:2; 1 Tim 2:8) "toward" the sanctuary, i.e., toward the Most Holy Place, in accordance with Solomon's instructions (cf. 1 Kings 8:30). Dahood understands by "sanctuary" the "heavenly sanctuary" (*Psalms,* 3:255) on the ground that the priests were already standing in the sanctuary. However, the similar phraseology in 28:2 as well as the central significance of the ark of the covenant in the "Most Holy Place" as God's footstool (cf. 132:7) makes the reference to a heavenly sanctuary somewhat strained.

Notes

For a brief discussion of the technical words and phrases in the superscription, see the Introduction.

1 The particle הִנֵּה (*hinnēh,* "behold," untr. in NIV) is an "emphatic call to attention" (Briggs, 2:477) and may be rendered: "Come!" (Dahood, *Psalms,* 3:254; Allen, p. 216; "Nun auf!" Kraus, *Psalmen,* 2:892).

The additional phrase in the LXX, "who minister . . . in the courts of the house of the LORD," may be an explanatory phrase from 135:2.

II. Priestly Benediction

134:3

[3]May the LORD, the Maker of heaven and earth,
bless you from Zion.

3 These words are reminiscent of the actual words spoken on the occasion of blessing by the priests (cf. Num 6:24–25). The blessing extends to all of life, wherever the people of God may go or live, because Yahweh, the covenant God ("LORD"), is "the Maker of heaven and earth," i.e., the Great King of the universe (see 121:2).

Psalm 135: Yahweh Is Free in His Marvelous Acts

The status of Psalms 135 and 136 in relation to the Great Hallel psalms (see introduction to Ps 120) in ancient Judaism is not clear. Some Jewish authorities include Psalms 135 and 136 as a part of the collection of Psalms 120–136, whereas others limit the Great Hallel psalms to 135–136, or even to Psalm 136 alone. Like the Songs of Ascents, Psalm 135 is related to one of the great feasts; but it is far from clear at which feast it was sung.

This psalm is a hymn of descriptive praise of God the Creator (vv.5–7) and Lord of history (vv.8–12). The reader will be struck by the many allusions as well as direct citations to other passages of Scripture. The end result of the psalmist's artistry is that the inspired creation stands on its own, even though it is dependent on other Scriptures for its poetic, liturgical, and idiomatic expressions.

Structurally the psalm divides into five strophes, four of which are symmetric; the central one (vv.8–14) is most important as it gives the reason why Israel should praise his "name" (v.13; cf. vv.3–4) as the God of the covenant community (see appendix to Ps 7: The Name of Yahweh).

- A. Israel's Praise (vv.1–4)
  - B. Yahweh's Greatness as Creator (vv.5–7)
    - C. Yahweh's Acts in Redemptive History (vv.8–14)
      1. In Egypt (vv.8–9)
      2. In conquest (vv.10–12)
      3. In all affairs (vv.13–14)
  - B′. The Inability of Idols (vv.15–18)
- A′. Israel's Praise (vv.19–21)

I. Israel's Praise

135:1–4

1 Praise the LORD.

Praise the name of the LORD;
  Praise him, you servants of the LORD,
2 you who minister in the house of the LORD,
  in the courts of the house of our God.

3 Praise the LORD, for the LORD is good;
  sing praise to his name, for that is pleasant.
4 For the LORD has chosen Jacob to be his own,
  Israel to be his treasured possession.

1–2 Verse 1 is identical to 113:1, except for the transposition of the colons, and together with v.2 is a continuation of 134:1–2. The priests and Levites (cf. vv.19–20) were charged with the worship of the Lord in "the house of the LORD" (= the temple; see 134:1) and with leading all Israel (cf. vv.20b–21), assembled "in the courts of the house of our God" (v.2; cf. 116:19), in the praise of his holy name (see appendix to Ps 7: The Name of Yahweh).

The "praise" of God included a recitation of his mighty acts in creation (vv.5–7) and in redemptive history (vv.8–14). It was an expression of devotion to the covenant God, referred to as "our God" (v.2; cf. 113:5; 118:27–28), whose name was revealed to Israel (see appendix to Ps 78: The Mighty Acts of Yahweh).

3–4 The praise of the Lord celebrates the goodness and pleasantness of the Lord (v.3). He is "good" (*ṭôḇ*) in his beneficent acts to his covenant people (cf. 23:6; 118:1, 29;

136:1). He is also "pleasant" (*nā'îm*) to those who have experienced his electing love (v.4).

The joyous proclamation of the name of the Lord evolves out of a relationship initiated and maintained by him. He "has chosen Jacob to be his own," i.e., "his treasured possession" (*s^e^gullāh*, v.4; cf. Exod 19:5; Deut 7:6; 14:2). They are his one nation on earth to serve him, and to this end he made them to be his "sanctuary" and "dominion" (114:2). The designation "treasured possession" must be associated with the complementary concepts of "rule" and "holy service" (cf. Exod 19:5–6; Mal 3:17).

Notes

3 The word נָעִים (*nā'îm*, "pleasant") could refer back to "the LORD" and be a synonym of "good": "for the LORD is good . . . for [the LORD] is pleasant" (A.A. Anderson, 2:890). It may also refer back to "his name": "sing praise to his name, for it is pleasant" (Allen, pp. 221–22; so NIV).

II. Yahweh's Greatness as Creator

135:5–7

5 I know that the LORD is great,
   that our Lord is greater than all gods.
6 The LORD does whatever pleases him,
   in the heavens and on the earth,
   in the seas and all their depths.
7 He makes clouds rise from the ends of the earth;
   he sends lightning with the rain
   and brings out the wind from his storehouses.

5 The confession of God's greatness is expressed in the personal language of faith—"I know" (*'^a^nî yāḏa'tî*, with emphatic "I"), as in the hymn "I know whom I have believed, and am persuaded." The public praise of the Lord's being "good and pleasant" (v.3) finds personal expression in a confession of his greatness: "the LORD is great" (v.5). The greatness of the Lord pertains to his rule over all creation, to the exclusion of any other deities (cf. Exod 15:11–12).

6 God's greatness also extends to his powers over earth, the sea, and in heaven. He is not limited to a particular sphere assigned to him by his creatures, as is the case with pagan deities. The Lord is God over all realms by virtue of his being the Creator. The realm of his dominion extends to everything, and his authority is unlimited ("The LORD does whatever pleases him"; see 115:3) in his acts in heaven, on the earth, in the seas, and in "all the depths" (MT), i.e., the subterranean waters rather than the depths of the sea (as implied by the NIV's "all their depths").

7 His greatness even extends to the elements and powers of nature: rain, lightning, and wind (cf. Jer 10:13; 51:16). The Canaanites believed that these powers belonged to Baal, but the psalmist confesses rightly that only Yahweh has powers to "the ends of the earth" and even to the "storehouses," from which any of the elements could be brought forth (cf. 33:7; 65:9–10; Job 38:22–23).

III. Yahweh's Acts in Redemptive History

135:8–14

8 He struck down the firstborn of Egypt,
the firstborn of men and animals.
9 He sent his signs and wonders into your midst, O Egypt,
against Pharaoh and all his servants.
10 He struck down many nations
and killed mighty kings—
11 Sihon king of the Amorites,
Og king of Bashan
and all the kings of Canaan—
12 and he gave their land as an inheritance,
an inheritance to his people Israel.

13 Your name, O LORD, endures forever,
your renown, O LORD, through all generations.
14 For the LORD will vindicate his people
and have compassion on his servants.

8–14 The power of the Lord is displayed in nature and in Israel's history. The connection lies in the participles (v.7) translated by "makes . . . rise" (*ma'ᵃleh,* "brings up" and "brings out"; *môṣē',* an alternate form of *môṣî'*) are identical to the participles employed in the story of the miraculous exodus from Egypt (cf. Lev 11:45; Josh 24:17; Jer 2:6). Though the psalmist does not detail the Exodus itself, the participles of v.7 are suggestive enough to make the mental association. Hence the psalmist continues on the theme of God's power in vv.8–12 without any further introduction. The particle *še* (an alternate form of *'ᵃšer,* "who," untr. in NIV; see Allen, "He is the one who," p. 222) at the beginning of v.8 further connects vv.8–12 with vv.5–7.

The greatness of the Lord's power in the Exodus and Conquest motif is portrayed in climactic strokes: the tenth plague (v.8; cf. 78:51; 105:36; Exod 12:29) as the last of his "signs and wonders" in Egypt (v.9; cf. 65:8), the conquest of Transjordan and of Canaan. He showed his sovereignty over "Pharaoh and all his servants" (v.9) and over "many nations" (cf. Deut 7:1) and "mighty kings" (v.10), namely Sihon, Og, and "all the kings [lit., 'kingdoms'] of Canaan" (v.11; cf. 136:19–20; Num 21:21–26, 33–35; Deut 2:30–33; 3:1–6; Josh 12:2–24). The lands of the nations he sovereignly gave to his people Israel to be their "heritage" (v.12, twice: *naḥᵃlāh;* cf. Deut 4:38).

The greatness and power of the Lord extends to Egypt (vv.8–9) and to Canaan (vv.10–12) and is manifest throughout redemptive history (vv.13–14). This last aspect climaxes this section. The psalmist celebrates "the name" (*šēm*) and "the remembrance" (*zēḵer;* NIV, "renown") of the Lord in this liturgical conclusion, reminiscent of Exodus 3:15. The "name" of the God of Israel is Yahweh, as revealed to Moses (Exod 3:15; 6:3, 6–8). The name was to increase in significance, as the Lord increased his activities in the history of redemption and revealed more of himself in history and revelation. The "name" connotes the "fame" of God (A.A. Anderson, 2:892), and the "remembrance" (NIV, "renown") connotes Israel's response in celebration and proclamation (Brevard S. Childs, *Memory and Tradition in Israel* [Naperville:

Allenson], pp. 71–72) "through all generations" (cf. "Yahweh, your name will endure forever, / Yahweh, proclamation of you for generations," Allen, p. 222).

Because of this confidence in the Lord, the people of the Lord have a proper perspective on the future. They know him, because he has revealed his power in history. He had promised to vindicate them from their adversaries and thus to "have compassion on his servants" (v.14; cf. Deut 32:36).

IV. The Inability of Idols

135:15–18

15 The idols of the nations are silver and gold,
made by the hands of men.
16 They have mouths, but cannot speak,
eyes, but they cannot see;
17 they have ears, but cannot hear,
nor is there breath in their mouths.
18 Those who make them will be like them,
and so will all who trust in them.

15–18 The affirmations of God's acts in creation and in redemption—together with the conviction that, for the sake of "his servants," the Lord will continue to act in history and to engender praise for his name—are set in the polemical context of the exclusive powers of Yahweh vis à vis idols (vv.5, 15–18). The psalmist returns to the motif of vanity of idolatry by an extensive quotation from Psalm 115:4–8 (q.v.). Zimmerli has expressed the superiority of Israel's God well: "Whenever a hymn speaks of those other divine powers, whose existence is by no means denied on theoretical grounds, it can only be with reference to the One who will call their actions to judgment (Ps. 82), or in the spirit of superiority that mocks their impotence (Pss. 115:4–8; 135:15–18)" (OTTO, p. 155).

V. Israel's Praise

135:19–21

19 O house of Israel, praise the LORD;
O house of Aaron, praise the LORD;
20 O house of Levi, praise the LORD;
you who fear him, praise the LORD.
21 Praise be to the LORD from Zion,
to him who dwells in Jerusalem.

Praise the LORD.

19–21 The psalm concludes on a call to praise the Lord. This section is symmetric with the beginning (vv.1–4) and employs the language of 115:9–11 and 118:2–4 (q.v.) with the addition of "O house of Levi." The appropriate response is "praise" (*b-r-k*, "bless," five times in vv.19–21), as he is the source of Israel's blessing (cf. 133:3; 134:3). As a part of the liturgical significance of this psalm, the psalmist celebrates the promise of the Lord to be present in Zion (= Jerusalem, v.21; cf. 132:13–16; see appendix to Ps 46: Zion Theology).

Psalm 136: Yahweh Is Good!

This is the last of the Great Hallel psalms (see the introduction to Ps 120) or, according to some Jewish authorities, the only Hallel psalm. It, too, was associated with one of the great annual feasts, especially with the Feast of Passover. The literary form (genre) is that of an antiphonal hymn.

Structurally the psalm is simple. The focus is on the Lord's continuous involvement in redemptive history, beginning with the Exodus and the Conquest. However, the Lord's majesty and "love" (*ḥesed*) are not to be limited to his people, as they extend to all of his creation by virtue of his being the Creator (vv.4–9, 25). The unfolding pattern reveals a beautiful symmetry, beginning and ending with a call to praise the Lord. Claus Schedl gives an impressive literary analysis of this psalm in "Die alphabetisch-arithmatische Struktur von Psalm CXXXVI," VetTest 36 (1986): 489–94.

The expository structure of the psalm is as follows:

A. Hymnic Introit (vv.1–3)
  B. Creation Hymn (vv.4–9)
    C. Redemption Hymn (vv.10–22)
    C′. Redemption Hymn (vv.23–24)
  B′. Creation Hymn (v.25)
A′. Hymnic Conclusion (v.26)

(see Pierre Auffret, "Note sur la Structure littéraire du Psaume CXXXVI," VetTest 27 [1977]: 1–12; Jacob Bazak, "The Geometric-Figurative Structure of Psalm cxxxvi," VetTest 35 [1985]: 129–38).

I. Hymnic Introit

136:1–3

1 Give thanks to the LORD, for he is good.
His love endures forever.
2 Give thanks to the God of gods.
His love endures forever.
3 Give thanks to the Lord of lords:
His love endures forever.

1–3 The hymn opens on a note of thanksgiving familiar from other psalms (for virtually identical verses see 106:1; 107:1; 118:1). However, this psalm is different in that it repeats the liturgical formula "His love [*ḥesed*] endures forever" after every colon. The reason for praising the Lord lies in his beneficent acts. Since he is "the God of gods" (v.2) and "the Lord [*'ᵃḏōnê*] of lords" (v.3; cf. Deut 10:17), he alone is to be thanked for all the acts in creation and in redemption (vv.4–25). (See the appendix to Ps 25: The Perfections of Yahweh.)

II. Creation Hymn

136:4–9

4 to him who alone does great wonders,
His love endures forever.
5 who by his understanding made the heavens,
His love endures forever.
6 who spread out the earth upon the waters,
His love endures forever.

7 who made the great lights—
His love endures forever.
8 the sun to govern the day,
His love endures forever.
9 the moon and stars to govern the night;
His love endures forever.

4–6 Since Yahweh alone is God and King, he alone is to be praised for the "great wonders" (*nip̱lā'ôt g^{e}ḏōlôṯ,* v.4; cf. 72:18; 86:10; see 9:1; and see appendix to Ps 78: The Mighty Acts of Yahweh). His work of creation reveals his great wisdom ("understanding," *t^{e}ḇûnāh,* v.5; cf. 104:24; Prov 3:19; Jer 10:12). In his wisdom he made the heavens and "spread out" (cf. Isa 42:5; 44:24) the earth on the waters. Like a tent or a curtain (Briggs, 2:483) or a thin sheet of metal (A.A. Anderson, 2:895) may be spread out to cover something, so the poetic imagery portrays the earth as resting on the waters of creation (cf. 24:2). This is not scientific but poetic language!

7–9 The work of creation focuses particularly on God's handiwork in space: the great lights of the sun, moon, and stars (vv.7–9; cf. Gen 1:16). Though God's creation on earth reflects great glory, his work in space is overwhelming to man in all ages (cf. 8:1, 3; 19:1–6). Heaven (vv.7–9), with the sun and moon, affects life on earth and hence is evidence of God's goodness to all creatures on earth (v.25), especially to his people (vv.10–24).

III. Redemption Hymn

136:10–22

10 to him who struck down the firstborn of Egypt
His love endures forever.
11 and brought Israel out from among them
His love endures forever.
12 with a mighty hand and outstretched arm;
His love endures forever.

13 to him who divided the Red Sea asunder
His love endures forever.
14 and brought Israel through the midst of it,
His love endures forever.
15 but swept Pharaoh and his army into the Red Sea;
His love endures forever.

16 to him who led his people through the desert,
His love endures forever.
17 who struck down great kings,
His love endures forever.
18 and killed mighty kings—
His love endures forever.
19 Sihon king of the Amorites
His love endures forever.
20 and Og king of Bashan—
His love endures forever.
21 and gave their land as an inheritance,
His love endures forever.
22 an inheritance to his servant Israel;
His love endures forever.

10–15 Verses 10–22 repeat the motifs of 135:8–12: the Exodus and the Conquest. Of the many wonders in Egypt, the tenth plague receives particular mention (v.10; cf. 135:8). The Lord brought Israel out of Egypt (v.11) "with a mighty hand and an outstretched arm" (v.12), a metaphor for God's great and personal strength on behalf of his people (cf. Exod 6:1, 6; Deut 4:34; 5:15; 7:19; 11:2; 26:8). The Lord showed himself to be the Divine Warrior in Egypt and, particularly, at the Red Sea. There he showed up Pharaoh and his forces by judging them (v.15; cf. Exod 14:27), while he delivered the Israelites (vv.13–14; cf. 106:7; Exod 4:23).

16–20 The Lord guided his people through the wilderness (v.16; cf. Deut 8:15; Jer 2:6; Amos 2:10). The psalmist makes no mention of the giving of the law and the making of the covenant at Mount Sinai. Neither does he mention Israel's many rebellions. Care must be taken not to introduce critical thought in the investigation of Israel's history by taking these poetic reflections as complete. They witness to the traditions of Israel by a selective representation of a few motifs.

Not only did the Lord strike down the firstborn in Egypt, he also struck down the great and mighty kings (vv.16–17; cf. v.10). Sihon and Og are representative of the long list of Canaanite kings who were subdued (vv.19–20; see 135:11).

21–22 The conquered land became Israel's "inheritance" (cf. 135:12). In 135:12 Israel is called "his people Israel," whereas here she is affectionately called "his servant Israel." This latter designation is especially found in Isaiah (cf. 41:8; 44:1–2).

IV. Redemption Hymn

136:23–24

23 to the One who remembered us in our low estate
His love endures forever.
24 and freed us from our enemies,
His love endures forever.

23–24 Whenever Israel suffered, the history of redemption continued. The mighty acts of God in Egypt, in the wilderness, and in the conquest of the land are a sampling of his power and his purpose. Israel hereby confesses that the Lord is their Great King, who alone is able to deliver them from their enemies. He remembers (*z-k-r*) his covenant people in their distress, whether in the Exodus, in the period of exile (Kirkpatrick, p. 779), or in any other low point in the history of redemption. The Lord's remembrance is based on the covenant and has as its purpose the full redemption of his people (cf. Exod 6:5).

V. Creation Hymn

136:25

25 and who gives food to every creature.
His love endures forever.

25 The hymn returns to a reflection of God's goodness as the Creator. His "love" to all of creation is evident in that he continually cares for his creatures. He promised to Noah and to all "flesh" to sustain it with his grace (cf. Gen 9:8–17). Here the psalmist makes use of the word "flesh" (*bāśār;* NIV, "creature") and thus makes an allusion to God's promise (cf. Gen 9:11, 15–17; NIV, "creatures").

VI. Hymnic Conclusion

136:26

26 Give thanks to the God of heaven.
His love endures forever.

26 The hymn concludes on a note of thanksgiving (cf. vv.1–3). In vv.2–3 the psalmist referred to the Lord as "the God of gods" and "the Lord of lords." Here he adds a related concept: "the God of heaven." The phrase occurs only here in the Book of Psalms and is a relatively late designation of the Great King (cf. Ezra 1; 2; Neh 1:4; 2:4; Dan 2:44).

Psalm 137: If I Forget You, O Jerusalem

This is one of the imprecatory psalms (see appendix following). The formal classification of the genre of the psalm has been more difficult, as it has mixed types: communal lament (vv.1–4), a song of Zion (vv.5–6), and a curse (vv.7–9). A.A. Anderson rightfully observes that it is a *communal lament,* the genre being determined by the opening of the psalm (2:897). Cursing (execration) is not uncommon in the lament genre, in which the psalmist prays for God's vengeance on those who are responsible for his misery. Allen opts, after a thorough discussion, in favor of "a modified version of a Song of Zion" (p. 241). Graham S. Ogden associates the national psalm of lament with the prophetic oracles of judgment in "Prophetic Oracles Against Foreign Nations and Psalms of Communal Lament: The Relationship of Psalm 137 to Jeremiah 49:7–22 and Obadiah," *Journal for the Study of the Old Testament* 24 (1982): 88–97.

The expository structure of the psalm is as follows:

A. The Lament (vv.1–4)
B. The Confession of Confidence (vv.5–6)
C. Prayer for Divine Intervention (vv.7–9)

On the structure see D.N. Freedman, "The Structure of Psalm 137," *Near Eastern Studies in Honor of W.F. Albright,* ed. H. Goedicke (Baltimore: Johns Hopkins, 1971), pp. 187–205; Morris Halle and John J. McCarthy, "The Metrical Structure of Psalm 137," JBL 100 (1981): 161–67; Allen, pp. 239–40. For a concentric structural analysis, see Jonathan Magonet, "Some Concentric Structures in Psalms," *The Heythrop Journal* 23 (1982): 373–76.

The date of the psalm reflects a situation in between the return of the exiles from Babylon (vv.1, 3) and the rebuilding of the second temple (c. 537–515 B.C.). Ulrich Kellermann places it between 520 and 445 B.C. ("Psalm 137," ZAW 90 [1978]: 43–58).

I. The Lament

137:1–4

1 By the rivers of Babylon we sat and wept
when we remembered Zion.

2 There on the poplars
we hung our harps,
3 for there our captors asked us for songs,
our tormentors demanded songs of joy;
they said, "Sing us one of the songs of Zion!"

4 How can we sing the songs of the LORD
while in a foreign land?

1–2 The psalmist reflects on the time when the Judeans lived by "the rivers of Babylon" (v.1). For many Judeans life in Babylon was good. They lived by the Tigris and Euphrates rivers and enjoyed regular harvests due to a complex system of irrigation canals. The very tokens of life ("rivers") and verdancy ("poplars," v.2) brought material benefits on captors and captives alike. One such community was settled by the river Kebar (Ezek 1:1; 3:15). But all was loss for the godly in exile. Babylon may have been a pleasant country, but the Judeans were aliens in a foreign land, being far removed from Jerusalem.

The exiled population was settled (*yāšabnû*, "we sat" or "dwelled"). The prophet Jeremiah had encouraged them to make a living, to increase in number, and to seek the peace and prosperity of the land (Jer 29:4–9). Even in the midst of plenty, they "wept" (*bāḵînû*), mourning the loss of Zion.

3 The dainties of Babylon were tainted with the taunts of the captors, who "demanded songs of joy" (v.3). The lamenting community could not respond joyously. The taunts of the "tormentors" were like the question"Where is your God?" (42:3, 10; 79:10; 115:2). In this context the taunt may have focused on the magnificent "songs of Zion," celebrating the majesty and protection of the Lord over his people (46; 48; 76; 84; 87; 122). How could they sing the songs of Zion proclaiming the victories and deliverances of Yahweh throughout the history of redemption?

4 The Israelites could not sing of the glories of Zion and the strength and protection of their God, because the city lay in ruins and the people were captive in a "foreign land." Instead, they had hung up their "harps" (v.2; see appendix to Ps 150: Musical Instruments) on the many "poplars" growing on the banks of the canals (vv.1–2). How could they dwell in a foreign land without constantly mourning the loss of Zion? Though they were close to water, used for ritual cleansing, they still felt themselves unclean. They could not sing any of the holy songs on foreign, unclean soil. It is with these words that the psalmist creates the mood of desperate and seemingly hopeless lament and thus sets up vv.5–6, a song of Zion and the confidence and hope of Israel.

Notes

1–3 The inspired poet uses in a majestic way several literary features: assonance and alliteration (vv.1–4) by a repetition of the sibilants (sin, shin, zayin, tsadhe), repetition (עַל, *'al*, "by" or "on," vv.1–2; the suffix *nû* for the first person plural "we" as many as nine times), and wordplay (see note on v.3).

3 The words for the Babylonians are שׁוֹבֵינוּ (*šôḇênû*, "our captors") and תוֹלָלֵינוּ (*tôlālênû*, "our tormentors"). The latter word is a *hapax legomenon,* whose meaning is contextually derived from being a synonym of "our captors." It appears that the word is chosen to form a wordplay with תָּלִינוּ (*tālînû,* "we hung"; Allen, p. 236). Some suggest that the etymology is from *y-l-l* ("to howl," Kraus, *Psalmen,* 2:904) and others from *h-l-l* ("make a fool of," "mock," Dahood, *Psalms,* 3:270–71). Interesting as these etymologies are, we stick with Dahood's observation that this is "one of the most recalcitrant *hapax legomena* of the Psalter" (p. 270). The Targum reads שׁוֹלְלֵינוּ (*šōlᵉlênû,* "our plunderers"; BHS).

4 A.A. Anderson translates this verse: "How can we who are unclean (in that we are punished) sing Yahweh's praises to an unclean people in an unclean land?" (2:899).

II. The Confession of Confidence

137:5–6

5 If I forget you, O Jerusalem,
may my right hand forget ⌊its skill⌋.
6 May my tongue cling to the roof of my mouth
if I do not remember you,
if I do not consider Jerusalem
my highest joy.

5–6 Lament and sorrow focus on the profound love for Zion. Love for Zion is not separate from love for God. For the exiles the love for God and for Jerusalem were intertwined because of the temple. Though the temple was in ruins, the godly community focused its attention on Jerusalem, possibly remembering Solomon's prayer for those in exile (1 Kings 8:48–49).

Loyalty lies in remembering (v.1) instead of forgetting (v.5). The godly could not forget Jerusalem and everything it stands for: covenant, temple, presence and kingship of God, atonement, forgiveness, and reconciliation. They vowed never to forget God's promises and to persevere, waiting for the moment of redemption. As part of the vow, the godly took on themselves a formula of self-cursing: "may my right hand wither" (NIV, "forget its skill") and "May my tongue cling to the roof of my mouth" (v.6; cf. Lam 4:4; Ezek 3:26)!

The center of the psalm focuses on "Jerusalem." The remembrance of Jerusalem leads to a renewed devotion to the Lord. The self-malediction ("my right hand" and "my mouth") includes acts and speech. The self-malediction may also extend to the playing of musical instruments with one's "right hand" and of singing the songs of Zion with one's mouth (Weiser, p. 796; Allen, p. 242).

Notes

5–6 The play on words in the phrases אִם־אֶשְׁכָּחֵךְ (*'im-'eškāḥēḵ,* "if I forget you") and תִּשְׁכַּח (*tiškah,* "may my right hand forget") is set within an ABB′A′ structure:

A. If I forget . . .
  B. my right hand . . .
  B′. my tongue . . .
A′. if I do not remember

It is not entirely clear what the meaning of "may my right hand forget" is. The NIV adds an interpretive addition: "forget [its skill]." A number of exegetes have opted in favor of another meaning suggested by the wordplay, "wither" in the following translation: "Should I forget you, / O Jerusalem, / Let my right hand wither!" (Dahood, *Psalms*, 3:268; see discussion in A.A. Anderson, 2:899). It is possible that the object of the verb may have been deleted (haplography), but there is no evidence to support this proposal. See the extensive discussion in Allen (p. 236).

6 The exaltation of Jerusalem is favorite with the psalmists. Rare, however, is this psalmist's form: "If I do not consider [lit., 'bring up'] Jerusalem my highest joy [lit., 'on head of my joy']." Freedman ("Structure," pp. 197–98) gives a different rendering by emending the Hiphil to a Qal imperfect (*'e'eleh*): "I will ascend Jerusalem with joy upon my head."

III. Prayer for Divine Intervention

137:7–9

7 Remember, O LORD, what the Edomites did
on the day Jerusalem fell.
"Tear it down," they cried,
"tear it down to its foundations!"

8 O Daughter of Babylon, doomed to destruction,
happy is he who repays you
for what you have done to us—
9 he who seizes your infants
and dashes them against the rocks.

7 As the psalmist reflects on the moments of Judah's fall, he remembers the Edomite involvement. The Edomites had done everything to disgrace Judah and to keep the Judeans from escaping (cf. Lam 4:21; Ezek 25:12–14; 35:5–15; Obad 11–14; for background see B. Oded, "Judah and the Exile," in *Israelite and Judean History*, edd. John H. Hayes and J. Maxwell Miller [Philadelphia: Westminster, 1977], pp. 469–76). Not only did the Edomites do everything to frustrate the desperate people of Judah, they also encouraged the Babylonians to "tear it down to its [Jerusalem's] foundations!" The word "foundations" (*y^esôḏ*, from *y-s-d*) implies more than the actual foundations of the walls of Jerusalem, as it also pertains to the God-established order (*y-s-d*) in creation, in his rule, and in his election of a people to himself (cf. 24:2; 78:69; 89:11; 104:5). The Edomites were hoping for the destruction of the "foundations," of Yahweh's rule on earth. This interpretation receives its validation in Obadiah's prophecy against Edom.

8 The psalmist also turns to Babylon (cf. v.1). Babylon is personified as the "Daughter of Babylon" (cf. Isa 47:1; TWOT, 1:115). The psalmist prays that Babylon and all that Babylon represents will come to an end.

The blessing (*'ašrê;* see 1:1; NIV, "happy") lies on anyone used in bringing down Babylon. The idiom of blessing is used here for the purpose of imprecation ("curse"). The curse on Babylon is an expression of the lex talionis ("principle of retribution"; cf. Jer 51:56). The issue of retribution is complex, but Brueggemann observes, "On reflection it [Ps 137] may be the voice of a seasoned religion which knows profoundly what it costs to beat off despair. . . . It is an act of profound faith to entrust one's most precious hatreds to God, knowing they will be taken seriously" (*Message of the Psalms,* p. 77).

9 The psalmist repeats the beatitude in "blessed is he who seizes" (MT) as he brings the psalm to a climactic and shocking end. He prays that the Lord will bring on Babylon's head the atrocities they themselves had committed in Judah and elsewhere. Since Babylon had no "rocks," it is most likely that the psalmist expressed hereby the importance of divine retribution and the terrible wrong the Babylonians had done and had to be punished for. Wars were very cruel in the OT (cf. 2 Kings 8:12; Isa 13:16; Hos 1:4; 13:16; Amos 1:3, 13; Nah 3:10), and the Babylonians were famed for their cruelties (see Ogden, "Prophetic Oracles," pp. 89–97). The psalmist relishes the thought that some day the proud Babylonian captors will taste the defeat they have dished out and that they will be rendered to such a state of desolation and defenselessness that they are unable to defend even their infants.

Notes

7–9 For an approach to this psalm as a war oracle, see the study by Christensen, pp. 112–27. For other psalms, see 12; 60; 74; 79; 80; 83; 85; 90, 94:1–11; 123; 126.

7 The verb זְכֹר (*zᵉḵōr,* "remember") has a legal connotation (see Brevard S. Childs, *Memory and Tradition,* p. 32). The psalmist invokes the name of the covenant Lord (Judge) to secure his judgment on the Edomites.

On the order and disorder of God's kingdom on earth, see H.H. Schmid, "Creation, Righteousness, and Salvation: 'Creation Theology' as a Broad Horizon of Biblical Theology," in *Creation in the Old Testament,* ed. Bernard W. Anderson (Philadelphia: Fortress, 1984), pp. 102–17.

8–9 The assonance in these verses is symmetric with that of v.3:
הַשְּׁדוּדָה [הַשּׁוֹדְדָה] אַשְׁרֵי שֶׁיְשַׁלֶּם־לָךְ (*haššᵉḏûḏāh* [or *haššôḏᵉḏāh*] *'ašrê šeyšallem-lāḵ*, "doomed to destruction ['devastator'], happy is he who repays you") and אַשְׁרֵי שֶׁיֹּאחֵז וְנִפֵּץ (*'ašrê šeyyō'ḥēz wᵉnippēṣ,* "[happy is] he who seizes . . . and dashes"). The usage of the ayin may form an inclusion with vv.1–2: עֹלָלַיִךְ אֶל־הַסָּלַע (*'ōlālayiḵ 'el-hassāla',* "your infants . . . against the rock," v.9); cf. vv.1–2: עַל . . . עַל (*'al. . . . 'al,* "by . . . on"), especially considering the interchangeability of *'al* ("on," "by," "to") and *'el* ("to," "on"; cf. KB, p. 705).

8 The idiom שְׁדוּדָה (*šᵉḏûḏāh,* "doomed to destruction") has caused problems in interpretation. The MT literally reads, "Daughter of Babylon, the destroyed one." Since Babylon was not destroyed by Cyrus upon its capture in 539 B.C. (cf. Cyrus Cylinder, in D.W. Thomas, ed., *Documents from Old Testament Times* [Edinburgh: T. & T. Clark, 1958], pp. 92–94), the NIV proposed an alternate reading: "doomed to destruction." Critics et al. emend the text to an active participle: "devastator," based on the Targum and the Syriac (BHS; Allen, p. 237). It seems that the emendation makes a good deal of sense, as the imprecation only begins with the words "happy is" and not before (cf. "O Daughter Babylon, you Devastator," Dahood, *Psalms,* 3:268).

Appendix: Imprecations in the Psalms

Many of the *lament* psalms include an imprecatory prayer (3:7; 5:10; 6:10; 7:14–16; 28:4–5; 31:17–18; 37:2, 9–10, 15, 20, 35–36; 40:14–15; 54:5; 55:9, 15,

23; 59:12–13; 63:9–11; 64:7–9; 71:13; 79:6, 12; 139:19–22; 140:9–10). These psalms are ascribed to David (35; 58; 69; 109), to Asaph (83), and to an unknown writer (137). The expression of hatred and the desire for vindication is not to be limited to the Psalms. It is also found in the prayers of Jeremiah (11:18–20; 15:15–18; 17:18; 18:19–23; 20:11–12) and Nehemiah (6:14; 13:29).

In these prayers the people of God prayed for the Lord's judgment, vengeance, and curse (execration) on their enemies. Their hatred for their enemies seems so opposed to the teaching of Jesus Christ and to the Christian emphasis on love that we must ask, How can a Christian read, sing, or pray the imprecatory psalms? How do these expressions of hatred correspond to Christ's teaching on love? These psalms force us to look at prayer against the enemies of God and of the psalmists' relationship between the Old and the New testaments.

The Old and New testaments hold in tension the requirement of love and the hatred of evil. The requirement of love, including one's enemy, comes from the OT (Lev 19:17–18; Prov 25:21). God is constant in his expectations, as he exemplifies love for his creation (Ps 145; Matt 5:45), even by the giving of his Son (John 3:16). But the NT also teaches that people are accountable to the Lord for their deeds (Acts 17:30–31) and as such are subject to God's wrath. The Lord Jesus proclaimed a judgment on Korazin and Capernaum (Matt 11:21–24; Luke 10:13–15) and strongly rebuked the leaders and the unbelief of the Jews (Matt 7:23; cf. Ps 6:8; Mark 11:14; 12:9). The apostles counted the heretics and evildoers likewise accursed (1 Cor 5:5; 16:22; Gal 1:8–9; 5:12; 2 Tim 4:14 [cf. Ps 62:12]; 2 Peter 2; 2 John 7–11; Jude 3–16). In the parable of the unjust judge, our Lord encouraged the godly to persevere in prayer, confirming the conviction that God is just, as he will "bring about justice for his chosen ones, who cry out to him day and night" (Luke 18:7).

In this spirit we must appreciate the cry of the martyrs in heaven, as they pray for God's vindication (Rev 6:10) and rejoice in the judgment of the wicked (18:20; 19:1–6). The apostle Paul also encouraged oppressed Christians to look forward to the return of our Lord as the time appointed for God's vindication of the church (2 Thess 1:6–10; cf. Ps 79:6). In this light we may appreciate the perspective of the psalms. Brueggemann writes,

> The Psalms are resources for spirituality. . . . That is, the spirituality of the Psalms is shaped, defined, and characterized in specific historical, experiential categories and shuns universals. Such recognition does not require a fresh exegesis of each psalm, so much as hermeneutical insistence about the categories through which the psalms are to be understood. But if I read it rightly, these Psalms characteristically subordinate "meaning" to "justice." The Psalms regularly insist upon equity, power, and freedom enough to live one's life humanely. (*Message of the Psalms*, pp. 175–76)

But indiscriminate hatred is wrong. The psalmists wrote under the inspiration of God regarding the nature of evil. They were intoxicated with God's character and name (9:16–20; 83:16–17) and were concerned with the manifestation of God's righteousness and holiness on earth. Since evil contrasts in every way with God's nature and plan, the psalmists prayed for divine retribution, by which God's order would be reestablished (109:6–21) and God's people would be reassured of his love (109:21, 26). C.S. Lewis, too, was sensitive to the piety of the psalter when he wrote on the place of justice and judgment in the Psalms. He observes that the cry of the psalmists may be explained, because they "took right and wrong more seriously" (*Reflections on the Psalms*, p. 31).

Thus the imprecatory psalms focus on the reality of evil and the hope of restoration. This is a very relevant question. C.S. Lewis rightly asks us to use the Psalms as a way of seeing this world as it is: "Against all this the ferocious parts of the Psalms serve as a reminder that there is in the world such a thing as wickedness, and that it . . . is hateful to God" (ibid., pp. 19, 33). Further, we caution against a wooden interpretation of the imprecations, as Kidner observes, "Here we should notice that invective has its own rhetoric, in which horror may be piled up on horror more to express the speaker's sense of outrage than to spell out the penalties he literally intends" (*Psalms*, 1:27).

For the Christian it is most important to uproot any selfish passions, judgmentalism, and personal vindictiveness, because those who practice these come under the judgment of God (Gal 5:15; James 4:13–16). These psalms help us to pray through our anger, frustrations, and spite to a submission to God's will. Only then will the godly man or woman be able to pray for the execration of evil and the full establishment of God's kingdom.

Texts: For an expository study of the imprecatory psalms, the reader is invited to read the expositions on Pss 35; 58; 69; 83; 109; 137; cf. 3:7; 5:10; 6:10; 7:14–16; 28:4–5; 31:17–18; 37:2, 9–10, 15, 20, 35–36; 40:14–15; 54:5; 55:9, 15, 23; 59:12–13; 63:9–11; 64:7–9; 69; 71:13; 79:6, 12; 139:19–22; 140:9–10.

Related Topics: See the appendixes to Pss 3 (Yahweh Is My God); 7 (The Name of Yahweh); 25 (The Perfections of Yahweh); 46 (Zion Theology); 78 (The Acts of Yahweh); 85 (Anger in the Psalms); 88 (Sheol-Grave-Death); 98 (Yahweh Is the Divine Warrior); 119 (Yahweh Is My Redeemer).

Bibliography: Herbert Chanan Brichto, "The Problem of 'Curse' in the Hebrew Bible," JBLMS 13 (Philadelphia: Society of Biblical Literature, 1963); H.A. Brongers, "Die Rache- und Fluchpsalmen im Alten Testament," *OudTestamentische Studien* 13 (1963): 21–43; Walter Brueggemann, "Vengeance: Human and Divine," *Praying the Psalms* (Winona Lake: St. Mary's Press, 1982), pp. 67–80; id., *The Message of the Psalms,* pp. 175–76; C.M. Cherian, "Attitude to Enemies in the Psalms," *Biblebhashyam* 8 (1982): 104–17; Erhard S. Gerstenberger, "Enemies and Evildoers in the Psalms: A Challenge to Christian Preaching," *Horizons in Biblical Theology* 4/5 (1982/83): 61–77; Karl Heinen, "Die Psalmen—Gebete für Christen?" *Bibel und Liturgie* 51 (1978): 232–35; Page H. Kelly, "Prayers of Troubled Saints," *Review and Expositor* 81 (1984): 377–83; C.S. Lewis, *Reflections on the Psalms;* Chalmers Martin, "Imprecations in the Psalms," *Classical Evangelical Essays in Old Testament Interpretation,* ed. Walter C. Kaiser, Jr. (Grand Rapids: Baker, 1972), pp. 113–32; George E. Mendenhall, "The 'Vengeance' of Yahweh," in *The Tenth Generation: The Origins of the Biblical Tradition* (Baltimore: Johns Hopkins University Press, 1973), pp. 69–104; Benedikta Strole, "Psalmen—Lieder der Verfolgten," *Bibel und Kirche* 35 (1980): 42–47; Martin J. Ward, "Psalm 109: David's Poem of Vengeance," *Andrews University Seminary Studies* 18 (1980): 163–68; Claus Westermann, "Die Bitte gegen die Feinde," *Ausgewählte Psalmen* (Göttingen: Vandenhoeck & Ruprecht, 1984), pp. 1208–9.

Psalm 138: Yahweh Delivers the Humble

This psalm has the distinctive features of the *individual thanksgiving* psalms: declaration of thanksgiving, reason for thanksgiving, summons to praise, and an expression of confidence in the Lord (Allen, p. 245). Kirkpatrick (p. 783) and A.A. Anderson (p. 901) favor the *communal* thanksgiving genre and locate the psalm in a postexilic setting. Eaton, on the other hand, defines it as a royal psalm. (See the appendix to Ps 89: The Messianic King.)

The structural elements move from the language of praise in the first person imperfect (vv.1–2) to the cause of praise in the first person perfect (v.3) to the summons to praise in the third person jussive (vv.4–5) to the cause of communal praise (vv.6–7) to finally an interchange between the third and second person singular as a part of a prayer to the Lord (vv.7–8).

A. Individual Thanksgiving (vv.1–3)
B. Communal Thanksgiving (vv.4–6)
C. Confidence in the Lord's Presence (vv.7–8)

I. Individual Thanksgiving

138:1–3

Of David.

1 I will praise you, O LORD, with all my heart;
before the "gods" I will sing your praise.
2 I will bow down toward your holy temple
and will praise your name
for your love and your faithfulness,
for you have exalted above all things
your name and your word.
3 When I called, you answered me;
you made me bold and stouthearted.

1–3 Typical of the thanksgiving psalms is the repetition of verbs for praise: "I will praise . . . sing. . . . bow down . . . praise." The first and last verbs form an inclusion by the use of the same root *y-d-h* ("praise"). The praise of the Lord is both an expression of devotion ("with all my heart"; cf. 119:2) and a witness against the impotence of idols ("before the 'gods,'" v.1). Praise belongs to the Lord alone and not to the gods of the nations, whose kings will have to submit to the Lord (vv.4–5).

Praise of the "name" of the Lord ("Yahweh," v.2) involves a personal experience of God's covenant perfections: his "love" (*ḥesed*) and "faithfulness" (*'emeṯ;* see Exod 34:6; cf. Pss 25:10; 57:3; 61:7). The Lord is constant in his love toward his children, and so great is his faithfulness to his "promise-name" ("your name and your word," v.2) that the psalmist exclaims that whatever the Lord has done in the past is dwarfed by what he is still doing! For him the "name" of God evokes the connotation of the promises of the covenant.

Praise is appropriate in the forms of song and liturgical prostration in the direction of the Lord's "holy temple" (v.2; cf. 5:7; 28:2; 134:2). The Lord is faithful and good. The formal praise (vv.1–2) ends on a personal confession as to what the Lord has done. The psalmist has experienced distress and called on the Lord for help. He not only answered his prayer but strongly encouraged him, revitalizing his life ("bold and stouthearted," v.3).

Notes

For a brief discussion of the technical words and phrases in the superscription, see the Introduction.

1 The NIV adds "O LORD," following a number of MSS, versions, and 11QPs[a]. The emendation is unnecessary (see Dahood, *Psalms*, 3:276; Allen, p. 244).

3 The LXX reads a form from *r-b-b* ("increase") instead of the MT's "you made me bold" (*r-h-b*). See the RSV's "thou didst increase." The BHS favors this emendation: תַּרְבֵּנִי (*tarbēnî*, "you increase me"), but the more difficult reading of the MT is preferable. See Allen: "and made me exultant, putting strength within me" (p. 243).

II. Communal Thanksgiving

138:4–6

4 May all the kings of the earth praise you, O LORD,
  when they hear the words of your mouth.
5 May they sing of the ways of the LORD,
  for the glory of the LORD is great.

6 Though the LORD is on high, he looks upon the lowly,
  but the proud he knows from afar.

4–5 The nations together with their gods and kings will pay homage to the Lord. From the personal vantage point of the knowledge of God, the psalmist expects the "kings of the earth" (v.4; cf. 68:32; 96:1, 3, 7–8; 97:1; 98:4; 100:1; 102:15) to lead their peoples in the praise and adoration of the Lord. The reason for his confidence lies in his conviction of the Lord's fidelity to "the words" of promise with regard to his people. The fulfillment is evident in "the ways of the LORD" (v.5; cf. 103:7) at the sound of which the nations will respond with song. The "words" and "the ways" reveal how great is "the glory of the LORD" (cf. 57:5; Isa 40:5; 60:1).

6 One particular application lies in the example of God's fidelity to the "lowly." Exalted as the Lord is in his kingship ("the LORD is on high"; cf. 113:4–9), he is the Redeemer-King. He deals favorably with "the lowly" (cf. Luke 1:48, 52) so as to deliver them out of their affliction (Isa 57:15; 66:2). But in delivering he also avenges "the proud." Pride is offensive to the Lord because he alone is the Exalted One (cf. Exod 15:1; Ps 94). He "knows" (*y-d-'*), that is, he cares for his own by delivering them and by keeping them from destruction (see 1:6).

III. Confidence in the Lord's Presence

138:7–8

7 Though I walk in the midst of trouble,
  you preserve my life;
you stretch out your hand against the anger of my foes,
  with your right hand you save me.
8 The LORD will fulfill ⌊his purpose⌋ for me;
  your love, O LORD, endures forever—
  do not abandon the works of your hands.

7–8 The psalm ends on a personal reflection even as it began on a personal note of thanksgiving. Confident of his God, to whom the nations must one day submit themselves, the believer confesses his indubitable faith in the Savior-King. He anticipates more "trouble" in life because the life of a believer is not immune from adversities. However, despite the hardships, he rests assured. He knows the difference between being self-assured and assured, between pride and lowliness. The difference lies in his two confessions. The first is couched in the second person: "you preserve . . . you stretch out . . . you save me" (imperfect in Heb., v.7), and the other in the third person: "The LORD will" (v.8). These expressions are the language of faith.

The Lord will keep his saint alive (v.7; cf. 119:25; 143:11), delivering him from danger and from his "foes." The psalmist portrays the Lord as reaching out his "hand" as an expression of help, while dealing in judgment with those who cause his adversity (cf. 144:7; Exod 3:20; 9:15). His "right hand" signifies strength (cf. 60:5; 139:10).

Confidence also comes from a recognition that the Lord has a purpose. This purpose also includes individuals ("purpose for me," v.8; cf. 57:2; Rom 8:28). Confidence is not misplaced, because the Lord has shown an interest in his creation and in his people ("the works of your hands"; cf. 90:16; 92:5; 143:5; Isa 60:21; 64:8). His concern is of the most profound and lasting kind, as it is nothing less than his enduring "love" (*ḥeseḏ*).

Psalm 139: Yahweh Knows Me!

The various components—hymn, thanksgiving, lament—of this psalm expose us to the intensely personal relationship between the psalmist and his God. The psalm defies the canons of genre criticism, as scholarship is divided on the genre and *Sitz im Leben* (Allen, pp. 254–60). Siegfried Wagner finds in this psalm a coming together of a variety of motifs: meditation, confession, prayer, and reflection ("Zur Theologie des Psalms CXXXIX," Supplements to VetTest 29 [1978]: 357–76). Helen Schüngel-Straumann argues in favor of a wisdom context ("Zur Gattung und Theologie des 139. Psalms," *Biblische Zeitschrift* 17 [1973]: 39–51).

The structure reveals an obvious break between v.18 and v.19. The first part (vv.1–18) consists mainly of thanksgiving for God's discernment, perception, and purpose of the individual. The second part (vv.19–24) is in the form of a prayer made during a period of distress. The reflections of the past and the present situation express a profound knowledge of God and a conviction that this God has a concern for individuals. Yahweh loves and knows his people, and they, in turn, need not be afraid of his scrutiny. (For a structural analysis see L.C. Allen, "Faith on Trial: An Analysis of Psalm 139," *Vox Evangelica* 10 [1977]: 5–23.)

The expository structure of Psalm 139 is as follows:

A. The Lord's Discernment of Individuals (vv.1–6)
B. The Lord's Perception of Individuals (vv.7–12)
C. The Lord's Purpose for Individuals (vv.13–18)
D. Prayer for Vindication (vv.19–24)

I. The Lord's Discernment of Individuals

139:1–6

For the director of music. Of David. A psalm.

1 O LORD, you have searched me
and you know me.
2 You know when I sit and when I rise;

you perceive my thoughts from afar.
3 You discern my going out and my lying down;
you are familiar with all my ways.
4 Before a word is on my tongue
you know it completely, O LORD.

5 You hem me in—behind and before;
you have laid your hand upon me.
6 Such knowledge is too wonderful for me,
too lofty for me to attain.

1–6 The Lord "knows" his own. The knowledge of God is relational. He knows his own (see 1:6), as he discerns the righteous from the wicked (cf. vv.19–20). The root *y-d-'* ("know") occurs throughout this section: "you know me. . . . you know when. . . . you know it completely. . . . Such knowledge." It signifies here divine discernment. The Lord discerns the actions of his own (v.1), whether they sit or stand (v.2; see 1:6). This discernment belongs uniquely to God, who alone is the Judge of all flesh. Hence the psalmist exclaims that this divine prerogative is beyond him: "Such knowledge is too wonderful for me" (v.6).

In his prayer (vv.23–24), which gives expression to his recommitment, the psalmist prayed for the Lord's justification of his acts against those who maligned him. He prayed for the Lord to examine him as in a judicial case and to declare him to be innocent of the charges (vv.23–24; see below). Now that the ordeal is over and he has been justified by the Lord, the psalmist testifies that the Lord is a righteous judge. He has come to a new level of relationship with the Lord who knows him through and through: "you have searched me" (v.1; cf. 7:9; 17:3; 26:2; Jer 17:10), "you know" (vv.1–2, 4; see above), "you perceive" (v.2; or "you have an understanding of," from *b-y-n*), "you discern" (v.3, or "you have winnowed me"), and "you are familiar with." The Lord knows his every move ("when I sit and when I rise," v.2).

However, the accused is not afraid of his judge. The divine Judge is more than an arbiter, because he is also the one in whom the psalmist has found protection. He hedges in his own for the purpose of protection ("behind and before," v.5). This thought receives further amplification in v.5b: "you have laid your hand upon me." The placement of the divine hand signifies protection and blessing (cf. Gen 48:14, 17; Exod 33:22).

This knowledge of God is nothing less than a knowledge that discerns and discriminates in favor of those who are loyal to the Lord. The discerning and favorable acts of God are gracious. It is grace that justifies, and it is by grace that humans are blessed. Though the psalmist has not taken his responsibilities lightly in all of his ways (his sitting, rising, going out, lying down, and speaking; cf. vv.2–4), he exclaims that God's favorable acts toward him are "too wonderful" and "too lofty" to apprehend (v.6; cf. Rom 11:33; see appendix to Ps 78: The Mighty Acts of Yahweh).

Notes

For a brief discussion of the technical words and phrases in the superscription, see the Introduction.

II. The Lord's Perception of Individuals

139:7–12

7 Where can I go from your Spirit?
Where can I flee from your presence?
8 If I go up to the heavens, you are there;
if I make my bed in the depths, you are there.
9 If I rise on the wings of the dawn,
if I settle on the far side of the sea,
10 even there your hand will guide me,
your right hand will hold me fast.

11 If I say, "Surely the darkness will hide me
and the light become night around me,"
12 even the darkness will not be dark to you;
the night will shine like the day,
for darkness is as light to you.

7–12 The presence of God is everywhere; hence he perceives all things in all places. Man cannot hide himself from the all-seeing eye of the Lord, whether in the highest heavens, the deepest recesses of the earth, or in the depths of the sea. The psalmist is not trying to evade God, but he further amplifies that God's knowledge is beyond the ability of humans to grasp. The knowledge or discernment of God can never be limited to any particular place, because God's sovereignty extends to the whole created universe.

The "Spirit" of God is parallel with "your presence" (v.7; cf. 51:11; Isa 63:9–10; Ezek 39:29) and is an indirect way of speaking about the Lord: "Where can I go from you. . . . flee from you." The interrogative language is an emphatic way of declaring that God's presence is everywhere to protect his children (cf. vv.5-6). Unlike the pagan deities, whose authority was defined to certain areas of operation, the Lord's authority extends to "the heavens . . . the depths. . . . the wings of the dawn . . . the sea" (vv.8–9). The extremities of heaven and the depths of the earth, of east ("the wings of the dawn," v.9) and west ("the far side of the sea"), and of "darkness" and "light" (vv.11–12) serve to strengthen the image of God's absolute sovereignty over creation (see J.L. Koole, "Quelques Remarques Sur Psaume 139," *Studia Biblica et Semitica: Theodoro Christiano Vriezen qui munere Professoris Theologiae per XXV Annos functus est, ab Amicis, Collegis, Discipulis dedicata* [Wageningen: Veenman, 1966], pp. 176–80).

The Lord's hand will protect God's child wherever he may be (v.10), even in "darkness" (vv.11–12). There is only light with God, and his light brightens up the darkness so that the psalmist can say affirmatively, "The night will shine like the day, for darkness is as light to you" (v.12).

III. The Lord's Purpose for Individuals

139:13–18

13 For you created my inmost being;
you knit me together in my mother's womb.
14 I praise you because I am fearfully and
wonderfully made;
your works are wonderful,
I know that full well.

15 My frame was not hidden from you
when I was made in the secret place.
When I was woven together in the depths of the earth,
16 your eyes saw my unformed body.
All the days ordained for me
were written in your book
before one of them came to be.

17 How precious to me are your thoughts, O God!
How vast is the sum of them!
18 Were I to count them,
they would outnumber the grains of sand.
When I awake,
I am still with you.

13 Confidence in the Lord's ability to discern and perceive the nature and needs of his people comes from a belief in God's purpose. He is the Creator, and his creative concerns include individuals!

In a sense this section continues the emphasis on divine involvement by an emphatic use of "you" (*'attāh*, vv.2, 13: "you know. . . . you created") and by the use of the pronominal prefixes and suffixes to the verbs and nouns in Hebrew (translated by "you" and "your"). The Lord has formed the individual as a spiritual ("you created [*q-n-h*; Gen 14:22; Prov 8:22] my inmost being ['kidneys']," v.13) and a physical being ("you knit me together"; cf. Job 8–11; Jer 1:5). All beings owe their existence to the Creator-God. How much more the individual who walks with God! He knows that the Lord has formed him for a purpose.

14 Creation is existential! The intensely personal language the psalmist returns to ("I" and "my") complements that of the second section. God is concerned with the individuals whom he has formed for his purpose. Therefore praise is the proper response to God's grace of discernment, perception, and purpose. The child of God sees God's presence everywhere (vv.7–12) and experiences the joy of God's watchful eye over him. All of God's "works" are "wonderful," but the believer senses more than any other part of God's creation that he is "fearfully and wonderfully made." Though God's grace to him is like a "knowledge . . . too wonderful for" him (v.6), he lives with a personal awareness of God's gracious purpose ("I know that full well"). The psalmist reveals a unique awareness of God's grace toward him and responds with a hymn of thanksgiving ("I praise you").

15–16 Even when unborn ("when I was made in the secret place," v.15) and little more than a physical being ("my frame"; lit., "my bone") in the womb ("when I was woven together in the depths of the earth"), the Lord had a purpose for the undeveloped embryo ("my unformed body," v.16).

The idea of purpose comes more clearly to expression in v.16. The Lord's writing in the book (cf. 51:1; 69:28) refers to God's knowledge and blessing of his child "all the days" of his life (cf. Eph 2:10). His life was written in the book of life, and each of his days was numbered.

17–18 In reflection the psalmist exclaims again in wonder and amazement the magnificence of God's purpose ("your thoughts," v.17; cf. 92:5; Job 42:3). The "thoughts" of God are too magnificent, too numerous, and too exalted for man, whose "thoughts" (v.2) are fully known to the Lord. It is impossible for the creature to comprehend the Creator! Yahweh's plans are beyond man's ability to comprehend, as they are more in number than the sand of the sea (vv.17–18; cf. Gen 22:17; 32:12). They are like a dream; but, unlike a dream, God's love is real. When awake the psalmist knows that he still enjoys God's presence (v.18).

Notes

14 The LXX, Syriac, and Jerome read "you are fearful and wonderful," suggesting a second person reading, rather than the first (see RSV: "for thou art fearful and wonderful"). This was possible in the pre-MT, which had no vowel markers. The MT is equally well possible; so too the NIV.

17 The NIV follows Dahood in translating רֵעֶיךָ (*rē'eykā*) "your thoughts" (3:296). The word *rēa'* is usually translated "friends," and so it was in the ancient versions. In vv.2, 17 of this psalm, another word seems to fit better: "intention" or "thought." Liudger Sabottka surveys the problem and concludes in favor of "your plans" or "your designs" ("*rē'ēkā* in Ps. 139,17: ein adverbieller Akkusativ," *Biblica* 63 [1982]: 558–59).

IV. Prayer for Vindication

139:19–24

19 If only you would slay the wicked, O God!
Away from me, you bloodthirsty men!
20 They speak of you with evil intent;
your adversaries misuse your name.
21 Do I not hate those who hate you, O LORD,
and abhor those who rise up against you?
22 I have nothing but hatred for them;
I count them my enemies.

23 Search me, O God, and know my heart;
test me and know my anxious thoughts.
24 See if there is any offensive way in me,
and lead me in the way everlasting.

The tone changes from thanksgiving and an overpowering gratitude to imprecation. The wicked have caused the psalmist great anguish. Though the Lord has been good to him, he prays that the Lord will remove the cause of evil in this world. (For the nature and theology of imprecation, see the appendix to Ps 137: Imprecations in the Psalms; Patrick D. Miller, Jr., "Psalm 139," *Interpreting the Psalms*, pp. 144–53.)

19–20 Overwhelmed as he was with gratitude for God's purpose in him (vv.13–18), the psalmist sees no purpose in the existence of the wicked (v.19). They foil God's purposes by their rebellious ways. The "wicked" (cf. 1:1, 6) are destructive, scheming, and rebellious to the rule of God in this world. In a few strokes the psalmist portrays evil. The ascription "bloodthirsty men" denotes a lack of respect for life and regard for justice and righteousness (cf. 5:6; Prov 29:10). They also scheme surreptitiously against God's authority ("speak of you with evil intent," v.20). They foreswear any allegiance to the Lord. He commits the wicked into God's just hands as he prays, "If only you would slay the wicked."

21–22 Devotion to the Lord excludes any loyalty to those who hate him. The psalmist manifests a spirit of discrimination. This type of discrimination reveals itself in an evident resolution to keep himself untainted from any relationship with evil. He hates, abhors (v.21; cf. 119:158), and shuns the enemies of God (v.22; cf. 1:1). The interrogative is again here a form of an emphatic: "Certainly, I hate those . . . ," and serves to express his commitment to the Lord over against those who forswear any loyalty to him. They are haters of God ("those who hate you") and rebels ("those who rise up against you"), whose enmity for God's rule he overturns by repugnance for God's enemies ("I count them my enemies") and by affirming his own devotion to the Lord.

23–24 The rejection of evil arises from the psalmist's spirit of commitment to the Lord and not from pride. This is clear from his prayer, asking for God to discern his motives and his actions. This prayer came out of a situation when evil men had accused him. Instead of directing himself to his adversaries, he raises up his voice in lament to God, who alone as the righteous Judge can discern his "heart" and "thoughts" (cf. vv.1–4; 26:2).

The psalmist desires nothing less than conformity to God's will. Therefore he prays for God's examination of his spiritual condition. He contrasts the two ways: the way of the world ("offensive way," v.24) and the way of God ("the way everlasting"). The one way leads to destruction and the other to life and fellowship with God (cf. 1:6; 16:11; Prov 12:28).

Notes

---

19 The MT has an imperative form reflected in the NIV's "Away from me." A number of MSS read a perfect סָרוּ (*sārû*, "have departed"). The Syriac and Targum continue the prayer with the form יָסוּרוּ (*yāsûrû*, "may they depart"; cf. the RSV: "that men of blood would depart from me").

20 This verse is exegetically difficult. First, thc LXX reads, "they rebel against you," intimating a variant Hebrew reading: יַמְרֻךָ (*yamrukā*; so BHS), for the MT's יֹאמְרֻךָ (*yō'mrukā*, "they speak of you"). Second, the translation "misuse your name" is interpretive for the MT's "lifted in vain." Instead of a passive participle נָשֻׂא (*nāśu'*, "lifted"), BHS and modern versions prefer an active form, נָשְׂאוּ (*nāś'û*, "they lift up"). The NIV accepts this emendation, taking "they lift up in vain" to be an allusion to the commandment not to take God's name in vain; hence, "misuse your name." The RSV offers an alternate rendering: "who lift themselves up." Gene Rice explains the line: "they have carried away the cities to destruction" ("The Integrity of the Text of Psalm 139:20b," CBQ 46 [1984]: 28–30). Allen has "who talk falsely, your foes" (p. 249). Third, the phrase "your adversaries" assumes the Aramaic meaning of *'ar* ("enemy"). The MT's עָרֶיךָ (*'āreykā*, "your cities") makes little sense. Some MSS read instead עָדֶיךָ (*'adeykā*, "on behalf of you"), but BHS proposes עָלֶיךָ (*'āleykā*, "against you"; cf. RSV). Allen favors the older view of adopting the Aramaic meaning (pp. 249, 253).

Psalm 140: You Are My God!

The psalmist has been falsely accused and turns to the Lord for deliverance, because he is the righteous Judge. Throughout the lament there is no expression of complaint against God for having permitted evil men to cause him so much pain. Instead, the poet commits his future to the Lord, whose very nature is just and righteous and who will intervene as the Deliverer of all the poor and oppressed.

The psalm exemplifies the spirit of the *individual lament*. The structure reflects the vacillation between lament and confidence. Prayer is the privilege of bringing one's concerns before God with the confident hope that he will respond.

The expository structure is as follows:

A. Prayer for Deliverance From Evil (vv.1–5)
  B. Confidence in God's Deliverance (vv.6–8)
A′. Prayer for Divine Justice (vv.9–11)
  B′. Confidence in God's Deliverance (vv.12–13)

I. Prayer for Deliverance From Evil

140:1–5

For the director of music. A psalm of David.

[1]Rescue me, O LORD, from evil men;
  protect me from men of violence,
[2]who devise evil plans in their hearts
  and stir up war every day.
[3]They make their tongues as sharp as a serpent's;
  the poison of vipers is on their lips. *Selah*

[4]Keep me, O LORD, from the hands of the wicked;
  protect me from men of violence
  who plan to trip my feet.
[5]Proud men have hidden a snare for me;
  they have spread out the cords of their net
  and have set traps for me along my path. *Selah*

1–5 The lament begins with a characteristic cry for help—"Rescue me . . . protect me" (v.1; cf. 41:4; 51:1; 57:1)—and ends on the confident conclusion that the Lord will help ("I know," v.12). The lament arises out of a real situation, in which wicked people perpetrate their evil. They are "evil men" because of their violent acts ("violence"; MT pl., "violent acts," v.1; cf. v.4; 2 Sam 22:49), which are delineated in vv.2–3. The evil men sow discord with their speech (v.2; 55:21; 109:3; Prov 15:18; 29:22). Their tongues are venomous, like the bite of a serpent (v.3; cf. 58:3–4; Rom 3:13). They devise wicked schemes in their evil hearts (21:11; 35:4), leading to intentional anarchy and perpetual ("every day") agitation (v.2).

The psalmist prays for God's deliverance, lest the wicked control him. Divine deliverance consists first of preservation ("rescue me . . . protect me") and then of vindication (vv.9–11). Because of the intensity of evil, the poet casts himself wholly on the Lord. The men of violence scheme and speak maliciously (vv.2–3) and act viciously (vv.4–5). They are intent on destroying the righteous, as they stretch forth their hands (v.4) and strive to make him collapse ("trip my feet"; cf. 118:13). In their arrogance ("proud men," v.5; cf. 94:2) they seek to entrap the righteous like a fowler ensnares animals with the "snare," the "net," and the "traps" (cf. 31:4; 119:110; 141:9; 142:3).

Notes

For a brief discussion of the technical words and phrases in the superscription, see the Introduction.

2 (3 MT) The MT's יָגוּרוּ (*yāg̱ûrû*, "attack") is emended to יְגָרוּ (*yᵉg̱ārû*, "stir up") in the NIV.

4–5 (5–6 MT) The description of the wicked abruptly ends with a renewed plea (v.4), only to be continued (vv.4b–5). Verse 4a is parallel with v.1 (with a repetition of "protect" [*n-ṣ-r*]), and the portrayal of the wicked (vv.4b–5) is symmetric with vv.2–3, forming an ABA′B′ pattern:

A. Plea for Help (v.1)
  B. Portrayal of Evil (vv.2–3)
A′. Plea for Help (v.4a)
  B′. Portrayal of Evil (vv.4b–5)

II. Confidence in God's Deliverance

140:6–8

6 O Lord, I say to you, "You are my God."
  Hear, O Lord, my cry for mercy.
7 O Sovereign Lord, my strong deliverer,
  who shields my head in the day of battle—
8 do not grant the wicked their desires, O Lord;
  do not let their plans succeed,
  or they will become proud. *Selah*

6–7 The previous expressions of lament (vv.1, 4) were addressed in the spirit of confidence in the Lord. In contrast to the lying speech of the wicked, the poet declares, "I say to you, 'You are my God' " (v.6; cf. 16:1; 31:14; 52:4). The phrase "my God" is parallel with "O Lord, my Lord" (v.7; NIV, "O Sovereign Lord"). He seeks protection from no other than the "Lord" who has made a covenant with his people, who alone is God, and who is Master over the world.

This God is the Divine Warrior, who will avenge and deliver his people, hence the allusions to war: "my strong deliverer, who shields my head in the day of battle" (v.7). The Divine Warrior (see Ps 98) is "strong" (*'ōz;* cf. 96:6; 99:4; 132:8) in his salvation (*yᵉšû'āh;* NIV, "deliverer"; see appendix to Ps 119: Yahweh Is My Redeemer). He protects the helpless (cf. 3:3; 60:7; Isa 59:17; Eph 6:17; 1 Thess 5:8).

8 The lament renews the plea for God to act, lest evil succeed and wickedness be lifted up arrogantly. The Divine Warrior cannot for long tolerate the infraction of his authority. The "wicked" may arrogantly desire, plan, and execute; but the Master of the universe cannot tolerate anarchy for long. To this end the plea changes into an imprecatory prayer (vv.9–11).

Notes

---

8 (9 MT) The NIV interprets the verbal phrase יָרוּמוּ (*yārûmû*, "they lift up") contextually as "or they will become proud." BHS and modern versions read it together with v.9, assuming several emendations, as in RSV's "Those who surround me lift up their head." M. Dahood's proposal of changing "never to rise" (*yārûmû*) to a divine epithet is largely based on a supposed parallel construction: "Yahweh . . . O Exalted" ("The Composite Divine Name in Psalms 89:16–17 and 140:9," *Biblica* 61 [1980]: 277–78; id., *Psalms*, 3:303–4). This phrase remains an exegetical crux.

III. Prayer for Divine Justice

140:9–11

9 Let the heads of those who surround me
be covered with the trouble their lips have caused.
10 Let burning coals fall upon them;
may they be thrown into the fire,
into miry pits, never to rise.
11 Let slanderers not be established in the land;
may disaster hunt down men of violence.

9–10 The imprecation is an expression of concern for God's just rule. It is not a personal vendetta. The psalmist prays that the Lord will boomerang on the heads of the wicked what they have spoken with their lips (v.9; cf. 141:10). The "burning coals," "fire," and "miry pits" (v.10) are metaphors for divine judgment. God's judgment will bring evil to its appropriate end, as the wicked will "rise" no more (cf. 1:5; 36:12). (See the appendix to Ps 137: Imprecations in the Psalms.)

11 The calumny of the wicked is one example of their evil. They are "slanderers" who with their slippery tongue create anarchy. As long as there are slanderers, justice is not established. Hence the psalmist prays that the evil men, whose tongues are venomous like snakes (cf. v.3), may not have a place among the people of God (cf. 1:5; 101:5, 7–8). The "men of violence" (cf. vv.1, 4) cannot find rest, as they have not given thought to leaving the righteous alone (cf. vv.4–5). They have done everything to entrap the godly, and hence the Lord must bring the disaster they had planned for others upon them (cf. 35:5–6; Prov 13:21).

Notes

---

11 (12 MT) Moshe Greenberg explains this verse mythopoetically. The word מַדְחֵפֹת (*madhēpōt*, "violence," NIV; "blow after blow," KB[3], 2:520) may denote a hunting corral, an enclosure used by hunters. The word may be a mythopoetic expression for the place of the dead ("Two New Hunting Terms in Psalm 140:12," *Hebrew Annual Review* 1 [1977]: 149–53).

IV. Confidence in God's Deliverance

140:12–13

12 I know that the LORD secures justice for the poor
and upholds the cause of the needy.
13 Surely the righteous will praise your name
and the upright will live before you.

12 The lament changes to a victory cry: "I know." In form this corresponds to v.6 ("I say") as both verbs are Qal perfect verbs, expressive of a present condition. In v.6 the psalmist speaks confidently, "You are my God," being fully persuaded in his whole being that the Lord is the just Judge (cf. 7:8–9; 9:4), who will interpose for his people (cf. 20:6; 56:9). His people are "the poor" (or "humble"), as they are dependent on him for deliverance.

13 At the time of the intervention and vindication, "the righteous" (pl. of *ṣaddîq;* see 1:6) will alter their prayers for deliverance (cf. vv.1, 4) to songs of triumph. Those who are "upright" (*yāšār*) in heart (see 32:11) will enjoy the presence of the Lord (cf. 23:6; 27:4). How blessed are the people whose God is the Lord!

Appendix: The Poor and Oppressed

The words *dak̲, dakkā'* ("oppressed" or "crushed") are synonyms with *'eb̲yôn* ("poor"), *'ānāw* ("afflicted," "humble"), *'ānî* ("poor," "afflicted"), *dal* ("poor"), and *yāt̲ôm* ("orphan"), as is clear from several passages:

You hear, O LORD, the desire of the afflicted [*'ānāw*];
you encourage them, and you listen to their cry,
defending the fatherless and the oppressed [*dak̲*],
in order that man, who is of the earth, may terrify no more.
(10:17–18)

He will take pity on the weak [*dal*] and the needy [*'eb̲yōn*]
and save the needy [*'eb̲yōn*] from death.
(72:13)

Do not let the oppressed [*dak̲*] retreat in disgrace;
may the poor [*'ānî*] and needy [*'eb̲yōn*] praise your name.
(74:21)

Defend the cause of the weak [*dal*] and fatherless;
maintain the rights of the poor and oppressed.
Rescue the weak [*dal*] and needy [*'eb̲yōn*];
deliver them from the hand of the wicked.
(82:3–4)

He raises the poor [*dal*] from the dust
and lifts the needy [*'eb̲yōn*] from the ash heap.
(113:7)

The oppressed are those who are persecuted for the sake of the kingdom. Originally the synonyms for "poor" may have referred to those without land and the destitute in society. But gradually the words for "poor" became a metaphor for the godly. The godly groaned, despaired, and lamented because their rights were trampled and because they longed for God's kingdom. They groan for redemption, praying for their Divine Warrior-Protector to arise, "Arise, O LORD, let not man triumph; / let the nations be judged in your presence" (9:19). The story of redemption is the history of God's acts toward those who await his deliverance:

> The poor [*ʿānāw*] will see and be glad [*ś-m-ḥ*]—
> you who seek [*d-r-š*] God, may your hearts live!
> The LORD hears the needy [*ʾeḇyōn*]
> and does not despise his captive people.
> (69:32–33)

The "poor" are overcome with joy, while awaiting his acts of deliverance:

> My whole being will exclaim,
> "Who is like you, O LORD?
> You rescue [*n-ṣ-l*] the poor [*ʿānî*] from those too strong for them,
> the poor [*ʿānî*] and needy [*ʾeḇyōn*] from those who rob them."
> (35:10; cf. 2 Thess 1:5–10; Rev 6:10; 7:10)

Even while they await his salvation, Yahweh assures them of his protection: "The LORD is a refuge [*miśgāḇ*] for the oppressed [*dak*], / a stronghold [*miśgāḇ*] in times of trouble" (9:9; cf. 14:6; 34:18). But they, in turn, must persevere in hope: "But the needy [*ʾeḇyōn*] will not always be forgotten, / nor the hope of the afflicted [*ʿānāw*] ever perish" (9:18). When the Lord vindicates his people (12:5; cf. 72:4, 12–13), they will be completely satisfied—bodily, spiritually, psychologically, and socially: "The poor [*ʿānāw*] will eat and be satisfied; / they who seek the LORD will praise him— / may your hearts live forever!" (22:26; cf. 68:10; 107:41; 113:7; 132:15; 146:7).

The psalms tell the story of how Yahweh has heard the prayers of his people as an encouragement: "This poor man [*ʿānî*] called, and the LORD heard him; / he saved him out of all his troubles" (34:6).

Hope shines through even in despair, as the righteous await the coming of the Divine Warrior:

> Yet I am poor [*ʿānî*] and needy [*ʾeḇyōn*];
> may the Lord think of me.
> You are my help [*ʿ-z-r*] and my deliverer [*p-l-ṭ*];
> O my God, do not delay.
> (40:17; cf. 82:3–4; 86:1; 129:1–2)

Hope focuses on the establishment of God's kingdom with justice and righteousness: "The LORD works righteousness [*ṣ-d-q*] and justice [*mišpāṭ*] for all the oppressed [*ʿ-ś-q*]" (103:6). So also, "I know that the LORD secures justice [*mišpāṭ*] for the poor [*ʿānî*] / and upholds the cause [*d-î-n*] of the needy [*ʾeḇyōn*]" (140:12).

Generosity characterizes God's dealings. He is kind, compassionate, and loving with his children. Since Yahweh has a concern for his troubled children, he expects them also to have regard for the outcast within the community of faith—"Blessed [*ʾašrê*] is he who has regard for the weak [*dal*]; / the LORD delivers [*m-l-ṭ*] him in times of trouble" (41:1; cf. 112:9).

Texts: 9:12, 18; 10:2, 14, 17–18; 12:5; 14:6; 18:27; 22:24, 26; 25:9, 16; 34:2, 6; 35:10, 13; 37:14; 40:17; 41:1; 44:9; 49:2; 68:5, 10; 69:32–33; 70:5; 72:2, 4, 12–13; 74:19, 21; 76:9; 82:3–4; 86:1; 88:15; 90:15; 94:5; 101:8; 107:39, 41; 109:9, 12, 16, 22, 31; 112:9; 113:7; 116:10; 119:67, 71, 75; 132:15; 140:12; 146:9; 147:6; 149:4.

Related Topics: See appendixes to Pss 7 (The Name of Yahweh); 25 (The Perfections of Yahweh); 98 (Yahweh Is the Divine Warrior); 119 (Yahweh Is My Redeemer).

Bibliography: Paul van der Berghe, "'*Ani* et '*Anaw* dans les Psaumes," *Le Psautier*, ed. Robert De Langhe (Leuven: Institut Orientaliste, 1962), pp. 273–95; Charles F. Fensham, "Widow, Orphan, and the Poor in Ancient Near Eastern Legal and Wisdom Literature," JNES 21 (1962): 129–39; Richard D. Patterson, "The Widow, the Orphan, and the Poor in the Old Testament and the Extra-Biblical Literature," BS 130 (1973): 223–34; J. Van der Ploeg, "Les Pauvres d'Israel et leur Piété," OTS 7 (1950): 236–70.

TDAT, 3:1075–79; TDOT, 1:27–41; 3:195–230; THAT, 1:23–25; 2:341–50; TWOT, 1:4–5, 188–91.

Psalm 141: May My Prayer Be Like Incense!

Reflecting a concern for wisdom, the poet prays for guidance in his speech and relations (vv.3–4) and for instruction by the righteous (v.5). He then cites a proverb (v.7) and sets up a clear contrast between the wicked and the righteous (as in Ps 1). The spirit of this lament resembles that of Psalm 140. Both psalms exemplify the *individual lament* genre, which includes the lament, confession of confidence, and imprecation. In addition they share linguistic similarities. The original life-situation is far from clear. In second-temple Judaism the psalm was associated with the evening sacrifice in the temple (v.2), and it may have been so originally.

The structural components of the psalm are as follows:

A. Prayer for Deliverance (vv.1–2)
B. Prayer for Wisdom (vv.3–5c)
C. Prayer for Vindication (vv.5d–7)
D. Prayer for Deliverance and Vindication (vv.8–10)

I. Prayer for Deliverance

141:1–2

A psalm of David.

1 O LORD, I call to you; come quickly to me.
Hear my voice when I call to you.
2 May my prayer be set before you like incense;
may the lifting up of my hands be like the
evening sacrifice.

1 With great urgency ("come quickly"; cf. 22:19; 38:22; 40:13; 70:1, 5; 71:12) the poet raises his prayer to God ("I call. . . . hear . . . when I call"). The repetition of "call" (*q-r-'*; cf. 17:6; 88:9; 130:1) and the different verbs for God's intervention ("come quickly. . . . hear my prayer") express the frequency of prayer and the urgency of the situation.

2 Though the psalmist is in a precarious situation, his "prayer" is like a pleasing offering before the Lord. Gradually incense and prayer had become associated. Incense was presented on the altar of incense every day (cf. Exod 30:7–8), usually together with the burnt offering (Lev 2:1–2) and often in connection with the evening sacrifice (cf. Exod 29:38–42). Its sweet smoke arose as a pleasing offering to the Lord (cf. 66:15; Rev 5:8). The association of evening prayers and evening sacrifice was postexilic. Certainly this poetic expression inspired the Jewish piety of later times (cf.

Ezra 9:5; Dan 9:21). The raising up of one's hands was symbolic of dependence on and praise of the Lord (cf. 28:2; 63:4; 1 Tim 2:8).

Notes

For a brief discussion of the technical words and phrases in the superscription, see the Introduction.

2 Von Rad views the language of prayer as incense as a stage in the process of spiritualization of OT rituals (OTT, 1:396). See also Steven R. Boguslawski, "The Psalms: Prophetic Polemics Against Sacrifices," *Irish Biblical Studies* 5 (1983): 14–41.

II. Prayer for Wisdom

141:3–5c

3 Set a guard over my mouth, O LORD;
keep watch over the door of my lips.
4 Let not my heart be drawn to what is evil,
to take part in wicked deeds
with men who are evildoers;
let me not eat of their delicacies.

5 Let a righteous man strike me—it is a kindness;
let him rebuke me—it is oil on my head.
My head will not refuse it.

3–4 The profligacy of evil is part of the existential situation. Evil is all around and temptations abound. The poet prays that he may be kept from evil. Evil comes in many forms: the sins of speech (v.3), of the heart (v.4), and of action. He asks the Lord to help him in his struggle with temptation ("set a guard . . . keep watch"). The "heart . . . is the wellspring of life" (Prov 4:23). The wise man carefully watches his heart, lest he succumb to sins of speech or action (see appendix to Ps 1: The Ways of Wisdom and Folly). Speech is an indicator of one's relationship to the Lord (cf. 34:13; 39:1; Prov 13:3; 21:23; James 3:1–12). The wicked use their tongues destructively (cf. 140:3), whereas the speech of the righteous expresses love and fidelity (cf. 15:2–3). When harassed the wise man trusts in the Lord to guard "over the door" of his lips (v.3; cf. Mic 7:5). By his assistance one may keep his heart from sin and temptation ("let not my heart be drawn") in order to do God's will (119:10, 36, 133).

Temptation to do evil was also real. The tempters were men of influence. The word "men" (*'îšîm*, v.4) denotes men of land, rank, and status within the community. However, these members of the aristocracy were nevertheless "evildoers" who practiced "wicked deeds" (cf. 28:3). Their riches permitted them the enjoyment of the finer things in life ("delicacies"; cf. Prov 4:17). Removal of oneself from their influence and from the enjoyment of their material benefits was the second step away from temptation; dependency on the Lord was the first.

5a–c Instead of receiving encouragement and privilege from the well-to-do but godless men, the righteous man receives joy from the discipline and words of rebuke by the wise. A wise man responds to wisdom (cf. Prov 9:8) as an expression of "love" (*ḥesed;* NIV, "kindness") and welcomes it like "oil," a symbol of honor extended to a welcome guest (cf. Prov 27:9). The allusions are to the banquet of the wicked, where he would have received acts of "love" and hospitality (cf. Amos 6:6), but the rebuke of the wise is as good or better than their attentiveness. The psalmist hopes to avoid the traps of pleasantry laid by the wicked, praying for their demise ("my prayer is ever against the deeds of the evildoers," v.5d; cf. vv.6–7, 10). Instead, he welcomes the rebukes of the righteous like "oil" poured out on the head (cf. 23:5).

III. Prayer for Vindication

141:5d–7

> Yet my prayer is ever against the deeds of evildoers;
> 6 their rulers will be thrown down from the cliffs,
> and the wicked will learn that my words were
> well spoken.
> 7 ⌞They will say,⌟ "As one plows and breaks up the earth,
> so our bones have been scattered at the mouth
> of the grave."

5d–7 The prayer ("my prayer," v.5d) is an imprecation against the godless aristocracy ("their rulers," v.6). The psalmist prays that they may die a cruel death, being thrown down the cliffs (cf. 2 Chron 25:12; Luke 4:29). The shock of God's judgment on their despotic regime will affect their followers and may bring them to their senses. They remind one another of the saying of the godly psalmist ("the wicked will learn that my words were well spoken") and the instruction of a popular proverb (v.7). The language of v.7 is difficult, but the sense seems to be thus: Even as a farmer breaks up the soil and brings up the rocks, so the bones of the wicked will be scattered without a decent burial.

Notes

7 R.J. Tournay argues from this verse—which he translates as "our bones are scattered at the mouth of Sheol"—and from 53:6 in favor of the desperate situation of Jerusalem's siege in 701 B.C. ("Psaume cxli: Nouvelle Interprétation," RB 90 [1983]: 321–23). If so, though this interpretation is dubious, the evildoers denote the Assyrians.

IV. Prayer for Deliverance and Vindication

141:8–10

> 8 But my eyes are fixed on you, O Sovereign LORD;
> in you I take refuge—do not give me over to death.
> 9 Keep me from the snares they have laid for me,
> from the traps set by evildoers.
> 10 Let the wicked fall into their own nets,
> while I pass by in safety.

8–10 The lament and imprecation give rise to a new height of faith (as in 140:4, 12). The psalmist's "eyes" of faith are toward the Lord (cf. 25:15). The "Sovereign LORD" ("Yahweh Adonai"; cf. 68:20; 71:5, 16; 73:28; 109:21; 140:7) has the power to provide "refuge" (cf. 7:1). The poet prays for deliverance on the one hand (vv.8–9) and for vindication on the other (v.10).

God's deliverance brings life. The poet prays that the Lord will not pour out his life, as one drains the blood out of slaughtered animals (cf. Isa 53:12). The wicked destroy life, as they set "traps" and "snares" for the righteous (v.9; cf. 38:12; 64:5; 91:3; 119:110; 140:5; 142:3). The precariousness of the situation is such that only the Lord can provide refuge and, ultimately, deliverance.

God's vindication comes in the form of retribution. The evil plots of the wicked will be foiled and will boomerang on themselves (cf. 5:10; 7:16; 9:16; 140:9). They will be caught, whereas the godly will escape. The Hebrew phraseology is terse and could be explained as the godly being singled out for deliverance (see NEB, "whilst I pass in safety, all alone") or as emphatic (see Allen: "while I myself escape," in loc.).

Psalm 142: Yahweh Alone Is My Portion in the Land of the Living

The psalmist speaks of the great distress he has found himself in. It is uncertain whether "prison" (v.7) is a metaphor for oppression or refers to actual imprisonment or exile. If the superscription is to be taken seriously, the "prison" may well refer to David's being in the cave when pursued by Saul, possibly at Adullam (1 Sam 22:1, 4) or at En Gedi (1 Sam 24:1–22).

This psalm is an *individual lament*. The expository structure is as follows:

A. Lament of the Individual (vv.1–2)
  B. Loneliness in Suffering (vv.3–7a)
A′. Public Thanksgiving (v.7b)

I. Lament of the Individual

142:1–2

A *maskil* of David. When he was in the cave. A prayer.

1 I cry aloud to the LORD;
  I lift up my voice to the LORD for mercy.
2 I pour out my complaint before him;
  before him I tell my trouble.

1–2 In two parallel expressions the psalmist makes his lament known to the Lord. These verbal expressions recur in the lament genre: "cry with my voice" ("cry aloud," v.1; cf. 3:4; 77:1), "lift up . . . for mercy" (cf. 30:8), "I pour out" (v.2; cf. 42:4; 62:8; 102, superscription); "my trouble" ("in distress"; cf. 77:2; 86:7). These phrases illustrate the tension between anguish of soul and dependence on the Lord.

II. Loneliness in Suffering

142:3–7a

3 When my spirit grows faint within me,
  it is you who know my way.

In the path where I walk
men have hidden a snare for me.
4 Look to my right and see;
no one is concerned for me.
I have no refuge;
no one cares for my life.

5 I cry to you, O LORD;
I say, "You are my refuge,
my portion in the land of the living."
6 Listen to my cry,
for I am in desperate need;
rescue me from those who pursue me,
for they are too strong for me.
7 Set me free from my prison,
that I may praise your name.

3a–b His adversity and his prayers have brought the psalmist to the point of total exhaustion (v.3a; cf. 76:12; 77:3; 143:4; Jonah 2:7). Nevertheless, even in this state of spiritual depression, he relies on his God, who knows his situation ("my way," v.3b). The "way" may signify here the present adversity or "the way out" of adversity. The second is more likely in the light of 143:7–8 (cf. 32:8). This also agrees with the contrast between "my spirit" and the emphatic use of "you," appropriately rendered "it is you" in the NIV.

3c–4 The path of the Lord is different from the present "path" the psalmist walks (v.3c). The path of the Lord leads to salvation (cf. vv.6–7), whereas the path of his opponents is repressive and full of entanglements (v.3d; cf. 141:9). But regardless of where the psalmist looks, the Lord is not at his "right" (*yāmîn*, v.4) hand. The "right" signifies the place where one's witness or legal council stood (cf. 16:8; 109:31; 110:5; 121:5). He has no one to defend him against the adversaries. He has no refuge. He is a refugee for whom no one cares (cf. v.7).

5–7 The lament resumes with a cry of the heart ("I cry . . . I say," v.5) and a petition for relief ("Listen . . . rescue me. . . . Set me free," vv.6–7). At the same time the psalmist develops the thoughts of vv.1–4, in confessing that the Lord is his "refuge" (*mānôs;* lit., "place of refuge," v.4; *maḥseh*, "refuge," v.5; cf. 91:2; Jer 17:17) and his hope ("my portion in the land of the living"; cf. 16:5; 73:26; 119:57; Lam 3:24).

The psalmist also resumes the existential need, as he refers to his present state: "I am in desperate need. . . . my prison" (vv.6–7). "Prison" may denote actual imprisonment but may also be a metaphor for his desperate condition in the light of the allusions to adversity and isolation (cf. 107:10; Isa 42:7).

The psalmist further prays that the Lord's deliverance will give him a renewed opportunity to give thanks to the covenant-faithful name of God (v.7a; cf. 18:49; 20:1; 140:13).

IV. Public Thanksgiving

142:7b

Then the righteous will gather about me
because of your goodness to me.

7b The resolution to his despair will not only bring him to thanksgiving (v.7a) but will serve as an encouragement to the righteous community. The "righteous" (*ṣaddîq;* cf. 1:5), too, will hear the psalmist's thanksgiving and will be edified. The psalmist envisions the godly crowding around him and listening to his thanksgiving for the great acts of God's deliverance. The acts of deliverance are acts of "goodness" or "bounty" (implied by the root *g-m-l;* see 13:6; cf. 116:7).

Psalm 143: Lead Me on Level Ground

This psalm is classified as one of the seven penitential psalms (6; 32; 38; 51; 102; 130; 143). Part of the reason for the designation lies in the confessional nature of certain psalms and part of the reason lies in its use within the Christian community. Because of its emphasis on the Lord's grace and favor, Luther called this psalm one of the "Pauline Psalms" (see also 32; 51; 130). The literary genre resembles that of an *individual lament.*

The structure of the psalm is as follows:

Part I:
- A. Prayer for God's Righteousness (vv.1–2)
  - B. Lament (vv.3–6)

Part II:
  - B′. Petitions (vv.7–11)
- A′. Prayer for God's Righteousness (v.12)

I. Prayer for God's Righteousness

143:1–2

A psalm of David.

1 O LORD, hear my prayer,
  listen to my cry for mercy;
in your faithfulness and righteousness
  come to my relief.
2 Do not bring your servant into judgment,
  for no one living is righteous before you.

1 The psalmist employs liturgical phrases in his prayer: "hear my prayer" (cf. 5:1; 17:1; 28:2; 54:2; 64:1), "listen" (cf. 5:2; 17:1; 55:1; 86:6; 140:6; 141:1), "my cry for mercy" (*taḥᵃnûnay;* cf. 28:2, 6; 31:22; 116:1; 130:2; 140:6), and "come to my relief" (lit., "answer me"; cf. v.7; 4:1; 13:3; 69:13, 16–17; 86:1; 102:2). In his appeal he throws himself on the "faithfulness" (*'ᵉmunāh*) and "righteousness" (*ṣᵉḏāqāh*) of the Lord (see appendix to Ps 25: The Perfections of Yahweh). Both qualities connote the absolute fidelity and perfection of God in keeping his covenant with his covenant children. The ground for answered prayer is the Lord's commitment to his people.

2 Another reason for the urgency of God's response lies in the psalmist's awareness of his unrighteousness. He knows that sin is to be found in him and that God's judgment could find him guilty and therefore condemn him to remain in his troubles (cf. 130:3). The psalmist is fully cognizant of God's righteousness and of his own sinfulness. Therefore he appeals to the Lord's faithfulness and righteousness (v.1).

How contrary is this spirit to the confession of innocence in several psalms (7:3–5)! Both expressions are valid, depending on the context in which one finds himself. The confession of innocence is appropriate when one is insulted and persecuted for righteousness's sake, and the confession of guilt is proper when confronted with one's own frailties. The recognition of worthlessness becomes an expression of full dependence on the Lord's mercy. Confidence may lead to spiritual pride and independence, whereas self-depreciation may lead to continual introspection and spiritual depression.

Notes

For a brief discussion of the technical words and phrases in the superscription, see the Introduction.

2 The theological position of man's sinfulness is further developed by the apostle Paul (Rom 3:20; Gal 2:16; see B. Lindars, *New Testament Apologetic; The Doctrinal Significance of the Old Testament Quotations* [Philadelphia: Westminster, 1961], pp. 224–25, 238–39; L.C. Allen, "The Old Testament in Romans I–VIII," *Vox Evangelica* 3 [1964]: 11–12).

II. Lament

143:3–6

3 The enemy pursues me,
he crushes me to the ground;
he makes me dwell in darkness
like those long dead.
4 So my spirit grows faint within me;
my heart within me is dismayed.

5 I remember the days of long ago;
I meditate on all your works
and consider what your hands have done.
6 I spread out my hands to you;
my soul thirsts for you like a parched land. *Selah*

3 The adversity is described in general terms, rendering the psalm suitable for universal application. The enemy hunts the psalmist down (see 7:5; cf. 88:3–6) so that he feels as if he lives "in darkness," i.e., in Sheol (cf. 88:6; Mic 7:8), like those who have been "dead" for a long time (cf. Jer 51:39; Lam 3:6). Robbed of life he exists as one abandoned by God and man (cf. 88:6–9, 12; see appendix to Ps 88: Sheol-Grave-Death in the Psalms).

4 Having no apparent reason for living, the psalmist is discouraged to the point of despair ("my spirit grows faint"; cf. 77:3; 142:3). The "spirit" is not the Holy Spirit but the spirit of life that sustains him (cf. 76:12; 142:3; Gen 6:3). The expression of despair is clarified by the metaphor of heart paralysis (NIV, "dismayed").

5 The psalmist's alienation and despair grows as he reflects on what God has done in the past. He does "remember" (*z-k-r;* 77:3, 11; 119:52), "meditate" (*h-g-h;* cf. 1:2;

77:12), and "consider" (*ś-y-ḥ;* cf. 77:3–12) the acts of God in creation and in the history of redemption (see 77:11–12). For "the days of long ago," see 77:5.

6 In his remembrance the psalmist can only turn to the Lord for help with outspread hands (cf. 28:2; 44:20; 88:9; Lam 1:17). His need for God and for his redemption increases as he deepens in his despair. His need is so great that he likens himself to "a parched land." As dry ground opens itself for rain, so is the psalmist longing for some evidence of his care (cf. 42:1–2; 63:1).

Notes

---

4 The idiom יִשְׁתּוֹמֵם לִבִּי (*yištômēm libbî,* "my heart . . . is dismayed") is a *hapax legomenon.* The verb means "be driven to consternation, numbness" (KB, p. 989). The sense is well reflected in the NEB: "and my heart is dazed with despair."

III. Petitions and Prayer (vv.7–12)

This section contains a mosaic of prayers for deliverance, guidance, and commitment to the Lord. We shall consider each motif separately. The language of these verses reveals a great dependence on the expressions of existing psalms.

A. *Petitions for Deliverance*

143:7–8a, 9a

7 Answer me quickly, O LORD;
my spirit faints with longing.
Do not hide your face from me
or I will be like those who go down to the pit.
8 Let the morning bring me word of your unfailing love,
. . . .
9 Rescue me from my enemies, O LORD,

7 Out of the depth of despair ("my spirit faints"; cf. 84:2), the psalmist calls on the Lord to deliver him speedily (cf. 40:13; 69:17; 102:2). As long as God hides his face (cf. 27:9; 102:2), the psalmist feels cast off from God's favor and is like "those who go down to the pit" (cf. 28:1; 88:4), i.e., as good as dead (cf. v.3).

8a Out of his despair the psalmist calls on the Lord to renew his "unfailing love" (*ḥeseḏ*). He waits for God's deliverance as a watchman waits for the dawn of day (130:6; cf. Lam 3:23). God's anger is like the darkness of night, and his favor is like the morning light (cf. 30:5).

9a In despair the psalmist calls on the Lord to deliver him from his adversaries (cf. 31:15; 59:1; 142:6). This prayer is further developed in the concluding prayers (cf. D below).

Notes

7–12 On the movement from lament to confidence, see Johannes Schildenberger, "Psalm 143. Von Verzagtheit zu Vertrauen," *Erbe und Auftrag* 57 (1981): 202–4.

B. *Expressions of Confidence*

143:8b–c, 9b, 10b

for I have put my trust in you.
Show me the way I should go,
for to you I lift up my soul.
. . . .
for I hide myself in you.
. . . .
for you are my God;

8b–c Despairing but confident—even in the depth of his despair—the psalmist is confident of the Lord. He has put his "trust" (*bāṭaḥtî,* v.8b; cf. 22:4; 78:22) in him. This expression is equivalent to "for to you I lift up my soul" (v.8c; cf. 25:1; 86:4).

9b, 10b The reason for the psalmist's trust is given in vv.9b and 10b. First, the Lord is his refuge ("for I hide myself in you," v.9b). Second, the Lord is his covenant God ("for you are my God," v.10b; cf. 31:14; 40:4; 86:3; 118:28; 140:6). He is sustained by the Lord's promise to be the God of his people (Exod 6:7).

Notes

9 The MT's כִּסִּתִי (*kissiṯî;* lit., "I covered"; NIV, "I hide myself") is problematic. The LXX reads, "I fled." Kraus has proposed an emendation, כְּסוּתִי (*kᵉsûṯî,* "my covering," *Psalmen,* 2:1116; so also BHS). The general idea of the NIV is derived from the other verses expressive of confidence in God. For other proposals see Allen (p. 281). Other renderings are, "I come for shelter" (Allen, p. 280); NEB, "with thee have I sought refuge"; Dahood (*Psalms* 3:321), "truly I am being submerged."

C. *Petitions for Guidance*

143:8b, 10a, c

Show me the way I should go,
for to you I lift up my soul.
. . . .
10 Teach me to do your will,
. . . .
may your good Spirit
lead me on level ground.

8b, 10a As an expression of humility and hope in the future, the psalmist asks for God's guidance out of the present and into the future so as to assure that he will continually enjoy the benefits of the covenant relationship (cf. 27:11). He desires to know "the way" he should go (v.8b; cf. 5:8; 25:4; 32:8; 142:3), i.e., the way of righteousness (cf. 1:6; Exod 33:13), so that he may do God's "will" (*rāṣôn*, v.10a; cf. 25:4–5; 40:8; 103:21).

Doing the will of God implies a complete submission to his will, as revealed in his word so that the deeds done in the flesh are acceptable to the Lord. Obedience here is an outgrowth of redemption, which itself is a work of God freely rendered to those who express faith in him. Obedience and sanctification grow out of a relationship of grace.

10c The psalmist believes that if the Lord instructs him and guides him, then he will experience divine illumination by the Spirit of God ("your good Spirit"; cf. Neh 9:20). The presence of the Spirit will further guarantee God's protection so that he will prepare "level ground" (lit., "a level land"). The psalmist anticipates God's blessing and protection as a consequence of his guidance (cf. 32:8–10).

Notes

10 The idiom אֶרֶץ מִישׁוֹר (*'ereṣ mîšôr*, "level ground") is unique. A number of MSS read אוֹרַח מִישׁוֹר (*'ôraḥ mîšôr*, "a level path"; cf. 27:11) or בְּדֶרֶךְ מִישׁוֹר (*bᵉderek mîšôr*, "on a level path"; see BHS). On Dahood's rendering of "meadow," see 36:10, and Elmer B. Smick, "Ugaritic and the Theology of the Psalms," *New Perspectives on the Old Testament*, ed. J. Barton Payne (Waco: Word, 1970), pp. 104–16.

D. Concluding Prayers

143:11–12

11 For your name's sake, O LORD, preserve my life;
in your righteousness, bring me out of trouble.
12 In your unfailing love, silence my enemies;
destroy all my foes,
for I am your servant.

11–12 These verses form a proper conclusion. First, the psalmist petitions the Lord for deliverance for his "name's sake" (v.11; cf. 31:3; 106:8), returning to the promises of his "faithfulness" (v.1; cf. "unfailing love," v.12) and "righteousness" (v.1; cf. v.11). After all, the Lord is the righteous King (see appendix to Ps 5: Yahweh Is King).

Second, the psalmist prays that his "life" may be delivered. All of "life" is before the Lord (v.2), but the psalmist is as dead in his experience of alienation (vv.3–4, 6–7). Therefore, he prays that the Lord will preserve his "life" (v.11; cf. 30:3; 119:25; 138:7) by delivering him from "trouble."

Third, the psalmist prays that the Lord may deal righteously with his adversaries (v.12). The spirit reflects hope as expressed in the imprecatory psalms. The psalmist prays that the Lord may "silence" ("exterminate"; cf. 54:5; 73:27; 94:23), i.e., "destroy," all his foes.

Only at the end does the psalmist call on the Lord to act for his "name's sake" (v.11) and for the sake of God's servant (v.12; cf. v.2). The "servant" (*'ebed;* see 19:11) who was in desperate need (v.2) is still the servant of the Lord. The relationship is still true, even in adversity and despair. His confidence lies, not in himself, but in the one who promised. He is true, faithful, and righteous.

Psalm 144: Yahweh Is My Warrior

In this psalm the monarch prays for the Lord's help for himself (vv.1–11) and for God's blessing on his people. While it is true that a shift from the individual to the community takes place in v.12, producing two units (vv.1–11, 12–15), the canonical unity reveals the need for God to act (a royal lament, vv.1–11) and the resultant blessings of his actions (a psalm of blessing, vv.12–15). The psalmist interweaves liturgical elements common to other psalms (esp. Ps 18). A.A. Anderson designates the resultant whole a "National Lamentation" (p. 931), but a good case may be made for reading it as a *royal psalm* (Kraus, *Psalmen,* 2:1123).

The structural elements reveal balance and movement. The expository structure is as follows:

A. Hymn of Praise (vv.1–2)
  B. Man's Need (vv.3–4)
    C. A Prayer for God's Involvement (vv.5–8)
A′. Hymn of Praise (vv.9–10)
  B′. Prayer for God's Involvement (v.11)
    C′. Prayer for Blessing on God's People (vv.12–15)

I. Hymn of Praise

144:1–2

Of David.

1 Praise be to the LORD my Rock,
who trains my hands for war,
my fingers for battle.
2 He is my loving God and my fortress,
my stronghold and my deliverer,
my shield, in whom I take refuge,
who subdues peoples under me.

1–2 The king praises the Lord his God in the language of Psalm 18: "my Rock" (*ṣûr,* v.1; cf. 18:46; 28:1; 42:9); "my fortress, my stronghold and deliverer" (v.2; cf. 18:2); and "my shield" (cf. 18:2). The Lord gives military success to his king ("who trains my hands for war"; cf. 18:34) so that the nations will be subject to him ("who subdues peoples"; cf. 18:47). In his acts of protection and victory, the Lord is loyal to his promises made to David ("my loving God"; cf. 59:10, 17).

The jubilant praise (vv.1–2), confessing God as the Redeemer-King, motivates an ephemeral human being to rouse the Divine Warrior to action! The psalmist does not present his petition before the Lord timidly but with boldness. He knows his God;

and despite human shortcomings, he is convinced that the Lord does "care for him" and "think of him" (v.3; see appendix to Ps 98: Yahweh Is the Divine Warrior).

Notes

For a brief discussion of the technical words and phrases in the superscription, see the Introduction.

2 The NIV margin calls attention to the textual issue. A number of MSS and ancient versions read here the plural עַמִּים (*'ammîm*, "peoples," as in 18:47), whereas the MT reads, "who subdues my people [*'ammî*] under me."

II. Man's Need

144:3–4

> 3 O LORD, what is man that you care for him,
> the son of man that you think of him?
> 4 Man is like a breath;
> his days are like a fleeting shadow.

3–4 In praise of God the royal psalmist exclaims that man, finite and unreliable, is unworthy of the love of the Lord (v.3; cf. 8:4; Job 7:17). Man is unstable, short-lived, and a momentary flicker ("a breath," v.4: cf. 39:5, 11; 62:9; "like a fleeting shadow," cf. 102:11; 109:23; Eccl 6:12). The strength of the Lord and the weakness of man accentuate divine grace and set the basis on which the king prays for divine intervention on behalf of his people.

Yet the Lord covenants with man. The "care" (*y-d-'*, v.3; see 1:6) of the Lord is nothing less than his covenantal commitment to be gracious and to fulfill his promises. See Herbert B. Huffmon, "The Treaty Background of Hebrew *Yada'*," BASOR 181 (1966): 31–37.

III. A Prayer for God's Involvement

144:5–8

> 5 Part your heavens, O LORD, and come down;
> touch the mountains, so that they smoke.
> 6 Send forth lightning and scatter ⌊the enemies⌋;
> shoot your arrows and rout them.
> 7 Reach down your hand from on high;
> deliver me and rescue me
> from the mighty waters,
> from the hands of foreigners
> 8 whose mouths are full of lies,
> whose right hands are deceitful.

5–8 The insistent prayer for God's immediate involvement is best felt by reading the verbs: "part . . . come down . . . touch. . . . send forth . . . scatter . . . shoot . . . rout. . . . reach down . . . deliver." He calls on the Lord to appear as he did at Mount

Sinai, where in the midst of smoke, lightning, and earthquake phenomena he came down to his people (cf. Exod 19:11, 18–19; cf. Ps 18:14). The purpose for the theophany is no other than God's coming as the Divine Warrior, by whose "hand" comes deliverance to the people of God and vengeance to the enemies. The enemies are the object of the "lightning," also called "arrows" (cf. 18:14), so that their power will be effectively eliminated. The people of God are the object of his deliverance, as he puts forth his right hand of deliverance (cf. 18:16) to "deliver . . . and rescue" (v.7; cf. vv.10–11). The marvel of grace is that the God who is so greatly exalted ("on high"; cf. 68:18) condescends to "come down" (v.5) to the aid of his own! (See the appendix to Ps 119: Yahweh Is My Redeemer.)

The adversaries are likened to "the mighty waters" (v.7) that, according to Canaanite legends, were under the rule of the god of the sea, Yamm. He caused havoc in the peaceful world of the gods but was eventually subjugated by Baal. Here it is the Lord who has quieted the stormy seas (cf. Gen 1:2; Ps 65:7), and his power still hovers over the stormy nations. The hegemony of the "foreigners" (cf. Isa 56:6; 61:5) is wholly contrary to the rule of God. Their words and intimating actions ("right hands," v.8) are nothing but "lies," i.e., unfaithful, treacherous, perfidious (cf. 140:1–3).

Notes

5–7 For an extensive study of the motif of water and divine warfare, see John Day, *God's Conflict with the Dragon and the Sea. Echoes of Canaanite Myth in the Old Testament* (Cambridge: Cambridge University Press, 1985). He interprets these verses as an example of the historization of the divine conflict (pp. 123–40). The same literary phenomenon occurs in the prophet Isaiah, as he speaks regarding the future deliverance in terms of God's victory over the "monster" (27:1; 51:9)

IV. Hymn of Praise

144:9–10

9 I will sing a new song to you, O God;
on the ten-stringed lyre I will make music to you,
10 to the One who gives victory to kings,
who delivers his servant David from the deadly sword.

9–10 Despite the present calamity the royal psalmist confidently sings praise to the Lord. He triumphantly expects him to be faithful in giving "victory" (v.10, from *y-š-ʿ*) to David and the Davidic "kings." He anticipates that subsequent to the victory, "a new song" (v.9) accompanied on "the ten-stringed lyre" (see appendix to Ps 150: Musical Instruments) will be raised to the Lord, celebrating the new acts of God (cf. 33:3; 96:1).

V. Prayer for God's Involvement

144:11

[11]Deliver me and rescue me
from the hands of foreigners
whose mouths are full of lies,
whose right hands are deceitful.

11 This verse is a repetition of vv.7–8 and appears to be here for the purpose of symmetry.

VI. Prayer for Blessing on God's People

144:12–15

[12]Then our sons in their youth
will be like well-nurtured plants,
and our daughters will be like pillars
carved to adorn a palace.
[13]Our barns will be filled
with every kind of provision.
Our sheep will increase by thousands,
by tens of thousands in our fields;
[14] our oxen will draw heavy loads.
There will be no breaching of walls,
no going into captivity,
no cry of distress in our streets.

[15]Blessed are the people of whom this is true;
blessed are the people whose God is the LORD.

12–15 David prays unselfishly for his people, asking that the Lord will richly bless their children, their lives, and their livelihoods. He prays that their "sons" may grow (cf. Isa 44:14) to be strong like verdant plants (cf. 128:3) and that their "daughters" may become aesthetically pleasing maidens, like richly decorated "pillars" adorning a Near-Eastern palace (v.12). He prays that the Lord may lavish riches on them and increase the fields, flocks, and herds without fear of foreign invaders (vv.13–14) or without the humiliation of captivity (cf. Amos 4:3).

The Lord had promised to bless his people with stalwart youth, productivity, and prosperity, and to protect them from enemy attacks and humiliation (cf. Lev 26:1–13; Deut 28:1–14; Ps 132:13–18). Blessed are the people that experience the Lord's ability to save, protect, and bless. They truly are "happy" (cf. 1:1), even in adversity, as Calvin writes, "We are to observe this, that while God in giving us meat and drink admits us to the enjoyment of a certain measure of happiness, it does not follow that those believers are miserable who struggle through life in want and poverty, for this want, whatever it be, God can counterbalance by better consolations" (5:271).

Notes

12 The MT's אֲשֶׁר (*'ašer*, "which" or "that") functions as an explication or result of the prayer. It is correctly rendered in the NIV by "Then." B.J. Tournay argues that this particle introduces a prophetic expectation by David ("Le Psaume CXLIV. Structure et Interprétation," RB 91 [1984]: 520–30).

Psalm 145: Great Is Yahweh's Universal Kingdom!

This psalm is an acrostic in which each verse begins with a letter of the Hebrew alphabet with the exception of the nun in the MT (v.13b). The NIV accepts the textual evidence from Qumran and several ancient versions, according to which v.13b has been accidentally omitted from the Hebrew text but may be reconstructed from these other witnesses.

The motif of the psalm is the praise of the Great King. The attributes and acts of God form the theme of this hymn. The poet was highly skilled as the acrostic form was no hindrance to the hymnic genre. All elements blend together well into an aesthetic whole (see Adele Berlin, "The Rhetoric of Psalm 145," in *Biblical and Related Studies Presented to Samuel Iwry*, edd. Ann Kort and Scott Morschauer [Winona Lake: Eisenbrauns, 1985], pp. 17–22). The structural elements are as follows:

A. In Praise of the Lord's Kingship (vv.1–3)
  B. In Praise of the Lord's Faithfulness to the Covenant (vv.4–9)
A′. In Praise of the Lord's Kingship (vv.10–13a)
  B′. In Praise of the Lord's Covenant Fidelity (vv.13b–21)

(For a concentric structural analysis, see Jonathan Magonet, "Some Concentric Structures in Psalms," *The Heythrop Journal* 23 [1982]: 365–69.)

I. In Praise of the Lord's Kingship

145:1–3

A psalm of praise. Of David.

1 I will exalt you, my God the King;
  I will praise your name for ever and ever.
2 Every day I will praise you
  and extol your name for ever and ever.

3 Great is the LORD and most worthy of praise;
  his greatness no one can fathom.

1–3 The synonyms for "praise ("I will exalt you . . . I will praise you. . . . I will praise you . . . and extol your name," vv.1–2) set the mood for the psalm. The object of the praise is "my God the King" (v.1; cf. 5:2; 68:24; 84:3) whose "name" (vv.1–2) signifies covenant fidelity. As the Lord is perpetually loyal to his covenant people, the poet calls on the covenant community to praise God unceasingly ("for ever and ever. . . . every day . . . for ever and ever," vv.1–2; cf. 115:18). In Jewish practice this psalm was recited twice in the morning and once in the evening service. The Talmud commends all who repeat it three times a day as having a share in the world to come (Ber 4b).

The reason for praise lies in God's greatness (v.3; cf. 48:1; 96:4; 147:5). He is the "great" King who deserves the "praise" of man. After all, no one can fully understand his purposes and his ways. In the presence of the divine King, man must admit his limitations (cf. Job 5:9; 9:10; Isa 40:28).

Notes

For a brief discussion of the technical words and phrases in the superscription, see the Introduction.

II. In Praise of the Lord's Faithfulness to the Covenant

145:4–9

4 One generation will commend your works to another;
they will tell of your mighty acts.
5 They will speak of the glorious splendor of your majesty,
and I will meditate on your wonderful works.
6 They will tell of the power of your awesome works,
and I will proclaim your great deeds.
7 They will celebrate your abundant goodness
and joyfully sing of your righteousness.

8 The LORD is gracious and compassionate,
slow to anger and rich in love.
9 The LORD is good to all;
he has compassion on all he has made.

4–9 These verses give more specifics on God's greatness. The unceasing praise of the Lord comes from the grateful instruction of the new generation by the older generation (v.4). The process of transmission of salvation history from one generation to another is by the telling (22:30–31) of God's "mighty acts" of deliverance (cf. 106:2). The "works" (v.5) of the Lord (see appendix to Ps 78: The Mighty Acts of Yahweh) reveal his "might" (*g^e^bûrāh*); his "glorious splendor"; his inscrutable nature ("wonderful"; cf. vv.11–12; 105:27); his "power" (*'^e^zûz*, v.6; cf. 62:11; 63:2); his awe-inspiring nature ("awesome"; cf. 65:5); his greatness ("great deeds"; cf. 1 Chron 17:19, 21); his "abundant goodness" (v.7; lit., "the great fame of your goodness"; cf. 31:19); his "righteousness" (cf. 51:14; 143:1); and his relational perfections, as he is "gracious and compassionate, slow to anger and rich in love" (v.8; cf. Exod 34:6–7; Neh 9:17, 31; Pss 86:15; 103:8; Joel 2:13; Jonah 4:2). Even to all his creation he is "good" and has "compassion" (v.9). God's kingship is magnificent, his sovereignty beneficent, and his redemptive acts manifold (see appendix to Ps 25: The Perfections of Yahweh).

These perfections are the object of education, proclamation, celebration, and meditation (v.5; for "meditate," see 119:15). The psalmist enjoins all God's people to share in the extension of God's kingdom by private meditation, discussion, and public speaking about God's mighty acts. They are inspiring in the sense that one's own accomplishments became dwarfed in comparison with the mighty acts of God. His is the kingdom, the power, and the glory!

III. In Praise of the Lord's Kingship

145:10–13a

10 All you have made will praise you, O LORD;
your saints will extol you.

[11]They will tell of the glory of your kingdom
and speak of your might,
[12]so that all men may know of your mighty acts
and the glorious splendor of your kingdom.
[13]Your kingdom is an everlasting kingdom,
and your dominion endures through all generations.

10–13a The meditation on the mighty acts of God (vv.4–9) occasions a renewed praise of the Lord's kingship (vv.10-13). His acts benefit the covenant community and all his creation. All his works ("all you have made"; lit., "all your works," v.10, as in v.4), including the "saints" (*ḥasîd,* v.10), praise the Lord for his covenant love (*ḥesed*). They give thanks for the many expressions of his kingship, all of which reveal his "glory" (vv.11–12; cf. v.5), "might" (cf. v.4), and stability ("everlasting . . . through all generations," v.13; cf. Dan 4:3). How different is his kingdom! He condescends to the needs of his creatures. Von Rad calls this revelation of God's identification the *kenosis* of the OT: the beauty of Yahweh's condescension to the needs of his people (OTT, 1:367). The marvel of divine condescension lies in his magnificence and eternal dominion (v.13; cf. Exod 15:18; Pss 10:16; 29:10; Jer 10:10; 1 Tim 1:17).

Notes

11–13 Wilfred G.E. Watson's study ("Reversed Rootplay in Ps 145," *Biblica* 62 [1981]: 101–2) highlights the ingenuity and creativity of the psalmist. Watson notes the chiastic repetition of the words "glory" and "might" (vv.11–12):

v.11 *k^eḇôḏ ("glory")*
g^eḇûrāṯ^eḵā ("your might")

v.12 *g^eḇûrōṯāyw* ("your mighty acts")
k^eḇôḏ ("glorious")

In addition Watson observes how the psalmist ingeniously used the acrostic letters K, L, and M to be read backwards, spelling M-L-K: *meleḵ* ("king") in reverse.

IV. In Praise of the Lord's Covenant Fidelity

145:13b–21

The LORD is faithful to all his promises
and loving toward all he has made.
[14]The LORD upholds all those who fall
and lifts up all who are bowed down.
[15]The eyes of all look to you,
and you give them their food at the proper time.
[16]You open your hand
and satisfy the desires of every living thing.

17 The LORD is righteous in all his ways
and loving toward all he has made.
18 The LORD is near to all who call on him,
to all who call on him in truth.
19 He fulfills the desires of those who fear him;
he hears their cry and saves them.
20 The LORD watches over all who love him,
but all the wicked he will destroy.

21 My mouth will speak in praise of the LORD.
Let every creature praise his holy name
for ever and ever.

13b–16 The psalmist returns to a more concrete description of God's fidelity in his kingship. He is "faithful" (v.13b; from *'-m-n,* related to *'ᵉmeṯ*) and "loving" (*ḥasîḏ,* related to *ḥeseḏ*) to all his "works" (NIV, "all he has made"; cf. v.4). His royal love extends to the whole domain of his rule, including his creation. His love evidences itself in his acts of restoration (v.14). He restores those who are dependent on him ("all who are bowed down"; see 146:8; Isa 58:5). His royal love also evidences itself in acts of provision (vv.15–16). He royally satisfies the needs of every living creature (cf. 104:27–28) as the master of a house opens his hand to all who are dependent on him (cf. Matt 6:26). The creatures are satiated with his provisions.

17 These observations lead the psalmist to a renewed reflection on the nature of God. He is "righteous" and "loving" (cf. vv.7, 13b). His "righteous" acts are those of restoration, redemption, and vindication. They are acts of "love" toward his whole creation (cf. vv.4, 10, 13b). Because of the celebration of Yahweh in and over his creation, Brueggemann treats Psalm 145 together with Psalms 8, 33, and 104 as "Songs of Creation" (*Message of the Psalms,* pp. 28–38). He comments, "We take Psalm 145 to be the fullest representative of those psalms that understand creation as a mode of equilibrium, coherence, and reliability" (p. 31).

18–20 Since the Lord is so good to his creation, how much more does he care for his covenant people! This is essentially what Jesus taught in the Sermon on the Mount (Matt 6:25–34). Those who are members of his covenant fellowship are distinguished from the rest of his creation, because they "call on him," "fear him," and "love him" (vv.18–20). He hears the prayers of those of his children who submit to his will ("call on him," v.18) "in truth" (*'ᵉmeṯ;* cf. 25:5; John 4:24), i.e., they respond to his fidelity with fidelity. He acknowledges the longings and cries of his children who "fear him" (cf. 85:9) by delivering them in their time of need. He preserves ("watches over," v.20; cf. 121:4) his own who love (*'-h-b*) him, but he will avenge the "wicked" (cf. 1:6; 104:35; 143:12).

21 In response to this hymnic ascription of praise, the psalmist appropriately concludes this section as well as the whole psalm with a vow to praise the Lord (cf. vv.1–2). Because the kingdom of God extends to all creation and because the Lord's acts are to all his creation, it is only appropriate that all mankind (*bāśār;* NIV, "every creature," but cf. Isa 40:5) must respond to his "holy name" (cf. 106:47; Matt 6:9).

Notes

13b On the addition of this line, see the introduction to this psalm.

Psalm 146: Yahweh Reigns Forever and Ever

Psalms 146–150 constitute the last Hallel ("praise") collection. These five Hallelujah psalms have the characteristic genre of the *hymn of descriptive praise.* These psalms were used at some point as a part of the daily prayers in the synagogue worship. The other two collections are the Egyptian Hallel psalms (113–118) and the Great Hallel (120–136).

The LXX and Vulgate attribute Psalm 146 and Psalm 147 (which is divided into two psalms [147/148]) to Haggai and Zechariah. Though linguistic criteria and literary references to earlier materials witness to a postexilic date of the composition, internal evidence does not corroborate prophetic authorship.

Structurally, the psalm is true to its hymnic genre with an opening and concluding imperatival call to praise the Lord (vv.1–2, 10b). The hymn describes the many ways in which the Lord, the Creator (vv.5–6) and King (v.10), sustains the individuals who have faith in him, particularly the needy.

A. Call to Praise (vv.1–4)
  B. God the Creator (vv.5–6)
    C. God the Sustainer (vv.7–9)
  B′. God the Great King (v.10a)
A′. Call to Praise (v.10b)

I. Call to Praise

146:1–4

1 Praise the LORD.

Praise the LORD, O my soul.
2 I will praise the LORD all my life;
I will sing praise to my God as long as I live.

3 Do not put your trust in princes,
in mortal men, who cannot save.
4 When their spirit departs, they return to the ground;
on that very day their plans come to nothing.

1–2 The call to praise consists of three elements: (1) an imperatival call to praise (v.1), (2) a personal commitment to praise (v.2), and (3) an encouragement to praise (vv.3–4). The communal call ("praise the LORD," v.1; see 104:35) is the ground for the psalmist's determination to join in. He speaks to his own soul, "Praise the LORD, O my soul" (cf. 103:1, 22; 104:1, 35). The personal commitment to praise the Lord (v.2) is also expressed by the cohortative in Hebrew ("let me praise . . . let me sing"), which is reflected in the NIV: "I will praise . . . I will sing." Life is to be lived for the purpose of praising the Lord (see 104:33).

3–4 The commitment to praise the Lord requires a dissociation from dependency on man. The negative exhortation ("Do not put your trust in princes," v.3) is a positive way of renouncing humanism and of abandonment to a God-centered way of life. Similar to Psalm 118:8–9, the psalmist uses the device of merismus: "princes" and "man" (*'āḏām;* NIV, "mortal men") to call on the community not to trust (*b-ṭ-ḥ*) in human beings. Mankind is unable to provide "salvation" (*tᵉšû'āh;* cf. 33:16; 35:3; 60:11), because man may die at any time (cf. 104:29; Isa 2:22), whenever God removes the "spirit" of life (v.4; cf. 104:30; Gen 6:3). He is "man" (*'āḏām*) and to the "ground" (*'ᵃḏāmāh*) he must return (cf. Gen 3:19; Ps 104:29). When man is no more, all of his "plans" for help and "salvation" will go down with him. The same thought is expressed in 1 Maccabees 2:63: "Today he may be high in honour, but tomorrow there will be no trace of him, because he will have returned to the dust and all his schemes come to nothing."

Notes

---

4 The phrase עֶשְׁתֹּנֹתָיו (*'eštōnōṯāyw*, "his plans") appears to be an Aramaism. Dahood argues that Aramaisms do not necessarily give grounds for dating a psalm late, because this word also occurs in the eighth-century Sefire Inscription (*Psalms*, 3:341).

II. God the Creator

146:5–6

5 Blessed is he whose help is the God of Jacob,
  whose hope is in the LORD his God,
6 the Maker of heaven and earth,
  the sea, and everything in them—
  the LORD, who remains faithful forever.

5 The blessing of God rests on those who look to him for "help" (*'ēzer*). Their hope (*śēḇer*, only here and in 119:116) is in "the God of Jacob." The designation "God of Jacob" is somewhat strange, but it may be a purposeful allusion to the Songs of Zion, as it reminds God's people that the Lord, whose dwelling is in Zion (cf. 46:7, 11; 76:6; 84:8), is their "help" (see appendix to Ps 46: Zion Theology). The "God of Jacob" is the God of Zion (v.10), whose kingship is established (cf. 47:8; 48:2), and who blesses those who trust in him (cf. 84:12). Those who trust in him are "blessed" (*'ašrê;* see 1:1; cf. 33:12; 144:15).

6 The "God of Jacob" is "the Maker of heaven and earth" (cf. 115:15; 121:2; 124:8; 134:3). He uses his power and control over all of his created universe, including the sea, to bless every creature (cf. 136:25) with the constancy of his love. He is "faithful" (*'ᵉmeṯ*). His fidelity to creation encourages God's people. His covenant with his people is "forever" (cf. 107:8–9). They believe that since he cares for creation at large, his care for them will be so much greater!

Notes

6 The NIV renders this verse as a unit by the inclusion of "the LORD" (not in the MT); but if our literary structuring is correct, v.6 should be read thus:

> The Maker of heaven and earth,
> the sea, and everything in them—
> is he who remains faithful.

The nature of the fidelity of the Lord is explicated and the identity of the Maker of heaven and earth is five times affirmed by the emphatic position of the term "the LORD" (vv.7b–9a). Thus the psalmist builds up his argument from the general verity that God is the Maker to the climactic theological truth: Yahweh is the Maker and the Sustainer.

III. God the Sustainer

146:7–9

> 7 He upholds the cause of the oppressed
> and gives food to the hungry.
> The LORD sets prisoners free,
> 8 the LORD gives sight to the blind,
> the LORD lifts up those who are bowed down,
> the LORD loves the righteous.
> 9 The LORD watches over the alien
> and sustains the fatherless and the widow,
> but he frustrates the ways of the wicked.

7–9 In hymnic style the psalmist celebrates the many acts of God. By the use of participles in the Hebrew text, the psalmist explicates that the Maker of heaven and earth (v.6) "upholds . . . and gives. . . . sets free . . . gives sight . . . lifts up . . . loves. . . . watches" (vv.7–9). The nature of his faithfulness is hence explained by participial phrases and in the end by two contrastive imperfects: He "sustains the fatherless and the widow, / but he frustrates the ways of the wicked" (v.9b).

The fivefold emphatic position of the Lord (Yahweh in vv.7b–9a) further suggests a symmetric literary structuring:

> He upholds [participle] the cause of the oppressed and
> gives [participle] food to the hungry:
> The LORD sets [participle] the prisoners free,
> The LORD gives sight [participle] to the blind,
> The LORD lifts up [participle] those who are bowed down,
> The LORD loves [participle] the righteous.
> The LORD watches [participle] over the alien
> and sustains [imperfect] the fatherless and the widow,
> but he frustrates [imperfect] the ways of the wicked.

The psalmist does not introduce anything new in this description of the Lord's mighty acts (v.7; cf. 68:6; 103:6; 107:9, 10–16; Isa 42:7; 61:1; v.8, cf. Deut 28:29; Ps 145:14–15; Isa 59:9–10; v.9, cf. 39:12; 94:6; see appendix to Ps 78: The Mighty Acts of Yahweh), but the manner in which he brings the various ways of divine sustenance together is most creative, including the conclusion (v.9b, suggestive of 1:6).

IV. God the Great King

146:10a

> 10 The LORD reigns forever,
> your God, O Zion, for all generations.

10a The reference to Yahweh's rule in Zion has already been anticipated by the allusions to the Songs of Zion (cf. v.5). The Lord is the Great King who has promised to dwell in the midst of his people, purposing to deliver them (cf. Exod 15:17; Pss 29:10; 132:13–15). The joyous expectation of God's people is that he is faithful (cf. v.6), so that he will sustain them "forever" (*leʿôlām*, vv.6, 10).

V. Call to Praise

146:10b

> Praise the LORD.

10b The hymn appropriately concludes with a renewed call to "praise the LORD" (cf. v.1).

Psalm 147: The Blessedness of the People of God

See the introduction to Psalm 146.

Because of the division of this psalm into two separate psalms in the LXX (vv.1–11: Ps 146; vv.12–20: Ps 147) and because of internal differences, the unity of this psalm has been assailed. Allen makes a good defense for the unity by a careful analysis of the structural components, repetition, and parallelism (pp. 307–8).

The psalm may be divided into three strophes (vv.1–6, 7–11, 12–20), whose subject matter reveals parallelism and whose language shows similarity with other sections of Scripture (Deut 4; Job 37–39; Pss 33; 104; Isa 40–66). Its dependence on Scripture as well as its allusions to the Exile (vv.2, 13) may indicate a postexilic composition.

The psalm consists of three major parts:

Part One: In Praise of God's Restoration, Creation, and Redemption (vv.1–6)
- A. Call for Praise (v.1)
  - B. God's Work of Restoration (vv.2–3)
  - B′. God's Rule Over Creation (vv.4–5)
- A′. God's Delight in the Humble (v.6)

Part Two: In Praise of God's Creation and Love for His People (vv.7–11)
- A. Call for Praise (v.7)
  - B. God's Sustenance of Creation (vv.8–9)
- A′. God's Delight in Praise (vv.10–11)

Part Three: In Praise of God's Restoration, Sovereignty, and Revelation (vv.12–20)
- A. Call for Praise (v.12)
  - B. God's Restoration, Sovereignty, and Revelation (vv.13–20a)
- A′. Concluding Call to Praise (v.20b)

I. In Praise of God's Restoration, Creation, and Redemption

147:1–6

1 Praise the LORD.

How good it is to sing praises to our God,
how pleasant and fitting to praise him!

2 The LORD builds up Jerusalem;
he gathers the exiles of Israel.
3 He heals the brokenhearted
and binds up their wounds.

4 He determines the number of the stars
and calls them each by name.
5 Great is our Lord and mighty in power;
his understanding has no limit.
6 The LORD sustains the humble
but casts the wicked to the ground.

1 The invocation to praise the Lord is familiar from 104:35; 106:1; and 146:1 as well as from the Egyptian Hallel psalms (113–118). The motif of praise is reworked as in 135:3–4 by the imperatival call to praise ("Sing praises to our God") and the ground for praising God ("he is good . . . pleasant"). The sheer joy in the praise of God lies in the response to God's fatherly "goodness" toward his children, as well as to all his creation. The psalmist celebrates the acts of God's goodness by the hymnic participle (cf. 146:6–9a).

Our analysis of 135:3, 5, where the psalmist ascribed to the Lord goodness, pleasantness, and greatness, has a bearing on understanding 147:1, 5, at variance from the NIV:

Praise the LORD.
Truly (for) he is good.
Sing praises to our God.
Truly (for) he is pleasant.
It is fitting to praise him!
. . . .
Great is our LORD.

2–3 First, the Lord is good in bringing the experience of "restoration" to his people (vv.2–3). It is the Lord who "builds . . . heals . . . and binds up" (participles). He restores "Jerusalem" by permitting its walls and institutions to be rebuilt when they had been lying in ruins (cf. Pss 51:18; 102:16; Isa 64:8–12; cf. Neh 6:15–7:3; 12:27–43) in accordance with his word (cf. Jer 31:38–40). He will see to it that his people prosper within the walls of Jerusalem (cf. Isa 60:17–18; 61:4–6), even as Isaiah prophesied (Isa 65:18).

The prophetic word is being fulfilled in the restoration of Jerusalem and in the return of the scattered "exiles" (v.2; cf. Deut 30:1–4; Isa 11:12; 56:8), who are further described as those who are "brokenhearted" (v.3; cf. Ps 126; Isa 61:1) and "wounded." The Lord not only "gathers" them, he also "heals" (cf. 30:2; Isa 57:18–19; Jer 30:17; Hos 6:1) the wounds of his grief-stricken children (Hos 14:4). What a joy to have lived in an age when "restoration" was taking place! What a joy to live in an age when the prophetic word is still being fulfilled, when God's kingdom is being built up!

4–5 Second, the Lord is good to his creation (vv.4–5). True encouragement and joy flood the hearts of the godly as they widen their perspectives from their own situations to consider God's creation at large. The Lord is faithful to all that he has created in that the Great Creator "determines" (*môneh,* i.e., takes an interest in and knows) the number of the stars (v.4; cf. Isa 40:26–29). The "stars" are not forces or deities as in the ancient Near East but created entities over which the Lord is sovereign.

The two motifs of restoration and creation are sufficient to bring God's people to worship. The psalmist exclaims how "great" (*gāḏôl;* cf. 48:1; 96:4; 145:3) God's royal sovereignty ("our Lord," *'ᵃḏônênû*) is in "power" and wisdom ("understanding," v.5; see 136:5)! This conclusion relates primarily to his creative and sustaining powers over the universe (cf. Isa 40:26–28). By inference God's royal power and greatness extended to the world of creation are small in comparison to the depth of God's love for his people (cf. Isa 40:26 with Isa 40:27–31). This brings the psalmist to a renewed consideration of God's care for his own (v.6).

6 Third, the Lord is a good judge in the vindication of his people. This verse resembles the structure and thought of 146:9, as it affirms that the Lord "sustains" (*mᵉʿôḏēḏ;* cf. 146:9) the needy ("humble"; cf. 149:4) but judges the wicked (cf. 1:6; 145:20; 146:9; Luke 1:52).

Notes

1 Verse 1 is problematic because of the ambiguity of כִּי (*kî,* "truly," "for") and of the adjectives "good" and "pleasant." Dahood is correct that "good" and "pleasant" are parallel (*Psalms,* 3:344; cf. 133:1); but at issue is the syntactic crux, whether to read "it is" or "he is." His suggestion makes good sense and is syntactically possible: "How good to hymn our God! / How pleasant to laud" (*Psalms,* 3:343; similarly Kraus, *Psalmen,* 2:954).

1, 7, 12 The psalm employs several synonyms for praise: "praise" (*h-l-l;* vv.1, 12), "sing praises," "make music" (*z-m-r;* vv.1, 7), "sing" (*ʿ-n-h;* v.7; lit., "respond"), and "extol" (*š-b-ḥ;* v.12):

a. *z-m-r*	b. *h-l-l* (v.1)
c. *ʿ-n-h*	a′. *z-m-r* (v.7)
d. *š-b-ḥ*	b′. *h-l-l* (v.12)

II. In Praise of God's Creation and Love for His People

147:7–11

7 Sing to the LORD with thanksgiving;
  make music to our God on the harp.
8 He covers the sky with clouds;
  he supplies the earth with rain
  and makes grass grow on the hills.
9 He provides food for the cattle
  and for the young ravens when they call.

[10]His pleasure is not in the strength of the horse,
nor his delight in the legs of a man;
[11]the LORD delights in those who fear him,
who put their hope in his unfailing love.

7 The psalmist renews the imperatival call to praise with the emphasis on "thanksgiving" (*tôḏāh*) and the instrumental accompaniment ("on the harp" or "lyre"; see appendix to Ps 150: Musical Instruments; cf. 33:2; 98:5). The verb for "sing" (*ʿenû*) is an imperative of a verb meaning "answer" or "respond." It belongs to the semantic field of praise, as the verbs used synonymously in 119:172 bear out.

8–9 The praise of God is due him because he is the good King over hiscreation (cf. 104:13–14). He sustains everything that he has created: "the cattle" and "the ravens" (v.9)—representatives of two realms of the animal kingdom. This stanza is complementary to v.4, where the psalmist praised the Lord's concern for space ("the stars"). The Lord is sovereign over and concerned with all his creation, not only the magnificent stars, but also the lowly creatures on earth. How different is the God of Israel from Baal, whose powers of rain and fertility were nothing in comparison!

10–11 The praise of God is due him because he justifies those who look to him in faith. Even though the words "faith" and "justification" are not used in these verses, the idea is there. The Lord rewards those who "fear him," i.e., those "who put their hope in his unfailing love" (*ḥeseḏ*, v.11; cf. 33:18). They look for victory and vindication (cf. 149:4; Exod 14:13–14). Those who depend on the Lord know the vanity of military, logistical, or human power, because the "strength" of "the horse" or "man" (v.10) is nothing in comparison to the Lord's "power" (v.5). In fact, the Lord hates those who depend on human conventions for security (cf. 20:7; 33:17; Amos 2:14–15). He disappoints those who depend on themselves, but he justifies those who have faith in him. Therefore, the "humble" have hope in his sustenance (cf. v.6).

III. In Praise of God's Restoration, Sovereignty, and Revelation

147:12–20

[12]Extol the LORD, O Jerusalem;
praise your God, O Zion,
[13]for he strengthens the bars of your gates
and blesses your people within you.
[14]He grants peace to your borders
and satisfies you with the finest of wheat.

[15]He sends his command to the earth;
his word runs swiftly.
[16]He spreads the snow like wool
and scatters the frost like ashes.
[17]He hurls down his hail like pebbles.
Who can withstand his icy blast?
[18]He sends his word and melts them;
he stirs up his breezes, and the waters flow.

[19]He has revealed his word to Jacob,
his laws and decrees to Israel.
[20]He has done this for no other nation;
they do not know his laws.

Praise the LORD.

12–14 The praise of the Lord begins with Zion, because the Lord has promised to be her God, to dwell in her (cf. 132:13–16), and to rule over her (cf. 146:10; see appendix to Ps 46: Zion Theology). The motif of the Lord's benefits toward his people finds further development in vv.13–14 (cf. vv.2–3, 6, 10–11). He "builds up Jerusalem" (v.2) by fortifying her ("he strengthens the bars of your gates," v.13; cf. Neh 3:3, 6, 13–15), by blessing her population with secure borders ("peace," v.14; cf. Isa 60:17–22), and with prosperity ("the finest of wheat"; cf. 81:16; Deut 32:14).

15–18 The praise of God is evoked by a further reflection on his power in the world of nature. All nature is at his command. When the sovereign Lord speaks, his word is effective. He orders and ordains everything in his created order, whether it be "snow," "frost," "ice," or "water" (cf. Isa 55:10–11). The contrastive imagery of snow and water is related to the regularity of nature, as the Lord ordains winter and summer. Indirectly, it is also related to the prophetic motif of exile and restoration, as the Lord sent the adversity of exile and also initiates the blessings of restoration (cf. Isa 55:9–13). His "word" (*'imrāh,* v.15) is true in nature, as witnessed by the powerful effects of the natural elements and the seasonal changes. Therefore God's people have hope! They, too, have received his word.

19–20 The people of God praise him because he has given them his "word" (*dāḇār*) of revelation (v.19). This word is first and foremost the "law of the LORD" by which Israel had to order their ways: "his laws and decrees." The law was God's distinct gift to make Israel a distinct nation (cf. Deut 4:7–8) in relation to the other nations (v.20). God's word is to have the same affect on his people as it has on nature. They must be responsive to his royal will. In the praise of Israel, a grateful and responsive heart is created as the people reflect on their unique status and the wonder of the involvements of God the Creator in their daily and national existence. (See the appendix to Ps 19: The Word of God.)

Psalm 148: Praise to Yahweh, the Wise Creator

See the introduction to Psalm 146.

Each of the two major components (vv.1–6, 7–14) of the hymn begins with a call to worship (vv.1, 7), and the whole of the hymn is framed between the call "Praise the LORD" (vv.1a, 14c). The psalmist develops the praise of God in relation to the worship in heaven (vv.1–6), on earth (vv.7–12), and by his people (vv.13–14). Von Rad compares this with other ancient Near Eastern hymns, cataloging the wonders of nature (*onomasticon*, cf. OTT, 1:425). D.H. Hiller's attempt at tracing the hymn tradition in its ancient Near Eastern setting bears further investigation ("A Study of Psalm 148," CBQ 40 [1978]: 323–34).

A. Call on Heaven to Praise the Lord (vv.1–6)
B. Call on Earth to Praise the Lord (vv.7–12)
C. Rationale for Praising the Lord (vv.13–14)

(See Lothar Ruppert, "Aufforderung an die Schöpfung zum Lob Gottes, Zur Literar-, Form-, und Traditionskritik von Psalm 148," *Freude an der Weisung des Herrn, Beiträge zur Theologie der Psalmen, Festgabe zum 70. Geburtstag von Heinrich*

Gross, edd. Ernst Haag and Frank-Lothar Hossfeld [Stuttgart: Katholisches Bibelwerk, 1986], pp. 275–96.)

I. Call on Heaven to Praise the Lord

148:1–6

1 Praise the LORD.

Praise the LORD from the heavens,
  praise him in the heights above.
2 Praise him, all his angels,
  praise him, all his heavenly hosts.
3 Praise him, sun and moon,
  praise him, all you shining stars.
4 Praise him, you highest heavens
  and you waters above the skies.
5 Let them praise the name of the LORD,
  for he commanded and they were created.
6 He set them in place for ever and ever;
  he gave a decree that will never pass away.

1 The psalm begins and ends on the familiar call, "Praise the LORD" (vv.1a, 14c; see 147:1). While Psalm 147:4 makes a brief mention of God's creative activities in heaven, this psalm develops extensively the participation of heaven in the worship of the Lord. The very "heights above," where God rules (68:18), together with outer space and the atmosphere of the earth, are invoked to join in Israel's praise. In their order of closeness to the Lord, the psalmist addresses rhetorically the "angels" (v.2), the starry hosts (v.3), and the elements (v.4). Kirkpatrick wrote, "The anthem of praise is to ring out from heaven above, and to be answered from the earth below" (p. 825).

2 Though the phrase "his hosts" may denote both the angelic as well as the starry hosts (cf. Job 38:7), it most likely refers to the angelic hosts that surround the throne of God (cf. 103:20–21; hence the NIV amplification, his "heavenly hosts").

3 The "sun and moon" and "shining stars" were created by the Lord (cf. Gen 1:14–19). The "shining stars" (*kôḵ*^{e}*ḇê 'ôr*, "stars of light") could well be "the morning stars" (compare the NIV in Job 38:7: "morning stars"; see Dahood, *Psalms*, 3:353). These are the planets visible at dawn.

4 Further, the "waters above the skies," a phenomenal expression for the source of the various forms of precipitation (cf. Gen 1:7), join in God's praise. The phrase "above the skies" is a synonymous expression for "the highest heavens." The twofold expression of heaven is symmetric with that of v.1, forming a chiastic inclusion: "from the heavens . . . in the heights above" (v.1); "highest heavens . . . above the skies" (v.4).

5–6 The sequence of imperatives ("praise him," vv.1–4) is followed by a jussive, "let them praise" (v.5). Praise of the Lord is due him because he is the Creator. The creative acts of God are marked by three characteristics. The Lord created everything by his word ("for he commanded"; cf. Gen 1; Pss 33:9; 147:15). Second, he permanently ordered and regulated the world of nature (v.6). The order and regularity of the heavenly bodies and of the forms of precipitation is because of his creative involvement. There is nothing due to a chance happening.

II. Call on Earth to Praise the Lord

148:7–12

7 Praise the LORD from the earth,
 you great sea creatures and all ocean depths,
8 lightning and hail, snow and clouds,
 stormy winds that do his bidding,
9 you mountains and all hills,
 fruit trees and all cedars,
10 wild animals and all cattle,
 small creatures and flying birds,
11 kings of the earth and all nations,
 you princes and all rulers on earth,
12 young men and maidens,
 old men and children.

The psalmist further develops the theme begun in v.1b by calling on "the earth" (v.7) to join in the praise of the Lord. Whatever has been said of God's creative activities of the heavenly beings and starry hosts (vv.5–6) is, to to large extent, true of the earth. Therefore he calls on the creatures and the formative features of the earth to praise the Lord:

A. sea creatures (v.7b)
A′. weather phenomena (v.8)
 B. geographical features (v.9a)
 B′. vegetation (v.9b)
  C. larger animals (v.10a)
  C′. smaller animals and birds (v.10b)
   D. kings and nations (v.11a)
   D′. princes and rulers (v.11b)
    E. male and female (v.12a)
    E′. young and old (v.12b)

The above organization reflects the general order of the days of Creation in Genesis 1 but also reveals a poetic freedom.

7–8 By poetic license the psalmist put the "sea creatures" (*tannînîm,* v.7; cf. Gen 1:21; Ps 104:26: "leviathan") at the beginning of this list. The "sea" and its mysterious depths were associated in the Canaanite religion with the powers of Baal. They believed that he had been victorious over Yamm (the sea god) and had demonstrated his powers in lightning, storms, and precipitation (v.8). The association of the meteorological phenomena with the "sea" may be explained by a polemical concern of demonstrating the supremacy of Yahweh over all objects of pagan worship, whether they be the starry hosts above or the "depths" (*tehōmôṯ,* 104:6) of the sea. He is in control over "the waters above the skies" (v.4) as well as the thunderstorms (v.8; cf. 18:12). The powers of nature are subject to his word ("bidding," *dāḇār,* v.8; cf. 147:15–16).

9–10 The Lord has also fashioned the relief of the earth (mountains and hills, v.9). On it he has planted fruit trees and the majestic cedars. They are good for food, for building materials, and for nesting (cf. 104:16–17). He has made the animals that may find refuge and food on the mountains and hills (v.10; cf. 104:11–18). Apparently the psalmist reflects on the same motifs as 104:10–18 but condenses the material.

11–12 Finally, the psalmist climactically portrays the world of people, consisting of kings and nations, old and young, male and female (vv.11–12). The Lord created them all, and all owe him praise, whether they belong to the household of Israel or not. He is the Creator of mankind and not only of Israel! Mankind is the crown of his creation (cf. Gen 1:26) and is subject to his bidding.

Notes

7 The translation "netherworld" (Dahood, *Psalms,* 3:351) for אֶרֶץ (*'ereṣ,* "earth") is highly dubious and has been criticized by D.H. Hillers ("A Study of Psalm 148," CBQ 40 [1978]: 328).

8 The meaning of קִטּוֹר (*qiṭṭôr;* NIV, "clouds") is dubious. The usual meaning is "smoke"; and it could be the "smoke" associated with "lightning," forming a chiastic structure: "lightning and hail," "snow and smoke." Allen is guided by the association with "snow" and translates it "mist" (p. 312). The NEB is influenced by the wintry weather motif: "snow and ice" (so also LXX).

III. Rationale for Praising the Lord

148:13–14

13 Let them praise the name of the LORD,
for his name alone is exalted;
his splendor is above the earth and the heavens.
14 He has raised up for his people a horn,
the praise of all his saints,
of Israel, the people close to his heart.

Praise the LORD.

13–14 The imperative "praise the LORD" (v.7) is here also followed by a jussive ("let them praise") and a causal connection (vv.13–14; cf. vv.5–6). By the use of the jussive, the psalmist restates the universal obligation of all of God's creation to demonstrate their allegiance by praising him. The praise is to be given to the God who revealed himself by the "name" Yahweh ("LORD," vv.5, 13; Exod 3:15): "let them praise the name of the LORD" (see appendix to Ps 7: The Name of Yahweh). The reasons for the praise are two. First, he is the exalted Ruler, who is not subject to the limitations of "the earth" (vv.7–12) or the "heavens" (vv.2–4) but is sovereign over all. His kingship is endowed with "splendor" (*hôḏ,* v.13, i.e., "majesty" or "glory"). Second, he is also to be praised because of his unique concern for his covenant people. Thus far the psalmist has not said anything about the people of God. He has made reference to the "angels" of God (v.2) in heaven but has left out any reference to the people who do his bidding on earth until the very end. This is a climactic development of the psalm. God loves and cares for all his creation, but he has a special affinity for "his people," "his saints" (*ḥasîḏ*, v.14; see 4:3), "Israel," also known as "the people close to his heart" (lit., "who are near him"; cf. Lev 10:3). He has endowed them with glory, symbolized by "a horn" (v.14; cf. 89:17, 24; 92:10; 112:9). He has raised them up for the purpose of giving him "the praise" (v.14b; cf. 65:1; 119:171; Deut 10:21).

Notes

14 The note in the NIV ("*Horn* here symbolizes strong one, that is, king") is interpretive because it is a metaphor for victory and prosperity (see Dahood, *Psalms*, 3:355). Though the metaphor is applied to David and the Davidic dynasty elsewhere (see 132:17), there is no warrant for the messianic interpretation. (See the appendix to Ps 98: Yahweh Is the Divine Warrior.)

Psalm 149: Yahweh Delights in His People

See the introduction to Psalm 146.

Psalm 149 celebrates a victory. Westermann holds that the victory has already been accomplished (*Praise of God*, pp. 90–92; so also Anthony R. Ceresko, "Psalm 149: Poetry, Themes [Exodus and Conquest], and Social Function," *Biblica* 67 [1986]: 177–94; Notger Füglister, "Ein garstig Lied—Ps 149," *Freude an der Weisung des Herrn, Beiträge zur Theologie der Psalmen, Festgabe zum 70. Geburtstag von Heinrich Gross*, edd. Ernst Haag and Frank-Lothar Hossfeld [Stuttgart: Katholisches Bibelwerk, 1986], pp. 81–105). Since the psalm also shares the language and hope of the imprecatory psalms—features not uncommon in Isaiah 40–66—it seems best to take it as an eschatological hymn (cf. Kidner, 2:489; Allen, pp. 319–20).

Structurally the psalm has been divided into two (vv.1–5, 6–9) or three (vv.1–3, 4–6, 7–9) strophes (Allen, p. 320). The expository structure is as follows:

A. The Present Joy of the Saints (vv.1–5)
B. The Hope of the Saints (vv.6–9)

I. The Present Joy of the Saints

149:1–5

1 Praise the LORD.

Sing to the LORD a new song,
his praise in the assembly of the saints.

2 Let Israel rejoice in their Maker;
let the people of Zion be glad in their King.
3 Let them praise his name with dancing
and make music to him with tambourine and harp.
4 For the LORD takes delight in his people;
he crowns the humble with salvation.
5 Let the saints rejoice in this honor
and sing for joy on their beds.

1–5 The psalm opens with the characteristic ascription of praise: "Praise the LORD" and closes on the same note (cf. 148:1, 14). Unlike the other Hallel psalms (but similar to 33:3; 96:1), the psalmist calls on the people to sing "a new song" (v.1). The "new"ness pertains to the present occasions for praising the Lord: restoration and eschatological expectation of the Lord's full victory over evil (vv.6–9; cf. Rev 14:3). The beneficiaries of the mighty acts of God are the "assembly of the saints" (*ḥasîdîm;* cf. 30:4, a designation for the godly within the larger covenant fellowship; cf. 22:22, 25; 107:32). The phrase is equivalent to "congregation of the righteous" (1:5), and it may be that Psalm 149 is a formal closure of the psalter, climaxed by the great praise psalm, Psalm 150.

In addition to the formal similarity of the "new song" to Psalm 148, the vocabulary for the people of God shows a loose connection with 148:14. There the people of God are called "his people . . . his saints . . . Israel, the people close to his heart." In 149:1–5 they are known as "the assembly of the saints. . . . Israel . . . the people of Zion. . . . his people . . . the humble. . . . the saints." These various designations make a colorful mosaic of the salvific relationship between the Lord and his people. The word "saints" emphasizes their loyalty (see 4:3). The former use of "the assembly" (*qāhāl*) as a denotation of Israel in the wilderness (cf. Num 14:5; 20:4, 6) is narrowed to a specific group within Israel, also known as "the humble" (see 9:12) or "the people of Zion" (lit., "the sons of Zion," a unique designation found only in Lam 4:2; Joel 2:23; see appendix to Ps 46: Zion Theology).

The object of praise is "the LORD" (Yahweh, v.1; cf. "his name," v.3), who is "the Maker" and "King" of his people. As their "Maker" he has elected, redeemed, and fashioned the descendants of Jacob (cf. 95:6; 100:3; Isa 44:2; 51:13) into a community characterized by holiness and royalty (cf. Exod 19:5–6).

In making a covenant with Israel, the Lord has become their "King" (v.5; see appendix to Ps 5: Yahweh Is King). He has established his residence among his people, symbolized by "Zion." Even when Israel had no king in the postexilic period, they knew that the Lord was King and that their well-being ("salvation," *yešû'āh;* see 132:9, 16) was secure. He "takes delight [*rôṣeh*] in his people" (v.4; cf. "the Lord delights [*rôṣeh*] in those who fear him," 147:11). The "delight" of the Lord guarantees his forgiveness, blessing, and restoration, as expressed in the idiom "the year of the LORD's favor" (*rāṣôn,* Isa 61:2). The "favor" of the Lord extends here to their enjoyment of "salvation" (see above) and God-given "honor" (v.5; *kāḇôḏ,* "glory"; cf. 91:15–16; 112:9). He "crowns" (v.4; *yepā'ēr,* "he adorns," "he endows") them with glory and splendor (Isa 44:23; 55:5; 61:3), thus sharing the benefits of his victory. The words "salvation" and "honor" are synonymous (cf. 85:9; 91:15–16).

The resultant expression on the part of the godly can only be joy. When the Lord "takes delight in his people" (v.4), they are fully assured that all the benefits of the covenants and the promises will be fulfilled. They are portrayed as "dancing" (v.3; cf. 150:4). The people of God regularly celebrated the Lord's victory and blessing in dance (cf. Exod 15:20; Judg 11:34; 2 Sam 6:14; Jer 31:4). The musicians would play the "tambourine and harp [lyre]" (v.3; see appendix to Ps 150: Musical Instruments). Also at home "on their beds," they rejoice in the glory and honor bestowed on them by the Lord. The "beds," which had before been soaked with tears, share in the joy of the Lord's deliverance (cf. 4:4; 6:6; 63:6; Hos 7:14).

Notes

---

5 Emendations and semantic changes have been proposed for עַל־מִשְׁכְּבוֹתָם (*'al-miškᵉḇôṯām,* "on their beds") to עַל־מִשְׁפְּחוֹתָם (*'al-mišpᵉḥôṯām,* "by their families" or "clans," BHS), עַל־מִשְׁכְּנוֹתָם (*'al-miškᵉnôṯām,* "by their great tabernacle," Briggs, 2:543), "prayer mats" (A.A. Anderson, 2:953), or "where they lie prostrate" (Allen, pp. 317–18).

II. The Hope of the Saints

149:6–9

6 May the praise of God be in their mouths
  and a double-edged sword in their hands,
7 to inflict vengeance on the nations
  and punishment on the peoples,
8 to bind their kings with fetters,
  their nobles with shackles of iron,
9 to carry out the sentence written against them.
  This is the glory of all his saints.

Praise the LORD.

6–9 The victory and "honor" (v.5) granted the saints is further developed in the form of an eschatological hymn. The saints are jubilant. "The praise of God" (cf. 66:17) goes together with "a double-edged sword" (v.6), as the one denotes a spirit of trust and confidence and the other a spirit of watchfulness. In this state of mind, the Lord will grant victory to his people, as he did to Nehemiah and his men who worked with "sword and trowel" while praying to the Lord (Neh 4:9, 16–23), believing that "Our God will fight for us!" (Neh 4:20).

Verses 7–9 are connected by the use of infinitives: "to inflict. . . . to bind. . . . to carry." It is not clear who is the subject of the actions, whether the Lord or his people. The reference to the sword might favor the latter. However, the psalms ascribing kingship to the Lord make it clear that the victory is the Lord's (cf. 96:13; 98:1–3, 8). He will avenge, punish, and bind in accordance with his "sentence written against them" (v.9). The "sentence" (*mišpāṭ,* "judgment") decrees that on the day of the Lord, the wicked (individuals, nations, and kings) will be fully judged for the deeds done against God and against his people (cf. Isa 24:21–22; 41:15–16; 45:14; 65:6; Ezek 38–39 Joel 3:9–16, 19–21; Mic 4:13; Zech 14; 2 Thess 1:5–10).

The Lord will "inflict vengeance" (v.7; cf. Isa 61:2; 62:1; 63:4; Ezek 25:14) by punishing the nations and by defeating their kings and dishonoring the nobles of the nations (v.8; cf. Isa 23:8–9; 45:14; 49:7, 23; Nah 3:10; see R.J. Tournay, "Le Psaume 149 et la 'Vengeance' des Pauvres de YHWH," RB 92 [1985]: 349–58).

The psalmist returns to the motif of "glory" as a reminder of the occasion for rejoicing (v.9; cf. vv.4–5: "salvation. . . . honor"). All the acts of God in judgment are to assure his own of his love (cf. 91:16) and must evoke a response of divine praise.

Notes

6 It is not unlikely that the psalmist refers here to a kind of sword-dance (cf. S of Songs 7:1; Dahood, *Psalms*, 3:354), symbolic of the attitude of joyous expectation.

Psalm 150: Praise Yahweh

See the introduction to Psalm 146.

In contrast to other hymns, Psalm 150 is an enlarged introit, lacking the descriptive praise. It functions as a final doxology, bringing the Psalter to a solemn and joyful conclusion. Brueggemann observes that while Psalm 1 is an intentional introduction to the Psalter, Psalm 150 is an appropriate conclusion, as it

> states the outcome of such a life under torah. Torah-keeping does arrive at obedience, yet obedience is not the goal of torah-keeping. Finally, such a life arrives at *unencumbered praise*. . . . In this light the expectation of the Old Testament is not finally *obedience*, but *adoration*. The Psalter intends to lead and nurture people to such a freedom that finds its proper life in happy communion that knows no restraint of convention or propriety. (*Message of the Psalms*, p. 167)

The psalm falls into the following sections: the subjects of praise (v.1), the object of praise (vv.1–2), the manner of praise (vv.3–5), and the subjects of praise (v.6).

A. Praise the Lord in Heaven (v.1)
  B. Praise the Greatness of God (v.2)
  B′. Praise the Lord With Great Intensity (vv.3–5)
A′. Praise the Lord on Earth (v.6)

I. Praise the Lord in Heaven

150:1

1 Praise the LORD.

Praise God in his sanctuary;
  praise him in his mighty heavens.

1 The psalm begins and concludes with "Praise the LORD" (Hallelujah, vv.1, 6) like so many other Hallel psalms (113–118; 120–136; 146–150). The angels (cf. 148:2) in his heavenly "sanctuary" (cf. 11:4) and in the heavenly bodies together with the waters "above the skies" (cf. 148:3–4) are summoned to praise "God" (El). The "mighty heavens" (lit., "firmament of his might") have been made by him and assure the order and well-being of man on earth (cf. Gen 1:6–7).

II. Praise the Greatness of God

150:2

2 Praise him for his acts of power;
  praise him for his surpassing greatness.

2 The voices in heaven and on earth (v.6) join together in the praise of the Lord's mighty acts. Weiser writes, "To praise the abundance of his power is the purpose which links together the most diverse voices in heaven and on earth in a tremendous symphonic hymn of praise" (p. 841). His "firmament" (NIV, "heavens") together with "his acts of power" (cf. 106:2; 145:4, 12) reveal how great he is (cf. 145:3; 147:5; 1 Chron 29:11).

III. Praise the Lord With Great Intensity

150:3–5

> 3 Praise him with the sounding of the trumpet,
> praise him with the harp and lyre,
> 4 praise him with tambourine and dancing,
> praise him with the strings and flute,
> 5 praise him with the clash of cymbals,
> praise him with resounding cymbals.

3–5 The greatness of the Lord is celebrated with a corresponding devotion to him by the instrumentality of the "trumpet," "harp and lyre," "tambourine and dancing" (cf. 149:3), "strings and flute," "the clash of cymbals," and "resounding cymbals."

IV. Praise the Lord on Earth

150:6

> 6 Let everything that has breath praise the LORD.
>
> Praise the LORD.

6 All of God's creation that "has breath" (*n^{e}šāmāh*)—particularly mankind (cf. Isa 2:22)—is summoned to praise the Lord (cf. 148:7–12). The word *n^{e}šāmāh* denotes all living creatures, endowed with life by the Creator (Gen 1:24–25; 7:21–22), but always in distinction from the Creator (cf. Isa 2:22; see Eichrodt, TOT, 2:242; TWOT, 2:605).

Appendix: Musical Instruments

The worship of God in the OT was accompanied with a variety of musical instruments. The people of God celebrated in dance and song the mighty acts of God (in creation and in redemption) to the accompaniment of percussion, wind, and string instruments.

Percussion Instruments

The percussion instruments were the tambourine (or "timbrel") and cymbals. The "tambourine" (*tōp̱*) was played at many occasions and by certain groups of players, women (Exod 15:20–21), military bands, and groups of prophets (1 Sam 10:5); for example, "In front are the singers, after them the musicians; / with them are the maidens playing tambourines" (68:25). The instrument comprised a relatively simple frame covered with skin. From its rare mention in connection with the temple (1 Chron 13:8), it appears that its use was restricted to outside the temple worship, possibly because of its association with Baal worship.

The "cymbal" (*ṣelṣelîm*) consisted of two bronze plates that when clashed together produced a ringing sound. The cymbals had a more clearly defined place in the temple worship, judging from the mention in Chronicles and in Psalm 150. The difference between "cymbals" and "resounding cymbals" (150:5) is not clear. Keel suggests that the two types may have made different levels of sound: soft and loud playing (p. 340).

Wind Instruments

The wind instruments known in the psalms are the ram's horn, the trumpet, and the flute. The "horn" (*šôp̱ār*) makes few sounds and was useful for giving a signal, as on special holy days: "Sound the ram's horn at the New Moon, / and when the moon is full, on the day of our Feast" (81:3). The coronation of a king may have been broadcast by the blowing of the horn at designated places (1 Kings 1:34, 39–42; 2 Kings 9:13). The psalms also celebrate Yahweh's rule with the blowing of the horn and trumpets: "God has ascended amid shouts of joy, / the LORD amid the sounding of trumpets [lit., 'ram's horn']" (47:5; cf. 98:6).

The blowing of the "trumpet" (*ḥaṣōṣerāh*) signified a convocation (cf. Num 10:1–10) of any type, whether for worship, coronation of a king (1 Kings 1:34, 39, 41–43; 2 Kings 12:13), or battle (Hos 5:8). This instrument was regularly used in the temple worship, as recorded in Chronicles.

The "flute" (*'ûgāḇ*) was a "pipe," commonly used in ancient Egypt, but more rarely in Israel's worship. Psalm 150 includes it among the instruments: "praise him with the strings and flute" (150:4). A.A. Anderson comments that the flute may have been restricted to a secular use (2:956). The more usual appearance of the "flute" is the *ḥālîl*, a "double flute," whose sound was much more pleasant than the single flute (or "pipe"). It was used at festive occasions or celebrations (cf. 1 Kings 1:40; Isa 5:12).

String Instruments

The string instruments mentioned in the Psalms are the "harp" (*kinnôr*) and the *nēḇel*. The string instruments were used in the temple worship. The *kinnôr* (NIV, "harp") is in fact a kind of lyre, a curved or rectangularly shaped instrument. The NIV distinguishes between the *kinnôr* and the "lyre" (*nēḇel*), but the parallel use in the psalms suggests that they refer to the same instrument: the lyre (cf. 57:8; 71:22; 81:2; 92:3; 108:2; 150:3). Some lyres had as many as ten strings: "Praise the LORD with the harp; / make music to him on the ten-stringed lyre" (33:2; cf. 92:3; 144:9).

Texts: 33:2; 43:4; 47:5; 49:4; 57:8; 68:24–25; 71:22; 81:2–3; 92:3; 98:5–6; 108:2; 137:2; 144:9; 147:7; 149:3; 150:3–5.

Related Topics: See the appendixes to Pss 25 (The Perfections of Yahweh); 78 (The Acts of Yahweh); 98 (Yahweh Is the Divine Warrior); 119 (Yahweh Is My Redeemer); 122 (The Praise of Yahweh); 132 (The Ark of the Covenant and the Temple: Symbols of Yahweh's Presence and Rule).

Bibliography: B. Blumenkranz, "Music," *Encyclopaedia Judaica*, 12:564–66; S.B. Finesinger, "Musical Instruments in the OT," HUCA 3 (1926): 21–27; P. Gradenwirtz, *The Music of Israel: Its Rise and Growth Through 5000 Years* (New York: Norton, 1949); Othmar Keel, *The Symbolism of the Biblical World. Ancient Near Eastern Iconography and the Book of Psalms*, tr. Timothy J. Hallett (New York: Crossroad, 1985), pp. 335–52; Curt Sachs, *The History of Musical Instruments* (1940); Hans Seidel, "Untersuchungen zur Aufführungspraxis der Psalmen in altisraelitischen Gottesdienst," VetTest 33 (1983): 503–9; A. Sendrey, *Music In Ancient Israel* (New York: Philosophical Library, 1969); E. Werner, "Musical Instruments," IDB, 3:469–76.

PROVERBS

Allen P. Ross

PROVERBS

Introduction

1. Background
2. Authorship and Date
3. Literary Forms
4. Theological Values
5. Canon and Text
6. Bibliography
7. Outline
8. Topical Index

1. Background

The Book of Proverbs is a marvelous collection of wise sayings and instructions for living a useful and effective life. The collection forms part of the larger group of biblical writings known as wisdom literature. This literature gives instructions for living while pondering the difficulties of life. Proverbial wisdom is characterized by short, pithy statements; but the speculative wisdom, such as Ecclesiastes or Job, uses lengthy monologues and dialogues to probe the meaning of life, the problem of good and evil, and the relationship between God and people.[1]

The genre of wisdom literature was common in the ancient world, and a copious amount of material comes from ancient Egypt (see Bryce, *A Legacy of Wisdom*). From the Old Kingdom (2686–2160 B.C.) we find pieces of wisdom in the "Instruction of Kagemni" and the "Instruction of Ptah-hotep" (2450 B.C.), which advise the proper decorum for a court official. Like Proverbs, Ptah-hotep counsels on persuasive speech: "Good speech is more hidden than the emerald, but it may be found with maidservants at the grindstones" (ANET, p. 412). He further warns against going after a woman like a fool, for "one attains death through knowing her" (ANET, p. 413). The "Instruction of Merikare" (2160–2040 B.C.) records a monarch's advice for his son on the wise qualities needed by a king, including this saying: "The tongue is a sword . . . and speech is more valorous than any fighting" (ANET, p. 415).

In the New Kingdom period (1580–1100 B.C.), the "Instruction of Amenemope" stands out. Amenemope instructs his son regarding proper conduct. This work, arranged in thirty sections, contains many instructions that resemble in form and content various laws of the Pentateuch and teachings of Proverbs. These instructions are generally seen as forming the background of Proverbs 22:17–24:22. Although the two collections are not identical, they are similar enough to attest direct influence. General knowledge of wisdom sayings across the ancient Near East as well as specific interchange between Egypt and Solomon's court make a literary connection likely.

[1] See D.A. Hubbard, "Wisdom Literature," NBD, p. 1334.

Because of the dates involved, it is unlikely that Amenemope borrowed from Solomon. Similar teachings in the Pentateuch might suggest a greater antiquity for biblical wisdom sayings, but there is insufficient material to draw a firm conclusion. Many ancient laws, sayings, songs, poetic couplets, and proverbs found their way into inspired Scripture. Inspiration does not exclude the divine use of existing material; but in Scripture it takes on a new force, a higher meaning, and becomes authoritative.

In the Instructions morality is defined as what is pleasing to the god, and it forms the basis for life and prosperity. For example, the instructions include these: "Do not associate to thyself the heated man, / Nor visit him for conversation" (ANET, p. 423; cf. Prov 22:24); "Do not strain to seek an excess, / When thy needs are safe for thee. / If riches are brought to thee by robbery. . . . / (Or) they have made themselves wings like geese / And are flown away to the heavens" (ANET, p. 422; cf. Prov 23:4–5).

After Amenemope, wisdom literature again surfaces with the "Instruction of Ani" (c. 1100 B.C.). Here a father instructs his son about personal piety, ritual purity, and appropriate speech. He enjoins fulfillment of religious and filial obligations, good manners, generosity, and reserve in speech; and he warns against adultery, clamor, and presumption before the god. He says, "Be on your guard against a woman from abroad. . . . a woman who is far away from her husband. . . . She has no witnesses when she waits to ensnare thee" (ANET, p. 420). And much later there is the "Instruction of 'Oncheheshongy" (c. 400–300 B.C.), a large collection of about five hundred sayings and precepts like those in the Book of Proverbs that reflect the practical and religious concerns of the community. But they do not have the poetic parallelism characteristic of Hebrew proverbs. For example, their instructions include: "Do not go to your brother if you are in trouble, go to your friend" (cf. Prov 27:10); and "Better [to have] a statue for a son than a fool" (cf. Prov 17:21) (see Scott, *Proverbs/Ecclesiastes*, p. xlv).

Mesopotamia also had collections of proverbial material (see Lambert, pp. 92–117). The "Instruction of Shuruppak" (c. 2000 B.C.) records the advice of a king to his son Ziusudra, the hero of the flood in the Sumerian version. For example, it says, "My son, let me give you instructions, may you pay attention to them," and, "[My] son, do not sit [alone] in a [chamber] with someone's wife."[2]

The "Counsels of Wisdom" (c. 1500–1000 B.C.) are a collection of moral exhortations about avoiding bad company and careless speech, being kind to the needy, and living in harmony with one's neighbor and in loyalty to the king. For example, it says, "Do not return evil to your adversary; Requite with kindness the one who does evil to you, / Maintain justice for your enemy" (ANET, p. 595).

The "Words of Ahiqar" (700–670 B.C.) is a collection of proverbs, riddles, short fables, and religious observations by a court official for the Assyrian kings Sennacherib and Esarhaddon, giving advice on disciplining children, guarding the tongue, respecting secrets, and being circumspect in dealing with the king. For example, it says, "Withhold not thy son from the rod" (ANET, p. 428; cf. Prov 13:24); and, "I have lifted sand, and I have carried salt; but there is naught which is heavier than [grief]" (ANET, cf. Prov 27:3).

Thus Proverbs has affinities with literature from other countries, and the Bible itself alludes to the wisdom of Egypt and Mesopotamia (1 Kings 4:30; Dan 1:4, 17, 20).

This literary background is helpful to understanding the biblical book. First, it

[2] See B. Alster, *The Instructions of Shuruppak: A Sumerian Proverb Collection* (Copenhagen: Akademisk Forlag, 1974), pp. 15, 37.

provides help in understanding the forms of wisdom literature—proverbs, maxims, fables, riddles, allegories, and instructions. Second, it indicates the antiquity of the forms used in the Bible, especially Proverbs 1–9, which was once considered to be the latest form. But it now can be demonstrated that the literary proverb of two lines may be as old as the Sumerian proverbs, and that collected instructions may be as ancient as the Old Kingdom of Egypt.

In making these comparisons, commentators find help in dating the various collections within the Book of Proverbs. Kitchen, for example, has argued for the plausibility of the Solomonic date for Proverbs 1:1–24:34 on the basis of its similarities with the instruction genre demonstrated in the first part of the second millennium. This form includes a title (cf. 1:1); a statement of purpose (cf. 1:2–7); a lengthy prologue exhorting and encouraging compliance to instruction (cf. 1:8–9:18); and a collection of maxims, proverbs, precepts, and admonitions (10:1–22:16). Kitchen also argues for the early inclusion of 22:17–24:34 based on the dating of the "Instruction of Amenemope."[3]

In addition to this comparison with the great collections of wise instructions, there is also value to be gained from tracing similar concepts. For example, paralleling the Hebrew concept of wisdom is the Egyptian presentation of *maat*—a fixed, eternal religious order, manifested in the stability of nature, in justice in society, and in the integrity of the individual's life (see Crenshaw, *Old Testament Wisdom*, p. 214). Another concept found in both Hebrew and Egyptian literature is the rhetorical use of personification to convey abstract concepts such as intelligence, understanding, justice, and skill. The biblical figure of personified wisdom (Prov 8) corresponds to the personification of *maat* in Egyptian art and literature.

Finally, many specific emphases in Proverbs find parallels in the wisdom literature of the ancient Near East. But even though the collections share some of the same interests, the biblical material is unique in its prerequisite of a personal faith in a personal God. To the Hebrews the success of wisdom did not simply require a compliance with wise instructions but trust in, reverence for, and submission to the Lord (Prov 1:7; 3:5–6; 9:10), who created everything and governs both the world of nature and human history (3:19–20; 16:4; 21:1). Any ancient wisdom used by the Hebrews had to harmonize with this religious world view, and any ancient wisdom used in this collection took on greater significance when subordinated to the true faith.

The biblical writers occasionally used literary forms and expressions that were common to their culture. While the fullness of the Yahwistic faith in all its distinctions came by direct revelation, God did include Semitic customs, standard laws, treaty forms, poetic expressions, and wise sayings that were compatible with the truth and useful in the communication of the divine will. One may speculate how and when concepts such as wisdom, justice, and holiness, or sacrifice, sanctuary, and priesthood—to name but a few—found their place in primitive societies. But apart from that, to recognize the biblical texts as divine revelation does not necessarily mean that all its contents had to be previously unknown information. On the contrary, before many of these facts and concepts were written down, they were passed on verbally from generation to generation and consequently could have circulated over vast distances and found their way into many diverse cultures. Therefore, whatever the

[3]Kenneth A. Kitchen, "Proverbs and Wisdom Books of the Ancient Near East: The Factual History of a Literary Form," *Tyndale Bulletin* 28 (1977): 69–114.

Spirit of God inspired the ancient writers to include became a part of the Word of the Lord. Such inclusions then took on a new and greater meaning when they formed part of Scripture; in a word, they became authoritative and binding, part of the communication of the divine will.

Very likely the writers deliberately used well-known concepts and expressions from the pagan world to subordinate them to the true religion. For example, while *Maāt* was a deity of justice and order in Egypt, no such deity existed in Israel. Rather, *ḥoḵmāh* ("wisdom") was personified and spoke its message in the first person—something *maat* did not do. By incorporating wise sayings and motifs (in addition to producing new and unparalleled sayings) and investing them with the higher religious value, the Hebrew sages were in a sense putting new wine into old wine skins. They could forcefully teach, then, that true wisdom was from above and not from below.

2. Authorship and Date

The traditional view that Solomon wrote the entire Book of Proverbs is supported by the titles in 1:1; 10:1; and 25:1. Moreover, Solomon was a wise man, writing proverbs and collecting sayings from other wise men (see 22:17–24:34). Proponents of this view have also frequently assumed that Agur (30:1) and Lemuel (31:1) were pseudonyms of Solomon.

This general view, however, stands in need of some revision. It is now recognized that Agur and Lemuel were probably not pseudonyms for Solomon and that 22:17–24:34 forms a separate collection of proverbs because it has a distinct form, separate title and purpose, and seems to be directly related to the "Instruction of Amenemope." It would be impossible to determine who added this material to the collection of Proverbs. Furthermore, on closer examination the title of 1:1, which has generally been taken to head up 1:1–9:18, may not actually refer to these chapters; it may simply be the heading of the whole book in its final form and may not necessarily indicate that the first nine chapters are from Solomon.

It would be unreasonable, however, to deny that the largest portion of the proverbs were Solomon's, as older critical scholars often did. Otto Eissfeldt is only willing to say that "one or another of the sayings" are Solomon's and that "one or another of the quite small collections" go back to Solomon.[4] More and more scholars, however, acknowledge that the earlier period is an appropriate setting for the composition and collection of such wisdom sayings. The age of Solomon was characterized by national consolidation, the organization and development of the temple staff, and the collection of traditional literary works, including wisdom sayings. It was also a period of broad international exchange; for through his many alliances and trade contacts, Solomon would have had scribes of foreign lands in his courts. It is easy to see how similarities between Proverbs and other ancient Near Eastern literature could have developed.

Yet it is not possible to date the Book of Proverbs only on the basis of literary style or content. All the literary forms and perhaps the overall structure can be demonstrated in early parallels as well as late parallels (see Waltke, pp. 223–26). In addition, the same sociological, theological, and educational background can be demonstrated

[4] *The Old Testament: An Introduction*, tr. by P.R. Ackroyd (New York: Harper and Row, 1965), p. 476.

for much of the wisdom literature in the ancient Near East. The instruction frequently came from a royal father concerned with preparing his son to replace him in court and teaching self-control in temperament, speech, and action so that his son might be successful. Also, the theology of Proverbs is consistent with the theology of the Law and the Prophets, making parallel references as a basis for dating rather difficult.[5] Moreover, even the earlier attempts to parallel motifs such as the personification of wisdom with the later Greek philosophical thought are no longer definite, for examples of such personification have been discovered all over the ancient world.[6]

An examination of the titles in the book is important to the study of its authorship. The heading in 10:1 clearly credits Solomon for the subsequent material. In 10:1–22:16 there may be two collections (chs. 10–15; 16:1–22:16) due to the difference in style, the second collection having greater variety of parallelism. The heading in 25:1 also affirms that Solomon was the author (or editor) of a larger collection from which the scribes of Hezekiah's court excerpted the proverbs in chapters 25–29. Once again there are differences of style between chapters 25–27 and chapters 28–29, the former having more illustrative parallelism and more grouping by topics.

The title in 1:1 has been taken variously as the heading (1) to the book as a whole, (2) to 1:1–9:18, and (3) to other delimited sections such as 1:1–24:34.[7] The title probably cannot be limited to 1:1–9:18, for then we might have expected the heading in 10:1 to be like that in 25:1—"these *also* are the Proverbs of Solomon" (Kidner, *Proverbs*, p. 22). In addition, the term *mišlê* ("proverbs") does not describe any of the sayings in 1:8–9:18; so the title would be inappropriate if specifically introducing just that section. Finally, 1:2–7, which belongs with the heading of 1:1 by its grammatical construction, best expresses the general purpose of the whole collection of the Proverbs; as an introduction it forms part of the prologue (1:8–9:18) to the major collection of 10:1–24:34.

This introductory section (1:1–7), however, could have functioned as the introduction to an earlier collection as well. Since the expression "the proverbs of Solomon" fits the dominant form found in the collections of 10:1–22:16 and 25:1–29:27, the introduction of 1:1–7 could have formerly introduced a collection now found in 10:1–31:31. And yet, since there seems to be no reason for dating 1:8–9:18 any later than the first Solomonic collection, this prologue could have been written for the core collection.

There are also titles in the book that are non-Solomonic. Any borrowing that took place might have been based on firsthand knowledge of the Egyptian material.[8] This dependence, confined to similarity of concepts and similarity of figures and not to precise wording, seems to be limited to 22:17–23:11. Since Amenemope dates from at least as early as 1000 B.C., the time could fit the Solomonic era. Scott thinks the "Instruction of Amenemope" was still being copied centuries later and "may well have been studied during his training by an Israelite scribe of the prophetic period" (*Proverbs/Ecclesiastes*, p. xxxv).

The title in 31:1 credits Lemuel with the sayings that follow. Although the NIV

---

[5] Ibid., pp. 302–17.

[6] See Kenneth A. Kitchen, "Some Egyptian Background to the Old Testament," *Tyndale Bulletin* 5–6 [1960]: 4–6.

[7] Kitchen, "Proverbs and Wisdom Books," pp. 98–99.

[8] For the connection of "the sayings of the wise" (22:17; 24:23) to the "Instruction of Amenemope," see J. Ruffle, "The Teaching of Amenemope and Its Connection With the Book of Proverbs," *Tyndale Bulletin* 28 (1977): 65.

translates *maśśā'* as "an oracle," it may be that this refers to a kingdom named Massa that is attested in the annals of the Assyrian kings from the time of Hezekiah (roughly 715–687 B.C.). The poem in 31:10–31 has no heading and cannot be readily connected with Lemuel. The heading in 30:1, "The sayings of Agur son of Jakeh—an oracle ['*of Massa*,' NIV mg.], is also obscure. These will be discussed in the commentary.

In conclusion, then, Solomon is responsible for 10:1–22:16 and perhaps all or part of chapters 25–29. Most scholars, including many conservatives, see some dependence of 22:17–24:34 on the Instruction of Amenemope. The nature of this dependence is debatable, but it may be that Israel knew these sayings by the time of Solomon. Most scholars also see chapters 30–31 as non-Solomonic and from a later date, perhaps from a time contemporary with Hezekiah.[9] The prologue to the book (1:8–9:18) would have been added to form an introduction, certainly by the time of Hezekiah, and possibly in Solomon's time. The old title and introductory purpose (1:1–7) then headed up the final collection.

3. Literary Forms

A casual reading of the Book of Proverbs reveals the general form of a proverb. A proverb, as Scott says, is a short, pregnant sentence or phrase whose meaning is applicable in many situations (*Way of Wisdom*, p. 58). A thorough analysis of the Proverbs reveals that these short sayings follow many patterns and constructions that have bearing on the meanings.

As with all Hebrew poetic discourse, the Proverbs use the different types of parallelism. *Synonymous* parallelism expresses one idea in parallel but slightly different expressions: "A fool's mouth is his undoing, / and his lips are a snare to his soul" (18:7). In *antithetical* parallelism the second line contrasts with the first: "The plans of the righteous are just, / but the advice of the wicked is deceitful" (12:5). This is the most common type of parallelism in the book; in 12:5 it sets before the reader the choice between the wise and profitable way and the foolish and disastrous way. *Emblematic* parallelism uses a figurative illustration as one of the parallel units: "As vinegar to the teeth and smoke to the eyes, / so is a sluggard to those who send him" (10:26). Another helpful category is the general one of *synthetic* parallelism. This is used for passages where the second line amplifies the first in some way: "The LORD works out everything for his own ends— / even the wicked for a day of disaster" (16:4). Lastly, proverbs whose second line simply completes the idea begun in the first are said to exhibit *formal* parallelism. One part may contain the subject and the second the predicate (15:31); the first line may state a condition and the second its consequences (16:7), its cause (16:12), or its purpose (15:24); and one part may state a preferred value or course over the other: "Better a little with the fear of the LORD / than great wealth with turmoil" (15:16).

Proverbs are essentially didactic, whether they follow the pattern of a formal instruction using imperatives or prohibitions (16:3; 23:9), are expressed in didactic sayings that observe traits and acts that are to be followed or avoided (14:31), tell an example story (7:6–23), make a wisdom speech (8:1–36), or develop numerical sayings (6:16–19).

Instructions, whether commands or admonitions, use motivations—reasons for

[9] Kitchen, "Proverbs and Wisdom Books," pp. 100–102.

complying. The most common form of motivation is a subordinate clause stating the purpose, result, or reason for the instruction: "Listen to advice and accept instruction, /and in the end you will be wise" (19:20). Sometimes the motivation is implied in a general observation: "My son, do not despise the LORD's discipline / and do not resent his rebuke, / because the LORD disciplines those he loves, / as a father the son he delights in" (3:11–12).

In general proverbs draw lessons by reflecting on the way things are in relation to right values and right conduct. Scott lists seven ways that this is done in the book: proverbs may present (1) things that appear distinct but are similar (14:4a), (2) things that seem the same but are different (27:7b), (3) things that are similar (using similes as in 25:25), (4) things that are absurd or futile (17:16), (5) sayings that classify types of people (14:15), (6) sayings that indicate relative values (27:3), and (7) sayings that set forth consequences (27:18) (*Way of Wisdom,* pp. 59–63).

Finally, it should be noticed that the structure of the entire book uses different forms. Proverbs 1:8–9:18 appears to be an organized introduction to the book with many admonitions and prohibitions as well as example stories and personified wisdom-speech. This section runs in cycles: the purpose of Proverbs is to give wisdom (1:1–7), but folly may interrupt this purpose (1:8–33); there are advantages to seeking wisdom (2:1–4:27), but folly may prevent one from seeking it (5:1–6:19); there are advantages to finding wisdom (6:20–9:12), but folly may prevent this too (9:13–18).

Proverbs 10:1–22:16 is a collection of some 375 unrelated proverbs. Then, after the sayings patterned after the "Instruction" (22:17–24:22), another collection of proverbs is included (chs. 25–29). The last two sections include among other things the numerical sayings of the wise (30:10–33) and the acrostic poem on wisdom (31:10–31).

4. Theological Values

This collection of wise sayings is not exclusively religious; its teachings apply to human problems in general and not primarily to the problems of the religious community or to major theological themes such as election, redemption, and covenant. Rather the teacher of wisdom "concerns himself with people as plain, ordinary individuals who live in the world, and with the wisdom and folly of their attitudes and actions in the common things of life" (Aitken, p. 4). Accordingly, the sayings exhibit several distinctive characteristics. First, they focus attention on individuals rather than on the nation, setting forth the qualities needed and the dangers to be avoided by people seeking to find success with God. Second, they are applicable to all people at any period in history who face the same types of perils and have the same characteristics and abilities (1:20; 8:1–5). Third, they are based on respect for authority, traditional values and teachings, and the wisdom of mature teachers (24:21). Fourth, they are immensely practical, (1) giving sound advice for developing personal qualities that are necessary to achieve success in this life and to avoid failure or shame and (2) warning that virtue is rewarded by prosperity and well-being but that vice leads to poverty and disaster.

It would be wrong, however, to conclude that Proverbs is a secular book; its teachings are solidly based on the fear of the Lord (1:7), making compliance with them in reality a moral and spiritual matter. In fact, the book teaches that this fear of the Lord is the evidence of faith; for the wise teacher enjoins people to trust in the Lord whose counsel stands (19:21) and not their own understanding (3:5–7). The purpose of proverbial teaching, then, is to inspire faith in the Lord (22:19). Such reverential fear requires a personal knowledge of the Lord ("fear" and "knowledge" are parallel in 9:10)—to find this fear is to find knowledge (2:5), a knowledge that comes by revelation (3:6). Ultimately, however, the fear of the Lord is manifested in a life of obedience, confessing and forsaking sin (28:18), and doing what is right (21:3), which is the believer's task before God (17:3). Since the motivation for faith and obedience comes from the Scripture, Proverbs relates the way of wisdom to the law (28:4; 29:18). In the final analysis we must conclude with Plaut, "There are no 'secular' proverbs which can be contrasted with 'religious' ones; everything on earth serves the purposes of God and is potentially holy" (p. 7).

According to Jeremiah 18:18, prophets, priests, and sages molded the cultural life of Israel, the sages being an ancient and influential group (Isa 29:14). In the early days their wisdom was probably declared in the gates for all to hear (Job 29:7–25). Their teachings were preeminently concerned with truth that had stood the test of experience—it had to ring true (Crenshaw, *Old Testament Wisdom*, pp. 68–69). They classified people into two groups—those who were wise, who possessed moral qualities to which wisdom makes her moral appeal, and those who are deficient in the same (R.K. Harrison, IOT, p. 1019). Accordingly, the teachings of Proverbs are of the highest ethical quality, relating virtue to the will of God. The disaster that comes to folly and vice is part of divine retribution—a more immediate concern than the question of immortality.

Finally, it may be observed that the religious value of the book is endorsed by its being in the canon. Furthermore, Jesus' recognition of the wisdom of Solomon recorded in Scripture was further evidence of its place in the developing plan of redemption.

5. Canon and Text

The Book of Proverbs is in all the Jewish lists of the books of the canon. It is quoted in the NT nine times (Rom 3:15 [1:16]; 12:16 [3:7], 20 [25:21–22]; Heb 12:5–6 [3:11–12]; James 4:6 [3:34], 13 [27:1]; 1 Peter 2:17 [24:21]; 4:8 [10:12], 18 [11:31]; 2 Peter 2:22 [26:11]). So the book is unquestionably an integral part of the Holy Scriptures. It was placed in the last section of the Hebrew canon, the *Kethubim* (the "Writings"), but it occupies different positions in different lists. According to Rabbinic literature, Proverbs follows Psalms and Job (*Baba Bathra* 14b, 15a); but the LXX grouped Proverbs, Ecclesiastes, and Song of Solomon on the basis of their authorship.

The Hebrew text is arguably in fair condition. Where the LXX differs in a number of places, the MT is usually far more satisfying. Harrison estimates that there are about twenty-five difficult readings in the Hebrew, along with some obscure words (IOT, p. 1018). But the LXX has greater problems. It is fairly close to the Hebrew in chapters 1–9, but in 10–31 the differences are great. The LXX retained the title in 1:1, omitted the title in 10:1, and changed the titles in 30:1 and 31:1. Throughout the book the LXX adds proverbs (which may be from a different Hebrew *Vorlage* [underlying text]) but deletes others. Moreover, the position of 30:1–31:9 differs in the Greek. Proverbs 30:1–14 is placed after 24:22, and 30:15–33 and 31:1–9 are placed after chapter 24. Possibly separate traditions of these chapters were in existence with differing orders; but it is also possible that the arrangement was the resolution of the LXX to show the Solomonic authorship (see Toy, pp. xxxi–xxxiv).

6. Bibliography

a. *Commentaries*

Alden, Robert L. *Proverbs: A Commentary on an Ancient Book of Timeless Advice.* Grand Rapids: Baker, 1984.

Alonso Schökel, Luis, and J. Vilchez Lindez. *Proverbios.* Nueva Biblia Española. Madrid: Ediciones Cristiandad, 1984.

Aitken, Kenneth T. *Proverbs.* Philadelphia: Westminster, 1986.

Cohen, A. *Proverbs: Hebrew Text and English Translation With Introduction and Commentary.* Soncino Bible. London: Soncino, 1946.

Delitzsch, Franz. *Biblical Commentary on the Proverbs of Solomon.* 2 volumes. Reprint. Translated by M.G. Easton. Grand Rapids: Eerdmans, 1970.

Greenstone, Julius H. *Proverbs With Commentary.* Philadelphia: The Jewish Publication Society of America, 1950.

Kidner, Derek. *The Proverbs: An Introduction and Commentary.* Tyndale Old Testament Commentary. Downers Grove: InterVarsity, 1964.

McKane, William. *Proverbs: A New Approach.* Old Testament Library. Philadelphia: Westminster, 1970.

Martin, G. Currie. *Proverbs, Ecclesiastes, and Song of Songs.* The New Century Bible. Edited by Walter F. Adney. New York: Henry Frowde; Edinburgh: T.C. and E.C. Jack, 1908.

Oesterley, William Oscar Emil. *The Book of Proverbs.* The Westminster Commentary. London: Methuen, 1929.

Perowne, T.T. *The Proverbs.* Cambridge Bible for Schools and Colleges. Cambridge: Cambridge University Press, 1899.

Plaut, W. Gunther. *Book of Proverbs.* Union of American Hebrew Congregations: Jewish Commentary for Bible Readers. New York, 1961.

Plöger, Otto. *Sprüche Salomos (Proverbia).* Biblischer Kommentar Alten Testament. Volume 17. Neukirchen-Vluyn: Neukirchener Verlag, 1984.

Ringgren, Helmer. *Sprüche Salomos.* Das Alte Testament Deutsch. 16/1. 3d edition. Göttingen: Vandenhoeck and Ruprecht, 1981.

Scott, Robert Balgarnie Young. *Proverbs/Ecclesiastes.* The Anchor Bible. Volume 18. Garden City: Doubleday, 1965.

Stuart, Moses. *A Commentary on the Book of Proverbs.* Andover: Warren F. Draper, 1852.

Toy, Crawford Howell. *A Critical and Exegetical Commentary on the Book of Proverbs.* The International Critical Commentary. Edinburgh: T. and T. Clark; New York: Charles Scribner's Sons, 1899.

van Leeuwen, Raymond C. *Context and Meaning: Proverbs 25–27.* Atlanta: Scholars, 1988.

b. *Selected Studies on the Book of Proverbs*

Dahood, Mitchell. *Proverbs and Northwest Semitic Philology.* Scripta Pontificii Instituti Biblici. Volume 113. Rome: Pontifical Biblical Institute, 1963.

Gerlemann, Gillis. *Studies in the Septuagint, III: Proverbs.* Lunds Universitets Arsskrift, 52:3. Lund: C.W.K. Gleerup, 1956.

Gladson, Jerry A. "Retributive Paradoxes in Proverbs 10–29." Ph.D. dissertation, Vanderbilt University, 1978.

Kayatz, Christa. *Studien zu Proverbien 1–9.* Wissenschaftliche Monographien zum Alten und Neuen Testament. Volume 22. Neukirchen-Vluyn, 1966.

Nel, Philip Johannes. *The Structure and Ethos of the Wisdom Admonitions in Proverbs.* Beihefte zur Zeitschrift für die alttestamentliche Wissenschaft. Volume 158. Berlin: Walter de Gruyter, 1982.
Postel, Henry John. "The Form and Function of the Motive Clause in Proverbs 10–29." Ph.D. dissertation, University of Iowa, 1976.
Schachter, J. *The Book of Proverbs in Talmudic Literature.* Jerusalem, 1963.
Thompson, John Mark. *The Form and Function of Proverbs in Ancient Israel.* The Hague: Mouton, 1974.
Waltke, Bruce K. "The Book of Proverbs and Ancient Wisdom Literature," *Bibliotheca Sacra* 136 (1979): 221–38.
Whybray, Roger N. *The Book of Proverbs.* Cambridge Bible Commentary on the New English Bible. Cambridge: Cambridge University Press, 1972.
______. *The Intellectual Tradition in the Old Testament.* Beihefte zur Zeitschrift für die alttestamentliche Wissenschaft. Volume 135. Berlin: Walter de Gruyter, 1974.
______. *Wisdom in Proverbs: The Concept of Wisdom in Proverbs 1–9.* Studies in Biblical Theology, I/45. London: SCM, 1965.
Williams, James G. *Those Who Ponder Proverbs: Aphoristic Thinking and Biblical Literature.* Sheffield: Almond, 1981.

c. *Selected Studies on Wisdom Literature*

Beaucamp, Evode. *Man's Destiny in the Book of Wisdom.* Staten Island: Alba House, 1970. A translation by J. Clarke of *La Sagesse et la Destin des Elus.* Paris: Editions Fleurus, 1957.
Bergant, Dianne. *What Are They Saying About Wisdom Literature?* New York: Paulist, 1984.
Blenkinsopp, Joseph. *Wisdom and Law in the Old Testament: The Ordering of Life in Israel and Early Judaism.* The Oxford Bible Series. Oxford: Oxford University Press, 1983.
Bryce, Glendon E. *A Legacy of Wisdom: The Egyptian Contribution to the Wisdom of Israel.* Lewisburg, Penn.: Bucknell University Press; London: Associated University Presses, 1979.
Camp, Claudia V. *Wisdom and the Feminine in the Book of Proverbs.* Bible and Literature Series. Volume 11. Sheffield: Almond, 1985.
Crenshaw, James L. *Old Testament Wisdom: An Introduction.* Atlanta: John Knox, 1981.
______ ed. *Studies in Ancient Israelite Wisdom.* The Library of Biblical Studies. Edited by Harry M. Orlinsky. New York: KTAV, 1976.
Cross, Thurman L. "The Fear of the Lord in Hebrew Wisdom." Ph.D. dissertation, Drew University 1957.
Gammie, John G., et al., edd. *Israelite Wisdom: Theological and Literary Essays in Honor of Samuel Terrien.* Missoula, Mont.: Scholars, 1978.
Gordis, Robert. *Poets, Prophets, and Sages: Essays in Biblical Interpretation.* Bloomington: Indiana University Press, 1971.
Gordon, Eckmund I. *Glimpses of Everyday Life in Ancient Mesopotamia.* Westport, Conn.: Greenwood, 1969.
Kevin, Robert Oliver. *The Wisdom of Amen-em-apt and Its Possible Dependence Upon the Hebrew Book of Proverbs.* Volume 14, Number 4. Reprint. Philadelphia: Journal of Society of Oriental Research, 1931.
Kidner, Derek. *The Wisdom of Proverbs, Job, and Ecclesiastes: An Introduction to Wisdom Literature.* Downers Grove, Ill.: InterVarsity, 1985.
Lambert, Wilfred G. *Babylonian Wisdom Literature.* London: Oxford University Press, 1960.
Langdon, Stephen. *Babylonian Wisdom.* London: Luzac, 1972.
Lange, H.O. *Das Weisheitsbuch des Amenemope: Aus Papyrus 10, 474 des British Museum.* Copenhagen: Andr. Fred. Høst and Son, 1925.
Morgan, Donn F. *Wisdom in the Old Testament Traditions.* Atlanta: John Knox, 1981.
Murphy, Roland E. *Introduction to the Wisdom Literature of the Old Testament.* Collegeville, Minn.: Liturgical Press, 1965.

Noth, Martin, and David Winton Thomas, edd. *Wisdom in Israel and in the Ancient Near East.* Supplement to *Vetus Testamentum.* Volume 3. Leiden: E.J. Brill, 1955.

Perdue, Leo G. *Wisdom and Cult: A Critical Analysis of the Views of Cult in the Wisdom Literature of Israel and the Ancient Near East.* Society of Biblical Literature Dissertation Series. Volume 30. Missoula, Mont.: Scholars, 1977.

Rad, Gerhard von. *Wisdom in Israel.* London: SCM; Nashville: Abingdon, 1972. A translation by James D. Martin of *Weisheit in Israel.* Neukirchen: Neukirchen Verlag, 1970.

Scott, Robert Balgarnie Young. *The Way of Wisdom in the Old Testament.* New York: Macmillan, 1971.

Simpson, W.K., ed. *The Instruction of Amenemope: The Literature of Ancient Egypt.* New Haven: Yale University Press, 1972.

Williams, Ronald J. "The Alleged Semitic Original of the Wisdom of Amenemope," *Journal of Egyptian Archaeology* 47 (1961): 100–106.

7. Outline

I. Introduction to the Book of Proverbs (1:1–7)
   A. Title: The Proverbs of Solomon (1:1)
   B. Purposes: To Develop Moral Skill and Mental Acumen (1:2–6)
   C. Motto: The Fear of the Lord (1:7)

II. A Father's Admonition to Acquire Wisdom (1:8–9:18)
   A. Introductory Exhortation (1:8–9)
   B. Admonition to Avoid Easy But Unjust Riches (1:10–19)
   C. Warning Against Disregarding or Despising Wisdom (1:20–33)
   D. The Benefits of Seeking Wisdom (2:1–22)
      1. The admonition to receive wisdom (2:1–4)
      2. Consequences of receiving wisdom (2:5–22)
         a. Knowledge of God and his protection (2:5–8)
         b. Moral discernment (2:9–22)
            1) Discernment for living (2:9–11)
            2) Protection from the evil men (2:12–15)
            3) Protection from the evil woman (2:16–19)
            4) Enablement for righteous living (2:20–22)
   E. Admonition to Follow the Way of Wisdom in Relationships With God and People (3:1–35)
      1. Introductory exhortation (3:1–4)
      2. Admonition to be faithful to the Lord (3:5–12)
      3. Commendation of the way of wisdom (3:13–26)
         a. Wisdom the most valuable possession (3:13–18)
         b. Wisdom essential to creation (3:19–20)
         c. Wisdom and a long and safe life (3:21–26)
      4. Warning to avoid unneighborliness (3:27–30)
      5. Warning against emulating the wicked (3:31–35)
   F. Admonition to Follow Righteousness and Avoid Wickedness (4:1–27)
      1. Traditional teaching and its benefits (4:1–9)
         a. Exhortation to acquire traditional wisdom (4:1–4a)
         b. Benefits of acquired wisdom (4:4b–9)
      2. Admonition to live righteously (4:10–19)
         a. Pursuit of a righteous life style (4:10–13)
         b. Avoidance of a wicked life style (4:14–19)
      3. Admonition to concentrate on righteous living (4:20–27)
         a. Exhortation to the father's teaching (4:20–22)
         b. Concentration on righteousness (4:23–27)
   G. Admonition to Avoid Seduction to Evil (5:1–23)
      1. A father's warning about deadly seduction (5:1–6)
         a. Exhortation for discretion (5:1–2)
         b. Motivation: With wisdom seduction may be avoided (5:3–6)
      2. A father's warning to avoid ruin and regret (5:7–14)
         a. Exhortation for prevention (5:7–8)
         b. Motivation: Obedience will avoid ruin and regret (5:9–14)
      3. Advice to find satisfaction at home (5:15–23)

a. Avoiding sharing love with strangers (5:15–17)
b. Finding satisfaction with one's wife (5:18–19)
c. Motivation: Adultery is sinful folly (5:20–23)

H. Admonition to Seek Release From a Foolish Indebtedness (6:1–5)
1. Conditions of indebtedness (6:1–2)
2. Exhortation to obtain release (6:3–5)

I. Admonition to Avoid Laziness (6:6–11)
1. Lesson in diligence (6:6–8)
2. Danger of poverty (6:9–11)

J. Warning Against Deviousness (6:12–15)
1. Description (6:12–14)
2. Destruction (6:15)

K. Conduct the Lord Hates (6:16–19)
1. Introductory statement (6:16)
2. Delineation (6:17–19)

L. Warning About Immorality (6:20–35)
1. Reminder to heed instruction (6:20–24)
2. Warning to avoid seduction (6:25–35)

M. Admonition to Avoid the Wiles of the Adulteress (7:1–27)
1. Important teaching of the father (7:1–5)
2. Description of seduction (7:6–23)
a. The victim (7:6–9)
b. The temptress (7:10–12)
c. The seduction (7:13–20)
d. The capitulation (7:21–23)
3. Deadly results of consorting (7:24–27)

N. The Appeal of Wisdom (8:1–36)
1. Introduction (8:1–3)
2. First cycle (8:4–9)
a. Invitation: Listen and gain understanding (8:4–5)
b. Motivation: Wisdom is noble, just, and true (8:6–9)
3. Second cycle (8:10–21)
a. Invitation (8:10)
b. Motivation (8:11–21)
4. Third cycle (8:22–36)
a. Motivation: Wisdom preceded and delights in Creation (8:22–31)
b. Invitation: Listen to wisdom and be blessed (8:32–36)

O. Consequences of Accepting the Invitations of Wisdom or Folly (9:1–18)
1. Accepting wisdom (9:1–12)
a. Invitation to wisdom (9:1–6)
1) Preparations for the invitation (9:1–3)
2) Wisdom's invitation (9:4–6)
b. Description of responses (9:7–11)
1) The scoffer (9:7–8a)
2) The wise man (9:8b–11)
c. Consequence: Reward (9:12)

2. Accepting the invitation of folly (9:13–18)
    a. Invitation (9:13–17)
        1) Situation of the invitation (9:13–15)
        2) Invitation (9:16–17)
    b. Consequence: Death (9:18)

III. The First Collection of Solomonic Proverbs (10:1–22:16)
(For a more detailed treatment of chapters 10–29, see the Topical Index.)

IV. The Sayings of the Wise (22:17–24:34)
  A. Thirty Precepts of the Sages (22:17–24:22)
  B. Further Sayings of the Wise (24:23–34)

V. Proverbs of Solomon Collected by Hezekiah (25:1–29:27)

VI. The Words of Agur (30:1–33)
  A. The Title (30:1)
  B. Agur's Confession and Petition (30:2–9)
    1. Confession of ignorance (30:2–4)
    2. Affirmation of the reliability of God's word (30:5–6)
    3. Prayer (30:7–9)
  C. The Admonitions of Agur (30:10–33)
    1. Noninterference in domestic situations (30:10)
    2. Four evil things (30:11–14)
      a. Disrespect for parents (30:11)
      b. Self-righteousness (30:12)
      c. Pride (30:13)
      d. Oppressing the poor (30:14)
    3. Insatiable things (30:15–16)
    4. Punishment for parental disrespect (30:17)
    5. Amazing things in nature (30:18–19)
    6. The brazen woman (30:20)
    7. Abuse of position (30:21–23)
    8. Wisdom the key to success (30:24–28)
    9. Leadership qualities (30:29–31)
    10. A final admonition (30:32–33)

VII. The Words of Lemuel (31:1–9)
  A. Title: The Words Taught to Lemuel by His Mother (31:1)
  B. First Warning (31:2–3)
  C. Second Warning (31:4–7)
  D. Instruction: Defend the Defenseless (31:8–9)

VIII. The Wife of Noble Character (31:10–31)
  A. Praise in General (31:10–12)
  B. Industrial Pursuits of the Household (31:13–15)
  C. Financial Enterprise (31:16–18)
  D. Provision for the Family and the Poor (31:19–21)
  E. Distinction by Industry (31:22–24)
  F. Wisdom and Prosperity (31:25–27)
  G. Merits Recognized (31:28–29)
  H. Laudatory Summation (31:30–31)

8. Topical Index

This index covers the short sayings of the book as well as the longer discourses. Since the passages are most frequently complex, i.e., showing a contrast, a "better than" statement, a consequence, or a development of ideas, it is clear that they could each be listed under several topics. However, the headings chosen here for the verses attempt to focus on the main teaching of each passage, i.e., one central idea, even though it may be elucidated by contrasts and causes. A more thorough topical study in the Proverbs would use several different types of listings. A very good index can be found in Plaut, pp. 333–36; and an excellent series of subject studies is included in Kidner, *Proverbs*, pp. 31–56.

Ability
  better than privilege, 17:2
Adversity
  test of, 24:10
Advice
  following, 23:26–28
  of a friend, 27:9
Associations
  dangerous, 12:26; 17:12; 22:24–25
  evil, 16:29; 24:1–2
  poor, 23:20–21
  unprofitable, 14:7
  with wise or fools, 13:20
Attention
  renewed call to, 23:12, 19
Avarice
  effect of, 28:22
Bribery
  success of, 17:8
Business
  foolish indebtedness, 6:1–5
  socially responsible, 11:26
Character traits (negative)
  anger, 29:22
  antisocial, 18:1
  beauty without discretion, 11:22
  blaming God, 19:3
  distasteful, 14:17
  greed versus trust, 28:25
  hatred, 29:27
  hot temper, 19:19
  inappropriate positions, 19:10
  jealousy, 27:4
  laziness, 26:13–15
  need versus desire, 27:7
  pride, 21:4, 24; 29:23; 30:13
  quarrelsomeness, 26:21
  self-conceit, 26:12, 16
  self-deceit, 28:11
  self-glory, 25:27
  self-righteousness, 30:12
  stubbornness, 29:1
  unfaithfulness, 25:19
  unmerciful, 21:13
  wicked, 21:10
  wicked expressions, 16:30
Character traits (positive)
  compassion for animals, 12:10
  faithful love, 20:6
  faithfulness, 28:20
  humility, 29:23
  integrity, 25:26
  leadership, 30:19–31
  loyalty, 19:22
  noble wife, 12:4
  praiseworthy, 27:21
  reflected in thoughts, 27:19
  self-control, 17:27; 25:28; 29:11
  strength and honor, 20:29
  strength in adversity, 24:10
  teachable, 15:31
Conduct (negative)
  cursing parents, 20:20
  disrespect for parents, 30:11
  gossip, 26:20
  hated by God, 6:16–19
  inappropriate, 25:20
  malicious, 16:27
  meddling, 26:17; 30:10
  rejoicing over misfortune, 24:17–18
  robbing parents, 28:24
  wicked, 17:20
Conduct (positive)
  acceptable to God, 15:9
  avoiding strife, 20:3
  avoid unneighborliness, 3:27–30
  beneficial for life, 15:24
  brings life or death, 11:19
  careful consideration, 14:8
  consequence of, 16:25
  develop moral skill and mental acumen,
    1:2–6

good and evil, 10:11–14; 14:22
hating falsehood or acting shamefully, 13:5
kindness to enemies, 25:21–22
moderation, 26:16–17
obedient versus profligate, 28:7
peaceful, 16:7
pleasing to God, 11:20; 12:2
righteous and wicked, 11:5–6
righteous versus self-sufficiency, 28:26
sinlessness, 20:9
straight course, 15:21
wise and foolish, 10:8–10
Confidence
in calamity, 10:25; 14:32
of the righteous, 28:1
Conscience
searching motives, 20:27
Contentment
healthy benefit of, 14:30
opposite of greed, 15:27
reward for righteous, 13:25
Counsel
king's, 25:3
needed for victory, 24:5–6
Criticism
helpful, 27:17
Desires
insatiable, 27:20; 30:15–16
Deviousness
warning against, 6:12–15
Diligence
better than daydreaming, 13:4
lesson in, 6:6–8
motivation of, 16:26
opposite of idleness, 10:5
profitable, 14:23
progress of, 15:19
prospers, 12:11
results of, 28:19; 31:22–24
rewarded, 20:13
rules, 12:24
successful, 12:27
Discernment
brings favor, 13:15
for living, 2:9–11
moral, 2:9–22
motives, 20:5
opposite of gullibility, 14:15
Discipline
acceptance of, 12:1; 13:1
affect of, 19:25
benefit of, 10:17; 13:18; 15:32; 19:18
concentration on plans, 17:24
effect of, 21:11; 29:15, 17
evidence of love, 13:24
lack of, 29:21
method of, 29:19
necessity of, 15:10; 23:13–14
parental, 22:15
physical, 26:3
rejected, 15:12; 19:27
spiritual value, 20:30
value of to the discerning, 17:10
wisely heeded, 15:5
Dishonesty
effects of, 20:17
false witnesses, 24:28
Disputes
divinely arbitrated, 18:18
their effect, 18:19
Divine omniscience
15:3, 11; 16:2; 17:3
Drink
effects of, 20:1
excessive, 23:29–35; 31:4–7
Emotions
affect on health, 17:22
joy and sorrow, 15:13, 15
joy when righteousness prevails, 11:10
love/hate, 10:12
mixed, 14:13
of a king, 19:12; 20:2
personal, 14:10
Encouragement
from rulers, 16:15
Envying
the wicked, 24:19–20
Evil
cautious avoidance, 14:16
disapproval, 24:8–9
protection from, 2:12–19
Faithfulness
admonished, 3:5–12; 5:15–17
appreciation of, 25:13
blessing of, 16:10
Family
child training, 22:6
mistreatment of parents, 19:26; 30:17
peaceful relationships, 21:9, 19; 25:24
provisions for, 31:19–21
prudent wife, 19:14
ruin of, 19:13
Family relationships
quarrelsome wife, 27:15–16

Fear of the Lord
advised, 23:17–18
beginning of knowledge, 1:7; 9:10–11
God and king, 24:21–22
godly, 28:14
life, 14:27
life giving, 10:27
safety and contentment, 19:23
security, 14:26
uprightness, 14:2
wisdom and honor, 15:33
Finances,
conditions of indebtedness, 6:1–2
release from indebtedness, 6:3–5
stability, 24:27
Folly
a grief to others, 17:21
death its consequence, 9:18
effect of on parents, 17:25
invitation of, 9:13–17
of adultery, 5:20–23
unalterable, 27:22
Fools
dangerous, 26:10
dense, 24:7; 26:7
persist in folly, 26:11
provocation of, 27:3
responding to, 26:4–5
useless as messengers, 26:6
use of proverbs, 26:9
Friend(s)
helpful, 27:10
loyal in adversity, 17:17
Friendship
influential, 19:6
loyal, 18:24
marked by truthfulness, 24:26
Generosity
evidence of righteousness, 21:26
nature of, 22:9
versus indifference, 28:27
Gifts
their influence, 18:16
Guilt
effects of, 28:17
Honesty
approved by leaders, 16:13
better than pretension, 13:7
in business, 11:1; 16:11; 20:10, 14, 23
Honor
inappropriate to fools, 26:1, 8
in family relationships, 17:6
parents, 23:22
Hospitality
unpleasant, 23:6–8
Human nature
God's creation, 20:12
Humility
better than plunder, 16:19
better than pretension, 12:9
confession of ignorance, 30:2–4
praise from others, 27:2
reward of, 18:12
wisdom of, 25:6–7
wise and honorable, 11:2; 29:23
Immorality
results of, 7:24–27
warning against, 6:20–35
Injustice
abuse of position, 30:21–23
bribery, 21:14; 28:21
denounced, 18:5
extortion and bribery, 22:16
Instruction
acceptance of, 19:20
benefits for life, 13:14
obedience to, 19:16
rejected for opinion, 18:2
reward for heeding, 13:13
Integrity
a preservation, 11:3
heritage of, 20:7
Judgment
certainty of, 21:12; 29:16
divine, 22:14
just, 21:18
partiality in, 24:23–25
Justice
a king's discernment, 20:8
corrupted, 17:15
corrupt witnesses, 19:28
cross-examination, 18:17
divine, 15:25
effects of, 21:15
for ingratitude, 17:13
for the poor, 29:7
from God, 29:26
perceived, 28:5
perverted by bribes, 17:23
removing wickedness, 20:26
Kindness
better than cruelty, 11:17
brings respect, 11:16
Knowledge
basis of prudent acts, 13:16
divine, 21:2

evidence of prudence, 14:18
of God, 2:5–8
sought, 18:15
sought by the discerning, 15:14
stored up, 10:13–14
Law
respect for, 28:4
Laziness
avoidance of, 6:6–11
consequences of, 19:15
effect of, 18:9
excuses of, 22:13; 26:13
nature of, 19:24
outcome of, 21:25
results of, 20:4; 24:30–34
trouble and poverty, 11:29
Life
amazing things in nature, 30:18–19
avoid ruin and regret, 5:7–14
from God, 29:13
preservation of, 24:11–12
Love
shown by discretion, 17:9
Marriage
finances before, 24:27
Misfortune
of enemy, 24:17–18
Neighbors
avoid unneighborliness, 3:27–30
proper treatment of, 14:21
Obligations
fulfilled, 20:16; 27:13
Parents
honoring, 23:22
obey father's teaching, 4:20–22; 7:1–5
Patience
affect of on strife, 15:18
more effective than power, 16:32
nature of, 19:11
opposite of quick temper, 14:29
Peace
value of, 17:1
Piety
reward of, 22:4
Plans
committed to God, 16:3
for evil or peace, 12:20
just and unjust, 12:5
pleasing to God, 15:26
sound advice, 20:18
uncertain future, 27:1
Pleasure
cost of, 21:17
good and evil, 10:23
Poor
susceptible to injustice, 13:23
treatment of, 14:31; 22:22–23; 28:3; 29:14; 30:14; 31:8–9, 20
Poverty
better than folly, 19:1
danger of, 6:9–11
effect of, 19:7; 22:7
Power
political, 14:28
Prayer
God's response to, 15:29
of Agur, 30:7–9
of the lawless unanswered, 28:9
Pride
consequences of, 16:18
fall of, 16:5
Property
respect for, 22:28; 23:10–11
Prospect for life
discouraging and encouraging, 13:12
endurance of the righteous, 13:9
fulfilled, 13:19
good or bad, 11:23; 16:22
hopes and fears, 10:24
joy and ruin, 10:28
of the wicked, 11:7
realized desires, 11:27
Prosperity
by fraud, 21:6
ensured, 14:11
for generosity, 11:24–25
for righteous pursuits, 12:12
honest investment, 13:11
in business, 14:4; 31:16–18
in the household, 14:1
patient planning, 21:5
reward of righteous, 13:21
sudden but unsatisfying, 20:21
through words and works, 12:14
Protection
from the evil men, 2:12–15
from the evil woman, 2:16–19
Providence
divine, 20:24
searched out, 25:2
Punishment
certain, 22:8
unjust, 17:26
Quarrels
private, 25:9–10
Reparation, 14:9

Repentance
effectual, 28:13
Reproof
a part of love, 27:5
preferable to flattery, 28:23
value of, 27:6
Reputation
good, 10:7; 22:1
Restitution
by divine intervention, 13:22
Retribution
certainty of, 11:21, 31; 17:11; 19:29; 26:26–27
divine, 16:4
God's work, 20:22
just, 11:8; 21:7
present in deeds, 14:14
vengeance, 24:29
Revelation
obedience to, 29:18
reliable, 30:5–6
Rewards
contentment for righteous, 13:25
for charity, 19:17
for righteousness, 15:6
for service, 27:18
just, 28:10
justly earned, 11:18
life or ruin, 10:16
long life, 16:31
satisfaction of needs, 10:3
victory over the wicked, 14:19
words of blessing, 10:6
Righteous,
enablement for living, 2:20–22
treatment of, 24:15–16
Righteousness
affect of on morale, 29:2
better than unjust wealth, 16:8; 28:6
better than wealth, 11:4
brings life, 11:30
brings security, 13:6
brings stability, 12:3
concentration on, 4:23–27
displayed in actions, 20:11
enablement for living, 2:20–22
genuineness of, 21:29
hated by the wicked, 29:10
in government, 28:12
leads to immortality, 12:28
national, 14:34
prevention of evil, 16:17
priority of, 21:3
pursuit of, 4:10–13, 23–27
revealed in works, 21:8
rewards of, 21:21
security, 11:5–6
stability in government, 16:12
value of, 10:2
Rulers
caution before, 23:1–2
emotions of, 20:2
good versus bad, 28:16
oppressive, 28:3
wicked, 28:15
Security
abandoned, 27:8
based on integrity, 28:18
faith in the Lord, 29:25
knowledge of God and his protection, 2:5–8
object of faith, 11:28
of the righteous, 10:30; 12:7, 21; 29:6
the name of the Lord, 18:10
the way of the Lord, 10:29
through justice, 29:4
through wisdom, 22:5
wealth, 18:11
Seduction
avoided with wisdom, 5:3–6; 7:1–27
deadly results of, 2:24–27
description of, 7:6–23
prevention of, 5:7–14
warning against, 5:1–6; 6:25–35
Servants
clever or incompetent, 14:35
lazy, 10:26
wicked or faithful, 13:17
Sin
adultery, 30:20
effect of, 18:3
entanglements of, 29:24
freedom from, 16:6
Skill
benefits of, 22:29
Sovereignty of God
16:9, 33; 19:21; 21:1, 30–31; 22:2, 12
Speech (general)
effects of, 14:3
helpful or harmful, 11:11; 13:2; 15:4
humble or harsh, 18:23
pleasing or perverse, 10:32
true and false witnesses, 12:17; 14:5, 25; 21:28
wise or foolish, 10:13–14; 15:2
wise or perverse, 10:31

wounding and healing, 12:18
Speech (negative)
arrogant and contentious, 17:19
bragging, 25:14
consequences of, 18:7, 21
dangerous, 12:13
deceptive, 26:18–19, 23, 28; 29:5
dishonest, 17:7
divisive, 16:28
false witnesses, 19:5; 24:28; 25:18
foolish, 10:10
gossip, 18:8; 20:19; 26:22
harmful, 15:4
hypocritical, 26:24–25
inappropriate greeting, 27:14
lies, 29:12
lies and slander, 10:18
malicious, 17:4
mocking the poor, 17:5
perjury, 19:9
premature, 18:13
rash vows, 20:25; 22:26–27; 29:20
sly words, 25:23
that invites trouble, 18:6
the scoffer, 9:7–8
undeserved curse, 26:2
Speech (positive)
appropriate, 15:23
avoid pledges, 11:15
beneficial, 16:24
carefully planned, 15:28
cautious testimony, 25:8
competent, 16:21
conciliatory, 15:1
controlled, 10:19; 21:23
discretion, 12:23
divine enablement, 16:1
edifying, 10:21
encouraging, 12:25
good advice, 11:14
good news, 15:30; 25:25
helpful, 15:4
honest and graceful, 22:11
keeping confidence, 11:13
patient and mild, 25:15
productive, 18:20
profound, 18:4; 25:11
rebuke, 9:8–9; 25:12
responsible, 16:10
safety from slander, 11:9
silence rather than derision, 11:12
skillful defense, 12:6
spreading knowledge, 15:7
truth outlasts lies, 12:19
truth pleases God, 12:22
valuable, 10:20
value of advice, 15:22
wisdom of discretion, 13:3
wisdom of silence, 17:28
wise, 16:23
wise and joyful, 23:15–16
wise words, 20:15
Stability
financial, 24:27
in government, 20:28; 28:2
righteous government, 28:28
through righteousness, 25:4–5
Spirit
healthy, 18:14
Strife
controlled, 17:14
exacerbated, 29:9
source of, 22:10
Teaching
vindicated, 27:11
Truthfulness
a mark of friendship, 24:26
Vengeance
avoid, 24:29
Vows,
rash, 22:26–27
Wealth
a benefit for the wise, 14:24
a blessing, 10:22
avoid easy but unjust, 1L10–19
disadvantages of, 13:8
effect of, 19:4
fleeting, 23:4–5
popularity of, 14:20
security, 10:15
spiritual better than physical, 15:16–17
through diligence, 10:4
transitory, 27:23–27
unjustly gained, 1:10–19; 28:8
Wickedness
avoid, 4:14–19
brazen woman, 30:20
not to be emulated, 3:31–35; 4:14–19
Wife
a blessing, 18:22
focus of attention, 5:15–19
noble, 31:10–31
satisfaction with, 5:18–19
Wisdom
accepts discipline, 13:1
accepts rebuke, 9:8–9

acquire traditional, 4:1-4a
admonished, 1:8–9; 2:1–4; 3:1–4; 4:1–4a, 20–22
affect of on others, 10:1; 15:20
affect of on the family, 29:3
appeal of, 8:1–36
appreciation of, 12:8
averting anger, 29:8
avoiding trouble, 22:3
benefits of acquiring, 4:4b–9
benefits of seeking, 2:1–22; 8:32–36
better than wealth, 16:16
consequences of receiving, 2:5–22
description of responses to, 9:7–11
essential to creation, 3:19–20; 8:22–31
estimation of, 23:23–25
exemplified in noble woman, 31:10–31
frugality of, 21:20
future of, 24:13–14
greater than strength, 21:22; 24:5–6
importance of, 21:16
inaccessible to fools, 17:16; 24:7
in appeasing wrath, 16:14
in business, 17:18
invitation of, 8:1–5, 10, 32–36; 9:1–6
longevity, 3:21–26
most valuable possession, 3:13–18
motivation for, 8:10–21
noble, just, and true, 8:6–9
obedient, 10:8
overlooks insults, 12:16
possessor of, 14:33
practicality of, 24:3–4
profitable, 19:8
response of the scoffer, 9:7–8a
response of the wise man, 9:8b–11
reward of, 9:12
takes advice, 12:15; 13:10
the purpose of Proverbs, 1:2–6
those who acquire it, 14:6
warning against despising, 1:20–33
wary of evil, 27:12
wasted on a fool, 23:9
Witness
false, 24:28, 25:18
Worldliness
destruction of, 14:12
Worship
acceptable, 15:8a
unacceptable, 15:8b; 21:27
Zeal
without knowledge, 19:2

Text and Exposition

I. Introduction to the Book of Proverbs (1:1–7)

A. *Title: The Proverbs of Solomon*

1:1

[1]The proverbs of Solomon son of David, king of Israel:

1 This verse provides the general heading for the entire book, even though the proverbs of Solomon probably do not begin until chapter 10.

What is a proverb? The usage of *māšāl* (here *mišlê šelōmōh,* "proverbs of Solomon") suggests the idea of likeness. Toy, referring to the Niphal, suggests the meaning "to become like, be comparable with" (p. 3). For example, Psalm 49:12 [13 MT] says that the one who lives only for this life is "like [*nimšal*] the beasts that perish"; and v.4 [5 MT] of the psalm identifies the poem as a wisdom psalm (*lemāšāl;* "to a proverb"). The word appears also in 1 Samuel 10:12, to report how a proverb (*māšāl,* "a saying") came into being: "Is Saul also among the prophets?" His prophesying invited comparison with the prophets. This idea for *māšāl* is also supported by the Akkadian *mišlu* ("of like portions") and the Arabic *miṯlu* ("likeness").

A proverb may then be described as an object lesson based on or using some comparison or analogy. It may be a short saying that provides a general truth (Ezek 16:44), a lesson drawn from experience (Ps 78:2–6), a common example (Deut 28:37), or a pattern of future blessing or cursing (Ezek 21:1–5). The purpose of a proverb is to help one choose the best course of action among those available—the foolish way is to be avoided and the wise way followed (A.R. Johnson, *Wisdom in Israel and in the Ancient Near East,* edd. Martin Noth and D. Winton Thomas [Leiden: E.J. Brill, 1955], pp. 162–69).

B. *Purposes: To Develop Moral Skill and Mental Acumen*

1:2–6

[2]for attaining wisdom and discipline;
for understanding words of insight;
[3]for acquiring a disciplined and prudent life,
doing what is right and just and fair;
[4]for giving prudence to the simple,
knowledge and discretion to the young—
[5]let the wise listen and add to their learning,
and let the discerning get guidance—
[6]for understanding proverbs and parables,
the sayings and riddles of the wise.

2 The Book of Proverbs has two purposes: to give moral skillfulness and to give mental discernment. The first purpose is developed in vv.3–4; then, after a parenthetical exhortation in v.5, the second purpose is developed in v.6.

The first purpose is that the disciple will develop skillfulness and discipline in holy living (v.2a). "Attaining," from the infinitive *da'aṯ* (lit., "to know"), encompasses an intellectual and experiential acquisition of wisdom and discipline.

"Wisdom" (*ḥoḵmāh*) basically means "skill." This word describes the "skill" of the craftsmen who worked in the tabernacle (Exod 31:6), the "wits" of seasoned mariners (Ps 107:27), administrative abilities (1 Kings 3:28), and the "wise advice" of a counselor (2 Sam 20:22). In the Book of Proverbs "wisdom" signifies skillful living—the ability to make wise choices and live successfully according to the moral standards of the covenant community. The one who lives skillfully produces things of lasting value to God and to the community.

The other object to be acquired is "discipline" (*mûsār;* cf. 3:5), the necessary companion of wisdom. *Mûsār* denotes the training of the moral nature, involving the correcting of waywardness toward folly and the development of reverence to the Lord and personal integrity.

The second major purpose of the Book of Proverbs is for the disciple to acquire discernment (v.2b). The meaning of the Hiphil infinitive *hāḇîn* ("to understand, discern") can be illustrated by the cognate preposition *bên* ("between"—"to discern" means to distinguish *between* things, to compare concepts, form evaluations, or make analogies).

The object of this infinitive is cognate to it: "words of insight" (*'imrê ḇînāh*). Proverbs will train people to discern lessons about life, such as distinguishing permanent values from immediate gratifications.

3 The first purpose statement is now developed. Once again an infinitive is used—the disciple will receive (*lāqaḥ,* "acquire") something worth having. In Proverbs 2:1 the verb *lāqaḥ* ("to accept") is parallel with *ṣāpan* ("to treasure, store up"). What the student receives is discipline (*mûsār*) and prudence (*haśkēl*). The Hiphil infinitive *haśkēl* indicates the (genitive of) result: discipline produces prudent living. To act prudently means "to act circumspectly." The concept may be illustrated by the actions of Abigail, the wife of the foolish Nabal (1 Sam 25).

The three terms that follow—*ṣeḏeq, mišpāṭ,* and *mêšārîm*—are adverbial accusatives of manner, expressing how the prudent acts manifest themselves. The first term, "rightness" or "righteousness," means basically conformity to a standard, as in Deuteronomy 25:15, where weights and measures were required to be right. The religious use of the term signifies what is right according to the standard of God's law (see Deut 16:18–20); viz., conduct that conforms to the moral standards of the covenant community (see Jer 22:13; Hos 10:12).

Prudent acts will also exhibit justice. *Mišpāṭ* (NIV, "just") essentially signifies a "decision" like that of an arbiter (see Deut 16:18). It is applied to litigation (2 Sam 15:2) and the precedent established by such (Exod 21:9; used of a custom in 1 Kings 18:18). The term also connotes that which is fitting or proper (Judg 13:12). Proverbs will develop a life that has a sense of propriety in making decisions.

The third quality is "equity" (NIV, "fair"). *Mêšārîm,* related to *yāšār* ("upright," "straight"), can describe that which is pleasing (Judg 14:3 ["right one"], 7 ["liked"; lit., "she was right"]). The book will instruct a life style that is equitable, one that incorporates the most pleasing aspects (see Ps 9:8 [9 MT]).

So the disciple of the Book of Proverbs will acquire discipline that will produce a prudent life, and that prudent life will be demonstrated by "doing what is right and just and fair."

4 The first purpose statement is now developed from the teacher's point of view—he will give shrewdness to the naive or "simple." (For a discussion of the simple person, see Kidner, *Proverbs,* p. 39). This naive person (*p^{e}ṯî*) is one who is gullible (14:15), easily enticed (9:4, 16), and falls into traps (22:3). The instructor wants to give such a one a sense of shrewdness (*ʿormāh;* NIV, "prudence"), the ability to foresee evil and prepare for it (13:16; 22:3). With *ʿormāh* the naive will be able to avoid the traps in life (see Matt 10:16).

The second half of the verse parallels "simple" or "naive" with "[immature] youth" (*naʿar*) and "shrewdness" or "prudence" with "knowledge" (*daʿaṯ*) and "discretion" (*mᵉzimmāh,* from *zāmam,* "to devise"). This latter expression refers to devising plans or perceiving the best course of action for gaining a goal (Toy, p. 7). *Daʿaṯ* and *mᵉzimmāh* may form a hendiadys, to be translated "purposive knowledge"; viz., the perceptive ability to make workable plans. Such ability is crucial for the immature youth in this world.

5 Before elaborating on the second purpose statement for the book, the writer digresses to make an exhortation. The first verb advises the wise to hear and the second gives the purpose—"[to] add to [*wᵉyôsep̱*] their learning."

Parallel to this advice is the counsel for the "discerning" (*nāḇôn,* part. of *bîn*) to get guidance. This person has the capacity of *bînāh*—he is one who is discerning. The "guidance" to be obtained is *taḥbulôṯ,* from *ḥāḇal,* meaning "to bind" (see *ḥeḇel,* "rope," "cord"). The term may be illustrated with the cognate *ḥōḇēl,* the rope-pulling done by sailors to steer or guide a ship. Cohen says *taḥbulôṯ* is the discernment to steer a right course through life (*Proverbs,* p. 2). Proverbs is not simply for the naive and the gullible; everyone can grow by its teachings. Discerning people can obtain guidance from this book so that they might continue in the right way.

6 The second major purpose of the book is to give mental acumen to the student (see under v.2). The repetition of *lᵉhāḇîn* from v.2b shows that this line expands that one. The point is that one needs to develop the ability to understand the language of the sages.

The teachings will develop one's ability in discerning "proverbs" (*māšāl*) and "parables" (*mᵉlîṣāh*). This latter term can refer to a satire, a mocking-poem, or an alluding saying. The verb *lîṣ,* related to the Arabic *lâṣa* ("to turn aside"), may have the idea of speaking indirectly. It may have included the idea of a spokesman, for *mēlîṣ* is an interpreter (Gen 42:23). *Mᵉlîṣāh* may then refer to a saying that has another sense to it that needs uncovering (see H. Neil Richardson, "Some Notes on ליץ and Its Derivatives," VetTest 5 [1955]: 163–79).

The disciple must understand also the "sayings" of the wise. *Dîḇrê* is a general term, but with the genitive *ḥᵃḵāmîm* ("the wise") it becomes specific—the words come from the sages. Their teachings at times take the form of "riddles" (*ḥîḏôṯ*). This word, if related to the Arabic *ḥâda* ("to turn aside, avoid"), may refer to what is obscure or indirect, such as the riddles of Samson (Judg 14:13–14) or of the queen of Sheba (1 Kings 10:1).

C. *Motto: The Fear of the Lord*

1:7

7 The fear of the LORD is the beginning of knowledge,
but fools despise wisdom and discipline.

7 Reverential fear of the Lord is the prerequisite of knowledge. The term *yir'āh* can describe dread (Deut 1:29), being terrified (Jonah 1:10), standing in awe (1 Kings 3:28), or having reverence (Lev 19:3). With the Lord as the object, *yir'āh* captures both aspects of shrinking back in fear and of drawing close in awe. It is not a trembling dread that paralyzes action, but neither is it a polite reverence (Plaut, p. 32). "The fear of the LORD" ultimately expresses reverential submission to the Lord's will and thus characterizes a true worshiper. In this context it is the first and controlling principle of knowledge. Elsewhere in Proverbs the fear of the Lord is the foundation for wisdom (9:10) or the discipline leading to wisdom (15:33); it is expressed in hatred of evil (8:13), and it results in a prolonged life (10:27).

On the other hand, fools disdain wisdom and discipline. Verse 7b is the antithesis of v.7a. The term *'ᵉwîlîm* ("fools") describes those who are thick-brained or stubborn (Greenstone, p. 6). They lack understanding (10:21), do not store up knowledge (10:14), fail to attain wisdom (24:7), talk loosely (14:3), are filled with pride (26:5), and are contentious (20:3). They are morally unskilled and refuse any correction (15:5; 27:22).

Fools are people who "despise" (*bāzû*) wisdom and discipline; they treat these virtues as worthless and contemptible. This attitude is illustrated in Genesis 25:34, where Esau despised the birthright, and in Nehemiah 4:4, where Sanballat and Tobiah belittled the Jews.

II. A Father's Admonition to Acquire Wisdom (1:8–9:18)

A. *Introductory Exhortation*

1:8–9

> 8 Listen, my son, to your father's instruction
> and do not forsake your mother's teaching.
> 9 They will be a garland to grace your head
> and a chain to adorn your neck.

8 The disciple is exhorted to heed parental guidance. "My son," the customary form of address for a disciple, derives from the idea that parents are primarily responsible for moral instruction (Prov 4:3–4; Deut 6:7). Here the disciple is to respond to (*šᵉma';* NIV, "Listen," with the attitude of "taking heed to") "discipline" (*mûsār;* NIV, "instruction") that is normally the father's responsibility (except in 31:1, where it is the warning of the mother).

The son is also to follow his mother's teaching. *Tôrāh* ("teaching") may be cognate to a verb meaning "to point or direct" (cf. BDB, pp. 434–35), so that the idea of teaching might be illustrated as pointing in the right direction (see Gen 46:28). At any rate, in Proverbs this instruction is for ordering the life (see also 6:20; 31:26).

9 For heeding the instruction of the law, the disciple is promised an attractiveness of life. "Grace," the charm that teaching brings to the disciple, refers to those qualities that make him agreeable. The metaphor compares these qualities to an attractive wreath worn round the head.

Obedience will also improve the disciple, the metaphor of the neck pendant speaking of adorning the life. The one who loses the rough edges through disciplined training will present a pleasing presence to the world (McKane, p. 268).

B. *Admonition to Avoid Easy But Unjust Riches* 1:10–19

10 My son, if sinners entice you,
do not give in to them.
11 If they say, "Come along with us;
let's lie in wait for someone's blood,
let's waylay some harmless soul;
12 let's swallow them alive, like the grave,
and whole, like those who go down to the pit;
13 we will get all sorts of valuable things
and fill our houses with plunder;
14 throw in your lot with us,
and we will share a common purse"—
15 my son, do not go along with them,
do not set foot on their paths;
16 for their feet rush into sin,
they are swift to shed blood.
17 How useless to spread a net
in full view of all the birds!
18 These men lie in wait for their own blood;
they waylay only themselves!
19 Such is the end of all who go after ill-gotten gain;
it takes away the lives of those who get it.

10 The summary statement warns the son not to consent to the enticement of moral misfits (see Notes). The term for "entice," related to the root of "simple" or "naive" (*peṯî,* from *pāṯāh*) mentioned in v.4, means "to allure, persuade, entice, or seduce." Here the enticement is to do evil because it comes from "sinners" (*ḥaṭṭā'îm* in this context describes professional criminals, a gang of robbers).

11 The nature of the enticement is that the young man is offered a part with professional criminals in a life of crime. The text explains how they waylay the unwary (vv.11–12). The ambush he is asked to join is vicious; the verb *'āraḇ* ("to lie in wait") is used elsewhere of hostile purposes such as murder (Deut 19:11), kidnapping (Judg 21:20), or seduction (Prov 23:28). Here the aim is bloodshed.

The attack is also evil. The wicked lie in wait for the innocent (*nāqî;* NIV, "harmless soul"), and their attack is without a cause (*ḥinnām* [untr. in NIV] is often used this way; see 1 Sam 25:31; Ps 35:7).

12–14 The criminals assure the novice of swift success: they will swallow up victims who are in the vitality of life (*tāmîm,* meaning "full of health," "whole") as surely and swiftly as death opens and swallows its victims (v.12; cf. Num 16:32–33); they determine to remove them from the living (see Notes). They are confident that by sharing the wealth (v.13), they will fill their houses with "plunder" (*šālāl*). The use of *šālāl* elsewhere for spoils from war suggests that theirs was a life of crime (Cohen, *Proverbs,* p. 4). So the offer made to the youth is to pursue with the roustabouts a life of easy but ill-gotten gain (v.14).

15–16 The young man's parents strongly advise him to avoid such evil companions because their life style, though it may appear prosperous, leads to destruction. The advice "do not go" (v.15) counters the allurement of the wicked—"Come along with us" (v.11). The primary reason for not going is that the sinners' purpose is bloodthirsty (v.16); therefore their retribution is sure (cf. v.18). In the final analysis, then, the trap the wicked lay for others in reality will catch them.

17–19 There are two ways to interpret v.17 within the context. One is to see a comparison with the folly of birds who fall into a snare even though forewarned—likewise the wicked fall into the snare God lays because they are driven by lust. The other is to see a contrast between the natural behavior of birds when forewarned and the irrational greed of robbers. In other words, it is futile to spread out a net for birds that are watching, but these men are so blinded by evil that they fail to recognize the trap (v.18). The blind folly of greed leads to their doom—retribution is the law that will take away their lives (v.19; see also G.R. Driver, "Problems in the Hebrew Text of Proverbs," *Biblica* 32 [1951]: 173–74).

Notes

10 For the conditional clause in the MT ("if sinners entice you"), the LXX has rendered a volitive: "Let not impious men lead you astray."

12 The LXX has an editorial variation for v.12b patterned after Ps 34:16 (17 MT) and 109:15—"Let us take away the remembrance of him from the earth."

C. *Warning Against Disregarding or Despising Wisdom*

1:20–33

20 Wisdom calls aloud in the street,
she raises her voice in the public squares;
21 at the head of the noisy streets she cries out,
in the gateways of the city she makes her speech:

22 "How long will you simple ones love your simple ways?
How long will mockers delight in mockery
and fools hate knowledge?
23 If you had responded to my rebuke,
I would have poured out my heart to you
and made my thoughts known to you.
24 But since you rejected me when I called
and no one gave heed when I stretched out my hand,
25 since you ignored all my advice
and would not accept my rebuke,
26 I in turn will laugh at your disaster;
I will mock when calamity overtakes you—
27 when calamity overtakes you like a storm,
when disaster sweeps over you like a whirlwind,
when distress and trouble overwhelm you.

28 "Then they will call to me but I will not answer;
they will look for me but will not find me.
29 Since they hated knowledge
and did not choose to fear the Lord,
30 since they would not accept my advice
and spurned my rebuke,
31 they will eat the fruit of their ways
and be filled with the fruit of their schemes.

32 For the waywardness of the simple will kill them,
and the complacency of fools will destroy them;
33 but whoever listens to me will live in safety
and be at ease, without fear of harm."

20–21 The first two verses introduce a lengthy appeal from wisdom (see Phyllis Trible, "Wisdom Builds a Poem: The Architecture of Proverbs 1:20–33," JBL 94 [1975]: 509–18). Wisdom personified stands in the public space, exhorting the ignorant and the scornful to listen, warning of destruction if they refuse (Toy, p. 20). The book has three such personifications—in 1:20–33; 8:1–36; and 9:1–6. Here the term "wisdom" is in the plural (*ḥoḵmôṯ,* v.20) to signify the intensity and comprehensiveness of it all—the "all-embracing, eloquent, veracious, and elevated wisdom" (McKane, p. 272). In addition, the verb for "crying out" (*rānan,* "to give a ringing cry"; NIV, "calls aloud") expresses an excited exhortation.

The location of this exhortation is in the public places—"in the street, . . . the public squares; . . . the gateways"—suggesting that wisdom is readily available for the business of living: it is for the common person, not the scholar exclusively (see Notes). These places were the centers for all activities: daily affairs (2 Kings 7:1), justice (Ruth 4:1), employment (Matt 20:3), and even playing (Zech 8:5 et al.). Since wisdom touches all aspects of life, the setting is appropriate. In this setting wisdom, like a prophet, calls out (McKane, p. 273).

22 Wisdom offers a complaint–"How long . . . ?" (see Notes). Three types of people are addressed by this: the "simple" (*p*ᵉ*ṯāyim*), the scoffers or "mockers" (*lēṣîm*), and the dullards or "fools" (*k*ᵉ*sîlîm*). The first is the naive person or the simpleton, the second the defiant and cynical freethinker, and the third the morally insensitive fool (Kidner, *Proverbs,* p. 40). Each is satisfied with his ways and does not listen to reason (see J.A. Emerton, "A Note on the Hebrew Text of Proverbs 1:22–23," JTS 19 [1968]: 609–14).

23 The invitation takes the form of a conditional clause—"If only you would respond" (NEB). Wisdom is firmly resolved to pour out her spirit, her active power, on those who respond. Like a copious spring she will gush forth to them.

24–28 There is grave danger, however, in disregarding the invitation. If the call has been extended for some time—"How long?" (v.22; see also Isa 65:2)—then this warning is given for a prolonged refusal. Because wisdom has been continually rejected, wisdom will laugh at the calamity of those who have rejected it. This retributive justice is expressed figuratively in vv.26–27 as wisdom's mocking at their distress. But then v.28 explains the meaning of the mocking—wisdom will not be there to help when the fools cry out from their distress. The figure of laughing reveals the absurdity of choosing a foolish way of life and being totally unprepared for disaster.

29–33 The section closes with a denunciation for despising wisdom. Not only had these foolish ones preferred their folly, but they had also despised the knowledge of ethical and religious principles for life (v.29; cf. Cohen, *Proverbs,* p. 7). Moreover, they continually spurned wisdom's reproofs (v.30).

The punishment for such indifference and antagonism takes the form of retribution (vv.31–33). The term "fruit" (v.31) is used metaphorically for the consequence of actions—likened to growth that culminates in produce (McKane, pp. 275–76). Their way—their life and what it produces—stands in contrast to the way of wisdom that they had spurned.

The teaching of retribution is confirmed in v.32. The "turning away" (NIV, "waywardness") and the "complacency" will be the ruin of these people. But those who heed the teachings of wisdom will live in safety and security (v.33). The expressions used suggest a permanent, settled condition free from the sense of danger or dread. Such is the contrast between the false security of the wicked and the true and lasting peace of the righteous.

Notes

---

21 Instead of "at the head of the noisy streets she cries out" (MT), the LXX reads, "She proclaims on the summits of the walls." It then expands the verse to read, "sits at the gates of the princes, at the gates of the city she boldly says." הֹמִיּוֹת (*hōmîyôṯ*, "noisy") is the feminine plural active participle from הָמָה (*hāmāh*, "to murmur, roar"). רֹאשׁ הֹמִיּוֹת (*rōʾš hōmîyôṯ*) then describes the head of bustling streets, or as Perowne says, the place where the street branches off or has its beginning (*Proverbs*, p. 45). The LXX reads "wall" as if from the word חֹמָה (*ḥōmāh*).

22–23 The LXX turns the questions into declarative sentences: "So long as the guileless hold fast to righteousness, they shall not be shamed; but the foolish, being lovers of insolences, have become impious, have hated knowledge . . ."

D. *The Benefits of Seeking Wisdom (2:1–22)*

1. *The admonition to receive wisdom*

2:1–4

1 My son, if you accept my words
and store up my commands within you,
2 turning your ear to wisdom
and applying your heart to understanding,
3 and if you call out for insight
and cry aloud for understanding,
4 and if you look for it as for silver
and search for it as for hidden treasure,

This chapter appears to be a long poem in six parts: the appeal for wisdom followed by a fivefold blessing. McKane argues that the formal structure is more complicated and follows the *instruction* pattern of Amenemope, because there is no concrete instruction about specific matters; the language of the chapter is set in the frame of religious commitment and its derivative, morality (p. 281).

1–4 The teacher again makes the appeal: To attain wisdom requires constant meditation and a rigid discipline. Charles T. Fritsch refers to it as a receptive spirit and an ardent search (IB, 4:793).

The requirement of meditation begins with receiving the teaching. "Accept" is paralleled with "store up" (v.1), a figure that implies that most teaching cannot be used immediately but that some time will pass before education's effects are felt (Plaut, p. 43). In the meantime the teachings will develop attitudes in their pupils that will influence their future actions. Such a perspective calls for patience by the students, making both heart and mind attentive ("ear" and "heart" [v.2] represent the mental faculties).

The other requirement is the diligent search for wisdom (v.3). On his own initiative the disciple is to summon or "call out . . . for" (*qārā'* + *l* [lamed]) understanding. The elevation in the lines from "call out" to "cry aloud" suggests that, if understanding does not come immediately, one should put forth greater efforts (Greenstone, p. 17). So the ear hears the teaching, the mind understands what is said, and the voice is used to inquire for true knowledge. This search for wisdom and understanding should be as diligent as the search for precious metal (v.4, "silver"), the simile suggesting both the value of the treasure and the diligence of the search. The starting point is revelation—specific words and commandments—and the method is not one of free speculation but of exploring and treasuring the teachings (Kidner, *Proverbs*, p. 61).

2. *Consequences of receiving wisdom (2:5–22)*

a. *Knowledge of God and his protection*

2:5–8

5 then you will understand the fear of the LORD
and find the knowledge of God.
6 For the LORD gives wisdom,
and from his mouth come knowledge and
understanding.
7 He holds victory in store for the upright,
he is a shield to those whose walk is blameless,
8 for he guards the course of the just
and protects the way of his faithful ones.

5 The point of this first consequence is direct: When you seek wisdom, you find God. The "knowledge of God" refers to more than intellectual opinion; it also encompasses religion and ethics. Coupled with the fear of the Lord, this knowledge means that the disciple will follow God's moral code; for to know God is to react ethically to his will, to follow his principles (Greenstone, p. 18).

6–8 The reason the one who seeks knowledge will find God is that God is the source of wisdom and knowledge (v.6). Moreover, God has stored wisdom up as a protection for his saints (vv.7–8). The word translated "victory" is *tûšîyāh*, meaning "sound wisdom"; the LXX translated it "salvation." The term includes the ideas of both sound wisdom and its effect: viz., abiding success, i.e., achievement and deliverance. So the verse states that God holds in store sound wisdom that is powerful for his saints.

b. *Moral discernment (2:9–22)*

1) *Discernment for living*

2:9–11

9 Then you will understand what is right and just
and fair—every good path.

10 For wisdom will enter your heart,
and knowledge will be pleasant to your soul.
11 Discretion will protect you,
and understanding will guard you.

9 The thought of this second consequence is introduced with *tāḇîn*—"you will understand"; this same verb is used in 1:2 and 2:5. The disciple will develop the intellectual capacity and moral insight to discern what is "right" (*ṣeḏeq*), "just" (*mišpāṭ*), and "fair" (*mêšārîm*)—viz., every good path (cf. 1:3). *Ma'gāl* ("path") is used metaphorically for the course of a person's actions. The word is related to the verb *gālal* ("to roll") and the noun *'ᵃgālāh* ("cart"); so the noun *ma'gāl* literally means "the track of a wagon wheel." It therefore would be a parallel idea to the idiomatic "way." Thus "every good path" is a life style that regularly leads in the direction of what is morally good (Toy, p. 39).

10–11 Verses 10–11 explain the basis for this understanding. Wisdom will take up its abode in the inner life, and knowledge will be pleasant to the soul. *Nā'ām* ("pleasant," v.10) describes a quality that attracts one to an object—so knowledge is attractive and attracting. When a person assimilates wisdom, doing right becomes attractive and delightful; for he sees the advantage of it (Toy, p. 41).

In addition, this assimilated wisdom will manifest itself in discretion and discernment that protect from evil or, as McKane says, save the good man from the consequences of naiveté (p. 283).

2) *Protection from the evil men*

2:12–15

12 Wisdom will save you from the ways of wicked men,
from men whose words are perverse,
13 who leave the straight paths
to walk in dark ways,
14 who delight in doing wrong
and rejoice in the perverseness of evil,
15 whose paths are crooked
and who are devious in their ways.

12–15 These verses present the first of two specific examples of protection from evil—from the "wicked men" (v.12). The adjective "wicked" (*ra'*) describes what is unpleasant, bringing pain and misery. Evil ways bring harm to others. The parallel colon clarifies how they harm others—they speak perverse things, things contrary to what is right and proper (Cohen, *Proverbs*, p. 10). Perverse speech is the inevitable expression of the evil within.

Verses 13–15 describe the wicked's purpose, pleasure, and perverted paths. Their purpose is to walk in the ways of darkness (v.13); they abandon the straight way to follow an evil way that can only be described as "dark." Their way is uncertain, devoid of ethical illumination (see 4:18 and Eccl 2:13). Their "delight" (v.14) is in doing what is morally evil. This activity may not be due to an abnormal or sadistic delight but rather to dullness of conscience (Greenstone, p. 21). Verse 15 then describes their perverted ways, using a variation of the expressions of the preceding verses—evil men are twisted and devious in the path they follow, constantly turning aside to the wrong ways. The disciple needs wisdom for protection from those who turn the Lord's ways upside down and try to draw others in by creating ethical chaos.

3) *Protection from the evil woman*

2:16–19

> 16 It will save you also from the adulteress,
> from the wayward wife with her seductive words,
> 17 who has left the partner of her youth
> and ignored the covenant she made before God.
> 18 For her house leads down to death
> and her paths to the spirits of the dead.
> 19 None who go to her return
> or attain the paths of life.

16–19 The second class of evil persons from whom wisdom delivers is the licentious woman. Whereas the evil man brings pain and perversion, the evil woman brings moral ruin through a more subtle temptation. Prostitutes and adulteresses existed in Israel from the earliest times (Judg 11:1; 1 Kings 3:16; Hos 3:1; notice also laws against adultery in Exod 20:14; Lev 20:10). In this passage the licentious woman is first described (vv.16–17); then her ruin and that of those who submit to her are presented as a warning (vv.18–19).

The descriptive term "strange" (*zārāh;* NIV, "adulteress") describes this woman as outside the framework of the covenant community (see L.A. Snijders, "The Meaning of זָר in the Old Testament: An Exegetical Study," OTS 10 [1954]: 85–86). The term does not necessarily mean that she is a foreigner; rather she is estranged from the corporate life of the community with its social and religious conventions (McKane, p. 285). An Israelite woman is probably in view because her marriage is called a "covenant" (v.17; see Notes), and she offers communion sacrifices (cf. 7:5, 14). Such a woman is acting outside the legal bounds of marriage within the covenant.

The subtlety of the appeal comes from flattering speech—the adulteress talks smoothly (see 5:3). An example of such talk is found in 7:14–20. Acquiring discernment will protect the disciple from the smooth, seductive speech of a temptress. Seductive talk is evil, not only because it reveals a brazen character, but also because the adulteress is guilty of marital infidelity: she leaves the companion of her youth (here and in Jer 3:4 for the husband) and is unmindful of the covenant.

"Covenant" (v.17) probably refers to the temptress's marriage vows (Mal 2:14) but could mean the covenant law that prohibited adultery (Exod 20:14). If the marriage vows are meant, such a covenant was entered into at betrothal, when the dowry was established. The adulteress violates her pledge of fidelity.

The effective warning against this type of evil derives from understanding the result of such infidelity—it leads to destruction, the very opposite of the happy and prosperous life. The syntax of v.18 is difficult. "Her house" could be taken in the construction as "she *with her house* sinks down to death," but "she sinks down to death, *which is her house*," may have better support; for 9:18 states that the dead are in her house and that her guests are in the nether world (see Notes). Not only does she sink down to death, but her paths lead to the "shades" (NIV, "the spirits of the dead"). The "shades" are the inhabitants of Sheol; the term describes the shadowy continuation of those who have lost their vitality and strength (see R.F. Schnell, IDB, 4:35, s.v. "Rephaim"). So the inevitable fate of her course of life is to be among the departed in the realm of the dead. The expressions may carry a figurative rather than a literal meaning: Get entangled with her, and you may find only estrangement from the living community, among outcasts, moral lepers who have taken a journey into the land of no return (McKane, p. 288).

Notes

---

17 The MT reads "covenant of her God," בְּרִית אֱלֹהֶיהָ (*b^e^rîṯ 'ᵉlōheyhā*). The LXX simply has "covenant of God," *διαθήκην θείαν* (*diathēkēn theian*). The editors, recognizing the reference is to marriage, suggest "covenant of her tent," אָהֳלָהּ (*'ohᵒlāh*, "her tent, hut") = חֻפָּתָהּ (*ḥuppāṯāh*, "her covering, tent").

18 The difficulty in this passage concerns the relationship of בֵּיתָהּ (*bêṯāh*, "her house") to the rest of the sentence. The MT literally reads, "she sinks down to death her house." The verb שָׁחָה (*šāhāh*) is the third feminine singular perfect tense of שׁוּחַ (*šûᵃḥ*, "to sink, bow down"). בַּיִת (*bayiṯ*, "house") is not normally a feminine noun; so it is probably not the subject of the verb. The editors suggest an emendation to נְתִיבָתָהּ (*nᵉṯîḇāṯāh*, "her path") in comparison with 7:27. But all the versions support the consonantal text of the MT. The LXX seems to have read a verb שָׁתָה (*šāṯāh*, third fem. sing. perf. of שִׁית [*šîṯ*, "to set, place"]) and made *bêṯāh* the object: "she has established her house near death." But we are left with the explanation of the more difficult verb form in the MT. Toy suggests taking the verb from שָׁחָה (*šāḥāh*, "to sink"), but that verb normally means "bow down" (p. 48). Delitzsch suggests that *bêṯāh* is a permutative noun that qualifies the subject—"she together with all that belongs to her" (KD, 1:83). Perhaps Kidner's solution is the simplest; he takes *bêṯāh* in apposition to מָוֶת (*māweṯ*), meaning that "death" is her house (*Proverbs*, p. 62).

---

4) *Enablement for righteous living*

2:20–22

20 Thus you will walk in the ways of good men
   and keep to the paths of the righteous.
21 For the upright will live in the land,
   and the blameless will remain in it;
22 but the wicked will be cut off from the land,
   and the unfaithful will be torn from it.

20–22 The passage ends on the more positive note that wisdom will enable people to do what is right and to enjoy God's blessing (see Notes). Here the text brings in the Deuteronomic emphasis on the land—God's supreme gift being the fulfillment of the promises. The upright will enjoy security and prosperity in it, but the wicked will be rooted out in divine judgment.

Notes

---

20 The LXX reads v.20 as a conditional sentence and connects it with v.19: "for if they had gone in good paths, they would have found the paths of righteousness easy." Toy thinks that v.20 interrupts the flow of v.19 and v.20; so he joins vv.9 and 20 and then follows with vv.10–19 (pp. 38–40).

E. *Admonition to Follow the Way of Wisdom in Relationships With God and People (3:1–35)*

1. *Introductory exhortation*

3:1–4

1 My son, do not forget my teaching,
but keep my commands in your heart,
2 for they will prolong your life many years
and bring you prosperity.

3 Let love and faithfulness never leave you;
bind them around your neck,
write them on the tablet of your heart.
4 Then you will win favor and a good name
in the sight of God and man.

1–2 The first exhortation is to follow the father's "teaching" (*tôrāh*) because it will bring a long and peaceful life. Kidner observes that where *tôrāh* occurs in the book unqualified, it refers to divine law; but when qualified, as here, it refers to home teachings (*Proverbs,* p. 63). Here the verbs "do not forget" and "keep" remind the disciple of general educational discipline. The result is a life worth living, free from danger and trouble (so *ḥayyîm* and *šālôm;* NIV, "life" and "prosperity").

3 The second exhortation is to be faithful and trustworthy because it brings honor with God and man (v.4). "Love" (*ḥeseḏ*) and "faithfulness" (*'emeṯ*) are the two basic covenant terms in Israel. *Ḥeseḏ* is essentially fidelity to obligations arising from a relationship (see Nelson Glueck, *Ḥeseḏ in the Bible,* tr. Alfred Gottschalk [Cincinnati: The Hebrew Union College Press, 1967], p. 55). *'emeṯ* is essentially that which can be relied on, that which is stable (Stuart, p. 167). The two words together form a hendiadys: "faithful love." These words, coupled with the allusion to Deuteronomy 6:8 and even Jeremiah 31:3, show that the content of this disciplined life is the Yahwistic faith. By "binding" and "writing" the teacher is stressing that the teachings become a part of the disciple's nature (Toy, p. 58). The ramifications of this terminology are that the disciple is actually subject to the Lord, not the teacher, and that the requisite "discipline" (*mûsār,* v.11) is respect and obedience for the Lord and his teaching and not merely for a human instructor (see McKane, pp. 290–91; but he thinks that Deuteronomy was influenced by Proverbs).

4 Verse 4 provides the final motivation: favor and a good name. Parallel to 13:15, this difficult line probably signifies that the disciple will have a reputation for good understanding, meaning that he will be respected by God and man (see Notes).

Notes

---

4 The MT reads literally, "You will find favor and good understanding in the sight of God and men." The word "understanding," שֵׂכֶל (*śēḵel*), seems not to form a good parallel with "favor," חֵן (*ḥēn*). The LXX attaches the first two words of v.4—וּמְצָא־חֵן (*ûmeṣā'-ḥēn*, "Then you will win favor")—to v.3 and then reads v.4 as "and devise excellent things in the sight of the LORD and of men" (cf. Rom 12:17; 2 Cor 8:21). The Targum and the Peshitta list the words separately—"favor and good and understanding." Toy (p. 58) suggests changing the word שֵׂכֶל (*śēḵel*) to שֵׁם (*šēm*, "name"), an emendation followed by the NIV. There is no MS evidence for such a change, however. It is possible that *śēḵel* has a derived meaning from understanding that would be akin to "success," i.e., a reputation for good understanding.

---

2. *Admonition to be faithful to the Lord*

3:5–12

5 Trust in the LORD with all your heart
  and lean not on your own understanding;
6 in all your ways acknowledge him,
  and he will make your paths straight.

7 Do not be wise in your own eyes;
  fear the LORD and shun evil.
8 This will bring health to your body
  and nourishment to your bones.

9 Honor the LORD with your wealth,
  with the firstfruits of all your crops;
10 then your barns will be filled to overflowing,
  and your vats will brim over with new wine.

11 My son, do not despise the LORD's discipline
  and do not resent his rebuke,
12 because the LORD disciplines those he loves,
  as a father the son he delights in.

5–6 Several specific instructions compose this general admonition to be faithful. The first is to trust in the Lord and not in oneself, because he grants success. *Bāṭaḥ* ("trust," v.5) carries the force of relying on someone for security; the confidence is to be in the Lord and not in human understanding. The call is for a trust characterized by total commitment—"with *all* your heart" (v.5), "in *all* your ways" (v.6). *Bînāh* ("understanding") is now cast in a sinful mode (cf. 1:2, 6); so there is to be a difference between the *bînāh* that wisdom brings and the natural *bînāh* that undermines faith. What these beautiful expressions call for is "absolute obedience and surrender in every realm of life" (Fritsch, IBC, 4:799). When obedient faith is present, the Lord will guide the believer along life's paths in spite of difficulties and hindrances. The idea of "straight" (v.6) contrasts to the crooked and perverse ways of the wicked.

7–8 The second instruction is to revere the Lord and avoid evil. Here too there is a difference between human wisdom and the new wisdom from above (cf. Isa 5:21). There must be a higher source, and v.7b clarifies it—"fear the LORD and shun evil." Compliance with this is therapeutic: it will be health to the body and nourishment for the frame (v.8; see Notes). The healing that the fear of the Lord and avoidance of evil bring is first and foremost spiritual. Scripture often uses the physical body to describe inner spiritual or psychical feelings (see A.R. Johnson, *The Vitality of the Individual in the Thought of Ancient Israel* [Cardiff: The University of Wales Press, 1949], pp. 67–68).

9–10 The third piece of advice is to give back to God some of one's wealth as a sacrifice in recognition that God gave it. Here we find a cultic verse in the admonition (see Exod 23:19; Num 28:26–27; Deut 18:4; 26:1–2). The admonition reminds the faithful of their religious duties to God. Kidner poignantly puts it, "To 'know' God in our financial 'ways' is to see that these honour Him" (*Proverbs*, p. 64). Then follows the promise of blessing in the "barns" and the "vats."

11–12 The final specific instruction warns the disciple not to rebel against the Lord's discipline, because it is an evidence of his love (see Notes on v.11). Wisdom literature knows that the righteous do not enjoy uninterrupted blessing; suffering remains a problem to the sages, and this text records one of their solutions (see Scott, *Proverbs/Ecclesiastes*, p. 47). This motivation recalls the language of the Davidic covenant (2 Sam 7:14; Ps 89:32–33), which mentions discipline in love. Indeed, it is the father-son relationship that provides insight into the nature of that discipline (see Notes on v.12). These verses are quoted in Hebrews 12:5–6 to show that suffering is a sign of sonship.

Notes

---

8 The MT has לְשָׁרֶּךָ (*lešārrekā*), which is "to your navel," instead of NIV's "to your body." The difficulty is that שָׁר (*šār*, "navel") is never used for "body" in the OT. The BHS editors suggest a slight change either to לִבְשָׂרֶךָ (*libśārekā*, "to your flesh") or לִשְׁאֵרֶךָ (*liš'ērekā*, "to your body"). Such changes run contrary to the canons of textual criticism; for they prefer a common reading over the rare and difficult one. Since *šār* only occurs twice in the Bible, it would be hard to conclude how it was or was not used. And since the words here must be synechdoches (i.e., the part representing the whole) anyway, *šār* would work as well as בָּשָׂר (*bāśār*, "flesh").

11 The LXX has "faint not" (see Heb 12:5). This appears to be either an interpretation (for "despise not" // "resent not") or a translation of another reading.

12 וּכְאָב (*ûke'āb*, "as a father") is slightly difficult in that it is the only place in Proverbs that identifies God as Father. The LXX reads a Hiphil verb here, וְיַכְאִב (*weyak'ib*, "and scourges"), yielding, "Whom the LORD loves, he reproves, and scourges every son whom he receives." The reading "scourges" (= afflicts) fits the parallelism; however, there is not sufficient difficulty with אָב (*'āb*, "father") to reject it in favor of a reading with better parallelism.

---

3. *Commendation of the way of wisdom (3:13–26)*

a. *Wisdom the most valuable possession*

3:13–18

13 Blessed is the man who finds wisdom,
the man who gains understanding,
14 for she is more profitable than silver
and yields better returns than gold.
15 She is more precious than rubies;
nothing you desire can compare with her.
16 Long life is in her right hand;

in her left hand are riches and honor.
17 Her ways are pleasant ways,
and all her paths are peace.
18 She is a tree of life to those who embrace her;
those who lay hold of her will be blessed.

13 Verses 13–18 appear to be following a hymnic style, for "blessed" (*'ašrê*) replaces the imperative (McKane, p. 289). The statement "Blessed is the man," which begins the section, is followed by a series of motive clauses giving the reasons for this happy estate. "Blessed" describes heavenly bliss stemming from being right with God; it depicts the human condition of well being that comes with God's blessing or as a divine reward for righteousness (see S.H. Blank, s.v. "Happiness," IDB, 2:523).

14–18 The statement concerning the blessedness of finding wisdom is now validated. Wisdom (personified) is better than wealth and riches (vv.14–15); for her yield is power, influence, and respect—the gifts of life (McKane, p. 295). She is also compared to "a tree of life" (v.18), the symbol of vitality and fullness of life (v.16). This figure, drawing on Genesis 2–3 (cf. Gen 3:22), signifies that wisdom is the source of a long and beneficial life (v.16; see Ralph Marcus, "The Tree of Life in Proverbs" JBL 62 [1943]: 117–20). Consequently, those who obtain wisdom will be "blessed" (v.18, forming an inclusio with v.13).

Notes

16 The LXX adds an ethical element that is out of place in the passage: "Out of her mouth proceeds righteousness, and law and mercy she bears on her tongue."

b. *Wisdom essential to creation*

3:19–20

19 By wisdom the LORD laid the earth's foundations,
by understanding he set the heavens in place;
20 by his knowledge the deeps were divided,
and the clouds let drop the dew.

19–20 Wisdom, understanding, and knowledge are also valuable to God; for by them he created the universe. How wisdom was used in Creation and how it pictures Christ, the Wisdom of God, is discussed in the comments on 8:22–23. (In addition see J. Emerton, "Spring and Torrent in Ps. 74:15," VetTest Suppl. 15 [1965]: 125.) This section shows that the wisdom that directs life is the same wisdom that created the universe (see discussion on 8:20–31); to surrender to God's wisdom is to put oneself in harmony with creation, the world around one (Fritsch, IBC, 4:804). The two verses concentrate first on the foundation of heaven and earth and then on the provision of waters on earth and from heaven, making a fine parallel to the nature of wisdom as the foundation and blessing of life.

c. *Wisdom and a long and safe life*

3:21–26

21 My son, preserve sound judgment and discernment,
do not let them out of your sight;
22 they will be life for you,
an ornament to grace your neck.
23 Then you will go on your way in safety,
and your foot will not stumble;
24 when you lie down, you will not be afraid;
when you lie down, your sleep will be sweet.
25 Have no fear of sudden disaster
or of the ruin that overtakes the wicked,
26 for the LORD will be your confidence
and will keep your foot from being snared.

21–26 This section forms an admonition to keep on the way of wisdom (v.21) along with promises for such compliance (vv.22–26). If the disciple diligently preserves sound judgment and discernment, he can be confident that the Lord will guide and protect him. But he cannot let them out of his sight for a moment, as *yālūzû* (lit., "depart") indicates (v.21). Whoever trusts and follows sound judgment in his life of righteousness will find not only strength and beauty in wisdom (v.22) but also preservation in action and repose (vv.23–24)—in normal life and in times of disaster (vv.25–26). In other words, his life will be enriched (v.22), safe and secure (vv.23–24), and without fear (v.25). True spiritual discernment that places its confidence in the Lord will not be disappointed (v.26).

Notes

21 In the MT the clauses are in reverse order, making the first line difficult since no subject is expressed: "My son, let them not depart from your eyes, keep sound judgment and discernment." The simplest solution is to reverse the clauses (so NIV), instead of inserting a subject (cf. 4:20).

4. *Warning to avoid unneighborliness*

3:27–30

27 Do not withhold good from those who deserve it,
when it is in your power to act.
28 Do not say to your neighbor,
"Come back later; I'll give it tomorrow"—
when you now have it with you.

29 Do not plot harm against your neighbor,
who lives trustfully near you.
30 Do not accuse a man for no reason—
when he has done you no harm.

27–30 A succession of instructions now follows with regard to neighborliness. These ideas, expressed in the negative, follow naturally from the emphasis on love and faithfulness in v.3. Verses 27–28 exhort doing acts of kindness to those in need (see Notes); for it is wrong to withhold help from a needy neighbor—people ought to be good neighbors. The father also prohibits plotting maliciously against an unsuspecting neighbor (v.29). Malice is a crime; it ruins community. Neither should anyone bring a groundless litigation against an innocent neighbor (v.30). The reference may have in mind people who take others to court on the flimsiest accusations (see McKane, p. 300).

Notes

---

27 The MT has "from its possessors"; the LXX has "from the poor" (as if the poor possessed the "good"). The Peshitta and Targum leave it out. Toy (p. 77) suggests reading "neighbor" instead, רעיך (*r'yk*) having some similarity to בעליו (*b'lyw*). This change seems gratuitous.

---

5. *Warning against emulating the wicked*

3:31–35

31 Do not envy a violent man
  or choose any of his ways,
32 for the LORD detests a perverse man
  but takes the upright into his confidence.

33 The LORD's curse is on the house of the wicked,
  but he blesses the home of the righteous.
34 He mocks proud mockers
  but gives grace to the humble.
35 The wise inherit honor,
  but fools he holds up to shame.

31–35 In dealing with neighbors, one should avoid envying or emulating (LXX) a violent person (cf. Ps 73:3–5). This warning is followed by the reasons, expressed in a series of contrasts. On the one side, the Lord detests the perverse (v.32), curses the house of the wicked (v.33), mocks proud mockers (v.34; see Notes), and holds fools up to shame (v.35). But the upright he is pleased with (v.32), blesses their home (v.33), gives grace to the humble (v.34), and bequeaths honor to the wise (v.35). So wise and upright behavior pleases God and results in his blessing.

Notes

---

34 The verse uses a strong anthropomorphic idea: "He mocks the proud mockers." The LXX has a softened interpretation: "The Lord resists the proud" (cf. James 4:6; 1 Peter 5:5).

F. *Admonition to Follow Righteousness and Avoid Wickedness (4:1–27)*

1. *Traditional teaching and its benefits (4:1–9)*

a. *Exhortation to acquire traditional wisdom*

4:1–4a

1 Listen, my sons, to a father's instruction;
pay attention and gain understanding.
2 I give you sound learning,
so do not forsake my teaching.
3 When I was a boy in my father's house,
still tender, and an only child of my mother,
4 he taught me and said,
"Lay hold of my words with all your heart;

This chapter is comprised of three discourses on the value of wisdom, each including the motifs of instruction, exhortation, command, and motivation.

1 The first discourse begins with a double call, stressing the importance of receiving the teaching. This "instruction" (*mûsar*) is the moral instruction introduced previously (cf. 1:2); it adds self-control and guidance to the wisdom.

The significant feature of this first discourse is that the teaching is traditional. The plural "sons" suggests that disciples are in view and that the father is a teacher (Toy, p. 84). However, the use of "mother" in v.3 and the fact that the teacher-pupil relationship was modeled on the parent-child relationship suggest that this is a father-children relationship. But Alden perhaps goes too far in identifying David and Bathsheba as the parents (p. 45).

2 The tradition being passed on is "sound"—it is the voice of experience. But it must be received, the term *leqaḥ* ("learning") implying that it requires taking (Plaut, p. 66). Accordingly, this teaching is designated better as tradition.

3–4a The concern that these traditional teachings be received is reinforced by personal experience—they were lovingly handed down by his parents. They were ingrained in his soul; he has seen them shape his life and prove reliable. So the home continues to be the prominent arena of learning as the parents in turn pass on the traditions (see Deut 6:6–9). In this section, then, the one teaching strengthens his credibility by informing his sons that it is a shared experience.

Notes

3 The LXX introduces the ideas of "obedient" and "beloved" for רַךְ וְיָחִיד (*rak̲ wᵉyāḥîd̲*, "still tender, and an only child"): viz., "I also was a son, obedient to a father, beloved in the presence of a mother." This seems to be a free interpretation, if not a translation, of a different Hebrew reading. The MT has "tender" and "only one"; although *rak̲* could be "alone" or "only." The Hebrew makes good sense and requires no emendation.

b. *Benefits of acquired wisdom*

4:4b–9

keep my commands and you will live.
5 Get wisdom, get understanding;
do not forget my words or swerve from them.
6 Do not forsake wisdom, and she will protect you;
love her, and she will watch over you.
7 Wisdom is supreme; therefore get wisdom.
Though it cost all you have, get understanding.
8 Esteem her, and she will exalt you;
embrace her, and she will honor you.
9 She will set a garland of grace on your head
and present you with a crown of splendor."

4b Receiving this traditional wisdom wholeheartedly will bring life. "You will live" must mean experiencing life with all its blessings, life as opposed to the whole realm of death with which it is in conflict (Kidner, *Proverbs*, p. 55). Deuteronomy 30 captures the contrast forcefully—people are in a life-and-death struggle; choosing life means obeying the commandments in order to enjoy God's bounty. This theme of life appears in each of the discourses (4:4, 10, 22–23). Of course, the sage uses this motivation in the general sense, for there are always exceptions like Job (Scott, *Proverbs/Ecclesiastes*, p. 52).

5–6 A second benefit of traditional wisdom is security. After reiterating the exhortation to acquire wisdom and understanding, the teacher uses feminine verbs to promise protection and safety. Here we find wisdom personified as a woman, at first reading like a bride that is to be loved and embraced (v.8), but also having the qualities of an influential patron who can protect (v.6; cf. McKane, p. 306). Wisdom personified as a virtuous woman contrasts to the strange woman. If the novice gives her wholehearted devotion, she will watch over him. Proverbs elaborates on how wisdom protects from the evil man (2:12–15), the evil woman (2:16–19; 5:1–20; ch. 7), and catastrophe (5:22–23).

7–9 A third benefit is honor (v.8). Using an implied comparison here with a valuable object (cf. 3:14–15), the teacher implores the disciple to obtain this wisdom at all costs; for it is of supreme value (v.7 is not in the LXX; see Notes). The personification continues in these verses, showing that embracing wisdom will bring honor like a wreath on the head. This honor essentially has to do with the character that wisdom produces; such virtue will be readily recognized in the community (11:10–11).

So there are several benefits to be gained from embracing this teaching. The first step is the earnest determination to have it (Greenstone, p. 39).

Notes

---

7 Toy, on the basis of its omission in the LXX, deletes v.7 as an impossible gloss that interrupts vv.6 and 8 (p. 88).

---

2. *Admonition to live righteously (4:10–19)*

a. *Pursuit of a righteous life style*

4:10–13

> 10 Listen, my son, accept what I say,
> and the years of your life will be many.
> 11 I guide you in the way of wisdom
> and lead you along straight paths.
> 12 When you walk, your steps will not be hampered;
> when you run, you will not stumble.
> 13 Hold on to instruction, do not let it go;
> guard it well, for it is your life.

10 The section begins with the repeated admonition to listen carefully to the instruction so that the life might be extended. The parallelism explains that the disciple must appropriate (*qaḥ;* NIV, "accept") wisdom's life principles.

11–12 That this teaching must be appropriated is underscored by the use of *hōrēṯîḵā* ("I guide you"), a verb related to the noun *tôrāh* (see further G.R. Driver, "Hebrew Notes," VetTest 1 [1951]: 241–50). James L. Crenshaw notes how wisdom taught that laws governed the universe and ensured prosperity and harmony ("The Acquisition of Knowledge in Israelite Wisdom Literature," *Word and World* 7 [1986]: 9).

The figure of a road is now used to make a comparison. Living according to wisdom is like walking or running on a safe road, a course that will be free of obstacles, so that progress will be certain (see comment on 3:5–6). Verse 12 uses two synonymous, temporal clauses to fill out the image: when one lives by this teaching (walking and running), nothing will impede progress.

13 Not only is wisdom the means of making progress in life, it is life itself. Anything so essential must be enthusiastically maintained.

b. *Avoidance of a wicked life style*

4:14–19

> 14 Do not set foot on the path of the wicked
> or walk in the way of evil men.
> 15 Avoid it, do not travel on it;
> turn from it and go on your way.
> 16 For they cannot sleep till they do evil;
> they are robbed of slumber till they make
> someone fall.
> 17 They eat the bread of wickedness
> and drink the wine of violence.
>
> 18 The path of the righteous is like the first gleam of dawn,
> shining ever brighter till the full light of day.
> 19 But the way of the wicked is like deep darkness;
> they do not know what makes them stumble.

14–15 The warning is to avoid evil ways and evil men by not even starting on the wicked path of life. Plaut rightly paraphrases: "Don't take the first step, for you may not be master of your destiny thereafter" (p. 69).

The rapid sequence of imperatives in these verses stresses the urgency of the matter. And the expressions used continue the comparison of life style with a path that can be traveled—only now the life style is evil.

16–17 The first reason that one should avoid such a life style is that it is enslaving. By using hyperboles the teacher portrays the character of the wicked as those who are addicted to evil (v.16; cf. Ps 36:4). They are so completely devoted to evil conduct that they cannot sleep until they find expression for it. Alden comments, "How sick to find peace only at the price of another man's misfortune!" (p. 47).

Moreover, evil is the diet of the wicked (v.17). This hyperbole stresses how powerful the influence of evil is in their life—it is like food and wine to the wicked (contrast Phil 4:8). Verse 17 has been taken also to mean that violence is the way the wicked sustain themselves.

18–19 In addition to being enslaved by evil, one should realize that becoming involved with evil is dangerous. Similes are now used to make the contrast vivid. The path of righteousness is secure and clear like the bright light of the daytime that shines brighter and brighter (dawn and day may form a merism to express that this light is constant, v.18). On the other hand, the way of the wicked is insecure and dangerous, like darkness in which people stumble (v.19).

Notes

18 For the noun "dawn" the LXX has a verbal translation: "The ways of the righteous shine like light." However, the contrast in v.19 is with a nominal form: "darkness." The editors of BHS propose transposing v.18 and v.19 because of the וְ (*w*[e]) at the beginning of v.18.

3. *Admonition to concentrate on righteous living (4:20–27)*

a. *Exhortation to the father's teaching*

4:20–22

20 My son, pay attention to what I say;
listen closely to my words.
21 Do not let them out of your sight,
keep them within your heart;
22 for they are life to those who find them
and health to a man's whole body.

20–21 The exhortation in this third discourse uses several terms for parts of the body: the disciple must use the ears to listen closely to the teacher's words, the eyes to watch them closely, and the heart to determine to do them. By using ears, eyes, and heart, the teacher is exhorting the whole person to receive the traditions.

22 The reason for giving heed to instruction once again is that the words of wisdom provide life—a life of health. The health that is promised here is physical, emotional, and spiritual—the whole person. It is made possible because of God's words that bring deliverance from the evils that harm and hinder life.

b. *Concentration on righteousness*

4:23–27

> 23 Above all else, guard your heart,
> for it is the wellspring of life.
> 24 Put away perversity from your mouth;
> keep corrupt talk far from your lips.
> 25 Let your eyes look straight ahead,
> fix your gaze directly before you.
> 26 Make level paths for your feet
> and take only ways that are firm.
> 27 Do not swerve to the right or the left;
> keep your foot from evil.

23 In this instruction for righteousness, the parts of the body that are used are those involved with expression or action. First, the "heart" (i.e., the mind) must be guarded diligently. Verse 21 instructed the disciple to guard wisdom in the heart. Now the heart must be guarded; for it is the wellspring of life. The heart is the starting point of the activities of life (16:9; 23:19); it determines the course of life (see R.J. Bouffier, "The Heart in the Proverbs of Solomon," *The Bible Today* 52 [1971]: 249–51).

24 Righteousness will control the tongue, avoiding twisted and crooked speech. This is the next logical step; for words flow out of the heart. Wisdom produces truthful speech (8:13; 10:32; et al.). Scott (*Proverbs/Ecclesiastes,* p. 52) reminds us that "falsehood and dissimulation are repeatedly condemned by Wisdom teachers"; he refers to Amenemope (ch. 10) and Ahiqar (ix) (ANET, pp. 423, 429).

25 Next, the eyes must be focused on proper goals. The wise person will have an unswerving directness, but the fool is easily distracted (17:24).

26–27 The imagery of the level, firm, and straight path is used again in these final verses to advise the disciple to avoid evil actions.

Notes

27 The LXX adds, "For the way of the right hand God knows, but those of the left are distorted; and he himself will make straight your paths and guide your goings in peace." For a brief discussion on the question of whether this addition is Jewish or early Christian, see Toy, p. 99.

G. *Admonition to Avoid Seduction to Evil (5:1–23)*

1. *A father's warning about deadly seduction (5:1–6)*

a. *Exhortation for discretion*

5:1–2

> 1 My son, pay attention to my wisdom,
> listen well to my words of insight,

2 that you may maintain discretion
and your lips may preserve knowledge.

1–2 In this chapter we have a man-to-man warning to avoid liaisons with loose women, a theme that is fairly common in the wisdom literature of the ancient Near East (McKane, p. 312; for an analysis of the arrangement of the chapter, see John E. Goldingay, "Proverbs V and IX," RB 84 [1977]: 80–93). The initial exhortation is for the son to listen carefully to this warning that he may keep discretion and knowledge. This knowledge and "discretion" (*m*^e*zimmôṯ*, elsewhere in a bad sense, signifies wise, prudential consideration here) will be basic for avoiding temptation to such disastrous folly.

b. *Motivation: With wisdom seduction may be avoided*

5:3–6

3 For the lips of an adulteress drip honey,
and her speech is smoother than oil;
4 but in the end she is bitter as gall,
sharp as a double-edged sword.
5 Her feet go down to death;
her steps lead straight to the grave.
6 She gives no thought to the way of life;
her paths are crooked, but she knows it not.

3 The reason that the disciple should guard discretion is that the adulteress is seductive. *Zārāh* ("strange woman" or "harlot" elsewhere) is taken here, as in chapter 7, to be a married woman. But the main point the text makes is that her words are flattering. The images of dripping honey and smooth oil refer to her words, not her kisses (cf. S of Songs 4:11; see also M. Dahood, "Honey That Drips. Notes on Proverbs 5:2–3," *Biblica* 54 [1973]: 65–66).

4 The teacher uncovers corruption under the adulteress's charm, as Kidner puts it, noting that Proverbs does not allow us to forget that there is an afterward (*Proverbs*, p. 65). Afterward she is "bitter" (*mārāh*) as "wormwood" (*la'*^a*nāh*). The reference in the MT is to the aromatic plant in contrast to the sweetness of honey. Some, however, follow the LXX with "gall" (so NIV). Plaut keenly observes that there was sweetness when the tryst had alluring glamour, but afterwards it has an ugly ring (p. 74). The image of the two-edged sword, literally a sword with more than one mouth, signifies that a liaison with this woman brings pain and destruction. The flattery conceals for a time the harmful side of this sin.

5–6 In fact, the wayward woman's life style is the pathway to death. Sheol (NIV, "grave," v.5) in this passage is not just the realm of the unblessed; for it is paralleled with "death" (*māweṯ*). Although these terms could be hyperbolic for a ruined life, they probably convey a note of the real consequences that exist for a life of debauchery. The sadder part of this description is that she does not know how unstable her life is (v.6; but see D.W. Thomas for the interpretation "she is not tranquil" in "A Note on *lō' ṯēḏā'* in Proverbs 5:6," JTS 37 [1936]: 59).

2. *A father's warning to avoid ruin and regret (5:7–14)*

a. *Exhortation for prevention*

5:7–8

7 Now then, my sons, listen to me;
do not turn aside from what I say.
8 Keep to a path far from her,
do not go near the door of her house,

7–8 The second discourse begins with a warning not to turn aside from the father's teaching. Going to the adulteress would be such a turning aside, and so the writer clearly warns against that—"Keep clear" (as Moffatt has it); do not even go near her door (there is a wordplay between *rāḥaq* ["Keep . . . far"] and *qāraḇ* ["go near"] in these verses).

b. *Motivation: Obedience will avoid ruin and regret*

5:9–14

9 lest you give your best strength to others
and your years to one who is cruel,
10 lest strangers feast on your wealth
and your toil enrich another man's house.
11 At the end of your life you will groan,
when your flesh and body are spent.
12 You will say, "How I hated discipline!
How my heart spurned correction!
13 I would not obey my teachers
or listen to my instructors.
14 I have come to the brink of utter ruin
in the midst of the whole assembly."

9–10 The first part of the writer's motivation is the warning that consorting with an adulteress will rob a person of health and prosperity (v.9). The theme here is that the hard-earned substance could pass over to "strangers" (*zārîm*, v.10). The "strength" (*hôḏ*, v.9) may refer to health and vigor that might be relinquished to a cruel enemy, perhaps an offended husband as in chapter 7 (although husband is not mentioned here). The "years," the best years in the prime of life, would signify what those years produced, what he had worked for. Likewise the "wealth" (*kōaḥ*) in v.10 would refer to the produce that laborious toiling had gained. The point of these verses is clear: The price of infidelity may be high; for everything one works for—position, power, prosperity—could be lost either through the avaricious demands of the woman or the outcry for restitution by the community.

11–14 When the foolish participant is ruined in such a way, there will be regret for not heeding the warnings. This theme is introduced with "You will groan" (v.11, from *wenāhamtā*), a term used elsewhere for the loud groaning of the poor and distressed (Ezek 24:23). Here the verb conveys an elemental, animal cry of anguish when the guilty finds himself destitute (McKane, p. 317). The use of both "flesh" and "body" underscores the fact that the whole body is exhausted.

Next begins what Alden calls a long litany of "if only"s (p. 51). The condemned conscience too late will realize that instruction and reproof have been ignored. If the disciple listens to his teacher and takes his warnings, he will be spared of "utter ruin" (*kol-rāʿ*, v.14) and the remorse of wrong choices.

Notes

11 The LXX has interpreted נָהַמְתָּ (*nāhamtā*, "groan," "mourn") as נִחַמְתָּ (*niḥamtā*, "repent"); viz., "And you repent at the last when the flesh of your body is consumed." Without vocalization they apparently thought of the common word נחם (*nḥm*) with an ethical emphasis.

3. *Advice to find satisfaction at home (5:15–23)*

a. *Avoiding sharing love with strangers*

5:15–17

15 Drink water from your own cistern,
running water from your own well.
16 Should your springs overflow in the streets,
your streams of water in the public squares?
17 Let them be yours alone,
never to be shared with strangers.

15–17 By using high figures the wise teacher instructs the son to find sexual satisfaction with his own wife and not strange women (see Notes). These figures have troubled commentators because they are not common in instruction material (see McKane, p. 317). But Kruger develops the section as an allegory consisting of a series of metaphors, and this seems satisfactory. He contends that what is at issue is private versus common property. The images of a cistern, well, or fountain are used of a wife (see S of Songs 4:15) because she, like water, satisfies desires. Channels of water in the street would then mean sexual contact with a lewd woman. According to Proverbs 7:12, she never stays at home but is in the streets and the property of many (Paul A. Kruger, "Promiscuity or Marriage Fidelity? A Note on Prov. 5:15–18," JNSL 13 [1987]: 61–68). So the young man is advised to spend his sexual energy at home, producing children (see Ecclus 26:19–21), rather than giving himself to "strangers" (*zārîm*, v.17).

Notes

15 For "cistern" the LXX has "vessel." While the change might be only slight and retain the basic idea of the passage, the Hebrew imagery means that the wife is to be a source of pleasure, not a useful conveyance of pleasure.

b. *Finding satisfaction with one's wife*

5:18–19

18 May your fountain be blessed,
and may you rejoice in the wife of your youth.
19 A loving doe, a graceful deer—
may her breasts satisfy you always,
may you ever be captivated by her love.

18 The advice is now plainly given—the proper course of action is to find pleasure in a fulfilling marriage. The first line, calling for the "fountain" to be blessed, indicates that sexual delight is God-given. Therefore one should rejoice in the wife who has from the vigor of youth shared the excitement and satisfaction, the joy and the contentment of a divinely blessed, monogamous relationship (see Mal 2:15).

19 The imagery for intimate love in marriage is now drawn from the animal world. The "doe" and the "deer" illustrate the exquisite gracefulness of a loving wife. The translation "gazelle" also is used (see ZPEB, 2:665). (Women frequently were named after pretty and graceful animals, such as the corresponding Tabitha and Dorcas.) The husband should be "captivated" by the love of his wife. The word *šāgāh* signifies a staggering gait and so here expresses the ecstatic joy of a "captivated" lover. It may even suggest "be intoxicated always with her love."

Notes

---

18 For the Hebrew "let your fountain be blessed," the LXX reads, "Let your fountain be your own," possibly reading לְבַדֶּךָ (*l*[e]*baddekā*) for בָּרוּךְ (*bārûk*).

---

c. *Motivation: Adultery is sinful folly*

5:20–23

20 Why be captivated, my son, by an adulteress?
Why embrace the bosom of another man's wife?

21 For a man's ways are in full view of the LORD,
and he examines all his paths.
22 The evil deeds of a wicked man ensnare him;
the cords of his sin hold him fast.
23 He will die for lack of discipline,
led astray by his own great folly.

20 Now the teacher shows the folly of adultery by raising rhetorical questions. Here he repeats the verb *šāgāh* ("captivated"; cf. v.19) but with the connotation of foolish delirium: "Why be captivated, my son, by an adulteress [*zārāh*]?" Common sense would say that such brief liaisons with strangers give no time for intimacy—that requires a lifelong bonding with the wife of one's youth.

21 Moreover, a man's ways are in clear view of the Lord who examines them. No matter how careful someone might be to conceal sin, he cannot conceal anything from God. Anyone who does not reckon on God's omniscience will get entangled in sin.

22–23 In sum, the lack of discipline and control in the area of sexual gratification is destructive. The one who plays with this kind of sin will become ensnared by it and led off to ruin (see Notes). Verse 23 uses *šāg̱āh* again (NIV, "led astray"), only this time to underscore that the crime spawns the punishment: "in the greatness of his folly he will *reel*" (pers. tr.). In other words, if the young man is not *captivated* by his wife but becomes *captivated* with a stranger in sinful acts, then his own iniquities will *captivate* him; and he will be led to ruin.

Notes

---

22 The Hebrew line is difficult; it literally reads, "his iniquities shall catch him, the wicked." Since אֶת־הָרָשָׁע (*'eṯ-hārāšā'*, "the wicked") is not represented in the LXX, it could be an old scribal error; or the LXX may have simply smoothed out the sentence. Toy suggests turning the sentence into a passive idea: "The wicked shall be caught in his iniquities" (p. 117). The NIV rearranges it to read, "The evil deeds of a wicked man ensnare him."

H. *Admonition to Seek Release From a Foolish Indebtedness (6:1–5)*

1. *Conditions of indebtedness*

6:1–2

1 My son, if you have put up security for your neighbor,
 if you have struck hands in pledge for another,
2 if you have been trapped by what you said,
 ensnared by the words of your mouth,

1–2 It was fairly common for someone to put up security for someone else, that is, to underwrite another's debts. Here the guarantee of surety is graphically represented by the image of striking hands (v.1; cf. 11:15; 17:18; 22:26). But the pledge is foolish because the debtor is a neighbor who is a misfit (*rē^{a}'* . . . *zār*, lit., "neighbor . . . stranger"). He would be under no obligation to do this—it was merely an impulsive act of generosity. A gullible young man might lack judgment and be easily swept in, only to realize too late that he was "trapped" (*yāqaš*, v.2) and "ensnared" (*lāḵaḏ*). Such a rash act of generosity might take a lifetime to pay.

2. *Exhortation to obtain release*

6:3–5

3 then do this, my son, to free yourself,
 since you have fallen into your neighbor's hands:
Go and humble yourself;
 press your plea with your neighbor!
4 Allow no sleep to your eyes,
 no slumber to your eyelids.

> [5]Free yourself, like a gazelle from the hand of the hunter,
> like a bird from the snare of the fowler.

3–4 The advice for an indebted person is to try to get released from the pledge as soon as possible (*'ēpô'*, signifying "here and now"; NIV, "then"). Freeing oneself (*hinnāṣēl* has the force of rescuing or delivering oneself from a situation) may be a humiliating process, but it is far better than the debt. The verb "humble yourself" (*hiṯrappēs*) may have behind it the literal idea of allowing oneself to be trampled on (which Gesenius interpreted to mean "prostrate yourself" [*Hebrew and Chaldee Lexicon* (London: Samuel Bagster and Son, 1847), p. 777]). G.R. Driver related it to the Akkadian *rapāsu* ("trample") and interpreted it in the sense of trampling oneself, or swallowing pride, with the implication of being unremitting in the effort ("Some Hebrew Verbs, Nouns, and Pronouns," JTS 30 [1929]: 374). This purpose for the humbling is "to press [the] plea" (*rᵉhaḇ*, from *rāhaḇ*, "to act stormily, boisterously," here "to importune"). The pledge can be released if one begs the creditor, but one should lose no time in pressing the appeal.

5 The exhortation is then repeated and enhanced by two similes that retrieve the motif of the person's being entrapped by the pledge.

I. *Admonition to Avoid Laziness (6:6–11)*

1. *Lesson in diligence*

6:6–8

> [6]Go to the ant, you sluggard;
> consider its ways and be wise!
> [7]It has no commander,
> no overseer or ruler,
> [8]yet it stores its provisions in summer
> and gathers its food at harvest.

6 The teacher next directs a lesson to the sluggard (*'āṣēl*, "to be sluggish, lazy"), using the activities of the ant to make the point (cf. the parallel section in 24:30–34, where the emphasis is on the neglected field of the sluggard). Since the ant is a lowly creature, this comparison is somewhat degrading. But the sluggard can learn diligence from its ways.

7–8 The description of the ant's activities shows that although it appears to have no leader (even though it actually does have organization and cooperation), it provides for the future with great industry (see Notes). The classic example of such foresight and industry is Joseph in Genesis 41. (For a treatment of wisdom motifs in the story of Joseph, see Gerhard von Rad, *God at Work in Israel*, tr. John H. Marks [Nashville: Abingdon, 1980], pp. 19–35.)

Notes

---

8 The LXX adds a lengthy section at the end of this verse on the lesson from the bee: "Or, go to the bee and learn how diligent she is and how seriously she does her work—her products kings and private persons use for health—she is desired and respected by all—though feeble in body, by honoring wisdom she obtains distinction." Toy surmises that the LXX translator thought the other insect ought to be mentioned and so elaborated on the point (p. 124).

---

2. *Danger of poverty*

6:9–11

9 How long will you lie there, you sluggard?
When will you get up from your sleep?
10 A little sleep, a little slumber,
a little folding of the hands to rest—
11 and poverty will come on you like a bandit
and scarcity like an armed man.

9–11 These verses provide the motivation for the admonition—there is the danger of poverty. The rhetorical question—"How long [*'aḏ-māṯay*] will you lie there, you sluggard?" (v.9)—is designed to rebuke the laziness in a forceful manner. Then, using effective irony, the instructor mimics the lazy person's speech (v.10). His point is that too much sleep will lead to poverty—it will rob the lazy person of potential increase.

Two similes in v.11 illustrate the onslaught of poverty. The first—"like a bandit"—uses *m^ehallēḵ*. This difficult term has been interpreted as a "dangerous assailant" or a "highwayman," i.e., a bandit that robs (see Notes). McKane, however, takes the view that it means a "vagrant" (p. 324). The other term, "an armed man" (*'îš māḡēn*) is probably connected to the military ideas of "shield" and "deliver" (s.v. *gānan*, "to cover, surround, defend"). G.R. Driver connects it with the Arabic word for "bold," "insolent," interpreting its use here as "beggar" or "insolent man" ("Studies in the Vocabulary of the Old Testament, IV," JTS 33 [1932]: 38–47).

Notes

---

11 The MT has "your poverty will come like a wayfarer"; the LXX has "swiftness of a traveler." The parallelism suggests that one traveling swiftly would be a robber or an assailant. The imagery, then, is of a swift attack that brings poverty.

J. *Warning Against Deviousness (6:12–15)*

1. *Description*

6:12–14

12 A scoundrel and villain,
who goes about with a corrupt mouth,
13 who winks with his eye,
signals with his feet
and motions with his fingers,
14 who plots evil with deceit in his heart—
he always stirs up dissension.

12–14 The subject matter is now the "scoundrel" (*'āḏām beliya'al*) and the "villain" (*'îš 'āwen*). These terms describe one who is both wicked and worthless. Gesenius, followed by BDB, analyzes *beliya'al* as a compound of the negative *belî* and a noun *ya'al* ("worth," "profit"). But there are many other proposals for its etymology as well, such as a compound with *ba'al* ("lord of goats" related to *'azazel*), a derivative of *bāla'* with reduplication ("confusion" or "engulfing ruin"), or a proper name from Babylonian Bililu. (See בְּלִיַּעַל [*beliya'al*] in TDOT, 2:131–36, by Benedikt Otzen; and see D.W. Thomas, "בְּלִיַּעַל in the Old Testament," in *Biblical and Patristic Studies in Memory of Robert Pierce Casey*, edd. J. Neville Birdsall and Robert W. Thomson [New York: Herder, 1963], pp. 11–19.) Whatever the etymology, a survey of use shows the word to describe people who violate the law (Deut 15:9; Judg 19:22; 1 Kings 21:10, 13; Prov 16:27; et al.) or act in a contemptuous and foolish manner against cultic observance or social institutions (1 Sam 10:27; 25:17; 30:22). The instruction will focus on the devious activities of this type of person.

The description moves from the scoundrel's corrupt or perverse sayings (v.12) to his sinister sign language (v.13) to his disruptive plots developed through deceit. The expressions in v.13 seem to refer to any look or gesture that is put on and therefore a form of deception if not a way of making insinuations. McKane thinks there is even a reference here to magic, "plots" (*ḥōrēš*, v.14) being used elsewhere to devise magic (p. 325).

2. *Destruction*

6:15

> 15 Therefore disaster will overtake him in an instant;
> he will suddenly be destroyed—without remedy.

15 Disaster will befall the troublemaker suddenly. It is uncertain whether *yiššāḇēr* ("he will be . . . destroyed") refers to death or not. Probably the line means that a character like this will be ruined when exposed.

K. *Conduct the Lord Hates (6:16–19)*

1. *Introductory statement*

6:16

> 16 There are six things the LORD hates,
> seven that are detestable to him:

16 The verses that follow condemn certain characteristics and activities; the terms "hate" and "detestable" show that these are taboo. Plaut perceives that these vices deny the divine element in humanity (p. 89). Verse 16 uses what is known as a numerical ladder, paralleling "six things" with "seven things" (see also 30:15, 18, 21, 24, 29; Job 5:19; Eccl 11:2; Amos 1:6, 9, 13; 2:1, 4, 6; Mic 5:5). The point of such a poetic arrangement is that the present enumeration does not exhaust the list (cf. Toy, p. 127; W.M. Roth, "The Numerical Sequence x / x + 1 in the Old Testament," VetTest 12 [1962]: 300–311; id., "Numerical Sayings in the Old Testament," VetTest 13 [1965]: 86).

2. *Delineation*

6:17–19

17 haughty eyes,
a lying tongue,
hands that shed innocent blood,
18 a heart that devises wicked schemes,
feet that are quick to rush into evil,
19 a false witness who pours out lies
and a man who stirs up dissension among brothers.

17–19 The seven things that the Lord hates are specific, personal attitudes and actions. There is something of a contrasting parallel arrangement with the Beatitudes in Matthew 5. It has seven blessed things to answer these seven hated things; moreover, the first beatitude ("Blessed are the poor in spirit," Matt 5:5) contrasts with the first hated thing ("haughty eyes," v.17; i.e., "a proud look") and the seventh ("peacemakers," Matt 5:7) with the seventh abomination ("stirs up dissension," v.19).

The first in the list, "haughty eyes" (*'ênayim rāmôṯ*, v.17a), refers to a proud look suggesting arrogant ambition. This term "high" is similarly used in Numbers 15:30 for the sin of the high hand, i.e., willful rebellion or defiant sin. Usage of "haughty eyes" in the OT is telling: it describes the pompous Assyrian invader in Isaiah 10:12–14 as well as the proud king in Daniel 11:12 (NIV, "pride"). God will not tolerate anyone who thinks so highly of himself (see Prov 21:4; Isa 2:11–17).

The second description is "a lying tongue" (*l^e^šôn šāqer*, lit., "a tongue of deception") (v.17b). The term is used in Jeremiah 14:14 to portray false prophets who deceive people and in Psalm 109:2 to describe the deceiver who betrays—a passage that the disciples applied to Judas in Acts 1:20. Deception in speech is harmful (Prov 26:28), but in the end truth will overcome it (Prov 12:19).

The third description focuses on the hands as the instruments of murder (v.17c). Genesis 9:6 prohibited shedding human blood because people are made in the image of God—no matter what one might think of them. But shedding "innocent blood" (*dām-nāqî*) was an even greater crime. King Manasseh had filled the streets with innocent blood (2 Kings 21:16; 24:4). Princes did it for gain according to Ezekiel (22:27). Even King David was prohibited from building the temple because he had shed much blood (1 Chron 22:8).

The fourth phrase (v.18a) concerns the heart that "devises [*ḥōrēš*] wicked schemes [*maḥš^e^ḇôṯ 'āwen*]." The heart represents the will most often. Here it plots evil. God early on declared that the human heart was capable of this (Gen 6:5); and Proverbs elaborates on the theme, showing that the heart that schemes wickedness is also deceitful (12:20; 14:22).

The fifth description uses the figure of "feet that are quick to rush into evil" (v.18b; see Notes). This captures the enthusiastic and complete involvement in activities that bring pain to all concerned.

The sixth abomination (v.19a) returns to the theme of deception. Here the focus is on perjury (*'ēḏ šāqer;* NIV, "a false witness"), a direct violation of the Decalogue. This character pours out "lies" (*k^e^zāḇîm*), a term found also in Psalm 40:4; Amos 2:4; and Micah 1:14 (where the wordplay on the city Achzib also carries the idea of a false expectation) (cf. Jer 15:18, where the adjective *'aḵzāḇ* describes a mirage; see also a helpful portrayal of this idea in Job 6:15–20).

The final description is general—God hates one "who stirs up dissension" (v.19b).

"Dissension" is attributed in Proverbs to contentious, quarreling people (21:9; 26:21; 25:24) who have a short fuse (15:18). Paul, on the other hand, warns against envy, malice, and strife (1 Tim 6:4). These things, then, God will not tolerate. If he hates these things, then conversely he must love and desire (1) humility, (2) truthful speech, (3) preservation of life, (4) pure thoughts, (5) eagerness to do good things, (6) honest witnesses, and (7) peaceful harmony.

Notes

18b The MT has literally "make haste to run," the idea being to make haste to begin to run, i.e., eager to seize the opportunity. The LXX omits "run," yielding the idea of feet hastening to do evil. The word "run" is unnecessary in the line, if the analogy of 1:16 holds, where only one verb is in each clause.

L. *Warning About Immorality (6:20–35)*

1. *Reminder to heed instruction*

6:20–24

20 My son, keep your father's commands
and do not forsake your mother's teaching.
21 Bind them upon your heart forever;
fasten them around your neck.
22 When you walk, they will guide you;
when you sleep, they will watch over you;
when you awake, they will speak to you.
23 For these commands are a lamp,
this teaching is a light,
and the corrections of discipline
are the way to life,
24 keeping you from the immoral woman,
from the smooth tongue of the wayward wife.

20–21 The youth is exhorted to cling fast to the teachings of his parents (see P.W. Skehan, *Studies in Israelite Poetry and Wisdom: Proverbs 5:15–19 and 6:20–24* [Washington: Catholic Biblical Association of America, 1971], pp. 1–8). Implicit in these verses is the basic understanding that a good home life—i.e., father and mother sharing the rearing of the children together—will go a long way to prevent the youth from falling into immorality.

22–24 The motivation for keeping these commands is that they will bring protection from the adulteress. Verse 22 strengthens the instruction by using language similar to Deuteronomy 6:7. And v.23 uses metaphors that are also used of the law (see Ps 119:105). But beside the general ideas of protection and direction, the specific benefit of the teaching will be in keeping the youth from the loose woman. She is described in v.24 as an "immoral woman" (*'ēšeṯ rā'*) and a "wayward wife" (*noḵrîyāh;* some commentators follow the variant reading *'ēšeṯ rēa'* to obtain "wife of another man," as in the LXX and v.29). The context shows that this immoral woman is another man's wife (see Notes).

Notes

24 The parallelism supports the reading "wife of another," i.e., a married woman, as in the LXX. The difference in readings is but one vowel change.

2. *Warning to avoid seduction*

6:25–35

25 Do not lust in your heart after her beauty
or let her captivate you with her eyes,
26 for the prostitute reduces you to a loaf of bread,
and the adulteress preys upon your very life.
27 Can a man scoop fire into his lap
without his clothes being burned?
28 Can a man walk on hot coals
without his feet being scorched?
29 So is he who sleeps with another man's wife;
no one who touches her will go unpunished.

30 Men do not despise a thief if he steals
to satisfy his hunger when he is starving.
31 Yet if he is caught, he must pay sevenfold,
though it costs him all the wealth of his house.
32 But a man who commits adultery lacks judgment;
whoever does so destroys himself.
33 Blows and disgrace are his lot,
and his shame will never be wiped away;
34 for jealousy arouses a husband's fury,
and he will show no mercy when he takes revenge.
35 He will not accept any compensation;
he will refuse the bribe, however great it is.

25 The admonition warns against lusting in one's heart for the immoral woman's beauty or charm. The verb *ḥāmaḏ* ("to lust") is used in the Decalogue to warn against coveting. Lust, according to Jesus, is a sin of the same kind as the act, not just the first step toward sin (Matt 5:28). Playing with temptation is only the heart reaching out after sin. So one should not dwell on the woman's seductive charms in one's heart. "Eyes" are singled out here because the painted eyes and the luring glances are symptoms of seduction (see 2 Kings 9:30).

26 The summary motivation for the admonition is that such sin has a high price—it may even ruin one's life. The parallelism in this verse is difficult. It is not meant to say that whoring is better than adultery because it only impoverishes whereas adultery preys on the very life. Both are costly sins to be avoided (see Notes).

27–35 The motivation now elaborates on the motif that punishment is inevitable. (For the use of questions, see James L. Crenshaw, "Impossible Questions, Sayings, and

Tasks," *Semeia* 17 [1980]: 19–34.) Playing on the word *'îš* ("man") and *'iššāh* ("woman" in v.26), the instructor introduces the figure of "fire" (*'ēš*, v.27). Scooping coals into one's lap would represent holding the adulteress, and walking on coals (v.28) would signify further sexual contact with her. The self-evident answer to the questions is that the adulterer will "get burned"; he will not go "unpunished" (v.29; "touches her" is probably a euphemism as in Gen 20:6). The rest of the passage then reasons that there is no restitution acceptable for adultery as there might be with thievery. The thief, when caught, has to pay dearly (v.31). But the adulterer will be humiliated and ruined. Nothing will satisfy the husband but revenge.

The expression "destroys himself" (*mašḥîṯ napšô*) in v.32 stresses that the guilty one destroys his own life. He could be given the death penalty (Deut 22:22); but he apparently continues to live in ignominy, destroyed spiritually and socially (see 2:18; 1 Tim 5:6). Kidner observes that in a morally healthy society the adulterer would be a social outcast (*Proverbs*, p. 75).

Notes

26 In the first clause of the verse, בְּעַד (*beʿaḏ*) may be taken either as "on account of" (= by means of) a harlot or "for the price of" a harlot. Most expositors take the first reading—though that use of the preposition *b* is unattested—and supply "one is brought down." The verse would then say that a harlot brings a man to poverty, but the married woman seeks death. If the second reading is taken (with the support of the ancient versions), then it would be saying that there is a small price for the one and a greater price for the other.

M. *Admonition to Avoid the Wiles of the Adulteress (7:1–27)*

1. *Important teaching of the father*

7:1–5

1 My son, keep my words
  and store up my commands within you.
2 Keep my commands and you will live;
  guard my teachings as the apple of your eye.
3 Bind them on your fingers;
  write them on the tablet of your heart.
4 Say to wisdom, "You are my sister,"
  and call understanding your kinsman;
5 they will keep you from the adulteress,
  from the wayward wife with her seductive words.

Once again the theme of seduction surfaces in the instructions of the father (see 2:16–19; 5:1–23; 6:20–35). Here the instruction takes the form of a narrative about an individual woman who draws a youth into adultery. It is a didactive narrative that serves to make an earnest warning. The adulteress is probably not a personification of evil in this chapter; that is fully developed in chapter 9. However, referring to wisdom as a sister certainly prepares for the personifications of chapters 8 and 9. Wisdom will obviate temptations, the greatest being the sexual urge.

1–4 The section begins by repeating the instruction for the son to preserve and practice the authoritative teachings in order to "live" (*weḥyēh,* v.2; see Notes). The expression "the apple of your eye" (*'îšôn 'êneyḵā*) is literally "the little man" in the eye, having reference to the pupil, where the object focused on is reflected. The point is that the teaching is so precious it must be guarded that closely. Verse 3 strengthens the admonition by alluding to the instruction for heeding the law given in Deuteronomy 6:8.

5 The reason for following these teachings carefully is to give protection from the wiles of the loose woman. She is called an "adulteress" (*'iššāh zārāh*) and a "wayward wife" (*noḵrîyāh;* cf. 6:24). There is some debate over the status of the woman, McKane contending that she is a foreigner and false god devotee (p. 334). Snijders, however, argues that she is an outsider because of her loose morals ("The Meaning of זָר," pp. 85–86). The distinction makes little practical difference; for she is a wayward wife with "seductive words" (*'^{a}māreyhā heḥ^{e}lîqāh,* lit., "smooth words"). Helmer Ringgren and Walther Zimmerli suggest that she is also a promoter of a pagan cult (*Sprüche/Prediger* [Göttingen: Vandenhoeck and Ruprecht, 1980], p. 19).

Notes

1 Before v.2 the LXX inserts, "My son, fear the Lord and you shall be strong, and besides him fear no other." Although this addition has the precedent of 3:7 and 9 and harmonizes with 14:26, it does not fit here. The advice is to listen to the teacher.

2. *Description of seduction (7:6–23)*

a. *The victim*

7:6–9

6 At the window of my house
  I looked out through the lattice.
7 I saw among the simple,
  I noticed among the young men,
  a youth who lacked judgment.
8 He was going down the street near her corner,
  walking along in the direction of her house
9 at twilight, as the day was fading,
  as the dark of night set in.

6–9 The narrative unfolds with the observation of an unwary youth strolling along the streets at night. He is described as one of the "simple" (*p^{e}ṯā'yim,* v.7; cf. 1:4) ones, i.e., "a youth who lacked judgment" (*na'ar ḥ^{a}sar-lēḇ;* lit., "a youth lacking of heart," i.e., one void of common sense or understanding). He is young, inexperienced, featherbrained (as Kidner puts it, *Proverbs,* p. 75). His evening stroll takes him intentionally (as *ṣā'ad,* "to step, march," suggests; NIV, "walking along") down the street to her house (v.8). And then, if all this activity of the naive young man takes place under the cover of night, only trouble can follow (v.9).

b. *The temptress*

7:10–12

10 Then out came a woman to meet him,
dressed like a prostitute and with crafty intent.
11 (She is loud and defiant,
her feet never stay at home;
12 now in the street, now in the squares,
at every corner she lurks.)

10 The narrative next introduces the seductress who comes out to meet the innocent youth. She has the "attire of a prostitute" (*šîṯ zônāh;* NIV, "dressed like a prostitute") and has "crafty intent" (*neṣuraṯ lēḇ*). This latter expression is difficult; the ancient versions took it with the meaning of causing the youth's heart to flutter or of bewildering or capturing his heart (see Notes). The expression literally means "guarded in heart," but Driver has shown semantic development from "guarded" to "crafty" or "sly." She has locked up her plans and gives nothing away. This, interestingly, contrasts with her attire, which gives her away.

11–12 The text further describes this wayward woman as "loud and defiant" (v.11a), with a roving desire (vv.11b–12). "She lurks" (*te'erōḇ*, from *'āraḇ*, "to lie in wait, ambush, with a hostile purpose") at every street corner, waiting for the gullible young man to pass her way. Plaut astutely warns, "Woe to the marriage whose partners cannot find values in their home and must constantly seek outside stimulation!" (p. 102).

Notes

---

10 The translation "crafty" or "wily" (RV) for נְצֻרַת (*neṣuraṯ*) is uncertain. Toy lists the commentators' suggestions: false, malicious, secret, subtle, excited, hypocritical (p. 149). If the root נָצַר (*nāṣar*) is the same as that found in Isa 48:6, נְצֻרוֹת (*neṣurôṯ*, "hidden," "secret"), then a sense such as "wily" fits. The LXX has "causes the hearts of the young men to fly away" (νέων [*neōn*, "young men"] is added for explanation).

---

c. *The seduction*

7:13–20

13 She took hold of him and kissed him
and with a brazen face she said:

14 "I have fellowship offerings at home;
today I fulfilled my vows.
15 So I came out to meet you;
I looked for you and have found you!
16 I have covered my bed
with colored linens from Egypt.
17 I have perfumed my bed
with myrrh, aloes and cinnamon.
18 Come, let's drink deep of love till morning;
let's enjoy ourselves with love!

[19] My husband is not at home;
he has gone on a long journey.
[20] He took his purse filled with money
and will not be home till full moon."

13–15 The steps in the seduction are carefully calculated to ensnare the inexperienced youth. First, she boldly grabs him and kisses him (v.13). This is followed, in the second step, by her flattering invitation (vv.14–15), in which she explains that she has "fellowship" offerings at home and came out especially looking for him (only a fool would believe that she was that interested in him). These fellowship offerings refer to the meat leftover from the votive offerings made in the sanctuary (see Lev 7:11–21). Apparently the sacrificial worship meant as little to her spiritually as does Christmas to modern hypocrites who follow in her pattern. By expressing that she has fellowship offerings, she could be saying nothing more than that she has fresh meat for a meal or that she is ceremonially clean, perhaps after her period. At any rate, it is all probably a ruse for winning a customer.

16–17 The third step is the report of her careful preparation. She is not poor; for she has a bed, and it is ready.

18 The fourth step is the direct proposition: "Come, let's drink deep of love." Her invitation speaks of complete satiety (*nirweh,* "let's drink deep") and sheer enjoyment (*niṯ'all^{e}sāh,* "let's enjoy ourselves") in physical love (*dōḏîm,* from *dôḏ,* found frequently in the Song of Songs for "loved one" or "beloved").

19–20 The final step is the adulteress's disarming reassurance. She explains that "the man" (i.e., "my husband," as the LXX actually interprets it) is not at home. He conveniently is gone on a journey; and judging from his taking a money bag and staying till the next full moon, they would be perfectly safe in their escapade (he might even be gone for a fortnight, if a comparison of v.9 and v.20 can give clues to the chronology). At any rate, her appeal is bold, exciting, and apparently safe. It would take someone with the wisdom and integrity of a Joseph to resist such an appeal (cf. the important motifs in Gen 39, esp. v.8).

d. *The capitulation*

7:21–23

[21] With persuasive words she led him astray;
she seduced him with her smooth talk.
[22] All at once he followed her
like an ox going to the slaughter,
like a deer stepping into a noose
[23] till an arrow pierces his liver,
like a bird darting into a snare,
little knowing it will cost him his life.

21–23 The fall of the simpleton (see *p^{e}ṯā'yim,* v.7), after a brief pondering, is sudden (*piṯ'ōm,* "at once," v.22), because she seduces him with her enticing speech. There is irony in the fact that *leqaḥ* (used earlier for wise instruction ["sound learning," 4:2]) is now used for "enticement" (*liqḥāh;* NIV, "persuasive words," v.21). D. Winton Thomas interprets this as the adulteress's taking ways ("Textual and Philological

Notes on Some Passages in the Book of Proverbs," VetTest Suppl. 3 [1955]: 280–92). Using the similes of an ox for the slaughter and a deer for the noose, the teacher warns of the complete ruin that can come to one guilty of allowing himself to bẹ seduced (v.22; see Notes). This sin could "cost him his life" (v.23; lit., "that it is his life"; as in Num 16:38)—he needs to know this. The meaning of the verse very well may refer to moral corruption rather than a literal death. The arrow piercing the liver may refer to the pangs of a guilty conscience that the guilty must reap along with spiritual and physical ruin.

Notes

---

22 The third clause is difficult. It traditionally has been translated as "fetters to the chastening of a fool." But there is no support that the word עֶכֶס (*ʿeḵes*) means "fetters." It appears in Isa 3:16 as "anklets." The parallelism here suggests that animal imagery is required. Thus the versions have "as a dog to bonds." Scott takes the emendation of the MT's וּכְעֶכֶס אֶל־מוּסַר אֱוִיל (*ûḵeʿeḵes 'el-mûsar 'ewîl*) to כְּעַכֵּס אֶל־מֹסֵר אַיָּל (*keʿakkēs 'el-mōsēr 'ayyāl*), yielding "like a stag prancing into captivity" (*Proverbs and Ecclesiastes*, p. 64).

---

3. *Deadly results of consorting*

7:24–27

24 Now then, my sons, listen to me;
   pay attention to what I say.
25 Do not let your heart turn to her ways
   or stray into her paths.
26 Many are the victims she has brought down;
   her slain are a mighty throng.
27 Her house is a highway to the grave,
   leading down to the chambers of death.

24–27 With a final flurry of exhortations, the teacher warns his sons to stay away from the seductress's paths (vv.24–25) because consorting with her leads to death (vv.26–27). The language is startling in its force; but the ruin that such evil brings is as devastating as death and may, of course, end in actual punishment. He stresses that she has been the death of many and that her house is the way that leads to the "chambers of death" (*ḥaḏrê-māweṯ*, v.27). Her house is not the grave. It is, however, surely the way to it, and the one who takes that way is pathetic indeed. A man's life is not destroyed in one instant; it is taken from him gradually as he enters into a course of life that will leave him as another victim of the wages of sin.

N. *The Appeal of Wisdom (8:1–36)*

In this chapter wisdom continues to be represented as a person (cf. ch.7). The material combines 1:20–33, in which wisdom proclaims her value, and 3:19–26, in which wisdom is the agent of Creation. This personification of wisdom has affinities with other ancient Near Eastern wisdom literature and, in fact, may have drawn on various mythological ideas (for a good survey of the literature on the subject, see

Claudia V. Camp, *Wisdom and the Feminine in the Book of Proverbs* [Sheffield: JSOT, 1985], pp. 23–70). Wisdom in Proverbs 8, however, is not a deity like Egypt's *maat* or the Assyrian-Babylonian *Ishtar*. Rather, it is presented as if it were a self-conscious divine being distinct but subordinate to Yahweh; but, in fact, it is a personification of the attribute of wisdom displayed by God (see further Scott, *Proverbs and Ecclesiastes*, pp. 69–72; Ralph Marcus, "On Biblical Hypostasis of Wisdom," HUCA 23 [1950–51]: 157–71).

Many have equated wisdom in this chapter with Jesus Christ. This connection works only so far as Jesus reveals the nature of God the Father, including his wisdom, just as Proverbs presents the personification of the attribute. Jesus' claims included wisdom (Matt 12:42) and a unique knowledge of God (Matt 11:25–27). He even personified wisdom in a way that was similar to Proverbs (Matt 11:19; Luke 11:49). Paul saw the fulfillment of wisdom in Christ (Col 1:15–20; 2:3) and affirmed that Christ became our wisdom in the Crucifixion (1 Cor 1:24, 30). So the bold personification of wisdom in Proverbs certainly provides a solid foundation for the revelation of divine wisdom in Christ. But because wisdom appears to be a creation of God in 8:22–31, it is unlikely that wisdom here is Jesus Christ.

1. *Introduction*

8:1–3

1 Does not wisdom call out?
  Does not understanding raise her voice?
2 On the heights along the way,
  where the paths meet, she takes her stand;
3 beside the gates leading into the city,
  at the entrances, she cries aloud:

1–3 Plaut introduces this chapter by observing that it is now wisdom's turn to exhibit her attractions—in the open, not lurking in secret (p. 107). Wisdom continually attests to her value: the rhetorical questions of v.1 show that she is ready to call out. But this crying out is in the high roads, at the doors of the city where people gather (v.2). Kidner comments, "A chapter which is to soar beyond time and space, opens at street level . . . relevant here as heaven" (*Proverbs*, p. 76).

2. *First cycle (8:4–9)*

a. *Invitation: Listen and gain understanding*

8:4–5

4 "To you, O men, I call out;
  I raise my voice to all mankind.
5 You who are simple, gain prudence;
  you who are foolish, gain understanding.

4–5 The invitation from wisdom embraces all classes of people: v.4 includes "men" (*'îšîm*) and "mankind" (*bᵉnê 'ā<u>d</u>ām*, lit., "sons of adam"); v.5 uses *pᵉ<u>t</u>ā'yim* ("simple") and *kᵉsîlîm* ("foolish"). The invitation for the "simple" and the "foolish" is to gain "prudence" (*'ormāh*) and "understanding" (*lē<u>b</u>*, lit., "heart").

b. *Motivation: Wisdom is noble, just, and true*

8:6–9

6 Listen, for I have worthy things to say;
I open my lips to speak what is right.
7 My mouth speaks what is true,
for my lips detest wickedness.
8 All the words of my mouth are just;
none of them is crooked or perverse.
9 To the discerning all of them are right;
they are faultless to those who have knowledge.

6 Wisdom begins her motivation by declaring that she has noble things to say. The term *n^eg̱îḏîm* is "noble," "princely," meaning literally excellent things. Moreover, when wisdom opens her mouth, she speaks what is upright (*mêšārîm*). So what she has to say is excellent and right.

7 The things that wisdom says are also reliable (*'^emeṯ,* lit., "true"; so NIV). The sense of truth here refers to what is firm and dependable; it is the reflection within the heart before the speech. This speaking truth is derived from detesting wickedness (e.g., wickedness is taboo for wisdom).

8 The motivation now includes *ṣeḏeq* (with a beth of essence), indicating wisdom's appeal is right or "just" (so NIV). *Ṣeḏeq* is contrasted with *nip̱tāl* ("crooked") and *'iqqēš* ("perverse"). There is no hidden agenda and no deception in wisdom's teachings.

9 Wisdom's words are "right" (*n^eḵōḥîm*) and "faultless" (*y^ešārîm*). The teachings are in plain view, intelligible to all who have some discernment or who find knowledge (the theme of "to find," *māṣā'*, is introduced here; NIV, "have").

3. *Second cycle (8:10–21)*

a. *Invitation: Receive instruction and knowledge*

8:10

10 Choose my instruction instead of silver,
knowledge rather than choice gold,

10 The second cycle begins with the invitation to receive (*q^eḥû,* lit., "take"; NIV, "choose") "instruction" (*mûsār*) and "knowledge" (*da'aṯ*) over silver and gold. True wealth derives from the former, not the latter.

b. *Motivation: Wisdom is valuable*

8:11–21

11 for wisdom is more precious than rubies,
and nothing you desire can compare with her.

12 "I, wisdom, dwell together with prudence;
I possess knowledge and discretion.
13 To fear the LORD is to hate evil;
I hate pride and arrogance,

evil behavior and perverse speech.
14 Counsel and sound judgment are mine;
I have understanding and power.
15 By me kings reign
and rulers make laws that are just;
16 by me princes govern,
and all nobles who rule on earth.
17 I love those who love me,
and those who seek me find me.
18 With me are riches and honor,
enduring wealth and prosperity.
19 My fruit is better than fine gold;
what I yield surpasses choice silver.
20 I walk in the way of righteousness,
along the paths of justice,
21 bestowing wealth on those who love me
and making their treasuries full.

11 The reason one should choose wisdom over wealth is because wisdom is more "precious" (*ṭôḇāh*), more desirable than anything else. The goodness of wisdom is based on its incomparable value in life.

12–16 The value of wisdom may be found in its practical use, especially by those in power. Wisdom claims now to dwell with "prudence" (*ʿormāh,* v.12), that is, right knowledge in special cases. She also has (*'emṣā';* NIV, "possess") knowledge and discretion. Parallel to this quality is the fear of the Lord, which leads to rejection (*śānē';* NIV, "hate," v.13) of evil, pride, and perverse speech. In vv.14–17, then, the pronouns are pronounced, although the English does not fully reflect it. Counsel, judgment, and understanding belong to wisdom; and that is power (v.14). Power naturally forms the transition to the practical side of these qualities—people in power use wisdom to govern the earth (see Isa 11:1–4, which prophesies how the Messiah will use wisdom in governing the world). The point is made forcefully with the use of paronomasia: *mᵉlāḵîm yimlōḵû* ("kings reign," v.15) and *śārîm yāśōrû* ("princes govern," v.16). Their government must be "just" (*ṣeḏeq,* v.15) if it derives from godly wisdom (see Notes).

17–21 Wisdom rewards those who love her. The emphasis of this section is that wisdom is accessible only to those who seek it. Loving (*'āhaḇ*) and seeking (*šāḥar*) point up the means of finding (*māṣā'*) wisdom (v.17). Those who find it obtain honor and wealth (vv.18, 21; see Notes). This honor and wealth come along the way of righteousness (v.20).

Notes

16 Many of the MT MSS have נְדִיבִים כָּל־שֹׁפְטֵי אָרֶץ (*nᵉḏîḇîm kol-šōp̱ᵉṭê 'āreṣ,* "sovereigns, all the judges of [the] earth"); the LXX reads, τύραννοι . . . κρατοῦσι γῆς (*tyrannoi kratousi gēs,* "sovereigns . . . rule the earth"). Toy suggests that the Hebrew here has assimilated to Ps 148:11 in its construction (p. 167).

21 At the end of this verse, the LXX adds a transition: "If I declare to you the things of daily occurrence, I will remember to recount the things of old."

4. *Third cycle (8:22–36)*

a. *Motivation: Wisdom preceded and delights in Creation*

8:22–31

22 "The LORD brought me forth as the first of his works,
before his deeds of old;
23 I was appointed from eternity,
from the beginning, before the world began.
24 When there were no oceans, I was given birth,
when there were no springs abounding with water;
25 before the mountains were settled in place,
before the hills, I was given birth,
26 before he made the earth or its fields
or any of the dust of the world.
27 I was there when he set the heavens in place,
when he marked out the horizon on the face of the
deep,
28 when he established the clouds above
and fixed securely the fountains of the deep,
29 when he gave the sea its boundary
so the waters would not overstep his command,
and when he marked out the foundations of the earth.
30 Then I was the craftsman at his side.
I was filled with delight day after day,
rejoicing always in his presence,
31 rejoicing in his whole world
and delighting in mankind.

22–23 In this third cycle, the motivation for receiving wisdom precedes the invitation. The first two verses provide a summary: Yahweh possessed wisdom before the creation of the world (v.23). The verb *qānāh* can mean either "possess" or "create." The older versions chose "possess"; otherwise it might sound as if God lacked wisdom and so created it before the world began. They wanted to avoid saying that wisdom was not eternal. Arius liked the idea of Christ as the meaning of wisdom and chose "create" as the verb. Athanasius read "constituted me as the head of creation." The verb *qānāh* occurs twelve times in Proverbs with the idea of acquire; but the LXX and Syriac have the idea of "create." Although the idea is that wisdom existed before Creation, the parallel ideas in these verses (*qānānî* ["brought me forth," v.22]; *nissaktî* ["I was appointed," v.23]; and *ḥôlāltî* ["I was given birth," v.24]) argue for the idea of "create/establish" (see R.N. Whybray, "Proverbs 8:22–31 and Its Supposed Prototypes," VetTest 15 [1965]: 504–14; W.A. Irwin, "Where Shall Wisdom Be Found," JBL 80 [1961]: 133–42).

24–31 The summary statement is now developed in a lengthy treatment of wisdom as the agent of Creation. Verses 24–26 reiterate that wisdom was established before Creation (*tᵉhōmôṯ*, "oceans" [v.24] or "deeps," recalling Creation); vv.27–29 declare that wisdom was present when God created (notice the same progress of preexistence to world-creating acts for the Logos in the NT [John 1:1–3; Col 1:15–16]); and vv.30–31 tell how wisdom rejoiced in God's creation ("delight day after day" [v.30] recalls that "God saw that it was good," Gen 1 *passim*).

Critical to the interpretation of this section is the meaning of *'āmôn* ("craftsman") in v.30. R.B.Y. Scott surveys the various possible interpretations, rejecting "master craftsman," "nursing child," "foster father," etc., and choosing rather the idea of "faithful"—a binding or living link ("Wisdom in Creation: The *'Āmōn* of Proverbs 8:30," VetTest 10 [1960]: 213–23). The image of "child" does fit the metaphor of birth. But "workman/craftsman" has the most support (LXX; Vul.; Syr.; Targ.; S of Songs 7:1 [2 MT]; Jer 52:15; see also Patrick W. Skehan, "Structures in Poems on Wisdom: Proverbs 8 and Sirach 24," CBQ 41 [1979]: 365–79).

b. *Invitation: Listen to wisdom and be blessed*

8:32–36

32 "Now then, my sons, listen to me;
blessed are those who keep my ways.
33 Listen to my instruction and be wise;
do not ignore it.
34 Blessed is the man who listens to me,
watching daily at my doors,
waiting at my doorway.
35 For whoever finds me finds life
and receives favor from the LORD.
36 But whoever fails to find me harms himself;
all who hate me love death."

32–36 Verses 32–33 offer the explanation to the sons to listen, for a blessing is in store for all who live by wisdom's teachings. The explanation of this follows in vv.34–36. The alternatives could not be more striking—it is a choice between life and favor (vv.34–35) and harm and danger (v.36). This contrast is further marked out by the verb "finds me" (*māṣā'*, v.35) and "fails to find me" (*ḥāṭā'*, lit., "misses me," v.36).

O. *Consequences of Accepting the Invitations of Wisdom or Folly (9:1–18)*

Chapter 9 forms the conclusion of the lengthy nine-chapter introduction to the book. Both wisdom and folly will make their final appeals; and both appeal to the simpletons, those who need to live by wisdom but who are most easily influenced by folly. Wisdom offers life with no mention of pleasure; folly offers pleasure with no mention of death.

1. *Accepting wisdom (9:1–12)*

a. *Invitation to wisdom (9:1–6)*

1) *Preparations for the invitation*

9:1–3

1 Wisdom has built her house;
she has hewn out its seven pillars.
2 She has prepared her meat and mixed her wine;
she has also set her table.
3 She has sent out her maids, and she calls
from the highest point of the city.

1 The text makes a transition now from the previous passage; wisdom was last seen as the director of work on the cosmic level (8:30–31), but now she is portrayed among humans. She has prepared a house and established it on seven pillars. This is probably a reference to the habitable world (8:31), which is spacious and enduring. For the equation of a house with the world, see 8:29; Job 38:6; and Psalm 104:5 (see Gustav Boström, *Proverbia Studien: die Weisheit and des fremde Weib in Spr. 1–9* [Lunds Universitetets Arsskrift, N.F., 1935], Aud. I, Bd. 30, Nr. 3, pp. 1–14). The seven "pillars" (*'ammûḏeyhā*) have been variously interpreted (Boström even suggests the seven planets). They seem to be part of the imagery of the house but may have cosmic references. The phrase has given rise to expressions like "the seven pillars of wisdom" or "the house that wisdom builds." Since seven is a sacred or ominous concept, the point seems to be that wisdom produces a perfect world.

2–3 Wisdom has prepared a sumptuous banquet in this house and sends out her maids to call the simple to come and eat (M. Lichtenstein, "The Banquet Motif in Keret and in Proverbs 9," JANES 1 [1968/69]: 19–31). The figures of meat and wine represent the good teaching of wisdom that will be palatable and profitable. Compare Isaiah 55:1–2 and John 6:51, 55 for similar uses of the figures. It is uncertain whether the mixing of wine here refers to the practice of mixing wine with spices or mixing it with water as the Greeks did (see the LXX of v.2, which introduces the Greek custom with the word *krater* ["bowl"]; cf. Prov 23:30; Isa 5:22). So just as one would prepare a banquet and invite guests, wisdom prepares to press her appeal. All this imagery lets the simpleton know that what wisdom has to offer is marvelous.

2) *Wisdom's invitation*

9:4–6

4 "Let all who are simple come in here!"
she says to those who lack judgment.
5 "Come, eat my food
and drink the wine I have mixed.
6 Leave your simple ways and you will live;
walk in the way of understanding.

4–6 The call goes out to the simple (*mî-p̱eṯî;* NIV, "who are simple"), to those "who lack judgment" (*ḥ^asar-lēḇ*), to turn aside to wisdom (v.4). Carrying the figure of eating forward, the writer invites people to eat the food and drink the wine, i.e., to appropriate the teaching of wisdom (v.5). This acceptance would necessarily prompt the simpleton to abandon the "simple ways" (*p^eṯā'yim*) and live (v.6). Some translations have interpreted this plural as simpletons—do not keep company with simpletons. The proper direction is on the way of understanding.

b. *Description of responses (9:7–11)*

The connection of these verses to the context is not immediately apparent, and so various commentators attempt different reconstructions. For example, Scott suggests that vv.10–12 continue the invitation and form the original end of vv.1–9 (*Proverbs/Ecclesiastes*, p. 76). Others regard vv.7–12 entirely as a later insertion. As the text stands one can see the descriptions of the scoffer (vv.7–8a) and the wise man (vv.8b–11) as samples of the two responses to the invitation of wisdom.

1) *The scoffer*

9:7–8a

[7]"Whoever corrects a mocker invites insult;
whoever rebukes a wicked man incurs abuse.
[8]Do not rebuke a mocker or he will hate you;

7–8a The scoffer has been met before in the book. He is the person who will not live by wise and moral teachings and is not content to let others do so without his cynical mocking. The warning is that anyone who tries to correct a mocker is asking for trouble. "Strife" or "insult" (*qālôn*) and "abuse" (*mûmô*) are second nature to this cynical heckler (v.7). The only response such rebuke will receive is hatred; so the warning is put in the form of a negative jussive: "Do not rebuke" (*'al-tôḵah*, v.8a). The idea of hatred is a spontaneous rejection as well as a dislike for the one trying to correct the mocker.

2) *The wise man*

9:8b–11

rebuke a wise man and he will love you.
[9]Instruct a wise man and he will be wiser still;
teach a righteous man and he will add to his learning.

[10]"The fear of the LORD is the beginning of wisdom,
and knowledge of the Holy One is understanding.
[11]For through me your days will be many,
and years will be added to your life.

8b–11 The authentically parallel idea forms the contrast—the wise person will love the one trying to correct him (v.8b). "Love" (*'āhaḇ*), conversely, has the idea of choosing and embracing; so this is the profitable response to corrective teaching. The parallelism of "wise" (*ḥāḵām*) and "righteous" (*ṣaddîq*) in v.9 underscores the interrelationship between these qualities and shows the predisposition of those who are teachable. Moreover, the theme of the fear of the Lord (v.10) is brought forward here, because this is the foundation of all wisdom and all righteousness (1:7). The epithet "Holy One" is the plural *qᵉḏōšîm;* although translated "holy men" by the Targum, the plural probably is meant to signify the majestic nature of the Lord—he is "All-holy" (Greenstone, p. 94). In the final analysis those who fear the Lord, add to their learning, and receive discipline, will look forward to a long and productive life.

c. *Consequence: Reward*

9:12

[12]If you are wise, your wisdom will reward you;
if you are a mocker, you alone will suffer."

12 The conclusion of the matter is expressed by the antithetically parallel ideas: Wisdom rewards the wise, but mockery suffers alone. "Your wisdom will reward you" (*ḥāḵamtā lāḵ*) is literally "you are wise to yourself," meaning that wisdom brings its own reward; it is sufficiently satisfying to be worth pursuing. Conversely, "if you are a mocker [*wᵉlaṣtā*], you alone must bear it [*lᵉḇaddᵉḵā tiśśā'*; NIV, 'you alone will suffer']." These words anticipate the teachings of James (cf. James 3:1–12), that words we speak will haunt us through life (see Notes).

Notes

12 The LXX has this expansion: "Forsake folly, that you may reign forever; and seek discretion and direct understanding in knowledge."

2. *Accepting the invitation of folly (9:13–18)*

a. *Invitation (9:13–17)*

1) *Situation of the invitation*

9:13–15

13 The woman Folly is loud;
she is undisciplined and without knowledge.
14 She sits at the door of her house,
on a seat at the highest point of the city,
15 calling out to those who pass by,
who go straight on their way.

13 Now the rival "woman Folly" presses her appeal for the naive to come and eat from her provision. The translation "the woman Folly" for *'ēšeṯ kᵉsîlûṯ* is better than "foolish woman"; she is the counterpart of the personification of wisdom. Her character is described as "loud" (*hōmîyāh*), "undisciplined" (*pᵉṯayyûṯ*), and "without knowledge" (see Notes). "Loud" comes close to the idea of riotous: McKane defines her as restless and rootless (p. 366). *Pᵉṯayyûṯ* portrays her as foolish and simplistic. To these troubling qualities is added the idea of ignorance, which must be moral ignorance in Proverbs. (See D. Winton Thomas, though, for the idea of *yāḏa'* meaning "become still," "be at rest," yielding here "restless" ["A Note on *bal yadᵉ'ā* in Prov. 10:13," JTS 4 (1953): 23–24].)

14–15 Folly's position (v.14) is prominent in the city streets. Here we must notice how she often imitates wisdom (cf. v.3) so that only the cautious and discerning will make the right choice. Her invitation, likewise, is to the passersby (v.15), here described as those "who go straight" (*hamyaššᵉrîm*) on their ways. This would identify them as quiet and unwary.

Notes

13 The text of v.13 is uncertain. The MT has "The foolish woman is boisterous, simplicity, and knows not what." The LXX reads: "A foolish and impudent woman comes to lack a morsel, she who knows not shame." The Syriac has "a woman lacking in discretion, seductive." The Targum translates it "a foolish woman and a gadabout, ignorant, and she knows not good."

The Vulgate has "a woman foolish and noisy, and full of wiles, and knowing nothing at all." The point of the passage seems to be a description of this woman who is seductive and without knowledge of moral integrity (see Toy, p. 189).

---

2) *Invitation*

9:16–17

16 "Let all who are simple come in here!"
she says to those who lack judgment.
17 "Stolen water is sweet;
food eaten in secret is delicious!"

16–17 Folly's invitation parrots wisdom's *mî-p̱eṯî* (see v.4): "all who are simple." This competing voice, albeit louder and more appealing to those who "lack judgment," likewise invites people to eat. "Stolen water" (*mayim-g^enûḇîm,* v.17) is now offered to passersby instead of mixed wine from wisdom. The "water" is only sweeter than "wine" because it is stolen, much as food seems more delicious because it is unjustly gained—the idea of getting away with something is appealing to the baser instincts. Of course, the figures here are similar to those in the section of wisdom: the words and ways of folly are compared to food and drink. Compare Proverbs 5:15–16 (water) and 30:20 (bread) to see the specification as sexual folly (see Notes on v.18).

b. *Consequence: death*

9:18

18 But little do they know that the dead are there,
that her guests are in the depths of the grave.

18 The contrast with Wisdom's banquet continues, but now the consequence for Folly's "guests" is startling. The naive who enter her banquet hall do not know that the dead are there. These "dead" are the *r^ep̱ā'îm,* often translated "shades." It refers to the dead who lead a shadowy existence in Sheol (see comment on 2:18–19; cf. Job 3:13–19; Ps 88:5; Isa 14:9–11). The verse approximates the "as–if" motif of wisdom literature—those ensnared by folly are as good as in hell, for that house is a throat to hell. Many "eat" on earth what they "digest" in hell. For a similar motif of death, see the sayings of Ptah-hotep (ANET, pp. 412–14). The point is that the life of folly—a life style of undisciplined, immoral, riotous living—runs counter to God's plan of life and inevitably leads to death. Jesus will warn people to avoid this broad way and follow the straight and narrow path of righteous, wise living.

Notes

---

18 The LXX adds to the end of v.18: "But turn away, linger not in the place, neither set your eye on her: for thus will you go through alien water; but abstain from alien water, drink not from an alien fountain, that you may live long, that years of life may be added to you."

III. The First Collection of Solomonic Proverbs (10:1–22:16)

Beginning with chapter 10 there is a notable change in the form of the material. No longer do we find the forceful admonitions to seek wisdom, the lengthy poems, or the developed pictures and personifications. Instead we find what more closely corresponds to the title "Proverbs"—a collection of independent, miscellaneous aphorisms, dealing mostly with the consequences of right or wrong actions on various topics. McKane classifies these topics generally into old wisdom sayings that are concerned with the education of the individual, community-life topics that address harmful effects of antisocial behavior, and expressions of religious piety that express moralism from the Yahwistic faith (p. 415).

Each saying falls into one of a number of parallel patterns. Whybray lists and explains the most common of these: *antithetical parallelism*, pointing to a contrast between the wise and the foolish ("A wise son brings joy to his father / a foolish son is his mother's bane," cf. 10:1); *synonymous parallelism*, giving the statement greater comprehensiveness and authority ("Pride comes before disaster / and arrogance before a fall," cf. 16:18); the *continuous sentence*, preserving the twofold shape of the saying but simply running the thought on to the second line ("A strong man who trusts in the fear of the LORD / will be a refuge for his sons," cf. 14:26); *comparisons*, in which comparative value judgments are offered instead of black and white decisions ("If the righteous in the land get their deserts / how much more the wicked and the sinner!" cf. 11:31); and the *statement and explanation* ("A king's threat is like a lion's roar / one who ignores it is his own worst enemy," cf. 20:2) (Whybray, *Book of Proverbs*, pp. 57–59).

Notes

The proverbs in chs. 10:1–22:16 seem to defy an orderly arrangement or outline but are indeed a "collection" of proverbs. With this in mind, yet still endeavoring to make this section as accessible and useable as possible to the reader, I gave a topical heading to each of the proverbs and then arranged a topical index (see the Introduction).

Wisdom, its affect on others

10:1

[1]The proverbs of Solomon:

A wise son brings joy to his father,
but a foolish son grief to his mother.

1 This antithetical saying declares that the consequences of wisdom or folly in the child ("son" is idiomatic) affects the parents accordingly (cf. 17:21, 25; 23:24–25; 28:7; 29:3; also Ptah-hotep in ANET, p. 413).

Righteousness, its value

10:2

[2]Ill-gotten treasures are of no value,
but righteousness delivers from death.

2 The sage asserts that righteousness has far greater value than ill-gotten wealth. *Ṣᵉḏāqāh* takes on the meaning of honesty in this contrast (NIV, "righteousness"). Wealth in general can only be enjoyed for a while, but righteousness delivers from mortal danger (*māweṯ*, "death").

Rewards, satisfaction of needs

10:3

[3]The LORD does not let the righteous go hungry
but he thwarts the craving of the wicked.

3 In another antithetical saying, the general observation is that the Lord rewards the righteous with the satisfaction of their needs. The text literally says that he will not leave unsatisfied "the appetite [*nep̱eš*, lit., 'soul'] of the righteous," which here includes the inner urge toward success. Conversely, McKane says, "The wicked are condemned to live forever with their unfulfilled, and so sterile, desires, which cannot be transformed into practical attainment" (p. 426).

Wealth, through diligence

10:4

[4]Lazy hands make a man poor,
but diligent hands bring wealth.

4 This saying attributes wealth to diligence. "Lazy hands" (*kap̱-rᵉmîyāh*, lit., "slack hand") refers to the careless work that such hands produce. See further Norman C. Habel, "Wisdom, Wealth, and Poverty Paradigms in the Book of Proverbs," *Bible Bhashyam* 14 (1988): 28–49.

Diligence, opposite of idleness

10:5

[5]He who gathers crops in summer is a wise son,
but he who sleeps during harvest is a disgraceful son.

5 Once again idleness, which leads to ruin, is contrasted with diligence. The wise son seizes the opportunities with keen insight into the importance of the season.

Rewards, words of blessing

10:6

[6]Blessings crown the head of the righteous,
but violence overwhelms the mouth of the wicked.

6 The focus of this contrast is on rewards. We would expect a curse to be the antithesis of "blessings." But the point is rather that behind the speech of the wicked is aggressive "violence" (*ḥāmās*); so he cannot be trusted (McKane, p. 422).

Reputation, good

10:7

[7]The memory of the righteous will be a blessing,
but the name of the wicked will rot.

7 Likewise, a reputation is determined by righteousness or wickedness. "Name" (*šēm*) and "memorial" (*zēker*) are often paired as synonyms. "Name" refers to fame; the name of the wicked will eventually disappear, and it will leave a bad memory that excites abhorrence. See also Meri-ka-re (ANET, p. 415).

Conduct, wise and foolish

10:8–10

[8]The wise in heart accept commands,
but a chattering fool comes to ruin.

[9]The man of integrity walks securely,
but he who takes crooked paths will be found out.

[10]He who winks maliciously causes grief,
and a chattering fool comes to ruin.

8–10 Next are three sayings contrasting the wise with the fool. The first exhorts compliance with "commands" (*miṣwōṯ* may refer to scriptural commands) from superiors—a fool talks too much to be attentive to them. The second holds out the promise that security goes with those who have "integrity" (*tōm*), but the insecurity of retribution awaits the perverse. Verse 10 departs from the normal antithetical pattern to form a comparison: shifty signs, although grievous, are not as ruinous as foolish talk (v.10b is identical to v.8b). Both are to be avoided.

Conduct, good and evil

10:11–12

[11]The mouth of the righteous is a fountain of life,
but violence overwhelms the mouth of the wicked.

[12]Hatred stirs up dissension,
but love covers over all wrongs.

11–12 Two pairs of sayings (vv.11–12, 13–14) contrast good and evil and wisdom and folly (see R.B.Y. Scott, "Wise and Foolish, Righteous and Wicked" VetTest 29 [1972]: 146–65). What the righteous say is beneficial to life, unlike the aggressive violence of the fool (cf. v.8b). The idea of the "fountain of life" (v.11) may come from Psalm 36:9 (see also Prov 13:14; 14:27; 16:22; Ezek 47:1–12; John 7:38). The second proverb (v.12) of the first pair compares the attitudes behind the two types: the wicked are motivated by hatred that brings dissension but the righteous by love that is harmonious. Love's covering wrongs is harmonious with forgiveness (see 1 Peter 4:8).

Speech, wise or foolish

10:13–14

[13]Wisdom is found on the lips of the discerning,
but a rod is for the back of him who lacks judgment.

[14]Wise men store up knowledge,
but the mouth of a fool invites ruin.

13–14 In the second pair of sayings, attention turns to wisdom and folly. In v.13 the critically perceptive person (*nāḇôn;* NIV, "discerning") speaks wisdom, unlike the fool who constantly needs correction (cf. Ps 32:8–9). The other proverb extols the wisdom of silently storing knowledge rather than foolishly talking prematurely (see James 3:13–18; Ptah-hotep and Amenemope in ANET, pp. 414, 423).

Wealth, security

10:15

[15]The wealth of the rich is their fortified city,
but poverty is the ruin of the poor.

15 A contrast is provided here between rich and poor: Security comes with wealth. The image used is of a "fortified city" (*qiryaṯ ʿuzzô*), protecting its inhabitants against all adversity.

Rewards, life or ruin

10:16

[16]The wages of the righteous bring them life,
but the income of the wicked brings them punishment.

16 Rewards are determined by moral choices—righteousness bringing life, wickedness punishment (see Rom 6:23). The point seems to be that what one receives in life depends on a wise use of gifts and a righteous character. Kidner admonishes to not blame poverty for the quality of life (*Proverbs,* pp. 87–88). The point again is to live righteously. (See also D.W. Thomas, "The Meaning of *ḥaṭṭāʾṯ* in Proverbs 10:16," JTS 15 [1964]: 295–96.)

Discipline, its benefit

10:17

[17]He who heeds discipline shows the way to life,
but whoever ignores correction leads others astray.

17 Learning to "accept" discipline is wise because it will benefit others. The participle *šômēr* means holding fast to discipline as a path of life (NIV, "heeds"). Abandoning (*ʿōzēḇ;* NIV, "ignores") correction also influences others, unfortunately.

Speech, lies and slander

10:18

[18]He who conceals his hatred has lying lips,
and whoever spreads slander is a fool.

18 In this comparison two errors are given, the second being climactic: hypocrisy is bad enough, slander is worse. At least in the first one—the "lying lips"—one keeps hatred to himself. In the ancient world there is much in wisdom literature that condemns lying and slander (see Amenemope, ANET, p. 423, and Ahiqar, ANET, p. 429).

Speech, controlled

10:19

[19] When words are many, sin is not absent,
but he who holds his tongue is wise.

19 Controlling the tongue helps avoid sin (see James 3:1–12 for a discussion of the loose tongue).

Speech, valuable

10:20

[20] The tongue of the righteous is choice silver,
but the heart of the wicked is of little value.

20 What the righteous say is infinitely more valuable than what the wicked intend. The contrast is between the tongue (i.e., what is said) and the mind ("heart," i.e., what is determined). Righteous speech, like silver, is valuable and treasured.

Speech, edifying

10:21

[21] The lips of the righteous nourish many,
but fools die for lack of judgment.

21 Moreover, what the righteous say is edifying—it enhances (*yirʿû;* NIV, "nourishes") common life. "Fools" (*'ᵉwîlîm*), characterized by a lack of discipline and little wit, ruin their lives and others as well.

Wealth, a blessing

10:22

[22] The blessing of the LORD brings wealth,
and he adds no trouble to it.

22 God brings wealth to those whom he blesses—and without anxiety (*ʿeṣeḇ;* NIV, "trouble"). Psalm 127:1–3 too stresses how the Lord gives to his beloved prosperity and safety as well as peace of mind. The proverb is also a warning against self-sufficiency.

Pleasure, good and evil

10:23

[23]A fool finds pleasure in evil conduct,
but a man of understanding delights in wisdom.

23 One's character is revealed in what one enjoys. Evil conduct to the fool is "like sport" (*kiśḥôq;* NIV, "pleasure"), literally, like a laugh; like child's play, it is so easy (Plaut, p. 132). This evil conduct is contrasted with wisdom, the delight of those who have understanding.

Prospect for life, hopes and fears

10:24

[24]What the wicked dreads will overtake him;
what the righteous desire will be granted.

24 This little contrast declares the working out of the fear of the wicked and the desire of the righteous. The "terror of the wicked" (*m^e^g̱ôraṯ rāšā';* NIV, "wicked dread") will come on them, so that there is no security for them; the "desire" (*ta'^a^wāh*) of the righteous, that which they long for in their righteous life style, will be given to them.

Confidence in calamity

10:25

[25]When the storm has swept by, the wicked are gone,
but the righteous stand firm forever.

25 Survival in catastrophes of life is reserved for the righteous; for they are properly prepared to meet the real tests of life (Plaut, p. 132). Matthew 7:24–27 addresses the same point: If people base their lives on temporal values, they must know that they can be quickly swept away.

Servants, lazy

10:26

[26]As vinegar to the teeth and smoke to the eyes,
so is a sluggard to those who send him.

26 Vinegar to the teeth is an irritant that is unpleasant to experience, and smoke to the eyes is a hindrance to progress. This little proverb portrays the aggravation in sending a lazy servant on a mission—it could be a confusing, unpleasant ordeal.

Fear of the Lord, life giving

10:27

[27]The fear of the LORD adds length to life,
but the years of the wicked are cut short.

27 The fear of the Lord, which is the beginning of wisdom (1:7), contributes to a long and prosperous life. This is a general saying. Why the righteous suffer and even die young is a problem that perplexed Israel's sages (cf. Job; Pss 49; 73).

Prospect for life, joy and ruin

10:28

> 28 The prospect of the righteous is joy,
> but the hopes of the wicked come to nothing.

28 This is a contrast of expectations: the righteous will experience the joyful fulfillment of their hopes, but what the wicked hope for will be dashed. The proverb is a general maxim based on God's justice.

Security, the way of the Lord

10:29

> 29 The way of the LORD is a refuge for the righteous,
> but it is the ruin of those who do evil.

29 The "way of the LORD" refers to God's providential administration of life. Thus divine justice will be security for the righteous and disaster for the wicked.

Security, of the righteous

10:30

> 30 The righteous will never be uprooted,
> but the wicked will not remain in the land.

30 This proverb concerns the enjoyment of covenantal promises—dwelling in the land of Israel. It is promised to the righteous (see Lev 26; Ps 92). If the people lived in righteousness, they would enjoy the land; if not, they would be exiled.

Speech, wise or perverse

10:31

> 31 The mouth of the righteous brings forth wisdom,
> but a perverse tongue will be cut out.

31 Righteous speech can be beneficial to others and pleasing to God; if it is perverse, it is a complete waste of words—no one wants to listen to the latter. The bold image of cutting out the tongue is hyperbolic.

Speech, pleasing or perverse

10:32

> 32 The lips of the righteous know what is fitting,
> but the mouth of the wicked only what is perverse.

32 The righteous speak words that produce pleasure or delight (*rāṣôn;* NIV, "what is fitting"). Proverbs teaches that good people use few words and choose them well. The wicked say things that are worthless or perverse, generally without prior consideration and beyond prudent limits.

Honesty, in business

11:1

> [1]The LORD abhors dishonest scales,
> but accurate weights are his delight.

1 Honesty pleases the Lord. This contrast between what the Lord abhors and delights in elaborates on the point. The Scriptures throughout condemn dishonesty in business (see Lev 19:35–36; Deut 25:13–16; Amos 8:5; et al.). Likewise, the law codes of the ancient world ruled against it (see ANET, pp. 388, 423). Whatever the Lord "abhors" (*tôʻᵃḇaṯ*) must be avoided. Thus to be accepted by God in one's transactions, one must deal honestly (see 16:11; 20:10, 23).

Humility, wise and honorable

11:2

> [2]When pride comes, then comes disgrace,
> but with humility comes wisdom.

2 Humility avoids disgrace and leads to wisdom (notice the sounds of the first colon: *bā'-zāḏôn wayyāḇō' qālôn,* "when pride comes, then comes disgrace"). "Pride" (*zāḏôn*) is literally a boiling up; and so hubris, an overstepping of the boundaries and insubordination, is meant. Humility describes those who know their place; but those who are proud, Plaut says, are inflated to the level of self-bestowed divinity (p. 136). The proud will have their egos deflated (*qālôn,* "made light of," "disgrace").

Integrity, a preservation

11:3

> [3]The integrity of the upright guides them,
> but the unfaithful are destroyed by their duplicity.

3 Here is another proverb affirming the value of integrity. The contrast is between the upright and the unfaithful; those who use treachery (*seleḇ bôgᵉḏîm,* lit., "the crookedness of the unfaithful") are destroyed rather than guided by it.

Righteousness, better than wealth

11:4

> [4]Wealth is worthless in the day of wrath,
> but righteousness delivers from death.

4 The focus of this saying is on what is most useful when disaster strikes: righteousness or wealth. Whybray is correct in taking the "day of wrath" as divine punishment in this life (*Book of Proverbs,* p. 67; see further Job 21:30; Ezek 7:19; Zeph 1:18). Righteousness, therefore, which is pleasing to God, is more valuable than riches when anticipating divine justice.

Conduct, righteous and wicked

11:5–6

> 5 The righteousness of the blameless makes a straight way
> for them,
> but the wicked are brought down by their own
> wickedness.
>
> 6 The righteousness of the upright delivers them,
> but the unfaithful are trapped by evil desires.

5–6 Here are two proverbs contrasting the righteous with the wicked. The first teaches that the righteous enjoy security and serenity through life (*t^e^yaššēr darkô;* NIV, "makes a straight way," v.5). The second one states that the wicked are caught by their own evil desires—their sins catch up with them (v.6).

Prospect for life, of the wicked

11:7

> 7 When a wicked man dies, his hope perishes;
> all he expected from his power comes to nothing.

7 The subject of the "hope" (*tiqwāh*) of the wicked is developed in this proverb, showing its consequences—his expectations perish with him (see Ps 49). Any hope for long life or success borne of wickedness will be disappointed. The LXX adds an antithesis to this: "When the righteous dies, hope does not perish." The LXX translators apparently wanted to see the fulfillment of the hope of the righteous as the world to come. But this proverb is not antithetical.

Retribution, just

11:8

> 8 The righteous man is rescued from trouble,
> and it comes on the wicked instead.

8 Here is an expression of confidence in God's justice in bringing recompense into the world. The antithesis shows the consequences of actions with an unusual twist—the "trouble" (*ṣārāh*) the righteous escape falls on the wicked.

Speech, safety from slander

11:9

> 9 With his mouth the godless destroys his neighbor,
> but through knowledge the righteous escape.

9 This antithetical verse stresses that a righteous person can escape devastating slander through knowledge. The "godless" (*ḥānēp̱*, i.e., the hypocrite or flatterer) is the one who "destroys" (*yašḥiṯ*) a neighbor. The righteous will have sufficient knowledge and experience to identify and end the slander.

Emotions, joy when righteousness prevails

11:10

10When the righteous prosper, the city rejoices;
when the wicked perish, there are shouts of joy.

10 The common theme of this line is joy; it comes from either the success of the righteous or the ruin of the wicked (so an antithetical idea is present). Samples are 2 Kings 11:20 and Esther 8:15. Kidner notes: "However drab the world makes out virtue to be, it appreciates the boon of it in public life" (*Proverbs*, p. 91).

Speech, helpful or harmful

11:11

11Through the blessing of the upright a city is exalted,
but by the mouth of the wicked it is destroyed.

11 This is a similar contrast expressing the social effects of words (see also Meri-ka-re in ANET, p. 415). The "blessing of the upright" (*birkaṯ yešārîm*) are the beneficent words and deeds that bring enrichment to a community. But the words of the wicked have a disastrous effect on society, endangering, weakening, and ruining it with demoralizing, slanderous, and malicious criticism.

Speech, silence rather than derision

11:12

12A man who lacks judgment derides his neighbor,
but a man of understanding holds his tongue.

12 The next four proverbs (vv.12–15) follow the theme of talking. The first advises that it is proper to hold one's tongue rather than deride a neighbor. The wise man is a "man of discernment" (*'îš tebûnôṯ;* NIV, "man of understanding"); the other man lacks "judgment" (*lēḇ*). How one treats a neighbor is significant in Proverbs—one was expected to be a good neighbor. To despise (*bāz;* NIV, "derides") a neighbor was contemptible.

Speech, keeping confidence

11:13

13A gossip betrays a confidence,
but a trustworthy man keeps a secret.

13 Verse 13 is a contrast between the gossip and the "trustworthy man" (*ne'eman-rûaḥ;* lit., "trustworthy spirit"). The talebearer goes from one to another and speaks disparagingly about someone in a malicious manner—he cannot wait to share secrets that should be kept (see Lev 19:16; Jer 9:3). The talebearer is despised in society because he cannot be trusted.

Speech, good advice

11:14

14 For lack of guidance a nation falls,
but many advisers make victory sure.

14 Verse 14 is framed in a contrast as well, showing that advice is essential for the stability of a nation. The term *taḥbulôṯ* ("guidance") is comparable to steering a ship, here a ship of state (see Whybray, *Book of Proverbs,* p. 67; Prov 1:5)—without it the nation is in danger. Of course, the saying assumes that the counselors are wise and intelligent, if "victory" (*tešû'āh*) is sure.

Speech, avoid pledges

11:15

15 He who puts up security for another will surely suffer,
but whoever refuses to strike hands in pledge is safe.

15 The fourth saying instructs people to avoid pledges with strangers if they want to remain financially solid. The point of this proverb is to focus on the consequences of an action. The "stranger" (*zār;* NIV, "another") could refer to an individual from a different nation or merely to an unknown person; but it may here refer to someone from another clan or family (see Toy, p. 228).

Kindness, brings respect

11:16

16 A kindhearted woman gains respect,
but ruthless men gain only wealth.

16 Two contrasts are here juxtaposed: "a kindhearted woman" (*'ēšeṯ-ḥēn*) and "ruthless men," and "honor" (*kāḇôḏ;* NIV, "respect") and "wealth" (*'ōšer*). The idea seems to be that one can seize wealth by any means, but "honor" is the natural reward for the gracious person. Two additional lines are found in the LXX, but they do not seem to provide the full sense (see Notes).

Notes

16 The LXX adds: "She who hates virtue makes a throne for dishonor / the idle will be destitute of means." The NEB follows this and inserts the readings. Toy thinks that the MT records remnants but that the LXX does not provide the full meaning (p. 229).

Kindness, better than cruelty

11:17

17 A kind man benefits himself,
but a cruel man brings trouble on himself.

17 This saying contrasts the consequences of dispositions: "kindness" (*heseḏ*) is healthy, but anger brings trouble. One's health and well being are at risk if the personality is volatile. We may say such raging works against a person as a part of divine justice. The word "trouble" may recall Joshua 7:25–26—Achan troubled Israel.

Rewards, justly earned

11:18

> [18]The wicked man earns deceptive wages,
> but he who sows righteousness reaps a sure reward.

18 Ultimately, rewards are appropriate for different character traits. The line extols the benefits for one "who sows righteousness," i.e., one who inspires righteousness in others while practicing it himself. What is sown will yield fruit (1 Cor 9:11; 2 Cor 9:6; James 3:18). Scott suggests that this verse teaches that one answer to the prosperity of the wicked is that it does not last (*Proverbs/Ecclesiastes,* p. 88). Notice the paronomasia in the line: "deceptive" is *šāqer* and "reward" is *śeḵer.*

Conduct, brings life or death

11:19

> [19]The truly righteous man attains life,
> but he who pursues evil goes to his death.

19 Since life and death result from moral choices, righteousness must be pursued. Some versions have "son of righteousness," an idiom meaning "having the quality of righteousness." The MT has *kēn,* which KB[2] identifies as a participle from *kûn* and interprets to mean "steadfast in righteousness," while Toy (pp. 231–32) and McKane (p. 435) read it as *kān* and interpret it to mean "strive after, pursue" (see also Notes). "Life" and "death" describe the vicissitudes of this life but can also refer to beyond the grave.

Notes

---

19 The form כֵּן (*kēn,* "truly") is in one MS, the LXX, and the Syriac as בֵּן (*bēn,* "son"), giving the reading "son of righteousness." The use of the idiom, however, usually introduces evil qualities ("son of Belial," "son of death"). The participle *kēn,* meaning "steadfast," would serve to modify the word following.

Conduct, pleasing to God

11:20

> [20]The LORD detests men of perverse heart
> but he delights in those whose ways are blameless.

20 This contrast records other things that the Lord either detests or delights in. The "perverse heart" is a twisted mind, i.e., the whole spiritual being is influenced toward evil. This is an abomination to the Lord. Conversely, to please God one should follow a blameless course of life (see 2:21; 17:20).

Retribution, its certainty

11:21

21 Be sure of this: The wicked will not go unpunished,
but those who are righteous will go free.

21 God's just retribution is certain. The initial expression, "Be sure of this" (lit., "hand to hand"), means that it is settled; one can depend on it (see M. Anbar, "Proverbs 11:21; 16:15: *yd lyd* «sur le champ»," *Biblica* 53 [1972]: 537–38). Those who escape are called, literally, the "seed of the righteous," a phrase that describes a class of people—the righteous and their kind (cf. Isa 1:4; 65:23) (Whybray, *Book of Proverbs*, p. 69).

Character traits, beauty without discretion

11:22

22 Like a gold ring in a pig's snout
is a beautiful woman who shows no discretion.

22 This proverb uses emblematic parallelism to describe a beautiful woman without "discretion." The word is literally "taste" (*ṭāʿam*); this can mean physical taste (Exod 16:31), intellectual discretion (1 Sam 25:33—Abigail had it), or ethical judgment (Ps 119:66). Here the description is probably of a woman with no moral sensibility, no propriety—unchaste. She is compared to a pig with an ornament. Why join a beautiful ornament and an unworthy body? The pig will not know its value. So is a woman who has no discretion.

Prospect for life, good or bad

11:23

23 The desire of the righteous ends only in good,
but the hope of the wicked only in wrath.

23 The consequences of hope are determined by moral character. God rewards the righteous with prosperity; wrath eventually comes on the wicked.

Prosperity, for generosity

11:24–25

24 One man gives freely, yet gains even more;
another withholds unduly, but comes to poverty.

25 A generous man will prosper;
he who refreshes others will himself be refreshed.

24 The paradox presented here does not refer to financial investments. Rather, in God's economy generosity often determines prosperity: one must give in order to gain (see Ps 112:9; 2 Cor 9:6–9).

25 There are rewards for being generous—the person who is generous toward others will be provided for himself. The two lines are in synonymous parallelism. The first description, "a generous man," is literally "the soul of blessing" (*nep̱eš-berāḵāh*). "Blessing" is used in the Bible to describe a "present" (Gen 33:11) or "special favor" (Josh 15:19). The verb "made rich" (*ṯeḏuššān;* NIV, "prosper") is literally "to be made fat," drawing on the standard comparison between fatness and abundance or prosperity (Deut 32:15). The second line makes a comparison between providing water for the thirsty with generously providing for those in need (see Jer 31:25; cf. Lam 3:15). The kind act will be reciprocated.

Business, socially responsible

11:26

> 26 People curse the man who hoards grain,
> but blessing crowns him who is willing to sell.

26 This proverb reveals how a merchant's response to supply and demand will influence the customer's opinion of him. Some merchants hoard up the produce to raise the prices when there is a great need for the produce. Merchants must have a social conscience, too.

Prospect for life, realized desires

11:27

> 27 He who seeks good finds good will,
> but evil comes to him who searches for it.

27 One generally receives the consequences of the kind of life he pursues, whether good or evil. The line stresses that there is a divine justice. The expression "seeks [NIV, 'finds'] good will" (*yeḇaqqēš rāṣôn*) could refer to seeking God's favor (see Ps 5:12; Isa 49:8): whoever diligently seeks good is seeking divine favor.

Security, object of faith

11:28

> 28 Whoever trusts in his riches will fall,
> but the righteous will thrive like a green leaf.

28 Security and prosperity are determined by the object of faith. The righteous trust in the Lord and flourish. The image of the "green leaf" is a figure of prosperity and fertility throughout the ancient Near East. The image of falling uses the analogy of the physical act to portray coming to ruin in life.

Laziness, trouble and poverty

11:29

29 He who brings trouble on his family will inherit
only wind,
and the fool will be servant to the wise.

29 This proverb describes an avaricious man who deprives his family of livelihood and brings them to nothing but distress. He gains nothing for his efforts, "wind" signifying that which cannot be grasped (27:16; Eccl 1:14, 17). The second line suggests that one who foolishly mismanages his accounts may have to sell himself into slavery to the wise. So the ideas in the verse are complementary.

Righteousness, brings life

11:30

30 The fruit of the righteous is a tree of life,
and he who wins souls is wise.

30 Righteousness brings life. Both "fruit" and "tree of life" are metaphorical, the first image signifying what the righteous produce and the second identifying that as a healthy, long life. The second half of the verse refers to "winning souls." If the reading stands (see Notes), it would refer to capturing (*lōqēaḥ*, "to lay hold of, seize, conquer") people with ideas or influence (2 Sam 15:6). This is the wise course of action. (See further Daniel C. Snell, "'Taking Souls' in Proverbs 11:30," VetTest 33 [1983]: 362–65; he interprets this as "comprehends souls.")

Notes

---

30 The alternative reading is "he who takes away lives is violent." חָמָס (*ḥāmās*, "violent"), instead of חָכָם (*ḥāḵām*, "wise"), is reflected in the LXX and Syriac. If לֹקֵחַ נְפָשׁוֹת (*lōqēaḥ nepāśôṯ*) were interpreted positively ("winning souls"), "wise" could have easily been read through orthographic confusion. If the phrase were read negatively ("captures souls"), then "violent" fits well as the predicate. The line would then form an antithetical idea to the first line.

Retribution, its certainty

11:31

31 If the righteous receive their due on earth,
how much more the ungodly and the sinner!

31 Retribution for sin is certain, for the righteous and especially for the sinner. The proverb uses a "how much more" argument—if this be true, how much more this (argument from the lesser to the greater). The point is that divine justice deals with all sin; and if the righteous suffer for their sins, certainly the wicked will. The LXX introduces a new idea to the verse: "If the righteous be scarcely saved"; this is recorded in 1 Peter 4:18. See J. Barr, "בארץ— μόλις: Prov. 11:31 and 1 Pet. 4:18," JSS 20 (1975): 149–64 (see Notes).

Notes

31 The MT has בָּאָרֶץ (*bā'āreṣ*, "in the land"). The LXX's "scarcely" could have come from a *Vorlage* of בַּצָּרָה (*baṣṣārāh*, "deficiency," "want") or בַּצֹּר (*baṣṣōr*, "to cut off, shorten"), perhaps arising from confusion over letters. The verb יְשֻׁלָּם (*yᵉšullām*, "receive due") means "be recompensed" and could be only indirectly interpreted "be saved."

Discipline, its acceptance

12:1

1 Whoever loves discipline loves knowledge,
but he who hates correction is stupid.

1 Those who wish to improve themselves must learn to accept correction and learn from it. This proverb adds the contrast that to refuse it is brutish ("stupid" is *bā'ar*, descriptive of a dumb animal). It is almost as if one distinction between the human and the brute is this rational feature of receiving discipline.

Conduct, pleasing to God

12:2

2 A good man obtains favor from the LORD,
but the LORD condemns a crafty man.

2 Obtaining the Lord's favor is the result of virtue. Here the "good man" is contrasted with the "crafty man" (*'îš mᵉzimmôṯ*). The term *mᵉzimmāh* is used of "plans" in a good sense in Proverbs 1–9 but in a bad sense in chapters 10–24.

Righteousness, brings stability

12:3

3 A man cannot be established through wickedness,
but the righteous cannot be uprooted.

3 Only righteousness brings stability in life. This is true of society as well as individuals. Society cannot long endure if established on evil principles (see 10:25).

Character traits, noble wife

12:4

4 A wife of noble character is her husband's crown,
but a disgraceful wife is like decay in his bones.

4 The moral character of a woman affects her husband's enjoyment of life. The contrast is between a wife of noble character (*'ēšet̲-ḥayil,* as in 31:10) and a "disgraceful wife" (*m^e^b̲îšāh,* lit., "one who puts to shame," i.e., lowers his standing in the community). A "crown" is a symbol of honor and renown; but the negative side, using the figure of "decay in his bones," is that the disgrace will eat away her husband's strength and destroy his happiness.

Plans, just and unjust

12:5

> [5]The plans of the righteous are just,
> but the advice of the wicked is deceitful.

5 Righteous people are fair and honest. This verse shows that the thoughts (i.e., intentions) of good people are directed toward what is right, to simple justice. The adverse describes the wicked whose advice is deceitful and can lead only to evil.

Speech, skillful defense

12:6

> [6]The words of the wicked lie in wait for blood,
> but the speech of the upright rescues them.

6 The righteous will be able to make a skillful defense against false accusations. The vivid picture of "lying in wait for blood" conveys that the wicked make a trap by their false accusations (Whybray, *Book of Proverbs,* p. 73). The righteous, who through discipline and instruction have gained knowledge and perception, are able to avoid this danger.

Security, of the righteous

12:7

> [7]Wicked men are overthrown and are no more,
> but the house of the righteous stands firm.

7 Here is another saying on the stability of the righteous in the times of trouble (cf. Matt 7:24–27). The image of the fate of the wicked being "overthrown" (*hāp̲ôk̲*) is forceful and may allude to Genesis 19:21—they will be destroyed completely.

Wisdom, its appreciation

12:8

> [8]A man is praised according to his wisdom,
> but men with warped minds are despised.

8 This saying makes a point about the appreciation of clear thinking. The verse says that in proportion to or "according to" (*l^e^p̲î,* from *peh,* which is literally "mouth") wisdom is praise. The term for "wisdom" (*śek̲el,* lit., "intelligent," as in 1 Sam 25:3) refers to the capacity to think straight. The "warped mind" is *na'^a^wēh-lēb̲,* viz., the crooked heart that lacks the ability to see things as they really are and so makes wrong choices. No praise exists for this.

Humility, better than pretension

12:9

> 9 Better to be a nobody and yet have a servant
> than pretend to be somebody and have no food.

9 One should be satisfied with comfort at the expense of pretension. The point seems to be that some people live beyond their means in a vain show (*mi<u>tk</u>abbē<u>d</u>*, "pretend to be somebody," a Hithpael participle from *kā<u>b</u>ē<u>d</u>*, "to be weighty, honored"), whereas, if they lived modestly, they could have some of the conveniences of life, e.g., a servant. Another way to read v.9a is "Better is the lowly that serves himself" (see Notes).

Notes

---

9 The reading "and yet have a servant" is the reading of the LXX, Vulgate, Syriac, and RSV. וְעֶבֶד לוֹ (*w^{e}'e<u>b</u>e<u>d</u> lô*) is ambiguous, the preposition *lô* being either possessive ("have a servant") or indirect object ("servant for himself").

Character traits, compassion for animals

12:10

> 10 A righteous man cares for the needs of his animal,
> but the kindest acts of the wicked are cruel.

10 Compassion for animals is an indication of one's character. The righteous are kind to all God's creation (see Deut 25:4) because they have received his bounty. Toy suggests the analogy that if one is kind to the lower animals, he will surely be kind to humans (p. 248). Greenstone adds that even when the wicked are moved to compassion, they often manifest it in a cruel way (p. 129).

Diligence, prospers

12:11

> 11 He who works his land will have abundant food,
> but he who chases fantasies lacks judgment.

11 One ensures income through diligent work and not through unfounded speculation. *Rêqîm* means "vain things" or "empty things"; here it refers to "fantasies" (so NIV). Plaut advises that on the basis of this people should do their work and not run after some dream of a quick profit (p. 145).

Prosperity, for righteous pursuits

12:12

[12]The wicked desire the plunder of evil men,
but the root of the righteous flourishes.

12 The proverb is difficult to interpret as the many variant readings for it show. The text of v.12a says that "the wicked desire the net of evil men." Toy surveys all the readings and proposals; and while he finds the LXX reading clear, he prefers the emendation "wickedness is the net of bad men" (see Notes). The verse seems to be saying that there are good rewards for the righteous, but the wicked are dangerous and perhaps get caught in their own devices.

Notes

12 The MT in the first colon reads, "The wicked desires the net of evil men"; the LXX has "the desires of the wicked are evil"; the Syriac has "the wicked desire to do evil"; and the Latin has "the desire of the wicked is a defense of the worst [things or persons]." For a full discussion, see Toy, pp. 249–50.

Speech, dangerous

12:13

[13]An evil man is trapped by his sinful talk,
but a righteous man escapes trouble.

13 Righteous people avoid evil talk because it is dangerous. The point of the parallel expression is that the evil man catches himself in his words (lit., "the rebellion / transgression of his lips"). People who are righteous will not get themselves into a bind (*ṣārāh;* NIV, "trouble") by what they say.

Prosperity, through words and work

12:14

[14]From the fruit of his lips a man is filled with good
things
as surely as the work of his hands rewards him.

14 The verse teaches that proper speech and diligent work result in good things. If one's conversation is wise, intelligent, and honoring to God, it will result in blessing, i.e., good things will come of it.

Wisdom, takes advice

12:15

[15]The way of a fool seems right to him,
but a wise man listens to advice.

15 People demonstrate their maturity by how well they respond to sound advice. Reasonable people (i.e., "wise") will recognize and accept good advice, even if they themselves often give advice to others. "Advice" (*ʿēṣāh*) is an application of wisdom and knowledge to a specific situation, either by astute observation or well thought out opinion. The fool, on the other hand, is set in his own way and will not listen to advice. "The way of a fool" (*dereḵ ʾᵉwîl*) describes the headlong course of actions that are not abandoned even when good advice is offered.

Wisdom, overlooks insults

12:16

> [16]A fool shows his annoyance at once,
> but a prudent man overlooks an insult.

16 Those who are mature are able to handle criticism without responding instinctively and irrationally. McKane says that the fool's reaction is "like an injured animal and so his opponent knows that he has been wounded" (p. 442). The wise man does not give the enemy that satisfaction. It is not so much that the wise man represses anger or feelings but that he is more shrewd in dealing with it.

Speech, true and false witnesses

12:17

> [17]A truthful witness gives honest testimony,
> but a false witness tells lies.

17 The true witness (*ʾᵉmûnāh;* NIV, "truthful witness") is reliable because he tells the truth; he always utters what is right. The contrast is with the false witness and his lies.

Speech, wounding and healing

12:18

> [18]Reckless words pierce like a sword,
> but the tongue of the wise brings healing.

18 Those who are wise do not cause harm by their reckless talk. "Reckless words" (*bôṭeh*) has the idea of speaking hastily and unadvisably (see Lev 5:4; Num 30:7). Such talk is like a piercing sword—it wounds. Conversely, the tongue of the wise (metonymy for what the wise say) is "healing" (*marpēʾ*, which is metonymy of the effect, showing the opposite of the cutting, irresponsible words). The words are healing because they are faithful and true, gentle and kind, and uplifting and encouraging.

Speech, truth outlasts lies

12:19

> [19]Truthful lips endure forever,
> but a lying tongue lasts only a moment.

19 Truthfulness will outlive lies—forever. Or, conversely, as Plaut says, "Lies have generally limited staying power" (p. 147). The LXX saw the setting for this proverb in the courts of law: "True lips establish testimony, but a hasty witness has an unjust tongue." The little expression "only a moment" is literally "till I wink again" (*'argî'āh,* a denominative verb from *rega'*); it forms a circumlocution for the idea.

Plans, for evil or peace

12:20

20 There is deceit in the hearts of those who plot evil,
but joy for those who promote peace.

20 The contrast here is between plotting evil and promoting peace with a view to the consequences. The effect of plotting evil can only be sorrow and trouble, because "evil" (*rā'*) has the idea of pain in it. "Peace" (*šālôm*), on the other hand, refers to social wholeness and well being (see Pss 34:14; 37:37). The "counselors of peace," as the text literally reads, will reap the inner contentment from doing what is right as well as the pleasure of seeing positive results.

Security, of the righteous

12:21

21 No harm befalls the righteous,
but the wicked have their fill of trouble.

21 Here is a relative truth about the contrast between the righteous and the wicked with respect to calamity. "No harm befalls the righteous" means that decent people do not have frequent trouble of their own making, although Rashi took it to mean that the righteous do no evil even unintentionally (Greenstone, p. 134). *'Āwen* is "evil," "harm," "misfortune," or "calamity" and probably not sin in this instance. See also Genesis 50:20 and Romans 8:28, 35–39.

Speech, truth pleases God

12:22

22 The LORD detests lying lips,
but he delights in men who are truthful.

22 Truthfulness rather than falsehood pleases the Lord. The contrast in consequences is strong: "pleasure," "delight" (*rāṣôn*) versus "abomination" (*tô'ēḇāh;* NIV, "detests"). To speak falsehood is a misuse of a God-given faculty. The point the verse teaches is to act in good faith (*'āśāh* + *'emûnāh* in the OT carry this meaning, i.e., "the ones doing truth"; the NIV has "men who are truthful").

Speech, discretion

12:23

23 A prudent man keeps his knowledge to himself,
but the heart of fools blurts out folly.

23 Wisdom is distinguishable from folly in speech. The "prudent" (*'āḏām 'ārûm*, lit., "a shrewd man") restrain themselves from displaying knowledge. The verb "conceal" (*kōseh;* NIV, "keeps") does not mean that he never speaks; rather, it means he uses discretion. Conversely, the intent of "fools" (*kesîlîm*) is to call out "folly" (*'iwwelet*). McKane notes that the more one speaks the less likely he is able to speak effectively (p. 422).

Diligence, rules

12:24

> 24 Diligent hands will rule,
> but laziness ends in slave labor.

24 Diligence at work determines success and advancement. To put it bluntly, the diligent rise to the top and the lazy sink to the bottom. At the bottom they may be forced to work as if they owed it. For other proverbs extolling the virtue of industry, see 6:6–11; 10:4; 12:27; 13:4; 19:15; and 21:5.

Speech, encouraging

12:25

> 25 An anxious heart weighs a man down,
> but a kind word cheers him up.

25 Words of encouragement will lift the spirits of someone who is depressed through anxious fear. "Anxious" (*de'āḡāh*) is literally "anxiety" and "fear" (see Jer 49:23; Ezek 4:16; and for the verb *dā'aḡ*, see Ps 38:18 [19 MT]; Jer 17:8 [NIV, "worries"]). Anxiety in the heart bows the person down—bowing in the sense of physical mourning (Pss 35:14; 38:6). The "kind word" (*dāḇār ṭôḇ*) probably includes encouragement, kindness, and insight—saying that which the person needs to gain the proper perspective and renew hope and confidence. There is an effective wordplay in the verse: "weighs down" (*yašḥennāh*) and "cheers up" (*yeśammeḥennāh*). One should seek to turn depression into rejoicing by saying the right things.

Associations, dangerous

12:26

> 26 A righteous man is cautious in friendship,
> but the way of the wicked leads them astray.

26 The righteous cautiously avoid dangerous friendships. There is a great variety of ways this verse has been translated and interpreted. The verb *yāṯēr* ("is cautious") can be taken to mean "spy out," "examine," which makes a fine contrast to the "leading astray" (from *nā'āh*) of the "way of the wicked." Emerton takes *ytr* from *ntr* in the Hiphil, "to set free"; *yuttar* in the Hophal would yield the meaning "the righteous is delivered from harm [reading *mērā'āh*]" (J.A. Emerton, "A Note in Proverbs 12:26," ZAW 76 [1964]: 191–93). Another possibility is to interpret the line thus: "the righteous guides his friend aright." The proverb, at least, is advising correct action in friendships.

Diligence, successful

12:27

> 27 The lazy man does not roast his game,
> but the diligent man prizes his possessions.

27 Diligence leads to success. The negative image in this antithetical line is of the lazy person who cannot bring a project to completion. The verb *yaḥ^{a}rōk̲* is rare; in Aramaic it means "to roast" (i.e., "to scorch or singe by burning"). The use of it here is metaphorical: just as one who might hunt but never cook what he finds, so the lazy person never completes a project. The Midrash (Gen R 67:2) sees here an allusion to the Jacob and Esau story in Genesis 25. (But see Mitchell Dahood, "The Hapax *ḥarak* in Proverbs 12:27," *Biblica* 63 [1982]: 60–62; he translates "The languid man will roast no game for himself, but the diligent will come upon the wealth of the steppe.")

Righteousness, leads to immortality

12:28

> 28 In the way of righteousness there is life;
> along that path is immortality.

28 A righteous life style leads to immortality. The verse probably means that those who enter righteousness by faith and seek to live righteously are on the way to eternal life. "No death" (*'al-māwet̲*) may be taken to mean "immortality" (so NIV); but it could also mean permanence and stability in this life (see M. Dahood, "Immortality in Proverbs 12:28," *Biblica* 41 [1960]: 176–81). Some MSS and versions take the second colon of this verse as "there is a path that leads to death." McKane opts for this reading, noting that the MT was probably prejudiced toward the doctrine of immortality (pp. 451–52). In Proverbs and in the early OT, the teachings on immortality are not clear; and, specifically, unless there is an exception, *ḥayyîm* (NIV, "there is life") is not used in Proverbs of eternal life. So many prefer the antithetical parallelism to the synonymous.

Discipline, its acceptance

13:1

> 1 A wise son heeds his father's instruction,
> but a mocker does not listen to rebuke.

1 Those who are wise will respond properly to discipline. The point of this antithetical saying is teachability. The "scorner" (*lēṣ;* NIV, "mocker") is the highest level of a fool. He has no respect for authority, reviles religion, and, because he thinks that he knows what is best, is not teachable (Whybray, *Book of Proverbs,* p. 77). The change to a stronger word in the second line—*g^{e}'ārāh* ("rebuke")—shows that he does not respond to any level of discipline. The contrast is the wise son who listens to his father / teacher. Driver suggests the reading *m^{e}yussār,* "allows himself to be disciplined" (G.R. Driver, "Hebrew Notes on Prophets and Proverbs," JTS 41 [1940]: 174). The LXX has "a wise son listens to his father."

Speech, helpful or harmful

13:2

> [2]From the fruit of his lips a man enjoys good things,
> but the unfaithful have a craving for violence.

2 Words and wishes find their just rewards. This saying concerns the outcome of conduct; as Alden says, it is a common theme in Proverbs that you get what you deserve (pp. 104–5). The clauses in this verse do not fit very well; the LXX, therefore, has for the second line "the souls of the wicked perish untimely." More likely the second line is saying that the desire of the "unfaithful" (*bōgᵉḏîm* or "treacherous") is to obtain what does not belong to them. The "violence" that is their appetite refers to the violence that is done to others.

Speech, wisdom of discretion

13:3

> [3]He who guards his lips guards his life,
> but he who speaks rashly will come to ruin.

3 It is safest to hold one's tongue. The lesson is that a tight control over what one says prevents trouble. Here is a perfect antithesis on the subject of speech. For similar ideas see Proverbs 10:10; 17:28; James 3:1–12; and Ecclesiasticus 28:25; see also Amenemope (ch. 3, 5:15), who advises to "sleep a night before speaking." The old Arab proverb is appropriate: "Take heed that your tongue does not cut your throat" (O. Zöckler, *Proverbs*, ed. Charles Aiken, *Lange's Commentary on the Holy Scriptures* [Grand Rapids: Zondervan, n.d.], p. 134).

Diligence, better than daydreaming

13:4

> [4]The sluggard craves and gets nothing,
> but the desires of the diligent are fully satisfied.

4 The fulfillment of dreams demands diligence. The contrast is between the "soul of the slothful" (*napšô ʿāṣēl;* NIV, "the sluggard") and the "soul of the diligent" (*nepeš ḥāruṣîm;* NIV, "the desires of the diligent"). Rather than spend all day hoping for things that they do not have, the diligent will work toward realizing their dreams. McKane says, "Laziness is barren and encourages escapism; the illusory world of desire unrelated to attainment is a prison" (p. 458).

Conduct, hating falsehood or acting shamefully

13:5

> [5]The righteous hate what is false,
> but the wicked bring shame and disgrace.

5 Here is another contrast between the moral conduct of the righteous and the wicked: the righteous hate the way that is "false" (*šeqer*), but the wicked act vilely and shamefully. The verbs *yaḇʾîš* ("shame") and *yaḥpîr* ("disgrace") could be taken as a hendiadys: "spread the smell of scandal" (McKane, p. 460). For the usage of the idea of "stink" for *bā'aš*, see Exodus 5:21 and Ecclesiastes 10:1 (see Notes). Plaut notes: "Unhappily, the bad odor adheres not only to the liar but also to the one about whom he lies—especially when the lie is a big one" (p. 152).

Notes

5 There is a variety in the translations: The LXX has "is ashamed and without confidence"; the Targum has "is ashamed and put to the blush"; the Latin has "confounds and shall be confounded" (Toy, p. 263). The variety may be due in small part to the relation of בָּאַשׁ (*bā'aš*, "offensive to smell") to בּוֹשׁ (*bôš*, "shame") and how these are interpreted.

Righteousness, brings security

13:6

[6]Righteousness guards the man of integrity,
but wickedness overthrows the sinner.

6 Security in life resides with righteousness. This little contrast shows that righteousness, like a fortress, protects the man of integrity (see 2:11; 4:6). This may work through divine intervention or natural causes. "Righteousness" (*ṣ^e^d̲āqāh*) refers to that which conforms to the law and to order; so it would be natural to expect that the perfect walk (*tām-dārek̲*, lit., "the way of integrity"; NIV, "the man of integrity") would be safe. On the other side, perverse and malicious activity (*riš'āh*, "wickedness") plunges one into sinful activity.

Honesty, better than pretension

13:7

[7]One man pretends to be rich, yet has nothing;
another pretends to be poor, yet has great wealth.

7 People may not be what they seem to be. Some who are poor pretend to be rich, perhaps to save face; some who are rich pretend to be poor, perhaps to conceal wealth and avoid responsibilities. Although there are times when such pretending may not be wrong, the proverb seems to be instructing that people should be honest and unpretentious. An empty display or a concealing of means can come to no good. "Pretending to be rich" is like "pretending to be somebody" (cf. 12:9).

Wealth, its disadvantages

13:8

[8]A man's riches may ransom his life,
but a poor man hears no threat.

8 There are disadvantages to having possessions. On the surface the verse appears to be saying that only the rich are susceptible to kidnapping and robbery. The second line, however, says that the poor does not heed rebuke—he does not have money to buy off oppressors. The rich person is exposed to legal and powerful assaults and uses his wealth as ransom. The poor person is free from blackmail and so ignores the attack and endures the consequences of difficulties—he does not have money to buy off oppressors (see McKane, p. 458).

Prospect for life, endurance of the righteous

13:9

9 The light of the righteous shines brightly,
but the lamp of the wicked is snuffed out.

9 The righteous can anticipate a long and prosperous life. The images of light and dark are used effectively: "light" represents life, joy, and prosperity; and "dark" signifies adversity and death. The verb *yiśmāḥ* carries the meaning of "shines" rather than "rejoices" (KJV, NASB) (see Driver, "Problems in the Hebrew Text," p. 180; he shows the relation between bright and joy in Ugaritic). The figure of the light may very well be drawn from the enduring flame of the temple light.

Notes

9 The LXX adds, "Deceitful souls go astray in sins, but the righteous are pitiful and merciful."

Wisdom, takes advice

13:10

10 Pride only breeds quarrels,
but wisdom is found in those who take advice.

10 Those who are wise listen to advice rather than argue out of stubborn pride. The idea of "pride" (*zāḏôn*) here describes contempt for other opinions, a clash of competing and unyielding personalities (Kidner, *Proverbs*, p. 102). This kind of conceited person creates strife, enflames passions, and wounds feelings (McKane, p. 454). Only strife (*raq* goes with strife) can come from him. But the wise are "those who take advice" (*nô'āṣîm*).

Prosperity, honest investment

13:11

11 Dishonest money dwindles away,
but he who gathers money little by little makes it grow.

11 Steady and wise investment produces prosperity. This is a warning against wild speculation. The image of "hand by hand" (NIV, "little by little") stresses the diligent activity and the gradual growth of one's investment. But if the riches come quickly through some unfounded means, one could lose them just as easily. There is some question whether the text should read "in haste" (quick scheme) or "in vanity" (meaning either "dishonest" [so NIV] or transitory) (see Notes). The MT reads the latter; it could simply mean that the gain comes from something transitory or nonexistent, which may imply dishonesty.

Notes

---

11 The LXX, Vulgate, and RSV prefer "in haste." The change would be from מֵהֶבֶל (*mēhebel*, "in vanity") to מְבֹהָל (*m^ebōhāl*). The idea of "vanity" does not make a very good parallel antithetical with the idea of the gradual labor, and this no doubt led to the reading "in haste," which is easier.

Prospect for life, discouraging and encouraging

13:12

12 Hope deferred makes the heart sick,
but a longing fulfilled is a tree of life.

12 It is invigorating to realize hopes; to fail to do so can be discouraging or depressing (*mah^alāh-lēb*, "makes the heart sick"). This is a general saying, applicable to believers or unbelievers alike. Plaut elaborates that people can bear frustration only so long; they must have encouragement to continue (p. 153). Perhaps believers should make it part of their task to help others realize their hopes whenever possible.

Instruction, reward for heeding

13:13

13 He who scorns instruction will pay for it,
but he who respects a command is rewarded.

13 Safety lies in obedience to proper "instruction." The word *dābār* (lit., "word," "thing") signifies teaching in general and the word *miṣwāh* the more forceful instruction, viz., "a command." The use of these two terms has religious significance: they most often refer to Scripture. Kidner says that their use is a "reminder that revealed religion is presupposed in Proverbs" (*Proverbs*, p. 103). The vivid point made in *yēḥābel* ("will pay"; BHS suggests *y^eḥubbāl*, "be broken by") is that whoever despises the teaching will be treated as a debtor—he will pay for it if he offends against the law. The LXX adds three lines (see Notes).

Notes

---

13 The LXX adds, "A crafty son will have no good thing, but the affairs of a wise servant will be prosperous; and his path will be directed rightly."

Instruction, benefits for life

13:14

> [14]The teaching of the wise is a fountain of life,
> turning a man from the snares of death.

14 The teaching of wisdom is life giving. The second line is the consequence of the first: not only does it give life, it turns one from the snares of death. "Snares of death" suggests that death is like a hunter; McKane compares the idea to the Ugaritic god of death, Mot, carrying people off to the realm of the departed (p. 455). At least the line conveys mortal peril. The image of the "fountain of life" is used of "the mouth of the righteous" in 10:11 and "the fear of the LORD" in 14:27.

Discernment, brings favor

13:15

> [15]Good understanding wins favor,
> but the way of the unfaithful is hard.

15 Wisdom and intelligence add to one's social esteem. *Śēḵel-ṭôḇ* ("good understanding") describes the capacity for good sense, sound judgment, and wise opinions. The second line is a bit problematic; it says that the way of treachery passes away. Driver ("Problems in the Hebrew Text," p. 181) supports the idea with the reading "is not lasting" (see Notes).

Notes

---

15 Driver suggests that אֵי (*'ê,* "not") was dropped before אֵיתָן (*'êṯān;* NIV, "hard") by haplography and so the reading should be "is not lasting." The LXX, Syriac, and Targum have "are destroyed."

Knowledge, basis of prudent acts

13:16

> [16]Every prudent man acts out of knowledge,
> but a fool exposes his folly.

16 Actions either display wisdom or expose folly. The wise will study the facts and then make decisions. The "prudent" here is *'ārûm,* one who knows the circumstances, the dangers, and the pitfalls. This makes him cautious. Not so the fool! He will eventually make a fool of himself because it is his nature. McKane sees in *yip̄rōś* ("exposes") the figure of a peddler displaying his wares: "he spreads out folly" (McKane, p. 456).

Servants, wicked or faithful

13:17

17 A wicked messenger falls into trouble,
but a trustworthy envoy brings healing.

17 The faithfulness of the messenger determines the success of the mission. Wisdom literature in the ancient world was frequently concerned with instructing ambassadors. Here the faithful envoy (*ṣîr 'ᵉmûnāh;* NIV, "trustworthy envoy," the expression suggesting government service—see Isa 18:2; Jer 49:14) ensures success (*marpē'*; lit., "brings healing"). The "wicked messenger" (*mal'ā<u>k</u> rāšā'*) falls into trouble, perhaps as a punishment. The RSV reads a causative *yappîl*, yielding "plunges men into trouble," perhaps by betraying trusts.

Discipline, its benefit

13:18

18 He who ignores discipline comes to poverty and shame,
but whoever heeds correction is honored.

18 Responding correctly to discipline can bring honor and success. The contrast is with poverty and shame. The key is "discipline" (*mûsār*) and "correction" (*tô<u>k</u>aḥa<u>t</u>*). The point seems to refer to commercial success: control and caution bring results. The verse has a powerful little wordplay: "shame" is *qālôn* (lit., "lightness") and "honor" is *yᵉ<u>k</u>ubbā<u>d</u>* (lit., "made heavy"). McKane observes that it is a difference between the man of weight (power and wealth) and the man of straw (lowly esteemed and impoverished) (p. 456).

Prospect for life, fulfilled

13:19

19 A longing fulfilled is sweet to the soul,
but fools detest turning from evil.

19 The lines here are very difficult. Toy suggests that each line has lost its parallel line (p. 274). Perowne may offer the best summary for the difficult verse: "In spite of the sweetness of good desires accomplished, fools will not forsake evil to attain it" (*Proverbs*, p. 103; cf. 13:12; 29:27). One can surely say that Proverbs teaches people to make their desires good so that fulfilling them is cause for joy.

Associations, with wise or fools

13:20

20 He who walks with the wise grows wise,
but a companion of fools suffers harm.

20 Proper company contributes to safety and growth. The verse advises association with the wise and not with the fools. The wordplay in the second line stresses the power of association: "a companion [*rō'eh*] of fools suffers harm [*yērôaʻ*]." Several have attempted to parallel the wordplay. A. Guillaume has "he who associates with fools will be left a fool" ("A Note on the Roots ריע, ירע, and רעע in Hebrew," JTS 15 [1964]: 294). Kidner cites Knox translating the Vulgate as saying: "Fool he ends that fool befriends" (*Proverbs*, p. 104). For further teachings on associations, see 1:10; 2:12; 4:14; 16:29; 23:20; et al. The point cannot be missed: Examine who is influencing you.

Prosperity, reward of righteous

13:21

> 21 Misfortune pursues the sinner,
> but prosperity is the reward of the righteous.

21 Here is teaching on recompense in absolute terms. It is this idea that Job's friends applied (incorrectly) to his situation. "Good" (*ṭôḇ*) is the general idea of "good fortune" or "prosperity" (so NIV); "evil" (*rāʿāh*) is likewise "misfortune" (so NIV) or "calamity."

Restitution, by divine intervention

13:22

> 22 A good man leaves an inheritance for his children's
> children,
> but a sinner's wealth is stored up for the righteous.

22 Divine justice determines the final disposition of one's inheritance. In Israel the idea of bequeathing an inheritance was a sign of God's blessing; blessings extended to the righteous and not to the sinners. See Psalm 49:10, 17 for the idea of the wicked leaving their estates for others.

Poor, susceptible to injustice

13:23

> 23 A poor man's field may produce abundant food,
> but injustice sweeps it away.

23 Injustice can take away what hard labor produces. Plaut makes this application: there is no need for poverty; the earth yields enough if justice and decency prevail (p. 155). The verse may also be saying that anything produced through unjust means will not endure. The lesson concerns the proper way to deal with produce, not the size of one's resources. For the variant readings, see the Notes.

Notes

---

23 The versions give evidence that the verse is hard to understand. The LXX has "the great enjoy wealth many years, but some men perish little by little." The Peshitta has "those who have no habitation waste wealth many years, and some waste it completely." The Targum has "the great man devours the land of the poor, and some men are taken away unjustly." The Latin reads "there is much food in the fresh land of the fathers, and for others it is collected without judgment." Toy concludes that the Hebrew text is corrupt beyond emendation (pp. 277–78).

Discipline, evidence of love

13:24

> [24] He who spares the rod hates his son,
> but he who loves him is careful to discipline him.

24 Parental love is displayed in disciplining the children responsibly. The powerful verbs "hates" and "loves" stress the point—hating a son probably means, in effect, abandoning or rejecting him. Whybray cites an Egyptian text that says that "boys have their ears on their backsides; they listen when they are beaten" (*Book of Proverbs*, p. 80). For the general biblical teaching on this, see Ephesians 6:4 and Hebrews 12:5–11; see Proverbs 4:3–4, 10–11 for the balanced tenderness. Too much lenience and too much harsh discipline are equally problematic. The balance comes when the child has room to grow while learning the limits. In this verse the word *šiḥ^{a}rô* has two possibilities. It may be translated "is careful in disciplining" (so NIV) but may be better rendered "treats him early with discipline" (see Driver, "Hebrew Notes on Prophets and Proverbs," p. 170).

Contentment, reward for righteous

13:25

> [25] The righteous eat to their hearts' content,
> but the stomach of the wicked goes hungry.

25 Righteousness is rewarded by the satisfaction of one's physical needs. This is another general saying based on the teachings in the law of God's blessings (Lev 26). It could also be implying that what the righteous acquire will prove satisfying to them because they are righteous.

Prosperity, in the household

14:1

> [1] The wise woman builds her house,
> but with her own hands the foolish one tears hers down.

1 A woman's wisdom enables the household to thrive. The contrast is between wisdom and folly; wisdom builds the house, but folly tears it down (cf. 9:1a). The text has *ḥaḵmôṯ nāšîm*, which could mean "wise ones among women" or "wisdom of women." To see these ideas worked out, contrast the wise woman (31:10–31) with the foolish one (7:10–23). The Midrash uses Jochebed, the mother of Moses, as an example of wisdom, and Zeresh, Haman's wife, for the foolish (Plaut, p. 158). But of course it is wisdom, not merely the woman, that brings the prosperity.

Fear of the Lord, uprightness

14:2

2 He whose walk is upright fears the LORD,
but he whose ways are devious despises him.

2 Here is a contrast between those who fear the Lord and those who despise him—the distinction is in the conduct produced: uprightness versus perversion (see 2:15; 3:32; 10:19).

Speech, its effects

14:3

3 A fool's talk brings a rod to his back,
but the lips of the wise protect them.

3 What people say has a great bearing on how they are received. The fool's conversation brings punishment. The text literally says that it is a "rod of pride" (*ḥōṭer ga'ᵃwāh*), the genitive being objective, viz., "a rod for pride." This line may seem only to be saying that his language is proud; but the contrast of the second line clarifies that his talk harms him, that he brings trouble on himself, for the speech of the righteous brings safety. Many commentators have emended the text from *ga'ᵃwāh* to *gēwōh* (cf. BHS) to read "a rod for his back." This makes the punishment seem stronger.

Prosperity, in business

14:4

4 Where there are no oxen, the manger is empty,
but from the strength of an ox comes an abundant
harvest.

4 To be productive one must use the appropriate means. For the farmer, oxen are indispensable; so the wise farmer will see to it that his oxen are numerous and in good condition. Whybray connects the two lines by observing that the farmer has to balance grain consumption with the work his oxen do (*Book of Proverbs*, p. 83).

Speech, true and false witnesses

14:5

5 A truthful witness does not deceive,
but a false witness pours out lies.

5 This short saying explicates true and false testimony. A faithful witness does not lie (*yᵉkazzēḇ*), but a false witness pours out lies (*kᵉzāḇîm*). The saying addresses the age-old problem of false witnesses in court that slow down the quest for the truth (see 12:17 and 16:10).

Wisdom, those who acquire it

14:6

[6]The mocker seeks wisdom and finds none,
but knowledge comes easily to the discerning.

6 Those who are serious and discerning acquire wisdom. The contrast is between the scorner (*lēṣ*) and the "discerning man" (*nāḇôn*). The scorner is intellectually arrogant; he lacks any serious interest in knowledge or religion. One can only guess that he pursues wisdom in a superficial way so that he might have the appearance of being wise. Plaut offers one application of this: those who want to read and learn will not be heard saying, "I have no time to read"—that is said only by those wishing to inflate their egos (p. 159).

Associations, unprofitable

14:7

[7]Stay away from a foolish man,
for you will not find knowledge on his lips.

7 One cannot increase in knowledge by associating with a fool—nothing comes from nothing, as many can affirm. The first clause advises to go out from the presence of a fool. The second clause is problematic; it literally reads, "You did not know the lips of knowledge" (see Notes). The verse is teaching people to get away from fools because they did not receive knowledge from what the fools said. If you want to learn, seek out the wise.

Notes

7 The MT has "you did not know lips of knowledge." The Targum freely interprets this as "for there is no knowledge on his lips." The LXX has several variations of the line, including "wise lips are weapons of discretion." Toy wants to emend to "for his lips do not utter knowledge" as in 15:7 (p. 285). But the Hebrew line makes sense as it is, even though the construction ("know lips") is not found elsewhere.

Conduct, careful consideration

14:8

[8]The wisdom of the prudent is to give thought
to their ways,
but the folly of fools is deception.

8 Biblical wisdom is practical theology. While the wise give careful consideration (*hāḇîn*) to their conduct, the way of the fool is "deception." The word *mirmāh* certainly means "deception," but some question whether it can mean "self-deception" (see McKane, p. 466, and D. Winton Thomas, "Textual and Philological Notes on Some Passages in the Book of Proverbs," VetTest Suppl. 3 [1955]: 286). The parallelism of this line would favor that, but there is little support elsewhere for it, as the word usually means craft practiced on others (see Toy, p. 285). If the line is saying that the fool is deceitful, then there is only a loose antithesis.

Reparation

14:9

[9] Fools mock at making amends for sin,
but good will is found among the upright.

9 Folly offends, but wisdom makes amends. This verse is difficult but is concerned with offending others. The first line has "fools mock reparation ['*āšām*]"; but the verb "mock" (*yālîṣ*) is singular, and the subject "fools" ('*ᵉwilîm*) is plural. This had led to the suggested reading "guilty / guilt offering mocks fools" (Toy [p. 287] offers Isa 1:14 and Amos 5:22 as examples). The versions are not very much help here; the LXX has something like "houses of transgressors will owe purification." The parallelism suggests that the idea is that fools ridicule reparation whereas the upright show good will.

Emotions, personal

14:10

[10] Each heart knows its own bitterness,
and no one else can share its joy.

10 There are joys and sorrows that cannot be shared. People in their deepest emotional feelings of "bitterness" (*mārāh*) or "joy" (*śimḥāh*) alone can understand those feelings. The proverb forewarns against any unnatural or forced attempts to express empathy.

Prosperity, ensured

14:11

[11] The house of the wicked will be destroyed,
but the tent of the upright will flourish.

11 Personal integrity ensures domestic stability and prosperity. The contrast is a simple one and the sentiment general. For comparison see 12:7 and Job 18:15.

Worldliness, its destruction

14:12

[12] There is a way that seems right to a man,
but in the end it leads to death.

12 Vice is a course of action that leads to ruin. One should be warned that any evil activity that seems successful and safe could take any number of turns to destruction (the expression is in the plural—"roads of death"). The proverb recalls the ways of the adulterous woman in chapters 1–9. The first half of the verse does not state that the way that seems right is a vice, but the second half clarifies that. The image used is of a traveler on a straight road; it seems safe, but it is fatal, because the destination is wrong. "Death" signifies mortal ruin (see 7:27; 16:25; also Matt 7:13–14). The LXX adds "Hades," but the verse seems to be concerned with this life's events. The issue then is how deceptive evil is. It might promise and deliver happiness, power, and the good life, but it cannot sustain what it gives.

Emotions, mixed

14:13

13 Even in laughter the heart may ache,
and joy may end in grief.

13 Life is filled with bittersweet things—no joy is completely free of grief. At first reading this proverb sounds pessimistic. The point must be the alternating emotions of life. On the other hand, the verse may be saying that in some superficial joyfulness there is underlying pain (*yik̲'ab̲;* NIV, "ache") and that once the joyfulness leaves, the "grief" (*tûg̲āh*) is still present.

Retribution, present in deeds

14:14

14 The faithless will be fully repaid for their ways,
and the good man rewarded for his.

14 This saying reminds the reader that retribution is at work: one's deeds determine the rewards. The faithless (*sûg̲ lēb̲*) are those whose heart turns aside; they will partake of their own evil ways (*yiśba'*, "be satisfied"; NIV, "be fully repaid"). The good man will be satisfied from his ways—his deeds are rewarding.

Discernment, opposite of gullibility

14:15

15 A simple man believes anything,
but a prudent man gives thought to his steps.

15 Wisdom prevents gullibility. The verse contrasts the simpleton (*pet̲î*) with the prudent (*'ārûm*), i.e., the youth who is untrained intellectually and morally with the wise one who has the ability to make critical discriminations. The saying shows that the *pet̲î* is gullible; he believes every word, probably because he hears what he wants to hear. The prudent person, however, discerns every step.

Evil, cautious avoidance

14:16

16 A wise man fears the Lord and shuns evil,
but a fool is hotheaded and reckless.

16 Wise people are cautious and not reckless. The first line of the verse simply says that "a wise man fears and turns from evil." Since the holy name is not used, the verse probably does not mean that he fears the Lord but fears the consequences of his actions—the wise person is thus cautious (Greenstone, p. 153). On the other hand, the fool is reckless, self-assured, and overconfident (as McKane defines the words, p. 465). The fool is arrogantly confident, when he of all types of people should be cautious.

Character traits, distasteful

14:17

[17] A quick-tempered man does foolish things,
and a crafty man is hated.

17 Two character traits that are distasteful to others are the quick temper (*q*ᵉ*ṣar-'appayim*) and craftiness (*m*ᵉ*zimmāh*). The "crafty man" may be the counterpart of the quick-tempered person, although Toy thinks it is antithetical and translates it "but a wise man endures" (p. 292). The quick-tempered person acts foolishly and loses people's respect, but the malicious plotter is hated (see Notes).

Notes

17 The LXX reads "endures" (יִשָּׂא, *yiśśā'*) rather than "is hated" (יִשָּׂנֵא, *yiśśānē'*). This change seems to have arisen on the assumption that a contrast was needed; the LXX reads "a man of thought endures." Many versions likewise have taken *m*ᵉ*zimmāh* in a good sense. However, the MT offers a contrast as well, albeit not a very strong one.

Knowledge, evidence of prudence

14:18

[18] The simple inherit folly,
but the prudent are crowned with knowledge.

18 The kind of honor one receives in life is based on the amount of wisdom used. The contrast is between the simple who "inherit" (*nāḥ*ᵃ*lû*) folly and the prudent who are crowned with knowledge. The meaning of *kāṯar* ("crowned") is a little difficult; it may not mean "are crowned" or "crown themselves" but "encircle" or "embrace." For the verb "inherit" Driver proposes "are adorned" from *hālāh* ("Problems in the Hebrew Text," p. 181).

Rewards, victory over the wicked

14:19

[19] Evil men will bow down in the presence of the good,
and the wicked at the gates of the righteous.

19 Ultimately the wicked will acknowledge and serve the righteous. The figure used here is of a conquered people kneeling before their victors awaiting their commands. Greenstone suggests that the expression "at the gates" may also imply that they are begging for favors (p. 154). While this proverb has its primary focus on triumphs in this life, one cannot help but think of the ultimate fulfillment of the thought in Philippians 2:10.

Wealth, its popularity

14:20

> 20 The poor are shunned even by their neighbors,
> but the rich have many friends.

20 Possessions determine popularity. This is just a statement of the reality of life. The poor are avoided and shunned (*yiśśānē'*, lit., "hated") as useless by their neighbors, but "the lovers of the rich are many" (lit. Heb.).

Neighbors, proper treatment of

14:21

> 21 He who despises his neighbor sins,
> but blessed is he who is kind to the needy.

21 One cannot sin against a neighbor and hope to enjoy God's blessings. The line contrasts the sin of despising (*bāz*) a neighbor with showing favor (*mᵉḥônēn;* NIV, "is kind") to the needy. In this line the neighbor is assumed to be poor or at least in need. Despising (*bāzāh*) means treating with contempt, discarding one as worthless. To ignore a neighbor in this cold-hearted fashion is just as much a sin as showing favor to the poor is an act of righteousness.

Conduct, good and evil

14:22

> 22 Do not those who plot evil go astray?
> But those who plan what is good find love and
> faithfulness.

22 One's moral behavior is usually the result of planning. The image bound up in *ḥāraš* is that of an artisan's skill. The contrast is between "those who plot evil" (*ḥōrᵉšê rā'*) and "those who plan good" (*ḥōrᵉšê ṭôḇ*). The result of the first is going astray and of the second showing faithful love (NIV mg., "show love and faithfulness"; "mercy and truth" [lit. Heb.] usually describe the Lord's intervention, but here they refer to the faithful and kind dealings of the righteous).

Diligence, profitable

14:23

> 23 All hard work brings a profit,
> but mere talk leads only to poverty.

23 Profits come from hard work and not idle talk. The "hard work" here is *'eṣeḇ* (lit., "painful toil"), a term introduced in Genesis 3:19. The empty talk (NIV, "mere talk"; lit., "words of lips") leads to poverty (see Job 11:2; 15:3 Isa 36:5). People should be more afraid of idle talk than of hard work. Or, to put it another way, do not just talk about it—Do it!

Wealth, a benefit for the wise

14:24

> [24]The wealth of the wise is their crown,
> but the folly of fools yields folly.

24 Wisdom has its own rewards. This verse is very difficult. The first line reads "the crown of the wise is their riches." Toy suggests it means that wealth is an ornament to those who use it well (p. 296). The second line seems to be saying that fools only have their folly. Consequently many follow the BHS proposal to read *w*^{e}*liwyaṯ* instead of *'iwweleṯ* to form a better parallel with the first half: "the wealth of fools is their folly" (McKane, p. 466). The point would be that the fool can only expect greater exposure of his folly, rather than merely saying his folly is his folly.

Notes

24 Commentators find both parts of the verse improbable, even though they make good sense as they appear in the Hebrew. Toy wishes to change the first colon to read "The crown of the wise is their wisdom" because he finds the idea in the MT farfetched (p. 296). The second line then following the LXX makes the change from folly to "wreath." For additional material on the Hebrew word, see M. Rotenberg, "The Meaning of *'iwweleṯ* in Proverbs," *Leshônênu* 25 (1960/61): 201.

Speech, true and false witnesses

14:25

> [25]A truthful witness saves lives,
> but a false witness is deceitful.

25 Telling the truth in court effects swift justice in the outcome of the trial. The person who tells the truth "saves lives" (*maṣṣîl n*^{e}*p̱āšôṯ*)—he is a true witness (*'ēḏ '*^{e}*meṯ*). The point is that this person will deliver someone else from death in a false charge by coming forward with the truth. On the other hand, a false testimony deceives the court and brings ruin. To make this point clearer, several commentators have changed *mirmāh* ("deceit") to *m*^{e}*rammeh* ("destroys"), a change that is not necessary, however. The point stands that nothing good is gained by perjury. Moreover, as Kidner says, anyone who will trim the facts for you is just as likely to do it against you (*Proverbs*, p. 110).

Fear of the Lord, security

14:26

> [26]He who fears the LORD has a secure fortress,
> and for his children it will be a refuge.

26 The reverential fear of the Lord leads to security. The image is of a "secure fortress" (*mibṭaḥ-'ōz*) for the God-fearer and his children. The "fear" finds expression in obedience to the law with all its rewards and punishments, and this ensures the safety. The children mentioned here are the God-fearer's children and not worshipers in general. Exodus 20:5–6 declares that children will reap the benefits of the righteous parents if they love the Lord too; so if fear gives the parents security in the Lord, it will be a refuge for their children.

Fear of the Lord, life

14:27

27 The fear of the LORD is a fountain of life,
turning a man from the snares of death.

27 Reverential fear of the Lord brings life. This line is similar to 13:14 except "fear of the LORD" replaces "the teaching of the wise."

Power, political

14:28

28 A large population is a king's glory,
but without subjects a prince is ruined.

28 A prince's power varies with the size of his empire. This statement is generally true of empires; from a human viewpoint political power is based on the number of people in the party.

Patience, opposite of quick temper

14:29

29 A patient man has great understanding,
but a quick-tempered man displays folly.

29 Patience is the evidence of understanding. The one who is patient has "great understanding" (*raḇ-tᵉḇûnāh*); the one who has a quick temper (*qᵉṣar-rûᵃḥ;* lit., "hasty of spirit") exalts folly, i.e., he brings it to a full measure. So one should cultivate understanding.

Contentment, its healthy benefit

14:30

30 A heart at peace gives life to the body,
but envy rots the bones.

30 It is healthy to find contentment, for envy brings constant turmoil. Literally the verse says, "the life of the flesh [*ḥayyê ḇᵉśārîm*] is a heart of healing [*lēḇ marpē'*]." The point is that a healthy spirit is the life of the body—it soothes. On the other hand, envy brings pain and problems. The word *qin'āh* ("envy") describes passionate zeal, a violent excitement that is never satisfied. The one who is "consumed with envy" has no tranquility.

Poor, treatment of

14:31

31 He who oppresses the poor shows contempt
for their Maker,
but whoever is kind to the needy honors God.

31 How people treat the poor displays their faith in the Creator. Here is the doctrine of the Creation in its practical outworking. Anyone who oppresses the "poor" (*'ōšēq*) shows contempt for his Maker, for that poor person also is the image of God. Showing favor for the poor (*ḥōnēn*) honors God because God commanded this to be done (see Matt 25:31–46; cf. Prov 14:21; 17:5; 19:17). See also J.A. Emerton, "Notes on Some Passages in the Book of Proverbs," JTS NS 20 (1969): 202–22, for a meaning of *'šq* as "slander."

Confidence, in calamity

14:32

32 When calamity comes, the wicked are brought down,
but even in death the righteous have a refuge.

32 Those who trust and obey the Lord have a sense of security in catastrophe. The contrast is with the wicked who are cast down (*yiddāḥeh;* NIV, "brought down") in the time of calamity; the righteous even in death have a "refuge" (*ḥōseh*). So the idea is that the righteous hope in a just retribution. A problem often raised is that nowhere in the Book of Proverbs is hope for immortality found. Rather death is seen as a misfortune (see Notes). Nevertheless, this verse may be a shadowy forerunner of that truth.

Notes

32 The LXX has "in his integrity," as if from בְּתֻמּוֹ (*b*^{e}*ṯûmmô*), in place of "in his death," which is from בְּמוֹתוֹ (*b*^{e}*môṯô*). Those who do not wish to see hope in immortality at this point favor this variant reading.

Wisdom, its possessor

14:33

33 Wisdom reposes in the heart of the discerning
and even among fools she lets herself be known.

33 The greatest amount of wisdom resides with those who have discernment. The second colon is a little difficult. It is normally translated "even among fools she lets herself be known." This may be ironic or sarcastic: the fool, anxious to appear wise, blurts out what he thinks is wisdom but in the process turns it to folly. The LXX, however, negates the clause: "not known in fools." D. Winton Thomas connects the verb to the Arabic root *wd'* and translates it "in fools it is suppressed" ("The Root *yd'* in Hebrew," JTS 35 [1934]: 302–3).

Righteousness, national

14:34

[34] Righteousness exalts a nation,
but sin is a disgrace to any people.

34 The prosperity and the power of a nation depends on its righteousness. The verb "exalt" (*rûm*) means that the people's condition in that nation is elevated. On the other hand, widespread sin is a disgrace (cf. *ḥassēḏ* in Aramaic [BDB, s.v.]).

Servants, clever and incompetent

14:35

[35] A king delights in a wise servant,
but a shameful servant incurs his wrath.

35 A servant's competence will affect the king's attitude toward him: the wise servant is a delight, for he is the skillful, clever one (*maśkîl*). But the incompetent one (*mēḇîš;* NIV, "shameful") is the bungler who botches the king's business and whose indiscretions and incapacity expose his master to scandal and criticism (McKane, p. 470).

Speech, conciliatory

15:1

[1] A gentle answer turns away wrath,
but a harsh word stirs up anger.

1 The way one answers another person will have an effect on the response. This antithetical proverb stresses that it is wise to use a gentle answer to turn away wrath. More than merely gentle or soft, the idea seems to be conciliatory, i.e., an answer that restores good temper and reasonableness (McKane, p. 477). To use a "harsh" (*'eṣeḇ*) word is to cause pain (same Heb. word) and bring an angry response. The incident of David and Nabal in 1 Samuel 25 is an illustration of this; Gideon in Judges 8:1–3 is a classic example of the soft answer that brings peace, whereas Jephthah illustrates the harsh answer that leads to war (Judg 12:1–6; see the Mishnah, *Berakoth* 17a).

Speech, wise or foolish

15:2

[2] The tongue of the wise commends knowledge,
but the mouth of the fool gushes folly.

2 How wise people are can often be determined by what they say: knowledge comes from the wise and folly from the fools, according to this contrast. The verb *têṭîḇ* of the first colon is a little difficult. Although translated "commends," the Hebrew word is literally "makes good" or "treats in a good or excellent way" (Toy, p. 303).

M. Dahood, however, suggests a change to *yṭp*, a cognate of *nṭp* ("drip") and offers the reading "tongues of the sages drip with knowledge" ("Proverbs and Northwest Semitic Philology," pp. 32ff.).

Divine omniscience

15:3

> [3]The eyes of the LORD are everywhere,
> keeping watch on the wicked and the good.

3 The Lord knows everyone completely. The thought is continuous in the two lines of this verse; it uses anthropomorphic language to stress God's exacting knowledge. But as Plaut says, the verse is not meant as a statement of theology but an incentive for conduct (p. 169). Of course, for the righteous divine omniscience is a great comfort. See also 2 Chronicles 16:9; Psalm 11:4; and Hebrews 4:13 (which shows that God's purpose in this is salvific).

Speech, helpful or harmful

15:4

> [4]The tongue that brings healing is a tree of life,
> but a deceitful tongue crushes the spirit.

4 What a person says can bring either healing or harm. The teaching here affirms that healing words bring life to the spirit but perverse words crush the spirit. The Greek has *iasis* for *marpē'*, giving the idea of therapy. This fits well with the image of the tree of life that signifies a source of vitality to others (see McKane, p. 483). The contrast is the perverse, twisted, or "deceitful" (*selep̱*) words that crush the spirit. The same idea appears in Isaiah 65:14.

Discipline, wisely heeded

15:5

> [5]A fool spurns his father's discipline,
> but whoever heeds correction shows prudence.

5 How well one responds to discipline reveals his character. The contrast here is between the fool who spurns it and the prudent individual who heeds it. The latter shows good sense. See also v.20 and 13:1 and 18.

Reward, for righteousness

15:6

> [6]The house of the righteous contains great treasure,
> but the income of the wicked brings them trouble.

6 Prosperity is one reward for righteousness. This verse contrasts great treasure with the prospects of the wicked. The Hebrew of the second line says that the income of the wicked is "a thing troubled" (*ne'kāreṯ*). The word "trouble" (*'āḵar*) is usually calamity that one man brings on another (as illustrated by Achan, whose name [*'āḵān*] seems to reflect the word in 1 Chron 2:7 [see NIV mg.]). The LXX for this verse, however, has no reference to wealth but talks about amassing righteousness.

Speech, spreading knowledge

15:7

7 The lips of the wise spread knowledge;
not so the hearts of fools.

7 Wise people will spread knowledge when they speak—their words are profitable. This verse is concerned with teaching, but the verb of the first clause ("spread") does not fit the idea of the parallel clause; for a mind does not scatter. So the idea of the second colon simply should be interpreted to mean that the fool has no comprehension of knowledge (see Notes).

Notes

7 Because the idea of יְזָרוּ (*yᵉzārû*, "spread" or "scatter") does not work with both lines of the verse, Toy (p. 305) suggests, with the support of the LXX, the verb יִצְּרוּ (*yiṣṣᵉrû*, "preserve," from נָצַר [*nāṣar*]). The Greek evidence (Symm.) for this, however, is not strong. For the second line the LXX has "hearts of fools are not safe," apparently taking לֹא־כֵן (*lō'-ḵēn*, "not so") as "unstable." McKane prefers the interpretation of "warped" or "perverse" instead (p. 478).

Worship, acceptable and unacceptable

15:8

8 The LORD detests the sacrifice of the wicked,
but the prayer of the upright pleases him.

8 The spiritual condition of the worshiper will determine the acceptability of the worship. Here, as well as throughout the Bible, sacrifices from wicked people are unacceptable because they are insincere and blasphemous (cf. v.29; 21:3, 27; 28:9, et al.; see also 1 Sam 15:22; Ps 40:6–8; Isa 1:10–17). On the other hand, prayer from the righteous pleases God. Greenstone observes (p. 162) that if God accepts the prayers of the righteous, he will accept their sacrifices. Sacrifice is an outward ritual and easily performed by the wicked, but prayer is a private and inward act and not usually fabricated by unbelievers.

Conduct, acceptable to God

15:9

9 The LORD detests the way of the wicked
but he loves those who pursue righteousness.

9 God is pleased with the righteous. Parallel to the preceding verse, this verse uses *tô'ᵃḇaṯ* ("detests" or "abominates") to describe the life of the wicked, in contrast to the verb *ye'ehāḇ* ("loves"), which describes God's approval of the righteous. The refinements of this verse should be carefully noted: God hates *the way* of the wicked, i.e., the sin but not the sinner; and God loves those *who follow after* righteousness (the Piel signifying persistent pursuit). Plaut says, "He who loves God will be moved to an active, persistent, and even dangerous search for justice" (p. 170).

Discipline, its necessity

15:10

10 Stern discipline awaits him who leaves the path;
he who hates correction will die.

10 Discipline must be used for those who go astray, but in this discipline they may die prematurely. The "way" (*'ōraḥ;* NIV, "path") here is the life of righteousness stressed throughout the book. The relationship of the two lines is probably synonymous: the "stern discipline" (*mûsār rā'*) of the first line is parallel to the death (*yāmûṯ*) in the second. The point of the verse is that it is one thing to sin and find forgiveness but another altogether to refuse correction and receive such stern discipline. See also Romans 8:13.

Divine omniscience

15:11

11 Death and Destruction lie open before the LORD—
how much more the hearts of men!

11 The Lord knows every intent of every individual. The development of thought in these two lines is an argument from the lesser to the greater ("how much more"). Sheol and Abaddon represent the remote underworld and all the mighty powers that reside there (see 27:20; Job 26:6; Ps 139:8; Amos 9:2; Rev 9:11). If that remote region with its inhabitants is open before the Lord (*neḡeḏ YHWH,* "before the LORD," signifies irresistible omniscience), how much more the hearts of the people! The word "hearts" in this verse is a metonymy for motives and thoughts (see Ps 44:21).

Discipline, rejected

15:12

12 A mocker resents correction;
he will not consult the wise.

12 The scoffer resists all efforts to reform him. This individual is fixed in his ways and will not change to live according to the wise; literally, he will not "walk with" the wise. The MT has "to the wise" (*'el-ḥaḵāmîm*), but the LXX has "with." If "to" is correct, it means that he does not seek their advice. For an illustration see the account of Ahab and Micaiah in 1 Kings 22:8.

Emotions, joy and sorrow

15:13

13 A happy heart makes the face cheerful,
but heartache crushes the spirit.

13 The emotional condition of a person has an obvious effect on body and soul. This verse uses an antithesis: joy is inspiring and is expressed by a cheerful face (*yêṭiḇ pānîm*), but "heartache" (*bᵉʿaṣṣᵉḇaṯ-lēḇ*) is depressing, i.e, "crushes the spirit" (*rûaḥ nᵉḵēʾāh*). The words used here stress the pain and the depression with a note of despair. Toy observes that the implication is also that a broken spirit is expressed by a sad face and that a cheerful face shows a courageous spirit (p. 308). See also 17:22; 18:14; and Isaiah 66:2. A good illustration is Genesis 40:6.

Knowledge, sought by the discerning

15:14

14 The discerning heart seeks knowledge,
but the mouth of a fool feeds on folly.

14 Those who are wise and discerning desire knowledge. This verse is similar to v.7; throughout the book knowledge is linked with righteousness, and ignorance goes with sinfulness. The idea of the second colon, "feeds on folly" (*yirʿeh ʾiwweleṯ*), does not make a strong parallel to the verb "seeks" of the first half (see Notes). But the poetic image of feeding would signify the acquisition of folly.

Notes

14 D. Winton Thomas suggests that instead of יִרְעֶה (*yirʿeh*, "feeds") we read יִדְעֶה (*yiḏʿeh*), with the one slight change from *r* to *d*. This would then be connected to the Arabic *daʿā* ("sought," "demanded") to form a better parallel ("Textual and Philological Notes," p. 285).

Emotions, joy and sorrow

15:15

15 All the days of the oppressed are wretched,
but the cheerful heart has a continual feast.

15 Life can be delightful or difficult, depending on one's circumstances and disposition. The contrast is between the "oppressed" (*ʿānî*) and the "cheerful heart" (*ṭôḇ-lēḇ*). The parallelism of the second line suggests that the *ʿānî* is one who is inwardly oppressed. Obviously the proverb recommends the cheerful frame of mind, for the image of the feast signifies enjoyment of life's offerings. This is far better than the evil (*rāʿîm;* NIV, "wretched") days. See Ruth 1:20–21 and Habakkuk 3:17–18.

Wealth, spiritual better than physical

15:16–17

16 Better a little with the fear of the LORD
than great wealth with turmoil.

17 Better a meal of vegetables where there is love
than a fattened calf with hatred.

16–17 These two verses stress that spiritual things are far better than material wealth. In v.16 the idea is that the fear of the Lord brings more satisfaction than wealth with discontentment or, as Moffat has it, wealth with worry (Kidner, *Proverbs*, p. 115). "Turmoil" (*m^e^hûmāh*) is anxiety; the reverential fear of the Lord alleviates such anxiety; for it causes contentment and tranquility, the very opposite of "turmoil." Not all wealth has this disadvantage, but when it does, it is undesirable. The tone of the proverb is caught in *Aboth* 2:7 of the Mishnah: "The more possessions, the more anxiety."

Verse 17 affirms that happy, loving relationships are more desirable than a great meal where there is hatred (contrasting *'ah^a^ḇāh* ["love"] with *śin'āh* ["hatred"]). Again the teaching concerns the negative side of wealth—it is often the case that wealth replaces love in a family. The ideal would be to have a loving family, friends, and great food; but short of that, a humble meal with love is preferable.

Patience, its affect on strife

15:18

18 A hot-tempered man stirs up dissension,
but a patient man calms a quarrel.

18 It takes great patience and calmness to maintain peaceful relationships. The contrast is with the "hot-tempered man" (*'îš ḥēmāh*) who stirs up dissension and the person who is "long or slow of anger" (*'ereḵ 'appayim;* i.e., "patient"). McKane, seeing here a reference to litigiousness, writes: "There is the kind of person who thrives on acrimony and who seeks a pretext to transform every difference or disagreement into a bitter legal contest, and there is his opposite who will do everything in his power to minimize contention and to obviate the acerbities of litigation" (p. 482). See also 14:29 and 15:1.

Diligence, its progress

15:19

19 The way of the sluggard is blocked with thorns,
but the path of the upright is a highway.

19 Diligence normally determines progress in life. This proverb says that the slothful person seems to find obstacles along the way—his way is like a hedge of thorns (*kimśuḵaṯ ḥāḏeq;* NIV, "blocked with thorns"; the LXX has "strewn with thorns"; see Hos 2:6). The way of the upright is like a well-made road; viz., a "highway" (*s^e^lulāh*, lit., "to heap up")—they have no reason to detour or swerve. For parallelism of the slothful and upright, see 28:19; cf. 6:10; 10:26.

Wisdom, its affect on others

15:20

20 A wise son brings joy to his father,
but a foolish man despises his mother.

20 Wise children affect their parents' joy. See 10:1, which is almost the same, except that "despises" replaces "is a source of anxiety" (NIV, "grief"). The contribution of this verse, according to Kidner (*Proverbs*, p. 116), is that it describes the callousness of the one who inflicts grief on his mother.

Conduct, straight course

15:21

21 Folly delights a man who lacks judgment,
but a man of understanding keeps a straight course.

21 A valuable life style must be maintained by wise decisions. The proverb shows the importance of good judgment and "understanding" (*t^e^b̲ûnāh*). The fool follows any whim of fancy, and it is a delight to him because he lacks "judgment" (*ḥ^a^sar-lēb̲*) to see the folly in it. The one who has insight follows in a "straight course" (*y^e^yaššer-lāk̲et̲*). So once again, as Toy reminds us, knowledge is the foundation of character (p. 312).

Speech, value of advice

15:22

22 Plans fail for lack of counsel,
but with many advisers they succeed.

22 The success of plans requires using good advice. See 11:14. This is a general observation that is of value on the personal and national level.

Speech, appropriate

15:23

23 A man finds joy in giving an apt reply—
and how good is a timely word!

23 It is most satisfying to be able to give timely and fitting advice. The parallelism is synonymous. The topic concerns the well thought out and appropriate reply. To say the right thing at the right time is satisfying; it requires knowledge and wisdom. Even to say the right thing at the wrong time is counterproductive.

Conduct, beneficial for life

15:24

24 The path of life leads upward for the wise
to keep him from going down to the grave.

24 A life of wisdom preserves life. The first colon reads, "The way of life is upward to the wise man." This is clarified by the second clause—it prevents him from going downward to Sheol (NIV mg.). There is some disagreement over the meaning of "upward" (*l^e^ma'lāh*). The verse generally is taken to mean that "upward" is a reference to this physical life and "going down to the Sheol" is a reference to physical death, viz., "the grave," because the idea of immortality is not clearly revealed in the book. The point here then would be that the righteous expect to live long and healthy lives (2:20–22; 3:18; 5:6; 10:17; 13:14). McKane argues that "upwards" does not fit this worldly pattern of conduct and that it is only intelligible if taken as a reference to immortality (see Notes). We may at least say that the language anticipates what later Scripture will clearly teach about the ultimate destination of the way of life.

Notes

3 The translation "upwards" and "downwards" are not found in the LXX. This has led some to speculate that these words were not in the original but were added afterward when the idea of immortality became prominent (see McKane, p. 480).

Justice, divine

15:25

25 The LORD tears down the proud man's house
but he keeps the widow's boundaries intact.

25 The Lord administers his justice through righteousness. He brings down the proud but protects the needy. Scripture amply confirms that the Lord champions the cause of the widow, the orphan, the poor, and the needy. These people were often the prey of the proud, who would take their lands and houses (cf. 1 Kings 21 and the story of Naboth; cf. also Prov 16:19; Isa 5:8–10).

Plans, pleasing to God

15:26

26 The LORD detests the thoughts of the wicked,
but those of the pure are pleasing to him.

26 The Lord is pleased with plans that have righteous intentions. On the one hand, the intentions or "thoughts of the wicked" (*maḥšᵉḇôṯ rāʿ*) are thoughts that will harm other people—these are an abomination to the Lord. The contrasting clause is very difficult, the MT having *ṭᵉhōrîm ʾimrê-nōʿam* ("pleasant words are pure"). Usually "to him" is inserted to make the connection (see Notes). The NIV words the clause to say "but those of the pure are pleasing to him."

Notes

26 The LXX has "the sayings of the pure are held in honor." The Vulgate has "pure speech will be confirmed by him as very beautiful."

Contentment, opposite of greed

15:27

> 27 A greedy man brings trouble to his family,
> but he who hates bribes will live.

27 Those who are secure in their circumstances will not succumb to the evil devices of greed. The "greedy man" is the *bôṣēaʿ bāṣaʿ*, the one who wants a big cut, who is in a hurry to get rich, and who is not particular how it happens (McKane, p. 485). The verse is actually a warning against taking bribes. "Gifts" (lit. Heb. of *mattānōṯ*) could be innocent enough, but they may alter one's values (Kidner, *Proverbs,* p. 117). So hating bribes is the safest path to follow. For an example of avoiding this danger, see Genesis 14:22–24, where Abram refused to take anything for himself. See also the story of Elisha's refusal of Naaman's gift and Gehazi's ruinous greed for it (2 Kings 5:16, 20, 27).

Speech, carefully planned

15:28

> 28 The heart of the righteous weighs its answers,
> but the mouth of the wicked gushes evil.

28 Those who are wise are cautious in how they answer, as opposed to the wicked who blurt out vicious things. The text says literally that the mind of the righteous "weighs" (*yehgeh,* "considers," "muses," "meditates," or "studies") how to answer. The advice is to say less but better things. The LXX in the first colon has "the hearts of the righteous meditate faithfulness." What the wicked say, on the other hand, is painfully "wicked" (*rāʿôṯ;* NIV, "evil").

Prayer, God's response to

15:29

> 29 The LORD is far from the wicked
> but he hears the prayer of the righteous.

29 God's response to prayer is determined by the righteousness of the one who prays. The wicked keep a distance from him; so he is "far" (*rāḥôq*) from them, an idea that signifies that he is inaccessible or deaf to their appeal (see the motif repeated in Ps 22). Of course, a prayer of repentance by the wicked is the exception, for by it they would become the righteous (Toy, p. 316).

Speech, good news

15:30

> 30 A cheerful look brings joy to the heart,
> and good news gives health to the bones.

30 It is uplifting to hear good news. These two lines form a synonymous parallelism with slight variation. The *meʾôr-ʿênayim* (lit., "light of the eyes"; NIV, "cheerful look") may indicate the gleam in the eyes of the one who tells good news, as the parallel second clause suggests (see Notes). The idea of "health to the bones" comes from a Hebrew expression that is literally "makes the bones fat," a symbol of health and prosperity. See also 17:22; 25:25; Genesis 45:27–28; and Isaiah 52:7–8.

Notes

30 The LXX has "the eye that sees beautiful things." For מְאוֹר (*me'ôr*, "light"), D. Winton Thomas suggests pointing a Hophal participle *mōr'ê* and reading "a fine sight cheers the mind" ("Textual and Philological Notes," p. 285).

Character traits, teachable

15:31

[31] He who listens to a life-giving rebuke
will be at home among the wise.

31 A teachable person will become wise. The proverb forms a single sentence; it shows how the one who listens to reproof that is beneficial to life will be at home with the wise.

Discipline, its benefit

15:32

[32] He who ignores discipline despises himself,
but whoever heeds correction gains understanding.

32 Accepting discipline is important to personal development. The antithesis, the person who despises discipline, slights or "despises himself" (*mô'ēs napšô* means that he rejects himself as if he were of little value and so fails to grow). One must acquire understanding, especially about oneself, to grow spiritually, intellectually, and emotionally.

Fear of the Lord, wisdom and honor

15:33

[33] The fear of the LORD teaches a man wisdom,
and humility comes before honor.

33 Humble submission in faith to the Lord brings wisdom and honor. The exact connection between the clauses is difficult. The idea of the first clause is similar to 1:7 and 9:10. Here it may mean that "the discipline of wisdom [teaches] the fear of the LORD," just as easily as the reverse, since the sentence is without a finite verb. The second clause has its contrast in 18:12, where pride leads to destruction. Here humility brings honor. See also 22:4, where fear and humility are connected.

Speech, divine enablement

16:1

[1]To man belong the plans of the heart,
but from the LORD comes the reply of the tongue.

1 God sovereignly enables people to put their thoughts into words. The verse is in the form of a contrast—"the plans of the heart" (*ma'arkê-lēḇ*) and the "reply of the tongue" (*ma'anēh lāšôn*) are contrasted by the prepositions "belong" and "from." The verse can be taken in one of two ways: (1) the thoughts and the speech are the same, or (2) the speech differs from what the person had intended to say. The second view fits the contrast better. This proverb then is actually giving the reader a glimpse of how God confounds even the wise. The word "reply" (*ma'anēh*) in the book seems to refer to a verbal answer to another person (15:1, 23; Job 32:3, 5); so when someone is trying to speak before others, the Lord directs the words according to his sovereign will.

Divine omniscience

16:2

[2]All a man's ways seem innocent to him,
but motives are weighed by the LORD.

2 The Lord alone can evaluate our behavior because he knows our motives. The proverb is arranged in antithetical parallelism to express the only true evaluation of moral behavior. People might seem "innocent" (*zaḵ*) in their own estimation, but self-deception and rationalization make this estimation unreliable. The word *zaḵ* is used for pure oils, undiluted liquids; here it signifies unmixed actions. The proverb suggests that such a premature opinion of oneself is naive at best and smug at the worst. The person may be far from pure when the Lord weighs the motives (*tōḵēn rûḥôṯ*). The figure of "weighing" signifies evaluation (see Exod 5:8 ["require"]; 1 Sam 2:3; Prov 21:2; 24:12; cf. 1 Sam 16:7). There may be a faint allusion to the Egyptian belief of weighing the heart after death to determine righteousness. The word *rûḥôṯ* is a metonymy for the motives, as in Proverbs 21:2 and 24:12 (where it is parallel to "heart"). The conclusion of the matter is that we deceive ourselves so easily and therefore cannot fully evaluate ourselves. God, by his Spirit and through his Word, provides the penetrating evaluation.

Plans, committed to God

16:3

[3]Commit to the LORD whatever you do,
and your plans will succeed.

3 For our plans to succeed, we must depend on the Lord. This is an instruction proverb that includes the result for compliance. The verb "commit" is literally "roll" (*gōl*, from *gālal;* although the LXX and Targum assume *gal*, "reveal"). The figure of rolling, as in rolling one's burdens onto the Lord, is found also in Psalms 22:8 (9 MT); 37:5; and 55:22. It portrays complete dependence on God. This would be accomplished with a spirit of humility and by means of a diligent season of prayer; but the plan also must have God's approval. The syntax of the second clause shows that there is subordination: the waw on *yikkōnû*, coming after the imperative of the first clause, expresses that this clause is the purpose or result of the first. People should commit their plans to the Lord so that he may establish them. Not every plan we have is pleasing to him; but for those that are, this verse is a great comfort. Greenstone says, "True faith relieves much anxiety and smoothens many perplexities" (p. 172).

Retribution, divine

16:4

> [4]The LORD works out everything for his own ends—
> even the wicked for a day of disaster.

4 God in his sovereignty ensures that everything in life receives its appropriate retribution. On the surface the verse strikes an immediate impression for God's sovereignty: all God's acts are part of his plan. Kidner says that ultimately there are no loose ends in God's world (*Proverbs*, p. 118). Since the wicked are punished in the end, this proverb adds that that is his plan for them. Whybray suggests that this saying could have grown up in answer to the question, "Why did God create the wicked?" (*Book of Proverbs*, pp. 93–94). The line of poetry is arranged with synthetic parallelism; it affirms the truth and then expands it with the specific application about the wicked. The verb *pā'al* means "to work out, bring about, accomplish"; it is naturally used of God's sovereign control of life (see Num 23:23; Isa 26:12; et al.). The interpretive difficulty concerns *lamma'ᵃnēhû;* it has been taken to mean "for his purpose" or "for its answer." The word is *ma'ᵃneh* ("answer" or "response") and is not from *lᵉma'an* ("purpose"). So the suffix likely refers to *kol* ("everything"). The point is that God ensures that everyone's actions and their consequences correspond—certainly the wicked for the day of calamity. In God's order there is just retribution for every act, for every act includes its answer or consequence.

Pride, its fall

16:5

> [5]The LORD detests all the proud of heart.
> Be sure of this: They will not go unpunished.

5 The Lord will surely bring down those who are arrogantly proud. The idea continues from the first colon to the second, but the second explains what it means by the Lord hating the proud. "Proud of heart" (*gᵉḇah-lēḇ*) describes the arrogance of the one who sets himself presumptuously against God (see 2 Chron 26:16; Ps 131:1; Prov 18:12). One can be absolutely sure (lit., "hand to hand," again used to signify something that is guaranteed, as in a confirming handshake; see comment on 11:21) that these arrogant people will not go free. *Lō' yinnāqeh* ("will not go unpunished") is probably a tapeinosis here, an understatement to stress, first, that they will be punished and, second, to imply that those who humble themselves before God in faith will go free (see E.W. Bullinger, *Figures of Speech Used in the Bible*, reprint ed. [Grand Rapids: Baker, 1968], p. 159). The LXX adds several lines to this verse (see Notes).

Notes

5 The LXX has inserted two couplets: The beginning of a good way is to do justly, and it is more acceptable with God than to offer sacrifices; he who seeks the Lord will find knowledge with righteousness, and they who rightly seek him will find peace. Toy notes that there were many proverbs and sayings in existence that sound like the Proverbs; these are in the LXX of the book and in Ecclesiasticus (pp. 321–22).

Sin, freedom from

16:6

> 6Through love and faithfulness sin is atoned for;
> through the fear of the LORD a man avoids evil.

6 Faithfulness to the Lord brings freedom from sin. This verse uses synonymous parallelism with a variant. One half speaks of atonement for sin and the other of avoidance of sin—so from both sides the stress is on complete freedom from sin. In the first colon we have *ḥeseḏ* and *'emeṯ* joined together; these form a hendiadys expressing "faithful covenant love" (NIV, "love and faithfulness"). The couplet often characterizes the Lord, but here in parallel to the fear of the Lord (as in 3:3–7) it refers to the faithfulness of the believer. Such faith and faithfulness bring atonement for sin (*yekuppar 'āwōn,* the technical term for expiation of sin). Toy explains the verbal idea by saying it affirms that the divine anger against sin is turned away and man's relation to God is as though he had not sinned (p. 322). In the second colon we read that the person who fears the Lord "avoids evil" (*sûr mērā'*). The word *rā'* can mean calamity or disaster, but it probably means sin or evil doing because it is parallel to *'āwōn* (see also v.17; 3:7; 4:27; 13:19). So reverential fear of the Lord prompts the believer to turn from evil doing.

Conduct, peaceful

16:7

> 7When a man's ways are pleasing to the LORD,
> he makes even his enemies live at peace with him.

7 A life style pleasing to God disarms social hostility. This verse uses formal parallelism with a protasis and an apodasis. The subject matter of the verse is "a man's ways" (*darkê-'îš*) that are "pleasing" (*birṣôṯ*) to the Lord. The question is who is the subject of the second clause: "he makes even his enemies live at peace [*yašlim*] with him"? The appropriate choice is the "man" and his "ways"—it is his life style that disarms the enemies. McKane comments that the righteous have the power to mend relationships (p. 491; see also 10:13; 14:9; 15:1, 4, 18; 25:21–22). The life that is pleasing to God will be above reproach and find favor with others. This is part of God's plan for rewards. But we must remember that this proverb, as well as 2 Timothy 3:12, must not be pressed to universal applications.

Righteousness, better than unjust wealth

16:8

> [8] Better a little with righteousness
> than much gain with injustice.

8 Few possessions with righteousness is better than much gain with dishonesty. The form follows the "better" sayings and so presents a contrast. There are of course other options (such as wealth with justice), but this line does not consider them. The "little" (*mᵉʿaṭ*) is not necessarily abject poverty; it could refer to modest income. To have little with righteousness is better than unjust wealth; but the contrast is between righteousness and "injustice" (*bᵉlōʾ mišpāṭ*). *Mišpāṭ* is used for both legal justice and ethical conduct. In 12:5 and 21:7 it is contrasted with righteousness; in 21:3 it describes ethical behavior. Here unethical conduct tarnishes the great gain and will be judged by God. See a similar saying in Amenemope, chapter 6, 8:19–20 (ANET, p. 422).

Sovereignty of God

16:9

> [9] In his heart a man plans his course,
> but the LORD determines his steps.

9 The Lord sovereignly determines the outworking of our plans. The Bible in general teaches that only those plans that are approved by him will succeed. The verse is antithetical—the human heart "plans" (*yᵉḥaššēḇ*) "his course" (*darkô*), but the Lord fulfills or "determines his steps" (*yāḵîn ṣaʿᵃḏô*). The verb *kûn* with *ṣaʿaḏ* (and similar expressions) means "to direct" (see Ps 119:133; Jer 10:23). The point is the contrast between what we actually plan and what actually happens—God determines that. As Paul later said, God is able to do abundantly more than we ask or think (Eph 3:20). See v.1; 19:21; and 20:24; see also Amenemope, chapter 18, 19:16–17 (ANET, p. 423).

Speech, responsible

16:10

> [10] The lips of a king speak as an oracle,
> and his mouth should not betray justice.

10 Next is a series of proverbs about kings. This first one teaches that kings must speak righteously in their official capacities. The parallelism is loosely synonymous, perhaps forming a cause-effect arrangement. The first part states that when the king speaks officially, it is as if it were "an oracle." The word *qesem* is used throughout the Bible in the negative sense of "divination"; here it seems merely to mean his words from an oracular sentence, as if he speaks for God (see Num 22:7; 23:23; and, for a popular opinion of such, 2 Sam 14:20). The effect of this is that his mouth "should not betray" (*lōʾ yimʿal*) justice. For a portrayal of the ideal king, see Psalm 72 and Isaiah 11:1–5. (For a comparison with Ezek 21:23–26, see E.W. Davies, "The Meaning of *qesem* in Prv 16:10," *Biblica* 61 [1980]: 554–56.)

Honesty, in business

16:11

> [11] Honest scales and balances are from the LORD;
> all the weights in the bag are of his making.

11 The Lord is the source of honesty and justice in all human enterprises. This proverb concerns weights and balances; the law of the Lord prescribed that they be just (see Lev 19:36; Deut 25:13; Amos 8:5; Mic 6:11). Shrewd people kept light and heavy weights to make dishonest transactions—as a modern individual might keep two sets of books. But the verse, using synonymous parallelism to stress the point, affirms that righteous and just measures are from the Lord. Toy, noting that the affirmation is unique in the OT, wants to change "LORD" to "king" within this context; he thinks some scribe might have thought it was a reference to the Divine King (p. 324).

Righteousness, stability in government

16:12

> [12] Kings detest wrongdoing,
> for a throne is established through righteousness.

12 A righteous administration determines the stability of a government. The verse is formal parallelism with an explanation coming in the second colon: kings detest criminal acts (*reša'*; NIV, "wrongdoing") because their thrones are "established" (*yikkôn*) in righteousness. This saying stresses the ideal that righteousness characterizes the administration in God's theocracy (see Deut 17:19–20; 2 Sam 7:13–16; Isa 32:1). McKane includes a lengthy discussion probing the parallel in Egyptian practices, i.e., a pedestal is portrayed under the throne that resembles the hieroglyph for *Maāt* ("justice" or "the divine order"), indicating that the throne was founded on justice. Solomon likewise used pedestals (1 Kings 10:18–20). McKane is not convinced that the parallel is helpful since the idea of a righteous basis for government was common (p. 492). Interestingly, if this proverb had been written later, after the monarchy had disintegrated, there would have been a greater variance between the ideal and the real. But coming from the golden age of Solomon, the ideal was still credible.

Honesty, approved by leaders

16:13

> [13] Kings take pleasure in honest lips;
> they value a man who speaks the truth.

13 People who are honest and candid are valuable to governments. Political leaders know that without such their domains would become anarchic. This little saying uses synonymous parallelism to make the point. Those who speak uprightly please (*reṣôn;* NIV, "take pleasure in") kings—they love (*ye'ehāḇ;* NIV, "value") those who speak uprightly. The ideal rulers love righteousness and not flattery (Plaut, p. 179).

Wisdom, in appeasing wrath

16:14

> [14] A king's wrath is a messenger of death,
> but a wise man will appease it.

14 The wise person knows how to pacify the unexpected or irrational anger of leaders. This proverb introduces the danger of becoming a victim of such caprice. By using formal parallelism, it presents a dictum and then a consequence. The first colon describes the "wrath" (*ḥ^{a}maṯ*) of the king as "messengers of death" (*mal'^{a}ḵê-māweṯ*). One good example of this is Solomon's assassinations of Adonijah, Joab, and Shimei in 1 Kings 2:25, 29–34, and 46. Some commentators suggest that this is a reference to the Ugaritic tablets where two messengers of Baal were sent to the god *Mot* ("Death") (see H.L. Ginsberg, "Baal's Two Messengers," BASOR 95 [1944]: 25–30). If there is a reference, it is obscure. This verse simply says that when the wrath of the king so threatens, a wise man will try to pacify or "appease it" (*y^{e}ḵapp^{e}rennāh*).

Encouragement, from rulers

16:15

> [15] When a king's face brightens, it means life;
> his favor is like a rain cloud in spring.

15 Favor from a king is encouraging to his people. This proverb is the antithesis of v.14. By using two figures the saying describes the benefits of having a king who is pleased with his subjects. The king's brightened face signifies his delight and thus means life for those around him (as opposed to his wrath). The favor this symbolizes is like the "rain cloud"—the latter rain or harvest rain, which is necessary for a successful harvest. Some of the ideas here are similar to Psalm 72:15–17, which portrays the prosperity of the land as a blessing on account of the ideal king, whose righteous reign seems to ensure prosperity.

Wisdom, better than wealth

16:16

> [16] How much better to get wisdom than gold,
> to choose understanding rather than silver!

16 Wisdom is more valuable than money. This didactic saying follows the pattern of the "better" sayings. Wisdom and wealth are not incompatible; but this comparison is between wealth without wisdom and wisdom without wealth. McKane says, "Wealth without wisdom may be vulgarity or greed or ruthless individualism" (p. 489). The point of the verse is to encourage people to acquire wisdom and understanding (cf. 3:14).

Righteousness, prevention of evil

16:17

> [17] The highway of the upright avoids evil;
> he who guards his way guards his life.

17 Righteous living is a safeguard against calamity. The parallelism of these lines is probably synthetic: the first asserts that integrity avoids evil, and the second explains further that the person who guards his way protects his life. In the first colon the point of righteous living is made with the image of a "highway" (*m[e]sillāh*), a raised and well-graded road. This well-cared-for life, this integrity, turns from or "avoids evil" (*sûr mērā'*, with *rā'* in the sense of "sinful living"). The metaphor of the "way" (*m[e]sillāh // darkô*) is carried into the second colon: he "guards" (*nōṣēr*) his way and thereby safeguards (*šōmēr;* NIV, "guards") his life. The LXX adds several lines here too (see Notes).

Notes

17 The LXX adds three lines after v.17a and one after v.17b:

> The paths of life turn aside from evils, and the ways of righteousness are length of life; he who receives instruction will be prosperous, and he who regards reproofs will be made wise; he who guards his ways preserves the soul, and he who loves his life will spare his mouth.

Pride, its consequences

16:18

> 18 Pride goes before destruction,
> a haughty spirit before a fall.

18 Pride leads inevitably to a downfall. In fact, pride is the first step down. The lines are synonymous. "Pride" (*gā'ôn*) and the "haughty spirit" (*gōḇah rû[a]ḥ*) are paired; and "destruction" (*šeḇer*) and "fall" (*kiššālôn*, lit., "a tottering, falling") are matched. Many similar sayings have appeared to warn against pride and arrogance. An Arabic proverb says, The nose is in the heavens, the seat is in the mire. McKane sees another implication in the words of this proverb. He writes, "'Disintegration' suggests a contrast with the man who has achieved wholeness [*šālôm*] by submitting to *mûsār* and learning wisdom; and 'stumbling' a contrast with the safe road along which the teacher directs his attentive and receptive pupils" (p. 490).

Humility, better than plunder

16:19

> 19 Better to be lowly in spirit and among the oppressed
> than to share plunder with the proud.

19 Better to be oppressed than to oppress. This, another "better" saying, presents a contrast of relative values. It is better to have a low spirit (*š[e]p̱al-rû[a]ḥ*) and be among the poor than to share the "plunder" (*šālāl*), or "loot" as Whybray translates it (*Book of Proverbs*, p. 95), with the "proud" (*gē'îm*). The "lowly" and the "proud" are here ethical and religious descriptions for the proud rebel against God, who is overbearing and oppressive, and for the humble, who submits to God and is unassuming and inoffensive (cf. Toy, p. 328). One should cultivate a humble spirit regardless of economic status; but one should never share the loot of those antagonistic to God.

Faithfulness, its blessing

16:20

> [20] Whoever gives heed to instruction prospers,
> and blessed is he who trusts in the LORD.

20 Faithfulness to the Lord brings his blessing. This simple proverb uses synonymous parallelism to make the basic point about the reward for the righteous. The person who trusts in the Lord and "gives heed to instruction" (*maśk̲îl 'al-dāb̲ār* specifically) "will be blessed by him" (*'ašrāyw*); he will find earthly prosperity and heavenly bliss from living a life that is right with God.

Speech, competent

16:21

> [21] The wise in heart are called discerning,
> and pleasant words promote instruction.

21 Wise speech will build a reputation for competence and enhance influence. It leads to the reputation of being "discerning" (*nāb̲ôn*), and its influence coming from sweet or "pleasant words" (*met̲eq śepāt̲ayim,* i.e., gracious and friendly words) is to "promote instruction" (*yōsîp̲ leqaḥ,* or increase appropriation)—viz., the teaching will be well received because it is persuasive.

Prospect for life, good or bad

16:22

> [22] Understanding is a fountain of life to those who have it,
> but folly brings punishment to fools.

22 An individual's prospects in life are determined by his wisdom. Here is another antithetical saying. "Understanding" (*śēk̲el*) is a "fountain of life" (see 10:11; 13:14; 14:27; 18:4), but "folly" (*'iwwelet̲*) brings "punishment" to fools. This "punishment" (*mûsar*) is essentially a requital for sin. Once again the Book of Proverbs affirms that there is very little that can be done for or with the fool. Alden astutely notes, "It is highly unlikely that Solomon would accept the idea that all men are created equal and thus deserve education at government expense" (p. 129).

Speech, wise

16:23

> [23] A wise man's heart guides his mouth,
> and his lips promote instruction.

23 Those who are wise ensure that they say wise things. The parallelism is synthetic, the first asserting that the wise heart "guides" (*yaśkîl*) the mouth and the second line adding that he increases the reception of what he says (see v.21).

Speech, beneficial

16:24

> [24] Pleasant words are a honeycomb,
> sweet to the soul and healing to the bones.

24 Pleasant words are comforting and encouraging. The subject matter here is *'imrê-nō'am* ("pleasant words"). They are first described as "a honeycomb" (see Ps 19:10 [11 MT]). Then the added predicates are "sweet" (*mā<u>t</u>ôq*) and "healing" (*marpē'*). One might recall, in line with the use of this imagery, how Jonathan's eyes brightened when he ate the honeycomb (1 Sam 14:27); such is the uplifting effect of pleasant words.

Conduct, its consequence

16:25

> [25] There is a way that seems right to a man,
> but in the end it leads to death.

25 Conduct that seems to be right may end in disaster. This proverb is identical to 14:12 (q.v.). The formal parallelism develops a continuous idea; but the contrast is with the "way" that seems right and the "ways of death" (*dar<u>k</u>ê-māwe<u>t</u>;* NIV, "leads to death"), which in the end provide the reality for the short-sighted evaluation.

Diligence, its motivation

16:26

> [26] The laborer's appetite works for him;
> his hunger drives him on.

26 Hunger drives people to work diligently. Here is a classification of labor and its primary incentive—need. "Labor" (*'āmēl*) is boring drudgery; motivations are necessary to its continuance, and hunger is the most frequent motivation. The word "appetite" is literally "soul" (*ne<u>p</u>eš*), that part of human nature that craves food; for the "life" (*ne<u>p</u>eš*) is a bundle of appetites. The second clause adds an explanatory idea: his "mouth" (*pîhû;* NIV, "his hunger") presses him on. The sense of the passage seems clear enough (although there are variant readings; see Notes); compare Ephesians 4:28; 6:7; and 2 Thessalonians 3:10–12. Also see Ecclesiastes 6:7, which says, "All man's efforts are for his mouth."

Notes

26 The LXX has misread פִּיהוּ (*pîhû,* "his hunger") and inserted the idea of "ruin" for the laborer—he drives away ruin. This influenced the Syriac to some degree; however, its first clause understands suffering instead of labor—the person who causes suffering suffers.

Conduct, malicious

16:27

27 A scoundrel plots evil,
and his speech is like a scorching fire.

27 Scoundrels plan ways to slander people. This verse is in formal parallelism, the thought continuing from one colon to the next. The "scoundrel" is literally a "man of belial" (*'îš bᵉlîya'al*). The meaning of "worthless" has been frequently given to *bᵉlîya'al*, but that is too weak. The term describes deep depravity and wickedness (see Toy, pp. 125–26, where he first discusses the term). This is a wicked person, for "he digs up evil." The meaning of *kōreh* (NIV, "plots") is that of bringing evil to the surface (cf. 26:27; Jer 18:20). What he finds he spreads; his speech is like scorching fire—the simile speaks of the devastating effect of his words. McKane says that he "digs for scandal and . . . propagates it with words which are ablaze with misanthropy" (p. 494).

Speech, divisive

16:28

28 A perverse man stirs up dissension,
and a gossip separates close friends.

28 Slanderers and gossips cause divisions. The wicked is described as "a perverse man" (*'îš tahpuḵôṯ*, "a man of falsehoods," "a liar") and a "gossip" (*nirgān*), viz., one who whispers and murmurs (18:8; 26:20, 22). This kind of person will destroy close friendships (*'allûp̱*) by what he says. Rashi took *'allûp̱* in the sense of "a prince," saying that such speech alienates the Prince, namely, God. But that is an unnecessary interpretation of the line.

Associations, evil

16:29

29 A violent man entices his neighbor
and leads him down a path that is not good.

29 Violent people influence others toward violence (synthetic parallelism, the second part adding to the first). The man of violence (*ḥāmās*) will influence his acquaintances toward violence. *Ḥāmās* often refers to sins against society, social injustices, and crimes. The "path that is not good" must refer to habits of crime. The point is to warn people to keep away from such villains.

Character traits, wicked expressions

16:30

30 He who winks with his eye is plotting perversity;
he who purses his lips is bent on evil.

30 Often people who are planning wicked things betray themselves with malicious expressions. Two expressions are depicted here: winking the eye and pursing the lips.

Facial expressions often reveal whether someone is plotting something evil (see 6:13–14). Mannerisms and character are closely linked. Plaut suggests that there may be another way to understand this verse, namely, that a person who sees no evil and hears no evil is a social detriment and by his passivity brings evil to pass (p. 182). Probably the verse is associating the expressions with malicious intent.

Rewards, long life

16:31

31 Gray hair is a crown of splendor;
it is attained by a righteous life.

31 Righteousness is rewarded with longevity. This proverb presents the ideal, of course, for the saying does not include evil old men. The equity envisioned in Proverbs is that the wicked come to an early end but the righteous endure. Toy suggests that the NT clarified this teaching by explaining how immortality guaranteed the long-lasting reward (p. 333). Proverbs is concerned with longevity in this life, however. "Gray hair" (*śêḇāh*) is the "crown of splendor"; it can only be attained through righteousness. While the proverb presents a simplified observation, there is something commendable about old age that can remember a long walk with God through life and can anticipate unbroken fellowship with him in glory.

Patience, more effective than power

16:32

32 Better a patient man than a warrior,
a man who controls his temper than one who
takes a city.

32 Patience is preferable to physical power. A "patient" (*'ereḵ 'appayim*, lit., "long of anger") man rules or "controls" (*mōšēl*) his "spirit" (*rûaḥ;* NIV, "temper"). Normally *'ereḵ 'appayim* is an attribute of God (see Exod 34:6). Here it describes a patient person. "Controls his spirit" means that he has his emotions under control. This saying would have significant meaning in the times when military prowess was held in high regard. *Aboth* 4:1 in the Mishnah uses this proverb to answer the question, Who is a true hero? Greenstone records the account from Nachmias about the pious man who said to the king, "You are the servant of my servant." He meant by this, "You are the slave of your evil inclinations, while I am its master" (p. 180).

Sovereignty of God

16:33

33 The lot is cast into the lap,
but its every decision is from the LORD.

33 The Lord controls the decisions that are submitted to him. The passage concerns the practice of seeking divine leading through casting lots. "Every decision" (*kol-mišpāṭô*) is from the Lord. See also Amenemope (18, 19:16–17, ANET, p. 423). So the chapter ends as it began, with a word about God's sovereignty.

Peace, its value

17:1

> [1]Better a dry crust with peace and quiet
> than a house full of feasting, with strife.

1 Poverty with peace is better than prosperity with strife. This contrast makes a preference for the better of two circumstances. On one side is the "dry crust" with quietness. *Pat̲ ḥ*ᵃ*rēḇāh* is like bread without butter, a morsel of bread not dipped in vinegar, or some such mix (cf. Ruth 2:14). In this humble setting there is "quiet" (*šalwāh;* the LXX reads *šālôm*, "peace"), which is better than a house of feasting with "sacrifices of strife" (*ziḇḥê-rîḇ;* cf. NIV mg.). The use of *ziḇḥê* suggests a connection with the temple (as in 7:14; see comment in loc.) in which the people may have made their sacrifices and had abundant meat to eat. It is also possible that the reference is simply to a sumptuous feast, for the term could refer to this as well (see Deut 12:15; Isa 34:6; Ezek 39:17). It would be rare for Israelites to have meat apart from sacrificial occasions. The contrast formed is not between the morsel and the meat but peace and strife (*rîḇ*). Abundance often brings a deterioration of moral and ethical standards as well as an increase in envy and strife.

Ability, better than privilege

17:2

> [2]A wise servant will rule over a disgraceful son,
> and will share the inheritance as one of the brothers.

2 Faithful and prudent servants are more highly honored than disgraceful sons. The verse expresses one continuous thought, although the two lines do reflect parallel ideas with "ruling" and "inheriting." The setting is the ancient world where servants rarely advanced beyond their station in life. Notable exceptions are the servant of Abram who would have been Abram's heir if there had been no son (Gen 15:3), the slave who married into the line of Judah and became an heir (1 Chron 2:35), and Ziba the servant of Mephibosheth (2 Sam 16:1–4; 19:24–30). This proverb focuses on the prudent or "wise servant" (*ʿeḇeḏ-maśkîl*) who uses all his abilities effectively. This one rules over the "disgraceful son" (*bēn mēḇîš*), becoming a joint heir with the brothers. The meaning is that the worthless son will be disinherited.

Divine omniscience

17:3

> [3]The crucible for silver and the furnace for gold,
> but the LORD tests the heart.

3 The Lord examines every thought and every motive. The parallelism is emblematic: one side is the imagery of silver and gold being purified; the other is the Lord "testing" (*bōḥēn*) human hearts. Such examinations are always constructive; they are designed to improve the value of the one being purified.

Speech, malicious

17:4

> [4]A wicked man listens to evil lips;
> a liar pays attention to a malicious tongue.

4 The wicked find destructive speech appealing. The synonymous parallelism stresses the point that those who listen to malicious talk are in fact malicious themselves—birds of a feather. The "wicked man" (*mēra'*) listens to wicked or "evil" (*'āwen*) lips, the "liar" (*šeqer*) pays attention to the "malicious tongue" (*lešôn ḥawwōṯ*). The metonymies "lips" and "tongue" signify speech, and the qualifications show this speech to be destructive. Leviticus 19:17 warns people to rebuke those with such malicious words and not to bear evil with them. Plaut explains that people are just as guilty of gossip if they listen to it (p. 186).

Notes

---

4 The verb מֵזִין (*mēzîn*) is from זין (*zîn*, "to feed"). The suggested emendation is to take it from אֹזֶן (*'ōzen*, "ear"), as a denominative verb, "pay attention to."

Speech, mocking the poor

17:5

> [5]He who mocks the poor shows contempt for their Maker;
> whoever gloats over disaster will not go unpunished.

5 Anyone who mocks the misfortune of the poor holds the Creator in contempt and will be punished. The parallel clauses identify the subject matter: "mocking the poor" (*lō'ēg lārāš*) and "gloating over disaster" (*śāmēaḥ le'êḏ*, although the proposed reading is *le'ōḇēḏ*, "to the one perishing"; cf. BHS mg.). The "disaster" is meant to explain the poverty.

The second part of each colon diverges: the first explains that whoever does this reproaches or "shows contempt for" (*ḥērēp*) his Maker, and the second line affirms that he will be punished. The idea of reproaching the Creator may be mistaking and blaming God's providential control of the world (Toy, p. 337). Plaut explains it just a little differently; he says that whoever mocks the poor holds up their poverty to them as a personal failure and so offends their dignity and their divine nature (as in 14:31). He adds that it is easier to rejoice over calamity than over good fortune (p. 187).

Honor, in family relationships

17:6

> [6]Children's children are a crown to the aged,
> and parents are the pride of their children.

6 People treasure their family heritage. The synonymous parallelism here focuses on this point from two sides—grandchildren are a crown to the aged, and parents are an honor to children. This idea comes from a culture that places great importance on the family in society—the elders have the preeminence in the family and receive the appropriate respect. On the clause that affirms that parents are an honor to children,

Plaut wryly comments, "Except, perhaps, in adolescence. Indeed, a family without full self-acceptance is in a state of perpetual immaturity" (p. 187). The LXX has an addition to this text (see Notes).

Notes

6 The LXX has inserted "To the faithful belongs the whole world of wealth, but to the unfaithful not an obolus." It was apparently some popular sentiment.

Speech, dishonest

17:7

> 7 Arrogant lips are unsuited to a fool—
> how much worse lying lips to a ruler!

7 A dishonest leader is worse than an arrogant fool. A comparison shows which of two things is worse. The first thesis lays the point for comparison: "Arrogant lips are unsuited to a fool." The word *yeṯer* ("arrogant") could also be rendered "excellent" (see Notes). It describes lofty speech, and this does not suit the fool. *Nāḇāl* ("fool") occurs only here, in v.21, and in 30:22 in the Book of Proverbs. It describes someone who is godless and immoral in an overbearing way (see 1 Sam 25:25; Ps 14:1). Lofty speech, whether great claims or arrogant opinions, is simply out of character for the fool. The second line makes the point: "how much worse lying lips to a ruler!" This *nāḏîḇ* ("ruler") is a gentleman with a code of honor, to whom truthfulness is almost second nature (McKane, p. 507). Lies simply are not suited to him. So the lesson is that if fools should not speak lofty things, then certainly honorable people should not lie.

Notes

7 There is some question over the best translation of יֶתֶר (*yeṯer*). The basic idea of "remainder" or "excess" has yielded derived meanings of "excellence," "heightened," and "arrogance." The LXX, using πιστά (*pista*), seems to reflect the idea of excellence and makes a contrast: "Words that are excellent do not fit a fool." The concept of "arrogance" works if it is taken in the sense of lofty, heightened, or excessive language.

Bribery, its success

17:8

> 8 A bribe is a charm to the one who gives it;
> wherever he turns, he succeeds.

8 Those who use bribery meet with widespread success. This line is a little troubling; but as Toy clarifies, the sage is merely affirming a point of reality without making a comment (p. 341). The first colon says that a bribe is a "stone of grace" (*'eḇen-ḥēn;* NIV, "charm"); and the second line adds to the thought that everywhere the briber turns with it, "he succeeds" (*yaśkîl*, or "deal wisely"). The word for "bribe" (*šōḥaḏ*) could simply refer to "a gift" that opens doors, the explanation being that it was the custom to offer a gift for most occasions. This would not be as problematic as a bribe and would fit well in this positive statement (Whybray, *Book of Proverbs*, p. 100). The Law clearly prohibited taking bribes (Exod 23:8); true bribery is described in v.23. But *šōḥaḏ* is never used of a disinterested gift; so there is always something of the bribe to it (see Ps 15:5; Isa 1:23). The proverb is expressing this reality from the viewpoint of the one giving the bribe—it works. *'Eḇen-ḥēn* indicates that it is a stone that brings "favor"; McKane says that it has magical properties and works like a charm (p. 502). It is a "lucky" stone.

Love, shown by discretion

17:9

[9]He who covers over an offense promotes love,
but whoever repeats the matter separates close friends.

9 How people respond to the faults of others reveals whether or not they have compassion. This proverb is an antithetical statement: the contrast is between "he who covers over an offense" (*m^e^ḵasseh-peša'*) of a friend and the one who "repeats" (*šōneh*) the news about it; the former promotes love and the latter separates friends. There can be no friendship without such understanding and discretion. Plaut says that such friendship requires the ability to forget; harping on the past has destroyed many friendships and marriages (p. 188). The point, as McKane sees it, is that the true friend buries the wrong done for the sake of love; he describes the antithesis as follows:

> On the one hand the person who believes that love is better served by a charitable silence than by a campaign of exposure and, on the other, the person who breaks up friendships—other men's friendships, not his own—by scandalous gossip. Even if this is done with a kind of zeal for the welfare of the community, the means are not justified by the end, for it is an activity which will destroy love and trust and so destroy what it sets out to preserve. And those who begin as crusaders will be degraded by what they supposed to be their mission in life and will become common informers and persecutors. (pp. 508–9)

Discipline, of value to the discerning

17:10

[10]A rebuke impresses a man of discernment
more than a hundred lashes a fool.

10 Discipline will benefit the wise but not the foolish. This verse contrasts the wise and the fool over the matter of "rebuke" (*g^e^'ārāh*). Those who are wise will be humbled by a rebuke and learn from it; but not even a hundred lashes will make such an impression on the "fool" (*k^esîl* here). The proverb may also be saying that in general physical punishment is less effective than criticism.

Retribution, its certainty

17:11

[11] An evil man is bent only on rebellion;
a merciless official will be sent against him.

11 Those bent on rebellion will surely meet with severe retribution. The formal parallelism lines up a cause and effect relationship. The cause is that evil people seek rebellion, and its effect is that retribution will be sent in the form of a "merciless official" (*mal'āk̲ 'ak̲zārî*). This expression could refer to a pitiless messenger that the king would send; but it also could refer to storms, pestilence, or any misfortune that was God's messenger of retribution.

Associations, dangerous

17:12

[12] Better to meet a bear robbed of her cubs
than a fool in his folly.

12 It is dangerous to encounter a fool engaged in folly. A contrast stresses this point. The first clause literally says, "Let a bear robbed of her whelps meet a man" (see 2 Sam 17:8; Hos 13:8). The contrast explains that this would be less dangerous than meeting a "fool" (*k^esîl*) engaged in "his [wicked] folly" (*'iwwaltô*). The human, who is supposed to be intelligent and rational, in such folly becomes more dangerous than the beast that in this case acts with good reason. As Alden comments, "Consider meeting a fool with a knife, or gun, or even behind the wheel of a car" (p. 134) (cf. Samuel E. Loewenstamm, "Remarks on Proverbs 17:12 and 20:27," VetTest 37 [1987]: 221–24).

Justice, for ingratitude

17:13

[13] If a man pays back evil for good,
evil will never leave his house.

13 Acts of ingratitude will be punished accordingly. This saying presents a condition and its consequences: the condition is when someone repays "evil" (*rā'āh*) for "good" (*ṭôb̲āh*); and the consequences are that the punishment fits the crime—"evil" (*rā'āh*) will never leave his house. The verse does not explain whether God will turn evil back on him directly or whether people will begin to treat him as he treated others. Moreover, the verse does not justify rewarding evil for evil.

Strife, controlled

17:14

[14] Starting a quarrel is like breaching a dam;
so drop the matter before a dispute breaks out.

14 Conflicts must be stopped before they get out of control. The proverb presents a cause and its effect. The first line says that starting a "quarrel" (*māḏôn*) is like "letting out water" (*pôṭēr mayim;* NIV, "breaching a dam"). The image is of a small leak, perhaps in a dam, that starts slowly to spurt water. The problem will only get worse. The second line gives the advice: stop it before "strife" (*rîḇ;* NIV, "a dispute") breaks out. McKane notes that there is probably a reference here to litigation (see 15:18, where both *māḏôn* and *rîḇ* are used). The lesson is to stop the quarrel before it gets to court, for a legal victory makes a disagreement permanent (p. 505).

Notes

14 The lines are difficult. The LXX has "The outpouring of words is the beginning of strife." Toy says that this is a warning against thoughtless talk as in 10:19 and 17:27 (p. 345).

Justice, corrupted
17:15

15 Acquitting the guilty and condemning the innocent—
the LORD detests them both.

15 The Lord hates any miscarriage of justice. This proverb uses effective wordplays to express the two things the Lord hates—declaring "righteous" (*maṣdîq;* NIV, "acquitting") the person who is a "guilty [criminal]" (*rāšā'*) and "declaring guilty" (*maršîa';* NIV, "condemning") the person who is "righteous" (*ṣaddîq;* "innocent"). Such reversals are an abomination for the righteous Judge of the whole earth.

Wisdom, inaccessible to fools
17:16

16 Of what use is money in the hand of a fool,
since he has no desire to get wisdom?

16 The fool has no interest in obtaining wisdom in the way that it must be obtained. This continuous sentence asks a rhetorical question. In effect it asks, What good is money, for what is needed cannot be bought. The person under consideration here is the "fool" (*kᵉsîl*), the one who lacks the intellect to gain wisdom in the first place (Toy, p. 346). He may desire the reputation of the wise, but he will not live up to its demands. McKane envisions a situation in which a *kᵉsîl* comes to a sage with a fee in hand, supposing that he can assure a career as a sage, and this gives rise to the biting comment presented here: Why does the fool have money in his hands? To buy wisdom when he has no brains? (p. 505).

Friends, loyal in adversity
17:17

17 A friend loves at all times,
and a brother is born for adversity.

17 The love of a true friend is constant. The verse is synonymous parallelism; i.e., the "friend" and the "brother" are equated. Faithful "love" (*'ōhēḇ*) is present at all times, even in times of "adversity" (*ṣārāh*), when it might be severely tested. Some take the two lines as antithetical. Plaut represents this view by arguing that friendship is a spiritual relationship, but a brother's ties are based on a blood relationship. He adds, "No wonder that adversity is frequently the only unifying force in many families" (p. 189). But the line is not implying that the brother confines his kindness to times of adversity; moreover, the brother does not always come forward at such times (see 18:19, 24; 19:7; 27:10). Here the true friend is the same as a brotherly relation. *Leṣārāh* may be translated "of adversity"—it is in such times of adversity that this strong friendship is displayed.

Wisdom, in business

17:18

18 A man lacking in judgment strikes hands in pledge
and puts up security for his neighbor.

18 It is foolish to pledge security for someone else's loans. The parallelism is synthetic. The lack of judgment is introduced with the idea of striking hands and then clarified by "puts up security" (*'ōrēḇ 'arubbāh*). The point is similar to 6:1–5.

Speech, arrogant and contentious

17:19

19 He who loves a quarrel loves sin;
he who builds a high gate invites destruction.

19 Arrogant and contentious speech ends in destruction. The double focus is on the one who "loves a quarrel [*maṣṣāh*]" in 19a and the one who "builds a high gate" in 19b. Some have taken the latter expression literally and interpreted it to mean pretentious house building, but that would be an unusual expression in the OT. Probably it is figurative; the gate is the mouth, and so to make it high is to say lofty things—he brags too much (see 1 Sam 2:3; Prov 18:12; 29:23). The figure would be comparable to the use of "trap" for mouth in American English. Toy wishes to emend the text to *pîw* ("his mouth") for clarity, but there is no need to do that; the figure can be properly interpreted that way. So the proverb is about a quarrelsome and arrogant individual who loves "sin" (*peša'*) and invites "destruction" (*šāḇer*). The destruction could be what he inflicts on others but may also mean what he brings on himself. The latter fits the parallel *peša'* a little better (although Toy wishes to emend *peša'* to "wounds" for the sake of parallelism, p. 348).

Conduct, wicked

17:20

20 A man of perverse heart does not prosper;
he whose tongue is deceitful falls into trouble.

20 Wicked ways and words lead to trouble. The synonymous parallelism makes this verse fairly easy to understand. The wicked person has a "perverse" (*ʿiqqeš*) heart, meaning he is morally crooked, and a "deceitful tongue" (*nehp̄aḵ bilšônô*), meaning he has turned away from the truth. Everyone who is wicked in his plans and speech can expect only trouble ahead. The idea of "trouble" (*rāʿāh*) refers to calamity or adversity in this life; he faces a life without good (= prosperity in this life).

Folly, a grief to others

17:21

> 21 To have a fool for a son brings grief;
> there is no joy for the father of a fool.

21 It is a grief to parents to have children become fools. It is not always a completely joyous experience to have children, not with the world and human nature as they are. Here *kᵉsîl* and *nāḇāl* are put in synonymous parallelism—they are almost the same. However, the first one, *kᵉsîl,* a term that occurs about fifty times in the book, portrays a slow-witted dullard, whether it be in spiritual, intellectual, or moral matters; and the latter, the *nāḇāl,* a term that is rare in the book, primarily focuses on religious folly, one who is morally and religiously indifferent (Toy, p. 348). In this situation a father who hoped for a son who would be a credit to the family and the faith may find only disappointment.

Emotions, affect on health

17:22

> 22 A cheerful heart is good medicine,
> but a crushed spirit dries up the bones.

22 One's psychological condition affects one's physical condition: a healthy attitude fosters good health but a depressed spirit ruins health. The antithetical idea, describing the two effects, stresses the importance of a cheerful heart. The first line presents the ideal: a "cheerful heart" (*lēḇ śāmēᵃḥ*) causes "good healing" (*yêṭîḇ gēhāh;* NIV, "is good medicine"). The heart, as with the spirit in v.22b, refers to the mind, the psyche. The positive and healthy outlook on life brings healing. On the other hand, a "crushed spirit" (*rûᵃḥ nᵉḵēʾāh*), i.e., one that is depressed or dejected, has an adverse effect on the health of the body. "Bones" figuratively represents the body (encased in the bony frame): fat bones means a healthy body (3:8; 15:30; 16:24), but dry bones signify unhealthiness and lifelessness (cf. Ezek 37:1–14).

Notes

22 The word גֵּהָה (*gēhāh,* "healing" or "health") is found in the MT. A suggested emendation is to "face," after the Arabic *jihatu,* and another is to גְּוִיָּה (*gᵉwîyāh,* "body"), as in the Syriac and Targum. The Hebrew, although a *hapax legomenon,* makes good sense in the verse.

Justice, perverted by bribes

17:23

23 A wicked man accepts a bribe in secret
to pervert the course of justice.

23 Bribery perverts justice. This single sentence uses a purpose clause to explain the intent of a bribe. The "wicked" who accepts the "gift" is a corrupt judge or some other official with similar power. The fact that he accepts it in secret (lit., "from the bosom," *mēḥêq*) indicates it is not proper. The purpose clause clarifies that the bribe is "to pervert the course of justice."

Discipline, concentration on plans

17:24

24 A discerning man keeps wisdom in view,
but a fool's eyes wander to the ends of the earth.

24 The wise persist in following a course of wisdom. They comprehend the true issues of life and concentrate on the path of wisdom. The "fool" (*k^esîl*), however, lacks any serious concentration and is unable to fix his attention on anything—so he drifts in the limitless sea of uncertainty (Toy, p. 351). McKane vividly depicts these distinctions; he says:

> The eyes of the *mēḇîn* ["discerning man"] are riveted on the teacher, for he is fascinated by her instruction and is a picture of unbroken concentration. The *k^esîl* ["fool"] has the wandering eye and the vacant distracted mind, and his condition is expressed by a hyperbole. As a student who is hearing nothing of what his teacher says might let his eyes rove to every corner of the classroom, so the fool who is inattentive to the instruction of Wisdom is said to have his eyes on the ends of the earth. (p. 504)

Folly, its effect on parents

17:25

25 A foolish son brings grief to his father
and bitterness to the one who bore him.

25 It is a bitter grief to have a child turn out to be a fool. See v.21; 10:1; and 15:20.

Punishment, unjust

17:26

26 It is not good to punish an innocent man,
or to flog officials for their integrity.

26 It is a mistake to punish people who are innocent. The two halves of this verse appear to be in synonymous parallelism, but the exact relation between them is a little more complicated. Rather than simply being two examples of injustice, the second part perhaps is being used to show how wrong the former is: viz., punishing the righteous makes about as much sense as flogging an official for his integrity. But if the two lines are simply synonymous, then the "officials" (*nᵉḏîḇîm*) are the good people. *Nāḏîḇ* ("noble") is used elsewhere in contrast to the fool (see comment on v.7; cf. Isa 32:5–8). The verse clearly affirms that punishing (lit., "fining") the righteous is "improper" (*'al-yōšer;* lit., "contrary to what is right"; NIV, "for integrity").

Character traits, self-control

17:27

27 A man of knowledge uses words with restraint,
and a man of understanding is even-tempered.

27 The wise restrain their speaking and control their actions. The text literally says that he is "sparing" (*ḥôśēḵ*) of words and "cool of spirit" (*qar-rûaḥ;* NIV, "even-tempered"). The one who restrains his speech is the truly knowledgeable person, and the one who has cool composure has understanding. So the instruction is that to gain composure and restraint one must develop knowledge and understanding.

Speech, wisdom of silence

17:28

28 Even a fool is thought wise if he keeps silent,
and discerning if he holds his tongue.

28 Silence is one evidence of wisdom. Even a fool appears wise in silence—at least he conceals his folly by keeping silent. Kidner says that a fool who takes this advice is no longer a complete fool (*Proverbs,* p. 127). He does not, of course, become wise; he just hides his folly. An old saying explains that no one knows that he nothing knows, unless he talks too much (Plaut, p. 192).

Character traits, antisocial

18:1

1 An unfriendly man pursues selfish ends;
he defies all sound judgment.

1 An antisocial person is self-centered and unreasonable. This verse does not describe someone who is merely unfriendly or unsociable but one who is an enemy of society; its message is a warning against being a schismatic (Toy, p. 354). The Mishnah uses this passage to teach the necessity of not separating from the community, because people have responsibilities as social beings (*Aboth* 2:4). The first line of the verse is difficult and complicated by a textual problem. Instead of reading "the one who separates himself seeks his own desires [*ta'ᵃwāh;* NIV, 'selfish ends']," Frankenberg follows the LXX and reads, "seeks his own occasion" (*tō'ᵃnāh*), viz., "his own pretext" (cited by Toy, p. 354). The change seems unnecessary to the point of the proverb, differing only in the reason behind the separation. Lot, for example, chose the best land out of his desires (Gen 13:11). The proverb also describes the antisocial person as one who contends against all sound judgment. The verb *yiṯgallā'* ("defies," from *gāla'*) means "burst out in contention" (lit., "snarl," "show the teeth"). He is indeed in opposition to society and its decisions. See also 17:14 and 20:3.

Instruction, rejected for opinion

18:2

[2]A fool finds no pleasure in understanding
but delights in airing his own opinions.

2 A fool prefers to give his opinion rather than acquire wisdom. Kidner says, "Closed mind, open mouth" (*Proverbs,* p. 127). By means of antithetical parallelism, we learn what the "fool" (*k^{e}sîl*) does and does not do. He "finds no pleasure in understanding" (a tapeinosis; the opposite is the point—he detests understanding). Instead of gaining "understanding" (*t^{e}ḇûnāh*), he loves telling what is on his mind (*b^{e}hiṯg̱allôṯ libbô;* NIV, "delights in airing his own opinions"; the verb *gālāh* means "to uncover, reveal, betray"; see 20:19; Ps 98:2). McKane observes that this kind of person is in love with his own ideas and enjoys spewing them out (pp. 515–16). This is the kind of person who would ask questions to show how clever he is rather than to learn.

Sin, its effect

18:3

[3]When wickedness comes, so does contempt,
and with shame comes disgrace.

3 Contempt and disgrace come with wickedness. This verse displays step parallelism: wickedness (see Notes) leads to contempt, and shame (parallel to contempt) leads to reproach. The point is that punishment for wickedness comes naturally from the community: *bûz* is "contempt"; *qālôn* is "shame"; and *ḥerpāh* is "disgrace." The disgrace, for example, would be the critical rebukes of the community against the wicked person. Of course, communities may not do this. Plaut notes, "Many a country club welcomes members whose contempt for the community and its needs should make them social outcasts" (p. 195). See Malachi 2:9, where the Lord made the wicked priests base and contemptible before the people.

Notes

3 Many commentators (McKane, p. 521; Scott, p. 112; Toy, p. 355) find the change from רָשָׁע (*rāšā'*, "wicked") to רֶשַׁע (*reša'*, "wickedness") a better parallel in the line: with wickedness comes contempt, etc.

Speech, profound

18:4

[4]The words of a man's mouth are deep waters,
but the fountain of wisdom is a bubbling brook.

4 The words of the wise are an inexhaustible supply of blessing and counsel. The question in this verse is whether v.4b is an antithesis to v.4a or a continuation. Normally a waw would begin an antithetical clause; the structure and the ideas suggest that the second part continues the idea of the first half. The metaphors in the verse normally describe the wise (see 10:11; 13:14; 16:22), and so that is the meaning of the verse (although v.4a only says "man"). The figure of "deep waters" suggests either the idea of an inexhaustible supply of words or that they are deep, profound. The figures of "fountain of wisdom" (see Notes) and "bubbling brook" describe the speech of the wise as a continuous source of refreshing and beneficial ideas. Consequently the idea of profound fits better.

Notes

4 The LXX has "life" instead of wisdom (i.e., "fountain of life"). This may have been influenced from 10:11. There is no reason for the change.

Injustice, denounced

18:5

> 5 It is not good to be partial to the wicked
> or to deprive the innocent of justice.

5 It is reprehensible to pervert justice. The second line complements the thesis presented in the first line. The image in the first part, "lifting up the face," means showing partiality in judgments (cf. Deut 10:17; Mal 2:9). The predicate "not good" is an understatement (tapeinosis)—it is reprehensible, vile, and wrong. The second clause may illustrate this crime: *l^e^haṭṭôṯ* signifies "to turn aside," i.e., to turn people from their rights (NIV, "deprive"). Compare 17:26; 28:21.

Speech, that invites trouble

18:6

> 6 A fool's lips bring him strife,
> and his mouth invites a beating.

6 Foolish people get themselves into trouble by what they say. The second line, almost identical in thought to the first, parallels the result ("beating") with the cause ("strife"). The fool's (*k^e^sîl*) speech brings him into (legal?—the term is *rîḇ*) controversies; and since he is wrong, he is punished. The "beating" is probably physical, given either by a father or by society (see for *mah^a^lumôṯ*, 19:25; Ps 141:5).

Speech, consequences of

18:7

> 7 A fool's mouth is his undoing,
> and his lips are a snare to his soul.

7 What a fool says can ruin him. This proverb continues the point of the former. What a fool says is his "undoing" (*m^e^ḥittāh-lô*); it is a "snare" (*môqēš*) to his life. Calamity and misfortune can come to the person who makes known his lack of wisdom by his speech.

Speech, gossip

18:8

> [8]The words of a gossip are like choice morsels;
> they go down to a man's inmost parts.

8 People delight in listening to gossip. This sad observation, developed in synthetic parallelism, simply affirms the common trait of human nature. The words of the "gossip" (*nirgān*) are like "choice morsels" (the word is related to a verb meaning "to swallow greedily"). When such tasty bits are taken into the innermost being, they stimulate the desire for more. Whybray summarizes, "There is a flaw in human nature that assures slander will be listened to" (*Book of Proverbs*, p. 105).

Laziness, its effect

18:9

> [9]One who is slack in his work
> is brother to one who destroys.

9 Laziness is destructive. The lines form a comparison to express that the lazy person and the destructive person are equally detrimental to society. The first is "slack" (*mitrappeh*) in his work; the other is called *ba'al mašḥîṯ* ("possessor [= dealer] in/of destruction"; NIV, "one who destroys"). The link between these two is the term "brother"; it signifies that they belong to the same classification, that they are of similar nature. For example, the one who is slack may look for shortcuts and may make things that fall apart. His destruction may be indirect and slow in coming, but it is just as problematic.

Security, the name of the Lord

18:10

> [10]The name of the LORD is a strong tower;
> the righteous run to it and are safe.

10 The Lord is fully able to protect those who trust in him. The first line establishes this truth, and the second focuses on the trust of the righteous. This is the only place in Proverbs where "the name of the LORD" is found; it signifies the attributes of God, here the power to protect (cf. Exod 34:5–7). The metaphor of "strong tower" (*migdal-'ōz*) sets up the imagery of the second clause: "running" metaphorically describes a wholehearted trust in God's protection (see Isa 40:31); and "safely on high" (*niśgāḇ;* NIV, "safe"), a military term, stresses the effect. Other Scriptures delineate how God actually protects his people in the different circumstances.

Security, wealth

18:11

> [11]The wealth of the rich is their fortified city;
> they imagine it an unscalable wall.

11 Wealthy people often assume that their wealth brings security. The imagery of safety (*niśgāḇāh;* NIV, "unscalable") links this proverb to the preceding; and since security is from God, this proverb is simply reporting a common assumption without commenting on it. Any protection wealth may bring is limited; for, as Psalm 49 teaches, money cannot bring ultimate security. The first metaphor, the "fortified city," suggests protection from all outsiders and outside elements; and the second, "unscalable wall," expresses their thoughts about being invincible.

Humility, its reward

18:12

> 12 Before his downfall a man's heart is proud,
> but humility comes before honor.

12 The way to honor is through humility. For a similar teaching see 11:2; 15:33; and 16:18. The humility and exaltation of Jesus provides the classic example of this truth (see Isa 52:13–53:12; Phil 2:1–10). An antithesis makes the point: pride (*yigbah*) in the heart is the way to a downfall, but "humility" (*ʿanāwāh*) is the prelude to "honor" (*kāḇôḏ*).

Speech, premature

18:13

> 13 He who answers before listening—
> that is his folly and his shame.

13 Speaking too hastily leads to shame. The formal parallelism completes the thought that premature answering is "folly" (*'iwweleṯ*) and "shame" (*kelimmāh*). Poor listening reveals that the person has a low regard for what the other is saying or is too absorbed in self-importance. The Mishnah lists this as the second characteristic of the uncultured person (*Aboth* 5:7). McKane adds, "It is impossible to speak to the point if the point has not been taken, and effective speaking is inseparable from high relevance and a sensitive regard for all views which are being expressed" (p. 515).

Spirit, healthy

18:14

> 14 A man's spirit sustains him in sickness,
> but a crushed spirit who can bear?

14 A healthy spirit brings healing to the body. This is affirmed by contrasting a healthy spirit with a "crushed spirit" (*rûaḥ nekē'āh*): the healthy attitude sustains a person, but depression is unbearable. In physical sickness one can fall back on the will to live; but in depression the will to live may be gone, and there is no reserve for physical strength. The figure of a "crushed" spirit suggests a broken will, loss of vitality, despair, and emotional pain. Few things in the human experience are as difficult to cope with as this.

Knowledge, sought

18:15

[15]The heart of the discerning acquires knowledge;
the ears of the wise seek it out.

15 Those who are wise eagerly search for knowledge. By paralleling "heart" and "ears," the verse stresses the full acquisition of knowledge: the ear of the wise listens to instruction, and the heart of the wise discerns what is heard to acquire knowledge. It is instructive to observe that it is the wise in Proverbs who continually seek knowledge. Kidner says, "Those who know most know best how little they know" (*Proverbs,* p. 129).

Gifts, their influence

18:16

[16]A gift opens the way for the giver
and ushers him into the presence of the great.

16 One may gain influence through gifts. The poetry is synthetic: the gift opens the way and gives "entrance" (*yanḥennû;* NIV, "ushers") to nobles. *Mattān* ("gift") is more general than "bribe" (*šōḥad̲,* as in 17:8, 23). But it too has danger (see 15:27; 21:14); for by offering such gifts one may learn how influential they are and start to make bribes. Here the proverb simply says that a gift can expedite matters but says nothing about bribing judges. See Genesis 43:11 and the appeasing gift for Joseph.

Justice, cross-examination

18:17

[17]The first to present his case seems right,
till another comes forward and questions him.

17 There must be cross-examination to settle legal disputes. The proverb is a continuous sentence. The first half affirms that the one side in a dispute may seem right, but it must be challenged by the other (*ḥ*ᵃ*qārô,* meaning "investigate"; NIV, "questions him"). The proverb reminds us that there are two sides in any dispute (legal, domestic, or religious) and that all sides in a dispute must be given a hearing.

Disputes, divinely arbitrated

18:18

[18]Casting the lot settles disputes
and keeps strong opponents apart.

18 Serious disputes may be prevented through divinely inspired arbitration. The assumption behind this saying is that providence played the determining role in the casting of lots. If both parties recognized this, the matter could be resolved, no matter how strong the "opponents" (*ʿ*ᵃ*ṣûmîm*). Today God's word and spiritual leaders figure prominently in divine arbitration (1 Cor 6:1–8).

Disputes, their effect

18:19

19 An offended brother is more unyielding than a
fortified city,
and disputes are like the barred gates of a citadel.

19 Serious disputes create insurmountable barriers among friends. The Hebrew is difficult; it seems to say that "an offended brother is [more isolated] than a strong city, and disputes are like the barred gates of the city"; but see the textual variations (see Notes). The proverb is talking about changing a friend into an enemy by abuse (McKane, p. 520). Kidner notes that these walls are easy to erect and hard to demolish (*Proverbs*, p. 130).

Notes

19 The LXX has a clear antithetical proverb here: "A brother helped [not offended] is like a stronghold, but disputes are like bars of a citadel." Accordingly the editors of BHS propose מוֹשִׁיעַ (*môšîaʿ*) or שׁוֹעַ (*šôaʿ*) instead of נִפְשָׁע (*nip̱šāʿ*, "offended"). This is followed by the Syriac, Targum, and Vulgate as well as the RSV. But since both lines use the comparison with a citadel (fortified/barred city), the antithesis seems problematic.

Speech, productive

18:20

20 From the fruit of his mouth a man's stomach is filled;
with the harvest from his lips he is satisfied.

20 Productive speech is satisfying. The lines are synonymous: the "fruit of his mouth" and "the harvest from his lips" both express the idea of productive speech. Such speech is satisfying (*tiśbaʿ* ["is filled"] and *yiśbāʿ* ["is satisfied"] are used in the two lines). In Proverbs words can bring good or evil; "fruit" and "harvest" have good connotations, and so constructive and beneficial speech is in view here.

Speech, consequences of

18:21

21 The tongue has the power of life and death,
and those who love it will eat its fruit.

21 What people say can lead to life or death. This proverb affirms this point and then explains it: "those who love it [*'ōhᵃḇeyhā*] will eat its fruit." The referent of "it" must be "the tongue," i.e., what the tongue says. So those who enjoy talking, i.e., indulging in it, must bear its fruit, whether good or bad. The lesson is to be warned, especially if you love to talk. The Midrash mentions this point, showing one way it can cause death: "The evil tongue slays three, the slanderer, the slandered, and the listener"

(*Midrash Tehillim* 52:2). (See further James G. Williams, "The Power of Form: A Study of Biblical Proverbs," *Semeia* 17 [1980]: 35–38.)

Wife, a blessing

18:22

> 22 He who finds a wife finds what is good
> and receives favor from the LORD.

22 A good marriage is a good gift from God. The parallelism is formal, the second line explaining the first: finding a mate is the sign of favor from God (see Notes). Although it does not say it, the verse clearly means a "good" wife. Proverbs 31:10–31 develops this idea more fully, whereas other passages lament a bad wife (e.g., 12:4 or Eccl 7:26, which says, "I find more bitter than death / the woman who is a snare"). But whoever finds a good wife—or, as it could be broadened, a good marriage—finds "good" (*ṭôḇ*, meaning "fortune" or "favor," not a "good thing"). The background of the saying may be Genesis 2:18, which affirms that it was "not good for the man to be alone." The word "good" describes that which is pleasing to God, beneficial to life, and abundantly enjoyable.

Notes

22 The LXX saw fit to embellish the line for the complete thought: "Whoever puts away a good wife puts away good, and whoever keeps an adulteress is foolish and ungodly."

Speech, humble or harsh

18:23

> 23 A poor man pleads for mercy,
> but a rich man answers harshly.

23 One's social status determines the tone of voice. The contrast is between the poor man and the rich man. The poor man "pleads for mercy" (*taḥ^{a}nûnîm*) because he has no choice—he has to ask. The rich man, however, often speaks "harshly" (*ʿazzôṯ*); he has hardened himself against such appeals because of relentless demands. It is a general view of the way of the world.

Friendship, loyal

18:24

> 24 A man of many companions may come to ruin,
> but there is a friend who sticks closer than a brother.

24 It is better to have one good, faithful friend than numerous unreliable ones. The first line of the contrast says, "A man of many friends [NIV, 'companions'] comes to ruin." The Hebrew *l^{e}hiṯrōʿē^{a}ʿ* is difficult. It means "for being crushed" or "to be shattered" but not "to show oneself friendly" (cf. KJV). The idea may be that there are friends to one's undoing (if we read *yēš* ["there is"] instead of *'îš* ["a man"] with Toy, p. 366). If a person has friends who are unreliable, he may still come to ruin, especially if these nominal friends use him. The second line is clearer: "there is a friend [*'ōhēḇ*] who sticks closer than a brother." This indeed is a rare treasure!

Poverty, better than folly

19:1

> 1 Better a poor man whose walk is blameless
> than a fool whose lips are perverse.

1 Personal integrity, even with poverty, is far better than foolish perversion. This proverb provides a contrast between two selected situations. One is poverty with integrity (*beṯummô;* NIV, "blameless") and the other is "perverse [speech]" (*'iqqēš* is "twisted") of a "fool" (*kesîl*). Some would change "fool" to "rich" to make a better parallel and to match 28:6, but the change is unnecessary for the point. The verse teaches people to follow honesty, even if it leads to poverty. See also 18:23 and 19:22.

Zeal, without knowledge

19:2

> 2 It is not good to have zeal without knowledge,
> nor to be hasty and miss the way.

2 Ill-advised and thoughtless zeal leads to failure. The lines are loosely synonymous. In the first the word *nep̄eš* means "vitality," "drive"—so it describes the eager "zeal" of a person. Without knowledge this will be unsuccessful ("not good"). Neither is there success for those who are "hasty" (*'āṣ beraḡlayim*, lit., "hasty with the feet") and "miss the way" (*ḥôṭē'*; see Judg 20:16; Job 5:24). Kidner underscores "how negative is the achievement of the man who wants tangible and quick rewards"—he will miss the way (*Proverbs*, p. 132). The passage reminds us that we must know the time and the direction for action, or zealous effort will be a futile activity.

Character traits, blaming God

19:3

> 3 A man's own folly ruins his life,
> yet his heart rages against the LORD.

3 Fools will try to blame God when they ruin their lives. The first line establishes the fact that it is a man's "folly" (*'iwweleṯ*) that ruins his life; the second adds that he "rages" (*yiz'ap̄*) against God. The fool is not willing to accept failure as his own. Of course, to blame God is also folly. Ecclesiasticus 27:25 says, "He who throws a stone into the air is throwing it on his own head."

Wealth, its effect

19:4

> 4 Wealth brings many friends,
> but a poor man's friend deserts him.

4 People run after the wealthy. Like 18:23–24, this proverb simply makes the observation on the reality of life. It does so with a contrast between the rich and the poor; wealth adds many friends, but a poor man is deserted by his friends. People will run after the rich, hoping to gain something; but they will avoid the poor, fearing that the poor might be trying to gain something from them.

Speech, false witnesses

19:5

> 5 A false witness will not go unpunished,
> and he who pours out lies will not go free.

5 Those who bear false witness will be punished. The lines are in synonymous parallelism: "false witness" (*'ēḏ š*^{e}*qārîm*) is parallel to "pours out lies" (*yāp̱î*^{a}*ḥ*). These will be punished. The saying is general, because sometimes a perjurer gets away with the crime. The Talmud affirms, "False witnesses are contemptible even to those who hire them" (*Sanhedrin* 29b). (See also v.9; 6:19; and 14:5, 25.)

Friendship, influential

19:6

> 6 Many curry favor with a ruler,
> and everyone is the friend of a man who gives gifts.

6 People seek the friendship of influential people. The verse's two ideas are loosely synonymous. The first uses the image of "stroking the face" (*y*^{e}*ḥallû p̱*^{e}*nê*); this means "to mollify," "to make the face soft," or "to curry favor" (NIV; cf. Ps 45:12). The second line introduces "gifts" again (*mattān;* lit., "gift"). As with 18:23–24, this proverb acknowledges the value of gifts in life, especially in business and politics.

Poverty, its effect

19:7

> 7 A poor man is shunned by all his relatives—
> how much more do his friends avoid him!
> Though he pursues them with pleading,
> they are nowhere to be found.

7 People avoid those who are poor. This verse is difficult; it has three parallel units, but the third is unclear. As the text stands in the MT, the first two lines are loosely synonymous: "A poor man is hated [*ś*^{e}*nē'uhû;* NIV, 'shunned'] by all his relatives— / how much more do his friends avoid him!" But the third line adds, "He pursues them [*m*^{e}*raddēp̱*] with pleading ['^{a}*mārîm*], / but they are nowhere to be found." The last line of the verse is open to various translations, none of which is completely satisfactory. Toy argues that it is probably the remnant of a lost couplet and thus hardly possible to restore the full meaning (p. 370). The basic meaning of the passage is fairly clear, however; the idea of "hate," taken in the sense of "reject," tells how superficial friends and relatives will abandon the poor man. The plight of Job captures such an abandonment.

Wisdom, profitable

19:8

> [8]He who gets wisdom loves his own soul;
> he who cherishes understanding prospers.

8 Those who choose wisdom will prosper. The lines are loosely synonymous: "gets wisdom [lit., 'a heart']" parallels "cherishes understanding," and "loves his own soul" (i.e., has regard for his own interests) parallels "prospers" (lit., "finds good"). Loving life states the cause, and finding good adds its effect. Toy notes that "intellectual insight (= clearness of thought, good sense) is profitable in this life, the moral as well as the physical life being probably included" (p. 371).

Speech, perjury

19:9

> [9]A false witness will not go unpunished,
> and he who pours out lies will perish.

9 Those who bear false witness will be punished. This proverb is the same as v.5, except that the last line changes to the verb *yō'b̲ēd̲* ("will perish").

Character traits, inappropriate positions

19:10

> [10]It is not fitting for a fool to live in luxury—
> how much worse for a slave to rule over princes!

10 A servant who gains power is worse than a fool who obtains wealth. Two thoughts here present unbearable conditions, one being slightly worse than the other. The operative word is *nā'weh*—"It is *not fitting* [italics mine] for a fool to live in luxury." Of course, if the fool changed and earned it, that is one thing. But this verse is about a misfit. The second thought is a slave who takes command over princes (see 12:24; 17:2). In these reversals the fool would only make worse his bad qualities—boorishness, insensitivity, and lack of discipline—and the slave would become arrogant and cruel. Toy says, "Wealth and power befit only the wise and the free" (p. 371). For other unbearable things, see 11:22; 17:7; 26:1; and 30:21–23.

Patience, its nature

19:11

> [11]A man's wisdom gives him patience;
> it is to his glory to overlook an offense.

11 Patience is prudent and honorable. The first line declares that "prudence" or "wisdom" causes patience. This *śēk̲el* is good sense; it makes the man even tempered. McKane says:

> The virtue which is indicated here is more than a forgiving temper; it includes also the ability to shrug off insults and the absence of a brooding hypersensitivity. It is the ability to deny to an adversary the pleasure of hearing a yelp of pain even when his words have inflicted a wound, of making large allowances for human frailties and keeping the lines of communication open. It contains elements of toughness and self-discipline; it is the capacity to stifle a hot, emotional rejoinder and to sleep on an insult. (p. 530)

This is the person who prudently lengthens anger (*he'ᵉrîḵ 'appô;* NIV, "gives him patience") and passes over an offense. Patience like this is "his glory" (*tip̱'artô;* lit., "his honor," signifying more the idea of beauty or adornment). Kidner explains that such patience "brings out here the glowing colours of a virtue which in practice may look drably unassertive" (*Proverbs,* p. 133).

Emotions, of a king

19:12

> [12]A king's rage is like the roar of a lion,
> but his favor is like dew on the grass.

12 A king has the power to terrify or to refresh. By the use of two similes, the verse contrasts the king's "rage" (*za'ap̱*) with his "pleasure" or "favor" (*rᵉṣônô*). The first simile, the roar of a lion, presents him at his most dangerous attitude (see 20:2; Amos 3:4). But the second portrays him as benevolent. For similar teachings see 16:14–15; 20:2; and 28:15. For a picture of the ideal king, see 2 Samuel 23:3–4. This proverb would advise the king's subjects to use tact and the king to cultivate kindness.

Family, its ruin

19:13

> [13]A foolish son is his father's ruin,
> and a quarrelsome wife is like a constant dripping.

13 Folly and strife destroy a home. There are two problems that bring chaos to a family. The first is a foolish son (lit., "son of a fool," meaning a son who is a fool), and the second is a "quarrelsome wife" (*miḏyᵉnê 'iššāh*). The foolish son brings "ruin" (*hawwōṯ*) to the father (cf. 10:1; 17:21, 25), but the quarrelsome wife is merely annoying (cf. 27:15–16). The LXX adds to the verse to fill out the complaint (see Notes).

Notes

---

13 The LXX adds to v.13b: "vows paid out of hire of a harlot are not pure." This is undoubtedly a moralistic addition.

Family, prudent wife

19:14

> [14] Houses and wealth are inherited from parents,
> but a prudent wife is from the LORD.

14 A prudent wife, unlike property, is God's special gift. The verse contrasts wealth that can be inherited from a father with a "prudent" (*maśkālet*) wife who is from the Lord. The verse does not answer questions about unhappy marriages or bad wives; rather, it simply affirms that when a marriage turns out well, one should credit God. See also 18:22 and 31:10–31.

Laziness, its consequences

19:15

> [15] Laziness brings on deep sleep,
> and the shiftless man goes hungry.

15 Those who are lazy waste time and lose money. These clauses are loosely synonymous, stressing one basic point. "Laziness" (*'aṣlāh*) brings on a "deep sleep." *Tardēmāh* is used to describe complete inactivity (see Gen 2:21; John 1:5); here it probably signifies lethargy (Whybray, *Book of Proverbs*, p. 110). This individual wastes time that is needed to provide for himself and his family. Parallel is the "shiftless man" (*remîyāh*) who goes hungry. Once again the first line presents the cause ("deep sleep") and the second the effect ("goes hungry").

Instruction, obedience to

19:16

> [16] He who obeys instructions guards his life,
> but he who is contemptuous of his ways will die.

16 Obedience to instruction is a safeguard of life. Another antithetical parallelism stresses this point: obedience contrasts with contempt and life with death. The first line affirms that obedience to instruction safeguards life. This "instruction" (*miṣwāh*) may refer to the teaching of the sages or to God's law. If it refers to God's commandments, then there is a stronger guarantee of safety for life. The second line announces that the one who holds in contempt his ways will die (see Notes). "His ways" could refer to the conduct of the individual or to the divine instruction (parallel to *miṣwāh*). If the latter is the case, then the punishment is more certain (even if through the courts). Toy offers the emendation from "his ways" to "his word" (as in 13:13), but this is not necessary (p. 374).

Notes

16 "Will die" represents the Qere reading יָמוּת (*yāmûṯ*), which harmonizes best with the Book of Proverbs. The Kethiv, יוּמָת (*yûmāṯ*), is "he will be put to death," which is a stronger reading.

Rewards, for charity

19:17

[17]He who is kind to the poor lends to the LORD,
and he will reward him for what he has done.

17 The Lord rewards those who are charitable. This proverb teaches that the Lord will reward those who give to the poor. The one who is gracious or "kind" (*hônēn*) to the poor is actually lending to the Lord, for the Lord will repay or "reward" (*y*^{e}*šallem*) him for his deed. This promise of reward does not necessarily signify that he will get his money back; the rewards in Proverbs involve life and prosperity in general. In the NT such kindness is viewed as kindness to the Lord (Matt 25:40); see also the reward for following Jesus (Matt 19:27–28).

Discipline, its benefit

19:18

[18]Discipline your son, for in that there is hope;
do not be a willing party to his death.

18 It is necessary to discipline children to prevent their premature death. Proverbs here and elsewhere teaches that to refrain from discipline allows a child to grow up stupid or wicked and thereby possibly incur death as a result of bad behavior (Whybray, *Book of Proverbs*, p. 110). The text teaches, "Discipline" (*yassēr*) your child. The motivation for this is "there is hope" (*tiqwāh*), an excellent reason to keep at it. The clause in the second half of the verse literally reads, "Do not lift up your life to kill him," meaning not to make the kind of decisions that will lead to his death (allowing him to go astray through neglect). The verb *yassēr* would include chastisement as well as instruction.

Character traits, hot temper

19:19

[19]A hot-tempered man must pay the penalty;
if you rescue him, you will have to do it again.

19 The second line of this proverb presents the consequence of the action of the first. Although the text is difficult (see Notes), the point is that a hot-tempered person will be constantly in trouble. "Pay the penalty" suggests paying a fine; so the trouble could be legal. In the second line the warning is given that if you save this person from his legal troubles, you will have to do it again and again. Unless he changes, he will always need bailing out.

Notes

19 There are many renderings of this verse that makes its true meaning elusive (see Toy, pp. 376–77). For example, the second clause could be: "If you save (your enemy), you will add (good to yourself); If you save (your son by chastisement), you may continue (chastisement and so educate him)"; etc. However, as Toy says (p. 377), all such attempts must supply a good deal.

Instruction, acceptance of

19:20

20 Listen to advice and accept instruction,
and in the end you will be wise.

20 By accepting advice and discipline, one becomes wise. This proverb is one continuous thought, the second half providing the purpose of the advice. The vocabulary reminds the reader of the first nine chapters of the book: "Listen to advice [*'ēṣāh*] and accept instruction [*mûsār;* lit., 'discipline']." This advice is in all probability the teachings of the sages that will make one wise. "In the end" there will be maturity from all the discipline, and there will be a steadfast perseverance in the path of life.

Sovereignty of God

19:21

21 Many are the plans in a man's heart,
but it is the LORD's purpose that prevails.

21 The success of our plans depends on the will of God. In the form of a contrast, the proverb teaches that only those plans that God approves will succeed (see 16:1, 9). People have many "plans" (*maḥ[a]šāḇôṯ*), but the Lord's counsel or "purpose" (*'[a]ṣaṯ*) will stand. Humans are diverse and uncertain; God is absolutely wise and sure, as Toy reminds us (p. 378). Midrash *Mishle* applies this passage to the accounts of Pharaoh, Absalom, and Haman.

Character traits, loyalty

19:22

22 What a man desires is unfailing love;
better to be poor than a liar.

22 Loyal love is better than wealth. According to the MT (see Notes), what is desired is "unfailing love" (*ḥasdô*). *Ḥeseḏ* refers to the bond of loyal love between members of the covenant. It was expected that covenanters would be faithful in their words and deeds of kindness. The second line may present the logical inference from this: "a liar" would be without *ḥeseḏ* entirely, and so poverty would be better than that character trait. *Kāzāḇ* ("liar") can be used in the sense of a mirage; so perhaps there is a closer antithesis between faithful love and false friend.

Notes

22 The MT has תַּאֲוַת (*ta'ᵃwaṯ*, "desire," "lust") and yields "What is desired in a man is loyalty." The LXX has καρπός (*karpos*, "fruit," probably from תְּבוּאַת [*tᵉḇû'aṯ*, "produce"]). It reads, "The fruit of man is mercy." "Desire" is the preferable reading in this couplet, which is an attempt to inspire loyal love.

Fear of the Lord, safety and contentment

19:23

23 The fear of the LORD leads to life:
Then one rests content, untouched by trouble.

23 Piety brings a life of contentment and safety. The saying uses synthetic parallelism, the second part carrying the idea of life further. "Life" is probably a metonymy for all the blessings and prosperity in life. Its essential feature is "contentment" (*śāḇēaʿ*; NIV, "content") that lodges without being visited by calamity or "trouble" (*rāʿ*). The vocabulary is vivid: "rests" is metaphorical for abide, and "untouched" means without any intervention to alter one's destiny. When one lives a life of piety, the Lord provides a quality of life that cannot be disrupted by such evil.

Laziness, its nature

19:24

24 The sluggard buries his hand in the dish;
he will not even bring it back to his mouth!

24 Some people are too lazy to eat. This humorous portrayal is certainly an exaggeration. It probably was meant more widely for anyone who starts a project but lacks the energy to complete it (Whybray, *Book of Proverbs*, p. 111). The sluggard "buries" (*ṭāman*, perhaps a cleverly chosen metaphor) his hand in the dish and is too lazy to pull it out—even to feed himself! See also 26:15.

Discipline, its affect

19:25

25 Flog a mocker, and the simple will learn prudence;
rebuke a discerning man, and he will gain knowledge.

25 Discipline affects people differently. The antithetical proverb shows the different ways that discipline works. There are three types of people here: the "mocker" (*lēṣ*) with a closed mind, the "simple" or simpleton (*peṯî*) with an empty mind, and the "discerning" (*nāḇôn*) with an open mind (Kidner, *Proverbs*, p. 135). The simpleton learns by observing punishment given to the scoffer. Although the punishment will have no effect on the scoffer, it should still be given; for the *peṯî* will learn what the *lēṣ* does not (McKane, pp. 525–26). But the discerning person will learn from verbal rebuke, even if it is painful truth. This is the more rational way. The contrast is caught in a wordplay in the Midrash: "For the wise a hint [*r'mizo*], for the fool a fist [*kurmezo*]" (*Mishle* 22:6).

Family, mistreatment of parents

19:26

26 He who robs his father and drives out his mother
is a son who brings shame and disgrace.

26 The one who abuses his parents is a disgrace. The saying portrays this ingrate as one who "robs" (*mešaddēḏ*) his father and "drives out" his mother. Father/mother may be taken as a poetic stereotypical word pair rather than as two ideas separating what is done to the father and then to the mother (see 10:1; 17:21; 23:24). The proverb may have in mind the son who wishes to take over his father's lands prematurely.

Discipline, its rejection

19:27

27 Stop listening to instruction, my son,
and you will stray from the words of knowledge.

27 Rejecting discipline leads to disobedience. The verse includes an admonition and its motivation (a result). The admonition uses irony (it is not a conditional clause): "Stop listening to instruction, my son." Of course, it means "Do not cease." The result of ceasing to listen is that the son will stray from the words of knowledge.

Notes

27 The LXX rewords the line to read, "A son who ceases to attend to discipline is likely to stray from words of knowledge." McKane argues for the MT on the form-critical considerations (p. 525).

Justice, corrupt witnesses

19:28

28 A corrupt witness mocks at justice,
and the mouth of the wicked gulps down evil.

28 Corrupt witnesses are a mockery to justice. The portrayal of the wicked witnesses in this proverb is arranged in loose synonymous parallelism. The wicked are first described as *ʿēḏ belîyaʿal*. *Belîyaʿal* does not mean "worthless" but wicked; they are witnesses who wilfully distort the facts (NIV, "corrupt"). Such activity certainly "mocks" (*yālîṣ*, from *lîṣ*, "to scorn") justice. The second line says that the mouth of the wicked "gulps down evil" (*yeḇallaʿ-ʾāwen*). The verb "gulps down" or "swallow" does not seem to fit the line very well. Some have emended the verb to *yabbîaʿ* ("gushes"; cf. BHS mg.). Driver, on the basis of the Arabic *balağa*, reads "enunciates," which makes a fine parallel for the idea of false witnesses (cited by McKane,

p. 529). However the last verb is translated, the proverb clearly decries wilfully corrupting justice through false witnessing.

Retribution, its certainty

19:29

[29] Penalties are prepared for mockers,
and beatings for the backs of fools.

29 Fools will be punished. The lines are almost identical. *Šᵉp̱āṭîm* (lit., "judgments") is a metonymy and may be rendered "penalties." This parallels "beatings" closely and makes the emendation to *šᵉḇāṭîm* ("rods") unnecessary (cf. BHS mg.; see Notes).

Notes

29 The variant is drawn from the LXX's "scourges," which may have read שׁוֹטִים (*šôṭîm*).

Drink, its effects

20:1

[1] Wine is a mocker and beer a brawler;
whoever is led astray by them is not wise.

1 The use of alcohol can lead to foolish behavior. The formal parallelism shows first the effects of intoxication and then makes an evaluation. The drinks are wine and beer, made from grapes and grains (see Lev 10:9; Deut 14:26; Isa 28:7). The terms "wine" and "beer" may be metonymies for those who drink them, or they may be personifications. In either case the point is the conduct of the inebriated person—mocking (*lēṣ*) and brawling (*hōmeh*). The excessive use of intoxicants excites the drinker to boisterous behavior and aggressive and belligerent attitudes; it confuses the senses so that he is out of control. The only evaluation possible is that whoever imbibes is unwise—it just is not sensible to drink to excess (Toy, p. 382). Moreover, given the ease with which one may make a habit of this, it is wise to avoid alcohol entirely. In the OT the use of alcohol was not prohibited; in fact, it was regularly used at festivals and celebrations. But intoxication was considered out of bounds for a member of the covenant community (see 23:20–21, 29–35; 31:4–7).

Emotions, of a king

20:2

[2] A king's wrath is like the roar of a lion;
he who angers him forfeits his life.

2 It is unsafe to provoke the anger of a king. The verse begins with a comparison and then offers an explanation. The "wrath" (*'êmaṯ*) of a king is compared to a lion's roar, indicating imminent judgment. Anyone who angered a king would "forfeit" (*hôṭē';*

lit., "misses" or "sins against") his life. The verb *mit'abb^erô* is problematic. The Hebrew form suggests "is angry with," but the LXX more appropriately has "angers"; the word has also been taken to mean "vent anger against" (see Notes). The simple idea is that one would do well to stay away from any angry person, especially a king who cannot be treated like other men (Whybray, *Book of Proverbs,* p. 113). See also 16:14 and 19:12.

Notes

---

2 McKane (pp. 543–44) surveys several suggestions for מִתְעַבְּרוֹ (*mit'abb^erô*): the LXX has "he who irritates (the king)"; Driver has "he that is negligent," connecting to the Arabic *ğabara*; KB² has "he who loses his temper."

Conduct, avoiding strife

20:3

> ³It is to a man's honor to avoid strife,
> but every fool is quick to quarrel.

3 Honorable people find ways to avoid strife. A contrast is presented here between avoiding "strife" (*rîb*) and jumping at a chance for a "quarrel" (*yitgallā'* includes the idea of snarling like a dog). The former is the way of honor and dignity; the latter, the manner of a "fool" (*'^ewîl* here). One cannot avoid strife entirely but should avoid every unnecessary confrontation. As McKane says, the honorable person stops short of undignified and unedifying wrangling; this is the person who has the capacity of preserving a working relation with even the most difficult people (p. 537). See also 17:14, 28, and 18:2.

Laziness, its results

20:4

> ⁴A sluggard does not plow in season;
> so at harvest time he looks but finds nothing.

4 A farmer who is too lazy to plant at the right time will find no harvest. The parallel lines present the cause and the effect. The first line describes the lazy man or "sluggard" (*'āṣēl*) who does not plant in the autumn (see Notes). The right time for planting was the rainy season (see Gen 8:22). It was cold, wet, and unpleasant. Perhaps such discomfort was his excuse. The effect is that at harvest time, when he "looks" (*y^ešā'al*; lit., "asks"), there is "nothing" (*wā'āyin*). The verse suggests that he did plant but perhaps at the wrong time or half-heartedly (contrast Ps 126:5–6); he actually looks for some harvest. It is also possible to take the verb *y^ešā'al* to mean that he begs others for a share of their income. This character is typical of all who want excellence without putting forth the effort.

Notes

---

4 Toy rejects translations of "winter" (RV) or the "cold" (Latin) because the point is laziness (p. 384). But such interpretations of "autumn" are not far from the point.

Discernment, motives

20:5

> [5]The purposes of a man's heart are deep waters,
> but a man of understanding draws them out.

5 Those who are wise can discern the motives of the heart. This saying is one continuous sentence, although there is a bit of an antithesis. The counsel or purpose (*'ēṣāh*) in the heart is first compared to "deep waters." This figure probably means that one's motives are difficult to "fathom"—it takes a counselor with "understanding" (*t^e^ḇûnāh*) to "draw them out" (*yiḏlennāh* continuing the figure). The line shows how important good counseling is. Plaut notes that if we are not aware of our motivations, then others who are wise may enable us to discover them (p. 209). Of course, there is always the need for discernment as to how much should be dredged from within the heart. McKane takes a slightly different approach, interpreting the "deep waters" to mean profound ideas (as in 18:4). Accordingly, it would take the wise to use their skills of clarification and interpretation (p. 536).

Character traits, faithful love

20:6

> [6]Many a man claims to have unfailing love,
> but a faithful man who can find?

6 It is rare to find a truly faithful friend. A contrast is offered here between many who claim to have faithful love and the rarity of one who actually has it (see Notes). Many people profess "love" (*ḥeseḏ*), but such professions are often hollow. The shift to *'^e^mûnîm* ("faithful") in the second clause makes this clear and captures the truth—it is rare to find one on whom you may actually depend.

Notes

---

6 There are various renderings offered for this verse. The Targum makes it passive: many are called kind. Some take the line to read, "Most men meet people who will do them occasional kindnesses" (Greenstone, p. 213).

Integrity, its heritage

20:7

> 7 The righteous man leads a blameless life;
> blessed are his children after him.

7 The integrity of parents will extend to the lives of their children. Two terms portray this integrity—*ṣaddîq* and *b^e^tummô. Ṣaddîq* introduces the "righteous" man as a member of the believing community who strives to live according to God's standards, and *b^e^tummô* shows his life style to be "blameless." The line describes a parent who believes in the Lord and lives out the claims of his faith. Based on this the second clause anticipates a blessing on the children. In God's economy the nature and actions of parents have an effect on children (Exod 20:4–6); here the parents' legacy is righteousness, and so the children reap the benefits. See 14:26.

Justice, a king's discernment

20:8

> 8 When a king sits on his throne to judge,
> he winnows out all evil with his eyes.

8 The righteous king discerns right from wrong. The first clause lays the foundation, and the second explains its out-working. The king in the ancient world was a judge, one whose counsel stood (see 2 Sam 15:2–4; 1 Kings 3:28; Ps 72:4; Isa 11:3–4). This proverb names justice (*dîn*; NIV, "to judge") as the basis of his administration and then uses the image of winnowing to show that he removes evil from his realm (see Ps 101). The verse could apply to any person in authority, but certainly the principle stands that a just government roots out the evils of society (Plaut, p. 210). Unfortunately, no government has ever lived up to this ideal.

Conduct, sinlessness

20:9

> 9 Who can say, "I have kept my heart pure;
> I am clean and without sin"?

9 No one can say that he is pure in thought and deed. The two ideas are similar, but there is a development in thought with the second part. Using a rhetorical question, the sage affirms that no one is sinless. To claim to have kept the heart "pure" (*zikkîṯî*) would be to say that all decisions and motives were faultless; and to claim "I am clean" (*ṭāhartî*) would be to say that moral perfection was attained and that one was therefore acceptable to God (*ṭāhar,* "clean," in the Levitical laws of purification means "purged of all sin"). Many passages affirm the inevitability of our sinfulness (Gen 6:5; 1 Kings 8:46; Ps 143:2), and Psalm 51:7 teaches that one can claim to be pure only if made pure by divine forgiveness. The sages here reflect the weakness of humanity. McKane says that one "can never be certain that his mind is pure and that he is without alloy of sin. Even when he has no good reason to believe otherwise, and might draw such a conclusion in good faith, he cannot be certain that he is not self-deceived and has failed to plumb unsuspected depths of duplicity and perversion which Yahweh will take into account" (p. 548). So this proverb should bring us to personal humility and engender in us an understanding of the failures of others.

Honesty, in business

20:10

[10] Differing weights and differing measures—
the LORD detests them both.

10 The Lord detests dishonesty in business. See v.23 and 11:1, which are based on Deuteronomy 25:13–16.

Righteousness, displayed in actions

20:11

[11] Even a child is known by his actions,
by whether his conduct is pure and right.

11 Righteous conduct reveals righteous character. The verse develops through synthetic parallelism the idea that a young child's character can be recognized by his actions. The *na'ar* in the first nine chapters referred to a young man, one whose character is formed in his early life; but here it refers to a younger boy. Parents can recognize (*yiṯnakker;* NIV, "is known") certain traits in a child's conduct. If it is pure and upright, they can cultivate this; if it is not, they must try to develop it through teaching, disciplining, and personal example.

Human nature, God's creation

20:12

[12] Ears that hear and eyes that see—
the LORD has made them both.

12 The Lord has prepared people with the capacity to see and hear. The statement "ears that hear and eyes that see" refers to the two basic senses, although Toy thinks that they represent all the God-given faculties. Certainly Scripture affirms that (see Exod 4:11). By usage hearing also means obeying (see 1 Sam 15:22; Prov 15:31; 25:12) and seeing also means perceiving or understanding (as in Isa 6:9–10). The verse not only credits the Lord with creating these senses but reminds everyone of their spiritual use in God's service.

Diligence, rewarded

20:13

[13] Do not love sleep or you will grow poor;
stay awake and you will have food to spare.

13 Diligence leads to prosperity. The verse is antithetical parallelism, the ideas of loving sleep and staying awake being contrasted, as well as their results of growing poor and being satisfied. Just as "sleep" can be used for slothfulness (see Ps 121), so opening the eyes and staying awake can represent vigorous, active conduct. The second line uses two imperatives to stress the point: "stay awake . . . and [in order that you may] be satisfied" (NIV, "you will have food to spare"). See also 6:9–11 and 19:15.

Honesty, in business

20:14

> [14]"It's no good, it's no good!" says the buyer;
> then off he goes and boasts about his purchase.

14 Some people falsely appraise a deal to gain a bargain. This humorous but realistic point may be looked at in several ways. It presents a buyer who complains about how bad the deal is for him: "It's no good, it's no good" (*raʿ raʿ*) and then goes away bragging about it. This may simply reflect normal procedure in a world where haggling for prices was common, but it may also be a warning to the inexperienced on how things are done and probably also evaluates it as a questionable business practice. Shrewdness is one thing, but deceitful misrepresentation in the deal in order to buy under value becomes unethical.

Speech, wise words

20:15

> [15]Gold there is, and rubies in abundance,
> but lips that speak knowledge are a rare jewel.

15 It is rare to find someone who speaks knowledgeably. The verse is normally taken as antithetical parallelism, "gold" and "rubies" being contrasted with "lips that speak knowledge." Toy, however, would arrange it as follows: "store of gold and wealth of corals and precious vessels—all are wise lips" (p. 388). "Lips that speak knowledge" should be taken to mean "lips that impart knowledge," viz., wise speech.

Obligations, fulfilled

20:16

> [16]Take the garment of one who puts up security for
> a stranger;
> hold it in pledge if he does it for a wayward woman.

16 People should be held to their obligations. Two synonymous lines teach that a person who foolishly becomes responsible for another person's debts should be made to keep his word. Taking the garment was the way of holding someone responsible to pay debts. The "one" for whom this person took responsibility is called "a stranger" (*zār // noḵrîyāh;* see Notes). The reference may be to other members of society in general. Dahood tries to argue that the cloak was given in pledge for a harlot; so two crimes are here: taking a cloak and going to a wayward woman, reading *noḵrîyāh* (M. Dahood, "To Pawn One's Cloak," *Biblica* 42 [1961]: 359–66; see also Snijders, "The Meaning of זָר," pp. 85–86).

Notes

16 The text involves a *Kethiv-Qere* reading for נָכְרִיָּם (*nokrîyām*). The text has the plural, "strangers" or "other men," but the marginal note has "strange woman" or "another man's wife" (as in 27:13). The parallelism suggests "strangers" is the correct reading, although theories have been presented with regard to the idea of the wayward woman (NIV). Plaut moderately says that willful foolishness must be paid for, especially when it involves another man's wife (p. 211).

Dishonesty, its effects

20:17

17 Food gained by fraud tastes sweet to a man,
but he ends up with a mouth full of gravel.

17 Good things that were acquired dishonestly will not bring satisfaction. The before and after scenes are presented in the two lines. "Food gained by fraud" means anything that is obtained through dishonest means: "food" harmonizes with the image of "sweet" (*'ārēb*) in the initial response. The imagery is advanced in the second line: "he ends up with a mouth full of gravel" (a mass of small particles; see Job 20:14–15; Lam 3:16). One thinks immediately of the bitterness after eating the forbidden fruit (Gen 3), but this verse applies to anything wrongfully acquired.

Plans, sound advice

20:18

18 Make plans by seeking advice;
if you wage war, obtain guidance.

18 Effective plans incorporate sound advice. This verse is written as an injunction; it presents a continuous idea of first making the plans and then waging the war. Sound "advice" (*'ēṣāh*) and "guidance" (*taḥbulôt*) are indispensable to the success of the mission. There have been many attempts to offer figurative interpretations of "war" as life struggles, litigation, or even evil inclinations (Rashi); but there is no reason or justification for this—it likely describes preparation for going to war, and in that there is wisdom in the consensus of leaders (see 24:6).

Speech, gossip

20:19

19 A gossip betrays a confidence;
so avoid a man who talks too much.

19 It is dangerous to associate with a gossip. The first line pictures the gossip as one who goes about revealing secrets, and the second line warns against associating with the person who opens his mouth too much. The idea of "opens his lips" is that such a one is always ready to talk; and if he is willing to talk to you about others, he will be willing to talk to others about you. McKane observes that these people are not necessarily malicious; they just lack discernment and are too garrulous (p. 537). The less contact one has with a gossip, the better off he will be.

Conduct, cursing parents

20:20

> 20 If a man curses his father or mother,
> his lamp will be snuffed out in pitch darkness.

20 Whoever curses his parents will be destroyed. Under the law (Exod 21:17; Lev 20:9; Deut 27:16), whoever cursed his parents was cursed with death. That judgment seems to be caught poetically in this single sentence proverb. The topic is cursing (*m*^{e}*qallēl*, "treating lightly, contemptuously") parents. Plaut reminds us that this can be done in a number of ways, including denying and disparaging one's origin and background (p. 212). The punishment is that "his lamp [*nērô*] will be snuffed out [*yiḏʿaḵ*]," and he will be left in pitch darkness. The lamp is metaphorical for the life; for the lamp to go out would mean death (see 13:9) and possibly also removal of posterity (see Whybray, *Book of Proverbs*, p. 115). In actual practice this may have been a social punishment only, that he be considered as one who is dead (see Toy, p. 390).

Prosperity, sudden but unsatisfying

20:21

> 21 An inheritance quickly gained at the beginning
> will not be blessed at the end.

21 Sudden prosperity may not prove satisfying. The statement that prosperity gained suddenly will not be blessed in the end seems rather general. The implication is that what is "quickly gained" (*m*^{e}*ḇōḥeleṯ*) is either unlawful or unrighteous. The verb describes a hurried or hastened activity; perhaps a wayward son seizes the inheritance quickly (cf. Luke 15:12) or even drives out his parents (cf. Prov 19:26). In either case divine justice is at work—this enterprise "will not be blessed" (*lō' ṯ*^{e}*ḇōrāḵ*); rather than prosper, it will probably be wasted.

Retribution, God's work

20:22

> 22 Do not say, "I'll pay you back for this wrong!"
> Wait for the LORD, and he will deliver you.

22 Leave retribution to the Lord. Let him bring about a just deliverance. The verse uses two imperatives to make the point; there is a slight antithesis between the two since one is negative ("Do not say") and the other positive ("Wait"). The righteous should not take vengeance on evil, for only God can repay evil justly (cf. Rom 12:19–20). The response of the righteous must be to "wait" (*qawwēh*) on the Lord; this involves belief in and reliance on him. The work of the Lord here focuses on the positive side—he is a deliverer (*yōšaʿ*) rather than an avenger, although to deliver the righteous would involve judgment on the wicked. The spirit of the verse is caught in *Gittin* 7a (b Tal): "Do not even ask him to inflict punishment on them."

Honesty, in business

20:23

[23]The LORD detests differing weights,
and dishonest scales do not please him.

23 The Lord detests dishonesty in business. See the idea in v.10 as well as in 11:1.

Providence, divine

20:24

[24]A man's steps are directed by the LORD.
How then can anyone understand his own way?

24 God's control of our lives is beyond human comprehension. The proverb contains an affirmation and then a rhetorical question based on it: the "steps of a mighty man [*miṣʿadê-gāḇer;* NIV, 'A man's steps']" are from the Lord—how, then, can anyone discern or "understand" (*yāḇîn*) his way? How can anyone delude himself into thinking that he does not need the Lord when even a strong man's activities are divinely prepared. (See, for example, Gen 50:20; see also Prov 3:6 for the proper advice in view of this truth.) McKane says: "No man can walk with enlightened assurance along the path of life by reason of a well-cultivated nicety of judgment and power of intellectual penetration. He is dependent at every step of the way on Yahweh, and without his light on his path his journey is deprived of safe guidance and enlightened purposiveness" (pp. 546–47).

Speech, rash vows

20:25

[25]It is a trap for a man to dedicate something rashly
and only later to consider his vows.

25 Do not get caught in a rash vow. This single sentence warning about making a rash vow addresses what was a common problem. Dedicating rashly, literally declaring something sacred (as in Mark 7:11), is considered a "trap" (*môqēš*) because it leads the person into financial difficulties (Lev 27 explains that Israelites could buy themselves out of rash vows—it was expensive). Whybray broadens the warning to the avoidance of all unconsidered action (*Book of Proverbs*, p. 116). After making a vow, one must consider how he will fulfill it. Too many people will make promises under the inspiration of the hour only later to realize that they have strapped themselves; they then try to go back on their word.

Justice, removing wickedness

20:26

[26]A wise king winnows out the wicked;
he drives the threshing wheel over them.

26 A wise king purges his kingdom of the wicked. Using a loose synonymous parallelism, the sage draws on the image of winnowing to explain how the king removes evil from his empire. The metaphor implies that the king can identify and rightly judge evildoers. The figure of driving the wheel over them represents a threshing process; the sharp iron wheels of the threshing cart would easily serve the purpose (cf. Isa 28:27–28). So this image also expresses the king's discrimination and ability to destroy evil from his domain. See also D. Winton Thomas, "Proverbs 20:26," JTS 15 (1964): 155–56.

Conscience, searching motives

20:27

27 The lamp of the LORD searches the spirit of a man;
it searches out his inmost being.

27 God provided everyone with a spirit that can evaluate actions and motives. The Hebrew literally says that the "breath" (*nišma<u>t</u>;* NIV, "spirit") is the lamp of the Lord, although the NIV interprets it differently and supplies "searches" to v.27a from v.27b. (Loewenstamm reads *nîr* ["to plow"] instead of *nēr* ["lamp"] to say that God "ploughs and examines the soul" ["Remarks on Proverbs 17:12 and 20:27," p. 223].) The *n*e*šāmāh* is that inner spiritual part of human life that was inbreathed at the Creation (Gen 2:7) and that constitutes humans as spiritual beings with moral, intellectual, and spiritual capacities. This spiritual nature includes the capacity to know and please God—it serves as the functioning conscience (the metaphor of "lamp"). This point is further developed in the second part; the searching makes it possible for people to know themselves. If one's spiritual life is functioning properly (i.e., yielded to God through salvation and controlled by his word [Heb 4:12]), then there should be increasingly less self-deception or indifference to righteousness.

Stability, in government

20:28

28 Love and faithfulness keep a king safe;
through love his throne is made secure.

28 Faithful covenant-love brings stability in society. The parallel ideas stress the security of the king's administration. The first line uses "love and faithfulness [lit., 'truth']" (*ḥese<u>d</u> we'*e*me<u>t</u>*), two terms that often form a hendiadys to express reliable love. *Ḥese<u>d</u>* is singled out of this couplet to form the parallel idea that the throne is secure. These are covenant terms. In the Davidic covenant (cf. 2 Sam 7:11–16) God promised not to take his covenant love (*ḥese<u>d</u>*) from the king (cf. v.15) but to make his house stable (*ne'*e*man*, "will endure," v.16). The two ideas are reiterated in Psalm 89:19–37, which expresses the covenant in poetry. It is the Lord and his faithfulness to his covenant that ultimately makes the empire secure; but the enjoyment of divine protection requires the king to rule with loyalty to the covenant.

Character traits, strength and honor

20:29

29 The glory of young men is their strength,
gray hair the splendor of the old.

29 Both youth and old age have their glory. This little observation reminds us that there are different commendations in life. For young men it is strength; for old men it is gray hair. This verse must be taken in the context of ancient Israel and not modern civilization, which often has little respect for the elderly. "Gray hair" symbolizes everything valuable about age: dignity, wisdom, honor, experience. At the very least one could say that since the elderly have survived, they must know something. At the most, they were the sages and wise elders of the people.

Discipline, spiritual value

20:30

30 Blows and wounds cleanse away evil,
and beatings purge the inmost being.

30 Physical punishment may prove spiritually valuable. Loosely synonymous, the clauses focus on corporeal punishment: "blows and wounds" // "beatings." These "cleanse" (*tamrîq*, "rub away") the soul of evil (see Notes). Other proverbs have explained that certain people will never learn from such discipline, but in general this saying is true. Kidner says that where the conscience is slow to work (see v.27), this intervention may be necessary (*Proverbs*, p. 141). He then reminds us of the bruising and stripes of the Suffering Servant, through which we are healed—an interesting turn of the sentiment here (Isa 53:5).

Notes

30 This verse is difficult. The LXX has "blows and contusions fall on evil men, and stripes penetrate their inner beings"; the Latin has "the bruise of a wound cleanses away evil things." Toy suggests adopting the LXX or emending the line to read "Stripes cleanse the body, and blows the inward parts" or "cosmetics purify the body, and blows the soul" (p. 397).

Sovereignty of God

21:1

1 The king's heart is in the hand of the LORD;
he directs it like a watercourse wherever he pleases.

1 A king's decisions are controlled by God. The verse uses synthetic parallelism to develop the point: the first line affirms that the decisions ("heart") of the king are under the Lord's control ("in the hand"), and the second explains that he directs the king as he pleases. What clarifies the second line is the simile the heart is "like a watercourse." As a farmer channels the water where he wants and regulates its flow, so does the Lord with the king. No human ruler, then, is supreme; or, to put it another way, the Lord is truly the King of kings. Scripture offers many examples (Ezra 7:21; Isa 10:6–7; 41:2–4; Dan 2:21; John 19:11).

Knowledge, divine

21:2

[2]All a man's ways seem right to him,
but the LORD weighs the heart.

2 The Lord evaluates our motives and not merely our actions. The verse, in antithetical parallelism, reiterates the point that we think we know ourselves; but the Lord knows our hearts, and his knowledge is evaluative. The verse is similar to 16:2.

Righteousness, its priority

21:3

[3]To do what is right and just
is more acceptable to the LORD than sacrifice.

3 The Lord requires righteousness before religious service. This single sentence affirms that to do what is "right" (*ṣ^e^ḏāqāh*) and "just" (*mišpāṭ*) is more acceptable to the Lord than sacrifice. The theme appears elsewhere (15:8; 21:29; 1 Sam 15:22; Ps 40:6–8; Isa 1:11–17; et al.). It does not teach that ritual acts of worship are to be avoided; rather, it stresses that religious acts are valueless without righteous living.

Character traits, pride

21:4

[4]Haughty eyes and a proud heart,
the lamp of the wicked, are sin!

4 Arrogant pride is sin. The verse is one continuous sentence, but the Hebrew is difficult. The MT reads, "Haughty eyes and a proud heart, the tillage of the wicked [*nir r^e^šā'îm*] is sin [*ḥaṭṭā'ṯ*]." The meaning of the line seems clear enough, but the relationship of the clauses needs explanation. The problem is *nir* ("tillage"); this figure indicates that the product of the wicked is sin. McKane explains that the wicked cannot be cultivated; they are not amenable to educational discipline (p. 559). But the difficulty remains in the line: Are pride and arrogance the product of the wicked? Even if one accepts the reading *nēr* ("lamp"), based on the LXX and the Aramaic, forming a nice contrast with 20:27—here it is the lamp of the wicked—there is still no clear connection in the verse. Toy suggests that the recovery of the text or its meaning seems impossible (p. 399). In general we may say that the verse portrays pride as sin.

Prosperity, patient planning

21:5

[5]The plans of the diligent lead to profit
as surely as haste leads to poverty.

5 Patience and planning lead to prosperity. By antithetical parallelism the verse exhorts industriousness. On the one hand, the "plans of the diligent" (*maḥš^e^ḇôṯ ḥārûṣ*) lead to profit; but on the other, "haste" (*'āṣ*) leads to poverty. Toy thinks that the contrast between the diligent and hasty is not precise and suggests changing hasty to "slothful" (p. 399). To make such a change, however, would be to level out the line to what McKane calls a pedestrian antithesis: the text contrasts calculated expeditiousness and unproductive haste (p. 550). The text here warns about the danger of hasty shortcuts. See also 10:4 and 28:20.

Prosperity, by fraud

21:6

6 A fortune made by a lying tongue
is a fleeting vapor and a deadly snare.

6 A fortune gained by fraudulent means will be a fleeting treasure. Here again the Hebrew lines are difficult. The subject, expressed in the first part, is clear—it concerns a "fortune" (*'ôṣārôṯ*) made by a "lying" (*šāqer*) tongue. Two ideas comprise the predicate: "fleeting vapor" and "deadly snare." The *heḇel niddāp̱* is more properly a "driven vapor" or "driven vanity"; it is as if the treasure disappears into thin air (Greenstone, p. 223). The second idea, "deadly snare" (lit., "snares of death"), is derived from a change based on the LXX; for the Hebrew has "seekers of death," which seems meaningless (see Notes). "Snares of death" occurs also in Psalm 18:5. The point of the verse, then, is that ill-gotten gain is a fleeting pleasure and a crime for which punishment is prepared.

Notes

6 The MT's מְבַקְשֵׁי־מָוֶת (*m*[e]*ḇaqšê-māweṯ*, "seekers of death") presumably would fit as follows: "a fleeting vapor for those who seek death." The variant reading מוֹקְשֵׁי (*môq*[e]*šê*, "snares of") is supported by the LXX and Latin. This reading does not make a more credible metaphor, and one must explain the loss of the letter beth. Nonetheless it is a little easier to interpret within the verse—the fortune is a deadly snare (as opposed to the fortune is a vapor for those who seek death).

Retribution, just

21:7

7 The violence of the wicked will drag them away,
for they refuse to do what is right.

7 The wicked will be destroyed in their own devices. The sentence affirms this truth and then explains it. It is the "violence" (*šōḏ*) of the wicked that destroys them—it "drags them away" (*y*[e]*ḡôrēm*), probably to more sin, but ultimately to their punishment. But they are not passive victims of their crimes or circumstances—"they refuse" (*mē'*[a]*nû*) to do justice. In the final analysis they can blame only themselves, for they chose to persist in evil rather than do what is right.

Righteousness, revealed in works

21:8

> [8]The way of the guilty is devious,
> but the conduct of the innocent is upright.

8 Righteous behavior reveals righteous character. The antithetical clause asserts that it is also true that sinful acts betray the wicked. The first line is difficult: "The way of the guilty [*'îš wāzār*] is devious." Since *wāzār* occurs only here, it has received much attention. The idea of "guilty" is drawn from an Arabic cognate meaning "bear a burden" and so "sin laden" or "guilty." Driver prefers the idea that "a man crooked of way is false [*zār*]" (Driver, "Problems in the Hebrew Text," p. 185). Toy adopts the idea of "proud." Whether they are here described as guilty, false, or proud, the point is that the men described are devious. Toy says that bad men are underhanded, whereas good men are above board (p. 400).

Another way to analyze the line is to take *zār* to mean "strange" or "stranger," yielding, "The way of a man and a stranger is perverse." But this would form no satisfactory contrast to v.8b. Another suggestion is "the way of (usual) man is changeable and strange, but the pure fellow leads a straight and even course" (Greenstone, p. 244). The second line is clear: "The conduct of the innocent is upright." This is the antithesis of the deviousness of the wicked.

Family, peaceful relationships

21:9

> [9]Better to live on a corner of the roof
> than share a house with a quarrelsome wife.

9 Simplicity with peace is better than prosperity with strife. The line is formal parallelism, framed as one of the "better" sayings. The situation presented is sharing a house with a quarrelsome wife. The *bêṯ ḥāḇer* (lit., "house of company") has received numerous interpretations (see the discussion in McKane, p. 554). According to this verse it would be better to live on the corner of the roof. The reference is probably to a little guest room that would be built on the roof (see 1 Kings 17:19; 2 Kings 4:10). It would be cramped and lonely—but peaceful in avoiding strife. The LXX removes all reference to a quarrelsome wife in favor of the idea of injustice in a common house.

Character traits, wicked

21:10

> [10]The wicked man craves evil;
> his neighbor gets no mercy from him.

10 The wicked pursue evil and not mercy. The saying gives the observation, "the wicked . . . craves [*'iwwᵉṯāh*] evil [*rā'*]," and its consequence, "his neighbor gets no mercy [*lō'-yuḥan*, 'favor']." See also 4:16; 10:23; 12:10; and Isaiah 1:16–17. The person who lives to satisfy his craving for evil thinks only of himself. McKane observes that since humanity consists of reaching out to help others, "the man who cannot transcend his own self-assertiveness is in a prison and is dehumanized" (p. 556). It is the propensity for evil that constitutes him as "wicked."

Discipline, its effect

21:11

[11]When a mocker is punished, the simple gain wisdom;
when a wise man is instructed, he gets knowledge.

11 How mature one is determines how easily he will learn. The contrast is between the wise and the simple; the former learns by instruction, the latter by example. The wise person will gain knowledge through "instruction" (*behaśkîl*). This instruction not only causes him to know but gives insight into the issues of life. The wise person never stops learning. By contrast the "mocker" (*lēṣ*) is unteachable. Nevertheless he should be punished, because the "simple" (*peṯî*) will "gain wisdom" (*yeḥkam*) through seeing his punishment. See also 19:25.

Judgment, its certainty

21:12

[12]The Righteous One takes note of the house of the wicked
and brings the wicked to ruin.

12 Righteousness will be satisfied when the wicked are punished. There are two very different ways that this proverb can be taken. The easiest interpretation is to take *ṣaddîq* to refer to God, "The Righteous One." God observes the house of the wicked and then hurls them to ruin (see 22:12; Toy, p. 402; Plaut, p. 220; Kidner, *Proverbs*, p. 143). But Proverbs does not refer to God in this way. The other interpretation takes *ṣaddîq* to refer to a "righteous man" (see NIV mg.), presumably a judge or ruler, who, although he might be kindly disposed to the family of the wicked, is obliged to condemn him (Greenstone, p. 225).

Character traits, unmerciful

21:13

[13]If a man shuts his ears to the cry of the poor,
he too will cry out and not be answered.

13 Those who show no mercy will not obtain mercy. Measure for measure justice is expressed by this cause and effect statement: The one who shuts his ears from the cry of the poor (i.e., refuses to help) will not be listened to when he cries out for help. So talionic justice is meted out for the omission of a commandment as well as for evil acts. See Luke 16:19–31 for a sample.

Injustice, bribery

21:14

[14]A gift given in secret soothes anger,
and a bribe concealed in the cloak pacifies great wrath.

14 Bribes can effectively pacify an angry person. The two clauses are synonymous; the first uses the more neutral word *mattān* ("gift") and the second the word *šōḥaḏ* ("bribe"). Kidner notes that their parallelism in the proverb underscores how hard it often is to discern the difference (*Proverbs*, p. 143). The verse does not condemn or condone; it merely observes the effectiveness of the practice. Although the verb "soothes" (*yikpeh*) is satisfactory, various commentators attempt to emend it to forms such as *yekappēr* ("covers") or *yekabbeh* ("extinguishes") (see BHS). The point of the verse is clear without the change (see Notes). The idea of the gift given in secret influenced the interpretation of the verse in the Talmud as a righteous act of charity (see *Baba Bathra* 9b: "Whoever does this in secret is greater than Moses our teacher").

Notes

14 The LXX offers a moralizing interpretation not too closely tied to the MT: "He who withholds a gift stirs up violent wrath."

Justice, its effects

21:15

15 When justice is done, it brings joy to the righteous
but terror to evildoers.

15 How people respond to justice reveals their character. The occasion—"When justice is done"—could refer specifically to a legal decision or to doing right in general. The point is that people who are law-abiding citizens are pleased with justice; those who are not are terrified by it, tend to ridicule it, and try to get around it in some way. *Mehittāh* means "terror," although some commentators prefer to change it to "dismay" to make a better parallel with *śimḥāh* ("joy"). But the idea of "terror" heightens the contrast (Toy, p. 404); the wicked may be shaken into reality when justice is carried.

Wisdom, its importance

21:16

16 A man who strays from the path of understanding
comes to rest in the company of the dead.

16 Those who abandon the way of wisdom inevitably ruin their lives. The verse is a single sentence with the second part providing the predicate. The subject matter is one who wanders (*tô'eh*) away from the "path of understanding" or prudence (*haśkēl*), i.e., one who does not live according to the knowledge, discipline, and insight of wisdom. This one "comes to rest" (*yānûaḥ*) in the "company of the shades" (*qehal repā'îm;* NIV, "dead"). The verb "rest" does not carry with it the comforting idea of repose but merely that of "dwell," for to rest among the "shades" is to be numbered among the dead. Physical death is once again presented as the punishment for folly, which is sin. Plaut remarks, "Errant man will destroy himself before his time"

(p. 221); he will follow the broad way that leads to destruction and find himself among the dead (Matt 7:13–14).

Pleasure, its cost

21:17

> [17]He who loves pleasure will become poor;
> whoever loves wine and oil will never be rich.

17 Living a life of self-indulgent pleasure leads to poverty. By two synonymous lines the sage makes his point that the unbridled love of the finest things of life is very costly. "Joy" (*śimḥāh;* NIV, "pleasure") represents the effect of the good life; "wine and oil" represent the cause for joy (so the metonymies work together). "Oil" signifies the anointing that goes with the luxurious life (see Pss 23:5; 104:15; Amos 6:6). There is nothing wrong with joy or with enjoying the finest things in life. The "love" that is here portrayed must be excessive or uncontrolled, because it brings one to poverty. Perhaps other responsibilities are being neglected or the people are trying to live above their means.

Judgment, just

21:18

> [18]The wicked become a ransom for the righteous,
> and the unfaithful for the upright.

18 Divine justice will be administered righteously. In what way are the wicked a "ransom" (*kōp̱er*) for the righteous? "Ransom" normally refers to the price paid to free a prisoner. Whybray puts the verse in perspective: If it means that the wicked obtain good things that should go to the righteous, it is then a despairing plea for justice (which would be unusual in Proverbs); but if it is taken to mean that the wicked suffers the evil he has prepared for the righteous, then it harmonizes with Proverbs (e.g., 11:8) (*Book of Proverbs*, p. 121). The saying is either a general statement or an ideal that in calamity the righteous escape but the wicked perish in their stead (example, Haman in the Book of Esther). We must think, as Toy puts it, when God punishes a community, it is the bad, not the good, that he is directing his anger against (p. 406). Believers have a wholehearted trust in the justice of God (see Gen 18:23–25).

Family, peaceful relations

21:19

> [19]Better to live in a desert
> than with a quarrelsome and ill-tempered wife.

19 Being alone is preferable to enduring domestic strife. This verse reiterates the theme of v.9 (see also 25:24), with one change—"a desert," which would be sparsely settled and quiet. These verses surely advise one to be careful in choosing a marriage partner and then to be diligent in cultivating the proper graces to make the marriage enjoyable.

Wisdom, its frugality

21:20

> [20] In the house of the wise are stores of choice food
> and oil,
> but a foolish man devours all he has.

20 With keen foresight and appropriate frugality, the wise prepare for the future. The verse makes the point by contrasting the wise and the fool (*k*ᵉ*sîl*). In the wise person's house are "precious treasure and oil" (*'ôṣār neḥmāḏ wāšemen;* NIV, "choice food and oil"), but the foolish man "devours it" (*y*ᵉ*ḇall*ᵉ*'ennû*). The verse basically means that the wise gain wealth but the foolish squander it. The mention of "oil" is problematic—How can a fool devour oil? Toy suggests dropping "oil" from the verse on the basis of the LXX (p. 406); but the LXX seems too free for any support: "precious treasure will rest on the mouth of the sage." McKane adopts the view that *šemen* should be repointed *šāmîm* after an Arabic word *ṯamīn* ("expensive") and the line rendered "desirable and rare wealth" (p. 552). This idea does not match the metaphor any better; the figure of "devouring" simply means that the fool uses up whatever substance there is. McKane says that the fool lets money run through his fingers and does not use it to create a material environment for gracious living (ibid.).

Righteousness, its rewards

21:21

> [21] He who pursues righteousness and love
> finds life, prosperity and honor.

21 Virtue will be rewarded. In fact, the idea may be that virtue has its own rewards. "Righteousness" (*ṣ*ᵉ*ḏāqāh*) and "love" (*ḥāseḏ*) depict the life style of the faithful covenant-believer who is pleasing to God and a blessing to others. Whoever pursues righteousness will be filled with "life, prosperity and honor." "Prosperity" is *ṣ*ᵉ*ḏāqāh* again; so there is a wordplay on the term, the first use giving the basic meaning of conduct that conforms to God's standard and the second the effect of such righteousness. The idea of the proverb is renewed in the words of Jesus: "Blessed are those who hunger and thirst for righteousness, / for they will be filled" (Matt 5:6; see also Matt 6:33).

Wisdom, greater than strength

21:22

> [22] A wise man attacks the city of the mighty
> and pulls down the stronghold in which they trust.

22 It is more effective to use wisdom than to rely on strength. This proverb uses a military scene to describe the superiority of wisdom; the lines are loosely synonymous. It tells how the wise can scale the walls of the city of the "mighty" (*gibbōrîm*) and pull down their trusted stronghold. In a war the victory is credited not so much to the infantry as to the tactician, the general who plans the attack. Brilliant strategy wins wars, even over apparently insuperable odds. See also Proverbs 24:5–6; Ecclesiastes

9:13–16; and 2 Corinthians 10:4, which explains that wisdom from above is necessary for spiritual victory.

Speech, controlled

21:23

23 He who guards his mouth and his tongue
keeps himself from calamity.

23 People who control what they say are more likely to avoid trouble than those who speak freely. The verse is a continuous sentence offering the consequences of an action—guarding the mouth and the tongue. The "calamity" (*ṣārôṯ*) may refer to social and legal difficulties into which careless talk might bring someone (see 13:3; 18:21). Therefore one should say only what is true, helpful, pleasant, and kind and avoid what is false, destructive, painful, and damaging to others.

Character traits, pride

21:24

24 The proud and arrogant man—"Mocker" is his name;
he behaves with overweening pride.

24 The two lines of v.24, loosely synonymous, portray the godless attitude and the scornful arrogance of the "mocker" (*lēṣ*). He is "proud" (*zēḏ*) and "arrogant" (*yāhîr*), acting with "overweening pride" (*beʿeḇraṯ zāḏôn*). Pride may refer to the refusal to submit to the Lord or describe the refusal to learn from wisdom (McKane, p. 551). While the latter may be in view here, the two are not unrelated. This verse describes the nature ("name") of the irreligious mocker as insolent and proud. He is a most unpleasant fellow, disliked even by his own family, the Talmud observes (*Aboda Zarah* 18b; *Sotah* 47b).

Laziness, its outcome

21:25

25 The sluggard's craving will be the death of him,
because his hands refuse to work.

25 The lazy come to ruin because they desire the easy way out. The "sluggard's desire [*taʾawaṯ;* NIV, 'craving']" must be coupled with "his hands refuse to work [*mēʾanû*]" to understand the point. Living in a world of wishful thinking and not working will bring ruin (*temîṯennû* ["will be the death of him"] probably is used hyperbolically). Plaut suggests that there may be more to this idea: the sluggard might set his goals too high, far out of reach, thus paralyzing himself and producing nothing (p. 223). At any rate, the verse teaches that doing rather than desiring brings success.

Generosity, evidence of righteousness

21:26

26 All day long he craves for more,
but the righteous give without sparing.

26 Generosity reveals righteousness. This verse has been placed with the preceding because of the literary connection with "desire"—"he craves for more" (*hiṯ'awwāh ta'awāh*), but it provides an independent thought. The verse contrasts the one who craves with the righteous who give generously. The Bible teaches that the righteous person is a giving person. One thinks of the contrast between Abram and Lot in Genesis 13; Lot chose the most desirable land for himself, but Abram gave Lot his preference. To be generous in that way requires walking by faith and not by sight.

Worship, unacceptable

21:27

[27] The sacrifice of the wicked is detestable—
how much more so when brought with evil intent!

27 God abhors worship without righteousness. The verse affirms that the "sacrifice" (*zeḇaḥ*) of the wicked is an abomination to the Lord and then intensifies the idea ("how much more") by referring to "evil intent" (*zimmāh*) with the sacrifice. Hypocritical worship is bad enough; worship with evil intent is deplorable. God does not want acts of worship without repentance; but he certainly detests them from someone still bent on wickedness, who thinks a sacrifice will buy continued acceptance with God. In popular religion people soon came to think that sacrifices could be given for any offense and without genuine submission to God. This happens with all religious acts. But God first requires of the worshiper true repentance and resolution to live righteously.

Speech, true and false witnesses

21:28

[28] A false witness will perish,
and whoever listens to him will be destroyed forever.

28 False witnesses will be discredited and destroyed. The verse is obscure, although it contrasts true and false witnesses. The first line affirms that the "false witness" (*'ēḏ-kezāḇîm*) "will perish" (*yō'ḇēḏ*), meaning that either his testimony will be destroyed or that he will be punished. The second line literally says, "A man who listens shall speak forever." The NIV following cognates saw a homonym meaning "perish." "The man who listens" contrasts with the false witness of the preceding line and probably describes a witness who knows and understands what the truth is (Kidner, *Proverbs*, p. 146). The idea of speaking forever (*lāneṣaḥ yeḏabbēr*) does not make a precise parallel. Toy expected an idea like "will be established" to contrast with "will perish" (p. 411). McKane's suggestion, even though it strains the meanings of the words, probably fits the best: the truthful witness "will speak to the end" without being put down or refuted (in cross-examination) (p. 556).

Righteousness, its genuineness

21:29

[29] A wicked man puts up a bold front,
but an upright man gives thought to his ways.

29 Those who are truly righteous cultivate a consistent life style that is pleasing to God. Kidner summarizes the verse to say that a bold front is no substitute for sound principles (*Proverbs,* p. 146). The verse contrasts the wicked person who puts up a "bold front" (*hē'ēz b^e^p̄ānāyw*) with the upright person who solidifies (*yāḵîn,* "gives thought") righteous conduct. The image of the hardened face reflects a hardened heart (Plaut, p. 224); it portrays one who holds the opinions and views of others in contempt (see Isa 48:4; Jer 5:3; Ezek 3:7).

Sovereignty of God

21:30

30 There is no wisdom, no insight, no plan
that can succeed against the LORD.

30 Human "wisdom" (*ḥoḵmāh*), "insight" (*t^e^ḇûnāh*), and "counsel" (*'ēṣāh;* NIV, "plan") must be in conformity to the will of God to be successful. The verse uses a single sentence to declare that if these qualities are in defiance of God, they cannot succeed; for human wisdom is nothing in comparison to the wisdom of God (Greenstone, p. 232; see Job 5:12–13; see also Isa 40:13–14). McKane reminds us that these qualities are the claims of the sages who present themselves as the intellectual elite, adding, "But the sages do not in fact possess the prescience and control which are indicated by these high-sounding words; their vocabulary and claims make shipwreck on Yahweh, to whom alone the vocabulary which the wise men use of themselves and their intellectual powers really applies" (p. 558).

Sovereignty of God

21:31

31 The horse is made ready for the day of battle,
but victory rests with the LORD.

31 Ultimate success comes from God and not from human efforts. The contrast here is between the plans and efforts for the battle ("the horse is made ready for the day of battle") and the true acknowledgment of the source of victory—the Lord. See Psalms 20:7 and 33:17.

Reputation, good

22:1

1 A good name is more desirable than great riches;
to be esteemed is better than silver or gold.

1 A good reputation is more valuable than wealth. The verse is not disparaging wealth; it is merely noting that a good name is worth more than silver or gold. The lines are synonymously parallel, "name" being matched by "to be esteemed." In the first line "good" is understood. Only a good name would be desired; for it brings praise, influence, and prosperity. *Ḥēn ṭôḇ* in the second line means "good favor," i.e., one well thought of, who has engaging qualities. The point is that a good reputation excels other blessings in life (see *Aboth* 4:17). Kidner says that our proper joy is "not in the power we wield, but in the love in which we are held" (*Proverbs,* p. 146).

Sovereignty of God

22:2

[2]Rich and poor have this in common:
The LORD is the Maker of them all.

2 Regardless of status in life, all are equally God's creation. The line uses synthetic parallelism to make this point. Both the rich and the poor live side by side in this life (*nip̱gāšû* expresses this sharing; NIV, "have this in common"), but they both are part of the order of God's creation (McKane, p. 570). People often forget this and make value judgments; they would do well to treat all people with respect, for God can as easily reduce the rich as raise the poor.

Wisdom, avoiding trouble

22:3

[3]A prudent man sees danger and takes refuge,
but the simple keep going and suffer for it.

3 Those who are shrewd avoid the dangers of life. The contrast is between the "prudent" (*'ārûm*) and the naive or "simple" (*peṯayîm*). The prudent know where the dangers and pitfalls are in life; they are wary. They are the product of training in wisdom and discipline, for one of the purposes of this book was to make the naive (*peṯî*) wary (*'ārûm;* see 1:4). The simple person is unwary, uncritical, and credulous; he is not equipped to survive in this world and so blunders into trouble (McKane, p. 563). This verse develops the contrast: the prudent avoid danger, but the naive do not see it and "suffer" (*wene'enāšû;* the word describes a fine in 17:26 and 19:19; here it is more general). See 27:12.

Piety, its reward

22:4

[4]Humility and the fear of the LORD
bring wealth and honor and life.

4 God will reward reverential piety. The verse simply lists two spiritual qualifications (humility and fear) and then three rewards (wealth, honor, and life). The relationship between the clauses is expressed by *'ēqeḇ* ("consequence" or "reward"; NIV, "bring"). "Humility" (*'anāwāh*) is used here in the religious sense for piety and so fits well with "the fear of the LORD" (*yir'aṯ YHWH*). For the idea of life as the product of piety, see 21:21; for the reward, see 3:2, 16.

Security, through wisdom

22:5

[5]In the paths of the wicked lie thorns and snares,
but he who guards his soul stays far from them.

5 Those who have the discipline of wisdom avoid life's dangers. The two parts are loosely antithetical. The first clause informs us that the "wicked" (*'iqqēš*) is on a path to death. The way is covered with "thorns and snares." "Thorns" (*ṣinnîm*) seems out of place in the line; therefore many emend the text to *ṣammîm* ("traps"), making a better match—"traps and snares" (see Notes). In contrast to the wicked person is the one who guards his life and in so doing avoids the snares. This person is obviously the prudent who has learned to avoid the traps.

Notes

---

5 The word צִנִּים (*ṣinnîm*, "thorns") is obscure. It is supported by the LXX *τρίβολοι* (*triboloi*, "prickly plants") and an apparent cognate צְנִינִים (*ṣ[e]nînîm*, "thorns") in Num 33:55 and Josh 23:13. The idea of thorns in the way is found in Prov 15:19. Some commentators suggest צַמִּים (*ṣammîm*, "traps"; see Job 18:9). McKane traces a possible development from the idea of *ṣen* ("basket," "trap") to support this change (p. 565).

Family, child training

22:6

> [6]Train a child in the way he should go,
> and when he is old he will not turn from it.

6 Proper training of a child will endure throughout his life. The parallelism is formal; the second clause provides the consequence of the first. The imperative is "train" (*ḥ[a]nōḵ*); the verb includes the idea of "dedicate," and so the training should be with purpose. The "child" (*na'ar*) presumably is in the youngest years, although the Talmud would place him between sixteen and twenty-four. The NEB captures the point of early instruction: "Start a boy on the right road." The right road is expressed "in the way he should go" (*'al-pî ḏarkô*). The way the verse has been translated shows that there is a standard of life to which he should go. Of course, he would have to be young enough when change for the better was still possible. The consequence is that when he is old (*yazqîn*), he will not depart from it. Whybray notes that the sages were confident of the character-forming quality of their teaching (*Book of Proverbs*, p. 125).

In recent years it has become popular to interpret this verse to mean that the training should be according to the child's way. The view is not new; over a thousand years ago Saadia suggested that one should train the child in accordance with his ability and potential. The wise parent will discern the natural bent of the individual child and train it accordingly. Kidner acknowledges that the wording implies respect for the child's individuality but not his self-will; he reminds us that the emphasis is still on the parental duty of training (*Proverbs*, p. 147). Training in accordance with a child's natural bent may be a practical and useful idea, but it is not likely what this proverb had in mind. In the Book of Proverbs there are only two "ways" a child can go, the way of the wise and the righteous or the way of the fool and the wicked. Moreover, it is hard to explain why a natural bent needs training. Ralbag, in fact, offered a satirical interpretation: "Train the child according to his evil inclinations (let him have his will) and he will continue in his evil way throughout life" (cited in Greenstone, p. 234).

Toy summarizes the ways that one might take "according to his way": "not exactly 'in the path of industry and piety' (which would require *in the right way*), nor 'according to the bodily and mental development of the child' (which does not agree with the second cl.), but 'in accordance with the manner of life to which he is destined,' the implication being that the manner of life will not be morally bad" (p. 415). McKane agrees that "according to his way" must mean the way he ought to go; he says, "There is only one right way—the way of life—and the educational discipline which directs young men along this way is uniform" (p. 564).

Poverty, its effect

22:7

7 The rich rule over the poor,
and the borrower is servant to the lender.

7 Poverty makes people dependent on others. The parallel is synonymous. The verse simply states a fact that the poor or the borrowers become subservient to the rich. The verse may be referring to the apparently common practice of Israelites selling themselves into slavery to pay off debts (see Exod 21:2–7). It is not appreciably different from the modern debtor who is working to pay off bills.

Punishment, certain

22:8

8 He who sows wickedness reaps trouble,
and the rod of his fury will be destroyed.

8 God will surely destroy the power of the wicked. The first clause declares the truth that the one who sows "wickedness" (*'awlāh*) reaps "trouble" (*'āwen*). The second clause appears to carry this idea further to reveal how it works: "The rod of his fury [*šēḇeṭ 'eḇrāṯô*] will be destroyed" (see Notes). The symbol of the rod here represents his power for doing evil. One would conclude that in reaping trouble this fellow will no longer be able to unleash his fury. The LXX adds, "A man who is cheerful and a giver God blesses." So the idea is expressed in 2 Corinthians 9:7.

Notes

8 The expression שֵׁבֶט עֶבְרָתוֹ (*šēḇeṭ 'eḇrāṯô*, translated "the rod of his fury") has a variant in the LXX: "the punishment of his deeds." So Toy emends to *šeḇer* to read, "the produce of his work" (p. 416). But the Hebrew text is not obscure, and *šeḇer* does not actually mean "produce." Although "rod of his fury" may not follow closely the imagery of v.8a, it is understandable in the verse.

Generosity, its nature

22:9

9 A generous man will himself be blessed,
for he shares his food with the poor.

9 There is a reward for being generous to the poor. The generous person is here *ṭôḇ-ʿayin* ("a good eye") as opposed to the "evil eye" that is stingy and covetous. This person has a benevolent disposition, keen social conscience, and concern for the poor. The irony is that because he is not the prisoner of his selfish desires, he achieves the highest degree of self-fulfillment (McKane, p. 569).

Strife, its source

22:10

[10]Drive out the mocker, and out goes strife;
quarrels and insults are ended.

10 The mocker causes quarrels and strife. Written in loosely synonymous parallelism, this verse advises us to expel the "mocker" (*lēṣ*). One can think of a heckler who is present only to disrupt a meeting; before serious discussions can begin, he will have to be removed. The LXX freely expresses "when he sits in a council [*synedriō*], he insults everyone." The MT does not suggest that the setting is in a court of law; so there is probably no reference to the Sanhedrin.

Speech, honest and graceful

22:11

[11]He who loves a pure heart and whose speech
is gracious
will have the king for his friend.

11 Honest and gracious speech will be highly respected. The syntax of this verse is not easy to understand. The text seems to say, "He who loves purity of heart, the grace of his lips the king is his friend" (see Notes). The simplest interpretation is that someone who is honest and gracious will be welcomed in the courts of the palace. The same theme is found in 16:13.

Notes

11 The LXX reads, "The Lord loves the pure in heart; all who are blameless in their ways are acceptable to him." The LXX has very little correspondence with the MT; nevertheless commentators attempt to reconstruct the verse using it.

Sovereignty of God

22:12

[12]The eyes of the LORD keep watch over knowledge,
but he frustrates the words of the unfaithful.

12 The Lord ensures that truth—and not deception—succeeds. The lines are in antithetical parallelism, contrasting how God deals with truth and error: He "frustrates" (*yᵉsallēp̱*) the words of the "traitor" (*bōḡēḏ*; NIV, "unfaithful"); but he keeps "watch over knowledge." The point is clear enough—the Lord acts to vindicate the truth. D. Winton Thomas suggests a change of meaning from "knowledge" to "lawsuit" based on an Arabic cognate ("A Note on דַעַת in Proverbs 22:12," JTS NS 14 [1963]: 93–94). This is one possible solution to the difficulty that the abstract idea of "knowledge" is not used with the verb "watch" (*nāṣ^erû*). Toy's additional change is too radical; he has "The eyes of Yahweh are on the righteous," because this would fit normal usage (p. 418).

Laziness, its excuses

22:13

13 The sluggard says, "There is a lion outside!"
or, "I will be murdered in the streets!"

13 The lazy person makes absurd excuses for not working. The verse humorously portrays the sluggard as not going out because he might be eaten by a lion in the streets (cf. 26:13). The LXX changes it to "murderers in the street" to form a better parallelism, possibly because *rāṣaḥ* is used only of humans in the Bible.

Judgment, divine

22:14

14 The mouth of an adulteress is a deep pit;
he who is under the LORD's wrath will fall into it.

14 Divine judgment brings ruin on the adulterer. The topic is the "mouth of an adulteress," perhaps a reference to her seductive speech (see 2:16–22 and chs. 5; 7). It is described as a "deep pit" where the guilty fall under God's judgment. The pit is like the hunter's snare—it is difficult to escape. So to succumb to the adulteress—or to any such folly—is both a sin and its punishment.

Discipline, parental

22:15

15 Folly is bound up in the heart of a child,
but the rod of discipline will drive it far from him.

15 Discipline will remove a child's bent to folly. A general contrast first explains that "folly" (*'iwwelet*) is in the child and then instructs how to get rid of it—"the rod of discipline." Whybray suggests that this idea might be described as a doctrine of "original folly" (*Book of Proverbs*, p. 125). The child is morally immature; the training must suppress folly and develop potential (see also 13:24; 23:13, 16; 29:15).

Injustice, extortion and bribery

22:16

16 He who oppresses the poor to increase his wealth
and he who gives gifts to the rich—both come to poverty.

16 The punishment for extortion and bribery is poverty. The Hebrew is a little cryptic: Oppressing the lowly, it is gain; he who gives to the rich, it is loss. Perhaps both are to be seen as folly and resulting in poverty, the first being an immoral act (*ʿōšēq*, "oppresses") that God will punish and the second being a waste of money. McKane says that "giving money to a person who is already rich is an example of squandermania" (p. 572). Perhaps the verse is simply observing that it is easy to oppress the poor for gain, but it is a waste of money to try to buy a patron (Kidner, *Proverbs*, p. 149).

IV. The Sayings of the Wise (22:17–24:34)

A. *Thirty Precepts of the Sages (22:17–24:22)*

Introductory call to attention

22:17–21

17 Pay attention and listen to the sayings of the wise;
apply your heart to what I teach,
18 for it is pleasing when you keep them in your heart
and have all of them ready on your lips.
19 So that your trust may be in the LORD,
I teach you today, even you.
20 Have I not written thirty sayings for you,
sayings of counsel and knowledge,
21 teaching you true and reliable words,
so that you can give sound answers
to him who sent you?

A new collection of sayings begins here, forming the fourth section of the book. This collection is not like that of 1:1–9:18; here the introductory material is more personal than 1:1–7 and the style differs, showing great similarity to the Instructions of Amenemope in Egypt (see McKane, pp. 369–74).

17–21 In the introductory call to attention, the sage urges greater trust in the Lord and promises solid teachings that will prove reliable. This extended introduction reminds us that the wise sayings were not curiosity pieces; they were revelation, and revelation demands a response. The call is laid out with the exhortation to learn and pass on the teaching (v.17), followed by three motivations: (1) there will be a pleasing store of wisdom (v.18); (2) there will be a deeper trust in the Lord—a distinctively Israelite aspect of wisdom literature (v.19); and (3) it will build reliability—he will grasp the truth (v.20) and see himself as a special envoy to keep wisdom in his heart and on his lips (v.21) (Kidner, *Proverbs*, p. 149).

Two connections with the Instruction of Amenemope in this introductory section are striking. First, the purpose of Amenemope was "To know how to return an answer to him who said it, and to direct a report to one who has sent him, in order to direct him to the ways of life" (intro., 1:5–7). Likewise, our "Sayings of the Wise" were words of truth that would provide reliable answers to the sender. Whybray explains that court officials were entrusted with conveying messages and obtaining answers; the ability to discharge this important function in a reliable manner was a test of character (*Book of Proverbs*, p. 133).

Second, the reference to "thirty" (*šālîšîm*, v.20) is significant, for Amenemope also had thirty sayings (ANET, pp. 421–24). So this section of the Book of Proverbs is very close in contents with the Egyptian; but the sayings are not direct borrowings or mere imitations. Nonetheless the influence is certainly there. (See Whybray, *Book of Proverbs*, p. 132; Bryce, *A Legacy of Wisdom;* Ruffle, "The Teaching of Amenemope," pp. 29–68; William Kelly Simpson, tr., "The Instruction of Amenemope," in *Literature of Ancient Egypt*, ed. W.K. Simpson [New Haven: Yale University Press, 1972]; and John A. Wilson, "Egyptian Instructions," in ANET, pp. 412–25; see also A. Cody, "Notes on Proverbs 22:21 and 22:23b," *Biblica* 61 [1980]: 418–26.)

The general thought of the introductory paragraph is, as Toy says, that "the pupil is to devote himself to study, in order that his religious life may be firmly established, and that he may be able to give wise counsel to those who seek advice" (pp. 424–25).

First saying: Treatment of the poor

22:22–23

22 Do not exploit the poor because they are poor
and do not crush the needy in court,
23 for the LORD will take up their case
and will plunder those who plunder them.

22–23 This passage warns people not to oppress the poor, because the Lord avenges them (cf. Amenemope, ch. 2, 4:4–5). The jussives *'al-tigzol* and *'al-tᵉḏakkē'* prohibit exploiting or crushing the poor. McKane observes that because the poor are defenseless, they can be robbed easily; and this makes the crime contemptible but tempting as well (p. 377). The oppression pictured here may be in bounds legally, but it is out of bounds morally (e.g., similar to modern business ethics). The motivation is that the Lord will plead or "take up their case" (*yārîḇ rîḇām*) and turn the plundering back on the guilty. Here again the Lord will champion the defenseless.

Second saying: Dangerous associations

22:24–25

24 Do not make friends with a hot-tempered man,
do not associate with one easily angered,
25 or you may learn his ways
and get yourself ensnared.

24–25 The warning is to avoid associating with a hothead because his influence could prove fatal (see Amenemope, ch. 9, 11:13–14). The saying is close to the teaching in 1:10–19 as well as 14:17, 29, and 15:1. The "one easily angered" (*'îš ḥēmôṯ;* lit., "a man of heat" // *ba'al 'āp̱*, "a hot-tempered man") is denounced here primarily because such conduct is injurious, although the implication would be that it is also morally bad (Toy, p. 426).

Third saying: Rash vows

22:26–27

26 Do not be a man who strikes hands in pledge
or puts up security for debts;
27 if you lack the means to pay,
your very bed will be snatched from under you.

26–27 If people foolishly pledge what they have, they could lose it all (see 6:1–5; 11:15; 17:18; 20:16; there is no parallel in the Egyptian material). The risk is that if someone lacks the means to pay, his creditors may take his bed, i.e., his last possession (cf. our expressions "the shirt off his back" or "the kitchen sink"). "Bed" may be a metonymy for the garment that covers the bed (cf. Exod 22:26).

Fourth saying: Respect for property

22:28

> 28 Do not move an ancient boundary stone
> set up by your forefathers.

28 The sage warns against appropriating someone else's property (see also Amenemope, ch. 6, 7:12–13). Removing an "ancient boundary" (*g^e^bûl ʿôlām*) was always an issue; the general teaching is that ancient traditions, if right, were to be preserved. But violations were frequent. Kidner says, "No law will protect people when integrity is absent" (*Proverbs*, p. 150; see Deut 19:14; 27:17; 1 Kings 21:16–19; Isa 5:8; Hos 5:10). The boundaries were sacred because God owned the land and had given it to the fathers as their inheritance; to extend one's land at another's expense was a major violation of covenant and oath. Of course, property disputes and wars ancient and modern arise because both sides can point to times when their ancestors owned the land.

Fifth saying: Benefits of skill

22:29

> 29 Do you see a man skilled in his work?
> He will serve before kings;
> he will not serve before obscure men.

29 Skill earns recognition and reward of advancement (see also Amenemope, ch. 30, 27:16–17). The saying anticipates that a person "skilled" (*māhîr*) in his work will serve kings. The person might be a scribe or an official (Whybray, *Book of Proverbs*, p. 134), like the keen-witted statesman in the Sayings of Ahiqar (see McKane, p. 380); but the description would apply to all craftsmen. Kidner notes: "Anyone who puts his workmanship before his prospects towers above the thrusters and climbers of the adjacent paragraphs" (*Proverbs*, p. 150). Such will find the proper setting where his skill will be appreciated and not have to waste it on an ignoramus (Plaut, p. 235).

Sixth saying: Caution before rulers

23:1–3

> 1 When you sit to dine with a ruler,
> note well what is before you,
> 2 and put a knife to your throat
> if you are given to gluttony.
> 3 Do not crave his delicacies,
> for that food is deceptive.

1–3 Amenemope (ch. 23, 23:13–18) also warns about getting too close and too familiar with a ruler—he probably has ulterior motives. Plaut reminds the reader that these sayings are set in the ancient history and culture; the courtiers had to learn how to deal with an all-powerful tyranny, surviving while not losing their self esteem (p. 237). This passage warns against overindulging in the ruler's food, because that could ruin one's chances for advancement. The expression "put a knife to your throat" (v.2) means "to curb your appetite" or "to control yourself" (like "bite your tongue"; see Delitzsch, 2:104). The reason is that the ruler's food may be "deceptive" (*keẓāḇîm*)—it is not what it seems. So the warning is not to indulge in his impressive feast—the ruler wants something from you or is observing you (Delitzsch, 2:105). The Mishnah (*Aboth* 2:3) quotes Gamaliel as warning that a ruler only draws you into court for his purpose, but in your day of trouble he will not be there.

Seventh saying: Fleeting wealth

23:4–5

4 Do not wear yourself out to get rich;
have the wisdom to show restraint.
5 Cast but a glance at riches, and they are gone,
for they will surely sprout wings
and fly off to the sky like an eagle.

4–5 People should not wear themselves out trying to get rich, because riches disappear quickly. Amenemope (ch. 7, 9:10–11) says, "They have made themselves wings like geese and are flown away to the heavens." In the ancient world the figure of a bird flying off symbolized fleeting wealth. It is therefore folly to be a slave to it (see also Luke 12:20; 1 Tim 6:7–10). Besides, as *Aboth* 2:8 warns, this will only add to the anxiety.

Eighth saying: Unpleasant hospitality

23:6–8

6 Do not eat the food of a stingy man,
do not crave his delicacies;
7 for he is the kind of man
who is always thinking about the cost.
"Eat and drink," he says to you,
but his heart is not with you.
8 You will vomit up the little you have eaten
and will have wasted your compliments.

6–8 It would be a mistake to accept hospitality from a stingy person, for his lack of sincerity would make the evening unpleasant. The person considered here has an "evil eye" (*ra' 'āyin;* NIV, "a stingy man," v.6). This miser (v.7; see 28:22) is ill-mannered and inhospitable; he is up to no good (contrast the "bountiful eye" in 22:9 [NIV, "generous man"]). Eating and drinking with him will be irritating and disgusting (see Notes). Any unpleasant conversation attempted would be lost (although Toy connects "lose sweet words" [NIV, "wasted your compliments"] with v.9 [pp. 430–31]).

Notes

7 The LXX has "Eating and drinking [with him] is as if one should swallow a hair; do not introduce him to your company nor eat bread with him." The Hebrew כְּמוֹ־שָׁעַר בְּנַפְשׁוֹ (*k^emô-šā'ar b^enap̱šô*, lit., "as he has calculated in his soul"), with a slight change from *šā'ar* to *šē'ār*, would give this picture of an irritating and sickening experience. Amenemope uses "blocking the throat" in the same saying (ch. 11, 14:7). Other attempts to explain v.7 are somewhat paraphrastic.

Ninth saying: Wisdom wasted on a fool

23:9

9 Do not speak to a fool,
for he will scorn the wisdom of your words.

9 A "fool" (*k^esîl*) despises wisdom; so it would be a waste of time to try to teach him. There is no specific connection to Egyptian literature, but the general concept was there that a fool rejected discipline and instruction, often scorning the teacher who tried to change him. Plaut suspects that "some hate the critic in direct proportion to the justification of the criticism" (p. 239).

Tenth saying: Respect property

23:10–11

10 Do not move an ancient boundary stone
or encroach on the fields of the fatherless,
11 for their Defender is strong;
he will take up their case against you.

10–11 Once again the instruction warns against removing a boundary stone and encroaching on the property of the defenseless (v.10; see 22:22–23, 28). The motivation is that their "Defender" (*gō'^alām*) is strong and will plead their cause. The Redeemer/Avenger (*gō'ēl*) was usually a powerful relative who would champion the rights of the defenseless; but if there was no human *gō'ēl*, God would take up their cause (see Gen 48:16; Exod 6:6; Job 19:25; Isa 41–63).

Renewed call to attention

23:12

12 Apply your heart to instruction
and your ears to words of knowledge.

12 The disciple is to apply his heart to discipline and listen carefully to knowledge. This introductory verse may have been added later, based on 22:17.

Eleventh saying: Necessity of discipline

23:13–14

13 Do not withhold discipline from a child;
if you punish him with the rod, he will not die.

14 Punish him with the rod
and save his soul from death.

13–14 The sage instructs the continued use of "discipline" (*mûsār*), for the one punished will not die. Ahiqar 6:82 also says, "If I strike you my son, you will not die." The idea is that discipline helps the child to live a full life; if he dies (prematurely), it would be a consequence of not being trained. In Proverbs such a death might be moral and social as well as physical.

Twelfth saying: Wise and joyful speech

23:15–16

15 My son, if your heart is wise,
then my heart will be glad;
16 my inmost being will rejoice
when your lips speak what is right.

15–16 Children bring joy to their parents by showing that they make wise choices. The quatrain is arranged in a chiastic pattern, using "if your heart is wise" and "when your lips speak what is right" to bracket the verses. The wise heart means one makes wise choices; the "right" (*mêšārîm*) speech refers to direct and honest speech—there is no discrepancy between the speech and the intentions. McKane summarizes: "[The] function of speech is then always to clarify and never to deceive" (p. 387); to speak *mêšārîm* is to speak in contrast to deception that uses ambiguity to darken counsel.

Thirteenth saying: Fear the Lord

23:17–18

17 Do not let your heart envy sinners,
but always be zealous for the fear of the LORD.
18 There is surely a future hope for you,
and your hope will not be cut off.

17–18 These lines advise us always to be zealous for the fear of the Lord rather than envious of sinners. The contrast is between right and wrong envy; the one is spiritual exercise and the other a disease. The difficulty, of course, is that the sinful world seems more attractive. Thus the motivation provided is that the future belongs to the righteous. Kidner remarks that the remedy for envying sinners is to look up (fear the Lord in v.17) and look ahead (there is a "future hope," v.18) (*Proverbs*, p. 152).

Renewed call to attention

23:19

19 Listen my son, and be wise,
and keep your heart on the right path.

19 The disciple is to listen, be wise, and keep his decisions right. For a fuller treatment, see comment on 4:25–27.

Fourteenth saying: Poor associations

23:20–21

20 Do not join those who drink too much wine
or gorge themselves on meat,
21 for drunkards and gluttons become poor,
and drowsiness clothes them in rags.

20–21 If one associates with drunkards and gluttons, he will become poor. The "drunkard" (*sōḇ^e'ê-yāyin*) and the "glutton" (*zōl^{a}lê ḇāśār*) represent the epitome of the lack of discipline. Drunkenness and gluttony are used to measure a stubborn and rebellious son in the Mishnah (*Sanhedrin* 8). Plaut observes that excessive eating and drinking are usually symptoms of deeper problems; we usually focus more on the drinking because it is a dangerous social problem with far-reaching consequences (pp. 241–42).

Fifteenth saying: Honoring parents

23:22

22 Listen to your father, who gave you life,
and do not despise your mother when she is old.

22 Because of parents' position and experience, their wise counsel should be heeded. The idea of honoring here takes on the precise nuance of listening to instructions (Toy, p. 436).

Sixteenth saying: Wisdom's estimation

23:23–25

23 Buy the truth and do not sell it;
get wisdom, discipline and understanding.
24 The father of a righteous man has great joy;
he who has a wise son delights in him.
25 May your father and mother be glad;
may she who gave you birth rejoice!

23–25 The instruction is to acquire truth and gain wisdom, discipline, and understanding—this is the life that pleases God and brings joy to parents. Getting truth would mean acquiring training in the truth, and gaining understanding would mean developing the perception and practical knowledge of the truth (Toy, p. 436).

Seventeenth saying: Following advice

23:26–28

26 My son, give me your heart
and let your eyes keep to my ways,
27 for a prostitute is a deep pit
and a wayward wife is a narrow well.
28 Like a bandit she lies in wait,
and multiplies the unfaithful among men.

26–28 It is imperative to follow the teacher's warnings about temptation because Dame Folly is lurking. The teacher calls for the pupil to imitate him, to follow his ways (v.26), i.e., to shun the temptress. The passage portrays two types of harlots: unmarried (*zônāh*, "prostitute") and married (*nokrîyāh*, "wayward wife") (v.27). In either case there is danger, for their way is a "pit," the gateway to Sheol; and those who enter are as good as dead. But the danger is active—"like a bandit she lies in wait" (v.28; see 7:12) and multiplies the unfaithful among men. Dahood reinterprets *bôgᵉdîm* (NIV, "a bandit") to mean "garments," saying that she collects garments in pledge for her service (Dahood, "To Pawn One's Cloak," pp. 359–66). The change is unnecessary; the line makes good sense meaning that her victims prove "unfaithful" to the law of God or that she is unfaithful to her husband repeatedly.

Eighteenth saying: Excessive drinking

23:29–35

29 Who has woe? Who has sorrow?
   Who has strife? Who has complaints?
   Who has needless bruises? Who has bloodshot eyes?
30 Those who linger over wine,
   who go to sample bowls of mixed wine.
31 Do not gaze at wine when it is red,
   when it sparkles in the cup,
   when it goes down smoothly!
32 In the end it bites like a snake
   and poisons like a viper.
33 Your eyes will see strange sights
   and your mind imagine confusing things.
34 You will be like one sleeping on the high seas,
   lying on top of the rigging.
35 "They hit me," you will say, "but I'm not hurt!
   They beat me, but I don't feel it!
 When will I wake up
   so I can find another drink?"

29–35 One should avoid the temptation to excessive drinking, for it leads to trouble when the senses are dulled. The change of style shows that the sage could break into a vivid use of his imagination (Whybray, *Book of Proverbs*, p. 138). M.E. Andrews charts the developing ideas here: v.29 is a riddle and v.30 its answer; instruction follows in v.31, with the consequences described in v.32; the direct address continues in vv.33–34; and the conclusion is in the drunk's own words (v.35) ("Variety of Expression in Proverbs 23:29–35," VetTest 28 [1978]: 102–3). The sage gives a vivid picture of the one who drinks too much: he raves on and on, picks quarrels and fights, poisons his system with alcohol, gets bloodshot eyes, loses control, is confused, is unable to speak clearly, imagines things, and is insensitive to pain. While alcoholism is a medical problem, it is also a moral problem because it involves choices and brings danger to other people.

Nineteenth saying: Evil associations

24:1–2

1 Do not envy wicked men,
   do not desire their company;

2for their hearts plot violence,
and their lips talk about making trouble.

1–2 One should not envy or desire the company of evil men, for they are obsessed with violence. See also 1:10–19; 3:31; and 23:17. Kidner observes that a close view of sinners is a good antidote to envying them (*Proverbs*, p. 153).

Twentieth saying: Practicality of wisdom

24:3–4

3By wisdom a house is built,
and through understanding it is established;
4through knowledge its rooms are filled
with rare and beautiful treasures.

3–4 The use of wisdom is essential for domestic enterprises. In Proverbs 9:1 wisdom is personified as a woman who builds a house, but here the emphasis is primarily on the building—it is a sign of security and prosperity (Toy, p. 442). One could make a secondary application to building a family (cf. Ps 127). Plaut observes: "The replacement of book shelves by television sets and of the study by the 'den' in modern homes (regressing from human to bestial habitats!) is a sad commentary on our times" (p. 247). It certainly is true that if it takes wisdom to build a house, it also takes wisdom to build a household.

Twenty-first saying: Wisdom is greater than strength

24:5–6

5A wise man has great power,
and a man of knowledge increases strength;
6for waging war you need guidance,
and for victory many advisers.

5–6 Wise counsel is necessary for war. The point is that for victory strategy is more important than strength—but that strategy must be wise. See on this theme 11:14; 20:18; and 21:22.

Twenty-second saying: Fools

24:7

7Wisdom is too high for a fool;
in the assembly at the gate he has nothing to say.

7 Fools cannot obtain wisdom. The text is difficult here (see Notes). The verse portrays a fool out of his element: in a serious moment in the gathering of the community, he does not even open his mouth. Wisdom is beyond the ability of the "fool" (*'ᵉwîl*).

Notes

7 רָאמוֹת (*rā'môṯ*, "too high") would normally be "corals"—"Wisdom to the fool is corals," i.e., an unattainable treasure. With the slight change in the word to *rāmôṯ*, "high" is formed (so NIV).

Twenty-third saying: Disapproval of evil men

24:8–9

8 He who plots evil
  will be known as a schemer.
9 The schemes of folly are sin,
  and men detest a mocker.

8–9 The general public disapproves of a wicked person who plots evil things. The picture of the wicked is graphic: he devises evil and is a schemer, a sinner, and a scorner (*lēṣ*). *Zimmāh* is "scheme"; elsewhere it describes outrageous and lewd schemes (see Lev 18:17; Judg 20:6). Here the description "schemer" (*ba'al-mezimmôṯ*) portrays him as a cold, calculating, active person: "the fool is capable of intense mental activity (*mezimmāh*) but it adds up to sin" (McKane, p. 399). This type of person flouts all morality, and sooner or later the public will have had enough of him. The only way out for such wickedness is repentance and forgiveness.

Twenty-fourth saying: Test of adversity

24:10

10 If you falter in times of trouble,
  how small is your strength!

10 How well one does under adverse conditions reveals how strong that person is. The verse uses a paronomasia to stress the connection: "If you falter in the times of trouble [*ṣārāh*], / how small [*ṣar*] is your strength!" One never knows his strength until he is put into situations that demand much from him. Of course, a weak person will plead adverse situations or conditions in order to quit (Kidner, *Proverbs*, p. 154).

Twenty-fifth saying: Preservation of life

24:11–12

11 Rescue those being led away to death;
  hold back those staggering toward slaughter.
12 If you say, "But we knew nothing about this,"
  does not he who weighs the heart perceive it?
Does not he who guards your life know it?
  Will he not repay each person according to what he
    has done?

11–12 God holds people responsible for rescuing those who are in mortal danger. The use of "death" and "slaughter" seems rather strong in this passage; one might expect the verse to stress the need to rescue through teaching those who by their vice or imprudence are hastening toward destruction (see Toy, p. 445). The idea of "staggering" to the slaughter may need emendation to "at the point of" (G.R. Driver, "Problems in 'Proverbs'," ZAW 50 [1932]: 146). The references could be general, viz., to any who are in mortal danger, or specific, referring to those convicted. If the latter is meant, the sage would be saying not to abandon the convicted to prison, for they need all the help they can get (McKane, p. 401). The general application would include any who are in mortal danger, through disease, hunger, war—we cannot dodge responsibility, even by ignorance.

Twenty-sixth saying: Future of wisdom

24:13–14

13 Eat honey, my son, for it is good;
honey from the comb is sweet to your taste.
14 Know also that wisdom is sweet to your soul;
if you find it, there is a future hope for you,
and your hope will not be cut off.

13–14 One should develop wisdom because it has a profitable future. The proverb draws on the image of honey; its health-giving properties make a good analogy to wisdom. While the literal instruction is to eat and enjoy honey, the point is to know wisdom (D.W. Thomas argues for "seek" instead of "know"; see "Notes on Some Passages in the Book of Proverbs," JTS 38 [1937]: 401). The motivation is that wisdom will have a long future to it ("hope"—*'aḥ*ᵃ*rîṯ* and *tiqwāh*).

Twenty-seventh saying: Treatment of the righteous

24:15–16

15 Do not lie in wait like an outlaw against a righteous man's house,
do not raid his dwelling place;
16 for though a righteous man falls seven times, he rises again,
but the wicked are brought down by calamity.

15–16 It would be futile and self-defeating to mistreat God's people, for they survive—the wicked do not! The warning is against attacking the righteous; to attack them is to attack God and his program, and that will fail (see Matt 16:18). The consequence, and thus the motivation, is that if the righteous suffer misfortune any number of times (= "seven times," v.16), they will rise again; for virtue triumphs in the end (Whybray, *Book of Proverbs*, p. 140). Conversely, the wicked will not survive—without God they have no power to rise from misfortune. The point then is that ultimately the righteous will triumph and those who oppose them will stumble over their evil.

Twenty-eighth saying: Misfortune of enemy

24:17–18

17 Do not gloat when your enemy falls;
when he stumbles, do not let your heart rejoice,
18 or the LORD will see and disapprove
and turn his wrath away from him.

17–18 It would be dishonoring to God for us to rejoice over the misfortune of our enemies. The prohibitions "Do not gloat" (*'al-tiśmāḥ*) and "do not . . . rejoice" (*'al-yāgēl*) extend even to the inner satisfaction (the "heart") at the calamity of the wicked; that person is still the image of God. The motivation for this instruction is the fear of the Lord's displeasure. God might even take pity on them! The point is a little complicated. It is the property of God to judge, and it is not to be taken lightly or personalized. God's judgment should strike a note of fear in the hearts of everyone (see Lev 19:17–18; Matt 5:44). So if we want God to continue his anger on the wicked, we better not gloat. These are personal enemies; the imprecatory psalms for the enemies of God and his program provide a different set of circumstances.

Twenty-ninth saying: Envying the wicked

24:19–20

19 Do not fret because of evil men
or be envious of the wicked,
20 for the evil man has no future hope,
and the lamp of the wicked will be snuffed out.

19–20 It is foolish to envy the wicked, because they are doomed (see 3:31; 23:17–18; 24:1–2). Two jussives—"Do not fret" (*'al-tiṯhar*) and "do not be envious" (*'al-teqannē'*)—form the warning. The motivation is that the wicked have no "future hope" (*'aḥarîṯ*), or as Toy explains, there will be no good outcome for their lives (p. 449). Their lives ("lamp") will be suddenly "snuffed out" (*yiḏ'āḵ*).

Thirtieth saying: Fearing God and the king

24:21–22

21 Fear the LORD and the king, my son,
and do not join with the rebellious,
22 for those two will send sudden destruction upon them,
and who knows what calamities they can bring?

21–22 People should fear both God and the government, for both punish rebels. The positive instruction is followed by the warning "do not join" (*'al-tiṯ'ārāḇ;* lit., "do not get mixed-up") with "the rebellious" (*šônîm;* lit., "people who change," i.e., political agitators; see Notes). Verse 21a is used in 1 Peter 2:17, and v.22 is used in Romans 13:1–7 (v.4). The reward for living in peace under God in the world is that those who do will escape the calamities that will fall on the rebellious.

Notes

21 The word שׁוֹנִים (*šônîm*, "the rebellious") has been given various translations. The idea of "change" is caught in the RV's "political agitators." The Syriac and Targum have "fools"; the Latin has "distractors"; the LXX has "do not disobey either of them," referring to God and the king in the first line. Accordingly the ruin predicted in the next line would be the ruin that God and the king can inflict (see a full discussion in Toy, p. 450).

B. *Further Sayings of the Wise (24:23–34)*

Partiality in judgment

24:23–25

23 These also are sayings of the wise:

To show partiality in judging is not good:
24 Whoever says to the guilty, "You are innocent"—
peoples will curse him and nations denounce him.
25 But it will go well with those who convict the guilty,
and rich blessing will come upon them.

23–25 These verses contain several ethical teachings for judges: "To show partiality" (*hakkēr-pānîm*) is not good (v.23), calling the "guilty" (*rāšā'*, lit., "the wicked") "innocent" (*ṣaddîq*, lit., "righteous") will bring strong denunciation (v.24); but "those who convict the guilty" (*lammôḵîḥîm*) will be richly blessed (v.25). All these sayings set the standard that righteousness and evil be clearly distinguished by the courts (see 18:5; Lev 19:15; Deut 16:19).

Truthfulness

24:26

26 An honest answer
is like a kiss on the lips.

26 A truthful answer is the mark of friendship. The symbol of specifically kissing on the lips is mentioned only here in the Bible. Herodotus (*History* 1.134) shows that among the Persians this was a sign of true friendship. The metaphor signifies that friendship is characterized by truth (cf. the NT practice of greeting; Rom 16:16; 1 Cor 16:20; et al.).

Financial stability

24:27

27 Finish your outdoor work
and get your fields ready;
after that, build your house.

27 A man should be financially secure before he starts a family. This verse is just good sense. Before entering marriage one should have a well-ordered life. Whybray thinks that the meaning is not restricted to marriage but in general teaches us to keep first things first (*Book of Proverbs*, p. 153).

False witness

24:28

28 Do not testify against your neighbor without cause,
or use your lips to deceive.

28 This saying may be directed to the false accuser—an actual friend says the right thing. There should be very solid reasons before one ever goes to testify against a friend.

Vengeance

24:29

29 Do not say, "I'll do to him as he has done to me;
I'll pay that man back for what he did."

29 Rather than give in to the old spirit of vengeance, one should avoid retaliation. The same teaching is used in 20:22; Matthew 5:43–45; and Romans 12:9. Hillel said, "Do not do unto others what you would not have them do unto you" (*Shabbath* 31a).

Laziness

24:30–34

30 I went past the field of the sluggard,
past the vineyard of the man who lacks judgment;
31 thorns had come up everywhere,
the ground was covered with weeds,
and the stone wall was in ruins.
32 I applied my heart to what I observed
and learned a lesson from what I saw:
33 A little sleep, a little slumber,
a little folding of the hands to rest—
34 and poverty will come on you like a bandit
and scarcity like an armed man.

30–34 The teacher makes several observations of the state of the sluggard that reveal that his continued laziness will result in poverty. The reminiscence used here may be a literary device to draw a fictional but characteristically true picture of the lazy person.

V. Proverbs of Solomon Collected by Hezekiah (25:1–29:27)

Introduction

25:1

1 These are more proverbs of Solomon, copied by the men of Hezekiah king of Judah:

1 This section of the book contains additional proverbs attributed to Solomon that were collected by the men of King Hezekiah (715–687 B.C.). These scribes or scholars "copied out" the sayings, i.e., transcribed them from one book to another. Critical scholars like Toy assert that this superscription has no historical value other than to report the later disposition that people attributed many proverbs to Solomon (p. 457).

The proverbs in these chapters differ in that there are more multiple line sayings and more similes; chapters 28–29 are similar to chapters 10–16, but chapters 25–27 differ in having few references to God.

Providence, searched out

25:2

2 It is the glory of God to conceal a matter;
to search out a matter is the glory of kings.

2 Kings must make things understandable to people, but God's providence is beyond knowing. This first saying expresses a contrast between God and kings. On the one hand, it is the glorious nature of God to "conceal" (*hastēr*) things. God's government of the universe is beyond human understanding—humans cannot fathom the divine intentions and operations. McKane rightly observes that this is appropriate to God: "When it is supposed that everything is known about God, it is no longer possible to worship him" (p. 579). He explains further that religion becomes ordinary and flat if there is no boundary to our understanding of him. On the other hand, it is the glory of kings to "uncover" or "search out" (*ḥ^a^qōr*) things. Plaut says that human government cannot claim divine secrecy (p. 257). Kings have to investigate everything, even divine government as far as possible; then they must make things open and intelligible to their subjects, especially judicial matters (Greenstone, p. 263). The juxtaposition of these two lines is basically forming a contrast; but kings who rule as God's representatives must also try to represent his will in human affairs—they must inquire after God to reveal his will. For more general material on vv.2–27, see G.E. Bryce, "Another Wisdom 'Book' in Proverbs," JBL 91 (1972): 145–57.

Counsel, king's

25:3

3 As the heavens are high and the earth is deep,
so the hearts of kings are unsearchable.

3 The king's decisions are beyond the knowledge of the people. Using formal parallelism—almost emblematic—the sage records a simple political fact. While a king ought to make judicial matters clear to the people (v.2), many things cannot be made known, being "unsearchable" because, perhaps, of his superior wisdom, his caprice, or the necessity of maintaining confidentiality. But the comparison with the heavens being high and the earth deep capture the nature of the king—he must be resourceful, inscrutable, always one step ahead, to keep a firm grip on power and to enhance his perception by the people.

Stability, through righteousness

25:4–5

4 Remove the dross from the silver,
and out comes material for the silversmith;
5 remove the wicked from the king's presence,
and his throne will be established through
righteousness.

4–5 These two verses offer first an illustration and then its application (so emblematic parallelism). The lines are written with imperatives, forming instructive lessons. The first verse is problematic; removing "dross" (*sîḡîm*) from silver does not produce "a vessel" (*kelî;* cf. NIV mg.) for the silversmith. Some versions render it "material" (so NIV) for the silversmith. The LXX states that it will be entirely pure. Following this, D. Winton Thomas reads *kālîl* and renders it "purified completely" ("Notes on Some Passages in the Book of Proverbs," VetTest 15 [1965]: 271–79). McKane simply rearranges the line to say that the smith can produce a work of art (p. 580). Whatever the exact reading for *kelî* is, the point is clear: Remove the wicked, and the throne will be established in righteousness (v.5). Greenstone says, "The king may have perfect ideals and his conduct may be irreproachable, but he may be misled by unscrupulous courtiers" (p. 264). When these are purged, then the government will be left with righteous counselors and therefore "established through righteousness."

Humility, its wisdom

25:6–7

6 Do not exalt yourself in the king's presence,
and do not claim a place among great men;
7 it is better for him to say to you, "Come up here,"
than for him to humiliate you before a nobleman.
What you have seen with your eyes

6–7 It is wiser to wait to be promoted than to risk demotion by self-promotion. The lesson is straightforward: Promoting oneself in court may risk a public humiliation; but it would be an honor to have everyone in court hear the promotion from the king himself. The lesson is also taught in Luke 14:8–11. The last line—"What you have seen with your eyes"—is attached to v.8 by the LXX, Syriac, Vulgate, and most modern translations.

Speech, cautious testimony

25:8

8 do not bring hastily to court,
for what will you do in the end
if your neighbor puts you to shame?

8 One must not be too eager to testify, lest he be put to shame publicly. "What you have seen with your eyes" (v.7c) fits well here, referring to a neighbor's affairs (so the reference may be to a private matter). When this information is known, it would be risky to go "hastily" (*mahēr*) to court; for if the case had no valid claim, then one would be in public disgrace (see Notes). This is a warning to be cautious in divulging information. McKane urges that the verse speaks more of broken confidence than of hasty legal action and that it would also apply to an administration that sees and hears things it must not divulge (p. 581).

Notes

8 פֶּן (*pen*, "lest"; NIV, "for") seems out of place in this line. Toy suggests changing it to כִּי (*kî*, "for"; cf. BHS mg.) to make a better connection, instead of supplying an ellipsis: "lest it be said what . . ." (p. 461).

Quarrels, private

25:9–10

9 If you argue your case with a neighbor,
do not betray another man's confidence,

10 or he who hears it may shame you
and you will never lose your bad reputation.

9–10 It is best to keep personal quarrels private to avoid public shame. These verses also are in the form of an instruction with a motivation. The thought runs that if in an argument with your neighbor you reveal another man's confidence, he who hears you will shame you and you will always have a bad reputation. To put it more directly, do not divulge secrets in order to clear yourself in an argument. The point involves damaging a friendship by involving others in a private quarrel. Plaut warns to stay in bounds if one must fight, for no success is achieved at the price of one's integrity or someone's hurt (p. 258). Kidner brings the application forward: "To run to the law or to the neighbours is usually to run away from the duty of personal relationship—see Christ's clinching comment in Matthew 18:15b" (*Proverbs,* p. 157).

Speech, profound

25:11

11 A word aptly spoken
is like apples of gold in settings of silver.

11 The emblematic parallelism uses the simile of "apples of gold in settings of silver." The meaning is not entirely certain; but it does speak of beauty, value, and artistry. The "apples of gold" (possibly apricots, citrons, quinces, or oranges) may refer to carvings of fruit in gold on columns. The point is obviously the immense value and memorable beauty of words used skillfully (Whybray, *Book of Proverbs,* p. 148). The expression translated "aptly" is *'al-'opnāyw* (lit., "on its wheels"). Noting the meaning of the term and the dual form of the word, McKane explains the view that the expression is metaphorical for the balancing halves of a Hebrew parallel wisdom saying: "The *stichos* is a wheel, and the sentence consisting of two wheels is a 'well-turned' expression" (p. 584). The line then would be describing a balanced, "well-turned" saying, a proverb (see 8:19; 15:23); it is skillfully constructed, beautifully written, and of lasting value.

Speech, rebuke

25:12

12 Like an earring of gold or an ornament of fine gold
is a wise man's rebuke to a listening ear.

12 A wise rebuke that is properly received is of lasting value. Another emblematic parallelism compares the rebuke to ornamental jewelry—it is pleasing and complimentary. The verse presents the ideal combination of wise teacher and willing student ("listening ear" means that the disciple is obedient to the rebuke).

Faithfulness, its appreciation

25:13

13 Like the coolness of snow at harvest time
is a trustworthy messenger to those who send him;
he refreshes the spirit of his masters.

13 A faithful messenger lifts up the spirits of those who sent him on the mission. The emblem in this verse is the "coolness of snow at harvest." Various attempts have been made to explain this idea: snow at harvest would be rare, so it may refer to snow brought down from the mountains and kept in an ice hole (Whybray, *Book of Proverbs*, p. 148); it may be the cool air with the snow, i.e., a "refreshing breeze that comes from the snow-capped mountains" (Greenstone, p. 266); it could be a snow-cooled drink (Toy, p. 464) or an application of ice water to foreheads (McKane, p. 585); or perhaps it is an imagined pleasure—snow at harvest (Plaut, p. 260). These suggestions, and others, attempt to clarify the simile; but the lesson itself is clear enough—a faithful messenger is refreshing. To "refresh the spirit" is literally *wᵉnep̱eš . . . yāšîḇ*, the idea being that someone who sends the messenger entrusts his life (i.e, his soul) to him; and a mission faithfully accomplished "restores" it to him. Faithfulness is always refreshing.

Speech, bragging

25:14

> 14 Like clouds and wind without rain
> is a man who boasts of gifts he does not give.

14 The promises of a boaster are empty. The illustration here is clouds and wind that lead one to expect rain but do not produce it—they gain attention but prove to be disappointing and hence deceitful. Similar is the windbag who brags of gifts to be bestowed, but the promise is deceitful (*šāqer*, "he does not give")—there are none. The lesson, of course, is not to make false promises.

Speech, patient and mild

25:15

> 15 Through patience a ruler can be persuaded,
> and a gentle tongue can break a bone.

15 Calm and patient speech can break down insurmountable opposition. The lines are loosely synonymous. By patience one can persuade a ruler. McKane suggests that the verb *yᵉp̱utteh* ("be persuaded") suggests the idea of "made to act like a *peṯî* ['a simple one']," but the parallelism with "break a bone" argues for *pāṯāh* II ("to persuade") (p. 585). By soft speech a bone can be broken, the figure meaning stiff opposition can be broken down. The verse recommends "conciliatory and persuasive advocacy which succeeds in the end over against the most determined and studied recalcitrance" (ibid.). See also 14:29 and 15:1, 18. Toy suggests changing "ruler" to "anger," arguing that princes are not shown forbearance; he then changes the verb as well to match (p. 464). But these changes seem gratuitous.

Conduct, moderation

25:16

> 16 If you find honey, eat just enough—
> too much of it, and you will vomit.

16 Anything that is over indulged can become distasteful. The verse is formal parallelism, giving the condition and then its consequences. It teaches that moderation ("just enough") is necessary in the pleasures of life (see 16:24). Kidner says, "Since Eden, man has wanted the last ounce out of life, as though beyond God's 'enough' lay ecstasy, not nausea" (*Proverbs,* p. 159).

Conduct, moderation

25:17

17 Seldom set foot in your neighbor's house—
too much of you, and he will hate you.

17 Do not wear out your welcome with frequent visits. Verses 16 and 17 are similar in their words and ideas, both advising moderate actions. The instruction "Seldom set foot" is literally "make your foot rare" (*hōqar rag̲lᵉk̲ā;* from *yāqar,* "rare," "precious"). Thomas suggests that *hōqar* is related to the Arabic *waqara* ("to overload, weigh heavily"), thus meaning here "make your foot heavy" (in keeping away) ("Notes on Some Passages in the Book of Proverbs," JTS 38, p. 402). The motivation for the warning is that familiarity breeds contempt.

Speech, false witnesses

25:18

18 Like a club or a sword or a sharp arrow
is the man who gives false testimony against his
neighbor.

18 False witnesses are deadly in society. The emblem line compares false witnesses to a club, a sword, and a sharp arrow—all deadly weapons. False witnesses can cause the death of innocent people. See the law in Exodus 20:16 and Deuteronomy 5:20. See also Proverbs 14:5.

Character traits, unfaithfulness

25:19

19 Like a bad tooth or a lame foot
is reliance on the unfaithful in times of trouble.

19 An unfaithful person is useless and painful. The verse also uses emblematic parallelism, starting with the similes of a bad tooth and a lame foot. Both are incapable of performing—they are painful and ineffective. The second line makes the point: "is reliance [*mib̲ṭāḥ*] on the unfaithful [*bôg̲ēd̲*] in times of trouble." The verse has been taken two ways, with "reliance" (*mib̲ṭāḥ*) referring either to reliance on an unfaithful person or to what the unfaithful person relies on. Toy argues that what the faithless relies on will fail him in the time of trouble (p. 466). Thus *mib̲ṭaḥ* refers to the ground of hope, e.g., wealth or power (as in 14:26: "has a secure fortress"). This view requires a slight change in pointing. The other view, which fits the Hebrew without changes, is that trusting a faithless person is like a decaying tooth or lame foot.

Conduct, inappropriate

25:20

[20] Like one who takes away a garment on a cold day,
or like vinegar poured on soda,
is one who sings songs to a heavy heart.

20 Irresponsible attempts to cheer people up only make matters worse. This verse has some serious textual difficulty; the first line may be a dittogram—it is not in the LXX (see Notes). As the MT stands, the verse is in emblematic parallelism, offering two similes for the point to be made. The first line refers to one who takes away a garment on a cold day. The verb usually means "adorn," but here it must mean "lay off." Removing a garment would be inappropriate. The second simile mentions pouring vinegar on soda (*ḥōmeṣ* on *nāṯer*). The LXX has "scab" (*neṯeq*), but that does not fit as a sensitive thing. The reference is to sodium carbonate, natural in Egypt (see also Jer 2:22), which is neutralized with vinegar. This would be counterproductive. It would be inappropriate and counterproductive to "sing songs" (*šār bašširîm*) to a "heavy heart" (*leḇ-rāʿ*). One needs to develop sensitivity to others; songs may only irritate the grief. However, see the example of David serenading Saul (1 Sam 19:9); that was an exceptional case, but even there Saul's response was unpredictable.

Notes

20 The Hebrew consonants מעדה בגד ביום קרה (*mʿdh bgd bywm qrh*) of this verse are similar to the consonants מועדת מבטח בוגד ביום צרה (*mwʿdt mbṭḥ bwgd bywm ṣrh*) in v.19. The LXX has a much longer reading: "Like vinegar is bad for a wound, so a pain that afflicts the body afflicts the heart. Like a moth in a garment and a worm in wood, so the pain of a man wounds the heart." The idea that v.20 is a dittogram is not that convincing; and the LXX is too far removed to be of help in the matter.

Conduct, kindness to enemies

25:21–22

[21] If your enemy is hungry, give him food to eat;
if he is thirsty, give him water to drink.
[22] In doing this, you will heap burning coals on his head,
and the LORD will reward you.

21–22 People who treat their enemies with kindness will bring remorse to them and blessing from God. The saying includes an instruction and consequences. The imagery of the "burning coals" represents pangs of conscience, more readily effected by kindness than by violence. These burning coals produce the sharp pain of contrition through regret (see 18:19; 20:22; 24:17; Gen 42–45; 1 Sam 24:18–20). Paul uses the expression in Romans 12:20.

The other consequence is that the Lord "will reward you" (*yešallem-lāḵ*)—although the rabbis took this in the causative sense: "will cause him to make peace with you" (Greenstone, p. 270). There being a reward from the Lord shows that this instruction belongs to the religious traditions of Israel. Plaut records a Chinese proverb on the same theme: "Meet good with good that good can be maintained; meet evil with good that good may be created" (p. 262). See also G.R. Driver, "Problems and Solutions," VetTest 4 (1954): 225–45.

Speech, sly words

25:23

> 23 As a north wind brings rain,
> so a sly tongue brings angry looks.

23 Sly words will infuriate people. The north wind that brings the rain is compared with the "sly tongue" (*l^e šôn sāṯer*) that brings angry looks. One problem in the verse concerns the north wind—it is the west wind that brings rain to Palestine (1 Kings 18:41–44). Toy suggests that the expression is general, meaning a northwest wind (possibly even an error; cf. Toy, p. 468). McKane summarizes and refutes the view of van der Ploeg, that the saying may have originated outside of the land, perhaps in Egypt; this would imply its currency was where it made no sense (J.P.M. van der Ploeg, "Prov. 25:23," VetTest 3 [1953]: 189–92; McKane, p. 583). Whybray suggests the solution lies with the verb *t^e ḥôlēl*; rather than mean "brings forth," perhaps it is more literally "distresses," i.e., "repels," "holds back." His interpretation then is that as the north wind holds back the rain, so an angry glance prevents slander (*Book of Proverbs*, p. 149). In this case *l^e šôn sāṯer* ("sly tongue") would mean a "quiet tongue" that drives anger away. I prefer the basic meaning that as northerly winds bring rain, the sly tongue brings angry looks. The verse stresses inevitable results.

Family, peaceful relationship

25:24

> 24 Better to live on a corner of the roof
> than share a house with a quarrelsome wife.

24 Better to have peaceful solitude than companionship with strife. The verse is the same as 21:9.

Speech, good news

25:25

> 25 Like cold water to a weary soul
> is good news from a distant land.

25 Good news refreshes the wearied soul. The point of the verse is transparent (see also 15:30). It is true of love; it is true of spiritual realms. Toy notes that the difficulty at that time of getting news from a distant place heightened the refreshment of it (p. 469). See for an illustration Genesis 45:27.

Character traits, integrity

25:26

> 26 Like a muddied spring or a polluted well
> is a righteous man who gives way to the wicked.

26 A righteous man who loses his position is useless. The images of the "muddied spring" (fouled perhaps by crossing animals) and the "polluted well" suggest an action that is unforgivable. The comparison is with the righteous person who "gives way" (*māṭ*, lit., "moved") before the wicked. This verse has often been interpreted to refer to the integrity of the righteous being lost. Perowne says, "To see a righteous man moved from his steadfastness through fear or favour in the presence of the wicked is as disheartening, as to find the stream turbid and defiled, at which you were longing to quench your thirst" (*Proverbs*, p. 161). But the line may refer to the loss of social standing and position by plots of the wicked (Toy, p. 470). For the righteous to so fall indicates that the world is out of joint (see also McKane, p. 593).

Character traits, self-glory

25:27

27 It is not good to eat too much honey,
nor is it honorable to seek one's own honor.

27 To seek one's own glory is dishonorable. The second line of this verse is problematic; it should make an analogy to honey—glory is good, like honey, but not to excess; so McKane translates, "Be sparing in your encouraging words" (pp. 587–88). The Hebrew *w^eḥēqer k^eḇōḏām kāḇôḏ* says that "the investigation of their glory is glory." This was rendered in the LXX as "it is proper to honor notable sayings." A.A. MacIntosh suggested, "He who searches for glory will be distressed" ("A Note on Prov. 25:27," VetTest 20 [1970]: 112–14); Bryce has "to search out difficult things is glorious" ("Another Wisdom 'Book'," pp. 145–57); Raymond C. Van Leeuwen suggests "to seek difficult things is as glory" ("Proverbs 25:27 Once Again," VetTest 36 [1986]: 105–14); but Toy argues that the text is doubtful, each line having lost its original companion (p. 470).

Character traits, self-control

25:28

28 Like a city whose walls are broken down
is a man who lacks self-control.

28 Without self-control a person is vulnerable. The point of the comparison to a broken-down city is that one who lacks self-control has no defenses.

Honor, inappropriate to fools

26:1

1 Like snow in summer or rain in harvest,
honor is not fitting for a fool.

1 Honor is out of place with a fool. Toy calls vv.1–12 the Book of Fools (p. 472). Verse 1 draws a comparison with snow in summer and rain in harvest to show that honor does not "belong" (*nā'weh*) to the fool. The "fool" (*k^esîl*) is the stupid person who is worthless and vain (just the kind of person popular culture seems to honor). *Kāḇôḏ* in this verse probably refers to the external recognition of worth, i.e., respect, advancement to high position, accolades, but could also include intrinsic worth. All the incongruities mentioned would mean that life was topsy-turvy (McKane, p. 595). The sage warns against elevating and acclaiming those who are worthless. See also J.A. Emerton, "Notes on Some Passages in the Book of Proverbs," VetTest 15 (1965): 271–79.

Speech, undeserved curse

26:2

2 Like a fluttering sparrow or a darting swallow,
an undeserved curse does not come to rest.

2 An "undeserved curse" (*qillaṯ ḥinnām*) is ineffective. Like a fluttering sparrow or darting swallow, it does not settle down; it does not reach its destination (see 1 Kings 4:33 for Solomon's interest in animals). It was commonly believed that blessings and curses had objective existence—that once uttered, the word was effectual. Scriptures make it clear that the power of a blessing or a curse depends on the power of the one behind it (e.g., Balaam could not curse what God had blessed; cf. Num 22:38; 23:8). This proverb underscores the correction of superstition. The Word of the Lord is powerful because it is the word of the Lord—he will fulfill it.

Discipline, physical

26:3

3 A whip for the horse, a halter for the donkey,
and a rod for the backs of fools!

3 A fool must be controlled by physical force. The point of this verse is that the "fool" (*k^esîl*) is as difficult to manage as a donkey or horse. Neither the fool nor these animals respond to reason but must be driven by whip, halter, or rod—in the case of the fool.

Fools, responding to

26:4

4 Do not answer a fool according to his folly,
or you will be like him yourself.

4 The one who responds to a fool appears like a fool. The instruction is that one should not answer a "fool" (*k^esîl*) according to "his folly" (*k^e'iwwaltô;* see Rotenberg, "The Meaning of *'iwweleth* in the Proverbs," p. 201). One should not descend to his level of thought. To get into an argument with a fool like that would only make one look like a fool as well (*pen-tišweh-lô* is the consequence of the instruction; NIV, "or you will be like him"). See v.5.

Fools, responding to

26:5

5 Answer a fool according to his folly,
or he will be wise in his own eyes.

5 The one who rebukes a fool will discourage him from thinking too highly of himself. The inclusion of both v.4 and v.5 posed a major problem for the rabbis; they solved it by saying that v.4 referred to secular things but v.5 to religious controversies. While this does not resolve the issue, it does present a sound application of the point being made—in negligible issues one should just ignore the stupid person; but in issues that matter, he must be dealt with lest credence be given to what he says (Plaut, p. 266). The text presents two sayings together that each contain an aspect of the whole truth. Whybray says they are put together to show that human problems are often complicated and cannot always be solved by appealing to a single rule (*Book of Proverbs,* p. 152). The meaning of the two together is that one should not lower himself to the level of a fool but that there are times when the lesser evil is to speak out than be silent. We are reminded that Paul talked like a fool to correct the foolish thoughts of the Corinthians (2 Cor 11:16–17; 12:11).

Fools, useless as messengers

26:6

> 6 Like cutting off one's feet or drinking violence
> is the sending of a message by the hand of a fool.

6 To use a fool as a messenger is to invite trouble. The similes of "cutting off one's feet" and "drinking violence" are difficult to comprehend. Sending a messenger is like having another pair of feet; sending a fool on the mission is not only no help, it is like cutting off the pair of feet one has—it is a setback! "Violence" (*ḥāmās*) is injustice or violent social wrongs; "drinking violence" is metaphorical for suffering violence—sending a fool on a mission will only have injurious consequences. The verse gives the consequences in line one and the condition that causes them in line two. The teaching is that it would be better not to send a message in the first place than to use a fool.

Fools, dense

26:7

> 7 Like a lame man's legs that hang limp
> is a proverb in the mouth of a fool.

7 Proverbs are useless to fools. In this verse the emblem is a little unclear, but the point is not. The first line gives the simile: "Like a lame man's legs that hang limp" (*dalyû šōqayim mippissēaḥ*). There are various attempts to interpret *dalyû,* but the idea must include that the lame man's legs are useless to him; they hang down, preventing him from going too far. Likewise, the fool is a "proverb-monger" (as Toy puts it, p. 474); he handles an aphorism about as well as a lame man walks. Plaut says that learning wisdom from a fool is like learning to dance from a lame man (p. 267). But of course a lame man could have intelligence and explain things. The fool does not understand the "proverb" (*māšāl*), has not implemented it, and cannot use it or teach it correctly and profitably.

Honor, inappropriate to fools

26:8

> 8 Like tying a stone in a sling
> is the giving of honor to a fool.

8 Honoring a fool is not only counterproductive, it is absurd. It is like "tying a stone" (*ṣ^{e}rôr 'eḇen*) in a sling. Various attempts to explain this picture have been made. One, based on the Latin, sees it referring to casting a stone into the heap of stones of (the god) Mercury (see Plaut, p. 267). Another explains it as hiding a precious stone among a heap of stones, i.e., a waste (Perowne, *Proverbs*, p. 163). But *margēmāh* is a "sling" (LXX, *sphendonē*) and not Mercury or a heap; and "bind" fits the idea the best. Whybray explains that only someone who does not know how a sling works would do such a stupid thing (*Book of Proverbs*, p. 152). So to honor a fool would be absurd, because what was intended could not be accomplished—he would still be a fool.

Fools, use of proverbs

26:9

> 9 Like a thornbush in a drunkard's hand
> is a proverb in the mouth of a fool.

9 It is painful to hear fools use proverbs. The illustration is that of a "thornbush in a drunkard's hand." Toy interprets this to be more than a thorn; he pictures a half-crazy, drunken man brandishing a stick (p. 475). But if in taking a thornbush the thorn pierces the hand (lit., "comes into the hand," *'ālāh ḇ^{e}yaḏ*), then the picture is one of a drunk who does not know how to handle the thornbush because he cannot control his movements and so gets hurt (see McKane, p. 599). A fool can read or speak a proverb but will be intellectually and spiritually unfit to handle it; he will misuse it and misapply it. It is at just such a time as this that he should be answered (see v.5).

Fools, dangerous

26:10

> 10 Like an archer who wounds at random
> is he who hires a fool or any passer-by.

10 Hiring a fool or a stranger is a dangerous thing to do. The one who hires such is compared to "an archer who wounds at random" (*raḇ m^{e}ḥôlēl-kōl*). The line is difficult because it can be translated in different ways: *raḇ* can mean "archer," "master," or "much"; and *m^{e}ḥôlēl* could mean "wound" or "bring forth." The possibilities include the following: "A master performs all"; "A master injures all"; "An archer wounds all"; or simply "Much produces (wounds) all" (see Toy, p. 476, for the variety of interpretations). The line must express something that is negative—an archer/master who injures/wounds everything. Anyone who hires a fool or a stranger gives them ample opportunity to do great damage. The undisciplined hireling will have the same effect as an archer's shooting at random.

Fools, persist in folly

26:11

[11]As a dog returns to its vomit,
so a fool repeats his folly.

11 Fools repeat their disgusting mistakes. No matter how many times a fool is warned, he never learns, not even from experience, but "repeats his folly" (*šôneh b̲ᵉʾiwwaltô*). The simile of a dog returning to his vomit is graphic and debasing; it was used in 2 Peter 2:22 to forestall returning to sin.

Character traits, self-conceit

26:12

[12]Do you see a man wise in his own eyes?
There is more hope for a fool than for him.

12 Those who think they are wise are almost impossible to help. The saying uses a comparison to stress how difficult it is to curb self-conceit—a fool has more hope. Kidner observes that there is more for an able man's vanity to feed on and thus more damage that he can do (*Proverbs*, p. 163). Self-conceit is actually a part of the folly the book decries, because for someone to think that he is wise when he is not makes him a "conceited ignoramus" (Plaut, p. 268).

Laziness, its excuses

26:13

[13]The sluggard says, "There is a lion in the road,
a fierce lion roaming the streets!"

13 The sluggard uses absurd excuses to get out of work (see 22:13). This verse begins the Book of Sluggards (vv.13–16). Kidner provides a helpful overview of the section by explaining that the sluggard does not think he is lazy and so is self-deceived: he would say that he is a realist and not a shirker (v.13), that he is below his best in the morning and not self-indulgent (v.14), that his inertia is an objection to being hustled (v.15), and that he is sticking to his guns and not mentally indolent (v.16) (*Proverbs*, p. 163).

Character traits, laziness

26:14

[14]As a door turns on its hinges,
so a sluggard turns on his bed.

14 The sluggard does not like to get out of his bed. The humor in this verse is based on the analogy with a door—it moves but goes nowhere. Likewise the sluggard is hinged to his bed. McKane says that his turning in his bed "is the greatest degree of movement to which he aspires" (p. 601). See also 6:9–10 and 24:33.

Character traits, laziness

26:15

[15]The sluggard buries his hand in the dish;
he is too lazy to bring it back to his mouth.

15 The sluggard is too lazy to eat. See 19:24.

Character traits, self-conceit

26:16

[16]The sluggard is wiser in his own eyes
than seven men who answer discreetly.

16 The sluggard is filled with self-conceit. This fellow is self-satisfied; in his own opinion he is wiser than any number of people who "answer good sense," i.e., "discreetly." He thinks that he has life all figured out and has chosen the wise course of action—but he is basically lazy. Greenstone says, for example, "Much anti-intellectualism may be traced to such rationalization for laziness" (p. 269).

Conduct, meddling

26:17

[17]Like one who seizes a dog by the ears
is a passer-by who meddles in a quarrel not his own.

17 Anyone who interferes in a fight is asking for trouble. The subject matter concerns the one who "meddles" in someone else's quarrel. The Hebrew verb literally means "become excited" (*mit̲ʿabbēr*); the Vulgate and the Syriac have "meddle" (reading *mit̲ʿārēb̲*). The Hebrew could fit the line—someone who gets angry over the fight of another. The comparison is with grabbing a dog by the ears. This would be a dangerous thing to do; for dogs in the ancient world were not domesticated but wild, like jackals. So the person who makes trouble for himself cannot complain when he gets hurt.

Speech, deceptive

26:18–19

[18]Like a madman shooting
firebrands or deadly arrows
[19]is a man who deceives his neighbor
and says, "I was only joking!"

18–19 It is dangerous to deceive someone out of jest. Anyone who "deceives" (*rimmāh*) his neighbor and then protests that he was "joking" (*m^{e}śaḥēq*) is like a "madman" (*mit̲lahlē^{a}h*) shooting deadly arrows. The practical joker is immature, thinking only of his own laughs. Plaut advises that "the only worthwhile humor is that which laughs with, not at others" (p. 270). By comparing the joker to a madman, the sage describes him as irresponsible and dangerous—he may hurt people while thinking it is all good fun. McKane says, "Liberties cannot be taken with dangerous weapons, nor can they be taken with the confidence of a friend" (p. 602).

Conduct, gossip

26:20

20 Without wood a fire goes out;
without gossip a quarrel dies down.

20 Gossip fuels strife. The instruction of the verse is to prevent a "quarrel" (*māḏôn*) by restricting "gossip" (*nirgān*), just as one would end a fire by withholding the wood. For more on the talebearer, see 18:8.

Character traits, quarrelsomeness

26:21

21 As charcoal to embers and as wood to fire,
so is a quarrelsome man for kindling strife.

21 Quarrelsome people start fights. The "quarrelsome man" (*'îš miḏwānîm*) in this instance is not unlike the *nirgān* ("gossip") of v.20. His quarreling is like piling fuel on the fire—strife flairs up again and again.

Speech, gossip

26:22

22 The words of a gossip are like choice morsels;
they go down to a man's inmost parts.

22 Gossip is appealing. Here the words of a "gossip" (*nirgān*) are compared to choice morsels—they are eagerly and thoroughly "devoured" by those who hear them. See 18:8.

Speech, deceptive

26:23

23 Like a coating of glaze over earthenware
are fervent lips with an evil heart.

23 Fervent speech may conceal evil plans. The sage compares hypocritical speech to the glazing over of an earthen pot. The Hebrew has *kesep̱ sîḡîm* ("silver dross"), which makes little sense, in spite of the attempts by commentators to explain it. Ugaritic turned up a word for "glaze" (*spsg*), and this found a parallel in Hittite *zapzaga(y)a*. H.L. Ginsberg repointed the Hebrew text to *kᵉsapsaḡîm* ("like glaze"), and this has been adopted by many modern interpretations (so NIV) (see H.L. Ginsberg, "The North-Canaanite Myth of Anat and Aqht," BASOR 98 [1945]: 21; id., "Ugaritic Studies and the Bible," *Biblical Archaeologist* 8 [1945]: 57–58; W.F. Albright, "A New Hebrew Word for 'Glaze' in Proverbs 26:23," BASOR 98 [1945]: 24–25; Driver, "Problems in the Hebrew Text," pp. 173–97; and Kenneth L. Barker, "The Value of Ugaritic for Old Testament Studies," BS 133 [1976]: 128–29). Glaze covering a vessel makes it look dazzling and certainly different from the clay that it actually is. The analogy fits the second line very well: "fervent" (*dōlᵉqîm*, lit., "burning," "glowing") lips concealing an evil heart (the LXX reads "flattering lips," as if from *ḥōlᵉqîm*). On the surface he fervently says things that may be pleasing, perhaps protestations of affection; but they merely cover his true nature as one plotting evil.

Speech, hypocritical

26:24

24 A malicious man disguises himself with his lips,
but in his heart he harbors deceit.

24 Hypocritical words may hide a wicked heart. This verse repeats the sentiment of v.23 (and continues through v.27). Here the "malicious man" (*śônē'*) "disguises" (*yinnāḵēr*) the "deceit" (*mirmāh*) in his heart by what he says.

Speech, hypocritical

26:25

25 Though his speech is charming, do not believe him,
for seven abominations fill his heart.

25 Charming words might merely cover evil thoughts. The sage warns the disciple, "Do not believe" (*'al-ta'ᵃmen*) the one who has "charming" (*yᵉḥannēn*) speech, because there are countless (seven) abominations he has planned. It will take great shrewdness and wisdom to discern who can be believed. This verse may have in mind a person who has already proven untrustworthy but who now is using speech to conceal and to put into action his evil plans.

Retribution, certain

26:26

26 His malice may be concealed by deception,
but his wickedness will be exposed in the assembly.

26 Concealed malice will inevitably be made known. The proverb is concerned with how evil will be exposed. The lines are in antithetical parallelism, the first stating that "malice" (*śin'āh*) may be concealed "by deception" (*bᵉmaššā'ôn*) and the second affirming that his evil will be exposed publicly. The assumption that righteousness will ultimately be victorious informs this saying.

Retribution, certain

26:27

27 If a man digs a pit, he will fall into it;
if a man rolls a stone, it will roll back on him.

27 Whatever a man sows he shall reap. The lines are synonymous parallelism, giving two illustrations of the point—digging a pit and rolling a stone. The digging refers to laying a trap for someone; and rolling a stone is probably on someone for greater force. Measure for measure justice is in view—he will fall into his own pit, or the stone will roll on him. For samples consider Haman (Esth 7:10) and Daniel's enemies (Dan 6:24–28). Also see the saying in the Mishnah (drowning for drowning, *Aboth* 2:7).

Speech, deceptive

26:28

> 28 A lying tongue hates those it hurts,
> and a flattering mouth works ruin.

28 Deceptive speech brings ruin without regard for those it may hurt. The two lines, loosely synonymous, portray the evil person who deceives ("lying tongue" // "flattering mouth") as one who ruthlessly ruins people. The "ruin" (*miḏḥeh*) that he works could be on himself (an idea that fits the context) or on others (which seems to be the point of the verse). The introduction of the motif of the tongue that "hates those it hurts" (*yiśnā' ḏakkāyw*) suggests that expressions or sentiments of hatred help the deceiver justify what he is doing (Plaut, p. 271). In any case, only pain and ruin can come from deception. Kidner says, "Truth is vital, and pride fatal, to right decisions" (*Proverbs*, p. 164). (See Driver, "Hebrew Notes on Prophets and Proverbs," pp. 162–75.)

Plans, uncertain future

27:1

> 1 Do not boast about tomorrow,
> for you do not know what a day may bring forth.

1 Presumption about the future is dangerous because the future is uncertain. Line one is the instruction and line two the reason. The warning is, "Do not boast ['*al-tiṯhallēl*] about tomorrow" (i.e., a metonymy for what you will do in the future). The verse is not ruling out wise planning for the future, only one's overconfident sense of ability to control the future—and no one can presume on God's future. Rather, humility is required; one "must live from day to day, grateful for the life which he has from God, with the awareness that it may be withdrawn at any time and that he must not speak or plan as if he himself had full disposal of his destiny and power over the future" (McKane, p. 607). See the development of the idea in James 4:13–16 and in Matthew 6:34 with the instruction not to worry; see also Luke 12:20. A second application of the verse would be not to postpone to an uncertain future what is in one's power to do at once (Greenstone, p. 282, citing *Aboth* 2:8).

Humility, praise from others

27:2

> 2 Let another praise you, and not your own mouth;
> someone else, and not your own lips.

2 It is best to let other people praise you. The verse is another instruction but now in synonymous parallelism. Self-praise is a form of pride, even if it begins with little things (such as who you know, where you have been, etc.), and it does not establish a reputation. The reputation comes from what others think of you. "Someone else" in this proverb is literally "stranger"—a person who may speak more objectively about your accomplishments and abilities. On a practical level, the rabbis permitted one to make his virtues and achievements known where he was not known (*Nedarim* 62a).

Fools, provocation of

27:3

> 3 Stone is heavy and sand a burden,
> but provocation by a fool is heavier than both.

3 The provocation of a fool is unbearable. Emblematic parallelism is used to make the comparison: stone and sand are heavy, and whoever carries them knows the work is exhausting and painful. But more tiring is the fool's provocation, for the mental effort it takes to deal with it is more wearying than physical work—the fool brings a spiritual malaise for others to endure (McKane, p. 609). Toy does not think that "provocation by a fool" would be given the epithet "heavy"; so he proposes "anger"—"the anger of a fool is heavier than them both" (p. 482). This is not very compelling.

Character traits, jealousy

27:4

> 4 Anger is cruel and fury overwhelming,
> but who can stand before jealousy?

4 Jealousy is more unbearable than anger. The parallelism is formal, the comparison being drawn with a rhetorical question. The sage focuses attention first on anger that is ruthless and destructive (lit., "a flood of anger"; see Job 38:25; Ps 32:6; Nah 1:8 for the imagery used for destruction). In contrast "jealousy" (*qin'āh*), here probably in the negative sense (as opposed to the positive sense of zeal to defend a threatened institution for the right reasons), is a raging emotion that defies reason at times and takes the form of destructive violence, like a consuming fire (McKane, p. 611). See Proverbs 6:32–35 and Song of Songs 8:6–7.

Reproof, a part of love

27:5

> 5 Better is open rebuke
> than hidden love.

5 Direct reproof is better than unexpressed love. The verse is a single sentence forming a "better" saying of relative values. "Open rebuke" (*tôḵaḥaṯ mᵉgullāh*) is a frank, direct word of honest criticism or disapproval (from either a friend or foe). "Hidden love" (*'ahᵃḇāh mᵉsuttāreṯ*) is a love that is too timid, too afraid, or not trusting enough to admit that reproof is a part of genuine love (McKane, p. 610). A love that manifests no rebuke is morally useless (Toy, p. 483). In fact, one might question whether or not it is sincere. See also 28:23 and 29:3.

Reproof, its value

27:6

> 6 Wounds from a friend can be trusted,
> but an enemy multiplies kisses.

6 Reproof given in love is superior to insincere expressions of affection. The lines are in antithetical parallelism, contrasting the faithful (*ne'emānîm;* NIV, "can be trusted") wounds of a "friend" (*'ôhēḇ*) with the profuse (*na'tārôṯ;* NIV, "multiplies") kisses of an "enemy" (*śônē'*). The wounds of a friend "can be trusted" because they are meant to correct (see 25:12; Deut 7:9; Job 12:20). But an enemy's kisses are deceptive (e.g., the deceitful kiss of Judas [Mark 14:43–45]), in spite of their profusion (for the word *na'tārôṯ*, the versions have a variety of translations—confused, fraudulent, bad, etc.).

Character traits, need versus desire

27:7

> 7 He who is full loathes honey,
> but to the hungry even what is bitter tastes sweet.

7 Those who have great needs are more appreciative than those who are satisfied (Toy remarks, "Hunger is the best sauce," p. 483). The verse contrasts the one who is "full" (*nep̱eš śeḇē'āh*) with the one who is "hungry" (*nep̱eš re'ēḇāh*); the former loathes honey, and the latter finds even bitter things sweet. The word *nep̱eš* in each half refers to the whole person with all his appetites. Most agree that the proverb is capable of wider application than eating; it could apply to possessions, experiences, education, etc. Toy suggests the idea of praise—it is nauseous to one who is much praised but greatly appreciated by one who seldom receives it (p. 483). Greenstone suggests that one who thinks he is fully competent rejects rebuke (p. 284).

Security, abandoned

27:8

> 8 Like a bird that strays from its nest
> is a man who strays from his home.

8 To stray from home is to lose security. The parallelism compares a bird that "strays" (*nôḏeḏeṯ*) from a nest with the man who "strays" (*nôḏēḏ*) from home. The reason for his straying is not given, but it could be because of exile, eviction, business, or irresponsible actions. Kidner thinks the sage condemns the one wandering because he has deserted his charge and forfeited his prospects; he is a rolling stone, but not a pilgrim or fugitive (*Proverbs*, p. 165). The saying may be more general, simply asserting that those who wander lack the security of their home and can no longer contribute to their community life (e.g., the massive movements of refugees). The verse could be portraying the wandering as an unhappy plight without condemning the wanderer as irresponsible.

Advice, of a friend

27:9

> 9 Perfume and incense bring joy to the heart,
> and the pleasantness of one's friend springs from his
> earnest counsel.

9 Advice from a friend is pleasant. The emblem is the joy that perfume and incense bring to people, and the point is the value of the advice of a friend. Line two of the verse is difficult. Toy suggests that it is unintelligible as it appears in the Hebrew (p. 484), which reads: "The sweetness of his friend from the counsel of soul." Many interpreters take it to mean the advice or counsel of a friend sweetening the soul (see Notes).

Notes

9 The Latin has "the soul is sweetened by the good counsels of a friend." Thomas suggests "counsels of a friend make sweet the soul" ("Notes on Some Passages in the Book of Proverbs," VetTest 15, p. 275). G.R. Driver suggests "the counsel of a friend is sweeter than one's own advice" (lit., "more than the counsel of the soul"). He also suggests "more than of fragrant wood." See "Hebrew Notes," ZAW 52 (1934): 54; and "Suggestions and Objections," ZAW 55 (1937): 69–70. The LXX reads "and the soul is rent by misfortunes."

Friend, helpful

27:10

[10] Do not forsake your friend and the friend of your father,
and do not go to your brother's house when disaster strikes you—
better a neighbor nearby than a brother far away.

10 A friend who is available is better than a relative who is not. The verse is very difficult. Toy suggests that the three lines have been put together but have no immediate connection: 10a instructs people to maintain relationships; 10b says not to go to their brother's house (only?) when disaster strikes; and 10c observes that a neighbor nearby is better than a brother far away (pp. 485–86). Toy thinks a connection may have been there once but has long since disappeared; he also wonders whether 10b is a gloss (see 17:17) from someone opposed to brothers (removing 10b, however, would not make the verse any clearer). The conflict between 17:17 and 10b may be another example of presenting two sides of the issue, showing that such a matter cannot be resolved with one simple teaching. If the verse is preserved as it appears in the MT, it teaches us to maintain relationships with family and friends but to realize that a neighbor who is near will be more help than a relative far away ("nearby" and "far away" referring to space, not feelings).

Teaching, vindicated

27:11

[11] Be wise, my son, and bring joy to my heart;
then I can answer anyone who treats me with contempt.

11 A wise son (disciple) enables a father (teacher) to defend himself against his critics. The verse gives an instruction ("Be wise") with its consequence ("then I can answer anyone who . . ."). The expression "treats me with contempt" (*ḥōrᵉp̱î*) refers to the taunting or criticizing of the instructor as a poor teacher. Teachers are usually held responsible for the faults and weaknesses of their pupils; but any teacher criticized that way takes pleasure in pointing to those who have learned as proof that he has not labored in vain. Along this concern, see 1 Thessalonians 2:19–20 and 3:8.

Wisdom, wary of evil

27:12

> 12 The prudent see danger and take refuge,
> but the simple keep going and suffer for it.

12 Avoiding the pitfalls in life requires wisdom. The contrast is between the "prudent" (*ʿārûm*) and the "simple" (*pᵉṯā'yim*); the first is the mature person who has developed a wariness (1:4), and the latter is the inexperienced and untrained youth who stumbles into things. The verse is a motivation for the naive to be trained; for life would be far less painful for them if they knew how to avoid life's dangers. See 22:3.

Obligations, fulfilled

27:13

> 13 Take the garment of one who puts up security for a
> stranger;
> hold it in pledge if he does it for a wayward woman.

13 People must be held to their obligations, no matter how foolishly they were made. The verse is essentially the same as 20:16.

Speech, inappropriate greeting

27:14

> 14 If a man loudly blesses his neighbor early in the
> morning,
> it will be taken as a curse.

14 Loud and untimely greetings are not appreciated. At the least the verse tells us that how, when, and why we say what we say is important (see Kidner, *Proverbs*, p. 166). But there are a few ways to interpret this verse. On the surface it appears to be describing one who comes in early and loud with his blessing or greeting; he is considered a nuisance ("it will be taken as a curse" [*qᵉlālāh tēḥāšeḇ lô*]). But "blesses" and "curse" could mean more; it could refer to the loud adulation of a hypocrite, the person who goes to great length to create the impression of piety and friendship but is considered a curse by the one who hears him. Another possibility, though less likely, is that the blessing is given prematurely, before the fortune is known, and that God, offended by the premature assumption, will reckon it a curse.

Family, quarrelsome wife

27:15

> 15 A quarrelsome wife is like
> a constant dripping on a rainy day;

15 A quarrelsome mate is an unbearable irritant. See 19:13. The LXX interprets: "Drops drive a man out of his house on a wintry day; so a railing woman also drives him out of his own house."

Family, quarrelsome wife

27:16

> [16]restraining her is like restraining the wind
> or grasping oil with the hand.

16 This verse would be completely obscure if it were not connected with v.15; so it adds the idea that the quarrelsome wife is also uncontrollable. The first line says that "restraining her is like restraining the wind" (*ṣōp̱eneyhā ṣāp̱an-rûaḥ*). The wind is elusive; it can gust at any moment. So too is the woman who may burst out at any moment. The second line is "grasping oil with the hand," an expression Scott compares to our idiomatic "butterfingers" (*Proverbs / Ecclesiastes*, p. 163). The point is that the husband would be dealing with a woman who was as unpredictable and uncontrollable as a gust of wind or a hand grasping oil. Greenstone presents another view that may be too subtle: "oil" represents fatness, and that means power, i.e., she has to be restrained by force (p. 288). The LXX also takes an etymologizing approach and arrives at "the north wind is a severe wind but by its name is termed auspicious."

Criticism, helpful

27:17

> [17]As iron sharpens iron,
> so one man sharpens another.

17 Constructive criticism between friends develops character. The simile focuses on the use of iron to "sharpen" (*yāḥaḏ*, from the root *ḥdd*, "to sharpen," as in the versions) iron. Possibly *yāḥaḏ* is to be translated "together," yielding the idea that they go together. But the point of line two is that a man sharpens the face of his fellow (*'îš yaḥaḏ penê-rē'ēhû;* NIV, "one man sharpens another"). The word *penê* ("face") must mean here the personality or the character of the individual. McKane suggests the idea of wits, i.e., that the interaction makes them sharp as a razor (p. 615). The Talmud applied it to study: two students sharpening each other in the study of Torah (*Taanith* 7a). See also A. Sperber, "Biblical Exegesis," JBL 64 (1945): 39–140.

Rewards, for service

27:18

> [18]He who tends a fig tree will eat its fruit,
> and he who looks after his master will be honored.

18 Those who faithfully serve will be rewarded in kind. Another emblematic parallelism, this verse uses the illustration that one who takes care of a fig tree will eat its fruit. The fig tree needed closer attention than other plants; so the point would include the diligent tending of it. A. Cohen suggests that *nōṣēr* refers to planting figs ("He Who Tends a Fig Tree Will Eat Its Fruit [Prov 27:18]," BM 25 [1979]: 81–82); see Jeremiah 31:5–6. The second line says that the servant "looks after" (*šōmēr*) his master, i.e., a meticulous service, anticipating the needs and watching over his charge. Such a servant need not worry about his efforts going unrecognized and unrewarded. See also 22:29 and 2 Timothy 2:6, 15.

Character traits, reflected in thoughts

27:19

> 19 As water reflects a face,
> so a man's heart reflects the man.

19 Thoughts reflect one's true character. This verse is very cryptic, and so there are several suggestions as to its meaning. It is emblematic parallelism, the first line forming the similitude. The verse literally says, "As water face to face / so a man's heart to a man." The simplest way to take the verse is to say that as clear water gives a reflection of the face, so the heart reflects the true nature of the man (NIV). Toy's suggestion that it is through the observation of another that a man can know himself is not convincing, for that would require another man's face in line one to make the parallel (p. 490). Kopf's idea is that "water of face" (a construct) means shame or modesty; i.e., a face is not really human without shame, and a man without heart is likewise not human. This view is rather forced and unnecessary (L. Kopf, "Arabische Etymologien und Parallelen Zum Bibelwörterbuch," VetTest 9 [1959]: 260–61). The point seems to be that it is through looking at our heart attitudes that we come to true self-awareness.

Desires, insatiable

27:20

> 20 Death and Destruction are never satisfied,
> and neither are the eyes of man.

20 The desires of human beings are as insatiable as "Death" and "Destruction." *Šᵉʾôl* and *ʾᵃḇaddōh* are expressions for the underworld (see 15:11). Generations of people have gone headlong into the world below; yet it is never satisfied. This observation forms the emblem of the point that the eyes of man "are never satisfied" (*lōʾ ṯiśbaʿnāh*). The Midrash (Eccl. R 1:34) says, "No man dies and has one-half of what he wanted." The LXX has a scribal addition: "He who fixes his eye is an abomination to the Lord, and the uninstructed do not restrain their tongues."

Character traits, praiseworthy

27:21

> 21 The crucible for silver and the furnace for gold,
> but man is tested by the praise he receives.

21 Public praise is usually a good measure of the qualities and contributions of a person. The comparison of the point is with the crucible for silver and the furnace for gold—they refine and reveal the pure metals. So the idea is that a person "is tested by the praise he receives [*lᵉp̄î mahᵃlālô*, lit., 'by his praise']." Public praise formed a test for Saul and David (1 Sam 18:7), David coming out the better for it. Public opinion, or the praise of others, is normally a good barometer; but there is the other side of the matter as well, that righteousness will be denounced (Matt 5:11). Another way to interpret *mahᵃlālô* is "the praise he gives"—we often stand revealed by what we praise (Kidner, *Proverbs*, p. 168). The LXX again adds a couplet: "The heart of the transgressor seeks evil; / but the upright heart seeks knowledge."

Folly, unalterable

27:22

> 22 Though you grind a fool in a mortar,
> grinding him like grain with a pestle,
> you will not remove his folly from him.

22 Folly cannot be removed by force. The verse is in formal parallelism but is highly metaphorical, using the imagery of grinding grain in a mortar with a pestle, i.e., pulverizing, to talk about physical punishment for the fool. Since folly is his nature, it will not be removed from him. The LXX paraphrases the line: "If you scourge a fool in the assembly, dishonoring him, you would not remove his folly," removing the imagery from the line. Many commentators think that the second line ("grinding him like grain with a pestle") is a gloss anyway (see Toy, p. 491).

Wealth, transitory

27:23–27

> 23 Be sure you know the condition of your flocks,
> give careful attention to your herds;
> 24 for riches do not endure forever,
> and a crown is not secure for all generations.
> 25 When the hay is removed and new growth appears
> and the grass from the hills is gathered in,
> 26 the lambs will provide you with clothing,
> and the goats with the price of a field.
> 27 You will have plenty of goats' milk
> to feed you and your family
> and to nourish your servant girls.

23–27 People should preserve what income they have because it does not long endure. The last few verses of the chapter form a little poem about the preservation of income. Verse 23 provides the main instruction—take care of your livelihood ("appearance" meaning condition). The motivation for this is that riches do not last long (v.24). The reasoning for wise care of income continues in the second half of the poem—the protasis is in v.25 and the apodasis in vv.26–27—if the growth is removed, then they can sell and use their livestock. The poem shows the proper interplay between human labor and divine provision.

Confidence, of the righteous

28:1

> 1 The wicked man flees though no one pursues,
> but the righteous are as bold as a lion.

1 The faith of the righteous builds confidence. This observation is presented in contrast to the fear of the wicked who flee when "no one pursues." The proverb implies that the wicked, prompted by a guilty conscience or a fear of judgment, become fearful and suspicious of everyone. But the righteous, who seek to find favor with God and man, have a clear conscience and thus no need to look over their shoulders, as it were (Kidner, *Proverbs*, p. 168). The righteous can have the confidence (*yiḇṭāḥ;* NIV, "are bold") to live righteously under God's providence.

Stability, in government

28:2

> [2]When a country is rebellious, it has many rulers,
> but a man of understanding and knowledge maintains order.

2 A nation's stability comes with a discerning and knowledgeable ruler. The verse uses antithetical parallelism to contrast the chaos of a sinful nation with the stability brought by a righteous order. In the first line the reference to "many rulers" (*rabbîm śāreyhā*) indicates that during rebellious times a nation has many changes of power or many people vying for power. Plaut adds that people generally get the governments they deserve (p. 281). The period of the judges and the days of the northern kingdom of Israel with its nine dynasties are examples of political instability due to sin.

The second line of the verse is difficult: "by a man who is discerning and knowledgeable right lasts long" (*ûḇeʾāḏām mēḇîn yōḏēaʿ kēn yaʾarîḵ;* NIV, "but a man of understanding and knowledge maintains order"). Toy suggests that this part of the verse may not belong with line one; for a detailed survey of all the proposed emendations, see Toy, p. 495, and McKane, p. 630. The LXX reads (probably from a different text): "It is the fault of a violent man that quarrels start, but they are settled by a man of discernment." For a study of the verses in chapters 28 and 29 concerning kings and governments, see Bruce V. Malchow, "A Manual for Future Monarchs," CBQ 47 (1985): 238–45.

Ruler, oppressive

28:3

> [3]A ruler who oppresses the poor
> is like a driving rain that leaves no crops.

3 A ruler who oppresses the poor destroys his own dominion. The first line introduces the subject matter—one who oppresses the poor—and the second line, by a simile, tells of the effect—like a driving rain he destroys and leaves nothing in the land (i.e., only the hardiest survive). The Hebrew has "a poor man" (*geḇer rāš*) "oppresses the poor" (*weʿōšēq dallîm*). The problem is that the poor in the Book of Proverbs is not an oppressor and does not have the power to be such. So commentators assume *rāš* is incorrect. By slight changes the reading "ruler" can be obtained, and this seems to fit the verse and the book better (see Notes). If the reading "poor man" is retained, then the oppression includes betrayal—one would expect a poor man to have sympathy for others who are impoverished, but in fact that is not the case.

Notes

3 The word רָשׁ (*rāš*, "poor"; NIV mg.) is emended to רָשָׁע (*rāšā'*, "wicked"); so גֶּבֶר רָשָׁע (*geber rāšā'*) is "a wicked ruler." There is no textual support for this. McKane suggests *rō'š* ("principal") (p. 629). The LXX has "A courageous man oppresses the poor with impieties."

Law, respect for

28:4

> 4Those who forsake the law praise the wicked,
> but those who keep the law resist them.

4 Obedience to the law determines one's attitude toward law-breakers. The contrast is between "those who forsake the law" (*'ōz^e bê tôrāh*) and "those who keep the law" (*šōm^e rê tôrāh*). Toy does not think that *tôrāh* refers to the law but to instruction because the verb "forsake" would be unexpected with the law (p. 495). But "keeping the law" implies that *tôrāh* is binding—which would not be true of teaching in general (see John Bright, "The Apodictic Prohibition: Some Observations," JBL 92 [1973]: 185–204). Moveover, Proverbs 28:9 and 29:18 refer to the law, and this chapter has a stress on the piety of God. The verse gives the consequences of those who forsake the law as those who "praise the wicked" (*ye hal^e lû rāšā'*) and of those who keep it as those who "resist them" (*yitgārû bām*), to which the Targum adds, "so as to induce them to repent." Praising the wicked may mean calling them good, i.e., no longer able to discern good from evil. Kidner says, "Without revelation, all is soon relative; and with moral relativity, nothing quite merits attack" (*Proverbs*, p. 169; he suggests the correlation with Rom 1:18–32).

Justice, perceived

28:5

> 5Evil men do not understand justice,
> but those who seek the LORD understand it fully.

5 Piety alone fully comprehends justice. This contrast between those who are evil and those who seek the Lord concerns the perception of justice. *Mišpāṭ* refers to the legal rights of people; but there are always those who believe justice is that which benefits them—otherwise it is not justice (Plaut, p. 282). To "seek the LORD" (*m^e baqšê YHWH*) originally meant trying to obtain an oracle from God (see 2 Sam 21:1) but then came to refer to devotion to God (i.e., seeking to learn and to do his will). Only people attuned to the divine will can fully perceive what justice is. Without that standard, legal activity can easily become self-serving.

Righteousness, better than unjust wealth

28:6

> 6Better a poor man whose walk is blameless
> than a rich man whose ways are perverse.

6 Honest poverty is better than dishonest wealth (Toy, p. 497). The verse is formal parallelism, presenting another "better" saying. The verse only contrasts a poor man with integrity and a perverse rich man (see 19:1)—there are rich people with integrity, and there are poor people who are perverse. The word for "ways" (*d^erāḵayim*) is dual, suggesting that the person has double ways, i.e., he is hypocritical, a double dealer. Toy does not like the interpretation that *d^erāḵayim* means good and bad ways (one way to interpret the dual); but his emendation to the plural is gratuitous. This chapter gives attention to the contrast between the rich man and the poor man, assuming an integrity to the poor that is not there in the rich; the subject is addressed in vv.6, 8, 11, 20, 22, 25, and 27 (see further Gordon A. Chutter, "Riches and Poverty in the Book of Proverbs," *Crux* 18 [1982]: 23–28).

Conduct, obedient versus profligate

28:7

> 7 He who keeps the law is a discerning son,
> but a companion of gluttons disgraces his father.

7 One who is obedient to the law will be discerning enough to lead an untarnished life. The antithesis is between the "discerning son" (*bēn mēḇîn*, meaning one having perception or moral illumination) and the "profligate" (NIV, "companion of gluttons"). Again, "law" could mean instruction, perhaps originally for this verse a father's instructions; but in this chapter that stresses religious piety, it probably refers to the law. Besides, in the Book of Proverbs a father's instruction would harmonize with the law any way. Obviously the son who becomes a "companion of gluttons" has not kept the law. He shames his father because such profligacy is unruly and antisocial—it brings disrespect on the family (Greenstone, p. 296).

Wealth, unjustly gained

28:8

> 8 He who increases his wealth by exorbitant interest
> amasses it for another, who will be kind to the poor.

8 Wealth amassed by unjust means will eventually go to the poor. The law prohibited making a commission or charging interest (see Exod 22:25; Lev 25:36–37; Deut 23:20; Ps 15:5). These laws were concerned with the necessities of life; if the poor needed help, the wealthy should give it to them as charity—they were not to take advantage of another Israelite's plight. This proverb assumes that wealth gained unjustly will eventually find its way to the poor. Greenstone says that the divine punishment for this activity would be the loss of wealth and its revision to those who "will be kind to the poor" (*l^eḥônēn dallîm*) and who will distribute it among those from whom it was taken (p. 297).

Prayer, of the lawless unanswered

28:9

> 9 If anyone turns a deaf ear to the law,
> even his prayers are detestable.

9 God will not listen to the prayers of those who will not listen to him. Toy says, "If a man, on his part, is deaf to instruction, then God, on His part, is deaf to prayer" (p. 499). The prayer certainly will not be a proper prayer; someone who refuses to obey God will not pray according to God's will—he will pray for some physical thing, perhaps even making demands on God. Plaut suggests that one implication of this is that adult education is a prerequisite for meaningful worship (p. 284). Of course, a prayer of repentance would not be an abomination to the Lord. But in general, McKane observes, "Yahweh's *rāṣōn* ['favor'] is enjoyed by the *ṣaddîq* ['righteous'], and his *tō'ēḇāh* ['abomination'] is incurred by the *rāšā'* ['wicked']. Hence one who fails to attend to Yahweh's *tōrāh* ['law'] is a *rāšā'*, even if he is a man of prayer" (p. 623).

Rewards, just

28:10

10 He who leads the upright along an evil path
will fall into his own trap,
but the blameless will receive a good inheritance.

10 Destruction awaits those who corrupt others; rewards await those who have integrity. Judgment is certain for those who lead the upright into evil—they will fall into their own trap (McKane wishes to emend *bišḥûṯô* ["his own trap"] to *šaḥṯô* ["his pit"][p. 623]). The line shows that the wicked will be caught in their own devices; but it also shows that the righteous are corruptible—they can be led into morally bad conduct ("an evil path"). See 26:27; see also Matthew 23:15.

Character trait, self-deceit

28:11

11 A rich man may be wise in his own eyes,
but a poor man who has discernment sees
through him.

11 Here is another contrast between the rich and the poor. In this one the rich man is filled with self-conceit, but the discerning poor man "sees through him" (*yaḥqᵉrennû*). With religious insight, i.e., "discernment" (*mēḇîn*), the poor man searches out the flaws of the rich man—he sees through the pretension. Some argue that the verb *yaḥqᵉrennû* is to be derived from the Arabic *ḥqr* ("despise"; see Thomas, "Notes on Some Passages in the Book of Proverbs," JTS 38, pp. 402–3); that would be predictable and flat.

Righteousness, in government

28:12

12 When the righteous triumph, there is great elation;
but when the wicked rise to power, men go
into hiding.

12 People flourish under righteous administrations. The contrast is between the situation when the wicked come to power and when the righteous triumph. The

Hebrew literally has "when the righteous rejoice, great is the glory; but when the wicked arise to power, men are sought out." Toy thinks that the translation derived from this has to be strained: "rejoice" = triumph = arise, i.e., come to power; and "are sought" = must be sought = have gone into hiding. Toy then constructs his own translation: "When the righteous are exalted there is great confidence, but when the wicked come into power men hide themselves" (p. 500). For *yeḥuppaś* Driver posits an Arabic cognate *ḫafaša* ("prostrated," "trampled on"; cf. "Problems in the Hebrew Text," pp. 192–93), which gives a more direct result of the rule of the wicked but is perhaps an unnecessary change. See also v.28; 29:2; and Emerton, "Notes on Some Passages in the Book of Proverbs," JTS 20, pp. 202–20.

Repentance, effectual

28:13

13 He who conceals his sins does not prosper,
but whoever confesses and renounces them
finds mercy.

13 Repentance and renunciation of sin bring God's mercy and blessing. This verse is unique in the Book of Proverbs; it captures the theology of forgiveness found in passages such as Psalm 32:1–5 and 1 John 1:6–9. The contrast is between the one who "conceals" (*mekasseh*) his sins and the one who "confesses and renounces them" (*môdeh we'ōzēb*). The former will not prosper; the latter will find God's "mercy" (*yeruḥām*). Every part of this verse is essential to the truth: "confession must be coupled with true return in order to assure God's mercy" (Plaut, p. 285). Would that the people of God were half as faithful in showing mercy as God is!

Fear of the Lord, godly

28:14

14 Blessed is the man who always fears the LORD,
but he who hardens his heart falls into trouble.

14 One's prospects in this life depend on reverential fear. The verse contrasts the one who "always fears" (*mepaḥēd tamîd*) with the one who hardens his heart. The first is blessed, and the second falls into trouble. The verse gives no object for "fear": various translations have assumed that it would be the Lord (so NIV), especially in the Book of Proverbs. But *yir'āh* ("fear") is not used here. It may be that the verse means fear of sin. In other words, the one who is always apprehensive about sin and its results will be more successful at avoiding it and finding God's blessing. Or perhaps the blessing is the avoidance of sin, for *'ašrê 'ādām* (cf. Ps 1:1, *'ašrê hā'îš*, "Blessed is the man") would describe the heavenly bliss of the one who is right with God.

Rulers, wicked

28:15

15 Like a roaring lion or a charging bear
is a wicked man ruling over a helpless people.

15 Political tyrants are dangerous and destructive. The wicked man who rules over "helpless people" (*ʿam-dāl*) is compared to a "roaring lion" and a "charging bear"—subhuman, beastly, powerful, insensitive, in search of victims (prey). Because tyrants are like this, animal imagery (beast imagery?) is used in Daniel 7:1–8 for the series of ruthless world rulers. The poor crumple under such tyrants because they cannot meet their demands.

Rulers, good versus bad

28:16

> 16 A tyrannical ruler lacks judgment,
> but he who hates ill-gotten gain will enjoy a long life.

16 The righteous ruler, not the tyrant, will remain in power. The first line literally reads, "The prince who lacks understanding is also a great tyrant" (*nāg̱îḏ ḥ^{a}sar t^{e}ḇûnôṯ w^{e}raḇ ma'^{a}šaqqôṯ*). The LXX has "lacks income" (reading *t^{e}ḇû'ōṯ* or *t^{e}nûḇōṯ* instead). Toy suggests deleting *nāg̱îḏ* ("prince") altogether (p. 501). This ruler, assuming *nāg̱îḏ* belongs, will face the danger of rebellion and even assassination. The second line describes the one who rules with integrity—he "will enjoy a long life" (*ya'^{a}rîḵ yāmîm*, lit., "extends days"). A righteous administration pleases the people and God, who preserves it.

Guilt, its effects

28:17

> 17 A man tormented by the guilt of murder
> will be a fugitive till death;
> let no one support him.

17 The guilty fugitive will be isolated. This verse has some difficulties for the interpreter. The first line literally says, "A man tormented by the blood of a life" (*'āḏām ʿāšuq b^{e}ḏam-nāp̱eš*); Toy thinks the words make no sense but may have at one time been part of a law book and were inserted here by mistake (p. 502). Other commentators try to emend *ʿāšuq* (lit., "oppressed"). Greenstone draws from the cognate in Syriac the meaning "accused," which may be reflected in the Targum as "suspected" or "charged with." This would yield the reading "A man charged with murder shall flee to the pit" (p. 300). Driver suggests *ʿōśēq* ("busied himself") in Aramaic or *ʿašiga* ("clung to") in Arabic as possible links: "a man given to bloodshed" ("Problems in the Hebrew Text," p. 192). But it may be that if the motive for this saying is religious and not legal (as Toy says), then the idea of "oppressed" is workable. At any rate, the second line of the verse is either saying that it is futile to try to support a murderer on the run or that one should not interfere.

Security, based on integrity

28:18

> 18 He whose walk is blameless is kept safe,
> but he whose ways are perverse will suddenly fall.

18 Integrity brings security; perversion brings insecurity. A life of integrity (*hôlēk tāmîm;* NIV, "walk is blameless") is contrasted with the one "whose ways [dual; see v.6] are perverse [*ne'qaš*]"; the result of the righteous life style is being "kept safe" (*yiwwāšēa'*), whereas the wicked will fall. The last word, *be'eḥāt* ("at one [once]"), may indicate a sudden fall (cf. NIV); for "will fall in one" makes little sense. McKane wishes to emend to "into a pit [*šaḥat*]" based on v.10b, which he emended there first (p. 622).

Diligence, its results

28:19

> 19 He who works his land will have abundant food,
> but the one who chases fantasies will have his fill of poverty.

19 Prosperity depends on diligent work. This verse is essentially the same as 12:11. There is a meaningful repetition here: the diligent person will have "plenty [*yiśba'*] of bread," but the lazy person will have "plenty [*yiśba'*] of poverty" (RSV).

Character traits, faithfulness

28:20

> 20 A faithful man will be richly blessed,
> but one eager to get rich will not go unpunished.

20 Faithfulness determines success. The "faithful man" (*'îš 'emûnôṯ*) is contrasted with the one who is "eager to get rich" (*'āṣ leha'ašîr*). The idea is that the first is faithful to his obligations to God and to other people; but the one who hastens to make riches is at the least doing it without an honest day's work and at the worst dishonestly. In a hurry to acquire wealth, he falls into dishonest schemes and bears the guilt of it—he will not be unpunished. The Targum adds an interpretation—probably a correct one—that he hastens through deceit and wrongdoing.

Injustice, bribery

28:21

> 21 To show partiality is not good—
> yet a man will do wrong for a piece of bread.

21 Partiality in judgment is wrong, even though easily acquired. To show partiality (*hakkēr-pānîm*) destroys justice (see Lev 19:15; Deut 1:17; 16:19; Prov 18:5; 24:23). The second line of this verse has several possibilities. It could mean that a man can be bribed for a very small price (a piece of bread being the figure for it) or that some might steal for a piece of bread so the judgment should show a little more compassion on the crime of desperation or that even in such a desperate act one should show no partiality. The first interpretation harmonizes best with the law. Kidner adds poignantly that the price can go even lower than a piece of bread and that what is true of judges is true of preachers as well (*Proverbs*, p. 172; see also Mal 2:9).

Avarice, its effect

28:22

22 A stingy man is eager to get rich
and is unaware that poverty awaits him.

22 Avarice inevitably leads to poverty. Here we meet the man with the "evil eye" again (*'îš ra' 'āyin*). The expression was used in 23:6 for the selfish, "stingy man" (so NIV) who looks at all the wrong things in life. Here he is eager for wealth; the presumption is that greed involves sin, for which he will be punished with poverty. In 22:9 we had the "good eye" (NIV, "generous man"). McKane terms the "bad eye" as the misanthropic person (greed being one expression of misanthropy) and the "good eye" as the philanthropic person (p. 627).

Reproof, preferable to flattery

28:23

23 He who rebukes a man will in the end gain more favor
than he who has a flattering tongue.

23 In the final analysis rebuke will be better received than flattery. The flattering tongue (*maḥ^{a}lîq lāšôn*) may be pleasing for the moment, but it will offer no constructive help like the "rebuke" (*môḵî^{a}ḥ*). There is a difficulty with the word rendered "in the end" (*'aḥ^{a}ray*). It literally means "after me" (e.g., "after my instructions"), but that would be awkward here. Toy suggests simply changing it to "after" or "afterward," i.e., "in the end" (p. 504). Driver suggested an Akkadian cognate *ahurru* ("common man"), reading, "As a rebuker an ordinary man" ("Hebrew Notes," ZAW 52, p. 147). See also 15:5, 12; 25:12; 27:5–6; and 29:5.

Conduct, robbing parents

28:24

24 He who robs his father or mother
and says, "It's not wrong"—
he is partner to him who destroys.

24 Whoever robs his parents, no matter how he seeks to justify it, is a destroyer. The point of *gôzēl 'āḇîw* ("he who robs his father") seems to be that of prematurely trying to gain control of the family property through some form of pressure and in the process reduce the parents' possessions and standing in the community. He can say, "It's not wrong" (*'ên-pāša'*), because he could reason that it would be his some day anyway. The proverb classifies this type of greedy person as a companion to one "who destroys" (*mašḥîṯ*).

Character traits, greed versus trust

28:25

25 A greedy man stirs up dissension,
but he who trusts in the LORD will prosper.

25 One's object of faith determines the direction of his life. The antithetical parallelism pits the "greedy man" (*r^e^ḥab-nep̱eš*, "large appetite"; lit., "wide of soul") against the one "who trusts" (*bôṭē^a^ḥ*) the Lord. The first one is completely selfish and usually ruthless. His attitudes and actions stir up strife because people do not long tolerate him. He pushes so hard for the things he wants that his zeal becomes a hinderance to obtaining them. Conversely, the true believer, who is blessed by God, "will prosper" (*y^e^ḏuššān;* lit., "will be made fat," i.e., abundantly prosperous).

Conduct, righteous versus self-sufficiency

28:26

> 26 He who trusts in himself is a fool,
> but he who walks in wisdom is kept safe.

26 Security comes from a life of wisdom and not from self-sufficiency. Some commentators think the lines of v.25 and v.26 got mixed up; they would arrange them as follows: 25a, 26b, 25b, 26a (Toy, pp. 505–6). As it stands, v.26 in the Hebrew is antithetical parallelism, contrasting the one who trusts in himself (*bôṭē^a^ḥ b^e^libbô*) with the one who "walks in wisdom." Toy says that trusting in one's own heart means to follow the untrained suggestions of the mind or to rely on one's own mental resources (p. 505). That being the case, the idea forms a fitting contrast to walking in wisdom, i.e., the wisdom from above that this book has been teaching. McKane observes that the end of the process of education is none other than to make the person rely on his own intellect *once it has been informed and disciplined* (so v.26a presumes impiety) (cf. McKane, p. 621; emphasis mine).

Generosity versus indifference

28:27

> 27 He who gives to the poor will lack nothing,
> but he who closes his eyes to them receives many
> curses.

27 Generosity is rewarded but indifference is cursed. See also 22:9 and 11:24–26. The one who is generous will not miss what he gives away (Greenstone, p. 303), but the one who is indifferent to the needs of the poor will be cursed often—by them no doubt.

Stability, righteous government

28:28

> 28 When the wicked rise to power, people go into hiding;
> but when the wicked perish, the righteous thrive.

28 The righteous flourish when wickedness is removed from government. The verse is essentially the same as 28:12; see also 11:10 and 29:2, 16. For "go into hiding" (*yissāṯēr*), Driver suggests the Akkadian *satāru* ("demolish"), cognate to the Aramaic *s^e^tar* ("destroyed") ("Problems in the Hebrew Text," pp. 192–93).

Character traits, stubbornness

29:1

[1]A man who remains stiff-necked after many rebukes
will suddenly be destroyed—without remedy.

1 Destruction comes swiftly to those who stubbornly refuse to change. The verse is a warning about the peril of persisting in sin; it uses the image of the "stiff neck" (*maqšeh-'ōrep̱*) to portray the obstinate person who disregards all rebukes (see Exod 32:9). The opposite of the stiff neck would be a bending neck, i.e., submission. The stubborn person does not foresee misfortune and so will suddenly "be destroyed" (*yiššāḇēr*) without any healing. Whybray illustrates this with the fable of the oak and the bulrush; the latter bends with the wind and survives, but the former is too rigid and breaks (*Book of Proverbs*, p. 167). For similar proverbs see 6:15; 13:18; and 15:10.

Righteousness, its affect on morale

29:2

[2]When the righteous thrive, the people rejoice;
when the wicked rule, the people groan.

2 Good people can enjoy life when righteousness predominates in government. The antithetical parallelism supports the interpretation of the righteous increasing to mean that they gain control (Greenstone, p. 305). When the righteous are in authority, there is rejoicing; but people always suffer under wicked regimes (see 11:10–11; 28:12, 28).

Wisdom, its affect on the family

29:3

[3]A man who loves wisdom brings joy to his father,
but a companion of prostitutes squanders his wealth.

3 Wisdom ensures joy and prosperity for the family. Here again the lines are antithetical: in contrast to the wise person who brings "joy" (*y^eśammaḥ*) to his father is the son who brings grief by squandering (*y^e'abbeḏ*) his wealth on "prostitutes" (*zônôṯ*). Whybray notes that since wealth was a sign of God's blessing, it was essential for an honorable standing in the community; to waste it would be a shameful betrayal of the family (*Book of Proverbs*, p. 168). Moreover, it would break a father's heart to see his son become a pauper through vice (McKane, p. 653). For the financial consequences of vice, see chapters 1–9 (esp. 5:10 and 6:31).

Security, through justice

29:4

[4]By justice a king gives a country stability,
but one who is greedy for bribes tears it down.

4 A nation is secure when justice prevails. This verse contrasts a king who makes the nation secure (lit., "stand," *ya'^amîḏ*) with one who "tears it down" (*yehersennāh*). The first brings prosperity by championing "justice" (*mišpāṭ*); the second is a "man of bribes" (*'îš t^{e}rûmôṯ*; NIV, "one who is greedy for bribes"). The term *t^{e}rûmāh* usually refers to "ritual offering"; here it refers to exactions or taxes. The idea of "bribes" is not the point; this king breaks the backs of the people with demands for monetary gifts (see 1 Sam 8:11–18), and this causes divisions and strife.

Speech, deceptive

29:5

> [5]Whoever flatters his neighbor
> is spreading a net for his feet.

5 False flattery is self-destructive. The subject is one who "flatters his neighbor." This flattering (*maḥ^{a}lîq*) works by deception and guile, for the word literally means "deals smoothly." McKane says, "The sycophant is not to be trusted, for words which are too smooth and too obviously designed to gratify are a form of premeditated malice and a cloak for evil conduct" (p. 636). There is some uncertainty of the referent in the second line: "he spreads [*pôrēś*] a net for his steps." This could be a net spread for the one flattered or for the flatterer himself. The latter would make the verse more powerful (see also 2:16; 7:5; 26:28; 28:23).

Security, of the righteous

29:6

> [6]An evil man is snared by his own sin,
> but a righteous one can sing and be glad.

6 Only the righteous can enjoy a sense of security. By means of another antithetical saying, the sage observes that the evil man is caught in his own sin (similar to v.5), but the righteous sing and are glad—two expressions that signify their confidence. The first line literally says "in the transgression of a bad man is a snare"; the Syriac simplifies this and makes the verb passive (see also NIV; Toy, p. 508). The second line makes the contrast that the righteous have no fear of snares and so can sing. The verbs *yārûn* ("sing") and *śāmē^{a}ḥ* ("be glad") present some problem. Because Proverbs does not usually duplicate verbal ideas like this, and because *yārûn* is irregular, some commentators change it to *yārûṣ* ("will rush"; BHS). Toy suggests "run" (p. 508), but McKane emends to "exult" to form a hendiadys: "is deliriously happy" (p. 638). Driver, changing *môqēš* ("snare") to *mûqāš* ("is snared") after the Peshitta and Targum, changes *yārûn* to *yāḏôn* ("remains") based on two MSS (Arabic *dāna,* "continue"). He then translates, "The evil man is snared, but the righteous remains and rejoices" ("Problems in the Hebrew Text," pp. 193–94).

Justice, for the poor

29:7

> [7]The righteous care about justice for the poor,
> but the wicked have no such concern.

7 Only the righteous champion justice for the poor. This, another antithetical parallelism, pits the righteous against the wicked. The righteous cares (*yōḏē^{a}',* "knows," meaning "has sympathetic knowledge of" or "considers favorably," Toy, p. 508) about justice (their rights; see 20:8; 31:5, 8) for the poor; but the wicked do not "discern knowledge" (*yāḇîn dā'aṯ*)—they have no such interest or insight into the problems of the people. See Job 29:12–17.

Wisdom, averting anger

29:8

> 8 Mockers stir up a city,
> but wise men turn away anger.

8 The wise maintain peace and harmony in society. This contrast tells how the wise "turn away anger" (*yāšîḇû 'āp̱*) rather than stir up strife. The "men of scoffing" or "mockers" are "men who laugh at moral obligations and stir up the baser passions of their fellow citizens (Isa. 28:14)" (Toy, pp. 508–9). The idea of "stir up" is from the Hebrew *yāp̱îḥû* ("blow," as in "blow up a flame," i.e., kindle a fire). It is also used of words in 6:19 and 12:17—viz., to "puff out" words. Such scoffers make dangerous situations worse, whereas the wise calm things down and ensure peace in the community. See the account of the rebellion of Sheba the son of Bicri and how the wise woman averted disaster (2 Sam 20).

Strife, exacerbated

29:9

> 9 If a wise man goes to court with a fool,
> the fool rages and scoffs, and there is no peace.

9 It is a waste of time to try to settle a dispute calmly or rationally with a fool. The first line presents the condition and the second the effect. To go into court with a fool, you have to reckon "with unreasonable and objectionable behavior and a complete lack of proportion" (McKane, p. 636). Whether this "fool" (*'ewîl*) is angry or laughing, there is no possible resolution to the matter (*'ên nāḥaṯ;* NIV, "no peace"). One can only cut the losses and have no further dealings with him (see Whybray, *Book of Proverbs*, p. 168; see also Prov 26:4 and its warning not to answer a fool).

Righteousness, hated by the wicked

29:10

> 10 Bloodthirsty men hate a man of integrity
> and seek to kill the upright.

10 Bloodthirsty men loathe the integrity of the upright. Because the wicked despise all sense of decency or "integrity" (*tām*), they seek to destroy it. The second line forms a contrast; literally it reads, "as for the upright, they seek his life [*nap̱šô*]." "Seeking a life" was usually a hostile act, but here the contrast requires the idea of "seek to preserve a life" (NIV interprets differently). McKane is satisfied that here "seek" means to seek the welfare of someone; so it would mean that the upright "have regard for" men of integrity (p. 637).

Character traits, self-control

29:11

> 11 A fool gives full vent to his anger,
> but a wise man keeps himself under control.

11 It takes wisdom to restrain anger. The antithesis is between the "fool" (*k^{e}sîl*) who lets out all his anger and the wise who "stills it back" (*'āḥôr*). The line is difficult but does make sense as it stands (see Notes). The wise man holds back anger, but the fool is the "slave of impulse and is at the mercy of every moment when he chances to feel irritation" (McKane, p. 635). See also 16:32 and 25:28.

Notes

11 The clause וְחָכָם בְּאָחוֹר יְשַׁבְּחֶנָּה (*w^{e}ḥāḵām b^{e}'āḥôr y^{e}šabb^{e}ḥennāh*) literally reads "but a wise man stills it back." Because *'āḥôr* does not fit well with the verb, most commentators offer some change. Toy reads "anger" for "back" and translates the verb "restrain" after the LXX, which has "has self-control" (p. 510). The idea of "keeps it back" (implied in the line; cf. NIV) and "stills it" is a possible interpretation however.

Speech, lies

29:12

> 12 If a ruler listens to lies,
> all his officials become wicked.

12 Once a ruler begins to listen to lies, his court will be corrupted. The point is, as Toy expresses it, that courtiers adjust themselves to the prince (p. 510)—when they see that deception and court flattery win the day, they learn how the game is played. Plaut reminds of the Roman saying, *Qualis rex, talis grex* ("like king, like people," p. 292; see 16:10; 20:8; 25:2).

Life, from God

29:13

> 13 The poor man and the oppressor have this in common:
> The LORD gives sight to the eyes of both.

13 Regardless of status or circumstances, all people receive their life from God. These lines are in synthetic parallelism. The first links the poor man and the oppressor (the LXX has debtor and creditor), and the second explains what they have in common: "The LORD gives sight [*mē'îr*] to the eyes of both." The imagery of giving sight means that God gives the light of life (see Job 33:30; Ps 13:3). God creates and controls them all. See 22:2.

Poor, treatment of

29:14

[14]If a king judges the poor with fairness,
his throne will always be secure.

14 The duration of an administration depends on its moral character. This verse shows the importance of guaranteeing that fair and just treatment is given to all (judging with "fairness" [*'emeṯ;* lit., "truth"]), especially the poor. To fail to do so is immoral. See 16:12; 20:28; 25:5; and 31:5.

Discipline, its effect

29:15

[15]The rod of correction imparts wisdom,
but a child left to himself disgraces his mother.

15 Discipline makes a child's behavior enjoyable. The lines form a contrast: "a rod of correction" ("rod" and "correction" form a hendiadys; viz., "a correcting rod") versus leaving a child alone (*meššullāḥ*). The focus on the mother in the last part is probably a rhetorical variation for the parent (see 17:21; 23:24–25) and not meant to assume that she will do the training. See also 13:24 and 23:13.

Judgment, its certainty

29:16

[16]When the wicked thrive, so does sin,
but the righteous will see their downfall.

16 No matter how much wickedness spreads in the land, righteousness will live to see it destroyed. The verse teaches that righteousness will prevail, but it does not say when or how. The first part merely affirms the equation that when the "wicked thrive" (*birḇôṯ rešā'îm*), then sin thrives. But one day the righteous will prevail over them (*yir'û be*, signifying to "see their downfall" triumphantly).

Discipline, its effect

29:17

[17]Discipline your son, and he will give you peace;
he will bring delight to your soul.

17 A disciplined child will bring contentment to parents. The parallelism is synthetic, the second line adding the thought of "delight" (*ma'adannîm*) to that of "giving peace" (*wînîḥeḵā*, "giving rest," "relieving anxiety," as in Deut 12:10). See 19:18.

Revelation, obedience to

29:18

[18]Where there is no revelation, the people cast off
restraint;
but blessed is he who keeps the law.

18 A nation's well-being depends on obedience to divine revelation. This popular verse refers to two forms of divine revelation, vision and law. The first line is worded negatively—if there is "no revelation" or "vision" (*ḥāzôn*), the people "throw off restraint" (*yippāra'*). The word *ḥāzôn* refers to divine communication to prophets (as in 1 Sam 3:1) and not to individual goals that are formed. Toy sees a problem with this meaning here: the most calamitous period of Israel's history was when prophetic vision was at its height, whereas people were obedient at times when God hid his face. He also notes that in Proverbs there is no mention of prophetic teaching with wisdom as a guide. Toy emends to "guidance" after the LXX (p. 512). The TEV has "guidance"; the NIV has "revelation." It should be stated, however, that the prophetic ministry was usually in response to the calamitous periods, calling the people back to God—*ḥāzôn* meaning revelatory vision should be retained. If there is no revelation from God, people can expect spiritual and political anarchy (Alden, p. 202). The meaning "cast off restraint" is assumed for *yippāra'*, based on Exodus 32:25. In contrast to the first line, the second provides the positive wording: there is a blessing for the one who keeps the law.

Discipline, its method

29:19

> 19 A servant cannot be corrected by mere words;
> though he understands, he will not respond.

19 It is not sufficient to train servants by words alone. The verse shows that slaves had to be treated like sons (i.e., they frequently had to be corrected), for they were naturally unresponsive (McKane, p. 634). The second line gives the explanation—it says literally that "though he understands, there is no answer." This means he does not obey when spoken to—he has to be trained. The LXX says that he is a stubborn servant. The verse is probably a general observation on the times; doubtless there were slaves who did better (e.g., Joseph in Egypt; Daniel in Babylon).

Speech, rash

29:20

> 20 Do you see a man who speaks in haste?
> There is more hope for a fool than for him.

20 It is easier to train a fool than to correct rash speech. The focus in this verse is on the one who is hasty (*'āṣ*) with his words—to speak before thinking something through is foolishness. The prospects (*tiqwāh*, "hope") of the fool are better, for rash speech cannot easily be remedied. See 26:12; see also James 3:8.

Discipline, lack of

29:21

> 21 If a man pampers his servant from youth,
> he will bring grief in the end.

21 An undisciplined servant causes nothing but grief. The proverb says that if someone pampers his servant from youth, in the end (of this procedure) he will have "grief" (*mānôn*). The word *mānôn,* a *hapax legomenon,* has been given a variety of translations; the idea of "grief" comes from the LXX. Reider takes the word to mean "weakling" from an Arabic root *na'na* ("to be weak"), with a noun/adjective *muna'ana'* ("weak," "feeble") (J. Reider, "Etymological Studies in Biblical Hebrew," VetTest 4 [1954]: 276–95).

Character traits, anger

29:22

22 An angry man stirs up dissension,
and a hot-tempered one commits many sins.

22 Anger brings strife. The lines, in synonymous parallelism, focus on the "angry man" (*'îš-'ap̱*)—one who is given to anger and not merely temporarily angry. Not only does such a one stir up "dissention" (*māḏôn*), but in so doing he also causes sin in himself and in others. See also 14:17, 29; 15:18; 16:32; and 22:24.

Character traits, pride and humility

29:23

23 A man's pride brings him low,
but a man of lowly spirit gains honor.

23 A humble spirit brings honor and respect. The verse contrasts consequences: pride leads to abasement, but humility brings exaltation. The lines are tied together with a paronomasia between "brings low" (*tašpîlennû*) and "lowly [*šᵉp̱al*] in spirit." McKane explains that the lowly one can learn, but "pride is a way of descent to mediocrity or worse" (p. 633). See Luke 14:11 and 18:14.

Sin, its entanglements

29:24

24 The accomplice of a thief is his own enemy;
he is put under oath and dare not testify.

24 An accomplice in crime will find no easy way out of his dilemma. This verse is a little confusing; it describes the accomplice of a thief (*ḥôlēq 'im-gannāḇ*) as his own enemy (lit., "he hates [*śônē'*] himself")—he hears a curse (*'ālāh yišma'*) and will not speak up. According to Leviticus 5:1, if a witness does not speak up, he is held accountable for the crime. The case here might be where the guilty person is unknown; and when a curse is pronounced on that unknown culprit, the accomplice hears it but cannot speak up. So the curse attaches itself to him as well (see Toy, p. 514). Another way to explain the verse is that the accomplice, when called as a witness (translating *'ālāh yišma'* as "he is put under oath"), perjures himself. The saying may have been aimed at some official who used crooks and then shielded them in legal inquiries.

Security, faith in the Lord

29:25

> 25 Fear of man will prove to be a snare,
> but whoever trusts in the LORD is kept safe.

25 True security is the result of trusting God and not humans. The contrast is between "trusting" (*bôṭēaḥ*) the Lord and "fearing man" (*ḥerdaṯ 'āḏām*). Such fear becomes a snare when it gets to the point of letting others control your life—their opinions and attitudes put subtle pressure on you, even hindering you from speaking the truth or doing what is right (Whybray, *Book of Proverbs*, pp. 169–70). Release from such bondage comes when people put their faith in the Lord alone. See 10:27; 12:2; and the example of the apostles in Acts 5:29.

Justice, from God

29:26

> 26 Many seek an audience with a ruler,
> but it is from the LORD that man gets justice.

26 True justice ultimately comes from God. The contrast is between seeking the face (grace) of a ruler and finding justice from the Lord. The great miscalculation is to assume that true justice depends on some ruler and that supplication must be directed first to him. Toy writes, "Proverbs deplores immoral (cringing or corrupt) reliances on human (especially political) power" (p. 515).

Character traits, hatred

29:27

> 27 The righteous detest the dishonest;
> the wicked detest the upright.

27 The righteous and the wicked detest the life styles of each other. The righteous "detest" (*tô'aḇaṯ*) the "dishonest" (*'îš 'āwel*), and the wicked detest those who try to live uprightly.

VI. The Words of Agur (30:1–33)

A. *The Title*

30:1

> 1 The sayings of Agur son of Jakeh—an oracle:
>
> This man declared to Ithiel,
> to Ithiel and to Ucal:

1 The heading for this section identifies the words that follow as those of Agur, the son of Jakeh, for Ithiel and Ucal. There have been many attempts to interpret these names. They have been translated as appellatives (Latin, assembler = teacher) and interpreted as sentences such as "I am weary, O God, I am weary and faint" (LXX; see NIV mg.) or "I am not a God, I am not a God that I should have power" (C.C. Torrey,

"Proverbs Chapter 30," JBL 73 [1954]: 93–96) or taken as names of unknown sages in Solomon's times (as there were others; see 1 Kings 4:30–31). The Midrash attempts to credit the section to Solomon through a clever but contrived etymology: "Agur is really Solomon because the latter girt his loins (*ogar*) with wisdom; he is called Bin Jakeh because he was free (*noki*) from sin; and the words, the burden, are added because he bore the yoke of God" (Plaut, p. 299, summarizing *Midrash Mishle*). It is most likely that someone other than Solomon wrote these sayings; they have a different, almost nonproverbial, tone to them. For the unity of the section, see Paul Franklyn, "The Sayings of Agur in Proverbs 30: Piety or Scepticism," ZAW 95 (1983): 239–52.

The section is also entitled a "burden" or "oracle" (*hammaśśā'*). It is possible that Massa might be a place; the idea of a "burden" normally describes a prophetic oracle of some kind.

This heading may not represent all the contents of chapter 30: there is much diversity in the chapter, and the arrangement differs somewhat between the LXX and the MT. Nonetheless, the heading ascribes most, if not all, of the passages to one Agur.

B. *Agur's Confession and Petition (30:2–9)*

1. *Confession of ignorance*

30:2–4

2 "I am the most ignorant of men;
I do not have a man's understanding.
3 I have not learned wisdom,
nor have I knowledge of the Holy One.
4 Who has gone up to heaven and come down?
Who has gathered up the wind in the hollow of his hands?
Who has wrapped up the waters in his cloak?
Who has established all the ends of the earth?
What is his name, and the name of his son?
Tell me if you know!

2–3 Agur confesses that he is ignorant of the ways of God. He begins by lamenting that he has not learned wisdom (vv.2–3), i.e., that he is not one of those who profess to understand the Holy One (Toy thinks this is a bit sarcastic [p. 521]). "Ignorant" refers to his intellectual dullness; he is like the lower animals (Pss 49:10–12; 73:22). The "Holy One" in this section is in the plural (*qᵉḏōšîm*) as in 9:10.

4 To make his point Agur includes five questions. These, like Job 38–41 or Proverbs 8:24–29, focus on divine acts to show that it is absurd for a mortal to think that he can explain God's works or to compare himself with God. These questions display man's limitations; they may have a sarcastic tone, implying that some people think they understand the phenomena of the universe. The first question, accordingly, could refer to a human ("Who has gone up to heaven?") but may simply refer to God as the other questions do. The final question seeks to identify this sovereign God. To know a person's name is to exhibit power over and closeness to him. The parallel reference to "son" was identified as Israel in the Midrash or in other places as the demiurge, the Logos, or a simple poetic parallelism for "his name." Christian interpreters have seen here a reference to the Son of God (a subtle anticipation of the full revelation in the NT).

2. *Affirmation of the reliability of God's word*

30:5–6

5 "Every word of God is flawless;
he is a shield to those who take refuge in him.
6 Do not add to his words,
or he will rebuke you and prove you a liar.

5 Agur affirms that God's word is pure (*ṣᵉrûpāh;* NIV, "flawless"); the point of the predicate, used elsewhere of purifying metal, is that God's word is trustworthy: there is nothing deceitful or false in it. The second half of the verse explains this meaning: it is safe to take refuge in the Lord (see Pss 12:6; 18:31).

6 This confidence is followed by a warning not to add to the Lord's words (see Deut 4:2), a tendency that is all too common. Man's danger, Plaut says, is conceit and the ascription of divinity to himself (p. 300).

3. *Prayer*

30:7–9

7 "Two things I ask of you, O LORD;
do not refuse me before I die:
8 Keep falsehood and lies far from me;
give me neither poverty nor riches,
but give me only my daily bread.
9 Otherwise, I may have too much and disown you
and say, 'Who is the LORD?'
Or I may become poor and steal,
and so dishonor the name of my God.

7–9 Agur prays that God will prevent him from becoming deceitful (v.8a) and self-sufficient (vv.8b–9). He wants to be honest in all his dealings, and he wants a life of balanced material blessings. He reasons that if he has too much, he might become independent of God (see Deut 8:11–14); and if he has too little, he might steal and thus profane God's name.

So acknowledging his own ignorance, relying on God's word for security in life, and praying that God will keep him from falling into temptation, Agur is ready to offer his words.

C. *The Admonition of Agur (30:10–33)*

1. *Noninterference in domestic situations*

30:10

10 "Do not slander a servant to his master,
or he will curse you, and you will pay for it.

10 The advice here is literally "not to slander" (*'al-talšēn*) a servant to his master, "lest he curse you" (*pen-yᵉqallelḵā*) and "you pay for it" (*wᵉ'āšāmtā*). The verse is not very clear on first reading. The verb *lāšan* (lit., "wag the tongue") means "defame," i.e., "slander," if the charge is untrue. Toy suggests that the warning is not limited to slaves (p. 525). The warning could be taken literally: Do not slander a servant to his master; for if it is not true, then he will make you look small (for this sense of *qālal,* see McKane, p. 650), and you will be found guilty (*'āšām*)—if you are not guilty, then the curse would have no effect. Another view is that the verse refers to the delivery of a fugitive slave to his master (Greenstone, p. 319). "Slander" in this case would refer to denouncing, i.e., accusing to authorities (see Deut 23:15–16). The advice then would be not to meddle in the affairs of someone else.

2. *Four evil things (30:11–14)*

Possibly there was a heading for this section at one time ("Three things, yea four . . ."). All the things listed here begin with the word *dôr* ("generation," meaning a class or group of people; see also Matt 11:16).

a. *Disrespect for parents*

30:11

11 "There are those who curse their fathers
  and do not bless their mothers;

11 The first observation is that there is a segment of society that lacks respect for parents, in spite of the law (cf. Exod 21:17; Prov 20:20). In the parallelism the negative (*lō' y^{e}bārēk,* "do not bless") follows the positive (*y^{e}qallēl,* "who curse"); "cursing" a parent could refer to defaming, treating lightly, or showing disrespect in general.

b. *Self-righteousness*

30:12

12 those who are pure in their own eyes
  and yet are not cleansed of their filth;

12 These are they who are "pure" (*ṭāhôr*) but are "not cleansed" (*lō' ruḥāṣ*) from their "filth" (*ṣō'āh*). "Filth" often refers to physical uncleanness, but here it is moral defilement (cf. Isa 36:12; Zech 3:3–4). There is a generation, a group of people, who may observe all outer ritual but pay no attention to inner cleansing (see Isa 1:16; Matt 23:27). Such hypocrisy is harmful in every walk of life.

c. *Pride*

30:13

13 those whose eyes are ever so haughty,
  whose glances are so disdainful;

13 The eyes of the proud are "high" (*rāmû;* NIV, "haughty") and their eyelids "disdainful" (*yinnāśē'û*). The expressions refer to their arrogant attitude—the lofty view of themselves and the corresponding contempt for others. See also 6:17 and Psalm 131:1.

d. *Oppressing the poor*

30:14

> 14 those whose teeth are swords
> and whose jaws are set with knives
> to devour the poor from the earth,
> the needy from among mankind.

14 The imagery of the first half of the verse captures the rapacity of their power—their teeth and their jaws are swords and knives. The second part explains that they devour, like a ravenous and insensitive beast, the poor and the needy (see 31:8–9). Those who exploit and destroy other people are beasts.

3. *Insatiable things*

30:15–16

> 15 "The leech has two daughters.
> 'Give! Give!' they cry.
>
> "There are three things that are never satisfied,
> four that never say, 'Enough!':
> 16 the grave, the barren womb,
> land, which is never satisfied with water,
> and fire, which never says, 'Enough!'

15a Things that seem never to be satisfied are problematic for the normal enjoyment of life. The meaning of v.15a and its relationship to vv.15b–16 has been debated for some time. The "leech" (*ʿᵃlûqāh*) is the symbol of greed because it sucks blood through its two suckers (here called its "two daughters" who cry "Give! Give! [*haḇ haḇ*]"). Various attempts to identify the two daughters have been made, none too satisfactory. The Zohar describes a dog in Gehenna that barks, "*Haḇ, haḇ.*" J.J. Glück suggests that what is in view is erotic passion (and not the leech) with its two maidens of burning desire crying out for more ("Proverbs 30:15a," VetTest 14 [1964]: 367–70). F.S. North rightly criticizes this view as gratuitous; he argues for the view that a leech with two suckers is what is intended ("The Four Insatiables," VetTest 15 [1965]: 281–82).

15b–16 There probably is a relationship in the numbering between v.15a and vv.15b–16: two daughters, three insatiable things, and four things that never say enough (see Roth, "Numerical Sequence," pp. 300–311, and "Numerical Sayings"). McKane suggests that the series builds to the climax, that the focus of attention is on the barren woman, and that insatiable death, the thirsty land, and the greedy fire are all metaphors of her sexual desire (p. 656). But this is not convincing.

The four insatiable things are then listed: *Šᵉʾôl* ("Sheol," or the "grave" in the NIV), the abode of the dead (see also 27:20); the barren womb (*ʿōṣer rāḥam,* lit., "the closing of the womb") of one whose desire for children is all consuming (see Gen 16:2; 30:1); land that is not satisfied with water; and fire that continues until stopped.

There is no clearly stated ethical lesson; these are basic observations of life. But one point that could be made is that greed, symbolized by the leech, is as insatiable as these other things.

4. *Punishment for parental disrespect*

30:17

[17]"The eye that mocks a father,
that scorns obedience to a mother,
will be pecked out by the ravens of the valley,
will be eaten by the vultures.

17 Severe punishment awaits those who show disrespect for their parents. The sentence focuses on the "eye" that "mocks" (*til'ag*) a father and despises or "scorns" (*tāḇûz*) obedience to a mother (see Notes). The point is that the eye manifests the inner heart attitude—so the contemptuous look runs deep. The punishment is talionic—the eye that mocks will be pecked out by the birds. By these images the sternest punishment is held out for one who holds his parents in such contempt.

Notes

17 "Obedience" is לִיקֲּהַת (*lîqqᵃhaṯ*), used only here and in Gen 49:10. Toy makes a change to *lᵉziqnaṯ*, thus reading, "the old age of the mother" (p. 530). The LXX's *gēras* suggests that a root *lhq* had something to do with "white hair." D. Winton Thomas suggests a form of *lᵉhāqāh* or *lᵉhîqāh*. This would have involved a corruption of *lhyqt* to *lyqht*. It would read, "The eye that mocks a father and despises an aged mother" ("A Note on לִיקֲּהַת in Proverbs 30:17," JTS 42 [1941]: 154–55).

5. *Amazing things in nature*

30:18–19

[18]"There are three things that are too amazing for me,
four that I do not understand:
[19]the way of an eagle in the sky,
the way of a snake on a rock,
the way of a ship on the high seas,
and the way of a man with a maiden.

18–19 Many things in nature are amazing but incomprehensible. This little observation also begins with the numerical formula "There are three things that are too amazing [*nip̄lᵉ'û*] for me, four that I do not understand [*lō' yᵉḏa'tîm*]." The verb "amazing" (*pālē'*) basically describes what is wonderful, surpassing, incomprehensible (cf. Gen 18:14; Judg 13:18; Ps 139:6; Isa 9:6 [5 MT]). The sage can only admire the wonders of nature—he is at a loss to explain it all.

It is not easy to discover what the four things have in common. They all are linked by the use of the word "way" (*dereḵ*, meaning a course of action) and by a sense of mystery in each area. Suggestions for a common theme include the following: all four things are hidden from continued observation, for they are there in majestic form and then are gone, not leaving a trace; they all have a mysterious means of propulsion or motivation; they all describe the movement of one thing within the sphere or domain of another; or the first three serve as illustrations of the fourth and greatest wonder—it concerns human relations and is slightly different than the first three. Whybray observes that if the author intended to be mysterious and keep us guessing, he has certainly succeeded (*Book of Proverbs*, p. 177).

The first entry is the way of the eagle in the sky, a marvelous creature soaring with apparent ease but certain determination and purpose, all hidden from the observer. Next is the way of the serpent on a rock. Here is the mysterious but smooth and efficient movement of a reptile without feet. The way of a ship in the sea portrays the magnificent movement of a vessel through a trackless sea. All these are marvelous to observe; they focus our attention on the majestic and mysterious movements in the sky, on the land, and on the sea.

The fourth mystery is "the way of a man with a maiden" (see Notes). The term *'almāh* ("maiden") does not in and of itself mean "virgin" but rather describes a young woman who is sexually ready for marriage. What is in view here is the wonder of human sexuality, for the preposition *b*ᵉ suggests that the "way of a man" is either "with" or "in" the *'almāh*. This mystery might begin with the manner of obtaining the love of the woman but focuses on the most intimate part of human relationships. So the most intimate moments of love are at the heart of what the sage considers to be wonderful. All of it is part of God's marvelous plan for his creation and therefore can be fully enjoyed and appreciated without fully comprehending it.

Notes

19 For an alternate view, see Gregorio Del Olmo Lete, "Nota Sobre Prov 30:19," *Biblica* 67 (1986): 68–74. He takes עַלְמָה (*'almāh*) as "darkness," reading, "the way of the courageous man in the dark."

6. *The brazen woman*

30:20

> 20 "This is the way of an adulteress:
> She eats and wipes her mouth
> and says, 'I've done nothing wrong.'

20 Equally amazing is the insensitivity of the adulteress to sin. That this verse was placed here lends support to the idea that the previous verse is focusing on sexual intimacy in marriage; for just as that is incomprehensible (filling one with wonder), so is the way that human nature has distorted and ruined it. Carrying forward the use of *dereḵ*, the verse describes "the way of an adulteress." She is *'iššāh mᵉnā'āp̱eṯ;* she may be married but certainly is unchaste. The portrayal is one of an amoral woman more than an immoral one (McKane, p. 658). Kidner notes that the act of adultery is as unremarkable to her as a meal (*Proverbs*, p. 180). The imagery of eating and wiping her mouth is euphemistic for sexual activity (see 9:17). It is incredible that human beings can engage in sin and then so easily dismiss any sense of guilt or responsibility, perhaps by rationalizing the deeds or perhaps through a calloused indifference to what the will of the Lord is for sexuality.

7. *Abuse of position*

30:21–23

21 "Under three things the earth trembles,
under four it cannot bear up:
22 a servant who becomes king,
a fool who is full of food,
23 an unloved woman who is married,
and a maidservant who displaces her mistress.

21–23 Certain people who are suddenly elevated in their status in life can be unbearable. The sage says that under these things the earth trembles and cannot bear it (v.21)—obviously using humorous or satirical hyperbole to say that these changes shake up the order of life. This assumes that the elevated status was not accompanied by a change of nature. For example, it was not uncommon for a servant to become a king in the ancient Near East (v.22). It would be possible that once he became king, he would develop the mentality and disposition of a king and perhaps be better than the preceding ruler. But the "earth trembles" when a servant is king; unaccustomed to such dignity, he might become a power-hungry tyrant and oppressive ruler (Greenstone suggests the example of Hitler, p. 324). The second, a fool who is full of food, describes a fool who becomes prosperous but continues to be boorish and irreligious; but now he is overbearing and, worse yet, finds time hanging heavy on his hands. The third is the unloved woman who is married (v.23). Perhaps she is unattractive or odious, but also perhaps she is married to someone incapable of showing love. Being unloved, not sought or wooed, she is actually hated (see Gen 29:31, 33). The fourth is the maid who displaces her mistress. The tension from the threat of Hagar in Genesis 16:5 and 21:10 shows how unbearable this could be. Such upheavals in the proper order of things make life intolerable.

8. *Wisdom the key to success*

30:24–28

24 "Four things on earth are small,
yet they are extremely wise:
25 Ants are creatures of little strength,
yet they store up their food in the summer;
26 coneys are creatures of little power,
yet they make their home in the crags;
27 locusts have no king,
yet they advance together in ranks;
28 a lizard can be caught with the hand,
yet it is found in kings' palaces.

24–28 These verses focus on four things that are small but "extremely wise" (*ḥ*^{a}*ḵāmîm m*^{e}*ḥukkāmîm*): ants, rock badgers, locusts, and lizards. The wisdom exhibited in the ants concerns their forethought and organization to make provision for food; the wisdom of the rock badgers (NIV, "coneys") is found in their ingenuity to find a place of security; the wisdom of the locust consists in its cooperation and order, which when massed in military division becomes a force for man to reckon with (see D.W. Thomas, "Notes on Some Passages in the Book of Proverbs," VetTest 15, p. 271–79); and the wisdom of the lizard is in its elusiveness and boldness (for a survey of lessons from nature, see S.P. Toperoff, "The Ant in the Bible and Midrash,"

Dor le Dor 13 [1985]: 179–83). In God's creation wisdom manifests itself in a variety of ways, and humans can learn the value of wisdom over size and numerical strength.

9. *Leadership qualities*

30:29–31

29 "There are three things that are stately in their stride,
four that move with stately bearing:
30 a lion, mighty among beasts,
who retreats before nothing;
31 a strutting rooster, a he-goat,
and a king with his army around him.

29–31 Leaders exhibit majestic qualities. There is a simple point to this observation: three things are "stately in their stride" (*mêṭiḇê ṣā'aḏ*), four that move with "stately being" (*mêṭiḇê lāḵeṯ*). Three examples come from the animal world, leading up to the fourth, the king, who has his army about him to defend against revolt (see Notes).

Notes

31 The text has אַלְקוּם עִמּוֹ (*'alqûm 'immô*, "with his army around him"). This has been emended to read *'immô lō' qām* ("against whom there is no rising up") or *qām 'el 'ammô* ("standing over his people") (Driver, "Problems in the Hebrew Text," p. 194). The LXX has "a king haranguing his people." While a slight change makes it a little easier to offer a translation, the exact meaning is far from certain. The point must focus on the stately appearance of the king.

10. *A final admonition*

30:32–33

32 "If you have played the fool and exalted yourself,
or if you have planned evil,
clap your hand over your mouth!
33 For as churning the milk produces butter,
and as twisting the nose produces blood,
so stirring up anger produces strife."

32–33 The sage advises those who have "exalted" (*b^{e}hiṯnaśśē'*) themselves and "played the fool" (*nāḇaltā*) and those who have "planned deception" (*zammôṯā*) to cease their efforts and control what they say; viz., "clap your hand over our mouth!" (*yāḏ l^{e}p̱eh;* cf. Job 40:4–5). The explanation for this warning is that it only causes strife. Two similes are used in the last verse, churning the milk and twisting the nose—both involve a pressing, the first producing butter from milk and the second drawing blood from the nose. In the same way stirring up anger (through pride and evil planning) produces "strife" (*rîḇ*). There is also a subtle wordplay here, for "nose" (*'ap̱*) is related to "anger" (*'appayim*). So the intent of this concluding advice is to strive for peace and harmony through humility and righteousness.

VII. The Words of Lemuel (31:1–9)

A. *Title: The Words Taught to Lemuel by His Mother*

31:1

1 The sayings of King Lemuel—an oracle his mother taught him:

1 Nothing is known about King Lemuel. The same question of translation occurs here with *maśśā'* that occurred in 30:1, whether it is "oracle" or a place "Massa." Jewish legend identifies Lemuel as Solomon and the advice as from Bathsheba from a time when Solomon indulged in magic with his Egyptian wife and delayed the morning sacrifices (see Greenstone, p. 329). But there is no evidence for this. The passage is the only direct address to a king in the book—something that was the norm in the wisdom literature of the other countries (see Leah Leila Brunner, "King and Commoner in Proverbs and Near Eastern Sources," *Dor le Dor* 10 [1982]: 210–19, 259; Brunner shows that the advice is religious and not secular). The instruction includes two warnings and then sound advice.

B. *First Warning*

31:2–3

2 "O my son, O son of my womb,
O son of my vows,
3 do not spend your strength on women,
your vigor on those who ruin kings.

2–3 The king is warned not to spend his strength on sensual lust. The repetition of "son" shows the seriousness of the warning; and the twofold motivation adds to this impact—he is her son, and she has vowed him (cf. 1 Sam 1:11). (See F. Deist, "Prov. 31:1, A Use of Constant Mistranslation" *Journal of Northwest Semitic Languages* 6 [1978]: 1–3; Deist argues that "son of my womb" should be "own son.") She advises him not to spend "his strength" (*ḥêleḵā*) or "his ways" (*d^e^rāḵeyḵā*) on women. The term *d^e^rāḵeyḵā* ("vigor" in NIV) may allude to sexual intercourse (see 30:19) or in general refer to the heart's affection or attention (Toy, p. 540). "Women" in this passage are qualified as those who "ruin" (*lamḥôṯ*) kings. Commentators note that this difficult term is close to an Aramaic word for concubine (see Greenstone, p. 330) and an Arabic word that is an indelicate description of women. Whatever the precise meaning, the point of the verse is that while it would be easy for a king to spend his time and energy enjoying women, that would be unwise.

C. *Second Warning*

31:4–7

4 "It is not for kings, O Lemuel—
not for kings to drink wine,
not for rulers to crave beer,
5 lest they drink and forget what the law decrees,
and deprive all the oppressed of their rights.
6 Give beer to those who are perishing,
wine to those who are in anguish;
7 let them drink and forget their poverty
and remember their misery no more.

4–7 Drinking wine and craving beer is not for kings. If this literally prohibits any use of such drinks, it would be unheard of in the ancient courts. Either excessive use of alcohol or troubling need for it (reflecting deeper problems) is what is meant. The danger, of course, would be to cloud the mind and deprive the oppressed of true justice.

Verses 6–7 explain that a better use for strong drink is to relieve bodily suffering and mental distress. People in those conditions need to forget.

D. *Instruction: Defend the Defenseless*

31:8–9

> 8 "Speak up for those who cannot speak for themselves,
> for the rights of all who are destitute.
> 9 Speak up and judge fairly;
> defend the rights of the poor and needy."

8–9 The king is to open his mouth (*p^{e}ṯaḥ-pîḵā*, i.e., "speak up for") those who are dumb (*'illēm* probably signifying "those who cannot speak for themselves"). It is the responsibility of the king to champion the rights of the poor and the needy, those who are left desolate by the cruelties of life (see 2 Sam 14:4–11; 1 Kings 3:16–28; Pss 45:3–5; 72:4; Isa 9:6–7).

VIII. The Wife of Noble Character (31:10–31)

The Book of Proverbs comes to a close with the addition of this poem about the woman of valor. A careful reading of the passage will show that her value is derived from her character of godly wisdom that is beneficial to her family and to the community as a whole. Traditionally this poem was recited by husbands and children at the Sabbath table on Friday night (see Y. Levin, " 'The Woman of Valor' in Jewish Ritual [Prov. 31:10–31]," *Beth Mikra* 31 [1985/86]: 339–47). Christians too have seen it as a paradigm for godly women.

The theme of the poem, the wife of noble character, captures the ideals of wisdom that have filled the book (see T.P. McCreesh, "Wisdom as Wife: Proverbs 31:10–31," RB 92 [1985]: 25–46). It may well be that this is more the point of the composition than merely a portrayal of the ideal wife. The woman here presented is a wealthy aristocrat who runs a household estate with servants and conducts business affairs—real estate, vineyards, and merchandise—domestic affairs, and charity. It would be quite a task for any woman to emulate this pattern. Camp describes the woman as an idealized wife, in an ideal home, in an ideal society—she is not just some man's dream woman but represents a universal type of woman (Claudia V. Camp, *Wisdom and the Feminine in the Book of Proverbs* [Sheffield: JSOT, 1985], pp. 92–93; see also Andre Barucq, *Le Livre des Proverbs* [Paris: LeCoffre, 1964], p. 233). Others have also recognized that more is going on here than a description of the ideal wife or instructions for the bride to be (that parallel the instructions for the young man in the book). Kidner allows that "this lady's standard is not implied to be in reach of all" (*Proverbs*, p. 184) but rather reveals the flowering of wisdom in domestic life. Aitken likewise affirms that "as a whole it cannot be read as a kind of blueprint of the ideal Israelite housewife, either for men to measure their wives against or for their wives to try to live up to" (p. 158). Moreover, the work says nothing about the woman's personal relationship with her husband, her intellectual or emotional strengths, or her religious activities. In general it appears that the woman of Proverbs 31 is a symbol of wisdom (see E. Jacob, "Sagesse et Alphabet: Pr. 31:10–31," in *Hommages à A. Dupont-Sommer*, edd. A. Caquot and M. Philonenko [n.p.: Adrien–Maisonneuve, 1971], pp. 287–95). If this is so, then the poem plays an important part in the personification of wisdom in the ancient Near Eastern literature. Indeed, many commentators rightly invite a contrast to the earlier portrayals of Dame Folly lurking dangerously in the streets—she was to be avoided—and Lady Wisdom, who is to be embraced. The Lady Wisdom in this chapter stands in the strongest contrast to the adulterous woman in the earlier chapters.

Several characteristics of this poem should be noted in order to appreciate its impact on the teaching of wisdom (on this subject see Murray H. Lichtenstein, "Chiasm and Symmetry in Proverbs 31," CBQ 44 [1982]: 202–11). First, the entire poem is arranged alphabetically (a pattern known as an acrostic). This means the first word of each line begins with a letter of the Hebrew alphabet in sequence. Most commentators recognize that such a pattern makes the work uneven and somewhat random in its organization. Nevertheless, the arrangement made memorization easier and perhaps also served to organize the thoughts. We may say, then, that the poem is an organized arrangement of the virtues of the wise wife—the ABC's of wisdom.

Second, the passage has striking similarities with hymns (see Al Wolters, "*Ṣôpiyyâ* [Prov. 31:27] as Hymnic Participle and Play on Sophia," JBL 104 [1985]: 577–87). Usually a hymn is written to God, but here apparently it was written to the wife of noble character. A comparison with Psalm 111, a hymn to God, illustrates some of the similarities. The psalm begins with *halᵉlû yāh* ("Hallelu Yah" [NIV mg.] or "Praise the LORD"); this is reflected in Proverbs 31:31, which says, "Her works bring her praise [*wîhalᵉlûhā*]." Psalm 111:2 speaks of God's works; Proverbs 31:13 speaks of her works. Psalm 111:2 says that the works of the Lord are searched or "pondered" (*dᵉrûšîm*); Proverbs 31:13 says that she "selects" (*dārᵉšāh*) wool and flax. Psalm 111:3 says that the Lord's work is honorable (*hāḏār;* NIV, "majestic"); Proverbs 31:25 ascribes strength and "dignity" (*hāḏār*) to the woman. Psalm 111:4 says that the Lord is gracious and full of compassion; Proverbs 31:26 ascribes the law of compassion to the woman. Psalm 111:5 says that the Lord gives "food" (*ṭerep̱*); Proverbs 31:15 says that the woman provides "food" (*ṭerep̱*) for her house. Psalm 111:10 says that the fear of the Lord is the beginning of wisdom—the motto of Proverbs; Proverbs 31:30 describes the woman as fearing the Lord. Psalm 111:10 says that the Lord's praise will endure; Proverbs 31:31 says that the woman will be praised for her works. It is clear that Proverbs 31 is patterned after the hymn to extol the works of wisdom.

Third, the passage has similarities with heroic literature. The vocabulary and the expressions in general have the ring of an ode to a champion. For example, "woman of valor" (*'ēšeṯ-ḥayil* in v.10; NIV, "woman of noble character") is the same expression one would find in Judges for the "mighty man of valor" (*gibbôr heḥayil*, Judg 6:12; NIV, "mighty warrior")—the warrior aristocrat; "strength" (*'ôz*, in vv.17 [NIV, "vigorously"], 25) is elsewhere used for powerful deeds and heroics (e.g., Exod 15:2, 13; 1 Sam 2:10); "value" (v.11) in "lacks nothing of value" is actually the word for "plunder" (*šālāl*, as used in the name "Maher-Shalal-Hash-Baz" in Isa 8:1, 3; cf. NIV mg. in loc.); "food" (v.15) is actually "prey" (*ṭerep̱*); "she holds" (*šillᵉḥāh*, in v.19) is an expression also used in military settings (cf. Judg 5:26, "reached for," for Jael's smiting Sisera); "surpass them all" (v.29) is an expression that signifies victory.

Putting these observations together, one would conclude that Proverbs 31:10–31 is a hymn to Lady Wisdom, written in the heroic mode. Wisdom is personified as a woman because the word "wisdom" is a feminine noun and naturally suggests it, and because the woman is an excellent example of wisdom by virtue of the variety of applications it receives—at home, in the market, with charity, in business. There are several reasons why the writer would use these literary features to present his description of wisdom: a personification of wisdom allows the writer to make all the lessons concrete and not abstract (we can see them in action in everyday life); it provides a polemic against the literature of the ancient world that saw women as decorative—charm and beauty without substance—and it depicts the greater heroism as moral and domestic rather than only exploits in battle.

The poem certainly presents a pattern for women who want to develop a life of wisdom; but since it is essentially about wisdom, its lessons are for both men and women to develop. The passage teaches that the fear of the Lord will inspire people to be faithful stewards of the time and talents that God has given; that wisdom is productive and beneficial for others, requiring great industry in life's endeavors; that wisdom is best taught and lived in the home—indeed, the success of the home demands wisdom—and that wisdom is balanced living, giving attention to domestic responsibilities as well as business enterprises and charitable service.

The poem can be arranged into eight stanzas; this arrangement generally follows Toy, albeit without some of the rearrangement of verses.

A. *Praise in General*

31:10–12

10 A wife of noble character who can find?
She is worth far more than rubies.
11 Her husband has full confidence in her
and lacks nothing of value.
12 She brings him good, not harm,
all the days of her life.

10 The introductory rhetorical question establishes the point that the wife of noble character is not easily found; but when she is, she is a treasure. Her description as "a wife of noble character" (*'ēšeṯ-ḥayil*) signifies that she possesses all the virtues, honor, and strength to do the things that the poem will set forth. It is interesting to notice that this woman, like wisdom, is worth more than rubies (cf. 3:15; 8:11).

11–12 The noble woman's husband lacks nothing of value. The term *šālāl* ("value," v.11) usually means "plunder"; the point may be that the gain will be as rich and bountiful as the spoils of war. The capable woman inspires the confidence of her husband because in her business and domestic enterprises she proves able (v.12; cf. 1 Sam 24:2). In any marriage, but especially when a large household is involved, such trust in the wife's abilities is essential.

B. *Industrial Pursuits of the Household*

31:13–15

13 She selects wool and flax
and works with eager hands.
14 She is like the merchant ships,
bringing her food from afar.

15 She gets up while it is still dark;
she provides food for her family
and portions for her servant girls.

13–15 Now the cataloging of activities begins. The picture presented is of a large household that requires supervision. All indicators suggest that it is a wealthy and honorable household. This noble woman takes the responsibility to see that food and clothing are provided, making the choices, working with her hands, and ensuring that the food for the day will be there. The simile with the merchant ships suggests that she brings a continual supply of abundance.

C. *Financial Enterprise*

31:16–18

16 She considers a field and buys it;
out of her earnings she plants a vineyard.
17 She sets about her work vigorously;
her arms are strong for her tasks.
18 She sees that her trading is profitable,
and her lamp does not go out at night.

16–18 This part of the account portrays the noble wife as a shrewd business woman, making wise investments from her earnings. There is no foolish purchasing nor indebtedness here. Verse 17 literally says that she "girds her loins with strength"—she is a vigorous and tireless worker, for girding is an expression for preparation for serious work. Consequently she learns by experience that her efforts are profitable. The last line of v.18 may simply mean that she burns the midnight oil in following through a business opportunity (McKane, p. 668), although it might signify that her house was flourishing without calamity (cf. Job 18:6; Jer 25:10).

D. *Provision for the Family and the Poor*

31:19–21

19 In her hand she holds the distaff
and grasps the spindle with her fingers.
20 She opens her arms to the poor
and extends her hands to the needy.
21 When it snows, she has no fear for her household;
for all of them are clothed in scarlet.

19 Verse 19 focuses on the domestic activity of spinning: the "distaff" is the straight rod, and the "spindle" is the round or circular part. She "stretches out" (NIV, "holds") her hand to the work to provide clothing.

20 The noble wife also provides for the poor. The text literally says that she "opens her palm" to the poor; i.e, she gives to the poor with liberality (Ps 112:9). This was the hand that was diligently at work in the previous verse with an acquired skill; it is not the hand of a lazy, wealthy woman. She uses her industry in charitable ways.

21 Moreover, the noble wife is well prepared for the future. When faced with cold, her family has warm clothes to wear. The word "scarlet" could be read also as "two cloaks," suggesting double garments for warmth (see Notes).

Notes

21 For the MT's שָׁנִים (*šānîm*, "scarlet"), the LXX and the Vulgate read שְׁנָיִם (*šᵉnāyim*, "two" or "double") and hence render "a double garment," having *šᵉnāyim* in pause with the word that follows, מַרְבַדִּים (*marḇaddîm*, "cover"). The question asked is whether scarlet would keep one as warm as a "double garment"?

E. *Distinction by Industry*

31:22–24

22 She makes coverings for her bed;
she is clothed in fine linen and purple.
23 Her husband is respected at the city gate,
where he takes his seat among the elders of the land.
24 She makes linen garments and sells them,
and supplies the merchants with sashes.

22 The word rendered "coverings" (*marḇaddîm*) appears also in 7:16, where it is rendered "covered." Delitzsch suggests "pillows" or "mattresses" (2:335). The LXX renders it "lined overcoats," bringing over the word *šānîm* (NIV, "scarlet" but see Notes on v.21), thus harmonizing with the second part of the verse, which clearly has attire in view.

The noble woman's clothing is "fine linen and purple," i.e., costly and luxurious. Garments dyed with purple indicated wealth and high rank (cf. Exod 25–37, passim; S of Songs 3:10). One is reminded of the rich man in Luke 16:19, who also was clothed in purple and fine linen. The problem was not with the clothing he wore but that he was not charitable.

23 The woman's husband was important. The "gate" was the place of the assembly of the elders who had judicial responsibilities (Ruth 4:1–12). The man was a prominent, well-known leader. Toy suggests that "it is assumed by the people that the head of so well-ordered a household must be a worthy man" (p. 546).

24 The woman's industry finds expression in business. The poet did not think it strange or unworthy for a woman to engage in honest trade. In fact, weaving of fine linens was a common trade for women in Palestine from antiquity.

F. *Wisdom and Prosperity*

31:25–27

25 She is clothed with strength and dignity;
she can laugh at the days to come.
26 She speaks with wisdom,

and faithful instruction is on her tongue.
27 She watches over the affairs of her household
and does not eat the bread of idleness.

25 The noble wife is diligent and prudent in her work; her strength and honor come from her solid financial and economic position, as v.25b shows (Toy, p. 547); so the result is that she is confident in facing the future.

26–27 She is wise and gracious in her speech. She uses good, practical common sense in her discussions; and her instruction is reliable. The last phrase of v.26 literally says "law of kindness" (*tôraṯ-ḥeseḏ*): kind and faithful instruction comes from her.

Finally, the wife's supervision of the household is alert, as a watchman (v.27).

G. *Merits Recognized*

31:28–29

28 Her children arise and call her blessed;
her husband also, and he praises her:
29 "Many women do noble things,
but you surpass them all."

28 The wisdom of the noble woman inspires praise from her family—from those who know her the best. Unfortunately, praise often comes from outside the home, from those who do not know the person very well. This woman is of such worth that her children "rise up" (*qāmû*) to praise her, an expression that describes an activity in preparation for such an utterance (see Gen 37:35 [NIV, "came"]).

29 This woman surpasses all other women. These words are probably the praise of the husband who speaks for the rest of the family.

H. *Laudatory Summation*

31:30–31

30 Charm is deceptive, and beauty is fleeting;
but a woman who fears the LORD is to be praised.
31 Give her the reward she has earned,
and let her works bring her praise at the city gate.

30 These words could be the husband's but may better form the poet's summation of the matter. In any case, what is valued in the wife is her domestic efficiency and her piety rather than charm and beauty. Physical appearance is not necessarily dismissed—it simply does not endure as do those qualities that the fear of the Lord produces (see Notes). Beauty is deceitful, and one who pursues beauty may very well be disappointed by the character of the "beautiful" person.

31 Once again there is a reference to the city gate, where all manner of business was conducted. The woman's works bring her praise in her own rights and not merely as an appendage of her husband (Toy, p. 549).

With the emphasis on the "fear of the LORD" (cf. v.30) at the close of the book, Perowne observes, "Thus does Wisdom, true even to herself, return in her last utterance to her first (1:7), and place once again the crown on the head of the godly" (*Proverbs*, p. 193). Plaut concludes by saying:

> Let all know about this kind of woman who, in piety, in devotion and with skill and diligence builds her home. Here is the foundation of society as Judaism sees it; for in Hebrew, house and woman are often used synonymously. . . . Over both man and wife stands God in whose honor these proverbial collections were made and reverently placed into the Biblical canon, so that later generations might listen, learn, and live more richly. (pp. 315–16)

Notes

30 The LXX has *συνετή* (*synetē*, "intelligence") in addition to "fears the LORD."

ECCLESIASTES

J. Stafford Wright

ECCLESIASTES

Introduction

1. Background
2. Unity
3. Authorship
4. Date
5. Place of Origin
6. Destination
7. Occasion
8. Purpose
9. Literary Form
10. Theological Values
11. Canonicity
12. Text
13. Bibliography
14. Outline

1. Background

Ecclesiastes is one of the most puzzling books of the Bible. Its apparently unorthodox statements and extreme pessimism caused its inclusion in the canon of Scripture to be questioned.[1] However, because historically it has been thought to have been the work of Solomon (see Authorship), its place in the canon of Scripture was generally secure (see Canonicity).

The correct interpretation of the Book of Ecclesiastes will harmonize with the rest of the OT even though, as always, we need to consider the fuller revelation of the NT. Rather than treating texts and verses in isolation from the total argument of the book, this commentary shows how the book may be taken as a whole in a way that is worthy of its inclusion in Scripture.

2. Unity

It is always wise to accept the unity of any book unless it is absolutely clear that more than one hand has been at work in its writing. Early in the present century, numerous literary scholars were busily engaged in trying to determine the sources of many books, whether they were the work of one or more writers and redactors. This activity included the works of Homer and Shakespeare as well as books of the Bible.

Two factors led some Bible scholars to surmise that Ecclesiastes had more than one

[1] See R. Beckwith, *The Old Testament Canon in the New Testament Church* (Grand Rapids: Eerdmans, 1985), pp. 297–304.

writer: (1) the literary forms, especially the groups of proverbs, and, more significantly, (2) the apparent blend of unorthodox and orthodox statements. Thus the author(s) seemed to regard man as caught in blind destiny, with his only sensible course being to make the most of life and enjoy himself (ch. 3). Yet periodically what could be an orthodox corrective appears (e.g., 2:26), and the book is rounded off with a wholly orthodox summary.

Among the multiple authorship theories, the simplest postulates three writers (so McNeile and Barton). The original writer (*Qoheleth*, "the Preacher") was a rebel against piety and held a pessimistic view of life in relation to God. His thoughts were toned down—or even contradicted—by an orthodox redactor who emended the text. He belonged to the *Ḥasîḏîm* ("holy ones," "saints"), who were forerunners of the Pharisees. Another writer of the regular Wisdom school, a *ḥāḵām* ("wise man"), incorporated a series of traditional proverbs. This is the simplest division of the book, but others claim to have discovered more writers at work.[2]

On the other hand, many commentators (e.g., Delitzsch) always have maintained the unity of the book—with the possible exception of the closing comments. Recent commentators have paid more attention to psychological understanding than to purely literary features.

Gordis, for example, believes that the alleged differences do not need the explanation of different authors: "Reared in the bosom of Jewish tradition and seeking to express in Hebrew a unique philosophic world-view possessing strong overtones of skepticism, Koheleth falls back upon the only abstract vocabulary he knows, that of traditional religion, which he uses in his own special manner" (p. 74).

Gerhard von Rad writes:

> There is, to be precise, an inner unity which can find expression otherwise than through a linear development of thought or through a logical progression in the thought process, namely through the unity of style and topic and theme, a unity which can make a work of literature into a whole and which can in fact give it the rank of a self-contained work of art. This is all the more so in the domain of ancient Near Eastern literature which, in any case, must be measured by different standards. A specific, unifying function is fulfilled by a small number of leading concepts to which Koheleth returns again and again, concepts such as "vanity", "striving after wind", "toil", "lot" etc. Nor can the modern reader escape the quite dispassionate—in contrast to Job—restrained solemnity and weight of his diction. Thus the book is more than a secondarily edited collection. No other collection of proverbs, not even that of Sirach, presents such clearly defined intellectual characteristics.[3]

Currently, the growing consensus favors viewing the book as having an identifiable literary integrity. Crenshaw observes that "both forms and content give the impression of a sustained argument" and that the content "proclaims a coherent message, a single point, which it declares again and again with complete abandon" (p. 35). For those who support the literary integrity of the book, there are four possible approaches: (1) some view the book as primarily the work of a single author that has been augmented by editorial glosses along the way; (2) others view the author as presenting the claims of traditional wisdom only to refute them from his wealth of experience; (3) still others believe that the apparent differences of perspective in the book can be accounted for by an author who records his changing

[2]E.g., D.C. Siegfried (*Prediger und Ḥoheslied*, 1898) has nine.

[3]*Wisdom in Israel* (Nashville: Abingdon, 1972), p. 227.

viewpoints over the years; and (4), finally, a fourth group suggests that the book represents a dialogue between the author and a philosophical antagonist.

Though it is common for the literary integrity of the book to be defended in scholarly circles, one should not confuse this with single authorship. Whybray concludes that "the wise commentator will assume that the material comes in its entirety from the hands of Qoheleth alone . . . and will attempt to understand it as such before resorting to theories of interpolations" (p. 19). Fox, however, has raised the interesting question of whether Qoheleth is presented as the author of the book at all. He contends that the author is quoting Qoheleth as a form of instruction to his son (12:12) ("Frame Narrative," pp. 83–106):

> The frame-narrator presents himself not as the creator of Qoheleth's teachings, but as their transmitter. He keeps himself well in the background, but he does not disappear. Insofar as the frame-narrator presents himself as having selected certain of Qoheleth's teachings to transmit, he is indeed analogous to an editor . . . [but] the frame-narrator is composing the sayings, not merely gathering them. (Fox, *Qoheleth and His Contradictions,* pp. 311–12)

In this sense perhaps the author's presenting the sayings of Qoheleth is much like the Gospel writers who gathered, composed, and presented the words of Jesus. As Fox observes, however, there are numerous examples of this type of frame-narrative in the wisdom literature of the ancient Near East (ibid., pp. 312–13).

Certainly whether one considers the author to be Qoheleth or not, the cohesiveness of the book is now well established and widely accepted. While the issue of editorial activity remains somewhat open, Fox sensibly observes that "even if we could identify certain glosses, we could not credibly associate them with specific types of thought" (e.g., allocating some verses to a *ḥāsîḏ* and others to a *ḥāḵām*) (ibid., p. 163). [JHW][4]

This commentary assumes a single writer, Qoheleth, except possibly for the closing verses (see introduction to comments on 12:9–12). It recognizes that the author looks at life from several angles, deliberately at times raising the arguments that would occur to his readers. Nevertheless, he is always firm in his conclusions. A central argument emerges throughout the book, and we point this out in section 8, as well as in the commentary itself.

3. Authorship

Traditionally, the authorship of the book has been ascribed to Solomon. This is implied in the opening verse, where the author, Qoheleth, is described as the "son of David, king in Jerusalem." Again at 1:12 he states, "I, the Teacher [Qoheleth], was king over Israel in Jerusalem." Yet commentators of all schools till recently emphasized that the Hebrew belongs to a time considerably later than that of Solomon (see discussion in section 4). Here, however, we first want to see how far the contents of the book tally with Solomon's authorship.

The tradition of David as singer and psalmist is borne out by an early reference at Amos 6:5 and is taken seriously in the light of the lament for Saul and Jonathan (2 Sam

[4]The editors wish to express their appreciation for the helpful contributions made by John H. Walton (associate professor of Old Testament at Moody Bible Institute), the major ones of which are identified by [JHW] (passim). See also his *Ancient Israelite Literature in Its Cultural Context* (Grand Rapids: Zondervan, 1989), esp. pp. 187–89.

1:17–27). We ought to take Solomon's reputation for wisdom equally seriously and see his court as the center that drew wise men from all quarters to discuss problems of living in a difficult world (1 Kings 4:34).

Solomon was on the highroad of trade and culture. He had important contacts with Egypt, including an Egyptian wife, and Egypt had a wealth of wisdom literature. This literature includes poems that reason about the problems of life.[5] Other known writings of a similar type come from Babylon.[6] Presumably, Solomon too listened, collected, and added to the literature by facing the realities of life and showing the way through for the God-fearing person.

So we begin by treating Solomonic authorship seriously. Since many modern commentators, however, completely reject such authorship, their reasons for doing so must be considered. Apart from the linguistic objections, it is suggested that certain passages cannot have come from Solomon's pen: e.g., sorrow for the oppression of the weak (4:1) and for corruption in government (5:8–9), the proper attitude to the king from the subject's point of view (8:2–5; 10:20), and unworthy rulers who do not properly distinguish good subjects from bad (9:1–2). If Solomon felt so strongly about these wrongs, surely he would have put them right.

The style of writing suggests that it was the subject who had suffered rather than the king. This is far from conclusive. A king or president may be aware of mismanagement by local authorities, however much he may want to rectify it. Solomon had a number of local officers (1 Kings 4:7–19); and, as always happens, complaints from his subjects would come to his notice from time to time. Unfortunately, he sagged in his moral actions as he grew older, both in the concessions he made to his pagan wives (1 Kings 11:4–6) and in his treatment of his subjects (cf. 1 Kings 12:14). Some men know what is wrong and make a profession of repentance but never clinch a decision by putting things right. With local rulers of considerable influence, Solomon probably found himself in the position of his father, David, who excused a murder with words: "These sons of Zeruiah are too strong for me" (2 Sam 3:39). On the positive side, according to a fair translation of 5:8–9, the rule of a king is contrasted favorably with the rule of power-hungry governors and their servants.

Some scholars support a late date for Ecclesiastes by a possible reference at 2:8 and 5:8 to the Persian provincial system (see Notes on 5:8). Solomon, however, could use the word translated "province" (cf. 1 Kings 20:14–15, 17) of the areas he had divided his kingdom into (1 Kings 4:7). Doubtless, the twelve officers directly responsible to him arranged with local suppliers, who in turn fixed things with juniors, somewhat like the system of tax gathering in Roman times.

Others see a reference at 7:19 to the committees of Ten who governed the cities of Palestine in Greek times. All the verse says, however, is that "Wisdom makes one wise man more powerful than ten rulers in a city," *ten* being an obvious round number, as we might say "a dozen" (cf. Lev 26:26; Num 14:22; Job 19:3; Isa 5:10; et al.).

There are, in fact, no passages in the book that rule out the possibility of Solomonic authorship. Commentators who look for a later date cannot agree on criteria for dating in any of the rather general references to contemporary situations and events.

---

[5]E.g., A Dispute Over Suicide (also referred to as The Dispute Between a Man and His Soul, ANET, pp. 405–7) and A Song of the Harper (ANET, p. 467).

[6]E.g., The Epic of Gilgamesh (ANET, pp. 72–99) and A Pessimistic Dialogue Between Master and Servant (ANET, pp. 437–38).

Although this commentary holds that Solomon was Qoheleth, the author, it would not be fair to force this view on the reader. Certainly it is not out of the realm of possibility that a later author is presenting the words and teachings of Qoheleth (= Solomon). (For the non-Solomonic authorship view, see E.J. Young, *An Introduction to the Old Testament* [Grand Rapids: Eerdmans, 1960].)

> On the other hand, granting that Solomonic authorship cannot be ruled out, one must fairly ask how strong is the case that Solomon should be equated with Qoheleth? Certainly his identification as the "son of David, king in Jerusalem" (1:1) strengthens the identification. However, it must be realized that any king of Judah could be identified as a "son of David." Though the claim in 1:16 of being wiser than all who ruled Jerusalem before him initially appears practically moot in the mouth of Solomon (who was preceded only by his father, David), the possibility that he is including non-Israelite kings over Jerusalem and the unlikelihood of a successor to Solomon plausibly making such a claim would favor identification of Solomon as Qoheleth. It must still be asked, though, why the name of Solomon was avoided. If Solomon was Qoheleth, why not just say so? If there is some attempt to conceal Solomon's identity, it certainly was not totally successful—nor was it very heartily attempted. Perhaps the title was a well-known one for Solomon and no other identification was necessary. [JHW]

Given all the uncertainty and difference of opinion regarding authorship, this commentary will treat Qoheleth anonymously. Thus, except when there are intentional references to Solomon, as at chapter 2, the Notes use the title that stands at the head of 1:1. Older versions have familiarized readers with the translation "Preacher," but the note on 1:1 explains a preference for "Teacher" in this commentary.

4. Date

Although, as it has already been suggested, the contents of the book do not demand a date later than Solomon, its language has been treated by most modern commentators as conclusive of a later period. All quote the dictum of Delitzsch: "If the Book of Koheleth were of old Solomonic origin, then there is no history of the Hebrew language" (p. 190). While this categorical statement may need some correction in the light of more recent discoveries, it obviously must be taken seriously.

The question is not one of the inclusion of a few Aramaic words, which by themselves are now recognized as unreliable criteria for dating. Aramaic had succeeded Hebrew as the spoken language of Israel by the time of Christ. Although it uses the same script and is closely related to Hebrew in vocabulary and constructions, it is not a derivative of Hebrew. Aramaic is used at Genesis 31:47; Ezra 4:8–6:18; 7:12–26; Jeremiah 10:11; and Daniel 2:4–7:28. It had become a trade language as early as the time of Isaiah (2 Kings 18:26).

It has been held that Ecclesiastes contains so much Aramaic influence that it cannot be dated before the Persian period (SOTI, p. 464). The problem is not so much that the author introduced Aramaic words and constructions but rather that to the expert ear he expressed himself often in a sort of Hebraized Aramaic. Gordis sums the book up as "written in Hebrew, by a writer who, like all his contemporaries, knew Aramaic and probably used it freely in daily life" (p. 61). One might compare him to a preacher who quotes the KJV but modernizes it as he goes along—viz., changing, e.g., "saith" to "says," "him that cometh" to "him who comes," "they did all eat" to "all of them ate," etc.

Some commentators have gone further than this, supposing the book to be a translation from an Aramaic original.[7] If this had been the case, one would have expected that all the Aramaisms would have been smoothed out. Moreover, a writer who wished to pass off his work as Solomonic would certainly have composed his original in Hebrew, not Aramaic.

It also has been argued that the book uses Hebrew words that are transitional between classical and Mishnaic Hebrew (Crenshaw, p. 31). The Mishnah is the collection of Jewish oral laws and traditions that were reduced to writing during the second century B.C. Although this contention is often accepted as a mark of a late date, it has been questioned by S.D. Margoliouth (JE, 5:33).[8]

The relationship to Mishnaic Hebrew has been called into question in a recent monograph by Fredericks, who argues that the language is a preexilic northern dialect. He suggests that features of this dialect were later incorporated in Mishnaic Hebrew, thus the similarity with Qoheleth. [JHW]

In yet another approach, an article by M.J. Dahood called attention to linguistic and other resemblances between Ecclesiastes and Phoenician literary forms and suggested that the book was written by a Jew or Jews living in Phoenicia soon after the Fall of Jerusalem in 587 B.C.[9]

Although this was attacked by Gordis (e.g., in an appendix to his commentary), it has been taken up by G.L. Archer in "The Linguistic Evidence for the Date of Ecclesiastes." He concludes:

1. There is no known Hebrew writing with which Ecclesiastes as a whole can be matched linguistically.

2. Comparative evidence shows that the original Hebrew text of Ecclesiastes was singularly lacking in vowel letters (*matres lectionis*). These were inserted more frequently in later Hebrew to assist pronunciation but are not found in Phoenician inscriptions.

3. Certain inflections, pronouns, and participles are characteristic of Phoenician.

4. Certain words and phrases resemble Phoenician usage—e.g., "under the sun" (used twenty-seven times in Ecclesiastes) is found elsewhere only in two Phoenician inscriptions. The series "seven . . . eight" (11:2) is typical of Phoenician usage.

Archer holds that Solomon himself wrote the book, adopting the standard linguistic presentation expected for a work of this kind. He compares the development of choral poetry among the Greeks; since the Dorian Greeks were the most famous original writers of this kind of poetry, it became a tradition for all subsequent choral poetry to be composed in this dialect. Since at present, however, we have no Phoenician parallels to the wisdom type found in Ecclesiastes, we must treat this part of Archer's theory as a hypothesis that could be clinched by further discoveries.

Archer does not suggest a further possibility—viz., that Solomon used a scribe with a Phoenician background, just as he used the Phoenician, Hiram of Tyre, in constructing the temple (1 Kings 7:13–14). A similar suggestion is often held to

[7] F. Zimmermann, JQR 36 [1945]; H.L. Ginsberg.

[8] Hebraists will find a list of Aramaisms and Mishnaic words in Barton, pp. 52–53.

[9] *Biblica* 33 (1952). The validity, however, of Dahood's conclusions that Qoheleth's use of vowel letters suggests Phoenician connections has been seriously undermined by Anton Schoors, "The Use of Vowel Letters in Qoheleth," *Ugarit Forschungen* 20 (1988): 277–86.

account for variations of style and language in Paul's epistles. The thoughts would then be Solomon's, which he gave to his scribes, but the form of the Hebrew would be colored by the scribe's Phoenician background.

Dahood and Archer have presented a strong case, but they are still very much a minority. We, therefore, must consider how far the standard view of lateness of language necessarily rules out Solomon as the original author. All that the language shows on this view is that the book in its present form was written later than Solomon's day. This need not be the date of its composition, any more than the language of the Mishnah indicates that all its material was first composed in the second century B.C.

As well as priest and prophet, there were wise men (Jer 18:18). Their task and joy would have been to treasure and discuss specialized sayings and discussions of what we call the wisdom type (cf. 12:9–12). Some of their conclusions would be written, others oral. From what we know of the gathering of the rabbis to debate the application of the laws to specific situations, we can similarly imagine gatherings of wise men to study and thrash out the problems of life.

As the living language inevitably changed, the language of a popular treatise like Ecclesiastes would keep step in the discussion groups, until eventually the book was seen more and more to have a place in the inspired canon and its form then fixed in writing.

Folk songs offer a modern analogy. Collectors of old songs in America and Britain are fully aware of changes in diction and expression down the ages, and it would be difficult to date a modern presentation of any folk song on linguistic grounds, which is what some try to do with Ecclesiastes.

If we then follow the tradition of the Bible that Solomon was the hero of the wise, his bequests would represent for the circles of the wise what Moses and the Law were for the rabbis.

Those who believe that one cannot make out a fair case for Solomonic authorship may well follow E.J. Young, a firm believer in the full inspiration of the Bible. Young holds that a later writer put his own thoughts into Solomon's mouth and indicates this by adopting a strange title for himself, without ever saying, "I, Solomon." One might go a step further than Young and hold that Solomon was traditionally known to have said, "Meaningless! Meaningless! . . . Utterly meaningless! Everything is meaningless." These may be the only words that come directly from the "son of David, king in Jerusalem" (1:1–2). The new Teacher takes up where Solomon left off, uses the words as a text, and puts himself in Solomon's place so as to discover how he came to reach his conclusion about life.

It is, therefore, entirely plausible that the words of Solomon (Qoheleth), preserved by wise men over several centuries, were eventually recorded by a new Teacher (the author of the book?) in his own dialect or in the Hebrew of his time period. Whether this scenario or another is true, given our state of knowledge, it is best to conclude with Eaton:

> Our conclusion must be that the language of Ecclesiastes does not at present provide an adequate resource for dating. It is possible that a particular style was adopted for pessimism literature. The possibility that a northern dialect of Hebrew was used must be left open. Equally it is possible that its dialect is Phoenicianizing. Certainly no other document possesses precisely the same characteristics, and no reliable date can be given this way. (p. 19) [JHW]

5. Place of Origin

One naturally assumes Palestine as the place of origin for the Book of Ecclesiastes, and most scholars accept this. Based on references to the weather (1:5–7) and anatomy (11:5; 12:1–7), some have suggested Alexandria as the book's place of origin (e.g., Plumptre, E. Sellin); but the references are too general to be specifically Egyptian. Also, one would expect a resident of Alexandria to show some Greek influence in his style, since the Alexandrian Jews were Greek speaking and were responsible for the translation of the LXX. Arguments for Greek influence, however, are not strong. (For Dahood's theory that the book was written in Phoenicia, see section 4 above.)

Certainly the author gives the impression of writing from Jerusalem (1:1, 16). In default of any other compulsive evidence, we may accept Jerusalem as the place of origin for the Book of Ecclesiastes.

6. Destination

Ecclesiastes was clearly written as a discussion guide for people prepared to think out their response to God's unseen hand in life and history. Although it contains practical advice, it would appeal to a different public than Proverbs. One may rather link it to Job. The Wisdom writings have a twofold scope. First, they set out the rules of life for an individual who wishes to be a member of a prosperous society and who looks for the right way to build up a God-fearing conscience. These rules form the Book of Proverbs.

Society, however, is not ideal; mankind has a fundamental twist, and there will always be cases where a person finds things happening to him that he cannot reconcile with the promises of Proverbs. He may suffer when he expects the temporal blessings of God, and others who deserve punishment may prosper. This second scope of Wisdom writings is taken up by Job and Ecclesiastes, each in its own way. Job shows the nature of testing and something of Satan's challenge, but Ecclesiastes explores these things more widely (see section 8).

7. Occasion

If the Book of Ecclesiastes was written by Solomon, the occasion of its writing was in his last years. In 2:1–11 he describes a lifetime of accumulating wealth, and in chapters 11–12 he writes as one beginning to experience the onset of old age. He writes for young men who might learn from his experiences (11:9; 12:1; cf. Prov 1:8 et al.).

8. Purpose

The theme of the book appears in the prologue: "Meaningless! Meaningless! . . . Everything is meaningless." The general conclusion comes in the epilogue, which speaks of fearing God and keeping his commandments because we must one day give account to him. The meaning and purpose of the book must be discovered within this framework. Life in the world is subject to frustration; but man can still accept his circumstances, even enjoy them, and find strength to live life as it comes.

Where does one start to build a way of life that transcends the meaninglessness of the world? Can purpose for life be found in nature, money, self-indulgence, property, position, intelligence, philosophy, and religious observances? Obviously, some of these pursuits are better than others, but all encounter some crowning frustration that invalidates them as solutions to the problem of living. The world does not contain the key to itself. It can be found only in God. Roughly speaking, this is the theme of chapters 1–6.

If God exists and is concerned for man's response to him, why has he made life so frustrating? The answer is that God originally made man perfect, but man fell and thus brought frustration into the human race (7:29).

How much does this frustration prevent us from recognizing God's plan in every circumstance? God does not show anyone what only he can know (3:11; 7:14). Indeed, the attempt to discover this brought about the Fall (Gen 3:5). But God has implanted in man the sense of an eternal existence (3:11), and in this man rises above the rest of the animal world. Since there is a total plan, there must be some way that man can fit into it; but how can he do so if he does not know what the plan is?

The book tells man to begin where he is, with the assumption that God has his purpose for today. To fulfill this purpose man must use his God-given sense as well as his own experience of himself and that of others. God has a proper time for each thing to be done (3:1–8), and recognizing this allows man to accept life as it comes (3:11a), even though he knows he has fitted no more than one piece in the great puzzle.

Thus we are directed from speculation (e.g., 8:16–17) to observation. It is right to meditate on the total work of God, but we are to glorify God in the common things of life; i.e., we are to make the fullest use of the present moment. There may be times of stress and strain and special calling; but the norm is to eat, drink, and live our daily life as those who gladly rejoice in God's good gifts and intend to use them to his glory. This is the theme of the refrains (2:24–26; 3:12–13, 22; 5:18–19; 8:15; 9:7–9).

In all this there is nothing unworthy. In fact, it tallies with the NT teaching that we are to eat and drink and do all our actions to the glory of God (1 Cor 10:31; Col 3:17), since he has generously given us everything for our enjoyment (1 Tim 6:17).

Several comments must be made, however:

1. The book offers insight to thoughtful readers who want to know how to develop a God-centered worldview. Its advice is compatible with the Sermon on the Mount, in which Christ said that we are to accept food, drink, and clothing as the gifts of God and are to seek God's kingdom and righteousness (Matt 6:25–33). In the same sermon he referred to those who would be called to undergo suffering precisely because they sought to fulfill God's righteous commands (Matt 5:10–12). Ecclesiastes also faces the fact of the suffering of the righteous but sees it in relation to the frustration in the world rather than as part of the witness to God's righteousness (e.g., 5:8). It teaches that we need not do something out of the ordinary in order to do God's will. Similarly, Paul advised the zealous convert to remain in the sphere in which God called him (1 Cor 7:17) though later he may be called to some special service.

2. Interestingly, the book makes no suggestion of living a life of self-sacrifice, so as to spur the reader on to a life of philanthropy or self-deprivation. Qoheleth would most likely identify self-sacrifice as meaningless if it is motivated by any degree of self-satisfaction. We need to remember that the author is not trying to describe the life of faith or what our faith responsibilities are. Rather, he is contrasting a self-centered

life style with a God-centered one. It is needless for the person of faith to be glum about life's anomalies or adversities. The Teacher's approach is through philosophy, not through an assumed source of revelation (much like C.S. Lewis's *Mere Christianity*). He does not discuss moral obligation to the law of God, though that is no reason to think that he was ignorant of the law [JHW]. Ecclesiastes expresses this faith as "I see" (2:24) and "I know" (3:14; 8:12). One may compare this with Paul's words in Romans 8 where, after speaking about how the whole creation is subject to frustration (v.20), he declares, "We know that in all things God works for the good of those who love him, who have been called according to his purpose" (v.28).

3. The book is not against serious thinking; it is itself a deep and thoughtful work. But it demands a recognition of the limitations of human philosophy (e.g., 3:11; 8:16–17).

4. The refrains do not mean "Do what you will." Man is accountable to God, not simply to himself; he has a duty to work and moral responsibilities to society. The book contains warnings against self-indulgence that exploits others for personal advantage (e.g., 8:8–9).

Christians may ask how the stress on using and enjoying life tallies with the NT command "Do not love the world" (1 John 2:15). The answer is that the Teacher (Ecclesiastes) would have agreed fully with John's next statement that "everything in the world—the cravings of sinful man, the lust of his eyes and the boasting of what he has and does—comes not from the Father but from the world. The world and its desires pass away" (vv.16–17). One could hardly find a better statement than this of the whole theme of Ecclesiastes (e.g., 2:1–11; 5:10). Life in the world has significance only when man remembers his Creator (12:1).

There always have been two kinds of teaching about the way to holiness. One is by withdrawal as far as possible from the natural in order to promote the spiritual. The other is to use and transform the natural into the expression of the spiritual. While each kind of teaching has its place, some people need one emphasis rather than the other. Ecclesiastes definitely teaches the second.

9. Literary Form

While the Book of Ecclesiastes is unanimously included in the larger literary category of wisdom literature, the specific literary genre of the book is somewhat uncertain. It has been likened to the so-called pessimism literature known from the ancient Near East (see footnotes 5 and 6). But these are not works of the same genre; they merely include observations about the meaninglessness of life and some advice concerning the enjoyment of life that show some similarity to the content of Ecclesiastes. So, for instance, a section from the Egyptian "A Song of the Harper" commends enjoyment of life:

> Hence rejoice in your heart!
> Forgetfulness profits you,
> Follow your heart as long as you live!
> Put myrrh on your head,
> Dress in fine linen,
> Anoint yourself with oils fit for a god.
> Heap up your joys,
> Let not your heart sink:

grounds, mostly resting on superficial contradictions; e.g., joy is commended at 8:15 but spoken of critically at 2:2 and 7:3.[10]

The book apparently was in the canon at the time of Christ, since the Jewish Council of Jamnia in A.D. 90 did not meet to put books into the canon but to discuss whether a few disputed books, already regarded as canonical, should remain in it. Undoubtedly, the association of Ecclesiastes with Solomon aided its retention, whereas Ecclesiasticus (cf. "The Apocrypha and Pseudepigrapha," EBC, 1:161–75) was not under consideration, because it was written by Ben Sira after God's direct inspiration was believed to have ceased.

Jamnia, however, did not close the debate. When Jerome made his Latin translation of the Bible in the fourth century, he noted that many Jews were still not happy about some theology in the book.

If we look for confirmation of Ecclesiastes by quotation in the NT, there is little doubt that Paul referred to it in Romans 8:20, where he spoke about the complete futility of the world system. Other parallels with the NT, though not quotations, are noted in the commentary.

12. Text

The Hebrew text of the Book of Ecclesiastes is in good condition. There are only a few places where one needs to give serious attention to the possibility of error by a copyist. The LXX is a rather formal Greek translation of the Hebrew and was possibly made in the first half of the second century B.C. There is also a Syriac translation, likewise quite formal. Its date, while uncertain, is later than the LXX.

The recent finds of fragments of the Hebrew text at Qumran show only very slight variants, chiefly in spelling. Therefore, we may accept the conclusion of Gordis that "fundamentally we read Koheleth today in the form in which it left its author's hands" (p. 128).

13. Bibliography

Commentaries

Barton, G.A. *A Critical and Exegetical Commentary on the Book of Ecclesiastes.* International Critical Commentary. Edinburgh: T. & T. Clark, 1908.
Bridges, C. *An Exposition of the Book of Ecclesiastes.* London: Banner of Truth Trust, 1960.
Crenshaw, James L. *Ecclesiastes.* Philadelphia: Westminster, 1987.
Delitzsch, Franz. *Commentary on the Song of Songs and Ecclesiastes.* KD. Grand Rapids: Eerdmans, n.d.
Eaton, Michael A. *Ecclesiastes.* London: Tyndale, n.d.
Fox, Michael V. *Qoheleth and His Contradictions.* Sheffield: Almond, 1989.
Fredericks, Daniel C. *Qoheleth's Language.* Lewiston, N.Y.: Mellen, 1988.
Ginsberg, Michael A. *Studies in Koheleth.* New York: Jewish Theological Society of America, 1950.
Ginsburg, Christian D. *Qoheleth, Commonly Called the Book of Ecclesiastes.* London: Longman, Green, Longman, and Roberts, 1861.

[10] Beckwith, *Old Testament Canon,* pp. 297–304.

Gordis, R. *Koheleth: The Man and His World.* New York: Bloch, 1955.
Hendry, G.S. "Ecclesiastes." *New Bible Commentary Revised.* Edited by D. Guthrie et al. Grand Rapids: Eerdmans, 1973.
Hengstenberg, E.W. *Commentary on Ecclesiastes.* Grand Rapids: Kregel, n.d.
Jones, E. *Ecclesiastes.* Torch Commentary. London: SCM, 1961.
Kidner, Derek. *A Time to Mourn and a Time to Dance.* London: Inter-Varsity, 1976.
Leupold, H.C. *Ecclesiastes.* Grand Rapids: Baker, 1966.
Loader, J.A. *Ecclesiastes.* Grand Rapids: Eerdmans, 1986.
Loretz, O. *Qohelet und der Alte Orient.* Freiburg: Herder, 1964.
MacDonald, James H. *The Book of Ecclesiastes.* Minneapolis: Klock and Klock, n.d.
McNeile, A.H. *An Introduction to Ecclesiastes.* Cambridge: Cambridge University Press, 1904.
Plumptre, E.H. *Commentary on Ecclesiastes.* CBSC. Cambridge: University Press, 1881.
Rankin, O.S. "Ecclesiastes." *Interpreter's Bible.* Edited by G.A. Buttrick. New York and Nashville: Abingdon, 1962.
Ryder, E.T. "Ecclesiastes." *Peake's Commentary on the Bible.* Edited by M. Black and H.H. Rowley. London: Thomas Nelson and Sons, 1962.
Rylaarsdam, J.C. *Ecclesiastes.* Layman's Bible Commentaries. London: SCM, 1964.
Scott, R.B.Y. *Ecclesiastes.* Anchor Bible. AB. Garden City, N.Y.: Doubleday, 1965.
Whybray, R.N. *Ecclesiastes.* Grand Rapids: Eerdmans, 1989.
Wright, J. Stafford. "The Interpretation of Ecclesiastes." *Classical Evangelical Essays in Old Testament Interpretation.* Edited by W.C. Kaiser, Jr. Grand Rapids: Baker, 1972.

Wisdom Literature

Henshaw, T. *The Writings.* London: George Allen & Unwin, 1963.
McKane, William. *Prophets and Wise Men.* Naperville, Ill.: Allenson, 1965.
Monro, M.T. *Enjoying the Wisdom Books.* London: Longmans, Green and Co., 1964.
Noth, M., and Thomas, D.W., edd. *Wisdom in Israel and in the Ancient Near East.* Leiden: E.J. Brill, 1955.
Rankin, O.S. *Israel's Wisdom Literature.* Edinburgh: T. & T. Clark, 1936.
Ranston, Harry. *The Old Testament Wisdom Books and Their Teaching.* London: Epworth, 1930.
Rylaarsdam, J. Coert. *Revelation in Jewish Wisdom Literature.* Chicago: University Press, 1957.
Wood, James. *Wisdom Literature.* London: Gerald Duckworth & Co., 1967.

Periodicals

Archer, Gleason L., Jr. "The Linguistic Evidence for the Date of Ecclesiastes," *Journal of Evangelical Theological Society* 12 (1969).
______. "Ecclesiastes," *Zondervan Pictorial Encyclopedia of the Bible.* Edited by M.C. Tenney. Grand Rapids: Zondervan, 1975, 2:184–90.
Fox, Michael V. "Frame Narrative and Composition in the Book of Qoheleth," *Hebrew Union College Annual* 48 (1977): 83–106.
Shank, H.C. "Qoheleth's World and Life View as Seen in His Recurring Phrases," *Westminster Theological Journal* 37 (1974/75): 57–73.

14. Outline

The following outline recognizes the twofold question that lies behind Ecclesiastes: (1) Is the world system so subject to frustration that it cannot offer any satisfying key to life? and (2) If a believer tries to rise above the world system and wishes to mold his life according to the will of God, how can he do so if he cannot grasp the whole plan?

I. The Meaninglessness of Nature, Wisdom, and Wealth (1:1–2:23)
   1. The Theme: All Is Frustration (1:1–3)
   2. The Frustration in Nature and History (1:4–11)
   3. The Frustration of Wisdom (1:12–18)
   4. The Frustration of Unlimited Wealth (2:1–11)
   5. The Ultimate Frustration: Death (2:12–23)

II. The Divine Order of Life (2:24–3:22)
   1. Daily Life to Be Enjoyed (2:24–26)
   2. God's Plan for Living (3:1–8)
   3. The Pieces and the Whole (3:9–15)
   4. The Consequences of Mortality (3:16–22)

III. The Frustration of Politics (4:1–16)

IV. The Frustration of Life (5:1–7:29)
   1. Quiet Before God (5:1–7)
   2. Money and Mortality (5:8–20)
   3. The Unfulfilled Life (6:1–9)
   4. What Is Good? (6:10–12)
   5. Practical Advice for Daily Living (7:1–14)
   6. Moderation Commended (7:15–22)
   7. Bad Relationships (7:23–29)

V. Life in View of Death (8:1–9:18)
   1. The Inevitability of Death (8:1–14)
   2. Life to Be Enjoyed (8:15–9:10)
   3. Uncertainty and Inequity (9:11–18)

VI. Proverbs (10:1–20)
   1. Wise Relationships (10:1–7)
   2. Wise Planning (10:8–11)
   3. Wise Speech and Thought (10:12–20)

VII. Wisdom for the Future and the Present (11:1–10)
   1. The Uncertain Future and Present Behavior (11:1–6)
   2. The Certain Future and Present Behavior (11:7–10)

VIII. The Frustration of Old Age (12:1–8)

IX. Epilogue (12:9–14)
   1. The Credibility of the Author (12:9–12)
   2. The Conclusion of the Matter (12:13–14)

Text and Exposition

I. The Meaninglessness of Nature, Wisdom, and Wealth (1:1–2:23)

1. *The Theme: All Is Frustration*

1:1–3

1 The words of the Teacher, son of David, king in Jerusalem:

2 "Meaningless! Meaningless!"
says the Teacher.
"Utterly meaningless!
Everything is meaningless."

3 What does man gain from all his labor
at which he toils under the sun?

1–3 The Teacher, writing as a wise and observant king of David's line, set out his theme. He lived in a world riddled through with vanity, futility, and frustration. He anticipated what Paul said in Romans 8:20, that the whole created order has been subjected to this futility. Human beings, struggling to live, meet frustration at every turn (v.3). One looks back to the record of sin's entry into man's life (7:29; Gen 3). Man chose to become self-centered and self-guided rather than remaining God-centered and God-guided. Thus man became earthbound and frustrated, and this book demonstrates that there is no firm foundation under the sun for earthbound man to build on so as to find meaning, satisfaction, and the key to existence. "Under the sun" is used twenty-nine times in this book and nowhere else (cf. "under heaven," 1:13; 2:3; 3:1), which shows that the writer's interest was universal and not limited to only his own people and land.

Notes

1 קֹהֶלֶת (*qōhele<u>t</u>*) is the feminine participial form, which is generally taken to denote the function of one who addresses a קָהָל (*qāhāl*, "assembly"). Another possibility is that it is not people who are being collected but proverbs (Crenshaw, p. 33), though the noun use suggests more the sense of convening than compiling. The LXX has ἐκκλησιαστής (*ekklēsiastēs*, i.e., a member of an assembly). In this commentary, and following the NIV, we use "Teacher," which is less pietistic than "Preacher."

2 הֲבֵל הֲבָלִים (*hᵃ<u>b</u>ēl hᵃ<u>b</u>ālîm*, "breath" or "vapor") commonly has the figurative use of that which is evanescent and unstable, hence in this book "meaningless," "frustration," or "futility." The whole phrase here means "utter meaninglessness," "utter frustration," "utter futility." The LXX has ματαιότης (*mataiotēs*) as in Rom 8:20, and the thought of futility may be read into most occurrences of the word in Ecclesiastes.

On the other hand, a few of the passages that use the term present problems for the translation "futility." In 11:8 it is difficult to maintain that one's existence after death is futile, and in 8:14 the work of God in the destiny of the righteous and the wicked could not easily be considered futility. Fox has built a plausible case for the translation "absurdity" (*Qoheleth and His Contradictions*, pp. 29–48). The essence of the absurd is a contrasting difference between two things that are supposed to be joined by a link of harmony or causality but are actually disjunct or even conflicting. The absurd is irrational, an affront to reason, in the broad sense of the human faculty that seeks and discovers order in the world about us. The quality of absurdity does not inhere in a being, act, or event in and of itself (though these may, by extension, be called absurd) but rather in the tension between a certain reality and a framework of expectations (ibid., p. 31). [JHW]

---

2. *The Frustration in Nature and History*

1:4–11

4 Generations come and generations go,
but the earth remains forever.
5 The sun rises and the sun sets,
and hurries back to where it rises.
6 The wind blows to the south
and turns to the north;
round and round it goes,
ever returning on its course.
7 All streams flow into the sea,
yet the sea is never full.
To the place the streams come from,
there they return again.
8 All things are wearisome,
more than one can say.
The eye never has enough of seeing,
nor the ear its fill of hearing.
9 What has been will be again,
what has been done will be done again;
there is nothing new under the sun.
10 Is there anything of which one can say,
"Look! This is something new"?
It was here already, long ago;
it was here before our time.
11 There is no remembrance of men of old,
and even those who are yet to come
will not be remembered
by those who follow.

4–11 The Teacher plunged straight into the search for ultimate truth and stability in nature and in human history. Here is the observation of the scientist, working with the phenomena of the world. He must reduce everything to a mutually dependent round of cause and effect. The Teacher cited examples of research into repetitive phenomena, choosing first four basic facts of the created order: (1) the solid earth, (2) the rising and setting of the heavenly bodies, (3) air currents, and (4) the flow and evaporation of water (vv.4–7). South and north (v.6) are selected as a balance to the east and west of the sun (v.5). Solomon was interested in nature generally (cf. 1 Kings 4:33).

The scientist defines physical laws that have always operated; but if we ask him about origins or some ultimate end or purpose, there is nothing he can tell us from nature that will give the meaning of life. The biblical view of nature, however, is that it testifies to a Creator, though it does not compel belief in him (e.g., Ps 19; Rom 1:20). But the Teacher is concerned with proof rather than testimony and rightly maintains that meaning and security cannot be found in nature alone. If everything is endlessly cyclical, how can man break out of the temporal circle into a state that leads somewhere? We may also ask, What is the true meaning to be found in nature—if there is a meaning, is it found in the beauty of spring or in the violence of the storm and the earthquake?

There is a similar impasse in the study of history. If the solid earth gives no stability, what help is there in an endless succession of birth and death (v.4)? History shows men and women struggling to find meaning in their experiences, but all in vain (v.8). Every generation looks for some satisfying novelty, but each novelty can be analyzed as only a variant on the past (v.9). Obviously, there have been many inventions; but in the context the Teacher probably has in mind any invention that enables man to break out of nature and the succession of history into *meaning,* which transcends the sense of futility. Man has not found it; and each generation, regarding itself as the greatest, still reaches no conclusion.

3. *The Frustration of Wisdom*

1:12–18

12 I, the Teacher, was king over Israel in Jerusalem. 13 I devoted myself to study and to explore by wisdom all that is done under heaven. What a heavy burden God has laid on men! 14 I have seen all the things that are done under the sun; all of them are meaningless, a chasing after the wind.

> 15 What is twisted cannot be straightened;
> what is lacking cannot be counted.

16 I thought to myself, "Look, I have grown and increased in wisdom more than anyone who has ruled over Jerusalem before me; I have experienced much of wisdom and knowledge." 17 Then I applied myself to the understanding of wisdom, and also of madness and folly, but I learned that this, too, is a chasing after the wind.

> 18 For with much wisdom comes much sorrow;
> the more knowledge, the more grief.

12–13 The Teacher has confronted us with a situation that today might be called "existential." Man exists in a series of experiences and cannot discover any onward meaning in them. All he can do is exist and make the best of what comes—or drop out altogether. Yet most people still believe that life has some meaning if only they could find it. In his first mention of God (v.13), the Teacher stated what comes out again later (e.g., 3:11)—viz., that God has given something to man that he has denied to the rest of the animal world: the constant, though often worrying, urge to make sense of life and to work toward a transcendent ideal. An animal lives within the circle of its instincts and drives. Man, in the likeness of God, looks for meanings so that he can control and direct his instinctive desires. Someone has said that it is better to be Socrates discontented (because he cannot solve his problems) than a contented pig. It may sound easy to abandon the search for ultimates and to drop to an animal level, but even the dropout often knows the restlessness and the pricks of conscience that belong to him as man. We are fallen beings who need the life and illumination that come from God.

14–15 Even Christians, with a fuller revelation than Solomon had, still cannot see the whole plan, though faith enables them to see that in everything God works for good to those who love him (Rom 8:28). There is so much people cannot understand. Not only are people aiming at unsubstantial ideals, which blow away like the wind (v.14), but their efforts to straighten things out and supply what seems to be lacking are continually disappointed (v.15). Today we have straightened out many of the twists of the past and added many comforts to life; but as many of us have seen in our lifetime, in one moment a whole generation or some dominant group of rulers can revive the horrors of the past and destroy what is truly good and meaningful in life.

16–18 The Teacher was remorseless in his effort to make us think, but even the wisdom of Solomon (v.16) could not break through on the basis of human reason. We observe that those who have struggled to wrest the secret of the universe and those who have abandoned any attempt to understand it both find frustration (v.17). Those who take life seriously can never take it lightly (v.18). At the end of this section (vv.12–18), the Teacher is frustrated because his thinking is earthbound under heaven (v.13), for he depends wholly on his own great wisdom and increased knowledge.

Notes

---

12 The perfect tense הָיִיתִי (*hāyîṯî*) can be translated either as "I was [and am no longer]" or "I have been [and still am]." The second meaning would be applicable at the end of Solomon's life when he cited the fruit of his experiences. The former meaning would show that a later author deliberately or inadvertently indicated that he himself was not Solomon.

16 This is often said to be a slip by the author, who forgot that David had been the only king in Jerusalem before Solomon. David was only the start of Israelite kings in Jerusalem. It was a very ancient city whose kings are mentioned in the Bible and elsewhere (cf. Melchizedek in Gen 14:18; Adoni-Zedek in Josh 10:3; and Abdu-Hepa in the Amarna Letter, ANET, pp. 487–88). Solomon was speaking here of all kingships over Jerusalem and was not saying that he was greater than previous kings *over Israel* in Jerusalem (cf. v.12).

---

4. *The Frustration of Unlimited Wealth*

2:1–11

1 I thought in my heart, "Come now, I will test you with pleasure to find
out what is good." But that also proved to be meaningless. 2 "Laughter,"
I said, "is foolish. And what does pleasure accomplish?" 3 I tried
cheering myself with wine, and embracing folly—my mind still guiding
me with wisdom. I wanted to see what was worthwhile for men to do
under heaven during the few days of their lives.
4 I undertook great projects: I built houses for myself and planted
vineyards. 5 I made gardens and parks and planted all kinds of fruit trees
in them. 6 I made reservoirs to water groves of flourishing trees. 7 I
bought male and female slaves and had other slaves who were born in
my house. I also owned more herds and flocks than anyone in
Jerusalem before me. 8 I amassed silver and gold for myself, and the
treasure of kings and provinces. I acquired men and women singers,
and a harem as well—the delights of the heart of man. 9 I became
greater by far than anyone in Jerusalem before me. In all this my wisdom
stayed with me.

> 10 I denied myself nothing my eyes desired;
> I refused my heart no pleasure.

> My heart took delight in all my work,
> and this was the reward for all my labor.
> 11 Yet when I surveyed all that my hands had done
> and what I had toiled to achieve,
> everything was meaningless, a chasing after the wind;
> nothing was gained under the sun.

To most people unlimited money suggests unlimited satisfaction and a life filled with happiness and meaning. We may criticize the extravagant luxuries of others, being sure that we would be more spartan and generous if we had as much money. Thank God for those men and women of wealth who accept their responsibilities for using money wisely. But there are only too many who envy the wealthy and wish they had money to spend on the vain pleasures of the "good life."

1–2 We notice that this description of Solomon omits mention of immorality but is concerned with the joys of luxury. No serious thinker supposes that a Casanova is on the way to discover the purpose of living (cf. 7:26). The Teacher set his sights on those pleasures that many people considered worthwhile in themselves. He surrounded himself with happy people who kept him amused, but even the jokes and laughter grew stale (cf. 7:1–6).

3 The Teacher turned to sensual pleasures, such as the enjoyment of drink, which so easily becomes the folly of overindulgence. Yet he still kept a hold of himself so that he could analyze his experiences and see whether they proved to be the answer to all human desires. In other words, is the true philosophy of life "Let us eat and drink, for tomorrow we die" (Isa 22:13)?

4–8 A sensible use of money may be a form of creativity; so Solomon expressed himself in extensive buildings and the planting of vineyards, fruit trees, and gardens (vv.4–6). In this he resembled the monarchs of Egypt, Assyria, Babylon, and Persia, whose achievements in building and planting were the wonder of the world. Naturally Solomon did no more than supervise the work. He had only to give the word, and slaves did his bidding (cf. 1 Kings 9:17–22). The service of others is something that money can buy. (For references to Solomon's public works, see 1 Kings 7:1–9; 9:15–19; S of Songs 8:11. Three pools near Bethlehem are said to have been constructed by him. They dam the Urtas Valley, and each of the first two can overflow into the pool below it. It is claimed that altogether these pools hold over forty million gallons.)

Solomon also determined to be the largest owner of cattle and sheep in the land (v.7b). He did not lose sight of the need for an ever-increasing income; and his position of holding the trading bridge between Egypt and Asia made him one of the wealthiest monarchs of the day (1 Kings 10:21–29). As a connoisseur of music, he collected at court the finest soloists and choirs (v.8). The final item in the list may well refer to Solomon's wives and concubines, but the Hebrew word does not occur elsewhere in the Bible (see Notes).

9–11 How are the experiences of this rich man to be summed up? More than any other man, he was able to buy every single thing he imagined could satisfy him. He kept his sense of discernment intact (vv.3, 9). A critic might say that this prevented him from making a fair sampling of pleasure because constant analysis of one's feelings hinders complete enjoyment. But if Solomon had allowed himself to be swept off his feet by sensual pleasures, he would doubtless have sunk to the despair of a slave of immorality. He wanted to determine to what extent one could find the key to life in a varied use of great wealth.

In the end money and the pleasures it can buy do not lift us out of the realm of earthbound frustration. The Teacher will later amplify this conclusion in terms of death and the handling of one's possessions (see 5:8–17). Meanwhile, he faces us with the question of whether money can bring us to the fulfillment we were made for. Despite riches we may still be empty shells and our gains only as substantial as the wind (v.11).

Notes

---

8 The Aramaic term מְדִינָה (*m*e*d̲înāh*, "provinces") is frequently used of governmental areas from the Exile onward but also of organized districts in Israel in Ahab's time (1 Kings 20:14–15). See further note on 5:8.

Various translations have been suggested for שִׁדָּה וְשִׁדּוֹת (*šiddāh w*e*šiddôt̲*) since the term occurs nowhere else in the Bible. Some suggestions follow:

1. "Harem" (cf. "Concubines," RSV) is the NIV's rendering. The word is perhaps connected with שַׁד (*šad̲*, "breast"). A Canaanite word of similar form is used to translate the Egyptian word for "concubine" in a letter of Amenophis III (ANET, p. 487a). We note that concubinage was considered a legal relationship and not fornication or adultery by the people. Although it was looked on as a normal convention in OT times, it is nowhere ordered by the Lord.

2. "Musical instruments" (KJV) is a traditional Jewish interpretation (so Kimchi in his lexicon), but its derivation is uncertain.

3. Connected with the Aramaic root שְׁדָא (*š*e*d̲ā'*, "to pour"), the LXX has "male and female cupbearers."

4. The Talmud (*Gittin* 78a) says that in Palestine the word meant "chests" or "sedan chairs"; hence JB's "every human luxury, chest on chest of it."

---

5. *The Ultimate Frustration: Death*

2:12–23

12 Then I turned my thoughts to consider wisdom,
  and also madness and folly.
What more can the king's successor do
  than what has already been done?
13 I saw that wisdom is better than folly,
  just as light is better than darkness.
14 The wise man has eyes in his head,
  while the fool walks in the darkness;
but I came to realize
  that the same fate overtakes them both.

15 Then I thought in my heart,

"The fate of the fool will overtake me also.
  What then do I gain by being wise?"
I said in my heart,
  "This too is meaningless."

> 16 For the wise man, like the fool, will not be long
> remembered;
> in days to come both will be forgotten.
> Like the fool, the wise man too must die!

17 So I hated life, because the work that is done under the sun was
grievous to me. All of it is meaningless, a chasing after the wind. 18 I
hated all the things I had toiled for under the sun, because I must leave
them to the one who comes after me. 19 And who knows whether he will
be a wise man or a fool? Yet he will have control over all the work into
which I have poured my effort and skill under the sun. This too is
meaningless. 20 So my heart began to despair over all my toilsome labor
under the sun. 21 For a man may do his work with wisdom, knowledge
and skill, and then he must leave all he owns to someone who has not
worked for it. This too is meaningless and a great misfortune. 22 What
does a man get for all the toil and anxious striving with which he labors
under the sun? 23 All his days his work is pain and grief; even at night
his mind does not rest. This too is meaningless.

12–16 A critic may object that the pursuit of luxury is the aim of a fool, but what of wisdom as a proper guide to life? Nobody who follows in Solomon's steps will ever have greater opportunities than he had for combining wisdom and wealth (v.12). Some see a specific reference to Solomon's son, Rehoboam, whose behavior divided the kingdom (1 Kings 12). I prefer a more general application, though Rehoboam may be in mind at vv.18–19. Delitzsch, however, is not justified in using v.18 against Solomonic authorship on the ground that Solomon "would not thus express himself indefinitely and unsympathetically regarding his son and successor on the throne" (p. 248). A father may be dubious about his son's abilities; moreover, Solomon no doubt had other sons who might have seized the throne.

Granted that wisdom is more worthwhile than folly and gives light in the darkness of life (vv.13–14); yet both wise and foolish have to face the ultimate fate of dying, and death is the ultimate frustration (v.15). The Teacher did not go back on his conclusion that wisdom is better than folly but asked how much better it is in the light of the fact that both wise man and fool will be forgotten in future ages? Their names may or may not be remembered in the school books, but they are thought of as little more than characters of fiction, cut off from the new generations who have their own lives to live (vv.15–16). This is the way of the world, and it is profoundly depressing as the next section shows. For the Christian the depression is overridden by the new revelation in Jesus Christ, not by wisdom's arguments (e.g., Rev 14:13).

17–23 The Teacher found no security and purpose in the rewards of his labor. A man may not be so rich as Solomon but may live wisely and accumulate wealth in a perfectly legitimate way. He may wear himself out in the process (v.17). Then comes death and the sharing of the estate. What sort of person will the heir be? He too may be wise; but he may also be a fool, especially if he has imbibed his father's materialistic values without having had to struggle for a living (vv.18–19; see comment on v.12).

Suppose the heir is wise. Surely the Teacher cannot complain of frustration then! He pointed out that men who have worked hard to build up their financial security often feel it unfair that everything should go to someone who has not earned it as they themselves have done (vv.20–21). It is frustration of pride in one's own achievements.

It is almost a warning of the life that is overburdened by the anxieties of laying up treasure on earth (vv.22–23).

II. The Divine Order of Life (2:24–3:22)

1. *Daily Life to Be Enjoyed*

2:24–26

> [24]A man can do nothing better than to eat and drink and find satisfaction in his work. This too, I see, is from the hand of God, [25]for without him, who can eat or find enjoyment? [26]To the man who pleases him, God gives wisdom, knowledge and happiness, but to the sinner he gives the task of gathering and storing up wealth to hand it over to the one who pleases God. This too is meaningless, a chasing after the wind.

24–26 This is the first of similar refrains that, if taken out of their context, might seem to advocate a life of mere pleasure seeking. (They have been discussed as a group in the Introduction, under Purpose.) This first one urges us to find the joy of serving God in the ordinary round of daily life. Thus it rounds off this section of the book. You can wear yourself out by trying to find the solution of life in nature and history (ch. 1). You can make the pursuit of luxury or money your chief aim (ch. 2). But you will end up in frustration because you are grounding yourself in this material world, which does not hold the key to satisfaction. Why not simply take your daily life from the hand of God (v.24)?

The Teacher was clearly speaking to normal people in normal circumstances. He was not at this point discussing physical and social evils that needed to be put right. Up to now he had considered life from the angle of the person who tried to have his own knowledge of good and evil (cf. Gen 2:16–17) without being accountable to God for his standards of thought or behavior. The alternative is the life of faith, which does not understand everything (see ch. 3) but looks for the hand of God in the events of daily life. A useful parallel is 1 Timothy 6:6–19, with its reminder that we are to be content with food and clothing, realizing that God gives us richly everything to enjoy.

The walk with God means that we can ask for his wisdom to use life rightly and his knowledge to understand such of his ways as he may disclose to us, and thus experience the joy of fulfillment despite life's difficulties (v.26; cf. Matt 25:21; Rom 12:2; Heb 12:2; James 1:5; 3:13–18). Yet are God's rewards and punishments as clear as v.26 suggests? The Wisdom writings speak of life in a stable society where individuals and authorities should be carrying out the will of God. Normally such a society prospers. It is God's will that the sinner who is here something more than the fool and who, because he is a sinner, does not mind what means he uses for "gathering and storing up" should hand over his ill-gotten gains.

The Wisdom writings also recognize that in the world as it is righteous individuals may suffer as Job did for a time and that individual sinners may prosper, as Job also pointed out. The Teacher will take this up later (7:15–18; 8:10–14). Meanwhile, he stated God's general plan, which, if not fulfilled through society on earth, must be rectified by God in the future judgment (3:16–22; 12:14; cf. Matt 25:28–30). The final sentence at v.26 obviously refers to the frustration for the sinner.

Notes

24 The terms "good" and "better" always take their significance from their context. Here the reference is not to moral goodness but to functional behavior; i.e., this is the best way for man to pass along the road of life.

25 The reading חוּץ מִמֶּנִּי (*ḥûṣ mimmennî*, lit., "without me") is meaningless here. Modern scholars usually follow the LXX and other versions, emending the final letter to ו (*w*), thus giving "without him," i.e., God.

---

2. *God's Plan for Living*

3:1–8

1 There is a time for everything,
and a season for every activity under heaven:

2 a time to be born and a time to die,
a time to plant and a time to uproot,
3 a time to kill and a time to heal,
a time to tear down and a time to build,
4 a time to weep and a time to laugh,
a time to mourn and a time to dance,
5 a time to scatter stones and a time to gather them,
a time to embrace and a time to refrain,
6 a time to search and a time to give up,
a time to keep and a time to throw away,
7 a time to tear and a time to mend,
a time to be silent and a time to speak,
8 a time to love and a time to hate,
a time for war and a time for peace.

1 Verses 1–8 have an important connection with the theme of the book and relate closely to what precedes and to what follows. Man is to take his life day by day from the hand of God (2:24–26; 3:12–13), realizing that God has a fitting time for each thing to be done (v.1). The significance of this section is that man is responsible to discern the right times for the right actions; and when he does the right action according to God's time, the result is "beautiful" (v.11). A parallel is Ephesians 2:10, where it is said that God created us in Christ Jesus for good works, which he has "prepared in advance for us to do." The Teacher did not say that everything was imposed on man against his will, even though some events go beyond his understanding.

2 Birth and death, the boundaries of life under the sun, are mentioned first. The issues they raise are important for us today. The so-called population explosion has led some to consider whether it is God's will to limit the number of children in a family. If so, how is God's plan to be achieved? When have the Scriptures on being fruitful and multiplying (Gen 1:28; 9:1; cf. 1 Tim 5:14) been abrogated? Children have always been looked upon as a blessing from God (cf. Ps 127:3–5), whereas barrenness has been considered a judgment from him (Gen 30:22–23; 1 Sam 1:6–7; 2:1–11; Isa 4:1; Luke 1:25). On the other hand, increased medical knowledge enables life to be extended far beyond the limits of threescore years and ten. So we look for God's plan, not for euthanasia, to determine when and whether to resuscitate lives that are ready to slip away.

Planting and uprooting have both a natural and a metaphorical sense. The natural sense is taken up at 11:6, the metaphorical in Jeremiah's call to break up the fallow ground and uproot the thorns (Jer 4:3) and also in Christ's parable of the wheat and the tares (Matt 13:24–30).

3 Killing and healing involve the question of a so-called just war and capital punishment (see Notes). A commentary of this type cannot present a full discussion of these problems. It must ask, however, what is God's plan for our time and for the specific situations that confront us? When should aggression be met by resistance and when should there be some healing compromise? When does an offender need a life sentence, and when does he need psychiatric treatment?

Tearing down and building up, while involving plans for building development, also have a metaphorical meaning. The Christian life has its negative and positive sides (1 Cor 3:10–15; Gal 2:18).

4–5 There are appropriate occasions for tears and laughter (v.4; Rom 12:15). Biblical society had a healthier attitude toward the use of weeping and mourning as a meaningful and healing part of life (cf. Ps 6:6–7; John 11:35). A Christian should not be perpetually facetious, but neither should he avoid occasions of social happiness. There is a time to clear the ground of loose stones before collecting other stones for building (v.5; see Notes). There are also times for expressing or refraining from love, a relevant reminder for many people today that there are standards of sex.

6–8 Acquisition and sacrifice form part of life (v.6), as do tearing up and repairing, silence and speech (v.7). Love and hate are both needed, provided we love and hate the proper things (v.8; Rom 12:9; 1 John 4:20). When must we protest against evil? When must we war against those who promote evil? With whom are we to be in happy agreement?

Notes

3 Significantly, the Hebrew word used here for "to kill," הָרַג (*hārag*), is not the word reserved for murder in the sixth commandment, where premeditation seems to be in view (cf. Exod 20:13; Deut 5:17).

5 The interpretation of v.5a in the commentary is that of the Targum and is straightforward. Even if it is rather similar to v.3b, there are other similarities here (e.g., vv.3a, 8). Other suggestions include the following:

1. Scattering stones on an enemy's land to make it hard for him to work it (2 Kings 3:19, 25).

2. A magical practice to symbolize the casting out of evil, but there is no parallel in this book to such superstition.

3. A symbolic reference to the sex act in the light of the second part of the verse (so the Midrash Eccles. R and Gordis). This seems too obscure to be correct.

3. *The Pieces and the Whole*

3:9–15

[9]What does the worker gain from his toil? [10]I have seen the burden
God has laid on men. [11]He has made everything beautiful in its time. He
has also set eternity in the hearts of men; yet they cannot fathom what
God has done from beginning to end. [12]I know that there is nothing
better for men than to be happy and do good while they live. [13]That
everyone may eat and drink, and find satisfaction in all his toil—this is
the gift of God. [14]I know that everything God does will endure forever;
nothing can be added to it and nothing taken from it. God does it so that
men will revere him.

> [15]Whatever is has already been,
> and what will be has been before;
> and God will call the past to account.

9–11 Admittedly, God has his proper time for every event, but we naturally want to grasp the whole plan he has for our lives. What is the point of it all (v.9)? We have to accept two facts that belong to man as he is.

First, we have to take steps to discover and fulfill the duties to be done each day (v.10). Doing the right thing at the right time yields a beautiful sense of fulfillment (v.11a).

Second, one thing that elevates us above the animal world, in addition to the God-given sense of eternity, is the desire to understand the whole. This accounts for all science, philosophy, and human knowledge, as well as theology. However much we see things as units of knowledge and experience, we must try to bring these units into a meaningful whole. This is an aspect of our creation in the likeness of God, who alone embraces the whole. Before the Fall God communicated to our original progenitors all they needed for living. The Fall occurred when they chose to have their own knowledge of good and evil and to be in charge of their own lives. By cutting themselves off from God, they were left to go along day by day without clear direction, no longer living in the light of God's whole plan.

In this fallen world the believer must ask, "Lord, what would you have me do now? I know my life has an eternal purpose, and I desire to understand how all things work together for good. But I realize that I am not as you and cannot say just why such-and-such a thing has come to me" (cf. v.11).

12–14 The Teacher is not a total pessimist about life. There is much to be enjoyed, especially as one goes through life doing good. It requires an act of faith to declare that there is a permanency about all God-inspired good deeds (vv.12–13). Therefore, one must walk in humble fear lest he miss the will of God in his life (v.14). The fuller Christian revelation enriches these principles. Treasure may be laid up in heaven (Matt 6:20), works of gold and silver will survive the fire test (1 Cor 3:10–15), and a Christian's works in the Lord follow him (Rev 14:13). But the unbelieving humanist, however earnest, cannot plan his life in the light of eternity.

15 If we look for further guidance as to the will of God, we may find it in his working in history. We naturally give prominence to the biblical records; once we accept the fact of God, we can see that history is more than a record of one generation after another (1:4). History does repeat itself. We may discard the lessons of history, but

God confronts us with them again and again (v.15b; cf. 1:10). We have no basis for complaining that he has not warned us that he will call the past to account.

Notes

11 The Hebrew הָעֹלָם (*hā'ōlām*, "eternity") represents "everness" and occurs also at 1:4 and 12:5. The use of the definite article here implies that it is the whole in contrast to units (viz., eons). Hence the NEB translates it "a sense of time and future."

15 The NIV's "God will call the past to account" is a rendering that fits the context. Some make the object personal; viz., "God cares for the persecuted" (JB). The LXX has ζητήσει τὸν διωκόμενον (*zētēsei ton diōkomenon*, "[God] will seek the one who has been driven out"). This would be abrupt, even if it forms the introduction to v.16.

Since Ecclesiastes is often compared with *The Rubaiyat of Omar Khayyam*, it is worth noting the contrast between the two. The Teacher's acceptance of God's beautiful plan differs from Omar Khayyam's nonaccepting attitude:

> Ah Love! Could thou and I with Him conspire
> To grasp this sorry Scheme of Things entire,
> Would not we shatter it to bits—and then
> Re-mould it nearer to the Heart's Desire!
> (4.99)

4. *The Consequences of Mortality*

3:16–22

16 And I saw something else under the sun:

> In the place of judgment—wickedness was there,
> in the place of justice—wickedness was there.

17 I thought in my heart,

> "God will bring to judgment
> both the righteous and the wicked,
> for there will be a time for every activity,
> a time for every deed."

18 I also thought, "As for men, God tests them so that they may see
that they are like the animals. 19 Man's fate is like that of the animals; the
same fate awaits them both: As one dies, so dies the other. All have the
same breath; man has no advantage over the animal. Everything is
meaningless. 20 All go to the same place; all come from dust, and to dust
all return. 21 Who knows if the spirit of man rises upward and if the spirit
of the animal goes down into the earth?"

22 So I saw that there is nothing better for a man than to enjoy his
work, because that is his lot. For who can bring him to see what will
happen after him?

16–17 One of the greatest problems in understanding the total plan of God is that reward and punishment sometimes seem conspicuously absent. People have a tendency to grab for themselves, and some are able to do this because they are in positions of power (v.16). Hence believers, admittedly by an act of faith, hold that God will redress the wrong assessments made on earth (v.17; Mal 3:16–4:3; Rev 22:11–12).

18–22 Meanwhile, the Teacher centered his thoughts on the inevitability of death. In their context these verses say that God makes all sensible people realize that they are as much subject to death as is the animal world. Both are animated by a similar breath of life that sustains them while living and is withdrawn at death (vv.19–21). The same word for "spirit" or "breath" (*rū^{a}ḥ*) is used in v.19 and v.21. People and animals also resemble each other in having bodies made of vegetable and mineral substances that revert to dust at death (v.20). The Teacher is speaking phenomenologically, i.e., as things appear to the senses. There is no reference here to any personal spirit or soul, but the spirit or breath is the sustaining life that comes from God (Gen 6:17; Ps 104:29–30).

How does v.21 fit the theme of the book? An author must be interpreted by himself, and we find a clue in two other passages concerning mortality. In 9:4–10 the theme is the need for us to work with all our power in this life, since we will have no further opportunity for this sort of work after we have left our bodies. In 11:9–12:8 there is the call for us to serve God from our earliest days, since old age brings increasing handicaps as it tends toward death. Both these ideas are latent here. Most of us behave as though we had endless time and close our eyes to the fact of death. God wants us to face that fact (v.18). Even in our Christian service of God, there may be the underlying idea that there is still plenty of time tomorrow, and what we fail to do here can be made up in our service in paradise. So the Teacher challenges those who live as though they are immortal and are never to be accountable to God (vv.16–17).

The conclusion is a further summary of the refrain that God has his day-by-day plan for our lives and that we can find the joy of fulfillment in it. We shall not be brought back again for a second chance to cooperate with God in doing his will on this side of eternity (v.22). The context suggests that we cannot be brought back from the state of death at some future time (cf. 9:4–6). An alternative interpretation is that we must make the most of the present in order to please God. We cannot count on the future, since we do not know what it is.

Notes

---

17 Literally, this verse reads, "For there is a time for every matter and for every work there." Some (e.g., RSV) read the final word שָׁם (*šām*, "there will be") as שָׂם (*śām*, "he appointed").

III. The Frustration of Politics

4:1–16

[1] Again I looked and saw all the oppression that was taking place under the sun:

I saw the tears of the oppressed—
  and they have no comforter;
power was on the side of their oppressors—

and they have no comforter.
2 And I declared that the dead,
who had already died,
are happier than the living,
who are still alive.
3 But better than both
is he who has not yet been,
who has not seen the evil
that is done under the sun.

4 And I saw that all labor and all achievement spring from man's envy of his neighbor. This too is meaningless, a chasing after the wind.

5 The fool folds his hands
and ruins himself.
6 Better one handful with tranquillity
than two handfuls with toil
and chasing after the wind.

7 Again I saw something meaningless under the sun:

8 There was a man all alone;
he had neither son nor brother.
There was no end to his toil,
yet his eyes were not content with his wealth.
"For whom am I toiling," he asked,
"and why am I depriving myself of enjoyment?"
This too is meaningless—
a miserable business!

9 Two are better than one,
because they have a good return for their work:
10 If one falls down,
his friend can help him up.
But pity the man who falls
and has no one to help him up!
11 Also, if two lie down together, they will keep warm.
But how can one keep warm alone?
12 Though one may be overpowered,
two can defend themselves.
A cord of three strands is not quickly broken.

13 Better a poor but wise youth than an old but foolish king who no
longer knows how to take warning.
14 The youth may have come from
prison to the kingship, or he may have been born in poverty within his
kingdom.
15 I saw that all who lived and walked under the sun followed
the youth, the king's successor.
16 There was no end to all the people
who were before them. But those who came later were not pleased with
the successor. This too is meaningless, a chasing after the wind.

Although this chapter may seem to be composed of several isolated themes—oppression, envy, individualism—these are linked by the overarching theme of the power complex common among humans and ways of reacting to it.

1–3 The Teacher returned to the theme of injustice (3:16–17). He had seen that God must inevitably redress the wrong judgments of unjust rulers (3:17) and that high and low must face the fact that they are but mortals (3:18–22). The Teacher met the valid objection that some people find it very hard to take their lives each day from the hand of God and enjoy them (3:22). Granted that average persons in settled circumstances may not find much difficulty in aiming at this, but observation shows that the simple ways of life may be wrecked by leaders who misuse their power (v.1).

There are times when we thank God for delivering some poor tortured sufferer through death (v.2). Anyone who feels deeply, like the Teacher, may wish on occasion that he had never been born into all the sufferings of the world (v.3). Observe how Jesus Christ comments on the misusers of power in Matthew 18:1–9; it is they, not their victims, who will wish that they had never been born.

4 How then can the bad state of the world be either remedied or resisted? This verse gives a profound diagnosis when it says that all achievement comes through a drive toward superiority. This was the basic idea of the psychologist Adler, who propounded the concept of the inferiority complex. The desire for achievement is good in itself, since God never intended man to be static or simply passive. The challenge to be the best and to be breaking fresh ground always involves some rivalry of ideas and has led to notable scientific progress; but rivalry between individuals and nations may divert healthy competition into bitter envy. In industry, moreover, where the average worker has little scope for creativity, there is envy for another man's money or status. So a healthy drive becomes yet another frustration and a chasing after the wind.

5–6 Two proverbs follow. To ignore the drive for achievement and become a dropout is foolish self-destructiveness. But the drive must be harnessed to what is compatible with inner peace.

7–8 Again, the drive may turn inward into miserliness—the overaccumulation of money or other possessions. Collecting possessions can become an obsession, which kills sane thinking and prevents a person from following the advice of 3:22. Here is another form of the power complex—wherein one's success gives him a feeling of triumphant superiority.

9–12 The drive to succeed is mature when it has its interplay with the whole of society. Society begins with one's neighbor. Two acting together are better than one selfish individual; they can support each other when there is need for support. This proverb applies to all relationships and is certainly relevant for members of the body of Christ. Individualism and divisions make for weakness. There is a proper complex of power in a three-strand rope, provided the strands are good and support one another.

13–16 Finally, the power complex is seen in the struggle between tradition and revolution. A political leader or business executive may fight to keep his position when he is no longer capable of making wise decisions; yet he will not take advice. The young revolutionary who has been imprisoned or kept down may indeed be wiser. But if he comes to power, he too may succumb to the desire to lord it over everyone else; and those under him will be glad to be rid of him (see Notes).

So, after reviewing man's twisted craving for power, the Teacher concludes that power all too often brings only frustration. It does not hold the key to life. First Corinthians illustrates the wise sayings in this chapter. The first-century Corinthian church knew too well how powerful leaders and powerful gifts could divide rather than strengthen the body of Christ.

Notes

4 The KJV has another possible translation: "that for this a man is envied of his neighbor." This would fit the theme equally well. Many would like power without having to work for it.

11 The Eastern custom was not to undress at night. The outer robe (Exod 22:26–27) and a coverlet (Isa 28:20) normally were sufficient for warmth, but if people slept on mats on the floor, others close by would add to the warmth (cf. Luke 17:34).

13–16 The Teacher may have some definite case in mind, and commentators have made guesses according to the period when they think the book was written. It is not clear whether only the king and the youth are spoken of. In v.15 the Hebrew reads, "the youth, the second"; this probably means that the king is the first in line and that his successor is the second. Or there may be yet another revolutionary who in turn will put down the young man who succeeded the original king; so NEB: "I saw his place taken by yet another young man." Solomon himself, threatened by at least one revolutionary (1 Kings 11:26–39), may have feared that he would be known as the foolish old king.

IV. The Frustration of Life (5:1–7:29)

1. *Quiet Before God*

5:1–7

[1]Guard your steps when you go to the house of God. Go near to listen rather than to offer the sacrifice of fools, who do not know that they do wrong.

[2]Do not be quick with your mouth,
do not be hasty in your heart
to utter anything before God.
God is in heaven
and you are on earth,
so let your words be few.
[3]As a dream comes when there are many cares,
so the speech of a fool when there are many words.

[4]When you make a vow to God, do not delay in fulfilling it. He has no pleasure in fools; fulfill your vow. [5]It is better not to vow than to make a vow and not fulfill it. [6]Do not let your mouth lead you into sin. And do not protest to the ⌊temple⌋ messenger, "My vow was a mistake." Why should God be angry at what you say and destroy the work of your hands? [7]Much dreaming and many words are meaningless. Therefore stand in awe of God.

Ecclesiastes presents a number of interludes as the Teacher reviews various attempts to find the satisfying and unifying key to life and its purpose. He has already said that the only satisfaction comes from accepting God's plan for one's life, even though the whole blueprint is not spread out to view. Life should be marked by acceptance, not by making demands on God. Indeed, the God-fearer must continually draw near to God if he is to be sensitive to his will.

1–2 In contrast to the power complexes of the previous chapter, we are brought quietly into the presence of God. Jesus may have had these verses in mind when he told the story of the two who went to the temple to pray (Luke 18:9–14). Here is a keen analysis of motives in prayer and worship. We come before God in humility, recognizing his majesty and his right to our lives. We seek his guidance and listen to his words.

The alternative is to suppose that offerings can be a substitute for a God-ordered life (v.1b). There may be an attempt to bribe God (e.g., Isa 1:11–20). Sometimes extreme concern over one issue is an unconscious screen against facing other issues. It is as though we call God's attention to the sacrifice we are making while being blind to some essential command that he makes. Thus we often find it easier to make sacrificial efforts to demonstrate against some evil in far distant lands than to face evil here at home and in our own lives. This is the point of v.1.

Yet we are meant to speak to God in prayer. The emphasis in v.2 is on rashness and haste. Prayer is not reciting a list as quickly as possible so as to rush once more into the round of daily life. Christ's words about many empty words in prayer (Matt 6:7–8) may be read as a commentary on this verse.

3 As personal and business cares produce dreams, which are unsubstantial things; so many words produce foolish and empty prayer. The proverb may speak of the false thinking that comes through preoccupation with one's own affairs. When we come before God, our minds are full of our own business rather than with the worship of God. When we talk too much, we usually talk like fools. This can be especially bad in the house of God.

4–6 There is, however, a place for making resolutions (vows) before God. The challenge that comes through a sermon or a book and, above all, from Scripture itself should be clinched by definite commitment. The same follow-up is vital if in time of trouble we make a promise to do something if only God will deliver us. If we do not carry it through, it would be better to have made no commitment at all. Our promise may involve giving to some special work of God or pledging prayer and other support for a missionary. When the representative of the work looks for the fulfillment of our promise, we must not draw back and make an excuse about not having understood what we were required to do. This can only arouse God's displeasure, and he may well take away what we were thinking of keeping for ourselves.

7 The section concludes with the reminder that our approach to God must be a realistic response to what he has shown us to be his will—not a wordy presentation of what we dream of for ourselves. In other words, we should try to put ourselves in a position to discover God's way to use what he has given us in our daily life.

Notes

---

1 In the Hebrew this verse is 4:17. Hence the Hebrew is numbered one verse behind the English all through the chapter.

6 מַלְאָךְ (*mal'āk*) means primarily "messenger" and in the OT is used some one hundred times each of a human messenger and of a divine messenger, translated "angel." This is one of the few places where it is impossible to say for certain which meaning is intended. The human messenger would be the person who comes to claim the fulfillment of the vow, probably the

priest. An angel here would be either one invisibly present as a witness or the recording angel at the Judgment Day.

---

2. *Money and Mortality*

5:8–20

8 If you see the poor oppressed in a district, and justice and rights
denied, do not be surprised at such things; for one official is eyed by a
higher one, and over them both are others higher still. 9 The increase
from the land is taken by all; the king himself profits from the fields.

10 Whoever loves money never has money enough;
whoever loves wealth is never satisfied with his
income.
This too is meaningless.

11 As goods increase,
so do those who consume them.
And what benefit are they to the owner
except to feast his eyes on them?

12 The sleep of a laborer is sweet,
whether he eats little or much,
but the abundance of a rich man
permits him no sleep.

13 I have seen a grievous evil under the sun:

wealth hoarded to the harm of its owner,
14 or wealth lost through some misfortune,
so that when he has a son
there is nothing left for him.
15 Naked a man comes from his mother's womb,
and as he comes, so he departs.
He takes nothing from his labor
that he can carry in his hand.

16 This too is a grievous evil:

As a man comes, so he departs,
and what does he gain,
since he toils for the wind?
17 All his days he eats in darkness,
with great frustration, affliction and anger.

18 Then I realized that it is good and proper for a man to eat and drink,
and to find satisfaction in his toilsome labor under the sun during the
few days of life God has given him—for this is his lot. 19 Moreover, when
God gives any man wealth and possessions, and enables him to enjoy
them, to accept his lot and be happy in his work—this is a gift of God.
20 He seldom reflects on the days of his life, because God keeps him
occupied with gladness of heart.

8–9 With the thoughts of power still ringing in his ears, the Teacher again spoke of the use and abuse of money in daily life. These transitional verses point to various authorities. Too often the struggle for power brings suffering for the underdog. Each shows servility toward the man above and waits to take his place while lording it over those below him. The Teacher does not say that this always happens. On the whole he sees an advantage in a supreme ruler truly concerned for the welfare of the land. One hopes for a wise person at the head of the country or a business or an institution—one who has both ability and humility.

10 Struggle for power comes from the desire for more and more money. It is not wrong to have a proper concern for a living wage, but the prestige of perquisites and greed for luxuries make this verse as relevant as ever. These insatiable desires also bring frustration. Not money itself, but a love of money is a root of all kinds of evil (1 Tim 6:10).

11–12 The man who has an abundance of material possessions may become a miser (4:7–8) or may never know real friendship because of the numbers of acquaintances who want to share his wealth. On the other hand, assuming that he has a living wage, the honest worker can sleep peacefully at night. But the anxieties of the man of money drive him to sleeping pills and tranquilizers.

12–17 A note of even deeper sadness is that a man may accumulate money, even to the extent of warping his character. Then a miscalculation or an unfortunate turn of events destroys everything. What he had hoped to leave to his son is gone. Perhaps the son has been counting on inheriting his father's money and has done nothing for himself (cf. 2:18–21). So the father has wasted the driving desire of his life. He had measured success by wrong standards; and when his long struggle for money came to nothing, he died a poor, frustrated man (cf. Matt 6:19–21).

18–19 So the refrain comes again. The highwayman traditionally demanded, "Your money or your life!" The Teacher has described those who aim for money and lose real life. Can we then have life first and secondarily find a place for money? The refrain says yes, if we take life day by day from God and seek to know his plan, so far as it may be known. We must be willing to work (v.18). Once most work was constructive and often creative. Today many of us are involved in monotonous activity, which a modern Solomon would cite as another example of frustration. We must also look for constructive uses of leisure—activity that may not bring much money but will bring the added enjoyment that the Teacher has in mind. Therefore, it is right to pray and to look for work that will produce enough to live on and possessions we can enjoy with a good conscience, because they are things God has given us to enjoy (1 Tim 6:17).

20 In summary, the ideal for the man of God is that he not brood over the past or worry about the future; for God fills his heart with joy (cf. Matt 6:25–34; Phil 4:4–7).

Again we remember that the Teacher in this section has in mind the average person with a living wage. Elsewhere, as we have seen, he takes up the frustration of the suffering and despised.

Notes

---

8 The word מְדִינָה (*m*^{e}*d̲înāh*, "district") is not necessarily a mark of a late date. Solomon divided his kingdom into areas (1 Kings 4:5, 7–27) for purposes of supply for the royal

household. Doubtless the twelve officials directly responsible to him worked with local suppliers, who in turn fixed things with juniors, an arrangement somewhat like the tax-gathering system in Roman times. See also the note on 2:8.

9 The commentary gives one interpretation of this difficult sentence. Williams prefers "The profit of the land is among the whole of them: the field when cultivated has a king"; i.e., all the officials have a share in the profits, and the moment someone cultivates a piece of land, representatives of the king descend on it. עָבַד (*ʿāḇaḏ*) is used in the Niphal, as here, of cultivated land in Deut 21:4 and Ezek 36:9. Its regular meaning is "serve" or "work," hence the KJV's "The king himself is served by the field." The NIV captures this thought with "the king himself profits from the fields."

20 The general sense of the final clause is clear, but the exact force of מַעֲנֶה (*maʿaneh;* NIV, "occupied") is uncertain. Literally it means "answers." God's response comes in inner joy.

---

3. *The Unfulfilled Life*

6:1–9

1 I have seen another evil under the sun, and it weighs heavily on men:
2 God gives a man wealth, possessions and honor, so that he lacks
nothing his heart desires, but God does not enable him to enjoy them,
and a stranger enjoys them instead. This is meaningless, a grievous evil.
3 A man may have a hundred children and live many years; yet no
matter how long he lives, if he cannot enjoy his prosperity and does not
receive proper burial, I say that a stillborn child is better off than he. 4 It
comes without meaning, it departs in darkness, and in darkness its
name is shrouded. 5 Though it never saw the sun or knew anything, it
has more rest than does that man— 6 even if he lives a thousand years
twice over but fails to enjoy his prosperity. Do not all go to the same
place?

7 All man's efforts are for his mouth,
   yet his appetite is never satisfied.
8 What advantage has a wise man
   over a fool?
 What does a poor man gain
   by knowing how to conduct himself before others?
9 Better what the eye sees
   than the roving of the appetite.
 This too is meaningless,
   a chasing after the wind.

1–2 There is an obvious contrast between the wording of 5:19 and 6:2. The former speaks of enjoyment of what God has given, the latter of the breakdown of this enjoyment. This is a realistic facing of the sort of thing that happens. Yet we need to see the difference of emphasis in the two verses. Without straining the interpretation, it seems that 5:19 describes the person who accepts a standard of living for which he has worked, without continually craving for more (cf. 5:10; 6:9). The man in 6:2 is more concerned with having everything he wants, and his God-given status in life allows this. But inasmuch as his heart is centered on his accumulated wealth, his tragedy comes when God allows this wealth to be taken over by a stranger. This may happen when the man has no children or when he loses his property through war, violence, or some other act of injustice. Many have been broken by such calamities. Others, particularly refugees, have refused to succumb to what the Teacher sees as vanity but have rebuilt a new life, often with less regard for the intrinsic value of possessions (Heb 10:34).

3–6 Many children and long life were looked upon by the Hebrews as a mark of God's blessing, but neither guarantees a satisfying life (v.3). It is tempting to read this in the light of modern times. Some parents think they have to decide how many children they ought to have, in view of the population explosion (see comment on 3:2). The exaggeration here may suggest that the large number of children keeps the whole family in poverty so that life cannot be enjoyed properly and so that at the end there is not enough to pay for the funeral. Or possibly, since children are considered in the Scriptures a blessing from the Lord, this verse may mean that a man may have double blessings—children and wealth—and yet not have the capacity to enjoy them and at the end die either in poverty or unloved or both. A life of total misery, which might have been avoided, is worse than natural abortion, by which a life never sees the light of day and never has to struggle in the arena of life (vv.4–5; cf. Job 3:16). The death of the fetus reminds the Teacher of the death that awaits every man, even though he lives to more than twice the age of the patriarchs (v.6).

7–9 This section speaks of another possible frustration. Man has to work to live but has an insatiable appetite for more. This is common to both wise and foolish. Today the business world contains many clever men who work hard because they are obsessed with piling up money, while on the other side there are those who are ever alert for a quick profit—honest or dishonest. In between come the average men and women who, though poor in material things, have come to terms with life (v.8b). They also work for their living but are content with what they have ("what the eye sees"), without the wandering desire that tries to grasp the elusive wind (v.9).

4. *What Is Good?*

6:10–12

10 Whatever exists has already been named,
and what man is has been known;
no man can contend
with one who is stronger than he.
11 The more the words,
the less the meaning,
and how does that profit anyone?

12 For who knows what is good for a man in life, during the few and meaningless days he passes through like a shadow? Who can tell him what will happen under the sun after he is gone?

10–12 The Teacher was prepared to listen to objections. He said that man should do the will of God by being content to take his daily life from God's hand. But is man really free to choose? Since God is supreme, he has surely predestined everything and has made man too weak to resist (v.10). Reasoning, complaining, and arguing bring no answer and lead to further frustration (v.11). What value are categories such as "good"? Life is too short to worry about behavior. Even if moral standards have some bearing on the future, no one knows what the future will bring (v.12).

Today we too are challenged about the grounds of moral behavior. Do they depend on some remote God who has issued a code of binding commands? How can one demonstrate what is right and what is wrong? Life is so short and the future so uncertain that surely we can be content with a permissive morality.

Many people today, Christian and non-Christian, know that this kind of argument, propagated by a vociferous minority, is not the true answer. They are puzzled, however, about how they should behave as members of a sick and suffering humanity. So the Teacher goes on to make a fresh approach in the next chapter.

5. *Practical Advice For Daily Living*

7:1–14

1 A good name is better than fine perfume,
and the day of death better than the day of birth.
2 It is better to go to a house of mourning
than to go to a house of feasting,
for death is the destiny of every man;
the living should take this to heart.
3 Sorrow is better than laughter,
because a sad face is good for the heart.
4 The heart of the wise is in the house of mourning,
but the heart of fools is in the house of pleasure.
5 It is better to heed a wise man's rebuke
than to listen to the song of fools.
6 Like the crackling of thorns under the pot,
so is the laughter of fools.
This too is meaningless.

7 Extortion turns a wise man into a fool,
and a bribe corrupts the heart.

8 The end of a matter is better than its beginning,
and patience is better than pride.
9 Do not be quickly provoked in your spirit,
for anger resides in the lap of fools.

10 Do not say, "Why were the old days better than these?"
For it is not wise to ask such questions.

11 Wisdom, like an inheritance, is a good thing
and benefits those who see the sun.
12 Wisdom is a shelter
as money is a shelter,
but the advantage of knowledge is this:
that wisdom preserves the life of its possessor.

13 Consider what God has done:

Who can straighten
what he has made crooked?
14 When times are good, be happy;
but when times are bad, consider:
God has made the one
as well as the other.
Therefore, a man cannot discover
anything about his future.

Ultimately the Teacher will return to the theme that obedience is possible even though we cannot discover the whole plan of God for us. The Latin saying *Solvitur ambulando* ("It is solved by walking") suggests that some problems are elucidated only as one goes forward in practical action (cf. Isa 30:21; as we go, the Lord guides).

So we now have some practical proverbs for daily living, showing that God's will for man is not a set of meaningless rules but a walk that brings a sense of fulfillment. The advice is clearly an answer to the petulant objection of 6:12. Here are some of the things known to be good for man both for the present and for the future.

1–6 The first group of proverbs speaks of a serious view of life. They are intended to give some answer to 6:10–12 and do not mean that there is no place for laughter and social entertainment.

First of all, the Teacher says that a good and well-deserved reputation is better than a mask of perfumed cosmetics. Preserve your good name until the day of your death and you achieve the potentiality of your birth inheritance (v.1; cf. v.8a).

If we are looking for signposts for living, we are more likely to gain insight when face to face with eternal things than in noisy company where the deeper realities of life are drowned in food, drink, and levity. Remembering that life on earth does not go on forever, we are moved to look below its surface (v.2). The two following verses continue the theme. A sorrow shared may bring more inner happiness than an evening with back-slapping jokers (vv.3–4).

Moreover, if we are in earnest about God's good plan (cf. 6:10–12), we must be ready for serious conversation with men and women who are experienced in life and be open to criticism from them. They may not answer all our problems, but their advice will be worth far more than popular songs devoid of serious moral content and the shallow humor of comedians (vv.5–6).

7 The next proverbs are not so closely linked, though each relates to the question of how to live an acceptable life. If you hold an influential position, do not use it for personal advantage. In particular, a bribe erodes character, making it susceptible to other forms of corruption. Thus a reputation can be destroyed in a moment.

8–9 The thought of v.1 is next amplified. Patience is needed to see our resolutions and enterprises through to the end. How often we embark on something with pride in our ability to carry it through but abandon it because of a few discouragements (v.8)! Then we may become angry and hit out at other people as an excuse for our own incompetence (v.9).

10–12 People have always looked back to the good old days (v.10). "If only we had lived then," they say, "we might have done better!" Even Christians sometimes overestimate the early church, the Reformation, or periods of revival. Wise people certainly learn from the past, but they live in the present with all its opportunities. Overmuch dwelling on the past can prevent us from overcoming the world, which often seems so much more wicked today than ever before.

Many suppose that sudden wealth, which would relieve them of having to earn their living, would solve all problems. If money comes like this, e.g., by inheritance, one needs wisdom to use it properly (v.11). The security that wisdom gives can be compared with the security associated with money; in fact, wisdom is a better guarantee of the good life (v.12).

13–14 God's name so far has not been mentioned in this section. The Teacher has set out advice that commends itself to any sensible person, even a humanist. But he is looking for the God-guided life that does not contradict the true wisdom of the ages but rather goes beyond it. The believer must look for the hand of the personal God.

The reference to God's "making crooked" (cf. v.13) does not make a moral judgment on God (cf. 1:15). It is meant to stress his sovereign control over all events. There are some things that we cannot alter, at least for the time being. This does not mean that we should not try to right wrongs and relieve suffering; the Teacher frequently protests against those who permit oppression (e.g., vv.7–8). It is easy to blame God when things go wrong and to forget to thank him when good things come (v.14). As children of God, we commonly experience both good and bad and may even thank God for allowing hardships rather than giving us an entirely smooth passage (cf. Matt 8:20; Luke 10:38; 2 Cor 1:4–7). Part of the life of faith is accepting prosperity and adversity from God's hand without being able to explain just how everything will be worked out for the future (v.14; Rom 8:28).

Notes

---

11 The Hebrew עִם (*'im*) may be translated "together with," thus giving "Wisdom together with an inheritance." It is also possible to translate this as a comparison, as NEB: "Wisdom is better than possessions."

---

6. *Moderation Commended*

7:15–22

15 In this meaningless life of mine I have seen both of these:

a righteous man perishing in his righteousness,
and a wicked man living long in his wickedness.
16 Do not be overrighteous,
neither be overwise—
why destroy yourself?
17 Do not be overwicked,
and do not be a fool—
why die before your time?
18 It is good to grasp the one
and not let go of the other.
The man who fears God will avoid all ⌊extremes⌋.

19 Wisdom makes one wise man more powerful
than ten rulers in a city.

20 There is not a righteous man on earth
who does what is right and never sins.

21 Do not pay attention to every word people say,
or you may hear your servant cursing you—
22 for you know in your heart
that many times you yourself have cursed others.

14–15 We have been told to live the good life. But if goodness is not rewarded in this life, why be good? The Teacher is sympathetic. His life, like everyone else's, is lived in a world subject to frustration, where temporal rewards and punishments are not neatly packaged. It is all very well to talk of accepting prosperity and adversity (v.14); yet it is strange when a righteous man dies while he has still much to offer while a villain survives to carry on his misdeeds (v.15).

16 This verse is not intended as an answer. In fact, its continuation at v.17 says that being a fool may bring on an early death, whereas the problem of v.15 is that a fool may live beyond his proper time. Therefore, these verses may be taken as a further contribution to the meaning of the good life. There may be unknown factors in the length of life of the good man and the bad (v.15), but there are some factors that are controllable. Being "overrighteous" is an obvious synonym for that type of Pharisaism that Christ warned against (Matt 5:20; 23:1–36). "Overwise" may be the subtle casuistry that such righteousness needs to support it (Matt 23:16–22), or it may be the substitute of a vast knowledge of facts for the knowledge needed for practical living (cf. 12:12). Even among Christians a passion for theology may obscure goodness and love.

17–19 We need not suppose that the Teacher means at v.17 that we may be a little wicked so long as we do not plunge headlong into folly. By balancing the two verses, we have the advice not to model ourselves after either the prig or the villain. Neither can lead us to the full life. We need to take both pieces of advice to heart and to act on them (v.18a). The way of victory is to keep God in the forefront of life (v.18b); compare the NT teaching about justification by faith, which is based on God's acceptance of Christ's righteousness, not on our offering to God our own righteousness (Phil 3:4b–9), wisdom (1 Cor 1:18–25), or the foolishness that supposes that freedom in Christ means freedom to sin (Rom 6:1–14).

Two further comments follow. Wisdom is not the knowledge of accumulated facts but the inner strength that comes from a God-instructed conscience. Hence we see the link between the fear of God (v.18) and the true wisdom that gives inner strength (v.10; cf. Prov 9:10), which is here contrasted with mere power.

20–22 The second comment is that the good life has to be lived with the awareness that there is no such thing as sinless perfection (v.20). There may be a side reference to v.17, where wickedness refers to a general way of life in which acts of sin are the norm. Here, however, righteousness is the settled way, though sins certainly occur and need to be repented of. The godly person should be genuine and sincere. He should not listen to gossip, especially if he is hoping to hear himself criticized or cursed especially by those who can observe him closely, such as his servant. An old saying is that "no man is a hero to his valet" (cf. v.21). The criticism may not be deserved, but again it may be. At any rate, it is a reminder that at some time everyone has been guilty of critical gossip (v.22; see Notes).

Notes

---

19 Some see a reference to the ten rulers in the Greek city-state, but ten is a perfectly normal round number (e.g., Gen 31:41; Neh 4:12).

21–22 קָלַל (*qālal*, "cursed") describes various grades of criticism; and the commentary has made the verse applicable to today, when actual cursing in the Oriental sense is less common. The NEB has "disparage."

---

7. *Bad Relationships*

7:23–29

23 All this I tested by wisdom and I said,

"I am determined to be wise"—
  but this was beyond me.
24 Whatever wisdom may be,
  it is far off and most profound—
  who can discover it?
25 So I turned my mind to understand,
  to investigate and to search out wisdom and the
    scheme of things
and to understand the stupidity of wickedness
  and the madness of folly.

26 I find more bitter than death
  the woman who is a snare,
whose heart is a trap
  and whose hands are chains.
The man who pleases God will escape her,
  but the sinner she will ensnare.

27 "Look," says the Teacher, "this is what I have discovered:

"Adding one thing to another to discover the scheme of
    things—
28 while I was still searching
  but not finding—
I found one ⌊upright⌋ man among a thousand,
  but not one ⌊upright⌋ woman among them all.
29 This only have I found:
  God made mankind upright,
  but men have gone in search of many schemes."

23–29 The main point of this section is about finding wisdom that the Teacher feels is very rare among humans (cf. Job 28). From a discussion of the good life, the Teacher passes to the intense depression he has felt when seeing men and women at their worst. Wise people admit that the problem of evil is insoluble (vv.23–24), but practical evil is a horrible reality for which men and women can be held responsible. As in modern times, the Teacher faced the evil of unrestrained sex (v.26; cf. Prov 7). As an example of human folly, he warned against the opportunities offered by women of easy morals. Verse 27 follows the general theme of vv.23–25, where the subject is about finding wisdom. So v.27 is not about "upright" men and women but about "wise" men and women. The NIV's "upright" is not in the MT. He found that an absolutely wise man is exceedingly rare, one in a thousand; but so far he had not found even this tiny percentage among women (v.28). One cannot blame God for this; so the fault lies in man's misuse of his freedom (v.29; the pronoun is masculine, referring to mankind generally).

Verse 26 may reflect Solomon's experiences with his hundreds of wives and concubines (1 Kings 11:3–4). Though Solomon's desire to compete with other

Oriental potentates may in large measure account for his building up a royal harem, he found that a harem did not provide the appropriate companion for man. How much better he would have been with one good wife, such as he speaks of in 9:9 and Proverbs 31!

V. Life in View of Death (8:1–9:18)

1. *The Inevitability of Death*

8:1–14

> 1 Who is like the wise man?
> Who knows the explanation of things?
> Wisdom brightens a man's face
> and changes its hard appearance.

2 Obey the king's command, I say, because you took an oath before
God. 3 Do not be in a hurry to leave the king's presence. Do not stand up
for a bad cause, for he will do whatever he pleases. 4 Since a king's word
is supreme, who can say to him, "What are you doing?"

> 5 Whoever obeys his command will come to no harm,
> and the wise heart will know the proper time and procedure.
> 6 For there is a proper time and procedure for every matter,
> though a man's misery weighs heavily upon him.
> 7 Since no man knows the future,
> who can tell him what is to come?
> 8 No man has power over the wind to contain it;
> so no one has power over the day of his death.
> As no one is discharged in time of war,
> so wickedness will not release those who practice it.

9 All this I saw, as I applied my mind to everything done under the sun.
There is a time when a man lords it over others to his own hurt. 10 Then
too, I saw the wicked buried—those who used to come and go from the
holy place and receive praise in the city where they did this. This too is
meaningless.

11 When the sentence for a crime is not quickly carried out, the hearts
of the people are filled with schemes to do wrong. 12 Although a wicked
man commits a hundred crimes and still lives a long time, I know that it
will go better with God-fearing men, who are reverent before God. 13 Yet
because the wicked do not fear God, it will not go well with them, and
their days will not lengthen like a shadow.

14 There is something else meaningless that occurs on earth: righteous men who get what the wicked deserve, and wicked men who get what the righteous deserve. This too, I say, is meaningless.

1 Chapter 7 concluded with a pessimistic view of man's attainment of wisdom. Great teachers sometimes use exaggerated language to make their point (cf. Matt 19:24). Here the Teacher shakes himself out of his depression. There are true wise men; and while true wisdom must be realistic, it need not make a person perpetually gloomy.

2–7 If you aim to please God, you are like a courtier who tries to please his king. Obey the king's commands, recognizing that you are pledged to serve him (v.2). If you displease him, you must accept the fact that there will be a rift between you. He says what you should do (v.3). He is not accountable to you for what he does (v.4). When you know his will, you will be wise to do it at the right time and in the right way (v.5), even though you cannot see his full purpose (vv.6–7).

8 The analogy of the king illustrates the concept of God's total plan. Like the king, God has the power of life and death; and, when the time comes for a person to die, he cannot insist that he should retain the breath of life (v.8a; see Notes). Meanwhile, one must press on until the end. There is no escape from the battle by treacherously joining the enemies of the king (v.8b).

9–13 Very probably v.9 belongs to the section that follows, since it is not an obvious comment on what has just been said. Powerful oppressors who made a show of religious observances have had magnificent funerals and public orations in their honor (v.10; see Notes). This has had its effect on society by creating an attitude of "If I can get away with it, I will do it." The only crime is in being found out (v.11). The servant of God knows that he lives in a fallen world, where bad men often escape punishment. Nevertheless, the servant of God looks for the enduring approval of his Lord, for this is the purpose of living (v.12).

Up to the time when Ecclesiastes was written, God had revealed little about the future life. The superficial contradiction between v.12 and v.13 can best be resolved by the Teacher's realization that living a long time is not necessarily the same as prolonging one's days—a concept made meaningful by the revelation of eternal life in Christ. Such life is both qualitatively and quantitatively beyond any number of years on earth. The Teacher obviously believes in a future judgment (11:9). The day of the wicked, however long it lasts, will not be the normal day that closes with the lengthening of the evening shadows (v.13; see Notes).

14 Yet the sense of frustration is not wholly removed so long as good and evil do not meet their just reward on earth. The Teacher does not hint again at the thought of the final assessment, because he intends to concentrate on life as it is meant to be lived now. The entire section should be compared with Malachi 3:13–4:3.

Notes

8 Is רוּחַ (*rûaḥ*) here "spirit" or "wind"? In either case the general sense of the verse would be much the same; the point of the second meaning is that a man cannot hold back the day of death anymore than he can grasp the wind. In the sense here we could interpret the verse to mean that "when the time of death comes, man cannot insist that he should retain the breath of life."

10 There are many translations and emendations of this verse. The literal Hebrew is "and they came and from the holy place they went and they were forgotten [or 'praised'] in the city who [or 'where they'] had so done [or 'had done well']." כֵּן (*kēn*) is usually taken as "so" or "thus" (BDB, p. 485), and the whole verse then refers to the wicked. But another word, with the same spelling, can mean "well" (BDB, p. 467); and this is adopted by RV, Delitzsch, and Williams, who thus find a contrast between the wicked who have an honorable burial and the welldoers who are led into exile from the holy place and are forgotten in the city. This accounts for the RV's "I saw the wicked buried, and they came to the grave; and they that had done right went away from the holy place, and were forgotten in the city."

To make sense of the former meaning of *kēn*, an unusual rendering is given to יִשְׁתַּכְּחוּ (*yištakhû*, lit., "they are forgotten"), following the LXX's ἐπηνέθησαν (*epēnethēsan*, "they were praised"); thus the NIV's "those . . . receive praise."

13 Normally a shadow is a simile of unsubstantial brevity (Job 14:2; Ps 102:11). Hence some (e.g., Delitzsch) translate the last part of the verse with a comma: "He shall not live long, like a shadow," or see Kidner (in loc.): "Prolong his days, which are like a shadow" (cf. 6:12).

---

2. *Life to Be Enjoyed*

8:15–9:10

15 So I commend the enjoyment of life, because nothing is better for a man under the sun than to eat and drink and be glad. Then joy will accompany him in his work all the days of the life God has given him under the sun.

16 When I applied my mind to know wisdom and to observe man's
labor on earth—his eyes not seeing sleep day or night—
17 then I saw all
that God has done. No one can comprehend what goes on under the sun. Despite all his efforts to search it out, man cannot discover its meaning. Even if a wise man claims he knows, he cannot really comprehend it.

9:1 So I reflected on all this and concluded that the righteous and the wise and what they do are in God's hands, but no man knows whether
love or hate awaits him.
2 All share a common destiny—the righteous
and the wicked, the good and the bad, the clean and the unclean, those who offer sacrifices and those who do not.

> As it is with the good man,
> so with the sinner;
> as it is with those who take oaths,
> so with those who are afraid to take them.

3 This is the evil in everything that happens under the sun: The same destiny overtakes all. The hearts of men, moreover, are full of evil and there is madness in their hearts while they live, and afterward they join
the dead.
4 Anyone who is among the living has hope—even a live dog is
better off than a dead lion!

> 5 For the living know that they will die,
> but the dead know nothing;
> they have no further reward,
> and even the memory of them is forgotten.
> 6 Their love, their hate
> and their jealousy have long since vanished;
> never again will they have a part
> in anything that happens under the sun.

7 Go, eat your food with gladness, and drink your wine with a joyful
heart, for it is now that God favors what you do.
8 Always be clothed in
white, and always anoint your head with oil.
9 Enjoy life with your wife,
whom you love, all the days of this meaningless life that God has given you under the sun—all your meaningless days. For this is your lot in life
and in your toilsome labor under the sun.
10 Whatever your hand finds to
do, do it with all your might, for in the grave, where you are going, there is neither working nor planning nor knowledge nor wisdom.

15 Once more the Teacher advocates the joy of life. As in 2:24–25, the gifts that God has given can be properly enjoyed only if they are accepted as God's gifts for use, not misuse. Both passages speak of the toil, or work, that God has given us to do to provide for our food and drink (cf. Gen 3:19; Ps 104:23). The verses say much the same as Jesus said in the Sermon on the Mount. Do not let your life be burdened with anxiety; relaxed enjoyment comes through seeking first the kingdom of God and taking food, drink, and clothing from the hands of your Father (Matt 6:25–34). So the Teacher refers to God-given work, God-given food and drink, and God-given joy. It is the realization of this that he commends.

16–17 In the Sermon on the Mount, Jesus spoke of anxiety about the future (Matt 6:34). Similarly, the Teacher recognizes the tendency toward worry of people who want to know what lies ahead (vv.16–17). To some this worry is more acute than it is to others. The more capacity one has for thinking things out, the more one is puzzled by the apparent meaninglessness of life. So man must be content to take the pieces one by one, without being able to fit them (past, present, and future) into the plan that he knows must be there (3:11).

1 The Teacher returns to the theme of the inevitability of death. In 3:16–22 he thought especially of the way man has oppressed man for his own advantage, as though he were establishing himself comfortably in this life forever. Here the emphasis is slightly different.

The righteous and the wise try to act according to the plan of God, as far as they can determine it. But they have to accept both the good and the bad. Some things, of course, can and should be changed; others must be taken as they are and made stepping stones to higher things. The vital thing is to realize that there is a purpose beyond happiness and sorrow. In fact, you cannot use good and bad events as criteria to decide whether God loves you or hates you. Your future may be a mixture of two. When trouble comes, it is easy to ask, "What have I done to deserve this?" It is less easy to ask the same question when happiness comes.

2–4 When people try to estimate the quantity of God's love by what happens to them, they have to face the final fact of death and its significance. Death is the final "reward" that God gives to good and bad persons alike. It almost seems as though God does not care whether people are good or bad (v.2). So why be good? If evil pays in this life, why should they not fling themselves into whatever they want to do? The end is only death, after all, and good people die just as others do (v.3). The contrast is between a man who is ready to speak the truth on oath and the guilty person who refuses to be put on oath.

The Teacher will not accept this. He is leading up to the way we ought to live in view of the finality of death. Instead of living the rotten life of drifting self-indulgence (v.3b), we should ask the further question, "What is the real purpose of life?" While there is life, there is hope—but hope for what? Surely, in the light of this book, there is hope for using life to the full. A dog that is alive can respond in a way that is impossible for the king of beasts when he is dead (v.4).

5–6 The contrast between the dead lion and the living dog supplies the meaning for v.5. The Teacher believes in a future judgment (12:14); so here he cannot be teaching the nonexistence of the departed. The context concerns the ability to plan and work. The living at least know that death must come, but from man's perspective the dead have not had it revealed to them what future there may be for them. The Teacher is not teaching soul-sleep here, that the dead have no consciousness. Rather his emphasis is on the contrast between the carnal knowledge of the living and the dead.

To fully understand this passage, it is important to realize that our knowledge of the hereafter depends on how much God reveals to us. Attempts to discover the state of the departed through mediums is forbidden in Scripture (e.g., Isa 8:19–20). The OT speaks of the patriarchs being "gathered to [their] people" (Gen 25:8; 49:33). The significance of this expression is shown in Christ's answer to the Sadducees concerning God as the continuing God of Abraham, Isaac, and Jacob: "He is not the God of the dead but of the living" (Matt 22:32). The spirits in Sheol can be roused to address the king of Babylon when he dies and joins them (Isa 14:9). Yet they clearly have not the capacities that they once had on earth. There is nothing corresponding to the temple worship in which they can join in singing the praises of God (Ps 115:17). Occasionally God speaks of a future resurrection, but this is linked to the coming of the Messiah (e.g., Ps 16:9–11; cf. Isa 25:7–8; 26:19; Dan 12:2–3; Acts 2:24–35).

So the dead at that time did not know what future they could expect. They had to wait for this till after the resurrection of Jesus Christ. They are soon forgotten on earth, and memorial inscriptions are obliterated with time (v.5b). "For them love, hate, ambition, all are now over" (NEB), and they cannot return to this life to do or undo (v.6).

7–9 In the refrain that follows once again (cf. 2:24; 3:12–13; 5:18–20; 8:15), the Teacher is not afraid to speak of God as concerned with our present life. We should start with the assumption that our circumstances have come to us with God's approval. We have already noticed that the Teacher is writing to ordinary people in average society. Let us make the most of life (v.7), though not in the way described in v.3. Let each day be a festal day, such as when we put on our best clothes. Our hair must not be unkempt like that of mourners (cf. Ezra 9:3) but should be neat (v.8; cf. Ps 23:5; Amos 6:6). God's approval is not inconsistent with life in a world of frustration (v.9). If God has given us the blessings of a wife and, presumably, a family, we are to find happiness in the precious gift of love. This is what Solomon himself failed to find (see comment on 7:23–29).

Food, drink, clothing, and family union form a God-given basis for the good life; and governments today regard them as human rights. But the breadwinner is to be indeed the bread*winner* and is to live the good life with an honest day's work. One knows the degrading feelings that come through continued unemployment and the dangers that surround the son who can become a playboy through his father's money (2:19). The Bible has a firm doctrine of work, summed up in 2 Thessalonians 3:6–13.

10 Now comes the climax. It may be that Jesus Christ was paraphrasing v.10 when he said, "As long as it is day, we must do the work of him who sent me. Night is coming, when no one can work" (John 9:4). The Teacher is not saying anything sub-Christian here. The Bible knows nothing of a purgatory where one can pick up the things neglected in this life. The NT agrees that it is deeds done in the body that count (e.g., 2 Cor 5:10).

Notes

1–2 The Hebrew is literally "Everything is before them. Everything comes alike to all." The LXX evidently read הֶבֶל (*heḇel*, "vanity") for the opening word of v.2, הַכֹּל (*hakōl*, "everything"; NIV, "all"), and some prefer this (e.g., Barton, Williams). Thus the NEB has: "Is it love or hatred? No man knows. Everything that confronts him, everything is empty, since one and the same fate befalls every one."

7–9 The Teacher may have known the Gilgamesh Epic, which was popular in the Near East from about 2000 B.C. In a fragment from this epic, Gilgamesh, king of Uruk, is told:

> Make thou merry by day and by night.
> Of each day make thou a feast of rejoicing.
> Day and night dance thou and play!
> Let thy garments be sparkling fresh,
> Thy head be washed; bathe thou in water.
> Pay heed to the little one that holds on to thy hand.
> Let thy spouse delight in thy bosom!
> (ANET, p. 90)

---

3. *Uncertainty and Inequity*

9:11–18

11 I have seen something else under the sun:

> The race is not to the swift
> or the battle to the strong,
> nor does food come to the wise
> or wealth to the brilliant
> or favor to the learned;
> but time and chance happen to them all.

12 Moreover, no man knows when his hour will come:

> As fish are caught in a cruel net,
> or birds are taken in a snare,
> so men are trapped by evil times
> that fall unexpectedly upon them.

13 I also saw under the sun this example of wisdom that greatly
impressed me: 14 There was once a small city with only a few people in it.
And a powerful king came against it, surrounded it and built huge
siegeworks against it. 15 Now there lived in that city a man poor but wise,
and he saved the city by his wisdom. But nobody remembered that poor
man. 16 So I said, "Wisdom is better than strength." But the poor man's
wisdom is despised, and his words are no longer heeded.

> 17 The quiet words of the wise are more to be heeded
> than the shouts of a ruler of fools.
> 18 Wisdom is better than weapons of war,
> but one sinner destroys much good.

11–12 It may seem strange that the Teacher can maintain faith in God's plan while accepting the factor of chance. His theme, however, is that we live in a world where we cannot calculate the future precisely but must share the day-by-day events that come to good and bad alike (cf. Matt 5:45). What we must look for is the plan of God for us today, whatever apparently chance factors have brought us to this day and will affect us for the future. At the same time the concept of chance in v.11 is not exactly the English usage (see Notes). It contains less the idea of haphazard occurrence than an event that we meet, whether anticipated or unanticipated.

The Teacher has just spoken of the need to use our capacities to work (vv.9–10). But the mere possession of speed, strength, wisdom, cleverness, and skill does not in itself guarantee success. We cannot bulldoze our way through life. The capacities must be used against a background of intelligent anticipation and a sense of uncertainty (v.11). All of us have to face life as it is; and humanity, of which we are a part, cannot foresee the future when it transcends what can reasonably be expected. There is more of this in 11:1–6. There is certainly a proper time for each action (3:1–11), and we naturally try now to use our gifts in the light of what we think the future will bring. Yet we cannot foresee every threat or obstacle (v.12). Few of us have not known what it means to be caught in the web of circumstance. We need not give up, but we must continue to ask, In what respect are we to accept God's plan and go forward from here?

13–15 The Teacher gives an interesting example, perhaps from his own experience. Time and chance struck a peaceful city when a powerful king came against it. Time and chance also ensured that the battle was not won by the strong (v.11) but by a poor man who happened to have a wiser plan than anyone else in the city. But then the poor man encountered something unexpected: the people just forgot him. It was all part of the vanity and frustration of a self-centered world. Moreover, it was undoubtedly humiliating for the people to admit that they had been saved by a nobody.

16 What are we to conclude from this illustration? Certainly not that in view of the changes and chances of life we are better off not to use our gifts. It was right for the poor man to come forward and use his wisdom to thwart the king; it would have been right for him to do so even if he had known that his fellow citizens would not ask his advice in the future.

17–18 The citizens were the real losers. The wise man's quiet words in their councils would have been worth more than the chairman's shouting for order in a meeting of people who had nothing to say but insisted on saying it (v.17). Yet, though the poor man's wisdom proved more effective than the king's armies, some loud-mouthed counselor was afterwards allowed to undo much of the good that had been gained (v.18).

Notes

---

11 פֶּגַע (*pega'*, "chance") is used elsewhere only in 1 Kings 5:4, where it is qualified by "evil," i.e., some adversity that has happened. The corresponding verb is used in the sense of "meet," as in the old English "I chanced upon" (e.g., 1 Sam 10:5).

11–18 We have found a thread of thought, but the verses can be divided into disconnected units.

VI. Proverbs (10:1–20)

1. *Wise Relationships*

10:1–7

1 As dead flies give perfume a bad smell,
so a little folly outweighs wisdom and honor.

[2]The heart of the wise inclines to the right,
but the heart of the fool to the left.
[3]Even as he walks along the road,
the fool lacks sense
and shows everyone how stupid he is.
[4]If a ruler's anger rises against you,
do not leave your post;
calmness can lay great errors to rest.

[5]There is an evil I have seen under the sun,
the sort of error that arises from a ruler:
[6]Fools are put in many high positions,
while the rich occupy the low ones.
[7]I have seen slaves on horseback,
while princes go on foot like slaves.

1 The Teacher has returned to the subject of wisdom being superior to folly, even when it fails to gain the recognition it deserves (9:13–18). So this is an appropriate place for another series of wise sayings (cf. 7:1–12) relating to guidance for life. Since few of us are wholly wise or wholly foolish, we must be careful that such wisdom as we have is not spoiled by apparently insignificant unwise behavior, just as dead flies in a pot of ointment may turn it into a foul-smelling mass (cf. S of Songs 2:15).

2–3 "Right" and "left" are natural symbols for the strong and good, on the one hand, and for the weak and bad, on the other hand. The Latin word *sinister* means "left," but it also has the unpleasant metaphorical meaning that it has in English. A wise man gravitates toward the good, the foolish toward the bad (v.2). Even when the foolish tries to keep in the middle of the road, his encounters with normal people show him up for what he is (v.3). Again, this may be taken as metaphorical.

4 Sometimes our encounters are with authorities. These may be tax officials, employers, or any "rulers" to whom we have to submit. If we clash with them, we should not walk out in a temper. Neither if we are at cross purposes with our supervisor should we resign at once. We should rather take an objective look at ourselves, and maybe we will find that we should apologize. Unwise people, however, lose their temper and suffer accordingly.

5–7 Unfortunately, the man at the top is not always right. He too may lack wisdom and enjoy manipulating people and situations. He finds jobs for his supporters and enjoys humiliating anyone of influence (vv.5–6). There are also many little manipulators in the world of business who have undeservedly risen to the top (v.7).

2. *Wise Planning*

10:8–11

[8]Whoever digs a pit may fall into it;
whoever breaks through a wall may be bitten by a
snake.
[9]Whoever quarries stones may be injured by them;
whoever splits logs may be endangered by them.

[10]If the ax is dull
and its edge unsharpened,

more strength is needed
  but skill will bring success.

11 If a snake bites before it is charmed,
  there is no profit for the charmer.

8–10 There is a song that says, "If you climb a mountain, you may break your legs; and you can't make an omelet without breaking eggs." The Teacher uses other illustrations. Despite difficulties and risks, you cannot sit back to avoid facing them in the daily round of life. If you dig a hole in your garden, remember it is there when you go out at night. If you have to pull down an old wall, watch out for snakes (v.8). You need stones and wood for building; then make sure that a boulder does not fall on you or a piece of wood fly in your face (v.9). Whenever you decide to do a certain piece of work, you will find your task easier if you make proper preparations. Sharpen your ax before you chop wood (v.10), or, to adapt the proverb to today, Sharpen your knife before carving the chicken. Or, Don't blame the class for not listening if you haven't sharpened your wits with proper preparation.

Finally, you may find yourself having to undertake a really dangerous task involving life or death. Do not keep putting it off. There is nothing for the snake charmer to do once the victim is dead (v.11). The early Christians were eager to charm the serpent and rescue his victims before it was too late (e.g., 1 Cor 9:22; 2 Tim 2:24–26).

Notes

8 Our interpretation follows Delitzsch. Some (e.g., Barton) treat the verse as referring to punishment for the man who digs a trap for his neighbor or breaks into a house to steal. Our interpretation is linked with the general theme of v.9.

3. *Wise Speech and Thought*

10:12–20

12 Words from a wise man's mouth are gracious,
  but a fool is consumed by his own lips.
13 At the beginning his words are folly;
  at the end they are wicked madness—
14 and the fool multiplies words.

No one knows what is coming—
  who can tell him what will happen after him?

15 A fool's work wearies him;
  he does not know the way to town.

16 Woe to you, O land whose king was a servant
  and whose princes feast in the morning.
17 Blessed are you, O land whose king is of noble birth
  and whose princes eat at a proper time—
  for strength and not for drunkenness.

18 If a man is lazy, the rafters sag;
  if his hands are idle, the house leaks.

19 A feast is made for laughter,

and wine makes life merry,
but money is the answer for everything.

20 Do not revile the king even in your thoughts,
or curse the rich in your bedroom,
because a bird of the air may carry your words,
and a bird on the wing may report what you say.

12–14 Our ignorance of the future should not eliminate common sense. Sensible talk meets with approval in a stable society, but there is destructive talk that degrades (vv.12–13). Unfortunately, much of the mass media is dominated by those who pull down moral standards rather than build them up. Again, there are clever arguments that try to interpret the significance—or nonsignificance—of human existence, with concepts that can only be uncertain (v.14). The multiplication of arguments that ignore the revelation of God in Jesus Christ can end only in foolishness (1 Cor 1:18–25).

15 In the context "work" may relate to the many arguments of v.14 (cf. 12:12). In a fine note of sarcasm, this proverb says that a person may be so involved in arguing about the universe that he misses what the ordinary person is concerned about, namely, finding the way home (cf. Isa 35:8–10).

16 The Teacher lived in days when kings were more common than they are today, but this does not make his theme irrelevant. There must always be leaders in every country and every enterprise (Rom 13:1), and much that is said here of kings can be applied in measure to other kinds of rulers.

It is hard to decide what sort of a king is described in v.16. Translations for the word *na'ar* vary among "servant" (NIV), "slave" (NEB), "child" (RSV), and "lad" (JB). The word certainly designates an inexperienced person in this context. The first two indicate that the king is someone who has suddenly come to the top by others and who keeps his power by letting his deputies do what they want. The other two indicate that the real power is that of the deputies. In any event, those under the influence of such leaders get no benefit from them. Lack of self-control in a leader, shown by feasting at breakfast (cf. Isa 5:11; Acts 2:15), sets an example that lesser men and women soon follow.

17 The contrast in v.17a suggests that the rendering "servant" is the more likely in v.16. The king here described is born to rule and has been trained for his task since his youth. His close associates have the self-control that gives their lives strength and not dissipation.

18–19 These two verses may be isolated proverbs, or they may well continue the preceding references to good and bad authorities. Lazy rulers bring down the great house of the nation, as a lazy householder lets the beams of his house collapse so that the roof sags and lets in the rain.

In v.19 the Teacher apparently returns to the thought of extravagant feasting (cf. v.16). Food and wine occupy the minds of lazy rulers, and they behave as though money can buy everything (see Notes).

20 When all is said and done, the average citizen must retain some respect for authority. The Teacher does not distinguish between good and bad leaders; he has spoken of both, and probably his advice here includes both. How far would he draw the line regarding bad authorities? He has just criticized them in the same strong terms that the prophets use. Since this verse speaks of wishing someone ill in the privacy of one's own home, it is a warning that malice toward the powers that be may lead to ultimate confrontation with them. If there is something wrong in your town or in the place where you work, you must either keep totally silent or be prepared for your proper criticisms to come to the ears of those at the top.

There are useful comparisons with this section in Isaiah 5:11–12; Amos 6:4–6; and 2 Peter 2:13–19.

Notes

18–19 Most commentators think that these proverbs refer to careless rulers. Williams, however, treats v.19 as an isolated encouragement to work and earn money rather than to sit and feast.

VII. Wisdom for the Future and the Present (11:1–10)

1. *The Uncertain Future and Present Behavior*

11:1–6

1 Cast your bread upon the waters,
for after many days you will find it again.
2 Give portions to seven, yes to eight,
for you do not know what disaster may come upon the land.

3 If clouds are full of water,
they pour rain upon the earth.
Whether a tree falls to the south or to the north,
in the place where it falls, there will it lie.
4 Whoever watches the wind will not plant;
whoever looks at the clouds will not reap.

5 As you do not know the path of the wind,
or how the body is formed in a mother's womb,
so you cannot understand the work of God,
the Maker of all things.

6 Sow your seed in the morning,
and at evening let not your hands be idle,
for you do not know which will succeed,
whether this or that,
or whether both will do equally well.

At last the Teacher is approaching the climax of his book. We cannot see God's whole plan, and there is nothing in this world that we can build on so as to find satisfaction or the key to the meaning of things. Yet we are to fulfill God's purpose by accepting our daily lot in life as from him and by thus pleasing him make each day a good day. But how can we please him when there is so much we cannot understand?

The Teacher has already shown that certain things stand out as right or wrong, and a sensible conscience will see these as an indication of what God desires. This section gives further wise advice in the light of an uncertain future. We must use common sense in sensible planning and in eliminating as many of the uncertainties as we can.

1–2 Interpreters differ over the pictures in vv.1–2. Barton sees them as an exhortation to charity. The Eastern flat bread is light enough to float, and what you give in charitable gifts will be washed back to you as a reward. But this idea of investment in charity does not belong to the Teacher's thought elsewhere. So (with Delitzsch and Williams) we may prefer the alternative that links the meaning with vv.4–6. "Nothing ventured, nothing gained," as a proverb says. Be like the merchant who uses his capital for trade, including trade across the seas. But be sensible, and do not gamble everything on one venture.

3–4 We are bound to recognize the God-given laws of nature (v.3), but we cannot always forecast how they will operate. We often have to act before we can foresee all we would like to know about the future. The farmer who waits till he is completely certain of perfect weather conditions will never reap anything at all (v.4).

5 Life begins in mystery with the baby's conception and prenatal growth and continues with the mystery of the working of God's total plan. Few parents understand precisely how a baby is formed, but most follow the rules of common sense for the welfare of the mother and the unborn child. This is exactly the application that the Teacher makes here to the plan of God. Indeed, it illustrates the whole theme of the book. We cannot understand all the ways God works to fulfill his plan, but we can follow God's rules for daily living and thus help bring God's purpose to birth.

6 Verse 6 sums up this section. Because the future is unknown, we must accept calculated risks and believe that though some of our ventures may fail, a sufficient number of them will succeed. The Teacher has been drawing his illustrations from trade and agriculture, and some of us may find difficulty in applying it to our situation today. It would be wrong, however, to spiritualize the verses. They are intended to be practical. One thinks of making an unwise investment in a single project that promises large profits or of the restlessness that risks the family's welfare by moving to some distant field that looks greener or of the indecision that loses an opportunity because of timidity.

Notes

3 Jerome's strange interpretation of the fallen tree has persisted, and some Christians have quoted it out of context. The tree, he said, is the dead person, and his destiny is fixed at death. But while this is true enough, it cannot be proved from this verse.

Both parts of the verse when taken together likely speak of the inevitable laws of nature, to which we must submit even if we also must allow for chance. McNeile and Barton, however, object, saying that a tree can be moved after it has fallen. They prefer to translate עֵץ (*ʿēṣ*) as "stick," in which sense it is used some fifteen times in the OT (e.g., Num 15:32).

The reference then would be to rhabdomancy, or divination by the position of rods that have been tossed into the air (Ezek 21:21). If a man seeks guidance by tossing sticks into the air, he has no control over the result (Barton). Or it might be an allusion to the futility of divination for discovering the will of God, since all one has is a stick lying on the ground. But the idea of divination is not obvious to the ordinary reader, and the usual translation is therefore preferable. The fact that a man can move a fallen tree if he gets help is immaterial in the simile.

5 Translators naturally differ about rendering הָרוּחַ (*hārûaḥ*) as "the spirit" or "the wind," as in 8:8. The literal translation of the Hebrew is "As you do not know what is the way of the spirit [wind], like bones in the womb." The RSV, the NEB, Williams, and Kidner adopt the translation "the spirit," with the slight emendation of "like" to "with," i.e., the initial letter כ (*k̠*) changed to ב (*b̠*); hence "the way of the spirit with the bones." But the RV, the JB, the NIV, Delitzsch, and Barton prefer to translate as "wind." Thus Delitzsch has "As you have no knowledge what is the way of the wind, like as the bones in the womb," i.e., "you do not know how the wind goes any more than you know how the bones are formed." But the comparison is abrupt and far from obvious. It is likely that Jesus Christ had this verse in mind when he told Nicodemus, "The wind blows wherever it pleases. You hear its sound, but you cannot tell where it comes from or where it is going" (John 3:8). This does not tie us to a particular interpretation here, since the Greek word πνεῦμα (*pneuma*) also can have either meaning, and some translate Christ's words as "The spirit breathes where he will."

6a In the light of v.5, some give this a sexual meaning; but the word "plant" in v.4 is literally *sow*, making this unlikely.

---

2. *The Certain Future and Present Behavior*

11:7–10

[7] Light is sweet,
and it pleases the eyes to see the sun.
[8] However many years a man may live,
let him enjoy them all.
But let him remember the days of darkness,
for they will be many.
Everything to come is meaningless.

[9] Be happy, young man, while you are young,
and let your heart give you joy in the days of your youth.
Follow the ways of your heart
and whatever your eyes see,
but know that for all these things
God will bring you to judgment.
[10] So then, banish anxiety from your heart
and cast off the troubles of your body,
for youth and vigor are meaningless.

The Teacher has discussed how we should act in view of the uncertainties of life. We must recognize the certainties but must plan in such a way as not to be thrown off balance when the unexpected happens. Now the Teacher goes on to speak of the certainty of growing up and growing old.

7–8 First there is the happiness of life when vitality is high, when all things seem possible and the sun shines all the time (v.7; cf. 12:2). The joy of living should continue throughout life. Yet one must face the inevitable restrictions (ch. 12) that old age brings just as he sees the sun going down toward evening and eventually setting, bringing the final darkness of night (v.8). Life is lived in a world of vanity, and part of the vanity is the process of aging. On the day Adam and Eve disobeyed God, their bodies began to die (Gen 2:17; 3:19).

It is usual to refer "the days of darkness" only to death, and we have allowed for this in the commentary. But there is no real reason to include death at all, in view of the use of darkness to describe the effects of old age in 12:2–3. God-given vitality is good and is meant to be used and enjoyed; but, as v.9 shows, each age must recognize that the succession of sunrise, noon, afternoon, evening, and night is reflected in the rhythm of life.

9 So the young man has vitality at its fullest; and if he cannot feel the sense of fulfillment in it, something is wrong. To older people it may seem to be too risky to advise a young person to walk in the ways of his heart and the sight of his eyes. Yet the advice is coupled with a reminder of responsibility before God. This is not to take away with one hand what is given with the other because a sense of responsibility belongs to youth just as vitality does. Though crushed or warped, a sense of responsibility to the group, society, or humanity is something all have at some time or another. The Teacher adds the further reminder of responsibility to God, who is the Supreme Assessor. Taken by themselves, the words could present a picture of God as a grim condemning judge, but this would be out of keeping with what the Teacher says elsewhere of God's approval of our enjoyment (e.g., 9:7). Rab, a Jewish teacher of the third century A.D., commented, "Man will have to give account for all that he saw and did not enjoy."

10 Obviously, young people face strong temptations, and vanity and frustration are as much a part of adolescence as vitality. So youth must say no as well as yes and must discard whatever damages mind or body (cf. Col 3:8–14). It is possible to take v.10 as advocating hedonism: e.g., "Banish care from your mind, do not burden your body" (Scott, in loc.). However, the next verse (12:1), with its advice to remember the Creator while one is young, makes it more likely that the other interpretation is correct. So we have to decide from the context and the general purport of the book whether the Teacher is referring to things that disturb us because they bring limitations from which life should be free or whether he is speaking of indulgences that bring guilt to the mind and damage to the body.

VIII. The Frustration of Old Age

12:1–8

Remember your Creator
  in the days of your youth,
before the days of trouble come
  and the years approach when you will say,
"I find no pleasure in them"—
2 before the sun and the light
  and the moon and the stars grow dark,
  and the clouds return after the rain;
3 when the keepers of the house tremble,
  and the strong men stoop,
when the grinders cease because they are few,

and those looking through the windows grow dim;
4 when the doors to the street are closed
and the sound of grinding fades;
when men rise up at the sound of birds,
but all their songs grow faint;
5 when men are afraid of heights
and of dangers in the streets;
when the almond tree blossoms
and the grasshopper drags himself along
and desire no longer is stirred.
Then man goes to his eternal home
and mourners go about the streets.

6 Remember him—before the silver cord is severed,
or the golden bowl is broken;
before the pitcher is shattered at the spring,
or the wheel broken at the well,
7 and the dust returns to the ground it came from,
and the spirit returns to God who gave it.
8 "Meaningless! Meaningless!" says the Teacher.
"Everything is meaningless!"

Remembering one's Creator in the time of one's youth, which is the theme at the end of the previous chapter, is shown to be especially important in view of the gradual loss of vitality as age takes its toll of the body and brain. Old age and death are the supreme frustration and vanity that we experience. We naturally wonder what the aging process would have been if we had not fallen. The Transfiguration probably indicates what would have happened. Jesus Christ, being without sin, had the opportunity of receiving a transformation of his ordinary body and of passing to heaven without dying. Instead of this, he deliberately chose to go forward and die for the sins of mankind (see Luke 9:30–31). We have mentioned this because it is sometimes argued that aging is natural for humanity and that the earth would soon have become overcrowded if there had been no death.

The description in the verses that follow ranks among the finest of the world's literature, especially when it is read aloud by a good reader. The onset of old age is pictured under a wide variety of metaphors, most of obvious application.

1 The passage begins with a nonmetaphorical statement so as to make it clear to the reader what is to follow. The thrill of youth fades into a lack of zest for life. The statement is a general one and certainly allows for varying degrees of experience, since some people retain their zest in extreme old age. Indeed, few today in the advanced nations of the world suffer from blindness, deafness, and other physical disabilities described in this chapter. The point is that as we grow older, we all have some traces of these marks of age, even if they do not develop to the extremes that this chapter describes. So the Teacher is justified in reminding young people that they cannot afford to put off faith in God their Creator until they are older. God wants the best of their lives.

2 The rhythm of life is like the rhythm of the year. Spring and summer give place to the clouds of autumn and winter. The showers that so quickly come and go in youth are succeeded by rain and clouds and then more rain. It becomes progressively harder to throw off troubles and anxieties.

3 The arms and hands that minister to the body begin to tremble, and the legs that once carried the body so strongly weaken and sag at the knee. The loss of teeth makes it hard to grind solid food, and the eyes are dimmed.

4 The other doors of the senses, the organs of hearing, gradually close, marooning the owner within the cramped house of his own body (v.4a.). The next picture is difficult to interpret; but, since in v.3 the grinders must be the teeth, it is likely that here it is the voice that comes out softly and often indistinguishably through the toothless gums. Delitzsch interprets it as the sucking noise that an old person makes as he tries to chew his food.

The next phrase in v.4 is also variously translated and interpreted. On the one hand, there is the rendering of the NIV (similar to KJV, RSV): "Men rise up at the sound of birds," meaning that in spite of deafness the old person sleeps badly and wakes at the first bird call. This translation requires no emendation. An alternative is "he shall rise up to the voice of a bird"; i.e., the voice rises in pitch and grows thin and squeaky like the twitter of a bird. One emendation gives "The voice of a bird is silent" (so basically NEB, JB, Scott); i.e., the old man no longer hears high-pitched sounds (see Notes).

The final clause of v.4 must also refer to sounds. It may be a straightforward statement that singing women no longer move him, since their voices do not come to him with any clearness. Or just as he wakes early at the first song of the birds, so he dozes off in the evening as the voices of the singers fade in his ears, or as today he loses the thread of the television story. But if the whole verse is symbolic, the meaning could be that while the old man's voice is squeaky in conversation, when he tries to sing he can make only a dreary, low, moaning noise.

5 We need not treat all the descriptions as metaphorical, since v.5 mentions two very concrete experiences that frighten old people. They have a fear of heights and are afraid of the traffic in the streets. The latter is specially applicable today in our big cities; but the narrow streets of an Eastern town, with camels, donkeys, and bustling traders, were doubtless almost as terrifying to a slow-moving pedestrian.

The Teacher returns to remorseless metaphor. The almond tree pictures the white hair of age. To us it is usually the harbinger of spring, and the blossom is pink. In Palestine, however, the tree begins to blossom in midwinter; and although the petals are pink at their base, they are white towards the tip. The general impression of the tree in flower is of a white mass (HDB, 1:67). But the old man has no spring to follow so as to enjoy the fruit.

Now the lively, leaping grasshopper can only drag itself along, as happens when the days grow cold, an obvious picture of old age. The Hebrew may also be translated, "The grasshopper shall be a burden" (KJV, RV). The meaning of the latter translation would be that even a small thing like a grasshopper seems unduly heavy, although it is difficult to see why a grasshopper should be singled out in this way. Gordis takes this translation but sees an allusion to the decline of sexual vitality. This would seem an unnecessary repetition of the sentence that follows, if, as Gordis and most commentators hold, the caperberry is mentioned here as a sexual stimulant. Some translations indeed bring out this meaning by rendering the Hebrew for caperberry as "desire," which, if translated literally, would be obscure to the ordinary reader today. Williams, however, points out that references to the caperberry in the classics treat it as an appetizer, not as an aphrodisiac. But one would expect some reference to declining sexual potency in these descriptions.

The Teacher has exhausted his description of the failing faculties, omitting little. It only remains to speak of the inevitable end, the long home of Sheol, inaugurated with the wailing of the professional mourners.

6 "Before" takes us back to v.1: "before the days of trouble come." Thus the NIV repeats the understood imperative: "Remember him." The young person must remember his Creator before the end draws near. The pictures in this verse have met with a variety of interpretations, but they certainly describe total collapse. The silver chain from which the lamp hangs is snapped. The golden lamp bowl is crushed. The clay pitcher is broken to pieces so that no water can be brought from the well. The wooden wheel that lowers the bucket into the well has itself been broken. Another interpretation links the pictures with parts of the body. The silver cord could be the spine, the golden bowl the head, the pitcher the heart, and the wheel the organs of digestion. Delitzsch is perhaps oversubtle when he interprets silver cord as the soul, which at death can no longer support the body. He sees the pitcher as the heart, drawing in and sending out the blood, and the wheel as the lungs and throat.

7 Whatever the interpretation of the details, the fixed fact is that of death. The body returns to its component parts (cf. Gen 2:7; 3:19). The OT consistently teaches that at death the life principle in humans and animals alike (3:19–21; Ps 104:29–30) returns to God, the Giver of life, and that we must one day give account to God (11:9).

8 So having warned the young man to make the most of life while he has the faculties to enjoy it, remembering that he is accountable to God for the use of God's gifts, the Teacher reminds him that these gifts and life itself are fleeting. At the moment his faculties are flexible, but as he grows older they will harden and decay. One day all will cease in death, the supreme frustration and apparent meaningless end to life.

Notes

Detailed notes on this superb passage may seem out of place. It may be asked how the idea of inspiration can be held when there are so many possible interpretations of individual pictures. The answer is that, while attention to detail is important, the total description is what matters; and whatever the interpretation of phrases, the whole picture of decrepit old age is conveyed clearly. In these notes we call attention to a few interpretations that have not been mentioned in the commentary.

1 The form בּוֹרְאֶיךָ (*bôr*^{e}*'eyḵā*, "your Creator") has often been identified either as a plural of majesty (e.g., Eaton, p. 147) or as an error for a singular form (GKC 124k). Others suggest emendation to words that would make allusion either to one's wife or to the grave (Crenshaw, pp. 184–85). Fox (pp. 299–300) follows Gordis in considering it an example of a final א (') being treated as a final ה (*h*) verb (cf. GKC 93ss).

4 The verb קוּם (*qûm*) means "arise" or "stand up." The suggestion "rise up to the voice of a bird," i.e., grows thin or high-pitched, is attractive, if we could be certain that the Hebrews had the metaphor of *up* and *down* with the scale. If so, it could be contrasted with "brought low" (NIV, "grow faint") in the following clause (see commentary). Suggested emendations for וְיָקוּם (*w*^{e}*yāqûm*) include וְיִקְמַל (*w*^{e}*yiqmal*, "the voice of the bird decays"; cf. Isa 19:6, 33:9) and וְיִדּוֹם (*w*^{e}*yiddôm*, "is silent").

5 Although there is sometimes a doubt whether one of several Hebrew words refers to a locust in a mature or immature state, there is no doubt that חָגָב (*ḥāgāḇ*) is "a small grasshopper," since it is used as a picture of smallness in Num 13:33.

Two famous passages from literature come to mind. Shakespeare (*As You Like It* 2.7) concludes his seven ages of man thus:

His big manly voice,
Turning again toward childish treble, pipes
And whistles in his sound. Last scene of all,
That ends this strange eventful history,
Is second childishness and mere oblivion;
Sans teeth, sans eyes, sans taste, sans everything.

This fine poem by Charles Kingsley appears in his children's book, *The Water Babies*, chapter 2.

When all the world is young, lad,
  And all the trees are green;
And every goose a swan, lad,
  And every lass a queen:
Then hey for boot and horse, lad,
  And round the world away;
Young blood must have its course, lad,
  And every dog his day.

When all the world is old, lad,
  And all the trees are brown;
And all the sport is stale, lad,
  And all the wheels run down;
Creep home, and take your place there,
  The spent and maimed among:
God grant you find one face there,
  You loved when all was young.

IX. Epilogue (12:9–14)

1. *The Credibility of the Author*

12:9–12

9 Not only was the Teacher wise, but also he imparted knowledge to the people. He pondered and searched out and set in order many proverbs. 10 The Teacher searched to find just the right words, and what he wrote was upright and true.

11 The words of the wise are like goads, their collected sayings like firmly embedded nails—given by one Shepherd. 12 Be warned, my son, of anything in addition to them.

Of making many books there is no end, and much study wearies the body.

Although it is usual to treat these words as the comment of a disciple, they could be by the Teacher himself, even by Solomon, who, in spite of personal failings, must have retained the gift of wisdom, which he had asked for and obtained for the benefit of his people (2:9; cf. 1 Kings 3:9–12; 4:29–34). The claim here is no more boastful than are the words of the prophets who claim to be speaking the words of the Lord.

God had various ways of inspiring his chosen writers. Prophets received direct communications through vision or voice. Historians were prompted to select and set down those records and estimates that were important for the understanding of God's plans for his people (see Luke 1:3). Wise men were given discernment in observing the experiences of mankind and sifting the conclusions that others, whether theists or humanists, had deduced about sensible behavior that would please God and bring maturity to individuals and society.

So, whether written by the Teacher or by a disciple, these verses put the imprimatur on the book. They show that it is not to be read as the chronicles of skepticism or an advocacy of hedonism.

9–10 It is possible to be a miser in accumulating knowledge instead of using it for the benefit of mankind, but this was not the way of this Teacher (v.9). He taught others with full regard for his responsibility as one in a position of authority. He took great care in sifting wise sayings (cf. Luke 1:1–4). He did not confuse truth with dullness (v.10a) but wrote "in an attractive style" (JB). On the other hand, he did not let his brilliance run away with him so as to cause him to write less than the truth—the danger of all popular speakers and writers (v.10b).

11 Verse 11 claims God's inspiration for the Wisdom writers and hence is very important. It is their equivalent of "Thus saith the Lord." There is some dispute over the precise translation but none over the basic claim (see Notes). The wise draw their wisdom from the Shepherd of Israel, the one true God (Gen 49:24; Pss 23:1; 80:1). Their wise teachings are to goad their readers to action and are to be seen as wholly dependable and worthy to be collected as Scripture. We can hardly read less into this verse.

12 Next comes a warning against the vast amount of literature that is a waste of time for the reader who is really concerned to find the truth. If we take the first sentence of v.12 as warning the disciple against going beyond the inspired words of the wise (NIV, RSV), this incorporates the theme of the book. In this world there will always be mystery, and human beings can fall into all sorts of error if they try to prove what cannot be proved (e.g., 3:11, 14; 7:14). There will always be books pouring off the presses, some helpful, some agnostic, some downright anti-God. Students who have to study them for examinations, and those mature Christians who need to understand modern trends, know how wearisome they can be and yet at times how attractive. The verse is certainly not intended to discourage Christian writers or even modern wise men who are not committed Christians if they can write constructively and expound in modern terms those truths of life that are there in the Scriptures. Nor should older Christians forget the great Christian classics that expounded the same truths in their own day.

Notes

---

11 בַּעֲלֵי אֲסֻפּוֹת (*ba'ₐlê 'ₐsuppôṯ*) is literally "masters of collections," but a personal meaning is difficult here. The NEB interprets this as the collections of assembled people: "They [the sayings] lead the assembled people, for they come from one shepherd." In spite of the unusual terminology, others make the phrase refer to the books that contain the assembled sayings and translate it as "collected sayings" (NIV, RSV, Gordis, and, in effect, Delitzsch and Barton).

12 The opening sentence is literally "And further than [or 'from'] those, my son, be warned." "Further" may be simply a repetition as in v.9, or the warning is not to pry beyond what the divinely given wisdom reveals.

---

2. *The Conclusion of the Matter*

12:13–14

13 Now all has been heard;
here is the conclusion of the matter:
Fear God and keep his commandments,
for this is the whole ⌊duty⌋ of man.
14 For God will bring every deed into judgment,
including every hidden thing,
whether it is good or evil.

13–14 A good author usually summarizes the main points that he has been making when he comes to the end of his book. The summary here is especially important, since commentators have tried to interpret the book as the thoughts of a skeptic.

Obviously, the Teacher is sometimes skeptical; but God is real to him, and he believes that God has revealed his will to mankind. If God had not done so, man could not be held accountable for his actions (v.14). Thus, although he would like to know more of the total plan of God, man knows enough to be held responsible for what he does or fails to do. His life day by day is to be lived as in the sight of God, who has given him the opportunity to fulfill God's purpose for that day. His actions, as well as the secret intentions of his heart, are open to God and one day will be opened up for reward or punishment (cf. 3:17; 11:9b).

Notes

13b The literal Hebrew, "This is (for) all mankind," is the equivalent of "This is what man is made for" or "This is the whole duty of man."

13–14 It is worth comparing these verses with the closing verse of Ecclesiasticus: "Work your work before the time comes, and in his time he will give you your reward" (51:30). Some find a parallel between v.12 and Ecclus 43:27: "We may say many things, yet shall we not attain: and the sum of our words is, He is all."

The Jews did not like ending a reading with a word of judgment, and in public they repeat v.13 after v.14. They follow the same practice at the end of Isaiah and Malachi.

SONG OF SONGS

Dennis F. Kinlaw

SONG OF SONGS

Introduction

1. Background

   a. The importance of the introduction
   b. Two primary issues
      1) The book's existence
      2) The book's interpretation
   c. Approaches to interpretation
      1) Allegorical
      2) Natural
      3) Dramatic
      4) Cultic
   d. Some history of a misunderstanding
   e. Purpose and message

2. Date
3. Authorship
4. Special Problems
5. Bibliography
6. Outline

1. Background

a. *The importance of the introduction*

The introduction to the Book of Song of Songs is perhaps more important than that of any other book in the Bible because of the problem that the church has had in interpreting its meaning. To a non-Christian that may seem strange. Song of Songs is patently a collection of ancient Hebrew love poems celebrating the experiences of a lover and his beloved as they taste the beauty, power, agony, and joys of human sexual love. Is that appropriate, however, for a book that is part of the Hebrew-Christian Scriptures?

b. *Two primary issues*

1) *The book's existence*

Why is the Book of Song of Songs included in the canon of Scriptures? If a MS of this little book were found alone, detached from biblical context and tradition, it undoubtedly would be viewed as secular. The book has no obvious religious content. Its few references to a historically identifiable person (Solomon) and to known places (Jerusalem, En Gedi, Tirzah) show its Jewish provenance. But the usual marks of biblical literature—its religious themes, institutions, and practices—are absent. There are no references to law, grace, sin, salvation, or prayer. In fact, there is not a single, indisputable reference to Yahweh in the text.

Yet Song of Songs is in our Bible. Furthermore, it has held a significant place in the affections of the synagogue and the church. In Israel the book came to be associated liturgically with the greatest Hebrew festival, being read on the eighth day of Passover. During the first fifteen centuries of the Christian church, most major Christian writers turned their attentions to this little work. Neither Jews nor Christians have been able to ignore it. Pope, with reason, says that no other composition of comparable size (117 verses) in world literature "has provoked or inspired such a volume and variety of comment and interpretation" (p. 17). His commentary amply documents his statement.

2) *The book's interpretation*

Since the Book of Song of Songs is in the sacred canon, how is it to be interpreted? No book in Scripture has had such varied treatment. The options are so broad that some have despaired. Saadia, the medieval Jewish commentator, said that it is like a lock for which the key has been lost (cited in Pope, p. 17). Pope counters that there is no key because the door is open to all who are willing to enter (ibid.). Yet Delitzsch called it "the most obscure book in the Old Testament" (p. 1).

c. *Approaches to interpretation*

1) *Allegorical*

The oldest documented interpretation of the Song of Songs sees it as an allegory. This position was well established by the first century of the Christian era and has had a long and illustrious history in both Judaism and Christianity.

An allegory is an extended metaphor. Allegory normally is not rooted in history or the real world but is drawn from the mind and imagination of the author. Its purpose is not to present real events related to identifiable places and persons, but rather to communicate spiritual truth of an abstract nature. Allegory, used from the earliest days of Greek literature, is an old device in which there is a divorce between the obvious literal meaning and the "high" spiritual message.

Theogenes of Rhegium (520 B.C.) used allegory to make some of the capers of the gods recorded in Homer and Hesiod more acceptable to the Greek public. He insisted that the stories were not to be taken literally but contained concealed meanings of a more acceptable nature. Allegorical interpretation of religious literature was picked up by a distinguished line of successors. Philo, Origen, Jerome, Bernard, Calvin, and many other illustrious figures stand in that train.

The Jews saw in the Song of Songs a depiction of the relationship of Yahweh to his chosen people, Israel. This is found from the earliest known Jewish interpreters such as Rabbi Aqiba (*Tosephta* Yad. 2.4) in the first century to the interpretations found in the Targum (*Ta'anith* 4.8), the Midrash, the great medieval commentators such as Saadia, Rashi, and Ibn Ezra, down to some present day orthodox scholarship. Early Christian interpreters took a similar tack. Hippolytus, who lived about 200 A.D., is our first known example of allegorical interpretation. He was soon followed by Origen (who wrote a ten-volume commentary and a series of homilies on the Song), Gregory of Nyssa, Ambrose of Milan, Jerome, and a host of other noteworthies, including some in our own century. These have seen the Song primarily as a statement of the love of Christ and his church. One of the most significant variations on that theme is the Roman Catholic identification of the bride with the Virgin Mary.[1] Pope, in the lengthy introduction to his commentary (q.v.), has an extended and helpful history of the interpretation of the Song.

There are problems, however, in accepting the Song of Songs as an allegory.

First, nothing in the text indicates that the intention of the author was to allegorize. There is an ingenuousness in style and content that belies the artfulness essential to good allegory. The text includes no clues that the author had any allegorical intent. The result is that the meanings in the text, if it is taken as allegory, are left to the imagination of every interpreter.

Second, the people, places, and experiences recorded seem to be real, not literary devices. The use of names like Solomon, Jerusalem, Lebanon, En Gedi, Tirzah, and others do not have the ring of metaphor about them. There is little here akin to a work like *Pilgrim's Progress.*

A third reality is that this little book does not have the narrative character—viz., the clear progressive story-line—that we usually expect in allegory.

The result of the use of the allegorical approach is that the Song of Songs has become to an unusual degree a field for fertile imaginations. There have been few or no hermeneutical controls. The boundaries of interpretation have tended to be as wide as the creative fancies of the scholars. Illustrative of this is the interpretation of the references in 4:5 and 7:8 to the breasts of the bride.

Jewish scholars have seen in the bride's breasts Moses and Aaron; the two Messiahs, Messiah Son of David and Messiah son of Ephraim; Moses and Phinehas; and Joshua and Eleazar. Christian interpreters have been equally ingenious. They have seen the bride's breasts as the church from which we feed; the two testaments, Old and New; the twin precepts of love of God and neighbor; and the Blood and the Water. Gregory of Nyssa found in them the outer and the inner man, united in one sentient being. Little wonder that the allegorical interpretation has come under increasing attack in the last two centuries. It is not difficult to understand Luther when he insisted that the literal sense

> alone holds the ground in trouble and trial, conquers the gates of hell [Matt 16:18] along with sin and death, and triumphs for the praise and glory of God. Allegory, however, is too often uncertain, unreliable, and by no means safe for supporting faith. Too frequently it depends upon human guesswork and opinion; and if one leans on it, one will lean on a staff made of Egyptian reed [Ezek 29:6].[2]

Yet Luther himself had difficulty admitting the literal sense of the Song. Rather, he saw in the bride a happy and peaceful Israel under Solomon's rule. The Song was for Luther a hymn in which Solomon "commends his own government to us and composes a sort of encomium of peace and of the present state of the realm."[3] The modern reader though finds few references in this text to provoke meditation on political philosophy.

---

[1] *Patrologia Latina,* 16, cols. 326f.; 67, col. 978; 196, col. 482.

[2] Heinrich Bornkamm, *Luther and the Old Testament* (Philadelphia: Fortress, 1969), p. 91.

[3] Jaroslav Pelikan, ed., *Luther's Works* (Saint Louis: Concordia Publishing House, 1972), 15:195.

2) *Natural*

Occasionally through history someone has become unhappy with the allegorical treatment and has raised a voice for a more natural approach to the plain sense of the text. Until the modern era a price was usually exacted for such bravery.

In the first century apparently some Jewish readers understood the Song of Songs literally. Some were even singing portions of it in their drinking houses. This evoked the wrath of Rabbi Aqiba who pronounced an anathema on such. For Aqiba this was blasphemous.

None can question Aqiba's love for the Song of Songs. Notice his famous saying: "The entire history of the world from its beginning to this very day does not outshine that day on which this book was given to Israel. All the Scriptures, indeed, are holy . . . ; but the Song of Songs is the Holy of Holies."[4] But it was for Aqiba, not the goodness of faithful married love that made it holy, but God's choice of Israel to be his bride.

Theodore of Mopsuestia, at the end of the fourth century, rejected the allegorical meaning and read Song of Songs in its plain sense (IOT, p. 1055). His commentary did not survive, and the Council of Constantinople in 553 condemned his views. In the same era Jovinian, a Roman monk, proposed that the book be used to demonstrate that virginity and celibacy were not more virtuous than a holy marriage. He even dared to question the perpetual virginity of Mary. This was too much for Augustine, who responded hostilely to him in the treatise *Adversus Jovinianum.*

In Reformation times in Geneva, Sabastian Castellio revived the view of Theodore of Mopsuestia. Castellio saw in it "a colloquy of Solomon with his lady friend." Such, he felt, should not have a place in the Scriptures. Calvin was distressed by this and assisted in Castellio's departure from Geneva.

Often those who dared to reject the allegorical approach questioned the spiritual value of the book. A welcome relief came in the work of Robert Lowth, the eighteenth-century Anglican bishop who put all biblical scholarship in his debt with the discovery of a key to biblical poetry (parallelism). He suggested that the book actually tells us about the marriage feast of Solomon (see Pope, pp. 130–31). The bride, he felt, may well have been the daughter of Pharaoh. He accepted the Song as historical but was willing to see something typological here. Solomon, the king of Israel, took a Gentile bride and made her a part of the people of God. Lowth felt that there might be reason to see here a foreshadowing of that other King, the Prince of Peace, who would take from among the Gentiles a bride, the church. This approach helped prepare the way for the stance most commonly taken among biblical expositors in our own time. As Horace Hummel points out, modern scholarship has moved "massively and almost unanimously away from allegory, at least in any strict sense of the term."[5]

3) *Dramatic*

In the last century Delitzsch revived a suggestion of Origen, a suggestion largely undeveloped in the period, that the Song was a drama (p. 8). A number of writers have picked this up and elaborated it. There has been no consistency though in the development of this view. Absence of stage directions, lack of agreement on how

[4] M *Yadaim* 3.5.

[5] *The Word Becoming Flesh* (Saint Louis: Concordia, 1979), p. 499.

many characters or who said what, the lack of any clear signs of division into "acts" or "scenes," and the fact that dramatic form never really caught on in the East have prevented this approach from gaining any extensive support.

4) *Cultic*

Recent studies of comparative literature of the ancient Near East have given us another approach to the interpretation of our text, the cultic-mythological. According to this view the poem does not really speak of human love at all; rather, it is either the celebration of the sacred marriage of a goddess in the person of a priestess with the king, or else it is the celebration of the victory of the divine king over death and drought. The origins of the Song are thus seen in Canaanite mythology and ritual where the sexual union of the goddess and her once-lost lover were seen as restoring fertility and well-being to the land. Of course, our text, so the argument goes, reflects Hebrew adaptations to cover the pagan origins. A careful reading of the text is, for this writer, enough to refute this view. Arthur Weiser is right when he says such a view can only be maintained by reading into the text what is not patently there or else by amending the text to fit the hypothesis. He sees it as based on ill-founded conjectures and thinks it difficult to believe that heathen cultic songs were admitted "without further ado into the religious life of Israel and into its canon."[6]

The conclusion to all this is that today the majority of commentators, regardless of their theological position, tend to begin their approach to the text with the assumption that this is first of all Hebrew love poetry that originated in an ancient experience, or experiences, of human love. They find that they cannot accept the divorce of literal and spiritual meanings so often assumed by the allegorist. They feel that the baseline here is in history. There may be more than the literal, but that is not up for discussion until the meaning of the plain sense of the text is accepted.

A factor that cannot be ignored that has its influence here is that allegory as a method for interpretation of Scripture has fallen out of honor in most scholarly circles. Louth explains: "Basically, I think we felt that there is something dishonest about allegory. If you interpret a text by allegorizing it, you seem to be saying that it means something which it patently does not. It is irrelevant, arbitrary: by allegory it is said, you can make a text mean anything you like" (p. 97). Louth makes a strong appeal for a reconsideration of allegory. As of now, he is largely a voice crying in a wilderness.

d. *Some history of a misunderstanding*

Early in the history of the church, a negative attitude arose toward marriage. In 325 at the Council of Nicea, a proposal was made that all clergy give up cohabitation with their wives. The proposal did not carry. The perspective represented in the proposal did. Pope Siricius in 386 commanded that all priests live celibately. Later this order was extended to sub-deacons. Many of the priests were married when they were ordained. Leo the Great (440–61) had a concern for these wives. He did not permit the priests to put their wives away, but he insisted that the priest and his wife live together as brother and sister.

Next the church insisted that a married man could not be ordained unless he and his wife exchanged vows of continence. This led ultimately to refusal to ordain anyone to the priesthood who had been married. Celibacy reigned as the symbol of supreme

[6] *The Old Testament: Its Formation and Development* (New York: Association, 1961), p. 301.

piety. (The Eastern Church permitted the ordination of married ordinands. Unmarried ordinands though are still forced to take a vow of celibacy.) Celibacy and chastity came close to being synonymous. So virginity became the way of special piety for women. Marriage was seen as a concession to human weakness and to the need to continue the human race. This could be done by weaker folk and more worldly believers. The more noble were the celibate and the virgin.

Augustine was a key influence in this. Notice his comments on marriage when addressing the subject of widowhood:

> Therefore the good of marriage is indeed ever a good: but in the people of God it was at one time an act of obedience unto the law; now it is a *remedy for weakness* [emphasis mine], but in certain a solace of human nature. Forsooth to be engaged in the begetting of children, not after the fashion of dogs by promiscuous use of females, but by honest order of marriage, is not an affection such as we are to blame in a man; yet this affection itself the Christian mind having thoughts of heavenly things, in a more praiseworthy manner surpasses and overcomes.[7]

Augustine's position basically was that since the Fall, man is unable to enter into a sexual relationship without concupiscence. Concupiscence is defiling. Marriage designed before the Fall is good. It was God's plan for the continuation of the race. Marriage is still good. The concupiscence that inevitably goes with it is not. Marriage and procreation were divine commands under the law. Since Christ has come, these are no longer commanded and are lesser goods. Celibacy should be urged on all as an escape from the inevitable sin of concupiscence. Sexuality should be sublimated. Christ should be our Bride. The Song of Songs is a picture of the ecstasy of that better way.

The result of this perspective was that the medieval church had a love affair with the Song of Songs. An eroticism precluded at the human level was permitted at the divine. No book of Scripture received such attention between Augustine and Luther. What Galatians was to the Reformers, the Song of Songs was to the church for a thousand years. That love affair was picked up by the Puritans and continues with many of those committed to the allegorical interpretation of the Song.

But is the position reflected here biblical? The irony is that Origen, Jerome, Augustine, and Bernard felt it was. A brief look at some biblical data will put this in a different perspective.

The OT certainly cannot be appealed to for support for this position. First of all, human sexuality was of divine design (Gen 1–2). Marriage was instituted by God (Gen 2) and was pronounced good. That evaluation never changes (Prov 5:15–20; Eccl 9:9; cf. Prov 31) and connubial joy is encouraged. No premium is ever placed on virginity or celibacy. Virginity and barrenness were seen rather as curses (Judg 11:34–40).

As for celibacy, OT Hebrew has no word for a bachelor. There were not supposed to be any. Every patriarch was married. The priests were all married. Every prophet was married, as far as we know, except for Jeremiah. He was commanded by God not to marry (Jer 16:2). Yahweh's wife (Israel) had forsaken him. Why should Yahweh's spokesman enjoy connubial bliss? The prophet's lonely life was to be seen as a parable of Yahweh's tragic divorcement from Israel. Even the high priest in Israel was

[7] "On the Good of Widowhood," *A Select Library of the Nicene and Post-Nicene Fathers of the Christian Church* (Grand Rapids: Eerdmans, 1980), 3:445.

to be married, since the office was to be hereditary. Instead of marriage and the cohabitation that normally goes with it being a hindrance to communion with God, this was a prerequisite for the person who was to enter the Most Holy Place on the Day of Atonement. Only a married man could experience the most intimate communion with Yahweh. Perhaps the most symbolical fact of all is that from Abraham to Paul, circumcision, the mark that a man was in covenant with Yahweh, was at the point of intimate contact of his body with his wife.

Nor does the NT change that picture. Jesus reaffirms the sanctity of marriage in Matthew 19:3–9. Hebrews 13:4 tells us that the marriage bed is pure and that marriage itself should be honored by all. Paul insists that it is desirable for elders and bishops to be married and to be model family men (1 Tim 3:4; Titus 1:6–7). History began with a wedding (Gen 2:18–25) and will climax with the Marriage Supper of the Lamb (Rev 19:6–10). It would seem no accident then that the Lord began his earthly ministry blessing a wedding. John the Baptist, when quizzed about Jesus' ministry, described it in nuptial terms (John 3:29–30). Jesus himself, when interrogated as to why his disciples did not fast, pictured his stay among us in terms of a wedding announcement party. A case can easily be made that the biblical philosophy of history is to be described in nuptial terms. Thus idolatry and adultery are used synonymously across the length of Scripture. Jesus spoke of eunuchs and that such a state could be good (Matt 19:11–12). Clearly he was speaking of exceptional cases. Paul in 1 Corinthians 7 may *appear* to be promoting an unmarried state. There is a question though about one's hermeneutics if a single debatable passage that may be addressing a particular situation is used to counter the clear thrust of the rest of Scripture.

e. *Purpose and Message*

Why is this seemingly erotic little book included in the sacred canon? What is its message? Part of the answer is that it speaks of an order of creation that is both pedagogical and eschatological. It speaks of marriage as it ought to be.

The Bible does not see marriage as an inferior state, a concession to human weakness. Nor does it see the normal physical love within that relationship as necessarily impure. Marriage was instituted before the Fall by God with the command that the first couple become one flesh. Therefore physical love within that conjugal union is good, is God's will, and should be a delight to both partners (Prov 5:15–19; 1 Cor 7:3).

The prospect of children is not necessary to justify sexual love in marriage. Significantly, the Song of Solomon makes no reference to procreation. It must be remembered that the book was written in a world where a high premium was placed on offspring and a woman's worth was often measured in terms of the number of her children. Sex was often seen with reference to procreation; yet there is not a trace of that here. The Song is a song in praise of love for love's sake and for love's sake alone. This relationship needs no justification beyond itself.

In a sense there is almost an Edenic quality to much of the Song of Songs, almost as if it were a commentary on Genesis 2:18–25. The psalmist looked at the awesome beauty and order of the heavens and saw in them subjects fit for Scripture. They were a declaration of the glory of God. This writer looked at and experienced the beauty of human love and wrote about it. The explicit references to the Creator found in the OT's praise of the heavens are not found in the Song of Songs. They were though the unchallenged assumption of whoever gave us this text.

Song of Songs, however, is more than a declaration that human sexual love in itself is good. Historically Judaism and Christianity have agreed. Have they been wrong so long? Their argument was allegorical. Their intuition may have been correct even if their exegetical method left something to be desired. This writer concurs with their position and believes there is biblical support for that intuition. That support rests in the analogical nature of the relationship between biblical election and human marriage.

The use of the marriage metaphor to describe the relationship of God to his people is almost universal in Scripture. From the time that God chose Israel to be his own in the Sinai Desert, the covenant was pictured in terms of a marriage. Idolatry was equated with adultery (Exod 34:10–17). Yahweh is a jealous God. Monogamous marriage is the norm for depicting the covenant relationship throughout Scripture, climaxing with the Marriage Supper of the Lamb. God has chosen a bride.

We tend to view the covenant-marriage relationship as an example of how human, created, historical realities can be used analogically to explain eternal truths. Thus human marriage is the original referent, and the union of God with his people is seen as the union of a loving husband and wife. The earthly and the temporal are used to explain the divine and the eternal. Human love is thus a good pedagogical device to cast light on divine love.

In reality there is much in Scripture to suggest that we should reverse this line of thought. Otherwise the union of Christ with his bride is a good copy of a bad original. The reality is, as Bromiley insists, that earthly marriage, as it is now lived, is "a bad copy of a good original" (p. 77). The original referent is not human marriage. It is God's elect love, first to Israel and then to the church.

If divine love is the pattern for marriage, then there must be something pedagogical *and* eschatological about marriage. It is an earthly institution that in itself images something greater than itself.

This reversal of type and antitype should not be difficult for us to understand since orthodox theology has always recognized this in the parent-child relationship. The first father was not Adam. Human parenthood is a finite "copy" of a divine original that eternally exists in the nature of the Triune Godhead. God was Father before the Creation. The original referent is in the Creator's own being, not in the Creation. So this natural-human relationship of parenthood is *like* the divine reality, not vice-versa.

Similarly it can be said that human marriage is an earthly institution designed to teach us about our intended eternal destiny. We are made for union with God; we are made for love. We may corrupt the vehicle and destroy its pedagogical value and its eschatological worth, but that speaks of our sin, not of his intent.

A question then must be raised. Did the author think of our eternal union with God or intend to communicate such thoughts when he wrote? There is no way to answer that question. There is certainly nothing within the text to make us think that he did. It is a song of human love. But when one sings of human love in a world that came from the hand of Love, can one only speak of human love? If we had found the Song of Songs in an archaeological dig with no Hebrew context, we could treat it as a secular song of love. The reality is that the Song originated among and was given to us, not by secularists, but by people whose model for love was election love. It would be wrong to separate the Song from its canonical context. It would be equally wrong to try to explain the beauty and the mystery of human love apart from the Creator God from whom it comes, who by definition is Love and love's source. Von Rad says, "Creation not only exists, it discharges truth" (p. 165).

Bromiley adds:

> In creating man—male and female—in his own image and joining them together so that they become one flesh, God makes us copies both of himself in his trinitarian unity and distinction as one God and three persons and of himself in relation to the people of his gracious election. Analogically, what is between Father and Son and Holy Spirit, and what ought to be and is and shall be between God and Israel and Christ and the Church, is also what is meant to be in the relation of man and woman and more specifically of husband and wife. Neither the intratrinitarian relationship nor the union between the heavenly bridegroom and his bride is a good copy of a bad original. Earthly marriage as it is now lived out is a bad copy of a good original.[8]

When we deal with human sexuality and married love, we are not dealing with simply biological and sociological by-products of an evolutionary process. We are dealing with realities within the created order that had divine origins and divine purposes. Earth is supposed to speak of heaven because it came from the Creator's hand. And to treat of sexual love apart from the divine intent would be to miss the glory. There is something proleptic and eschatological in human passion. We deal with symbols that image eternal realities here. Little wonder that this little book is in the canon.

2. Date

The tendency of liberal biblical criticism in the last two centuries has been to date most everything much later than the church had traditionally maintained. Otto Kaiser of Marburg illustrates this with his view of the date of the Song.

> The occurrence of the Persian loanword *pardēs* in 4:13, and of the either Greek or Iranian loanword *'appiryŏn* in 3:9 as well as the Aramaisms, which on a percentage basis are the most numerous in the Old Testament after Esther and Ecclesiastes, make a pre-exilic origin for Canticles impossible. . . . The fact that apart from the heading in 1:1 the relative particle *'ᵃšer* is never used, but in its stead always the relative *še*, argues unmistakably for a late post-exilic origin of the collection in the third century B.C.[9]

Archaeology, comparative linguistics, and the study of ancient Near Eastern literature have effected some changes here. The very data that for Kaiser made a preexilic origin of the Song impossible now is used to place its origin in or around the time of Solomon.

Chaim Rabin of the Hebrew University now points out that *pardēs* ("orchard," 4:13 ["garden"]) occurs in Greek as *parádeisos,* and Mycenean Greek predates the Exodus. The origins of *'appiryôn* ("carriage," 3:9) he considers dubious. Aramaic is as old as Hebrew, and *še* (e.g., 5:2 ["for," untr. in NIV], 9 ["so that," untr. in NIV]), the Hebrew relative, was common in familiar language in dialects over part of the Hebrew language area prior to the time of David and Solomon and disappeared from the written language "only with the emergence of the official classical Hebrew of the time of David and Solomon" (pp. 205–19).

---

[8] Ibid.

[9] *Introduction to the Old Testament* (Minneapolis: Augsburg, 1975), p. 365.

Rabin further states that the many references to aromatic spices and perfumes "suggest that the Song of Songs was written in the heyday of Judean trade with South Arabia and beyond (and this may include the lifetime of King Solomon)" (p. 211). The reference to Tirzah (6:4) supports such a date. This was an early capital of the northern kingdom. A favorable mention of it would seem most unlikely after the division of the monarchy in 922. Tirzah's successor as capital, Samaria, is never mentioned. All this makes a tenth-century date quite plausible.

3. Authorship

The question of authorship of the Song of Songs is a difficult one. Traditionally it was attributed to Solomon, due in part to the title, the six other explicit references to Solomon (1:5; 3:7, 9, 11; 8:11, 12), and the three references to an unnamed king (1:4, 12; 7:5 [6 MT]). The data, however, contains some ambiguities. The Hebrew construction in the heading (*lišlōmōh*) was once referred to as the *lamedh auctoris*. Now it is known that it was used for other purposes than the ascription of authorship (see Notes on 1:1).

Nor do the references to Solomon indisputably indicate authorship. These could be historical references to a royal prototype. There are no references anywhere else in Scripture to help us in this matter except the identification of Solomon in 1 Kings 4:29–34 with Hebrew wisdom, poetry, and knowledge of the flora and fauna of Israel. His multiplicity of wives and concubines means little in terms of his knowledge of the kind of love described in the Song of Songs, unless this is a product of his earlier and purer years.

The case for Solomon's authorship is not definitive, but the case against it is equally far from being sure. Arguments for a late dating, which would preclude Solomonic authorship, have been largely exploded. Even some liberal critical scholarship is now insisting that the book could have originated in the Solomonic era.

Fortunately, a knowledge of who wrote this little book is essential neither to its interpretation nor to an appreciation of its content. As a work of literature of singular beauty and power, it stands on its own feet. Like other works in the Bible, it is enough to know that it is part of our sacred canon.

4. Special Problems

Several problems confront the modern reader in the study of the text of the Song of Songs that make certainty in understanding and interpretation difficult to achieve. One of these is the matter of language.

Ancient Hebrew is a primitive tongue. The syntax is quite different from ours. Verb tenses are different so that time sequences are more difficult to establish. Word order can raise problems. There is an economy of language that can be tantalizing. And then it is poetry. There is a succinctness of style that makes it almost telegraphic. The result is that the text is often more suggestive than delineative, more impressionistic than really pictorial. Much is left to the imagination of the reader rather than spelled out for the curious modern, who wants to know the specific meaning of every detail.

Added to the preceding problems is that of vocabulary. In 117 verses there is an amazing number of rare words, words that occur only in the Song of Songs, many only once there, or else that occur only a handful of times in all the rest of the corpus of the OT. There are about 470 different words in the whole Song. Some 50 of these are *hapax legomena.* Since use is a major way of determining the meaning of words in another language, the result is that we are often uncertain as to the exact meaning of key terms and phrases.

Another problem is that the imagery used was a normal part of a culture that is very different from our modern world. The scene is pastoral and Middle Eastern. So the references to nature, birds, animals, spices, perfumes, jewelry, and places are not the normal vocabulary of the modern love story. The associations that an ancient culture gives to its vocabulary are difficult, if not impossible, for us to recapture. The list of plants and animals is illustrative: figs, apples, lilies, pomegranates, raisins, wheat, brambles, nuts, cedar, palms, vines, doves, ravens, ewes, sheep, fawns, gazelles, goats, lions, and leopards. So is that of spices and perfumes: oils, saffron, myrrh, nard, cinnamon, henna, frankincense, and aloes. The place names carried connotations some of which are undoubtedly lost to us: Jerusalem, Damascus, Tirzah, En Gedi, Carmel, Sharon, Gilead, Senir, and Heshbon. We understand the overtones of "bedroom," but when the lover refers to "the clefts of the rock, in the hiding places on the mountainside" (2:14), to gardens, parks, fields, orchards, vineyards, or valleys, we are aware that the places of rendezvous were different for lovers in that world than in ours.

The terms of endearment cause us problems. The metaphors used are often alien. When the lover likens his beloved to a mare in the chariot of Pharaoh (1:9), we are surprised. "Darling among the maidens" (2:2) or even "dove" (2:14; 5:2; 6:9) is understandable, or "a rose of Sharon" (2:1). "A garden locked up" (4:12), "a sealed fountain" (4:12), "a wall" (8:9–10), "a door" (8:9), "beautiful . . . as Tirzah" (6:4), and "lovely as Jerusalem" (6:4) are not our normal metaphors of love. Nor are our heroine's references to her lover as "an apple tree" (2:3), "a gazelle" (2:9, 17), "a young stag" (2:9, 17), or "a cluster of henna" (1:14).

To further complicate matters, it is not always certain who is speaking. One of the most difficult tasks is to determine who the speaker is in each verse. It is not even completely clear as to how many speakers there are. Our best clues are grammatical. Fortunately, pronominal references in Hebrew commonly reflect gender and number. In some cases, however, the masculine and the feminine forms are the same.

Nor are we fully comfortable with the literary genre of the whole or the parts. Is Song of Songs a single composition from a common source, or is it a collection of songs that originally circulated independently? Is there a progression of a story line in the material? Is it a drama? All these questions affect interpretation. Some of the text seems to be "stream of consciousness" material where the dialogue takes place as it might in dreamlike material. Or is it all to be taken as actually occurring in normal consciousness? We do not know enough about Hebrew literature in the second millennium to answer all these questions dogmatically. For this writer the Song does contain an inherent unity that causes him to see it as a body of material from a single source. There is a bit of a story line. In chapter 4 the lover begins to speak of his beloved as his bride. In ten verses (4:8–5:1) he calls her his bride six different times. This is climaxed in 5:1, which seems clearly to be a euphemistic account of the physical culmination of the relationship. It seems, furthermore, that much of the material represents the world of wonder in the imagination of the maiden rather than actual happenings. Thus a time line on the progress of the relationship is very difficult. But it all fits together to make a whole.

The passages starting at 3:1 and 5:2 may represent dream sequences. No theory answers all the questions. The above proposal is most helpful to this commentator.

So there are problems in understanding and interpretation. One thing is very clear. Song of Songs is a magnificent piece of literature that merits a place in our hearts as well as in the sacred canon. We may wonder at the title: The Song of Songs. This relates it to all other songs as the NT relates Jesus to all other kings: the King of kings. It is, to whoever gave us the title, the worthiest of all songs!

Whether we concur or not, we must be impressed with the great host of worthies in the history of the church who have paid Song of Songs the highest tribute. Notice John Wesley's comments:

> The most excellent of all songs. And so this might well be called, whether you consider the authority of it . . . ; or the subject of it . . . ; or the matter of it, which is most lofty, containing in it the noblest of all the mysteries contained in either the Old or the New Testament; . . . useful to all that read it with serious and Christian eyes. (p. 1927)

5. Bibliography

Books

Bernard of Clairvaux. *Song of Solomon.* Translated by Samuel J. Eales. Minneapolis: Klock and Klock, 1984.

Bromiley, Geoffrey W. *God and Marriage.* Grand Rapids: Eerdmans, 1980.

Carr, G. Lloyd. *The Song of Solomon.* Tyndale Old Testament Commentaries. Downer's Grove: InterVarsity, 1984.

Davidson, Robert. *Ecclesiastes and the Song of Solomon.* The Daily Study Bible. Philadelphia: Westminster, 1986.

Delitzsch, Franz. *Commentary on the Song of Songs and Ecclesiastes.* Translated from the German by M.G. Easton. Edinburgh: Clark's Foreign Theological Library, LIV, 1885.

Fuerst, Wesley J. *The Books of Ruth, Esther, Ecclesiastes, the Song of Songs, Lamentations.* The Cambridge Bible Commentary. New York: Cambridge University Press, 1975.

Glickman, S. Craig. *A Song for Lovers.* Downer's Grove: InterVarsity, 1976.

Gordis, Robert. *The Song of Songs and Lamentations.* New York: Ktav, 1954.

Lehrman, S.M. *The Song of Songs.* Soncino Books of the Bible, The Five Megilloth. London: Soncino, 1946.

Louth, Andrew. *Discerning the Mystery.* Oxford: Clarendon, 1983.

Luther, Martin. *Notes on Ecclesiastes, Lectures on the Song of Solomon, Treatise on the Last Words of David.* Works. Volume 15. Saint Louis: Concordia, 1972.

Meek, Theophile J. *The Song of Songs: Introduction and Exegesis.* Interpreter's Bible. Volume 5. Nashville: Abingdon, 1956.

Murphy, Roland E. *The Book of Ecclesiastes and the Canticle of Canticles.* Pamphlet Bible Series. Volume 38. New York: Paulist Fathers, 1961.

———. *Wisdom Literature: Job, Proverbs, Ruth, Canticles, Ecclesiastes, Esther.* The Forms of the Old Testament Literature. Volume XIII. Grand Rapids: Eerdmans, 1981.

Pope, Marvin H. *Song of Songs.* Anchor Bible. Garden City, N.Y.: Doubleday, 1977.

Rylaarsdam, J. Coert. *The Proverbs, Ecclesiastes, The Song of Solomon.* Layman's Bible Commentary. Volume 10. Richmond: John Knox, 1964.

Shideler, Mary McDermott. *The Theology of Romantic Love: A Study of the Writings of Charles Williams.* Grand Rapids: Eerdmans, 1966.

Trible, Phyllis. *God and the Rhetoric of Sexuality.* Philadelphia: Fortress, 1978.

Von Rad, Gerhard. *Wisdom in Israel.* Nashville: Abingdon, 1972.
Wesley, John. *Explanatory Notes Upon the Old Testament.* Volume 3. Bristol: William Pine, 1765.

Journals and Other Articles

Ginsberg, H. Louis. "Introduction to the Song of Songs." *The Five Megilloth and Jonah.* Philadelphia: Jewish Publication Society of America, 1969.
Kinlaw, Dennis. "Charles Williams's Concept of Imaging Applied to 'The Song of Songs.'" *Wesleyan Theological Journal* 16, 1 (1981): 85–92.
Rabin, Chaim. "The Song of Songs and Tamil Poetry." *Studies in Religion* 3 (1973).
Rowley, H.H. "The Interpretation of the Song of Songs." *The Servant of the Lord and Other Essays on the Old Testament.* London: Lutterworth, 1952, pp. 187–234.

6. Outline

I. The Title (1:1)
II. Courtship (1:2–3:5)
  A. A Maiden's Amorous Musings (1:2–4b)
  B. The Friends' Praise (1:4c)
  C. The Maiden's Self-Consciousness (1:4d–7)
  D. The Friends' Admonition (1:8)
  E. The Lover's Praise (1:9–11)
  F. The Fragrances of Love (1:12–14)
  G. Love's Exchanges (1:15–2:2)
  H. Faint With Love (2:3–7)
  I. Love's Rhythm (2:8–3:5)
    1. A lover's call (2:8–17)
    2. A lover's seeking (3:1–5)
III. The Bridal Procession (3:6–11)
IV. The Wedding (4:1–5:1)
  A. The Beauty and the Purity of the Bride (4:1–15)
  B. Love's Consummation (4:16–5:1)
    1. Invitation (4:16)
    2. Response (5:1a–d)
    3. Joy (5:1e–f)
V. The Life of Love (5:2–8:7)
  A. Its Hesitancies (5:2–8)
  B. The Friends' Concern (5:9)
  C. Love's Affirmations (5:10–6:10)
    1. The beloved's praise (5:10–16)
    2. The friends' inquiry (6:1)
    3. The beloved's praise (6:2–3)
    4. The lover's praise (6:4–10)
  D. Love's Questions (6:11–13)
  E. Love's Repetitions (7:1–9a)
  F. Love's Belonging and Giving (7:9b–13)
  G. Love's Longing and Liberty (8:1–4)
  H. Love's Seal and Strength (8:5–7)
VI. Conclusion (8:8–14)

Text and Exposition

I. The Title

1:1

[1]Solomon's Song of Songs.

1 The title for this little book, Solomon's Song of Songs, is taken from the opening line of the Hebrew text. It is the literal translation of the first two words: *šîr haššîrîm.* This construction carries more meaning in the Hebrew than it does in English. It is the regular form of the Hebrew superlative: "The song of songs" is "the greatest of all songs." Pope translates it "the sublime song" (p. 294).

A comparable expression is found in the term "the Holy of Holies" (cf. Exod 26:33 et al.). The NIV correctly translates this "the Most Holy Place." Similar superlatives are found in the expressions "King of kings" and "Lord of lords."

If this superscription is from the author, it immediately reveals the significance he attached to his subject. More likely the title was assigned by those responsible for the book's transmission to us. In that case it is an indication of their view of its worth.

Notes

1 The rest of the Hebrew superscription is אֲשֶׁר לִשְׁלֹמֹה (*'ašer lišlōmōh*). A literal translation of this would be "which (is) to / for / from / with reference to Solomon." The possessive element (actually the preposition *lᵉ*) has been known as the *lamedh auctoris* and has been translated "Solomon's." From comparative Semitics we now know that it can indicate far more than authorship. It can designate subject matter, literary genre, or who edited the text (cf. GKC, pars. 119r; 129c; Ronald J. Williams, *Hebrew Syntax* [Toronto: University of Toronto Press, 1967], pars. 265–84).

II. Courtship (1:2–3:5)

A. *A Maiden's Amorous Musings*

1:2–4b

[2]Let him kiss me with the kisses of his mouth—
for your love is more delightful than wine.
[3]Pleasing is the fragrance of your perfumes;
your name is like perfume poured out.
No wonder the maidens love you!
[4]Take me away with you—let us hurry!
Let the king bring me into his chambers.

2 The book begins with the girl expressing her deep desire for physical expressions of love by her lover. There is a fascinating shift of persons in the first two verses. The RSV covers this in translation and makes vv.2–4a direct address. The Hebrew, though, begins in the third person and then shifts: "Let him kiss me with the kisses of his mouth—for your love is better than wine." This change in persons is not unusual in Hebrew poetry. It is as if she begins with the wish in her own mind and then shifts almost unwittingly to speaking directly to him.

It is significant to this work that the girl speaks first. This young lady is not extremely diffident. She seems to see herself as of equal stature with the male. She longs to express her love to him, and she wants him to reciprocate. There is a sense in which she is the major character in this poem. This is one of the aspects of this work that makes it unique in its day. Much more of the text comes from her mouth and mind than from his. It is more her love story than it is his, though there is no failure on his part to declare his love and admiration for her.

3 We are quickly introduced to the association of love with the most pleasant tastes and smells. Love is so delightful that it should be accompanied with all that is pleasant. Oils are mentioned. We know that olive oil was used in the ancient Near East as a base for various perfumes.

The lover's name is like "perfume poured out." This is the only time in the Song that the word "name" occurs. It speaks of her lover as a person of repute. He is well known. The maidens love him. The Hebrew for "poured out" is *tûraq*. Pope translates this as a proper noun: "oil of Turaq." He feels that it refers to a particular high grade cosmetic oil. Most commentators, however, see *tûraq* as a causative-passive verb form. Gordis translates this line as "thy presence as oil wafted about" (p. 45). However we translate this, our lover is obviously the object of wide-scale affection.

4a The beloved longs for her lover to take her away with him, and speedily. Her emotion is intense, and she longs to be able to act on it.

4b The second part of v.4 can be significant to the story line in the Song. The NEB translates the Hebrew vocatively: "Bring me into your chamber, O King." This follows the Syriac and the Greek of Symmachus. The NIV and RSV follow the MT and read it as a declarative sentence in the third person. Ibn Ezra translated it: "Even if the king were to bring me into his chambers."

The reference to "the king" is variously interpreted. Ginsburg sees in this that the king is different from her lover. Most scholars do not concur. Some see it as evidence that it was customary in that day to speak of all brides and grooms in royal terms (Dentan, p. 325). The evidence for this is not definitive. Others find in this an indication that her lover was really a king. Notice the references in 1:12; 3:9, 11; and 7:5 to the king. The simplest solution is that we are really dealing here with a royal romance.

Notes

---

2 For דֹּדֶיךָ (*dōḏeyḵā*, "your love") the LXX has *μαστοί σου* (*mastoi sou*, "your breasts"), apparently reading דַּדַּיִךְ (*dadyḵ*) here and also in v.4c.

3 טוֹבִים (*ṭôḇîm*) is rendered "pleasing" by the NIV. The LXX strengthens the thought with ὑπερ παντα τὰ ἀρώματα (*hyper panta ta arōmata*, "better than all spices") by reading מִכָּל־בְּשָׂמִים (*mikkol-beśāmîm*). The word for "spices" is literally "balsam."

4 Instead of מָשְׁכֵנִי (*māšeḵēnî*, "take me"), the LXX has εἵλκυσάν σε (*eilkysan se*, "they drew you"), reading מְשָׁכוּךָ (*mešāḵuḵā*). The maiden's action seems to be more of a consequence than a request.

B. *The Friends' Praise*

1:4c

We rejoice and delight in you;
  we will praise your love more than wine.

4c The third part of v.4 confronts us with an annoying change of persons. Who are the "we" here? Delitzsch says they are the women of Jerusalem. He assigns the whole of this first section to them and sees in this unit their praise of Solomon. Murphy does not assign the whole first unit to the women of Jerusalem, but he does identify the "we" in this verse with them. Carr is willing to hear these words as coming from the mouth of the girl. Two things are clear enough: the love of these two merits praise, and the lover merits the popular affection in which he is held. We concur with the NIV in identifying them as the daughters of Jerusalem, i.e., the friends of the maiden.

C. *The Maiden's Self-Consciousness*

1:4d–7

How right they are to adore you!

5 Dark am I, yet lovely,
  O daughters of Jerusalem,
  dark like the tents of Kedar,
  like the tent curtains of Solomon.
6 Do not stare at me because I am dark,
  because I am darkened by the sun.
My mother's sons were angry with me
  and made me take care of the vineyards;
  my own vineyard I have neglected.
7 Tell me, you whom I love, where you graze your flock
  and where you rest your sheep at midday.
Why should I be like a veiled woman
  beside the flocks of your friends?

4d The NIV is helpful here in including the last line of v.4 with this segment. Our maiden turns her attention to his public again: "How right they are to adore you!" The consciousness of these "daughters of Jerusalem" (v.5) and their affection for the maiden's lover makes her apprehensive. Her question is not about his attractiveness. It is about hers.

5–6 The maiden is self-conscious about her darkness (v.5). Kedar was a territory southeast of Damascus where the Bedouin roamed. Their tents were made of the skins of black goats. She explains that her color is due to her exposure to the sun as she worked the vineyards for her brothers (v.6). She obviously is from a family where the girls had to work. Mention is made in the text of her brothers, a sister (see comment on 8:8–10), and her mother. There is no reference though to her father. She was compelled to care for her brother's concerns whether she cared for her own or not.

We notice a confidence in this maiden about her own loveliness (v.5). There is an appealing modesty in our heroine; yet she is not overly diffident. Several times, as Carr points out, the separate emphatic first personal pronoun "I" is used in the text rather than just depending on the more common and less forcible verbal ending (1:5–6; 2:1, 5; 5:2, 5–6, 8; 6:3; 7:10; 8:10). In every case it is the girl who is speaking. She is very much the appropriate match for the lover pictured here. The fullness with which the text presents her and the strength that she portrays make this little book most remarkable for its age and place in human history. The two lovers meet as equals.

7 The maiden next turns her attention to her lover and addresses him. The NIV loses a bit of the force of the Hebrew. The RSV is accurate in the phrase "whom my soul loves." The NIV is correct in that the Hebrew *nep̱eš* ("soul") can be used as an equivalent for the personal pronoun. When it is though, as here, it always carries with it a deep sense of personal emotional involvement. (Notice the use of this expression in 3:1–5.) Pope says that the term designates "the person or self including all its appetites and desires, physical and spiritual" (p. 328).

The maiden wants to know where her lover grazes his flock so that she can be near him, if not with him. Yet she does not want to unduly expose herself. She does not want to be like "a veiled woman" beside the flocks of his friends. The term *ʿōṭᵉyāh* occurs only once in the Song but some sixteen times elsewhere in the OT. The verbal root means "to cover" or "to veil." A number of attempts have been made to emend the text and find another reading. There is little need for this. The girl is saying that she does not want to be mistaken for a cult prostitute, a good picture of which is seen in Genesis 38:13–15. She is not a loose woman following the flocks looking for any lover. She has made a commitment to one. And she wants to know where she can find him.

Notes

---

7 The Syriac, Targum, and Vulgate read כְּטֹעִיָּה (*kᵉṭōʿîyāh*, "as a wandering, straying woman") for כְּעֹטְיָה (*kᵉʿōṭᵉyāh*, "as a veiled woman").

D. *The Friends' Admonition*

1:8

[8]If you do not know, most beautiful of women,
  follow the tracks of the sheep
and graze your young goats
  by the tents of the shepherds.

8 Next follows a response to the maiden: first, by the daughters of Jerusalem, to whom the maiden has spoken in the preceding segment (v.5); then by her lover (vv.9–11). Her uncertainty is met by the assurance that she is the "most beautiful" of all women. The pronominal elements are feminine singular; so we know there has been a shift in speaker, for the maiden would hardly be speaking to herself. Most expositors attribute v.8 to the daughters of Jerusalem (so Dentan, NIV), to whom she has spoken in the preceding segment (v.5). The NASB includes v.8 with the lover's words in vv.9–11.

The superlative used here, "most beautiful," occurs again in 5:9 and 6:1. In each of these the women of Jerusalem are describing her beauty. This supports the view that this verse is from them.

E. *The Lover's Praise*

1:9–11

9 I liken you, my darling, to a mare
harnessed to one of the chariots of Pharaoh.
10 Your cheeks are beautiful with earrings,
your neck with strings of jewels.
11 We will make you earrings of gold,
studded with silver.

9–11 If there is any question about the identity of the speaker in v.8, that is not so in vv.9–11. In v.9 we confront for the first time the Hebrew word *ra'yāh,* translated by the NIV as "darling," the NEB as "dearest," and the RSV and the JB as " love." The word occurs nine times in the Song. It is used each time by the lover of his beloved. Five of these occurrences are in the first two chapters. The root idea in the word is associate, companion, or friend. Thus the Vulgate translates it with *amica.* In the Song, however, it develops a strong connotation of commitment and delight.

Modern Western readers understand "most beautiful" and "darling." The next figure, though, is unexpected to us. The lover likens his loved one to a mare harnessed to one of Pharaoh's chariots. We have forgotten what a thing of beauty a horse can be when compared to other animals. We are also unaware what valuable creatures they were in that ancient world. They were beautiful in themselves, and the ancient royal courts insisted on brilliantly caparisoning the ones that pulled the king's chariot. The beloved's jewelry, earrings, and necklaces make him think of such.

We now know, as Pope points out (p. 338), that mares were never used after the middle of the second millennium B.C. to draw chariots. Pairs of stallions were used for the royal vehicles. The presence of a mare among such stallions could be the ultimate distraction. So our lover pays his beloved the ultimate compliment to her sexual attractiveness. That he relishes this thought is clear. He will provide her with the jewelry of silver and gold to match her natural charms.

Notes

10 For the MT's בַּתֹּרִים (*battōrîm,* "with earrings"), the LXX has ὡς τρυγόνες (*hōs trygones,* "as a turtle-dove"), apparently reading כַּתֹּרִים (*kattōrîm*).

F. *The Fragrances of Love*

1:12–14

12 While the king was at his table,

my perfume spread its fragrance.
13 My lover is to me a sachet of myrrh
resting between my breasts.
14 My lover is to me a cluster of henna blossoms
from the vineyards of En Gedi.

12 The maiden now muses in response to her lover's affection and praise. The ambience and the language change. The context up to now has been pastoral. The discussion has been of flocks, herds, shepherds, and vineyards. Now it is of a table, expensive and exotic perfumes, spices from far away places, and a king. The context is royal. This may be confusing to us because we do not usually associate shepherds and kings. That simply indicates how far our world is from the world of David's day. In the ancient Near East in the second and first millenniums B.C., kings from Greece to Egypt to Persia were called shepherds. Notice that the Lord calls Cyrus of Persia "my shepherd" (Isa 44:28). In Jeremiah 2:4–13 four classes of leaders are castigated: the priests, the legal authorities, the rulers, and the prophets. The Hebrew term for the rulers is *rōʿîm* (lit., "shepherds"). We must not forget that the application of this figure to the Lord had its royal overtones to the Hebrew as the supreme Shepherd-King.

The maiden ponders the impact of the presence or the memory of the one lover on the other and describes it in aromatic terms. She is like nard to him. It is as if his table is surrounded by the most delightful fragrance. She is that fragrance.

Nard (NIV, "perfume"; ASV, KJV, NEB, "spikenard") was an ointment derived from a plant that grew in northern and eastern India. It was considered very fragrant and quite expensive. It was used as a love charm in the ancient Near East, as were other aromatic oils (cf. Luke 7:36–50). Her presence as a reality in his life surrounded him like a choice perfume.

13–14 The beloved's impact on her lover was no greater than his on her. The consciousness of him brought sensations as real and as delightful as the smell of myrrh and henna blossoms. Myrrh, a resinous gum, came from trees in Arabia, Abyssinia, and India. It was highly prized in the ancient world and was a valuable article in international trade. It was used for incense (Exod 30:23), for perfuming garments of special people, for special occasions (Ps 45:8), for lover's beds (Prov 7:17), for preparing girls for visits with Oriental kings (Esth 2:12), and for embalming corpses (John 19:39).

Henna was a Palestinian shrub. Its leaves were used to produce a bright orange-red cosmetic dye. It has been used in the Near East to color the hair, hands, and feet. We still know it as a hair dye. Its blossoms, however, were quite fragrant. It is the smell of the blossoms the maiden refers to here.

En Gedi, an oasis on the western shore of the Dead Sea, was an extraordinarily fertile place because of its spring (cf. ZPEB, 2:307). Archaeological explorations indicate that a significant perfume business was located there (cf. E.M. Blaiklock and R.K. Harrison, edd., *The New International Dictionary of Biblical Archaeology* [Grand Rapids: Zondervan, 1983], p. 180).

The impact of the girl's lover on her is encompassing and inescapable. Her consciousness of him sweetens her life the way the aroma of a sachet of perfume placed between the breasts makes a girl move in a cloud of fragrance. The thought or sight of him is as pleasant as the aroma wafted from a field of henna blossoms. Love has its own hallowing touch on all of life.

In this section the maiden's pet name for her lover—*dôḏî*—appears for the first time (v.13). This is translated variously (NIV, "my lover"; NEB, "my love"; RSV and JB, "my beloved"). Apparently this word best expressed her joy in him. She uses it twenty-seven times as she speaks to him or about him. Five times it is used by the women of Jerusalem as they speak of him. Four additional occurrences are in the plural (1:2, 4; 4:10; 7:12). In each case it seems best, as Carr suggests, to translate the plural form as "love-making."

Notes

---

13 The root דוד (*dwd*) of the appellation דּוֹדִי (*dôḏî*, "lover") is a relatively common one in the larger Semitic world and is found in love poetry, fertility rituals, occasionally occurring as a euphemism for the genitals, as an epithet of a god, or perhaps even as the name of a deity. Its most familiar occurrence in Hebrew is in the name David (דָּוִיד, *dāwîḏ*), which in the consonantal text is identical with דּוֹד (*dôḏ* ; the *î* on *dôḏî* is the personal possessive pronoun "my").

G. *Love's Exchanges*

1:15–2:2

15 How beautiful you are, my darling!
Oh, how beautiful!
Your eyes are doves.

16 How handsome you are, my lover!
Oh, how charming!
And our bed is verdant.

17 The beams of our house are cedars;
our rafters are firs.

2:1 I am a rose of Sharon,
a lily of the valleys.

2 Like a lily among thorns
is my darling among the maidens.

1:15–2:2 Now the dialogue between the lovers quickens. Three times he speaks, and twice she responds. They are becoming more direct in their expressions of love. A common language is developing to show the mutuality of their love. He calls her "beautiful" (v.15); she responds with the masculine form of the same Hebrew word (*yāp̄āh* is feminine; *yāp̄eh* is masculine). The NIV translates the masculine form as "handsome" (v.16).

The lover compares his beloved's eyes to doves. She speaks of his manner as charming and delightful. We are aware that these lovers live in a different milieu from ours. It is pastoral; so their metaphors are drawn from nature. Notice the extensive references to animals, birds, trees, flowers, and mountains. The site of their love-making is among the cedars and firs, in all of their greenery. It hints of a return to Eden (Gen 2:18–25), with its simplicity, naïveté, equality, and purity. It is as if this were the original couple.

Notes

2:1 חֲבַצֶּלֶת (h^a^ḇaṣṣeleṯ, "rose") appears elsewhere only in Isa 35:1, where it is translated "crocus." TWOT has it as "meadow saffron or crocus" (p. 259). The crocus is a spring flower and not the "rose" familiar to us today. J.A. Balchin says that the flower "most likely is the *Tulipa sharonensis*, a bulbous plant related to the Syrian mountain tulip" (NBCrev, p. 581; cf. ZPEB, 5:172). Similarly, the "lily of the valley" is perhaps the hyacinth (NBCrev, p. 581; cf. ZPEB, 3:936; cf. also EBC, 6:221).

H. *Faint With Love*

2:3–7

3 Like an apple tree among the trees of the forest
  is my lover among the young men.
I delight to sit in his shade,
  and his fruit is sweet to my taste.
4 He has taken me to the banquet hall,
  and his banner over me is love.
5 Strengthen me with raisins,
  refresh me with apples,
  for I am faint with love.
6 His left arm is under my head,
  and his right arm embraces me.
7 Daughters of Jerusalem, I charge you
  by the gazelles and by the does of the field:
Do not arouse or awaken love
  until it so desires.

3–7 The maiden now responds with a longer speech. Her senses are being stirred by his presence and his affirmations of his love. She finds herself feasting on it all. It is as if he is a tree that provides relief from the sun and delicious fruit for her hunger (v.3). Her satisfaction lies in him. And yet his nearness and his offering of love only intensify her desire. She is faint from it all. Her solution is not the removal of the desire that torments her. It is more food—raisins and apples (v.5)—that will intensify that desire. She began with a desire for his kisses. Now she longs for his embrace. Here perhaps the RSV translation of v.6 is preferable: "O that his left hand were under my head, and that his right hand embraced me!"

The beloved is being carried away by her passions. She relishes the joy. Yet she knows that love should have its own rhythm and its proper progression. Too fast too soon would spoil it all. So she adjures the women of Jerusalem not to encourage love beyond its right and proper pace (v.7). With the attention turned to the world beyond the two of them, the spell is for the moment broken and the first section (1:2–2:7) ends.

Notes

7 The LXX renders בִּצְבָאוֹת אוֹ בְּאַיְלוֹת הַשָּׂדֶה (*bisḇā'ôṯ 'ô b^e^'aylôṯ haśśāḏeh*) as ἐν ταῖς δυνάμεσιν καὶ ἐν ταῖς ἰσχύσεσιν τοῦ ἀγροῦ (*en tais dynamesin kai en tais ischysesin tou agrou*, "by the powers and by the virtues of the field") as opposed to the NIV's "by the gazelles and by the does of the field" (cf. KJV, NASB) (cf. 3:5). The Hebrew supports either translation. The LXX adds this phrase as a gloss to the first line of 5:8.

I. *Love's Rhythm (2:8–3:5)*

1. *A lover's call*

2:8–17

8 Listen! My lover!
  Look! Here he comes,
 leaping across the mountains,
  bounding over the hills.
9 My lover is like a gazelle or a young stag.
  Look! There he stands behind our wall,
 gazing through the windows,
  peering through the lattice.
10 My lover spoke and said to me,
  "Arise, my darling,
  my beautiful one, and come with me.
11 See! The winter is past;
  the rains are over and gone.
12 Flowers appear on the earth;
  the season of singing has come,
 the cooing of doves
  is heard in our land.
13 The fig tree forms its early fruit;
  the blossoming vines spread their fragrance.
 Arise, come, my darling;
  my beautiful one, come with me."

14 My dove in the clefts of the rock,
  in the hiding places on the mountainside,
 show me your face,
  let me hear your voice;
 for your voice is sweet,
  and your face is lovely.
15 Catch for us the foxes,
  the little foxes
 that ruin the vineyards,
  our vineyards that are in bloom.

16 My lover is mine and I am his;
  he browses among the lilies.
17 Until the day breaks
  and the shadows flee,
 turn, my lover,
  and be like a gazelle
 or like a young stag
  on the rugged hills.

8–17 We have seen in the text thus far the beginnings of a very free expression of love between a maiden and a man. The courtship has begun, and the desire for each other is intense. She is weak with passion. It is at that point that the protagonist, the maiden, has appealed to the daughters of Jerusalem. She is concerned that the emotions of her and her lover not take them beyond the proper pace of pure love. So we now see them separated but longing for each other. Two poems (2:8–17; 3:1–5) make up this section. Again we find at the close of this division a plea for restraint.

This section is a good example of how tantalizing the Song can be for the interpreter. The maiden seems clearly (v.9) to be in her own home in the city. She hears her lover's voice as he comes to visit her. He is like a gazelle or a young stag in his energy and in his passionate desire to be with her. He stands outside and calls her to go into the country with him to enjoy the beauty of spring as nature erupts with the passing of winter (vv.10–13). Gordis says that this may be the most beautiful expression of love in the spring to be found anywhere in literature (p. 52).

But is it an actual visit by her lover? Or is this a poetic projection of the maiden's own consuming desires for his presence? Davidson feels it is a dream (p. 117). Regardless of how we interpret it, there is no way we can miss the trauma of true love with its ecstasy of longing and fear. The thought of his coming delights her. Her distance, like a dove in the clefts of the rocks (v.14), distresses him. He wants to see her form and hear her voice; for her voice is sweet, and her appearance is comely. Yet caution is called for.

Verse 15 raises questions. The verb "catch" (*'āḥaz*) is a masculine plural imperative. There is debate over who is speaking and to whom. It seems that here we find a characteristic common to the moments of passion in these early chapters. Just as the two lovers are about to surrender themselves to each other and forget the world, attention is turned to the larger world; so the addresses to "the daughters of Jerusalem" throughout the Song. The appeal is made here to outsiders to prevent "the foxes," those forces that could destroy the purity of their love, from defiling their vineyards, which are blossoming. In 1:6 the maiden uses "vineyard" as a metaphor for her own person (see Carr, p. 79; Murphy, p. 60). So they plead for protection for the love that blossoms between them that nothing will spoil it.

The lovers may accept restraint on the pace of love's development, but there is no denying that they belong to each other (v.16). Here we are tantalized by the questions of whether we are to understand the text literally or figuratively. There seems clearly to be a double entendre character that pulls a cloak over the details of the lovers' love-making—a metaphor in the service of the mystery and sanctity of sex! In 5:13 his lips are called "lilies." The verb *rā'āh* in v.16b means "to feed on." Thus Pope suggests that she is ready for him to "graze" on her lips as sheep "browse" in lush grasses. The ambiguity of the language of the Song is characteristic of lyric poetry. Here it certainly seems fair to look for more than one level of meaning (see Pope, pp. 405–7). Perhaps this is to be related to the opening wish of our young lady (1:2).

Notes

9 The LXX adds ἐπὶ τὰ ὄρη βαιθήλ (*epi ta orē baithēl*, "on the mountains of Bethel") as an apparent gloss to the first line of v.9. Compare the NIV margin on v.17.

10 The LXX adds περιστερά μου (*peristera mou*, "my dove") as a gloss to the end of this verse and also v.13. The phrase is found, however, in v.14 (q.v.). Compare 1:10 and 2:12, where a different word is used.

14 The word for "dove," יוֹנָה (*yônāh*), is the same as the name of the prophet from Gath Hepher, "Jonah" (2 Kings 14:25).

The LXX renders בְּסֵתֶר הַמַּדְרֵגָה (*b^eseṯer hammaḏrēḡāh,* "in the hiding places on the mountainside") as *ἐχόμενα τοῦ προτειχίσματος* (*echomena tou proteichismatos,* "near the wall").

17 The meaning of הָרֵי בָתֶר (*hārê ḇāṯer*) is unknown. The NIV renders it "the rugged hills" but has "the hills of Bether" in the margin. The LXX reads *ὄρη κοιλωμάτων* (*orē koilōmatōn,* "the mountains of the ravines"). Walter C. Kaiser, Jr., doubts whether the reference is to the city of Bether, which gained fame as the location of Bar Kochba's final battle and massacre (ZPEB, 1:535–36). The word בֶּתֶר (*beṯer*) means "disruption," i.e., a ravine or rugged terrain.

---

2. *A lover's seeking*

3:1–5

1 All night long on my bed
  I looked for the one my heart loves;
  I looked for him but did not find him.
2 I will get up now and go about the city,
  through its streets and squares;
 I will search for the one my heart loves.
  So I looked for him but did not find him.
3 The watchmen found me
  as they made their rounds in the city.
  "Have you seen the one my heart loves?"
4 Scarcely had I passed them
  when I found the one my heart loves.
 I held him and would not let him go
  till I had brought him to my mother's house,
  to the room of the one who conceived me.
5 Daughters of Jerusalem, I charge you
  by the gazelles and by the does of the field:
 Do not arouse or awaken love
  until it so desires.

1–5 Our next poetic unit seems clearly to be a dream sequence. The lover is the maiden's obsession night and day (v.1). So in a dream she seeks him. She goes about the city in the night querying those whom she meets about her beloved (vv.2–3). She finds him and will not let him go until she has brought him into her mother's home, into the very room where she was conceived (v.4). She is not looking for an illicit consummation of their love. Consummation she wants, but even in her dream she wants that consummation to be right. Where in human literature does one find a text so erotic and yet so moral as this?

It may be that the reference to the maiden's bringing her lover to her mother's home reflects Genesis 2:24, where the husband is to leave father and mother, but no like command is given to the woman. This passage may also reflect ancient Israelite marital customs now unknown to us. Perhaps we should notice that Isaac brought Rebekah into the tent of his mother, even though Sarah was deceased, and there consummated their marriage (Gen 24:67).

Notes

1 The LXX adds as a gloss to the end of this verse ἐκάλεσα αὐτὸν καὶ οὐχ ὑπήκουσέ μου (*ekalesa auton kai ouch hypēkouse mou,* "I called him but he did not respond to me"), intensifying the anxiety of the maiden. This phrase does appear in the MT at 5:6.

III. The Bridal Procession

3:6–11

6 Who is this coming up from the desert
like a column of smoke,
perfumed with myrrh and incense
made from all the spices of the merchant?
7 Look! It is Solomon's carriage,
escorted by sixty warriors,
the noblest of Israel,
8 all of them wearing the sword,
all experienced in battle,
each with his sword at his side,
prepared for the terrors of the night.
9 King Solomon made for himself the carriage;
he made it of wood from Lebanon.
10 Its posts he made of silver,
its base of gold.
Its seat was upholstered with purple,
its interior lovingly inlaid
by the daughters of Jerusalem.
11 Come out, you daughters of Zion,
and look at King Solomon wearing the crown,
the crown with which his mother crowned him
on the day of his wedding,
the day his heart rejoiced.

6–11 This unit is one of the most intriguing of all the Song. It obviously is a wedding procession. The first problem has to do with who rides in the procession (v.6). Many commentators are sure it is the groom. The Hebrew indicates otherwise (see Notes). There seems to be clear evidences in the Song that our protagonist comes from northern Israel, from Lebanon (v.9; cf. 4:8). The other geographical references support this. So our picture is of the groom and his men bringing his bride from her home to his city for the wedding.

The wedding "carriage" or palanquin (*miṭṭāh*) is identified as belonging to Solomon (v.7). In fact, it appears that he oversaw its building (vv. 9–10). His name has occurred only once before (1:5) in the text of the Song. It will not reappear until the last chapter (8:11–12). It occurs three times in this brief section. This forces the questions of the relationship of the Song to Solomon (see Notes).

For the fourth time the daughters of Jerusalem are addressed. This time they are called *b*[e]*nôṯ ṣîyôn* ("daughters of Zion," v.11). This expression occurs only here in the Song. It is found in Isaiah 3:16–17 and 4:4, where it is rendered "women of Zion." The singular "daughter of Zion" is used twenty-three times in the OT. It normally refers to Israel as a nation. This is the passage that most definitively attaches the Song to Israel. In fact, this is the only passage where the name "Israel" occurs (v.7).

In v.11 we are told that Solomon wears "the crown" with which his mother crowned him for his wedding day. This obviously is not a reference to his coronation, since the high priest presided at that (cf. 1 Kings 1:32–48; 2 Kings 11:11–20). Could it be that this is an indication that, if the Song did come from Solomon, it originated before his crowning in his most innocent period?

Notes

---

6 Several translations read v.6a as "What is this coming from the wilderness?" (JB, LXX, NEB, RSV). מִי זֹאת (*mî zō'ṯ*) is normally translated, "Who is this?" and "this" is feminine singular. Those who translate *mî* as "what" remind us that in Akkadian *mî* is ordinarily so translated. They see the feminine pronoun "this" as a reference to Solomon's carriage. The word translated "carriage" (RSV, NIV; JB reads "litter"), אַפִּרְיוֹן (*'appiryôn*) is feminine. There is no reason though why the *mî* should not be read as it normally is and refer to the maiden. If so, we have the scene where the groom has sent for his bride, and she comes properly perfumed in a magnificently appropriate carriage and with an impressive array of protecting attendants. It is a royal procession. In 1 Macc 9:39–41 we find a picture of an actual wedding procession remarkably like the one here, including the military characters with their weapons.

7 Some solve the problem of Solomonic authorship by simply excising his name from the text. This seems hardly satisfactory. Meek sees it as a reference to the god "Shalam" and thus an indication that the Song originated in Canaanite fertility-cult liturgy (pp. 119–20). Few modern scholars follow this. Some see in these references traces of an old Hebrew custom of making every bride a queen and every groom a king. Those who see the Song as simply a collection of unrelated love poems have no problem. So Gordis says this is the oldest, datable unit in the collection and was written for one of Solomon's many marriages to foreign princesses (p. 56). For those who see the Song as a literary unit, the problem remains. Carr expresses it by wondering how one so notoriously lascivious could appear in an account of love so holy and pure.

IV. The Wedding (4:1–5:1)

A. *The Beauty and the Purity of the Bride*

4:1–15

1 How beautiful you are, my darling!
Oh, how beautiful!
Your eyes behind your veil are doves.
Your hair is like a flock of goats
descending from Mount Gilead.
2 Your teeth are like a flock of sheep just shorn,
coming up from the washing.
Each has its twin;
not one of them is alone.
3 Your lips are like a scarlet ribbon;
your mouth is lovely.
Your temples behind your veil

are like the halves of a pomegranate.
4 Your neck is like the tower of David,
built with elegance;
on it hang a thousand shields,
all of them shields of warriors.
5 Your two breasts are like two fawns,
like twin fawns of a gazelle
that browse among the lilies.
6 Until the day breaks
and the shadows flee,
I will go to the mountain of myrrh
and to the hill of incense.
7 All beautiful you are, my darling;
there is no flaw in you.

8 Come with me from Lebanon, my bride,
come with me from Lebanon.
Descend from the crest of Amana,
from the top of Senir, the summit of Hermon,
from the lions' dens
and the mountain haunts of the leopards.
9 You have stolen my heart, my sister, my bride;
you have stolen my heart
with one glance of your eyes,
with one jewel of your necklace.
10 How delightful is your love, my sister, my bride!
How much more pleasing is your love than wine,
and the fragrance of your perfume than any spice!
11 Your lips drop sweetness as the honeycomb, my bride;
milk and honey are under your tongue.
The fragrance of your garments is like that of
Lebanon.
12 You are a garden locked up, my sister, my bride;
you are a spring enclosed, a sealed fountain.
13 Your plants are an orchard of pomegranates
with choice fruits,
with henna and nard,
14 nard and saffron,
calamus and cinnamon,
with every kind of incense tree,
with myrrh and aloes
and all the finest spices.
15 You are a garden fountain,
a well of flowing water
streaming down from Lebanon.

1–7 The bride has now come to the groom. The time for consummation has arrived. The bride in biblical fashion is veiled (v.1; cf. Gen 24:65; 29:23–25; 38:14). But her lover is now free to enjoy her physical charms. The result is an erotic physical inventory of the details of her beauty. The description of her is given in metaphors that may seem alien to moderns. But, even then, the power of this bit of love poetry is moving. Her sense of modesty is protected (vv.1, 3). His freedom is uninhibited. She is his, and what he sees is perfection (v.7). To him there is no flaw in her.

Eyes luminous as doves, hair glossy black, perfectly matched white teeth with none missing, lips scarlet, and cheeks touched with color like a sliced pomegranate make her an object of beauty that brings ecstasy touched with mystery (vv.1–3). All this was veiled, but now it is his.

A long neck (v.4), which made her stately in appearance, like a prominent nose, seems to have been a mark of beauty in this ancient world. As was the custom, her neck was ornamented with layers of jewelry. Often these contained row upon row of beads or platelets like shields covering a tower. Her breasts had the grace and beauty that evoked tenderness like that produced by two fawns at play (v.5).

The lover's metaphors permit a chasteness and a modesty that less poetic speech would preclude. So when he says that he will go to his mountain of myrrh and to his hill of incense (v.6), he is most probably referring to the breasts he has just described and the body that awaits him. The night gives covering for their love.

8–15 The beloved has come to her lover. Her beauty is overwhelming. She has captured his heart. He wants her to be his forever. The Hebrew of this invitation is even more impressive in its simplicity than our English. The "come with me" (v.8) of our translation is in Hebrew *'ittî* ("with me"), twice repeated, a simple prepositional phrase used as an invitation! He wants her with him. "With me" sums up his desire.

For the first time the lover calls the maiden his bride. In ten verses (4:8–5:1) he uses this term of her six times. It is found only twenty-eight times in the rest of the OT. Carr says that the focus of the word is on "the married status of the woman, particularly on the sexual element presupposed in that status as 'the completed one' " (p. 119). He obviously sees "bride" (*kallāh*) as derived from the Hebrew root *kll* ("to complete").

The lover also calls his beloved his "sister" four times (vv.9–10, 12; 5:1). This is not uncommon in ancient Near Eastern love poetry as a love epithet. Notice that Tobias and his father-in-law call their wives "sister" (Tobit 7:16; 8:4, 7).

The geographical references here are significant. They all speak of places in northern Israel. The indications are that the bride was originally from that area. Senir (v.8) is the Amorite name of the Hebrew Hermon, the tallest peak (over 9,200 ft.) in the anti-Lebanon range.

Notes

---

4 The meaning of the word תַּלְפִּיּוֹת (*talpîyô<u>t</u>*) is unknown. Most (BDB, TWOT) relate it to weapons of some kind, but with much uncertainty. The LXX has *θαλπίωθ* (*thalpiōth*) and renders it "armoury." Symmachus has *ὕψη* (*hypsē*, "high," "lofty"), which could convey the idea of "elegance" (so NIV).

10 See the note on 1:2 for the LXX's use of "your breasts" for the MT's "your love."

The LXX has *ἱματίων σου* (*imatiōn sou*, "your garments") apparently reading שַׂלְמֹתַיִךְ (*śalmō<u>t</u>ayi<u>k</u>*) instead of the MT's שְׁמָנַיִךְ (*šᵉmānayi<u>k</u>*, "your perfume").

B. *Love's Consummation (4:16–5:1)*

1. *Invitation*

4:16

16 Awake, north wind,
    and come, south wind!
Blow on my garden,

> that its fragrance may spread abroad.
> Let my lover come into his garden
> and taste its choice fruits.

16 The maiden now responds to her lover's praise and his cry for her to cast her lot with him. The language is figurative; she picks up the metaphor that he has used of the locked garden (4:12). She invites her lover to enter her garden, make it his own, and enjoy its fruits. She calls for the north wind and the south wind to make her fragrances the more enticing.

2. *Response*

5:1a–d

> [1] I have come into my garden, my sister, my bride;
> I have gathered my myrrh with my spice.
> I have eaten my honeycomb and my honey;
> I have drunk my wine and my milk.

1a–d The language used here of love's consummation is classic in its chasteness, a character possible only through use of symbolic language. The beauty of expression fits the holiest of all human relationships. Metaphor plays the same role here as the veil in the temple. Sinful man needs such to protect the mystery.

Notes

1c Instead of reading יַעַר (*ya'ar*, "honeycomb"), the LXX and the Latin versions have ἄρτον μου (*arton mou*, "my bread").

---

3. *Joy*

5:1e–f

> Eat, O friends, and drink;
> drink your fill, O lovers.

1e–f This brief unit is a problem to most commentators. Who is speaking? And to whom? Carr (p. 129) is convinced that these must be the words of onlookers or guests encouraging the couple to enjoy their love. The NIV concurs. Fuerst (p. 186), on the basis of a notation in Codex Sinaiticus, feels that the two lines are addressed to companions of the bride and groom. The LXX seems to have understood it this way; for it translates "friends" and "lovers" by "neighbors" (*plēsioi*) and "brothers" (*adelphoi*).

Regardless of who is speaking here, one thing is clear. The kind of relationship that our two lovers now have is more than a private affair. What one does with one's sexuality is from a biblical perspective always more than a private, personal thing. It has widespread social implications. Biblically, when a lover gives himself to his beloved as these two have done, the relationship of each has changed to all the rest of the human race. That is why traditionally in our culture a wedding cannot be performed without witnesses. That is the reason behind the publishing of wedding bans. The taking of a woman by a man is a public matter.

Furthermore, what one does with one's sexuality is of concern to God (Exod 20:14). Likewise, it is a concern to everyone else. The woman now belongs to the man and the man to the woman. This changes all other personal relationships. Thus the witnesses present at weddings represent the larger society. This is why weddings are considered legal matters.

The public aspect of marriage helps explain the presence of "the daughters of Jerusalem" (2:7; 3:5; 5:8, 16; 8:4). It also explains the role of the "friends" as seen in the NIV (1:4b, 8; 5:1c, 9; 6:1, 10, 13; 8:5, 8–9). Self-giving love between the sexes is of social significance. Society must know. How else can marriage be a witness and testimony to the relationship of Christ and the church? One Savior, one spouse! Again, one almost feels that the Song is a commentary on Genesis 2:18–25 (see comment on 1:15–2:2).

This little unit bears witness also to the appropriateness of the festive character of weddings normally. Such joy demands that others rejoice, too.

V. The Life of Love (5:2–8:7)

A. *Its Hesitancies*

5:2–8

2 I slept but my heart was awake.
   Listen! My lover is knocking:
 "Open to me, my sister, my darling,
   my dove, my flawless one.
 My head is drenched with dew,
   my hair with the dampness of the night."
3 I have taken off my robe—
   must I put it on again?
 I have washed my feet—
   must I soil them again?
4 My lover thrust his hand through the latch-opening;
   my heart began to pound for him.
5 I arose to open for my lover,
   and my hands dripped with myrrh,
 my fingers with flowing myrrh,
   on the handles of the lock.
6 I opened for my lover,
   but my lover had left; he was gone.
   My heart sank at his departure.
 I looked for him but did not find him.
   I called him but he did not answer.
7 The watchmen found me
   as they made their rounds in the city.
 They beat me, they bruised me;
   they took away my cloak,
   those watchmen of the walls!
8 O daughters of Jerusalem, I charge you—
   if you find my lover,
 what will you tell him?
   Tell him I am faint with love.

2–8 The ecstasy of the preceding section is replaced by deep apprehension. What has been won seems now to be lost.

This section most probably is to be taken like 3:1–5, as a dream sequence. Love brings its joys, but those joys are seldom unalloyed for long. We are such flawed and fragile creatures, and interpersonal relationships contain such subtleties. With our joys come fears. Often they surface in our dreams, arising from some sense of failure or fear of inadequacy.

So our maiden dreams that her lover comes for her. He comes knocking and calling. It is inconvenient for her to respond. She has already undressed, washed her feet, and is now in bed (vv.2–3). She is slow to acknowledge his overture. Her hesitancy reflects a paralysis that we often experience both in dreams and in real life. Then the opportunity is gone. She finally rises to open to him, but he has departed (vv.5–6). Love's chance is lost.

This is a remarkable picture of the kind of adjustments that are necessary in life style in marriage. Our natural sloth, the differences between a man and a woman, our uncertainty about the other's thinking, the variations in our life rhythms, our unwillingness to alter our preferred patterns for the other, our own self-consciousness—all contribute to the problem of reading each other's advances. The lover misunderstands and departs. She is sick now with longing for him. Carr suggests that the third line of v.6 could be translated, "I nearly died when I found he had gone" (p. 136).

The bride's remorse and her love drive her out into the darkened city to seek her groom (v.7). The watchmen find her just as they did in 3:1–5. This time they are hostile. They beat, wound, and shame her. Does this treatment by the watchmen reflect the girl's guilt and sense of failure at the slowness of her response to her husband?

There is a realism in the Song that merits our respect. The course of true love seldom runs smoothly for long. For every moment of ecstasy, there seems to be the moment of hurt and pain. The openness that lovers experience with each other makes possible both extremes. Not even love can guarantee perfect performance in personal relationships. Time and humility help. Our poet is dealing with such in this passage.

Rylaarsdam suggests that this text was in the mind of the author of the Book of Revelation (3:20) in his letter to the Laodicean church. He says that this is "the one instance in which the NT clearly uses the Song of Songs" (p. 153). He is receptive though to the possibility that Jesus alluded to this section when he spoke of a day when the bridegroom would be taken from his guests (Mark 2:19–20) and when he gave the parable of the foolish virgins (Matt 25:1–13).

The bride's consciousness of loss and perhaps her feeling of blameworthiness drive her to call for her friends, the daughters of Jerusalem, to help (v.8). She urges them that if they find her lover, they are to let him know of her love for him.

Notes

8 See the note on 2:7 for the LXX's gloss to the end of line 1.

B. *The Friends' Concern*

5:9

9 How is your beloved better than others,
most beautiful of women?
How is your beloved better than others,
that you charge us so?

9 The request of our hurting bride to the daughters of Jerusalem (v.8) evokes a query. They want to know what is so remarkable about her lover, how he differs from other grooms.

Our questions here are numerous. Does this report an actual conversation, or is this part of the dream? The probability of such a midnight conversation seems unlikely enough. Or are we dealing with a master poet who uses this literary device to give the maiden a chance to recount the attractions and charms of the groom?

C. *Love's Affirmations (5:10–6:10)*

1. *The beloved's praise*

5:10–16

10 My lover is radiant and ruddy,
outstanding among ten thousand.
11 His head is purest gold;
his hair is wavy
and black as a raven.
12 His eyes are like doves
by the water streams,
washed in milk,
mounted like jewels.
13 His cheeks are like beds of spice
yielding perfume.
His lips are like lilies
dripping with myrrh.
14 His arms are rods of gold
set with chrysolite.
His body is like polished ivory
decorated with sapphires.
15 His legs are pillars of marble
set on bases of pure gold.
His appearance is like Lebanon,
choice as its cedars.
16 His mouth is sweetness itself;
he is altogether lovely.
This is my lover, this my friend,
O daughters of Jerusalem.

10–16 Regardless of how we interpret the sequence of vv.9–16, the passage in vv.10–16 is most remarkable. This is one of the few poems that has come down to us from the ancient world in which the female gives an inventory of the male's features. Obviously it is her response to his description of her in 4:1–7. Her description witnesses to the uniqueness of this little book in its world in that it illustrates in its own way the equality of position and freedom that she enjoys. Carr points out that 80 of the 111 lines contained in 5:2—8:4 are spoken by the bride (p. 130). It is really her book. Again one thinks of Genesis 2:18–25.

The bride sings. She sings of the handsomeness of her lover. Beginning with his complexion, ruddy and golden, and his hair, black and wavy, she descends from his eyes to his cheeks to his lips to his arms to his torso to his legs. The metaphors are ancient Near Eastern ones, but the import is clear: he is one in ten thousand. She returns then to his mouth (v.16), which she finds to be a source of sweetness (cf. 1:2).

The Hebrew word translated as "mouth" (*ḥēḵ*) actually is the word for palate. So the RSV reads it "speech," the NEB "whispers," and JB "conversation." In Hebrew the palate is an organ of taste as well as speech. In 2:3 she spoke of his fruit as sweet to her palate. He has spoken of her lips as dropping sweetness and honey. So she counters with the delights of his kisses (cf. Prov 5:3). His conclusion about her was that she was beauty without flaw (4:7) and sweetness itself. She counters with the fact that he is altogether desirable.

All this is addressed to the daughters of Jerusalem (5:9–16). She is speaking of her lover, her "friend." The word "friend" (*rēaʿ*) is the masculine counterpart of his regular designation of her (*raʿyāh;* cf. 1:9, 15; 2:2, 10; 4:1, 7; 5:2). Its root meaning is "to associate with," and it came to mean "friend" or "companion" (cf. 1:9). The Song is unabashedly erotic. Yet it is never satisfied to be content with the physical alone. A normal person finds the erotic ultimately meaningful only if there is trust and commitment, delight in the other's person as well as in the body. The writer of the Song understands this. Our hero is her lover, but he is more: he is her friend.

2. *The friends' inquiry*

6:1

1 Where has your lover gone,
most beautiful of women?
Which way did your lover turn,
that we may look for him with you?

1 Now the daughters of Jerusalem inquire of the bride as to where her lover is. They want to assist her in finding him.

3. *The beloved's praise*

6:2–3

2 My lover has gone down to his garden,
to the beds of spices,
to browse in the gardens
and to gather lilies.
3 I am my lover's and my lover is mine;
he browses among the lilies.

2–3 The bride's response to the friends' inquiry assures them that she has not really lost him. The anxiety in her dream was without foundation in reality. She is her lover's, but he is also hers. And he now is browsing in his garden of spices among the lilies (v.2). In 5:13 she has described his lips as lilies that drip with myrrh. The erotic implications in this language seem clear. Her fears were unwarranted. As he possesses her, she possesses him (v.3).

4. *The lover's praise*

6:4–10

4 You are beautiful, my darling, as Tirzah,
lovely as Jerusalem,
majestic as troops with banners.
5 Turn your eyes from me;
they overwhelm me.
Your hair is like a flock of goats
descending from Gilead.
6 Your teeth are like a flock of sheep
coming up from the washing.
Each has its twin,
not one of them is alone.
7 Your temples behind your veil
are like the halves of a pomegranate.
8 Sixty queens there may be,
and eighty concubines,
and virgins beyond number;
9 but my dove, my perfect one, is unique,
the only daughter of her mother,
the favorite of the one who bore her.
The maidens saw her and called her blessed;
the queens and concubines praised her.

10 Who is this that appears like the dawn,
fair as the moon, bright as the sun,
majestic as the stars in procession?

4–10 The lover speaks again in poetic ode about his beloved's beauty. She is like a great city to be taken (v.4). Tirzah was an ancient Canaanite center that served as the capital of the northern kingdom before Omri (c. 879 B.C.) established Samaria as the capital. This reference is a strong indication of an early date for the origin of the Song. So some commentators are willing to accept a Solomonic date for at least this portion.

The reference to Jerusalem is the only time the name occurs except in the phrase "daughters of Jerusalem." It may seem strange at first for a lover to think of his bride as a great city. This figure is not unique though to the Song. The author of the Book of Revelation uses Babylon as a figure of a great harlot and Jerusalem as the Bride of Christ (Rev 18:2–19:3; 19:7–9; 21:1–2). Do we perhaps have in this metaphor an anticipation of the outcome of history for every believer?

The beloved is regal to the point of awesomeness. She appears like the dawn in its glory, fair as the moon, bright as the sun, terrible as an army with banners (vv.4, 10). She is more impressive than queens or royal concubines or virgins without number. The reference to queens, concubines, and virgins (v.8) may well be a reference to the royal harem. She is without equal among women. Even the ladies of the royal harem acknowledge her superiority.

D. *Love's Questions*

6:11–13

11 I went down to the grove of nut trees
to look at the new growth in the valley,
to see if the vines had budded
or the pomegranates were in bloom.
12 Before I realized it,

my desire set me among the royal chariots of my
people.

13 Come back, come back, O Shulammite;
come back, come back, that we may gaze on you!

Why would you gaze on the Shulammite
as on the dance of Mahanaim?

11–13 This is a tantalizing section. Verse 11 seems simple enough. The words are familiar. The meaning is another matter. Does this represent a momentary separation of the maiden from her lover as she or he goes to investigate the flowering of springtime? Or are we to look for a deeper, more erotic meaning here?

If v.11 is difficult to interpret, v.12 is more so. Many scholars consider this the most difficult verse in the book. The suggestions are almost as numerous as the commentators. The versions indicate by their trouble with it that the problem in the text antedates them.

Perhaps the best approach is to see in the unit a momentary separation that leaves the bride yearning again for her lover. So the daughters of Jerusalem call for her to return (v.13). Our lack of certain and detailed knowledge of the cultural context may make inexplicable to us what would have been very clear to a contemporary. Carr sees the appeal for the bride to return as originating with the wedding guests whom he distinguishes from the daughters of Jerusalem.

Whoever is speaking calls the girl "the Shulammite" (v.13). This verse with its two occurrences is the only place where this term is found in the OT. Some see in it a proper name. Others see a reference to her place of origin and link it with Shunem, the home of Abishag, the wife of David (1 Kings 1:1–4; cf. Josh 19:18). Others see in it a feminine form of the name of Solomon. Still others find here a reference to a pagan god or goddess of fertility. Pope is obviously right when he says that the final word on this has not yet been written (p. 600).

In v.13 the bride responds to the guests who want to see her. She is modestly reluctant. She questions their desire. If she wonders why anyone would want to see her, she is to get an answer from her lover. The next unit is his description of her charms. It is a response to her description of him in 5:10–16.

Notes

11 The LXX adds *ἐκεῖ δώσω τοὺς μαστούς μου σοί* (*ekei dōsō tous mastous mou soi*, "There I will give you my breasts") as a gloss to the end of this verse. Compare the last line of 7:12, where the MT has "love" for "breasts" (see Notes on 1:2).

13 An intriguing suggestion relates שׁוּלַמִּית (*šûlammîṯ*, "Shulammite") to the root שָׁלֵם (*šālēm*), which means "to be complete." Thus the Shulammite would be "the completed one" or "the peaceful one" (see Carr, p. 153).

Numerous attempts have been made to explain the closing line of v.13. The Hebrew כִּמְחֹלַת הַמַּחֲנָיִם (*kimḥōlaṯ hammaḥ[a]nāyim*, "as on the dance of Mahanaim") is rendered by the LXX as *ἡ ἐρχομένη ὡς χοροὶ τῶν παρεμβολῶν* (*hē erchomenē hōs choroi tōn parembolōn*, "she comes as bands of armies"), which seems to make little sense here, although *χορός* (*choros*) refers to a circular dance or an enclosure for dancing. Meek sees here a reference to a special dance, performed apparently in the nude, a part of a fertility rite (p. 134). Others see in the text a reference to a dance performed by the bride before her wedding guests. It is hard to escape the suspicion that most of these attempts to interpret some of these difficult lines tell us more about the presuppositions that we bring to the text than they do about the meaning contained in the text. Fortunately, the progression of the Song is not dependent on an accurate understanding of this line.

E. *Love's Repetitions*

7:1–9a

1 How beautiful your sandaled feet,
O prince's daughter!
Your graceful legs are like jewels,
the work of a craftsman's hands.
2 Your navel is a rounded goblet
that never lacks blended wine.
Your waist is a mound of wheat
encircled by lilies.
3 Your breasts are like two fawns,
twins of a gazelle.
4 Your neck is like an ivory tower.
Your eyes are the pools of Heshbon
by the gate of Bath Rabbim.
Your nose is like the tower of Lebanon
looking toward Damascus.
5 Your head crowns you like Mount Carmel.
Your hair is like royal tapestry;
the king is held captive by its tresses.
6 How beautiful you are and how pleasing,
O love, with your delights!
7 Your stature is like that of the palm,
and your breasts like clusters of fruit.
8 I said, "I will climb the palm tree;
I will take hold of its fruit."
May your breasts be like the clusters of the vine,
the fragrance of your breath like apples,
9 and your mouth like the best wine.

1–9a One of the problems in the Song, as has been said before, is identifying the speakers. The result is that scholars often differ. This next unit is illustrative. Carr (in loc.) sees it as the response of the wedding guests to the question of the bride in 6:13b. He sees this section as their song of praise to her charms. Gordis and Davidson concur. The JB, NEB, and NIV all attribute this section to the groom, the position taken here.

The groom's description of his bride begins with her sandals and feet and proceeds upward to the flowing locks of hair on her head. It should be compared with previous descriptions in 4:1–7; 5:10–16; and 6:4–10. This is the fullest detailing of her physical charms found in the Song.

It should be noticed that, though the Song is really the bride's song, there are three occasions when the groom describes her beauty in detail and only one where she reciprocates. If the Song has any allegorical significance, it should indicate that God finds us much more delightful than we find him. If this seems strange, it should be remembered that his love is pure and eternal. His capacity for love and joy is greater than ours even though the object of our affection is greater and infinitely more worthy.

This poem reflects the perpetual charm of the female form to the male. This song has been sung an almost infinite number of times. There is repetition here. Some of his figures are the same as those used in 4:1–15 and 6:4–10. But that is the nature of love. Our language has its limits. Our love pushes those limits and falls back in frustration at the inability of our words to communicate our ecstasy.

Even the beloved's feet are beautiful. Her rounded thighs, like the work of some more-than-human artist, capture him. Her navel has its own allure. He would like to fill it with spiced wine and drink from it. Her belly is round and wheat colored. The reference to the lilies that encircle the stomach reminds us that we are dealing with figures whose very ambiguity enrich the eroticism of the passage. Her breasts are symmetrical objects of grace and beauty that evoke tender and solicitous response. Her neck gives her stature and impressiveness. Her eyes are like pools—luminous, clear, and deep. The nose adds to her stateliness. Her head and hair crown her. She is awesome and majestic as Mount Carmel. A king is held captive by her tresses. She is an object of beauty and loveliness, a treasure of delights.

In v.7 the groom sees his bride as a palm tree loaded with luscious fruits. He turns again to her breasts and lips to enjoy his possession (vv.8–9a).

We should not miss the element of near-adoration in our lover's depiction of his beloved nor be unmindful of the high value placed on the flesh in Scripture. The body is not an unworthy shell to be shucked in death. It is destined for resurrection. It may be the occasion for sin, but it can also be the very clothing of Deity as in the Incarnation. If the devotion of our two lovers is but an imaging of the relationship of the true Bridegroom and his bride, it is fitting that there should be an almost noumenal air in the poetry. One is reminded of Charles Williams's discussion of Lancelot's perception of Queen Guinevere:

> The physical beauty of Guinevere appeared to him a thing literally transcendental. This is, no doubt, what the code [of chivalry] told him he ought to feel and in any case how he ought to behave. It will not do, however, to forget that a great number of lovers have felt like this. . . . The body of the beloved appears vital with holiness; the physical flesh is glorious with sanctity, not her sanctity, but its own. It is gay and natural to genuflect to it. ("The Figure of Arthur," in *Taliessin Through Logres, The Region of the Summer Stars, and Arthurian Torso* [Grand Rapids: Eerdmans, 1974], pp. 238–39)

The beauty of the imagery of the Song and the validity of its vision has had a profound influence on Christian poets through the centuries (cf. Edmund Spenser's "Epithalamion," in *Spensers Poetical Works*, edd. J.C. Smith and E. De Selincourt [London: Oxford University Press, 1966], p. 581).

F. *Love's Belonging and Giving*

7:9b–13

May the wine go straight to my lover,
  flowing gently over lips and teeth.
10 I belong to my lover,
  and his desire is for me.
11 Come, my lover, let us go to the countryside,
  let us spend the night in the villages.
12 Let us go early to the vineyards
  to see if the vines have budded,
if their blossoms have opened,

and if the pomegranates are in bloom—
there I will give you my love.
13 The mandrakes send out their fragrance,
and at our door is every delicacy,
both new and old,
that I have stored up for you, my lover.

9b–13 Now the maiden responds. There is no holding back. She belongs to him. There is a primeval Edenic purity about all of this. Once again we are reminded of that first couple that God gave to each other and commanded to be one flesh. We cannot keep from thinking of that context when she speaks of "his desire" for her (v.10). The Hebrew word is *t*ᵉ*šûqāh;* it is found in Genesis 3:16 in reference to Eve's desire for her husband. It is as if we are observing the Fall momentarily reversed. This word is found only three times in all of the OT. It occurs in Genesis 4:7 as well as in 3:16 and here. It obviously is a very strong, almost overpowering, urge. His desire for her easily equals hers for him. She is at no disadvantage. She relishes the security of her relationship to her husband.

The bride's joy and fulfillment are such that she is ready to get out into the fields and vineyards to let the common nature that flows in lovers and the cosmos rejoice together (vv.11–12). "Mandrakes" (v.13) were prized for their aphrodisiac properties. The joys the two now are experiencing in each other are but the beginning of raptures that she is prepared to bring to him.

G. *Love's Longing and Liberty*

8:1–4

1 If only you were to me like a brother,
who was nursed at my mother's breasts!
Then, if I found you outside,
I would kiss you,
and no one would despise me.
2 I would lead you
and bring you to my mother's house—
she who has taught me.
I would give you spiced wine to drink,
the nectar of my pomegranates.
3 His left arm is under my head
and his right arm embraces me.
4 Daughters of Jerusalem, I charge you:
Do not arouse or awaken love
until it so desires.

1–2 The bride continues to speak about leaving the security of their bed chamber and going into the fields and villages with him. Yet she is reluctant to leave the freedom that they have behind closed doors to express their love for each other. The proprieties demanded in public seem limiting. She would like the liberty in public that the brother and sister in that day had (v.1). So she wishes she could freely kiss him in public. She would like to take him to the house of her own mother and to the very chamber where she was conceived (v.2).

There is no sense of wrongness about their love. She is reminded of her mother, who in a similar relationship gave to her the life that she now enjoys with her groom. Her joy in him strengthens her identification with her own mother who taught her.

With all the strength of the union with her husband, there is still the consciousness that she is a woman. She longs for a woman with whom she can share, and the appropriate one is her mother. This is no indication of withdrawal from her spouse. She would like to take him to the place of her conception and there give herself to him.

3–4 The bride yearns for her lover's embrace. Apparently that yearning once more evokes the bride's remark to the daughters of Jerusalem. Again we are reminded that we are social creatures inextricably bound up in a web of human relations. In this moment of deepest intimacy, when no prying eyes are wanted, she thinks of her mother (v.2) and her friends (v.4). Her ecstasy she would share with her mother and her wisdom with the daughters of Jerusalem. Love has its ecstasy when it is right, but it also has its pain when it cannot freely express itself. It is the better part of wisdom, she informs her friends, not to permit love to be awakened until the time is right. Love like this should have no shadows or constraints.

Notes

2 The LXX adds *καὶ εἰς ταμίειον τῆς συλλαβούσης με* (*kai eis tamieion tēs syllabousēs me*, "into the chamber of her that conceived me") to the second line. This phrase appears in 3:4.

H. *Love's Seal and Strength*

8:5–7

5 Who is this coming up from the desert
  leaning on her lover?

Under the apple tree I roused you;
  there your mother conceived you,
  there she who was in labor gave you birth.
6 Place me like a seal over your heart,
  like a seal on your arm;
for love is as strong as death,
  its jealousy unyielding as the grave.
It burns like blazing fire,
  like a mighty flame.
7 Many waters cannot quench love;
  rivers cannot wash it away.
If one were to give
  all the wealth of his house for love,
  it would be utterly scorned.

5–7 The drama is now almost over. The couple have followed her desire and now return from the trip into the fields and the villages. The friends, daughters of Jerusalem, spot the couple and call attention to them as they return (v.5a). The bride leans on her lover.

The bride pays no attention to the call of the friends. She speaks only to her lover. She has not taken him to her mother's home. He has apparently taken her to the site of his conception (v.5b). There they have sealed more deeply their love. She speaks of the depth of that sealing (v.6).

An engraved stone or metal seal was a mark of ownership in the ancient world. Possession of another's seal indicated mutual access and possession. Her love is so total and so strong that she wants their mutual possession of each other to be as lasting as life. It is a strongly poetic demand for "until death do us part." Better to die than to experience the failure of love that produces jealousy. Love's demands are all consuming. External forces cannot quench or drown it. Its value is greater than all the possessions one might ever possess. In all of human literature there are few passages on the power of love compared with this unit.

Notes

6 One of the most interesting problems in all of the Song is found here. It is the Hebrew form שַׁלְהֶבֶתְיָה (*šalhebetyāh*). The JB translates this "a flame of Yahweh himself." Thus JB finds in the final syllable—יָה (*yāh*)—the short form of the divine name. That would then constitute the single reference in the text to the Lord. Gordis (p. 26) sees a reference in this to Yahweh but points out that this can be a Hebrew way of expressing the superlative. So a "flame of Yah" is really "a mighty flame," as the NIV translates it. The RSV does the same by reading it as "a most vehement flame." It does not seem necessary to struggle to find the divine name in this text. The Song obviously has a Hebrew provenance. The picture of human love found here is consistent with the noblest biblical teaching on human sexuality. It hardly demands the introduction of the name Yahweh to sanctify it. Where else in the ancient world but in Israel could such an Edenic picture of sexual love originate? It clearly comes from one who shares the OT view of creation at its best. The purity of the relationship pictured is one of the strong arguments for the fact of divine revelation.

VI. Conclusion

8:8–14

8 We have a young sister,
and her breasts are not yet grown.
What shall we do for our sister
for the day she is spoken for?
9 If she is a wall,
we will build towers of silver on her.
If she is a door,
we will enclose her with panels of cedar.

10 I am a wall,
and my breasts are like towers.
Thus I have become in his eyes
like one bringing contentment.
11 Solomon had a vineyard in Baal Hamon;
he let out his vineyard to tenants.
Each was to bring for its fruit
a thousand shekels of silver.
12 But my own vineyard is mine to give;
the thousand shekels are for you, O Solomon,
and two hundred are for those who tend its fruit.

[13] You who dwell in the gardens
with friends in attendance,
let me hear your voice!

[14] Come away, my lover,
and be like a gazelle
or like a young stag
on the spice-laden mountains.

8–10 The JB takes vv.7b–14 as appendixes to the Song. It sees v.7b as an aphorism, vv.8–12 as two epigrams, and vv.13–14 as final additions. This illustrates the problems that many have with this section. Many commentators actually feel that the Song ends with v.7.

There is no consensus on the division of these final verses. Nor is there agreement as to who is speaking. There is even a substantial difference as to who is being spoken about.

Pope and Lehrman identify the speakers in vv.8–9 as the brothers referred to in 1:6. The NIV calls them "friends" and the NEB "companions." Gordis sees them as suitors ready to lay siege to our heroine like an army to a city. Some take "the sister" as the bride, while others see her as an actual, younger sibling of our bride.

It seems most plausible to see vv.8–10 as coming from our heroine. She has now consummated her relationship with her beloved. She has tasted the mysteries of sexual love with her spouse. She is looking back with joy that she came to those sacred moments as a virgin. She thinks of her younger sister and longs for her to know the same joys that she now experiences. So she expresses her concern for the protection of her sibling.

This interpretation takes the expressions "wall" and "door" as antithetical rather than parallel. It sees "towers of silver" (v.9) and "panels of cedar" as protective rather than as primarily ornamental. She with her groom commit themselves to guard her sister from the loss of something precious. She affirms vigorously that she kept herself chaste for her husband. Thus by keeping herself a virgin, she was as one "bringing contentment" (v.10; see Notes).

11–12 Verses 11–12 are among the more tantalizing in the whole Song. Solomon is referred to again. This time though it seems clear that he is not the hero of the piece. The speaker, whether it is the bride or the groom, is contrasting his or her vineyard with that of Solomon's. Solomon's vineyard is large and fruitful, very impressive. It contains a thousand vines. Solomon must let it out to tenants to keep. They share in the produce. It is a very extensive operation.

Our hero or heroine is in a very different position. But he/she is not unhappy. His/her vineyard is his/hers alone. And that is enough to satisfy our spokesman. To possess one's beloved is enough. It is to be wealthy beyond measure.

Is this passage a reference to Solomon's harem with his 700 wives and 300 concubines? If so, the question then is as to the pay of the vineyard keepers. The probability is that references that were easily understandable when written have become problems for us because of distance and its accompanying ignorance of ancient customs.

Or is the reference here to an actual vineyard? Because of previous references to a vineyard, which seems clearly to have a symbolical meaning, one is tempted to see this as a reference to the sexual personage of the maiden. Vineyard and garden seem clearly to be used to speak of her self in previous passages (see 1:6; 2:15; 4:12; 5:1).

There is always the possibility, though difficult for us, that the reference to Solomon's vineyard is to be taken literally while the reference to the spouse's vineyard is metaphorical. Jesus did the same kind of thing when he said, "Destroy this temple, and I will raise it again in three days" (John 2:19). That would be consistent with the double entendres of the book. It would also be fitting that the text come to its climax with a passage of such ambiguity and possible double meaning. However we interpret this text, it is clear that the lover's concern is not for material wealth.

13–14 The closing two verses come from our groom and his bride. She seems to be in a garden with her friends (v.13). He calls to her. He wants to hear her voice. She who began the Song wishing for the kisses of his mouth answers. That response (v.14) is in language used previously (cf. 2:9, 17). She urges him to make haste and resume the delights of love. The figures of the deer and the mountain of spices symbolize for us for the last time the lover and his beloved. Restraints are gone. He is hers and she is his. They are free to pursue those delights of love that image a love to come for every believer.

The bride's call to her groom to hasten may find an interesting echo in the NT. Rylaarsdam (p. 160) suggests that the conclusion of the Book of Revelation contains an allusion to this. "The Spirit and the bride say, 'Come!' And let him who hears say, 'Come!' Whoever is thirsty, let him come; and whoever wishes, let him take the free gift of the water of life" (Rev 22:17).

Whether Rylaarsdam is right or not, the heavenly call has always been that of the Divine Groom for a human bride. In the Song she invites him to come. In human history he invites her to come. Love, Divine Love, calls to love, and love responds.

"Amen. Come, Lord Jesus!"

Notes

10 Two words in the MT are very significant. One is שָׁלוֹם (*šālôm*). The bride's purity and love have resulted in peace. This term carries with it the nuances of completion, fulfillment, contentment (NIV), and rest. Each shade of meaning carries its own witness to the richness of the experience here. The term "peace" also brings instant association with Solomon and the Shulammite since all three words come from the same Hebrew root, שלם (*šlm*).

The second significant term is מוֹצְאֵת (*môṣ^{e}'ēṯ*). It can have two different origins with equally different meanings resulting. If it comes from יָצָא (*yāṣā'*), it is a causative participle meaning "one who causes to go forth, produces." That would mean that her spouse saw her as the one who brought *šālôm* to him. It may rather be from the root מָצָא (*māṣā'*) and would mean "the one who finds" peace. One of the beauties of the poetry of the Song is just such multiple possibilities in the language. Either way the bride is rejoicing in the joyous consequences of chaste love. If it comes from *māṣā'*, it carries the sense of happy accident or unexpected but joyous discovery.

This approach creates problems for some commentators. Fuerst, for example (p. 196), sees nothing of "Christian love" or "moralism" here. Such a view for him would be to deny the erotic and sexual character of these poems. It is as if some of the potential mystery and joy in human sexual love is lost if restrained within the commitment implicit within Christian marriage. It seems, however, that this is the very point of this little passage. The purity of the relationship intensifies the richness of the experience. The Creator's ways and created joys are not antithetical. These joys only reach richest completeness when kept within his purposes and ways. His "walls" only deepen and enrich the mystery.